CIVIL PROCEDURE

CASES AND MATERIALS

Compact Thirteenth Edition for Shorter Courses

■ ■ ■

Jack H. Friedenthal
Edward F. Howrey Professor of Law Emeritus and Former Dean
George Washington University

Arthur R. Miller
University Professor and Chief Justice Warren E. Burger
Professor of Constitutional Law and the Courts
New York University

John E. Sexton
President Emeritus, Dean Emeritus, and
Benjamin Butler Professor of Law
New York University

Helen Hershkoff
Herbert M. and Svetlana Wachtell
Professor of Constitutional Law and Civil Liberties
New York University

Adam N. Steinman
University Research Professor of Law
University of Alabama

Troy A. McKenzie
Dean and Cecelia Goetz Professor of Law
New York University

AMERICAN CASEBOOK SERIES®

© 2010 Thomson Reuters
© 2013 LEG, Inc. d/b/a West Academic Publishing
© 2018 LEG, Inc. d/b/a West Academic
© 2022 LEG, Inc. d/b/a West Academic
    444 Cedar Street, Suite 700
    St. Paul, MN 55101
    1-877-888-1330

West, West Academic Publishing, and West Academic are trademarks of West Publishing Corporation, used under license.

Printed in the United States of America

ISBN: 978-1-63659-183-4

For Jo Anne

—Jack

In Ellen's memory

—Arthur

For Lisa

—John

For Stephen and Benjamin

—Helen

For Jenny, Isadola, and Syla

—Adam

In memory of Monica McKenzie

—Troy

PREFACE

This Compact Thirteenth Edition is designed to meet the needs of those teaching Civil Procedure courses shorter than the traditional assignment of three hours for each of two semesters. It responds to suggestions and requests that a book of this type be made available. The authors continue to believe that the larger Comprehensive Thirteenth Edition will prove advantageous for many teachers who have shorter courses of four or even three hours because it provides the maximum flexibility in terms of an individual classroom's coverage, depth, sensibility, and emphasis. With that in mind, we have included material in the Compact Thirteenth Edition that expands the range of choices available to you.

The Compact Thirteenth Edition offers an up-to-date and accessible approach to the study of Civil Procedure. Students tend to find Civil Procedure the most mysterious of their law school courses. Our goal is to present the material in a clear and simple environment, yet one that challenges and stimulates the student toward increasing critical understanding. This revised edition reflects up-to-date amendments to the Federal Rules of Civil Procedure, as well as the latest Supreme Court cases involving subject-matter jurisdiction, personal jurisdiction, and other topics pertinent to the first-year course. The edition addresses not simply doctrinal change, but also the still uncertain effects of new technology, globalism, and privatization on the system of civil justice. The edition also responds to the many helpful comments from judges, practitioners, colleagues, and students at the large number of schools in which earlier editions have been used. Our conversations confirm our own conclusion that the book is and will continue to be a highly successful teaching tool, and we have preserved in this volume the basic format of the prior edition. Along with traditional material, we include contemporary cases in which the facts are interesting, the conflicting policies seem to be in a state of equilibrium or context has extrinsic fascination, rather than materials that offer a tight monograph on various aspects of procedure.

As has been the practice with all of the past editions, this Compact Thirteenth Edition offers substantial emphasis on the operation of the Federal Rules and draws comparisons with state and international practice. The materials in this volume refer to and are augmented by a Supplement, which contains not only the federal statutes and rules governing procedure, but also selected state provisions for comparison. A number of other materials, such as Advisory Committee notes, proposed rule alterations, and local court rules, also are included. The Supplement contains a litigation flow chart and an illustrative litigation problem, showing how a case develops in practice and samples of the documents that actually might have formed a portion of the record. These samples are not designed as models to be emulated. To the contrary, they often contain defects intended to encourage criticism from students in light of knowledge they have obtained from the cases and classroom discussion. The Supplement also includes complaints from two principal cases and one note case.

The cases and excerpts from other materials have been edited carefully to shorten them and to clarify issues for discussion. With regard to footnotes, the same numbering appears in the casebook as appears in the original sources; our footnotes are indicated by letters. Our omissions are indicated with asterisks, and where there might be any ambiguity, we provide clarifying information in a footnote.

The authors are deeply grateful to a host of people who have assisted us in the preparation of this volume, the earlier editions, and the Supplements. Among our students deserving special mention for the aid they have provided in preparing earlier editions of the book are Sam L. Abram, Brandon Adoni, Christopher J. Asta, Alessandra Baniel-Stark, Kim Barry, Prudence C. Beatty, Gabriel Bedoya, James J. Beha, Jeffrey A. Benjamin, Lina Bensman, Adrienne Lee Benson, John M. Bentil, Richard B. Bernstein, Michael Blasie, Barry B. Boyer, André Brewster, James M. Brockway, Matt Brown, Michael Broyde, William M. Burns, Bertram Carp, Sanford Caust-Ellenbogen, Anna L. Cavnar, Jeffrey J. Chapman, Daniel Chazin, Tan Yee Cheung, Caroline P. Cincotta, Adam S. Cohen, Stephanie Cohen, Steven Cohen, Ellen K. Connell, Diane Costa, Thomas F. Coyle, Russell C. Crane, Stavan Shivraj Desai, Sarah Dowd, David Drueding, Devon Edwards, Gary Eisenberg, Seth K. Endo, Lisa Fair, David E. Firestone, Raymond Fisher, Grant H. Franks, Kelly A. Frawley, Amelia Frenkel, Monte Frenkel, Patrick P. Garlinger, Stacy Gershwind, Lisa E. Goldberg, Robert H. Goldman, Steven F. Goldman, Ashley K. Goodale, Amanda W. Goodin, Kurt Gosselin, Chelsea Goulet, Susanna R. Greenberg, Debra L. Greenberger, Kimberly M. Greene, Kevin A. Griffin, Edward Hartnett, Daniel M. Hennefeld, Nancy Louise Hoffman, Steve Hsieh, Wendy B. Jacobs, Colin Johnson, Drew Johnson-Skinner, Joe J. Kalo, Mary Kay Kane, Lonnie Keene, Christopher D. Kercher, Tarek M. Khanachet, Amy Kimpel, Jessica M. Kumm, Pearline M. Kyi, Nicolas Kyriakides, Daniel Laguardia, Fredrick W. Lambert, Joshua Lee, Judyann M. Lee, Susan S. Lee, Callie Lefevre, Xiang Li, Kevin J. Lynch, Alexandra A. Magness, Christopher Mahon, Shirin Malkani, Maureen P. Manning, Jeanette E. Markle, Claire Martirosian, Christen M. Martosella, John J. McGonagle, Matthew McGrath, Kiran H. Mehta, Lisabeth C. Meletta, Franklin N. Meyer, Gary Meyerhoff, Tara Mikkilineni, Joy E. Milligan, Andrew Moore, Chris C. Morley, Jennifer Nevins, Etan Newman, John Nichols, Greg G. Oehler, Marcy Oppenheimer, Jennifer Pariser, Dawn A.

SUMMARY OF CONTENTS

TABLE OF CONTENTS

TABLE OF CASES

The principal cases are in bold type.

TABLE OF AUTHORITIES

CIVIL PROCEDURE

CASES AND MATERIALS

Compact Thirteenth Edition
for Shorter Courses

CHAPTER 1

A SURVEY OF THE CIVIL ACTION

■ ■ ■

This chapter provides a thematic and doctrinal framework for studying civil procedure. The materials examine how adversarial assumptions about party autonomy influence the design of judicial procedures. They also explore the ways in which adversarial decision-making differs from other methods of resolving disputes. Another theme we consider is that of federalism: the relation between the federal government and its national court system and that of the states and their separate judicial systems. The materials then offer a nuts-and-bolts picture of a civil action, tracing a lawsuit from its commencement and the service of the summons to the entry of judgment and subsequent appeals. As you read these materials, keep in mind the historical context of your studies. Procedural doctrine dates back to medieval times, and its evolution reflects changes in social, economic, and political conditions. Likewise, changes in procedure have influenced public expectations about important concepts such as fairness, participation, and justice. The materials invite you to take a critical view of civil procedure and to ask how the rules and doctrine that you are studying can be improved.

A. THE CONCERN AND CHARACTER OF CIVIL PROCEDURE

Courts exist to provide a decision "by an agent of state power, [of] a controversy existing between two individuals (or the State and an individual), by rational (not merely personal) considerations, purporting to rest on justice and law (i.e., the community's general sense of order)." Wigmore, *The Judicial Function*, in Science of Legal Method xxvi, xxviii (1917). Although this definition contains some question-begging elements that need definition themselves, it provides a starting point for understanding the United States judicial system. For now, it will suffice to recognize the following points about courts:

(1) The judicial process deals with actual controversies between real parties and also helps to express abstract values for the society.

(2) Courts draw on public power to resolve controversies.

(3) This resolution proceeds not arbitrarily but according to some standards of general application.

(4) These standards are applied in a proceeding that follows some fixed lines set out by a system of rules known as procedure.

In resolving the legal disputes that are presented, courts apply two types of law—*substantive* and *procedural*. Other courses (such as Torts and Contracts) deal with the substantive rights and duties that regulate everyday relationships. This course, by contrast, will explore the procedures used by courts to resolve disputes about those substantive rights and duties. Our focus will be on how attorneys in the United States frame their cases in order to bring them properly before a particular court, and how the case proceeds from its commencement until a judgment is reached and enforced.

It is interesting but sometimes frustrating that the line separating the substantive law from the procedural law is not clear in every instance. Certainly a requirement that all papers filed with a particular court be on 8 1/2 by 14-inch paper is a procedural rule. Equally certain is that the elements of the law of assault and battery are substantive. But not every legal rule can be so easily classified. For example, a statute of limitations (which determines the length of time a party has to sue on a claim) may appear at first glance to be purely procedural. But upon closer examination, it becomes clear that the length of a jurisdiction's statute of limitations is as much a product of public policy, and will affect plaintiff's ability to recover, as any purely "substantive" provision of the jurisdiction's law. As a student of civil procedure, keep your eye on the substance-procedure dichotomy, but also remain wary of its rigid application.

This course deals with the procedural questions presented in *civil* suits; the procedures of criminal suits will not concern us. In analyzing questions of civil procedure, bear in mind how the goals of civil suits differ from those of criminal suits. The principal difference is that civil suits generally are initiated and litigated by private parties attempting to vindicate their legal rights vis-à-vis other private parties. The community thus is seeking to provide a method for resolving the disputes that arise out of private relations, which include commercial and personal interactions. Criminal suits are instituted and prosecuted by the government (on behalf of "the People") in an effort to punish those individuals whose conduct has violated the community's moral judgments as expressed in its penal law. Government involvement, however, is not always an indicator of a criminal suit for the government often is a party to civil suits (for example, when an agency brings an action to enforce regulations), and can be either a plaintiff or a defendant.

The most distinctive element of United States procedure for resolving legal controversies is the (adversary system.) The central feature of this system is the almost total responsibility placed on the parties to the controversy for beginning suit, for shaping issues, and for presenting evidence. The judge who presides over the proceeding is conceptualized as that of a passive umpire. By contrast, the courts in civil law countries employ what traditionally was known as an (inquisitorial system), although that term has fallen out of use as obscuring, rather than clarifying, important features. Under this model, the court conducts an active and independent inquiry into the merits of each case, which may include having the judge question and examine witnesses, as well as order certain fact finding.

It has been argued that the trend in the United States is toward increasing the affirmative functions of the court. This is evidenced by the participation of the judge as an active case manager with respect to such matters as pretrial discovery and the settlement process. Nonetheless, primary responsibility and control over almost all phases of the adversarial proceeding continue to reside in the parties.

Despite criticisms of the adversary system, this mode of decision-making continues to exist in many parts of the world. Four explanations typically are put forward to explain its perseverance:

(1) A truer decision is reached as the result of a contest directed by interested parties.

(2) The parties, who after all are the ones principally interested in the controversy's resolution, should bear the major burden of the time and energy required.

(3) Although impartial investigation may be better when no final decision need be reached, setting up sides makes easier the type of yes-or-no decision that is thought to be necessary in most lawsuits.

(4) Since resort to law has replaced the resort to force that characterized primitive ages, the (atavistic instinct) to do battle is better satisfied by a means of settling disputes that is very much in the hands of the parties.

When one reflects on the fact that the adversary system often means that victory will turn on considerations other than the justice or true merits of the cause, there is reason to believe that we have permitted it to assume an exaggerated place in our civil dispute resolution scheme. But the system remains and its presence will color every facet of this course. Full understanding of the materials in this book will require your constant attention to its existence, as well as critical analysis of its shortcomings.

What is the test of a good system of procedure? One answer is: *Does it tend to lead to the just and efficient determination of legal controversies?* In this regard, recognize that although this course is only an introduction to United States civil procedure, do not assume that your function is to digest uncritically the law you read. Instead, this course will play an integral part in your process of learning to examine, to question, and "to wash in cynical acid" each rule, each form, and each principle you learn. While doing so, keep in mind that the values informing a system of procedure are many, diverse, and complex.

NOTES AND QUESTIONS

1.   What are the values that ought to guide a system of civil procedure? The passages that follow offer different views on this issue.

(a) Solum, *Procedural Justice*, 78 S.Calif.L.Rev. 181, 321 (2004).

The Participation Principle requires that the arrangements for the resolution of civil disputes be structured to provide each interested party with a right to adequate participation. The Accuracy Principle requires that the arrangements for the resolution of civil disputes be structured to maximize the chances of achieving the legally correct outcome in each proceeding. Together, the two principles provide guidance where guidance is needed, both for the architects of procedural design and reform and for judges who apply general procedural rules to particular cases.

(b) Michelman, *The Supreme Court and Litigation Access Fees: The Right to Protect One's Rights—Part* I, 1973 Duke L.J. 1153, 1172–73 (footnotes omitted).

Dignity values reflect concern for the humiliation or loss of self-respect which a person might suffer if denied an opportunity to litigate. *Participation values* reflect an appreciation of litigation as one of the modes in which persons exert influence, or have their wills "counted," in societal decisions they care about. *Deterrence values* recognize the instrumentality of litigation as a mechanism for influencing or constraining individual behavior in ways thought socially desirable. *Effectuation values* see litigation as an important means through which persons are enabled to get, or are given assurances of having, whatever we are pleased to regard as rightfully theirs.

(c) Posner, Economic Analysis of Law § 22.1 (9th ed. 2014).

The objective of a procedure system, viewed economically, is to minimize the sum of two types of cost. The first is the cost of erroneous judicial decisions. Suppose the expected cost of a particular type of accident is $100 and the cost to the potential injurer of avoiding it is $90 (the cost of avoidance by the victim, we will assume, is greater than $100). If the potential injurer is subject to either a negligence or a strict liability standard, he will avoid the accident—assuming the standard is administered accurately. But suppose that in 15 percent of the cases in which an accident occurs, the injurer can expect to avoid liability because of erroneous factual determinations by the procedural system. The expected cost of the accident to him will fall to $85, and since this is less than the cost of avoidance to him ($90), the accident will not be prevented. The result will be a net social loss of $10—or will it?

We must not ignore the cost of operating the procedural system. Suppose that to reduce the rate of erroneous failures to impose liability from 15 percent to below 10 percent that would require an additional investment in procedure of $20 per accident. Then we should tolerate the 15 percent of probability of error, because the cost of error ($10) is less than the cost necessary to eliminate it ($20).

The author goes on to ask, "What if the purpose of the substantive rule in question is not to improve efficiency? In what sense could we still speak of the goal of procedure as being the minimization of the sum of error and direct costs?" Id. What are the consequences of giving one value precedence over another?

Is it clear that all of the values identified can be incorporated in a single procedural system? Will accommodation inevitably lead to tradeoffs? See Morrison, *The Necessity of Tradeoffs in a Properly Functioning Civil Procedure System*, 90 Or.L.Rev. 993 (2012). If there must be tradeoffs, how should they be determined and by whom? By the legislature? The parties? The courts? See Sward, *Values, Ideology and the Evolution of the Adversary System*, 64 Ind.L.J. 301, 303 (1988/1989). And should these tradeoffs be done on a case-by-case basis or through a formal process of rulemaking? See Mulligan & Staszewski, *The Supreme Court's Regulation of Civil Procedure: Lessons from Administrative Law*, 59 UCLA L.Rev. 1188 (2012).

2.   Judicial decisionmaking often is said to serve two distinct but interrelated social goals. The first goal is that of conflict resolution—"in the interests of preserving the peace, society offers through the courts a mechanism for the impartial judgment of personal grievances, as an alternative to retaliation or forcible self-help." The second goal is that of behavior modification—"courts and civil process [serve] as a way of altering behavior by imposing costs on a person. Not the resolution of the immediate dispute but its effect on the future conduct of others is the heart of the matter." Scott, *Two Models of the Civil Process*, 27 Stan.L.Rev. 937, 937–38 (1975).

3.   Studies show that acceptance of an unfavorable judgment often turns on the losing party's perception that the court reached its decision through a fair process. A leading commentary links the concept of fair process (sometimes called procedural fairness) with four principles: "voice," or the opportunity to present one's own side of a story; "neutrality," or the decisionmaker's lack of

bias and adherence to rules; "respect," or the system's treatment of the participants as important and valued, regardless of their social or economic status; and "trust," or the view that the court system is serving a public function and is committed to its mission. Tyler, *Procedural Justice and the Courts*, 44 Ct.Rev. 26, 28–31 (2007–2008); see Thibaut & Walker, *A Theory of Procedure*, 66 Calif.L.Rev. 541 (1978). Should the court's process differ depending on the substantive law underlying the dispute? See West, *The Limits of Process*, in Getting to the Rule of Law: Nomos L 32–51 (Fleming, ed. 2011).

Maryland and Florida?

4.   In Avista Mgmt., Inc. v. Wausau Underwriters Ins. Co., 2006 WL 1562246 (M.D.Fla. 2006), the parties could not agree on where to hold a deposition and sought the court's intervention. In response, the judge ordered the parties to meet on the front steps of the courthouse and to "engage in one (1) game of 'rock, paper, scissors.'" The winner would select the deposition's location, although the loser could appeal the outcome to the judge. Was it appropriate to use a children's game to resolve the parties' disagreement? What if the court had ordered the parties to draw lots? See Brown, *Casting Lots: The Illusion of Justice and Accountability in Property Allocation*, 53 Buff.L.Rev. 65 (2005).

5.   Beginning in 2020, courts throughout the United States made dramatic changes in response to the COVID-19 pandemic. Among other things, "the 'day in court' ideal took on new meaning as litigants found themselves outside the public space of a brick-and-mortar courthouse and instead required to participate remotely in electronic proceedings." Hershkoff & Miller, *Courts and Civil Justice in the Time of COVID: Emerging Trends and Questions to Ask*, 23 N.Y.U.J.Legis. & Pub.Pol'y 321, 411 (2021). What impact do such changes have on the procedural values discussed above? Although the pandemic made it especially imperative to deploy new technologies, technological advances have affected civil procedure in myriad ways independent of COVID's public health emergency. See Engstrom & Gelbach, Legal Tech, *Civil Procedure and the Future of Adversarialism*, 169 U.Pa.L.Rev. 1001 (2021); Koh, *The "Gants Principles" for Online Dispute Resolution: Realizing the Chief Justice's Vision for Courts in the Cloud*, 62 B.C.L.Rev. 2768 (2021).

B. AN OUTLINE OF THE PROCEDURE IN A CIVIL ACTION

Lawsuits do not begin themselves. Someone first must decide to sue someone else. If this decision is made intelligently, the person choosing to sue must have weighed several matters, among which at least three are basic. These three considerations are first, whether legal relief is available; second, what the probability of winning a lawsuit is; and third, whether what would be won is worth the burden of litigating.

A potential litigant obviously feels aggrieved or would not be thinking of a lawsuit, but before litigating must first consider whether the grievance is one for which the law furnishes relief. There are a great many hurts a person may feel that the law will not redress. A homeowner is offended by the paint on a neighbor's house; a manufacturer has worked for weeks to persuade a distributor to buy a product and sees the sale go to a competitor; a landowner has been holding a plot of ground for speculation, expecting industry to move in, and the area is zoned for residential use; a visitor slips on a spot of grease in the county courthouse but the county is immune from suit. A potential litigant often must consult an attorney before deciding whether there is a case to be litigated.

Even if the grievance is one for which the courts may grant relief, a potential litigant secondly must consider the probability of winning a lawsuit. The answer turns on a number of factors: whether the person who has caused the injury can be found and brought into court; whether witnesses and documents will be available to support the claims being sued on; whether this proof will be believed; whether the potential adversary can justify its conduct or establish any defenses to the action; and whether an accurate assessment of the law can be made ahead of time.

Thirdly, and perhaps most importantly of all, a potential litigant must consider whether what is won will be worth the time, the effort, and the expense that litigating it will cost. Most significantly, this includes the payment of fees to an attorney who provides representation in the case. In the United States, each litigating party typically bears the full costs of these attorney's fees—this is called the American Rule. These fees are calculated in several ways: by time (at an hourly rate); fixed (the attorney sets the fee prior to providing the services); task-based (the attorney charges a fee based on the nature of the tasks provided to the client); or on contingency (the attorney is paid a portion of the ultimate judgment awarding money damages or settlement). By contrast, the more widely accepted "English Rule" requires the losing party to pay the attorney's fees of the prevailing party. Congress has enacted "fee-shifting" statutes that require the losing party to pay the attorney's fees of the prevailing party in certain kinds of cases, such as antitrust and civil rights, and many states have enacted similar provisions. The purpose of these statutes is to create incentives for individuals to initiate lawsuits in a role described as that of "private attorneys general." See Maxeiner, *Cost and Fee Allocation in Civil Procedure*, 58 Am.J.Comp.L. 195, 201 (2010). A prospective litigant must weigh the costs of a lawsuit against other possibilities, among them settlement, arbitration, self-help, and letting matters rest. How easily will someone who lacks economic resources, and cannot retain counsel, be able to access judicial remedies through civil litigation? See Resnik, *Lawyers' Ethics Beyond the Vanishing Trial: Unrepresented Claimants, De Facto Aggregations, Arbitration Mandates, and Privatized Processes*, 85 Fordham

L.Rev. 1899, 1916–18 (2017) (noting that more than twenty-five percent of civil plaintiffs in federal court lack counsel at the trial level and more than fifty percent of federal civil appeals are filed without counsel); Steinberg, *A Theory of Civil Problem-Solving Courts*, 93 N.Y.U.L.Rev. 1579, 1596 (2018) ("According to the National Center for State Courts, seventy-six percent of cases in the civil courts now involve an unrepresented party.").

Further, attention must be given to the form that the relief will take. Most frequently the relief will be restricted to a judgment for damages. The potential litigant thus needs to consider whether the injury is one for which a monetary payment will be satisfactory. Assuming it is, will defendant be rich enough to pay? How difficult will a judgment be to collect? How expensive? Will the recovery be enough to pay the lawyer's fees and the other litigation expenses that undoubtedly will be incurred? Even in a context in which the court may grant specific relief—for example, an order directing the opposing party to do something or to stop doing something— will compliance by defendant be possible? Worthwhile? Sufficient? In the same vein, a potential litigant must consider whether there are risks not directly tied to the suit. Will filing a lawsuit antagonize people whose goodwill plaintiff needs? Will the action publicize an error of judgment on plaintiff's part or open private affairs to public gaze?

Only after considerable thought about the utility and expense of litigation will the prospective plaintiff be ready for the steps that a litigant must take to bring a lawsuit. Let us now consider these steps in the light of a relatively uncluttered hypothetical case:

> Aikin, while crossing the street in front of her private home, was struck and seriously injured by an automobile driven by Beasley. On inquiry, Aikin found that the automobile was owned by Cecil and that Beasley apparently had been in Cecil's employ. Beasley was predictably without substantial assets and a judgment against him for Aikin's injuries promised little material compensation. But Cecil was wealthy, and Aikin was advised that if she could establish that Beasley had indeed been working for Cecil and had been negligent, she then could recover from Cecil. Aikin decided to sue Cecil for $500,000.

1.   SELECTING A PROPER COURT

Aikin initially must determine in which court to bring the action. She might have some choice between filing her lawsuit in a state or a federal court, but her choice is not open-ended. This is because the court selected must have *jurisdiction over the subject matter* (that is, the constitution and statutes under which the court operates must have conferred upon it power to decide this type of case) and also must have *jurisdiction over the person* of Cecil (that is, Cecil must be subject or amenable to suit in the state in which the court is located so that a judgment may be entered against him).

Aikin probably will file suit in a state court, for the subject-matter jurisdiction of the federal courts is limited. If the court organization of Aikin's state is typical, there will be courts of original jurisdiction in which cases are brought and tried, and at least one court of appellate jurisdiction that sits, with rare exceptions, only to review the decisions of lower courts. (In most states, there also will be a group of intermediate courts of appellate jurisdiction.) The courts of original jurisdiction probably consist of one set of courts of general jurisdiction and several sets of courts of inferior jurisdiction. "General" in this sense refers to a court's power to decide any type of dispute that comes before it, as distinguished from jurisdiction that is limited to specific kinds of disputes.

Typically, a state's courts of general jurisdiction are organized into districts comprising one or more counties, or demarcated along other geographic lines. These district courts hear cases of many kinds and are competent to grant every kind of relief, but usually are authorized to hear claims for which the relief requested exceeds a statutorily fixed dollar amount. The courts of inferior jurisdiction can include municipal courts, which have jurisdiction resembling that of the district courts except that the claims are of smaller financial significance; justice-of-the-peace courts, which hear very minor matters; and specialized tribunals such as traffic courts. Since Aikin's injuries are quite serious and her claim is correspondingly large, she will, if she sues in a state court, bring the action in one of the district courts.

The federal government also operates a system of courts. The principal federal courts are the United States District Courts, courts of original jurisdiction of which there is at least one in every state; the United States Courts of Appeals, each of which reviews the decisions of federal district courts in the several states within its circuit (with the exception of the Courts of Appeals for the District of Columbia Circuit and the Federal Circuit); and the Supreme Court of the United States, which has discretionary authority to review the decisions of federal courts and decisions of state courts that involve a question of federal law. At all these levels, federal judges are appointed by the President and confirmed by the Senate, and they have lifetime tenure pursuant to Article III of the Constitution. Congress has also authorized other kinds of judicial personnel—including United States Magistrate Judges and United States Bankruptcy Judges—who do not enjoy the protections of Article III.

The subject-matter jurisdiction of the United States District Courts extends to many, but by no means all, cases involving federal law and also to many cases, similar to Aikin's, that do not involve federal law, but where there is *diversity of citizenship* (the parties are citizens of different states or one of them is a citizen of a foreign country) and the required *amount in controversy* (currently more than $75,000) is at stake. Diversity jurisdiction, in common with jurisdiction to hear cases arising under federal law, is not exclusive to the courts of the federal system. Rather, the state courts also are competent to hear these cases and have concurrent jurisdiction with the United States District Courts unless Congress has made jurisdiction exclusive to the federal courts. If Cecil is not a citizen of Aikin's state, Aikin may bring an action for $500,000 in a federal court even though it asserts only state law claims. Indeed, in these circumstances, if Aikin sued Cecil in a state court in Aikin's home state, Cecil could remove the action from the state court in which it was commenced to the federal district court in that state.[a]

It is not enough for the court selected by Aikin to have jurisdiction over the subject matter. That court, whether state or federal, also must be one in which Cecil can be required to appear so that it is appropriate for the legal system to enter a judgment against him. Traditionally, a court could enter a judgment only against a defendant who resided in the state or was physically in the state, even if temporarily. However, constitutional restrictions on a court's jurisdiction over the person have diminished in recent decades. If Cecil is not present in Aikin's state but he directed Beasley to drive there, Aikin probably will be able to bring the action in that state because of Cecil's prior contact with the state and the benefits that those contacts have brought him, assuming that a statute authorizes the court to exercise personal jurisdiction in these circumstances.

Not every court that has subject-matter jurisdiction and personal jurisdiction can hear the case. It also is necessary that an action be brought in a court having proper *venue*, which refers to where within the state or district the original proceeding is to be located. Thus, although every court in Aikin's state could assert personal jurisdiction over Cecil if he was within its boundaries, that state's statutes typically will provide that the case should be brought in a court in a particular district, such as the one that includes the county in which either Aikin or Cecil lives or where the relevant acts occurred. Similarly, if Aikin decides to sue in federal court based on diversity of citizenship, she must bring suit in a district that has venue as defined by federal statute (currently, the district in which Cecil resides, or in a district where a substantial part of the events giving rise to the claim occurred, or in any district where Cecil is subject to personal jurisdiction if there is no district in which the action otherwise may be brought).

---

[a] If Cecil is not a citizen of Aikin's state but Beasley is, then one of the considerations Aikin will have in deciding whether to join Beasley as a defendant is the effect on the availability of subject-matter jurisdiction in the federal courts. If Aikin wants to be in the federal court, she should not join Beasley; if Aikin wants to begin and stay in a state court, she should join him. In the latter case, there will not be complete diversity of citizenship between plaintiff and defendants.

A defect in a court's subject-matter jurisdiction cannot be waived by the parties. If Aikin and Cecil are both citizens of the same state, a federal court will refuse to hear the action even if both are anxious that it do so. By contrast, the requirements of personal jurisdiction and venue essentially are protections for defendant, who may waive them if he wishes.

Plaintiff, having decided to sue, must determine in which court to bring the action. In the following case, consider which two types of jurisdiction—subject-matter jurisdiction or personal jurisdiction—the United States Supreme Court is addressing in the context of a lawsuit filed in federal court. In reading the case, notice that the word "jurisdiction" is used without a modifier. But, from the context and information given above, you should be able to identify the kind of jurisdiction involved.

CAPRON V. VAN NOORDEN
Supreme Court of the United States, 1804.
6 U.S. (2 Cranch) 126, 2 L.Ed. 229.

Error to the [United States] Circuit Court of *North Carolina*. The proceedings stated *Van Noorden* to be late of *Pitt county*, but did not allege *Capron*, the plaintiff, to be an alien, nor a citizen of any state, nor the place of his residence.

Upon the general issue, in an action of trespass on the case, a verdict was found for the defendant, *Van Noorden*, upon which judgment was rendered.

The writ of Error was sued out by *Capron*, the plaintiff below, who assigned for error, among other things, first, "That the circuit court aforesaid is a court of limited jurisdiction, and that by the record aforesaid it doth not appear, as it ought to have done, that either the said *George Capron*, or the said *Hadrianus Van Noorden*, was an alien at the time of the commencement of said suit, or at any other time, or that one of the said parties was at that or any other time, a citizen of the state of *North Carolina* where the suit was brought, and the other a citizen of another state; or that they the said *George* and *Hadrianus* were for any cause whatever, persons within the jurisdiction of the said court, and capable of suing and being sued there."

And secondly, "that by the record aforesaid it manifestly appeareth that the said Circuit Court had not any jurisdiction of the cause aforesaid, nor ought to have held plea thereof, or given judgment therein, but ought to have dismissed the same, whereas the said Court hath proceeded to final judgment therein."

Harper, for the *plaintiff in error*, stated the only question to be whether the plaintiff had a right to assign for error, the want of jurisdiction in that court to which he had chosen to resort.

It is true, as a general rule, that a man cannot reverse a judgment for error *in process or delay*, unless he can shew that the error was to his disadvantage; but it is also a rule, that he may reverse a judgment for an error of *the Court*, even though it be for his advantage. As if a verdict be found for the debt, damages, and costs; and the judgment be only for the debt and damages, the defendant may assign for error that the judgment was not also for costs, although the error is for his advantage.

Here it was the duty of the Court to see that they had jurisdiction, for the consent of parties could not give it.

It is therefore an *error of the Court*, and the plaintiff has a right to take advantage of it. * * *

The defendant in error did not appear, but the citation having been duly served, the judgment was reversed.

NOTES AND QUESTIONS

1.   The Supreme Court regarded the defect in this case as extremely serious. Does the fact that it was plaintiff who sought review in the Supreme Court make this particularly clear? Did the defect in *Capron* concern subject-matter jurisdiction or personal jurisdiction? Why is such significance attached to this error?

2.   Read Article III, § 2 of the United States Constitution, which is set out in the Supplement. What specific language in that Section is pertinent to the Supreme Court's opinion in *Capron*?

3.   In what court was the *Capron* suit commenced? Under the First Judiciary Act of 1789, Congress established two levels of courts below the Supreme Court: the District Courts and the Circuit Courts. The circuit courts exercised both original and appellate jurisdiction, and had original jurisdiction over diversity cases when the amount in controversy exceeded $500.

4.   The Supreme Court reversed the judgment of the lower court. What was the effect of this reversal? Does it mean that Capron won the lawsuit? If not, why had he sought review in the appellate court?

2.   COMMENCING THE ACTION

Aikin must give Cecil notice of the commencement of the action by service of process. The process typically consists of a summons, which directs defendant to appear and defend under penalty of default; that is, unless defendant answers the summons, a judgment will be entered against that party. Service refers to the delivery of the process. Service of process generally is achieved by personal service, meaning that the summons is physically delivered to defendant or is left at defendant's home, sometimes by the plaintiff's attorney or someone in the attorney's office, sometimes by a private process-server hired for that purpose, and sometimes by a public official such as a sheriff or a United States marshal. If Cecil lives in another state, but the circumstances are such that a court in Aikin's state may assert jurisdiction over Cecil, the summons may be personally delivered to him out of state, or some form of substituted service, such as sending the papers by registered mail or delivering the summons to Cecil's agent within Aikin's state, may be employed. Even if Cecil cannot be located, service in yet another form, usually by publication in a newspaper for a certain length of time, may be allowed, although the validity of this kind of service in the type of case Aikin is bringing against Cecil is unlikely to be upheld. The Supreme Court repeatedly has emphasized that service must be of a kind reasonably calculated to bring the action to defendant's notice. In addition, before any court may proceed, it also must have the power to require defendant to appear in the action.

Unlike the federal courts, state courts of general jurisdiction have subject-matter jurisdiction over a very broad spectrum of lawsuits. Indeed, questions of the competence of those courts to decide a particular kind of case rarely arise. However, before any court may proceed, it also must have the power to require defendant to appear in the action. In the next case, the court must decide whether it has that power, and whether it will exercise it.

TICKLE V. BARTON

Supreme Court of Appeals of West Virginia, 1956.
142 W.Va. 188, 95 S.E.2d 427.

HAYMOND, JUDGE. The plaintiff, Richard Tickle, an infant, who sues by his next friend, instituted this action of trespass on the case in the Circuit Court of McDowell County in March, 1955, to recover damages from the defendants, Raymond Barton, a resident of Austinville, Virginia, and Lawrence Coleman, for personal injuries inflicted upon him by a motor vehicle, owned by the defendant Raymond Barton and operated by his agent the defendant Lawrence Coleman, on private property instead of a public highway, in that county which the plaintiff alleges were caused by the negligence of the defendants.

* * * [A first attempt to serve Barton had been made under a statute relating to actions by or against nonresident drivers involved in accidents on a public highway, and the validity of this service was still undecided at the time the instant decision was rendered.]

On December 5, 1955, one of the attorneys for the plaintiff caused an alias process to be issued against the defendants * * * and delivered it to a deputy sheriff for service upon the defendant Barton in McDowell County; and in the evening of December 6, 1955, that process was served by the deputy upon the defendant Barton in person at the War Junior High School in the town of War in that county where he appeared to attend a banquet which was held there at that time.

By his amended plea in abatement * * *, the defendant Barton challenged the validity of the service of the alias process upon him on the ground that he had been induced to come to that place in McDowell County by trickery, artifice and deceit practiced upon him by the attorney for the plaintiff.

The circuit court overruled the demurrer of the plaintiff to the amended plea in abatement and * * * certified its ruling upon the demurrer to this Court on the joint application of the plaintiff and the defendant Barton.

* * * [T]he amended plea in abatement alleges in substance that after procuring alias process for the purpose of causing it to be served upon the defendant Barton in McDowell County, and inducing him to come to the Junior High School in the town of War in that county, an attorney representing the plaintiff in this action, in the evening of December 5, 1955, called by telephone the defendant Barton at his home in Austinville, Virginia, and wrongfully and deceitfully represented that, in behalf of the sponsors of a banquet honoring a championship high school football team to be held at the Junior High School in the town of War, in McDowell County * * *, he extended an invitation to the defendant Barton, whose son had been a member of an earlier football team of that school, to attend the banquet; that during that telephone conversation between them the attorney, though requested to do so by the defendant Barton, did not disclose his identity except to say that he called him in behalf of the sponsors to extend the defendant Barton a special invitation to attend the banquet; that the defendant Barton before being so invited did not know that the banquet would be held and did not intend to attend it; that he did not know or suspect the identity of the attorney, or realize that the telephone call was a trick or device to entice, induce and inveigle him to come into McDowell County to be served with process in this action; that the attorney was not connected with any of the sponsors of the banquet and was not authorized by them to invite the defendant Barton to attend it; that the attorney called the defendant Barton and invited him to the banquet solely for the purpose of tricking, deceiving and inveigling him to come to the town of War in order to obtain personal service * * * upon him * * *; that the defendant Barton, believing that the invitation was extended in good faith, by a person authorized to extend it, and not suspecting the real purpose of the telephone call, accepted the invitation and informed the attorney that he would be present at the banquet and on December 6, 1955, left Austinville, Virginia, and went to the town of War with the intention of attending it; that, when he entered the high school where the banquet was held * * * he was served by the deputy sheriff with the alias process * * *; that the service of the alias process upon the defendant Barton,

having been procured by trickery, deceit and subterfuge which was not realized or suspected by him, is, for that reason, null and void and of no force or effect and does not confer upon the Circuit Court of McDowell County jurisdiction of the person of the defendant Barton in this action.

The amended plea in abatement also alleges, on information and belief, that after the defendant Barton had left his home * * * the attorney for the plaintiff * * * made a telephone call to the residence of the defendant Barton, or caused some other person to make such call, and inquired of the wife of the defendant Barton if he intended to attend the banquet and was informed by her that he had left his home to attend it and was then on his way to the town of War for that purpose.

The amended plea in abatement further avers that after the defendant Barton had been served with the alias process his attorney inquired of the attorney for the plaintiff if he had made either of the two telephone calls or had procured some person to make the second telephone call and that the attorney for the plaintiff denied that he had made, or procured any person to make, either of the foregoing telephone calls, and denied that he had any knowledge whatsoever of either of them.

The question certified to this Court for decision is whether the allegations of the amended plea in abatement, which insofar as they are material and are well pleaded must be considered as true upon demurrer, are sufficient to render invalid the personal service of process upon the defendant Barton in McDowell County because his presence in that county at the time of such service of process was induced or procured by trickery, artifice, or deceit practiced upon him by an attorney representing the plaintiff in this action.

The precise question presented by the certificate of the circuit court has not been determined in any prior decision of this Court. It has, however, been discussed in authoritative texts and treatises and considered and determined by appellate courts in other jurisdictions.

* * * In 42 Am. Jur., Process, Section 35, the general principle is stated thus: "Personal service of process, if procured by fraud, trickery, or artifice is not sufficient to give a court jurisdiction over the person thus served, and service will be set aside upon proper application. Relief is accorded in such cases not because, by reason of the fraud, the court did not get jurisdiction of the person of the defendant by the service, but on the ground that the court will not exercise its jurisdiction in favor of one who has obtained service of his summons by unlawful means. Thus, if a person resident outside the jurisdiction of the court and the reach of its process is inveigled, enticed, or induced, by any false representation, deceitful contrivance, or wrongful device for which the plaintiff is responsible, to come within the jurisdiction of the court for the purpose of obtaining service of process on him in an action brought against him in such court, process served upon

him through such improper means is invalid, and upon proof of such fact the court will, on motion, set it aside." * * *

The foregoing principle applies to the party when such service is procured by his agent or by someone acting for and in his behalf. * * *

In Economy Electric Company v. Automatic Electric Power and Light Plant, 185 N.C. 534, 118 S.E. 3, the court, discussing service of process by fraudulent means, used this language: "Where service of process is procured by fraud, that fact may be shown, and, if shown seasonably, the court will refuse to exercise its jurisdiction and turn the plaintiff out of court. The law will not lend its sanction or support to an act, otherwise lawful, which is accomplished by unlawful means. * * * Such a fraud is one affecting the court itself and the integrity of its process. * * * The objection, strictly, is not that the court is without jurisdiction, but that it ought not, by reason of the alleged fraud, to take or to hold jurisdiction of the action. * * *"

* * *

This Court approves and adopts the view supported by the above cited text, treatise and case authorities, which appears to be generally recognized as the law, and accordingly holds that when a person who resides outside the jurisdiction of a court and, for that reason, is beyond the reach of its process, is inveigled, enticed, or induced by fraud, trickery, artifice or wrongful device for which a party is responsible, by virtue of the action of his attorney or of any other person for and in his behalf, to come within the jurisdiction of the court for the purpose of enabling such party to obtain service of process upon such nonresident person in an action brought against him in such court, service of process which results from such fraud, trickery, artifice or wrongful device, is invalid and does not justify the exercise of jurisdiction by such court over the person so served with process; and upon proof that service of process has been so obtained, it will be vacated and set aside.

Under the material allegations of the amended plea in abatement which, as already indicated, must be considered as true upon demurrer, the defendant Barton was induced or enticed to come into McDowell County by the unauthorized invitation extended to him by the attorney for the plaintiff whose purpose at the time was to obtain personal service upon the defendant Barton * * *; the defendant Barton knew that the present action against him was pending in the circuit court by reason of the service of the original process upon him * * * but he did not suspect or realize that he would be served with process while present in McDowell County to attend the banquet; he was induced to come into that county by the invitation to the banquet; and he would not have come into that jurisdiction if the attorney for the plaintiff had disclosed his identity and his real purpose in extending the invitation, all of which he concealed from the defendant Barton.

* * *

The amended plea in abatement is sufficient on demurrer and the action of the circuit court in overruling the demurrer was correct.

It should perhaps be emphasized that, as the factual allegations of the amended plea in abatement have not been denied at this stage of this action by any pleading filed by the plaintiff, the question of the truth or the falsity of those allegations is not before this Court * * *.

Ruling affirmed.

GIVEN, JUDGE (dissenting).

My disagreement with the majority is not as to the rule of law laid down. I think the rule a salutary one, and masterfully stated. I do not believe, however, that the facts properly pleaded, and the inferences which may be rationally drawn therefrom, bring the facts of this case within the influence of the rule.

Stripped of all explanatory language, and of many allegations of conclusions of fact, * * * the plea in abatement charges no more than that the attorney, by telephone, inquired at defendant's home whether defendant intended to attend a certain social function to be held in McDowell County, to which defendant was then invited by the attorney; that the attorney, though requested to give his name, did not do so; that the attorney later, or someone for him, again by telephone, inquired whether defendant had decided to attend the social function, and was advised that defendant had made arrangements to attend; and that the attorney caused process to be served on defendant while attending the social function. * * * The principal, if not only, fact of wrongdoing, if wrongdoing, alleged against the attorney was his failure to inform defendant of the identity of the telephone caller. * * * It seems to me that the facts properly alleged can not be held to establish fraud or wrongdoing. At most, they would simply show that the attorney took advantage of an opportunity, the holding of the social function in McDowell County and the interest of defendant's son in the holding of the function, to try to obtain proper service of process, which was no more than a duty owed his client. In considering the questions arising, it should be kept in mind that defendant had full knowledge of the institution of the action against him in McDowell County, of the fact that he had questioned the validity of the service of other process issued in that action, and of the fact that the alleged cause of action arose in McDowell County, where ordinarily it would have been triable.

* * *

An examination of the cases cited by the majority discloses that, though they fully support the rule laid down, not one of them, in my opinion, requires, or even permits, the application of the rule in a case wherein the facts are comparable, in effect, with the facts alleged in the plea involved in the instant case. The majority opinion points out no such case, and I find none. * * *

* * *

Being of the views indicated, I respectfully dissent. I am authorized to say that Judge RILEY joins in this dissent.

NOTES AND QUESTIONS

1.   Did the appeals court in this case decide that West Virginia courts did not have personal jurisdiction over defendant (accepting defendant's story as true), or that those courts should not exercise jurisdiction in these circumstances even though they had it?

2.   In thinking about the cases you read, try to consider how the court might approach the problem if certain facts were different. For example, should service in West Virginia in the following situations be treated the same as under the facts alleged in the principal case?

(a)   Tickle had asked Barton to appear as a witness in a suit against a third party involved in the accident.

(b)   Tickle had asked Barton to come to West Virginia to discuss settling the case.

(c)   Tickle had telephoned Barton and falsely told him that his son lay critically injured in a West Virginia hospital.

(d)   Tickle (like the Sheriff of Nottingham) had scheduled a football banquet in West Virginia that he knew Barton (like Robin Hood) would be unable to resist attending, although he did not personally invite him.

3.   When the case is reconsidered by the West Virginia Circuit Court on remand, Barton's lawyer must prove his allegations if Barton is to avoid trial in West Virginia. What problems do you foresee in his being able to prove them, and how should he attempt to do so?

3.   PLEADING AND PARTIES

With the summons, Aikin usually will serve on Cecil the first of the pleadings, commonly called the complaint. This is a written statement that will contain Aikin's claim against Cecil. What should be required of such a statement? It may vary from a simple assertion that Cecil owes her $500,000, to a second-by-second narration of the accident, closely describing the scene and the conduct of each party, followed by a gruesome recital of Aikin's medical treatment and her prognosis for recovery. No procedural system insists upon either of these extremes, but systems do vary greatly in the detail required depending on the purposes that the pleadings are expected to serve. Three objectives are particularly relevant, and to the extent that a procedural system regards one rather than another as crucial, we may expect to find differing amounts of detail required.

First, the system may desire the pleadings to furnish a basis for identifying and separating the legal and factual contentions involved so that the legal issues—and hopefully through them the entire case—may be disposed of at an early stage. Thus, suppose that Cecil's liability for Beasley's driving depends upon the degree of independence with which Beasley was working at the time of the accident. A dispute on this issue might exist on either or both of two elements. The parties might disagree as to what Beasley's duties were, and they might disagree as to whether those duties put Beasley so much under the control of Cecil that the law will impose liability on Cecil for Beasley's actions. The first disagreement would be a question of fact, and there may be no alternative to trying the suit and letting the finder of fact (usually the jury) decide the truth. But if there was agreement on that first element, a question of law may be presented by the second issue, which could be determined by the judge without a trial. The court can resolve such legal questions at the pleading stage only if Aikin's complaint sets forth what Beasley's job required him to do. That objective could not be accomplished if Aikin's complaint states only that "Beasley was driving the car on Cecil's business."

Second, the pleadings may be intended to establish in advance what a party proposes to prove at trial so that the opponent will know the factual contentions and prepare to meet them. If this objective is regarded as very important, it will not be enough for the complaint to state that Beasley was negligent or that Aikin suffered serious bodily injuries. It must be more specific and say that Beasley was speeding, or was not keeping a proper look-out, or had inadequate brakes, or describe some other act of negligence and say that Aikin suffered a concussion, or a broken neck, or fractures of three ribs, or other injuries.

Third, the pleadings may be intended to give each party only a general notice of the opponent's contentions, in which event the system would rely upon subsequent stages of the lawsuit to identify the legal and factual contentions of the parties and to enable each to prepare to meet the opponent's case. If notice is the goal, then in a suit involving a car accident, it would be sufficient for the pleading to state the date and place of the incident; to describe the incident generally (for example, "defendant negligently drove a car into plaintiff"); and, to allege injury and a demand for relief.

It seems that each of the first two objectives is desirable. It is a waste of everybody's time to try lawsuits when the underlying legal claim is inadequate to support a judgment, and it is only fair that a person called upon to defend a judicial proceeding should know what defendant is alleged to have done. But to achieve the first objective fully may require pleading after pleading in order to expose and sharpen the issues; if detail is insisted upon, a long time may be consumed in producing it. Moreover, a single pleading oversight may eliminate a contention necessary to one party's case that easily could have been proven, but that will be held to have been waived. To achieve the second objective through the pleadings will mean that the parties must take rigid positions as to their factual contentions at the very beginning of the case when they may not know what they will learn by the time trial begins. It also assumes that plaintiff knows most if not all of the important facts pertinent to the claim at the time of filing the complaint, which is not always the case or even possible. Either the first or second objective, if fully pursued, requires that the parties adhere to the positions taken in the pleadings. They could not be permitted to introduce evidence in conflict with the pleadings or to change them. To the extent that variances between pleading and proof or amendments to the pleadings are permitted, the objectives will be lost. The court frequently will find itself forced either to depart from these objectives or to tolerate lawsuits turning on the skill of the lawyers rather than on the merits of the controversy.

The third objective, insofar as it allows the parties to use the later stages of the lawsuit to identify and flesh out the issues in the case, avoids the problems created by trying to decide the case based only on the pleadings. However, simple notice pleading potentially may be used to harass defendant when plaintiff has no real claim. More often, though, plaintiff will use notice pleading to subject defendant to pretrial discovery (discussed more fully below), and, in the process, to reveal information so that plaintiff can determine or confirm whether a bona fide claim actually exists. Lawyers often refer to such use of the pleadings as a "fishing expedition" or as a "springboard into litigation." However, if defendant controls access to the information that plaintiff needs to establish the claim, discovery may be essential for a meritorious complaint to be drafted and to avoid dismissal. One way that courts have dealt with these problems is to impose appropriate sanctions on parties and lawyers who bring baseless claims.

4. THE RESPONSE

Following the service of Aikin's complaint, Cecil must respond. He may challenge the complaint by a *motion to dismiss*. This motion may challenge the court's jurisdiction over the subject matter or Cecil's person, the service of process, or venue. It also may be a *motion to dismiss for failure to state a claim or cause of action* (the older term for this motion is a demurrer). For the purpose of this motion, the facts alleged in the complaint are accepted as true, and the court considers whether, on this assumption, plaintiff has shown that she is entitled to legal relief.

There are three general situations in which such a motion might be granted. First, the complaint may clearly show that the injury is one for which the law furnishes no redress; for example, when plaintiff simply alleges that "defendant has made faces at me." Second, plaintiff may have failed to include an allegation necessary to a part of the case; for example, Aikin might have alleged the accident, her injuries, and Beasley's negligence, but have forgotten to allege that Beasley was Cecil's servant. Third, the complaint may be so general or confusing that the court finds that it does not give adequate notice of what plaintiff's claim is (for example, a complaint in which Aikin merely alleged, "Cecil injured me and owes me $500,000," although complaints far more specific have been dismissed on this ground). The extent to which motions to dismiss will be granted on the second and third grounds will vary with the degree of detail that the particular system requires of its pleadings. A court generally has power to allow plaintiff an opportunity to amend the pleading to cure certain kinds of defects.

If the motion to dismiss is denied, or if none is made, Cecil must file an *answer*. In this pleading, he must admit or deny Aikin's factual allegations in the complaint. Moreover, if Cecil wishes to rely on certain legal contentions called *affirmative defenses*, he must plead them in the answer. Thus, if he wishes to contend that Aikin was negligent in the manner in which she tried to cross the street and that this negligence was also a cause of the accident, he must in many states plead this in the answer; if the answer only denied the allegations in Aikin's complaint, Cecil may not advance at trial the contention that Aikin's negligence caused the accident.

There may be further pleadings, particularly a *reply* by Aikin. But the tendency today is to close the pleadings after the answer, and if Cecil has raised new matters in his answer, they automatically are taken as denied by Aikin. There is one major exception: if Cecil has a claim against Aikin, particularly one that arises out of the same occurrence being sued upon by Aikin, Cecil may plead this claim as a *counterclaim* as part of the answer. This is in essence a complaint by Cecil, and Aikin will have to respond to it just as Cecil had to respond to the original complaint.

The original action between Aikin and Cecil may expand in terms of the number of parties, and this frequently will occur at the pleading stage. For example, although Aikin decided not to sue Beasley, Cecil might *implead* Beasley, asking that Beasley be held liable to him for whatever amount he may be found liable to Aikin, since his liability depends upon Beasley having been at fault. Cecil will decide whether to do this in light of a number of practical concerns, including the effect Beasley's presence will have on the jury in Aiken's suit against Cecil.

5. OBTAINING INFORMATION PRIOR TO TRIAL

Pretrial discovery is the procedure currently designed to allow the parties to exchange information about their claims and defenses and to prepare for trial. At earlier periods in history, the pleadings served this purpose. Currently, the federal system requires the parties, without a court order or a request from the opponent, to exchange certain types of information. The parties also then may initiate requests for information from the opponent and, in some situations, from persons who are not parties to the litigation. One method for obtaining information is to take *depositions* of parties and witnesses. In this procedure, the person whose deposition is to be taken is questioned by lawyers for each side through direct and cross-examination; the *deponent's* statements are taken down and transcribed. This device is useful for finding information that is relevant to the case, including unearthing leads as to other witnesses or documents; it also is useful for laying a basis for impeaching a witness who attempts to change his or her story at trial. The two parties almost certainly will want depositions taken of each other, as well as of Beasley; the depositions of Aikin and Cecil will be particularly important because they are treated as admissions and can be used by their adversaries as evidence at trial. In some circumstances, even the deposition of a nonparty witness who will be unavailable at trial may be used in place of live testimony.

Another device especially adapted to probing the content of an opponent's case is the written *interrogatory*, which usually may be addressed only to a party to the suit. (The availability of interrogatories may be one reason Aikin might wish to join Beasley as a defendant with Cecil or Cecil might wish to implead Beasley.) These interrogatories are answered by the party, presumably with counsel's aid, and the answers will not be as spontaneous as they would be in a deposition; on the other hand, interrogatories will require Cecil to supply some information that he does not carry in his head but can obtain, and may be even more valuable than the deposition in finding out what he will try to prove. Thus, information regarding Beasley's employment that Cecil cannot be expected to remember may best be exposed in this way.

Other discovery devices include *requests for production of documents*, such as the service record of Cecil's automobile, and *requests for admissions*, which will remove uncontested issues from the case. A particularly useful device for Cecil will be a court order directing Aikin to submit to a *physical examination* by a physician of Cecil's choice to determine the real extent of Aikin's alleged injuries.

The availability of discovery enables the parties to prepare for trial better than the pleadings ever did. Moreover, if a legal system permits broad discovery, the role of the pleadings will change. In particular, it may be senseless to make parties take rigid positions with respect to the issues at the very beginning of the lawsuit before they have had the chance to utilize these very useful devices for obtaining information. In addition, the availability of discovery does much to make summary judgment, which is discussed below, a viable and fair procedure, since it enables a party to ascertain those issues on which the opposing party has no evidence, while giving the opponent a chance to develop such evidence. On the other hand, if the costs of discovery are excessive, a defendant may be motivated to settle a lawsuit that satisfies a weak pleading standard yet would lack sufficient proof to prevail at trial.

6. SUMMARY JUDGMENT

One of the basic difficulties with attempting to resolve cases at the pleading stage is that the allegations of the parties must be accepted as true for the purpose of ruling on a motion to dismiss. Thus, if plaintiff tells a plausible story in the complaint, the court cannot dismiss the action even though it does not believe the allegations or think that plaintiff will be able to prove the tale. The pleading stage is not the time to resolve questions of fact.

However, in some cases it will be possible to provide additional material to show that an apparently decisive issue is spurious and that the case may therefore be decided without a trial. This is done by a motion for *summary judgment*. This motion can be supported by demonstrating that the crucial issue will have to be resolved in the movant's favor, because the opposing party will be unable to produce sufficient admissible evidence to create a genuine dispute regarding that issue. For example, suppose that it is Cecil's position that prior to the accident he had fired Beasley, but that Beasley had secretly acquired keys to Cecil's automobile and taken the car without permission shortly before the accident. On the face of the pleadings, we have only an allegation that Beasley was Cecil's employee and a denial of that allegation; thus, the pleadings seem to present a question of credibility that cannot be resolved at this stage. Cecil now moves for summary judgment, alleging that this issue is not a genuine one. He accompanies his motion with affidavits of his own and two other witnesses that he had fired Beasley; a deposition of the garage attendant indicating that he had been instructed not to allow Beasley to have the car and that it was taken without Cecil's knowledge; and a deposition of Beasley to the effect that he had been fired, but wanted to use the car once more for his own purposes. It is now incumbent upon Aikin to show that the issue is genuine; Aikin cannot rely simply upon her own assertion that all this is not so; after all, she has no personal knowledge of the facts. Aikin must convince the court that she can present admissible evidence at trial that Beasley still was acting as Cecil's employee in driving the car at the time of the accident. If Aikin fails to do so, summary judgment will be entered against her.

It should be noted that in ruling on a summary judgment motion, the judge does not decide which party is telling the truth. If Aikin presents an affidavit of a witness who claims to have been present when Cecil allegedly fired Beasley, and says that Cecil told Beasley that this was only a subterfuge and that he wanted him to continue to work for him but to pretend to steal the car, summary judgment will not be appropriate even though the judge is firmly convinced that Aikin's affiant is lying.

7. SETTING THE CASE FOR TRIAL

After discovery is completed, and if the case has not been terminated by dismissal, summary judgment, or settlement, it must be set for *trial*. Most cases already will have been disposed of prior to trial. If Aikin's lawsuit has not yet been resolved, typically either party may file a note of issue, at which time the case will be given a number and placed on a *trial calendar*. These calendars have become extremely long in many courts, and the case may have to wait a year, three years, or more before it is called for trial, especially if a jury trial has been requested.

8. THE JURY AND ITS SELECTION

In most actions for damages, the parties have a right to have the facts tried by a jury. This right is assured in the federal courts by the Seventh Amendment to the United States Constitution, and it is protected in the courts of most states by similar state constitutional provisions. If there is a right to a trial by jury, either party may assert it, but if neither wishes to do so, a judge will try the facts as well as the law. Largely for historical reasons growing out of a division of authority in the English court structure, there are many civil actions in which neither party has a right to a jury trial; these include most cases in which plaintiff wants an order directing or prohibiting specific action by defendant rather than a judgment for damages—a so-called equitable remedy.

If a jury has been demanded, the first order of business at trial will be to impanel the jurors. A large number of people, selected in an impartial manner from various lists, tax rolls, or street directories, will have been ordered to report to the courthouse for jury duty at a given term of court. The prospective jurors will be questioned—usually by the judge but sometimes by the lawyers—as to their possible biases. If one of the persons called has prior knowledge of the case or is a personal friend of one of the parties, he or she probably will be successfully challenged for cause and excused. But suppose Aikin is an architect and her lawyer finds that one of the jury panel has recently constructed a house and believes that he was greatly overcharged for its design and construction; this likely will not be enough to persuade the judge to excuse him. However, fearing the juror might be prejudiced against her client, Aikin's lawyer probably will exercise one of the small number of peremptory challenges a party is allowed for which no reason need be given. Ultimately, a panel of between six and 12 hopefully unbiased jurors will be selected.

9. THE TRIAL

After the jurors have been sworn, plaintiff's lawyer will make an *opening statement*, describing for the jury what the case is about, what contentions will be made, and how plaintiff plans to prove them. Defendant's lawyer also may make an opening statement at this time, but may reserve the right to do so until later when it is time to present defendant's case. Following the opening statement, plaintiff's lawyer calls her witnesses one by one. Each witness is first questioned by the lawyer who has called that witness—this is the *direct examination*; then the lawyer for the other side has the opportunity to *cross-examine* the same witness; this may be followed by *re-direct* and *re-cross* examination, and even further stages. The judge maintains some control over the length and tenor of the examination, and in particular will see to it that the stages beyond cross-examination are not prolonged.

Just as the primary responsibility for introducing evidence is on the lawyers, so too is the responsibility for objecting to evidence that is thought to be inadmissible under the rules of evidence. Suppose that Aikin's lawyer asks: "What happened while you were lying on the ground after the accident?" To which Aikin replies: "The driver of the car came over and said that he had been going too fast and he was sorry." Aikin's answer is objectionable because it contains hearsay evidence; that is, it repeats what someone else has said for the purpose of proving the truth of what was said. It is up to Cecil's counsel to object, and then the judge must rule on the objection. This particular issue is not an easy one, for Aikin's answer may well come within one of the exceptions to the rule excluding hearsay evidence. This kind of issue will recur continually throughout the trial and the judge must be prepared to make instantaneous rulings if the trial is to proceed with dispatch. Evidentiary rulings form a major source of the errors raised on appeal, but at the same time appellate courts are very reluctant to disturb the trial judge's ruling on the point. If the judge rules that Aikin's answer is inadmissible, the judge will instruct the jury to disregard the testimony. Can a juror who has heard such an important confession totally put it to the side?

Documents, pictures, and other tangible items may be put into evidence, but unless their admissibility has been stipulated to in advance, they will be introduced through witnesses. For example, if Aikin's lawyer has had pictures taken of the accident scene and wishes to get them to the jury, she will call the photographer as a witness, have him testify that he took pictures of the scene, and then show them to the photographer who will identify them as the pictures he took. At this point, they may be formally introduced into evidence.

When plaintiff's lawyer has called all of her witnesses and their examinations are over, plaintiff will *rest*. At this point, defendant's lawyer may ask for a *directed verdict* (in federal practice now called a judgment as a matter of law) for defendant on the ground that plaintiff has not established a prima facie case. The thrust of the motion is that plaintiff has not introduced enough evidence to permit the jury to find in plaintiff's favor. If the motion is denied, defendant may rest and choose to rely on the jury's agreeing with him, but in almost all cases he will proceed to present witnesses of his own, and these witnesses will be exposed to the same process of direct and cross-examination. When defendant has rested, plaintiff may present additional evidence to meet any new matter raised by defendant's witnesses. In turn, defendant, after plaintiff rests, may meet any new matter presented by plaintiff. This procedure will continue until both parties rest. Again, the trial judge will maintain considerable control to prevent the protraction of these latter stages.

When both parties have rested, either or both may move for a directed verdict, asking the trial judge to rule that under the evidence presented, viewed most favorably to the nonmoving party, there is no basis for a reasonable jury to find for that party with respect to that issue. If these motions are denied, the case must be submitted to the jury.

10. SUBMITTING THE CASE TO THE JURY

At this stage the judge and the lawyers will confer out of the jury's hearing with regard to the content of the judge's *instructions* or *charge* to the jury. Each lawyer may submit proposed instructions, which the trial judge will grant or deny, but the judge is under a duty to charge the jury on the basic aspects of the case in any event. If a party's lawyer has neither requested a particular instruction nor objected to the judge's charge, a later argument that the charge was erroneous generally will not be upheld on appeal.

Ordinarily, the lawyers will make their final arguments to the jury before the judge delivers the charge. The lawyers will review the evidence from their own points of view, and may suggest how the jury should weigh certain items and resolve specific issues, but it is improper for the lawyers to discuss a matter that has been excluded or never has been introduced. In other words, they are arguing, not testifying.

In the instructions the judge will summarize the facts and issues, tell the jury about the substantive law to be applied on each issue, give general information on determining the credibility of witnesses, and state who has the *burden of persuasion* on each issue of fact. The burden of persuasion in a civil case ordinarily requires that one party prove its contention on a given issue by a preponderance of the evidence. On most issues, Aikin will carry this burden, but on an affirmative defense such as contributory negligence, the burden probably will be on Cecil. The burden means that if a juror is unable to resolve an issue, then a finding on that issue should be made against the party who has the burden. In the federal courts and in some states, the judge may comment on the evidence, as it is clear that the judge's opinions are not binding on the jurors. However, judicial comment is rare, and in many states it is not permitted at all.

Following the charge, the jury retires to reach its decision, called a *verdict*. The verdict will be of a type chosen by the judge. There are three types, of which by far the most common is the *general verdict*. This verdict permits the jurors to determine the facts and apply the law on which they have been charged to those facts; it is simple in form in that only the conclusion as to who prevails, and the amount of damages, if that party is a claimant, is stated. A second type is the *general verdict with interrogatories*, which combines the form of the general verdict with several key questions that are designed to test the jury's understanding of the issues. Suppose that the accident occurred five miles away from Beasley's appointed route. Aikin's evidence is that Beasley detoured to have the vehicle's brakes fixed; Cecil's is that Beasley was going to visit his friend. The judge might charge the jury that in the former event, but not in the latter, Beasley was acting within the scope of his employment and Cecil would be liable for his negligence. The judge might direct the jury, in addition to rendering a verdict for Aikin or for Cecil, to answer the question, "Why did Beasley depart from his route?" If the general verdict was for Aikin, but the jury's answer was that Beasley was driving to his friend's home, the judge would order judgment for Cecil, for if the answer is inconsistent with the verdict, the answer controls. The third type of verdict is the *special verdict*, in which all of the factual issues in the case are submitted to the jury as questions without instructions as to their legal effect; the judge applies the law to the jury's answers and determines which party prevails.

Traditionally, only a unanimous jury verdict has been effective. However, in many states, and by consent of the parties in the federal courts, a nonunanimous verdict by the jurors may stand in a civil action. If the minimum number of jurors required for a verdict cannot reach agreement, the jury is said to be hung, and a new trial before a different jury is necessary.

11. POST-TRIAL MOTIONS

After the jury has returned its verdict, judgment will be entered thereon, but the losing party will have an opportunity to make certain post-trial motions. There may be a motion for a *judgment notwithstanding the verdict* (commonly called a motion for a *judgment n.o.v.*, from the Latin *non obstante veredicto,* but in federal practice now called a renewed motion for judgment as a matter of law). This motion raises the same question as a motion for a directed verdict. The losing party also may move for a *new trial*; the grounds for this motion are many, and may include assertions that the judge erred in admitting (or excluding) certain evidence, that the charge was defective, that attorneys, parties, or jurors have been guilty of misconduct, that the damages awarded are excessive, or that the jury's verdict is against the clear weight of the evidence. Should these motions fail, it sometimes is possible to reopen a judgment, even several months after the trial, on the grounds of clerical mistake, newly discovered evidence, or fraud, but the occasions on which such relief is granted are very rare.

12. THE JUDGMENT AND ITS ENFORCEMENT

The *judgment* is the final determination of the lawsuit, absent an appeal. Judgment may be rendered by default when defendant does not appear; or following the granting of a demurrer, a motion to dismiss, or a motion for summary judgment; or based on a settlement agreement of the parties; or upon the jury's verdict; or the findings of fact and conclusions of law of the trial judge in a non-jury case. The judgment may be in the form of an award of money to plaintiff, a declaration of rights between the parties, specific recovery of property, or an order requiring or prohibiting some future activity. When defendant has prevailed, the judgment generally will not be "for" anything or order anything; it simply will provide that plaintiff takes nothing by her complaint.

In most cases, a judgment for plaintiff will not order defendant to do anything; typically it will simply state that plaintiff shall recover a sum of money from defendant. This does not necessarily mean that defendant will pay. It is up to plaintiff to collect the money. Execution is the common method of forcing the losing party to satisfy a money judgment, if the loser does not do so voluntarily. A *writ of execution* is issued by the court commanding an officer—usually the sheriff—to seize property of the losing party and, if necessary, to sell it publicly and use the proceeds to satisfy plaintiff's judgment.

When plaintiff's recovery takes the form of an *injunction* requiring defendant to do something or to stop doing something, the judgment (in this context typically called a *decree*) is said to operate against defendant's person (in personam). Its sanction is direct, and if defendant fails to obey, he may be held in *contempt of court* and punished by fine or imprisonment.

Costs provided by statute and certain out-of-pocket disbursements are awarded to the prevailing party and included in the judgment. Usually, these costs are nominal in relation to the total expense of litigation and include only such items as the clerk's fee and witnesses' mileage. As previously mentioned, in the United States, attorney's fees are not recoverable as costs in ordinary litigation.

13. APPEAL

Every judicial system in the United States provides for review of a trial court's decisions by an appellate court. Generally a party has the right to appeal any judgment to at least one higher court. When the system contains two levels of appellate courts, appeal usually lies initially to one of the intermediate courts, and review at the highest level is only at the discretion of that court except in certain classes of cases. Under current practice in the federal courts, district court decisions are reviewed by the appropriate court of appeals, but review in the Supreme Court generally is discretionary and sought by a *petition for a writ of certiorari.* (In a few cases, a direct appeal lies from the district court to the Supreme Court.) The discretion of a higher-level appellate court generally is exercised so that only cases with legal issues of broad importance are taken.

The *record* on appeal will contain the pleadings, at least a portion of the *transcript of the trial* (the court reporter's verbatim record of the trial), and the orders and rulings relevant to the appeal. The parties present their contentions to the appellate court by *written briefs.* The appellate court will often hear *oral argument* as well, although many courts have increased their frequency of deciding appeals without oral argument—especially in certain categories of cases. The appellate court may review any ruling of law by the trial judge, although frequently it will limit the scope of its review by holding that particular matters were within the trial judge's discretion or that the error, if any, was not prejudicial—that is, it did not substantially affect the outcome of the case. There are constitutional limits to the review of a jury's verdict, but even when these limits do not apply— for example, when the judge has tried the case without a jury—it is unusual for an appellate court to re-examine a question of fact because a cold record does not convey the nuances of what the trier observed, notably the demeanor of the witnesses.

The appellate court has the power to *affirm, reverse,* or *modify* the judgment of the trial court. If it reverses, it may order that a new judgment be entered or it may *remand* the case to the trial court for a new trial or other proceedings not inconsistent with its decision. The decision of an appellate court usually is accompanied by a written opinion, signed by one of a panel of judges hearing the appeal; there is always more than one judge deciding an appeal. Concurring and dissenting opinions also may be filed. The opinions of a court are designed to set forth the reasons for a decision and to furnish guidance to lower courts, lawyers, and the public.

Keep in mind an important distinction between the *reviewability* of a particular ruling of a trial judge and its *appealability*. For example, a trial judge's ruling excluding certain evidence at trial as hearsay is reviewable; that is, when the judgment is appealed, that ruling may be assigned as error and the appellate court will consider whether it was correct. But trial would become excessively protracted if an appeal could be taken from every ruling at the time it is made. Thus, appeals lie only from judgments and from certain orders made in the course of litigation when immediate review is deemed so important that a delay in the action during appeal can be tolerated. Judicial systems differ in the extent to which interlocutory orders can be appealed. In the federal system, very little other than a final judgment can be taken to the Courts of Appeals; however, in some states, many kinds of interlocutory orders can be appealed even before a final judgment is entered.

A good example of the contrast between the two approaches can be seen by looking at the consequences of an order denying a motion to dismiss. Suppose that Cecil moves to dismiss Aikin's complaint on the ground that even on Aikin's view of the facts, Cecil is not responsible for the conduct of Beasley, and this motion is denied. In the federal courts, such an order would not be appealable since it does not terminate the lawsuit. Indeed, the disposition of the motion means that the action will continue. In some states, however, this question could be taken immediately to a higher court for a ruling, while the other stages of the litigation wait.

The question of which system is better is not easy to answer. One may argue in favor of the federal practice that everything should be done at one level before going to the next, that too much time is taken in waiting for appellate courts to decide these questions serially, and that no appeal may ever be necessary, since Cecil may prevail anyway. On the other hand, if the appellate court holds at this early stage that Aikin has no claim against Cecil, the time necessary for discovery and trial will be saved.

One point worth noting is that the resolution of the question of the appealability of interlocutory orders has an important bearing on the procedural developments within a given system. In the case of motions to dismiss, for example, if denials are not appealable, much of the law on this subject will be made in the trial courts. A trial judge who is in doubt may tend to deny such motions rather than to grant them, and the decision generally will not be disturbed. Although the ruling theoretically is reviewable after final judgment, by that time the significance of the ruling on the pleadings may have been displaced by more substantive questions, as well as by the development of a more robust evidentiary record through discovery and, perhaps, trial. When grants of motions to dismiss are immediately appealable, but denials are not, the appellate precedent will involve a skewed set of cases—those where the complaint was so weak that the trial judge believed dismissal was warranted.

Alternatively, if the denial is appealable, a tactical consideration is added and such motions will be resorted to more frequently, inasmuch as they will afford defendant an additional opportunity to delay trial and thus to wear down the opponent. With respect to other procedural rulings—as in the discovery area—the absence of an interlocutory appeal will strengthen the hand of the trial judge, who will, in fact if not in theory, exercise a wider range of discretion because fewer rulings will come before the appellate courts and when they do they will be enmeshed in a final judgment, making it easier to conclude that any error was not prejudicial.

14. THE CONCLUSIVENESS OF JUDGMENTS

Generally, a judgment becomes final after the appeal and whatever further proceedings may take place, or, if no appeal is taken, when the time for appeal expires. With very rare exceptions, the judgment cannot be [*once a judgment is decided, it is final*] challenged in another proceeding. It is res judicata, a thing decided, and now the matter is at rest. The concept of res judicata includes claim preclusion and issue preclusion, the latter traditionally known as collateral estoppel. Defining the scope and effect of this finality principle is one of the most complex tasks in the entire law of procedure.

C. A NOTE ON MOTION PRACTICE

Throughout the previous section, we frequently have used the term "motion," and for good reason. A motion is the procedural device by which a litigant asks a court for an order. For example, a request for an order to dismiss a complaint for failure to state a claim, a request for an order granting summary judgment, and a request for an order granting a new trial all are made formally to a court through a motion.

The usual practice is that a motion must be made in writing. Two [*word for word*] exceptions to this rule are when the court is recording a hearing verbatim or when a trial is taking place. A motion generally must state with particularity the reasons or grounds supporting the request and the relief sought. The written motion also must appear in a proper form, which typically is determined by local court rules.

The litigant must serve the motion on the opposing party. In addition, a notice of hearing regarding the motion, a brief or memorandum of law in support of the motion, a proposed order, and, if necessary, affidavits, generally accompany a motion, but not all courts require the movant to submit a proposed order and only certain motions require affidavits. Briefs usually have a maximum page limit.

All motions in federal court require the signature of the litigant's attorney or the litigant. The signature attests that the attorney or litigant has read the motion papers and that the motion has sufficient grounds and is made in good faith. Sanctions may be imposed if, for example, the papers are submitted for impermissible purposes or without a reasonable investigation into the supporting facts and law.

A party served with a motion may respond and usually must do so within a time period specified by the rules. A party also may move for an extension of time, either to make a cross-motion, to extend the time to respond to the motion, or both. In addition, making a motion may defer the next stage of litigation. Finally, making a particular motion may preserve other legal rights.

Motion practice involves the parties' strategic choices given the interrelationship among motions, their intended effects, their secondary effects, and their effects on the opposing party. A motion such as summary judgment usually is designed to win the lawsuit. A successful motion to exclude certain material from discovery may convince an adversary that information cannot be obtained that is needed to establish essential contentions and induce the party to end the lawsuit early without an unfavorable judgment. A motion to bring a third party into the lawsuit may help convince an adversary that the lawsuit will be more time consuming and costly than expected. A lawyer deciding to make a motion must consider carefully whether benefits will accrue to the movant and whether obstacles will be imposed on the adversary as a result of the motion.

Making a motion may have negative aspects. One of the drawbacks may be the time and expense of the motion, including drafting and serving multiple copies of papers, spending hours preparing the brief in support of the motion, and taking resources from other more fruitful pursuits. Repeated, unsuccessful motions will result in expense and delay that may reduce client satisfaction.

In addition, poor motion practice may leave the judge with the impression that the lawyer is sloppy, shoddy, and disorganized. Arguing motions at a hearing that the attorneys could have settled without a hearing may convince the judge that the movant is contentious by nature. In short, an unwise making of a motion may do more harm in the long run than not making the motion at all, even if the motion is granted.

Motion practice is a central part of a litigator's arsenal. When a particular motion can be made, how it must be made, and what its effect will be are questions that can be answered by studying the applicable procedural rules. Whether a motion should be made and how it can affect the course of the lawsuit are matters of judgment and experience.

D. A NOTE ON REMEDIES

The remedies that may be obtained in a modern civil action should be viewed principally as a part of the substantive law: contract law, tort law, commercial law, labor law, and so forth. Yet, because the goal of a lawsuit is the remedy and the means of securing it are procedural, there necessarily is a close relationship between them. For example, the range of available remedies in a case may be limited by the manner in which plaintiff has pleaded, and certain procedural aspects of the case, such as whether it is tried to a judge or a jury, may be determined by the remedy that is being sought; again, whether a person may be joined as a party may depend on the relief that is being sought, and conversely certain remedies may be available only if all interested persons can be joined.

Without question, the most important relationship between procedure and remedies grows out of the existence in English law of two great branches of jurisprudence administered in different courts: common law and equity; the latter was envisioned as complementary to the former. There are two special facts about equity that are important for our purpose. First, already alluded to, courts of equity had no jury. Second, the injunction was a creature of equity and remained in its sole custody when the two branches remained distinct.

From this heritage, two consequences of immense significance for the law of procedure result. One, whether a party has a right to a trial by jury in the federal courts often has been determined by inquiring whether the matter in question was a subject of a legal or equitable cognizance in 1791—the date of the adoption of the Seventh Amendment. To some extent, this question depends on the remedy sought, since the availability of injunctive relief was one form of equity's jurisdiction. Two, just as equity was regarded as a special legal system to be resorted to only when the common law was inadequate, so too the injunction and most forms of specific relief are regarded as exceptional, to be ordered only when the ordinary remedy of money damages is inadequate.

The most important types of relief that a court may award in a civil action fall into three categories: *declarative*, *specific*, and *damages*. Declaratory relief encompasses a court's defining the rights and duties of the parties in a particular legal context. Suppose a company believes that an agreement it has entered into is not a valid contract and that it is under no obligation to perform it. However, the company is reluctant to act on this belief in the face of another's insistence that it perform because if the contract is enforceable, the damages for the nonperformance will be great. In these circumstances, the company may seek a declaratory judgment asking the court to determine whether it is under a duty to perform. This type of relief is not as common as those discussed below and its availability often is limited by statute. In numerous situations, however, it is invaluable.

Specific relief generally consists of an order directing conduct. Defendant may be commanded to return a jewel taken from plaintiff, to stop operating a pig farm in a residential neighborhood, to deliver a car that was contracted for sale, or to refrain from opening a barbershop next door to a person to whom defendant sold a former barbershop. An order for such relief is often called an injunction. Specific relief is not possible in all cases. For example, no kind of injunction will compensate or cure Aikin in our hypothetical case; Beasley cannot retroactively be ordered not to run into her. On the other hand, a person who has contracted to sell a house or a piece of land ordinarily will be ordered to perform the agreement, for the law regards each bit of real property as unique. But beyond the real property context, specific relief will be given only if damages would be inadequate. Thus, if you order a special garment (for example, a tuxedo or an evening dress) from a tailor who fails to perform the promise to deliver it, it is unlikely that any remedy except damages will be forthcoming. The reasons for this are not purely historical. There is a burden on the court in ordering and supervising the performance of a decree of specific performance that is avoided if a simple judgment for money damages is entered. Moreover, specific performance might impose a hardship or at least an indignity on defendant not commensurate with the advantage to be gained by receiving this tailor's garment rather than one from another tailor. But it may well be asked whether our courts today are not being too reluctant to grant the form of relief that will most adequately redress plaintiff's grievance.

A damages remedy calls for a judgment that defendant pay plaintiff a certain sum of money. Keep in mind that when we speak of the court ordering that compensation be paid, we are speaking of one form of relief, but the amount of damages can be computed in accordance with many measures. In the action against the tailor, for example, if you had struck a good bargain, you might claim the difference between the price you agreed to pay and the value the special garment would have had if the tailor had performed the promise; or you might claim only the money you had advanced as a down payment; or you might claim the amount you paid for opera tickets you were unable to use without the special garment. The difference in amount that could be collected under these theories might be very substantial. In some circumstances, the law authorizes awards of punitive damages, which are designed to punish defendants or to deter more forcefully certain kinds of behavior.

There is a final point to be considered in evaluating the adequacy of any judicial remedy: How much of it will be consumed by the cost of litigation? As we have noted, the costs awarded to a successful plaintiff will not, in most cases, reimburse the fees incurred for legal representation or other substantial costs of a suit, such as the expense of investigation or the fees of expert witnesses. It is not possible to give any meaningful figure for the cost of an average trial, but it can be assumed that as the stakes rise the fees will be correspondingly higher.

In most personal injury and in many other types of damage actions, plaintiff's cost of recovery must be computed differently because the attorney will be litigating the case under a contingent-fee agreement; that is, the attorney will receive a percentage—one-third is common—of plaintiff's judgment. Thus, in a real sense, an adequate legal remedy is one that not simply compensates plaintiff for a loss but rather one that covers both the loss and the cost of recovering it. This distinction has not been ignored by many triers of fact. Indeed, it has been suggested that if damages for pain and suffering ever are abolished, defendants should be required explicitly to pay the legal fees of a plaintiff who prevails.

E. A NOTE ON PROCEDURAL RULES IN THE FEDERAL AND STATE COURTS

Federal and state rules of procedure derive from constitutional authority, statutes, and judicial decisions. The Federal Rules of Civil Procedure owe their genesis to the Rules Enabling Act, 28 U.S.C. § 2072, enacted in 1934, which vests power in the Supreme Court to promulgate rules of procedure for the district courts and to combine law and equity into one civil action. In 1935, the Supreme Court appointed an Advisory Committee composed of lawyers, judges, and law professors to draft federal procedural rules. The Advisory Committee proposed rules that the Court approved in 1937, and the Federal Rules became effective on September 16, 1938. See Burbank, *The Rules Enabling Act of* 1934, 130 U.Pa.L.Rev. 1015 (1982). The Federal Rules have undergone amendment since 1938, but certain core features persist.

An important hallmark of the Federal Rules is their applicability to all causes of action no matter how complex or simple—a feature referred to as "transsubstantivity." Some commentators question whether it is practical or even desirable to use the same procedural rules in lawsuits as different as a large antitrust action is from a simple contract dispute. See Cover, *For James Wm. Moore: Some Reflections on a Reading of the Rules*, 84 Yale L.J. 718, 732, 739–40 (1975). On the other hand, transsubstantivity reflects a principle of equality that is critical to procedural justice.

The Federal Rules generally do not bind state judicial systems. States have their own processes for adopting procedural rules, with one of two models typically predominating within a state. In one model, the state constitution grants exclusive rulemaking power to the state judiciary; in the other, state courts exercise inherent rulemaking authority but share this authority with the legislature. For a collection of state constitutional provisions as they bear on state rulemaking, see Main, *Reconsidering Procedural Conformity Statutes*, 35 W.St.U.L.Rev. 75, 84–85 (2007).

Currently no state's procedures completely track those of the federal, although some come close. However, the divergence between state and federal procedural rules appears to be growing, largely because state systems that earlier had modeled their procedures on those of the federal system are declining to change their rules when the Federal Rules are amended. See Subrin & Main, *Braking the Rules: Why State Courts Should Not Replicate Amendments to the Federal Rules of Civil Procedure*, 67 Case W.Res.L.Rev. 501 (2016).

CHAPTER 2

JURISDICTION OVER THE PARTIES
OR THEIR PROPERTY

■ ■ ■

This chapter explores the doctrine of personal jurisdiction: the power of a court to enter a judgment against a person or a thing. A court can assert personal jurisdiction only if the exercise of power is authorized by statute and is consistent with the Due Process Clause of the federal Constitution. The earliest recognized basis for a court's assertion of such power was the presence of defendant within the territorial boundaries of the state in which the tribunal sat. This rationale did not permit the state to exercise power over a defendant who caused injury within its borders but was not physically present within the territory when plaintiff sought to serve process on the party. As the national economy grew and technology fostered the movement of goods and people across state boundaries, new justifications developed for when a court could exercise power over a defendant who was out-of-state at the time of service but earlier had caused harm in the forum state. The law in this area continues to develop and today faces significant conceptual pressures from the "borderless" worlds of the global and virtual economy. The resulting doctrine is both significant and complex—what one federal judge, borrowing from Winston Churchill, called "a riddle wrapped in a mystery inside an enigma." Donatelli v. National Hockey League, 893 F.2d 459, 462 (1st Cir. 1990).

A. THE TRADITIONAL BASES FOR JURISDICTION

PENNOYER V. NEFF
Supreme Court of the United States, 1877.
95 U.S. (5 Otto) 714, 24 L.Ed. 565.

Error to the Circuit Court of the United States for the District of Oregon.

JUSTICE FIELD delivered the opinion of the court.

This is an action to recover the possession of a tract of land, of the alleged value of $15,000, situated in the State of Oregon. The plaintiff asserts title to the premises by a patent of the United States issued to him in [March] 1866, under the Act of Congress of September 27th, 1850, 9 Stat. at L., 496, usually known as the Donation Law of Oregon. The defendant claims to have acquired the premises under a sheriff's deed, made upon a sale of the property on execution issued upon a judgment recovered against the plaintiff in one of the circuit courts of the State. The case turns upon the validity of this judgment.

It appears from the record that the judgment was rendered in February, 1866, in favor of J.H. Mitchell, for less than $300, including costs, in an action brought by him upon a demand for services as an attorney; that, at the time the action was commenced and the judgment rendered, the defendant therein, the plaintiff here, was a non-resident of the State; that he was not personally served with process, and did not appear therein; and that the judgment was entered upon his default in not answering the complaint, upon a constructive service of summons by publication.

The Code of Oregon provides for such service when an action is brought against a non-resident and absent defendant, who has property within the State. It also provides, where the action is for the recovery of money or damages, for the attachment of the property of the non-resident. And it also declares that no natural person is subject to the jurisdiction of a court of the State, "unless he appear in the court, or be found within the State, or be a resident thereof, or have property therein; and in the last case, only to the extent of such property at the time the jurisdiction attached." Construing this latter provision to mean that, in an action for money or damages where a defendant does not appear in the court, and is not found within the State, and is not a resident thereof, but has property therein, the jurisdiction of the court extends only over such property, the declaration expresses a principle of general, if not universal, law. The authority of every tribunal is necessarily restricted by the territorial limits of the State in which it is established. Any attempt to exercise authority beyond those limits would be deemed in every other forum, as has been said by this court, an illegitimate assumption of power, and be resisted as mere abuse. * * * In the case against the plaintiff, the property here in controversy sold under the judgment rendered was not attached, nor in any way brought under the jurisdiction of the court. Its first connection with the case was caused by a levy of the execution. It was not, therefore, disposed of pursuant to any adjudication, but only in enforcement of a personal judgment, having no relation to the property, rendered against a non-resident without service of process upon him in the action, or his appearance therein. The court below did not consider that an attachment of the property was essential to its jurisdiction or to the validity of the sale, but held that the judgment was invalid from defects in the affidavit upon which the order of publication was obtained, and in the affidavit by which the publication was proved.

There is some difference of opinion among the members of this court as to the rulings upon these alleged defects. The majority are of opinion that, inasmuch as the statute requires, for an order of publication, that certain facts shall appear by affidavit *to the satisfaction of the court or judge,* defects in such affidavit can only be taken advantage of on appeal, or by some other direct proceeding, and cannot be urged to impeach the judgment collaterally. The majority of the court are also of opinion that the provision of the statute requiring proof of the publication in a newspaper to be made by the "affidavit of the printer, or his foreman, or his principal clerk," is satisfied when the affidavit is made by the editor of the paper. The term "printer," in their judgment, is there used not to indicate the person who sets up the type—he does not usually have a foreman or clerks—it is rather used as synonymous with publisher. * * *

If, therefore, we were confined to the rulings of the court below upon the defects in the affidavits mentioned, we should be unable to uphold its decision. But it was also contended in that court, and is insisted upon here, that the judgment in the State Court against the plaintiff was void for want of personal service of process on him, or of his appearance in the action in which it was rendered, and that the premises in controversy could not be subjected to the payment of the demand of a resident creditor except by a proceeding *in rem;* that is, by a direct proceeding against the property for that purpose. If these positions are sound, the ruling of the Circuit Court as to the invalidity of that judgment must be sustained, notwithstanding our dissent from the reasons upon which it was made. And that they are sound would seem to follow from two well established principles of public law respecting the jurisdiction of an independent State over persons and property. The several States of the Union are not, it is true, in every respect independent, many of the rights and powers which originally belonged to them being now vested in the government created by the Constitution. But, except as restrained and limited by that instrument, they possess and exercise the authority of independent States, and the principles of public law to which we have referred are applicable to them. One of these principles is, that every State possesses exclusive jurisdiction and sovereignty over persons and property within its territory. As a consequence, every State has the power to determine for itself the civil *status* and capacities of its inhabitants; to prescribe the subjects upon which they may contract, the forms and solemnities with which their contracts shall be executed, the rights and obligations arising from them, and the mode in which their validity shall be determined and their obligations enforced; and also to regulate the manner and conditions upon which property situated within such territory, both personal and real, may be acquired, enjoyed and transferred. The other principle of public law referred to follows from the one mentioned; that is, that no State can exercise direct jurisdiction and authority over persons or property without its territory. * * * The several States are of equal dignity and authority, and the independence of one implies the exclusion of power from all others. And so it is laid down by jurists, as an elementary principle, that the laws of one State have no operation outside of its territory, except so far as is allowed by comity; and that no tribunal established by it can extend its process beyond that territory so as to subject either persons or property to its decisions. * * *

But as contracts made in one State may be enforceable only in another State, and property may be held by non-residents, the exercise of the jurisdiction which every State is admitted to possess over persons and property within its own territory will often affect persons and property without it. To any influence exerted in this way by a State affecting persons resident or property situated elsewhere, no objection can be justly taken; whilst any direct exertion of authority upon them, in an attempt to give ex-territorial operation to its laws, or to enforce an ex-territorial jurisdiction by its tribunals, would be deemed an encroachment upon the independence of the State in which the persons are domiciled or the property is situated, and be resisted as usurpation.

Thus the State, through its tribunals, may compel persons domiciled within its limits to execute, in pursuance of their contracts respecting property elsewhere situated, instruments in such form and with such solemnities as to transfer the title, so far as such formalities can be complied with; and the exercise of this jurisdiction in no manner interferes with the supreme control over the property by the State within which it is situated. * * *

So the State, through its tribunals, may subject property situated within its limits owned by non-residents to the payment of the demand of its own citizens against them; and the exercise of this jurisdiction in no respect infringes upon the sovereignty of the State where the owners are domiciled. Every State owes protection to its own citizens; and, when non-residents deal with them, it is a legitimate and just exercise of authority to hold and appropriate any property owned by such non-residents to satisfy the claims of its citizens. It is in virtue of the State's jurisdiction over the property of the non-resident situated within its limits that its tribunals can inquire into that non-resident's obligations to its own citizens, and the inquiry can then be carried only to the extent necessary to control the disposition of the property. If the non-resident has no property in the State, there is nothing upon which the tribunals can adjudicate.

* * * If, without personal service, judgments *in personam,* obtained *ex parte* against non-residents and absent parties, upon mere publication of process, which, in the great majority of cases, would never be seen by the parties interested, could be upheld and enforced, they would be the constant instruments of fraud and oppression. Judgments for all sorts of claims upon contracts and for torts, real or pretended, would be thus obtained, under which property would be seized, when the evidence of the

transactions upon which they were founded, if they ever had any existence, had perished.

Substituted service by publication, or in any other authorized form, may be sufficient to inform parties of the object of proceedings taken where property is once brought under the control of the court by seizure or some equivalent act. The law assumes that property is always in the possession of its owner, in person or by agent; and it proceeds upon the theory that its seizure will inform him, not only that it is taken into the custody of the court, but that he must look to any proceedings authorized by law upon such seizure for its condemnation and sale. * * * In other words, such service may answer in all actions which are substantially proceedings *in rem*. But where the entire object of the action is to determine the personal rights and obligations of the defendants, that is, where the suit is merely *in personam*, constructive service in this form upon a non-resident is ineffectual for any purpose. Process from the tribunals of one State cannot run into another State, and summon parties there domiciled to leave its territory and respond to proceedings against them. Publication of process or notice within the State where the tribunal sits cannot create any greater obligation upon the non-resident to appear. Process sent to him out of the State, and process published within it, are equally unavailing in proceedings to establish his personal liability.

The want of authority of the tribunals of a State to adjudicate upon the obligations of non-residents, where they have no property within its limits, is not denied by the court below; but the position is assumed that, where they have property within the State, it is immaterial whether the property is in the first instance brought under the control of the court by attachment or some other equivalent act, and afterwards applied by its judgment to the satisfaction of demands against its owner; or such demands be first established in a personal action, and the property of the non-resident be afterwards seized and sold on execution. But the answer to this position has already been given in the statement, that the jurisdiction of the court to inquire into and determine his obligations at all is only incidental to its jurisdiction over the property. Its jurisdiction in that respect cannot be made to depend upon facts to be ascertained after it has tried the cause and rendered the judgment. If the judgment be previously void, it will not become valid by the subsequent discovery of property of the defendant, or by his subsequent acquisition of it. The judgment, if void when rendered, will always remain void; it cannot occupy the doubtful position of being valid if property be found, and void if there be none. Even if the position assumed were confined to cases where the non-resident defendant possessed property in the State at the commencement of the action, it would still make the validity of the proceedings and judgment depend upon the question whether, before the levy of the execution, the defendant had or had not disposed of the property. If, before the levy, the property should be sold, then, according to this position, the judgment would not be binding. This doctrine would introduce a new element of uncertainty in judicial proceedings. The contrary is the law; the validity of every judgment depends upon the jurisdiction of the court before it is rendered, not upon what may occur subsequently. * * *

The force and effect of judgments rendered against non-residents without personal service of process upon them, or their voluntary appearance, have been the subject of frequent consideration in the courts of the United States and of the several States, as attempts have been made to enforce such judgments in States other than those in which they were rendered, under the provision of the Constitution requiring that "Full faith and credit shall be given in each State to the public Acts, records and judicial proceedings of every other State;" and the Act of Congress providing for the mode of authenticating such Acts, records and proceedings, and declaring that, when thus authenticated, "They shall have such faith and credit given to them in every court within the United States as they have by law or usage in the courts of the State from which they are or shall be taken." In the earlier cases, it was supposed that the Act gave to all judgments the same effect in other States which they had by law in the State where rendered. But this view was afterwards qualified so as to make the Act applicable only when the court rendering the judgment had jurisdiction of the parties and of the subject-matter, and not to preclude an inquiry into the jurisdiction of the court in which the judgment was rendered, or the right of the State itself to exercise authority over the person or the subject-matter. * * *

Since the adoption of the 14th Amendment to the Federal Constitution, the validity of * * * judgments may be directly questioned, and their enforcement in the State resisted, on the ground that proceedings in a court of justice to determine the personal rights and obligations of parties over whom that court has no jurisdiction do not constitute due process of law. Whatever difficulty may be experienced in giving to those terms a definition which will embrace every permissible exertion of power affecting private rights, and exclude such as is forbidden, there can be no doubt of their meaning when applied to judicial proceedings. They then mean a course of legal proceedings according to those rules and principles which have been established in our systems of jurisprudence for the protection and enforcement of private rights. To give such proceedings any validity, there must be a tribunal competent by its constitution—that is, by the law of its creation—to pass upon the subject-matter of the suit; and, if that involves merely a determination of the personal liability of the defendant, he must be brought within its jurisdiction by service of process within the State, or his voluntary appearance.

Except in cases affecting the personal *status* of the plaintiff, and cases in which that mode of service may be considered to have been assented to in advance as hereinafter mentioned, the substituted service of process by publication allowed by the law of Oregon and by similar laws in other States, where actions are brought against non-residents, is effectual only where, in connection with process against the person for commencing the action, property in the State is brought under the control of the court, and subjected to its disposition by process adapted to that purpose, or where the judgment is sought as a means of reaching such property or affecting some interest therein; in other words, where the action is in the nature of a proceeding *in rem.* * * *

It is true that, in a strict sense, a proceeding *in rem* is one taken directly against property, and has for its object the disposition of the property, without reference to the title of individual claimants; but, in a larger and more general sense, the terms are applied to actions between parties, where the direct object is to reach and dispose of property owned by them, or of some interest therein. Such are cases commenced by attachment against the property of debtors, or instituted to partition real estate, foreclose a mortgage, or enforce a lien. So far as they affect property in the State, they are substantially proceedings *in rem* in the broader sense which we have mentioned.

* * *

It follows from the views expressed that the personal judgment recovered in the State Court of Oregon against the plaintiff herein, then a non-resident of the State, was without any validity, and did not authorize a sale of the property in controversy.

To prevent any misapplication of the views expressed in this opinion, it is proper to observe that we do not mean to assert, by anything we have said, that a State may not authorize proceedings to determine the *status* of one of its citizens towards a non-resident, which would be binding within the State, though made without service of process or personal notice to the non-resident. The jurisdiction which every State possesses to determine the civil *status* and capacities of all its inhabitants involves authority to prescribe the conditions on which proceedings affecting them may be commenced and carried on within its territory. The State, for example, has absolute right to prescribe the conditions upon which the marriage relation between its own citizens shall be created, and the causes for which it may be dissolved. One of the parties guilty of acts for which, by the law of the State, a dissolution may be granted, may have removed to a State where no dissolution is permitted. The complaining party would, therefore, fail if a divorce were sought in the State of the defendant; and if application could not be made to the tribunals of the complainant's domicile in such case, and proceedings be there instituted without personal service of process or personal notice to the offending party, the injured citizen would be without redress. * * *

Neither do we mean to assert that a State may not require a non-resident entering into a partnership or association within its limits, or making contracts enforceable there, to appoint an agent or representative in the State to receive service of process and notice in legal proceedings instituted with respect to such partnership, association or contracts, or to designate a place where such service may be made and notice given, and provide, upon their failure, to make such appointment or to designate such place that service may be made upon a public officer designated for that purpose, or in some other prescribed way, and that judgments rendered upon such service may not be binding upon the non-residents both within and without the State. * * * Nor do we doubt that a State, on creating corporations or other institutions for pecuniary or charitable purposes, may provide a mode in which their conduct may be investigated, their obligations enforced, or their charters revoked, which shall require other than personal service upon their officers or members. * * *

In the present case, there is no feature of this kind and, consequently, no consideration of what would be the effect of such legislation in enforcing the contract of a non-resident can arise. * * *

Judgment affirmed.

[The dissenting opinion of JUSTICE HUNT is omitted.]

NOTES AND QUESTIONS

1.   Justice Field's opinion in *Pennoyer* makes no mention of the unsavory characters and scandalous facts implicated in the dispute:

[The] story begins with a young man, Marcus Neff, heading across the country by covered wagon train, presumably to seek his fortune. Neff left Iowa in early 1848 * * * [and] was one of the earliest settlers to claim land under the Oregon Donation Act. * * *

Early in 1862 Neff made the unfortunate decision to consult a local Portland attorney, J.H. Mitchell. * * * Neff may have consulted Mitchell in an attempt to expedite the paperwork concerning his land patent. * * * "J.H. Mitchell" was actually the Oregon alias of one John Hipple. Hipple had been a teacher in Pennsylvania who, after being forced to marry the 15-year-old student whom he seduced, left teaching and took up law. * * * [I]n 1860 Hipple headed west taking with him four thousand dollars of client money and his then current paramour, a local school teacher. They made their way to California where Hipple abandoned the teacher * * * and moved on to Portland, Oregon. There, using the name John H. Mitchell, he quickly established himself as a successful lawyer, specializing in land litigation and railroad right-of-way cases. He also remarried without bothering to divorce his first wife. * * *

On November 3, 1865, Mitchell filed suit against Neff in Oregon state court [seeking payment for the legal services that had been rendered]. * * *

A default judgment * * * was entered against Neff on February 19, 1866. Although Mitchell had an immediate right to execute on the judgment, he waited until early June 1866 to seek a writ of execution, possibly waiting for the arrival of Neff's land patent. * * *

On August 7, 1866, the property was sold at a sheriff's auction * * *. Notably, the buyer was not Sylvester Pennoyer, as the Supreme Court opinion and commentators have implied. The property was purchased by none other than J. H. Mitchell, who three days later assigned the property to Sylvester Pennoyer. * * *

Following the litigation, Neff disappeared into obscurity; not so Pennoyer and Mitchell. Pennoyer went on to be Governor of Oregon * * *. Mitchell * * * was elected to the United States Senate in 1872, [but] lost his senate seat in 1879 * * *. * * * Shortly before the 1885 election, Judge Deady, the lower court judge in Pennoyer v. Neff, came into possession of a set of love letters which Mitchell had written to Mitchell's second wife's younger sister during the five years that he carried on an affair with her. Deady turned the love letters over to a newspaper, the *Oregonian* * * *. [However, in spite of] the scandal, Mitchell was [re]elected four days later * * *. In July of 1905, while still serving in the United States Senate, Mitchell was convicted [of land fraud] and sentenced to six months in jail, a $1,000 fine, and complete disbarment from public office.

Perdue, *Sin, Scandal and Substantive Due Process: Personal Jurisdiction and* Pennoyer *Reconsidered*, 62 Wash.L.Rev. 479, 481–90 (1987). Do the facts recounted by Professor Perdue affect whether the Oregon court properly exercised jurisdiction over Neff in Mitchell's initial lawsuit?

2.   Traditional analysis distinguishes three types of jurisdiction. In a proceeding in personam, the court exercises its power to render a judgment for or against a person by virtue of that party's presence within the state's territory or citizenship there. In a proceeding in rem, the court exercises its power to determine the status of property located within its territory, and the determination of the court is binding with respect to all possible interest holders in that property. In a proceeding quasi in rem, the court renders a judgment for or against a person, but recovery is limited to the value of property that is within the jurisdiction and thus subject to the court's authority. The dispute that gives rise to an action quasi in rem may be related to the property or unrelated to it, and the property may be used to satisfy any judgment assessed in the action. Each of these types of power, to be effective, required service of process over the person or property subject to the state's jurisdiction ("attachment" is the term used for service upon property). Which of these bases of jurisdiction were at issue in *Pennoyer*?

3. The concepts of jurisdiction found in the *Pennoyer* opinion were derived from nineteenth-century international law. In the traditional international model, a citizen of Country A might have been injured by a citizen of Country B in Country A. The citizen of Country A seeking relief had three options: proceed against the citizen of Country B in personam in Country A (with the likelihood that the paper called a judgment would be worthless because the courts of Country B would not enforce it against citizens of Country B); proceed against the citizen of Country B quasi in rem in Country A (with the advantage that the property of the citizen of Country B in Country A would be available to satisfy at least part (possibly all) of the judgment); or proceed against the citizen of Country B in the courts of Country B (in the hope of winning a judgment enforceable in Country B). Given these choices, it is understandable that the citizen of Country A probably would prefer the courts of Country A to the courts of Country B, the latter being farther away and possibly more disposed to find in favor of its own citizens, and would sue quasi in rem in Country A, so at least partial payment would be assured.

How much weight ought United States jurisdictional doctrine give to the international model? Are there significant differences between the 50 states that make up the United States and sovereign nations within an international order? Do the states have the same kind of interest in adjudicating claims brought by their citizens as, say, France might have relative to England or to Germany? Are there similar concerns that a state might favor its citizens over the citizens of another state? Does the Full Faith and Credit Clause of the federal Constitution require states to recognize and enforce valid judgments by other states?

4. According to the territorial principle identified in *Pennoyer*, does defendant's length of time in the forum state affect the court's power to assert in personam jurisdiction? Does the reason for the person's presence in the forum affect your answer to this question? In GRACE v. MacARTHUR, 170 F.Supp. 442 (E.D.Ark. 1959), defendant was served aboard a commercial flight from Tennessee to Texas when the plane was in air space over Arkansas. The federal court in Arkansas refused to quash the summons, holding that defendant was within the territorial limits of the state and so amenable to suit if properly served.

5. Does *Pennoyer*'s territorial theory allow a court to exercise jurisdiction over a domiciliary who is not present in the state at the time of service? Should it matter whether the complaint alleges that defendant caused harm within the forum state? In MILLIKEN v. MEYER, 311 U.S. 457, 462–64, 61 S.Ct. 339, 342–43, 85 L.Ed. 278, 283–84 (1940), Milliken sued Meyer, a Wyoming domiciliary, in Wyoming state court. Personal service was effected in Colorado under a Wyoming statute that permitted out-of-state service upon a state resident who was absent from the state under specified circumstances. Meyer did not appear in the Wyoming action and an in personam judgment was entered against him. Four years later, Meyer asked a Colorado court to restrain Milliken's enforcement of the Wyoming judgment. The United States

Supreme Court held that the Wyoming judgment was valid and entitled to Full Faith and Credit. According to the Court:

> * * * Domicile in the state is alone sufficient to bring an absent defendant within the reach of the state's jurisdiction for purposes of a personal judgment by means of appropriate substituted service. * * * [T]he authority of a state over one of its citizens is not terminated by the mere fact of his absence from the state. The state which accords him privileges and affords protection to him and his property by virtue of his domicile may also exact reciprocal duties. * * * [A domiciliary is amenable] to suit within the state even during sojourns without the state, where the state has provided and employed a reasonable method for apprising such an absent party of the proceedings against him.

The Court previously had held that a United States citizen living abroad is subject to in personam jurisdiction when served in a manner consistent with due process. In BLACKMER v. UNITED STATES, 284 U.S. 421, 52 S.Ct. 252, 76 L.Ed. 375 (1932), a United States citizen was served with a subpoena in France, requiring him to appear as a witness in the criminal trial arising from the Teapot Dome Scandal during President Harding's administration. The Supreme Court held that personal service effected through the consul's office satisfied due process.

6.   Suppose a plaintiff brings suit in a forum with which the party has no connection other than invoking its jurisdiction. Should that forum be able to entertain a suit against plaintiff if defendant asserts the claim as a part of the same proceeding? Consider the Court's analysis in ADAM v. SAENGER, 303 U.S. 59, 67–68, 58 S.Ct. 454, 458, 82 L.Ed. 649, 654–55 (1938):

> There is nothing in the Fourteenth Amendment to prevent a state from adopting a procedure by which a judgment *in personam* may be rendered in a cross-action against a plaintiff in its courts, upon service of process or of appropriate pleading upon his attorney of record. The plaintiff having, by his voluntary act in demanding justice from the defendant, submitted himself to the jurisdiction of the court, there is nothing arbitrary or unreasonable in treating him as being there for all purposes for which justice to the defendant requires his presence. It is the price which the state may exact as the condition of opening its courts to the plaintiff.

Does your analysis change if defendant—or some other third party—files a separate, unrelated action against the original plaintiff in the forum state? Would the court in the forum state have jurisdiction to hear the claim against the original plaintiff? Would such jurisdiction be based on plaintiff's presence in the state or on some other notion? Should a state be permitted to condition the use of its courts on consent to the jurisdiction of those courts in actions unrelated to the initial lawsuit?

7.   Justice Field in *Pennoyer* characterized territoriality as a "general, if not universal, law" that limits a state's exercise of jurisdiction. Despite that statement, the rules governing adjudicatory jurisdiction differ in legal systems around the world. Although defendant's presence was the cornerstone of British and United States practice, domicile was key in the Netherlands and Switzerland, plaintiff's nationality was important in France, and domicile and the situs of property were significant factors in Germany. See Juenger, *Judicial Jurisdiction in the United States and in the European Communities: A Comparison*, 82 Mich.L.Rev. 1195 (1984). Indeed, commentators have emphasized that "[i]n this area of law, differences among civil-law countries are as great as differences between given civil-law and common-law countries." de Vries & Lowenfeld, *Jurisdiction in Personal Actions—A Comparison of Civil Law Views*, 44 Iowa L.Rev. 306, 344 (1959). The increasing incidence of transnational litigation has spurred efforts to define a global law of personal jurisdiction, which so far has proven elusive. See Chase, Hershkoff, Silberman, Sorabji, Stürner, Taniguchi & Varano, Civil Litigation in Comparative Context 642–74 (Chase & Hershkoff, eds., 2d ed. 2017).

B. TOWARD A NEW THEORY OF JURISDICTION

The twentieth century witnessed important technological advances that indirectly but significantly affected the doctrine of personal jurisdiction. In particular, the growing popularity of the automobile led to increased interstate travel and with it, increased interactions between parties from different states that gave rise to litigation. Under *Pennoyer*'s territorial theory, could a court in State A exercise jurisdiction over an out-of-state defendant in a case involving an automobile accident in State A once the car and driver had exited the state and before personal service could be effected?

In KANE v. NEW JERSEY, 242 U.S. 160, 37 S.Ct. 30, 61 L.Ed. 222 (1916), the Supreme Court held that New Jersey could require an out-of-state motorist to file a formal instrument appointing a New Jersey agent to receive process as a condition of using the state's highways. Significantly, the statute limited the consent to matters arising from the party's motoring activity within the forum state.

HESS v. PAWLOSKI, 274 U.S. 352, 47 S.Ct. 632, 71 L.Ed. 1091 (1927), involved a car accident on a public highway in Massachusetts between a Massachusetts resident and a motorist from Pennsylvania. The nonresident driver owned no property in Massachusetts. Service was effected under Chapter 90, General Laws of Massachusetts, as amended by Stat. 1923, c. 431, § 2, the material parts of which follow:

> The acceptance by a nonresident of the rights and privileges conferred by section three or four, as evidenced by his operating a motor vehicle thereunder, or the operation by a nonresident of a motor vehicle on a public way in the commonwealth other than

under said sections, shall be deemed equivalent to an appointment by such nonresident of the registrar or his successor in office, to be his true and lawful attorney upon whom may be served all lawful processes in any action or proceeding against him, growing out of any accident or collision in which said nonresident may be involved while operating a motor vehicle on such a way, and said acceptance or operation shall be a signification of his agreement that any such process against him which is so served shall be of the same legal force and validity as if served on him personally. Service of such process shall be made by leaving a copy of the process with a fee of two dollars in the hands of the registrar, or in his office, and such service shall be sufficient service upon the said nonresident: Provided, that notice of such service and a copy of the process are forthwith sent by registered mail by the plaintiff to the defendant, and the defendant's return receipt and the plaintiff's affidavit of compliance herewith are appended to the writ and entered with the declaration. * * *

Id. at 354, 47 S.Ct. at 632–33, 71 L.Ed. at 1093–94.

Defendant made a special appearance to challenge jurisdiction. The trial court denied the motion and the Supreme Judicial Court of Massachusetts affirmed the order finding the statute to be a valid exercise of the police power of the state. The United States Supreme Court affirmed as a matter of due process. Justice Butler's opinion for a unanimous Court explained:

The process of a court of one state cannot run into another and summon a party there domiciled to respond to proceedings against him. Notice sent outside the state to a nonresident is unavailing to give jurisdiction in an action against him personally for money recovery. Pennoyer v. Neff * * *. There must be actual service within the state of notice upon him or upon some one authorized to accept service for him. * * * A personal judgment rendered against a nonresident, who has neither been served with process nor appeared in the suit, is without validity. * * * The mere transaction of business in a state by nonresident natural persons does not imply consent to be bound by the process of its courts. * * * The power of a state to exclude foreign corporations, although not absolute, but qualified, is the ground on which such an implication is supported as to them. * * * But a state may not withhold from nonresident individuals the right of doing business therein. The privileges and immunities clause of the Constitution (section 2, art. 4), safeguards to the citizens of one state the right "to pass through, or to reside in any other state for purposes of trade, agriculture, professional pursuits, or otherwise." And it prohibits state legislation discriminating against citizens of other states. * * *

Motor vehicles are dangerous machines, and, even when skillfully and carefully operated, their use is attended by serious dangers to persons and property. In the public interest the state may make and enforce regulations reasonably calculated to promote care on the part of all, residents and nonresidents alike, who use its highways. The measure in question operates to require a nonresident to answer for his conduct in the state where arise causes of action alleged against him, as well as to provide for a claimant a convenient method by which he may sue to enforce his rights. Under the statute the implied consent is limited to proceedings growing out of accidents or collisions on a highway in which the nonresident may be involved. It is required that he shall actually receive and receipt for notice of the service and a copy of the process. And it contemplates such continuances as may be found necessary to give reasonable time and opportunity for defense. It makes no hostile discrimination against nonresidents, but tends to put them on the same footing as residents. Literal and precise equality in respect of this matter is not attainable; it is not required. * * * The state's power to regulate the use of its highways extends to their use by nonresidents as well as by residents. * * * And, in advance of the operation of a motor vehicle on its highway by a nonresident, the state may require him to appoint one of its officials as his agent on whom process may be served in proceedings growing out of such use. Kane v. New Jersey * * *. That case recognized power of the state to exclude a nonresident until the formal appointment is made. And, having the power so to exclude, the state may declare that the use of the highway by the nonresident is the equivalent of the appointment of the registrar as agent on whom process may be served. * * * The difference between the formal and implied appointment is not substantial, so far as concerns the application of the due process clause of the Fourteenth Amendment.

Id. at 355–57, 47 S.Ct. at 633–34, 71 L.Ed. at 1094–95.

NOTES AND QUESTIONS

1. How did the statute authorizing service in *Hess* differ from that in *Kane*? How did it differ from the mode of service in *Tickle*, p. 13, supra?

2. Could the rationale of implied consent to jurisdiction created by driving within a state be employed to support jurisdiction over a nonresident in a matter unrelated to the driver's conduct within the state?

3.   The *Hess* opinion noted that the defendant had "appeared specially for the purpose of contesting jurisdiction." A "special appearance" allows a party to appear in the case in order to challenge the court's jurisdiction without thereby consenting to jurisdiction. See p. 171, infra.

The territorial theory of jurisdiction did not easily apply to corporations. A corporation, after all, is a fiction. It exists on paper and acts through its employees, directors, and shareholders. Well into the nineteenth century it was accepted that a corporation could "have no legal existence out of the boundaries of the sovereignty by which it is created." Bank of Augusta v. Earle, 38 U.S. (13 Pet.) 519, 588, 10 L.Ed. 274, 308 (1839) (Taney, J.). By analogy to a person, courts treated a corporation as a domiciliary of the state of its incorporation and held that a corporation was subject to the jurisdiction of that state when properly served. However, exercising jurisdiction over a "foreign" corporation—a corporation chartered by a state other than the forum state—raised difficult questions, even when the corporation's activity caused injury in the forum state.

Within the territorial principle, two theories predominated as justifications for a state court's exercise of in personam jurisdiction over a corporation that was not chartered by the forum state: consent and presence. The "consent" theory presupposed that a corporation could transact business in a state in which it was not incorporated only with that state's consent. Thus, as a condition of doing business, a state could require a foreign corporation to consent to service of process through the appointment of an in-state agent to receive process. Courts applied this principle when the corporation actually designated an agent to receive process, even if its consent was given under compulsion. However, some courts also applied this principle when the corporation did not designate an agent to receive process and, thus, could be said only to have granted implied consent to such a designation through its in-state activity.

The "presence" theory built on the notion that a corporation by engaging in activity within a state established a presence through those activities for jurisdictional purposes: "A foreign corporation is amenable to process * * * if it is doing business within the State in such manner and to such extent as to warrant the inference that it is present there." Philadelphia & Reading Ry. Co. v. McKibbin, 243 U.S. 264, 265, 37 S.Ct. 280, 280, 61 L.Ed. 710, 711–12 (1917) (Brandeis, J.). This doctrine measured the propriety of a state's assertion of jurisdiction over a foreign corporation in terms of the corporation's actual activities in the forum state. However, a court lost its power over a nonresident corporation once it ceased doing business in the state. How much activity was needed to establish presence was not easily defined; the term "presence" was conclusory and all too often was used by the courts without any meaningful analysis.

Under the theories of implied consent and presence, the court asked whether the corporation was "doing business" within the forum state. As the number of cases making this factual inquiry multiplied, "doing business" gradually came to be a test in and of itself. The cases became cluttered with refined and often senseless distinctions that sought to measure the quantity of defendant's activities within the state, but paid little or no attention to the burden imposed on the corporation by asserting jurisdiction over it or to the overall desirability of litigating in the particular forum.

> With doctrine in so bad a state of disrepair, the time had long since passed for the Supreme Court to acknowledge the truth of Holmes' dictum that "[t]he Constitution is not to be satisfied with a fiction." *International Shoe Co. v. Washington* afforded the Court an opportunity to begin to set its house in order in this field.

Kurland, *The Supreme Court, the Due Process Clause and the In Personam Jurisdiction of State Courts—From* Pennoyer *to* Denckla: *A Review*, 25 U.Chi.L.Rev. 569, 586 (1958).

INTERNATIONAL SHOE CO. v. WASHINGTON
Supreme Court of the United States, 1945.
326 U.S. 310, 66 S.Ct. 154, 90 L.Ed. 95.

Appeal from the Supreme Court of the State of Washington.

CHIEF JUSTICE STONE delivered the opinion of the Court.

The questions for decision are (1) whether, within the limitations of the due process clause of the Fourteenth Amendment, appellant, a Delaware corporation, has by its activities in the State of Washington rendered itself amenable to proceedings in the courts of that state to recover unpaid contributions to the state unemployment compensation fund exacted by state statutes * * * and (2) whether the state can exact those contributions consistently with the due process clause of the Fourteenth Amendment.

The [Washington] statutes in question set up a comprehensive scheme of unemployment compensation, the costs of which are defrayed by contributions required to be made by employers to a state unemployment compensation fund. The contributions are a specified percentage of the wages payable annually by each employer for his employees' services in the state. The assessment and collection of the contributions and the fund are administered by respondents. Section 14(c) of the Act, Wash. Rev. Stat. 1941 Supp., § 9998–114c, authorizes respondent Commissioner to issue an order and notice of assessment of delinquent contributions upon prescribed personal service of the notice upon the employer if found within the state, or, if not so found, by mailing the notice to the employer by registered mail at his last known address. That section also authorizes the Commissioner to collect the assessment by distraint if it is not paid within ten days after service of the notice. * * *

In this case notice of assessment for the years in question was personally served upon a sales solicitor employed by appellant in the State of Washington, and a copy of the notice was mailed by registered mail to appellant at its address in St. Louis, Missouri. Appellant appeared specially before the office of unemployment and moved to set aside the order and notice of assessment on the ground that the service upon appellant's salesman was not proper service upon appellant; that appellant was not a corporation of the State of Washington and was not doing business within the state; that it had no agent within the state upon whom service could be made; and that appellant is not an employer and does not furnish employment within the meaning of the statute.

The motion was heard on evidence and a stipulation of facts by the appeal tribunal which denied the motion and ruled that respondent Commissioner was entitled to recover the unpaid contributions. That action was affirmed by the Commissioner; both the Superior Court and the Supreme Court affirmed. * * * Appellant in each of these courts assailed the statute as applied, as a violation of the due process clause of the Fourteenth Amendment, and as imposing a constitutionally prohibited burden on interstate commerce.

* * * Appellant is a Delaware corporation, having its principal place of business in St. Louis, Missouri, and is engaged in the manufacture and sale of shoes and other footwear. It maintains places of business in several states, other than Washington, at which its manufacturing is carried on and from which its merchandise is distributed interstate through several sales units or branches located outside the State of Washington.

Appellant has no office in Washington and makes no contracts either for sale or purchase of merchandise there. It maintains no stock of merchandise in that state and makes there no deliveries of goods in intrastate commerce. During the years from 1937 to 1940, now in question, appellant employed eleven to thirteen salesmen under direct supervision and control of sales managers located in St. Louis. These salesmen resided in Washington; their principal activities were confined to that state; and they were compensated by commissions based upon the amount of their sales. The commissions for each year totaled more than $31,000. Appellant supplies its salesmen with a line of samples, each consisting of one shoe of a pair, which they display to prospective purchasers. On occasion they rent permanent sample rooms, for exhibiting samples, in business buildings, or rent rooms in hotels or business buildings temporarily for that purpose. The cost of such rentals is reimbursed by appellant.

The authority of the salesmen is limited to exhibiting their samples and soliciting orders from prospective buyers, at prices and on terms fixed by appellant. The salesmen transmit the orders to appellant's office in St. Louis for acceptance or rejection, and when accepted the merchandise for filling the orders is shipped f.o.b. from points outside Washington to the purchasers within the state. All the merchandise shipped into Washington is invoiced at the place of shipment from which collections are made. No salesman has authority to enter into contracts or to make collections.

The Supreme Court of Washington was of opinion that the regular and systematic solicitation of orders in the state by appellant's salesmen, resulting in a continuous flow of appellant's product into the state, was sufficient to constitute doing business in the state so as to make appellant amenable to suit in its courts. But it was also of opinion that there were sufficient additional activities shown to bring the case within the rule frequently stated, that solicitation within a state by the agents of a foreign corporation plus some additional activities there are sufficient to render the corporation amenable to suit brought in the courts of the state to enforce an obligation arising out of its activities there. * * * The court found such additional activities in the salesmen's display of samples sometimes in permanent display rooms, and the salesmen's residence within the state, continued over a period of years, all resulting in a substantial volume of merchandise regularly shipped by appellant to purchasers within the state. * * *

Appellant * * * insists that its activities within the state were not sufficient to manifest its "presence" there and that in its absence the state courts were without jurisdiction, that consequently it was a denial of due process for the state to subject appellant to suit. It refers to those cases in which it was said that the mere solicitation of orders for the purchase of goods within a state, to be accepted without the state and filled by shipment of the purchased goods interstate, does not render the corporation seller amenable to suit within the state. * * * And appellant further argues that since it was not present within the state, it is a denial of due process to subject it to taxation or other money exaction. It thus denies the power of the state to lay the tax or to subject appellant to a suit for its collection.

Historically the jurisdiction of courts to render judgment in personam is grounded on their de facto power over the defendant's person. Hence his presence within the territorial jurisdiction of a court was prerequisite to its rendition of a judgment personally binding him. Pennoyer v. Neff * * *. But now that the capias ad respondendum has given way to personal service of summons or other form of notice, due process requires only that in order to subject a defendant to a judgment in personam, if he be not present within the territory of the forum, he have certain minimum contacts with it such that the maintenance of the suit does not offend "traditional notions of fair play and substantial justice." Milliken v. Meyer * * * [p. 46, Note 5, supra]. * * *

Since the corporate personality is a fiction, although a fiction intended to be acted upon as though it were a fact * * *, it is clear that unlike an individual its "presence" without, as well as within, the state of its origin can be manifested only by activities carried on in its behalf by those who are authorized to act for it. To say that the corporation is so far "present" there as to satisfy due process requirements, for purposes of taxation or the maintenance of suits against it in the courts of the state, is to beg the question to be decided. For the terms "present" or "presence" are used merely to symbolize those activities of the corporation's agent within the state which courts will deem to be sufficient to satisfy the demands of due process. * * * Those demands may be met by such contacts of the corporation with the state of the forum as make it reasonable, in the context of our federal system of government, to require the corporation to defend the particular suit which is brought there. An "estimate of the inconveniences" which would result to the corporation from a trial away from its "home" or principal place of business is relevant in this connection. * * *

"Presence" in the state in this sense has never been doubted when the activities of the corporation there have not only been continuous and systematic, but also give rise to the liabilities sued on, even though no consent to be sued or authorization to an agent to accept service of process has been given. * * * Conversely it has been generally recognized that the casual presence of the corporate agent or even his conduct of single or isolated items of activities in a state in the corporation's behalf are not enough to subject it to suit on causes of action unconnected with the activities there. * * * To require the corporation in such circumstances to defend the suit away from its home or other jurisdiction where it carries on more substantial activities has been thought to lay too great and unreasonable a burden on the corporation to comport with due process.

While it has been held in cases on which appellant relies that continuous activity of some sorts within a state is not enough to support the demand that the corporation be amenable to suits unrelated to that activity * * * there have been instances in which the continuous corporate operations within a state were thought so substantial and of such a nature as to justify suit against it on causes of action arising from dealings entirely distinct from those activities. * * *

Finally, although the commission of some single or occasional acts of the corporate agent in a state sufficient to impose an obligation or liability on the corporation has not been thought to confer upon the state authority to enforce it, Rosenberg Bros. & Co. v. Curtis Brown Co., 260 U.S. 516, 43 S.Ct. 170, 67 L.Ed. 372, other such acts, because of their nature and quality and the circumstances of their commission, may be deemed sufficient to render the corporation liable to suit. Cf. Kane v. New Jersey * * *; Hess v. Pawloski * * * [p. 48, supra]. True, some of the decisions holding the corporation amenable to suit have been supported by resort to the legal fiction that it has given its consent to service and suit, consent being implied from its presence in the state through the acts of its authorized agents. * * * But more realistically it may be said that those authorized acts were of such a nature as to justify the fiction. * * *

It is evident that the criteria by which we mark the boundary line between those activities which justify the subjection of a corporation to suit, and those which do not, cannot be simply mechanical or quantitative. The test is not merely, as has sometimes been suggested, whether the activity, which the corporation has seen fit to procure through its agents in another state, is a little more or a little less. * * * Whether due process is satisfied must depend rather upon the quality and nature of the activity in relation to the fair and orderly administration of the laws which it was the purpose of the due process clause to insure. That clause does not contemplate that a state may make binding a judgment in personam against an individual or corporate defendant with which the state has no contacts, ties, or relations. * * *

But to the extent that a corporation exercises the privilege of conducting activities within a state, it enjoys the benefits and protection of the laws of that state. The exercise of that privilege may give rise to obligations; and, so far as those obligations arise out of or are connected with the activities within the state, a procedure which requires the corporation to respond to a suit brought to enforce them can, in most instances, hardly be said to be undue. * * *

Applying these standards, the activities carried on in behalf of appellant in the State of Washington were neither irregular nor casual. They were systematic and continuous throughout the years in question. They resulted in a large volume of interstate business, in the course of which appellant received the benefits and protection of the laws of the state, including the right to resort to the courts for the enforcement of its rights. The obligation which is here sued upon arose out of those very activities. It is evident that these operations establish sufficient contacts or ties with the state of the forum to make it reasonable and just according to our traditional conception of fair play and substantial justice to permit the state to enforce the obligations which appellant has incurred there. Hence we cannot say that the maintenance of the present suit in the State of Washington involves an unreasonable or undue procedure.

We are likewise unable to conclude that the service of the process within the state upon an agent whose activities establish appellant's "presence" there was not sufficient notice of the suit, or that the suit was so unrelated to those activities as to make the agent an inappropriate vehicle for communicating the notice. It is enough that appellant has established such contacts with the state that the particular form of substituted service adopted there gives reasonable assurance that the notice will be actual. * * *

Appellant having rendered itself amenable to suit upon obligations arising out of the activities of its salesmen in Washington, the state may maintain the present suit in personam to collect the tax laid upon the exercise of the privilege of employing appellant's salesmen within the state. For Washington has made one of those activities, which taken together establish appellant's "presence" there for purposes of suit, the taxable event by which the state brings appellant within the reach of its taxing power. The state thus has constitutional power to lay the tax and to subject appellant to a suit to recover it. * * *

Affirmed.

JUSTICE JACKSON took no part in the consideration or decision of this case.

JUSTICE BLACK delivered the following opinion.

* * *

I believe that the Federal Constitution leaves to each State, without any "ifs" or "buts," a power to tax and to open the doors of its courts for its citizens to sue corporations whose agents do business in those States. Believing that the Constitution gave the States that power, I think it a judicial deprivation to condition its exercise upon this Court's notion of "fair play," however appealing that term may be. Nor can I stretch the meaning of due process so far as to authorize this Court to deprive a State of the right to afford judicial protection to its citizens on the ground that it would be more "convenient" for the corporation to be sued somewhere else.

There is a strong emotional appeal in the words "fair play," "justice," and "reasonableness." But they were not chosen by those who wrote the original Constitution or the Fourteenth Amendment as a measuring rod for this Court to use in invalidating State or Federal laws passed by elected legislative representatives. No one, not even those who most feared a democratic government, ever formally proposed that courts should be given power to invalidate legislation under any such elastic standards. Express prohibitions against certain types of legislation are found in the Constitution, and under the long settled practice, courts invalidate laws found to conflict with them. This requires interpretation, and interpretation, it is true, may result in extension of the Constitution's purpose. But that is no reason for reading the due process clause so as to restrict a State's power to tax and sue those whose activities affect persons and businesses within the State, provided proper service can be had. * * *

NOTES AND QUESTIONS

1.   Historically, the writ of capias ad respondendum—referred to in *International Shoe*—directed the sheriff or other official to secure defendant's appearance in a civil suit by physically taking him into custody. Service of process on defendant, which does not require taking defendant into custody, is "the contemporary counterpart to that writ." Murphy Bros. v. Michetti Pipe Stringing, Inc., 526 U.S. 344, 350, 119 S.Ct. 1322, 1326–27, 143 L.Ed.2d 448, 456–57 (1999). In its brief to the Supreme Court, International Shoe argued, "It would be manifestly impolitic to uphold service upon a salesman in a case not involving a sale. It would require of mere soliciting salesmen, notoriously happy-go-lucky fellows, good mixers, a higher degree of judgment and responsibility than that for which they are selected." Quoted in Cameron & Johnson, *Death of a Salesman? Forum Shopping and Outcome Determination Under* International Shoe, 28 U.C. Davis L.Rev. 769, 795 (1995). Within the *Pennoyer* model, why was it important to serve the corporation's salesmen in the forum state?

2.   The opinion in *International Shoe* used contacts with the forum in two different ways. First, a defendant could have sufficient contacts with the forum to warrant asserting jurisdiction over it for all matters. This form of power now is termed "general jurisdiction," and we will study it in more detail later in this chapter. Second, a defendant could have sufficient contacts with the forum to warrant asserting jurisdiction over it for matters arising out of or related to its activity in the forum without having sufficient contact with the forum to warrant general jurisdiction. In such a case, the jurisdiction is termed "specific jurisdiction." See von Mehren & Trautman, *Jurisdiction to Adjudicate: A Suggested Analysis*, 79 Harv.L.Rev. 1121 (1966). Determining when a company has engaged in sufficient business within the state, or which of its activities count as a basis for the state's exercise of jurisdiction, often raises uncertain questions. See Brilmayer, *Related Contacts and Personal Jurisdiction*, 101 Harv.L.Rev. 1444 (1988).

C. THE GROWTH OF STATE LONG-ARM LAWS

———

Read the selected state jurisdiction statutes in the Supplement.

———

The Supreme Court's decision in *Hess*, p. 48, supra, encouraged states to enact statutes asserting jurisdiction based on the nonresident's engagement in a variety of activities or enterprises that, like driving a car, were considered hazardous. *International Shoe*—with its focus on defendant's contacts with the forum state—enabled states to further expand their jurisdictional reach in conformance with the Supreme Court's latest view of constitutional boundaries. This spate of legislative activity came largely in the form of "long-arm" or "single-act" statutes, which based jurisdiction over nonresidents upon defendant's general activity in the state, or the commission of one of a series of enumerated acts within the state, or, in some cases, the commission of a certain act outside the state causing consequences within it. The theory supporting the assertion of jurisdiction depended on *International Shoe*'s emphasis on the quantum and quality of defendant's in-state activity. In its 1957 Term, the Supreme Court handed down a pair of decisions that further elaborated on when a state's exercise of personal jurisdiction would comport with the Due Process Clause.

McGEE v. INTERNATIONAL LIFE INSURANCE CO., 355 U.S. 220, 222–24, 78 S.Ct. 199, 200–01, 2 L.Ed.2d 223, 225–26 (1957). Plaintiff, McGee, was the beneficiary of a life insurance policy issued by the Empire Mutual Insurance Co., an Arizona corporation, to Lowell Franklin, a resident of California. In 1948, defendant, International Life Insurance Co., assumed Empire Mutual's insurance obligations. Franklin and International Life transacted business by mail until Franklin's death in 1950. Neither Empire Mutual nor International Life ever had any office or agent in California, and, as far as the record disclosed, International Life had never solicited or done any insurance business in California other than the policy with Franklin.

When International Life refused to pay McGee upon Franklin's death, McGee sued in a California state court basing jurisdiction on the California Unauthorized Insurer's Process Act. The Act subjects out-of-state corporations to suits in California arising out of insurance contracts with in-state residents. After recovering a judgment in California, McGee sought to enforce the judgment in Texas. The Texas court refused to enforce the judgment, holding it to be void under the Fourteenth Amendment on the ground that the California courts could not assume jurisdiction over International Life without service of process within its boundaries. The Supreme Court held that the exercise of jurisdiction by California was proper.

The Court noted that, with the increased "nationalization of commerce," the tremendous growth "in the amount of business conducted by mail across state lines," and the frequency with which "commercial transactions touch two or more States," there had developed "a trend * * * clearly discernible toward expanding the permissible scope of state jurisdiction over foreign corporations and other nonresidents."

* * * [W]e think it apparent that the Due Process Clause did not preclude the California court from entering a judgment binding

on respondent. It is sufficient * * * that the suit was based on a contract which had substantial connection with that State. * * * The contract was delivered in California, the premiums were mailed from there and the insured was a resident of that State when he died. * * * California has a manifest interest in providing effective means of redress for its residents when their insurers refuse to pay claims. These residents would be at a severe disadvantage if they were forced to follow the insurance company to a distant State in order to hold it legally accountable. When claims were small or moderate individual claimants frequently could not afford the cost of bringing an action in a foreign forum— thus in effect making the company judgment proof. Often the crucial witnesses—as here on the company's defense of suicide— will be found in the insured's locality. Of course there may be inconvenience to the insurer if it is held amenable to suit in California * * * but certainly nothing which amounts to a denial of due process. * * * There is no contention that respondent did not have adequate notice of the suit or sufficient time to prepare its defenses and appear.

NOTES AND QUESTIONS

1.   Did the Court in *McGee* modify the *International Shoe* test? Is the exercise of jurisdiction over the insurance company in *McGee* consistent with *International Shoe*? In what way did the insurance company have "minimum contacts" with California?

2.   The Court said in *McGee* that improvements in transportation and communication make it less burdensome for out-of-state litigants to defend suits. Is it as reasonable to say that these advances make it easier for plaintiffs to sue out of state where the defendant is located? In assessing whether jurisdiction is to be exercised, should weight be given to the interests of the forum state in ensuring the enforcement of its state's laws?

———

In HANSON v. DENCKLA, 357 U.S. 235, 78 S.Ct. 1228, 2 L.Ed.2d 1283 (1958), service of process was effected on a Delaware trustee pursuant to a Florida statute that permitted service by publication for claims arising from the construction of a will. Dora Donner, a resident of Pennsylvania, had established a trust in Delaware, naming the Delaware bank as trustee. During her lifetime, the income from the trust would go to her and, upon her death, the remainder would pass to the persons she appointed as beneficiaries under her will. Donner retained the power to change the appointed beneficiaries at any time.

Later, Donner moved to Florida, and, several years before her death, she executed her last will and testament, leaving most of her estate to two of her daughters, Katherine and Dorothy. On the same day, she executed her power to change the appointed beneficiaries under the Delaware trust—this time, she designated two of her grandchildren (the children of a third daughter, Elizabeth) as beneficiaries of a significant portion of the trust's assets, with the remainder going to her estate.

After Donner's death, Katherine and Dorothy, the two daughters named in the will, brought an action in Florida against the trustee claiming that the appointment of their sister's children as beneficiaries of the trust had been ineffective. If that were true, the assets of the trust would pass under the will to the two daughters, as legatees.

The Florida court found that it had jurisdiction over the trustee, concluded that the trust was invalid and that the exercise of the power of appointment was ineffective to pass title, and held that the trust property therefore passed under the will and so to Katherine and Dorothy. Before the Florida judgment was rendered, Elizabeth, as executrix of the estate, commenced an action in Delaware to determine who was entitled to share the trust assets, which were situated in Delaware. With minor exceptions, the parties were the same as in the Florida action. When the Florida judgment was rendered, the legatees under the will—Katherine and Dorothy—unsuccessfully argued that the Florida judgment was entitled to Full Faith and Credit and thus barred the Delaware action. The Delaware court ultimately held that the trust and the exercise of the power of appointment were valid under Delaware law.

Accepting both cases for review, a divided Supreme Court found that because the Delaware trustee's contacts with Florida had been less than minimal, the Florida court could not assert personal jurisdiction over it. Moreover, because Florida law considered the trustee an indispensable party without whom the lawsuit could not continue, Delaware was justified in refusing to give Full Faith and Credit to the Florida decree. Writing for a majority of five, Chief Justice Warren explained that:

> * * * [T]he requirements for personal jurisdiction over nonresidents have evolved from the rigid rule of Pennoyer v. Neff * * * to the flexible standard of International Shoe Co. v. State of Washington * * *. But it is a mistake to assume that this trend heralds the eventual demise of all restrictions on the personal jurisdiction of state courts. * * * Those restrictions are more than a guarantee of immunity from inconvenient or distant litigation. They are a consequence of territorial limitations on the power of the respective States. However minimal the burden of defending in a foreign tribunal, a defendant may not be called upon to do so unless he has had the "minimal contacts" with that State * * *.

> We fail to find such contacts in the circumstances of this case. The defendant trust company has no office in Florida, and transacts

no business there. None of the trust assets has ever been held or administered in Florida, and the record discloses no solicitation of business in that State either in person or by mail. * * *

The cause of action in this case is not one that arises out of an act done or transaction consummated in the forum State. * * * From Florida Mrs. Donner carried on several bits of trust administration that may be compared to the mailing of premiums in McGee [p. 59, supra]. But the record discloses no instance in which the trustee performed any acts in Florida that bear the same relationship to the agreement as the solicitation in McGee. Consequently, this suit cannot be said to be one to enforce an obligation that arose from a privilege the defendant exercised in Florida. * * *

* * * The unilateral activity of those who claim some relationship with a nonresident defendant cannot satisfy the requirement of contact with the forum State. The application of that rule will vary with the quality and nature of the defendant's activity, but it is essential in each case that there be some act by which the defendant purposefully avails itself of the privilege of conducting activities within the forum State, thus invoking the benefits and protections of its laws. * * *

Id. at 251–53, 78 S.Ct. at 1238–40, 2 L.Ed.2d at 1296–98.

Justice Black dissented:

In light of the * * * circumstances it seems quite clear to me that there is nothing in the Due Process Clause which denies Florida the right to determine whether [the] appointment was valid as against its statute of wills. * * * Not only was the appointment made in Florida by a domiciliary of Florida, but the primary beneficiaries also lived in that State. In my view it could hardly be denied that Florida had sufficient interest so that a court with jurisdiction might properly apply Florida law, if it chose, to determine whether the appointment was effectual. * * * True, the question whether the law of a State can be applied to a transaction is different from the question whether the courts of that State have jurisdiction to enter a judgment, but the two are often closely related and to a substantial degree depend upon similar considerations. It seems to me that where a transaction has as much relationship to a State as * * * [this] appointment had to Florida its courts ought to have power to adjudicate controversies arising out of that transaction, unless litigation there would impose such a heavy and disproportionate burden on a nonresident defendant that it would offend what this Court has referred to as "traditional notions of fair play and substantial justice." * * * Florida, the home of the principal contenders * * *, was a reasonably convenient forum for all. Certainly there is nothing fundamentally unfair in subjecting the corporate trustee to the jurisdiction of the Florida courts. It chose to maintain business relations with [the settlor] in that State for eight years, regularly communicating with her with respect to the business of the trust including the very appointment in question.

Florida's interest in the validity of [the] appointment is made more emphatic by the fact that her will is being administered in that State. It has traditionally been the rule that the State where a person is domiciled at the time of his death is the proper place to determine the validity of his will, to construe its provisions and to marshal and distribute his personal property. Here Florida was seriously concerned with winding up [this] estate and with finally determining what property was to be distributed under her will. * * *

Id. at 258–59, 78 S.Ct. at 1242–43, 2 L.Ed.2d at 1300–01.

NOTES AND QUESTIONS

1.   Donner's estate plan appeared to have divided her property in three shares. Under the last appointment of trust beneficiaries, the children of Donner's third daughter, Elizabeth, received about $400,000. Donner's other two daughters, the residual legatees under the will, received over $1,000,000 from the estate, to be divided equally. The Florida decision would have invalidated the last appointment of trust beneficiaries, defeated Donner's estate plan, and added $400,000 to the amount received by Elizabeth's sisters at the expense of Elizabeth's family.

2.   Could the *Hanson* decision be justified on the ground that Delaware, as the state where the trust was validly established (at least under Delaware law), had a stronger interest in the disposition of the trust's funds than Florida did? Delaware's interest certainly is sufficient to support jurisdiction in Delaware, but was it sufficient to preclude jurisdiction in Florida? Compare California's interests in *McGee*, in which jurisdiction was upheld, with Florida's interests in *Hanson*, in which jurisdiction was denied. When is a state's "interest" sufficient to support jurisdiction? Is a legislative desire to provide a forum enough?

3.   In their opinions in *Hanson*, the Chief Justice and Justice Black agreed that whether a court may apply its own law to a dispute is subject to a different standard than whether the court can exercise jurisdiction over defendant and adjudicate the controversy at all.

In ALLSTATE INS. CO. v. HAGUE, 449 U.S. 302, 312–13, 101 S.Ct. 633, 640, 66 L.Ed.2d 521, 531 (1981), the plurality opinion held that "for a State's substantive law to be selected in a constitutionally permissible manner, that State must have a significant contact or significant aggregation of contacts, creating state interests, such that choice of its law is neither arbitrary nor fundamentally unfair." Under this test, the plurality upheld Minnesota's decision to apply its own law in an action by a former Wisconsin resident who moved to Minnesota just prior to filing suit to collect proceeds under an automobile insurance policy made in Wisconsin covering vehicles owned by a Wisconsin resident who had been killed in an accident in Wisconsin. After *Hague* it seems clear that the Due Process Clause allows states extraordinary latitude in developing choice of law rules. Why should the due process restrictions on a court's adjudicatory jurisdiction be greater than on its power to exercise local law?

The long-arm statutes at issue in *McGee* and *Hanson* dealt only with specialized kinds of litigation. The first truly comprehensive long-arm statute was enacted in Illinois and it was used as a model by a number of states. According to the Illinois Supreme Court, the statute was an attempt to assert jurisdiction to the fullest permissible constitutional limits. Under the Illinois statute, an individual or a corporation, whether a citizen or noncitizen of Illinois, is amenable to the jurisdiction of the state's courts if the person transacts any business within the state; commits a tort within the state; owns, uses, or possesses any real estate within the state; or contracts to insure any person, property, or risk located within the state. Several years after its enactment, the Illinois statute was amended to include jurisdiction over claims involving alimony, support, and property division against former residents. Other states soon followed the Illinois approach in expanding the jurisdictional reach of their courts. Contemporary long-arm statutes run the gamut from very broad ones that permit states to assert jurisdiction up to the limits allowed by the Constitution, to narrow ones that carve out small parts of their constitutionally permitted authority. See McFarland, *Dictum Run Wild: How Long-Arm Statutes Extended to the Limits of Due Process*, 84 B.U.L.Rev. 491 (2004).

GRAY V. AMERICAN RADIATOR & STANDARD SANITARY CORP.

Supreme Court of Illinois, 1961.
22 Ill.2d 432, 176 N.E.2d 761.

KLINGBIEL, JUSTICE. Phyllis Gray appeals from a judgment of the circuit court of Cook County dismissing her action for damages. The issues are concerned with the construction and validity of our statute providing for substituted service of process on nonresidents. Since a constitutional question is involved, the appeal is direct to this court.

The suit was brought against the Titan Valve Manufacturing Company and others, on the ground that a certain water heater had exploded and injured the plaintiff. The complaint charges, *inter alia,* that the Titan company, a foreign corporation, had negligently constructed the safety valve; and that the injuries were suffered as a proximate result thereof. Summons issued and was duly served on Titan's registered agent in Cleveland, Ohio. The corporation appeared specially, filing a motion to quash on the ground that it had not committed a tortious act in Illinois. Its affidavit stated that it does no business here; that it has no agent physically present in Illinois; and that it sells the completed valves to defendant, American Radiator & Standard Sanitary Corporation, outside Illinois. * * * American Radiator * * * (also made a defendant) filed an answer in which it set up a cross claim against Titan, alleging that Titan made certain warranties to American Radiator, and that if the latter is held liable to the plaintiff it should be indemnified and held harmless by Titan. The court granted Titan's motion, dismissing both the complaint and the cross claim.

Section 16 of the Civil Practice Act provides that summons may be personally served upon any party outside the State; and that as to nonresidents who have submitted to the jurisdiction of our courts, such service has the force and effect of personal service within Illinois. (Ill.Rev.Stat.1959, chap. 110, par. 16.) Under section 17(1)(b) a nonresident who, either in person or through an agent, commits a tortious act within this State submits to jurisdiction. * * * The questions in this case are (1) whether a tortious act was committed here, within the meaning of the statute, despite the fact that the Titan corporation had no agent in Illinois; and (2) whether the statute, if so construed, violates due process of law.

The first aspect to which we must direct our attention is one of statutory construction. Under section 17(1)(b) jurisdiction is predicated on the committing of a tortious act in this State. It is not disputed, for the purpose of this appeal, that a tortious act was committed. The issue depends on whether it was committed in Illinois, so as to warrant the assertion of personal jurisdiction by service of summons in Ohio.

The wrong in the case at bar did not originate in the conduct of a servant physically present here, but arose instead from acts performed at the place of manufacture. Only the consequences occurred in Illinois. It is well established, however, that in law the place of a wrong is where the last event takes place which is necessary to render the actor liable. Restatement, Conflict of Laws, sec. 377. A second indication that the place of injury is the determining factor is found in rules governing the time within which an action must be brought. In applying statutes of limitation our court has computed the period from the time when the injury is done. * * * We think it is clear that the alleged negligence in manufacturing the valve cannot be separated from the resulting injury; and that for present purposes, like those of liability and limitations, the tort was committed in Illinois.

Titan seeks to avoid this result by arguing that instead of using the word "tort," the legislature employed the term "tortious act"; and that the latter refers only to the act or conduct, separate and apart from any consequences thereof. We cannot accept the argument. To be tortious an act must cause injury. The concept of injury is an inseparable part of the phrase. In determining legislative intention courts will read words in their ordinary and popularly understood sense. * * * We think the intent should be determined less from technicalities of definition than from considerations of general purpose and effect. To adopt the criteria urged by defendant would tend to promote litigation over extraneous issues concerning the elements of a tort and the territorial incidence of each, whereas the test should be concerned more with those substantial elements of convenience and justice presumably contemplated by the legislature. As we observed in Nelson v. Miller, 11 Ill.2d 378, 143 N.E.2d 673 [(1957)], the statute contemplates the exertion of jurisdiction over nonresident defendants to the extent permitted by the due-process clause.

The Titan company contends that if the statute is applied so as to confer jurisdiction in this case it violates the requirement of due process of law. The precise constitutional question thus presented has not heretofore been considered by this court. * * *

Under modern doctrine the power of a State court to enter a binding judgment against one not served with process within the State depends upon two questions: first, whether he has certain minimum contacts with the State * * * and second, whether there has been a reasonable method of notification. See International Shoe Co. v. State of Washington * * *. In the case at bar there is no contention that section 16 provides for inadequate notice or that its provisions were not followed. Defendant's argument on constitutionality is confined to the proposition that applying section 17(1)(b), where the injury is defendant's only contact with the State, would exceed the limits of due process.

A proper determination of the question presented requires analysis of those cases which have dealt with the quantum of contact sufficient to warrant jurisdiction. Since the decision in Pennoyer v. Neff * * * the power of a State to exert jurisdiction over nonresidents has been greatly expanded, particularly with respect to foreign corporations. * * * [In International Shoe Co. v. Washington,] the court pointed out that the activities of the corporation in Washington were not only continuous and systematic but also gave rise to the liability sued on. It was observed that such operations, which resulted in a large volume of business, established "sufficient contacts or ties with the state of the forum to make it reasonable and just according to our traditional conception of fair play and substantial justice to permit the state to enforce the obligations which appellant has incurred there." * * *

Where the business done by a foreign corporation in the State of the forum is of a sufficiently substantial nature, it has been held permissible for the State to entertain a suit against it even though the cause of action arose from activities entirely distinct from its conduct within the State. * * * But where such business or other activity is not substantial, the particular act or transaction having no connection with the State of the forum, the requirement of "contact" is not satisfied. * * *

In the case at bar the defendant's only contact with this State is found in the fact that a product manufactured in Ohio was incorporated in Pennsylvania, into a hot water heater which in the course of commerce was sold to an Illinois consumer. The record fails to disclose whether defendant has done any other business in Illinois, either directly or indirectly; and it is argued, in reliance on the International Shoe test, that since a course of business here has not been shown there are no "minimum contacts" sufficient to support jurisdiction. We do not think, however, that doing a given volume of business is the only way in which a nonresident can form the required connection with this State. Since the International Shoe case was decided the requirements for jurisdiction have been further relaxed, so that at the present time it is sufficient if the act or transaction itself has a substantial connection with the State of the forum.

In McGee * * * [p. 59, supra] suit was brought in California against a foreign insurance company on a policy issued to a resident of California. The defendant was not served with process in that State but was notified by registered mail at its place of business in Texas, pursuant to a statute permitting such service in suits on insurance contracts. The contract in question was delivered in California, the premiums were mailed from there and the insured was a resident of that State when he died, but defendant had no office or agent in California nor did it solicit any business there apart from the policy sued on. After referring briefly to the International Shoe case the court held that "it is sufficient for purposes of due process that the suit was based on a *contract* which had substantial connection" with California. (Emphasis supplied.)[a]

* * *

In Nelson v. Miller * * * the commission of a single tort within this State was held sufficient to sustain jurisdiction under the present statute. The defendant in that case, a resident of Wisconsin, was engaged in the business of selling appliances. It was alleged that in the process of delivering a stove in Illinois, an employee of the defendant negligently caused injury to the plaintiff. In holding that the defendant was not denied due process by being required to defend in Illinois, this court observed * * *: "The defendant sent his employee into Illinois in the advancement of his own interests. While he was here, the employee and the defendant enjoyed

---

[a] Alteration in original.

the benefit and protection of the laws of Illinois, including the right to resort to our courts. In the course of his stay here the employee performed acts that gave rise to an injury. The law of Illinois will govern the substantive rights and duties stemming from the incident. Witnesses, other than the defendant's employee, are likely to be found here, and not in Wisconsin. In such circumstances, it is not unreasonable to require the defendant to make his defense here."

Whether the type of activity conducted within the State is adequate to satisfy the requirement depends upon the facts in the particular case. * * * The question cannot be answered by applying a mechanical formula or rule of thumb but by ascertaining what is fair and reasonable in the circumstances. In the application of this flexible test the relevant inquiry is whether defendant engaged in some act or conduct by which he may be said to have invoked the benefits and protections of the law of the forum. * * * The relevant decisions since Pennoyer v. Neff show a development of the concept of personal jurisdiction from one which requires service of process within the State to one which is satisfied either if the act or transaction sued on occurs there or if defendant has engaged in a sufficiently substantial course of activity in the State, provided always that reasonable notice and opportunity to be heard are afforded. * * * [T]he trend in defining due process of law is away from the emphasis on territorial limitations and toward emphasis on providing adequate notice and opportunity to be heard: from the court with immediate power over the defendant, toward the court in which both parties can most conveniently settle their dispute.

In the McGee case the court commented on the trend toward expanding State jurisdiction over nonresidents, observing that: 'In part this is attributable to the fundamental transformation of our national economy over the years. Today many commercial transactions touch two or more States and may involve parties separated by the full continent. With this increasing nationalization of commerce has come a great increase in the amount of business conducted by mail across state lines. At the same time modern transportation and communication have made it much less burdensome for a party sued to defend himself in a State where he engages in economic activity.'

It is true that courts cannot "assume that this trend heralds the eventual demise of all restrictions on the personal jurisdiction of state courts." Hanson * * * [p. 60, supra]. An orderly and fair administration of the law throughout the nation requires protection against being compelled to answer claims brought in distant States with which the defendant has little or no association and in which he would be faced with an undue burden or disadvantage in making his defense. * * * [P]rocedural rules must be designed and appraised in the light of what is fair and just to both sides in the dispute. Interpretations of basic rights which consider only those of a claimant are not consonant with the fundamental requisites of due process.

In the case at bar defendant does not claim that the present use of its product in Illinois is an isolated instance. While the record does not disclose the volume of Titan's business or the territory in which appliances incorporating its valves are marketed, it is a reasonable inference that its commercial transactions, like those of other manufacturers, result in substantial use and consumption in this State. To the extent that its business may be directly affected by transactions occurring here it enjoys benefits from the laws of this State, and it has undoubtedly benefited, to a degree, from the protection which our law has given to the marketing of hot water heaters containing its valves. Where the alleged liability arises, as in this case, from the manufacture of products presumably sold in contemplation of use here, it should not matter that the purchase was made from an independent middleman or that someone other than the defendant shipped the product into this State.

With the increasing specialization of commercial activity and the growing interdependence of business enterprises it is seldom that a manufacturer deals directly with consumers in other States. The fact that the benefit he derives from its laws is an indirect one, however, does not make it any the less essential to the conduct of his business; and it is not unreasonable, where a cause of action arises from alleged defects in his product, to say that the use of such products in the ordinary course of commerce is sufficient contact with this State to justify a requirement that he defend here.

As a general proposition, if a corporation elects to sell its products for ultimate use in another State, it is not unjust to hold it answerable there for any damage caused by defects in those products. Advanced means of distribution and other commercial activity have made possible these modern methods of doing business, and have largely effaced the economic significance of State lines. By the same token, today's facilities for transportation and communication have removed much of the difficulty and inconvenience formerly encountered in defending lawsuits brought in other States.

* * *

The principles of due process relevant to the issue in this case support jurisdiction in the court where both parties can most conveniently settle their dispute. The facts show that the plaintiff, an Illinois resident, was injured in Illinois. The law of Illinois will govern the substantive questions, and witnesses on the issues of injury, damages and other elements relating to the occurrence are most likely to be found here. Under such circumstances the courts of the place of injury usually provide the most convenient forum for trial. * * * In Travelers Health Association v.

Commonwealth of Virginia, 339 U.S. 643, 70 S.Ct. 927, 94 L.Ed. 1154 [(1950)], a Nebraska insurance corporation was held subject to the jurisdiction of a Virginia regulatory commission although it had no paid agents within the State and its only contact there was a mail-order business operated from its Omaha office. The court observed, by way of *dictum,* that "suits on alleged losses can be more conveniently tried in Virginia where witnesses would most likely live and where claims for losses would presumably be investigated. Such factors have been given great weight in applying the doctrine of *forum non conveniens.* * * * And prior decisions of this Court have referred to the unwisdom, unfairness and injustice of permitting policyholders to seek redress only in some distant state where the insurer is incorporated. The Due Process Clause does not forbid a state to protect its citizens from such injustice." 339 U.S. at page 649, 70 S.Ct. at page 930, 94 L.Ed. at 1161–1162. * * *

* * * We conclude accordingly that defendant's association with this State is sufficient to support the exercise of jurisdiction.

* * *

Reversed and remanded, with directions.

NOTES AND QUESTIONS

1.   As *Gray* illustrates, the application of a long-arm statute often entails difficult questions of statutory construction. Are you persuaded by *Gray*'s interpretation of the Illinois long-arm statute? How could the statute have been drafted differently to remove any ambiguity about whether it covered the scenario in that case?

2.   Is the *Gray* court's due process analysis consistent with the U.S. Supreme Court's case law? In what way did Titan establish minimum contacts with Illinois? Is its relationship with Illinois stronger or weaker than International Life's relationship with California in *McGee*? Can it be argued that Titan "purposefully avail[ed] itself of the privilege of conducting activities within [Illinois], thus invoking the benefits and protections of its laws," as the Court required in *Hanson*, p. 60, *supra*?

D. SPECIFIC JURISDICTION IN STATE COURT

In 1977, after a 20-year hiatus following its decisions in *McGee* and *Hanson*, the Supreme Court returned to questions of personal jurisdiction and in a single decade decided 11 major personal jurisdiction cases. In this period, the *Hanson* majority's emphasis on acts "by which the defendant purposefully avails itself of the privilege of conducting activities within the forum State," p. 62, *supra*, came to dominate the Court's analysis. The critical question in each ensuing decision focuses on the nature of the acts that will be treated as manifesting defendant's purposeful availment sufficient to support the constitutionality of a state's exercise of specific jurisdiction. "Specific jurisdiction," as discussed p. 58, Note 2, supra, is the term that describes the court's power when the alleged claims arise out of or relate to defendant's contacts with the forum. It is contrasted with "general jurisdiction," which can subject a defendant to jurisdiction in all matters. As will be seen in Section E, infra, general jurisdiction requires more pervasive contacts with the forum than specific jurisdiction.

WORLD-WIDE VOLKSWAGEN CORP. v. WOODSON
Supreme Court of the United States, 1980.
444 U.S. 286, 100 S.Ct. 559, 62 L.Ed.2d 490.

Certiorari to the Supreme Court of Oklahoma.

JUSTICE WHITE delivered the opinion of the Court.

The issue before us is whether, consistently with the Due Process Clause of the Fourteenth Amendment, an Oklahoma court may exercise *in personam* jurisdiction over a nonresident automobile retailer and its wholesale distributor in a products liability action, when the defendants' only connection with Oklahoma is the fact that an automobile sold in New York to New York residents became involved in an accident in Oklahoma.

I

Respondents Harry and Kay Robinson purchased a new Audi automobile from petitioner Seaway Volkswagen, Inc. (Seaway) in Massena, N.Y., in 1976. The following year the Robinson family, who resided in New York, left that State for a new home in Arizona. As they passed through the State of Oklahoma, another car struck their Audi in the rear, causing a fire which severely burned Kay Robinson and her two children.

The Robinsons subsequently brought a products liability action in the District Court for Creek County, Okla., claiming that their injuries resulted from defective design and placement of the Audi's gas tank and fuel system. They joined as defendants the automobile's manufacturer, Audi NSU Auto Union Aktiengesellschaft (Audi); its importer, Volkswagen of America, Inc. (Volkswagen); its regional distributor, petitioner World-Wide Volkswagen Corporation (World-Wide); and its retail dealer, petitioner Seaway. Seaway and World-Wide entered special appearances, claiming that Oklahoma's exercise of jurisdiction over them would offend the limitations on the State's jurisdiction imposed by the Due Process Clause of the Fourteenth Amendment.

The facts presented to the District Court showed that World-Wide is incorporated and has its business office in New York. It distributes vehicles, parts, and accessories, under contract with Volkswagen, to retail dealers in New York, New Jersey, and Connecticut. Seaway, one of these retail dealers, is incorporated and has its place of business in New York. Insofar as the record reveals, Seaway and World-Wide are fully independent corporations whose relations with each other and with Volkswagen and Audi are contractual only. Respondents adduced no evidence that either World-Wide or Seaway does any business in Oklahoma, ships or sells any products to or in that State, has an agent to receive process there, or purchases advertisements in any media calculated to reach Oklahoma. In fact, * * * there was no showing that any automobile sold by World-Wide or Seaway has ever entered Oklahoma with the single exception of the vehicle involved in the present case.

Despite the apparent paucity of contacts between petitioners and Oklahoma, the District Court rejected their constitutional claim and reaffirmed that ruling in denying petitioners' motion for reconsideration. Petitioners then sought a writ of prohibition in the Supreme Court of Oklahoma to restrain the District Judge, respondent Charles S. Woodson, from exercising *in personam* jurisdiction over them. They renewed their contention that, because they had no "minimal contacts" * * * with the State of Oklahoma, the actions of the District Judge were in violation of their rights under the Due Process Clause.

The Supreme Court of Oklahoma denied the writ, * * * holding that personal jurisdiction over petitioners was authorized by Oklahoma's "long-arm" statute, Okla.Stat., Tit. 12, § 1701.03(a)(4) (1971).[7] Although the court noted that the proper approach was to test jurisdiction against both statutory and constitutional standards, its analysis did not distinguish these questions, probably because § 1701.03(a)(4) has been interpreted as conferring jurisdiction to the limits permitted by the United States Constitution. The court's rationale was contained in the following paragraph * * *:

> "In the case before us, the product being sold and distributed by the petitioners is by its very design and purpose so mobile that petitioners can foresee its possible use in Oklahoma. This is especially true of the distributor, who has the exclusive right to distribute such automobile in New York, New Jersey and Connecticut. The evidence presented below demonstrated that goods sold and distributed by the petitioners were used in the State of Oklahoma, and under the facts we believe it reasonable to infer, given the retail value of the automobile, that the petitioners derive substantial income from automobiles which from time to time are used in the State of Oklahoma. This being the case, we hold that under the facts presented, the trial court

---

7   This subsection provides:

"A court may exercise personal jurisdiction over a person, who acts directly or by an agent, as to a cause of action or claim for relief arising from the person's * * * causing tortious injury in this state by an act or omission outside this state if he regularly does or solicits business or engages in any other persistent course of conduct, or derives substantial revenue from goods used or consumed or services rendered, in this state * * *." * * *

was justified in concluding that the petitioners derive substantial revenue from goods used or consumed in this State."

We granted certiorari * * * to consider an important constitutional question with respect to state-court jurisdiction and to resolve a conflict between the Supreme Court of Oklahoma and the highest courts of at least four other States. We reverse.

II

* * *

As has long been settled, and as we reaffirm today, a state court may exercise personal jurisdiction over a nonresident defendant only so long as there exist "minimum contacts" between the defendant and the forum State. *International Shoe Co. v. Washington* * * * [p. 52, supra]. The concept of minimum contacts, in turn, can be seen to perform two related, but distinguishable, functions. It protects the defendant against the burdens of litigating in a distant or inconvenient forum. And it acts to ensure that the States, through their courts, do not reach out beyond the limits imposed on them by their status as coequal sovereigns in a federal system.

The protection against inconvenient litigation is typically described in terms of "reasonableness" or "fairness." We have said that the defendant's contacts with the forum State must be such that maintenance of the suit "does not offend 'traditional notions of fair play and substantial justice.' " * * * The relationship between the defendant and the forum must be such that it is "reasonable * * * to require the corporation to defend the particular suit which is brought there." * * * Implicit in this emphasis on reasonableness is the understanding that the burden on the defendant, while always a primary concern, will in an appropriate case be considered in light of other relevant factors, including the forum State's interest in adjudicating the dispute * * *; the plaintiff's interest in obtaining convenient and effective relief, * * * at least when that interest is not adequately protected by the plaintiff's power to choose the forum * * *; the interstate judicial system's interest in obtaining the most efficient resolution of controversies; and the shared interest of the several States in furthering fundamental substantive social policies * * *.

The limits imposed on state jurisdiction by the Due Process Clause, in its role as a guarantor against inconvenient litigation, have been substantially relaxed over the years. As we noted in *McGee* * * * [p. 59, supra] this trend is largely attributable to a fundamental transformation in the American economy:

"Today many commercial transactions touch two or more States and may involve parties separated by the full continent. With this increasing nationalization of commerce has come a great increase in the amount of business conducted by mail across state lines. At the same time modern transportation and communication have made it much less burdensome for a party sued to defend himself in a State where he engages in economic activity."

The historical developments noted in *McGee,* of course, have only accelerated in the generation since that case was decided.

Nevertheless, we have never accepted the proposition that state lines are irrelevant for jurisdictional purposes, nor could we, and remain faithful to the principles of interstate federalism embodied in the Constitution. * * * [T]he Framers * * * intended that the States retain many essential attributes of sovereignty, including, in particular, the sovereign power to try causes in their courts. The sovereignty of each State, in turn, implied a limitation on the sovereignty of all of its sister States—a limitation express or implicit in both the original scheme of the Constitution and the Fourteenth Amendment.

* * *

* * * Even if the defendant would suffer minimal or no inconvenience from being forced to litigate before the tribunals of another State; even if the forum State has a strong interest in applying its law to the controversy; even if the forum State is the most convenient location for litigation, the Due Process Clause, acting as an instrument of interstate federalism, may sometimes act to divest the State of its power to render a valid judgment. *Hanson* * * * [p. 60, supra].

III

Applying these principles to the case at hand, we find in the record before us a total absence of those affiliating circumstances that are a necessary predicate to any exercise of state-court jurisdiction. Petitioners carry on no activity whatsoever in Oklahoma. They close no sales and perform no services there. They avail themselves of none of the privileges and benefits of Oklahoma law. They solicit no business there either through salespersons or through advertising reasonably calculated to reach the State. Nor does the record show that they regularly sell cars at wholesale or retail to Oklahoma customers or residents or that they indirectly, through others, serve or seek to serve the Oklahoma market. In short, respondents seek to base jurisdiction on one, isolated occurrence and whatever inferences can be drawn therefrom: the fortuitous circumstance that a single Audi automobile, sold in New York to New York residents, happened to suffer an accident while passing through Oklahoma.

It is argued, however, that because an automobile is mobile by its very design and purpose it was "foreseeable" that the Robinsons' Audi would cause injury in Oklahoma. Yet "foreseeability" alone has never been a sufficient benchmark for personal jurisdiction under the Due Process

Clause. In *Hanson v. Denckla* * * * it was no doubt foreseeable that the settlor of a Delaware trust would subsequently move to Florida and seek to exercise a power of appointment there; yet we held that Florida courts could not constitutionally exercise jurisdiction over a Delaware trustee that had no other contacts with the forum State. * * *

If foreseeability were the criterion, a local California tire retailer could be forced to defend in Pennsylvania when a blowout occurs there, * * * a Wisconsin seller of a defective automobile jack could be haled before a distant court for damage caused in New Jersey, * * * or a Florida soft-drink concessionaire could be summoned to Alaska to account for injuries happening there * * *. Every seller of chattels would in effect appoint the chattel his agent for service of process. His amenability to suit would travel with the chattel. * * *

This is not to say, of course, that foreseeability is wholly irrelevant. But the foreseeability that is critical to due process analysis is not the mere likelihood that a product will find its way into the forum State. Rather, it is that the defendant's conduct and connection with the forum State are such that he should reasonably anticipate being haled into court there. * * * The Due Process Clause, by ensuring the "orderly administration of the laws," * * * gives a degree of predictability to the legal system that allows potential defendants to structure their primary conduct with some minimum assurance as to where that conduct will and will not render them liable to suit.

When a corporation "purposefully avails itself of the privilege of conducting activities within the forum State," * * * it has clear notice that it is subject to suit there, and can act to alleviate the risk of burdensome litigation by procuring insurance, passing the expected costs on to customers, or, if the risks are too great, severing its connection with the State. Hence if the sale of a product of a manufacturer or distributor such as Audi or Volkswagen is not simply an isolated occurrence, but arises from the efforts of the manufacturer or distributor to serve, directly or indirectly, the market for its product in other States, it is not unreasonable to subject it to suit in one of those States if its allegedly defective merchandise has there been the source of injury to its owner or to others. The forum State does not exceed its powers under the Due Process Clause if it asserts personal jurisdiction over a corporation that delivers its products into the stream of commerce with the expectation that they will be purchased by consumers in the forum State. Cf. *Gray v. American Radiator* * * * [p. 64, supra].

But there is no such or similar basis for Oklahoma jurisdiction over World-Wide or Seaway in this case. Seaway's sales are made in Massena, N.Y. World-Wide's market, although substantially larger, is limited to dealers in New York, New Jersey, and Connecticut. There is no evidence of record that any automobiles distributed by World-Wide are sold to retail customers outside this tristate area. It is foreseeable that the purchasers of automobiles sold by World-Wide and Seaway may take them to Oklahoma. But the mere "unilateral activity of those who claim some relationship with a nonresident defendant cannot satisfy the requirement of contact with the forum State." *Hanson* * * *.

In a variant on the previous argument, it is contended that jurisdiction can be supported by the fact that petitioners earn substantial revenue from goods used in Oklahoma. * * * While this inference seems less than compelling on the facts of the instant case, we need not question the court's factual findings in order to reject its reasoning.

This argument seems to make the point that the purchase of automobiles in New York, from which the petitioners earn substantial revenue, would not occur *but for* the fact that the automobiles are capable of use in distant States like Oklahoma. Respondents observe that the very purpose of an automobile is to travel, and that travel of automobiles sold by petitioners is facilitated by an extensive chain of Volkswagen service centers throughout the country, including some in Oklahoma. However, financial benefits accruing to the defendant from a collateral relation to the forum State will not support jurisdiction if they do not stem from a constitutionally cognizable contact with that State. * * * In our view, whatever marginal revenues petitioners may receive by virtue of the fact that their products are capable of use in Oklahoma is far too attenuated a contact to justify that State's exercise of *in personam* jurisdiction over them.

Because we find that petitioners have no "contacts, ties, or relations" with the State of Oklahoma, *International Shoe* * * *, the judgment of the Supreme Court of Oklahoma is

Reversed.

[The dissenting opinions of JUSTICE MARSHALL and JUSTICE BLACKMUN are omitted.]

JUSTICE BRENNAN, dissenting.

* * *

I

The Court's opinions focus tightly on the existence of contacts between the forum and the defendant. In so doing, they accord too little weight to the strength of the forum State's interest in the case and fail to explore whether there would be any actual inconvenience to the defendant. The essential inquiry in locating the constitutional limits on state-court jurisdiction over absent defendants is whether the particular exercise of jurisdiction offends "'traditional notions of fair play and substantial justice.' " * * * The clear focus in *International Shoe* was on fairness and reasonableness. * * * The Court specifically declined to establish a mechanical test based on the quantum of contacts between a State and the defendant * * *. The existence of contacts, so long as there were some, was merely one way of giving content to the determination of fairness and reasonableness.

Surely *International Shoe* contemplated that the significance of the contacts necessary to support jurisdiction would diminish if some other consideration helped establish that jurisdiction would be fair and reasonable. The interests of the State and other parties in proceeding with the case in a particular forum are such considerations. *McGee* * * *, for instance, accorded great importance to a State's "manifest interest in providing effective means of redress" for its citizens. * * *

Another consideration is the actual burden a defendant must bear in defending the suit in the forum. * * * Because lesser burdens reduce the unfairness to the defendant, jurisdiction may be justified despite less significant contacts. The burden, of course, must be of constitutional dimension. Due process limits on jurisdiction do not protect a defendant from all inconvenience of travel * * *. Instead, the constitutionally significant "burden" to be analyzed relates to the mobility of the defendant's defense. For instance, if having to travel to a foreign forum would hamper the defense because witnesses or evidence or the defendant himself were immobile, or if there were a disproportionately large number of witnesses or amount of evidence that would have to be transported at the defendant's expense, or if being away from home for the duration of the trial would work some special hardship on the defendant, then the Constitution would require special consideration for the defendant's interests.

That considerations other than contacts between the forum and the defendant are relevant necessarily means that the Constitution does not require that trial be held in the State which has the "best contacts" with the defendant. * * * The defendant has no constitutional entitlement to the best forum or, for that matter, to any particular forum. Under even the most restrictive view of *International Shoe,* several States could have jurisdiction over a particular cause of action. We need only determine whether the forum States in these cases satisfy the constitutional minimum.

II

* * * I would find that the forum State has an interest in permitting the litigation to go forward, the litigation is connected to the forum, the defendant is linked to the forum, and the burden of defending is not unreasonable. Accordingly, I would hold that it is neither unfair nor unreasonable to require these defendants to defend in the forum State.

* * *

* * * [T]he interest of the forum State and its connection to the litigation is strong. The automobile accident underlying the litigation occurred in Oklahoma. The plaintiffs were hospitalized in Oklahoma when they brought suit. Essential witnesses and evidence were in Oklahoma. * * * The State has a legitimate interest in enforcing its laws designed to keep its highway system safe, and the trial can proceed at least as efficiently in Oklahoma as anywhere else.

The petitioners are not unconnected with the forum. Although both sell automobiles within limited sales territories, each sold the automobile which in fact was driven to Oklahoma where it was involved in an accident. It may be true, as the Court suggests, that each sincerely intended to limit its commercial impact to the limited territory, and that each intended to accept the benefits and protection of the laws only of those States within the territory. But obviously these were unrealistic hopes that cannot be treated as an automatic constitutional shield.

An automobile simply is not a stationary item or one designed to be used in one place. An automobile is *intended* to be moved around. Someone in the business of selling large numbers of automobiles can hardly plead ignorance of their mobility or pretend that the automobiles stay put after they are sold. It is not merely that a dealer in automobiles foresees that they will move. * * * The dealer actually intends that the purchasers will use the automobiles to travel to distant States where the dealer does not directly "do business." The sale of an automobile does *purposefully* inject the vehicle into the stream of interstate commerce so that it can travel to distant States. * * *

The Court accepts that a State may exercise jurisdiction over a distributor which "serves" that State "indirectly" by "deliver[ing] its products into the stream of commerce with the expectation that they will be purchased by consumers in the forum State." * * * It is difficult to see why the Constitution should distinguish between a case involving goods which reach a distant State through a chain of distribution and a case involving goods which reach the same State because a consumer, using them as the dealer knew the customer would, took them there. In each case the seller purposefully injects the goods into the stream of commerce and those goods predictably are used in the forum State.

* * *

III

It may be that affirmance of the judgments in these cases would approach the outer limits of *International Shoe*'s jurisdictional principle. But that principle, with its almost exclusive focus on the rights of defendants, may be outdated. * * *

International Shoe inherited its defendant focus from *Pennoyer v. Neff* * * * and represented the last major step this Court has taken in the long process of liberalizing the doctrine of personal jurisdiction. Though its flexible approach represented a major advance, the structure of our society has changed in many significant ways since *International Shoe* was decided in 1945. * * * As the Court acknowledges, * * * both the nationalization of commerce and the ease of transportation and communication have accelerated in the generation since 1957 [when the Court decided *McGee*]. The model of society on which the *International Shoe* Court based its opinion is no longer accurate. Business people, no matter how local their businesses, cannot assume that goods remain in the business' locality. Customers and goods can be anywhere else in the country usually in a matter of hours and always in a matter of a very few days.

In answering the question whether or not it is fair and reasonable to allow a particular forum to hold a trial binding on a particular defendant, the interests of the forum State and other parties loom large in today's world and surely are entitled to as much weight as are the interests of the defendant. The "orderly administration of the laws" provides a firm basis for according some protection to the interests of plaintiffs and States as well as of defendants. Certainly, I cannot see how a defendant's right to due process is violated if the defendant suffers no inconvenience. * * *

The conclusion I draw is that constitutional concepts of fairness no longer require the extreme concern for defendants that was once necessary. Rather, * * * minimum contacts must exist "among the *parties,* the contested transaction, and the forum State."[15] The contacts between any two of these should not be determinative. * * *

In effect the Court is allowing defendants to assert the sovereign rights of their home States. The expressed fear is that otherwise all limits on personal jurisdiction would disappear. But the argument's premise is wrong. I would not abolish limits on jurisdiction or strip state boundaries of all significance * * *; I would still require the plaintiff to demonstrate sufficient contacts among the parties, the forum, and the litigation to make the forum a reasonable State in which to hold the trial.

I would also, however, strip the defendant of an unjustified veto power over certain very appropriate fora—a power the defendant justifiably enjoyed long ago when communication and travel over long distances were slow and unpredictable and when notions of state sovereignty were impractical and exaggerated. * * *

---

[15] In some cases, the inquiry will resemble the inquiry commonly undertaken in determining which State's law to apply. That it is fair to apply a State's law to a nonresident defendant is clearly relevant in determining whether it is fair to subject the defendant to jurisdiction in that State. * * *

NOTES AND QUESTIONS

1.   At the time the suit was filed, Kay Robinson and her two children, Sam and Eva, were hospitalized with severe burns:

> Since Kay Robinson had been trapped in the burning car the longest, her burns were the most horrible of all. She had burns on forty-eight percent of her body—thirty-five percent of which were third degree. Kay was in the intensive care unit for seventy-seven days and was hospitalized in Tulsa for another several months. She underwent thirty-four operations, all but two of which were under general anesthetic, for skin grafts and other reconstructive surgery. Most of her fingers were amputated, and she had severe scarring over the entire part of her body. Eva and Kay also suffered severe psychological trauma both from the ordeal and from their permanent disfigurement.

Adams, World-Wide Volkswagen v. Woodson—*The Rest of the Story*, 72 Neb.L.Rev. 1122, 1126 (1993). The author continues: "Unfortunately for the Robinsons, [the driver], the person most responsible for their injuries, had no insurance and was judgment proof. Since they could not recover from [him], the Robinsons were forced to bring a difficult products liability suit that continued for fifteen years." Id. at 1156.

2.   In the course of its *World-Wide Volkswagen* opinion, the Court invoked notions of sovereignty and of convenience. Is there a tension between these two concepts? Is the Court promulgating a two-part test with a "sovereignty branch" and a "convenience branch"? Is this a new test or a refinement of the "minimum contacts" test announced in *International Shoe*?

3.   How might the Court have decided *World-Wide Volkswagen* if the Robinsons had been Oklahoma residents and purchased the ill-fated car while in New York on vacation? Would the Court have given more weight to plaintiffs' foreseeability argument? What if the driver of the other car had sued World-Wide and Seaway for injuries resulting from the exploding gas tank? What if that driver had never driven or even been outside the state of Oklahoma?

4.   Review the text of Oklahoma's long-arm statute, p. 72, n.7, supra. As a matter of statutory interpretation (as distinct from the constitutional issues addressed by the U.S. Supreme Court), does the text of that statute permit jurisdiction over World-Wide and Seaway? Would it permit jurisdiction over Audi and Volkswagen? What other information would be needed to analyze these questions?

———

The constraints on personal jurisdiction in state court can also be relevant when an action is brought in federal court. See p. 168, infra. In many federal cases the federal court's jurisdictional reach is limited to that of the state in which it sits. See Federal Rule 4(k)(1)(A). In KEETON v.

HUSTLER MAGAZINE, INC., 465 U.S. 770, 104 S.Ct. 1473, 79 L.Ed.2d 790 (1984), Keeton, a resident of New York, brought a libel suit in New Hampshire federal court against Hustler Magazine, an Ohio corporation. Keeton chose to sue in New Hampshire because it was the only state where the statute of limitations did not time-bar the action. Defendant's contacts with New Hampshire consisted "of the sale of some 10 to 15,000 copies of *Hustler* magazine in that state each month." Id. at 772, 104 S.Ct. at 1477, 79 L.Ed.2d at 796. Keeton herself had only one connection to New Hampshire: A magazine that she helped to produce was circulated there.

The district court dismissed Keeton's suit for lack of jurisdiction, and the First Circuit affirmed, holding that Keeton's lack of contacts with New Hampshire rendered the state's interest in redressing the libel, in a suit seeking nationwide damages, too attenuated to support jurisdiction. The Supreme Court unanimously reversed, saying:

> [R]egular monthly sales of thousands of magazines cannot by any stretch of the imagination be characterized as random, isolated, or fortuitous. It is, therefore, unquestionable that New Hampshire jurisdiction over a complaint based on those contacts would ordinarily satisfy the requirement of the Due Process Clause that a State's assertion of personal jurisdiction over a nonresident defendant be predicated on "minimum contacts" between the defendant and the State. * * * And, as the Court of Appeals acknowledged, New Hampshire has adopted a "long-arm" statute authorizing service of process on nonresident corporations whenever permitted by the Due Process Clause. * * * Thus, all the requisites for personal jurisdiction over Hustler Magazine, Inc., in New Hampshire are present.

Id. at 774–75, 104 S.Ct. at 1478, 79 L.Ed.2d at 797–98. The Court also found that "it is 'fair' to compel [defendant] to defend a multistate lawsuit in New Hampshire seeking nationwide damages * * * even though only a small portion of those copies were distributed in New Hampshire." Id. at 775, 104 S.Ct. at 1478–79, 79 L.Ed.2d at 798. It explained:

> [I]t is beyond dispute that New Hampshire has a significant interest in redressing injuries that actually occur within the State. * * * This interest extends to libel actions brought by nonresidents. False statements of fact harm both the subject of the falsehood and the readers of the statement. New Hampshire may rightly employ its libel laws to discourage the deception of its citizens. * * * New Hampshire also has a substantial interest in cooperating with other States * * * to provide a forum for efficiently litigating all issues and damage claims arising out of a libel in a unitary proceeding. This rule reduces the potential serious drain of libel cases on judicial resources. It also serves to

protect defendants from harassment resulting from multiple suits.

Id. at 776–77, 104 S.Ct. at 1479–80, 79 L.Ed.2d at 798–99.

Although the Court upheld jurisdiction in New Hampshire even though plaintiff was a nonresident, the Court recognized that a plaintiff's residence in the forum state could further strengthen the case for jurisdiction. In particular, a plaintiff's residence in the forum, "because of the defendant's relationship with the plaintiff, [may] enhance the defendant's contacts with the forum." Id. at 780, 104 S.Ct. at 1481, 79 L.Ed.2d at 801. The Court made clear, however, that "plaintiff's residence in the forum State is not a separate requirement, and lack of residence will not defeat jurisdiction established on the basis of defendant's contacts." Id.

What of the argument that it was unfair to allow suit to be brought in the only state where it was not time-barred? The Court did not treat that factor as relevant to the jurisdictional inquiry:

> * * * [A]ny potential unfairness in applying New Hampshire's statute of limitations to all aspects of this nationwide suit has nothing to do with the jurisdiction of the Court to adjudicate the claims. "The issue is personal jurisdiction, not choice of law." Hanson v. Denckla * * *. The question of the applicability of New Hampshire's statute of limitations to claims for out of state damages presents itself in the course of litigation only after jurisdiction over respondent is established, and we do not think that such choice of law concerns should complicate or distort the jurisdictional inquiry.

Id. at 778, 104 S.Ct. at 1480, 79 L.Ed.2d at 800.

NOTES AND QUESTIONS

1.   In CALDER v. JONES, 465 U.S. 783, 104 S.Ct. 1482, 79 L.Ed.2d 804 (1984), Jones, a professional entertainer who lived and worked in California, brought suit in California state court, claiming that she had been libeled by an article published in the National Enquirer, a national magazine having its largest circulation in California. Defendants were the writer and editor of the article, both residents of Florida, as well as the magazine. The writer and the editor moved to quash service of process for lack of personal jurisdiction, and the California state court granted the motion on the ground that First Amendment concerns weighed against an assertion of jurisdiction otherwise proper under the Due Process Clause.

Ultimately, the Supreme Court disagreed, saying: "We also reject the suggestion that First Amendment concerns enter into the jurisdictional analysis. The infusion of such concerns would needlessly complicate an already imprecise inquiry." See also Keeton ("[W]e reject categorically the suggestion that invisible radiations from the First Amendment may defeat jurisdiction otherwise proper under the Due Process Clause," 465 U.S. at 781 n.12, 104 S.Ct. at 1481 n.12, 79 L.Ed.2d at 801 n.12).

Applying the minimum contacts test to the writer and editor in *Calder*, the Court found that jurisdiction was proper in California given that they were "primary participants in an alleged wrongdoing intentionally directed at a California resident." 465 U.S. at 790, 104 S.Ct. at 1487, 79 L.Ed.2d at 813.

> The allegedly libelous story concerned the California activities of a California resident. It impugned the professionalism of an entertainer whose television career was centered in California. The article was drawn from California sources, and the brunt of the harm, in terms both of respondent's emotional distress and the injury to her professional reputation, was suffered in California. In sum, California, is the focal point both of the story and of the harm suffered. Jurisdiction over petitioners is therefore proper in California based on the "effects" of their Florida conduct in California.

Id. at 788–89, 104 S.Ct. at 1486–87, 79 L.Ed.2d at 812.

2.   KULKO v. SUPERIOR COURT, 436 U.S. 84, 98 S.Ct. 1690, 56 L.Ed.2d 132 (1978), was a suit for modification of a child support agreement. The mother lived in California and her ex-husband lived in New York. Initially, the couple's two children lived with the father in New York; later, the father permitted the daughter to live with the mother in California and purchased her a plane ticket to travel to that state. Soon afterwards, the son, without asking his father, joined his mother and sister in California using a ticket that his mother mailed to him. The California Supreme Court based jurisdiction on the ground that by consenting to his children's living in California, the father caused an effect in the state.

The Supreme Court reversed, six-to-three. The Court found that reliance on an effects test in the domestic context was "misplaced," emphasizing that use of the effects test should be limited to disputes involving commercial activity or to wrongful activity done outside the state but generating in-state negative effects: "To make jurisdiction in a case such as this turn on whether appellant bought his daughter her ticket or instead unsuccessfully sought to prevent her departure would impose an unreasonable burden on family relations, and one wholly unjustified by the 'quality and nature' of appellant's activities in or relating to the State of California." Id. at 98, 98 S.Ct. at 1700, 56 L.Ed.2d at 145.

———

BURGER KING CORP. v. RUDZEWICZ, 471 U.S. 462, 105 S.Ct. 2174, 85 L.Ed.2d 528 (1985), involved a diversity suit in Florida federal court against Michigan-based franchisees for breach of a franchise agreement with Burger King, a Florida company. The district court entered judgment on the merits against the franchisees (named John Rudzewicz and Brian MacShara), but the court of appeals reversed, holding that "[j]urisdiction under these circumstances would offend the fundamental fairness which is the touchstone of due process." Burger King Corp. v. MacShara, 724 F.2d 1505, 1513 (11th Cir. 1984). The Supreme Court, in an opinion by Justice Brennan, reversed, clarifying when a contract counts as a contact for jurisdictional purposes:

> * * * If the question is whether an individual's contract with an out-of-state party alone can automatically establish sufficient minimum contacts in the other party's home forum, we believe the answer clearly is that it cannot. * * * [W]e have emphasized the need for a "highly realistic" approach that recognizes that a "contract" is "ordinarily but an intermediate step serving to tie up prior business negotiations with future consequences which themselves are the real object of the business transaction." * * * It is these factors—prior negotiations and contemplated future consequences, along with the terms of the contract and the parties' actual course of dealing—that must be evaluated in determining whether the defendant purposefully established minimum contacts within the forum.
>
> In this case, no physical ties to Florida can be attributed to Rudzewicz other than MacShara's brief training course in Miami. * * * Rudzewicz did not maintain offices in Florida and, for all that appears from the record, has never even visited there. Yet this franchise dispute grew directly out of "a contract which had a substantial connection with that State." McGee * * * (emphasis added).[b] Eschewing the option of operating an independent local enterprise, Rudzewicz deliberately "reach[ed] out beyond" Michigan and negotiated with a Florida corporation for the purchase of a long-term franchise and the manifold benefits that would derive from affiliation with a nationwide organization. * * * Upon approval, he entered into a carefully structured 20-year relationship that envisioned continuing and wide-reaching contacts with Burger King in Florida. In light of Rudzewicz' voluntary acceptance of the long-term and exacting regulation of his business from Burger King's Miami headquarters, the "quality and nature" of his relationship to the company in Florida can in no sense be viewed as "random," "fortuitous," or "attenuated." * * * Rudzewicz' refusal to make the contractually required payments in Miami, and his continued use of Burger King's trademarks and confidential business information after his termination, caused foreseeable injuries to the corporation in Florida. * * *

---

[b] Alteration in original.

* * * Rudzewicz most certainly knew that he was affiliating himself with an enterprise based primarily in Florida. The contract documents themselves emphasize that Burger King's operations are conducted and supervised from the Miami headquarters, that all relevant notices and payments must be sent there, and that the agreements were made in and enforced from Miami. * * * Moreover, the parties' actual course of dealing repeatedly confirmed that decisionmaking authority was vested in the Miami headquarters and that the district office served largely as an intermediate link between the headquarters and the franchisees. * * *

Moreover, * * * provisions in the various franchise documents provid[ed] that all disputes would be governed by Florida law. * * * The Court in *Hanson* [p. 60, supra] and subsequent cases has emphasized that choice-of-law analysis—which focuses on all elements of a transaction, and not simply on the defendant's conduct—is distinct from minimum-contacts jurisdictional analysis—which focuses at the threshold solely on the defendant's purposeful connection to the forum. Nothing in our cases, however, suggests that a choice-of-law provision should be ignored in considering whether a defendant has "purposefully invoked the benefits and protections of a State's laws" for jurisdictional purposes. Although such a provision standing alone would be insufficient to confer jurisdiction, we believe that, when combined with the 20-year interdependent relationship Rudzewicz established with Burger King's Miami headquarters, it reinforced his deliberate affiliation with the forum State and the reasonable foreseeability of possible litigation there. * * *

Id. at 478–82, 105 S.Ct. at 2185–87, 85 L.Ed.2d at 544–47.

The Court went on to emphasize that neither Michigan's interest in protecting franchisees nor any inconvenience defendant might face in calling Michigan witnesses rendered the exercise of power unconstitutional: "We cannot conclude that Florida had no "legitimate interest in holding [Rudzewicz] answerable on a claim related to" the contacts he had established in that State. * * * Although the Court has suggested that inconvenience may at some point become so substantial as to achieve constitutional magnitude, * * * this is not such a case." Id. at 482–84, 105 S.Ct. at 2187–88, 85 L.Ed.2d at 547–48.

Finally, accepting the district court's finding that defendants were "experienced and sophisticated businessmen" who did not act under economic duress, the Court declined to overturn the exercise of jurisdiction as a "prophylactic measure":

[T]he Court of Appeals apparently believed * * * that an affirmance of the District Court's judgment would result in the exercise of jurisdiction over "out-of-state consumers to collect payments due on modest personal purchases" and would "sow the seeds of default judgments against franchisees owing smaller debts." * * * We share the Court of Appeals' broader concerns and therefore reject any talismanic jurisdictional formulas; "the facts of each case must [always] be weighed" in determining whether personal jurisdiction would comport with "fair play and substantial justice." * * *

Id. at 485–86, 105 S.Ct. at 2189, 85 L.Ed.2d at 549.

Justice Stevens dissented, joined in his opinion by Justice White:

In my opinion there is a significant element of unfairness in requiring a franchisee to defend a case of this kind in the forum chosen by the franchisor. It is undisputed that respondent maintained no place of business in Florida, that he had no employees in that State, and that he was not licensed to do business there. Respondent did not prepare his French fries, shakes, and hamburgers in Michigan, and then deliver them into the stream of commerce "with the expectation that they [would] be purchased by consumers in" Florida. * * * To the contrary, respondent did business only in Michigan, his business, property, and payroll taxes were payable in that State, and he sold all of his products there.

Throughout the business relationship, respondent's principal contacts with petitioner were with its Michigan office. Notwithstanding its disclaimer, * * * the Court seems ultimately to rely on nothing more than standard boilerplate language contained in various documents * * * to establish that respondent " 'purposefully availed himself of the benefits and protections of Florida's laws.' " * * * Such superficial analysis creates a potential for unfairness not only in negotiations between franchisors and their franchisees but, more significantly, in the resolution of the disputes that inevitably arise from time to time in such relationships.

Id. at 487–88, 105 S.Ct. at 2190, 85 L.Ed.2d at 550–51.

NOTES AND QUESTIONS

1. What guidance does *Burger King* provide for assessing personal jurisdiction in breach-of-contract cases? The First Circuit has described *Burger King* as mandating a "contract-plus" analysis: "[A] court is to look at all of the communications and transactions between the parties, before, during and after the consummation of the contract, to determine the degree and type of contacts

the defendant has with the forum, apart from the contract alone." Ganis Corp. of Cal. v. Jackson, 822 F.2d 194, 197–98 (1st Cir. 1987). What purpose does the "plus" factor serve? Is it constitutionally compelled?

2.   How important to the decision in *Burger King* was the fact that the franchise agreement included a choice-of-law term selecting Florida as the governing law? Is that type of provision appropriately considered a "contact" with the chosen forum? Is it a "plus" factor? What if the forum has no interest in the contract other than the parties' agreement to be bound by the law of that state? Would the court give more weight to a forum-selection clause? We consider this type of agreement later in this chapter, p. 138, infra.

ASAHI METAL INDUSTRY CO. V. SUPERIOR COURT
Supreme Court of the United States, 1987.
480 U.S. 102, 107 S.Ct. 1026, 94 L.Ed.2d 92.

Certiorari to the Supreme Court of California.

JUSTICE O'CONNOR announced the judgment of the Court and delivered the unanimous opinion of the Court with respect to Part I, the opinion of the Court with respect to Part II-B, in which THE CHIEF JUSTICE, JUSTICE BRENNAN, JUSTICE WHITE, JUSTICE MARSHALL, JUSTICE BLACKMUN, JUSTICE POWELL, and JUSTICE STEVENS join, and an opinion with respect to Parts II-A and III, in which THE CHIEF JUSTICE, JUSTICE POWELL, and JUSTICE SCALIA join.

This case presents the question whether the mere awareness on the part of a foreign defendant that the component it manufactured, sold, and delivered outside the United States would reach the forum state in the stream of commerce constitutes "minimum contacts" between the defendant and the forum state such that the exercise of jurisdiction "does not offend 'traditional notions of fair play and substantial justice.' " * * *

I

On September 23, 1978, on Interstate Highway 80 in Solano County, California, Gary Zurcher lost control of his Honda motorcycle and collided with a tractor. Zurcher was severely injured, and his passenger and wife, Ruth Ann Moreno, was killed. In September 1979, Zurcher filed a product liability action in the Superior Court of the State of California in and for the County of Solano. Zurcher alleged that the 1978 accident was caused by a sudden loss of air and an explosion in the rear tire of the motorcycle, and alleged that the motorcycle tire, tube, and sealant were defective. Zurcher's complaint named, *inter alia,* Cheng Shin Rubber Industrial Co., Ltd. (Cheng Shin), the Taiwanese manufacturer of the tube. Cheng Shin in turn filed a cross-complaint seeking indemnification from its codefendants and from petitioner, Asahi Metal Industry Co., Ltd. (Asahi), the manufacturer of the tube's valve assembly. Zurcher's claims against Cheng

Shin and the other defendants were eventually settled and dismissed, leaving only Cheng Shin's indemnity action against Asahi.

California's long-arm statute authorizes the exercise of jurisdiction "on any basis not inconsistent with the Constitution of this state or of the United States." * * * Asahi moved to quash Cheng Shin's service of summons arguing the State could not exert jurisdiction over it consistent with the Due Process Clause of the Fourteenth Amendment.

In relation to the motion, the following information was submitted by Asahi and Cheng Shin. Asahi is a Japanese corporation. It manufactures tire valve assemblies in Japan and sells the assemblies to Cheng Shin, and to several other tire manufacturers, for use as components in finished tire tubes. Asahi's sales to Cheng Shin took place in Taiwan. The shipments from Asahi to Cheng Shin were sent from Japan to Taiwan. Cheng Shin bought and incorporated into its tire tubes 150,000 Asahi valve assemblies in 1978; 500,000 in 1979; 500,000 in 1980; 100,000 in 1981; and 100,000 in 1982. Sales to Cheng Shin accounted for 1.24 percent of Asahi's income in 1981 and 0.44 percent in 1982. Cheng Shin alleged that approximately 20 percent of its sales in the United States are in California. Cheng Shin purchases valve assemblies from other suppliers as well, and sells finished tubes throughout the world.

In 1983 an attorney for Cheng Shin conducted an informal examination of the valve stems of the tire tubes sold in one cyclery in Solano County. The attorney declared that of the approximately 115 tire tubes in the store, 97 were purportedly manufactured in Japan or Taiwan, and of those 97, 21 valve stems were marked with the circled letter "A", apparently Asahi's trademark. Of the 21 Asahi valve stems, 12 were incorporated into Cheng Shin tire tubes. The store contained 41 other Cheng Shin tubes that incorporated the valve assemblies of other manufacturers. * * * An affidavit of a manager of Cheng Shin whose duties included the purchasing of component parts stated: " 'In discussions with Asahi regarding the purchase of valve stem assemblies the fact that my Company sells tubes throughout the world and specifically the United States has been discussed. I am informed and believe that Asahi was fully aware that valve stem assemblies sold to my Company and to others would end up throughout the United States and in California.' " * * * An affidavit of the president of Asahi, on the other hand, declared that Asahi " 'has never contemplated that its limited sales of tire valves to Cheng Shin in Taiwan would subject it to lawsuits in California.' " * * * The record does not include any contract between Cheng Shin and Asahi. * * *

Primarily on the basis of the above information, the Superior Court denied the motion to quash summons, stating that "Asahi obviously does business on an international scale. It is not unreasonable that they defend claims of defect in their product on an international scale." Order Denying Motion to Quash Summons * * *.

The Court of Appeal of the State of California issued a peremptory writ of mandate commanding the Superior Court to quash service of summons. The court concluded that "it would be unreasonable to require Asahi to respond in California solely on the basis of ultimately realized foreseeability that the product into which its component was embodied would be sold all over the world including California." * * *

The Supreme Court of the State of California reversed and discharged the writ issued by the Court of Appeal. * * * The court observed that "Asahi has no offices, property or agents in California. It solicits no business in California and has made no direct sales [in California]." * * * Moreover, "Asahi did not design or control the system of distribution that carried its valve assemblies into California." * * * Nevertheless, the court found the exercise of jurisdiction over Asahi to be consistent with the Due Process Clause. It concluded that Asahi knew that some of the valve assemblies sold to Cheng Shin would be incorporated into tire tubes sold in California, and that Asahi benefited indirectly from the sale in California of products incorporating its components. The court considered Asahi's intentional act of placing its components into the stream of commerce—that is, by delivering the components to Cheng Shin in Taiwan—coupled with Asahi's awareness that some of the components would eventually find their way into California, sufficient to form the basis for state court jurisdiction under the Due Process Clause.

We granted certiorari * * * and now reverse.

II

A

* * *

Applying the principle that minimum contacts must be based on an act of the defendant, the Court in *World-Wide Volkswagen* * * * [p. 71, supra,] rejected the assertion that a *consumer's* unilateral act of bringing the defendant's product into the forum State was a sufficient constitutional basis for personal jurisdiction over the defendant. It had been argued in *World-Wide Volkswagen* that because an automobile retailer and its wholesale distributor sold a product mobile by design and purpose, they could foresee being haled into court in the distant States into which their customers might drive. The Court rejected this concept of foreseeability as an insufficient basis for jurisdiction under the Due Process Clause. * * * The Court disclaimed, however, the idea that "foreseeability is wholly irrelevant" to personal jurisdiction, concluding that "[t]he forum State does not exceed its powers under the Due Process Clause if it asserts personal jurisdiction over a corporation that delivers its products into the stream of commerce with the expectation that they will be purchased by consumers in the forum State." * * *

In *World-Wide Volkswagen* itself, the state court sought to base jurisdiction not on any act of the defendant, but on the foreseeable unilateral actions of the consumer. Since *World-Wide Volkswagen,* lower courts have been confronted with cases in which the defendant acted by placing a product in the stream of commerce, and the stream eventually swept defendant's product into the forum State, but the defendant did nothing else to purposefully avail itself of the market in the forum state. Some courts have understood the Due Process Clause, as interpreted in *World-Wide Volkswagen,* to allow an exercise of personal jurisdiction to be based on no more than the defendant's act of placing the product in the stream of commerce. Other courts have understood the Due Process Clause and the above-quoted language in *World-Wide Volkswagen* to require the action of the defendant to be more purposefully directed at the forum State than the mere act of placing a product in the stream of commerce.

The reasoning of the Supreme Court of California in the present case illustrates the former interpretation of *World-Wide Volkswagen.* The Supreme Court of California held that, because the stream of commerce eventually brought some valves Asahi sold Cheng Shin into California, Asahi's awareness that its valves would be sold in California was sufficient to permit California to exercise jurisdiction over Asahi consistent with the requirements of the Due Process Clause. The Supreme Court of California's position was consistent with those courts that have held that mere foreseeability or awareness was a constitutionally sufficient basis for personal jurisdiction if the defendant's product made its way into the forum State while still in the stream of commerce. * * *

Other courts, however, have understood the Due Process Clause to require something more than that the defendant was aware of its product's entry into the forum State through the stream of commerce in order for the state to exert jurisdiction over the defendant. * * *

We now find this latter position to be consonant with the requirements of due process. The "substantial connection" * * * between the defendant and the forum State necessary for a finding of minimum contacts must come about by *an action of the defendant purposefully directed toward the forum State.* * * * The placement of a product into the stream of commerce, without more, is not an act of the defendant purposefully directed toward the forum State. Additional conduct of the defendant may indicate an intent or purpose to serve the market in the forum State, for example, designing the product for the market in the forum State, advertising in the forum State, establishing channels for providing regular advice to customers in the forum State, or marketing the product through a distributor who has agreed to serve as the sales agent in the forum State.

But a defendant's awareness that the stream of commerce may or will sweep the product into the forum State does not convert the mere act of placing the product into the stream into an act purposefully directed toward the forum State.

Assuming, *arguendo,* that respondents have established Asahi's awareness that some of the valves sold to Cheng Shin would be incorporated into tire tubes sold in California, respondents have not demonstrated any action by Asahi to purposefully avail itself of the California market. Asahi does not do business in California. It has no office, agents, employees, or property in California. It does not advertise or otherwise solicit business in California. It did not create, control, or employ the distribution system that brought its valves to California. * * * There is no evidence that Asahi designed its product in anticipation of sales in California. * * * On the basis of these facts, the exertion of personal jurisdiction over Asahi by the Superior Court of California exceeds the limits of due process.

B

* * *

We have previously explained that the determination of the reasonableness of the exercise of jurisdiction in each case will depend on an evaluation of several factors. A court must consider the burden on the defendant, the interests of the forum state, and the plaintiff's interest in obtaining relief. It must also weigh in its determination "the interstate judicial system's interest in obtaining the most efficient resolution of controversies; and the shared interest of the several States in furthering fundamental substantive social policies." * * *

A consideration of these factors in the present case clearly reveals the unreasonableness of the assertion of jurisdiction over Asahi, even apart from the question of the placement of goods in the stream of commerce.

Certainly the burden on the defendant in this case is severe. Asahi has been commanded by the Supreme Court of California not only to traverse the distance between Asahi's headquarters in Japan and the Superior Court of California in and for the County of Solano, but also to submit its dispute with Cheng Shin to a foreign nation's judicial system. The unique burdens placed upon one who must defend oneself in a foreign legal system should have significant weight in assessing the reasonableness of stretching the long arm of personal jurisdiction over national borders.

When minimum contacts have been established, often the interests of the plaintiff and the forum in the exercise of jurisdiction will justify even the serious burdens placed on the alien defendant. In the present case, however, the interests of the plaintiff and the forum in California's assertion of jurisdiction over Asahi are slight. All that remains is a claim for indemnification asserted by Cheng Shin, a Taiwanese corporation, against Asahi. The transaction on which the indemnification claim is based took place in Taiwan; Asahi's components were shipped from Japan to Taiwan. Cheng Shin has not demonstrated that it is more convenient for it to litigate its indemnification claim against Asahi in California rather than in Taiwan or Japan.

Because the plaintiff is not a California resident, California's legitimate interests in the dispute have considerably diminished. The Supreme Court of California argued that the State had an interest in "protecting its consumers by ensuring that foreign manufacturers comply with the state's safety standards." * * * The State Supreme Court's definition of California's interest, however, was overly broad. The dispute between Cheng Shin and Asahi is primarily about indemnification rather than safety standards. Moreover, it is not at all clear at this point that California law should govern the question whether a Japanese corporation should indemnify a Taiwanese corporation on the basis of a sale made in Taiwan and a shipment of goods from Japan to Taiwan. * * * The possibility of being haled into a California court as a result of an accident involving Asahi's components undoubtedly creates an additional deterrent to the manufacture of unsafe components; however, similar pressures will be placed on Asahi by the purchasers of its components as long as those who use Asahi components in their final products, and sell those products in California, are subject to the application of California tort law.

World-Wide Volkswagen also admonished courts to take into consideration the interests of the "several States," in addition to the forum state, in the efficient judicial resolution of the dispute and the advancement of substantive policies. In the present case, this advice calls for a court to consider the procedural and substantive policies of other *nations* whose interests are affected by the assertion of jurisdiction by the California court. The procedural and substantive interests of other nations in a state court's assertion of jurisdiction over an alien defendant will differ from case to case. In every case, however, those interests, as well as the Federal interest in its foreign relations policies, will be best served by a careful inquiry into the reasonableness of the assertion of jurisdiction in the particular case, and an unwillingness to find the serious burdens on an alien defendant outweighed by minimal interests on the part of the plaintiff or the forum State. "Great care and reserve should be exercised when extending our notions of personal jurisdiction into the international field." * * *

Considering the international context, the heavy burden on the alien defendant, and the slight interests of the plaintiff and the forum State, the exercise of personal jurisdiction by a California court over Asahi in this instance would be unreasonable and unfair.

III

Because the facts of this case do not establish minimum contacts such that the exercise of personal jurisdiction is consistent with fair play and substantial justice, the judgment of Supreme Court of California is reversed, and the case is remanded for further proceedings not inconsistent with this opinion.

It is so ordered.

JUSTICE BRENNAN, with whom JUSTICE WHITE, JUSTICE MARSHALL, and JUSTICE BLACKMUN join, concurring in part and concurring in the judgment.

I do not agree with the interpretation in Part II-A of the stream-of-commerce theory, nor with the conclusion that Asahi did not "purposely avail itself of the California market." * * * I do agree, however, with the Court's conclusion in Part II-B that the exercise of personal jurisdiction over Asahi in this case would not comport with "fair play and substantial justice" * * *. This is one of those rare cases in which "minimum requirements inherent in the concept of 'fair play and substantial justice' . . . defeat the reasonableness of jurisdiction even [though] the defendant has purposefully engaged in forum activities." * * * I therefore join Parts I and II-B of the Court's opinion, and write separately to explain my disagreement with Part II-A.

Part II-A states that "a defendant's awareness that the stream of commerce may or will sweep the product into the forum State does not convert the mere act of placing the product into the stream into an act purposefully directed toward the forum State." * * * Under this view, a plaintiff would be required to show "[a]dditional conduct" directed toward the forum before finding the exercise of jurisdiction over the defendant to be consistent with the Due Process Clause. * * * I see no need for such a showing, however. The stream of commerce refers not to unpredictable currents or eddies, but to the regular and anticipated flow of products from manufacture to distribution to retail sale. As long as a participant in this process is aware that the final product is being marketed in the forum State, the possibility of a lawsuit there cannot come as a surprise. Nor will the litigation present a burden for which there is no corresponding benefit. A defendant who has placed goods in the stream of commerce benefits economically from the retail sale of the final product in the forum State, and indirectly benefits from the State's laws that regulate and facilitate commercial activity. These benefits accrue regardless of whether that participant directly conducts business in the forum State, or engages in additional conduct directed toward that State. Accordingly, most courts and commentators have found that jurisdiction premised on the placement of a product into the stream of commerce is consistent with the Due Process Clause, and have not required a showing of additional conduct.

* * *

JUSTICE STEVENS, with whom JUSTICE WHITE and JUSTICE BLACKMUN join, concurring in part and concurring in the judgment.

The judgment of the Supreme Court of California should be reversed for the reasons stated in Part II-B of the Court's opinion. While I join Parts I and II-B, I do not join Part II-A for two reasons. First, it is not necessary to the Court's decision. An examination of minimum contacts is not always necessary to determine whether a state court's assertion of personal jurisdiction is constitutional. See *Burger King* * * * [p. 83, supra]. Part II-B establishes, after considering the factors set forth in *World-Wide Volkswagen Corp. v. Woodson,* * * * that California's exercise of jurisdiction over Asahi in this case would be "unreasonable and unfair." * * * This finding alone requires reversal; this case fits within the rule that "minimum requirements inherent in the concept of 'fair play and substantial justice' may defeat the reasonableness of jurisdiction even if the defendant has purposefully engaged in forum activities." *Burger King* * * *. Accordingly, I see no reason in this case for the plurality to articulate "purposeful direction" or any other test as the nexus between an act of a defendant and the forum State that is necessary to establish minimum contacts.

Second, even assuming that the test ought to be formulated here, Part II-A misapplies it to the facts of this case. The plurality seems to assume that an unwavering line can be drawn between "mere awareness" that a component will find its way into the forum State and "purposeful availment" of the forum's market. * * * Over the course of its dealings with Cheng Shin, Asahi has arguably engaged in a higher quantum of conduct than "[t]he placement of a product into the stream of commerce, without more. . . ." * * * Whether or not this conduct rises to the level of purposeful availment requires a constitutional determination that is affected by the volume, the value, and the hazardous character of the components. In most circumstances I would be inclined to conclude that a regular course of dealing that results in deliveries of over 100,000 units annually over a period of several years would constitute "purposeful availment" even though the item delivered to the forum State was a standard product marketed throughout the world.

NOTES AND QUESTIONS

1. Given the division among the Justices, on what particular issues do a majority of Justices agree? On what particular issues does Justice O'Connor's plurality opinion differ from the opinions filed by Justice Brennan and by Justice Stevens? Notice that Justice Scalia did not join Part II-B of the opinion of the Court. Why is that significant?

In the wake of *Asahi*, lower courts disagreed over which of the *Asahi* opinions to follow. The Sixth Circuit, for example, embraced Justice O'Connor's approach. See Bridgeport Music, Inc. v. Still N The Water Pub, 327 F.3d 472 (6th Cir. 2003) ("[W]e make clear today our preference for Justice O'Connor's stream of commerce 'plus' approach, for the reasons set forth in that opinion, and conduct the remainder of our analysis accordingly."). The Fifth Circuit, by contrast, reasoned as follows:

> This court has consistently held that mere foreseeability or awareness is a constitutionally sufficient basis for personal jurisdiction if the defendant's product made its way into the forum state while still in the stream of commerce. We adopted this position in an effort faithfully to interpret *World Wide Volkswagen* * * *, which holds that a state does not offend due process by exercising jurisdiction over an entity that delivers its products into the stream of commerce with the expectation that they will be purchased by consumers in the forum State. Where a defendant knowingly benefits from the availability of a particular state's market for its products, it is only fitting that the defendant be amenable to suit in that state. We have, therefore, declined to follow the suggestion of the plurality in *Asahi* * * * that some additional action on the part of the defendant, beyond foreseeability, is necessary to convert the mere act of placing the product into the stream into an act purposefully directed toward the forum State.

Luv N' care, Ltd. v. Insta-Mix, Inc., 438 F.3d 465, 470 (5th Cir. 2006) (footnotes, brackets, and internal quotation marks omitted).

2.   The Supreme Court did not disturb the California court's finding that "Asahi knew that some of the valve assemblies sold to Cheng Shin would be incorporated into tire tubes sold in California." Asahi Metal Industry Co., Ltd. v. Superior Court, 39 Cal.3d 35, 48, 702 P.2d 543, 549, 216 Cal.Rptr. 385, 392 (1985). Under Part II-A of Justice O'Connor's opinion, this knowledge alone could not serve as a basis for jurisdiction unless Asahi had taken some further action "purposefully directed toward the forum state." What additional action might satisfy that standard? Does Justice O'Connor's approach allow the nonresident manufacturer of a component part to avoid the safety standards of states in which the final product is sold? How would a supporter of Justice O'Connor's approach respond to this concern?

3.   Should the approach taken by Justice O'Connor apply only to foreign defendants? Does it affect your view that some bases of jurisdiction in the United States are regarded as "exorbitant" by other countries? See Clermont & Palmer, *Exorbitant Jurisdiction*, 58 Me.L.Rev. 474 (2006). Doesn't a United States plaintiff face a "substantial hardship" if required to litigate against a foreign defendant in a foreign court? Did the plurality give any weight to that concern?

4.   Does the reasoning in Justice O'Connor's plurality opinion support the exercise of jurisdiction in *Gray*, p. 64, supra? In *Calder*, p. 82, Note 1, supra?

———

After the *Asahi* Court's lack of a majority opinion regarding the proper approach to personal jurisdiction in cases where contacts occur via the "stream of commerce," more than two decades passed before the Supreme Court revisited the issue.

J. MCINTYRE MACHINERY, LTD. V. NICASTRO
Supreme Court of the United States, 2011.
564 U.S. 873, 131 S.Ct. 2780, 180 L.Ed.2d 765.

Certiorari to the Supreme Court of New Jersey.

JUSTICE KENNEDY announced the judgment of the Court and delivered an opinion, in which the CHIEF JUSTICE, JUSTICE SCALIA, and JUSTICE THOMAS joined.

* * * The rules and standards for determining when a State does or does not have jurisdiction over an absent party have been unclear because of decades-old questions left open in *Asahi* * * * [p. 87, supra].

* * * [T]he Supreme Court of New Jersey, relying in part on *Asahi*, held that New Jersey's courts can exercise jurisdiction over a foreign manufacturer of a product so long as the manufacturer "knows or reasonably should know that its products are distributed through a nationwide distribution system that might lead to those products being sold in any of the fifty states." *Nicastro v. McIntyre Machinery America, Ltd.*, 201 N.J. 48, 76, 77, 987 A.2d 575, 591, 592 (2010). Applying that test, the court * * * concluded that a British manufacturer of scrap metal machines was subject to jurisdiction in New Jersey, even though at no time had it advertised in, sent goods to, or in any relevant sense targeted the State.

That decision cannot be sustained. * * * As a general rule, the exercise of judicial power is not lawful unless the defendant "purposefully avails itself of the privilege of conducting activities within the forum State, thus invoking the benefits and protections of its laws." *Hanson v. Denckla* * * * [p. 60, supra]. There may be exceptions, say, for instance, in cases involving an intentional tort. But the general rule is applicable in this products-liability case, and the so-called "stream-of-commerce" doctrine cannot displace it.

I

This case arises from a products-liability suit filed in New Jersey state court. Robert Nicastro seriously injured his hand while using a metal-shearing machine manufactured by J. McIntyre Machinery, Ltd. (J. McIntyre). The accident occurred in New Jersey, but the machine was manufactured in England, where J. McIntyre is incorporated and operates.

The question here is whether the New Jersey courts have jurisdiction over J. McIntyre, notwithstanding the fact that the company at no time either marketed goods in the State or shipped them there. * * *

At oral argument in this Court, Nicastro's counsel stressed three primary facts in defense of New Jersey's assertion of jurisdiction over J. McIntyre. * * *

First, an independent company agreed to sell J. McIntyre's machines in the United States. J. McIntyre itself did not sell its machines to buyers in this country beyond the U.S. distributor, and there is no allegation that the distributor was under J. McIntyre's control.

Second, J. McIntyre officials attended annual conventions for the scrap recycling industry to advertise J. McIntyre's machines alongside the distributor. The conventions took place in various States, but never in New Jersey.

Third, no more than four machines (the record suggests only one, * * *), including the machine that caused the injuries that are the basis for this suit, ended up in New Jersey.

In addition to these facts emphasized by respondent, the New Jersey Supreme Court noted that J. McIntyre held both United States and European patents on its recycling technology. * * * It also noted that the U.S. distributor "structured [its] advertising and sales efforts in accordance with" J. McIntyre's "direction and guidance whenever possible," and that "at least some of the machines were sold on consignment to" the distributor. * * *

* * * Jurisdiction was proper, in that court's view, because the injury occurred in New Jersey; because petitioner knew or reasonably should have known "that its products are distributed through a nationwide distribution system that might lead to those products being sold in any of the fifty states"; and because petitioner failed to "take some reasonable step to prevent the distribution of its products in this State." * * *

Both the New Jersey Supreme Court's holding and its account of what it called "[t]he stream-of-commerce doctrine of jurisdiction," * * * were incorrect, however. This Court's *Asahi* decision may be responsible in part for that court's error regarding the stream of commerce, and this case presents an opportunity to provide greater clarity.

II

* * *

Asahi

The imprecision arising from *Asahi*, for the most part, results from its statement of the relation between jurisdiction and the "stream of commerce." * * * This Court has stated that a defendant's placing goods into the stream of commerce "with the expectation that they will be purchased by consumers within the forum State" may indicate purposeful availment. *World-Wide Volkswagen Corp.* * * * [p. 71, supra] (finding that expectation lacking). But that statement does not amend the general rule of personal jurisdiction. It merely observes that a defendant may in an appropriate case be subject to jurisdiction without entering the forum— itself an unexceptional proposition—as where manufacturers or distributors "seek to serve" a given State's market. * * * The principal inquiry in cases of this sort is whether the defendant's activities manifest an intention to submit to the power of a sovereign. In other words, the defendant must "purposefully avai[l] itself of the privilege of conducting activities within the forum State, thus invoking the benefits and protections of its laws." *Hanson* * * *; *Insurance Corp.* * * * [p. 135, infra] ("[A]ctions of the defendant may amount to a legal submission to the jurisdiction of the court"). Sometimes a defendant does so by sending its goods rather than its agents. The defendant's transmission of goods permits the exercise of jurisdiction only where the defendant can be said to have targeted the forum; as a general rule, it is not enough that the defendant might have predicted that its goods will reach the forum State.

In *Asahi*, an opinion by Justice Brennan for four Justices outlined a different approach. It discarded the central concept of sovereign authority in favor of considerations of fairness and foreseeability. As that concurrence contended, "jurisdiction premised on the placement of a product into the stream of commerce [without more] is consistent with the Due Process Clause," for "[a]s long as a participant in this process is aware that the final product is being marketed in the forum State, the possibility of a lawsuit there cannot come as a surprise." * * * It was the premise of the concurring opinion that the defendant's ability to anticipate suit renders the assertion of jurisdiction fair. In this way, the opinion made foreseeability the touchstone of jurisdiction.

The standard set forth in Justice Brennan's concurrence was rejected in an opinion written by Justice O'Connor; but the relevant part of that opinion, too, commanded the assent of only four Justices, not a majority of the Court. That opinion stated: "The 'substantial connection' between the defendant and the forum State necessary for a finding of minimum contacts must come about by an action of the defendant purposefully directed toward the forum State. The placement of a product into the stream of commerce, without more, is not an act of the defendant purposefully directed toward the forum State." * * *

Since *Asahi* was decided, the courts have sought to reconcile the competing opinions. But Justice Brennan's concurrence, advocating a rule based on general notions of fairness and foreseeability, is inconsistent with the premises of lawful judicial power. This Court's precedents make clear that it is the defendant's actions, not his expectations, that empower a State's courts to subject him to judgment.

* * * [W]ere general fairness considerations the touchstone of jurisdiction, a lack of purposeful availment might be excused where carefully crafted judicial procedures could otherwise protect the defendant's interests, or where the plaintiff would suffer substantial hardship if forced to litigate in a foreign forum. That such considerations have not been deemed controlling is instructive. * * *

Two principles are implicit in the foregoing. First, personal jurisdiction requires a forum-by-forum, or sovereign-by-sovereign, analysis. The question is whether a defendant has followed a course of conduct directed at the society or economy existing within the jurisdiction of a given sovereign, so that the sovereign has the power to subject the defendant to judgment concerning that conduct. Personal jurisdiction, of course, restricts "judicial power not as a matter of sovereignty, but as a matter of judicial liberty," for due process protects the individual's right to be subject only to lawful power. *Insurance Corp.* * * *. But whether a judicial judgment is lawful depends on whether the sovereign has authority to render it.

The second principle is a corollary of the first. Because the United States is a distinct sovereign, a defendant may in principle be subject to the jurisdiction of the courts of the United States but not of any particular State. This is consistent with the premises and unique genius of our Constitution. * * * For jurisdiction, a litigant may have the requisite relationship with the United States Government but not with the government of any individual State. That would be an exceptional case, however. If the defendant is a domestic domiciliary, the courts of its home State are available and can exercise general jurisdiction. And if another State were to assert jurisdiction in an inappropriate case, it would upset the federal balance, which posits that each State has a sovereignty that is not subject to unlawful intrusion by other States. Furthermore, foreign corporations will often target or concentrate on particular States, subjecting them to specific jurisdiction in those forums.

It must be remembered, however, that although this case and *Asahi* both involve foreign manufacturers, the undesirable consequences of Justice Brennan's approach are no less significant for domestic producers. The owner of a small Florida farm might sell crops to a large nearby distributor, for example, who might then distribute them to grocers across the country. If foreseeability were the controlling criterion, the farmer could be sued in Alaska or any number of other States' courts without ever leaving town. And the issue of foreseeability may itself be contested so that significant expenses are incurred just on the preliminary issue of jurisdiction. Jurisdictional rules should avoid these costs whenever possible.

* * *

III

In this case, petitioner directed marketing and sales efforts at the United States. It may be that, assuming it were otherwise empowered to legislate on the subject, the Congress could authorize the exercise of jurisdiction in appropriate courts. That circumstance is not presented in this case, however, and it is neither necessary nor appropriate to address here any constitutional concerns that might be attendant to that exercise of power. * * * Nor is it necessary to determine what substantive law might apply were Congress to authorize jurisdiction in a federal court in New Jersey. * * * A sovereign's legislative authority to regulate conduct may present considerations different from those presented by its authority to subject a defendant to judgment in its courts. Here the question concerns the authority of a New Jersey state court to exercise jurisdiction, so it is petitioner's purposeful contacts with New Jersey, not with the United States, that alone are relevant.

Respondent has not established that J. McIntyre engaged in conduct purposefully directed at New Jersey. Recall that respondent's claim of jurisdiction centers on three facts * * *. Indeed, after discovery the trial court found that the "defendant does not have a single contact with New Jersey short of the machine in question ending up in this state." * * * These facts may reveal an intent to serve the U.S. market, but they do not show that J. McIntyre purposefully availed itself of the New Jersey market.

* * *

JUSTICE BREYER, with whom JUSTICE ALITO joins, concurring in the judgment.

The Supreme Court of New Jersey adopted a broad understanding of the scope of personal jurisdiction based on its view that "[t]he increasingly fast-paced globalization of the world economy has removed national borders as barriers to trade." *Nicastro v. McIntyre Machinery America, Ltd.*, 201 N.J. 48, 52 * * * (2010). I do not doubt that there have been many recent changes in commerce and communication, many of which are not anticipated by our precedents. But this case does not present any of those issues. So I think it unwise to announce a rule of broad applicability without full consideration of the modern-day consequences.

In my view, the outcome of this case is determined by our precedents. Based on the facts found by the New Jersey courts, respondent Robert Nicastro failed to meet his burden to demonstrate that it was constitutionally proper to exercise jurisdiction over petitioner * * *. On that basis, I agree with the plurality that the contrary judgment of the Supreme Court of New Jersey should be reversed.

I

In asserting jurisdiction over the British Manufacturer, the Supreme Court of New Jersey relied most heavily on three primary facts as providing constitutionally sufficient "contacts" with New Jersey, thereby making it fundamentally fair to hale the British Manufacturer before its courts: (1) The American Distributor on one occasion sold and shipped one machine to a New Jersey customer, namely, Mr. Nicastro's employer, Mr. Curcio; (2) the British Manufacturer permitted, indeed wanted, its independent American Distributor to sell its machines to anyone in America willing to buy them; and (3) representatives of the British Manufacturer attended trade shows in "such cities as Chicago, Las Vegas, New Orleans, Orlando, San Diego, and San Francisco." * * * In my view, these facts do not provide contacts between the British firm and the State of New Jersey constitutionally sufficient to support New Jersey's assertion of jurisdiction in this case.

None of our precedents finds that a single isolated sale, even if accompanied by the kind of sales effort indicated here, is sufficient. Rather, this Court's previous holdings suggest the contrary. The Court has held that a single sale to a customer who takes an accident-causing product to a different State (where the accident takes place) is not a sufficient basis for asserting jurisdiction. See *World-Wide Volkswagen Corp.* * * *. And the Court, in separate opinions [in *Asahi*], has strongly suggested that a single sale of a product in a State does not constitute an adequate basis for asserting jurisdiction over an out-of-state defendant, even if that defendant places his goods in the stream of commerce, fully aware (and hoping) that such a sale will take place. * * *

Here, the relevant facts found by the New Jersey Supreme Court show no "regular . . . flow" or "regular course" of sales in New Jersey; and there is no "something more," such as special state-related design, advertising, advice, marketing, or anything else. Mr. Nicastro, who here bears the burden of proving jurisdiction, has shown no specific effort by the British Manufacturer to sell in New Jersey. He has introduced no list of potential New Jersey customers who might, for example, have regularly attended trade shows. And he has not otherwise shown that the British Manufacturer "purposefully avail[ed] itself of the privilege of conducting activities" within New Jersey, or that it delivered its goods in the stream of commerce "with the expectation that they will be purchased" by New Jersey users. *World-Wide Volkswagen* * * * (internal quotation marks omitted).

There may well have been other facts that Mr. Nicastro could have demonstrated in support of jurisdiction. And the dissent considers some of these facts. See [p. 104, infra] (opinion of GINSBURG, J.) (describing the size and scope of New Jersey's scrap-metal business). * * * But the plaintiff bears the burden of establishing jurisdiction, and here I would take the facts precisely as the New Jersey Supreme Court stated them. * * *

Accordingly, on the record present here, resolving this case requires no more than adhering to our precedents.

II

I would not go further. Because the incident at issue in this case does not implicate modern concerns, and because the factual record leaves many open questions, this is an unsuitable vehicle for making broad pronouncements that refashion basic jurisdictional rules.

A

The plurality seems to state strict rules that limit jurisdiction where a defendant does not "inten[d] to submit to the power of a sovereign" and cannot "be said to have targeted the forum." * * * But what do those standards mean when a company targets the world by selling products from its Web site? And does it matter if, instead of shipping the products directly, a company consigns the products through an intermediary (say, Amazon.com) who then receives and fulfills the orders? And what if the company markets its products through popup advertisements that it knows will be viewed in a forum? Those issues have serious commercial consequences but are totally absent in this case.

B

But though I do not agree with the plurality's seemingly strict no-jurisdiction rule, I am not persuaded by the absolute approach adopted by the New Jersey Supreme Court and urged by respondent and his *amici*. Under that view, a producer is subject to jurisdiction for a products-liability action so long as it "knows or reasonably should know that its products are distributed through a nationwide distribution system that *might* lead to those products being sold in any of the fifty states." * * * (emphasis added). In the context of this case, I cannot agree.

For one thing, to adopt this view would abandon the heretofore accepted inquiry of whether, focusing upon the relationship between "the defendant, the *forum*, and the litigation," it is fair, in light of the defendant's contacts *with that forum*, to subject the defendant to suit there. *Shaffer v. Heitner* * * * [p. 147, infra] (emphasis added).[c] It would ordinarily rest jurisdiction instead upon no more than the occurrence of a product-based accident in the forum state. But this Court has rejected the notion that a defendant's amenability to suit "travel[s] with the chattel." *World-Wide Volkswagen* * * *.

---

[c] Alteration in original.

[handwritten margin note: Can not hold big and small companies to different standards?]

For another, I cannot reconcile so automatic a rule with the constitutional demand for "minimum contacts" and "purposefu[l] avail[ment]," each of which rest upon a particular notion of defendant-focused fairness. * * * A rule like the New Jersey Supreme Court's would permit every State to assert jurisdiction in a products-liability suit against any domestic manufacturer who sells its products (made anywhere in the United States) to a national distributor, no matter how large or small the manufacturer, no matter how distant the forum, and no matter how few the number of items that end up in the particular forum at issue. What might appear fair in the case of a large manufacturer which specifically seeks, or expects, an equal-sized distributor to sell its product in a distant State might seem unfair in the case of a small manufacturer (say, an Appalachian potter) who sells his product (cups and saucers) exclusively to a large distributor, who resells a single item (a coffee mug) to a buyer from a distant State (Hawaii). I know too little about the range of these or in-between possibilities to abandon in favor of the more absolute rule what has previously been this Court's less absolute approach.

Further, the fact that the defendant is a foreign, rather than a domestic, manufacturer makes the basic fairness of an absolute rule yet more uncertain. I am again less certain than is the New Jersey Supreme Court that the nature of international commerce has changed so significantly as to require a new approach to personal jurisdiction.

It may be that a larger firm can readily "alleviate the risk of burdensome litigation by procuring insurance, passing the expected costs on to customers, or, if the risks are too great, severing its connection with the State." *World-Wide Volkswagen* * * *. But manufacturers come in many shapes and sizes. It may be fundamentally unfair to require a small Egyptian shirt maker, a Brazilian manufacturing cooperative, or a Kenyan coffee farmer, selling its products through international distributors, to respond to products-liability tort suits in virtually every State in the United States, even those in respect to which the foreign firm has no connection at all but the sale of a single (allegedly defective) good. And a rule like the New Jersey Supreme Court suggests would require every product manufacturer, large or small, selling to American distributors to understand not only the tort law of every state, but also the wide variance in the way courts within different states apply that law. * * *

C

At a minimum, I would not work such a change to the law in the way either the plurality or the New Jersey Supreme Court suggests without a better understanding of the relevant contemporary commercial circumstances. * * *

* * * Accordingly, though I agree with the plurality as to the outcome of this case, I concur only in the judgment of that opinion and not its reasoning.

JUSTICE GINSBURG, with whom JUSTICE SOTOMAYOR and JUSTICE KAGAN join, dissenting.

A foreign industrialist seeks to develop a market in the United States for machines it manufactures. It hopes to derive substantial revenue from sales it makes to United States purchasers. Where in the United States buyers reside does not matter to this manufacturer. Its goal is simply to sell as much as it can, wherever it can. It excludes no region or State from the market it wishes to reach. But, all things considered, it prefers to avoid products liability litigation in the United States. To that end, it engages a U.S. distributor to ship its machines stateside. Has it succeeded in escaping personal jurisdiction in a State where one of its products is sold and causes injury or even death to a local user?

Under this Court's pathmarking precedent in *International Shoe* * * * [p. 52, supra] and subsequent decisions, one would expect the answer to be unequivocally, "No." But instead, six Justices of this Court, in divergent opinions, tell us that the manufacturer has avoided the jurisdiction of our state courts, except perhaps in States where its products are sold in sizeable quantities. Inconceivable as it may have seemed yesterday, the splintered majority today "turn[s] the clock back to the days before modern long-arm statutes when a manufacturer, to avoid being haled into court where a user is injured, need only Pilate-like wash its hands of a product by having independent distributors market it." Weintraub, A Map Out of the Personal Jurisdiction Labyrinth, 28 U. C. Davis L.Rev. 531, 555 (1995).

I

* * *

The machine that injured Nicastro, a "McIntyre Model 640 Shear," sold in the United States for $24,900 in 1995 * * * and features a "massive cutting capacity" * * *.

Nicastro operated the 640 Shear in the course of his employment at Curcio Scrap Metal (CSM) in Saddle Brook, New Jersey. * * * "New Jersey has long been a hotbed of scrap-metal businesses." * * * In 2008, New Jersey recycling facilities processed 2,013,730 tons of scrap iron, steel, aluminum, and other metals—more than any other State—outpacing Kentucky, its nearest competitor, by nearly 30 percent. * * *

* * * McIntyre UK exhibited its products at * * * trade shows [in the United States], the company acknowledged, hoping to reach "anyone interested in the machine from anywhere in the United States." * * * [The convention where Nicastro's employer first learned about the shear

machine was sponsored by an organization with nearly 100 New Jersey members.]

Although McIntyre UK's U.S. sales figures are not in the record, it appears that for several years in the 1990's, earnings from sales of McIntyre UK products in the United States "ha[d] been good" in comparison to "the rest of the world." * * * In response to interrogatories, McIntyre UK stated that its commissioning engineer had installed the company's equipment in several States—Illinois, Iowa, Kentucky, Virginia, and Washington. * * *

From at least 1995 until 2001, McIntyre UK retained an Ohio-based company, McIntyre Machinery America, Ltd. (McIntyre America), "as its exclusive distributor for the entire United States." * * *[2] Though similarly named, the two companies were separate and independent entities with "no commonality of ownership or management." * * *

In a November 23, 1999 letter to McIntyre America, McIntyre UK's president spoke plainly about the manufacturer's objective in authorizing the exclusive distributorship: "All we wish to do is sell our products in the [United] States—and get paid!" * * * Notably, McIntyre America was concerned about U.S. litigation involving McIntyre UK products, in which the distributor had been named as a defendant. McIntyre UK counseled McIntyre America to respond personally to the litigation, but reassured its distributor that "the product was built and designed by McIntyre Machinery in the UK and the buck stops here—if there's something wrong with the machine." * * * Answering jurisdictional interrogatories, McIntyre UK stated that it had been named as a defendant in lawsuits in Illinois, Kentucky, Massachusetts, and West Virginia. * * * And in correspondence with McIntyre America, McIntyre UK noted that the manufacturer had products liability insurance coverage. * * *

* * * McIntyre UK's regular attendance and exhibitions at [scrap metal] conventions was surely a purposeful step to reach customers for its products "anywhere in the United States." At least as purposeful was McIntyre UK's engagement of McIntyre America as the conduit for sales of McIntyre UK's machines to buyers "throughout the United States." Given McIntyre UK's endeavors to reach and profit from the United States market as a whole, Nicastro's suit, I would hold, has been brought in a forum entirely appropriate for the adjudication of his claim. He alleges that McIntyre UK's shear machine was defectively designed or manufactured and, as a result, caused injury to him at his workplace. The machine arrived in Nicastro's New Jersey workplace not randomly or fortuitously, but as a result of the U.S. connections and distribution system that

---

[2] McIntyre America filed for bankruptcy in 2001, is no longer operating, and has not participated in this lawsuit. * * * After "the demise of . . . McIntyre America," McIntyre UK authorized a Texas-based company to serve as exclusive United States distributor of McIntyre UK shears. * * *

McIntyre UK deliberately arranged.[3] On what sensible view of the allocation of adjudicatory authority could the place of Nicastro's injury within the United States be deemed off limits for his products liability claim against a foreign manufacturer who targeted the United States (including all the States that constitute the Nation) as the territory it sought to develop?

II

* * * [T]he question * * * is one of specific jurisdiction, which turns on an "affiliatio[n] between the forum and the underlying controversy." *Goodyear Dunlop* * * * [p. 113, infra].

* * *

* * * [T]he plurality's notion that consent is the animating concept draws no support from controlling decisions of this Court. Quite the contrary, the Court has explained, a forum can exercise jurisdiction when its contacts with the controversy are sufficient; invocation of a fictitious consent, the Court has repeatedly said, is unnecessary and unhelpful. * * *[5]

III

This case is illustrative of marketing arrangements for sales in the United States common in today's commercial world.[6] * * * A foreign-country manufacturer engages a U.S. company to promote and distribute the manufacturer's products, not in any particular State, but anywhere and everywhere in the United States the distributor can attract purchasers. The product proves defective and injures a user in the State where the user lives or works. Often, as here, the manufacturer will have liability insurance covering personal injuries caused by its products. * * *

When industrial accidents happen, a long-arm statute in the State where the injury occurs generally permits assertion of jurisdiction, upon giving proper notice, over the foreign manufacturer. * * *

---

[3] McIntyre UK resisted Nicastro's efforts to determine whether other McIntyre machines had been sold to New Jersey customers. * * * McIntyre did allow that McIntyre America "may have resold products it purchased from [McIntyre UK] to a buyer in New Jersey," * * * but said it kept no record of the ultimate destination of machines it shipped to its distributor * * *. A private investigator engaged by Nicastro found at least one McIntyre UK machine, of unspecified type, in use in New Jersey. * * * But McIntyre UK objected that the investigator's report was "unsworn and based upon hearsay." * * * Moreover, McIntyre UK maintained, no evidence showed that the machine the investigator found in New Jersey had been "sold into [that State]." * * *

[5] * * * The plurality's notion that jurisdiction over foreign corporations depends upon the defendant's "submission," * * * seems scarcely different from the long-discredited fiction of implied consent. It bears emphasis that a majority of this Court's members do not share the plurality's view.

[6] Last year, the United States imported nearly $2 trillion in foreign goods. * * * Capital goods, such as the metal shear machine that injured Nicastro, accounted for almost $450 billion in imports for 2010. * * * New Jersey is the fourth-largest destination for manufactured commodities imported into the United States, after California, Texas, and New York. * * *

The modern approach to jurisdiction over corporations and other legal entities, ushered in by *International Shoe*, gave prime place to reason and fairness. Is it not fair and reasonable, given the mode of trading of which this case is an example, to require the international seller to defend at the place its products cause injury?[9] Do not litigational convenience * * * and choice-of-law considerations[11] point in that direction? On what measure of reason and fairness can it be considered undue to require McIntyre UK to defend in New Jersey as an incident of its efforts to develop a market for its industrial machines anywhere and everywhere in the United States?[12] Is not the burden on McIntyre UK to defend in New Jersey fair, *i.e.*, a reasonable cost of transacting business internationally, in comparison to the burden on Nicastro to go to Nottingham, England to gain recompense for an injury he sustained using McIntyre's product at his workplace in Saddle Brook, New Jersey?

McIntyre UK dealt with the United States as a single market. Like most foreign manufacturers, it was concerned not with the prospect of suit in State X as opposed to State Y, but rather with its subjection to suit anywhere in the United States. * * * As a McIntyre UK officer wrote in an e-mail to McIntyre America: "American law—who needs it?!" * * * If McIntyre UK is answerable in the United States at all, is it not "perfectly appropriate to permit the exercise of that jurisdiction . . . at the place of injury"? * * *

In sum, McIntyre UK, by engaging McIntyre America to promote and sell its machines in the United States, "purposefully availed itself" of the United States market nationwide, not a market in a single State or a discrete collection of States. McIntyre UK thereby availed itself of the market of all States in which its products were sold by its exclusive distributor. "Th[e] 'purposeful availment' requirement," this Court has explained, simply "ensures that a defendant will not be haled into a jurisdiction solely as a result of 'random,' 'fortuitous,' or 'attenuated' contacts." * * * Adjudicatory authority is appropriately exercised where "actions by the defendant *himself*" give rise to the affiliation with the forum. How could McIntyre UK not have intended, by its actions targeting

---

[9] The plurality objects to a jurisdictional approach "divorced from traditional practice." * * * But "the fundamental transformation of our national economy," this Court has recognized, warrants enlargement of "the permissible scope of state jurisdiction over foreign corporations and other nonresidents." *McGee* * * * [p. 59, *supra*].

[11] Historically, "tort cases were governed by the place where the last act giving rise to a claim occurred—that is, the place of injury." * * * Even as many jurisdictions have modified the traditional rule of *lex loci delicti*, the location of injury continues to hold sway in choice-of-law analysis in tort cases. * * *

[12] The plurality suggests that the Due Process Clause might permit a federal district court in New Jersey, sitting in diversity and applying New Jersey law, to adjudicate McIntyre UK's liability to Nicastro. * * * In other words, McIntyre UK might be compelled to bear the burden of traveling to New Jersey and defending itself there under New Jersey's products liability law, but would be entitled to federal adjudication of Nicastro's state-law claim. I see no basis in the Due Process Clause for such a curious limitation.

a national market, to sell products in the fourth largest destination for imports among all States of the United States and the largest scrap metal market? * * *

IV

A

While this Court has not considered in any prior case the now-prevalent pattern presented here—a foreign-country manufacturer enlisting a U.S. distributor to develop a market in the United States for the manufacturer's products—none of the Court's decisions tug against the judgment made by the New Jersey Supreme Court. * * *

World-Wide Volkswagen concerned a New York car dealership that sold solely in the New York market, and a New York distributor who supplied retailers in three States only: New York, Connecticut, and New Jersey. * * * Jurisdiction, the Court held, could not be based on the *customer's* unilateral act of driving the vehicle to Oklahoma. * * *

Notably, the foreign manufacturer of the Audi in *World-Wide Volkswagen* did not object to the jurisdiction of the Oklahoma courts and the U.S. importer abandoned its initially stated objection. * * * And most relevant here, the Court's opinion indicates that an objection to jurisdiction by the manufacturer or national distributor would have been unavailing. To reiterate, the Court said in *World-Wide Volkswagen* that, when a manufacturer or distributor aims to sell its product to customers in several States, it is reasonable "to subject it to suit in [any] one of those States if its allegedly defective [product] has there been the source of injury." * * *

* * *

[*Asahi*] * * * was not a close call. * * * All agreed on the bottom line: The Japanese valve-assembly manufacturer was not reasonably brought into the California courts to litigate a dispute with another foreign party over a transaction that took place outside the United States.

* * *

* * * Asahi, unlike McIntyre UK, did not itself seek out customers in the United States, it engaged no distributor to promote its wares here, it appeared at no tradeshows in the United States, and, of course, it had no Web site advertising its products to the world. Moreover, Asahi was a component-part manufacturer with "little control over the final destination of its products once they were delivered into the stream of commerce." * * * It was important to the Court in *Asahi* that "those who use Asahi components in their final products, and sell those products in California,

[would be] subject to the application of California tort law." * * * To hold that *Asahi* controls this case would, to put it bluntly, be dead wrong.[15]

B

The Court's judgment also puts United States plaintiffs at a disadvantage in comparison to similarly situated complainants elsewhere in the world. Of particular note, within the European Union, in which the United Kingdom is a participant, the jurisdiction New Jersey would have exercised is not at all exceptional. The European Regulation on Jurisdiction and the Recognition and Enforcement of Judgments provides for the exercise of specific jurisdiction "in matters relating to tort . . . in the courts for the place where the harmful event occurred." Council Reg. 44/2001, Art. 5, 2001 O.J. (L.12) 4. * * * The European Court of Justice has interpreted this prescription to authorize jurisdiction either where the harmful act occurred or at the place of injury. * * *

V

* * * [Academic commentary anticipated that] courts would differently appraise two situations: (1) cases involving a substantially local plaintiff, like Nicastro, injured by the activity of a defendant engaged in interstate or international trade; and (2) cases in which the defendant is a natural or legal person whose economic activities and legal involvements are largely home-based, *i.e.*, entities without designs to gain substantial revenue from sales in distant markets.[18] * * * [C]ourts presented with [the] * * * first scenario * * * have repeatedly confirmed that jurisdiction is appropriately exercised by courts of the place where the product was sold and caused injury. [Appendix of cases omitted.]

* * *

For the reasons stated, I would hold McIntyre UK answerable in New Jersey for the harm Nicastro suffered at his workplace in that State using McIntyre UK's shearing machine. While I dissent from the Court's judgment, I take heart that the plurality opinion does not speak for the Court, for that opinion would take a giant step away from the "notions of fair play and substantial justice" underlying *International Shoe*. * * *

---

[15] The plurality notes the low volume of sales in New Jersey * * *. A $24,900 shearing machine, however, is unlikely to sell in bulk worldwide, much less in any given State. By dollar value, the price of a single machine represents a significant sale. Had a manufacturer sold in New Jersey $24,900 worth of flannel shirts, see *Nelson v. Park Industries, Inc.*, 717 F.2d 1120 (C.A.7 1983), cigarette lighters, see *Oswalt v. Scripto, Inc.*, 616 F.2d 191 (C.A.5 1980), or wire-rope splices, see *Hedrick v. Daiko Shoji Co.*, 715 F.2d 1355 (C.A.9 1983), the Court would presumably find the defendant amenable to suit in that State.

[18] Assigning weight to the local or international stage on which the parties operate would, to a considerable extent, answer the concerns expressed by Justice Breyer. * * *

NOTES AND QUESTIONS

*Marks
test*

1.   *McIntyre* marks the Court's return to questions left open by *Asahi* and not addressed since 1987. Which opinion speaks for the Court? Under MARKS v. UNITED STATES, "[w]hen a fragmented Court decides a case and no single rationale explaining the result enjoys the assent of five Justices, 'the holding of the Court may be viewed as the position taken by those Members who concurred in the judgment on the narrowest grounds.'" 430 U.S. 188, 193, 97 S.Ct. 990, 993, 51 L.Ed.2d 260, 266 (1977) (quoting Gregg v. Georgia, 428 U.S. 153, 169 n.15, 96 S.Ct. 2909, 2923 n.15, 49 L.Ed.2d 859, 872 n.15 (1976)). Applying this test, which opinion states the Court's holding? Given the lack of a majority opinion, would lower courts be justified in giving *McIntyre* limited weight? For a comparison of the three opinions, see Steinman, *The Lay of the Land: Examining the Three Opinions in* J. McIntyre Machinery, Ltd. v. Nicastro, 63 S.C.L.Rev. 481 (2012).

2.   In his plurality opinion, Justice Kennedy insisted that determining whether jurisdiction may be exercised requires a "sovereign-by-sovereign" analysis. Is this approach at odds with *International Shoe*'s requirement that the exercise of jurisdiction comport with "traditional notions of fair play and substantial justice"? How does plaintiff show that defendant has submitted to the will of the sovereign as to support the court's exercise of jurisdiction? Does Justice Kennedy endorse the "stream of commerce plus" analysis? If so, why didn't Justice Kennedy treat the activities of McIntyre UK's Ohio distributor as a plus-factor to support jurisdiction in New Jersey? Would this showing have satisfied Justice O'Connor's plurality approach in *Asahi*?

3.   What are the major points of disagreement between Justice Ginsburg's dissenting opinion and that of the plurality? Do you agree with Justice Ginsburg's dissent that the plurality's view of jurisdiction is no different from "the long-discredited fiction of implied consent"? According to the dissent, is a manufacturer that markets its product nationwide amenable to suit in the state where the product is sold and causes injury? Is this approach consistent with the notion of purposeful availment?

4.   On what basis do Justices Breyer and Alito concur? What kind of additional factual information might have persuaded them to uphold jurisdiction in New Jersey?

5.   Which of the opinions in *McIntyre* would support the exercise of specific jurisdiction by a court in Idaho in a suit by a plaintiff injured in that state:

(a)   When defendant is a German component part manufacturer who markets its product throughout the United States.

(b)   When defendant is a California component part manufacturer who markets its product nationwide through an independent distributor.

(c)   When defendant is an Illinois component part manufacturer who markets its product to an end-product manufacturer whose principal place of business is in Washington State.

(d)   When defendant is a component part manufacturer who markets its product to an end-product manufacturer whose principal place of business is in Illinois.

(e)   When defendant is a foreign end-product manufacturer who markets its product throughout the United States.

See Noyes, *The Persistent Problem of Purposeful Availment*, 45 Conn.L.Rev. 41 (2012).

6.   After *McIntyre*, what advice would you give to a foreign company that sells component parts in the United States market about its amenability to suit in a state court in which the end-product causes injury? Does your advice depend on the company's mode of distribution? What if the foreign company directly sells an end-product within the United States market? Would one direct sale support the exercise of jurisdiction?

7.   Justice Kennedy suggests that Congress could enact a long-arm statute for the federal courts authorizing the exercise of jurisdiction based on contacts with the United States as a whole. Is this suggestion consistent with the plurality's theory of jurisdiction as an incident of sovereignty and not a matter of fairness or reasonableness? The topic of nationwide service of process is considered later in this chapter, p. 168, infra.

8.   In WALDEN v. FIORE, 571 U.S. 277, 134 S.Ct. 1115, 188 L.Ed.2d 12 (2014), a pair of professional gamblers filed suit in a federal court in Nevada, where they lived, alleging that an airport security officer had violated their Fourth Amendment rights by seizing their cash winnings, and then filing a false probable cause affidavit in support of the funds' forfeiture and delaying return of the cash. The seizure took place at the Atlanta, Georgia airport while plaintiffs were en route to Nevada. The Nevada district court dismissed for lack of personal jurisdiction and the Ninth Circuit reversed, finding that the officer had falsified the affidavit with the knowledge that it would have effects in Nevada where plaintiffs lived. The Supreme Court unanimously reversed, finding that the appeals court improperly focused on plaintiffs' contacts with the forum and not on the officer's contacts. Justice Thomas wrote:

A forum State's exercise of jurisdiction over an out-of-state intentional tortfeasor must be based on intentional conduct by the defendant that creates the necessary contacts with the forum.

Calder v. Jones * * * [p. 82, Note 1, supra] illustrates the application of these principles. * * *

* * *

The crux of *Calder* was that the reputation-based "effects" of the alleged libel connected the defendants to California, not just to the plaintiff. The strength of that connection was largely a function of the nature of the libel tort. However scandalous a newspaper article might be, it can lead to a loss of reputation only if communicated to (and read and understood by) third persons. * * * Accordingly, the reputational injury caused by the defendants' story would not have occurred but for the fact that the defendants wrote an article for publication in California that was read by a large number of California citizens. Indeed, because publication to third persons is a necessary element of libel, * * * the defendants' intentional tort actually occurred in California. * * *

* * *

* * * *Calder* made clear that mere injury to a forum resident is not a sufficient connection to the forum. Regardless of where a plaintiff lives or works, an injury is jurisdictionally relevant only insofar as it shows that the defendant has formed a contact with the forum State. The proper question is not where the plaintiff experienced a particular injury or effect but whether the defendant's conduct connects him to the forum in a meaningful way.

Respondents' claimed injury does not evince a connection between petitioner and Nevada. Even if we consider the continuation of the seizure in Georgia to be a distinct injury, it is not the sort of effect that is tethered to Nevada in any meaningful way. Respondents (and only respondents) lacked access to their funds in Nevada not because anything independently occurred there, but because Nevada is where respondents chose to be at a time when they desired to use the funds seized by petitioner. * * *

Id. at 290, 134 S.Ct. at 1125, 188 L.Ed.2d at 23.

E. GENERAL JURISDICTION IN STATE COURT

Pennoyer's principle of territoriality justified a court's exercise of personal jurisdiction over a defendant who was physically present in the forum at the time of service or was a domiciliary of the state. In those circumstances, the court's power was all-purpose and over any claim. *International Shoe* further recognized that all-purpose jurisdiction could be exercised in some cases over a corporate defendant incorporated by a state other than the forum when its "continuous corporate operations within a state were thought so substantial and of such nature as to justify suit against it on causes of action arising from dealings entirely distinct from those activities." *International Shoe*, p. 52, supra. This species of jurisdiction came to be known as "general" jurisdiction and consists of the "power to adjudicate any kind of controversy when jurisdiction is based on relationships, direct or indirect, between the forum and the person or persons whose legal rights are to be affected." von Mehren & Trautman, *Jurisdiction to Adjudicate: A Suggested Analysis*, 79 Harv.L.Rev. 1121 (1966).

In HELICOPTEROS NACIONALES DE COLOMBIA, S.A. v. HALL, 466 U.S. 408, 104 S.Ct. 1868, 80 L.Ed.2d 404 (1984), the Supreme Court observed:

> It has been said that when a State exercises personal jurisdiction over a defendant in a suit arising out of or related to the defendant's contacts with the forum, the State is exercising 'specific jurisdiction' over the defendant. * * * When a State exercises personal jurisdiction over a defendant in a suit not arising out of or related to the defendant's contacts with the forum, the State has been said to be exercising 'general jurisdiction' over the defendant.

Id. at 414 nn.8–9, 104 S.Ct. at 1872 nn.8–9, 80 L.Ed.2d at 411 nn.8–9.

GOODYEAR DUNLOP TIRES OPERATIONS, S.A. v. BROWN

Supreme Court of the United States, 2011.
564 U.S. 915, 131 S.Ct. 2846, 189 L.Ed.2d 796.

Certiorari to the Court of Appeals of North Carolina.

JUSTICE GINSBURG delivered the opinion for a unanimous Court.

This case concerns the jurisdiction of state courts over corporations organized and operating abroad. * * *

* * *

I

On April 18, 2004, a bus destined for Charles de Gaulle Airport overturned on a road outside Paris, France. Passengers on the bus were young soccer players from North Carolina beginning their journey home. Two 13-year-olds, Julian Brown and Matthew Helms, sustained fatal injuries. The boys' parents, respondents in this Court, filed a suit for wrongful-death damages in the Superior Court of Onslow County, North Carolina, in their capacity as administrators of the boys' estates. Attributing the accident to a tire that failed when its plies separated, the parents alleged negligence in the "design, construction, testing, and inspection" of the tire. * * *

Goodyear Luxembourg Tires, SA (Goodyear Luxembourg), Goodyear Lastikleri T.A.S. (Goodyear Turkey), and Goodyear Dunlop Tires France, SA (Goodyear France), petitioners here, were named as defendants. Incorporated in Luxembourg, Turkey, and France, respectively, petitioners are indirect subsidiaries of Goodyear USA, an Ohio corporation also named as a defendant in the suit. Petitioners manufacture tires primarily for sale in European and Asian markets. Their tires differ in size and construction from tires ordinarily sold in the United States. They are designed to carry significantly heavier loads, and to serve under road conditions and speed limits in the manufacturers' primary markets.[1]

In contrast to the parent company, Goodyear USA, which does not contest the North Carolina courts' personal jurisdiction over it, petitioners are not registered to do business in North Carolina. They have no place of business, employees, or bank accounts in North Carolina. They do not design, manufacture, or advertise their products in North Carolina. And they do not solicit business in North Carolina or themselves sell or ship tires to North Carolina customers. Even so, a small percentage of petitioners' tires (tens of thousands out of tens of millions manufactured between 2004 and 2007) were distributed within North Carolina by other Goodyear USA affiliates. These tires were typically custom ordered to equip specialized vehicles such as cement mixers, waste haulers, and boat and horse trailers. Petitioners state, and respondents do not here deny, that the type of tire involved in the accident, a Goodyear Regional RHS tire manufactured by Goodyear Turkey, was never distributed in North Carolina.

Petitioners moved to dismiss the claims against them for want of personal jurisdiction. The trial court denied the motion, and the North Carolina Court of Appeals affirmed. Acknowledging that the claims neither "related to, nor ... ar[o]se from, [petitioners'] contacts with North Carolina," the Court of Appeals confined its analysis to "general rather than specific jurisdiction," which the court recognized required a "higher threshold" showing: A defendant must have "continuous and systematic contacts" with the forum. * * * That threshold was crossed, the court determined, when petitioners placed their tires "in the stream of interstate commerce without any limitation on the extent to which those tires could be sold in North Carolina." * * *

Nothing in the record, the court observed, indicated that petitioners "took any affirmative action to cause tires which they had manufactured to be shipped into North Carolina." * * * The court found, however, that tires made by petitioners reached North Carolina as a consequence of a "highly-organized distribution process" involving other Goodyear USA subsidiaries. * * * Petitioners, the court noted, made "no attempt to keep these tires from reaching the North Carolina market." * * * As further support, the court invoked North Carolina's "interest in providing a forum in which its citizens are able to seek redress for [their] injuries," and noted the hardship North Carolina plaintiffs would experience "[were they] required to litigate their claims in France," a country to which they have no ties. * * *

---

[1] Respondents portray Goodyear USA's structure as a reprehensible effort to "outsource" all manufacturing, and correspondingly, tort litigation, to foreign jurisdictions. * * * Yet Turkey, where the tire alleged to have caused the accident-in-suit was made, is hardly a strange location for a facility that primarily supplies markets in Europe and Asia.

II

A

* * *

* * * For an individual, the paradigm forum for the exercise of general jurisdiction is the individual's domicile; for a corporation, it is an equivalent place, one in which the corporation is fairly regarded as at home. * * * [Academic commentary has identified] domicile, place of incorporation, and principal place of business as "paradig[m]" bases for the exercise of general jurisdiction[.] * * *

* * *

In only two decisions postdating *International Shoe* * * * has this Court considered whether an out-of-state corporate defendant's in-state contacts were sufficiently "continuous and systematic" to justify the exercise of general jurisdiction over claims unrelated to those contacts: *Perkins v. Benguet Consol. Mining Co.*, 342 U.S. 437, 72 S.Ct. 413, 96 L.Ed. 485 (1952) (general jurisdiction appropriately exercised over Philippine corporation sued in Ohio, where the company's affairs were overseen during World War II); and *Helicopteros* [p. 113, supra] (helicopter owned by Colombian corporation crashed in Peru; survivors of U.S. citizens who died in the crash, the Court held, could not maintain wrongful-death actions against the Colombian corporation in Texas, for the corporation's helicopter purchases and purchase-linked activity in Texas were insufficient to subject it to Texas court's general jurisdiction).

B

To justify the exercise of general jurisdiction over petitioners, the North Carolina courts relied on the petitioners' placement of their tires in the "stream of commerce." * * *

* * *

The North Carolina court's stream-of-commerce analysis elided the essential difference between case-specific and all-purpose (general) jurisdiction. Flow of a manufacturer's products into the forum, we have explained, may bolster an affiliation germane to *specific* jurisdiction. * * * But ties serving to bolster the exercise of specific jurisdiction do not warrant a determination that, based on those ties, the forum has *general* jurisdiction over a defendant. * * *

* * * Our 1952 decision in *Perkins v. Benguet Consol. Mining Co.* remains "[t]he textbook case of general jurisdiction appropriately exercised over a foreign corporation that has not consented to suit in the forum." * * *.

Sued in Ohio, the defendant in *Perkins* was a Philippine mining corporation that had ceased activities in the Philippines during World War II. To the extent that the company was conducting any business during and immediately after the Japanese occupation of the Philippines, it was doing so in Ohio: the corporation's president maintained his office there, kept the company files in that office, and supervised from the Ohio office "the necessarily limited wartime activities of the company." * * * Although the claim-in-suit did not arise in Ohio, this Court ruled that it would not violate due process for Ohio to adjudicate the controversy. * * *

We next addressed the exercise of general jurisdiction over an out-of-state corporation over three decades later, in *Helicopteros*. In that case, survivors of United States citizens who died in a helicopter crash in Peru instituted wrongful-death actions in a Texas state court against the owner and operator of the helicopter, a Colombian corporation. The Colombian corporation had no place of business in Texas and was not licensed to do business there. "Basically, [the company's] contacts with Texas consisted of sending its chief executive officer to Houston for a contract-negotiation session; accepting into its New York bank account checks drawn on a Houston bank; purchasing helicopters, equipment, and training services from [a Texas enterprise] for substantial sums; and sending personnel to [Texas] for training." * * * These links to Texas, we determined, did not "constitute the kind of continuous and systematic general business contacts . . . found to exist in *Perkins*," and were insufficient to support the exercise of jurisdiction over a claim that neither "ar[o]se out of . . . no[r] related to" the defendant's activities in Texas. * * *

Helicopteros concluded that "mere purchases [made in the forum State], even if occurring at regular intervals, are not enough to warrant a State's assertion of [general] jurisdiction over a nonresident corporation in a cause of action not related to those purchase transactions." * * * We see no reason to differentiate from the ties to Texas held insufficient in *Helicopteros*, the sales of petitioners' tires sporadically made in North Carolina through intermediaries. Under the sprawling view of general jurisdiction urged by respondents and embraced by the North Carolina Court of Appeals, any substantial manufacturer or seller of goods would be amenable to suit, on any claim for relief, wherever its products are distributed. But cf. *World-Wide Volkswagen* * * * (every seller of chattels does not, by virtue of the sale, "appoint the chattel his agent for service of process").

Measured against *Helicopteros* and *Perkins*, North Carolina is not a forum in which it would be permissible to subject petitioners to general jurisdiction. Unlike the defendant in *Perkins*, whose sole wartime business activity was conducted in Ohio, petitioners are in no sense at home in North Carolina. Their attenuated connections to the State * * * fall far short of * * * "the continuous and systematic general business contacts" necessary to empower North Carolina to entertain suit against them on claims unrelated to anything that connects them to the State. * * *

C

Respondents belatedly assert a "single enterprise" theory, asking us to consolidate petitioners' ties to North Carolina with those of Goodyear USA and other Goodyear entities. * * * In effect, respondents would have us pierce Goodyear corporate veils, at least for jurisdictional purposes. * * * Neither below nor in their brief in opposition to the petition for certiorari did respondents urge disregard of petitioners' discrete status as subsidiaries and treatment of all Goodyear entities as a "unitary business," so that jurisdiction over the parent would draw in the subsidiaries as well. * * * Respondents have therefore forfeited this contention, and we do not address it. * * *

Reversed.

NOTES AND QUESTIONS

1.   Under *Goodyear*, when can general jurisdiction be exercised by a forum other than the company's state of incorporation or principal place of business? In DAIMLER AG v. BAUMAN, 571 U.S. 117, 134 S.Ct. 746, 187 L.Ed.2d 624 (2014), Argentinian victims of human rights abuses sued Daimler, a German corporation, in California federal court alleging that defendant's wholly-owned Argentinian subsidiary had collaborated with Argentine security forces to kidnap, detain, torture, and kill plaintiffs or their relatives in Argentina. Personal jurisdiction was based on the California contacts of defendant's U.S. subsidiary (MBUSA), which was incorporated in Delaware and had its principal place of business in New Jersey. MBUSA was Daimler's exclusive importer in the United States, distributing Daimler vehicles to dealerships throughout the country. MBUSA had multiple facilities in California and was the largest supplier of luxury vehicles to the California market. MBUSA's sales in California amounted to 2.4 percent of Daimler's sales worldwide. See id. at 123, 134 S.Ct. at 752, 187 L.Ed.2d at 631.

Although the Ninth Circuit upheld general jurisdiction based on Daimler's agency relation with the United States subsidiary, the Supreme Court reversed, holding that Daimler was not amenable to suit "for claims involving only foreign plaintiffs and conduct occurring entirely abroad." Justice Ginsburg, writing for the majority, first rejected the Ninth Circuit's rationale for attributing MBUSA's contacts to Daimler: "The Ninth Circuit's agency theory * * * appears to subject foreign corporations to general jurisdiction whenever they have an in-state subsidiary or affiliate, an outcome that would sweep beyond even the 'sprawling view of general jurisdiction' we rejected in *Goodyear*." Id. at 136, 134 S.Ct. at 759–60, 187 L.Ed.2d at 639. Justice Ginsburg then explained that general jurisdiction would not be proper in California even if MBUSA's contacts were attributable to Daimler:

Goodyear made clear that only a limited set of affiliations with a forum will render a defendant amenable to all-purpose jurisdiction there. * * * With respect to a corporation, the place of incorporation and principal place of business are "paradig[m] . . . bases for general jurisdiction." * * * Those affiliations have the virtue of being unique— that is, each ordinarily indicates only one place—as well as easily ascertainable. * * * These bases afford plaintiffs recourse to at least one clear and certain forum in which a corporate defendant may be sued on any and all claims.

Goodyear did not hold that a corporation may be subject to general jurisdiction *only* in a forum where it is incorporated or has its principal place of business; it simply typed those places paradigm all-purpose forums. Plaintiffs would have us look beyond the exemplar bases *Goodyear* identified, and approve the exercise of general jurisdiction in every State in which a corporation "engages in a substantial, continuous, and systematic course of business." * * * That formulation, we hold, is unacceptably grasping.

* * * [T]he inquiry under *Goodyear* is not whether a foreign corporation's in-forum contacts can be said to be in some sense "continuous and systematic," it is whether that corporation's "affiliations with the State are so 'continuous and systematic' as to render [it] essentially at home in the forum State." * * *

Here, neither Daimler nor [the subsidiary] is incorporated in California, nor does either entity have its principal place of business there. If Daimler's California activities sufficed to allow adjudication of this Argentina-rooted case in California, the same global reach would presumably be available in every other State in which [the subsidiary's] sales are sizable. Such exorbitant exercises of all-purpose jurisdiction would scarcely permit out-of-state defendants "to structure their primary conduct with some minimum assurance as to where that conduct will and will not render them liable to suit." *Burger King* * * * [p. 83, supra].

Id. at 137–39, 134 S.Ct. at 760–62, 187 L.Ed.2d at 639–41.

In so holding, the Court relied upon the views of the Solicitor General that subjecting foreign corporations to suit under what was thought to be an expansive concept of general jurisdiction could create "international friction." Id. at 142, 134 S.Ct. at 763, 187 L.Ed.2d 642. The Court noted that it did "not foreclose the possibility that in an exceptional case" general jurisdiction could be exercised based on contacts "so substantial and of such a nature as to render the corporation at home" in the forum. Id. at 139 n.19, 134 S.Ct. at 761 n.19, 187 L.Ed.2d at 641 n.19. Justice Ginsburg clarified, however, that general jurisdiction cannot be based "solely on the magnitude of the defendant's in-state contacts":

General jurisdiction instead calls for an appraisal of a corporation's activities in their entirety, nationwide and worldwide. A corporation that operates in many places can scarcely be deemed at home in all of them. * * * Nothing in *International Shoe* and its progeny suggests that a particular quantum of local activity should give a State authority over a far larger quantum of activity having no connection to any in-state activity.

Id. at 139 n.20, 134 S.Ct. at 762 n.20, 187 L.Ed.2d at 641 n.20.

Justice Sotomayor concurred in the judgment. She would have rejected jurisdiction based on the reasonableness factors that were dispositive in *Asahi* [p. 87, supra], arguing that California's "exercise of jurisdiction would be unreasonable given that the case involves foreign plaintiffs suing a foreign defendant based on foreign conduct, and given that a more appropriate forum is available." Id. at 144–46, 134 S.Ct. at 764–65, 187 L.Ed.2d at 643–45. She disagreed, however, with the majority's conclusion that defendant's contacts with California were insufficient to make it at home in the forum state:

The Court acknowledges that Mercedes-Benz USA, LLC (MBUSA), Daimler's wholly owned subsidiary, has considerable contacts with California. It has multiple facilities in the State, including a regional headquarters. Each year, it distributes in California tens of thousands of cars, the sale of which generated billions of dollars in the year this suit was brought. And it provides service and sales support to customers throughout the State. Daimler has conceded that California courts may exercise general jurisdiction over MBUSA on the basis of these contacts, and the Court assumes that MBUSA's contacts may be attributed to Daimler for the purpose of deciding whether Daimler is also subject to general jurisdiction.

Are these contacts sufficient to permit the exercise of general jurisdiction over Daimler? The Court holds that they are not, for a reason wholly foreign to our due process jurisprudence. The problem, the Court says, is not that Daimler's contacts with California are too few, but that its contacts with other forums are too many. In other words, the Court does not dispute that the presence of multiple offices, the direct distribution of thousands of products accounting for billions of dollars in sales, and continuous interaction with customers throughout a State would be enough to support the exercise of general jurisdiction over some businesses. Daimler is just not one of those businesses, the Court concludes, because its California contacts must be viewed in the context of its extensive "nationwide and worldwide" operations. * * * In recent years, Americans have grown accustomed to the concept of multinational corporations that are supposedly "too big to fail"; today the Court deems Daimler "too big for general jurisdiction."

* * *

[T]he majority announces the new rule that in order for a foreign defendant to be subject to general jurisdiction, it must not only possess continuous and systematic contacts with a forum State, but those contacts must also surpass some unspecified level when viewed in comparison to the company's "nationwide and worldwide" activities.

* * *

[T]he majority's approach unduly curtails the States' sovereign authority to adjudicate disputes against corporate defendants who have engaged in continuous and substantial business operations within their boundaries. * * * Suppose a company divides its management functions equally among three offices in different States, with one office nominally deemed the company's corporate headquarters. If the State where the headquarters is located can exercise general jurisdiction, why should the other two States be constitutionally forbidden to do the same? Indeed, under the majority's approach, the result would be unchanged even if the company has substantial operations within the latter two States (and even if the company has no sales or other business operations in the first State). * * *

Id. at 142–57, 134 S.Ct. at 763–72, 187 L.Ed.2d at 643–52.

2.   In BNSF RAILWAY CO. v. TYRRELL, 581 U.S. ___, 137 S.Ct. 1549, 198 L.Ed.2d 36 (2017), railroad employees sued BNSF in Montana state court under the Federal Employers' Liability Act for injuries that occurred outside of Montana.

BNSF is incorporated in Delaware and has its principal place of business in Texas. * * * It operates railroad lines in 28 States. * * * BNSF has 2,061 miles of railroad track in Montana (about 6% of its total track mileage of 32,500), employs some 2,100 workers there (less than 5% of its total work force of 43,000), generates less than 10% of its total revenue in the State, and maintains only one of its 24 automotive facilities in Montana (4%).

Id. at ___, 137 S.Ct. at 1554, 198 L.Ed.2d at 42. The Supreme Court held that these contacts with Montana were not sufficient to support general jurisdiction:

BNSF * * * is not incorporated in Montana and does not maintain its principal place of business there. Nor is BNSF so heavily engaged in activity in Montana "as to render [it] essentially at home" in that State. * * * BNSF has over 2,000 miles of railroad track and more than 2,000 employees in Montana. But, as we observed in *Daimler*, "the general jurisdiction inquiry does not focus solely on the magnitude of the defendant's in-state contacts." * * * Rather, the inquiry "calls for an appraisal of a corporation's activities in their entirety"; "[a] corporation that operates in many places can scarcely be deemed at home in all of them." * * *

Id. at ___, 137 S.Ct. at 1559, 198 L.Ed.2d at 47–48.

Justice Sotomayor dissented from the Court's application of the "at home" test for general jurisdiction, and criticized using "a comparative analysis" to determine jurisdiction:

> The majority does even *Daimler* itself a disservice, paying only lipservice to the question the Court purported to reserve there—the possibility of an "exceptional case" in which general jurisdiction would be proper in a forum State that is neither a corporate defendant's place of incorporation nor its principal place of business. * * * Its opinion here could be understood to limit that exception to the exact facts of *Perkins* * * *. That reading is so narrow as to read the exception out of existence entirely * * *.

Id. at 1560–61, 198 L.Ed.2d at 49–50.

3.   A state may exercise general jurisdiction over a domiciliary, for that is the place where a natural person "at home." In ABKCO INDUSTRIES, INC. v. LENNON, 85 Misc.2d 465, 469, 377 N.Y.S.2d 362, 366 (N.Y.Co. 1975), affirmed in part, 52 A.D.2d 435, 384 N.Y.S.2d 871 (1st Dept. 1976), a New York trial court held that general jurisdiction could be exercised over Richard Starkey, better known as Ringo Starr of the Beatles, because Starkey did business in New York "pervasively, unmistakably, undeniably, continuously, and substantially." Does this result survive *Goodyear* and *Daimler*?

4.   Is the "at home" test a bright-line rule or can it ever be unreasonable to exercise general jurisdiction in defendant's state of incorporation or principal place of business? In *Daimler* [p. 117, Note 1, supra], Justice Ginsburg's majority opinion wrote that *Asahi*'s "multipronged reasonableness check" applied only "when *specific* jurisdiction is at issue." 571 U.S. at 139 n.20, 134 S.Ct. at 762 n.20, 187 L.Ed.2d at 641 n.20. For general jurisdiction, however, "[w]hen a corporation is genuinely at home in the forum State, * * * any second-step inquiry would be superfluous." Id. Before *Daimler*, some lower courts had subjected the exercise of general jurisdiction to the five-factor reasonableness test endorsed in *Asahi* and *World-Wide Volkswagen*. See Metropolitan Life Insurance Co. v. Robertson-Ceco Corp., 84 F.3d 560 (2d Cir. 1996), cert. denied, 519 U.S. 1006, 117 S.Ct. 508, 136 L.Ed.2d 398 (1996).

5.   A rationale for general jurisdiction is that it assures the availability of a forum "where a defendant may be sued on any cause of action." Twitchell, *The Myth of General Jurisdiction*, 101 Harv.L.Rev. 610, 632 (1988). Does general jurisdiction fulfill this purpose if defendant is not "at home" anywhere in the United States?

F. DISTINGUISHING SPECIFIC AND GENERAL JURISDICTION

Although the distinction between specific and general jurisdiction was alluded to *International Shoe*, see p. 58, Note 2, supra, the Supreme Court initially decided few cases in which the outcome hinged on the line between the two. In *Helicopteros*, p. 113, supra, the parties conceded that the case had to be evaluated under a general jurisdiction standard. Justice Brennan dissented, however, arguing against accepting that concession and emphasizing that specific jurisdiction should be available when defendant's forum contacts "relate to" the cause of action:

> Limiting the specific jurisdiction of a forum to cases in which the cause of action formally arose out of the defendant's contacts with the State would subject constitutional standards under the Due Process Clause to the vagaries of the substantive law or pleading requirements of each State. * * *

> Our interpretation of the Due Process Clause has never been so dependent upon the applicable substantive law or the State's formal pleading requirements. * * * [T]he principal focus when determining whether a forum may constitutionally assert jurisdiction over a nonresident defendant has been on fairness and reasonableness to the defendant. To this extent, a court's specific jurisdiction should be applicable whenever the cause of action arises out of *or* relates to the contacts between the defendant and the forum.

Id. at 427, 104 S.Ct. at 1879, 80 L.Ed.2d at 419.

In the wake of decisions like *Goodyear*, *Daimler*, and *BNSF*, p. 113, Section E, supra, which set a high threshold for when a defendant would be "essentially at home" in the forum state such that general jurisdiction would be available, the Supreme Court has addressed more directly the distinction between specific and general jurisdiction.

In BRISTOL-MYERS SQUIBB CO. v. SUPERIOR COURT OF CALIFORNIA, SAN FRANCISCO COUNTY, 582 U.S. ___, 137 S.Ct. 1773, 198 L.Ed.2d 395 (2017), consumers from California and 33 other states filed eight actions in California state court against a pharmaceutical company alleging that Plavix, a drug that defendant manufactured and distributed, had damaged their health. Of the 678 plaintiffs, 88 resided in California; defendant was incorporated in Delaware and headquartered in New York. The California Supreme Court held it was constitutional to exercise specific jurisdiction over the company. Although the nonresident plaintiffs had not purchased the drugs in the state or alleged an injury in the forum, due process could be met under a sliding-scale approach, which permitted a more attenuated connection between defendant's forum contacts and the claim when defendant otherwise had extensive contacts with the state. That connection was shown in this case because the nonresidents' claims were similar to the residents' claims and defendant had engaged in other in-state activity.

The Supreme Court, in an eight-to-one decision, reversed, rejecting the California court's sliding-scale approach and emphasizing that for the exercise of specific jurisdiction, "there must be an 'affiliation between the forum and the underlying controversy, principally, [an] activity or an occurrence that takes place in the forum state,'" quoting *Goodyear*, p. 113, supra. As the Court explained:

> The present case illustrates the danger of the California approach. The State Supreme Court found that specific jurisdiction was present without identifying any adequate link between the State and the nonresidents' claims. * * * [T]he nonresidents were not prescribed Plavix in California, did not purchase Plavix in California, did not ingest Plavix in California, and were not injured by Plavix in California. The mere fact that other plaintiffs were prescribed, obtained, and ingested Plavix in California—and allegedly sustained the same injuries as did the nonresidents—does not allow the State to assert specific jurisdiction over the nonresidents' claims. * * * Nor is it sufficient—or even relevant—that [defendant] conducted research in California on matters unrelated to Plavix. What is needed—and what is missing here—is a connection between the forum and the specific claims at issue.

582 U.S. at ___, 137 S.Ct. at 1781, 198 L.Ed.2d at 404–05. The majority insisted that the nonresident plaintiffs were not left without a forum; suit could be brought where defendant is incorporated and headquartered, and residents of a particular state "could probably sue together in their home States." The Court left open whether a different jurisdictional standard would apply in federal court. Id. at ___, 137 S.Ct. at 1783–84, 198 L.Ed.2d at 407.

Justice Sotomayor dissented, arguing that the requirements of specific jurisdiction were easily met. Defendant had purposefully availed itself of the benefits of California's pharmaceutical market through substantial employment, maintenance of production facilities, contracts with in-state distributors, and more than a $1 billion of sales of Plavix in the state during the relevant period. Moreover, the nonresidents' claims related to defendant's in-state conduct, because they had a "'connect[ion] with' that conduct," citing *International Shoe*, p. 52, supra. Finally, in the dissent's view, the exercise of jurisdiction was reasonable:

> [According to the majority, a] corporation that engages in a nationwide course of conduct cannot be held accountable in a state court by a group of injured people unless all of those people were injured in the forum State.

I fear the consequences of the Court's decision today will be substantial. The majority's rule will make it difficult to aggregate the claims of plaintiffs across the country whose claims may be worth little alone. It will make it impossible to bring a nationwide mass action in state court against defendants who are "at home" in different States. And it will result in piecemeal litigation and the bifurcation of claims. None of this is necessary. A core concern in this Court's personal jurisdiction cases is fairness. And there is nothing unfair about subjecting a massive corporation to suit in a State for a nationwide course of conduct that injures both forum residents and nonresidents alike.

Id. at ___, 137 S.Ct. at 1784, 198 L.Ed.2d at 407–08.

FORD MOTOR CO. v. MONTANA EIGHTH JUDICIAL DISTRICT COURT; FORD MOTOR CO. v. BANDEMER
Supreme Court of the United States, 2021.
592 U.S. ___, 141 S.Ct. 1017, 209 L.Ed.2d 225.[d]

JUSTICE KAGAN delivered the opinion of the Court, in which THE CHIEF JUSTICE, JUSTICE BREYER, JUSTICE SOTOMAYOR, and JUSTICE KAVANAUGH joined.

In each of these two cases, a state court held that it had jurisdiction over Ford Motor Company in a products-liability suit stemming from a car accident. The accident happened in the State where suit was brought. The victim was one of the State's residents. And Ford did substantial business in the State—among other things, advertising, selling, and servicing the model of vehicle the suit claims is defective. Still, Ford contends that jurisdiction is improper because the particular car involved in the crash was not first sold in the forum State, nor was it designed or manufactured there. We reject that argument. When a company like Ford serves a market for a product in a State and that product causes injury in the State to one of its residents, the State's courts may entertain the resulting suit.

I

Ford is a global auto company. It is incorporated in Delaware and headquartered in Michigan. But its business is everywhere. Ford markets, sells, and services its products across the United States and overseas. In this country alone, the company annually distributes over 2.5 million new cars, trucks, and SUVs to over 3,200 licensed dealerships. See App. 70, 100. Ford also encourages a resale market for its products: Almost all its dealerships buy and sell used Fords, as well as selling new ones. To enhance its brand and increase its sales, Ford engages in wide-ranging

---

d   All alterations that appear in the *Ford* opinions are in the original, except for the lettered footnote, omissions that are indicated with asterisks, and bracketed cross-references to pages in this casebook.

promotional activities, including television, print, online, and direct-mail advertisements. No matter where you live, you've seen them: "Have you driven a Ford lately?" or "Built Ford Tough." Ford also ensures that consumers can keep their vehicles running long past the date of sale. The company provides original parts to auto supply stores and repair shops across the country. (Goes another slogan: "Keep your Ford a Ford.") And Ford's own network of dealers offers an array of maintenance and repair services, thus fostering an ongoing relationship between Ford and its customers.

Accidents involving two of Ford's vehicles—a 1996 Explorer and a 1994 Crown Victoria—are at the heart of the suits before us. One case comes from Montana. Markkaya Gullett was driving her Explorer near her home in the State when the tread separated from a rear tire. The vehicle spun out, rolled into a ditch, and came to rest upside down. Gullett died at the scene of the crash. The representative of her estate sued Ford in Montana state court, bringing claims for a design defect, failure to warn, and negligence. The second case comes from Minnesota. Adam Bandemer was a passenger in his friend's Crown Victoria, traveling on a rural road in the State to a favorite ice-fishing spot. When his friend rear-ended a snowplow, this car too landed in a ditch. Bandemer's air bag failed to deploy, and he suffered serious brain damage. He sued Ford in Minnesota state court, asserting products-liability, negligence, and breach-of-warranty claims. * * *

II

A

The Fourteenth Amendment's Due Process Clause limits a state court's power to exercise jurisdiction over a defendant. The canonical decision in this area remains *International Shoe Co. v. Washington*, [p. 52, supra]. There, the Court held that a tribunal's authority depends on the defendant's having such "contacts" with the forum State that "the maintenance of the suit" is "reasonable, in the context of our federal system of government," and "does not offend traditional notions of fair play and substantial justice." * * * In giving content to that formulation, the Court has long focused on the nature and extent of "the defendant's relationship to the forum State." * * * That focus led to our recognizing two kinds of personal jurisdiction: general (sometimes called all-purpose) jurisdiction and specific (sometimes called case-linked) jurisdiction.

A state court may exercise general jurisdiction only when a defendant is "essentially at home" in the State. * * * General jurisdiction, as its name implies, extends to "any and all claims" brought against a defendant. * * * Those claims need not relate to the forum State or the defendant's activity there; they may concern events and conduct anywhere in the world. But that breadth imposes a correlative limit: Only a select "set of affiliations with a forum" will expose a defendant to such sweeping jurisdiction. *Daimler AG v. Bauman*, [p. 117, Note 1, supra]. In what we have called the "paradigm" case, an individual is subject to general jurisdiction in her place of domicile. * * * And the "equivalent" forums for a corporation are its place of incorporation and principal place of business. * * *; see *id.* * * * (leaving open "the possibility that in an exceptional case" a corporation might also be "at home" elsewhere). So general jurisdiction over Ford (as all parties agree) attaches in Delaware and Michigan—not in Montana and Minnesota. * * *

Specific jurisdiction is different: It covers defendants less intimately connected with a State, but only as to a narrower class of claims. The contacts needed for this kind of jurisdiction often go by the name "purposeful availment." * * * The defendant, we have said, must take "some act by which [it] purposefully avails itself of the privilege of conducting activities within the forum State." * * * The contacts must be the defendant's own choice and not "random, isolated, or fortuitous." * * * They must show that the defendant deliberately "reached out beyond" its home—by, for example, "exploi[ting] a market" in the forum State or entering a contractual relationship centered there. * * * Yet even then—because the defendant is not "at home"—the forum State may exercise jurisdiction in only certain cases. The plaintiff's claims, we have often stated, "must arise out of or relate to the defendant's contacts" with the forum. * * * Or put just a bit differently, "there must be 'an affiliation between the forum and the underlying controversy, principally, [an] activity or an occurrence that takes place in the forum State and is therefore subject to the State's regulation.' " * * *

These rules derive from and reflect two sets of values—treating defendants fairly and protecting "interstate federalism." * * * Our decision in *International Shoe* founded specific jurisdiction on an idea of reciprocity between a defendant and a State: When (but only when) a company "exercises the privilege of conducting activities within a state"—thus "enjoy[ing] the benefits and protection of [its] laws"—the State may hold the company to account for related misconduct. * * * Later decisions have added that our doctrine similarly provides defendants with "fair warning"—knowledge that "a particular activity may subject [it] to the jurisdiction of a foreign sovereign." * * * A defendant can thus "structure [its] primary conduct" to lessen or avoid exposure to a given State's courts. * * * And this Court has considered alongside defendants' interests those of the States in relation to each other. One State's "sovereign power to try" a suit, we have recognized, may prevent "sister States" from exercising their like authority. * * * The law of specific jurisdiction thus seeks to ensure that States with "little legitimate interest" in a suit do not encroach on States more affected by the controversy. * * *

B

Ford contends that our jurisdictional rules prevent Montana's and Minnesota's courts from deciding these two suits. In making that argument, Ford does not contest that it does substantial business in Montana and Minnesota—that it actively seeks to serve the market for automobiles and related products in those States. * * * Or to put that concession in more doctrinal terms, Ford agrees that it has "purposefully avail[ed] itself of the privilege of conducting activities" in both places. * * * Ford's claim is instead that those activities do not sufficiently connect to the suits, even though the resident-plaintiffs allege that Ford cars malfunctioned in the forum States. In Ford's view, the needed link must be causal in nature: Jurisdiction attaches "only if the defendant's forum conduct *gave rise* to the plaintiff's claims." * * * And that rule reduces, Ford thinks, to locating specific jurisdiction in the State where Ford sold the car in question, or else the States where Ford designed and manufactured the vehicle. * * * On that view, the place of accident and injury is immaterial. * * *

But Ford's causation-only approach finds no support in this Court's requirement of a "connection" between a plaintiff's suit and a defendant's activities. * * * That rule indeed serves to narrow the class of claims over which a state court may exercise specific jurisdiction. But not quite so far as Ford wants. None of our precedents has suggested that only a strict causal relationship between the defendant's in-state activity and the litigation will do. As just noted, our most common formulation of the rule demands that the suit "arise out of *or relate to* the defendant's contacts with the forum." * * * The first half of that standard asks about causation; but the back half, after the "or," contemplates that some relationships will support jurisdiction without a causal showing. That does not mean anything goes. In the sphere of specific jurisdiction, the phrase "relate to" incorporates real limits, as it must to adequately protect defendants foreign to a forum. But again, we have never framed the specific jurisdiction inquiry as always requiring proof of causation—*i.e.,* proof that the plaintiff's claim came about because of the defendant's in-state conduct. * * * So the case is not over even if, as Ford argues, a causal test would put jurisdiction in only the States of first sale, manufacture, and design. A different State's courts may yet have jurisdiction, because of another "activity [or] occurrence" involving the defendant that takes place in the State. * * *[3]

---

[3] In thus reiterating this Court's longstanding approach, we reject Justice GORSUCH's apparent (if oblique) view that a state court should have jurisdiction over a nationwide corporation like Ford on *any* claim, no matter how unrelated to the State or Ford's activities there. * * * On that view, for example, a California court could hear a claim against Ford brought by an Ohio plaintiff based on an accident occurring in Ohio involving a car purchased in Ohio. Removing the need for any connection between the case and forum State would transfigure our specific

* * *

To see why Ford is subject to jurisdiction in these cases * * *, consider first the business that the company regularly conducts in Montana and Minnesota. * * * Small wonder that Ford has here conceded "purposeful availment" of the two States' markets. * * * By every means imaginable— among them, billboards, TV and radio spots, print ads, and direct mail— Ford urges Montanans and Minnesotans to buy its vehicles, including (at all relevant times) Explorers and Crown Victorias. Ford cars—again including those two models—are available for sale, whether new or used, throughout the States, at 36 dealerships in Montana and 84 in Minnesota. And apart from sales, Ford works hard to foster ongoing connections to its cars' owners. The company's dealers in Montana and Minnesota (as elsewhere) regularly maintain and repair Ford cars, including those whose warranties have long since expired. And the company distributes replacement parts both to its own dealers and to independent auto shops in the two States. Those activities, too, make Ford money. And by making it easier to own a Ford, they encourage Montanans and Minnesotans to become lifelong Ford drivers.

Now turn to how all this Montana- and Minnesota-based conduct relates to the claims in these cases, brought by state residents in Montana's and Minnesota's courts. Each plaintiff's suit, of course, arises from a car accident in one of those States. In each complaint, the resident-plaintiff alleges that a defective Ford vehicle—an Explorer in one, a Crown Victoria in the other—caused the crash and resulting harm. And as just described, Ford had advertised, sold, and serviced those two car models in both States for many years. (Contrast a case, which we do not address, in which Ford marketed the models in only a different State or region.) In other words, Ford had systematically served a market in Montana and Minnesota for the very vehicles that the plaintiffs allege malfunctioned and injured them in those States. So there is a strong "relationship among the defendant, the forum, and the litigation"—the "essential foundation" of specific jurisdiction * * *.[4]

The only complication here, pressed by Ford, is that the company sold the specific cars involved in these crashes outside the forum States, with

___

jurisdiction standard as applied to corporations. "Case-linked" jurisdiction * * * would then become not case-linked at all.

[4] None of this is to say that any person using any means to sell any good in a State is subject to jurisdiction there if the product malfunctions after arrival. We have long treated isolated or sporadic transactions differently from continuous ones. * * * And we do not here consider internet transactions, which may raise doctrinal questions of their own. * * * So consider, for example, a hypothetical offered at oral argument. "[A] retired guy in a small town" in Maine "carves decoys" and uses "a site on the Internet" to sell them. * * * "Can he be sued in any state if some harm arises from the decoy?" * * * The differences between that case and the ones before us virtually list themselves. (Just consider all our descriptions of Ford's activities outside its home bases.) So we agree with the plaintiffs' counsel that resolving these cases does not also resolve the hypothetical. * * *

consumers later selling them to the States' residents. Because that is so, Ford argues, the plaintiffs' claims "would be precisely the same if Ford had never done anything in Montana and Minnesota." * * * Of course, that argument merely restates Ford's demand for an exclusively causal test of connection—which we have already shown is inconsistent with our caselaw. * * *

But in any event, that assumption is far from clear. For the owners of these cars might never have bought them, and so these suits might never have arisen, except for Ford's contacts with their home States. Those contacts might turn any resident of Montana or Minnesota into a Ford owner—even when he buys his car from out of state. He may make that purchase because he saw ads for the car in local media. And he may take into account a raft of Ford's in-state activities designed to make driving a Ford convenient there: that Ford dealers stand ready to service the car; that other auto shops have ample supplies of Ford parts; and that Ford fosters an active resale market for its old models. The plaintiffs here did not in fact establish, or even allege, such causal links. * * * Nor should jurisdiction in cases like these ride on the exact reasons for an individual plaintiff's purchase, or on his ability to present persuasive evidence about them.[5] But the possibilities listed above—created by the reach of Ford's Montana and Minnesota contacts—underscore the aptness of finding jurisdiction here, even though the cars at issue were first sold out of state.

For related reasons, allowing jurisdiction in these cases treats Ford fairly, as this Court's precedents explain. In conducting so much business in Montana and Minnesota, Ford "enjoys the benefits and protection of [their] laws"—the enforcement of contracts, the defense of property, the resulting formation of effective markets. * * * All that assistance to Ford's in-state business creates reciprocal obligations—most relevant here, that the car models Ford so extensively markets in Montana and Minnesota be safe for their citizens to use there. Thus our repeated conclusion: A state court's enforcement of that commitment, enmeshed as it is with Ford's government-protected in-state business, can "hardly be said to be undue." * * * An automaker regularly marketing a vehicle in a State * * * has "clear notice" that it will be subject to jurisdiction in the State's courts when the product malfunctions there (regardless where it was first sold). * * * Precisely because that exercise of jurisdiction is so reasonable, it is also predictable—and thus allows Ford to "structure [its] primary conduct" to lessen or even avoid the costs of state-court litigation. * * *

Finally, principles of "interstate federalism" support jurisdiction over these suits in Montana and Minnesota. * * * Those States have significant interests at stake—"providing [their] residents with a convenient forum for

---

[5]   It should, for example, make no difference if a plaintiff had recently moved to the forum State with his car, and had not made his purchasing decision with that move in mind—so had not considered any of Ford's activities in his new home State.

redressing injuries inflicted by out-of-state actors," as well as enforcing their own safety regulations. * * * Consider, next to those, the interests of the States of first sale (Washington and North Dakota)—which Ford's proposed rule would make the most likely forums. For each of those States, the suit involves all out-of-state parties, an out-of-state accident, and out-of-state injuries; the suit's only connection with the State is that a former owner once (many years earlier) bought the car there. In other words, there is a less significant "relationship among the defendant, the forum, and the litigation." * * * So by channeling these suits to Washington and North Dakota, Ford's regime would undermine, rather than promote, what the company calls the Due Process Clause's "jurisdiction-allocating function." * * *

* * *

Here, resident-plaintiffs allege that they suffered in-state injury because of defective products that Ford extensively promoted, sold, and serviced in Montana and Minnesota. For all the reasons we have given, the connection between the plaintiffs' claims and Ford's activities in those States—or otherwise said, the "relationship among the defendant, the forum[s], and the litigation"—is close enough to support specific jurisdiction. * * *

It is so ordered.

JUSTICE BARRETT took no part in the consideration or decision of these cases.

JUSTICE ALITO, concurring in the judgment.

These cases can and should be decided without any alteration or refinement of our case law on specific personal jurisdiction. To be sure, for the reasons outlined in Justice GORSUCH's thoughtful opinion, there are grounds for questioning the standard that the Court adopted in *International Shoe Co. v. Washington* * * *. And there are also reasons to wonder whether the case law we have developed since that time is well suited for the way in which business is now conducted. But there is nothing distinctively 21st century about the question in the cases now before us, and the answer to that question is settled by our case law.

Since *International Shoe,* the rule has been that a state court can exercise personal jurisdiction over a defendant if the defendant has "minimum contacts" with the forum—which means that the contacts must be "such that the maintenance of the suit does not offend 'traditional notions of fair play and substantial justice.' " * * *

That standard is easily met here. Ford has long had a heavy presence in Minnesota and Montana. It spends billions on national advertising. It has many franchises in both States. Ford dealers in Minnesota and Montana sell and service Ford vehicles, and Ford ships replacement parts to both States. In entertaining these suits, Minnesota and Montana courts have not reached out and grabbed suits in which they "have little legitimate interest." * * * *Their* residents, while riding in vehicles purchased within *their* borders, were killed or injured in accidents on *their* roads. Can anyone seriously argue that requiring Ford to litigate these cases in Minnesota and Montana would be fundamentally unfair?

* * *

Ford * * * asks us to adopt an unprecedented rule under which a defendant's contacts with the forum State must be proven to have been a but-for cause of the tort plaintiff's injury. The Court properly rejects that argument, and I agree with the main thrust of the Court's opinion. My only quibble is with the new gloss that the Court puts on our case law. Several of our opinions have said that a plaintiff's claims " 'must arise out of or relate to the defendant's contacts' " with the forum. * * * The Court parses this phrase "as though we were dealing with language of a statute," * * * and because this phrase is cast in the disjunctive, the Court recognizes a new category of cases in which personal jurisdiction is permitted: those in which the claims do not "arise out of " (*i.e.*, are not caused by) the defendant's contacts but nevertheless sufficiently "relate to" those contacts in some undefined way * * *.

This innovation is unnecessary and, in my view, unwise. To say that the Constitution does not require the kind of proof of causation that Ford would demand—what the majority describes as a "strict causal relationship," * * *—is not to say that no causal link of any kind is needed. And here, there is a sufficient link. It is reasonable to infer that the vehicles in question here would never have been on the roads in Minnesota and Montana if they were some totally unknown brand that had never been advertised in those States, was not sold in those States, would not be familiar to mechanics in those States, and could not have been easily repaired with parts available in those States. * * * The whole point of those activities was to put more Fords (including those in question here) on Minnesota and Montana roads. The common-sense relationship between Ford's activities and these suits, in other words, is causal in a broad sense of the concept, and personal jurisdiction can rest on this type of link without strict proof of the type Ford would require. When "arise out of " is understood in this way, it is apparent that "arise out of " and "relate to" overlap and are not really two discrete grounds for jurisdiction. The phrase "arise out of or relate to" is simply a way of restating the basic "minimum contacts" standard adopted in *International Shoe.*

* * *

JUSTICE GORSUCH, with whom JUSTICE THOMAS joins, concurring in the judgment.

Since *International Shoe Co. v. Washington* * * *, this Court's cases have sought to divide the world of personal jurisdiction in two. A tribunal with "general jurisdiction" may entertain any claim against the defendant. But to trigger this power, a court usually must ensure the defendant is " 'at home' " in the forum State. * * * Meanwhile, "specific jurisdiction" affords a narrower authority. It applies only when the defendant " 'purposefully avails' " itself of the opportunity to do business in the forum State and the suit " 'arise[s] out of or relate[s] to' " the defendant's contacts with the forum State. * * *

* * *

* * * Focusing on the phrase "arise out of or relate to" that so often appears in our cases, the majority asks us to parse those words "as though we were dealing with language of a statute." * * * In particular, the majority zeros in on the disjunctive conjunction "or," and proceeds to build its entire opinion around that linguistic feature. * * * The majority admits that "arise out of" may connote causation. But, it argues, "relate to" is an independent clause that does not.

Where this leaves us is far from clear. For a case to "relate to" the defendant's forum contacts, the majority says, it is enough if an "affiliation" or "relationship" or "connection" exists between them. * * * But what does this assortment of nouns *mean*? Loosed from any causation standard, we are left to guess. The majority promises that its new test "does not mean anything goes," but that hardly tells us what does. * * *

* * *

With the old *International Shoe* dichotomy looking increasingly uncertain, it's hard not to ask how we got here and where we might be headed.

Before *International Shoe*, * * * a court's competency normally depended on the defendant's presence in, or consent to, the sovereign's jurisdiction. But once a plaintiff was able to "tag" the defendant with process in the jurisdiction, that State's courts were generally thought competent to render judgment on any claim against the defendant, whether it involved events inside or outside the State. *Pennoyer v. Neff*, [p. 37, supra]; *Burnham v. Superior Court of Cal., County of Marin*, [p. 160, infra].e * * *

International Shoe's emergence may be attributable to many influences, but at least part of the story seems to involve the rise of corporations and interstate trade. * * * A corporation doing business in its

---

e   The Court's fractured decision in *Burnham*, p. 160, infra, upheld the traditional practice, recognized in *Pennoyer*, permitting personal jurisdiction over an individual defendant who is served with process while present in the forum state—regardless of whether the substance of the lawsuit has any connection to defendant's presence there.

State of incorporation is one thing; the old physical presence rules for individuals seem easily adaptable to them. But what happens when a corporation, created and able to operate thanks to the laws of one State, seeks the privilege of sending agents or products into another State?

* * *

* * * *International Shoe* sought to start over. * * * In place of nearly everything that had come before, the Court sought to build a new test focused on " 'traditional notions of fair play and substantial justice.' " * * *

It was a heady promise. But it is unclear how far it has really taken us. Even today, this Court usually considers corporations "at home" and thus subject to general jurisdiction in only one or two States. All in a world where global conglomerates boast of their many "headquarters." The Court has issued these restrictive rulings, too, even though *individual* defendants remain subject to the old "tag" rule, allowing them to be sued on any claim anywhere they can be found. *Burnham* * * *.[4] Nearly 80 years removed from *International Shoe*, it seems corporations continue to receive special jurisdictional protections in the name of the Constitution. Less clear is why.

Maybe, too, *International Shoe* just doesn't work quite as well as it once did. For a period, its specific jurisdiction test might have seemed a reasonable new substitute for assessing corporate "presence," a way to identify those out-of-state corporations that were simply pretending to be absent from jurisdictions where they were really transacting business. When a company "purposefully availed" itself of the benefits of another State's market in the 1940s, it often involved sending in agents, advertising in local media, or developing a network of on-the-ground dealers, much as Ford did in these cases. * * * But, today, even an individual retiree carving wooden decoys in Maine can "purposefully avail" himself of the chance to do business across the continent after drawing online orders to his e-Bay "store" thanks to Internet advertising with global reach. * * * A test once aimed at keeping corporations honest about their out-of-state operations now seemingly risks hauling individuals to jurisdictions where they have never set foot.

Perhaps this is the real reason why the majority introduces us to the hypothetical decoy salesman. Yes, he arguably availed himself of a new market. Yes, the plaintiff's injuries arguably arose from (or were caused by) the product he sold there. Yes, *International Shoe*'s old causation test would seemingly allow for personal jurisdiction. But maybe the majority resists that conclusion because the old test no longer seems as reliable a proxy for determining corporate presence as it once did. Maybe *that's* the intuition lying behind the majority's introduction of its new "affiliation"

---

[4] Since *Burnham*, some courts have sought to revive the tag rule for artificial entities while others argue that doing so would be inconsistent with *International Shoe*. * * *

rule and its comparison of the Maine retiree's "sporadic" and "isolated" sales in the plaintiff's State and Ford's deep "relationships" and "connections" with Montana and Minnesota. * * *

If that is the logic at play here, I cannot help but wonder if we are destined to return where we began. * * * Perhaps it was, is, and in the end always will be about trying to assess fairly a corporate defendant's presence or consent. * * * Perhaps, too, none of this should come as a surprise. New technologies and new schemes to evade the process server will always be with us. But if our concern is with " '*traditional* notions of fair play and substantial justice,' " * * * not just our personal and idiosyncratic impressions of those things, perhaps we will always wind up asking variations of the same questions.[5]

None of this is to cast doubt on the outcome of these cases. The parties have not pointed to anything in the Constitution's original meaning or its history that might allow Ford to evade answering the plaintiffs' claims in Montana or Minnesota courts. No one seriously questions that the company, seeking to do business, entered those jurisdictions through the front door. And I cannot see why, when faced with the process server, it should be allowed to escape out the back. * * * The real struggle here isn't with settling on the right outcome in these cases, but with making sense of our personal jurisdiction jurisprudence and *International Shoe's* increasingly doubtful dichotomy. On those scores, I readily admit that I finish these cases with even more questions than I had at the start. * * *

NOTES AND QUESTIONS

1.   According to Justice Kagan's majority opinion, what is the test for deciding whether specific jurisdiction satisfies due process? In what ways do the concurring opinions disagree with the majority about the test?

2.   Both *Bristol-Myers* and *Ford* involved large companies doing substantial business in the forum state. Why was specific jurisdiction proper in *Ford* but not proper in *Bristol-Myers*?

3.   Justice Kagan's majority opinion discusses "two sets of values—treating defendants fairly and protecting 'interstate federalism.' " How do these values factor into the requirements for specific jurisdiction? Do they play a different role under *Ford*'s test for specific jurisdiction than they did in

---

[5]   The majority worries that the thoughts expressed here threaten to "transfigure our specific jurisdiction standard as applied to corporations" and "return [us] to the mid-19th century." * * * But it has become a tired trope to criticize any reference to the Constitution's original meaning as (somehow) both radical and antiquated. Seeking to understand the Constitution's original meaning is part of our job. What's the majority's real worry anyway—that corporations might lose special protections? The Constitution has always allowed suits against *individuals* on any issue in any State where they set foot. * * * Yet the majority seems to recoil at even entertaining the possibility the Constitution might tolerate similar results for "nationwide corporation[s]," whose "business is everywhere." * * *

earlier decisions such as *World-Wide Volkswagen*, p. 71, supra, *Burger King*, p. 83, supra, and *Asahi*, p. 87, supra?

4.   Consider the scenario discussed in footnote 4 of the majority opinion. If such an individual sells one of his products to a Montana customer and it causes injury there, how would a court analyze whether he would be subject to personal jurisdiction in Montana? What additional information would be relevant?

5.   In footnote 3 of the majority opinion, Justice Kagan alludes to Justice Gorsuch's "apparent (if oblique) view that a state court should have jurisdiction over a nationwide corporation like Ford on *any* claim, no matter how unrelated to the State or Ford's activities there." In what way does Justice Gorsuch's opinion reflect that view? Would Justice Gorsuch conclude that the California court could exercise jurisdiction in *Daimler*, p. 117, Note 1, supra, or in *Bristol-Myers*, p. 122, supra? If not, why not?

G. CONSENT AS ANOTHER BASIS OF JURISDICTION

1. CONSENT BY APPEARANCE IN COURT

INSURANCE CORP. OF IRELAND, LTD. V. COMPAGNIE DES BAUXITES DE GUINEE, 456 U.S. 694, 102 S.Ct. 2099, 72 L.Ed.2d 492 (1982). Plaintiff, Compagnie des Bauxites de Guinee (CBG), a bauxite producer incorporated in Delaware but doing business only in the Republic of Guinea, purchased business-interruption insurance from a domestic insurer in Pennsylvania and from a group of foreign insurance companies through a London brokerage house. When a mechanical failure forced a halt in production, CBG filed a multi-million dollar claim, which the insurers refused to pay. CBG then sued in federal court in Pennsylvania, but most of the foreign insurance companies contested personal jurisdiction. CBG attempted to use discovery to establish the essential jurisdictional facts. After the companies failed to comply with the court's orders for production of the requested information despite repeated warnings, the district court, pursuant to Federal Rule 37(b)(2)(A)(i), imposed a sanction consisting of a presumptive finding that the insurers were subject to its jurisdiction because of their business contacts in Pennsylvania. The Supreme Court upheld the sanction in an opinion written by Justice White:

> Because the requirement of personal jurisdiction represents first of all an individual right, it can, like other such rights, be waived. * * *
>
> * * * By submitting to the jurisdiction of the court for the limited purpose of challenging jurisdiction, the defendant agrees to abide by that court's determination on the issue of jurisdiction[,] * * *

[and] the manner in which the court determines whether it has personal jurisdiction may include a variety of legal rules and presumptions, as well as straightforward factfinding. * * *

* * * CBG was seeking through discovery to respond to [the insurers'] contention that the District Court did not have personal jurisdiction. Having put the issue in question, [the insurers] did not have the option of blocking the reasonable attempt of CBG to meet its burden of proof. [They] surely did not have this option once the court had overruled [their] objections. Because of [the insurers'] failure to comply with the discovery orders, CBG was unable to establish the full extent of the contacts between [the insurers] and Pennsylvania, the critical issue in proving personal jurisdiction. [Their] failure to supply the requested information as to [their] contacts with Pennsylvania supports "the presumption that the refusal to produce evidence . . . was but an admission of the want of merit in the asserted defense." * * * The sanction took as established the facts—contacts with Pennsylvania—that CBG was seeking to establish through discovery. * * *

Id. at 703, 706–09, 102 S.Ct. at 2105–08, 72 L.Ed.2d at 502, 504–05. In a footnote, Justice White added:

It is true that we have stated that the requirement of personal jurisdiction, as applied to state courts, reflects an element of federalism and the character of state sovereignty vis-à-vis other States. * * * The restriction on state sovereign power * * * must be seen as ultimately a function of the individual liberty interest preserved by the Due Process Clause. That clause is the only source of the personal jurisdiction requirement and the Clause itself makes no mention of federalism concerns. Furthermore, if the federalism concept operated as an independent restriction on the sovereign power of the court, it would not be possible to waive the personal jurisdiction requirement: Individual actions cannot change the powers of sovereignty, although the individual can subject himself to powers from which he may otherwise be protected.

Id. at 702 n.10, 102 S.Ct. at 2104 n.10, 72 L.Ed.2d 502 n.10.

NOTE AND QUESTION

A defendant may waive objections to a court's exercise of personal jurisdiction, may forfeit an opportunity to raise objections to jurisdiction, or may be estopped from raising the issue. For example, Federal Rule 12(h)(1) provides that a defendant who fails to raise an objection to personal jurisdiction in the answer or in an initial motion under Rule 12 is precluded from raising the issue. See p. 428, Background Note on Federal Rule 12, infra. In these settings, is defendant's consent the basis for the court's power?

2.   CONSENT BY REGISTRATION IN STATE

Most states have statutes that require a foreign corporation to register as a condition of doing business in the state. By analogy to the motorist statute at issue in *Kane*, p. 48, supra, can it be argued that registration manifests consent to the general jurisdiction of the forum state? In PENNSYLVANIA FIRE INSURANCE CO. OF PHILADELPHIA v. GOLD ISSUE MINING & MILLING CO., 243 U.S. 93, 94–96, 37 S.Ct. 344, 345, 61 L.Ed. 610, 616 (1917), the Supreme Court held that due process permitted personal jurisdiction over an out-of-state insurance company based on its consent that service of process on an in-state official would be deemed personal service on the company. In FLEXNER v. FARSON, 248 U.S. 289, 293, 39 S.Ct. 97, 98, 63 L.Ed. 250, 253 (1919), however, it rejected such consent with respect to individual defendants, noting that the forum state "had no power to exclude the defendants" and therefore cannot attach consent-to-service as a condition of doing business in the state.

In RATLIFF v. COOPER LABORATORIES, INC., 444 F.2d 745 (4th Cir. 1971), cert. denied, 404 U.S. 948, 92 S.Ct. 271, 30 L.Ed.2d 265 (1971), the court of appeals held that an out-of-state drug manufacturer that regularly sent salesmen into South Carolina was not amenable to suit in that state even though it had filed an application and had been given authority to do business in the state, and had appointed an in-state agent for service of process. Plaintiffs were residents of Florida and Indiana that had purchased and consumed in their home states drugs manufactured by defendant; they sued in South Carolina to take advantage of that state's relatively long statute of limitations. The Fourth Circuit explained: "Applying for the privilege of doing business is one thing, but the actual exercise of that privilege is quite another. * * * The principles of due process require a firmer foundation than mere compliance with state domestication statutes." 444 F.2d at 748.

Would *Daimler* or *Goodyear* support the exercise of general jurisdiction based on registration to do business in the forum state? See Benish, Pennoyer's *Ghost: Consent, Registration Statutes, and General Jurisdiction after* Daimler AG v. Bauman, 90 N.Y.U.L.Rev. 1609 (2015). The Supreme Court has not addressed the issue, but lower courts have questioned whether that practice remains constitutionally permissible after the Court's recent decisions on general jurisdiction. See, e.g., Fidrych v. Marriott International, Inc., 952 F.3d 124, 135–37 (4th Cir. 2020) (recognizing earlier Supreme Court decisions supporting the view that "a foreign corporation obtaining a business license or appointing an agent for service of process in a state has consented to general jurisdiction in the state if state law so provides" but finding it "difficult to reconcile [that] approach with the modern view of general jurisdiction expressed in the Supreme Court's recent cases"). Some courts have avoided the constitutional question by construing the relevant statutes as not making registration the equivalent of consent to general jurisdiction. See, e.g., Aybar v. Aybar, 177 N.E.2d 1257, 37 N.Y.3d 274 (2021); Magna Powertrain de Mexico S.A. de C.V. v. Momentive Performance Materials USA LLC, 192 F.Supp.3d 824 (E.D.Mich. 2016). Other courts, however, have recognized consent-by-registration as an independent ground for general jurisdiction that survives the Supreme Court's recent case law. See, e.g., Cooper Tire & Rubber Co. v. McCall, 863 S.E.2d 81 (Ga. 2021) (reaffirming its prior case law holding "that Georgia courts may exercise general personal jurisdiction over any out-of-state corporation that is 'authorized to do or transact business in this state at the time a claim arises,'" despite its "tension with a recent line of United States Supreme Court cases addressing when state courts may exercise general personal jurisdiction over out-of-state corporations").

On April 25, 2022, the Supreme Court agreed to hear a case that presents the question whether due process allows a state to require a corporation to consent to personal jurisdiction in order to do business in that state. Mallory v. Norfolk Southern Railway Co., ___ U.S. ___, ___ S.Ct. ___, ___ L.Ed.2d ___, 2022 WL 1205835 (2022) (granting certiorari). The case will be argued during the Term that begins in October 2022.

3. CONSENT BY CONTRACT

A party may consent to the jurisdiction of a forum by assenting to a contractual choice-of-forum term. Contractual consent can apply to a dispute that already exists or to one that may arise later between the parties. Moreover, a party may agree to a forum-term that waives objections to jurisdiction in a forum, or purports to oust any but the designated forum of jurisdiction to hear the dispute. Traditionally, agreements to oust courts of jurisdiction were void as against public policy and were not judicially enforceable.

———

M/S BREMEN v. ZAPATA OFF-SHORE CO., 407 U.S. 1, 92 S.Ct. 1907, 32 L.Ed.2d 513 (1972). Plaintiff Zapata, a Houston-based American corporation, contracted with Unterweser, a German corporation, to tow Zapata's drilling rig from Louisiana to Italy. The contract contained a provision that all disputes were to be litigated before the "London Court of Justice." In the course of the towing, the rig was damaged in a storm off Florida and was towed to Tampa. Zapata commenced suit against Unterweser in a federal court in Florida. Unterweser, citing the forum-selection clause in the contract, moved to dismiss or, alternatively, to stay the action pending the submission of the dispute to the High Court of

Justice in London. On a parallel track, Unterweser sued Zapata for breach of contract in the English court.

The district court refused to dismiss or stay the American action, and the court of appeals affirmed. The Supreme Court reversed:

> We hold * * * that far too little weight and effect were given to the forum clause in resolving this controversy. * * * The expansion of American business and industry will hardly be encouraged if, notwithstanding solemn contracts, we insist on a parochial concept that all disputes must be resolved under our laws and in our courts. * * * We cannot have trade and commerce in world markets and international waters exclusively on our terms, governed by our laws, and resolved in our courts.

Id. at 8–9, 92 S.Ct. at 1912–13, 32 L.Ed.2d at 519–20.

———

CARNIVAL CRUISE LINES, INC. v. SHUTE, 499 U.S. 585, 111 S.Ct. 1522, 113 L.Ed.2d 622 (1991). Plaintiffs, Eulala and Russel Shute, purchased passage for a seven-day cruise on defendant's ship, the *Tropicale*, through a Washington State travel agent. Plaintiffs paid the fare to the agent, who forwarded the payment to defendant's headquarters in Florida. Defendant then prepared the tickets and sent them to plaintiffs in Washington. The ticket included a provision stating that:

> 8.   It is agreed by and between the passenger and the Carrier that all disputes and matters whatsoever arising under, in connection with or incident to this Contract shall be litigated, if at all, in and before a Court located in the State of Florida, U.S.A., to the exclusion of the Courts of any other state or country.

Plaintiffs boarded the *Tropicale* in Los Angeles, California and sailed for Puerto Vallarta, Mexico; off the coast of Mexico, Eulala Shute slipped on a deck mat and was injured. Plaintiffs filed suit in federal court in Washington, claiming that the negligence of defendant and its employees had caused the injuries. The district court held that defendant's contacts with Washington were constitutionally insufficient to exercise personal jurisdiction; the Ninth Circuit declined to enforce the forum-selection clause, but concluded that defendant did have sufficient contacts with Washington and reversed the lower court.

The Supreme Court did not consider defendant's "minimum contacts" argument; instead, it addressed the enforceability of the forum-selection clause. Rejecting the argument that *The Bremen* was limited to contracts between two business corporations, the Court stated:

> * * * Including a reasonable forum clause in a form contract of this kind well may be permissible for several reasons: First, a cruise

line has a special interest in limiting the fora in which it potentially could be subject to suit. Because a cruise ship typically carries passengers from many locales, it is not unlikely that a mishap on a cruise could subject the cruise line to litigation in several different fora. * * * Additionally, a clause establishing *ex ante* the forum for dispute resolution has the salutary effect of dispelling any confusion about where suits arising from the contract must be brought and defended, sparing litigants the time and expense of pretrial motions to determine the correct forum and conserving judicial resources that otherwise would be devoted to deciding those motions. * * * Finally, it stands to reason that passengers who purchase tickets containing a forum clause like that at issue in this case benefit in the form of reduced fares reflecting the savings that the cruise line enjoys by limiting the fora in which it may be sued. * * *

Id. at 593–94, 111 S.Ct. at 1527, 113 L.Ed.2d at 632.

NOTE AND QUESTIONS

The Bremen held that forum-selection clauses "are prima facie valid and should be enforced" by federal courts sitting in admiralty "unless enforcement is shown by the resisting party to be 'unreasonable' under the circumstances." 407 U.S. at 1, 10, 92 S.Ct. at 1907, 1913, 32 L.Ed.2d at 513, 520 (1972). Applying this test, *Carnival Cruise* emphasized that "forum-selection clauses contained in form passage contracts are subject to judicial scrutiny for fundamental fairness." 499 U.S. at 595, 111 S.Ct. at 1528, 113 L.Ed.2d at 633. What factors are relevant in determining whether a forum-selection clause is "unreasonable" or meets "fundamental fairness"? Are you convinced that *Carnival Cruise* engaged in the appropriate level of scrutiny? How does the reasonableness standard of contract doctrine differ from an inquiry under the Due Process Clause? See Davis & Hershkoff, *Contracting for Procedure*, 53 Wm. & Mary L.Rev. 507 (2011).

H. INTERNET AND OTHER TECHNOLOGICAL CONTACTS

A territorial approach to jurisdiction does not neatly fit activity conducted through the Internet. What does it mean to target a forum when a website is available to all online users? Do the operators of those websites have contacts wherever the Internet is available, i.e., everywhere? The Supreme Court has not yet resolved these questions. As Justice Thomas observed in *Walden*, p. 111 Note 8, supra, the Court has left "questions about virtual contacts for another day." Some of the justices alluded to these concerns in the *Ford* case as well. See p. 130, supra (noting that there are "reasons to wonder whether the case law we have developed since

[*International Shoe*] is well suited for the way in which business is now conducted") (Alito, J., concurring).

Without explicit guidance from the Supreme Court, lower courts have tried to adapt existing jurisdictional doctrine to Internet activity. Early cases tended to involve information posted on websites that lacked the capacity for interactive exchange with the user. INSET SYSTEMS, INC. v. INSTRUCTION SET, INC., 937 F.Supp. 161 (D.Conn. 1996), a trademark infringement action, held that advertising over the Internet counted as "solicitation of business" under the state long-arm statute, and that it was constitutional to exercise jurisdiction based on defendant's use of the Internet and its provision of a toll-free number to conduct business in the forum state. The court emphasized that defendant had "purposefully directed its advertising activity" to the forum state, and so "could reasonably anticipate the possibility" of being haled into court. Id. at 165. However, in BENSUSAN RESTAURANT CORP. v. KING, 937 F.Supp. 295 (S.D.N.Y. 1996), the district court declined to find that maintaining a website accessible in the forum state and providing a phone number satisfied the forum's long-arm statute, which authorized jurisdiction over a nondomiciliary who reasonably expects a tortious act to have consequences in the state and derives substantial revenue from in-state activity.

ZIPPO MANUFACTURING CO. v. ZIPPO DOT COM, INC., 952 F.Supp. 1119, 1124 (W.D.Pa. 1997), another trademark infringement case, explored whether the "conducting of electronic commerce"—use of a domain name and entering into contracts with 3,000 individuals and seven access providers to supply Internet news services—satisfied the state long-arm statute and showed defendant's purposeful availment. Zippo became an influential decision because it offered a taxonomy of digital contacts that could guide other courts:

> [T]he likelihood that personal jurisdiction can be constitutionally exercised is directly proportionate to the nature and quality of commercial activity that an entity conducts over the Internet. This sliding scale is consistent with well developed personal jurisdiction principles. At one end of the spectrum are situations where a defendant clearly does business over the Internet. If the defendant enters into contracts with residents of a foreign jurisdiction that involve the knowing and repeated transmission of computer files over the Internet, personal jurisdiction is proper. * * * At the opposite end are situations where a defendant has simply posted information on an Internet Web site which is accessible to users in foreign jurisdictions. A passive Web site that does little more than make information available to those who are interested in it is not grounds for the exercise [of] personal jurisdiction. * * * The middle ground is occupied by interactive

> Web sites where a user can exchange information with the host
> computer. In these cases, the exercise of jurisdiction is determined
> by examining the level of interactivity and commercial nature of
> the exchange of information that occurs on the Web site. * * *

In the wake of Zippo, interactivity became a central, although not
dispositive, factor in digital contact cases. See 4A Wright, Miller &
Steinman, Federal Practice and Procedure § 1073 (4th ed.). However, as
digital technology evolved, interactivity came to play a less prominent role
in the jurisdictional analysis. In HY CITE CORP. v.
BADBUSINESSBUREAU.COM, L.L.C., 297 F.Supp.2d 1154, 1160
(W.D.Wis. 2004), the district court treated interactivity as a relevant factor
in its purposeful-availment analysis, but declined to follow Zippo,
questioning whether a special test for jurisdiction was even needed for
disputes involving digital activity. The case was a defamation action
against the operator of an Internet website that posted negative comments
from customers. The court dismissed almost out of hand the argument that
general jurisdiction could be based on defendant's maintenance of a website
that permitted users to purchase ad space, when no in-state company had
purchased space. Likewise, although in-state solicitation could weigh as a
contact for purposeful availment, the court did not find defendant's
potential contacts with in-state users who had not yet used the site for
commercial activity sufficient to support the exercise of specific
jurisdiction. Nor could specific jurisdiction be based on the effects of
defendant's action: merely placing the name of a trademark on a website
was not sufficient evidence of targeting a forum; defendant had not created
the consumer complaints that it collected—consumers did—and there was
no showing that the "brunt" of the injury was suffered in the forum.

In JOHNSON v. THEHUFFINGTONPOST.COM, INC., 21 F.4th 314
(5th Cir. 2021), the court rejected personal jurisdiction in a libel case
against an online publisher, finding that interactivity and the ability to
access the publisher's website in the forum state (Texas) were not
sufficient. The majority reasoned:

> At bottom, the only reason to hale HuffPost into Texas is that
> Texans visited the site, clicking ads and buying things there. But
> * * * those visits reflect only HuffPost's universal accessibility, not
> its purposeful availment of Texas. Accessibility alone cannot
> sustain our jurisdiction. If it could, lack of personal jurisdiction
> would be no defense at all.

Id. at 326; see also id. at 320 ("Grannies with cooking blogs do not, and
should not, expect lawsuits from Maui to Maine."). The majority analogized
defendant's website to "a physical store in New York, where HuffPost is 'at
home,' " with users coming to defendant to visit its store—rather than
defendant reaching out to users in Texas and elsewhere. Id. at 322. It also

found that jurisdiction could not be based on either defendant's sales of merchandise to Texans or defendant's posting of ads from Texas-based advertisers, because those contacts with Texas did not "relate to" plaintiff's libel claim; they therefore could not support specific jurisdiction. Id. at 323 ("Exercising jurisdiction over HuffPost would collapse the distinction between specific and general jurisdiction."). Nor did those activities show that defendant was targeting Texas. Id. at 321 ("What matters is whether HuffPost aimed the *alleged libel* at Texas. * * * To target every user everywhere * * * is to target no place at all.").

The dissenting judge, however, argued that denying jurisdiction "ignores the Supreme Court's recent decision in *Ford Motor* [p. 124, supra]" and "all but nullifies the Supreme Court's decision in *Keeton* [p. 80, supra]." Id. at 327 (Haynes, J., dissenting). She wrote: "As in *Keeton*, HuffPost continuously and deliberately exploits the Texas market, so it should not be surprised if it is haled into court there for allegations of libel. * * * As in *Keeton*, it doesn't matter that the article did not expressly address Texas. As in *Keeton*, jurisdiction exists." Id. at 329–30 (internal quotation marks and brackets omitted). This theory of jurisdiction, according to the dissent, is "very similar to that of *Ford Motor*, albeit a different form of 'exploitation of a market.' " Id. at 328.

NOTES AND QUESTIONS

1.   Does the distinction among active, interactive, and passive websites still make sense given technological developments? Should the jurisdictional analysis for a product liability action against an online retailer be the same as for a libel action arising out of a social media post?

2.   Technology now allows a party to block individuals or entire regions from accessing a website. How should using or deciding not to use such technology affect the purposeful-availment argument? In TRIPLE UP LIMITED v. YOUKU TUDOU INC., 235 F.Supp.3d 15, 24–26 (D.D.C. 2017), affirmed 2018 WL 4440459 (D.C.Cir. 2018), plaintiff alleged that a foreign online streaming company purposefully availed itself of the benefits of the forum because it allowed access to videos although it had the ability to block videos from being viewed in certain countries and frequently did so. The court recognized that the possibility for "geoblocking" countered the common refrain that universal accessibility is an unavoidable side-effect of modern technology. However, it held that a failure to block cannot constitute purposeful availment. See Wandell, *Geolocation and Jurisdiction: From Purposeful Availment to Avoidance and Targeting on the Internet*, 16 J.Tech.L. & Pol'y 275, 297–304 (2011).

3.   In BE2 LLC v. IVANOV, 642 F.3d 555 (7th Cir. 2011), an online dating service brought a trademark infringement action in Illinois against a New Jersey businessman, alleging that defendant deliberately misled customers by using a domain name "confusingly similar" to "be2." Evidence

that 20 Illinois residents had accessed defendant's website was held insufficient to show that defendant had targeted the Illinois market or availed himself of the privilege of doing business in the state. To the contrary, the court explained, "the 20 Chicagoans who created free profiles on be2.net may have done so unilaterally by stumbling across the website and clicking a button that automatically published their dating preferences online." Id. at 559. Where would you advise plaintiff to file the lawsuit and what evidence would be best to show defendant's purposeful availment of the benefits of the forum?

4.   In MAVRIX PHOTO, INC. v. BRAND TECHNOLOGIES, INC., 647 F.3d 1218, 1230 (9th Cir. 2011), a Florida "celebrity photo" company brought a copyright infringement action in California against an Ohio company for allegedly posting plaintiff's photographs on a website that had a substantial viewer base in California. Defendant did not market its website in California's local media, but rather sold website space to third-party advertisers whose ads were directed to California. On this basis, the court found the requisite purposeful availment, emphasizing that defendant had caused harm knowing it would be suffered in California. The court found it "immaterial" for purposeful availment whether defendant or the third-party advertisers targeted the California residents. Is this approach consistent with Justice Kennedy's plurality opinion in *McIntyre*, p. 96, supra? Does it properly apply *Keeton*, p. 80, supra, in the context of a new technology? For a criticism of the Ninth Circuit approach, see *Recent Cases*, 125 Harv.L.Rev. 634 (2011).

5.   In ADVANCED TACTICAL ORDNANCE SYSTEMS, LLC v. REAL ACTION PAINTBALL, INC., 751 F.3d 796 (7th Cir. 2014), the Seventh Circuit reversed the district court's finding of specific jurisdiction based on the foreseeability that misleading emails would harm an in-state plaintiff. In its analysis, the appeals court did not cite *Zippo*, and instead asked whether the nonresident defendant "purposefully exploited" the forum market "beyond simply operating an interactive website accessible in the forum state and sending emails to people who may happen to live there." Id. at 802 (internal quotation omitted). As to the significance of the emails, the Seventh Circuit wrote:

> As a practical matter, email does not exist in any location at all; it bounces from one server to another, it starts wherever the account-holder is sitting when she clicks the "send" button, and it winds up wherever the recipient happens to be at that instant. The connection between the place where an email is opened and a lawsuit is entirely fortuitous. We note as well that it is exceedingly common in today's world for a company to allow consumers to sign up for an email list. We are not prepared to hold that this alone demonstrates that a defendant made a substantial connection to each state (or country) associated with those persons' "snail mail" addresses. * * * It may be different if there were evidence that a defendant in some way targeted residents of a specific state, perhaps through geographically-restricted online ads. But in such a case the focus would not be on the

users who signed up, but instead on the deliberate actions by the defendant to target or direct itself toward the forum state.

Id. at 803 (citations omitted).

6.   Consider how activity conducted on the Internet or through social media might affect the analysis in some of the canonical cases of personal jurisdiction doctrine:

(a)   In *International Shoe*, p. 52, supra, defendant posted ads on the social media pages of state residents to buy its shoes, rather than using in-state sales agents who displayed shoes at in-state show rooms.

(b)   In *McGee*, p. 59, supra, defendant's predecessor-in-interest did not mail the contract, but rather emailed it to the insured, who executed the contract using an electronic signature. Subsequently, premiums were paid online using a credit card.

(c)   In *World-Wide Volkswagen*, p. 71, supra, Audi cars were sold only through an Internet site, and were delivered to U.S.-based consumers through an independent distributor that was incorporated in Delaware and headquartered in New York. An Audi sold to a California resident was driven to Oklahoma, where it caused injury.

(d)   In *Carnival Cruise*, p. 139, supra, the forum-selection clause appeared on defendant's website, but was not imprinted on the physical ticket. Would it matter if the consumer was required to click "accept the terms" before printing the ticket?

(e)   In *Keeton*, p. 80, supra, instead of distributing print magazines, defendant operated an online magazine company selling subscriptions for digital versions only.

I.   JURISDICTION BASED ON POWER OVER PROPERTY

PENNINGTON v. FOURTH NATIONAL BANK, 243 U.S. 269, 271–72, 37 S.Ct. 282, 282–83, 61 L.Ed. 713, 714–15 (1917). Petitioner challenged the garnishment of his bank account to pay alimony. Although petitioner did not reside in the forum state, the Court held that attachment of his in-state bank account did not violate due process. In his opinion for the Court, Justice Brandeis explained:

The 14th Amendment did not, in guarantying due process of law, abridge the jurisdiction which a state possessed over property within its borders, regardless of the residence or presence of the owner. That jurisdiction extends alike to tangible and to intangible property. Indebtedness due from a resident to a nonresident—of which bank deposits are an example—is property within the state. * * * It is, indeed, the species of property which courts of the several states have most frequently applied in satisfaction of the obligations of absent debtors. * * * Substituted service on a nonresident by publication furnishes no legal basis for a judgment in personam. * * * But garnishment or foreign attachment is a proceeding quasi in rem. * * * The thing belonging to the absent defendant is seized and applied to the satisfaction of his obligation. The Federal Constitution presents no obstacle to the full exercise of this power.

NOTE AND QUESTION

What is the situs of corporate stock for purposes of attachment—the corporation's place of incorporation, the domicile of the shareholder, or the state in which the stock certificates actually are located? See Note, *Attachment of Corporate Stock: The Conflicting Approaches of Delaware and the Uniform Stock Transfer Act*, 73 Harv.L.Rev. 1579 (1960).

———

HARRIS v. BALK, 198 U.S. 215, 25 S.Ct. 625, 49 L.Ed. 1023 (1905). Harris, a citizen of North Carolina, owed Balk, also of North Carolina, $180. Epstein, a Maryland citizen, claimed that Balk owed him $344. On August 6, 1896, while Harris was visiting Baltimore, Epstein instituted a garnishee proceeding in a Maryland court, attaching the debt due Balk from Harris. Harris was personally served with the writ of attachment and summons, and notice of the suit was posted at the courthouse door, as required by Maryland law. Harris consented to the entry of judgment against him and paid the $180 to Epstein. On August 11, 1896, Balk commenced an action against Harris in a North Carolina court to recover the $180. Harris asserted that he no longer owed Balk the $180, having paid that sum to Epstein in partial satisfaction of Balk's debt to Epstein, since the Maryland judgment and his payment thereof was valid in Maryland, and was therefore entitled to Full Faith and Credit in the courts of North Carolina. The trial court ruled in favor of Balk, and the North Carolina Supreme Court affirmed on the ground that the Maryland court had no jurisdiction over Harris to attach the debt because Harris was only temporarily in the state, and the situs of the debt was in North Carolina. The Supreme Court reversed:

> * * * We do not see how the question of jurisdiction *vel non* can properly be made to depend upon the so-called original situs of the debt, or upon the character of the stay of the garnishee, whether temporary or permanent, in the state where the attachment is issued. Power over the person of the garnishee confers jurisdiction on the courts of the state where the writ issues. * * * If, while temporarily there, his creditor might sue him there and recover

the debt, then he is liable to process of garnishment, no matter where the situs of the debt was originally. We do not see the materiality of the expression "situs of the debt," when used in connection with attachment proceedings. If by situs is meant the place of the creation of the debt, that fact is immaterial. If it be meant that the obligation to pay the debt can only be enforced at the situs thus fixed, we think it plainly untrue. The obligation of the debtor to pay his debt clings to and accompanies him wherever he goes. He is as much bound to pay his debt in a foreign state when therein sued upon his obligation by his creditor, as he was in the state where the debt was contracted. * * * It would be no defense to such suit for the debtor to plead that he was only in the foreign state casually or temporarily. * * * It is nothing but the obligation to pay which is garnished or attached. This obligation can be enforced by the courts of the foreign state after personal service of process therein, just as well as by the courts of the domicil of the debtor. * * *

Id. at 222–23, 25 S.Ct. at 626–27, 49 L.Ed. at 1026. The Court indicated in dictum that the result might have been different had Balk not been given notice of the attachment and an opportunity to defend in the Maryland action.

NOTES AND QUESTIONS

1.   Professor Lowenfeld provides the following interesting information concerning Harris, Balk, and Epstein. Epstein was an importer of goods who regularly did business with Balk, a retailer. The $344 debt was for money owed on shipments of goods by Epstein to Balk. Harris was a dry goods merchant from the same town as Balk, and had borrowed money from Balk on several occasions, including a $10 loan just before the fateful trip to Baltimore. Harris carried with him on that trip a message from Balk to Epstein saying that Balk would be coming to Baltimore soon. Lowenfeld, *In Search of the Intangible: A Comment on* Shaffer v. Heitner, 53 N.Y.U.L.Rev. 102, 104–06 (1978).

2.   If the events leading up to Harris v. Balk were to occur today, would due process allow Epstein to file an in personam action against Balk in Maryland? Could Epstein have served Harris as Balk's agent? See Simowitz, *Siting Intangibles*, 48 N.Y.U.J.Int'l L. & Pol. 259 (2015).

SHAFFER V. HEITNER
Supreme Court of the United States, 1977.
433 U.S. 186, 97 S.Ct. 2569, 53 L.Ed.2d 683.

On Appeal from the Supreme Court of Delaware.

JUSTICE MARSHALL delivered the opinion of the Court.

* * *

I

Appellee Heitner, a nonresident of Delaware, is the owner of one share of stock in the Greyhound Corp., a business incorporated under the laws of Delaware with its principal place of business in Phoenix, Ariz. On May 22, 1974, he filed a shareholder's derivative suit in the Court of Chancery for New Castle County, Del., in which he named as defendants Greyhound, its wholly owned subsidiary Greyhound Lines, Inc.,[1] and 28 present or former officers or directors of one or both of the corporations. In essence, Heitner alleged that the individual defendants had violated their duties to Greyhound by causing it and its subsidiary to engage in actions that resulted in the corporations being held liable for substantial damages in a private antitrust suit and a large fine in a criminal contempt action. The activities which led to these penalties took place in Oregon.

Simultaneously with his complaint, Heitner filed a motion for an order of sequestration of the Delaware property of the individual defendants pursuant to Del.Code Ann., Tit. 10, § 366 (1975). This motion was accompanied by a supporting affidavit of counsel which stated that the individual defendants were nonresidents of Delaware. The affidavit identified the property to be sequestered as [shares of Greyhound Corporation stock and stock options] * * *. The requested sequestration order was signed the day the motion was filed. Pursuant to that order, the sequestrator "seized" approximately 82,000 shares of Greyhound common stock belonging to 19 of the defendants, and options belonging to another 2 defendants. These seizures were accomplished by placing "stop transfer" orders or their equivalents on the books of the Greyhound Corp. So far as the record shows, none of the certificates representing the seized property was physically present in Delaware. The stock was considered to be in Delaware, and so subject to seizure, by virtue of Del.Code Ann., Tit. 8, § 169 (1975), which makes Delaware the situs of ownership of all stock in Delaware corporations.

All 28 defendants were notified of the initiation of the suit by certified mail directed to their last known addresses and by publication in a New Castle County newspaper. The 21 defendants whose property was seized (hereafter referred to as appellants) responded by entering a special appearance for the purpose of moving to quash service of process and to vacate the sequestration order. They contended that the *ex parte* sequestration procedure did not accord them due process of law and that the property seized was not capable of attachment in Delaware. In addition, appellants asserted that under the rule of *International Shoe Co. v. Washington*, * * * [p. 52, supra], they did not have sufficient contacts with Delaware to sustain the jurisdiction of that State's courts.

---

[1] Greyhound Lines, Inc., is incorporated in California and has its principal place of business in Phoenix, Ariz.

The Court of Chancery rejected these arguments * * *.

On appeal, the Delaware Supreme Court affirmed the judgment of the Court of Chancery. * * * Most of the Supreme Court's opinion was devoted to rejecting appellants' contention that the sequestration procedure is inconsistent with the due process analysis developed in the *Sniadach* line of cases [pp. 203–207, Notes 1–5, infra]. The court based its rejection of that argument in part on its agreement with the Court of Chancery that the purpose of the sequestration procedure is to compel the appearance of the defendant, a purpose not involved in the *Sniadach* cases. The court also relied on what it considered the ancient origins of the sequestration procedure and approval of that procedure in the opinions of this Court, * * * Delaware's interest in asserting jurisdiction to adjudicate claims of mismanagement of a Delaware corporation, and the safeguards for defendants that it found in the Delaware statute. * * *

* * *

Appellants' claim that the Delaware courts did not have jurisdiction to adjudicate this action received much more cursory treatment. * * *[12] We reverse.

II

The Delaware courts rejected appellants' jurisdictional challenge by noting that this suit was brought as a *quasi in rem* proceeding. Since *quasi in rem* jurisdiction is traditionally based on attachment or seizure of property present in the jurisdiction, not on contacts between the defendant and the State, the courts considered appellants' claimed lack of contacts with Delaware to be unimportant. This categorical analysis assumes the continued soundness of the conceptual structure founded on the century-old case of *Pennoyer v. Neff*, * * * [p. 37, supra].

* * *

III

The case for applying to jurisdiction *in rem* the same test of "fair play and substantial justice" as governs assertions of jurisdiction *in personam* is simple and straightforward. It is premised on recognition that "[t]he phrase, 'judicial jurisdiction over a thing', is a customary elliptical way of referring to jurisdiction over the interests of persons in a thing." Restatement (Second) of Conflict of Laws § 56, Introductory Note * * *. This recognition leads to the conclusion that in order to justify an exercise of jurisdiction *in rem*, the basis for jurisdiction must be sufficient to justify exercising "jurisdiction over the interests of persons in a thing." The

---

[12] Under Delaware law, defendants whose property has been sequestered must enter a general appearance, thus subjecting themselves to *in personam* liability, before they can defend on the merits. * * *

standard for determining whether an exercise of jurisdiction over the interests of persons is consistent with the Due Process Clause is the minimum-contacts standard elucidated in *International Shoe.*

This argument, of course, does not ignore the fact that the presence of property in a State may bear on the existence of jurisdiction by providing contacts among the forum State, the defendant, and the litigation. For example, when claims to the property itself are the source of the underlying controversy between the plaintiff and the defendant, it would be unusual for the State where the property is located not to have jurisdiction. In such cases, the defendant's claim to property located in the State would normally indicate that he expected to benefit from the State's protection of his interest. The State's strong interests in assuring the marketability of property within its borders and in providing a procedure for peaceful resolution of disputes about the possession of that property would also support jurisdiction, as would the likelihood that important records and witnesses will be found in the State. The presence of property may also favor jurisdiction in cases, such as suits for injury suffered on the land of an absentee owner, where the defendant's ownership of the property is conceded but the cause of action is otherwise related to rights and duties growing out of that ownership.

It appears, therefore, that jurisdiction over many types of actions which now are or might be brought *in rem* would not be affected by a holding that any assertion of state-court jurisdiction must satisfy the *International Shoe* standard. For the type of *quasi in rem* action typified by *Harris v. Balk* and the present case, however, accepting the proposed analysis would result in significant change. These are cases where the property which now serves as the basis for state-court jurisdiction is completely unrelated to the plaintiff's cause of action. Thus, although the presence of the defendant's property in a State might suggest the existence of other ties among the defendant, the State, and the litigation, the presence of the property alone would not support the State's jurisdiction. If those other ties did not exist, cases over which the State is now thought to have jurisdiction could not be brought in that forum.

Since acceptance of the *International Shoe* test would most affect this class of cases, we examine the arguments against adopting that standard as they relate to this category of litigation. Before doing so, however, we note that this type of case also presents the clearest illustration of the argument in favor of assessing assertions of jurisdiction by a single standard. For in cases such as *Harris* and this one, the only role played by the property is to provide the basis for bringing the defendant into court. Indeed, the express purpose of the Delaware sequestration procedure is to compel the defendant to enter a personal appearance. In such cases, if a direct assertion of personal jurisdiction over the defendant would violate the Constitution, it would seem that an indirect assertion of that jurisdiction should be equally impermissible.

The primary rationale for treating the presence of property as a sufficient basis for jurisdiction to adjudicate claims over which the State would not have jurisdiction if *International Shoe* applied is that a wrongdoer

> "should not be able to avoid payment of his obligations by the expedient of removing his assets to a place where he is not subject to an in personam suit." Restatement [(Second) of Conflicts] § 66, Comment a.

* * * This justification, however, does not explain why jurisdiction should be recognized without regard to whether the property is present in the State because of an effort to avoid the owner's obligations. Nor does it support jurisdiction to adjudicate the underlying claim. At most, it suggests that a State in which property is located should have jurisdiction to attach that property, by use of proper procedures, as security for a judgment being sought in a forum where the litigation can be maintained consistently with *International Shoe.* * * * Moreover, we know of nothing to justify the assumption that a debtor can avoid paying his obligations by removing his property to a State in which his creditor cannot obtain personal jurisdiction over him. The Full Faith and Credit Clause, after all, makes the valid *in personam* judgment of one State enforceable in all other States.

It might also be suggested that allowing *in rem* jurisdiction avoids the uncertainty inherent in the *International Shoe* standard and assures a plaintiff of a forum.[37] * * * We believe, however, that the fairness standard of *International Shoe* can be easily applied in the vast majority of cases. Moreover, when the existence of jurisdiction in a particular forum under *International Shoe* is unclear, the cost of simplifying the litigation by avoiding the jurisdictional question may be the sacrifice of "fair play and substantial justice." That cost is too high.

We are left, then, to consider the significance of the long history of jurisdiction based solely on the presence of property in a State. Although the theory that territorial power is both essential to and sufficient for jurisdiction has been undermined, we have never held that the presence of property in a State does not automatically confer jurisdiction over the owner's interest in that property. This history must be considered as supporting the proposition that jurisdiction based solely on the presence of property satisfies the demands of due process * * *, but it is not decisive. * * * The fiction that an assertion of jurisdiction over property is anything but an assertion of jurisdiction over the owner of the property supports an

---

[37] This case does not raise, and we therefore do not consider, the question whether the presence of a defendant's property in a State is a sufficient basis for jurisdiction when no other forum is available to the plaintiff.

ancient form without substantial modern justification. Its continued acceptance would serve only to allow state-court jurisdiction that is fundamentally unfair to the defendant.

We therefore conclude that all assertions of state-court jurisdiction must be evaluated according to the standards set forth in *International Shoe* and its progeny.

IV

The Delaware courts based their assertion of jurisdiction in this case solely on the statutory presence of appellants' property in Delaware. Yet that property is not the subject matter of this litigation, nor is the underlying cause of action related to the property. Appellants' holdings in Greyhound do not, therefore, provide contacts with Delaware sufficient to support the jurisdiction of that State's courts over appellants. If it exists, that jurisdiction must have some other foundation.[40]

Appellee Heitner did not allege and does not now claim that appellants have ever set foot in Delaware. Nor does he identify any act related to his cause of action as having taken place in Delaware. Nevertheless, he contends that appellants' positions as directors and officers of a corporation chartered in Delaware provide sufficient "contacts, ties, or relations" * * * with that State to give its courts jurisdiction over appellants in this stockholder's derivative action. This argument is based primarily on what Heitner asserts to be the strong interest of Delaware in supervising the management of a Delaware corporation. That interest is said to derive from the role of Delaware law in establishing the corporation and defining the obligations owed to it by its officers and directors. In order to protect this interest, appellee concludes, Delaware's courts must have jurisdiction over corporate fiduciaries such as appellants.

This argument is undercut by the failure of the Delaware Legislature to assert the state interest appellee finds so compelling. Delaware law bases jurisdiction, not on appellants' status as corporate fiduciaries, but rather on the presence of their property in the State. Although the sequestration procedure used here may be most frequently used in derivative suits against officers and directors, * * * the authorizing statute

---

[40] Appellants argue that our determination that the minimum contacts standard of *International Shoe* governs jurisdiction here makes unnecessary any consideration of the existence of such contacts. * * * They point out that they were never personally served with a summons, that Delaware has no long-arm statute which would authorize such service, and that the Delaware Supreme Court has authoritatively held that the existence of contacts is irrelevant to jurisdiction under Del.Code Ann., Tit. 10, § 366 (1975). As part of its sequestration order, however, the Court of Chancery directed its clerk to send each appellant a copy of the summons and complaint by certified mail. The record indicates that those mailings were made and contains return receipts from at least 19 of the appellants. None of the appellants has suggested that he did not actually receive the summons which was directed to him in compliance with a Delaware statute designed to provide jurisdiction over non-residents. In these circumstances, we will assume that the procedures followed would be sufficient to bring appellants before the Delaware courts, if minimum contacts existed.

evinces no specific concern with such actions. Sequestration can be used in any suit against a nonresident * * * and reaches corporate fiduciaries only if they happen to own interests in a Delaware corporation, or other property in the State. But as Heitner's failure to secure jurisdiction over seven of the defendants named in his complaint demonstrates, there is no necessary relationship between holding a position as a corporate fiduciary and owning stock or other interests in the corporation. If Delaware perceived its interest in securing jurisdiction over corporate fiduciaries to be as great as Heitner suggests, we would expect it to have enacted a statute more clearly designed to protect that interest.

Moreover, even if Heitner's assessment of the importance of Delaware's interest is accepted, his argument fails to demonstrate that Delaware is a fair forum for this litigation. The interest appellee has identified may support the application of Delaware law to resolve any controversy over appellants' actions in their capacities as officers and directors. But we have rejected the argument that if a State's law can properly be applied to a dispute, its courts necessarily have jurisdiction over the parties to that dispute. * * *

Appellee suggests that by accepting positions as officers or directors of a Delaware corporation, appellants performed the acts [sufficient to justify the assertion of jurisdiction by Delaware courts under] *Hanson v. Denckla* [p. 60, supra]. He notes that Delaware law provides substantial benefits to corporate officers and directors, and that these benefits were at least in part the incentive for appellants to assume their positions. It is, he says, "only fair and just" to require appellants, in return for these benefits, to respond in the State of Delaware when they are accused of misusing their power. * * *

But like Heitner's first argument, this line of reasoning establishes only that it is appropriate for Delaware law to govern the obligations of appellants to Greyhound and its stockholders. It does not demonstrate that appellants have "purposefully avail[ed themselves] of the privilege of conducting activities within the forum State," *Hanson v. Denckla* * * *, in a way that would justify bringing them before a Delaware tribunal. Appellants have simply had nothing to do with the State of Delaware. Moreover, appellants had no reason to expect to be haled before a Delaware court. Delaware, unlike some States, has not enacted a statute that treats acceptance of a directorship as consent to jurisdiction in the State. And "[i]t strains reason * * * to suggest that anyone buying securities in a corporation formed in Delaware 'impliedly consents' to subject himself to Delaware's * * * jurisdiction on any cause of action." Folk & Moyer, [*Sequestration in Delaware: A Constitutional Analysis,* 73 Colum.L.Rev. 749, 785 (1973)] * * *. Appellants, who were not required to acquire interests in Greyhound in order to hold their positions, did not by acquiring those interests surrender their right to be brought to judgment only in States with which they had had "minimum contacts."

* * * Delaware's assertion of jurisdiction over appellants in this case is inconsistent with that constitutional limitation on state power. The judgment of the Delaware Supreme Court must, therefore, be reversed.

It is so ordered.

JUSTICE REHNQUIST took no part in the consideration or decision of this case.

JUSTICE POWELL, concurring.

* * *

I would explicitly reserve judgment * * * on whether the ownership of some forms of property whose situs is indisputably and permanently located within a State may, without more, provide the contacts necessary to subject a defendant to jurisdiction within the State to the extent of the value of the property. In the case of real property, in particular, preservation of the common law concept of *quasi in rem* jurisdiction arguably would avoid the uncertainty of the general *International Shoe* standard without significant cost to " 'traditional notions of fair play and substantial justice.' " * * *

Subject to the foregoing reservation, I join the opinion of the Court.

JUSTICE STEVENS, concurring in the judgment.

* * *

One who purchases shares of stock on the open market can hardly be expected to know that he has thereby become subject to suit in a forum remote from his residence and unrelated to the transaction. As a practical matter, the Delaware sequestration statute creates an unacceptable risk of judgment without notice. Unlike the 49 other States, Delaware treats the place of incorporation as the situs of the stock, even though both the owner and the custodian of the shares are elsewhere. Moreover, Delaware denies the defendant the opportunity to defend the merits of the suit unless he subjects himself to the unlimited jurisdiction of the court. Thus, it coerces a defendant either to submit to personal jurisdiction in a forum which could not otherwise obtain such jurisdiction or to lose the securities which have been attached. If its procedure were upheld, Delaware would, in effect, impose a duty of inquiry on every purchaser of securities in the national market. For unless the purchaser ascertains both the State of incorporation of the company whose shares he is buying, and also the idiosyncrasies of its law, he may be assuming an unknown risk of litigation. I therefore agree with the Court that on the record before us no adequate basis for jurisdiction exists and that the Delaware statute is unconstitutional on its face.

How the Court's opinion may be applied in other contexts is not entirely clear to me. I agree with Mr. Justice POWELL that it should not be read to invalidate *in rem* jurisdiction where real estate is involved. I would also not read it as invalidating other long-accepted methods of acquiring jurisdiction over persons with adequate notice of both the particular controversy and the fact that their local activities might subject them to suit. My uncertainty as to the reach of the opinion, and my fear that it purports to decide a great deal more than is necessary to dispose of this case, persuade me merely to concur in the judgment.

JUSTICE BRENNAN, concurring in part and dissenting in part.

I join Parts I–III of the Court's opinion. I fully agree that the minimum-contacts analysis * * * represents a far more sensible construct for the exercise of state-court jurisdiction than the patchwork of legal and factual fictions that has been generated from the decision in *Pennoyer v. Neff* * * *. It is precisely because the inquiry into minimum contacts is now of such overriding importance, however, that I must respectfully dissent from Part IV of the Court's opinion.

I

The primary teaching of Parts I–III of today's decision is that a State, in seeking to assert jurisdiction over a person located outside its borders, may only do so on the basis of minimum contacts among the parties, the contested transaction, and the forum state. The Delaware Supreme Court could not have made plainer, however, that its sequestration statute * * * does not operate on this basis, but instead is strictly an embodiment of *quasi in rem* jurisdiction, a jurisdictional predicate no longer constitutionally viable * * *. This state-court ruling obviously comports with the understanding of the parties, for the issue of the existence of minimum contacts was never pleaded by appellee, made the subject of discovery, or ruled upon by the Delaware courts. These facts notwithstanding, the Court in Part IV reaches the minimum-contacts question and finds such contacts lacking as applied to appellants. Succinctly stated, once having properly and persuasively decided that the *quasi in rem* statute that Delaware admits to having enacted is invalid, the Court then proceeds to find that a minimum-contacts law that Delaware expressly *denies* having enacted also could not be constitutionally applied in this case.

In my view, a purer example of an advisory opinion is not to be found. True, appellants do not deny having received actual notice of the action in question. * * * But notice is but one ingredient of a proper assertion of state-court jurisdiction. The other is a statute authorizing the exercise of the State's judicial power along constitutionally permissible grounds— which henceforth means minimum contacts. As of today, [Del. Code Ann.,

Tit. 8,] § 366 is not such a law.[1] Recognizing that today's decision fundamentally alters the relevant jurisdictional ground rules, I certainly would not want to rule out the possibility that Delaware's courts might decide that the legislature's overriding purpose of securing the personal appearance in state courts of defendants would best be served by reinterpreting its statute to permit state jurisdiction of the basis of constitutionally permissible contacts rather than stock ownership. Were the state courts to take this step, it would then become necessary to address the question of whether minimum contacts exist here. But in the present posture of this case, the Court's decision of this important issue is purely an abstract ruling.

My concern with the inappropriateness of the Court's action is highlighted by two other considerations. First, an inquiry into minimum contacts inevitably is highly dependent on creating a proper factual foundation detailing the contacts between the forum state and the controversy in question. Because neither the plaintiff-appellee nor the state courts viewed such an inquiry as germane in this instance, the Court today is unable to draw upon a proper factual record in reaching its conclusion; moreover, its disposition denies appellee the normal opportunity to seek discovery on the contacts issue. Second, it must be remembered that the Court's ruling is a constitutional one and necessarily will affect the reach of the jurisdictional laws of all 50 States. Ordinarily this would counsel restraint in constitutional pronouncements. * * * Certainly it should have cautioned the Court against reaching out to decide a question that, as here, has yet to emerge from the state courts ripened for review on the federal issue.

II

Nonetheless, because the Court rules on the minimum-contacts question, I feel impelled to express my view. While evidence derived through discovery might satisfy me that minimum contacts are lacking in a given case, I am convinced that as a general rule a state forum has jurisdiction to adjudicate a shareholder derivative action centering on the conduct and policies of the directors and officers of a corporation chartered by that State. Unlike the Court, I therefore would not foreclose Delaware from asserting jurisdiction over appellants were it persuaded to do so on the basis of minimum contacts.

It is well settled that a derivative lawsuit as presented here does not inure primarily to the benefit of the named plaintiff. Rather, the primary beneficiaries are the corporation and its owners, the shareholders. * * *

---

[1] Indeed, the Court's decision to proceed to the minimum-contacts issue treats Delaware's sequestration statute as if it were the equivalent of Rhode Island's long-arm law, which specifically authorizes its courts to assume jurisdiction to the limit permitted by the Constitution, R.I.Gen.Laws Ann. § 9–5–33 (1970), thereby necessitating judicial consideration of the frontiers of minimum contacts in every case arising under that statute.

Viewed in this light, the chartering State has an unusually powerful interest in insuring the availability of a convenient forum for litigating claims involving a possible multiplicity of defendant fiduciaries and for vindicating the State's substantive policies regarding the management of its domestic corporations. I believe that our cases fairly establish that the State's valid substantive interests are important considerations in assessing whether it constitutionally may claim jurisdiction over a given cause of action.

In this instance, Delaware can point to at least three interrelated public policies that are furthered by its assertion of jurisdiction. First, the State has a substantial interest in providing restitution for its local corporations that allegedly have been victimized by fiduciary misconduct, even if the managerial decisions occurred outside the State. The importance of this general state interest in assuring restitution for its own residents previously found expression in cases that went outside the then-prevailing due process framework to authorize state-court jurisdiction over nonresident motorists who injure others within the State. * * * More recently, it has led States to seek and to acquire jurisdiction over nonresident tortfeasors whose purely out-of-state activities produce domestic consequences. * * * Second, state courts have legitimately read their jurisdiction expansively when a cause of action centers in an area in which the forum State possesses a manifest regulatory interest. * * * Only this Term we reiterated that the conduct of corporate fiduciaries is just such a matter in which the policies and interests of a domestic forum are paramount. * * * Finally, a State like Delaware has a recognized interest in affording a convenient forum for supervising and overseeing the affairs of an entity that is purely the creation of that State's law. * * *

To be sure, the Court is not blind to these considerations. It notes that the State's interests "may support the application of Delaware law to resolve any controversy over appellants' actions in their capacities as officers and directors." * * * But this, the Court argues, pertains to choice of law, not jurisdiction. I recognize that the jurisdictional and choice-of-law inquiries are not identical. * * * But I would not compartmentalize thinking in this area quite so rigidly as it seems to me the Court does today, for both inquiries "are often closely related and to a substantial degree depend upon similar considerations." [Hanson v. Denckla, 357 U.S.] at 258, 78 S.Ct. at 1242 (Black, J., dissenting). * * * At the minimum, the decision that it is fair to bind a defendant by a State's laws and rules should prove to be highly relevant to the fairness of permitting that same State to accept jurisdiction for adjudicating the controversy.

Furthermore, I believe that practical considerations argue in favor of seeking to bridge the distance between the choice-of-law and jurisdictional inquiries. Even when a court would apply the law of a different forum, as a general rule it will feel less knowledgeable and comfortable in interpretation, and less interested in fostering the policies of that foreign jurisdiction, than would the courts established by the State that provides the applicable law. * * * Obviously, such choice-of-law problems cannot entirely be avoided in a diverse legal system such as our own. Nonetheless, when a suitor seeks to lodge a suit in a State with a substantial interest in seeing its own law applied to the transaction in question, we could wisely act to minimize conflicts, confusion, and uncertainty by adopting a liberal view of jurisdiction, unless considerations of fairness or efficiency strongly point in the opposite direction.

This case is not one where, in my judgment, this preference for jurisdiction is adequately answered. Certainly nothing said by the Court persuades me that it would be unfair to subject appellants to suit in Delaware. The fact that the record does not reveal whether they "set foot" or committed "acts related to [the] cause of action" in Delaware * * * is not decisive, for jurisdiction can be based strictly on out-of-state acts having foreseeable effects in the forum State. * * * I have little difficulty in applying this principle to nonresident fiduciaries whose alleged breaches of trust are said to have substantial damaging effect on the financial posture of a resident corporation. Further, I cannot understand how the existence of minimum contacts in a constitutional sense is at all affected by Delaware's failure statutorily to express an interest in controlling corporate fiduciaries. * * * To me this simply demonstrates that Delaware did not elect to assert jurisdiction to the extent the Constitution would allow. Nor would I view as controlling or even especially meaningful Delaware's failure to exact from appellants their consent to be sued. * * * Once we have rejected the jurisdictional framework created in *Pennoyer v. Neff*, I see no reason to rest jurisdiction on a fictional outgrowth of that system such as the existence of a consent statute, expressed or implied.

* * * Crucial to me is the fact that appellants voluntarily associated themselves with the State of Delaware, "invoking the benefits and protections of its laws," * * * by entering into a long-term and fragile relationship with one of its domestic corporations. They thereby elected to assume powers and to undertake responsibilities wholly derived from that State's rules and regulations, and to become eligible for those benefits that Delaware law makes available to its corporations' officials. E.g., Del.Code Ann., Tit. 8, § 143 (1975) (interest-free loans); § 145 (1975 ed. and Supp.1976) (indemnification). While it is possible that countervailing issues of judicial efficiency and the like might clearly favor a different forum, they do not appear on the meager record before us; and, of course, we are concerned solely with "minimum" contacts, not the "best" contacts. * * *

NOTES AND QUESTIONS

1.   Within 13 days after the decision in *Shaffer*, the Delaware legislature amended its laws to provide that every nonresident who is elected or appointed a director of a Delaware corporation after September 1, 1977, shall "be deemed" to have consented to the appointment of the corporation's registered agent in Delaware, or, if there is no registered agent, of the Secretary of State of Delaware, as his agent for service of process in any Delaware action based on violations of the director's duties as director after September 1, 1977. 10 Del. Code Ann. tit. 10, § 3114. The constitutionality of the section was upheld by the Supreme Court of Delaware in Armstrong v. Pomerance, 423 A.2d 174 (Del.1980), a suit against nonresidents whose sole contact with Delaware was their status as directors of a Delaware corporation. See also Stearn v. Malloy, 89 F.R.D. 421 (E.D.Wis.1981) (reaching the same conclusion under a similar Wisconsin statute). In 2004, the Delaware consent-to-service statute was extended to high officers of Delaware corporations (such as the president, treasurer, or CEO). Do you agree that statutes subjecting nonresident officers and directors to jurisdiction in the state of the company's incorporation comport with due process? Would it be constitutional to deem the purchase of a share of Delaware stock as consent to be sued in Delaware in suits pertaining to the corporation? See Hershkoff & Kahan, *Forum-Selection Provisions in Corporate "Contracts,"* 93 Wash.L.Rev. 101 (2018).

2.   How does *Shaffer* affect a court's power to enter a judgment in an action in which the cause of action relates to real property located in the forum state?

3.   In RUSH v. SAVCHUK, 444 U.S. 320, 100 S.Ct. 571, 62 L.Ed.2d 516 (1980), the Supreme Court settled the question of whether an insurance obligation can be attached to effect quasi in rem jurisdiction. In finding such an attachment unconstitutional, the Court separated the forum contacts of the defendant-tortfeasor from those of the insurer. Having done so, the Court held that sufficient contacts between defendant and the forum did not exist and that the Due Process Clause forbade the assertion of jurisdiction.

4.   Why would a plaintiff ever rely on quasi in rem jurisdiction if its validity is subject to the same constitutional standard as that of in personam jurisdiction?

J. TRANSIENT PRESENCE IN THE FORUM

BURNHAM V. SUPERIOR COURT
Supreme Court of the United States, 1990.
495 U.S. 604, 110 S.Ct. 2105, 109 L.Ed.2d 631.

Certiorari to the Court of Appeal of California, First Appellate District.

JUSTICE SCALIA announced the judgment of the Court and delivered an opinion in which THE CHIEF JUSTICE and JUSTICE KENNEDY join, and in which JUSTICE WHITE joins with respect to Parts I, II-A, II-B, and II-C.

The question presented is whether the Due Process Clause of the Fourteenth Amendment denies California courts jurisdiction over a nonresident, who was personally served with process while temporarily in that State, in a suit unrelated to his activities in the State.

I

Petitioner Dennis Burnham married Francie Burnham in 1976 in West Virginia. In 1977 the couple moved to New Jersey, where their two children were born. In July 1987 the Burnhams decided to separate. They agreed that Mrs. Burnham, who intended to move to California, would take custody of the children. Shortly before Mrs. Burnham departed for California that same month, she and petitioner agreed that she would file for divorce on grounds of "irreconcilable differences."

In October 1987, petitioner filed for divorce in New Jersey state court on grounds of "desertion." Petitioner did not, however, obtain an issuance of summons against his wife and did not attempt to serve her with process. Mrs. Burnham, after unsuccessfully demanding that petitioner adhere to their prior agreement to submit to an "irreconcilable differences" divorce, brought suit for divorce in California state court in early January 1988.

In late January, petitioner visited southern California on business, after which he went north to visit his children in the San Francisco Bay area, where his wife resided. He took the older child to San Francisco for the weekend. Upon returning the child to Mrs. Burnham's home on January 24, 1988, petitioner was served with a California court summons and a copy of Mrs. Burnham's divorce petition. He then returned to New Jersey.

Later that year, petitioner made a special appearance in the California Superior Court, moving to quash the service of process on the ground that the court lacked personal jurisdiction over him because his only contacts with California were a few short visits to the State for the purposes of conducting business and visiting his children. The Superior Court denied the motion, and the California Court of Appeal denied mandamus relief, rejecting petitioner's contention that the Due Process Clause prohibited

California courts from asserting jurisdiction over him because he lacked "minimum contacts" with the State. The court held it to be "a valid jurisdictional predicate for *in personam* jurisdiction" that the "defendant [was] present in the forum state and personally served with process." * * *

II

A

* * *

To determine whether the assertion of personal jurisdiction is consistent with due process, we have long relied on the principles traditionally followed by American courts in marking out the territorial limits of each State's authority. * * * In what has become the classic expression of the criterion, we said in *International Shoe Co. v. Washington* [p. 52, supra], * * * that a state court's assertion of personal jurisdiction satisfies the Due Process Clause if it does not violate " 'traditional notions of fair play and substantial justice.' " * * * Since *International Shoe,* we have only been called upon to decide whether these "traditional notions" permit States to exercise jurisdiction over absent defendants in a manner that deviates from the rules of jurisdiction applied in the 19th century. We have held such deviations permissible, but only with respect to suits arising out of the absent defendant's contacts with the State. * * * The question we must decide today is whether due process requires a similar connection between the litigation and the defendant's contacts with the State in cases where the defendant is physically present in the State at the time process is served upon him.

B

Among the most firmly established principles of personal jurisdiction in American tradition is that the courts of a State have jurisdiction over nonresidents who are physically present in the State. * * * Justice STORY believed the principle, which he traced to Roman origins, to be firmly grounded in English tradition * * *.

* * * [O]ne must conclude that Story's understanding was shared by American courts at the crucial time for present purposes: 1868, when the Fourteenth Amendment was adopted. * * *

Decisions in the courts of many States in the 19th and early 20th centuries held that personal service upon a physically present defendant sufficed to confer jurisdiction, without regard to whether the defendant was only briefly in the State or whether the cause of action was related to his activities there. * * * Although research has not revealed a case deciding the issue in every State's courts, that appears to be because the issue was so well settled that it went unlitigated. * * *

This American jurisdictional practice is, moreover, not merely old; it is continuing. It remains the practice of, not only a substantial number of the States, but as far as we are aware *all* the States and the Federal Government—if one disregards (as one must for this purpose) the few opinions since 1978 that have erroneously said, on grounds similar to those that petitioner presses here, that this Court's due process decisions render the practice unconstitutional. * * * We do not know of a single state or federal statute, or a single judicial decision resting upon state law, that has abandoned in-state service as a basis of jurisdiction. Many recent cases reaffirm it. * * *

C

Despite this formidable body of precedent, petitioner contends, in reliance on our decisions applying the *International Shoe* standard, that in the absence of "continuous and systematic" contacts with the forum, * * * a nonresident defendant can be subjected to judgment only as to matters that arise out of or relate to his contacts with the forum. This argument rests on a thorough misunderstanding of our cases.

The view of most courts in the 19th century was that a court simply could not exercise *in personam* jurisdiction over a nonresident who had not been personally served with process in the forum. * * *

* * * In the late 19th and early 20th centuries, changes in the technology of transportation and communication, and the tremendous growth of interstate business activity, led to an "inevitable relaxation of the strict limits on state jurisdiction" over nonresident individuals and corporations. * * * States required, for example, that nonresident corporations appoint an in-state agent upon whom process could be served as a condition of transacting business within their borders, * * * and provided in-state "substituted service" for nonresident motorists who caused injury in the State and left before personal service could be accomplished * * *. We initially upheld these laws under the Due Process Clause on grounds that they complied with *Pennoyer*'s rigid requirement of either "consent," * * * or "presence" * * * As many observed, however, the consent and presence were purely fictional. * * * Our opinion in *International Shoe* cast those fictions aside and made explicit the underlying basis of these decisions: Due process does not necessarily *require* the States to adhere to the unbending territorial limits on jurisdiction set forth in *Pennoyer*. * * * Subsequent cases have derived from the *International Shoe* standard the general rule that a State may dispense with in-forum personal service on nonresident defendants in suits arising out of their activities in the State. * * *

Nothing in *International Shoe* or the cases that have followed it, however, offers support for the very different proposition petitioner seeks to establish today: that a defendant's presence in the forum is not only unnecessary to validate novel, nontraditional assertions of jurisdiction, but is itself no longer sufficient to establish jurisdiction. That proposition is unfaithful to both elementary logic and the foundations of our due process jurisprudence. The distinction between what is needed to support novel procedures and what is needed to sustain traditional ones is fundamental * * *. The short of the matter is that jurisdiction based on physical presence alone constitutes due process because it is one of the continuing traditions of our legal system that define the due process standard of "traditional notions of fair play and substantial justice." That standard was developed by *analogy* to "physical presence," and it would be perverse to say it could now be turned against that touchstone of jurisdiction.

D

Petitioner's strongest argument, though we ultimately reject it, relies upon our decision in *Shaffer v. Heitner* * * * [p. 147, supra].

It goes too far to say, as petitioner contends, that *Shaffer* compels the conclusion that a State lacks jurisdiction over an individual unless the litigation arises out of his activities in the State. *Shaffer,* like *International Shoe,* involved jurisdiction over an *absent defendant,* and it stands for nothing more than the proposition that when the "minimum contact" that is a substitute for physical presence consists of property ownership it must, like other minimum contacts, be related to the litigation. Petitioner wrenches out of its context our statement in *Shaffer* that "all assertions of state-court jurisdiction must be evaluated according to the standards set forth in *International Shoe* and its progeny" * * *. When read together with the two sentences that preceded it, the meaning of this statement becomes clear * * *. *Shaffer* was saying * * * not that all bases for the assertion of *in personam* jurisdiction (including, presumably, in-state service) must be treated alike and subjected to the "minimum contacts" analysis of *International Shoe;* but rather that *quasi in rem* jurisdiction, that fictional "ancient form," and *in personam* jurisdiction, are really one and the same and must be treated alike—leading to the conclusion that *quasi in rem* jurisdiction, *i.e.,* that form of *in personam* jurisdiction based upon a "property ownership" contact and by definition unaccompanied by personal, in-state service, must satisfy the litigation-relatedness requirement of *International Shoe.* The logic of *Shaffer's* holding—which places all suits against absent nonresidents on the same constitutional footing, regardless of whether a separate Latin label is attached to one particular basis of contact—does not compel the conclusion that physically present defendants must be treated identically to absent ones. * * *

It is fair to say, however, that while our holding today does not contradict *Shaffer,* our basic approach to the due process question is different. We have conducted no independent inquiry into the desirability or fairness of the prevailing in-state service rule, leaving that judgment to the legislatures that are free to amend it; for our purposes, its validation is its pedigree, as the phrase *"traditional notions* of fair play and substantial justice" makes clear. *Shaffer* did conduct such an independent inquiry, asserting that " 'traditional notions of fair play and substantial justice' can be as readily offended by the perpetuation of ancient forms that are no longer justified as by the adoption of new procedures that are inconsistent with the basic values of our constitutional heritage." * * * Perhaps that assertion can be sustained when the "perpetuation of ancient forms" is engaged in by only a very small minority of the States. Where, however, as in the present case, a jurisdictional principle is both firmly approved by tradition and still favored, it is impossible to imagine what standard we could appeal to for the judgment that it is "no longer justified." * * *

III

A few words in response to Justice BRENNAN's opinion concurring in the judgment: It insists that we apply "contemporary notions of due process" to determine the constitutionality of California's assertion of jurisdiction. * * * The "contemporary notions of due process" applicable to personal jurisdiction are the enduring *"traditional* notions of fair play and substantial justice" established as the test by *International Shoe.* By its very language, that test is satisfied if a state court adheres to jurisdictional rules that are generally applied and have always been applied in the United States.

But the concurrence's proposed standard of "contemporary notions of due process" requires more: It measures state-court jurisdiction not only against traditional doctrines in this country, including current state-court practice, but also against each Justice's subjective assessment of what is fair and just. Authority for that seductive standard is not to be found in any of our personal jurisdiction cases. * * *

* * *

* * * The only reason for charging Mr. Burnham with the reasonable expectation of being subject to suit is that the States of the Union assert adjudicatory jurisdiction over the person, and have always asserted adjudicatory jurisdiction over the person, by serving him with process during his temporary physical presence in their territory. That continuing tradition, which anyone entering California should have known about, renders it "fair" for Mr. Burnham, who voluntarily entered California, to be sued there for divorce—at least "fair" in the limited sense that he has no one but himself to blame. * * *

* * * Justice BRENNAN's approach does not establish a rule of law at all, but only a "totality of the circumstances" test, guaranteeing what traditional territorial rules of jurisdiction were designed precisely to avoid: uncertainty and litigation over the preliminary issue of the forum's

competence. It may be that those evils, necessarily accompanying a freestanding "reasonableness" inquiry, must be accepted at the margins, when we evaluate *non*traditional forms of jurisdiction newly adopted by the States * * *. But that is no reason for injecting them into the core of our American practice, exposing to such a "reasonableness" inquiry the ground of jurisdiction that has hitherto been considered the very *baseline* of reasonableness, physical presence.

The difference between us and Justice BRENNAN has nothing to do with whether "further progress [is] to be made" in the "evolution of our legal system." * * * It has to do with whether changes are to be adopted as progressive by the American people or decreed as progressive by the Justices of this Court. Nothing we say today prevents individual States from limiting or entirely abandoning the in-state-service basis of jurisdiction. And nothing prevents an overwhelming majority of them from doing so, with the consequence that the "traditional notions of fairness" that this Court applies may change. But the States have overwhelmingly declined to adopt such limitation or abandonment, evidently not considering it to be progress. The question is whether, armed with no authority other than individual Justices' perceptions of fairness that conflict with both past and current practice, this Court can compel the States to make such a change on the ground that "due process" requires it. We hold that it cannot.

* * *

Affirmed.

JUSTICE WHITE, concurring in part and concurring in the judgment.

I join Parts I, II-A, II-B, and II-C of Justice SCALIA's opinion and concur in the judgment of affirmance. The rule allowing jurisdiction to be obtained over a nonresident by personal service in the forum State, without more, has been and is so widely accepted throughout this country that I could not possibly strike it down, either on its face or as applied in this case, on the ground that it denies due process of law guaranteed by the Fourteenth Amendment. * * *

JUSTICE BRENNAN, with whom JUSTICE MARSHALL, JUSTICE BLACKMUN, and JUSTICE O'CONNOR join, concurring in the judgment.

I agree with Justice SCALIA that the Due Process Clause of the Fourteenth Amendment generally permits a state court to exercise jurisdiction over a defendant if he is served with process while voluntarily present in the forum State. I do not perceive the need, however, to decide that a jurisdictional rule that " 'has been immemorially the actual law of the land,' " * * * automatically comports with due process simply by virtue of its "pedigree." * * * Unlike Justice SCALIA, I would undertake an "independent inquiry into the * * * fairness of the prevailing in-state service rule." * * * I therefore concur only in the judgment.

I

I believe that the approach adopted by Justice SCALIA's opinion today—reliance solely on historical pedigree—is foreclosed by our decisions in *International Shoe Co.* * * * and *Shaffer* * * *. * * * The critical insight of *Shaffer* is that all rules of jurisdiction, even ancient ones, must satisfy contemporary notions of due process. * * * I agree * * * and continue to believe that "the minimum-contacts analysis developed in *International Shoe* . . . represents a far more sensible construct for the exercise of state-court jurisdiction than the patchwork of legal and factual fictions that has been generated from the decision in *Pennoyer v. Neff*." * * *

While our *holding* in *Shaffer* may have been limited to *quasi in rem* jurisdiction, our mode of analysis was not. Indeed, that we were willing in *Shaffer* to examine anew the appropriateness of the *quasi in rem* rule—until that time dutifully accepted by American courts for at least a century—demonstrates that we did not believe that the "pedigree" of a jurisdictional practice was dispositive in deciding whether it was consistent with due process. * * * If we could discard an "ancient form without substantial modern justification" in *Shaffer*, * * * we can do so again. Lower courts, commentators, and the American Law Institute all have interpreted *International Shoe* and *Shaffer* to mean that *every* assertion of state-court jurisdiction, even one pursuant to a "traditional" rule such as transient jurisdiction, must comport with contemporary notions of due process. Notwithstanding the nimble gymnastics of Justice SCALIA's opinion today, it is not faithful to our decision in *Shaffer*.

II

Tradition, though alone not dispositive, is of course *relevant* to the question whether the rule of transient jurisdiction is consistent with due process. * * * Tradition is salient not in the sense that practices of the past are automatically reasonable today; indeed, under such a standard, the legitimacy of transient jurisdiction would be called into question because the rule's historical "pedigree" is a matter of intense debate. * * * For much of the 19th century, American courts did not uniformly recognize the concept of transient jurisdiction, and it appears that the transient rule did not receive wide currency until well after our decision in *Pennoyer v. Neff* * * *.

Rather, I find the historical background relevant because * * * the fact that American courts have announced the rule for perhaps a century * * * provides a defendant voluntarily present in a particular State *today* "clear notice that [he] is subject to suit" in the forum. * * * [Thus, t]he transient rule is consistent with reasonable expectations and is entitled to a strong presumption that it comports with due process. * * *

By visiting the forum State, a transient defendant actually "avail[s]" himself * * * of significant benefits provided by the State. His health and safety are guaranteed by the State's police, fire, and emergency medical services; he is free to travel on the State's roads and waterways; he likely enjoys the fruits of the State's economy as well. Moreover, the Privileges and Immunities Clause of Article IV prevents a state government from discriminating against a transient defendant by denying him the protections of its law or the right of access to its courts. * * * Without transient jurisdiction, an asymmetry would arise: A transient would have the full benefit of the power of the forum State's courts as a plaintiff while retaining immunity from their authority as a defendant. * * *

The potential burdens on a transient defendant are slight. * * * That the defendant has already journeyed at least once before to the forum—as evidenced by the fact that he was served with process there—is an indication that suit in the forum likely would not be prohibitively inconvenient. Finally, any burdens that do arise can be ameliorated by a variety of procedural devices. For these reasons, as a rule the exercise of personal jurisdiction over a defendant based on his voluntary presence in the forum will satisfy the requirements of due process. * * *

In this case, it is undisputed that petitioner was served with process while voluntarily and knowingly in the State of California. I therefore concur in the judgment.

JUSTICE STEVENS, concurring in the judgment.

As I explained in my separate writing, I did not join the Court's opinion in *Shaffer* * * * because I was concerned by its unnecessarily broad reach. * * * The same concern prevents me from joining either Justice SCALIA's or Justice BRENNAN's opinion in this case. For me, it is sufficient to note that the historical evidence and consensus identified by Justice SCALIA, the considerations of fairness identified by Justice BRENNAN, and the common sense displayed by Justice WHITE, all combine to demonstrate that this is, indeed, a very easy case.* Accordingly, I agree that the judgment should be affirmed.

NOTES AND QUESTIONS

1.   The Justices agreed on the result in *Burnham*, but could not agree on its theoretical underpinnings. Which approach do you find to be more persuasive?

2.   In which situations would all of the Justices agree that in-forum service of process is a constitutionally sufficient basis for personal jurisdiction? Are there any situations in which jurisdiction based on in-forum service of process would be constitutionally suspect? Would it be constitutional to

---

*   Perhaps the adage about hard cases making bad law should be revised to cover easy cases.

exercise general jurisdiction over a foreign defendant who is served while present in the forum for a two-hour lay-over at the airport? See Hay, *Transient Jurisdiction, Especially Over International Defendants: Critical Comments on Burnham v. Superior Court of California*, 1990 U.Ill.L.Rev. 593. Or over a foreign defendant served while in-flight over the forum state? See p. 46, Note 4, supra.

3.   Is in-state service upon a corporation by delivering process to a corporate officer who happens to be present in the state at the time of service an effective way to establish jurisdiction? How does the notion that general jurisdiction requires a corporation to be "at home" in the forum state affect your analysis? See p. 112, Section E, supra. Consider the concern expressed by Justice Gorsuch in his *Ford* concurring opinion that "even though *individual* defendants remain subject to the old 'tag' rule, allowing them to be sued on any claim anywhere they can be found * * * it seems corporations continue to receive special jurisdictional protections in the name of the Constitution. Less clear is why." See p. 133, supra.

K. JURISDICTIONAL REACH OF THE FEDERAL DISTRICT COURTS

———

Read Federal Rule of Civil Procedure 4 and the accompanying materials in the Supplement.

———

NOTE ON FEDERAL RULE 4

A federal court, like any court in the United States, can exercise personal jurisdiction over a defendant only if that power is authorized by statute and its exercise comports with due process. Some of the decisions covered earlier in this chapter—including *Keeton*, p. 80, supra, *Burger King*, p. 83, supra, *Daimler*, p. 117, Note 1, supra, and *Walden*, p. 111, Note 8, supra—involved cases filed initially in a federal district court.

Conventionally, discussions about personal jurisdiction in the federal courts focus on Federal Rule 4. Much of Rule 4 is concerned with the methods of serving process on defendants in federal court. See Chapter 3, Section B, infra. Rule 4(k), however, designates when service of process "establishes personal jurisdiction over a defendant" in a federal court action. As Rule 4(k) confirms, service of process is a precondition for obtaining personal jurisdiction.

Rule 4(k)(1) has three distinct provisions:

(a)   Rule 4(k)(1)(A) allows personal jurisdiction over a defendant "who is subject to the jurisdiction of a court of general jurisdiction in the state where the district court is located."

(b) Rule 4(k)(1)(B) allows personal jurisdiction over a party joined under Rules 14 or 19 who is served with process "within a judicial district of the United States and not more than 100 miles from where the summons was issued."

(c) Rule 4(k)(1)(C) allows personal jurisdiction when authorized by a federal statute.

By contrast to Rule 4(k)(1), Rule 4(k)(2) is a limited federal long-arm provision that establishes personal jurisdiction "for a claim that arises under federal law" if the "defendant is not subject to jurisdiction in any state's courts of general jurisdiction" and "exercising jurisdiction is consistent with the United States Constitution and laws." The requirement that the claim must "arise[ ] under federal law" means that Rule 4(k)(2) does not apply to claims that are based exclusively on state law. See Chapter 4, Section C, infra (discussing the federal question category of federal subject-matter jurisdiction).

As the Federal Circuit has explained:

Rule 4(k)(2) closed a loophole that existed prior to the 1993 amendments of the Federal Rules of Civil Procedure. Before the adoption of Rule 4(k)(2), a non-resident defendant who did not have "minimum contacts" with any individual state sufficient to support [any court's] exercise of jurisdiction, but did have sufficient contacts with the United States as a whole, could escape jurisdiction in all fifty states. Rule 4(k)(2) was adopted to ensure that federal claims will have a U.S. forum if sufficient national contacts exist. * * *

Touchcom, Inc. v. Bereskin & Parr, 574 F.3d 1403, 1414 (Fed.Cir. 2009) (footnotes omitted).

NOTES AND QUESTIONS

1. What is the constitutional test for determining whether a defendant is subject to personal jurisdiction in a federal court under Rule 4(k)(1)(A)? Does the state's long-arm statute play a role? Note that Rule 4(k)(1)(A)'s reference to "a court of general jurisdiction in the state" does not refer only to state courts with "general jurisdiction" over a defendant as that term is used in Section E, supra. Rather, it refers to state courts whose authority is not limited by subject matter.

2. Rule 4(k)(1)(B), the so-called "bulge" provision, was promulgated in order "to allow complicated controversies to be ended by a single lawsuit if all the necessary third parties could be found within 100 miles of the courthouse." Coleman v. American Export Isbrandsten Lines, Inc., 405 F.2d 250, 252 (2d Cir. 1968). When service is effected under Rule 4(k)(1)(B), is due process satisfied if defendant has minimum contacts with the state in which bulge service is effected?

3. Rule 4(k)(1)(C) applies when Congress has specifically authorized personal jurisdiction for a particular kind of case. These are sometimes

referred to as "nationwide service of process" provisions, such as those in the Commodity Exchange Act, 7 U.S.C. §§ 13a–1, 13a–2(4), 18(b); the Clayton Act § 12, 15 U.S.C. § 22; the Securities Exchange Act of 1934, § 27, 15 U.S.C. § 78aa; the False Claims Act, 28 U.S.C. § 3732(a); the Federal Debt Collection Procedures Act, 28 U.S.C. § 3004(b)(1); and Federal Trade Commission subpoenas, 15 U.S.C. § 49. Because such statutes provide independent federal authority for personal jurisdiction, their application in federal court is not subject to the limits imposed on state courts under the Fourteenth Amendment's Due Process Clause. Instead, they are governed by the Due Process Clause of the Fifth Amendment. See, e.g., Republic of Panama v. BCCI Holdings (Luxembourg) S.A., 119 F.3d 935, 942 (11th Cir. 1997) ("It is well established that when, as here, a federal statute provides the basis for jurisdiction, the constitutional limits of due process derive from the Fifth, rather than the Fourteenth, Amendment."). The Fifth Amendment test does not hinge on defendant's contacts with any particular state; rather it considers defendant's "contacts with the nation as a whole." Laurel Gardens, LLC v. McKenna, 948 F.3d 105, 122 (3d Cir. 2020).

Recall that in *McIntyre*, p. 96, supra, Justice Kennedy's plurality opinion raised the possibility of Congress authorizing jurisdiction over a foreign defendant on the basis of nationwide contacts. Is the argument in favor of nationwide service of process as strong when the federal court sits in diversity and hears a state law claim?

4. Service under Federal Rule 4(k)(2) generally is said to call for a two-step inquiry. At step one, the court determines whether defendant is subject to personal jurisdiction in any one of the 50 states; at step two, the court assesses whether defendant's contacts with the nation satisfy due process. As to the first step, an influential Seventh Circuit decision held that this requirement of Rule 4(k)(2) is satisfied if defendant acknowledges that he cannot be sued in the forum state but declines to identify a state in which jurisdiction is present. See ISI Intern. Inc. v. Borden Ladner Gervais LLP, 256 F.3d 548, 552 (7th Cir. 2001). The First Circuit instead requires the plaintiff to certify that defendant is not subject to jurisdiction in any state, and then the burden shifts to defendant to rebut the certification. See United States v. Swiss American Bank, Ltd., 191 F.3d 30 (1st Cir. 1999). As to the constitutional inquiry, jurisdiction under Rule 4(k)(2) is subject to the Fifth Amendment's constraints rather than the Fourteenth Amendment's (see Note 3, supra); thus, defendant's nationwide contacts may be aggregated to determine whether "there are sufficient minimum contacts with the nation as a whole." Abelesz v. OTP Bank, 692 F.3d 638, 660 (7th Cir. 2012).

5. How does Federal Rule 4(n) differ from the other service rules so far discussed? Under what circumstances may the federal court piggy-back on a state law authorizing jurisdiction based on the seizure of assets? In Office Depot, Inc. v. Zuccarini, 596 F.3d 696 (9th Cir. 2010), the appeals court affirmed that quasi in rem jurisdiction can be obtained under Rule 4(n) by attaching any form of property; the court held that domain names are personal property subject to attachment wherever the domain registry is located.

L. CHALLENGING A COURT'S EXERCISE OF JURISDICTION OVER THE PERSON OR PROPERTY

———

Read Federal Rules of Civil Procedure 12(b), (g), and (h) and the accompanying materials in the Supplement.

———

1. RAISING THE JURISDICTIONAL ISSUE DIRECTLY

The term "special appearance" refers to the procedure at common law by which a defendant presented a challenge to the court's exercise of personal jurisdiction without submitting to the court's jurisdiction for any other purpose. The rules varied from state to state on the technical requirements for making a special appearance. A defendant generally had to designate the appearance "special" and limit argument to raising the jurisdictional defense. If the party did anything else, such as argue the merits in any way, defendant would be deemed to have made a "general appearance," constituting a voluntary submission to the court's jurisdiction and a waiver of any defects in the court's jurisdiction. In YORK v. STATE OF TEXAS, 137 U.S. 15, 21 11 S.Ct. 9, 10 34 L.Ed. 604, 605 (1890), a divided Court held that the Fourteenth Amendment did not bar "legislation simply forbidding the defendant to come into court, and challenge the validity of service upon him in a personal action, without surrendering himself to the jurisdiction of the court."

Although substantial variation still may be encountered among different systems of state procedure, the general rules regarding objections to personal jurisdiction are illustrated by the federal scheme. The federal system does not use the term "special appearance"; but as discussed in Chapter 7, infra, a defendant who fails to argue a lack of personal jurisdiction early in the litigation may waive the defense and, effectively, consent to the court's jurisdiction.

2. COLLATERAL ATTACK ON PERSONAL JURISDICTION

If a defendant contests a court's exercise of personal jurisdiction and loses, may jurisdiction again be challenged in a later action to enforce the judgment? Consider BALDWIN v. IOWA STATE TRAVELING MEN'S ASS'N, 283 U.S. 522, 51 S.Ct. 517, 75 L.Ed. 1244 (1931), in which respondent attempted to attack a judgment rendered against it in a Missouri federal court. The company had made a special appearance in the prior suit and had moved to set aside service and dismiss the case for a lack of personal jurisdiction. In rejecting respondent's attempt to attack the first judgment collaterally, the Supreme Court stated:

> Public policy dictates that there be an end of litigation; that those who have contested an issue shall be bound by the result of the contest; and that matters once tried shall be considered forever settled as between parties. We see no reason why this doctrine should not apply in every case where one voluntarily appears, presents his case and is fully heard, and why he should not, in the absence of fraud, be thereafter concluded by the judgment of the tribunal to which he has submitted his cause.

Id. at 525–26, 51 S.Ct. at 517–18, 75 L.Ed. at 1247.

The *Baldwin* opinion repeats the established rule that a defendant who makes no appearance whatsoever remains free to challenge collaterally a default judgment for want of personal jurisdiction. The principle that a court has power to determine its own personal jurisdiction is limited to defendants who submit the question for resolution in that court. Would it be unthinkable to require a defendant to raise the jurisdictional objection in the initial forum or lose the opportunity to contest personal jurisdiction?

3. THE LIMITED-APPEARANCE PROBLEM

A "limited appearance" allows a defendant in an action commenced on a quasi in rem basis to appear for the limited purpose of defending the party's interest in the attached property without submitting to the full in personam jurisdiction of the court. See Dry Clime Lamp Corp. v. Edwards, 389 F.2d 590 (5th Cir. 1968). Without provision for a limited appearance, a defendant must choose between appearing, and thereby risking the possibility of an in personam judgment in excess of the value of the attached property, or not appearing, and thereby, as a practical matter, suffering the forfeiture of the attached property. See *Developments in the Law—State-Court Jurisdiction*, 73 Harv.L.Rev. 911, 954 (1960). Does the limited appearance have a constitutional basis after *Shaffer*, p. 147, supra? Note that the federal rules do not expressly allow for a limited appearance in cases where jurisdiction is based on the attachment of property under Rule 4(n).

CHAPTER 3

PROVIDING NOTICE AND AN OPPORTUNITY TO BE HEARD

■ ■ ■

This chapter examines two additional constitutional requirements for a judgment to be valid. The first requirement is that the parties receive adequate notice of the commencement of the action and the issues involved in it. This chapter addresses adequate notice in terms of both constitutional due process and the Federal Rules of Civil Procedure. The second requirement is that the parties have an adequate opportunity at an appropriate time to present their sides of the dispute. Both conditions are essential components of "due process of law," a concept that traces back to the Magna Carta: "No freeman shall be taken, or imprisoned, or disseized, or outlawed, or banished, or in anywise destroyed; nor will the king pass upon him, or commit him to prison, save by the lawful judgment of his peers, or the law of the land." Magna Carta (1297), 25 Edw. 1, c 29; see Russell, *Due Process of Law*, 14 Yale L.J. 322, 325–26 (1905). Due process is a bedrock constitutional principle, set out in the Fifth and Fourteenth Amendments of the United States Constitution, but courts often disagree about how to put the concept into practice.

A. THE REQUIREMENT OF REASONABLE NOTICE

MULLANE V. CENTRAL HANOVER BANK & TRUST CO.

Supreme Court of the United States, 1950.
339 U.S. 306, 70 S.Ct. 652, 94 L.Ed. 865.

Appeal from the Court of Appeals of New York.

JUSTICE JACKSON delivered the opinion of the Court.

This controversy questions the constitutional sufficiency of notice to beneficiaries on judicial settlement of accounts by the trustee of a common trust fund established under the New York Banking Law * * *. The New York Court of Appeals considered and overruled objections that the statutory notice contravenes requirements of the Fourteenth Amendment * * *. The case is here on appeal * * *.

Common trust fund legislation is addressed to a problem appropriate for state action. Mounting overheads have made administration of small trusts undesirable to corporate trustees. In order that donors and testators of moderately sized trusts may not be denied the service of corporate fiduciaries, the District of Columbia and some thirty states other than New York have permitted pooling small trust estates into one fund for investment administration. The income, capital gains, losses and expenses of the collective trust are shared by the constituent trusts in proportion to their contribution. By this plan, diversification of risk and economy of management can be extended to those whose capital standing alone would not obtain such advantage.

Statutory authorization for the establishment of such common trust funds is provided in the New York Banking Law, § 100–c * * *. Under this Act a trust company may, with approval of the State Banking Board, establish a common fund and, within prescribed limits, invest therein the assets of an unlimited number of estates, trusts or other funds of which it is trustee. Each participating trust shares ratably in the common fund, but exclusive management and control is in the trust company as trustee, and neither a fiduciary nor any beneficiary of a participating trust is deemed to have ownership in any particular asset or investment of this common fund. The trust company must keep fund assets separate from its own, and in its fiduciary capacity may not deal with itself or any affiliate. Provisions are made for accountings twelve to fifteen months after the establishment of a fund and triennially thereafter. The decree in each such judicial settlement of accounts is made binding and conclusive as to any matter set forth in the account upon everyone having any interest in the common fund or in any participating estate, trust or fund.

In January, 1946, Central Hanover Bank and Trust Company established a common trust fund in accordance with these provisions, and in March, 1947, it petitioned the Surrogate's Court for settlement of its first account as common trustee. During the accounting period a total of 113 trusts, approximately half *inter vivos* and half testamentary, participated in the common trust fund, the gross capital of which was nearly three million dollars. The record does not show the number or residence of the beneficiaries, but they were many and it is clear that some of them were not residents of the State of New York.

The only notice given beneficiaries of this specific application [for judicial settlement of the account] was by publication in a local newspaper [for four successive weeks] in strict compliance with the minimum requirements of New York Banking Law § 100–c(12) * * *. Thus the only notice required, and the only one given, was by newspaper publication setting forth merely the name and address of the trust company, the name and the date of establishment of the common trust fund, and a list of all participating estates, trusts or funds.

At the time the first investment in the common fund was made on behalf of each participating estate, however, the trust company, pursuant to the requirements of § 100–c(9), had notified by mail each person of full age and sound mind whose name and address was then known to it and who was "entitled to share in the income therefrom * * * [or] * * * who would be entitled to share in the principal if the event upon which such estate, trust or fund will become distributable should have occurred at the time of sending such notice." Included in the notice was a copy of those provisions of the Act relating to the sending of the notice itself and to the judicial settlement of common trust fund accounts.

Upon the filing of the petition for the settlement of accounts, appellant was, by order of the court pursuant to § 100–c(12), appointed special guardian and attorney for all persons known or unknown not otherwise appearing who had or might thereafter have any interest in the income of the common trust fund; and appellee Vaughan was appointed to represent those similarly interested in the principal. There were no other appearances on behalf of anyone interested in either interest or principal.

Appellant appeared specially, objecting that notice and the statutory provisions for notice to beneficiaries were inadequate to afford due process under the Fourteenth Amendment, and therefore that the court was without jurisdiction to render a final and binding decree. Appellant's objections were entertained and overruled [by] the Surrogate * * *. A final decree accepting the accounts has been entered, affirmed by the Appellate Division of the Supreme Court * * * and by the Court of Appeals of the State of New York * * *.

The effect of this decree, as held below, is to settle "all questions respecting the management of the common fund." We understand that every right which beneficiaries would otherwise have against the trust company, either as trustee of the common fund or as trustee of any individual trust, for improper management of the common trust fund during the period covered by the accounting is sealed and wholly terminated by the decree. * * *

We are met at the outset with a challenge to the power of the State—the right of its courts to adjudicate at all as against those beneficiaries who reside without the State of New York. It is contended that the proceeding is one *in personam* in that the decree affects neither title to nor possession of any *res*, but adjudges only personal rights of the beneficiaries to surcharge their trustee for negligence or breach of trust. Accordingly, it is said, * * * the Surrogate is without jurisdiction as to nonresidents upon whom personal service of process was not made.

Distinctions between actions *in rem* and those *in personam* are ancient and originally expressed in procedural terms what seems really to have been a distinction in the substantive law of property under a system quite unlike our own. * * * The legal recognition and rise in economic importance of incorporeal or intangible forms of property have upset the ancient simplicity of property law and the clarity of its distinctions, while new forms of proceedings have confused the old procedural classification. American courts have sometimes classed certain actions as *in rem* because personal service of process was not required, and at other times have held personal service of process not required because the action was *in rem*. * * *

Judicial proceedings to settle fiduciary accounts have been sometimes termed *in rem*, or more indefinitely *quasi in rem*, or more vaguely still, "in the nature of a proceeding *in rem*." It is not readily apparent how the courts of New York did or would classify the present proceeding, which has some characteristics and is wanting in some features of proceedings both *in rem* and *in personam*. But in any event we think that the requirements of the Fourteenth Amendment to the Federal Constitution do not depend upon a classification for which the standards are so elusive and confused generally and which, being primarily for state courts to define, may and do vary from state to state. Without disparaging the usefulness of distinctions between actions *in rem* and those *in personam* in many branches of law, or on other issues, or the reasoning which underlies them, we do not rest the power of the State to resort to constructive service in this proceeding upon how its courts or this Court may regard this historic antithesis. It is sufficient to observe that, whatever the technical definition of its chosen procedure, the interest of each state in providing means to close trusts that exist by the grace of its laws and are administered under the supervision of its courts is so insistent and rooted in custom as to establish beyond doubt the right of its courts to determine the interests of all claimants, resident or nonresident, provided its procedure accords full opportunity to appear and be heard.

Quite different from the question of a state's power to discharge trustees is that of the opportunity it must give beneficiaries to contest. Many controversies have raged about the cryptic and abstract words of the Due Process Clause but there can be no doubt that at a minimum they require that deprivation of life, liberty or property by adjudication be preceded by notice and opportunity for hearing appropriate to the nature of the case.

In two ways this proceeding does or may deprive beneficiaries of property. It may cut off their rights to have the trustee answer for negligent or illegal impairments of their interests. Also, their interests are presumably subject to diminution in the proceeding by allowance of fees and expenses to one who, in their names but without their knowledge, may conduct a fruitless or uncompensatory contest. Certainly the proceeding is one in which they may be deprived of property rights and hence notice and hearing must measure up to the standards of due process.

Personal service of written notice within the jurisdiction is the classic form of notice always adequate in any type of proceeding. But the vital interest of the State in bringing any issues as to its fiduciaries to a final settlement can be served only if interests or claims of individuals who are outside of the State can somehow be determined. A construction of the Due

Process Clause which would place impossible or impractical obstacles in the way could not be justified.

Against this interest of the State we must balance the individual interest sought to be protected by the Fourteenth Amendment. This is defined by our holding that "The fundamental requisite of due process of law is the opportunity to be heard." Grannis v. Ordean, 234 U.S. 385, 394, 34 S.Ct. 779, 783, 58 L.Ed. 1363 [(1914)]. This right to be heard has little reality or worth unless one is informed that the matter is pending and can choose for himself whether to appear or default, acquiesce or contest.

The Court has not committed itself to any formula achieving a balance between these interests in a particular proceeding or determining when constructive notice may be utilized or what test it must meet. Personal service has not in all circumstances been regarded as indispensable to the process due to residents, and it has more often been held unnecessary as to nonresidents. * * *

An elementary and fundamental requirement of due process in any proceeding which is to be accorded finality is notice reasonably calculated, under all the circumstances, to apprise interested parties of the pendency of the action and afford them an opportunity to present their objections. * * * The notice must be of such nature as reasonably to convey the required information * * * and it must afford a reasonable time for those interested to make their appearance * * *. But if with due regard for the practicalities and peculiarities of the case these conditions are reasonably met the constitutional requirements are satisfied. * * *

But when notice is a person's due, process which is a mere gesture is not due process. The means employed must be such as one desirous of actually informing the absentee might reasonably adopt to accomplish it. The reasonableness and hence the constitutional validity of any chosen method may be defended on the ground that it is in itself reasonably certain to inform those affected * * *, or, where conditions do not reasonably permit such notice, that the form chosen is not substantially less likely to bring home notice than other of the feasible and customary substitutes.

It would be idle to pretend that publication alone, as prescribed here, is a reliable means of acquainting interested parties of the fact that their rights are before the courts. It is not an accident that the greater number of cases reaching this Court on the question of adequacy of notice have been concerned with actions founded on process constructively served through local newspapers. Chance alone brings to the attention of even a local resident an advertisement in small type inserted in the back pages of a newspaper, and if he makes his home outside the area of the newspaper's normal circulation the odds that the information will never reach him are large indeed. The chance of actual notice is further reduced when as here the notice required does not even name those whose attention it is supposed to attract, and does not inform acquaintances who might call it to attention.

In weighing its sufficiency on the basis of equivalence with actual notice we are unable to regard this as more than a feint.

Nor is publication here reinforced by steps likely to attract the parties' attention to the proceeding. It is true that publication traditionally has been acceptable as notification supplemental to other action which in itself may reasonably be expected to convey a warning. The ways of an owner with tangible property are such that he usually arranges means to learn of any direct attack upon his possessory or proprietary rights. Hence, libel of a ship, attachment of a chattel or entry upon real estate in the name of law may reasonably be expected to come promptly to the owner's attention. When the state within which the owner has located such property seizes it for some reason, publication or posting affords an additional measure of notification. A state may indulge the assumption that one who has left tangible property in the state either has abandoned it, in which case proceedings against it deprive him of nothing * * *, or that he has left some caretaker under a duty to let him know that it is being jeopardized. * * * As phrased long ago by Chief Justice Marshall in The Mary, 9 Cranch 126, 144, 3 L.Ed. 678 [(1815)]: 'It is the part of common prudence for all those who have any interest in [a thing], to guard that interest by persons who are in a situation to protect it.'

In the case before us there is, of course, no abandonment. On the other hand these beneficiaries do have a resident fiduciary as caretaker of their interest in this property. But it is their caretaker who in the accounting becomes their adversary. Their trustee is released from giving notice of jeopardy, and no one else is expected to do so. Not even the special guardian is required or apparently expected to communicate with his ward and client, and, of course, if such a duty were merely transferred from the trustee to the guardian, economy would not be served and more likely the cost would be increased.

This Court has not hesitated to approve of resort to publication as a customary substitute in another class of cases where it is not reasonably possible or practicable to give more adequate warning. Thus it has been recognized that, in the case of persons missing or unknown, employment of an indirect and even a probably futile means of notification is all that the situation permits and creates no constitutional bar to a final decree foreclosing their rights. * * *

Those beneficiaries represented by appellant whose interests or whereabouts could not with due diligence be ascertained come clearly within this category. As to them the statutory notice is sufficient. However great the odds that publication will never reach the eyes of such unknown parties, it is not in the typical case much more likely to fail than any of the choices open to legislators endeavoring to prescribe the best notice practicable.

Nor do we consider it unreasonable for the State to dispense with more certain notice to those beneficiaries whose interests are either conjectural or future or, although they could be discovered upon investigation, do not in due course of business come to knowledge of the common trustee. Whatever searches might be required in another situation under ordinary standards of diligence, in view of the character of the proceedings and the nature of the interests here involved we think them unnecessary. We recognize the practical difficulties and costs that would be attendant on frequent investigations into the status of great numbers of beneficiaries, many of whose interests in the common fund are so remote as to be ephemeral; and we have no doubt that such impracticable and extended searches are not required in the name of due process. The expense of keeping informed from day to day of substitutions among even current income beneficiaries and presumptive remaindermen, to say nothing of the far greater number of contingent beneficiaries, would impose a severe burden on the plan, and would likely dissipate its advantages. These are practical matters in which we should be reluctant to disturb the judgment of the state authorities.

Accordingly, we overrule appellant's constitutional objections to published notice insofar as they are urged on behalf of any beneficiaries whose interests or addresses are unknown to the trustee.

As to known present beneficiaries of known place of residence, however, notice by publication stands on a different footing. Exceptions in the name of necessity do not sweep away the rule that within the limits of practicability notice must be such as is reasonably calculated to reach interested parties. Where the names and post office addresses of those affected by a proceeding are at hand, the reasons disappear for resort to means less likely than the mails to apprise them of its pendency.

The trustee has on its books the names and addresses of the income beneficiaries represented by appellant, and we find no tenable ground for dispensing with a serious effort to inform them personally of the accounting, at least by ordinary mail to the record addresses. * * * Certainly sending them a copy of the statute months and perhaps years in advance does not answer this purpose. The trustee periodically remits their income to them, and we think that they might reasonably expect that with or apart from their remittances word might come to them personally that steps were being taken affecting their interests.

We need not weigh contentions that a requirement of personal service of citation on even the large number of known resident or nonresident beneficiaries would, by reasons of delay if not of expense, seriously interfere with the proper administration of the fund. Of course personal service even without the jurisdiction of the issuing authority serves the end of actual and personal notice, whatever power of compulsion it might lack. However, no such service is required under the circumstances. This type of trust presupposes a large number of small interests. The individual interest does not stand alone but is identical with that of a class. The rights of each in the integrity of the fund and the fidelity of the trustee are shared by many other beneficiaries. Therefore notice reasonably certain to reach most of those interested in objecting is likely to safeguard the interests of all, since any objections sustained would inure to the benefit of all. We think that under such circumstances reasonable risks that notice might not actually reach every beneficiary are justifiable. * * *

The statutory notice to known beneficiaries is inadequate, not because in fact it fails to reach everyone, but because under the circumstances it is not reasonably calculated to reach those who could easily be informed by other means at hand. However it may have been in former times, the mails today are recognized as an efficient and inexpensive means of communication. Moreover, the fact that the trust company has been able to give mailed notice to known beneficiaries at the time the common trust fund was established is persuasive that postal notification at the time of accounting would not seriously burden the plan.

In some situations the law requires greater precautions in its proceedings than the business world accepts for its own purposes. In few, if any, will it be satisfied with less. Certainly it is instructive, in determining the reasonableness of the impersonal broadcast notification here used, to ask whether it would satisfy a prudent man of business, counting his pennies but finding it in his interest to convey information to many persons whose names and addresses are in his files. We are not satisfied that it would. Publication may theoretically be available for all the world to see, but it is too much in our day to suppose that each or any individual beneficiary does or could examine all that is published to see if something may be tucked away in it that affects his property interests. We have before indicated in reference to notice by publication that, 'Great caution should be used not to let fiction deny the fair play that can be secured only by a pretty close adhesion to fact.' McDonald v. Mabee, 243 U.S. 90, 91, 37 S.Ct. 343, 61 L.Ed. 608, L.R.A.1917F, 458.

We hold the notice of judicial settlement of accounts required by the New York Banking Law § 100–c(12) is incompatible with the requirements of the Fourteenth Amendment as a basis for adjudication depriving known persons whose whereabouts are also known of substantial property rights. * * *

Reversed.

JUSTICE DOUGLAS took no part in the consideration or decision of this case.

[The dissenting opinion of JUSTICE BURTON is omitted.]

NOTES AND QUESTIONS

1.   WUCHTER v. PIZZUTTI, 276 U.S. 13, 48 S.Ct. 259, 72 L.Ed. 446 (1928), concerned the constitutionality of a nonresident motorist statute similar to the one involved in *Hess*, p. 48, supra. The statute authorized in-state service on the Secretary of State and did not expressly require that notice of the action be given to the nonresident. A divided Court held that the statute violated due process, even though defendant had actual notice of the action and was served by the Secretary:

> Every statute of this kind * * * should require the plaintiff bringing the suit to show in the summons to be served the post office address or residence of the defendant being sued, and should impose either on the plaintiff himself or upon the official receiving service or some other, the duty of communication by mail or otherwise with the defendant.

Id. at 20, 48 S.Ct. at 261, 72 L.Ed. at 450. Would the result be the same under *Mullane*'s balancing test?

2.   What role did the "ancient" distinctions of in personam, quasi in rem, and in rem jurisdiction play in *Mullane*?

3.   Can the government ever resort to attachment of property followed by publication if it knows the party's name and address or the information is available from public records? The Supreme Court has considered this question in a number of contexts often involving property-related disputes.

In MENNONITE BOARD OF MISSIONS v. ADAMS, 462 U.S. 791, 103 S.Ct. 2706, 77 L.Ed.2d 180 (1983), a mortgagee challenged the state's use of publication and posting to give notice of a pending tax sale. A divided Court found that the procedure violated due process:

> Since a mortgagee clearly has a legally protected property interest, he is entitled to notice reasonably calculated to apprise him of a pending tax sale. * * * When the mortgagee is identified in a mortgage that is publicly recorded, constructive notice by publication must be supplemented by notice mailed to the mortgagee's last known available address, or by personal service. But unless the mortgagee is not reasonably identifiable, constructive notice alone does not satisfy the mandate of *Mullane*.

Id. at 798, 103 S.Ct. at 2711, 77 L.Ed.2d at 187. Justice O'Connor, joined by Justice Powell and Justice Rehnquist, dissented. In the dissent's view, the majority impermissibly had imposed a bright-line rule—at odds with *Mullane*'s balancing approach—requiring notice "by means certain to ensure actual notice as long as the party's identity and location are 'reasonably ascertainable.'" Id. at 800–01, 103 S.Ct. at 2712, 77 L.Ed.2d at 189.

Five years after *Mennonite*, a divided Court extended its holding in TULSA PROFESSIONAL COLLECTION SERVICES, INC. v. POPE, 485 U.S. 478, 108 S.Ct. 1340, 99 L.Ed.2d 565 (1988), but this time Justice O'Connor wrote for the majority. The case involved a provision in Oklahoma's probate code—known as a nonclaim statute—that barred creditors' claims against an estate if not filed within two months of publication of notice that probate proceedings had commenced. Claimant was an unsecured creditor for an unpaid hospital bill of the decedent. The Court held that if the creditor's identity "was known or 'reasonably ascertainable,' " then termination of the claim without actual notice violated due process, but that, as in *Mullane*, it would be "reasonable to dispense with actual notice to those with mere 'conjectural' claims." Id. at 490–91, 108 S.Ct. at 1347–48, 99 L.Ed.2d at 578–79.

4.   In GREENE v. LINDSEY, 456 U.S. 444, 102 S.Ct. 1874, 72 L.Ed.2d 249 (1982), a divided Court again invalidated the use of constructive notice—this time, the posting of eviction notices on the doors of apartments in public housing. The tenants claimed never to have seen the notices, and to have first learned of their eviction when served with writs of possession after default judgments had been entered against them. A divided Court held that in the circumstances of this case, the Due Process Clause required service by mail:

> As the process servers were well aware, notices posted on apartment doors in the area where these tenants lived were "not infrequently" re-moved by children or other tenants before they could have their intended effect. Under these conditions, notice by posting on the apartment door cannot be considered a "reliable means of acquainting interested parties of the fact that their rights are before the courts."

Id. at 453–54, 102 S.Ct. at 1879–80, 72 L.Ed.2d at 257–58. Justice O'Connor, joined by Chief Justice Burger and Justice Rehnquist, dissented. The dissent questioned whether mail notice was so far superior to posting as to be constitutionally required, adding that "unattended mailboxes are subject to plunder by thieves." Id. at 459–60, 102 S.Ct. at 1883, 72 L.Ed.2d at 261. Does the *Mullane* balancing test consider only the reliability of the notice provided, or does it also consider the private interest involved? Is the tenant's interest that of continued occupancy of an apartment? Might it also include a dignity interest in not having the household's financial troubles exposed to other tenants through the public posting of an eviction notice? See Weinberg, *The Right to be Taken Seriously*, 67 U. Miami L.Rev. 149 (2012).

5.   The Court again considered the constitutionality of constructive notice in DUSENBERY v. UNITED STATES, 534 U.S. 161, 122 S.Ct. 694, 151 L.Ed.2d 597 (2002), but this time held that personal notice was not required even though the recipient's name and address were known to the government. The case involved the notice given to a prisoner prior to the forfeiture of property under the Controlled Substances Act, 21 U.S.C. § 801—about $30,000 and a car registered in the name of the prisoner's step-mother. Dusenbery, the petitioner, moved for return of the seized property, alleging he had not received notice prior to the forfeiture. According to the government, the FBI had published notice in a newspaper and mailed certified letters addressed to petitioner in care of the federal prison where he was incarcerated, to his

residence at the time of arrest, and to an address where his step-mother lived. A divided Court held that the notice met *Mullane*'s reasonableness standard:

> * * * The Government here carried its burden of showing the following procedures had been used to give notice. The FBI sent certified mail addressed to petitioner at the correctional facility where he was incarcerated. At that facility, prison mailroom staff traveled to the city post office every day to obtain all the mail for the institution, including inmate mail. * * * The staff signed for all certified mail before leaving the post office. Once the mail was transported back to the facility, certified mail was entered in a logbook maintained in the mailroom. * * * A member of the inmate's Unit Team then signed for the certified mail to acknowledge its receipt before removing it from the mailroom, and either a Unit Team member or another staff member distributed the mail to the inmate during the institution's "mail call." * * *
>
> Petitioner does not seriously contest the FBI's use of the postal service to send its certified letter to him, a method our cases have recognized as adequate for known addressees when we have found notice by publication insufficient. * * * Instead, he argues that the notice was insufficient because due process generally requires "actual notice" to interested parties prior to forfeiture, which he takes to mean actual receipt of notice. * * * [*Mennonite*, upon which he relies,] is at best inconclusive dicta for the view petitioner espouses.
>
> We note that none of our cases cited by either party has required actual notice in proceedings such as this. * * *
>
> Petitioner argues that * * * the FBI could have made arrangements with the [Bureau of Prisons] to assure the delivery of the notice in question to him. * * * But it is hard to see why such a principle would not also apply, for example, to members of the Armed Forces both in this country and overseas. Undoubtedly the Government could make a special effort in any case (just as it did in the movie "Saving Private Ryan") to assure that a particular piece of mail reaches a particular individual who is in one way or another in the custody of the Government. It could, for example, have allowed petitioner to make an escorted visit to the post office himself in order to sign for his letter. But the Due Process Clause does not require such heroic efforts by the Government * * *.

Id. at 168–70, 122 S.Ct. 700–01, 151 L.Ed.2d at 605–07. A dissent, authored by Justice Ginsburg and joined by Justices Stevens, Souter, and Breyer, argued that the notice provided was "substantially less likely" to give notice than a "feasible alternative." Id. at 173–75, 122 S.Ct. at 702–03, 151 L.Ed.2d at 608–09. Is it significant that no Justice found the lack of actual notice constitutionally deficient?

6.   In JONES v. FLOWERS, 547 U.S. 220, 126 S.Ct. 1708, 164 L.Ed.2d 415 (2006), a divided Court held that when a mailed notice of a tax sale is

returned unclaimed by the owner-taxpayer, due process requires the state to take "reasonable additional steps" to attempt to notify the property owner, "if it is practicable to do so." Id. at 225, 126 S.Ct. at 1713, 164 L.Ed.2d at 425. Chief Justice Roberts explained:

> We do not think that a person who actually desired to inform a real property owner of an impending tax sale of a house he owns would do nothing when a certified letter sent to the owner is returned unclaimed. If the Commissioner prepared a stack of letters to mail to delinquent taxpayers, handed them to the postman, and then watched as the departing postman accidentally dropped the letters down a storm drain, one would certainly expect the Commissioner's office to prepare a new stack of letters and send them again. No one "desirous of actually informing" the owners would simply shrug his shoulders as the letters disappeared and say "I tried." Failure to follow up would be unreasonable, despite the fact that the letters were reasonably calculated to reach their intended recipients when delivered to the postman.

Id. at 229, 126 S.Ct. at 1716, 164 L.Ed.2d at 427–28. In the circumstances of this case, the Court identified a number of "reasonable additional steps" that the government could have taken once it knew that the notice had been returned unclaimed:

> The return of the certified letter marked "unclaimed" meant either that Jones still lived at 717 North Bryan Street, but was not home when the postman called and did not retrieve the letter at the post office, or that Jones no longer resided at that address. One reasonable step primarily addressed to the former possibility would be for the State to resend the notice by regular mail, so that a signature was not required. The Commissioner says that use of certified mail makes actual notice more likely, because requiring the recipient's signature protects against misdelivery. But that is only true, of course, when someone is home to sign for the letter, or to inform the mail carrier that he has arrived at the wrong address. * * * [T]he use of certified mail might make actual notice less likely in some cases—the letter cannot be left like regular mail to be examined at the end of the day, and it can only be retrieved from the post of-ice for a specified period of time. * * * Even occupants who ignored certified mail notice slips addressed to the owner (if any had been left) might scrawl the owner's new address on the notice packet and leave it for the postman to retrieve, or notify Jones directly.

> Other reasonable followup measures * * * would have been to post notice on the front door, or to address otherwise undeliverable mail to "occupant."

Id. at 234–35, 126 S.Ct. at 1718–19, 164 L.Ed.2d at 431. Significantly, the Court found that the government would not have been required to locate the taxpayer's new address by searching through the tax rolls or a current phone book, noting that "[a]n open-ended search for a new address—especially when the State obligates the taxpayer to keep his address updated with the tax collector * * *—imposes burdens on the State significantly greater than the several relatively easy options outlined above." Id. at 236, 126 S.Ct. at 1719, 164 L.Ed.2d at 432.

Justice Thomas dissented, joined by Justices Scalia and Kennedy. The dissent argued that notice by certified mail sent to the taxpayer's "record address" was constitutionally sufficient. Moreover, in the dissent's view, the state went further than due process required by publishing additional notice in a local newspaper. Underscoring "the well-established presumption that individuals, especially those owning property, act in their own interest" to guard that interest, the dissent criticized the majority for assessing the government's method of notice from an ex post, rather than an ex ante perspective:

> First, whether a method of notice is reasonably calculated to notify the interested party is determined ex ante, i.e., from the viewpoint of the government agency at the time its notice is sent. * * * [In] Mullane, * * * this Court rested its analysis on the information the sender had "at hand" when its notice was sent. * * * Relatedly, we have refused to evaluate the reasonableness of a particular method of notice by comparing it to alternative methods that are identified after the fact. * * *
>
> Second, implicit in our holding that due process does not require "actual notice," * * * is that when the "government becomes aware . . . that its attempt at notice has failed," * * * it is not required to take additional steps to ensure that notice has been received. * * * Under the majority's logic, each time a doubt is raised with respect to whether notice has reached an interested party, the State will have to consider additional means better calculated to achieve notice. Because this rule turns on speculative, newly acquired information, it has no natural end point, and, in effect, requires the States to achieve something close to actual notice.

Id. at 243–44, 126 S.Ct. at 1723–24, 164 L.Ed.2d at 436–37.

In your view, did *Flowers* break new ground in requiring the government to send a follow-up notice when practicable, or did it simply apply existing precedent? Under the *Mullane* balancing test, how would you assess the private interest in avoiding the permanent loss of one's home? Should it matter that the taxpayer did not actually live in the property?

7.   Another requirement of due process is that the recipient of notice must be given adequate time to respond to the threatened adverse action. In ROLLER v. HOLLY, 176 U.S. 398, 20 S.Ct. 410, 44 L.Ed. 520 (1900), defendant was required to defend an action in Texas five days after he received service of process in Virginia. The Supreme Court held that the procedure violated the Due Process Clause. Would seven days be sufficient? Twenty days? How much time is defendant given to respond to a complaint? See Federal Rule 12(a).

8. Due process concerns not only the form and timing of notice, but also the content of the information provided. In AGUCHAK v. MONTGOMERY WARD CO., 520 P.2d 1352 (Alaska 1974), a department store sold a snowmobile and freezer to the Aguchaks, which they took to a remote area where they lived. When the Aguchaks allegedly did not pay, the seller sent a summons to which the Aguchaks did not respond and a default judgment of $988.22 plus costs was entered against them. The summons did not inform the Aguchaks that they could appear by a written pleading, nor did it inform them that they had a right to request a change of venue. Travel to court would have required at least a one night stopover and cost of $186. On appeal, the Supreme Court of Alaska held that the summons in small claims cases had to tell the recipient of these options, and it set aside the default judgment.

9. A cognovit note is a written document that authorizes the entry of judgment against the party signing the note if an obligation is not paid when due. Effectively, the cognovit note waives the party's right to receive notice before litigation is commenced, bars the assertion of any defenses against the maker of the note, and forecloses any appeal from the judgment that is entered. In D.H. OVERMYER CO. v. FRICK, 405 U.S. 174, 92 S.Ct. 775, 31 L.Ed.2d 124 (1972), the Supreme Court held that the enforcement of a cognovit note does not per se violate the Due Process Clause and that its validity must be assessed on a case-by-case basis with regard to such factors as lack of consideration and inequality of bargaining power between the parties.

B. THE MECHANICS OF GIVING NOTICE

Read Federal Rule of Civil Procedure 4 and the comparable state statutes set out in the Supplement.

1. INTRODUCTION

Notice of a suit is given by the service of process upon the defendant. Service refers to the delivery of the notice; process refers to the document that is delivered. Each jurisdiction has a set of rules governing the correct methods of making service. Federal Rule 4 implements a uniform form of summons to be used by all federal courts. A summons will not issue until a complaint has been filed with the court, and under Federal Rule 3, the filing of the complaint "commences" the action. Be sure you are clear on the procedure that governs service of the summons. Under Rule 4(a), what information must a summons contain? Under Rule 4(b), how does plaintiff obtain a summons for service on defendant? Under Rule 4(c), when must a summons be served? Who is permitted to serve a summons?

2. SPECIFIC APPLICATIONS OF THE SERVICE PROVISIONS

Federal Rule 4, in several subdivisions, sets forth specific means of making personal service on different entities such as individuals, corporations, partnerships, and other associations subject to suit under a common name. Traditionally, service of process was made by personal delivery of the summons and complaint to the defendant. Other methods of service, however, have assumed greater importance since the advent of long-arm statutes. See p. 58, supra.

a. Federal Rule 4(d): "Waiving Service"

In 1982, the Supreme Court proposed, but Congress rejected, an amendment to the Rules that would have permitted service by registered or certified mail, with delivery restricted to the addressee and a return receipt required.

In 1983, Congress chose a system of service by mail that allowed the summons and complaint to be sent by ordinary first-class mail, together with a form for acknowledging receipt and accepting service. If the acknowledgment form was not returned, plaintiff had to effect service through some other means authorized by the Federal Rules. In order to encourage defendants to execute and return the form, the Rule directed the court to order a defendant who did not cooperate to pay the costs incurred by plaintiff in making personal service, unless defendant could show good cause for failing to return the acknowledgment form.

This system was not always successful because it relied on defendant's cooperation in returning the acknowledgment form. After a decade of use, Rule 4 was revised again in 1993. The most significant change was that the "service by mail" provision was replaced by Rule 4(d), which strongly encourages waiver of formal service. Under this modification, an action commences when plaintiff sends a form, entitled "Notice of a Lawsuit and Request to Waive Service of a Summons," or a similar document, by mail or some other "reliable" means. Domestic defendants have at least 30 days from the date on which the waiver was sent to return the waiver; otherwise—unless defendant had good cause for refusing to waive service— it will be charged with the costs associated with providing formal service. How did the amendment change the incentives for waiving service?

NOTES AND QUESTIONS

1. What steps must be taken for waiver of service to be effective?

2. What forms of transmittal are permitted in addition to first-class mail? The Advisory Committee Notes to the 1993 amendment specifically approved the use of "electronic means." Should transmittal by social media

satisfy Rule 4(d)? See p. 194, Note 4, infra, discussing use of social media to serve process abroad under Rule 4(f)(3).

3. What is the time period if the waiver is sent to a defendant outside the United States? See Rule 4(d)(1)(F).

4. If a plaintiff is confronting a filing deadline in a state in which the statute of limitations continues to run until a defendant is served, would formal service be the wisest course of action? Why? Would you advise a client in this circumstance to waive service?

b. Federal Rule 4(e): Personal Delivery on Natural Persons

Federal Rule 4(e) sets out the federal rule for service of process upon individuals. Rule 4(e)(2) provides methods of serving process that are authorized for any federal court action. One such method is the most direct form of service—"delivering a copy of the summons and of the complaint to the individual personally." Rule 4(e)(2)(A). Other methods authorized by Rule 4(e)(2) are discussed in the next two subsections.

Rule 4(e)(1) provides an alternative to these methods by broadly authorizing service in conformity with the law of the state in which the district court is sitting or the state where service is effected. Keep in mind that, although many state service statutes are modeled on the Rules, state statutes may differ in important ways, including the issuance of the summons, who may effect service, and the information that must appear in the summons. Comparative state provisions are set out in the Supplement.

c. Federal Rule 4(e)(2)(B): Service on a Person Residing in Defendant's Dwelling or Usual Place of Abode

As an alternative to personal delivery, Federal Rule 4(e)(2)(B) permits service of process to be made upon an individual by leaving a copy of the summons and complaint at the party's "dwelling or usual place of abode with someone of suitable age and discretion who resides there." The facts of a particular case often prove to be crucial.

NOTE AND QUESTIONS

What is the "usual place of abode" for a litigant with multiple dwellings? NATIONAL DEVELOPMENT CO. v. TRIAD HOLDING CORP., 930 F.2d 253 (2d Cir. 1990), cert. denied, 502 U.S. 968, 112 S.Ct. 440, 116 L.Ed.2d 459 (1991), concerned efforts to vacate a default judgment entered against a Saudi Arabian citizen who maintained 12 homes around the world and was described as "a frequent intercontinental traveler." Id. at 257. Service was effected by delivering papers to defendant's New York apartment, which was valued at $20–$25 million and contained 23,000 square feet, and leaving them with defendant's housekeeper. The Second Circuit upheld service, holding that "a person can have two or more 'dwelling houses or usual places of abode'" and that because defendant was "actually living" in the apartment on the day of service, "service there on that day was, if not the most likely method of ensuring that he received the summons and complaint, reasonably calculated to provide actual notice of the action." Id. at 257–58. Should it matter if defendant had been at one of his other dwellings on the day of service?

d. Federal Rule 4(e)(2)(C): Delivery to an Agent Authorized by Appointment

A third method of effecting personal service on an individual under the Federal Rules is by delivering a copy of the summons and complaint to an agent of defendant who is "authorized by appointment or by law" to receive process. Rule 4(e)(2)(C). The cases dealing with agency by appointment indicate that an actual appointment for the specific purpose of receiving process normally is expected. Consistent with this judicial construction of "appointment," the courts have held that a person's actual acceptance of process or purported authority to do so is not enough to bind defendant; there must be evidence that defendant intended to confer such authority upon the agent.

NOTES AND QUESTIONS

1.   In NATIONAL EQUIPMENT RENTAL, LTD. v. SZUKHENT, 375 U.S. 311, 84 S.Ct. 411, 11 L.Ed.2d 354 (1964), a divided Court held that the validity of a contractual provision appointing an agent to receive service of process is a matter of "well-settled general principles of the law of agency," subject to a "uniform federal standard" set forth in the Federal Rules, and that the appointment in that case was valid even though the contract did not explicitly require the agent to provide notice of the service of process or to mail a copy of the summons and complaint to defendant. The Court explained:

> We need not and do not in this case reach the situation where no personal notice has been given to the defendant. Since the respondents did in fact receive complete and timely notice of the lawsuit pending against them, no due process claim has been made. The case before us is therefore quite different from cases where there was no actual notice * * *.

Id. at 315, 84 S.Ct. at 414, 11 L.Ed.2d at 357. Justice Black dissented, arguing, first, that New York agency law ought to determine whether the appointment was valid, and second, that upholding service denied defendants due process of law. Justice Black further warned:

> The end result of today's holding is not difficult to foresee. Clauses like the one used against the Szukhents—clauses which companies have not inserted, I suspect, because they never dreamed a court would uphold them—will soon find their way into the "boilerplate" of everything from an equipment lease to a conditional sales contract. Today's holding gives a green light to every large company in this country to contrive contracts which declare with force of law that

when such a company wants to sue someone with whom it does business, that individual must go and try to defend himself in some place, no matter how distant, where big business enterprises are concentrated, like, for example, New York, Connecticut, or Illinois, or else suffer a default judgment. * * * The very threat of such a suit can be used to force payment of alleged claims, even though they be wholly without merit. This fact will not be news to companies exerting their economic power to wangle such contracts. * * *

Id. at 328–29, 84 S.Ct. at 421, 11 L.Ed.2d at 365. In a separate dissent, Justice Brennan, joined by Chief Justice Warren and Justice Goldberg, argued that federal standards and not state law ought to define who is an agent for purposes of service under Federal Rule 4 and questioned whether assent to the contract signified assent to the appointment.

Why did the majority look to the law of agency, and not to the Due Process Clause, in accessing the propriety of the waiver?

2.   Since *Szukhent*, e-commerce has generated new forms of agreement with such interesting names as "shrinkwrap," "clickwrap," and "browsewrap." Would a waiver of jurisdiction, notice, or service of process embedded in such an agreement and assented to through the click of a mouse or the tap of a phone be enforceable under the Court's analysis in *Szukhent*? Would it matter if the consumer could accept the clause only after scrolling down through the entire document? Should it matter that the waiver terms are boilerplate and not subject to arms-length negotiation? Should there be a clear prompt directing the user to read the waiver provisions before signing?

e.   Federal Rule 4(h): Serving a Corporation, Partnership, or Association

Rule 4(h) authorizes service upon corporations, partnerships, and unincorporated associations that are subject to suit under a common name. As with Rule 4(e)(1)'s provisions for serving process on an individual, Rule 4(h) allows service in accordance with the law of either the state where the district court is located or the state where service is made. See Rule 4(h)(1)(A). The most frequently invoked portion of the rule is subpart (h)(1)(B), permitting service by delivery of process to an officer, a managing agent, or a general agent. How do the requirements of this subpart differ from those of serving an individual?

––––––––––

In INSURANCE CO. OF NORTH AMERICA v. S/S "HELLENIC CHALLENGER", 88 F.R.D. 545 (S.D.N.Y. 1980), a United States Marshal deposited the summons and complaint with a claims adjuster at the office of defendant. The complaint stated an admiralty and maritime claim for nondelivery, shortage, loss, and damage relating to pickled sheepskins shipped to New York aboard defendant's vessel.

The adjuster who had accepted service of the summons and complaint was not expressly authorized by defendant to accept process; the only employees endowed with express authority to do so on behalf of defendant were all titled officers and the claims manager. At the time of service of the summons and complaint, the claims manager was absent due to illness and the adjuster, an assistant to the claims manager, accepted service.

Since the adjuster misplaced the summons and complaint, defendant remained unaware of the pendency of the lawsuit until its bank informed it that its account had been attached by plaintiff. Only then did defendant learn that plaintiff's counsel had filed a default judgment and that a writ of execution had been issued. The court denied defendant's motion to set aside the judgment on the basis of improper service of process:

> Rule * * * 4(d)(3)[a] has been liberally construed by the courts and, as interpreted, does not require rigid formalism. To be valid, service of process is not limited solely to officially designated officers, managing agents or agents appointed by law for the receipt of process. Rather, "[r]ules governing service of process [are] to be construed in a manner reasonably calculated to effectuate their primary purpose: to give the defendant adequate notice that an action is pending. * * * [T]he rule does not require that service be made solely on a restricted class of formally titled officials, but rather permits it to be made 'upon a representative so integrated with the organization that he will know what to do with the papers. Generally, service is sufficient when made upon an individual who stands in such a position as to render it fair, reasonable and just to imply the authority on his part to receive services.' " * * *

> Plaintiff's method of service of the summons and complaint was indeed "reasonably calculated" to alert defendants to the initiation of the suit. * * * [T]he adjuster served with the summons and complaint * * * can be categorized as a representative of defendant "well-integrated" into the organization and quite familiar with the formalities associated with the receipt of service of summonses and complaints. He had accepted service of summonses and complaints on behalf of defendant on at least two previous occasions * * * in connection with his ordinary duties of receiving and investigating new claims against defendant. Furthermore, it may be inferred from the facts presented on this motion that [the adjuster] had easy access to * * * the claims manager officially authorized to accept service of process, since the two men are separated from each other only by [the claims manager's] glass-walled office. * * * [The adjuster's] familiarity with service of process negates any and all suspicion that the U.S.

---

[a]   Rule 4(d)(3) now comprises part of Rule 4(h).

Marshal delivered the summons and complaint to a representative of defendant who had infrequent contact with summonses and complaints and whose unfamiliarity with service of process increased the risk of careless or improper handling. * * *

In the case at hand, the * * * adjuster's loss of the summons and complaint is a mistake in the ordinary course of the internal operations of defendant's business and thus does not merit remedial relief * * *.

Id. at 547–48.

NOTES AND QUESTIONS

1.   Given the language of the rule—now set out in Federal Rule 4(h)(1)(B)—was it appropriate for the court to disregard labels such as "general" and "managing" agent? Should the court have held that the claims adjuster could be regarded as defendant's "managing agent"? In determining whether the person served is "so integrated with the organization that he will know what to do with the papers," courts consider whether the person served is employed by defendant and whether actual notice was received, but the fact of actual notice will not inevitably cure a defect in service under this rule. See American Institute of Certified Public Accountants v. Affinity Card, Inc., 8 F.Supp.2d 372 (S.D.N.Y. 1998) (service on vice president of one corporation sharing office with defendant corporation was insufficient to create personal jurisdiction despite the fact that both corporations were owned by the same individual who had received actual notice).

2.   Could the court reasonably have reached the same result by finding that the claims adjuster was an agent authorized by appointment to receive process? In FASHION PAGE, LTD. v. ZURICH INS. CO., 50 N.Y.2d 265, 428 N.Y.S.2d 890, 406 N.E.2d 747 (1980), the process-server went to defendant's office where he was greeted by a receptionist. The receptionist told him to proceed down a certain corridor and to "see the girl sitting down there." Following instructions, the process-server went to the executive secretary of the vice president in charge of the New York office. She asked to see the papers and after perusing them said: "Okay, leave it with me. * * * I'll take it." When the process-server questioned her authority, she responded: "I can take it."

There was doubt that the executive secretary possessed sufficient discretionary authority to be a "managing agent" for purposes of service. The New York Court of Appeals, however, refused to be drawn into that issue, finding instead that the executive secretary was an "agent authorized by appointment * * * to receive service." The executive secretary testified that for at least five years she regularly accepted service whenever the vice president was not in the office, and during that period had accepted about half of the summonses brought to his office. The court explained:

Thus a corporation may assign the task of accepting process and may establish procedures for insuring that the papers are directed to those ultimately responsible for defending its interests. * * * The corporation however cannot escape the consequences of establishing alternative procedures which it may prefer. * * * Reliance may be based on the corporate employees to identify the proper person to accept service. * * *

Id. at 270–73, 428 N.Y.S.2d at 892–94, 406 N.E.2d at 749–51.

f.   Federal Rule 4(f): Serving an Individual in a Foreign Country

Rule 4(f) authorizes alternative methods by which an individual (other than a minor, an incompetent, or a person whose waiver has been filed) may be served outside the United States. International service of process also must comply with constitutional standards of due process. Rule 4(f) was amended in 1993 to afford United States attorneys a flexible framework that accommodates the widely divergent procedures for service of process employed by the various nations of the world. This accommodation is necessary both to avoid violating the sovereignty of other countries by committing acts within their borders that they may consider to be "official" and to maximize the likelihood that the judgment rendered in the action in this country will be recognized and enforced abroad. Most of the methods authorized by Rule 4(f)—discussed below—also apply to serving a corporation or other entity in a foreign country. See Rule 4(h)(2).

NOTES AND QUESTIONS

1.   Rule 4(f)(1) provides that "any internationally agreed means of service that is reasonably calculated to give notice, such as those authorized by the Hague Convention on the Service Abroad of Judicial and Extrajudicial Documents" may be used to effect service on those outside the United States. The Hague Service Convention contains the most important internationally agreed means of service of process; as of June 2021, 79 states were contracting parties. See *Convention on the Service Abroad of Judicial and Extrajudicial Documents in Civil or Commercial Matters*, The Hague, 1965, 20 U.S.T. 361, T.I.A.S. No. 6638, 658 U.N.T.S. 163, reproduced (with declarations by the contracting states) in 28 U.S.C.A. following Federal Rule 4. The heart of the Convention is a requirement that each Contracting State establish a Central Authority, which will receive and execute requests for service from judicial authorities in other Contracting States, and will see that a certification that service has been effected is returned to the court of origin. Service may be made either in accordance with the law of the nation in which service is to be made or (unless incompatible with that law) by a particular method requested by the applicant. For a discussion of modes of service in selected countries, see Chase, Hershkoff, Silberman, Sorabji, Stürner, Taniguchi & Varano, Civil Litigation in Comparative Context 234–51 (Chase & Hershkoff, eds., 2d ed. 2017).

2.   A question that had divided lower courts was whether the Hague Service Convention bars service by mail. In WATER SPLASH, INC. v. MENON, 581 U.S. ___, 137 S.Ct. 1504, 197 L.Ed.2d 826 (2017), the Supreme Court clarified that mail service is permissible if two conditions are met: "first, the receiving state has not objected to service by mail; and second, service by mail is authorized under otherwise-applicable law." Id. at ___, 137 S.Ct. at 1513, 197 L.Ed.2d at 836.

3.   There are several circumstances when the Hague Service Convention does not govern service on foreign-based defendants.

First, and most significantly, the Convention does not govern in those countries that are not Contracting States.

Second, the Supreme Court held in VOLKSWAGENWERK AK-TIENGESELLSCHAFT v. SCHLUNK, 486 U.S. 694, 108 S.Ct. 2104, 100 L.Ed.2d 722 (1988), that the Convention applies only if service actually is made abroad; service under the Convention is not required if service is effected in the United States. In this case, suit was brought against a German corporation, and service was made on a domestic subsidiary that was deemed to be the corporation's involuntary agent for service of process.

Third, because the Convention is only invoked by "service" abroad, an agreement to waive service, if voluntary and private, may be regarded as not implicating the Convention, although some other nations might well take a contrary position. Foreign defendants, like domestic defendants, are given incentives by Rule 4(d) to waive service in the form of longer times to respond, but they are not to be charged with the costs for formal service should they refuse to return the waiver; otherwise the waiver could be deemed compulsory and thus might violate the Convention.

4.   Rule 4(f)(3) authorizes forms of service "by other means not prohibited by international agreement, as the court orders." Even before the 1993 amendment to the Federal Rule, a federal trial court had ordered service of process on defendants in Iran by telex, then an innovative form of information-exchange. See New England Merchants National Bank v. Iran Power Generation and Transmission Co., 495 F.Supp. 73 (S.D.N.Y. 1980). Since then, new forms of technology have broadened the kinds of service a court might order. In RIO PROPERTIES, INC. v. RIO INTERNATIONAL INTERLINK, 284 F.3d 1007 (9th Cir. 2002), the court authorized email service on a foreign Internet business, after plaintiff was unsuccessful in effecting service in the United States, in Costa Rica, and on the international courier designated as an address when defendant registered its website. The Court of Appeals emphasized that service of process under Rule 4(f)(3) is neither extraordinary nor a last resort, but rather "one means among several which enables services of process on an international defendant," and its use is committed to the discretion of the district judge. Id. at 1015.

Given advances in technology, should service abroad be permitted through email or social media? Federal courts have continued to approve of such service under Rule 4(f)(3) in certain circumstances. See, e.g., Nagravision SA v. Gotech

Int'l Tech. Ltd., 882 F.3d 494, 498 (5th Cir. 2018) (approving of "court-ordered email service under Rule 4(f)(3)"); Elsevier, Inc. v. Siew Yee Chew, 287 F.Supp.3d 374, 379–80 (S.D.N.Y. 2018) ("Service through email is particularly appropriate here because, as the record reflects * * *, the defendants engage in online business and regularly communicate with customers through functional email addresses."); Nowak v. XAPO, Inc., 2020 WL 5877576, *4 (N.D.Cal. 2020) (authorizing service on an Indonesian defendant by email and via social media to its Facebook and Twitter accounts); Fisher v. Petr Konchalovsky Foundation, 2016 WL 1047394, *6 (S.D.N.Y. 2016) (authorizing service by email for a defendant residing in Russia, finding that no international agreement barred this mode of service, Russia had not objected to this specific mode of service, and plaintiff had provided "sufficient evidence" that sending email to a designated address was "likely to reach the defendant"). In other cases, however, courts have declined to authorize service by email or social media, finding that the requestor had failed to show that electronic service either was needed or would be sufficiently reliable. E.g., Keck v. Alibaba.com, Inc., 330 F.R.D. 255, 259–60 (N.D.Cal. 2018) (finding that plaintiff "has not sufficiently shown why she should be allowed to serve the Additional Defendants by the messaging system on Alibaba.com and AliExpress.com"); McGillvary v. Holom, 2019 WL 2124509, at *2 (D.N.J. 2019) (rejecting request to serve defendant via her Facebook account); SEC v. China Intelligent Lighting & Electronics, Inc., 2014 WL 338817, *2 (S.D.N.Y. 2014) (rejecting service via email because plaintiff had not shown that the email addresses were likely to reach defendants, noting that a spreadsheet purporting to associate one defendant with a particular email address "does not include a date or any other information from which the Court could infer that [defendant] continues to use the relevant e-mail address today"). In I.M. Wilson, Inc. v. Otvetstvennostyou "Grichko,", 2018 WL 6446601, *3 n.1 (E.D.Pa. 2018), the court authorized alternative service under Rule 4(f)(3) on two Russian defendants and a Czech defendant by serving hard copies of the summons and complaint on their United States counsel but rejected proposed service on their United States counsel by email: "Lest such a ubiquitous means of communication fall prey to a 'spam' filter, or worse, service shall be with hard copy material."

5.   A special provision of the Foreign Sovereign Immunities Act (FSIA) provides methods for serving process on foreign states, political subdivisions of foreign states, and agencies or instrumentalities of foreign states. In REPUBLIC OF SUDAN v. HARRISON, 587 U.S. ___, 139 S.Ct. 1048, 203 L.Ed.2d 433 (2019), the Supreme Court interpreted the provision allowing service "by any form of mail requiring a signed receipt, to be addressed and dispatched by the clerk of the court to the head of the ministry of foreign affairs of the foreign state concerned." 28 U.S.C. § 1608(a)(3). Victims of the bombing of the USS Cole, and their relatives, brought suit against the Republic of Sudan in federal district court under the FSIA. The clerk of the court, at plaintiffs' request, addressed the service packet to Sudan's minister of foreign affairs at the Sudan Embassy in the United States, and later certified that a signed receipt had been returned. Sudan failed to appear and the court entered a

default judgment plus orders to effect payment of the judgment. In an eight-to-one decision, the Court found that this method of service did not comply with Section 1608(a)(3), concluding that the service packet "must be addressed and dispatched to the foreign minister at the minister's office in the foreign state"— not to some office in the United States where the minister might rarely be found. Id. at ___, 139 S.Ct. at 1062, 203 L.Ed.2d at 447. Justice Thomas dissented on the ground that delivery of service to a country's embassy was within the terms of the statute and a reasonable means of notifying the country's foreign minister.

6.   In many cases, a court will reject a challenge to service of process when there is a showing that defendant had actual notice of the action. See Armco, Inc. v. Penrod-Stauffer Bldg. Sys., Inc., 733 F.2d 1087, 1089 (4th Cir. 1984) ("every technical violation of the rule or failure of strict compliance may not invalidate the service of process"). Is a different case presented if plaintiff uses "other means" of service under Rule 4(f)(3) without seeking prior court authorization? In this circumstance, should service be quashed even if defendant has actual notice of the action? See De Gazelle Group, Inc. v. Tamaz Trading Establishment, 817 F.3d 747 (11th Cir. 2016).

3.   RETURN OF SERVICE

The process-server, after delivering the papers, must file a "return," which should disclose enough facts to demonstrate that defendant has been served and given notice of the requirement to appear in court. The prerequisite for the court assuming jurisdiction is the actual service of process and not the proof of that act; however, courts have held a proper return ordinarily is necessary to enable the trial court to conclude it has jurisdiction. The specific form of the proof of service varies from state-to-state, as well as according to the method of service used. An affidavit from the person who performed the acts constituting service is the usual proof.

Should the process-server's return of service be considered conclusive or merely presumptive evidence that service has been effected? In MIEDREICH v. LAUENSTEIN, 232 U.S. 236, 34 S.Ct. 309, 58 L.Ed. 584 (1914), plaintiff sought to vacate a mortgage foreclosure judgment rendered in a prior suit arguing that the sheriff had made a false return of summons. Plaintiff, a state resident but not a resident of the county in which the action had been brought, was not served with process, and lacked knowledge of the prior proceeding. Nevertheless, the Supreme Court upheld the prior judgment, treating the return as conclusive:

> [A]lthough contrary to the fact, in the absence of any attack upon it, the court was justified in acting upon such return as upon a true return. If the return is false the law of the state * * * permitted a recovery against the sheriff upon his bond. We are of the opinion that this system of jurisprudence, with its provisions for safeguarding the rights of litigants, is due process of law.

Id. at 246, 34 S.Ct. at 312, 58 L.Ed. at 591. Would the result have been the same if plaintiff had not been a state resident?

In most American jurisdictions today, the return is treated as strong evidence of the fact of service, but is not given conclusive effect. Keep in mind that prior to 1983, only United States marshals or deputy marshals could serve process in federal civil actions. At least some courts held that it would be "demeaning to the dignity of the court" to hold a hearing into the truth of an official's document. Halpert v. Appeby, 23 F.R.D. 5, 6 (S.D.N.Y. 1958). Defendant's own testimony alone generally will not be sufficient to impeach the return of a private process server, but it is not clear whether a "strong and convincing evidence" or some lesser standard applies.

NOTE ON "SEWER" SERVICE

In UNITED STATES v. BRAND JEWELERS, INC., 318 F.Supp. 1293 (S.D.N.Y. 1970), noted in 37 Brooklyn L.Rev. 426 (1970–1971), 84 Harv.L.Rev. 1930 (1970–1971), 46 N.Y.U.L.Rev. 367 (1971), 20 J.Pub.L. 337 (1971), 24 Vand.L.Rev. 829 (1970–1971), 17 Wayne L.Rev. 1287 (1971), 1971 Wis.L.Rev. 665, it was held that the United States had standing to seek an injunction preventing defendant from systematically obtaining default judgments against economically disadvantaged people through use of so-called "sewer" service techniques, by which the process-server disposes the papers and makes a false affidavit of service. The actions were for the purchase price of consumer goods sold on "easy credit terms" by door-to-door salespersons. The court reasoned that continuously failing to make proper service of process or preparing false affidavits of service imposed "a burden on interstate commerce." Moreover, defendants' alleged conduct was held to be "state action"; the United States had standing to sue to end a widespread unconstitutional deprivation of property without due process of law.

In 1972, the case was settled, and a consent decree was issued. It vacated the default judgments obtained by Brand Jewelers from 1969 to 1971, established procedures to notify those who were not properly served that they could proceed to a trial on the merits, and placed upon Brand Jewelers' attorney the duty of ensuring that future service of process would be fair and in good faith. What are the advantages and disadvantages of placing that duty on an attorney?

In 1970, New York adopted procedural reforms aimed at stopping the practice of fraudulent service. Prior to the amendments, delivery of a summons to a person other than the defendant was not permitted unless the process-server had first exercised due diligence to locate the defendant. The burden of this requirement was viewed as the single most important cause of "sewer service." The revision adopted by the legislature allowed service by leaving one copy of the summons with a person of suitable age and discretion at the place where the defendant actually works, dwells, or usually abides and by mailing a second copy to defendant's last known address. N.Y.C.P.L.R. § 308(2). In

1973, the legislature took the additional step of requiring process servers to make more detailed statements relating to how the process was served.

In 1986, following a two-year investigation, the Attorney General of the State of New York and other government officials reported that fraudulent service of process continued to plague the New York City courts. The findings suggested that 48,000 (of 140,000) default judgments entered annually were tainted by sewer service. See N.Y. Attorney General, N.Y. City Dep't of Consumer Affairs, N.Y. City Dep't of Investigation City, A Joint Investigative Report into the Practice of Sewer Service in New York City (1986). In response, the legislature again amended the state's service rules and mandated that a copy of the summons be filed with the return of service. N.Y.C.P.L.R. §§ 306, 306–a.

In 2009, the Chief Administrative Judge of the New York State Unified Court System commenced a special proceeding against numerous debt collection attorneys seeking to vacate tens of thousands of default judgments that were alleged to have been based on false affidavits of service. See Matter of Pfau v. Forster & Garbus (Sup.Ct. Erie Co. No. 8236/09) (2009). The action was settled by a consent order. A part of the relief established a procedure for the vacating of a default judgment that had been illegally obtained. See Matter of Pfau v. Forster & Garbus (Sup.Ct. Erie Co. No. 2166/11) (2011). New York City also enacted legislation requiring licensed process-servers to maintain records of the location and date of attempts at service using global position system devices. See N.Y. City Code § 2–233. For an overview of problematic debt collection practices and some proposed solutions, see Stifler, *Debt in the Courts: The Scourge of Abusive Debt Collection*, 11 Harv.L. & Pol'y Rev. 91 (2017).

4.   SERVICE OF PROCESS AND STATUTES OF LIMITATIONS

All states have statutes of limitations that fix specific time limits within which various categories of actions must be brought. They are supplemented by bodies of law that define when various causes of action are said to "accrue"—the point when the limitations clock begins to run on an action, and the circumstances in which the running of the clock is suspended or "tolled" because a plaintiff for some reason has been prevented from timely assertion of her rights. See *Developments in the Law—Statutes of Limitations*, 63 Harv.L.Rev. 1177 (1950). Although statutes of limitations generally are deemed "procedural," their impact decidedly is "substantive"—a plaintiff loses the opportunity to invoke the assistance of the courts to obtain relief even for an otherwise valid claim. Almost the first duty of a lawyer for a potential plaintiff is to determine, by the most conservative estimates, the latest possible day for commencing an action.

When is a suit "commenced" for purposes of a statute of limitations? In federal court, if the underlying cause of action is based on federal law,

Rule 3 governs when the action is commenced. Thus, the suit is commenced when a copy of the complaint is filed with the federal district court. WEST v. CONRAIL, 481 U.S. 35, 107 S.Ct. 1538, 95 L.Ed.2d 32 (1987). However, if the underlying cause of action is based on state law, state law usually governs when the action is commenced—even if the action is in federal court. See Walker v. Armco Steel Corp., 446 U.S. 740, 100 S.Ct. 1978, 64 L.Ed.2d 659 (1980), at p. 342, infra. In some states, an action is not deemed "commenced" until process is served. In these states, a defect in service can be fatal to plaintiff's claim, because the statute of limitations may run before plaintiff has a chance to correct the error.

NOTES AND QUESTIONS

1.   Consider how the running of the statute of limitations interacts with the operation of Federal Rule 4(m). Rule 4(m) requires the federal court to dismiss an action without prejudice, or to order service to be made within a specified period if defendant is not served within 90 days of filing of the complaint. If plaintiff makes a showing of good cause for the failure, the court must extend the time for service. The rule does not define "good cause." What kind of showing ought to count as "good cause"? What if the statute of limitations expires during that period, the action is dismissed, and plaintiff seeks to refile the suit? Will the refiled action be defeated if challenged as untimely? When good cause is not shown, what factors ought to guide the court's discretion in granting an extension?

2.   What is the time limit for service of process in a foreign country under Rule 4(f)? By its terms, does Rule 4(m) apply to service abroad? Does this mean plaintiff has unlimited time to effect service abroad? The circuits are divided on this question.

3.   Does the 90-day limit in Rule 4(m) apply to service on a corporation, partnership, or association located outside the United States?

4.   The Federal Rules authorize two types of challenges to service of process. Rule 12(b)(4) allows defendant to move to dismiss the complaint for insufficiency of process. This motion attacks defects in the form of the summons. Rule 12(b)(5) allows defendant to move to dismiss the complaint for insufficiency of service of process. This motion attacks defects in the way in which process was delivered to defendant. Which motion would defendant use to challenge service that does not meet the time limits of Rule 4(m)?

C. IMMUNITY FROM PROCESS AND ETIQUETTE OF SERVICE

1. IMMUNITY FROM PROCESS

A court sometimes will immunize a party from service of process when the party's availability is thought to promote the administration of justice. The immunity is provided not for the benefit of the party, but for the benefit of the court. For example, witnesses, parties, and attorneys who come to a state to participate in a lawsuit often are granted immunity from service of process in other suits.

NOTES AND QUESTIONS

1.   The traditional rule is that a party or witness who is present in the forum for legal proceedings is immune from process in a different and unrelated action. The rationale for traditional immunity was explained by Justice Stone in LAMB v. SCHMITT, 285 U.S. 222, 52 S.Ct. 317, 76 L.Ed. 720 (1932):

> The general rule that witnesses, suitors, and their attorneys, while in attendance in connection with the conduct of one suit, are immune from service of process in another, is founded, not upon the convenience of the individuals, but of the court itself. * * * As commonly stated and applied, it proceeds upon the ground that the due administration of justice requires that a court shall not permit interference with the progress of a cause pending before it, by the service of process in other suits, which would prevent, or the fear of which might tend to discourage, the voluntary attendance of those whose presence is necessary or convenient to the judicial administration in the pending litigation. * * * In Stewart v. Ramsay, the court said at page 130, of 242 U.S., 37 S.Ct. 44, 46 [(1916),] * * * "The privilege which is asserted here is the privilege of the court, rather than of the defendant. It is founded in the necessities of the judicial administration, which would be often embarrassed, and sometimes interrupted, if the suitor might be vexed with process while attending upon the court for the protection of his rights, or the witness while attending to testify."

> It follows that the privilege should not be enlarged beyond the reason upon which it is founded, and that it should be extended or withheld only as judicial necessities require. * * * Limitations of it on this basis have been not infrequently made because the attendance upon the trial of a cause, however vital to the personal interests of those concerned, was not for the purpose of facilitating the progress of the cause * * *; or because the service was made on one whose attendance was not voluntary, and hence had no tendency to interfere with judicial administration * * *.

Id. at 225–26, 52 S.Ct. at 318, 76 L.Ed. at 722–23. See also Keefe & Roscia, *Immunity and Sentimentality*, 47 Cornell L.Q. 471 (1947).

2.   In certain situations, federal courts accord an immunity from service of process to representatives of foreign governments, as well as their families and members of their households. The scope of the immunity under a treaty called the United Nations Headquarters Agreement, reprinted at 22 U.S.C. § 287 note, was at issue in KADIC v. KARADZIC, 70 F.3d 232 (2d Cir. 1995), an action by Croat and Muslim human rights victims against the self-

announced president of the break-away Bosnian-Serb republic. Plaintiffs served defendant while he was in New York, and he claimed an official immunity. Whether immunity attached turned on two questions under the Headquarters Agreement: where defendant was served and whether he was a designated representative of the United Nations at the time of service. Plaintiffs' affidavits provided the following information about service:

> [P]laintiffs obtained from [District Court] Judge Owen an order for alternative means of service, directing service by delivering the complaint to a member of defendant's State Department security detail, who was ordered to hand the complaint to the defendant. The security officer's affidavit states that he received the complaint and handed it to Karadzic outside the Russian Embassy in Manhattan. * * * Appellants also allege that during his visits to New York City, Karadzic stayed at hotels outside the "headquarters district" of the United Nations and engaged in non-United Nations-related activities such as fundraising.

Id. at 246–47. The court of appeals held that defendant was not a designated representative of any member of the United Nations and was not entitled to immunity when served outside the area of the Headquarters District.

3.   Should service of process be invalidated if secured through artifice or trickery? In WYMAN v. NEWHOUSE, 93 F.2d 313 (2d Cir. 1937), cert. denied, 303 U.S. 664, 58 S.Ct. 831, 82 L.Ed. 1122 (1938), the Second Circuit Court of Appeals upheld a collateral attack on a default judgment entered in a Florida state court. The record showed that defendant had been induced to travel from New York to Florida after receiving a series of urgent messages from plaintiff, with whom he "had engaged in meretricious relations." The messages—including telegrams, letters, and telephone calls—recited plaintiff's love for defendant and her desire to see him before leaving the country to see her dying mother in Ireland. The appeals court recounted that upon defendant's arriving at the airport, he was met by a deputy sheriff who served him with process in a lawsuit seeking $500,000. Defendant returned to New York and a default judgment was entered against him. The appeals court refused to enforce the Florida judgment:

> This judgment is attacked for fraud perpetrated upon the appellee which goes to the jurisdiction of the Florida court over his person. A judgment procured fraudulently, as here, lacks jurisdiction and is null and void. * * * A fraud affecting the jurisdiction is equivalent to a lack of jurisdiction. * * * The appellee was not required to proceed against the judgment in Florida. His equitable defense in answer to a suit on the judgment is sufficient. A judgment recovered in a sister state, through the fraud of the party procuring the appearance of another, is not binding on the latter when an attempt is made to enforce such judgment in another state. * * *

> The appellee was not required to make out a defense on the merits to the suit in Florida. * * * An error made in entering judgment against

a party over whom the court had no jurisdiction permits a consideration of the jurisdictional question collaterally. The complaint was properly dismissed.

Id. at 315.

Reread Tickle v. Barton, p. 13, supra. Which case presents a stronger situation for quashing service: *Wyman* or *Tickle*? Why? Would the result have been the same in *Wyman* if Newhouse had been in Florida and the trickery had been used to "flush him out of hiding"? Do you think that the situations in which plaintiff will resort to fraud, force, or artifice are increasingly rare given long-arm statutes and the ability to serve process outside the state where the court is located? See Burnham v. Superior Court, p. 160, supra. Are these rules nevertheless justified because, even in the rare case, they will deter plaintiffs from engaging in trickery?

D. OPPORTUNITY TO BE HEARD

Recall that in *Mullane*, p. 173, supra, Justice Jackson stated: "Many controversies have raged about the cryptic and abstract words of the Due Process Clause but there can be no doubt that at a minimum they require *[the judgement given]* that deprivation of life, liberty or property by (adjudication) be preceded by notice and opportunity for hearing appropriate to the nature of the case." In simple terms, a defendant has an adequate opportunity to be heard when—in light of the interests at stake in the litigation—defendant is able to develop the facts and legal issues in the case and present that party's position to the court. Depending on the interests involved, an informal hearing may suffice, or a full trial may be required, or something in-between may pass muster.

In a series of cases beginning in the 1960s, the Court considered whether the Due Process Clause requires a hearing before the deprivation of liberty or property takes place, or whether a hearing after the fact sometimes suffices. The cases fell into two groups. The first group involved challenges to a private creditor's use of a provisional remedy at the commencement of a lawsuit. Provisional remedies today are largely statutory in nature but date back to the common law writs; traditionally they operated as an exception to the requirement of prior notice and hearing. In practice, a provisional remedy allowed plaintiff to request an order from the court at the commencement or during the pendency of the suit allowing the seizure or encumbrance of defendant-debtor's assets for the benefit of the creditor prior to a determination of liability or the entry of a final judgment.

The second group of cases concerned whether the Due Process Clause entitled a person who sought a government benefit (such as a welfare payment, civil service job, or pilot license) to an opportunity to be heard before being denied the benefit. Until the mid-twentieth century, benefits of this sort were not considered to be "property" and so the Due Process

4. The *Sniadach* line of cases did not articulate an overall test for determining when a provisional remedy would meet constitutional standards and when it would not. Was the Court in practice applying a rule that notice and a prior hearing were required before seizure of a defendant's property, absent a showing of extraordinary circumstances? Or was the court engaged in a balancing test that looked to the reasonableness of the procedure? If so, what factors counted in the overall balance? The cases gestured toward a number of factors critical to the Court's analysis, but did not assign weights to any one of them:

Who—whether a judge or a clerk is the decision-maker;

What—whether the party seeking relief has a pre-existing interest in the property to be seized or encumbered;

When—whether the seizure is effected before notice and hearing, or is followed by an immediate hearing after the seizure;

Why—whether the seizure is to establish jurisdiction or for security purposes, and if for security purposes, whether exceptional circumstances such as destruction of an asset are presented; and

How—whether the applicant must show probable cause or meet a lesser burden of proof; whether factual allegations must be sworn to under penalty of perjury and based on personal knowledge; and whether the dispute can be resolved by uncontested documentary evidence.

5. Should the *Sniadach* line of cases apply when an attachment is used to establish jurisdiction (as in *Shaffer*, see p. 147, supra)?

6. Parallel to the cases involving provisional remedies, the Supreme Court considered the applicability of the Due Process Clause to the administration of government benefit programs. In GOLDBERG v. KELLY, 397 U.S. 254, 90 S.Ct. 1011, 25 L.Ed.2d 287 (1970), the Court held that the recipient of government-funded public assistance is entitled to "the opportunity for an evidentiary hearing prior to termination" of those benefits. Id. at 255, 90 S.Ct. at 1014, 25 L.Ed.2d at 292. In reaching this decision, the Court emphasized the recipient's "brutal need" for assistance of this sort, observing that "termination of aid pending resolution of a controversy over eligibility may deprive an eligible recipient of the very means by which to live while he waits." Id. at 261, 264, 90 S.Ct. at 1017, 1018, 25 L.Ed.2d at 295, 297. The Court made clear that although a full-scale judicial trial was not required, the hearing had to be tailored "to the capacities and circumstances of those who are to be heard." Id. at 268–69, 90 S.Ct. at 1021, 25 L.Ed.2d at 299.

Goldberg appeared to link the "kind of hearing" that due process requires with the importance of plaintiff's interest in the benefit that was being withheld. See Friendly, *"Some Kind of Hearing,"* 123 U.Pa.L.Rev. 1267 (1975). On this basis, the Court in MATHEWS v. ELDRIDGE, 424 U.S. 319, 96 S.Ct. 893, 47 L.Ed.2d 18 (1976), held that the Due Process Clause does not require a hearing *before* the government terminates a recipient's Social Security disability benefits. The Court explained that the loss of disability benefits did not present as strong a showing of hardship as the loss of public assistance. The Court made clear, however, that "the degree of potential deprivation" is only one of a number of factors that affect what process is due. Other factors to be considered are "the fairness and reliability" of existing procedures and "the probable value, if any of additional procedural safeguards." Id. at 341–43, 96 S.Ct. at 906–07, 47 L.Ed.2d at 37–38. Determining what process is due also was to consider the "public interest," including any "administrative burden and other societal costs" involved with constitutionalizing the procedures to be provided. Id. at 347, 96 S.Ct. at 909, 47 L.Ed.2d at 40. Rather than looking exclusively to the individual interest at stake, the Court put forward a balancing test that considers three factors:

> First, the private interest that will be affected by the official action; second, the risk of an erroneous deprivation of such interest through the procedures used, and the probable value, if any, of additional or substitute procedural safeguards; and finally, the Government's interest, including the function involved and the fiscal and administrative burdens that the additional or substitute procedural requirement would entail.

Id. at 335, 96 S.Ct. at 903, 47 L.Ed.2d at 33.

7.   Would the application of the *Mathews* test have changed the outcome in *Fuentes*, p. 203, Note 2, supra? Can you reconcile the *Mathews*-balancing test with the factor-analysis of *Sniadach* and its progeny? Consider the factors listed in p. 207, Note 4, supra. How would you organize those factors to align with the *Mathews* test?

8.   In JONES v. GOVERNOR OF FLORIDA, 975 F.3d 1016 (11th Cir. 2020), the en banc Eleventh Circuit considered a challenge to Florida's statute permitting reenfranchisement of individuals convicted of felonies. After Florida voters voted to amend the state constitution to allow those who had been convicted of felonies and completed their sentences to vote—overall, about 1.4 million people—the legislature enacted a statute that (a) limited reenfranchisement to those who had paid all fees and costs incurred in connection with the convictions; and (b) imposed a penalty on persons who registered to vote without having met the specified financial conditions. There were significant practical difficulties, however, for any individual who wished to locate their prior criminal judgments, to determine whether fees were imposed because of felony or other offenses, or to identify how much of their debt remained. The district court issued an injunction against what it called the "pay-to-vote system," ordering as a remedy that an individual may request an opinion from the Division of Elections stating their total amount of outstanding fines and restitution and permitting any individual who did not receive an answer within 21 days to register to vote without the threat of penalty or prosecution.

In reversing the injunction, the Eleventh Circuit majority emphasized the distinction between legislative and adjudicative action; legislative action includes general laws that apply to "more than a few people" and are "prospective in nature"; adjudicative action applies to a "relatively small number of persons" who are "exceptionally affected, in each case upon individual grounds" by the action. Id. at 1048. Because the deprivation of the right to vote occurred "through legislative action, not adjudicative action," the majority concluded that the *Mathews* balancing test did not come into play. Rather, "the affected persons are not entitled to any process beyond that provided by the legislative process." Id. (citing Bi-Metallic Investment Co. v. State Board of Equalization, 239 U.S. 441, 445, 36 S.Ct. 141, 142, 60 L.Ed. 372, 375 (1915)). "The Due Process Clause does not require States to provide individual process to help citizens learn the facts necessary to comply with laws of general application." Id. at 1049.

Consider, by contrast, this example from one of the *Jones* dissenting opinions:

> [I]magine a state that requires, as a condition of renewing drivers' licenses and vehicle registrations, that drivers pay all outstanding citations for parking/traffic infractions. A driver goes to his county agency and is told that he may have some unpaid citations. He asks for information about the citations and their respective amounts so that he can verify their accuracy and pay whatever is outstanding. But the clerk tells him that the state can't give him the information because the debt for the citations has been sold to third-party collection agencies; those agencies charge certain fees (which vary by agency and year) on top of the citation amounts; and the county has no way of knowing what those fees are or what amounts have been paid or credited. The clerk tries to call other state agencies (and some of the collection agencies) to get answers, but to no avail, and tells the driver he will have to figure everything out on his own. So the driver has to leave without his license and car registration, and will need to risk driving in violation of the law—and face arrest—in order to get to work, take his children to school, and carry out the other tasks of daily life. Would this state of affairs be constitutionally permissible? Of course not.

Id. at 1094–95 (Jordan, J., dissenting).

———

In CONNECTICUT v. DOEHR, 501 U.S. 1, 111 S.Ct. 2105, 115 L.Ed.2d 1 (1991), the Supreme Court applied the *Mathews* test to assess a provisional remedy that authorized prejudgment attachment of real estate in a civil action unrelated to the property. The statute did not provide for notice or a hearing prior to the attachment, did not require the requestor to show extraordinary circumstances for the attachment, and did not mandate the posting of a bond. The statute provided:

> The court or a judge of the court may allow the prejudgment remedy to be issued by an attorney without hearing * * * upon

verification by oath of the plaintiff or of some competent affiant, that there is probable cause to sustain the validity of the plaintiff's claims and (1) that the prejudgment remedy requested is for an attachment of real property * * *.

Conn.Gen.Stat. § 52–278e (1991). The Court invalidated the provision:

Prejudgment remedy statutes ordinarily apply to disputes between private parties rather than between an individual and the government. * * * For this type of case, therefore, the relevant inquiry requires, as in *Mathews*, first, consideration of the private interest that will be affected by the prejudgment measure; second, an examination of the risk of erroneous deprivation through the procedures under attack and the probable value of additional or alternative safeguards; and third, in contrast to *Mathews*, principal attention to the interest of the party seeking the prejudgment remedy, with, nonetheless, due regard for any ancillary interest the government may have in providing the procedure or forgoing the added burden of providing greater protections.

501 U.S. at 10–11, 111 S.Ct. at 2112, 115 L.Ed.2d at 13.

The Court found the property interest affected by the attachment was significant even though not permanent; attachment could taint credit ratings and perhaps place a mortgage in technical default. Moreover, the risk of an erroneous deprivation was great because only a skeletal affidavit needed to be submitted to support the attachment, the supporting affidavit was likely to be conclusory and self-serving, the statute's standard of probable cause was "obscure": "Unlike determining the existence of a debt or delinquent payments, the issue does not concern 'ordinarily uncomplicated matters that lend themselves to documentary proof.' " Id. at 14, 111 S.Ct. at 2114, 115 L.Ed.2d at 15. The Court went on to explain that existing procedural safeguards did not adequately reduce the risk of error:

* * * Connecticut points out that the statute also provides an "expeditiou[s]" postattachment adversary hearing * * *; notice for such a hearing * * *; judicial review of an adverse decision * * *; and a double damages action if the original suit is commenced without probable cause * * *. Similar considerations were present in *Mitchell* * * *. But in *Mitchell*, the plaintiff had a vendor's lien to protect, the risk of error was minimal because the likelihood of recovery involved uncomplicated matters that lent themselves to documentary proof, * * * and plaintiff was required to put up a bond. None of these factors diminishing the need for a predeprivation hearing is present in this case. It is true that a later hearing might negate the presence of probable cause, but this would not cure the temporary deprivation that an earlier hearing might have prevented. * * *

Id. at 14–15, 111 S.Ct. at 2114–15, 115 L.Ed.2d at 16. Finally, the Court found that the interests in favor of attachment were too minimal given the absence of an existing interest in the real estate, of any threat that assets would be transferred or encumbered during the pendency of the action, and of any financial burden to the state in providing a predeprivation hearing, since the state already had in place a process for an immediate postdeprivation hearing.

A majority of the Court did not reach the issue of whether due process requires the party seeking the attachment to post a bond or other security. Justice White, joined by Justices Marshall, Stevens, and O'Connor, underscored the importance of a bond even though the state provided for double damages in suits commenced without probable cause:

> * * * The need for a bond is especially apparent where extraordinary circumstances justify an attachment with no more than the plaintiff's *ex parte* assertion of a claim. * * * Until a postattachment hearing * * *, a defendant has no protection against damages sustained where no extraordinary circumstance in fact existed or the plaintiff's likelihood of recovery was nil. Such protection is what a bond can supply. * * *

> But the need for a bond does not end here. A defendant's property rights remain at undue risk even when there has been an adversarial hearing to determine the plaintiff's likelihood of recovery. At best, a court's initial assessment of each party's case cannot produce more than an educated prediction as to who will win. * * *

> If a bond cannot serve to dispense with a hearing immediately after attachment, neither is it sufficient basis for not providing a preattachment hearing in the absence of exigent circumstances even if in any event a hearing would be provided a few days later. The reasons are the same: a wrongful attachment can inflict injury that will not fully be redressed by recovery on the bond after a prompt postattachment hearing determines that the attachment was invalid.

Id. at 19–23, 111 S.Ct. at 2117–19, 115 L.Ed.2d at 19–21. Chief Justice Rehnquist, joined by Justice Blackmun, concurred:

> * * * The Court's opinion is, in my view, ultimately correct * * *. But I do not believe that the result follows so inexorably as the Court's opinion suggests. All of [our prior decisions] dealt with personalty—bank deposits or chattels—and each involved the physical seizure of the property itself, so that the defendant was deprived of its use. * * * [I]n all of them the debtor was deprived of the use and possession of the property. In the present case, on the other hand, Connecticut's prejudgment attachment on real

property statute, which secures an incipient lien for the plaintiff,
does not deprive the defendant of the use or possession of the
property.

The Court's opinion therefore breaks new ground * * *. * * * I
agree with the Court, however, that upon analysis the deprivation
here is a significant one, even though the owner remains in
undisturbed possession. * * *

Id. at 26–27, 111 S.Ct. at 2121, 115 L.Ed.2d at 23–24. Justice Scalia also
concurred.

NOTES AND QUESTIONS

1.   SHAUMYAN v. O'NEILL, 987 F.2d 122 (2d Cir. 1993), involved the
same attachment statute at issue in *Doehr*, but applied in a contract dispute
between a homeowner and a contractor hired to do repairs. The homeowner
questioned the quality of the repair work and refused to pay the remainder of
the bill. The contractor moved ex parte in state court and obtained a
prejudgment attachment against the owner's home. While the state court
action was pending, the homeowner sued in federal court to enjoin enforcement
of the statute as violative of due process. Both the district court and the court
of appeals rejected the constitutional challenge. Although the homeowner had
a strong private interest, the likelihood of an erroneous deprivation was not
high because the evidence largely involved written documentation; moreover,
the contractor "had a substantial pre-existing interest" in the property once his
labor and materials had been incorporated into plaintiff's home. Id. at 127. See
Alquist, *Balancing the Checklist: Connecticut's Legislative Response to
Connecticut v. Doehr*, 26 Conn.L.Rev. 721 (1994).

2.   In the wake of *Doehr*, commentators questioned the constitutionality
of lis pendens statutes, which permit a plaintiff who claims an interest in real
property to file a "notice of pendency" that alerts potential buyers of the claim;
the property owner is not given an opportunity to contest imposition of the
notice. See Levy, *Lis Pendens and Procedural Due Process: A Closer Look After
Connecticut v. Doehr*, 51 Md.L.Rev. 1054 (1992). In DIAZ v. PATERSON, 547
F.3d 88 (2d Cir. 2008), a federal appeals court upheld the constitutionality of
New York's lis pendens statute under the *Mathews* factors as construed in
Doehr. Should the property owner be given an opportunity to challenge the
notice after it is imposed?

3.   In NELSON v. COLORADO, 581 U.S. ___, 137 S.Ct. 1249, 197
L.Ed.2d 611 (2017), the Court held that the Colorado Exoneration Act failed to
satisfy due process under the *Mathews* balancing test. The Court described the
statute as follows:

The Exoneration Act provides a civil claim for relief "to compensate
an innocent person who was wrongly convicted." * * * Recovery under
the Act is available only to a defendant who has served all or part of
a term of incarceration pursuant to a felony conviction, and whose

conviction has been overturned for reasons other than insufficiency of evidence or legal error unrelated to actual innocence. * * * To succeed on an Exoneration Act claim, a petitioner must show, by clear and convincing evidence, her actual innocence of the offense of conviction. * * * A successful petitioner may recoup, in addition to compensation for time served, "any fine, penalty, court costs, or restitution . . . paid . . . as a result of his or her wrongful conviction." * * *

Id. at ___, 137 S.Ct. at 254, 197 L.Ed.2d at 617.

Looking to the private interest, the Court found that the claimants had "an obvious interest in regaining the money the paid to Colorado," and that the state could not lay claim to the funds once innocence had been restored. Id. at ___, 137 S.Ct. at 1255–56, 197 L.Ed.2d at 618. Further, the Court found an unacceptable risk of erroneous deprivation; the claimants should be presumed innocent, and not "saddled with any proof burden," especially a burden as high as clear and convincing evidence. Id. at 1251, 1256, 197 L.Ed.2d at 614, 619. Finally, the Court found no countervailing interest in the state's retaining the funds—indeed, it found that the state had "no interest in withholding" the funds once the conviction had ben invalidated. Id. at ___, 137 S.Ct. at 1257–58, 197 L.Ed.2d at 620. Justice Thomas, dissenting, questioned whether due process even applied. To state a procedural due process claim, the dissent argued, plaintiff must first identify a protected property interest, and there had been no showing that plaintiffs actually were entitled to the funds they sought to recover.

4. Can a party's opportunity to be heard be meaningful without adequate legal representation? The Supreme Court repeatedly has held that the Due Process Clause does not mandate the appointment of counsel for civil litigants who are too poor to retain a lawyer; whether to appoint counsel instead depends on a balance of factors. In LASSITER v. DEPARTMENT OF SOCIAL SERVICES, 452 U.S. 18, 101 S.Ct. 2153, 68 L.Ed.2d 640 (1981), the Court underscored that there is "a presumption that an indigent litigant has a right to appointed counsel only when, if he loses, he may be deprived of his physical liberty." Id. at 26–27, 101 S.Ct. 2159, 68 L.Ed.2d at 649. Under that standard, the Court held that due process was not violated when a trial court failed to appoint counsel prior to terminating a mother's parental rights when the petition contained no allegations that would have exposed her to criminal liability. Later, in TURNER v. ROGERS, 564 U.S. 431, 131 S.Ct. 2507, 180 L.Ed.2d 452 (2011), the Court considered whether due process required the appointment of counsel for a father who was held in civil contempt and jailed after repeated failures to make court-ordered child support payments, or whether it was sufficient for the Court to determine his financial capacity to make the payments. Justice Breyer, writing for a divided Court, held that counsel was not necessarily required:

> Due Process Clause does not automatically require the provision of counsel at civil contempt proceedings to an indigent individual who is subject to a child support order, even if that individual faces

(margin annotation: "emphasize")

incarceration (for up to a year). In particular, that Clause does not require the provision of counsel where the opposing parent or other custodian (to whom support funds are owed) is not represented by counsel and the State provides alternative procedural safeguards [such as or equivalent to] * * * adequate notice of the importance of ability to pay, fair opportunity to present, and to dispute, relevant information, and court findings * * *.

Id. at 448, 131 S.Ct. at 2520, 180 L.Ed.2d at 466. In this case, however, the Court found that the state had failed to provide even those alternative safeguards; therefore, the contemnor's incarceration violated due process. Id. at 449, 131 S.Ct. at 2520, 180 L.Ed.2d at 466–67.

CHAPTER 4

JURISDICTION OVER THE SUBJECT MATTER OF THE ACTION—THE COURT'S COMPETENCY

■ ■ ■

This chapter considers subject-matter jurisdiction: the power of a court to hear a case given the nature of the dispute, as distinct from its power to enter a judgment against a particular defendant. Every court system has its own rules governing subject-matter jurisdiction. The United States comprises multiple court systems—including the federal and those of the states. State courts are subject not only to state rules but also, to a limited extent, federal rules. In the federal court system, subject-matter jurisdiction is governed by Article III of the federal Constitution, federal statutes, and judicial decisions. State and federal courts have overlapping jurisdiction in certain areas and this concurrent jurisdiction allows a plaintiff, when commencing a lawsuit, to choose from among courts of different systems. Removal jurisdiction, which allows defendant a limited right to transfer a case from state to federal court, creates additional strategic possibilities. These opportunities to "forum shop" help to promote litigant autonomy, but in practice may conflict with important public concerns.

A. SUBJECT-MATTER JURISDICTION IN STATE COURTS

State courts are considered to be courts of "general" jurisdiction, which in this context means they have authority to hear cases on any subject matter unless they are ousted of such power by state or federal law. This does not mean that every court in a state has power to hear all kinds of disputes. The jurisdiction of most state courts is distributed among a variety of courts. In many instances, this is accomplished by segregating certain types of controversies from the mainstream of litigation and giving special courts subject-matter jurisdiction over them, as usually is done with domestic relations and probate matters. Probably the most common method of limiting judicial power is by providing that the court can adjudicate only controversies involving more than a certain minimum or less than a stated maximum of money, or its equivalent. These rules are designed to direct the quantitative and qualitative flow of litigation into various courts within a jurisdiction.

NOTES AND QUESTIONS

1.   A state court of general jurisdiction is permitted and indeed may be under a duty to hear a cause of action arising under the laws of another state. This requirement flows from the Full Faith and Credit Clause, Article IV, § 1 of the United States Constitution. In HUGHES v. FETTER, 341 U.S. 609, 71 S.Ct. 980, 95 L.Ed. 1212 (1951), the Supreme Court held that under the "national policy" of the Full Faith and Credit Clause, Wisconsin could not "close the doors of its courts to the cause of action created by the Illinois wrongful death act," while keeping judicial doors open for analogous claims under Wisconsin law for deaths "caused locally." As the Court explained: "[A state] * * * cannot escape [its] constitutional obligation to enforce the rights and duties validly created under the laws of other states by the simple device of removing jurisdiction from courts otherwise competent." Id. at 611–13, 71 S.Ct. at 981–83, 95 L.Ed. at 1215–17.

2.   It is settled that a court can apply its own procedural law even when it hears a dispute involving a claim arising under the laws of another system. Can a state apply its own statute of limitations to a claim arising under the laws of another state? If so, does this mean that a court can dismiss a claim as untimely under its statute of limitations even though the claim would be timely under the law of the state creating the cause of action? The Supreme Court answered this question in the affirmative in WELLS v. SIMONDS ABRASIVE CO., 345 U.S. 514, 73 S.Ct. 856, 97 L.Ed. 1211 (1953), explaining that. "applying the statute of limitations of the forum to a foreign substantive right did not deny full faith and credit." Id. at 516, 73 S.Ct. at 857, 97 L.Ed. at 1215. Conversely, a state may apply its own longer statute of limitations to a cause of action created by another state's law even though the claim would have been time-barred under the law of the state where the cause of action arose. See Sun Oil Co. v. Wortman, 486 U.S. 717, 108 S.Ct. 2117, 100 L.Ed.2d 743 (1988).

3.   When Congress enacts a federal statute, the presumption is that both the federal and the state courts have power to enforce the law—referred to as the presumption of concurrent jurisdiction. Congress may confer jurisdiction exclusively on the federal courts, but the presumption of concurrency will be rebutted only "by an explicit statutory directive, by unmistakable implication from legislative history, or by a clear incompatibility between state-court jurisdiction and federal interests." Tafflin v. Levitt, 493 U.S. 455, 458–60, 110 S.Ct. 792, 795, 107 L.Ed.2d 887, 894 (1990) (internal quotation omitted). In ATLANTIC RICHFIELD CO. v. CHRISTIAN, 590 U.S. ___, 140 S.Ct. 1335, 206 L.Ed.2d 516 (2020), the Supreme Court noted the "deeply rooted presumption in favor of concurrent state court jurisdiction" in rejecting the argument that the federal Comprehensive Environmental Response, Compensation, and Liability Act ousted Montana state courts of jurisdiction

over claims by property owners against the owner of a smelter that was subject to an Environmental Protection Agency clean-up plan.

4.   If a state court has subject-matter jurisdiction to hear a claim that arises under federal law, is it required to exercise that power? In HOWLETT v. ROSE, 496 U.S. 356, 110 S.Ct. 2430, 110 L.Ed.2d 332 (1990), a unanimous Supreme Court held that the Florida courts could not invoke sovereign immunity as a ground for declining to hear a federal civil rights claim under 42 U.S.C. § 1983 when that defense would not bar the state court from hearing an analogous state law claim. The Court explained that the state's defense in this context "raise[d] the concern that the state court may be evading federal law and discriminating against federal causes of action":

> A state policy that permits actions against state agencies for the failure of their officials to adequately police a parking lot and for the negligence of such officers in arresting a person on a roadside, but yet declines jurisdiction over federal actions for constitutional violations by the same persons can be based only on the rationale that such persons should not be held liable for § 1983 violations in the courts of the State. That reason, whether presented in terms of direct disagreement with substantive federal law or simple refusal to take cognizance of the federal cause of action, flatly violates the Supremacy Clause.

Id. at 380–81, 110 S.Ct. at 2445, 110 L.Ed.2d at 356. In HAYWOOD v. DROWN, 556 U.S. 729, 129 S.Ct. 2108, 173 L.Ed.2d 920 (2009), the Court held, five-to-four, that it was impermissible for a New York court to invoke a jurisdictional rule as grounds for declining to hear a federal claim: "[H]aving made the decision to create courts of general jurisdiction that regularly sit to entertain analogous suits, New York is not at liberty to shut the courthouse door to federal claims that it considers at odds with its local policy." Id. at 740, 129 S.Ct. at 2117, 173 L.Ed.2d at 931. May a state court decline to enforce a federal statute for which there is no analogous state law claim?

NOTE ON IDENTIFYING JURISDICTIONAL CONDITIONS

The requirement of subject-matter jurisdiction is a nonwaivable defect and its absence may be raised at any time during a proceeding, including for the first time on appeal. It therefore is important to be able to distinguish a legal condition that pertains to subject-matter jurisdiction from one that involves the merits. In ARBAUGH v. Y & H CORP., 546 U.S. 500, 126 S.Ct. 1235, 163 L.Ed.2d 1097 (2006), plaintiff sued under a federal statute that bars employers with 15 or more employees from discriminating on the basis of race or gender. After a jury awarded damages to plaintiff for sexual harassment, defendant sought to establish that it was not subject to the statute because of the size of its workforce. The district court dismissed the claim for lack of subject-matter jurisdiction, and the court of appeals affirmed. The Supreme Court reversed, holding that the numerosity requirement was not jurisdictional, but rather "a substantive ingredient" of the claim. As a result, defendant was too late in raising the defect. Id. at 503, 126 S.Ct. at 1238, 163 L.Ed.2d at 1103. In so holding, the Court applied a "bright line" rule. The statute did not clearly state that the numerosity requirement is jurisdictional; to the contrary, the requirement appeared in a part of the statute separate from the provision pertaining to jurisdiction. Id. at 516, 126 S.Ct. at 1245, 163 L.Ed.2d at 1110. In a later decision, SEBELIUS v. AUBURN REGIONAL MEDICAL CENTER, 568 U.S. 145, 133 S.Ct. 817, 184 L.Ed.2d 627 (2013), the Court again addressed, in the context of a federal statute, how to distinguish jurisdictional from claim-processing rules:

> We inquire whether Congress has "clearly state[d]" that the rule is jurisdictional; absent such a clear statement, we have cautioned, "courts should treat the restriction as nonjurisdictional in character." * * * This is not to say that Congress must incant magic words in order to speak clearly. We consider "context, including this Court's interpretations of similar provisions in many years past," as probative of whether Congress intended a particular provision to rank as jurisdictional. * * *

Id. at 153–54, 133 S.Ct. at 824, 184 L.Ed.2d at 637 (citations omitted).

Would you characterize a statute of limitations as a jurisdictional bar or as a condition of relief? Ordinarily, a party is permitted to waive an objection to the statute of limitations, which is treated as an affirmative defense and not as a jurisdictional requirement. However, in JOHN R. SAND & GRAVEL CO. v. UNITED STATES, 552 U.S. 130, 128 S.Ct. 750, 169 L.Ed.2d 591 (2008), the Court held that the six-year limitations period for filing claims against the United States in the Court of Federal Claims is "more absolute" than a timeliness provision that merely bars the defense of stale claims and so may not be waived. Id. at 134, 128 S.Ct. at 753, 169 L.Ed.2d at 596. In reaching this result, the Court relied on earlier precedent that treated the limitations period in the statute plaintiff was seeking to enforce as jurisdictional, and observed that the condition appeared in a portion of the statute stating that " '[e]very claim of which' the Court of Federal Claims 'has *jurisdiction* shall be barred' " unless filed within the designated period. Id. at 135, 128 S.Ct. at 755, 169 L.Ed.2d at 597. The opinion underscores the importance of statutory text to resolving the question of whether a statutory condition is an aspect of the merits or a jurisdictional requirement. Indeed, the Supreme Court has found that other time periods are not jurisdictional. See, e.g., Boechler, P.C. v. Commissioner of Internal Revenue, 596 U.S. ___, 142 S.Ct. 1493, 212 L.Ed.2d 524 (2022) (26 U.S.C. § 6330(d)(1)'s 30-day deadline to file a petition for review in Tax Court); Hamer v. Neighborhood Housing Services of Chicago, 583 U.S. ___, 138 S.Ct. 13, 199 L.Ed.2d 249 (2017) (Federal Rule of Appellate Procedure 4(a)(5)(C)'s limit on extensions of time to file a notice of appeal); Henderson ex rel. Henderson v. Shinseki, 562 U.S. 428, 131 S.Ct. 1197, 179 L.Ed.2d 159 (2011) (38 U.S.C. § 7266(a)'s 120-day deadline for appealing a denial of federal benefits by the Board of Veterans' Appeals).

B. THE SUBJECT-MATTER JURISDICTION OF THE FEDERAL COURTS—DIVERSITY OF CITIZENSHIP

Read Article III, § 2 of the United States Constitution and 28 U.S.C. §§ 1332, 1359, and 1369 in the Supplement.

By contrast to state courts, federal courts are courts of limited jurisdiction. They may exercise subject-matter jurisdiction only over the kinds of "cases" and "controversies" identified in Article III, § 2 of the United States Constitution, and only if Congress has enacted a statute vesting such jurisdiction.[a]

Article III, § 2 of the Constitution extends the judicial power of the United States to controversies "between Citizens of different States * * * and between a State, or the Citizens thereof, and Foreign States, Citizens or Subjects." Since the First Judiciary Act in 1789, Congress has vested jurisdiction over so-called "diversity" cases in the federal courts. The current statute conferring diversity jurisdiction is set out in 28 U.S.C. § 1332. It may surprise you to learn that this grant of jurisdiction allows the federal courts to hear cases in which the claims arise solely under state law, so long as the parties to the dispute meet the constitutional and statutory conditions. The conferral of diversity jurisdiction raises important issues about federalism and the appropriate relation between unelected federal judges and the states.

It is not clear why the Framers authorized the grant of diversity jurisdiction in Article III, § 2, and scholars do not find clear answers to that question in the debates of the Constitutional Convention. See Wood, *The Changing Face of Diversity Jurisdiction*, 82 Temp.L.Rev. 593 (2009). Chief Justice Marshall offered an early and influential explanation in BANK OF THE UNITED STATES v. DEVEAUX, 9 U.S. (5 Cranch) 61, 87, 3 L.Ed. 38, 45 (1809):

> However true the fact may be, that the tribunals of the states will administer justice as impartially as those of the nation, * * * it is not less true that the constitution itself either entertains apprehensions on this subject, or views with such indulgence the possible fears and apprehensions of suitors, that it has established national tribunals for the decision of controversies * * * between citizens of different states.

---

[a] An exception is that the Supreme Court may exercise its original jurisdiction even without statutory authorization from Congress. See California v. Arizona, 440 U.S. 59, 99 S.Ct. 919, 59 L.Ed.2d 144 (1979).

The availability of diversity jurisdiction is said to have fostered a secure financial environment during a formative period of national development by extending a federal forum to investors and creditors. According to William Howard Taft (who served as President and then as Chief Justice of the United States): "[N]o single element in our governmental system has done so much to secure capital for the legitimate development of enterprises * * * as the existence of federal courts * * * with a jurisdiction to hear diverse citizenship cases." See Taft, *Possible and Needed Reform in Administration of Justice in Federal Courts*, 8 A.B.A.J. 601, 604 (1922). Among other factors, the bench and jury of the federal courts were differently constituted from those of the states. See Friendly, *The Historic Basis of the Diversity Jurisdiction*, 41 Harv.L.Rev. 483 (1928); Jones, *Finishing a Friendly Argument: The Jury and the Historical Origins of Diversity Jurisdiction*, 82 N.Y.U.L.Rev. 997 (2007).

The Rule of Complete Diversity

One of the most important limitations on federal diversity jurisdiction is the rule of "complete diversity" announced by Chief Justice Marshall in STRAWBRIDGE v. CURTISS, 7 U.S. (3 Cranch) 267, 2 L.Ed. 435 (1806). The Court affirmed the dismissal of a suit for lack of subject-matter jurisdiction, and explained:

> The words of the act of congress are, "where an alien is a party; or the suit is between a citizen of a state where the suit is brought, and a citizen of another state."

> The court understands these expressions to mean that each distinct interest should be represented by persons, all of whom are entitled to sue, or may be sued, in the federal courts. That is, that where the interest is joint, each of the persons concerned in that interest must be competent to sue, or liable to be sued, in those courts.

> But the court does not mean to give an opinion in the case where several parties represent several distinct interests, and some of those parties are, and others are not, competent to sue, or liable to be sued, in the courts of the United States.

Id. at 267–68, 2 L.Ed. at 435.

Courts have interpreted the *Strawbridge* rule to bar diversity jurisdiction under Section 1332(a) if any plaintiff is a citizen of the same state as any defendant, no matter how many parties are involved in the litigation. See, e.g., Lincoln Property Co. v. Roche, 546 U.S. 81, 82, 126 S.Ct. 606, 613, 163 L.Ed.2d 415, 424 (2005) (noting that since *Strawbridge*, "this Court has read the statutory formulation 'between . . . citizens of different States,' * * * to require complete diversity between all plaintiffs and all defendants"). Is the rule a construction of the Constitution? Could Congress abrogate the complete-diversity condition? Should it?

Diversity jurisdiction includes not only actions between citizens of different states within the United States (Section 1332(a)(1)), but also actions between citizens of the United States and foreign citizens and subjects (Section 1332(a)(2))[b] and actions between citizens of different U.S. states in which foreign litigants are "additional parties" (Section 1332(a)(3)). As with diversity jurisdiction involving United States citizens, a justification for foreign-party jurisdiction is protection of a discrete class of litigants from prejudice in state courts. See Johnson, *Why Alienage Jurisdiction? Historical Foundations and Modern Justifications for Federal Jurisdiction Over Disputes Involving Noncitizens*, 21 Yale J. Int'l L. 1, 2 (1996). For an empirical study of foreign litigant success rates in United States courts, see Clermont & Eisenberg, *Xenophilia or Xenophobia in U.S. Courts? Before and After* 9/11, 4 J. Empirical Legal Stud. 441 (2007). Another justification for foreign-party jurisdiction is to prevent state court rulings from interfering with foreign policy. See JPMorgan Chase Bank v. Traffic Stream (BVI) Infrastructure Limited, 536 U.S. 88, 94, 122 S.Ct. 2054, 2058, 153 L.Ed.2d 95, 101 (2002).

The Terms of the Debate

Granting the historic importance of diversity jurisdiction, does its current utility justify the expenditure of federal resources to hear disputes that pertain exclusively to state law? Whether to retain or enlarge the grant of diversity jurisdiction is a question that continues to engage scholars and policymakers. Here are some statistics from recent decades:

U.S. DISTRICT COURTS. CIVIL CASES FILED, BY JURISDICTION[c]			
FISCAL YEAR	TOTAL	FEDERAL QUESTION	DIVERSITY
1990	217,013	104,307	57,435
2000	259,517	139,624	48,626
2010	282,895	138,655	101,202
2020	470,581	138,455	284,603

---

[b] Some courts and commentators refer to this jurisdictional grant as "alienage jurisdiction." Consistent with the language of Article III and Section 1332 itself, we prefer "foreign-party jurisdiction."

[c] Source: United States Courts, Caseload Statistics Data Tables, Chiefly Table C-2, www.uscourts.gov/statistics-reports/caseload-statistics-data-tables. The large number of diversity cases reported in 2020 is greatly influenced by an enormous multidistrict litigation (MDL) proceeding, In re: 3M Combat Arms Earplug Products Liability Litigation, that began in 2019 and grew to include over 200,000 cases. See 2022 WL 504451, at *5 (N.D.Fla. 2022) (noting "the more than 200,000 cases in this MDL"). MDLs are studied in Chapter 5, Section B & Chapter 8, Section H, infra.

Proposals to curtail or abolish diversity jurisdiction have been made in Congress since the 1920s. See Shapiro, *Federal Diversity Jurisdiction: A Survey and a Proposal*, 91 Harv.L.Rev. 317 (1977). The Report of the Federal Courts Study Committee 38–43 (April 2, 1990), recommended limiting diversity jurisdiction in four ways: (1) prohibiting plaintiffs from invoking diversity jurisdiction in the federal courts of their home states; (2) treating corporations as citizens of every state in which they are licensed to do business; (3) excluding non-economic damages, such as punitive damages, from calculation of the amount-in-controversy; and (4) raising the amount-in-controversy threshold and indexing it to inflation. Looking at the current version of 28 U.S.C. § 1332, which of these proposals have been adopted?

Proposals also have been made to expand the scope of diversity jurisdiction by authorizing jurisdiction even when the *Strawbridge* rule of complete diversity is not met—a condition called minimal diversity. The interpleader statute, 28 U.S.C. § 1335, is the oldest of these legislative changes. Under the statute, the court may exercise diversity jurisdiction over an interpleader action provided a $500 amount-in-controversy requirement is met and at least one claimant is a citizen of a state different from that of the other claimants. In addition, Congress has authorized a federal forum based on minimal diversity for mass accident cases raising state law claims "where at least 75 natural persons have died" from "a single accident" and "at a discrete location." See Multiparty, Multiforum Trial Jurisdiction Act of 2002, 28 U.S.C. §§ 1369, 1441(e). Finally, the Class Action Fairness Act of 2005, 28 U.S.C. §§ 1332(d) and 1453, authorizes a federal forum for any class action in which the aggregate amount-in-controversy exceeds $5 million, when the class contains at least 100 members, and in which any plaintiff "is a citizen of a State different from any defendant," subject to some exceptions. These aggregation devices are studied in Chapters 8 and 9, infra.

Arguments in favor of diversity jurisdiction underscore the persistence of bias against out-of-state litigants and the threat it poses to the administration of justice. Although empirical evidence of parochial bias is sparse, there is concern that curtailing diversity jurisdiction would dampen investor willingness to enter markets in different parts of the country. What matters from this perspective is not whether out-of-state investors in fact receive fair treatment in state courts, but rather whether they *think* they will. See Flango, *Litigant Choice Between State and Federal Courts*, 46 S.C.L.Rev. 961, 965 (1995).

Retention of diversity jurisdiction also is urged as a way to encourage competition between the state and federal court systems and so to motivate judicial reform across the country. Federal courts historically were considered institutionally superior to state courts because of the independence that comes from the judicial life tenure and salary guarantees of Article III, § 1 of the United States Constitution. See Neuborne, *The Myth of Parity*, 90 Harv.L.Rev. 1105 (1977). However, many states now provide similar assurances of judicial independence and have undertaken significant modernization reforms, leading commentators to challenge suggestions of state judicial inferiority. Indeed, on some issues, litigators may prefer a state to a federal forum. See Rubenstein, *The Myth of Superiority*, 16 Const. Comment. 599 (1999). Nevertheless, proponents of diversity jurisdiction contend that out-of-state litigants, who have limited opportunity to work for the improvement of state courts, should be able to avoid exposure to them if they wish.

Finally, diversity jurisdiction is said to encourage substantive legal improvement within the federal system. The metaphor typically used to express this rationale is that of the "cross-pollination" of ideas so that each court system becomes alert to issues across jurisdictional boundaries. See Redish, *Reassessing the Allocation of Judicial Business Between State and Federal Courts: Federal Jurisdiction and "The Martian Chronicles,"* 78 Va.L.Rev. 1769, 1785 (1992).

Critics of diversity jurisdiction focus on the implications of channeling state law disputes to federal judges. Justice Frankfurter expressed concern that diversity jurisdiction contributes to docket congestion in the federal courts. See Frankfurter, *Distribution of Judicial Power Between United States and State Courts*, 13 Cornell L.Q. 499 (1928). Moreover, under the rule of *Erie R.R. Co.*, p. 314, infra, federal courts are required to apply state law to substantive issues in diversity cases, arguably making federal disposition of such cases unnecessary, wasteful, and inappropriate since the state courts are authoritative on matters of state substantive law. Indeed, disposition of state disputes in federal court may threaten nationalizing local concerns and federalizing state law. Far from encouraging legal reform, critics warn, the diversion of diversity-of-citizenship cases to federal courts may retard the development of state law by treating it as static or encouraging influential professional groups to exit the state judicial systems. Finally, it is suggested that the persistence of diversity jurisdiction supports gamesmanship that has little to do with the constitutional justification for authorizing a federal forum.

Assessing whether the federal court may exercise diversity jurisdiction requires a determination of (1) the citizenship of the parties and (2) the amount-in-controversy in the dispute. Both requirements of 28 U.S.C. § 1332 must be met.

1. DETERMINING CITIZENSHIP

MAS v. PERRY

United States Court of Appeals, Fifth Circuit, 1974.
489 F.2d 1396, cert. denied, 419 U.S. 842, 95 S.Ct. 74, 42 L.Ed.2d 70.

AINSWORTH, CIRCUIT JUDGE.

* * *

Appellees Jean Paul Mas, a citizen of France, and Judy Mas were married at her home in Jackson, Mississippi. Prior to their marriage, Mr. and Mrs. Mas were graduate assistants, pursuing coursework as well as performing teaching duties, for approximately nine months and one year, respectively, at Louisiana State University in Baton Rouge, Louisiana. Shortly after their marriage, they returned to Baton Rouge to resume their duties as graduate assistants at LSU. They remained in Baton Rouge for approximately two more years, after which they moved to Park Ridge, Illinois. At the time of the trial in this case, it was their intention to return to Baton Rouge while Mr. Mas finished his studies for the degree of Doctor of Philosophy. Mr. and Mrs. Mas were undecided as to where they would reside after that.

Upon their return to Baton Rouge after their marriage, appellees rented an apartment from appellant Oliver H. Perry, a citizen of Louisiana. This appeal arises from a final judgment entered on a jury verdict awarding $5,000 to Mr. Mas and $15,000 to Mrs. Mas for damages incurred by them as a result of the discovery that their bedroom and bathroom contained "two-way" mirrors and that they had been watched through them by the appellant during three of the first four months of their marriage.

At the close of the appellees' case at trial, appellant made an oral motion to dismiss for lack of jurisdiction. The motion was denied by the district court. Before this Court, appellant challenges the final judgment below solely on jurisdictional grounds, contending that appellees failed to prove diversity of citizenship among the parties and that the requisite jurisdictional amount is lacking with respect to Mr. Mas. Finding no merit to these contentions, we affirm. Under § 1332(a)(2), the federal judicial power extends to the claim of Mr. Mas, a citizen of France, against the appellant, a citizen of Louisiana. Since we conclude that Mrs. Mas is a citizen of Mississippi for diversity purposes, the district court also properly had jurisdiction under § 1332(a)(1) of her claim.

It has long been the general rule that complete diversity of parties is required in order that diversity jurisdiction obtain; that is, no party on one side may be a citizen of the same State as any party on the other side. Strawbridge v. Curtiss * * *. This determination of one's State citizenship for diversity purposes is controlled by federal law, not by the law of any

State. * * * As is the case in other areas of federal jurisdiction, the diverse citizenship among adverse parties must be present at the time the complaint is filed. * * * Jurisdiction is unaffected by subsequent changes in the citizenship of the parties. * * * The burden of pleading the diverse citizenship is upon the party invoking federal jurisdiction * * * and if the diversity jurisdiction is properly challenged, that party also bears the burden of proof.

To be a citizen of a State within the meaning of § 1332, a natural person must be both a citizen of the United States * * * and a domiciliary of that State. * * * For diversity purposes, citizenship means domicile; mere residence in the State is not sufficient. * * *

A person's domicile is the place of "his true, fixed, and permanent home and principal establishment, and to which he has the intention of returning whenever he is absent therefrom . . ." * * * A change of domicile may be effected only by a combination of two elements: (a) taking up residence in a different domicile with (b) the intention to remain there. * * *

It is clear that at the time of her marriage, Mrs. Mas was a domiciliary of the State of Mississippi. While it is generally the case that the domicile of the wife—and, consequently, her State citizenship for purposes of diversity jurisdiction—is deemed to be that of her husband, * * * we find no precedent for extending this concept to the situation here, in which the husband is a citizen of a foreign state but resides in the United States. Indeed, such a fiction would work absurd results on the facts before us. If Mr. Mas were considered a domiciliary of France—as he would be since he had lived in Louisiana as a student-teaching assistant prior to filing this suit * * *—then Mrs. Mas would also be deemed a domiciliary, and thus, fictionally at least, a citizen of France. She would not be a citizen of any State and could not sue in a federal court on that basis; nor could she invoke the alienage jurisdiction to bring her claim in federal court, since she is not an alien. * * * On the other hand, if Mrs. Mas's domicile were Louisiana, she would become a Louisiana citizen for diversity purposes and could not bring suit with her husband against appellant, also a Louisiana citizen, on the basis of diversity jurisdiction. These are curious results under a rule arising from the theoretical identity of person and interest of the married couple. * * *

An American woman is not deemed to have lost her United States citizenship solely by reason of her marriage to an alien. 8 U.S.C. § 1489. Similarly, we conclude that for diversity purposes a woman does not have her domicile or State citizenship changed solely by reason of her marriage to an alien.

Mrs. Mas's Mississippi domicile was disturbed neither by her year in Louisiana prior to her marriage nor as a result of the time she and her husband spent at LSU after their marriage, since for both periods she was a graduate assistant at LSU. * * * Though she testified that after her marriage she had no intention of returning to her parents' home in Mississippi, Mrs. Mas did not effect a change of domicile since she and Mr. Mas were in Louisiana only as students and lacked the requisite intention to remain there. * * * Until she acquires a new domicile, she remains a domiciliary, and thus a citizen of Mississippi. * * *

[The court's discussion of the jurisdictional amount is omitted.]

Thus the power of the federal district court to entertain the claims of appellees in this case stands on two separate legs of diversity jurisdiction: a claim by an alien against a State citizen; and an action between citizens of different States. We also note, however, the propriety of having the federal district court entertain a spouse's action against a defendant, where the district court already has jurisdiction over a claim, arising from the same transaction, by the other spouse against the same defendant. * * * In the case before us, such a result is particularly desirable. The claims of Mr. and Mrs. Mas arise from the same operative facts, and there was almost complete interdependence between their claims with respect to the proof required and the issues raised at trial. Thus, since the district court had jurisdiction of Mr. Mas's action, sound judicial administration militates strongly in favor of federal jurisdiction of Mrs. Mas's claim.

Affirmed.

NOTES AND QUESTIONS

(1) Determining State Citizenship of Natural Persons

The party invoking diversity jurisdiction has the burden of proving its existence. For purposes of diversity jurisdiction, a natural person is a citizen of a U.S. state only if the person is a citizen of the United States. The rule stems from DRED SCOTT v. SANDFORD, 60 U.S. (19 How.) 393, 15 L.Ed. 691 (1856), which held that persons descended from African slaves, even if born free, were not United States citizens and could not invoke diversity jurisdiction. The Fourteenth Amendment abrogated portions of *Dred Scott* by establishing the principle of birth-right citizenship, but did not eliminate the rule that "[a] person cannot be a 'citizen' of a state unless she is also a citizen of the United States." Coury v. Prot, 85 F.3d 244, 249 (5th Cir. 1996). Of course, diversity jurisdiction may reach foreign citizens if the requirements of Section 1332(a)(2) or (a)(3) are met. See Servicios Azucareros de Venezuela, C.A. v. John Deere Thibodaux, Inc., 702 F.3d 794 (5th Cir. 2012).

To determine a United States citizen's state of citizenship, the test looks to the party's domicile, which is different from residence. At the time of the *Mas* decision, federal courts applied the common law rule of "derivative domicile" to married women, meaning that a wife was deemed to have acquired her husband's domicile. Why did the *Mas* court resist applying this rule in determining whether the wife met the conditions of diversity jurisdiction?

Would its application have effectively stripped the wife of her United States citizenship? See Abrams & Barber, *Domicile Dismantled*, 92 Ind.L.J. 387 (2017). Modern cases have rejected this rule even when both spouses are United States citizens and the issue is state citizenship. See Holley v. Techtronic Indus. N. Am., Inc., 2016 WL 7474811 (N.D.Cal. 2016) ("[T]he common law rule has been rejected by modern cases; a spouse may establish a domicile separate from the other spouse."); 13E Wright & Miller, Federal Practice and Procedure § 3614 (3d ed.) ("It is difficult to find any justification for the retention of * * * what essentially is a sex-biased rule that certainly will disappear eventually.").

Determining a natural person's domicile may involve a fact-intensive inquiry. CONNECTU LLC v. ZUCKERBERG, 482 F.Supp.2d 3 (D.Mass. 2007), reversed by 522 F.3d 82 (1st Cir. 2008), involved the citizenship of Mark Zuckerberg, the founder of Facebook. The evidence showed that Zuckerberg was born in New York, graduated from a high school in New Hampshire, attended college in Massachusetts, and lived in California the summer after his sophomore year. After taking a leave of absence from college, defendant returned to California, where his company was incorporated. He continued to use his parents' New York address as a permanent residence. On these facts, how would you decide where defendant resided and whether he intended to change his domicile?

If the goal of diversity jurisdiction is to protect out-of-staters from bias in suits against in-staters, does it make sense to disregard residence in defining citizenship for diversity purposes? Should a party who is a United States citizen but is domiciled abroad be eligible to invoke diversity jurisdiction?

(2) Determining Citizenship of Corporations and Associations

Different rules for determining citizenship apply when the party is a corporation or an association. Like a natural person, a corporation is treated as an entity for purposes of determining citizenship; unlike a natural person, a corporation may have multiple states of citizenship. See 28 U.S.C. § 1332(c)(1). A corporation is a citizen "of every State and foreign state" in which it is incorporated, as well as *the* state or foreign state in which it has its principal place of business. For many years, it was unclear how to determine the location of a corporation's principal place of business. Three tests predominated: the "nerve-center" test, which located citizenship in the state in which corporate decisionmaking and overall control take place (normally, the corporation's headquarters); the "corporate activities" or "operating assets" test, which located citizenship in the state in which the corporation has its production or service activities; and the "total activity" test, which located citizenship in light of all of the facts and circumstances.

In HERTZ CORP. v. FRIEND, 559 U.S. 77, 130 S.Ct. 1181, 175 L.Ed.2d 1029 (2010), the Supreme Court resolved that the phrase "principal place of business" in 28 U.S.C. § 1332(c)(1) refers only to the corporation's nerve center. In reaching this result, the Court relied on three grounds: the terms of the statute; the legislative history; and the simplicity of a clear rule that could discourage gamesmanship. Under *Hertz*, how should a court determine the citizenship of a dissolved corporation? Would it be best to have a bright-line rule that looks only to the company's state of incorporation? Or for the dissolved corporation also to be treated as a citizen of the state of its former principal place of business? Or for the dissolved corporation not to have any principal place of business? The circuits currently are divided on this question. Which approach best serves the purposes of diversity jurisdiction?

Special rules govern the citizenship of banks chartered under federal law—so-called "national banks." The statute, 28 U.S.C. § 1348, provides that national banks are "deemed citizens of the States in which they are respectively located." How does this definition differ from the general rule for determining corporate citizenship? In WACHOVIA BANK, N.A. v. SCHMIDT, 546 U.S. 303, 126 S.Ct. 941, 163 L.Ed.2d 797 (2006), the Supreme Court interpreted the term "located" to mean that a national bank is a citizen of the state in which its main office is found, as set out in the articles of incorporation. The Court left open whether for diversity jurisdiction a national bank also is a citizen of the state in which it has its principal place of business. See Lund, *Federally Chartered Corporations and Federal Jurisdiction*, 36 Fla.St.U.L.Rev. 317 (2009).

Keep in mind that there are many different kinds of corporations—non-profit corporations, professional corporations, and cooperative corporations, to name a few. To complicate matters, some business groups that are not incorporated nevertheless function like a corporation (such as a limited partnerships). Generally, courts have applied a "bright line rule," Hoagland v. Sandberg, Phoenix & Von Gontard, P.C., 385 F.3d 737 (7th Cir. 2004), and held that for purposes of diversity jurisdiction, "a corporation is a corporation is a corporation." Cote v. Wadel, 796 F.2d 961, 963 (7th Cir. 1986). This means if a business organization is incorporated under state law, it is treated as a corporate entity and not as an unincorporated association.

The category of unincorporated association includes many different kinds of groups. These include partnerships, charitable organizations, and trade unions. Under the general diversity rules, an unincorporated association is not treated as an entity but rather takes on the citizenship of each and every one of the association's members. See Carden v. Arkoma Assocs., 494 U.S. 185, 110 S.Ct. 1015, 108 L.Ed.2d 157 (1990) (limited partnership); United Steelworkers of America v. R.H. Bouligny, Inc., 382 U.S. 145, 86 S.Ct. 272, 15 L.Ed.2d 217 (1965) (trade union). How are unincorporated associations treated for diversity purposes under the Class Action Fairness Act? See 28 U.S.C. § 1332(d)(10).

In AMERICOLD REALTY TRUST v. CONAGRA FOODS, INC., 577 U.S. 378, 136 S.Ct. 1012, 194 L.Ed.2d 71 (2016), the Supreme Court held that the citizenship of a real estate investment trust is based on the citizenship of its members, which includes its shareholders, rejecting the view that only the citizenship of the trustee was jurisdictionally significant. The Court emphasized that it intended to maintain a "doctrinal wall" between corporate and unincorporated entities. Id. at 384, 136 S.Ct. at 1017, 194 L.Ed.2d at 77.

(3) Determining Citizenship of Representatives, Guardians, and Insurance Companies

Some persons can appear in court only through a legal representative. Examples include a decedent's estate, an infant, and a person who lacks mental competence. In 1988, Congress amended 28 U.S.C. § 1332 to block parties from manufacturing diversity jurisdiction through the appointment of a representative. See Mullenix, *Creative Manipulation of Federal Jurisdiction: Is There Diversity After Death?*, 70 Cornell L.Rev. 1011 (1985) (discussing the uncertainty surrounding this issue prior to the 1988 amendment). How does the current statute determine citizenship when a representative is appointed? How can a representative show that a person who has been found incompetent wishes to change domicile? See Upchurch, *Can Granny Have a New Home? Resolving the Dilemma of Dementia and Domicile in Federal Diversity Jurisdiction Cases*, 79 U. Colo.L.Rev. 545 (2008).

Another special situation is presented by the "direct-action case," in which the victim of an accident sues the tortfeasor's insurance carrier without naming the insured party whose wrongdoing gave rise to the claim. How does the citizenship rule for insurers in direct-action cases differ from the rules that apply to guardians and other representatives? See 28 U.S.C. § 1332(c)(1).

(4) Determining Jurisdiction in Cases Involving Foreign Parties

Diversity jurisdiction also is available in actions involving citizens of foreign countries and parties who are United States citizens. See 28 U.S.C. § 1332(a)(2) and (3). Section 1332(a)(2) requires complete diversity between citizens of U.S. states and citizens of foreign countries. See Ruhrgas AG v. Marathon Oil Co., 526 U.S. 574, 580 n.2, 119 S.Ct. 1563, 1568 n.2, 143 L.Ed.2d 760, 768 n.2 (1999). Section 1332(a)(3) permits foreign citizens on opposing sides of the case, as long as there are citizens of U.S. states on opposing sides and complete diversity exists between those U.S. citizens. See 28 U.S.C. § 1332(a)(3) (authorizing jurisdiction in actions that are between "citizens of different States and in which citizens or subjects of a foreign state are additional parties"); see also Iraola & CIA S.A. v. Kimberly-Clark Corp., 232 F.3d 854, 860 (11th Cir. 2000) ("It is a standard rule that federal courts do not have diversity jurisdiction over cases where there are foreign entities on both sides of the action, without the presence of citizens of a state on both sides.").

Test your reading of the statute by explaining whether jurisdiction is present under any of Section 1332(a)'s subsections:

(a) Two plaintiffs [a company that is incorporated and has its principal place of business in Indiana] and [a company that is incorporated in Mexico] sue two defendants [a company that is incorporated in Delaware and has its principal place of business in Illinois] and [a natural person who is a citizen of Mexico].

(b) Two plaintiffs [a company that is incorporated and has its principal place of business in Indiana] and [a natural person who is a citizen of Canada] sue two defendants [a company that is incorporated and has its principal place of business in Michigan] and [a natural person who is a citizen of Canada].

(c)   Two plaintiffs [a natural person who is a citizen of New York] and [a natural person who is a citizen of France] sue one defendant [a natural person who is a citizen of France].

The statute's treatment of foreign citizens who are "permanent residents" of the United States has evolved over time. In 1988 Congress amended 28 U.S.C. § 1332(a) to add this language: "For the purpose of this section, section 1335, and section 1441, an alien admitted to the United States for permanent residence shall be deemed a citizen of the State in which such alien is domiciled." See Judicial Improvements and Access to Justice Act, Pub. L. No. 100–702, 102 Stat. 4642 (1988). Then, in 2011, Congress deleted this language and instead added at the end of 28 U.S.C. § 1332(a)(2): "except that the district courts shall not have original jurisdiction under this subsection of an action between citizens of a State and citizens or subjects of a foreign state who are lawfully admitted for permanent residence in the United States and are domiciled in the same State." See Section 105 of the Federal Courts Jurisdiction and Venue Clarification Act of 2011, Pub. L. 112–63, 125 Stat. 758 (2011). The legislative history states:

> The purpose of th[e 1988] change was to preclude Federal alienage jurisdiction . . . in suits between a citizen of a state and an alien permanently residing in the same state . . . . Section 101 of the [Clarification Act will] thus achieve the goal of modestly restricting jurisdiction, *which Congress sought to accomplish when it first enacted the resident alien proviso*, and would avoid the threat of the expansion of jurisdiction now posed by the proviso.

H.R.Rep. No. 112–10, at 7 (2011), quoted in H.K. Huilin International Trade Co., Ltd. v. Kevin Multiline Plymer Inc., 907 F.Supp.2d 284, 288 (E.D.N.Y. 2012) (alteration and emphasis added by the court); see also Tagger v. Strauss Grp. Ltd., 951 F.3d 124, 126–27 (2d Cir. 2020) (finding no jurisdiction over a suit brought by an Israeli citizen who was a permanent resident of the United States domiciled in New York against an Israeli corporation, because the 2011 amendment eliminated the provision that had deemed foreign-citizen permanent residents to be citizens of the U.S. state where they are domiciled).

Would there be a constitutional problem in extending diversity jurisdiction to a suit by a foreign-citizen permanent resident of the United States who is domiciled in State A against another foreign-citizen permanent resident of the United States who is domiciled in State B? Or by a permanent resident who is domiciled in a U.S. state against a foreign citizen who is domiciled abroad?

A separate question concerns whether diversity jurisdiction may include a "stateless" person—meaning an individual who is not a citizen of any country. In BLAIR HOLDINGS CORP. v. RUBINSTEIN, 133 F.Supp. 496 (S.D.N.Y.1955), defendant, Serge Rubinstein, held a "Nansen" passport issued after World War I by the League of Nations to stateless persons; he also had registered as a stateless person with the United States Department of Justice. In addition, the complaint described defendant as "not [being] a citizen of the United States." Id. at 498. The district court held that there was no jurisdiction under 28 U.S.C. § 1332(a)(2) because plaintiff failed to show he was a citizen of a foreign state. Does withholding a federal forum from a stateless person serve the purposes of foreign-party jurisdiction? Some critics argue that being stateless makes a litigant more vulnerable to bias in state court, heightening the need for a federal forum. See Chemerinsky, Federal Jurisdiction § 5.3 (8th ed.).

The term "stateless" can also refer to a person who is neither a citizen of a foreign state nor a citizen of a state of the United States. Consider citizens of the United States who are domiciled abroad. As United States citizens, such persons are not citizens or subjects of a foreign state. Yet they also are not citizens of any particular state of the United States, because they are not domiciled in any state. See Newman-Green, Inc. v. Alfonzo-Larrain, 490 U.S. 826, 828, 109 S.Ct. 2218, 2221, 104 L.Ed.2d 893, 899 (1989) ("In order to be a citizen of a State within the meaning of the diversity statute, a natural person must both be a citizen of the United States and be domiciled within the State."). As one court has explained, federal courts "lack jurisdiction over these so-called 'stateless' citizens if the only basis for subject matter jurisdiction is the diversity statute." Page v. Democratic Nat'l Comm., 2 F.4th 630, 636 (7th Cir. 2021); see also Cresswell v. Sullivan & Cromwell, 922 F.2d 60, 68 (2d Cir. 1990).

Finally, consider how the jurisdictional rules so far studied apply to a "dual national"—a person who is a citizen of the United States and of a foreign country. In SADAT v. MERTES, 615 F.2d 1176 (7th Cir. 1980), the court of appeals considered whether a litigant who was both a citizen of Egypt and a naturalized citizen of the United States met the requirements of diversity jurisdiction. Plaintiff was involved in a car accident while living in Pennsylvania. He returned to Egypt and later filed suit against the United States parties involved in the accident. The court of appeals held that plaintiff could not invoke Section 1332(a)(1) because he was domiciled in Egypt and so was not a citizen of any state; moreover, he could not invoke Section 1332(a)(2) because, although an Egyptian citizen, his United States citizenship was dominant given his voluntary naturalization and intent to return to the United States. The consensus view is that only the United States citizenship of a dual citizen should count in determining whether foreign-party jurisdiction may be invoked. The Seventh Circuit has explained:

> [T]he major purpose of alienage jurisdiction is to promote international relations by assuring other countries that litigation involving their nationals will be treated at the national level, and alienage jurisdiction is also intended to allow foreign subjects to avoid real or perceived bias in the state courts—a justification that should not be available to the dual citizen who is an American.

Buchel-Ruegsegger v. Buchel, 576 F.3d 451, 454 (7th Cir. 2009) (quotations omitted). Do you agree that a dual national "who is an American" is less likely to be subject to "real or perceived bias" in state courts?

(5) The Problem of Collusive Joinder and the Real Party in Interest

Sometimes a party may wish to litigate a state-law claim in federal court, but the requirement of complete diversity is not met. In KRAMER v. CARIBBEAN MILLS, INC., 394 U.S. 823, 89 S.Ct. 1487, 23 L.Ed.2d 9 (1969), a Panamanian corporation assigned its interest under a contract with a Haitian corporation to Kramer, a Texas attorney, for $1. By a separate agreement, Kramer reassigned 95 percent of any net recovery on the assigned cause of action to the Panamanian company. Kramer then commenced suit against the Haitian company invoking federal jurisdiction. The district court denied defendant's motion to dismiss for want of jurisdiction. The court of appeals reversed, holding that the assignment was "improperly or collusively made" within the meaning of 28 U.S.C. § 1359. The Supreme Court affirmed, holding that:

> If federal jurisdiction could be created by assignments of this kind, which are easy to arrange and involve few disadvantages for the assignor, then a vast quantity of ordinary contract and tort litigation could be channeled into the federal courts at the will of one of the parties. Such "manufacture of Federal jurisdiction" was the very thing which Congress intended to prevent when it enacted § 1359 and its predecessors.

Id. at 828–29, 89 S.Ct. at 1490, 23 L.Ed.2d at 14. See Collins, *Jurisdictional Exceptionalism*, 93 Va.L.Rev. 1829 (2007) (recounting the history of the Court's approach to jurisdiction by assignment). Should the motive for making the assignment be relevant to the jurisdictional inquiry, or should it be dispositive that the party making the assignment retains a significant financial interest in the transaction?

On the other hand, sometimes a party may wish to litigate a state-law claim in state court and not in federal court. In this situation, plaintiff may try to block defendant's right to remove the action to federal court. We study removal jurisdiction later in this chapter, but the basic rule is that the federal court can exercise removal jurisdiction if it could have exercised original jurisdiction on the day the suit was first filed in state court (however, when diversity jurisdiction is the basis for removal, generally an in-state defendant may not remove). In ROSE v. GIAMATTI, 721 F.Supp. 906 (S.D.Ohio 1989), Pete Rose, the manager of the Cincinnati Reds baseball team, filed a state court action to enjoin the Commissioner of Baseball from investigating whether Rose had wagered on ball games in violation of the Rules of Major League Baseball. Rose also named Major League Baseball and the Cincinnati Reds as defendants. The Commissioner removed the action to federal district court in Ohio. Rose, a citizen of Ohio, sought to remand the suit to Ohio state court, arguing that because he was a citizen of the same state as two of the defendants, complete diversity was lacking and removal was not proper. The district court rejected this argument:

> [I]t is * * * a long-established doctrine that a federal court in its determination of whether there is diversity of citizenship between the parties, must disregard nominal or formal parties to the action, and determine jurisdiction based solely upon the citizenship of the real parties to the controversy. * * * A real party in interest defendant is one who, by the substantive law, has the duty sought to be enforced or enjoined. * * * [A] formal or nominal party is one who, in a genuine legal sense, has no interest in the result of the suit, * * * or no actual interest or control over the subject matter of the litigation. * * *

Id. at 914. The court went on to explain:

> [T]he controversy in this case is between plaintiff Rose and defendant Giamatti; that they are the real parties in interest in this case; that the Cincinnati Reds and Major League Baseball, are, at best, nominal parties in this controversy; and that, consequently, the citizenship of the Cincinnati Reds and Major League Baseball may be disregarded for diversity of citizenship purposes. The Court determines that diversity of citizenship exists between Rose * * * and Commissioner Giamatti * * * and that the Court has diversity subject matter jurisdiction over this action.

Id. at 923–24. Do you agree that the Cincinnati Reds and Major League Baseball were "nominal" parties? Why was Rose so anxious to keep the case in state court? Is *Rose* the prototypical case in which diversity jurisdiction serves to protect an out-of-state defendant against local prejudice? See Case Note, *"Root, Root, Root for the Home Team": Pete Rose, Nominal Parties and Diversity Jurisdiction*, 66 N.Y.U.L.Rev. 148 (1991).

2. THE AMOUNT-IN-CONTROVERSY REQUIREMENT

Since the First Judiciary Act of 1789, Congress has conditioned the exercise of diversity jurisdiction on an amount-in-controversy requirement. Originally set at an amount that exceeds $500, today the amount must exceed $75,000, exclusive of interest and costs. See 28 U.S.C. § 1332(a). Article III of the federal Constitution does not impose this condition, and Congress eliminated the requirement from 28 U.S.C. § 1331 (the statute governing federal question jurisdiction, discussed in Section C, infra) in 1980. What do you think accounts for the persistence of the dollar condition on the exercise of diversity jurisdiction?

A.F.A. TOURS, INC. v. WHITCHURCH

United States Court of Appeals, Second Circuit, 1991.
937 F.2d 82.

KEARSE, CIRCUIT JUDGE. Plaintiff A.F.A. Tours, Inc., doing business as Alumni Flights Abroad ("AFA"), appeals from a final judgment of the

United States District Court for the Southern District of New York * * * dismissing for lack of subject matter jurisdiction this diversity action against defendant Desmond Whitchurch for misappropriation of trade secrets. The district court summarily dismissed the complaint on the ground that it would not be possible for AFA to prove damages amounting to more than $50,000. * * *

* * * AFA operates a travel and tour business, specializing in deluxe tours for United States residents to overseas destinations including Australia, New Zealand, and New Guinea. It expended large sums of money and invested significant time and labor to develop, *inter alia,* a client and customer list, marketing information, and tour information. It regarded this information as confidential trade secrets.

From 1972 through 1989, Whitchurch was employed by AFA as its exclusive tour escort in the above areas. In that position, Whitchurch was privy to certain of the above confidential information. The complaint alleged that in or about October 1989, Whitchurch resigned from AFA, misappropriated the confidential information known to him, and organized his own tour business. Since that time, he has offered or intends to offer tours that compete with those offered by AFA; in connection with his own tours, he has solicited or intends to solicit participants from AFA's customer list.

AFA commenced the present diversity action in the district court for misappropriation of its trade secrets, seeking an injunction against any use by Whitchurch of confidential AFA information, and damages "in an amount which is not presently ascertainable, but which is believed to exceed the sum of $50,000.00."[d] It also sought punitive damages of "no less than $250,000.00."

* * *

At the oral argument of Whitchurch's motion, Whitchurch's attorney began by characterizing the motion as "turn[ing] on a very narrow issue" of whether the AFA information constituted trade secrets * * *, and stating that the case was important to Whitchurch because "he may one day in the future wish to organize a tour, and write letters to individuals again" * * *. The court, however, asked whether it even had to reach the question of trade secrets, raising sua sponte the question of whether the value of AFA's claims exceeded $50,000, a jurisdictional prerequisite for a diversity action. In response to the court's jurisdictional question, Whitchurch's attorney stated that Whitchurch, in soliciting for his planned tour, had written to 100–200 former AFA tour participants but had received favorable responses from only two. * * *

---

[d] At the time of the lawsuit, the amount-in-controversy requirement was a sum that exceeded $50,000.

AFA's attorney argued that Whitchurch's lack of success on his first effort was hardly dispositive of the issue of the amount of damages AFA might suffer, in light of Whitchurch's desire to conduct other tours in the future. * * * AFA's attorney, noting that over the years Whitchurch had escorted some 1,500 AFA clients on tours and had indicated that he would conduct a number of tours, argued that AFA's damages would be substantial. He stated that a single 10-customer tour to the area in question would easily generate more than $50,000 * * *. * * *

At the close of this hearing, the court granted summary judgment in favor of Whitchurch * * *. * * * On appeal, AFA contends that the dismissal for lack of jurisdiction was improper because the court (1) failed to give AFA an appropriate opportunity to show that it satisfied the jurisdictional amount, and (2) failed to apply the proper standard to AFA's requests for (a) damages and (b) injunctive relief. * * *

The district courts have jurisdiction over civil diversity suits "where the matter in controversy exceeds the sum or value of $50,000, exclusive of interest and costs." 28 U.S.C. § 1332 (1988). The test for determining whether a plaintiff meets the jurisdictional amount, established by the Supreme Court in *St. Paul Mercury Indemnity Co. v. Red Cab Co.*, 303 U.S. 283, 58 S.Ct. 586, 82 L.Ed. 845 (1938), is as follows:

> The rule governing dismissal for want of jurisdiction in cases brought in the federal court is that, unless the law gives a different rule, the sum claimed by the plaintiff controls if the claim is apparently made in good faith. It must appear *to a legal certainty* that the claim is really for less than the jurisdictional amount to justify a dismissal.

303 U.S. at 288–89, 58 S.Ct. at 590 (emphasis added).

The amount of damages recoverable in an action for misappropriation of trade secrets may be measured either by the plaintiff's losses, * * * or by the profits unjustly received by the defendant * * *. In addition, if punitive damages are permitted under the controlling law, the demand for such damages may be included in determining whether the jurisdictional amount is satisfied. * * * New York law apparently allows the recovery of punitive damages in a trade secrets case if the defendant's conduct has been sufficiently "gross and wanton." * * *

Further, in appropriate circumstances, the owner of trade secrets may obtain an injunction against their use or disclosure by another in breach of his confidential relationship with the owner. * * * Where the plaintiff seeks injunctive relief, the value of his claim is generally assessed with reference to the right he seeks to protect and measured by the extent of the impairment to be prevented by the injunction. * * * In calculating that impairment, the court may look not only at past losses but also at potential harm. * * *

Before making a determination that the plaintiff's claim does not meet the jurisdictional minimum, the court must afford the plaintiff an "appropriate and reasonable opportunity to show good faith in believing that a recovery in excess of [the jurisdictional amount] is reasonably possible." * * * Under these substantive and procedural principles, although the record indicates that AFA has not yet suffered actual damages even approaching $50,000, we have difficulty with the district court's decision.

First, though AFA did not make an evidentiary showing in support of its contention that the value of its claims exceeded $50,000, it was not afforded a proper opportunity to do so. The issue of the jurisdictional amount was first raised by the district court sua sponte at the argument on the summary judgment motion, and the court rendered its decision at the end of that argument. To the extent that the court thought AFA could not meet the jurisdictional minimum, it should not have dismissed without giving AFA an opportunity to present substantiation directed toward that issue.

Second, despite AFA's lack of an opportunity to present evidence addressed directly to the jurisdictional question, there was evidence in the record to suggest that the matter could not be conclusively resolved against it, for the oral arguments made by AFA's attorney to show that its claims were worth more than $50,000 had some support from documents already before the court. For example, he said Whitchurch had the names of some 1,500 AFA customers; this was consistent with (a) Whitchurch's own statement that in the 17 years he was employed by AFA he had led approximately seven tours each year (thus totaling some 119 tours) and (b) his attorney's statement that there were usually 10–15 people per tour. * * * As to AFA's attorney's estimate that a single tour of this type "[i]s about seven to ten thousand dollars per customer," the evidence in the record as to the destination and deluxe nature of the tours, including evidence that some participants traveled first class and reserved preferred hotel accommodations, supports an inference that a 28-day tour could well cost $10,000 per person.

What this means in terms of loss of earnings to a tour operator, however, is not revealed by the present record. AFA's suggestion that the tour operator himself would earn $10,000 per tourist * * * does not have the same record support and seems questionable. The district court was also undoubtedly correct in its assumption that many of the persons who traveled to the South Pacific with Whitchurch during the 17 years he was with AFA are not likely to travel to that area again. But it could not be said to a legal certainty that no one would return to that area. There was ample support in the record for the proposition that AFA has the prospects for repeat customers. For example, AFA had submitted from one of its brochures two pages excerpting comments from participants in a recent

AFA tour * * *; nearly one-third of those quoted indicated that they either had been on other AFA tours or would hope to go on future AFA tours. * * * If a tour operator could earn 17% of the price of a tour, and if Whitchurch were eventually successful in soliciting even 30 of the approximately 1,500 AFA participants he has escorted (*i.e.*, 2%, which may reflect the ratio of his success on his first attempt), the profit he could siphon from AFA would total $51,000. Thus, on the present record, the court could not conclude to a legal certainty that the value of AFA's claims did not exceed the jurisdictional minimum.

Further, AFA requested injunctive relief not just against Whitchurch's solicitation of its customers but also against any use of the information. Presumably such an injunction would include a prohibition against Whitchurch's sale or disclosure of the names and addresses of AFA's customers to other tour operators who might be better equipped than Whitchurch to exploit the information and attract more than 2% of the persons whose names Whitchurch could provide them. In addition, AFA's request for punitive damages in the amount of $250,000 might provide a basis for satisfaction of the jurisdictional amount. Whether or not AFA will be able to prove that Whitchurch's conduct was "gross and wanton" and warrants the recovery of such damages under New York law is an open question. But the present record does not foreclose that possibility.

In all the circumstances, we conclude that the record as it existed in the district court did not permit the court to find with legal certainty that the value of AFA's claims did not exceed $50,000.

* * *

NOTES AND QUESTIONS

1.   The party invoking diversity jurisdiction has the burden of showing that the amount-in-controversy requirement is met at the time the suit commences. In meeting this burden, the Supreme Court has established a rule that "the sum claimed by the plaintiff controls if the claim is apparently made in good faith. It must appear to a legal certainty that the claim is really for less than the jurisdictional amount to justify dismissal." ST. PAUL MERCURY INDEMNITY CO. v. RED CAB CO., 303 U.S. 283, 288–89, 58 S.Ct. 586, 590, 82 L.Ed. 845, 848 (1938) (footnotes omitted). Under what circumstances could a court find to a legal certainty that a party's claim does not meet the amount-in-controversy requirement?

2.   Is diversity jurisdiction lost if plaintiff's recovery turns out to be less than the amount-in-controversy requirement? See 28 U.S.C. § 1332(b). Should events that take place after the filing of the complaint ever be relevant to the jurisdictional inquiry? Might some post-filing events suggest that an allegation about injuries or damages was made in bad faith? See Hall v. Earthlink Network, Inc., 396 F.3d 500 (2d Cir. 2005).

3.   The Federal Rules authorize the joinder of multiple parties and multiple claims in a single lawsuit. See Chapter 8, infra. Many joinder variations are possible. For example, a single plaintiff may wish to file multiple claims against a single defendant, or multiple plaintiffs may wish to file multiple claims against a single defendant, and so forth. Courts have developed a number of rules, referred to as rules of aggregation, for determining when the amount-in-controversy requirement is met in the complex situations that typically arise. See Gensler, *Diversity Class Actions, Common Relief, and the Rule of Individual Valuation*, 82 Or.L.Rev. 295 (2003).

Generally, when a single plaintiff sues a single defendant, plaintiff can aggregate the value of all of its claims against defendant to meet the amount-in-controversy requirement. The claims need not share common questions of law or fact; aggregation is permitted "even when those claims share nothing in common besides the identity of the parties." Everett v. Verizon Wireless, Inc., 460 F.3d 818, 822 (6th Cir. 2006). By contrast, when multiple plaintiffs sue a single defendant, they can aggregate their claims for purposes of meeting the amount-in-controversy requirement only if their claims are common and indivisible. Whether claims are common and indivisible turns on whether the parties seek "to enforce a single title or right." Troy Bank v. G.A. Whitehead & Co., 222 U.S. 39, 40, 32 S.Ct. 9, 9, 56 L.Ed. 81, 82 (1911). As the Fifth Circuit explained in an influential decision:

> To aggregate claims of several plaintiffs the plaintiffs must have a "common and undivided interest," though it may be separable as between themselves. But where their interests are distinct, and their only relationship is that "they form a class of parties whose rights or liabilities arose out of the same transaction, or have a relation to a common fund or mass or property sought to be administered, such distinct demands or liabilities cannot be aggregated * * *." Clay v. Field, 138 U.S. 464, 11 S.Ct. 419, 34 L.Ed. 1044 (1891).

Eagle Star Ins. Co. v. Maltes, 313 F.2d 778, 780 (5th Cir. 1963). On the other hand, if the claims of multiple plaintiffs are joint and severable, plaintiffs may not aggregate them to meet the jurisdictional amount. Typically, then, tort claims by multiple plaintiffs may not be aggregated to meet the amount-in-controversy requirement—even if they arise from the same transaction. See, e.g., Travelers Property Casualty v. Good, 689 F.3d 714, 720 (7th Cir. 2012) ("[W]here the plaintiffs' claims are cognizable, calculable, and correctable individually—say, personal injuries arising from mass torts—they are clearly separate and distinct and may not be aggregated to meet the amount in controversy." (citations and internal quotation marks omitted)).

4.   Consider whether the amount-in-controversy requirement for diversity jurisdiction is met in the following cases and whether you need additional information to answer the question:

(a)   One plaintiff sues one defendant, claiming $40,000 in property damage and $45,000 for personal injury resulting from the same accident.

(b)   One plaintiff sues one defendant on two unrelated claims, one
      for $40,000 and the other for $45,000.

(c)   Two plaintiffs sue one defendant, each seeking $40,000 in
      damages.

(d)   Two plaintiffs sue one defendant, jointly seeking $80,000 in
      damages.

(e)   One plaintiff sues two defendants, seeking $40,000 from each
      defendant.

(f)   Two plaintiffs sue one defendant on the same issue. One plaintiff
      seeks $45,000 in damages; the other seeks $35,000.

5.   The question of how to value non-damages relief such as a declaratory
judgment or injunction has divided the courts of appeals. The majority rule is
that the jurisdictional amount is tested by the value to plaintiff of the relief
sought, but some courts have held that the larger of either the worth of the
relief to plaintiff or its cost to defendant should control. See Pinahs, *Diversity
Jurisdiction and Injunctive Relief: Using a "Moving-Party Approach" to Value
the Amount in Controversy*, 95 Minn.L.Rev. 1930 (2011).

3.   JUDICIALLY CREATED EXCEPTIONS TO DIVERSITY JURISDICTION

Even if the requirements of diversity jurisdiction are met, a federal
court generally will decline to hear a case that involves domestic relations
or probate matters.

The Supreme Court addressed the source and scope of the domestic
relations exception in ANKENBRANDT v. RICHARDS, 504 U.S. 689, 112
S.Ct. 2206, 119 L.Ed.2d 468 (1992), in which a mother alleged that her
daughters had been physically and sexually abused by their father and his
female companion. The Court found that the Constitution "does not
mandate the exclusion of domestic relations cases from federal-court
jurisdiction," but that federal courts nevertheless should decline to hear
divorce, alimony, and child custody cases under 28 U.S.C. § 1332 as a
matter of policy and longstanding judicial practice. In so holding, the Court
underscored the fact that state judicial systems "are more eminently suited
to work of this type than are federal courts." Id. at 697, 704, 112 S.Ct. at
2212, 2215, 119 L.Ed.2d at 478, 482. Nevertheless, the Court held that the
exception did not warrant abstention in a suit involving an intra-familial
tort. See Resnik, *"Naturally" Without Gender: Women, Jurisdiction, and
the Federal Courts*, 66 N.Y.U.L.Rev. 1682 (1991).

The Supreme Court addressed and clarified the limited nature of the
probate exception in MARSHALL v. MARSHALL, 547 U.S. 293, 126 S.Ct.
1735, 164 L.Ed.2d 480 (2006), a bankruptcy proceeding concerning the
estate of J. Howard Marshall II. Marshall died in 1994, leaving his entire

estate to a son and nothing to his widow, who was not the son's mother and was significantly younger than decedent. Two years later, while the estate was subject to proceedings in a Texas probate court, the widow filed for bankruptcy in the U.S. Bankruptcy Court for the Central District of California. In that latter case, the son filed a claim, asserting that the widow had defamed him. The widow counterclaimed, alleging that the son had tortiously interfered with a substantial gift of money she expected from her husband. The bankruptcy court, finding it had authority to enter a final judgment on these claims, dismissed the son's claim and found for the widow, awarding her nearly $500 million. The son filed a post-trial motion, alleging that the widow's claim could only be heard in the Texas probate court. After review in the district court, the Ninth Circuit held that under the "probate exception" to federal court jurisdiction, federal courts cannot take subject-matter jurisdiction over claims that involve the validity of a decedent's estate planning instrument, and that this exception also includes tort claims that do not directly involve any probate issues.

The Supreme Court granted certiorari and reversed. Justice Ginsburg, writing for a unanimous Court, held that the widow's claim, seeking damages for a "widely recognized tort," id. at 312, 126 S.Ct. at 1748, 164 L.Ed.2d at 498, did not interfere with the state probate proceeding and was within the subject-matter jurisdiction of the federal bankruptcy court. She explained: "[N]o 'sound policy considerations' militate in favor of extending the probate exception to cover the case at hand. Trial courts, both federal and state, often address conduct of the kind * * * [the widow] alleges. State probate courts possess no 'special proficiency ... in handling [such] issues.'" Id. at 312, 126 S.Ct. at 1748–49, 164 L.Ed.2d at 498 (citations omitted). Justice Stevens separately concurred, urging the elimination of the probate exception as historically unjustified. See Graves, Marshall v. Marshall: *The Past, Present, and Future of the Probate Exception to Federal Jurisdiction*, 59 Ala.L.Rev. 1643 (2008).

C. THE SUBJECT-MATTER JURISDICTION OF THE FEDERAL COURTS—FEDERAL QUESTIONS

———

Read Article III, § 2 of the United States Constitution and 28 U.S.C. §§ 1331 and 1441 in the Supplement.

———

Article III, § 2 extends the judicial power of the United States "to all Cases, in Law and Equity, arising under this Constitution, the Laws of the United States, and Treaties made, or which shall be made under their Authority." This kind of jurisdiction is referred to as "federal question" or "arising under" jurisdiction, and the general statutory authority for such jurisdiction in federal district courts is currently set out in 28 U.S.C. § 1331. Congress did not enact federal question jurisdiction until the Midnight Judges Act of 1801, which Congress repealed the next year when the Federalists lost power. See LaCroix, *Federalists, Federalism, and Federal Jurisdiction*, 30 L. & Hist.Rev. 205 (2012). The current statute traces to the jurisdictional grant enacted in 1875, which was conditioned on an amount-in-controversy requirement. See Act of Mar. 3, 1875, § 1, 18 Stat. 470. Other than Congress's elimination of the amount-in-controversy condition in 1980, the statute has remained essentially unchanged.

The grant of jurisdiction in 28 U.S.C. § 1331 often is justified on three grounds: to promote the uniformity of federal law; to encourage judicial expertise in interpreting federal law; and to protect against possible state-court hostility to claims arising under federal law. See Preis, *Reassessing the Purposes of Federal Question Jurisdiction*, 42 Wake Forest L.Rev. 247, 248–60 (2007). A revisionist view casts the federal courts as a "franchising arrangement" characterized by "procedural homogeneity, cultural conformity, and technical competence." Seinfeld, *The Federal Courts as a Franchise: Rethinking the Justifications for Federal Question Jurisdiction*, 97 Calif.L.Rev. 95, 100 (2009). Why do you suppose Congress waited until the late nineteenth century to confer jurisdiction on the federal courts to hear cases arising under federal law?

MISHKIN, THE FEDERAL "QUESTION" IN THE DISTRICT COURTS, 53 Colum.L.Rev. 157, 157–59 (1953):

Although the framers of our Constitution could not agree upon whether there should be any federal trial courts at all, it was generally conceded at the Convention that the national judicial power should, in some form, extend to cases arising under the laws of the new government. However, though the first Congress did exercise its option to establish a system of "inferior" national tribunals, it did not assign to them general jurisdiction over cases of that type. With the exception of an extremely shortlived statute enacted just after the end of the eighteenth century, it was not until 1875 that the federal courts were given initial cognizance of all types of federal question cases. * * *

Whatever may have been the circumstances and needs during the first century of our country's history, there seems to be little doubt that today, with the expanding scope of federal legislation, the exercise of power over cases of this sort constitutes one of the major purposes of a full independent system of national trial courts. The alternative would be to rely entirely upon United States Supreme Court review of state court decisions. But, at least in our present judicial system, Supreme Court pronouncements as to any particular segment of national law are comparatively few. Consequently, sympathetic handling of the available Supreme Court rulings assumes a role of substantial importance in achieving widespread, uniform effectuation of federal law. Presumably judges selected and paid by the central government, with tenure during good behavior—and that determined by the Congress—and probably even somewhat insulated by a separate building, are more likely to give full scope to any given Supreme Court decision, and particularly ones unpopular locally, than are their state counterparts. By the same token, should a district judge fail, or err, a more sympathetic treatment of Supreme Court precedents can be expected from federal circuit judges than from state appellate courts.

Thus, the exercise of federal question jurisdiction by lower federal tribunals presumably permits the Supreme Court to confine itself (insofar as any such distinction can be drawn) to the solving of new problems rather than the policing of old solutions, without the loss that might otherwise be entailed in the effectuation of national rights. Further, the fact that the lower federal bench is chosen by officials of the national government under the same procedure as the members of the high Court suggests a greater similarity in the interpretation of national law, even on first impression, among the several parts of the national system than between the Supreme Court and any state system, or among the various state tribunals themselves. Insofar as this is true, it also promotes a more uniform, correct application of federal law in that significant group of cases where, either because of the novelty of the question, disproportionate expense or for other reasons, recourse to the Supreme Court has previously either not been attempted or been precluded. Finally, it might even be argued that the very existence of an alternative forum stimulates state courts to give a more attentive treatment to claims of federal right.

These factors suggest that it is desirable that Congress be competent to bring to an initial national forum all cases in which the vindication of federal policy may be at stake. However, it does not follow from this that at any given time all such cases should in fact be brought before the federal courts. There are other considerations which must enter into any decision as to the actual use of the national judiciary. For example, there are limits on the volume of litigation which they can handle without an expansion which might not be warranted by the advantages to be gained; the hardships which the geographic location of these courts may impose on the litigants and a willingness to trust that a party's self-interest will lead him to bring or remove an appropriate case to the federal courts might well justify the current rule that federal question jurisdiction is, for the most part, shared by the local courts; in some circumstances, such as where the validity of state action may be at issue, it may avoid friction and wasted effort, without sacrificing national authority, to allow the initial adjudication to be made by the state's tribunals subject to ultimate review by the United States Supreme Court. Other factors could easily be added.
* * *

In OSBORN v. BANK OF THE UNITED STATES, 22 U.S. (9 Wheat.) 738, 6 L.Ed. 204 (1824), the Bank of the United States sued in federal court to enjoin the state auditor of Ohio from collecting a tax from it. The court granted a temporary injunction restraining the state auditor from collecting the tax. Undeterred, the state auditor arranged to have the moneys that it claimed due forcibly removed from the Bank, and the court then ordered the state officials to return the money. The officials appealed on the ground that the federal court lacked subject-matter jurisdiction over the case.

The congressional act chartering the Bank authorized it "to sue and be sued * * * in any Circuit Court of the United States." First, Chief Justice Marshall held that this authorization was a grant by Congress to the federal courts of jurisdiction in all cases to which the Bank was a party. He then considered whether Congress had the constitutional power to confer jurisdiction over these cases, pursuant to the "arising under" language of Article III, § 2. That power clearly existed in the actual case, since the bank was alleging that Ohio's attempt to tax it violated the federal Constitution. The Chief Justice, however, undertook to support the validity of the jurisdictional grant in all cases to which the bank was a party. Chief Justice Marshall explained:

> When [the] Bank sues, the first question which presents itself, and which lies at the foundation of the cause, is, has this legal entity a right to sue? Has it a right to come, not into this Court particularly, but into any Court? This depends on a law of the United States. The next question is, has this being a right to make this particular contract? If this question be decided in the negative, the cause is determined against the plaintiff; and this question, too, depends entirely on a law of the United States. These are important questions, and they exist in every possible case. The right to sue, if decided once, is decided for ever; but the power of Congress was exercised antecedently to the first decision on that right, and if it was constitutional then, it cannot cease to be so, because the particular question is decided. It may be revived at the will of the party, and most probably would be renewed, were the tribunal to be changed. But the question respecting the right to make a particular contract, or to acquire a particular property, or to sue on account of a particular injury, belongs to every particular case, and may be renewed in every case. The question forms an original ingredient in every cause. Whether it be in fact relied on or not, in the defence, it is still a part of the cause, and may be relied on. The right of the plaintiff to sue, cannot depend on the defence which the defendant may choose to set up. His right

to sue is anterior to that defence, and must depend on the state of things when the action is brought. The questions which the case involves, then, must determine its character, whether those questions be made in the cause or not.

The appellants say, that the case arises on the contract; but the validity of the contract depends on a law of the United States, and the plaintiff is compelled, in every case, to show its validity. The case arises emphatically under the law. The act of Congress is its foundation. The contract could never have been made, but under the authority of that act. The act itself is the first ingredient in the case, is its origin, is that from which every other part arises. That other questions may also arise, as the execution of the contract, or its performance, cannot change the case, or give it any other origin than the charter of incorporation. The action still originates in, and is sustained by, that charter.

Id. at 823–25, 6 L.Ed. at 224–25.

NOTES AND QUESTIONS

1.   In LIGHTFOOT v. CEDANT MORTGAGE CORP., 580 U.S. ___, 137 S.Ct. 553, 196 L.Ed.2d 493 (2017), the Supreme Court clarified when a "sue-and-be-sued" clause of the sort involved in *Osborn* vests jurisdiction or instead simply confers capacity to sue. *Lightfoot* involved the Federal National Mortgage Association (known as "Fannie Mae"), which, by statute, is authorized "to sue and to be sued, and to complain and to defend, in any court of competent jurisdiction, State or Federal." 12 U.S.C. § 1723a(a). The Court interpreted the clause as permitting Fannie Mae to sue in any state or federal court but only if the court is "already endowed with subject-matter jurisdiction over the suit." Id. at ___, 137 S.Ct. at 560–61, 196 L.Ed.2d at 502.

2.   Petitioner argued in *Osborn* that even if the Bank's charter did vest federal jurisdiction, Congress lacked constitutional authority to make this grant of judicial power. On what basis did Chief Justice Marshall reject that view? Under his "ingredient" test, can Congress confer jurisdiction over disputes involving the Bank if claims arise under state law and no federal issue is involved? That question was raised in BANK OF THE UNITED STATES v. PLANTERS' BANK OF GEORGIA, 22 U.S. (9 Wheat.) 904, 6 L.Ed. 244 (1824). The Bank of the United States had purchased notes issued by a state bank, which refused to honor them. The Bank sued for payment, and the state bank contested the federal court's jurisdiction. The Supreme Court held that the question had been "fully considered" in *Osborn*, and that it was "unnecessary to repeat the reasoning used in that case." Id. at 905, 6 L.Ed. at 244. What was the federal "ingredient" that provided the constitutional basis for jurisdiction in both cases?

3.   The concept of "protective jurisdiction" draws from *Osborn's* broad interpretation of Article III and allows a federal court, in the absence of

diversity of citizenship, "to hear state law claims, even though the claims themselves neither incorporate an original federal ingredient nor seek to enforce rights conferred by federal law." Pfander, *Protective Jurisdiction, Aggregate Litigation, and the Limits of Article III*, 95 Calif.L.Rev. 1423 (2007). The Supreme Court has never embraced this species of jurisdiction, finding ways to sidestep the issue when it has been argued. See, e.g., Mesa v. California, 489 U.S. 121, 137, 109 S.Ct. 959, 969, 103 L.Ed.2d 99, 115 (1989) ("We have, in the past, not found the need to adopt a theory of 'protective jurisdiction' to support Art. III 'arising under' jurisdiction, * * * and we do not see any need for doing so here * * * ."). In TEXTILE WORKERS UNION v. LINCOLN MILLS, 353 U.S. 448, 474, 77 S.Ct. 912, 920, 1 L.Ed.2d 972, 990–91 (1957), Justice Frankfurter, dissenting, argued that the federal Constitution provides no basis for protective jurisdiction when the suit involves only state law claims, federal common law does not provide the rule of decision, and the requirements of diversity jurisdiction are not met.

The language of 28 U.S.C. § 1331, like its predecessor statute, tracks that of Article III, § 2 with the exception of referring to "civil actions" rather than to "cases." See Chadbourn & Levin, *Original Jurisdiction of Federal Questions*, 90 U.Pa.L.Rev. 639, 645 (1942) (the 1875 statute referred to "suits"). The statute's drafting history, although spare, shows Congress's intent to confer jurisdiction that runs the full scope of Article III. See Collins, *The Unhappy History of Federal Question Removal*, 71 Iowa L.Rev. 717, 723 & nn.32–35 (1986). Nevertheless, over time the Court has "more narrowly construed" the legislative grant than "its constitutional counterpart." Currie, *The Federal Courts and the American Law Institute, Part II*, 36 U.Chi.L.Rev. 268, 268–69 (1969). Why might the Court feel constrained to limit the flow of cases to the district courts?

LOUISVILLE & NASHVILLE R. CO. V. MOTTLEY

Supreme Court of the United States, 1908.
211 U.S. 149, 29 S.Ct. 42, 53 L.Ed. 126.

Appeal from the Circuit Court of the United States for the Western District of Kentucky * * *.

* * *

The bill alleged that in September, 1871, plaintiffs, while passengers upon the defendant railroad, were injured by the defendant's negligence, and released their respective claims for damages in consideration of the agreement for transportation during their lives, expressed in the contract. It is alleged that the contract was performed by the defendant up to January 1, 1907, when the defendant declined to renew the passes. The bill then alleges that the refusal to comply with the contract was based solely upon that part of the act of Congress of June 29, 1906, (34 Stat. 584) which forbids the giving of free passes or free transportation. The bill further alleges: First, that the act of Congress referred to does not prohibit the giving of passes under the circumstances of this case; and, second, that, if the law is to be construed as prohibiting such passes, it is in conflict with the 5th Amendment of the Constitution, because it deprives the plaintiffs of their property without due process of law. The defendant demurred to the bill. The judge of the circuit court overruled the demurrer, entered a decree for the relief prayed for, and the defendant appealed directly to this court.

MR. JUSTICE MOODY, after making the foregoing statement, delivered the opinion of the court:

Two questions of law were raised by the demurrer to the bill, were brought here by appeal, and have been argued before us. They are, first, whether * * * the act of Congress of June 29, 1906 * * * makes it unlawful to perform a contract for transportation of persons who, in good faith, before the passage of the act, had accepted such contract in satisfaction of a valid cause of action against the railroad; and, second, whether the statute, if it should be construed to render such a contract unlawful, is in violation of the 5th Amendment of the Constitution * * *. We do not deem it necessary, however, to consider either of these questions, because, in our opinion, the court below was without jurisdiction of the cause. Neither party has questioned that jurisdiction, but it is the duty of this court to see to it that the jurisdiction of the circuit court, which is defined and limited by statute, is not exceeded. * * *

There was no diversity of citizenship, and it is not and cannot be suggested that there was any ground of jurisdiction, except that the case was a "suit . . . arising under the Constitution or laws of the United States." * * * It is the settled interpretation of these words, as used in this statute, conferring jurisdiction, that a suit arises under the Constitution and laws of the United States only when the plaintiff's statement of his own cause of action shows that it is based upon those laws or that Constitution. It is not enough that the plaintiff alleges some anticipated defense to his cause of action, and asserts that the defense is invalidated by some provision of the Constitution of the United States. Although such allegations show that very likely, in the course of the litigation, a question under the Constitution would arise, they do not show that the suit, that is, the plaintiff's original cause of action, arises under the Constitution. * * *

* * * The application of this rule to the case at bar is decisive against the jurisdiction of the circuit court.

It is ordered that the judgment be reversed and the case remitted to the circuit court with instructions to dismiss the suit for want of jurisdiction.

NOTES AND QUESTIONS

1.   Some commentators question whether the Court in *Mottley* properly interpreted 28 U.S.C. § 1331, pointing to the statute's legislative history. See Chemerinsky, Federal Jurisdiction § 5.2 (8th ed.) (quoting the floor manager of the statute as saying the bill "gives precisely the power which the Constitution confers—nothing more, nothing less"). To what extent is statutory jurisdiction under *Mottley* narrower than the *Osborn* "ingredient" test for jurisdiction under Article III? If the *Mottley* test is not constitutionally required, does this mean the Supreme Court has discretion to give the statutory grant a more generous reading?

2.   Following the Court's decision, the Mottleys commenced an action in a Kentucky state court. The case ultimately was brought to the Supreme Court by appeal from the highest court in Kentucky on the question of the validity and construction of the 1906 Act; three years after the Supreme Court dismissed the federal, action it examined the merits of the Mottleys' contentions and decided in favor of the railroad. See 219 U.S. 467, 31 S.Ct. 265, 55 L.Ed. 297 (1911). What was gained by the original dismissal?

3.   After the Civil War, the number of lawsuits filed in the federal courts dramatically increased, but Congress was slow to increase judicial capacity or to meet the problems of court congestion. See Purcell, Jr., *Reconsidering the Frankfurterian Paradigm: Reflections on Histories of Lower Federal Courts*, 24 Law & Soc. Inquiry 679 (1999). In what way did *Mottley* help to resolve problems of federal docket overload?

4.   *Mottley* is said to stand for the "well-pleaded complaint" rule. Vaden v. Discover Bank, 556 U.S. 49, 60, 129 S.Ct. 1262, 1272, 173 L.Ed.2d 206, 218 (2009) (citing *Mottley* as establishing "the longstanding well-pleaded complaint rule"). That is, plaintiff must allege the federal issue as an element of the claim; if the federal issue is assigned to defendant as an affirmative defense, federal question jurisdiction cannot be asserted under Section 1331. Why was federal jurisdiction not present on the face of the Mottleys' complaint? Is it that the complaint anticipated a federal defense? What was that defense? The American Law Institute's Study of the Division of Jurisdiction Between State and Federal Courts, published in 1969, proposed a reform—never adopted— that would permit retention of jurisdiction whenever defendant has introduced a federal defense or a federal counterclaim. See Doernberg, *There's No Reason for It; It's Just Our Policy: Why the Well-Pleaded Complaint Rule Sabotages the Purposes of Federal Question Jurisdiction*, 38 Hastings L.J. 597 (1987). What problems might arise from adoption of the ALI proposal?

5.   A recurring question is whether jurisdiction under 28 U.S.C. § 1331 may be exercised over state law claims that implicate federal issues— sometimes referred to as hybrid cases. One approach to the question, announced by Justice Holmes in AMERICAN WELL WORKS CO. v. LAYNE & BOWLER CO., 241 U.S. 257, 36 S.Ct. 585, 60 L.Ed. 987 (1916), bars jurisdiction over every claim that arises under state law, even if the well pleaded complaint includes a federal issue. *American Well Works* involved a

claim by a pump manufacturer that a competitor had damaged its reputation by telling customers that plaintiff's pump infringed defendant's patent. The Supreme Court held that there was no federal jurisdiction over the suit because the claim did not arise under the federal patent law, but rather was a state cause of action. See Woolhandler & Collins, *Federal Question Jurisdiction and Justice Holmes*, 84 Notre Dame L.Rev. 2151 (2009).

In SMITH v. KANSAS CITY TITLE & TRUST CO., 255 U.S. 180, 41 S.Ct. 243, 65 L.Ed. 577 (1921), a shareholder sued to enjoin the Trust Company, a Missouri corporation, from investing in certain federal bonds on the ground that the Act of Congress authorizing their issuance was unconstitutional. Plaintiff claimed that under Missouri law an investment in securities, the issuance of which had not been authorized by a valid law was ultra vires, and so enjoinable. Although the cause of action was created by state law, the Supreme Court held that the action arose under federal law for purposes of 28 U.S.C. § 1331:

> The general rule is that where it appears from the bill or statement of the plaintiff that the right to relief depends upon the construction or application of the Constitution or laws of the United States, and that such federal claim is not merely colorable, and rests upon a reasonable foundation, the District Court has jurisdiction. * * *

Id. at 199, 41 S.Ct. at 245, 65 L.Ed. at 585. Justice Holmes dissented.

By contrast, in MOORE v. CHESAPEAKE & OHIO RY. CO., 291 U.S. 205, 54 S.Ct. 402, 78 L.Ed. 755 (1934), federal jurisdiction was not available in an action under Kentucky's Employer Liability Act. The statute provided that defendant could not invoke the defense of contributory negligence or assumption of risk if defendant had violated state or federal employee-safety laws. Plaintiff alleged defendant's failure to comply with the Federal Safety Appliance Act. The Supreme Court found that federal question jurisdiction did not exist, holding that:

> [A] suit brought under the state statute which defines liability to employees who are injured while engaged in intrastate commerce, and brings within the purview of the statute a breach of the duty imposed by the federal statute, should [not] be regarded as a suit arising under the laws of the United States and cognizable in the federal court in the absence of diversity of citizenship.

Id. at 214–15, 54 S.Ct. at 406, 78 L.Ed. at 763. Can *Moore* be reconciled with *Smith*?

6. In MERRELL DOW PHARMACEUTICALS INC. v. THOMPSON, 478 U.S. 804, 106 S.Ct. 3229, 92 L.Ed.2d 650 (1986), plaintiff sued a drug manufacturer in state court on a number of state law claims including per se negligence on the theory that defendant had failed to comply with labeling requirements under a federal statute. Defendant removed the action from state court to federal court on the basis of federal question jurisdiction. The Court of Appeals reversed and remanded. After granting certiorari, the Supreme Court affirmed. The Court stated that "determinations about federal jurisdiction

require sensitive judgments about congressional intent, judicial power, and the federal system," and found it jurisdictionally significant that Congress had not created a private right of action to enforce the federal labeling requirement. Id. at 810, 106 S.Ct. 3233, 92 L.Ed.2d at 659. On that basis, the Court held that the federal interest in the state negligence suit was too insubstantial to support § 1331 jurisdiction:

> We * * * conclude that the congressional determination that there should be no federal remedy for the violation of this federal statute is tantamount to a congressional conclusion that the presence of a claimed violation of the statute as an element of a state cause of action is insufficiently "substantial" to confer federal-question jurisdiction. * * *

Id. at 814, 106 S.Ct. at 3235, 92 L.Ed.2d at 662. In a footnote, the Court elaborated on the significance of "the nature of the federal interest at stake" to the jurisdictional determination:

> Focusing on the nature of the federal interest, moreover, suggests that the widely perceived "irreconcilable" conflict between the finding of federal jurisdiction in *Smith* * * * and the finding of no jurisdiction in *Moore* * * * is far from clear. For the difference in result can be seen as manifestations of the differences in the nature of the federal issues at stake. In *Smith*, as the Court emphasized, the issue was the constitutionality of an important federal statute. * * * In *Moore*, in contrast, the Court emphasized that the violation of the federal standard as an element of state tort recovery did not fundamentally change the state tort nature of the action. * * *

> The importance of the nature of the federal issue in federal-question jurisdiction is highlighted by the fact that, despite the usual reliability of the Holmes test as an inclusionary principle, this Court has sometimes found that formally federal causes of action were not properly brought under federal-question jurisdiction because of the overwhelming predominance of state-law issues.

Id. at 814 n.12, 106 S.Ct. at 3235 n.12, 92 L.Ed.2d at 662 n.12.

Justice Brennan dissented. In particular, the dissent questioned whether it was appropriate to equate Congress's decision not to create a private right of action to enforce a federal statute with a decision to withhold federal jurisdiction from an action to enforce the statute using state tort law. Justice Brennan also criticized the majority's emphasis on "the importance of the federal issue," characterizing this factor as "infinitely malleable" and based upon an "ad hoc evaluation" that was inevitably "vague and general." Id. at 820–21 n.1, 106 S.Ct. at 3238–39 n.1, 92 L.Ed.2d at 667 n.1 (Brennan, J., dissenting).

Does the test in *Merrell Dow* differ from that of *American Well Works*? In what way? Is it consistent with *Mottley*? *Merrell Dow* generated a serious division among the circuits on a number of issues, including whether *Smith* continued to support federal jurisdiction over a state cause of action; whether a federal right of action was a bright-line condition for jurisdiction under 28

U.S.C. § 1331; and whether the substantiality of the federal issue is a jurisdictional factor. The Supreme Court revisited these issues in the cases that follow.

GRABLE & SONS METAL PRODUCTS, INC. V. DARUE ENGINEERING & MANUFACTURING

Supreme Court of the United States, 2005.
545 U.S. 308, 125 S.Ct. 2363, 162 L.Ed.2d 257.

Certiorari to the United States Court of Appeals for the Sixth Circuit.

JUSTICE SOUTER delivered the opinion of the Court.

The question is whether want of a federal cause of action to try claims of title to land obtained at a federal tax sale precludes removal to federal court of a state action with nondiverse parties raising a disputed issue of federal title law. We answer no, and hold that the national interest in providing a federal forum for federal tax litigation is sufficiently substantial to support the exercise of federal-question jurisdiction over the disputed issue on removal, which would not distort any division of labor between the state and federal courts, provided or assumed by Congress.

I

In 1994, the Internal Revenue Service seized Michigan real property belonging to petitioner Grable & Sons Metal Products, Inc., to satisfy Grable's federal tax delinquency. Title 26 U.S.C. § 6335 required the IRS to give notice of the seizure, and there is no dispute that Grable received actual notice by certified mail before the IRS sold the property to respondent Darue Engineering & Manufacturing. Although Grable also received notice of the sale itself, it did not exercise its statutory right to redeem the property within 180 days of the sale, § 6337(b)(1), and after that period had passed, the Government gave Darue a quitclaim deed, § 6339.

Five years later, Grable brought a quiet title action in state court, claiming that Darue's record title was invalid because the IRS had failed to notify Grable of its seizure of the property in the exact manner required by § 6335(a), which provides that written notice must be "given by the Secretary to the owner of the property [or] left at his usual place of abode or business." Grable said that the statute required personal service, not service by certified mail.

Darue removed the case to Federal District Court as presenting a federal question, because the claim of title depended on the interpretation of the notice statute in the federal tax law. The District Court declined to remand the case at Grable's behest after finding that the "claim does pose a 'significant question of federal law,' " * * * and ruling that Grable's lack of a federal right of action to enforce its claim against Darue did not bar the exercise of federal jurisdiction. On the merits, the court granted summary judgment to Darue, holding that although § 6335 by its terms required personal service, substantial compliance with the statute was enough. * * *

The Court of Appeals for the Sixth Circuit affirmed. * * * We granted certiorari on the jurisdictional question * * * to resolve a split within the Courts of Appeals on whether *Merrell Dow* * * * always requires * * * a federal cause of action as a condition for exercising federal-question jurisdiction. We now affirm.

II

Darue was entitled to remove the quiet title action if Grable could have brought it in federal district court originally, 28 U.S.C. § 1441(a), as a civil action "arising under the Constitution, laws, or treaties of the United States," § 1331. This provision for federal-question jurisdiction is invoked by and large by plaintiffs pleading a cause of action created by federal law (e.g., claims under 42 U.S.C. § 1983). There is, however, another longstanding, if less frequently encountered, variety of federal "arising under" jurisdiction, this Court having recognized for nearly 100 years that in certain cases federal-question jurisdiction will lie over state-law claims that implicate significant federal issues. * * * The doctrine captures the commonsense notion that a federal court ought to be able to hear claims recognized under state law that nonetheless turn on substantial questions of federal law, and thus justify resort to the experience, solicitude, and hope of uniformity that a federal forum offers on federal issues, see ALI, Study of the Division of Jurisdiction Between State and Federal Courts 164–166 (1968).

The classic example is *Smith* * * * [pp. 247–248, Note 5, supra]. Although Missouri law provided the cause of action, the Court recognized federal-question jurisdiction because the principal issue in the case was the federal constitutionality of the bond issue. * * *

* * * *Smith* * * * has been subject to some trimming to fit earlier and later cases recognizing the vitality of the basic doctrine, but shying away from the expansive view that mere need to apply federal law in a state-law claim will suffice to open the "arising under" door. * * * [Justice Cardozo later explained] that a request to exercise federal-question jurisdiction over a state action calls for a "common-sense accommodation of judgment to [the] kaleidoscopic situations" that present a federal issue, in "a selective process which picks the substantial causes out of the web and lays the other ones aside." *Gully v. First Nat. Bank in Meridian*, 299 U.S. 109, 117–118, 57 S.Ct. 96, 81 L.Ed. 70 (1936). It has in fact become a constant refrain in such cases that federal jurisdiction demands not only a contested federal issue, but a substantial one, indicating a serious federal interest in claiming the advantages thought to be inherent in a federal forum. * * *

But even when the state action discloses a contested and substantial federal question, the exercise of federal jurisdiction is subject to a possible veto. For the federal issue will ultimately qualify for a federal forum only if federal jurisdiction is consistent with congressional judgment about the sound division of labor between state and federal courts governing the application of § 1331. * * * Because arising-under jurisdiction to hear a state-law claim always raises the possibility of upsetting the state-federal line drawn (or at least assumed) by Congress, the presence of a disputed federal issue and the ostensible importance of a federal forum are never necessarily dispositive; there must always be an assessment of any disruptive portent in exercising federal jurisdiction. * * *

These considerations have kept us from stating a "single, precise, all-embracing" test for jurisdiction over federal issues embedded in state-law claims between nondiverse parties. * * * We have not kept them out simply because they appeared in state raiment, as Justice Holmes would have done * * * [in *American Well Works*], but neither have we treated "federal issue" as a password opening federal courts to any state action embracing a point of federal law. Instead, the question is, does a state-law claim necessarily raise a stated federal issue, actually disputed and substantial, which a federal forum may entertain without disturbing any congressionally approved balance of federal and state judicial responsibilities.

III

A

This case warrants federal jurisdiction. Grable's state complaint must specify "the facts establishing the superiority of [its] claim," Mich. Ct. Rule 3.411(B)(2)(c) (West 2005), and Grable has premised its superior title claim on a failure by the IRS to give it adequate notice, as defined by federal law. Whether Grable was given notice within the meaning of the federal statute is thus an essential element of its quiet title claim, and the meaning of the federal statute is actually in dispute; it appears to be the only legal or factual issue contested in the case. The meaning of the federal tax provision is an important issue of federal law that sensibly belongs in a federal court. The Government has a strong interest in the "prompt and certain collection of delinquent taxes," * * * and the ability of the IRS to satisfy its claims from the property of delinquents requires clear terms of notice to allow buyers like Darue to satisfy themselves that the Service has touched the bases necessary for good title. The Government thus has a direct interest in the availability of a federal forum to vindicate its own administrative action, and buyers (as well as tax delinquents) may find it valuable to come before judges used to federal tax matters. Finally, because it will be the rare state title case that raises a contested matter of federal law, federal jurisdiction to resolve genuine disagreement over federal tax title provisions will portend only a microscopic effect on the federal-state division of labor. * * *

B

Merrell Dow * * * [p. 248, Note 6, supra], on which Grable rests its position, is not to the contrary. * * *

Because federal law provides for no quiet title action that could be brought against Darue, Grable argues that there can be no federal jurisdiction here, stressing some broad language in *Merrell Dow* * * * that on its face supports Grable's position * * *. But an opinion is to be read as a whole, and *Merrell Dow* cannot be read whole as overturning decades of precedent * * * and converting a federal cause of action from a sufficient condition for federal-question jurisdiction into a necessary one.

In the first place, *Merrell Dow* disclaimed the adoption of any bright-line rule, as when the Court reiterated that "in exploring the outer reaches of § 1331, determinations about federal jurisdiction require sensitive judgments about congressional intent, judicial power, and the federal system." * * * The opinion included a lengthy footnote explaining that questions of jurisdiction over state-law claims require "careful judgments," * * * about the "nature of the federal interest at stake," * * * (emphasis deleted). And as a final indication that it did not mean to make a federal right of action mandatory, it expressly approved the exercise of jurisdiction sustained in *Smith*, despite the want of any federal cause of action available to *Smith*'s shareholder plaintiff. * * * *Merrell Dow* then, did not toss out, but specifically retained, the contextual enquiry that had been *Smith*'s hallmark for over 60 years. At the end of *Merrell Dow*, Justice Holmes was still dissenting.

Accordingly, *Merrell Dow* should be read in its entirety as treating the absence of a federal private right of action as evidence relevant to, but not dispositive of, the "sensitive judgments about congressional intent" that § 1331 requires. The absence of any federal cause of action affected *Merrell Dow*'s result two ways. The Court saw the fact as worth some consideration in the assessment of substantiality. But its primary importance emerged when the Court treated the combination of no federal cause of action and no preemption of state remedies for misbranding as an important clue to Congress's conception of the scope of jurisdiction to be exercised under § 1331. The Court saw the missing cause of action not as a missing federal door key, always required, but as a missing welcome mat, required in the circumstances, when exercising federal jurisdiction over a state misbranding action would have attracted a horde of original filings and removal cases raising other state claims with embedded federal issues. For if the federal labeling standard without a federal cause of action could get a state claim into federal court, so could any other federal standard without a federal cause of action. And that would have meant a tremendous number of cases.

* * * "The violation of federal statutes and regulations is commonly given negligence per se effect in state tort proceedings." Restatement (Third) of Torts § 14 Reporters' Note, Comment *a*, p. 195 (Tent. Draft No. 1, March 28, 2001). * * * A general rule of exercising federal jurisdiction over state claims resting on federal mislabeling and other statutory violations would thus have heralded a potentially enormous shift of traditionally state cases into federal courts. Expressing concern over the "increased volume of federal litigation," and noting the importance of adhering to "legislative intent," *Merrell Dow* thought it improbable that the Congress, having made no provision for a federal cause of action, would have meant to welcome any state-law tort case implicating federal law "solely because the violation of the federal statute is said to [create] a rebuttable presumption [of negligence] . . . under state law." * * *e In this situation, no welcome mat meant keep out. *Merrell Dow*'s analysis thus fits within the framework of examining the importance of having a federal forum for the issue, and the consistency of such a forum with Congress's intended division of labor between state and federal courts.

As already indicated, however, a comparable analysis yields a different jurisdictional conclusion in this case. Although Congress also indicated ambivalence in this case by providing no private right of action to Grable, it is the rare state quiet title action that involves contested issues of federal law * * *. * * * Consequently, jurisdiction over actions like Grable's would not materially affect, or threaten to affect, the normal currents of litigation. Given the absence of threatening structural consequences and the clear interest the Government, its buyers, and its delinquents have in the availability of a federal forum, there is no good reason to shirk from federal jurisdiction over the dispositive and contested federal issue at the heart of the state-law title claim.

IV

The judgment of the Court of Appeals * * * is affirmed.

It is so ordered.

JUSTICE THOMAS, concurring.

The Court faithfully applies our precedents interpreting 28 U.S.C. § 1331 to authorize federal-court jurisdiction over some cases in which state law creates the cause of action but requires determination of an issue of federal law. * * * In this case, no one has asked us to overrule those precedents and adopt the rule Justice Holmes set forth in *American Well Works Co.* * * * [p. 247, Note 5, supra] limiting § 1331 jurisdiction to cases in which federal law creates the cause of action pleaded on the face of the

---

e   Alteration in original.

plaintiff's complaint. * * * In an appropriate case, and perhaps with the benefit of better evidence as to the original meaning of § 1331's text, I would be willing to consider that course. * * *

GUNN V. MINTON
Supreme Court of the United States, 2013.
568 U.S. 251, 133 S.Ct. 1059, 185 L.Ed.2d 72.

Certiorari to the Supreme Court of Texas.

CHIEF JUSTICE ROBERTS delivered the opinion of the Court.

Federal courts have exclusive jurisdiction over cases "arising under any Act of Congress relating to patents." 28 U.S.C. § 1338(a). The question presented is whether a state law claim alleging legal malpractice in the handling of a patent case must be brought in federal court.

I

* * *

[Minton was represented by attorney Gunn in a federal patent infringement action in which his patent was declared invalid. Minton later sued his attorney for malpractice and on appeal argued that the attorney had failed to raise the "experimental use" exception under federal patent law, which he alleged caused his infringement claim to fail. The Texas Supreme Court, reversing the trial and intermediate appeals courts, held that the case properly belonged in federal court because the success of Minton's malpractice claim turned on a question of federal patent law.]

II

* * *

* * * Adhering to the demands of "[l]inguistic consistency," we have interpreted the phrase "arising under" [as set forth in 28 U.S.C. § 1338(a)] * * * identically [as under 28 U.S.C. § 1331], applying our § 1331 and § 1338(a) precedents interchangeably. * * *

For statutory purposes, a case can "aris[e] under" federal law in two ways. Most directly, a case arises under federal law when federal law creates the cause of action asserted. * * * As a rule of inclusion, this "creation" test admits of only extremely rare exceptions * * * and accounts for the vast bulk of suits that arise under federal law * * *. * * *

But even where a claim finds its origins in state rather than federal law—as Minton's legal malpractice claim indisputably does—we have identified a "special and small category" of cases in which arising under jurisdiction still lies. In outlining the contours of this slim category, we do not paint on a blank canvas. Unfortunately, the canvas looks like one that Jackson Pollock got to first. See 13D C. Wright, A. Miller, E. Cooper, & R.

Freer, Federal Practice and Procedure § 3562, pp. 175–176 (3d ed. 2008) (reviewing general confusion on question).

In an effort to bring some order to this unruly doctrine several Terms ago, [in *Grable*, p. 250, supra,] we condensed our prior cases into the following inquiry: Does the "state-law claim necessarily raise a stated federal issue, actually disputed and substantial, which a federal forum may entertain without disturbing any congressionally approved balance of federal and state judicial responsibilities"? * * *

III

Applying *Grable*'s inquiry here, it is clear that Minton's legal malpractice claim does not arise under federal patent law. Indeed, for the reasons we discuss, we are comfortable concluding that state legal malpractice claims based on underlying patent matters will rarely, if ever, arise under federal patent law for purposes of § 1338(a). Although such cases may necessarily raise disputed questions of patent law, those cases are by their nature unlikely to have the sort of significance for the federal system necessary to establish jurisdiction.

A

To begin, we acknowledge that resolution of a federal patent question is "necessary" to Minton's case. Under Texas law, a plaintiff alleging legal malpractice must establish four elements: (1) that the defendant attorney owed the plaintiff a duty; (2) that the attorney breached that duty; (3) that the breach was the proximate cause of the plaintiff's injury; and (4) that damages occurred. * * * In cases like this one, in which the attorney's alleged error came in failing to make a particular argument, the causation element requires a "case within a case" analysis of whether, had the argument been made, the outcome of the earlier litigation would have been different. * * * To prevail on his legal malpractice claim, therefore, Minton must show that he would have prevailed in his federal patent infringement case if only petitioners had timely made an experimental-use argument on his behalf. * * *

B

The federal issue is also "actually disputed" here—indeed, on the merits, it is the central point of dispute. Minton argues that the experimental-use exception properly applied * * *; petitioners argue that it did not. This is just the sort of " 'dispute . . . respecting the . . . effect of [federal] law' " that *Grable* envisioned. * * *[f]

C

Minton's argument founders on *Grable*'s next requirement, however, for the federal issue in this case is not substantial in the relevant sense. In

---

[f]   Alteration in original.

reaching the opposite conclusion, the Supreme Court of Texas focused on the importance of the issue to the plaintiff's case and to the parties before it. * * * As our past cases show, however, it is not enough that the federal issue be significant to the particular parties in the immediate suit; that will *always* be true when the state claim "necessarily raise[s]" a disputed federal issue, as *Grable* separately requires. The substantiality inquiry under *Grable* looks instead to the importance of the issue to the federal system as a whole.

* * *

Here, the federal issue carries no such significance. Because of the backward-looking nature of a legal malpractice claim, the question is posed in a merely hypothetical sense: *If* Minton's lawyers had raised a timely experimental-use argument, would the result in the patent infringement proceeding have been different? No matter how the state courts resolve that hypothetical "case within a case," it will not change the real-world result of the prior federal patent litigation. Minton's patent will remain invalid.

Nor will allowing state courts to resolve these cases undermine "the development of a uniform body of [patent] law." * * * Congress ensured such uniformity by vesting exclusive jurisdiction over actual patent cases in the federal district courts and exclusive appellate jurisdiction in the Federal Circuit. * * * In resolving the nonhypothetical patent questions those cases present, the federal courts are of course not bound by state court case-within-a-case patent rulings. * * * In any event, the state court case-within-a-case inquiry asks what would have happened in the prior federal proceeding if a particular argument had been made. In answering that question, state courts can be expected to hew closely to the pertinent federal precedents. * * *

As for more novel questions of patent law that may arise for the first time in a state court "case within a case," they will at some point be decided by a federal court in the context of an actual patent case, with review in the Federal Circuit. If the question arises frequently, it will soon be resolved within the federal system, laying to rest any contrary state court precedent; if it does not arise frequently, it is unlikely to implicate substantial federal interests. * * *

Minton also suggests that state courts' answers to hypothetical patent questions can sometimes have real-world effect on other patents through issue preclusion. * * * He argues that, in evaluating this separate application, the patent examiner could be bound by the Texas trial court's interpretation of the scope of Minton's original patent. * * * In fact, Minton has not identified any case finding such preclusive effect based on a state court decision. But even assuming that a state court's case-within-a-case adjudication may be preclusive under some circumstances, the result would be limited to the parties and patents that had been before the state court. Such "fact-bound and situation-specific" effects are not sufficient to establish federal arising under jurisdiction. * * * [*Empire Healthchoice Assurance, Inc.* v. *McVeigh*, 547 U.S. 677, 701, 126 S.Ct. 2121, 2137, 165 L.Ed.2d 131, 138 (2006)].

Nor can we accept the suggestion that the federal courts' greater familiarity with patent law means that legal malpractice cases like this one belong in federal court. * * * [T]he possibility that a state court will incorrectly resolve a state claim is not, by itself, enough to trigger the federal courts' exclusive patent jurisdiction, even if the potential error finds its root in a misunderstanding of patent law.

* * *

D

It follows from the foregoing that *Grable*'s fourth requirement is also not met. * * * We have already explained the absence of a substantial federal issue within the meaning of *Grable*. The States, on the other hand, have "a special responsibility for maintaining standards among members of the licensed professions." * * * We have no reason to suppose that Congress—in establishing exclusive federal jurisdiction over patent cases—meant to bar from state courts state legal malpractice claims simply because they require resolution of a hypothetical patent issue.

The judgment of the Supreme Court of Texas is reversed, and the case is remanded for further proceedings not inconsistent with this opinion.

It is so ordered.

NOTE AND QUESTION

What is the test for jurisdiction under 28 U.S.C. § 1331 after *Grable* and *Gunn*? Do these opinions incorporate the tests from *Mottley*, *Smith*, *Moore*, and *Merrell Dow*, see pp. 245–250, supra, or do they abrogate the earlier decisions? Keep in mind that these cases all address the possibility of Section 1331 jurisdiction over state law causes of action. When a cause of action is provided by federal law and federal law provides the rule of decision, subject-matter jurisdiction clearly exists.

NOTE ON THE DECLARATORY JUDGMENT ACT AND ARTFUL PLEADING

The Declaratory Judgment Act, 28 U.S.C. §§ 2201–02, allows the federal court to issue a declaration of "rights and other legal relations" to an "interested party" in "a case of actual controversy within its jurisdiction." The statute creates a remedy but does not confer jurisdiction; a federal court can hear a declaratory judgment action only if the corresponding coercive action—meaning, an action seeking money damages or an injunction—could invoke jurisdiction under 28 U.S.C. § 1331 (or some other federal jurisdictional source).

In SKELLY OIL CO. v. PHILLIPS PETROLEUM CO., 339 U.S. 667, 673–74, 70 S.Ct. 876, 880, 94 L.Ed. 1194, 1201 (1950), suit was brought for a declaration that certain contracts were still in effect because a necessary federal certificate had been timely issued. Had the declaratory-plaintiff sued to enforce the contract following a breach, the complaint would not have raised a federal question, for the claim would have sounded in state contract law. However, defendant would have included in its answer to a post-breach complaint an affirmative defense derived from federal law. *Skelly Oil* asked whether the declaratory complaint, by anticipating the federal defense, satisfied the statutory test for federal jurisdiction. The Court held it did not: "[t]o sanction suits for declaratory relief as within the jurisdiction of the District Courts merely because, as in this case, artful pleading anticipates a defense based on federal law would contravene the whole trend of jurisdictional legislation by Congress, disregard the effective functioning of the federal judicial system and distort the limited procedural purposes of the Declaratory Judgment Act." *Skelly Oil* coined the phrase "artful pleading" to refer, as Professor Miller has put it, to "an attempt by the plaintiff to create federal question jurisdiction through the anticipation and inclusion of a federal defense on the face of its complaint in an action brought under the Declaratory Judgment Act." Miller, *Artful Pleading: A Doctrine in Search of Definition*, 76 Tex.L.Rev. 1781, 1784 (1998). For a criticism of *Skelly Oil*, see Doernberg, *The Trojan Horse: How the Declaratory Judgment Act Created a Cause of Action and Expanded Federal Jurisdiction While the Supreme Court Wasn't Looking*, 36 UCLA L.Rev. 529 (1989).

D. THE SUBJECT-MATTER JURISDICTION OF THE FEDERAL COURTS—SUPPLEMENTAL CLAIMS AND PARTIES

Read Article III, § 2 of the United States Constitution and 28 U.S.C. § 1367 in the Supplement.

In some cases, a transaction or series of occurrences will generate a dispute that involves multiple legal theories and claims for relief. In that situation, different patterns of party and claim joinder might arise. For example, a plaintiff may wish to assert multiple claims against a single defendant or against multiple defendants; relatedly, multiple plaintiffs may wish to assert multiple claims against a single defendant or multiple defendants. To complicate matters, original jurisdiction under 28 U.S.C. § 1331 might be available over some but not all of the claims and the rule of complete diversity of citizenship might not be met.

Whether claims and parties may be joined in a single lawsuit is a separate question from whether the federal court has subject-matter jurisdiction over the case. (The joinder rules are studied in Chapter 8, infra.) The doctrines of pendent and ancillary jurisdiction were judicially developed to deal with the jurisdictional issues posed by these different joinder situations. The term "pendent jurisdiction" was used when plaintiff, in her complaint, appended a claim lacking an independent basis for federal jurisdiction to a claim possessing such a basis. The term "ancillary jurisdiction" was used when either a plaintiff or a defendant injected a claim lacking an independent basis for federal jurisdiction by way of a counterclaim, crossclaim, or third-party complaint.

UNITED MINE WORKERS OF AMERICA V. GIBBS

Supreme Court of the United States, 1966.
383 U.S. 715, 86 S.Ct. 1130, 16 L.Ed.2d 218.

Certiorari to the United States Court of Appeals for the Sixth Circuit.

JUSTICE BRENNAN delivered the opinion of the Court.

Respondent Paul Gibbs was awarded compensatory and punitive damages in this action against petitioner United Mine Workers of America * * * ["UMW"] for alleged violations of § 303 of the Labor Management Relations Act, 1947, and of the common law of Tennessee. The case grew out of the rivalry between the United Mine Workers and the Southern Labor Union over representation of workers in the southern Appalachian coal fields. Tennessee Consolidated Coal Company, not a party here, laid off 100 miners of the UMW's Local 5881 when it closed one of its mines in southern Tennessee during the spring of 1960. Late that summer, Grundy Company, a wholly owned subsidiary of Consolidated, hired respondent as mine superintendent to attempt to open a new mine on Consolidated's property at nearby Gray's Creek through use of members of the Southern Labor Union. As part of the arrangement, Grundy also gave respondent a contract to haul the mine's coal to the nearest railroad loading point.

On August 15 and 16, 1960, armed members of Local 5881 forcibly prevented the opening of the mine, threatening respondent and beating an organizer for the rival union. The members of the local believed Consolidated had promised them the jobs at the new mine; they insisted that if anyone would do the work, they would. * * * George Gilbert, the UMW's field representative for the area including Local 5881, * * * [had] explicit instructions from his international union superiors to establish a limited picket line, to prevent any further violence, and to see to it that the strike did not spread to neighboring mines. There was no further violence at the mine site * * *.

Respondent lost his job as superintendent, and never entered into performance of his haulage contract. He testified that he soon began to lose other trucking contracts and mine leases he held in nearby areas. Claiming these effects to be the result of a concerted union plan against him, he sought recovery not against Local 5881 or its members, but only against petitioner, the international union. The suit was brought in the United States District Court for the Eastern District of Tennessee, and jurisdiction was premised on allegations of secondary boycotts under § 303. The state law claim, for which jurisdiction was based upon the doctrine of pendent jurisdiction, asserted "an unlawful conspiracy and an unlawful boycott aimed at him and [Grundy] to maliciously, wantonly and willfully interfere with his contract of employment and with his contract of haulage."

* * * The jury's verdict was that the UMW had violated both § 303 and state law. Gibbs was awarded $60,000 as damages under the employment contract and $14,500 under the haulage contract; he was also awarded $100,000 punitive damages. On motion, the trial court set aside the award of damages with respect to the haulage contract on the ground that damage was unproved. It also held that union pressure on Grundy to discharge respondent as supervisor would constitute only a primary dispute with Grundy, as respondent's employer, and hence was not cognizable under § 303. Interference with employment was cognizable as a state claim, however, and a remitted award was sustained on the state law claim. * * * The Court of Appeals for the Sixth Circuit affirmed. * * * We granted certiorari. * * *

I.

A threshold question is whether the District Court properly entertained jurisdiction of the claim based on Tennessee law. * * *

* * * The Court held in Hurn v. Oursler, 289 U.S. 238, 53 S.Ct. 586, 77 L.Ed. 1148, that state law claims are appropriate for federal court determination if they form a separate but parallel ground for relief also sought in a substantial claim based on federal law. The Court distinguished permissible from non-permissible exercises of federal judicial power over state law claims by contrasting "a case where two distinct grounds in support of a single cause of action are alleged, one only of which presents a federal question, and a case where two separate and distinct causes of action are alleged, one only of which is federal in character. In the former, where the federal question averred is not plainly wanting in substance, the federal court, even though the federal ground be not established, may nevertheless retain and dispose of the case upon the nonfederal *ground*; in the latter it may not do so upon the nonfederal *cause of action*." 289 U.S., at 246, 53 S.Ct., at 589. The question is into which category the present action fell.

Hurn was decided in 1933, before the unification of law and equity by the Federal Rules of Civil Procedure. At the time, the meaning of "cause of action" was a subject of serious dispute * * *. The Court in *Hurn* identified what it meant by the term by citation of Baltimore S. S. Co. v. Phillips, 274 U.S. 316, 47 S.Ct. 600, 71 L.Ed. 1069, a case in which "cause of action" had been used to identify the operative scope of the doctrine of *res judicata*. In that case the Court had noted that " 'the whole tendency of our decisions is to require a plaintiff to try his whole cause of action and his whole case at one time,' " 274 U.S., at 320, 47 S.Ct., at 602. It stated its holding in the following language, quoted in part in the *Hurn* opinion:

> "Upon principle, it is perfectly plain that the respondent [a seaman suing for an injury sustained while working aboard ship] suffered but one actionable wrong, and was entitled to but one recovery, whether his injury was due to one or the other of several distinct acts of alleged negligence, or to a combination of some or all of them. In either view, there would be but a single wrongful invasion of a single primary right of the plaintiff, namely, the right of bodily safety, whether the acts constituting such invasion were one or many, simple or complex.

> "A cause of action does not consist of facts, but of the unlawful violation of a right which the facts show. The number and variety of the facts alleged do not establish more than one cause of action so long as their result, whether they be considered severally or in combination, is the violation of but one right by a single legal wrong. The mere multiplication of grounds of negligence alleged as causing the same injury does not result in multiplying the causes of action. 'The facts are merely the means, and not the end. They do not constitute the cause of action, but they show its existence by making the wrong appear.' " Id., at 321, 47 S.Ct. at 602.

Had the Court found a jurisdictional bar to reaching the state claim in *Hurn*, we assume that the doctrine of *res judicata* would not have been applicable in any subsequent state suit. But the citation of *Baltimore S.S. Co.* shows that the Court found that the weighty policies of judicial economy and fairness to parties reflected in *res judicata* doctrine were in themselves strong counsel for the adoption of a rule which would permit federal courts to dispose of the state as well as the federal claims.

With the adoption of the Federal Rules * * * and the unified form of action * * * much of the controversy over "cause of action" abated. The phrase remained as the keystone of the *Hurn* test, however, and * * * has been the source of considerable confusion. Under the Rules, the impulse is toward entertaining the broadest possible scope of action consistent with fairness to the parties; joinder of claims, parties and remedies are strongly encouraged. Yet because the *Hurn* question involves issues of jurisdiction as well as convenience, there has been some tendency to limit its application to cases in which the state and federal claims are, as in *Hurn*, "little more than the equivalent of different epithets to characterize the same group of circumstances." 289 U.S., at 246, 53 S.Ct. at 590.

This limited approach is unnecessarily grudging. Pendent jurisdiction, in the sense of judicial *power*, exists whenever there is a claim "arising under [the] Constitution, the Laws of the United States, and Treaties made, or which shall be made, under their Authority * * *," U.S. Const., Art. III, § 2, and the relationship between that claim and the state claims made in the complaint permits the conclusion that the entire action before the court comprises but one constitutional "case." The federal claim must have substance sufficient to confer subject matter jurisdiction on the court. * * * The state and federal claims must derive from a common nucleus of operative fact. But if, considered without regard for their federal or state character, a plaintiff's claims are such that he would ordinarily be expected to try them all in one judicial proceeding, then, assuming substantiality of the federal issues, there is *power* in federal courts to hear the whole.

That power need not be exercised in every case in which it is found to exist. It has consistently been recognized that pendent jurisdiction is a doctrine of discretion, not of plaintiff's right. Its justification lies in considerations of judicial economy, convenience and fairness to litigants; if these are not present a federal court should hesitate to exercise jurisdiction over state claims, even though bound to apply state law to them, Erie R. Co. v. Tompkins * * * [p. 314, infra]. Needless decisions of state law should be avoided both as a matter of comity and to promote justice between the parties, by procuring for them a surer-footed reading of applicable law. Certainly, if the federal claims are dismissed before trial, even though not insubstantial in a jurisdictional sense, the state claims should be dismissed as well. Similarly, if it appears that the state issues substantially predominate, whether in terms of proof, of the scope of the issues raised, or of the comprehensiveness of the remedy sought, the state claims may be dismissed without prejudice and left for resolution to state tribunals. There may, on the other hand, be situations in which the state claim is so closely tied to questions of federal policy that the argument for exercise of pendent jurisdiction is particularly strong. In the present case, for example, the allowable scope of the state claim implicates the federal doctrine of preemption; while this interrelationship does not create statutory federal question jurisdiction, Louisville & N.R. Co. v. Mottley * * * [p. 245, supra] reasons independent of jurisdictional considerations, such as the likelihood of jury confusion in treating divergent legal theories of relief, that would justify separating state and federal claims for trial, Fed.Rule Civ.Proc. 42(b). If so, jurisdiction should ordinarily be refused.

The question of power will ordinarily be resolved on the pleadings. But the issue whether pendent jurisdiction has been properly assumed is one which remains open throughout the litigation. Pretrial procedures or even the trial may reveal a substantial hegemony of state law claims, or likelihood of jury confusion, which could not have been anticipated at the pleading stage. Although it will of course be appropriate to take account in this circumstance of the already completed course of the litigation, dismissal of the state claim might even then be merited. For example, it may appear that the plaintiff was well aware of the nature of his proofs and the relative importance of his claims; recognition of a federal court's wide latitude to decide ancillary questions of state law does not imply that it must tolerate a litigant's effort to impose upon it what is in effect only a state law case. Once it appears that a state claim constitutes the real body of a case, to which the federal claim is only an appendage, the state claim may fairly be dismissed.

We are not prepared to say that in the present case the District Court exceeded its discretion in proceeding to judgment on the state claim. * * *

It is true that the § 303 claims ultimately failed and that the only recovery allowed respondent was on the state claim. We cannot confidently say, however, that the federal issues were so remote or played such a minor role at the trial that in effect the state claim only was tried. Although the District Court dismissed as unproved the claims that petitioner's secondary activities included attempts to induce coal operators other than Grundy to cease doing business with respondent, the court submitted the § 303 claims relating to Grundy to the jury. The jury returned verdicts against petitioner on those § 303 claims, and it was only on petitioner's motion for a directed verdict and a judgment *n.o.v.* that the verdicts on those claims were set aside. * * * Although there was some risk of confusing the jury in joining the state and federal claims—especially since, as will be developed, differing standards of proof of UMW involvement applied—the possibility of confusion could be lessened by employing a special verdict form, as the District Court did. * * *

[The Court went on to hold that plaintiff could not recover damages for conspiracy under Tennessee common law on the basis of the record.]

Reversed.

THE CHIEF JUSTICE took no part in the decision of this case.

[A concurring opinion by JUSTICE HARLAN, joined by JUSTICE CLARK, agreed with "Part I of the Court's opinion relating to pendent jurisdiction."]

NOTES AND QUESTIONS

1. What is the constitutional and statutory basis for the jurisdiction recognized in *Hurn* and in *Gibbs*? Recall that the language of 28 U.S.C. § 1331 is virtually identical to that of Article III. Is the term "civil action" that appears in the statute coextensive with the Constitution's use of the term "case"?

2. In *Hurn*, discussed in *Gibbs*, the Supreme Court permitted a district court with original jurisdiction over a federal law claim to exercise pendent

jurisdiction over a nondiverse state law claim when the two claims presented a "single cause of action," but not when they were "separate and distinct causes of action." How did *Gibbs* change the test for determining when pendent jurisdiction may be exercised?

NOTE ON PENDENT AND ANCILLARY JURISDICTION AFTER GIBBS

In three cases after *Gibbs*, the Supreme Court considered whether pendent or ancillary jurisdiction could be asserted when the district court had original jurisdiction over a claim and plaintiff sought to join a state law claim against an *additional* nondiverse defendant.

1.   In ALDINGER v. HOWARD, 427 U.S. 1, 96 S.Ct. 2413, 49 L.Ed.2d 276 (1976), a Washington State citizen brought a federal civil rights action under 42 U.S.C. § 1983 against several state officials; jurisdiction was invoked under 28 U.S.C. § 1343(a)(3). Plaintiff sought to join Spokane County, Washington as an additional defendant, but under the then-prevailing construction of the civil rights statute, counties were not liable under it.[g] Therefore, plaintiff sued the county under state law. Although the new claim shared a "common nucleus of operative fact" with the federal civil rights claim, and so satisfied *Gibbs*, the Supreme Court held that pendent jurisdiction could not be exercised because it would be inconsistent with the statute authorizing original jurisdiction. However, the Court declined to lay down any "sweeping pronouncement upon the existence or exercise of [pendent party] jurisdiction":

> * * * Other statutory grants and other alignments of parties and claims might call for a different result. When the grant of jurisdiction to a federal court is exclusive, for example, as in the prosecution of tort claims against the United States * * *, the argument of judicial economy and convenience can be coupled with the additional argument that only in a federal court may all of the claims be tried together. * * *

Id. at 18, 96 S.Ct. at 2422, 49 L.Ed.2d at 288.

2.   In OWEN EQUIPMENT & ERECTION CO. v. KROGER, 437 U.S. 365, 98 S.Ct. 2396, 57 L.Ed.2d 274 (1978), Kroger, a citizen of Iowa, brought a diversity action in Nebraska against Omaha Public Power District (OPPD), a Nebraska corporation, for the wrongful death of her husband, who was electrocuted when the beam of a steel crane, next to which he was walking, came too close to a high-tension electric line. OPPD filed a third-party claim under Federal Rule 14(a) against the owner-operator of the crane, Owen Equipment and Erection Company (Owen), alleging that it was Owen's negligence that had been the proximate cause of the decedent's death. At the time, lower federal courts consistently held that an impleader complaint

---

g   Municipalities and other governmental units have since been held to be amenable to suit under 42 U.S.C. § 1983. See Monell v. Dep't of Soc. Servs., 436 U.S. 658, 98 S.Ct. 2018, 56 L.Ed.2d 611 (1978).

against a third party did not require an independent basis of federal jurisdiction.

Following OPPD's impleader of Owen, plaintiff was allowed to amend her complaint to name Owen as a defendant, which she alleged was a Nebraska corporation with its principal place of business in Nebraska. OPPD requested, and was granted, summary judgment, leaving Owen as the sole defendant. During the course of the trial, it was discovered that Owen's principal place of business actually was in Iowa.[h] Owen then moved to dismiss the case for a lack of subject-matter jurisdiction. The district court denied the motion and the court of appeals affirmed. The Supreme Court reversed on the ground that the exercise of ancillary jurisdiction would be inconsistent with the requirements of diversity jurisdiction.

3.   In FINLEY v. UNITED STATES, 490 U.S. 545, 109 S.Ct. 2003, 104 L.Ed.2d 593 (1989), plaintiff's husband and two of her children were killed when their plane struck electric power lines on its approach to a city-run airfield in San Diego, California. Plaintiff alleged that the Federal Aviation Administration had been negligent in its operation and maintenance of the runway lights and in its performance of air traffic control functions, and invoked jurisdiction under 28 U.S.C. § 1346(b). Later, plaintiff was allowed to amend her complaint to include state tort claims against the city of San Diego and the utility company that maintained the power lines. The court of appeals reversed the district court's decision to allow the amendment, and the Supreme Court affirmed, setting out a new rule requiring explicit congressional authorization for the exercise of pendent party jurisdiction.

> * * * *Aldinger* indicated that the *Gibbs* approach would not be extended to the pendent-party field, and we decide today to retain that line. Whatever we say regarding the scope of jurisdiction conferred by a particular statute can of course be changed by Congress. What is of paramount importance is that Congress be able to legislate against a background of clear interpretive rules, so that it may know the effect of the language it adopts. All our cases * * * have held that a grant of jurisdiction over claims involving particular parties does not itself confer jurisdiction over additional claims by or against different parties. Our decision today reaffirms that interpretive rule; the opposite would sow confusion.

Id. at 556, 109 S.Ct. at 2010–11, 104 L.Ed.2d at 606. In dissent, Justice Stevens characterized the Court's holding as a major departure from *Aldinger*, which, he stated, had "adopted a rule of construction that assumed the existence of pendent jurisdiction unless 'Congress in the statutes conferring jurisdiction

---

[h] The problem concerned the Missouri River, which generally marks the boundary between Iowa and Nebraska. Carter Lake, Iowa, where the accident occurred and where Owen had its main office, lies west of the river, adjacent to Omaha, Nebraska. Apparently, the river had avulsed at one of its bends, cutting Carter Lake off from the rest of Iowa. See Oakley, *The Story of* Owen Equipment v. Kroger: *A Change in the Weather of Federal Jurisdiction*, in Civil Procedure Stories 81–134 (Clermont ed., 2d ed. 2008).

has * * * expressly or by implication negated its existence' * * *." Id. at 573, 574–75, 109 S.Ct. at 2020–21, 104 L.Ed.2d at 617, 618 (Stevens, J., dissenting).

4.   Congress responded to *Finley* by enacting 28 U.S.C. § 1367, giving pendent and ancillary jurisdiction the shared name of supplemental jurisdiction. Does the statute codify the *Gibbs* test for determining when two claims "form part of the same case or controversy under Article III of the United States Constitution"? Is it clear that if two claims derive from a "common nucleus of operative fact" they satisfy the statutory test of subsection (a)? What is the significance of the words "so related" in Section 1367(a) and the statute's omission of the *Gibbs* language referring to a "common nucleus of fact"? Is the test set out in Section 1367(a) arguably broader than the *Gibbs* test? See Fletcher, *"Common Nucleus of Operative Fact" and Defensive Set-Off: Beyond the* Gibbs *Test*, 74 Ind.L.J. 171 (1998).

5.   Before the enactment of 28 U.S.C. § 1367, a permissive counterclaim under Federal Rule 13(b) was assumed to require an independent basis of federal jurisdiction, although not all judges agreed. See United States v. Heyward-Robinson Co., 430 F.2d 1077, 1088 (2d Cir. 1970) (Friendly, J., concurring). After the enactment of Section 1367, some courts held that Congress had codified the conventional view. See Iglesias v. Mutual Life Ins. Co. of New York, 156 F.3d 237, 241 (1st Cir. 1998). However, in JONES v. FORD MOTOR CREDIT CO., 358 F.3d 205, 209, 213–14 (2d Cir. 2004), the Second Circuit held that the statute "displaced, rather than codified" the traditional rule with respect to permissive counterclaims, finding that a district court may exercise supplemental jurisdiction whenever there exists a " 'logical relationship' between the counterclaim and the main claim." See Global Naps, Inc. v. Verizon New England Inc., 603 F.3d 71, 76 (1st Cir. 2010) ("§ 1367 supersedes case law on supplemental jurisdiction that had distinguished between compulsory and permissive counterclaims").

6.   The legislative history to 28 U.S.C. § 1367(b) indicates the intent to withhold supplemental jurisdiction when its exercise would circumvent traditional limitations on the grant of diversity jurisdiction. The *Strawbridge* rule of complete diversity is one judge-made limit. Explain whether supplemental jurisdiction is available in these situations:

(a)   P, a citizen of Virginia, sues D, a citizen of Texas. D moves under Federal Rule 14 to implead TP, a citizen of Texas.

(b)   P, a citizen of Virginia, sues D, a citizen of Texas. D moves under Federal Rule 14 to implead TP, a citizen of Virginia.

(c)   Assuming the facts of (b), P moves to amend her complaint to allege a state law claim against TP.

See Oakley, Kroger *Redux*, 51 Duke L.J. 663 (2001).

7.   Multiple plaintiffs suing one defendant are permitted to aggregate their claims to meet the amount-in-controversy requirement of diversity jurisdiction only if their claims are common and indivisible. See p. 238, Note 3, supra. Prior to the enactment of 28 U.S.C. § 1367, this rule prevented a party

(who met the citizenship requirement) from joining a lawsuit as a plaintiff under Federal Rule 20 when its claim did not exceed $75,000 and was separate and distinct from the claim of a diverse plaintiff whose claim did meet the dollar requirement. See CLARK v. PAUL GRAY, INC., 306 U.S. 583, 59 S.Ct. 744, 83 L.Ed. 1001 (1939). A similar rule applied to class actions under Rule 23; the named representative plaintiff and each and every unnamed class member were required to meet the amount-in-controversy requirement. See ZAHN v. INTERNATIONAL PAPER CO., 414 U.S. 291, 94 S.Ct. 505, 38 L.Ed.2d 511 (1973).

The enactment of 28 U.S.C. § 1367 presented two distinct but related problems. The first was whether Section 1367(a), in its reference to "any civil action of which the district courts have original jurisdiction," incorporates the judge-made rules of both *Strawbridge* and aggregation. The second problem concerned which parties and claims were excluded from § 1367(a)'s presumption of supplemental jurisdiction. The statute excludes "claims by plaintiffs against persons made parties under Rule 14, 19, 20, or 24," but does not mention claims by plaintiffs made parties under Rule 20 or 23. Did that omission reflect a congressional intent to abrogate both the *Clark* and the *Zahn* restrictions? See Pfander, *Supplemental Jurisdiction and Section* 1367: *The Case for Sympathetic Textualism*, 148 U.Pa.L.Rev. 109 (1999).

The Court addressed this set of questions in EXXON MOBIL CORP. v. ALLAPATTAH SERVICES, INC., 545 U.S. 546, 125 S.Ct. 2611, 162 L.Ed.2d 502 (2005), and held that "where the other elements of jurisdiction are present and at least one named plaintiff in the action satisfies the amount-in-controversy requirement, § 1367 does authorize supplemental jurisdiction over the claims of other plaintiffs in the same Article III case or controversy, even if those claims are for less than the jurisdictional amount specified in the statute setting forth the requirements for diversity jurisdiction." Id. at 549, 125 S.Ct. at 2615, 162 L.Ed.2d at 515. As the Court stated, "The natural, indeed the necessary, inference is that § 1367 confers supplemental jurisdiction over claims by Rule 20 and Rule 23 plaintiffs." Id. at 560, 125 S.Ct. at 2621, 162 L.Ed.2d at 522. In reaching this conclusion, the majority rejected the view, put forward in Justice Ginsburg's dissenting opinion, "that the inclusion of a claim or party falling outside the district court's original jurisdiction somehow contaminates every other claim in the complaint, depriving the court of original jurisdiction over any of these claims." Id. The majority acknowledged, however, that "[t]he contamination theory * * * can make some sense in the special context of the complete diversity requirement because the presence of nondiverse parties on both sides of a lawsuit eliminates the justification for providing a federal forum." Do you agree that the presence of a single nondiverse party "contaminates" diversity jurisdiction, such that the court lacks original jurisdiction and thereby defeats supplemental jurisdiction? Why isn't original jurisdiction destroyed by the presence of claims that do not meet the amount-in-controversy requirement?

8.   Recall that under *Gibbs*, p. 260, supra, the district court has discretion to decline or to exercise pendent jurisdiction, and the opinion set

forth a variety of factors to guide the decision. The circuits are divided on when supplemental jurisdiction may be declined under 28 U.S.C. § 1367(c). One approach holds that the statute displaced the *Gibbs* factors and narrowed the district court's scope of discretion. See EXECUTIVE SOFTWARE NORTH AMERICA, INC. v. UNITED STATES DISTRICT COURT, 24 F.3d 1545 (9th Cir. 1994), overruled on other grounds by California Dept. of Water Resources v. Powerex Corp., 533 F.3d 1087 (9th Cir. 2008). A competing approach holds that the statute codified *Gibbs* so that a district court is never required to exercise supplemental jurisdiction, at least when an enumerated factor does not apply. See Montana v. City of Chicago, 375 F.3d 593 (7th Cir. 2004). Alternatively, could the statute be read as channeling the court's discretion in light of the policies announced in *Gibbs*? See Enochs v. Lampasas County, 641 F.3d 155, 159 (5th Cir. 2011) (stating that courts should "look to the statutory factors set forth by 28 U.S.C. § 1367(c), and to the common law factors of judicial economy, convenience, fairness, and comity" and then "consider and balance each of the factors"). The Supreme Court has not yet decided this question.

9.   Section 1367(d) includes a tolling provision that enables a party to refile state claims in state court after some claims asserted under Section 1367(a) are dismissed. In ARTIS v. DISTRICT OF COLUMBIA, 583 U.S. ___, 138 S.Ct. 594, 199 L.Ed.2d 473 (2018), the Court, five-to-four, held that the provision stops the clock on the state statute of limitations, thus suspending the limitations period while the federal action is pending and for 30 days after dismissal.

10.   After the codification of pendent and ancillary jurisdiction in 28 U.S.C. § 1367, do federal courts retain any inherent authority to exercise jurisdiction when it is not conferred by statute? This question was presented in KOKKONEN v. GUARDIAN LIFE INSURANCE CO. OF AMERICA, 511 U.S. 375, 114 S.Ct. 1673, 128 L.Ed.2d 391 (1994). The action involved a dispute between an insurer and an insurance agent for breach of an agency agreement. The action was filed in state court and removed to federal court on the basis of diversity jurisdiction. Pursuant to Federal Rule 41(a)(1)(ii), the parties executed a Stipulation and Order of Dismissal, which the district court signed. Later, a dispute arose about the settlement agreement, and the insurer moved to enforce that agreement. The district court entered an enforcement order asserting it had "inherent authority" to do so, rejecting the argument that it lacked subject-matter jurisdiction over the settlement. The court of appeals affirmed, and the Supreme Court reversed and remanded. Significantly, the Supreme Court acknowledged that a residual category of ancillary jurisdiction—"over some matters (otherwise beyond their competence) that are incidental to other matters properly before them"—survives the enactment of 28 U.S.C. § 1367. Generally speaking, the assertion of ancillary jurisdiction is limited to two purposes: "(1) to permit disposition by a single court of claims that are, in varying respects and degrees, factually interdependent"; and "(2) to enable a court to function successfully, that is, to manage its proceedings, vindicate its authority, and effectuate its decrees." Id. at 380, 114 S.Ct. at 1676,

128 L.Ed.2d at 397. The Court found that neither basis was present in this case. Moreover, although parties are free to agree to the retention of judicial jurisdiction to enforce a settlement agreement, the agreement did not do so:

> If the parties *wish* to provide for the court's enforcement of a dismissal-producing settlement agreement, they can seek to do so. When the dismissal is pursuant to * * * Rule * * * 41(a)(2), which specifies that the action "shall not be dismissed at the plaintiff's instance save upon order of the court and upon such terms and conditions as the court deems proper," the parties' compliance with the terms of the settlement contract (or the court's "retention of jurisdiction" over the settlement contract) may, in the court's discretion, be one of the terms set forth in the order. Even when, as occurred here, the dismissal is pursuant to Rule 41(a)(1)(ii) (which does not by its terms empower a district court to attach conditions to the parties' stipulation of dismissal) we think the court is authorized to embody the settlement contract in its dismissal order (or, what has the same effect, retain jurisdiction over the settlement contract) if the parties agree. Absent such action, however, enforcement of the settlement agreement is for state courts, unless there is some independent basis for federal jurisdiction.

Id. at 381–82, 114 S.Ct. at 1677, 128 L.Ed.2d at 398.

E. THE SUBJECT-MATTER JURISDICTION OF THE FEDERAL COURTS—REMOVAL JURISDICTION

Read 28 U.S.C. §§ 1441, 1442, 1443, 1445, 1446, and 1447 in the Supplement.

Removal is a procedure that allows a suit filed in state court to be transferred to the federal court. Under the current general removal statute, only defendants can remove. The possibility of removal gives defendants a significant veto power over plaintiff's forum choice. As such, removal "runs directly contrary to one of the most deeply embedded, yet implicit, maxims of United States adversarial procedure: the plaintiff is the master of his or her claim." Bassett & Perschbacher, *The Roots of Removal*, 77 Brooklyn L.Rev. 1, 2 (2011). Generally, all defendants, other than nominal parties, must join in the petition for removal. See Chicago, R.I. & P. Ry. Co. v. Martin, 178 U.S. 245, 20 S.Ct. 854, 44 L.Ed. 1055 (1900). An exception to the rule of unanimity applies to the removal of multiparty "single accident" cases under 28 U.S.C. § 1369, see 28 U.S.C. § 1441(e), as well as to class actions under the Class Action Fairness Act, see 28 U.S.C. § 1453(b).

The United States Constitution does not mention removal, but Congress has conferred jurisdiction to hear removed cases since the First Judiciary Act of 1789. The general removal statute, 28 U.S.C. § 1441, traces to the Judiciary Act of 1875 and amendments enacted in 1887. See Collins, *The Unhappy History of Federal Question Removal*, 71 Iowa L.Rev. 717 (1986). Special removal statutes have been enacted for specific parties and claims. E.g., 28 U.S.C. § 1442 (removal by federal officers); 28 U.S.C. § 1443 (removal of certain cases involving civil rights); 28 U.S.C. § 1453 (removal of certain interstate class actions). Congress also has barred the removal of certain kinds of claims. E.g., 28 U.S.C. § 1445 (actions against railroads under the Federal Employers Liability Act).

The procedure for removal is justified on a number of grounds. From the perspective of litigant equality, removal ensures that defendants as well as plaintiffs have an opportunity to "decide which cases federal courts hear." Haiber, *Removing the Bias Against Removal*, 53 Cath.U.L.Rev. 609, 611 (2004). Moreover, in diversity actions, removal protects an out-of-state defendant from the threat of local bias. However, the use of removal jurisdiction does not always align with public goals. Instead, the decision to remove often is based on tactical factors, "such as jury verdicts, trial rules and procedure, and the availability, caseload and personality of federal judges in making the decision of whether to remove a case to federal court." Reggio, *Removal and Remand: A Guide to Navigating Between the State and Federal Courts,* 23 Miss.C.L.Rev. 97, 98 (2004). The strategic significance of removal is underscored by empirical studies of win-loss rates in removed actions. Plaintiff's win rate in diversity actions filed as an original matter is 71 percent, but drops to 34 percent for an action that is removed. See Clermont, *Litigation Realities Redux*, 84 Notre Dame L.Rev. 1919, 1927 (2009).

NOTES AND QUESTIONS

1.   Section 1441(a) authorizes removal "by the defendant or the defendants." SHAMROCK OIL & GAS CORP. v. SHEETS, 313 U.S. 100, 105–09, 61 S.Ct. 868, 871–72, 85 L.Ed. 1214, 1217–19 (1941), presented the question of whether plaintiff could remove a state court action on the basis of defendant's assertion of a federal law counterclaim. Justice Stone, writing for a unanimous Court, held no.

The Supreme Court revisited this aspect of the removal statute more recently in HOME DEPOT U.S.A., INC. v. JACKSON, 587 U.S. ___, 139 S.Ct. 1743, 204 L.Ed.2d 34 (2019). A bank filed a debt-collection action in state court, alleging that a consumer was liable for charges he had incurred on a Home Depot credit card. The consumer responded by filing third-party class-action claims against Home Depot, alleging that it had engaged in practices that violated state law. Home Depot removed the case to federal court, citing not only Section 1441(a) but also Section 1453(b) (the Class Action Fairness Act's specialized removal provision for certain interstate class actions).

Writing for a five-to-four majority, Justice Thomas concluded that removal was not proper because "in the context of these removal provisions the term 'defendant' refers only to the party sued by the original plaintiff." Id. at ___, 139 S.Ct. at 1746, 204 L.Ed.2d at 40. Although Justice Thomas recognized that "*Shamrock Oil* does not specifically address whether a party who was not the original plaintiff can remove a counterclaim filed against it," he saw "no textual reason to reach a different conclusion for a counterclaim defendant who was not originally part of the lawsuit." Id. at ___, 139 S.Ct. at 1749, 204 L.Ed.2d at 44.

> In that regard, *Shamrock Oil* did not view the counterclaim as a separate action with a new plaintiff and a new defendant. Instead, the Court highlighted that the original plaintiff was still "the plaintiff." * * * Similarly here, the filing of counterclaims that included class-action allegations against a third party did not create a new "civil action" with a new "plaintiff" and a new "defendant."

Id. The same reasoning applied to removal under Section 1453(b), which likewise permits only a "defendant" to remove. Id. at ___, 139 S.Ct. at 1750, 204 L.Ed.2d at 45 ("Congress did not expand the types of parties eligible to remove a class action under § 1453(b) beyond § 1441(a)'s limits."). Justice Alito wrote a dissent, joined by Chief Justice Roberts and Justices Gorsuch and Kavanaugh. The dissent emphasized that a third-party defendant, like an original defendant, did not choose to litigate in state court, and "might face bias there, and with it the potential for crippling unjust losses." Id. at ___, 139 S.Ct. at 1752, 204 L.Ed.2d at 47 (Alito, J., dissenting).

2. Just as plaintiff cannot create federal jurisdiction by anticipating defendant's federal responses, so plaintiff cannot block removal by disguising the federal nature of the claim. In BRIGHT v. BECHTEL PETROLEUM, INC., 780 F.2d 766 (9th Cir. 1986), a worker challenged his employer's practice of issuing paychecks net of state and federal income taxes, and styled the action as a state court breach of contract claim. The employer removed the case to federal court arguing that the complaint really was a challenge to the employer's compliance with federal tax law. The Ninth Circuit held that removal was proper: "Although the plaintiff is generally considered the 'master of his complaint' and is free to choose the forum for his action, this principle is not without limitation. * * * A plaintiff will not be allowed to conceal the true nature of a complaint through 'artful pleading.'" Id. at 769. See Miller, *Artful Pleading: A Doctrine in Search of Definition*, 76 Tex.L.Rev. 1781, 1783 (1998).

3. Defendant's pleading of a federal affirmative defense to a state law claim generally does not support removal. An important but complex exception involves the doctrine of complete preemption, when state claims are so exclusively federal in nature that only the federal remedy exists and federal jurisdiction is present. See, e.g., Avco Corporation v. Aero Lodge No. 735, 390

U.S. 557, 88 S.Ct. 1235, 20 L.Ed.2d 126 (1968). As the Supreme Court has explained, "[I]f a federal cause of action completely preempts a state cause of action any complaint that comes within the scope of the federal cause of action necessarily 'arises under' federal law." Franchise Tax Bd. of State of California v. Construction Laborers Vacation Trust for Southern California, 463 U.S. 1, 24, 103 S.Ct. 2841, 2854, 77 L.Ed.2d 420, 440 (1983).

4.   Traditionally, the doctrine of derivative jurisdiction barred the removal because, if the state court lacked subject-matter jurisdiction, "there was, legally speaking, no action pending in the state court and hence no action which could be removed to the federal court." See Bee Mach. Co. v. Freeman, 131 F.2d 190, 194 (1st Cir. 1942), affirmed, 319 U.S. 448, 63 S.Ct. 1146, 87 L.Ed. 1509 (1943). What is the current rule? See 28 U.S.C. § 1441(f).

5.   A number of special rules involving citizenship apply when defendant seeks to remove on the basis of diversity jurisdiction.

In-state defendant: Section 1441(b)(2) bars removal "solely" on the basis of diversity jurisdiction "if any of the parties in interest properly joined and served as defendants is a citizen of the State in which such action is brought." What is the rationale for preventing in-state defendants from removing based on diversity jurisdiction?

Fraudulent joinder: Another rule in diversity cases involves the judicial ban on fraudulent joinder, the situation when a plaintiff joins a nondiverse party in an effort to block removal in a case that otherwise would satisfy the rule of complete diversity. Removal is permitted if plaintiff has no cause of action against the nondiverse defendant; the district court may sever the nondiverse party from the action under Federal Rule 21. See Percy, *Making a Federal Case of It: Removing Civil Cases to Federal Court Based on Fraudulent Joinder*, 91 Iowa L.Rev. 189 (2005). Some courts will remand the case to allow the diverse defendant to move for severance and then to remove. See Osborn v. Metropolitan Life Ins. Co., 341 F.Supp.2d 1123 (E.D.Cal.2004). Which approach is preferable? See Marple, *Removal to Federal Court Based on Misjoinder of Parties*, 41 Tex.Tech L.Rev. 551 (2009).

Unrelated federal claim: Another rule pertains to a case in which plaintiff joins a nondiverse state law claim with an unrelated federal claim. See 28 U.S.C. § 1441(c). What is the constitutional significance of requiring the district court to sever and remand the "claim that has been made nonremovable by statute" to state court? See Belyea v. Florida Dept. of Revenue, 859 F.Supp.2d 1272 (N.D.Fla. 2012).

6.   In 2012, Congress amended the removal statute as it affects the jurisdictional amount. See 28 U.S.C. § 1446(c)(2)(a)(i)–(ii). The Supreme Court in DART CHEROKEE BASIN OPERATING CO., LLC v. OWENS, 574 U.S., 81, 135 S.Ct. 547, 554, 190 L.Ed.2d 495, 503 (2014), interpreted the changed provision in a case seeking to remove an action under the Class Action Fairness Act, 28 U.S.C. § 1332(d) and § 1453. The Court held that when defendant asserts an amount in controversy that exceeds plaintiff's allegation, and

plaintiff challenges the larger amount, "both sides submit proof and the court decides, by a preponderance of the evidence, whether the amount-in-controversy has been satisfied." Should *Dart Cherokee* apply when the suit does not involve CAFA? The Court emphasized the fact that "no antiremoval presumption attends cases invoking CAFA," but left open "whether such a presumption is proper in mine-run diversity cases." Id. at 89, 135 S.Ct. at 554, 190 L.Ed.2d at 504.

7.   Removal is subject to a number of different time limits:

(a)   What is the trigger date in an action involving multiple defendants who are served at different times? See 28 U.S.C. § 1446(b).

(b)   What is the time limit when removal is based on diversity of citizenship? See 28 U.S.C. § 1446(c).

(c)   Would it be proper for a defendant who has been joined but not yet served to seek removal—a practice known as "snap removal"? See 28 U.S.C. § 1446(b)(2)(A).

(d)   If a suit is not removable based on the initial pleading, what are defendant's options if a later filing in the suit indicates a basis for removal? See 28 U.S.C. § 1446(b)(3).

(e)   What is the time limit if plaintiff acts in bad faith to block removal, for example, by deliberately refusing to disclose the actual amount in controversy? See 28 U.S.C. § 1446(c)(3)(B).

8.   Supplemental jurisdiction, standing alone, may not be invoked as a basis for removal. However, in CITY OF CHICAGO v. INTERNATIONAL COLLEGE OF SURGEONS, 522 U.S. 156, 118 S.Ct. 523, 139 L.Ed.2d 525 (1997), the Supreme Court clarified that supplemental jurisdiction may be exercised to permit removal in state court cases that also include claims for which there would be original jurisdiction in federal court. The Court noted that "[t]he propriety of removal * * * depends on whether the case originally could have been filed in federal court," and that Section 1367(a) "applies with equal force to cases removed to federal court as to cases initially filed there." Id. at 163, 165, 118 S.Ct. at 529, 530, 139 L.Ed.2d at 534, 535. If the federal claim on which removal is based is dismissed, the district court has discretion to remand the supplemental state claims to state court. See Carnegie-Mellon Univ. v. Cohill, 484 U.S. 343, 108 S.Ct. 614, 98 L.Ed.2d 720 (1988); see also 28 U.S.C. § 1367(c)(3) (permitting a district court to "decline to exercise supplemental jurisdiction" when "the district court has dismissed all claims over which it has original jurisdiction").

F. CHALLENGING THE SUBJECT-MATTER JURISDICTION OF THE COURT

1. DIRECT ATTACK ON A COURT'S LACK OF SUBJECT-MATTER JURISDICTION

Read Federal Rules of Civil Procedure 8(a)(1), 12(b)(1), 12(h)(3), and 60(b)(4), Form 40, and 28 U.S.C. § 1653 in the Supplement.

NOTES AND QUESTIONS

1. A defect in subject-matter jurisdiction may be raised by any party and by the court sua sponte, at any time during the proceeding, including for the first time on appeal. Moreover, it is settled that the jurisdiction of a federal court may not be created by agreement or by consent. See Mansfield, C. & L. M. Ry. Co. v. Swan, 111 U.S. 379, 4 S.Ct. 510, 28 L.Ed. 462 (1884).

2. Must a district court determine that subject-matter jurisdiction exists before making any other decision in the suit? In STEEL CO. v. CITIZENS FOR A BETTER ENVIRONMENT, 523 U.S. 83, 118 S.Ct. 1003, 140 L.Ed.2d 210 (1998), the Court underscored that the "requirement that jurisdiction be established as a threshold matter 'spring[s] from the nature and limits of the judicial power of the United States' and is 'inflexible and without exception.'" Id. at 94–95, 118 S.Ct. at 1012, 140 L.Ed.2d at 227. It follows, the Court explained, that it is impermissible for a lower court to exercise "hypothetical" jurisdiction to resolve questions of law. See Steinman, *After Steel Co.: "Hypothetical Jurisdiction" in the Federal Appellate Courts*, 58 Wash. & Lee L.Rev. 855 (2001). However, in RUHRGAS AG v. MARATHON OIL CO., 526 U.S. 574, 119 S.Ct. 1563, 143 L.Ed.2d 760 (1999), the Supreme Court unanimously held that the lower court's inquiry into personal jurisdiction could precede that of subject-matter jurisdiction. The Court explained:

> Where * * * a district court has before it a straightforward personal jurisdiction issue presenting no complex question of state law, and the alleged defect in subject matter jurisdiction raises a difficult and novel question, the court does not abuse its discretion by turning directly to personal jurisdiction.

Id. at 588, 119 S.Ct. at 1572, 143 L.Ed.2d at 773. See Friedenthal, *The Crack in the* Steel *Case*, 68 Geo.Wash.L.Rev. 258, 259 (2000). Similarly, the Court has held that a district court may dismiss an action on grounds of forum non conveniens before resolving that subject-matter jurisdiction exists. See *Sinochem*, p. 308, Note 8, infra. For a criticism of post-*Steel* cases, see Idleman,

The Emergence of Jurisdictional Resequencing in the Federal Courts, 87 Cornell L.Rev. 1 (2001).

3.   Is a district court's remand order reviewable by appeal? The text of 28 U.S.C. § 1447(d) appears to bar appellate review of all remand orders other than in cases removed under 28 U.S.C. § 1442 (removal by federal officers) and 28 U.S.C. § 1443 (removal of certain cases involving civil rights). See Steinman, *Reinventing Appellate Jurisdiction*, 48 B.C.L.Rev. 1237 (2007). However, the Supreme Court has held that only remands based on grounds stated in Section 1447(c)—a lack of subject-matter jurisdiction or a procedural defect—are immune from review. See Powerex Corp. v. Reliant Energy Services, Inc., 551 U.S. 224, 127 S.Ct. 2411, 168 L.Ed.2d 112 (2007). In CARLSBAD TECHNOLOGY, INC. v. HIF BIO, INC., 556 U.S. 635, 129 S.Ct. 1862, 173 L.Ed.2d 843 (2009), the Court held that a remand order declining to exercise supplemental jurisdiction is reviewable by appeal notwithstanding Section 1447(d). Special rules apply to the review of remand orders in suits under the Class Action Fairness Act. See 28 U.S.C. § 1453(c).

In BP P.L.C. v. MAYOR & CITY COUNCIL OF BALTIMORE, 593 U.S. ___, 141 S.Ct. 1532, 209 L.Ed.2d 631 (2021), the Supreme Court addressed the provision of Section 1447(d) authorizing appellate review of "an order remanding a case to the State court from which it was removed pursuant to section 1442 or 1443." Plaintiffs in that case sued various energy companies in Maryland state court, asserting state causes of action alleging that defendants promoted fossil fuels while concealing their environmental impacts. Defendants removed the case to federal court on several grounds. They primarily argued for removal under 28 U.S.C. § 1441, on the theory that plaintiffs' claims necessarily arose under federal common law and, accordingly, federal subject-matter jurisdiction existed under 28 U.S.C. § 1331. But defendants asserted other grounds for removal as well—including federal officer removal under 28 U.S.C. § 1442. The district court rejected all of defendants' grounds for removal—including federal officer removal—and ordered the case remanded to state court.

On appeal, defendants argued that the exception in Section 1447(d) permitted appellate review not only of the district court's ruling on federal officer removal, but also its rulings on their other grounds for removal. In a 7–1 decision (Justice Alito did not participate), the Supreme Court agreed. As long as a defendant "premised removal in part on the federal officer removal statute, § 1442, or the civil rights removal statute, § 1443," the appellate court could review the district court's rulings on every ground for removal asserted. 593 U.S. at ___, 141 S.Ct. at 1536, 209 L.Ed.2d at 637. Justice Gorsuch's majority opinion reasoned that "the statute allows courts of appeals to examine the whole of a district court's 'order,' not just some of its parts or pieces." Id. at ___, 141 S.Ct. at 1537–38, 209 L.Ed.2d at 639.

The Court also addressed plaintiffs' argument that the majority's interpretation of Section 1447(d) would encourage "gamesmanship" by defendants, who "may frivolously add § 1442 or § 1443 to their other grounds for removal, all with an eye to ensuring appellate review down the line if the case is remanded":

> [T]hanks to § 1447(c) a district court may order a defendant to pay the plaintiff's costs and expenses (including attorney's fees) if it frivolously removes a case from state court. Additionally, the Federal Rules of Civil Procedure allow courts to sanction frivolous arguments made in virtually any context. Rules 11(b)–(c).

Id. at ___, 141 S.Ct. at 1542–43, 209 L.Ed.2d at 645.

Justice Sotomayor was the lone dissenter. She wrote that the majority's interpretation "lets defendants sidestep § 1447(d)'s bar on appellate review by shoehorning a § 1442 or § 1443 argument into their case for removal. In other words, it lets the exception swallow the rule." Id. at ___, 141 S.Ct. at 1543, 209 L.Ed.2d at 646 (Sotomayor, J., dissenting). Justice Sotomayor also cast doubt on the majority's view that the possibility of sanctions would deter gamesmanship by defendants seeking a federal forum, noting that "[a] federal-officer claim can be so weak it is not worth pursuing on appeal, but not so meritless as to warrant sanctions." Id. at ___, 141 S.Ct. at 1547, 209 L.Ed.2d at 649. In the *BP* case itself, defendants "no longer advance their argument under § 1442, * * * [y]et that argument somehow opens a back door to appellate review that would otherwise be closed to them." Id.

4.   What are the consequences if a district court fails to remand an action that was improperly removed, but the jurisdictional defect is cured before a judgment on the merits is entered? In considering this question, the Supreme Court has drawn a line between "jurisdictional cures" that involve a change in the parties to the action, and those that involve post-filing changes to a party's citizenship.

In CATERPILLAR INC. v. LEWIS, 519 U.S. 61, 117 S.Ct. 467, 136 L.Ed.2d 437 (1996), the district court mistakenly retained removal jurisdiction despite the absence of complete diversity. Diversity became complete prior to trial when the nondiverse party was formally dismissed from the action. The Sixth Circuit held it was error not to have remanded, and vacated the district court's judgment. The Supreme Court, in a unanimous decision, reversed, emphasizing the "overwhelming" effect of "considerations of finality, efficiency, and economy." Id. at 75, 117 S.Ct. at 476, 136 L.Ed.2d at 451. By contrast, in GRUPO DATAFLUX v. ATLAS GLOBAL GROUP, L.P., 541 U.S. 567, 124 S.Ct. 1920, 158 L.Ed.2d 866 (2004), complete diversity became present when the citizenship of plaintiff, a limited partnership, changed due to the withdrawal of two Mexican citizens who were members of the partnership at the time of filing. The Supreme Court, in a five-to-four decision, adhered to the time-of-filing rule and refused to extend the *Caterpillar* rationale to this situation. See Simpson-Wood, *Has the Seductive Siren of Judicial Frugality Ceased to Sing?:* Dataflux *and Its Family Tree*, 53 Drake L.Rev. 281 (2005).

2. COLLATERAL ATTACK ON A JUDGMENT FOR LACK OF SUBJECT-MATTER JURISDICTION

NOTES AND QUESTIONS

1.   An old and repeated maxim of jurisdiction doctrine is that a judgment rendered by a court that lacked jurisdiction over the subject matter (or the "cause," to use the older terminology) is void and a nullity. See, e.g., The Case of the Marshalsea, 10 Co. Rep. 68b, 77 Eng. Rep. 1027 (K.B. 1613). However, the subject is considerably more complex than the maxim would indicate and the question of when a judgment is vulnerable to collateral attack for lack of subject-matter jurisdiction remains vexing.

2.   Section 10 of the Restatement (First) of Judgments (1942) stated that if the court in the original action determined that it had subject-matter jurisdiction, the permissibility of collateral attack depended on weighing a non-exclusive list of factors:

(a)   the lack of jurisdiction over the subject matter was clear;

(b)   the determination as to jurisdiction depended upon a question of law rather than of fact;

(c)   the court was one of limited and not of general jurisdiction;

(d)   the question of jurisdiction was not actually litigated;

(e)   the policy against the court's acting beyond its jurisdiction is strong.

3.   Restatement (Second), Judgments §§ 12, 69 (1982), took the approach that the judgment in a contested action, whether or not the question of subject-matter jurisdiction actually was litigated, is beyond collateral attack unless there are no justifiable interests of reliance that must be protected, and:

(a)   the subject matter of the action was so plainly beyond the court's jurisdiction that its entertaining the action was a manifest abuse of authority; or

(b)   allowing the judgment to stand would substantially infringe the authority of another tribunal or agency of government; or

(c)   the judgment was rendered by a court lacking capability to make an adequately informed determination of a question concerning its own jurisdiction and as a matter of procedural fairness the party seeking to avoid the judgment should have opportunity belatedly to attack the court's subject-matter jurisdiction.

In addition, the Restatement (Second) of Judgments generally permits collateral attack on the original court's subject-matter jurisdiction, as well as on personal jurisdiction and inadequate notice, in default judgment situations. Id. at § 65. Does this approach go far enough, or too far, toward giving preclusive effect to the original court's judgment?

4. The Supreme Court has given mixed signals as to when a lack of subject-matter jurisdiction will support a collateral challenge. In CHICOT COUNTY DRAINAGE DISTRICT v. BAXTER STATE BANK, 308 U.S. 371, 60 S.Ct. 317, 84 L.Ed. 329 (1940), parties who had notice but chose not to appear in the original action attempted a collateral challenge to a judgment rendered by a district court sitting as a court of bankruptcy under a statute that was later declared unconstitutional. The Supreme Court refused to allow the attack. In TRAVELERS INDEMNITY CO. v. BAILEY, 557 U.S. 137, 129 S.Ct. 2195, 174 L.Ed.2d 99 (2009), the Court relied on *Chicot* to bar a collateral challenge to a bankruptcy court's order.

By contrast, a collateral challenge was allowed by the Court in KALB v. FEUERSTEIN, 308 U.S. 433, 60 S.Ct. 343, 84 L.Ed. 370 (1940), decided the same day as *Chicot*. The questions for decision in *Kalb* were whether a state court had jurisdiction to render a judgment confirming a foreclosure sale while the mortgagor's petition under the Bankruptcy Act was pending in a bankruptcy court, and, if not, whether the mortgagor was prohibited from attacking the state-court judgment collaterally. The Court answered both questions in the negative. Which of the categories in the two Restatements seems determinative of the *Kalb* case?

The Court again considered the question of collateral challenge for a defect in subject-matter jurisdiction in DURFEE v. DUKE, 375 U.S. 106, 84 S.Ct. 242, 11 L.Ed.2d 186 (1963), involving a dispute over title to a tract of bottom land on the Missouri River, which forms the boundary between Nebraska and Missouri. A Missouri federal district court allowed collateral attack on a Nebraska judgment quieting title, on the ground that considerations of territorial sovereignty outweighed the policies of res judicata. The Nebraska court's subject-matter jurisdiction depended on whether the land was within Nebraska, which "depended entirely upon a factual question—whether a shift in the river's course had been caused by avulsion or accretion." The question had been fully litigated in the Nebraska action. The Supreme Court reversed. The decision in *Durfee* was followed in UNDERWRITERS NATIONAL ASSURANCE CO. v. NORTH CAROLINA LIFE & ACC. & HEALTH INS. GUAR. ASS'N, 455 U.S. 691, 102 S.Ct. 1357, 71 L.Ed.2d 558 (1982). See generally 18A Wright, Miller & Cooper, Federal Practice and Procedure: Jurisdiction and Related Matters § 4428 (3d ed.).

CHAPTER 5

VENUE, TRANSFER, AND
FORUM NON CONVENIENS

■ ■ ■

This chapter considers venue, a doctrine that concerns the geographic location of a lawsuit. Venue plays an important administrative role by allocating cases among courts of the same type within a single judicial system, which can prevent docket congestion. Venue also helps to protect a defendant from having to litigate in a forum that has jurisdiction but nevertheless is inconvenient. Unlike personal jurisdiction and subject-matter jurisdiction, the venue of a civil action does not raise any federal constitutional questions. However, as an aspect of forum choice, the venue of an action holds great strategic significance for a party's litigation success.

A. VENUE

1. GENERAL PRINCIPLES

STEVENS, VENUE STATUTES: DIAGNOSIS AND PROPOSED CURE, 49 Mich.L.Rev. 307, 308–15 (1951):

* * * Given a cause of action, and having decided what court has jurisdiction over the subject matter, the lawyer must lay the venue, that is, select the place * * * [for litigating the case]. In making this decision, the lawyer in every state of the United States turns in the first instance, not to common law, but to statute, constitutional provision or rule of court. And he finds that the "proper" venue of his action depends upon the theory of his claim, the subject matter of his claim, the parties involved, or a combination of these factors.

Most codes make provision for the place of trial in local actions, and all codes provide in one way or another for venue in transitory actions arising both within and without the state. Many states make special provision for divorce actions, actions against executors, and actions for the specific recovery of personal property. Most states also provide for venue in actions against residents, against nonresidents, against corporations, domestic and foreign, against partnerships, associations and individuals doing business in the state, and against the state, or a county, or a city or public officers generally or specifically. The nature of the plaintiff, as a resident or nonresident, corporation, domestic or foreign, or political entity, is another factor frequently considered and provided for. * * *

A comparative study of contemporary venue provisions reveals some thirteen different fact situations upon which venue statutes are predicated.

A. *Where the subject of action or part thereof is situated.* The common law concept of actions which were local because the facts could have occurred only in a particular place still persists. As might well be expected, the proper venue for such actions is the county where the subject of the action is situated. There is, however, considerable variation from state to state as to what types of cases are local and fall into this category. * * *

This type of venue * * * is based upon the idea that the court of the county in which the res, which is the subject matter of the suit, is located is best able to deal with the problem. The local sheriff can attach, deliver or execute upon the property. The local clerk can make the necessary entries with a minimum of red tape where title to land is affected. Trial convenience is served where "a view" is necessary or of value in reaching a determination. Third parties can readily ascertain, at a logical point of inquiry, the status of a res in which they may be interested.

It is submitted that these factors are of sufficient importance in this type of case to outweigh other considerations such as convenience of parties or witnesses in the selection of place of trial. * * *

B. *Where the cause of action, or part thereof, arose or accrued.* Convenience of witnesses is the most logical reason for venue provisions allowing the action to be brought in the county where the cause of action, or part thereof, arose or accrued. And since convenience of witnesses is a very practical problem in the trial of a law suit, one would expect to find venue based upon the place where the cause of action arose or accrued a rather common, and general, provision. * * *

The idea behind this type of venue provision * * * is sound and popular. * * * However, its usefulness has been somewhat impaired by difficulties arising out of problems of statutory interpretation. First, what do the words "arose" and "accrued" mean? Second, what is the difference, if any, between "arose" and "accrued"? And, third, what is the meaning of the phrase "or part thereof"? * * *

C. *Where some fact is present or happened.* There is a sizeable group of statutes which provide for * * * [hearing] the action in the county where some particular fact or fact situation related to, but no part of, the cause of action is present or happened. * * *

If the purpose of venue is * * * convenience, either of parties, or witnesses, or the court or court officials, then it is hard to find any real justification for this group of venue provisions. Most if not all of them are examples of singling out certain specific types of actions for special treatment where a need for special treatment is not or at least no longer [is] apparent. * * *

D. *Where the defendant resides.* Convenience of the defendant is the reason usually given for venue statutes which provide for the place of trial in the county where the defendant resides—the theory probably being, as suggested by Professor E.R. Sunderland, "that since the plaintiff controls the institution of the suit he might behave oppressively toward the defendant unless restrained." * * *

E. *Where the defendant is doing business.* * * * Convenience of the defendant, and of witnesses, appears to be the reason behind such provisions where they are tied to causes of action arising out of the doing of business in the state. Convenience of the defendant, and even more clearly, convenience of the plaintiff, by providing a county in which to lay the venue against a nonresident individual, partnership, company or corporation without undue inconvenience to defendant, is served by the broader type of provision—against certain classes of defendants generally. * * *

F. *Where defendant has an office or place of business, or an agent, or representative, or where an agent or officer of defendant resides.* [These venue statutes] * * * are quite common where a corporation, company or some other type of business organization is the defendant. Convenience of the plaintiff, rather than the defendant, is the moving consideration behind such statutes in most instances. * * *

G. *Where the plaintiff resides.* * * *

Convenience of the plaintiff is the obvious reason behind venue statutes of this nature. Convenience of plaintiff's witnesses may or may not be served, depending upon the nature of the action. * * * In certain types of cases against certain classes of defendants—such as an action on a foreign cause of action against a nonresident—this type of provision is both logical and practical. * * *

H. *Where the plaintiff is doing business.* * * * Obviously the convenience of the plaintiff is the sole consideration behind such a provision. It is submitted that other * * * convenience [factors] such as convenience of witnesses and of the defendant are more important, and that in view of the number of adherents to this ground of venue, it would be wise to advocate its abandonment. * * *

I. *Where the defendant may be found.* Venue based upon the county where the defendant may be found is in accord with the common law doctrine that the right of action follows the person. * * *

It is difficult to find any sound reason for venue based upon where the defendant may be found. It serves no useful purpose—no * * * convenience of either witnesses or parties. It is a good example of a historical hangover—a type of provision which has long since outlived its usefulness. The problem which this type of provision was designed to solve was and is not one of venue but of service of process. * * *

J.   *Where the defendant may be summoned or served.* Another group of statutes, also based upon the common law doctrine that the right of action follows the person, provides that venue may be laid in the county where the defendant may be summoned, or served with process. * * *

The comments which were made with respect to venue based upon where the defendant may be found apply with equal force to this type of provision. * * *

K.   *In the county designated in the plaintiff's complaint.* * * *

Venue provisions of this type give the plaintiff an unnecessary economic advantage not warranted by convenience of parties or witnesses. In the interests of justice and trial convenience they should be eliminated.

L.   *In any county.* The broadest venue provision on the books is that which provides that the plaintiff may lay the venue in any county. * * *

M.   *Where the seat of government is located.* * * *

Statutes of this sort have a sound and practical reason behind them. With one exception, this type of provision is reserved for actions by or against governmental units or agencies. Convenience of the government appears to be the controlling factor. * * *

NOTES AND QUESTIONS

1.   Professor Stevens' explanation of venue is as relevant now as it was in 1951. However, in the decades since he wrote, venue largely has become the site of pretrial proceedings, leading to settlement or summary judgment, and not of a trial on the merits. Why is it necessary to superimpose venue requirements on a soundly conceived jurisdictional system, especially one that includes an analysis of party convenience? See Clermont, *Restating Territorial Jurisdiction and Venue for State and Federal Courts*, 66 Cornell L.Rev. 411 (1981). Does venue serve an additional function of protecting the judicial system from inconvenience?

2.   Should the rules governing venue in a state system differ from those in the federal system? Does the territorial size of the judicial system affect your analysis? Relatedly, the state and federal systems make use of specialized courts, such as the Surrogate's Court where the accounting in *Mullane* took place, see p. 173, supra.

2. LOCAL AND TRANSITORY ACTIONS

REASOR-HILL CORP. V. HARRISON

Supreme Court of Arkansas, 1952.
220 Ark. 521, 249 S.W.2d 994.

GEORGE ROSE SMITH, JUSTICE. Petitioner asks us to prohibit the circuit court of Mississippi County from taking jurisdiction of a cross-complaint filed by D.M. Barton. In the court below the petitioner moved to dismiss the cross-complaint for the reason that it stated a cause of action for injury to real property in the state of Missouri. When the motion to dismiss was overruled the present application for prohibition was filed in this court.

The suit below was brought by the Planters Flying Service to collect an account for having sprayed insecticide upon Barton's cotton crop in Missouri. In his answer Barton charged that the flying service had damaged his growing crop by using an adulterated insecticide, and by cross-complaint he sought damages from the petitioner for its negligence in putting on the market a chemical unsuited to spraying cotton. The petitioner is an Arkansas corporation engaged in manufacturing insecticides and is not authorized to do business in Missouri.

The question presented is one of first impression: May the Arkansas courts entertain a suit for injuries to real property situated in another State? For the respondent it is rightly pointed out that if the suit is not maintainable Barton has no remedy whatever. The petitioner cannot be served with summons in Missouri; so unless it is subject to suit in Arkansas it can escape liability entirely by staying out of Missouri until the statute of limitations has run. * * * The petitioner answers this argument by showing that with the exception of the Supreme Court of Minnesota every American court that has passed upon the question (and there have been about twenty) has held that jurisdiction does not exist.

We agree that the weight of authority is almost unanimously against the respondent, although in some States the rule has been changed by statute and in others it has been criticized by the courts and restricted as narrowly as possible. But before mechanically following the majority view we think it worthwhile to examine the origin of the rule and the reasons for its existence.

The distinction between local and transitory actions was recognized at the beginning of the fourteenth century in the common law of England. Before then all actions had to be brought where the cause of action arose, because the members of the jury were required to be neighbors who would know something of the litigants and of the dispute as well. But when cases were presented that involved separate incidents occurring in different communities the reason for localizing the action disappeared, for it was then impossible to obtain a jury who knew all the facts. Consequently the courts developed the distinction between a case that might have arisen anywhere, which was held to be transitory, and one that involved a particular piece of land, which was held to be local. * * *

As between judicial districts under the same sovereign the rule has many advantages and has been followed in America. As between counties our statutes in Arkansas require that actions for injury to real estate be brought where the land lies. * * * But we permit the defendant to be served anywhere in the State * * *; so the plaintiff is not denied a remedy even though the defendant is a resident of another county.

The English courts, in developing the law of local and transitory actions, applied it also to suits for injuries to real property lying outside England. If, for example, there had been a trespass upon land in France, the courts would not permit the plaintiff to bring suit in England, even though the defendant lived in England and could not be subjected to liability in France. The American courts, treating the separate States as independent sovereigns, have followed the English decisions.

In the United States the leading case is unquestionably Livingston v. Jefferson, Fed. Case No. 8411, 1 Brock 203. That suit was a part of the famous litigation between Edward Livingston and Thomas Jefferson * * *. The case was heard by Marshall as circuit justice and Tyler as district judge. Both agreed that the suit, which was for a wrongful entry upon land in Louisiana, could not be maintained in Virginia. In Marshall's concurring opinion he examined the English precedents and concluded that the law was so firmly established that the court was bound to follow it, though Marshall expressed his dissatisfaction with a rule which produced "the inconvenience of a clear right without a remedy."

Since then the American courts have relied almost uniformly upon the Livingston case in applying the rule to interstate litigation in this country. At least three reasons have been offered to justify the rule, but it is easy to show that each reason is more applicable to international controversies than to interstate disputes.

First, the ground most frequently relied upon is that the courts are not in a position to pass upon the title to land outside the jurisdiction. As between nations this reasoning may be sound. The members of this court have neither the training nor the facilities to investigate questions involving the ownership of land in France, in Russia, or in China. But the same difficulties do not exist with respect to land in another State. In our library we have the statutes and decisions of every other State, and it seldom takes more than a few hours to find the answer to a particular question. Furthermore, the American courts do not hesitate to pass upon an out-of-state title when the issue arises in a transitory action. If, for example, Barton had charged that this petitioner converted a mature crop in Missouri and carried it to Arkansas, our courts would decide the case even though it became necessary to pass upon conflicting claims of title to the land in Missouri. Again, a suit for damages for nonperformance of a contract to purchase land is transitory and may be maintained in another State, even though the sole issue is the validity of the seller's title. To put an extreme example, suppose that two companion suits, one local and one transitory, were presented to the same court together. In those States where the courts disclaim the ability to pass upon questions of title in local actions it might be necessary for the court to dismiss the local action for that reason and yet to decide the identical question in the allied transitory case.

Second, it has been argued that since the tort must take place where the land is situated the plaintiff should pursue his remedy before the defendant leaves the jurisdiction. This argument, too, has merit when nations are concerned. A sovereign, by its control of passports and ports of entry, may detain those who wish to cross its borders. But the citizens of the various States have a constitutional right to pass freely from one jurisdiction to another. * * * In the case at bar * * * Barton could hardly be expected to discover the damage and file an attachment suit before the pilot returned to his landing field in Arkansas.

Third, there is an understandable reluctance to subject one's own citizens to suits by aliens, especially if the other jurisdiction would provide no redress if the situation were reversed. * * * One may have some sympathy for this position in international disputes, but it has no persuasive effect when the States are involved. We do not feel compelled to provide a sanctuary in Arkansas for those who have willfully and wrongfully destroyed property, torn down houses, uprooted crops, polluted streams, and inflicted other injuries upon innocent landowners in our sister States. Yet every jurisdiction which follows the rule of the Livingston case affords that refuge to any person—whether one of its citizens or not—who is successful in fleeing from the scene of such misdeeds.

The truth is that the majority rule has no basis in logic or equity and rests solely upon English cases that were decided before America was discovered and in circumstances that are not even comparable to those existing in our Union. Basic principles of justice demand that wrongs should not go unredressed. * * * Under the majority rule we should have to tell Barton that he would have been much better off had the petitioner stolen his cotton outright instead of merely damaging it. And the only reason we could give for this unfortunate situation would be that English juries in the thirteenth century were expected to have personal knowledge of the disputes presented to them. We prefer to afford this litigant his day in court.

Writ denied.

GRIFFIN SMITH, C.J., concurs.

McFADDIN and WARD, J.J., dissent.

McFADDIN, JUSTICE (dissenting).

* * *

In the first place, the majority says that we have ample facilities to determine the land laws of other States in the United States. * * * This statement about the size of the law library seems rather weak, because land actions are tried in lower courts and not in the Supreme Court library. Just because we have a fine law library does not mean that we are prepared to determine the title to lands in Texas,[4] Missouri, Vermont, or any other State. But if we have the jurisdiction which the majority claims, then we could determine ejectment actions involving ownership of lands in other States. We might undertake to do this, but the Full Faith and Credit clause of the U.S. Constitution would not require the Sister State to recognize our judgment. * * *

Secondly, the majority says that the rule, requiring that an action be brought in the jurisdiction in which the land is situated, is a good rule between Nations, but is not good as between States in the American Union. For answer to this, I say: I have always understood that each of the American States is Sovereign; that the Federal Government is a government of delegated powers; and that all powers not delegated to the Federal Government are retained by the States and the People. Surely the majority is not attempting to reduce our American States to the level of mere local administrative units. Yet such, unfortunately, is the natural conclusion to which the majority opinion would carry us, when it concedes one rule for Nations and another for States.

Thirdly, the majority says that it does not desire to afford Arkansas Citizens a sanctuary from damage actions by citizens of other States. This is an argument that should be made—if at all—in the Legislative branch of Government, rather than in a judicial opinion. It is for the Legislative Department to determine when and where actions may be prosecuted. * * *

* * * [M]any, many cases * * * have considered the question here involved; and each Court—with the sole exception of Minnesota—has seen fit to follow the great weight of authority which has come down to us from the common law. In matters affecting real property particularly, we should leave undisturbed the ancient landmarks. * * *

---

[4] The writer knows by experience that only one skilled in Texas Land Law can successfully handle an action of Trespass to Try Title in the State of Texas.

NOTES AND QUESTIONS

1.   Why did the dissenting opinion in *Reasor-Hill* state that a judgment in ejectment rendered by the Arkansas courts involving land outside the state would not be entitled to Full Faith and Credit by a sister state? Does this suggest that it viewed the local action doctrine as a rule of subject-matter jurisdiction, and not of venue? If the rule is jurisdictional, would a court lack power to hear an action involving foreign land even if the parties did not raise an objection to venue? E.g., Taylor v. Sommers Bros. Match Co., 35 Idaho 30, 204 P. 472 (1922).

2.   In a state that recognizes the local action doctrine, could the court enforce a party-agreement locating a dispute about property in a district other than where the property is located? See Friedenthal, Kane, Miller & Steinman, Civil Procedure § 2.16 (6th ed.).

3.   Have the justifications for the local action rule eroded over time? Is it relevant that courts now have widely available access to electronic research systems including aerial maps? Should the doctrine be limited to in rem and quasi in rem actions when the lawsuit is brought to determine ownership or control of real property? The local action doctrine in federal court is discussed in p. 290, Note 3, infra.

3.   VENUE IN THE FEDERAL COURTS

Read 28 U.S.C. §§ 1390 and 1391 in the Supplement.

NOTES AND QUESTIONS

1.   Federal venue rules underwent significant revision in 1990 followed by other reforms in 1992 and 1995. The Jurisdiction and Venue Clarification Act of 2011 addressed additional problems that courts and litigants faced. Does the current version of 28 U.S.C. §§ 1390 and 1391 limit venue to a single geographic location or can there be multiple venues for civil actions within its scope?

2.   Unlike earlier versions of the statute, Section 1391(b) sets a unitary venue rule for diversity and federal question cases. Venue in both categories generally may be based on two criteria: defendant's residence, if all defendants reside in the same state, and the location of the events giving rise to the claim or a substantial part of the property that is the subject of the action. What is the default rule if no district meets the requirements of 28 U.S.C. § 1391(b)(1) or (2)?

Test your knowledge of the statute by identifying the provision that applies in the following situations:

(a) Determining the residence of a defendant-company that is incorporated in Delaware and has a principal place of business in Wilmington, Delaware.

(b) Determining the residence of a defendant-partnership that has its main office in Brooklyn, New York and members in every one of the fifty states.

(c) Determining the residence of a defendant-company that is incorporated in England and does business in Chicago, Illinois, in San Diego, California, and in Burlington, Vermont.

(d) Determining the residence of a plaintiff-company that is incorporated in South Dakota and has a principal place of business in Atlanta, Georgia.

(e) Determining the residence of a plaintiff-fraternal organization that has its main office in San Diego, California.

(f) Determining the residence of a defendant-corporation that is incorporated in a state that has more than one judicial district.

(g) Determining the residence of a natural person who is not a citizen but resides in the United States.

(h) Determining the residence of a natural person who is a citizen but resides outside the United States.

3.   Recall that many state venue rules incorporate a "local action" doctrine for lawsuits involving property. In LIVINGSTON v. JEFFERSON, 15 F.Cas. 660 (C.C.D.Va.1811), Chief Justice Marshall, sitting as Circuit Court Justice for Virginia, recognized the local action doctrine in the federal courts. See Degnan, Livingston v. Jefferson—*A Freestanding Footnote*, 75 Calif.L.Rev. 115 (1987). Does the federal venue statute continue to distinguish between local and transitory actions? See 28 U.S.C. § 1391(a)(2). To what extent does the location of property affect the venue determination? See 28 U.S.C. § 1391(b)(2). Does the current statute suggest that the rule, at least now, is one of venue and not of subject-matter jurisdiction? Not all courts agree with that conclusion. See Eldee-K Rental Properties, LLC v. DirecTV Inc., 748 F.3d 943 (9th Cir. 2014).

4.   Some federal statutes contain special venue rules for actions within their compass. For example, the Fair Debt Collection Practices Act provides that in an action by a debt collector on a debt not involving an interest in real property, venue is limited to either the district in which the consumer signed the contract giving rise to the debt or the district in which the consumer resides at the commencement of the action. See 15 U.S.C. § 1692i(a)(2). Another example of a special venue rule may be found in 42 U.S.C. § 2005e–5(f)(3), which defines the venue for an action under Title VII of the Civil Rights Act of 1964. Such actions may be brought:

[I]n any judicial district in the State in which the unlawful employment practice is alleged to have been committed, in the judicial district in which the employment records relevant to such practice are maintained and administered, or in the judicial district in which the aggrieved person would have worked but for the alleged unlawful employment practice, but if the respondent is not found within any such district, such an action may be brought within the judicial district in which the respondent has his principal office.

See James v. Verizon Services Corp., 639 F.Supp.2d 9, 12 (D.D.C. 2009). Does the general venue statute remain available to plaintiffs who bring suit under federal statutes with special venue rules? The Supreme Court has drawn a distinction that depends on whether the special venue rule is designed to be permissive or mandatory, restrictive or liberal. See Cortez Byrd Chips, Inc. v. Bill Harbert Construction Co., 529 U.S. 193, 204, 120 S.Ct. 1331, 1339, 146 L.Ed.2d 171, 181 (2000).

5.   In TC HEARTLAND LLC v. KRAFT FOOD GROUP BRANDS LLC, 581 U.S. ___, 137 S.Ct. 1514, 197 L.Ed.2d 816 (2017), the Supreme Court held that the definition of corporate residence set out in the general venue statute did not apply to the statute governing venue for patent infringement actions. 28 U.S.C. § 1400. Rather, for purposes of the patent venue statute, a domestic corporation resides only in its state of incorporation or "where the defendant has committed acts of infringement and has a regular and established place of business." The Court did not offer guidance regarding the latter basis for patent venue, but lower courts have interpreted it to require—among other things—a "physical place in the district" and the "regular, physical presence of an employee or other agent of the defendant." In re Google LLC, 949 F.3d 1338, 1344 (Fed. Cir. 2020). Prior to *TC Heartland*, a patent owner could bring an infringement action in almost any district where defendant's products were sold, and empirical studies showed that almost half of all patent suits in the period January 2014 through June 2016 were filed in only two federal districts. See Bone, *Forum Shopping and Patent Law—A Comment on* TC Heartland, 96 Tex.L.Rev. 141 (2017).

B.   TRANSFER OF VENUE IN THE FEDERAL COURTS

———

Read 28 U.S.C. §§ 1404, 1406, 1407, and 1631 in the Supplement.

———

NOTES AND QUESTIONS

1.   When may a court authorize a transfer of venue under 28 U.S.C. § 1404?

2.   In HOFFMAN v. BLASKI, 363 U.S. 335, 80 S.Ct. 1084, 4 L.Ed.2d 1254 (1960), the Court construed the statutory language "where it might have

been brought" in 28 U.S.C. § 1404 to bar the transfer of a case to a district that lacked personal jurisdiction over defendant even though he was willing to waive objections to the forum and it might be a better place to adjudicate the dispute. Does the current version of 28 U.S.C. § 1404(a) abrogate the *Hoffman* rule?

3.   Is a district court limited in its transfer analysis to the specified factors of party and witness convenience, or is the "interest of justice" factor a separate consideration that embraces a range of private and public interests? The Supreme Court noted in VAN DUSEN v. BARRACK, 376 U.S. 612, 84 S.Ct. 805, 11 L.Ed.2d 945 (1964), that the legislative history of Section 1404(a) treated the "interest of justice" as a separate consideration: "The new subsection requires the court to determine that the transfer is necessary for convenience of the parties and witnesses, and further, that it is in the interest of justice to do so." Id. at 634 n. 30, 84 S.Ct. at 818 n. 30, 11 L.Ed.2d at 960 n. 30 (quoting Revision of Title 28, United States Code, Report of the House Committee on Revision of the Laws on H.R. 7124, 79th Cong., 2d sess., p. A127).

Those courts that treat the interests of justice as a separate condition generally consider such factors as: (1) access to witnesses; (2) access to the forum; (3) docket congestion; (4) speed to trial; (5) relationship of the community to the dispute; (6) the court's familiarity with the governing law; (7) plaintiff's forum choice; (8) whether the original forum is where plaintiff resides; and (9) the existence of a presuit venue agreement. See Steinberg, *The Motion To Transfer and the Interests of Justice*, 66 Notre Dame L.Rev. 443 (1990).

4.   In VAN DUSEN v. BARRACK, Note 3, above, the Supreme Court held that, in diversity cases, the law of the transferor forum applies even after the defendant has transferred the action under 28 U.S.C. § 1404(a). "Where the defendants seek transfer," the Court explained, "the transferee district court must be obligated to apply the state law that would have been applied if there had been no change of venue." Id. at 639, 84 S.Ct. at 821, 11 L.Ed.2d at 962. The Court concluded, "[a] change of venue under § 1404(a) generally should be, with respect to state law, but a change of courtrooms." Id. at 639, 84 S.Ct. at 821, 11 L.Ed.2d at 962–63.

In FERENS v. JOHN DEERE CO., 494 U.S. 516, 110 S.Ct. 1274, 108 L.Ed.2d 443 (1990), the Court applied the *Van Dusen* rule to a plaintiff-initiated transfer. Plaintiff, a citizen of Pennsylvania, lost a hand when he accidentally caught it in a harvester manufactured by defendant, a Delaware corporation. Plaintiff failed to file suit within Pennsylvania's two-year tort limitations period. But, in the third year, plaintiff filed one suit in federal court in Pennsylvania, raising contract and warranty claims that were not yet time-barred, and a second suit in federal court in Mississippi, alleging tort claims. Mississippi had a six-year tort statute of limitations, which the federal court was required to apply. The federal court in Mississippi then granted plaintiff's motion to transfer the tort action to the Pennsylvania court under 28 U.S.C.

§ 1404(a). The Pennsylvania court refused to apply Mississippi's statute of limitations and dismissed the tort claims as time-barred under Pennsylvania's statute of limitations, and the court of appeals affirmed. Relying on *Van Dusen*, the Supreme Court reversed, holding that, in a diversity suit, the transferee forum is required to apply the law of the transferor court, including its choice-of-law rule, regardless of who initiates the transfer. Is this a sound result? See Bassett, *The Forum Game*, 84 N.C.L.Rev. 333, 352–70 (2006).

5.   Of what relevance is the *Van Dusen* rule when the district court transfers an action within its federal question jurisdiction? See Marcus, *Conflict Among Circuits and Transfers Within the Federal Judicial System*, 93 Yale L.J. 677, 721 (1984). The circuits currently are divided on this question. Because federal law is assumed to be unitary, some circuits have held that the transferee court should exercise its own judgment when determining the requirements of federal law and not be bound by the law of the transferor court. See Lanfear v. Home Depot, Inc., 536 F.3d 1217, 1223–24 (11th Cir. 2008). Other circuits have recognized a narrow role for *Van Dusen* in specific statutory contexts that, because of "unique language and purpose," contemplate "circuit disharmony." Olcott v. Delaware Flood Co., 76 F.3d 1538, 1546–47 (10th Cir. 1996).

6.   An empirical study found that plaintiffs won in 58 percent of nontransferred cases that went to judgment, but only in 29 percent of cases that were transferred. See Clermont & Eisenberg, *Exorcising the Evil of Forum-Shopping*, 80 Cornell L.Rev. 1507 (1995). The authors concluded that the reduced win rate can be explained by "a possibly less favorable set of local biases" and the "shifted balance of inconveniences," and not differences in the merits. Controlling for all variables, a later study found that the odds of a plaintiff prevailing went from 50 to 40 percent in a transferred action. See Clermont, *Litigation Realities Redux*, 84 Notre Dame L.Rev. 1919, 1928 (2009).

7.   When is a district court permitted to transfer under 28 U.S.C. § 1406(a), rather than under Section 1404(a)? When a case is transferred under Section 1406, the transferee court will treat the action as if it were started in that court as an initial matter. Under these circumstances, would it be appropriate to apply the *Van Dusen* rule, p. 292, Note 4, supra, to a case transferred under Section 1406? Do you agree that a party should benefit from the law that would have been applied in the original federal forum only if that court were "a proper one to begin with"? Manley v. Engram, 755 F.2d 1463, 1470 (11th Cir. 1985). See 14D Wright, Miller & Freer, Federal Practice & Procedure § 3827 (4th ed.) ("[W]henever the original venue is improper, so that transfer is under Section 1406(a), the transferee court should apply whatever law it would have applied had the action been properly commenced there.").

8.   In GOLDLAWR, INC. v. HEIMAN, 369 U.S. 463, 82 S.Ct. 913, 8 L.Ed.2d 39 (1962), the Supreme Court held that Section 1406 authorizes the transfer of an action even if the transferor court lacks personal jurisdiction. In 1982, Congress enacted 28 U.S.C. § 1631, permitting transfer of an action between any two federal courts when the original court lacks jurisdiction.

Section 1631 does not specify whether "jurisdiction" in this context means subject-matter jurisdiction, personal jurisdiction, or both. See Franco v. Mabe Trucking Co., 3 F.4th 788, 792–96 & n.5 (5th Cir. 2021) (describing what various courts have said about this issue and deciding that "the weight of circuit authority" has found that "the use of the term 'jurisdiction' in § 1631 encompasses both subject-matter and personal jurisdiction."). In some cases, courts have permitted transfer for a lack of venue under Section 1631. The better view is that venue is not a jurisdictional concept and so transfer should be limited to Section 1406. See Sorcia v. Holder, 643 F.3d 117, 122 (4th Cir.), cert. denied, 556 U.S. 1061, 132 S.Ct. 776, 181 L.Ed.2d 487 (2011).

9.   In cases where venue is improper or personal jurisdiction is lacking in plaintiff's initially chosen district, it is "within the sound discretion of the district court" whether to dismiss or transfer the case. Twin Flames Universe.com, Inc. v. Cole, 528 F.Supp.3d 708, 718 (E.D.Mich. 2021). "Unless evidence exists that the case was brought in the improper venue in bad faith or to harass the defendant, the interest of justice generally requires a transfer rather than a dismissal." Id. Courts have also observed that "the reasons for transferring a case to a proper forum rather than dismissing are especially compelling if the statute of limitations has run since the commencement of the action, so that dismissal might prevent the institution of a new suit by the plaintiff and a resolution on the merits." Jackson v. L & F Martin Landscape, 421 F. App'x 482, 484 (6th Cir. 2009). But compare McFarlane v. Esquire Mag., 74 F.3d 1296, 1301 (D.C.Cir. 1996) (affirming the district court's dismissal notwithstanding the expiration of the statute of limitations where defendant's answer put plaintiff on notice of his defense of lack of personal jurisdiction and plaintiff "failed to file a protective suit in [the proper forum]").

NOTE ON THE PANEL ON MULTIDISTRICT LITIGATION (MDL)

In 1968 Congress enacted the Multidistrict Litigation Act, 28 U.S.C. § 1407. See generally Bradt, *"A Radical Proposal": The Multidistrict Litigation Act of 1968*, 165 U.Pa.L.Rev. 831 (2017). It created a special venue procedure that authorizes the temporary transfer of related cases to one district when the cases involve common questions of fact and law and transfer would be for the convenience of the parties and witnesses and "will promote the just and efficient conduct of such actions." The statute established the Judicial Panel on Multidistrict Litigation ("JPML"), composed of seven judges from the federal district courts and courts of appeals who are appointed by the Chief Justice of the Supreme Court. The JPML decides whether cases should be transferred under the statute, which authorizes consolidation for pretrial purposes only. Since its enactment, the MDL statute has been used very frequently for coordinated discovery in cases involving environmental disaster, employment, trademark, mass tort, consumer, and other high stakes matters. See Gluck & Burch, *MDL Revolution*, 96 N.Y.U.L.Rev. 1 (2021); Miller, *What Are Courts For? Have We Forsaken the Procedural Gold Standard?*, 78 La.L.Rev. 739, 41–48 (2018).

In LEXECON INC. v. MILBERG WEISS BERSHAD HYNES & LERACH, 523 U.S. 26, 118 S.Ct. 956, 140 L.Ed.2d 62 (1998), the Supreme Court held that 28 U.S.C. § 1407 imposes a duty on the JPML to remand a transferred action to its original court for trial, and that a district court conducting such pretrial proceedings lacks authority to invoke 28 U.S.C. § 1404(a) "to assign a transferred case to itself for trial." Id. at 28, 118 S.Ct. at 959, 140 L.Ed.2d at 68. In so holding, the Court rejected a 30-year practice of self-assignment by the district courts that the JPML had sanctioned through its rulemaking authority. The Court declined to answer whether Section 1404(a) "permits self-transfer" by the transferee court "given that the statute explicitly provides for transfer only 'to any other district.'" Id. at 41 n.4, 118 S.Ct. at 964 n.4, 140 L.Ed.2d at 76 n.4.

The Judicial Conference of the United States has requested that the mandatory remand provision be eliminated from 28 U.S.C. § 1407, but Congress has not yet done so. See Marcus, *Cure-All For an Era of Dispersed Litigation? Toward a Maximalist Use of the Multidistrict Litigation Panel's Transfer Power*, 82 Tul.L.Rev. 2245 (2008). Because the procedure for multidistrict transfer is a rule of venue, may the parties waive the provision for mandatory remand? See Armstrong v. LaSalle Bank Nat. Ass'n, 552 F.3d 613 (7th Cir.2009). As a matter of first impression, the Fifth Circuit held that waiver is permissible, but it must be "clear and unambiguous." In re Depuy Orthopaedics, Inc., 870 F.3d 345, 357 (5th Cir. 2017).

Until *Lexecon*, the majority of courts applied the law of the transferee circuit to questions of federal law in cases transferred under 28 U.S.C. § 1407. In doing so, the courts were influenced by the decision authored by then-Judge Ruth Bader Ginsburg in In re Korean Air Lines Disaster of Sept. 1, 1983, 829 F.2d 1171, 1174 (D.C.Cir. 1987), affirmed on other grounds sub nom. Chan v. Korean Air Lines, Ltd., 490 U.S. 122, 109 S.Ct. 1676, 104 L.Ed.2d 113 (1989). Her opinion stressed that applying "divergent interpretations" of federal law "would surely reduce the efficiencies achievable through consolidated preparatory proceedings"; moreover, the parties could seek review by the Supreme Court if interpretations by lower courts diverged. Id. at 1175–76. In a concurrence, Judge Douglas H. Ginsburg emphasized the practical problems of resolving the choice of law question under the existing language of 28 U.S.C. § 1407, which is silent on whether the transferee court is to apply the law of the transferor court. In particular, he observed that "Congress contemplated that transferred cases might never return to the transferor courts," and that the majority of transferred cases do not return to the transferor courts. Id. at 1178. Does *Lexecon* undermine the rationale of applying the law of the transferee court? In a number of unpublished decisions, lower courts have been considering this question, but so far have concluded that they are compelled to follow existing circuit law and to apply the law of the transferee court until either Congress amends the statute or the Supreme Court announces a different rule. See, e.g., In re General Motors LLC Ignition Switch Litigation, 2016 WL 3920353 (S.D.N.Y.2016).

In IN RE: MF GLOBAL HOLDINGS LTD. INVESTMENT LITIGATION, 857 F.Supp.2d 1378, 1380–81 (Jud.Pan.Mult.Lit.2012), defendants in three actions and 12 "tag-along" actions pending in four districts moved for consolidation. The actions all followed in the wake of a holding company's filing for bankruptcy after announcing a shortfall of an estimated $1.6 billion in commodities futures customer accounts. The JPML held that transfer was appropriate even though the various actions involved multiple claims based on different legal theories:

> Plaintiffs opposing centralization of all actions together argue that claims under securities laws are separate and distinct from customer claims brought pursuant to the Commodities Exchange Act, 7 U.S.C. § 1, *et seq.* and related claims. They argue, *inter alia*, that centralization of both types of claims will be inefficient and inevitably slow the progress of the customer actions. We are not persuaded that the differences between these two types of claims weigh against centralizing all actions in a single proceeding. This is primarily because all actions arise from the common factual backdrop of the demise of MF Global Holdings, Ltd., and related entities and the reported shortfall in MF Global, Inc., commodities futures customer accounts. * * * [O]ur longstanding practice has been to leave the degree of coordination or consolidation of the different actions to the sound discretion of the transferee judge. * * * We see no reason to depart from this practice in these circumstances.

Why do you suppose some plaintiffs opposed the transfer? For some parties, won't transfer potentially increase administrative costs, decrease attorney control, reduce attorney's fees, and deflate settlement prospects? Did the JPML seriously consider these disparate effects? See Burch, *Financiers as Monitors in Aggregate Litigation*, 87 N.Y.U.L.Rev. 1273, 1288–91 (2012).

The use of multidistrict litigation for pretrial proceedings has increased significantly over the last decade, coinciding with a decline in the certification of national class actions. See Bradt, *Something Less and Something More: MDL's Roots as a Class Action Alternative*, 165 U.Pa.L.Rev. 1711 (2017). Some scholars have questioned whether MDL procedure produces optimal results or favors particular categories of litigants. See Burch & Williams, *Repeat Players in Multidistrict Litigation: The Social Network*, 102 Cornell L.Rev. 1445 (2017); Coleman, *One Percent Procedure*, 91 Wash.L.Rev. 1005 (2016).

C. FORUM NON CONVENIENS

GULF OIL CORP. v. GILBERT, 330 U.S. 501, 67 S.Ct. 839, 91 L.Ed. 1055 (1947), delineated the factors to be considered in deciding a motion based upon the principle of forum non conveniens:

> The principle of *forum non conveniens* is simply that a court may resist imposition upon its jurisdiction even when jurisdiction is authorized by the letter of a general venue statute. These statutes

are drawn with a necessary generality and usually give a plaintiff a choice of courts, so that he may be quite sure of some place in which to pursue his remedy. But the open door may admit those who seek not simply justice but perhaps justice blended with some harassment. A plaintiff sometimes is under temptation to resort to a strategy of forcing the trial at a most inconvenient place for an adversary, even at some inconvenience to himself.

Many of the states have met misuse of venue by investing courts with a discretion to change the place of trial on various grounds, such as the convenience of witnesses and the ends of justice. The federal law contains no such express criteria to guide the district court in exercising its power. But the problem is a very old one affecting the administration of the courts as well as the rights of litigants, and both in England and in this country the common law worked out techniques and criteria for dealing with it.

* * *

If the combination and weight of factors requisite to given results are difficult to forecast or state, those to be considered are not difficult to name. An interest to be considered, and the one likely to be most pressed, is the private interest of the litigant. Important considerations are the relative ease of access to sources of proof; availability of compulsory process for attendance of unwilling, and the cost of obtaining attendance of willing, witnesses; possibility of view of premises, if view would be appropriate to the action; and all other practical problems that make trial of a case easy, expeditious and inexpensive. There may also be questions as to the * * * [enforceability] of a judgment if one is obtained. The court will weigh relative advantages and obstacles to fair trial. It is often said that the plaintiff may not, by choice of an inconvenient forum, "vex," "harass," or "oppress" the defendant by inflicting upon him expense or trouble not necessary to his own right to pursue his remedy. But unless the balance is strongly in favor of the defendant, the plaintiff's choice of forum should rarely be disturbed.

Factors of public interest also have place in applying the doctrine. Administrative difficulties follow for courts when litigation is piled up in congested centers instead of being handled at its origin. Jury duty is a burden that ought not to be imposed upon the people of a community which has no relation to the litigation. In cases which touch the affairs of many persons, there is reason for holding the trial in their view and reach rather than in remote parts of the country where they can learn of it by report only. There is a local interest in having localized controversies decided at home. There is an appropriateness, too, in having the trial of a diversity case in a forum that is at home with the state law that must govern the case, rather than having a court in some other forum untangle problems in conflict of laws, and in law foreign to itself.

Id. at 507–09, 67 S.Ct. at 842–43, 91 L.Ed. at 1062–63.

PIPER AIRCRAFT CO. V. REYNO
Supreme Court of the United States, 1981.
454 U.S. 235, 102 S.Ct. 252, 70 L.Ed.2d 419.

Certiorari to the United States Court of Appeals for the Third Circuit.

JUSTICE MARSHALL delivered the opinion of the Court.

* * *

I

A

In July 1976, a small commercial aircraft crashed in the Scottish highlands during the course of a charter flight from Blackpool to Perth. The pilot and five passengers were killed instantly. The decedents were all Scottish subjects and residents, as are their heirs and next of kin. There were no eyewitnesses to the accident. At the time of the crash the plane was subject to Scottish air traffic control.

The aircraft, a twin-engine Piper Aztec, was manufactured in Pennsylvania by petitioner Piper Aircraft Co. (Piper). The propellers were manufactured in Ohio by petitioner Hartzell Propeller, Inc. (Hartzell). At the time of the crash the aircraft was registered in Great Britain and was owned and maintained by Air Navigation and Trading Co., Ltd. (Air Navigation). It was operated by McDonald Aviation, Ltd. (McDonald), a Scottish air taxi service. Both Air Navigation and McDonald were organized in the United Kingdom. The wreckage of the plane is now in a hangar in Farnsborough, England.

The British Department of Trade investigated the accident shortly after it occurred. A preliminary report found that the plane crashed after developing a spin, and suggested that mechanical failure in the plane or the propeller was responsible. At Hartzell's request, this report was reviewed by a three-member Review Board, which held a 9-day adversary hearing attended by all interested parties. The Review Board found no evidence of defective equipment and indicated that pilot error may have contributed to the accident. The pilot, who had obtained his commercial pilot's license only three months earlier, was flying over high ground at an altitude considerably lower than the minimum height required by his company's operations manual.

In July 1977, a California probate court appointed respondent Gaynell Reyno administratrix of the estates of the five passengers. Reyno is not related to and does not know any of the decedents or their survivors; she was a legal secretary to the attorney who filed this lawsuit. Several days after her appointment, Reyno commenced separate wrongful death actions against Piper and Hartzell in the Superior Court of California, claiming negligence and strict liability. Air Navigation, McDonald, and the estate of the pilot are not parties to this litigation. The survivors of the five passengers whose estates are represented by Reyno filed a separate action in the United Kingdom against Air Navigation, McDonald, and the pilot's estate. Reyno candidly admits that the action against Piper and Hartzell was filed in the United States because its laws regarding liability, capacity to sue, and damages are more favorable to her position than are those of Scotland. Scottish law does not recognize strict liability in tort. Moreover, it permits wrongful death actions only when brought by a decedent's relatives. The relatives may sue only for "loss of support and society."

On petitioners' motion, the suit was removed to the United States District Court for the Central District of California. Piper then moved for transfer to the United States District Court for the Middle District of Pennsylvania, pursuant to 28 U.S.C. § 1404(a). Hartzell moved to dismiss for lack of personal jurisdiction, or in the alternative, to transfer.[5] In December 1977, the District Court quashed service on Hartzell and transferred the case to the Middle District of Pennsylvania. Respondent then properly served process on Hartzell.

B

In May 1978, after the suit had been transferred, both Hartzell and Piper moved to dismiss the action on the ground of *forum non conveniens.* The District Court granted these motions in October 1979. It relied on the balancing test set forth by this Court in *Gulf Oil Corp. v. Gilbert* * * *.

* * * [T]he District Court analyzed the facts of * * * [this case]. It began by observing that an alternative forum existed in Scotland; Piper and Hartzell had agreed to submit to the jurisdiction of the Scottish courts and to waive any statute of limitations defense that might be available. It then stated that plaintiff's choice of forum was entitled to little weight. The court recognized that a plaintiff's choice ordinarily deserves substantial deference. It noted, however, that Reyno "is a representative of foreign citizens and residents seeking a forum in the United States because of the more liberal rules concerning products liability law," and that "the courts have been less solicitous when the plaintiff is not an American citizen or resident, and particularly when the foreign citizens seek to benefit from

---

[5]   The District Court concluded that it could not assert personal jurisdiction over Hartzell consistent with due process. However, it decided not to dismiss Hartzell because the corporation would be amenable to process in Pennsylvania.

the more liberal tort rules provided for the protection of citizens and residents of the United States." * * *

The District Court next examined several factors relating to the private interests of the litigants, and determined that these factors strongly pointed towards Scotland as the appropriate forum. Although evidence concerning the design, manufacture, and testing of the plane and propeller is located in the United States, the connections with Scotland are otherwise "overwhelming." * * * The real parties in interest are citizens of Scotland, as were all the decedents. Witnesses who could testify regarding the maintenance of the aircraft, the training of the pilot, and the investigation of the accident—all essential to the defense—are in Great Britain. Moreover, all witnesses to damages are located in Scotland. Trial would be aided by familiarity with Scottish topography, and by easy access to the wreckage.

The District Court reasoned that because crucial witnesses and evidence were beyond the reach of compulsory process, and because the defendants would not be able to implead potential Scottish third-party defendants, it would be "unfair to make Piper and Hartzell proceed to trial in this forum." * * * The survivors had brought separate actions in Scotland against the pilot, McDonald, and Air Navigation. "[I]t would be fairer to all parties and less costly if the entire case was presented to one jury with available testimony from all relevant witnesses." * * * Although the court recognized that if trial were held in the United States, Piper and Hartzell could file indemnity or contribution actions against the Scottish defendants, it believed that there was a significant risk of inconsistent verdicts.

The District Court concluded that the relevant public interests also pointed strongly towards dismissal. The court determined that Pennsylvania law would apply to Piper and Scottish law to Hartzell if the case were tried in the Middle District of Pennsylvania.[8] As a result, "trial in this forum would be hopelessly complex and confusing for a jury." * * * In addition, the court noted that it was unfamiliar with Scottish law and thus would have to rely upon experts from that country. The court also found that the trial would be enormously costly and time-consuming; that it would be unfair to burden citizens with jury duty when the Middle

---

[8]   Under *Klaxon* * * * [p. 358, infra], a court ordinarily must apply the choice-of-law rules of the State in which it sits. However, where a case is transferred pursuant to 28 U.S.C. § 1404(a), it must apply the choice-of-law rules of the State from which the case was transferred. *Van Dusen* * * * [p. 292, Notes 3 and 4, supra]. Relying on these two cases, the District Court concluded that California choice-of-law rules would apply to Piper, and Pennsylvania choice-of-law rules would apply to Hartzell. It further concluded that California applied a "governmental interests" analysis in resolving choice-of-law problems, and that Pennsylvania employed a "significant contacts" analysis. The court used the "governmental interests" analysis to determine that Pennsylvania liability rules would apply to Piper, and the "significant contacts" analysis to determine that Scottish liability rules would apply to Hartzell.

District of Pennsylvania has little connection with the controversy; and that Scotland has a substantial interest in the outcome of the litigation.

In opposing the motions to dismiss, respondent contended that dismissal would be unfair because Scottish law was less favorable. The District Court explicitly rejected this claim. * * *

C

On appeal, the * * * Third Circuit reversed and remanded for trial. The decision to reverse appears to be based on two alternative grounds. First, the Court held that the District Court abused its discretion in conducting the *Gilbert* analysis. Second, the Court held that dismissal is never appropriate where the law of the alternative forum is less favorable to the plaintiff.

The Court of Appeals began its review of the District Court's *Gilbert* analysis by noting that the plaintiff's choice of forum deserved substantial weight, even though the real parties in interest are nonresidents. It then rejected the District Court's balancing of the private interests. It found that Piper and Hartzell had failed adequately to support their claim that key witnesses would be unavailable if trial were held in the United States: they had never specified the witnesses they would call and the testimony these witnesses would provide. The Court of Appeals gave little weight to the fact that Piper and Hartzell would not be able to implead potential Scottish third-party defendants, reasoning that this difficulty would be "burdensome" but not "unfair" * * *. Finally, the court stated that resolution of the suit would not be significantly aided by familiarity with Scottish topography, or by viewing the wreckage.

The Court of Appeals also rejected the District Court's analysis of the public interest factors. It found that the District Court gave undue emphasis to the application of Scottish law: "the mere fact that the court is called upon to determine and apply foreign law does not present a legal problem of the sort which would justify the dismissal of a case otherwise properly before the court." * * * In any event, it believed that Scottish law need not be applied. After conducting its own choice-of-law analysis, the Court of Appeals determined that American law would govern the actions against both Piper and Hartzell. The same choice-of-law analysis apparently led it to conclude that Pennsylvania and Ohio, rather than Scotland, are the jurisdictions with the greatest policy interests in the dispute, and that all other public interest factors favored trial in the United States.

In any event, it appears that the Court of Appeals would have reversed even if the District Court had properly balanced the public and private interests. * * * [T]he court decided that dismissal is automatically barred if it would lead to a change in the applicable law unfavorable to the plaintiff.

We granted certiorari * * *.

II

The Court of Appeals erred in holding that plaintiffs may defeat a motion to dismiss on the ground of *forum non conveniens* merely by showing that the substantive law that would be applied in the alternative forum is less favorable to the plaintiffs than that of the present forum. The possibility of a change in substantive law should ordinarily not be given conclusive or even substantial weight in the *forum non conveniens* inquiry.

* * *

In fact, if conclusive or substantial weight were given to the possibility of a change in law, the *forum non conveniens* doctrine would become virtually useless. Jurisdiction and venue requirements are often easily satisfied. As a result, many plaintiffs are able to choose from among several forums. Ordinarily, these plaintiffs will select that forum whose choice-of-law rules are most advantageous. Thus, if the possibility of an unfavorable change in substantive law is given substantial weight in the *forum non conveniens* inquiry, dismissal would rarely be proper.

* * *

The Court of Appeals' approach is not only inconsistent with the purpose of the *forum non conveniens* doctrine, but also poses substantial practical problems. If the possibility of a change in law were given substantial weight, deciding motions to dismiss on the ground of *forum non conveniens* would become quite difficult. Choice-of-law analysis would become extremely important, and the courts would frequently be required to interpret the law of foreign jurisdictions. First, the trial court would have to determine what law would apply if the case were tried in the chosen forum, and what law would apply if the case were tried in the alternative forum. It would then have to compare the rights, remedies, and procedures available under the law that would be applied in each forum. Dismissal would be appropriate only if the court concluded that the law applied by the alternative forum is as favorable to the plaintiff as that of the chosen forum. The doctrine of *forum non conveniens,* however, is designed in part to help courts avoid conducting complex exercises in comparative law. As we stated in *Gilbert,* the public interest factors point towards dismissal where the court would be required to "untangle problems in conflict of laws, and in law foreign to itself." * * *

Upholding the decision of the Court of Appeals would result in other practical problems. At least where the foreign plaintiff named an American manufacturer as defendant, a court could not dismiss the case on grounds of *forum non conveniens* where dismissal might lead to an unfavorable change in law. The American courts, which are already extremely attractive to foreign plaintiffs, would become even more attractive. The flow of litigation into the United States would increase and further congest already crowded courts.

* * *

We do not hold that the possibility of an unfavorable change in law should *never* be a relevant consideration in a *forum non conveniens* inquiry. Of course, if the remedy provided by the alternative forum is so clearly inadequate or unsatisfactory that it is no remedy at all, the unfavorable change in law may be given substantial weight; the district court may conclude that dismissal would not be in the interests of justice.[22] In these cases, however, the remedies that would be provided by the Scottish courts do not fall within this category. Although the relatives of the decedents may not be able to rely on a strict liability theory, and although their potential damages award may be smaller, there is no danger that they will be deprived of any remedy or treated unfairly.

III

The Court of Appeals also erred in rejecting the District Court's *Gilbert* analysis. The Court of Appeals stated that more weight should have been given to the plaintiff's choice of forum, and criticized the District Court's analysis of the private and public interests. However, the District Court's decision regarding the deference due plaintiff's choice of forum was appropriate. Furthermore, we do not believe that the District Court abused its discretion in weighing the private and public interests.

A

The District Court acknowledged that there is ordinarily a strong presumption in favor of the plaintiff's choice of forum, which may be overcome only when the private and public interest factors clearly point towards trial in the alternative forum. It held, however, that the presumption applies with less force when the plaintiff or real parties in interest are foreign.

The District Court's distinction between resident or citizen plaintiffs and foreign plaintiffs is fully justified. * * * When the home forum has been chosen, it is reasonable to assume that this choice is convenient. When the plaintiff is foreign, however, this assumption is much less reasonable. Because the central purpose of any *forum non conveniens* inquiry is to ensure that the trial is convenient, a foreign plaintiff's choice deserves less deference.

---

[22] At the outset of any *forum non conveniens* inquiry, the court must determine whether there exists an alternative forum. Ordinarily, this requirement will be satisfied when the defendant is "amenable to process" in the other jurisdiction. *Gilbert* * * *. In rare circumstances, however, where the remedy offered by the other forum is clearly unsatisfactory, the other forum may not be an adequate alternative, and the initial requirement may not be satisfied. Thus, for example, dismissal would not be appropriate where the alternative forum does not permit litigation of the subject matter of the dispute. * * *

B

The *forum non conveniens* determination is committed to the sound discretion of the trial court. It may be reversed only when there has been a clear abuse of discretion; where the court has considered all relevant public and private interest factors, and where its balancing of these factors is reasonable, its decision deserves substantial deference. * * * Here, the Court of Appeals expressly acknowledged that the standard of review was one of abuse of discretion. In examining the District Court's analysis of the public and private interests, however, the Court of Appeals seems to have lost sight of this rule, and substituted its own judgment for that of the District Court.

(1)

In analyzing the private interest factors, the District Court stated that the connections with Scotland are "overwhelming." * * * This characterization may be somewhat exaggerated. Particularly with respect to the question of relative ease of access to sources of proof, the private interests point in both directions. As respondent emphasizes, records concerning the design, manufacture, and testing of the propeller and plane are located in the United States. She would have greater access to sources of proof relevant to her strict liability and negligence theories if trial were held here. However, the District Court did not act unreasonably in concluding that fewer evidentiary problems would be posed if the trial were held in Scotland. A large proportion of the relevant evidence is located in Great Britain.

The Court of Appeals found that the problems of proof could not be given any weight because Piper and Hartzell failed to describe with specificity the evidence they would not be able to obtain if trial were held in the United States. It suggested that defendants seeking *forum non conveniens* dismissal must submit affidavits identifying the witnesses they would call and the testimony these witnesses would provide if the trial were held in the alternative forum. Such detail is not necessary. Piper and Hartzell have moved for dismissal precisely because many crucial witnesses are located beyond the reach of compulsory process, and thus are difficult to identify or interview. Requiring extensive investigation would defeat the purpose of their motion. Of course, defendants must provide enough information to enable the District Court to balance the parties' interests. Our examination of the record convinces us that sufficient information was provided here. Both Piper and Hartzell submitted affidavits describing the evidentiary problems they would face if the trial were held in the United States.

The District Court correctly concluded that the problems posed by the inability to implead potential third party defendants clearly supported holding the trial in Scotland. Joinder of the pilot's estate, Air Navigation, and McDonald is crucial to the presentation of petitioners' defense. If Piper and Hartzell can show that the accident was caused not by a design defect, but rather by the negligence of the pilot, the plane's owners, or the charter company, they will be relieved of all liability. It is true, of course, that if Hartzell and Piper were found liable after a trial in the United States, they could institute an action for indemnity or contribution against these parties in Scotland. It would be far more convenient, however, to resolve all claims in one trial. The Court of Appeals rejected this argument. Forcing petitioners to rely on actions for indemnity or contributions would be "burdensome" but not "unfair." * * * Finding that trial in the plaintiff's chosen forum would be burdensome, however, is sufficient to support dismissal on grounds of *forum non conveniens.*

(2)

The District Court's review of the factors relating to the public interest was also reasonable. On the basis of its choice-of-law analysis, it concluded that if the case were tried in the Middle District of Pennsylvania, Pennsylvania law would apply to Piper and Scottish law to Hartzell. It stated that a trial involving two sets of laws would be confusing to the jury. It also noted its own lack of familiarity with Scottish law. Consideration of these problems was clearly appropriate under *Gilbert*; in that case we explicitly held that the need to apply foreign law pointed towards dismissal. The Court of Appeals found that the District Court's choice-of-law analysis was incorrect, and that American law would apply to both Hartzell and Piper. Thus, lack of familiarity with foreign law would not be a problem. Even if the Court of Appeals' conclusion is correct, however, all other public interest factors favored trial in Scotland.

Scotland has a very strong interest in this litigation. The accident occurred in its airspace. All of the decedents were Scottish. Apart from Piper and Hartzell, all potential plaintiffs and defendants are either Scottish or English. As we stated in *Gilbert,* there is "a local interest in having localized controversies decided at home." * * * Respondent argues that American citizens have an interest in ensuring that American manufacturers are deterred from producing defective products, and that additional deterrence might be obtained if Piper and Hartzell were tried in the United States, where they could be sued on the basis of both negligence and strict liability. However, the incremental deterrence that would be gained if this trial were held in an American court is likely to be insignificant. The American interest in this accident is simply not sufficient to justify the enormous commitment of judicial time and resources that would inevitably be required if the case were to be tried here.

* * *

Reversed.

[JUSTICE POWELL and JUSTICE O'CONNOR took no part in the decision of this case. JUSTICE WHITE concurred in part and dissented in part. JUSTICE STEVENS, with whom JUSTICE BRENNAN joined, dissented. Their dissent argued that remand was appropriate to the court of appeals, to determine "whether the District Court correctly decided that Pennsylvania was not a convenient forum in which to litigate a claim against a Pennsylvania company that a plane was defectively designed and manufactured in Pennsylvania."]

NOTES AND QUESTIONS

1. Lord Denning famously said: "As a moth is drawn to the light, so is a litigant drawn to the United States." Smith Kline & French Labs. Ltd. v. Bloch, [1983] 2 All E.R. 72, 72 (Eng.C.A.1982). On this account, foreign litigants choose to sue in the United States for strategic reasons: the Federal Rules are thought to be pro-plaintiff because they offer access to discovery and the possibility of class relief; litigation can be financed through contingency fees; and tort awards can include compensation for pain and suffering. See Robertson, *Transnational Litigation and Institutional Choice*, 51 B.C.L.Rev. 1081 (2010). Forum preferences have adapted somewhat given procedural developments abroad and here in the United States. See Bookman, *Litigation Isolationism*, 67 Stan.L.Rev. 1081, 1109 (2015) ("many nations have begun to recognize higher damages awards, aggregate litigation procedures, and third-party litigation funding").

2. In ISLAMIC REPUBLIC OF IRAN v. PAHLAVI, 62 N.Y.2d 474, 478 N.Y.S.2d 597, 467 N.E.2d 245 (1984), cert. denied, 469 U.S. 1108, 105 S.Ct. 783, 83 L.Ed.2d 778 (1985), the Islamic Republic of Iran sued the former ruler of Iran, Shah Mohammed Reza Pahlavi, and his wife to recover $35 billion dollars in Iranian funds that the couple were alleged to have misappropriated. The Shah and his wife had withdrawn these assets from Iran after a fundamental Islamist revolution deposed the Shah in 1979. Plaintiff served the couple in New York while the Shah was undergoing medical treatment at a New York hospital. The New York Court of Appeals affirmed the lower courts' dismissal on forum non conveniens grounds even though it appeared no alternative forum was available to plaintiff since the Shah would not return to Iran given the political situation under the Khomeini regime. Requiring proof of an alternative adequate forum, the court explained, "would place an undue burden on New York courts forcing them to accept foreign-based actions unrelated to this State merely because a more appropriate forum is unwilling or unable to accept jurisdiction." Id. at 481, 478 N.Y.S.2d at 601, 467 N.E.2d at 249. Are the facts of this case sui generis?

3. In TUAZON v. R.J. REYNOLDS TOBACCO CO., 433 F.3d 1163 (9th Cir. 2006), plaintiff, a Philippine citizen, filed a federal action in Washington State against a United States tobacco company, alleging defendant's "participation in a world-wide conspiracy to deny the addictive and harmful effects of smoking." Id. at 1167. The Ninth Circuit affirmed the district court's

denial of defendant's motion to dismiss on forum non conveniens, but rejected plaintiff's contention that the Philippines judicial system would be inadequate because of corruption, delay, or potential influence by wealthy corporate defendants. Plaintiff's only evidence on this issue consisted of a State Department Country Report and did not include "a single episode that [plaintiff] directly observed or of which he has personal knowledge" concerning civil litigation. Id. at 1179. Why would personal information be more probative than a State Department report? See id. ("[W]e note that the reports are focused on human rights in the Philippines, and the criminal justice system in particular. * * * [S]uch a general indictment provides insufficient substance to condemn the adequacy of Philippine courts in the face of the expert evidence offered by [defendant].").

4.　　The *Piper* decision indicated that appellate courts must review a district court's forum non conveniens ruling for abuse of discretion. That deference is not absolute, however. In NANDJOU v. MARRIOTT INTERNATIONAL, INC., 985 F.3d 135 (1st Cir. 2021), the court found that the district court's "assessment of the private interest factors * * * is clearly wrong." Id. at 143. The case was a wrongful death action by the estate of a father and child who died in a hotel swimming pool in Canada, and the district court found that Canada was a more appropriate forum. The appellate court concluded that "on this record, we do not agree that there is a supportable basis for saying that the defendants have met their heavy burden to show that concerns about private convenience justify depriving Nandjou of the forum she chose." Id. at 147. It emphasized "the critically important role that her young children may play at trial as witnesses, as they alone are in a position to testify about the conditions at the pool at the moment of the drownings," and found that "while the defendants have estimated that twenty-five non-party witnesses reside in Canada, they have not explained why live testimony from all of those witnesses is critical." Id.

5.　　Should an international tribunal—such as the International Court of Justice, the World Trade Organization, or the United Nations Compensation Commission—ever be an acceptable alternative forum for purposes of forum non conveniens? In NEMARIAM v. FEDERAL DEMOCRATIC REPUBLIC OF ETHIOPIA, 315 F.3d 390 (D.C.Cir. 2003), cert. denied, 540 U.S. 877, 124 S.Ct. 278, 157 L.Ed.2d 141 (2003), the D.C. Circuit held it was an abuse of discretion to dismiss on grounds of forum non conveniens when the alternative forum was a Claims Commission designed to resolve war-related suits involving Ethiopia and Eritrea. Relief in the Claims Commission was subject to offset by amounts due from one nation to the other. The court found that "it would be peculiar indeed to dismiss * * * [plaintiff's] claim in the United States District Court—a forum in which * * * she is certain to be awarded full relief if she wins on the merits of her claim—in favor of a forum in which she has no certainty of getting relief for a meritorious claim." Id. at 395.

6.　　Some courts have found that a foreign country's remedies can be adequate even if they require a plaintiff to proceed against a different defendant or through a nonjudicial compensation scheme. In IMAMURA v.

GENERAL ELECTRIC CO., 957 F.3d 98 (1st Cir. 2020), the First Circuit affirmed the district court's forum non conveniens dismissal of a putative class action in Massachusetts federal court against the designer of a nuclear power plant, seeking damages for injuries caused by an earthquake-induced tsunami and a resulting nuclear disaster at the Fukushima Daiichi Nuclear Power Plant in Japan. It reasoned that forum non conveniens is permissible when the alternative forum "offers adequate remedies for the exact same injuries alleged by the plaintiff in U.S. court but channels liability for those injuries to a third party who is not the same defendant in the U.S. case." Id. at 109. It also found that it was proper to consider the availability of Japan's "administrative compensation scheme" in assessing the adequacy of the alternative forum. Id. at 112. In what situations should a nonjudicial forum be sufficiently "adequate" to permit a forum non conveniens dismissal?

7.   How much weight should the court give to plaintiff's forum preference? In WIWA v. ROYAL DUTCH PETROLEUM CO., 226 F.3d 88 (2d Cir. 2000), three Nigerian émigrés living in the United States sued two foreign holding companies alleging that the companies had participated in human rights violations against them in retaliation for their political opposition to the companies' oil exploration activities in Nigeria. The district court dismissed on the basis of forum non conveniens and the Second Circuit reversed, holding that the deference due to the forum choice of a United States resident depends on the party's affiliation with the forum. "[T]he greater the plaintiff's ties to the plaintiff's chosen forum," the court explained, "the more likely it is that the plaintiff would be inconvenienced by a requirement to bring the claim in a foreign jurisdiction." Id. at 102. Conversely, absolute deference is not accorded to the forum choice of a United States citizen when the facts show a significant relationship with an alternative forum. See Carey v. Bayerische Hypo-Und Vereinsbank AG, 370 F.3d 234, 238 (2d Cir. 2004).

8.   In SINOCHEM INTERNATIONAL CO. LTD. v. MALAYSIA INTERNATIONAL SHIPPING CORP., 549 U.S. 422, 127 S.Ct. 1184, 167 L.Ed.2d 15 (2007), the Supreme Court affirmed the dismissal of an action against a Chinese company on the basis of forum non conveniens even though the district court had not first ascertained whether subject-matter or personal jurisdiction was present. Justice Ginsburg explained that when a district court does not intend to resolve the merits of a case, it "has leeway 'to choose among threshold grounds for denying audience to a case on the merits,'" id. at 431, 127 S.Ct. at 1191, 167 L.Ed.2d at 25 (quoting Ruhrgas, p. 275, Note 2, supra), and "may dispose of an action by a forum non conveniens dismissal, bypassing questions of subject-matter and personal jurisdiction, when considerations of convenience, fairness, and judicial economy so warrant." Id. at 432, 127 S.Ct. at 1192, 167 L.Ed.2d at 26. Prior to the Court's decision in Sinochem, district courts sometimes conditioned a forum non conveniens dismissal on defendant's waiver of a jurisdictional or limitations defense in the alternative forum. See In re Union Carbide Corp. Gas Plant Disaster at Bhopal, India in Dec., 1984, 809 F.2d 195 (2d Cir. 1987), cert. denied, 484 U.S. 871, 108 S.Ct. 199, 98 L.Ed.2d 150 (1987). May a district court that has not yet determined its

jurisdiction impose such conditions? May a district court exercising removal jurisdiction dismiss an action on grounds of forum non conveniens without first determining whether subject-matter jurisdiction is present? See Provincial Gov't of Marinduque v. Placer Dome, Inc., 582 F.3d 1083, 1088 (9th Cir. 2009), cert. denied, 562 U.S. 827, 131 S.Ct. 65, 178 L.Ed.2d 22 (2010).

9. Commentators have criticized the doctrine of forum non conveniens as a ground for dismissal in transnational cases. In this context, it has been argued that the doctrine affords district courts excessive discretion; its use subverts congressional policy; and it produces unfair results for plaintiffs. See Gardner, *Retiring Forum Non Conveniens*, 92 N.Y.U.L.Rev. 390 (2017).

D. VENUE-SELECTION AGREEMENTS

————

Read Federal Rule of Civil Procedure 12(b)(3) and 28 U.S.C. §§ 1404 and 1406 in the Supplement.

————

In ATLANTIC MARINE CONSTRUCTION COMPANY, INC. v. UNITED STATES DISTRICT COURT FOR THE WESTERN DISTRICT OF TEXAS, 571 U.S. 49, 134 S.Ct. 568, 187 L.Ed.2d 487 (2013), the Supreme Court addressed the proper mechanism for enforcing a contractually-valid venue-selection provision in federal court. It held that "a forum-selection clause does not render venue in a court 'wrong' or 'improper' within the meaning of Section 1406(a) or Rule 12(b)(3)." Id. at 59, 134 S.Ct. at 579, 187 L.Ed.2d at 499. Instead, a clause that selects another federal district as the location of litigation may be enforced using a motion to transfer under Section 1404(a). And a clause that points to a state or foreign forum may be enforced using a forum non conveniens motion.

The Court then outlined an approach to deciding such motions that is heavily weighted toward enforcing forum-selection clauses. The Court explained that in "the typical case, not involving a forum-selection clause, a district court considering a § 1404(a) motion (or a forum non conveniens motion) must evaluate both the convenience of the parties and various public-interest considerations." However, the "calculus changes" when the transfer motion is based on a forum-selection clause:

> [A] court evaluating a defendant's § 1404(a) motion to transfer based on a forum-selection clause should not consider arguments about the parties' private interests. When parties agree to a forum-selection clause, they waive the right to challenge the preselected forum as inconvenient or less convenient for themselves or their witnesses, or for their pursuit of the litigation.

A court accordingly must deem the private-interest factors to weigh entirely in favor of the preselected forum. * * *

As a consequence, a district court may consider arguments about public-interest factors only. * * * Because those factors will rarely defeat a transfer motion, the practical result is that forum-selection clauses should control except in unusual cases. * * *

Id. at 63–64, 134 S.Ct. at 581–82, 187 L.Ed.2d at 501. The district court is to accord a presumption in favor of enforcing a valid forum-selection clause "unless extraordinary circumstances unrelated to the convenience of the parties clearly disfavor a transfer." The Supreme Court also made clear that, if the motion is granted and the case is transferred to the contractually-designated forum, then the law of the transferee court, and not that of the transferor court, will govern the proceedings. Why doesn't the *Van Dusen* rule, p. 292, Notes 3 and 4, supra, control in this circumstance?

CHAPTER 6

ASCERTAINING THE APPLICABLE LAW

■ ■ ■

This chapter focuses on the ways in which federalism and separation of powers affect choice of law in United States courts. Civil actions involving citizens of a single state and a transaction that occurred entirely within the boundaries of that state do not present any problems of choosing the proper body of substantive law to be applied in determining the rights and liabilities of the parties. However, as soon as the litigation touches two or more states, one is likely to be confronted with the serious question of choosing between two or more sources of law. For example, suppose plaintiff and defendant, both citizens of State X, are involved in an automobile accident or agree to perform a contract or engage in a sale of property in State Y. Should questions pertaining to defendant's alleged negligence or failure to perform the contract or transfer the ownership of the property be decided under the law of State X or the law of State Y? Should the choice be made in the same way in tort, contract, and property actions? The complexity of these questions increases if plaintiff and defendant are citizens of different states and the event, relationship, or property that forms the predicate of the controversy can be traced to a third or perhaps even a fourth or fifth state. You will be exposed to problems of this type on numerous occasions. Formal education in the philosophy of choosing among the laws of two or more states is the focus of a course in Conflict of Laws.

This chapter is devoted to choice-of-law problems of a somewhat different dimension. Let us suppose that plaintiff is a citizen of State X and defendant is a citizen of State Y, and plaintiff has decided to litigate a tort or contract claim against defendant in a federal district court in State Y. What law should the federal court apply to adjudicate this action? The law of State X? Of State Y? Federal law? Would the answer be different if, assuming personal jurisdiction could be acquired, the action were commenced in a federal district court in State X? Conversely, the problem of choosing between federal and state law is present when a state court is called upon to decide cases arising under federal statutes or cases in which federal rights and liabilities are at issue. As one might surmise, the processes of choosing between the law of two states and that of choosing between federal and state law are analogous, but also involve important differences.

311

A. STATE LAW IN THE FEDERAL COURTS

1. THE RULE OF SWIFT V. TYSON

Although Article III of the Constitution sets limits on the jurisdiction of the federal court system, it does not establish any lower federal courts. The power to establish those "inferior" courts was left to Congress, which quickly used it. The Judiciary Act of 1789 established a lower federal court system and promulgated rules governing its jurisdiction and operation. Among those rules, in Section 34 of the Judiciary Act, was the so-called Rules of Decision Act. The modern version of this Act is found in 28 U.S.C. § 1652 and reads: "The laws of the several states, except where the Constitution or treaties of the United States or Acts of Congress otherwise require or provide, shall be regarded as rules of decision in civil actions in the courts of the United States, in cases where they apply."

For almost a century, the Supreme Court's decision in SWIFT v. TYSON, 41 U.S. (16 Pet.) 1, 10 L.Ed. 865 (1842), provided the basic interpretation of the Rules of Decision Act. Consider this account:

> The famous case of *Swift v. Tyson* arose from the following rather commonplace circumstances: Two persons, [Norton] and Keith, gave Swift a bill of exchange in payment of a promissory note. The bill was accepted, or guaranteed, by another person named Tyson who in so doing meant to pay for certain land which he was purchasing from Norton and Keith. Sadly enough for Tyson, he discovered that Norton and Keith could not sell him the land because they did not own it. Therefore, when Swift sued Tyson on the bill, Tyson defended on the ground that there had been a failure of consideration to him, and that Swift could not, under these circumstances recover as a bona-fide holder for valuable consideration because Swift had paid nothing for the bill—all he had done was to accept the bill as new evidence of an old debt. The controlling issue thus became whether a new bill of exchange for an old debt was an adequate consideration for Swift's acceptance of the bill.

> The bill was made in the State of Maine; it was accepted in New York. If governed by the laws of New York, which might have been thought applicable, Swift would probably have been found to have given no consideration.

Address of U.S. Supreme Court Associate Justice Hugo L. Black to the Missouri Bar Annual Banquet, Sept. 25, 1942, reprinted in 64 J.Mo.B. 26, 27 (2008). The principal question considered in *Swift* was whether the case was governed by New York decisional law, or whether the federal court could interpret principles of commercial law as it thought best.

Whether New York law applied turned upon the meaning of the phrase "laws of the several states" in the Rules of Decision Act. If the phrase encompassed state statutes and state decisional law involving commercial relations, then the federal court was required to apply the New York rule. Justice Story, writing for a unanimous Court, concluded that the Act did not command the federal courts to follow state judicial decisions in general commercial matters:

[T]he Courts of New York do not found their decisions upon this point upon any local statute, or positive, fixed, or ancient local usage: but they deduce the doctrine from the general principles of commercial law. It is, however, contended, that the thirty-fourth section of the judiciary act of 1789, ch. 20, furnishes a rule obligatory upon this Court to follow the decisions of the state tribunals in all cases to which they apply. * * * In order to maintain the argument, it is essential, therefore, to hold, that the word "laws," in this section, includes within the scope of its meaning the decisions of the local tribunals. In the ordinary use of language it will hardly be contended that the decisions of Courts constitute laws. They are, at most, only evidence of what the laws are, and are not of themselves laws. They are often reexamined, reversed, and qualified by the courts themselves, whenever they are found to be either defective, or ill-founded, or otherwise incorrect. The laws of a state are more usually understood to mean the rules and enactments promulgated by the legislative authority thereof, or long established local customs having the force of laws. In all the various cases, which have hitherto come before us for decision, this Court have uniformly supposed, that the true interpretation of the thirty-fourth section limited its application to state laws strictly local, that is to say, to the positive statutes of the state, and the construction thereof adopted by the local tribunals, and to rights and titles to things having a permanent locality, such as the rights and titles to real estate, and other matters immovable and intraterritorial in their nature and character. It never has been supposed by us, that the section did apply, or was designed to apply, to questions of a more general nature, not at all dependent upon local statutes or local usages of a fixed and permanent operation, as, for example, to the construction of ordinary contracts or other written instruments and especially to questions of general commercial law, where the state tribunals are called upon to perform the like functions as ourselves, that is, to ascertain upon general reasoning and legal analogies, what is the true exposition of the contract or instrument, or what is the just rule furnished by the principles of commercial law to govern the case. And we have not now the slightest difficulty in holding, that this section * * * is strictly limited to local statutes and local usages of the character before stated, and does not extend to contracts and other instruments of a commercial nature, the true interpretation and effect whereof are to be sought, not in the decisions of the local tribunals, but in the general principles and doctrines of commercial jurisprudence. * * *

Id. at 18–19, 10 L.Ed. at 871.

NOTES AND QUESTIONS

1. According to Justice Story, why are judicial decisions only evidence of law, and not law itself? On what basis did Justice Story distinguish judicial decisions interpreting state statutes or "matters immovable and intraterritorial" from other judicial decisions?

2. According to *Swift*, what is the source of the federal courts' authority to develop and apply general common law rules in commercial cases within the grant of diversity jurisdiction? Is Justice Story's reading of the words "the law of the several states" in the Rules of Decision Act the only plausible reading of the statute? What are the competing interpretations? See, e.g., Ritz, Holt & Larue, Rewriting the History of the Judiciary Act of 1789: Exposing Myths, Challenging Premises, and Using New Evidence (1990).

3. Does it make sense to have the federal courts promulgate general, uniformly applied commercial laws? Why should a person suing in federal court in Oklahoma not receive the same remedy as a person suing in federal court in Vermont? On the other hand, if a federal court sitting in diversity is forced to apply the forum state's court decisions, what advantage would a party have in going to federal court? How might a uniform federal rule of decision in commercial matters have affected the nation's economic development? See Freyer, Harmony & Dissonance: The *Swift* & *Erie* Cases in American Federalism (1981).

2. THE *ERIE* DOCTRINE: THE RULES OF DECISION ACT AND THE RULES ENABLING ACT

ERIE R. CO. V. TOMPKINS
Supreme Court of the United States, 1938.
304 U.S. 64, 58 S.Ct. 817, 82 L.Ed. 1188.

Certiorari to the United States Circuit Court of Appeals for the Second Circuit.

JUSTICE BRANDEIS delivered the opinion of the Court.

[Slightly after midnight on July 27, 1934, Harry James Tompkins was walking home along a well-trodden footpath running parallel to the Erie Railroad tracks in Hughestown, Pennsylvania, when he was struck by "a black object that looked like a door" protruding from a passing train. Tompkins' right arm was severed.

Under Pennsylvania law, a traveler like Tompkins on a parallel (or "longitudinal") path was regarded as a trespasser to whom the railroad merely owes a duty to avoid wanton negligence. The majority rule in most states, however, was that a railroad owes a duty of ordinary care to a traveler on a parallel footpath.

Tompkins' lawyers were well aware of the rule in *Swift* that, absent state statutory law, federal courts apply "general law," and thus they tried to avoid the harsh Pennsylvania rule by suing the New York-based railroad in federal court. As anticipated, the district court applied "general law," the majority rule, and the jury awarded Tompkins $30,000 in damages.

The court of appeals affirmed, holding that:

> [U]pon questions of general law the federal courts are free, in absence of a local statute, to exercise their independent judgment as to what the law is; and it is well settled that the question of the responsibility of a railroad for injuries caused by its servants is one of general law. * * * Where the public has made open and notorious use of a railroad right of way for a long period of time and without objection, the company owes to persons on such permissive pathway a duty of care in the operation of its trains. * * * It is likewise generally recognized law that a jury may find that negligence exists toward a pedestrian using a permissive path on the railroad right of way if he is hit by some object projecting from the side of the train.]

* * *

First. Swift v. Tyson * * * held that federal courts exercising jurisdiction on the ground of diversity of citizenship need not, in matters of general jurisprudence, apply the unwritten law of the state as declared by its highest court; that they are free to exercise an independent judgment as to what the common law of the state is—or should be * * *.

* * * The federal courts assumed, in the broad field of "general law," the power to declare rules of decision which Congress was confessedly without power to enact as statutes. Doubt was repeatedly expressed as to the correctness of the construction given section 34, and as to the soundness of the rule which it introduced. But it was the more recent research of a competent scholar, who examined the original document, which established that the construction given to it by the Court was erroneous; and that the purpose of the section was merely to make certain that, in all matters except those in which some federal law is controlling, the federal courts exercising jurisdiction in diversity of citizenship cases

would apply as their rules of decision the law of the state, unwritten as well as written.[5]

Criticism of the doctrine became widespread after the decision of Black & White Taxicab & Transfer Co. v. Brown & Yellow Taxicab & Transfer Co., 276 U.S. 518, 48 S.Ct. 404, 72 L.Ed. 681, 57 A.L.R. 426. There, Brown & Yellow, a Kentucky corporation owned by Kentuckians, and the Louisville & Nashville Railroad, also a Kentucky corporation, wished that the former should have the exclusive privilege of soliciting passenger and baggage transportation at the Bowling Green, Ky., railroad station; and that the Black & White, a competing Kentucky corporation, should be prevented from interfering with that privilege. Knowing that such a contract would be void under the common law of Kentucky, it was arranged that the Brown & Yellow reincorporate under the law of Tennessee, and that the contract with the railroad should be executed there. The suit was then brought by the Tennessee corporation in the federal court for Western Kentucky to enjoin competition by the Black & White; an injunction issued by the District Court was sustained by the Court of Appeals; and this Court, citing many decisions in which the doctrine of Swift v. Tyson had been applied, affirmed the decree.

Second. Experience in applying the doctrine of Swift v. Tyson, had revealed its defects, political and social; and the benefits expected to flow from the rule did not accrue. Persistence of state courts in their own opinions on questions of common law prevented uniformity; and the impossibility of discovering a satisfactory line of demarcation between the province of general law and that of local law developed a new well of uncertainties.

On the other hand, the mischievous results of the doctrine had become apparent. Diversity of citizenship jurisdiction was conferred in order to prevent apprehended discrimination in state courts against those not citizens of the state. Swift v. Tyson introduced grave discrimination by noncitizens against citizens. It made rights enjoyed under the unwritten "general law" vary according to whether enforcement was sought in the state or in the federal court; and the privilege of selecting the court in which the right should be determined was conferred upon the noncitizen. Thus, the doctrine rendered impossible equal protection of the law. In attempting to promote uniformity of law throughout the United States, the doctrine had prevented uniformity in the administration of the law of the state.

The discrimination resulting became in practice far-reaching. This resulted in part from the broad province accorded to the so-called "general law" as to which federal courts exercised an independent judgment. In addition to questions of purely commercial law, "general law" was held to

---

[5] Charles Warren, *New Light on the History of the Federal Judiciary Act of 1789,* 37 Harv. L. Rev. 49 (1923).

include the obligations under contracts entered into and to be performed within the state, the extent to which a carrier operating within a state may stipulate for exemption from liability for his own negligence or that of his employee; the liability for torts committed within the state upon persons resident or property located there, even where the question of liability depended upon the scope of a property right conferred by the state; and the right to exemplary or punitive damages. Furthermore, state decisions construing local deeds, mineral conveyances, and even devises of real estate, were disregarded.

In part the discrimination resulted from the wide range of persons held entitled to avail themselves of the federal rule by resort to the diversity of citizenship jurisdiction. Through this jurisdiction individual citizens willing to remove from their own state and become citizens of another might avail themselves of the federal rule. And, without even change of residence, a corporate citizen of the state could avail itself of the federal rule by reincorporating under the laws of another state, as was done in the Taxicab Case.

The injustice and confusion incident to the doctrine of Swift v. Tyson have been repeatedly urged as reasons for abolishing or limiting diversity of citizenship jurisdiction. Other legislative relief has been proposed. If only a question of statutory construction were involved, we should not be prepared to abandon a doctrine so widely applied throughout nearly a century. But the unconstitutionality of the course pursued has now been made clear, and compels us to do so.

Third. Except in matters governed by the Federal Constitution or by acts of Congress, the law to be applied in any case is the law of the state. And whether the law of the state shall be declared by its Legislature in a statute or by its highest court in a decision is not a matter of federal concern. There is no federal general common law. Congress has no power to declare substantive rules of common law applicable in a state whether they be local in their nature or "general," be they commercial law or a part of the law of torts. And no clause in the Constitution purports to confer such a power upon the federal courts. * * *

The fallacy underlying the rule declared in Swift v. Tyson is made clear by Mr. Justice Holmes. The doctrine rests upon the assumption that there is "a transcendental body of law outside of any particular State but obligatory within it unless and until changed by statute," that federal courts have the power to use their judgment as to what the rules of common law are; and that in the federal courts "the parties are entitled to an independent judgment on matters of general law":

> But law in the sense in which courts speak of it today does not exist without some definite authority behind it. The common law so far as it is enforced in a State, whether called common law or

not, is not the common law generally but the law of that State existing by the authority of that State without regard to what it may have been in England or anywhere else. * * *

The authority and only authority is the State, and if that be so, the voice adopted by the State as its own [whether it be of its Legislature or of its Supreme Court] should utter the last word.

Thus the doctrine of Swift v. Tyson is, as Mr. Justice Holmes said, "an unconstitutional assumption of powers by the Courts of the United States which no lapse of time or respectable array of opinion should make us hesitate to correct." In disapproving that doctrine we do not hold unconstitutional section 34 of the Federal Judiciary Act of 1789 or any other act of Congress. We merely declare that in applying the doctrine this Court and the lower courts have invaded rights which in our opinion are reserved by the Constitution to the several states.

Fourth. The defendant contended that by the common law of Pennsylvania * * * the only duty owed to the plaintiff was to refrain from willful or wanton injury. The plaintiff denied that such is the Pennsylvania law. In support of their respective contentions the parties discussed and cited many decisions of the Supreme Court of the State. The Circuit Court of Appeals ruled that the question of liability is one of general law; and on that ground declined to decide the issue of state law. As we hold this was error, the judgment is reversed and the case remanded to it for further proceedings in conformity with our opinion.

Reversed.

JUSTICE CARDOZO took no part in the consideration or decision of this case.

JUSTICE BUTLER (dissenting).

* * *

Defendant's petition for writ of certiorari presented two questions: Whether its duty toward plaintiff should have been determined in accordance with the law as found by the highest court of Pennsylvania, and whether the evidence conclusively showed plaintiff guilty of contributory negligence. Plaintiff contends that, as always heretofore held by this Court, the issues of negligence and contributory negligence are to be determined by general law against which local decisions may not be held conclusive * * *.

No constitutional question was suggested or argued below or here. And as a general rule, this Court will not consider any question not raised below and presented by the petition. * * * Here it does not decide either of the questions presented, but, changing the rule of decision in force since the foundation of the government, remands the case to be adjudged according to a standard never before deemed permissible.

* * *

The doctrine of * * * [Swift v. Tyson] has been followed by this Court in an unbroken line of decisions. * * *

* * *

So far as appears, no litigant has ever challenged the power of Congress to establish the rule as construed. It has so long endured that its destruction now without appropriate deliberation cannot be justified. There is nothing in the opinion to suggest that consideration of any constitutional question is necessary to a decision of the case. * * * Against the protest of those joining in this opinion, the Court declines to assign the case for reargument. It may not justly be assumed that the labor and argument of counsel for the parties would not disclose the right conclusion and aid the Court in the statement of reasons to support it. Indeed, it would have been appropriate to give Congress opportunity to be heard before divesting it of power to prescribe rules of decision to be followed in the courts of the United States. * * *

* * * Congress intended to give the United States the right to be heard in every case involving constitutionality of an act affecting the public interest. In view of the rule that, in the absence of challenge of constitutionality, statutes will not here be invalidated on that ground, the Act of August 24, 1937 extends to cases where constitutionality is first "drawn in question" by the Court. * * *

I am of opinion that the constitutional validity of the rule need not be considered, because under the law, as found by the courts of Pennsylvania and generally throughout the country, it is plain that the evidence required a finding that plaintiff was guilty of negligence that contributed to cause his injuries, and that the judgment below should be reversed upon that ground.

JUSTICE MCREYNOLDS concurs in this opinion.

JUSTICE REED (concurring in part).

I concur in the conclusion reached in this case, in the disapproval of the doctrine of Swift v. Tyson, and in the reasoning of the majority opinion except in so far as it relies upon the unconstitutionality of the "course pursued" by the federal courts.

* * *

To decide the case now before us and to "disapprove" the doctrine of Swift v. Tyson requires only that we say that the words "the laws" include in their meaning the decisions of the local tribunals. As the majority opinion shows, by its reference to Mr. Warren's researches and the first quotation from Mr. Justice Holmes, that this Court is now of the view that "laws" includes "decisions," it is unnecessary to go further and declare that the "course pursued" was "unconstitutional," instead of merely erroneous.

The "unconstitutional" course referred to in the majority opinion is apparently the ruling in Swift v. Tyson that the supposed omission of Congress to legislate as to the effect of decisions leaves federal courts free to interpret general law for themselves. I am not at all sure whether, in the absence of federal statutory direction, federal courts would be compelled to follow state decisions. There was sufficient doubt about the matter in 1789 to induce the first Congress to legislate. No former opinions of this Court have passed upon it. * * * If the opinion commits this Court to the position that the Congress is without power to declare what rules of substantive law shall govern the federal courts, that conclusion also seems questionable. The line between procedural and substantive law is hazy, but no one doubts federal power over procedure. * * * The Judiciary Article, 3, and the "necessary and proper" clause of article 1, § 8, may fully authorize legislation, such as this section of the Judiciary Act.

NOTES AND QUESTIONS

1.   Is *Erie* a constitutional decision or does it rest on other grounds? Is it significant to your answer that the Court found the rule of *Swift* to be unconstitutional, but did not invalidate the Rules of Decision Act? For efforts to explain the constitutional principle underlying *Erie*, see Clark, *Ascertaining the Laws of the Several States: Positivism and Judicial Federalism After* Erie, 145 U.Pa.L.Rev. 1459 (1997); Steinman, *What Is the* Erie *Doctrine? (and What Does It Mean for the Contemporary Politics of Judicial Federalism?)*, 84 Notre Dame L.Rev. 245 (2008). For a skeptical view of *Erie's* constitutional basis, see Green, *Repressing Erie's Myth*, 96 Calif.L.Rev. 595 (2008).

2.   What is the constitutional basis for the statement in *Erie* that "Congress has no power to declare substantive rules of common law applicable in a State" and that "no clause in the Constitution purports to confer such a power upon the federal courts"? Consider, first, Article I of the Constitution. Does Congress have power under that provision to regulate commercial activities that affect interstate commerce? Is it significant that by the time *Erie* was decided, Congress already had enacted legislation regulating railroads with respect to employment and tort liability, e.g., Federal Employers' Liability Act of 1908, 45 U.S.C. § 51? If Congress has power to legislate in this area, why can't the courts act, as well? See Clark, *State Law in the Federal Courts: The Brooding Omnipresence of* Erie v. Tompkins, 55 Yale L.J. 267, 278 (1946). Of what relevance to *Erie's* possible constitutional basis is the reservation of power to the states and the people in the Tenth Amendment of the Constitution?

3.   Does the statement that the rule in *Swift* "rendered impossible equal protection of the law" implicate constitutional or policy concerns? Does it matter that at the time of the decision the Court had not yet recognized an equal protection component to the Fifth Amendment to the United States Constitution? See Rutherglen, *Reconstructing* Erie*: A Comment on the Perils of Legal Positivism*, 10 Const. Comment. 285 (1993).

4.   If discrimination against in-state defendants really is a problem, could it be solved by allowing in-state defendants to remove to federal court? Does it make sense to require federal courts to apply state law in diversity cases simply out of a desire for parity between in-state defendants who cannot remove and out-of-state defendants who can? Justice Brandeis used the *Black & White Taxicab* case to illustrate the evils resulting from *Swift*. Could the problem in that case have been handled without overruling *Swift*?

5.   The *Erie* decision relied on research by Professor Warren, referenced in p. 316, footnote 5, supra, that revealed a previously unknown draft of what became the Rules of Decision Act of 1789. The draft read:

> And be it further enacted, That the Statute law of the several States in force for the time being and their unwritten or common law now in use, whether by adoption from the common law of England, the ancient statutes of the same or otherwise, except where the Constitution, Treaties or Statutes of the United States shall otherwise require or provide, shall be regarded as rules of decision in the trials at common law in the courts of the United States in cases where they apply.

Did Justice Brandeis properly interpret the Rules of Decision Act given this legislative history? Or, did the shorter final version reflect congressional intent to limit the definition of "laws of the several states" to statutory laws, thus expanding the law-making power of federal courts in diversity cases? Can we be sure that Congress even saw the draft discussed by Professor Warren?

6.   The Court in *Swift* associated law with transcendent principles that the judiciary discovered. See Ides, *The Supreme Court and the Law to Be Applied in Diversity Cases: A Critical Guide to the Development and Application of the* Erie *Doctrine and Related Problems*, 163 F.R.D. 19, 23 (1995). Consider how this concept of law differs from the view expressed by Justice Holmes, quoted by Justice Brandeis in *Erie*, that "law in the sense in which courts speak of it today does not exist without some definite authority behind it."

7.   Does the Rules of Decision Act require federal courts to follow state procedures as "rules of decision"? Justice Reed's concurring opinion in *Erie* emphasized the power of Congress to enact procedures for the federal courts. What constitutional provisions support that assertion? Until the adoption of the Federal Rules of Civil Procedure, the Process Act of 1792, as amended in 1872, required federal courts to conform their procedure in common law

disputes to those of the state in which the court sat. See Burbank, *The Rules Enabling Act of* 1934, 130 U.Pa.L.Rev. 1015 (1982).

8.   "It is impossible to overstate the importance of the *Erie* decision." Wright & Kane, Law of Federal Courts § 55 (7th ed.). Reactions to the *Erie* decision voiced shortly after it was handed down include Shulman, *The Demise of* Swift v. Tyson, 47 Yale L.J. 1336 (1938); and Tunks, *Categorization and Federalism: "Substance" and "Procedure" After* Erie Railroad v. Tompkins, 34 Ill.L.Rev. 271 (1939). Over time, *Erie* has been called " 'transcendently significant,' " Nelson, *A Critical Guide to* Erie Railroad Co. v. Tompkins, 54 Wm. & Mary L.Rev. 921, 922 (2013) (quoting Krock, *In the Nation: A Momentous Decision of the Supreme Court*, N.Y. Times, May 3, 1938, at 22), as well as "the worst decision of all time." Sherry, *Wrong, Out of Step, and Pernicious:* Erie *as the Worst Decision of All Time*, 39 Pepp.L.Rev. 129 (2011), to "a way of life." Young, Erie *As a Way of Life*, 52 Akron L.Rev. 193 (2018). For an excellent discussion of the decision and the context in which it was decided, see Purcell, Jr., *The Story of* Erie: *How Litigants, Lawyers, Judges, Politics, and Social Change Reshape the Law*, in Civil Procedure Stories 21 (Clermont ed., 2d ed. 2008).

GUARANTY TRUST CO. V. YORK
Supreme Court of the United States, 1945.
326 U.S. 99, 65 S.Ct. 1464, 89 L.Ed. 2079.

Certiorari to the United States Circuit Court of Appeals for the Second Circuit.

JUSTICE FRANKFURTER delivered the opinion of the Court.

[The Guaranty Trust Company served as trustee for some of the noteholders of Van Sweringen Corporation. In October 1930, Guaranty loaned money to corporations affiliated with and controlled by Van Sweringen. By October 1931, it was evident that Van Sweringen was having trouble meeting its financial obligations. Guaranty and several other banks worked out a plan by which Guaranty would offer to purchase the notes by paying $500 and twenty shares of Van Sweringen stock for each $1,000 note.

Respondent York received $6,000 of the notes from a donor who had not accepted Guaranty's offer. York brought a diversity suit alleging that Guaranty had breached its fiduciary duties. York's complaint involved allegations of fraud and misrepresentation, relief for which was governed by equitable principles. On appeal, the Circuit Court of Appeals, one judge dissenting, found that in a suit brought in equity the federal court was not required to apply the state statute of limitations that would govern similar suits in state courts, even though the exclusive basis of federal jurisdiction was diversity of citizenship. The Supreme Court granted review in order to decide whether federal courts should apply state statutes of limitations in such cases.]

* * *

Our starting point must be the policy of federal jurisdiction which Erie R. Co. v. Tompkins * * * embodies. In overruling Swift v. Tyson * * * *Erie* * * * did not merely overrule a venerable case. It overruled a particular way of looking at law which dominated the judicial process long after its inadequacies had been laid bare. * * * Law was conceived as a "brooding omnipresence" of Reason, of which decisions were merely evidence and not themselves the controlling formulations. Accordingly, federal courts deemed themselves free to ascertain what Reason, and therefore Law, required wholly independent of authoritatively declared State law, even in cases where a legal right as the basis for relief was created by State authority and could not be created by federal authority and the case got into a federal court merely because it was "between Citizens of different States" under Art. III, § 2 of the Constitution * * *.

In exercising their jurisdiction on the ground of diversity of citizenship, the federal courts, in the long course of their history, have not differentiated in their regard for State law between actions at law and suits in equity. Although § 34 of the Judiciary Act of 1789 * * * directed that the "laws of the several states * * * shall be regarded as rules of decision in trials of common law * * *," this was deemed, consistently for over a hundred years, to be merely declaratory of what would in any event have governed the federal courts and therefore was equally applicable to equity suits. * * * Indeed, it may fairly be said that the federal courts gave greater respect to State-created "substantive rights," Pusey & Jones Co. v. Hanssen, 261 U.S. 491, 498, 43 S.Ct. 454, 456, 67 L.Ed. 763, in equity than they gave them on the law side, because rights at law were usually declared by State courts and as such increasingly flouted by extension of the doctrine of Swift v. Tyson, while rights in equity were frequently defined by legislative enactment and as such known and respected by the federal courts. * * *

Partly because the States in the early days varied greatly in the manner in which equitable relief was afforded and in the extent to which it was available, * * * Congress provided that "the forms and modes of proceeding in suits * * * of equity" would conform to the settled uses of courts of equity. * * * But this enactment gave the federal courts no power that they would not have had in any event when courts were given "cognizance," by the first Judiciary Act, of suits "in equity." * * * In giving federal courts "cognizance" of equity suits in cases of diversity jurisdiction, Congress never gave, nor did the federal courts ever claim, the power to deny substantive rights created by State law or to create substantive rights denied by State law.

This does not mean that whatever equitable remedy is available in a State court must be available in a diversity suit in a federal court, or conversely, that a federal court may not afford an equitable remedy not available in a State court. * * * State law cannot define the remedies which a federal court must give simply because a federal court in diversity jurisdiction is available as an alternative tribunal to the State's courts. Contrariwise, a federal court may afford an equitable remedy for a substantive right recognized by a State even though a State court cannot give it. Whatever contradiction or confusion may be produced by a medley of judicial phrases severed from their environment, the body of adjudications concerning equitable relief in diversity cases leaves no doubt that the federal courts enforced State-created substantive rights if the mode of proceeding and remedy were consonant with the traditional body of equitable remedies, practice and procedure, and in so doing they were enforcing rights created by the States and not arising under any inherent or statutory federal law.

* * *

And so this case reduces itself to the narrow question whether, when no recovery could be had in a State court because the action is barred by the statute of limitations, a federal court in equity can take cognizance of the suit because there is diversity of citizenship between the parties. Is the outlawry, according to State law, of a claim created by the States a matter of "substantive rights" to be respected by a federal court of equity when that court's jurisdiction is dependent on the fact that there is a State-created right, or is such statute of "a mere remedial character," * * * which a federal court may disregard?

Matters of "substance" and matters of "procedure" are much talked about in the books as though they defined a great divide cutting across the whole domain of law. But, of course, "substance" and "procedure" are the same keywords to very different problems. Neither "substance" nor "procedure" represents the same invariants. Each implies different variables depending upon the particular problem for which it is used. * * * And the different problems are only distantly related at best, for the terms are in common use in connection with situations turning on such different considerations as those that are relevant to questions pertaining to *ex post facto* legislation, the impairment of the obligations of contract, the enforcement of federal rights in the State courts and the multitudinous phases of the conflict of laws. * * *

Here we are dealing with a right to recover derived not from the United States but from one of the States. When, because the plaintiff happens to be a non-resident, such a right is enforceable in a federal as well as in a State court, the forms and mode of enforcing the right may at times, naturally enough, vary because the two judicial systems are not identic.

But since a federal court adjudicating a State-created right solely because of the diversity of citizenship of the parties is for that purpose, in effect, only another court of the State, it cannot afford recovery if the right to recover is made unavailable by the State nor can it substantially affect the enforcement of the right as given by the State.

And so the question is not whether a statute of limitations is deemed a matter of "procedure" in some sense. The question is whether such a statute concerns merely the manner and the means by which a right to recover, as recognized by the State, is enforced, or whether such statutory limitation is a matter of substance in the aspect that alone is relevant to our problem, namely, does it significantly affect the result of a litigation for a federal court to disregard a law of a State that would be controlling in an action upon the same claim by the same parties in a State court?

It is therefore immaterial whether statutes of limitation are characterized either as "substantive" or "procedural" in State court opinions in any use of those terms unrelated to the specific issue before us. Erie R. Co. v. Tompkins was not an endeavor to formulate scientific legal terminology. It expressed a policy that touches vitally the proper distribution of judicial power between State and federal courts. In essence, the intent of that decision was to insure that, in all cases where a federal court is exercising jurisdiction solely because of the diversity of citizenship of the parties, the outcome of the litigation in the federal court should be substantially the same, so far as legal rules determine the outcome of a litigation, as it would be if tried in a State court. The nub of the policy that underlies Erie R. Co. v. Tompkins is that for the same transaction the accident of a suit by a non-resident litigant in a federal court instead of in a State court a block away should not lead to a substantially different result. * * * A policy so important to our federalism must be kept free from entanglements with analytical or terminological niceties.

Plainly enough, a statute that would completely bar recovery in a suit if brought in a State court bears on a State-created right vitally and not merely formally or negligibly. As to consequences that so intimately affect recovery or non-recovery a federal court in a diversity case should follow State law. * * *

Diversity jurisdiction is founded on assurance to non-resident litigants of courts free from susceptibility to potential local bias. The Framers of the Constitution, according to Marshall, entertained "apprehensions" lest distant suitors be subjected to local bias in State courts, or, at least, viewed with "indulgence the possible fears and apprehensions" of such suitors. Bank of the United States v. Deveaux, 5 Cranch 61, 87, 3 L.Ed. 38. And so Congress afforded out-of-State litigants another tribunal, not another body of law. The operation of a double system of conflicting laws in the same State is plainly hostile to the reign of law. Certainly, the fortuitous circumstance of residence out of a State of one of the parties to a litigation ought not to give rise to a discrimination against others equally concerned but locally resident. The source of substantive rights enforced by a federal court under diversity jurisdiction, it cannot be said too often, is the law of the States. * * *

The judgment is reversed and the case is remanded for proceedings not inconsistent with this opinion.

So ordered.

Reversed.

JUSTICE ROBERTS and JUSTICE DOUGLAS took no part in the consideration or decision of this case.

JUSTICE RUTLEDGE dissented in an opinion in which JUSTICE MURPHY joined.

* * * [T]he decision of today does not in so many words rule that Congress could not authorize the federal courts to administer equitable relief in accordance with the substantive rights of the parties, notwithstanding state courts had been forbidden by local statutes of limitations to do so. Nevertheless the implication to that effect seems strong, in view of the reliance upon Erie R. Co. v. Tompkins. * * * In any event, the question looms more largely in the issues than the Court's opinion appears to make it. For if legislative acquiescence in long-established judicial construction can make it part of a statute, it has done so in this instance. More is at stake in the implications of the decision, if not in the words of the opinion, than simply bringing federal and local law into accord upon matters clearly and exclusively within the constitutional power of the state to determine. It is one thing to require that kind of an accord in diversity cases when the question is merely whether the federal court must follow the law of the state as to burden of proof, * * * contributory negligence, * * * or perhaps in application of the so-called parol evidence rule. These ordinarily involve matters of substantive law, though nominated in terms of procedure. But in some instances their application may lie along the border between procedure or remedy and substance, where the one may or may not be in fact but another name for the other. It is exactly in this borderland, where procedural or remedial rights may or may not have the effect of determining the substantive ones completely, that caution is required in extending the rule of the Erie case by the very rule itself.

The words "substantive" and "procedural" or "remedial" are not talismanic. Merely calling a legal question by one or the other does not resolve it otherwise than as a purely authoritarian performance. * * * But they have come to designate in a broad way large and distinctive legal domains within the greater one of the law and to mark, though often indistinctly or with overlapping limits, many divides between such regions.

* * * This division, like others drawn by the broad allocation of adjective or remedial and substantive, has areas of admixture of these two aspects of the law. In these areas whether a particular situation or issue presents one aspect or the other depends upon how one looks at the matter. * * *

Whenever this integration or admixture prevails in a substantial measure, so that a clean break cannot be made, there is danger either of nullifying the power of Congress to control not only how the federal courts may act, but what they may do by way of affording remedies, or of usurping that function, if the Erie doctrine is to be expanded judicially to include such situations to the utmost extent.

It may be true that if the matter were wholly fresh the barring of rights in equity by statutes of limitation would seem to partake more of the substantive than of the remedial phase of law. But the matter is not fresh and it is not without room for debate. A long tradition, in the states and here, as well as in the common law which antedated both state and federal law, has emphasized the remedial character of statutes of limitations, more especially in application to equity causes, on many kinds of issues requiring differentiation of such matters from more clearly and exclusively substantive ones. * * * The tradition now in question is equally long and unvaried. I cannot say the tradition is clearly wrong in this case more than in that. Nor can I say, as was said in the Erie case, that the matter is beyond the power of Congress to control. If that be conceded, I think Congress should make the change if it is to be made. The Erie decision was rendered in 1938. Seven years have passed without action by Congress to extend the rule to these matters. That is long enough to justify the conclusion that Congress also regards them as not governed by Erie and as wishing to make no change. This should be reason enough for leaving the matter at rest until it decides to act. * * *

Applicable statutes of limitations in state tribunals are not always the ones which would apply if suit were instituted in the courts of the state which creates the substantive rights for which enforcement is sought. The state of the forum is free to apply its own period of limitations, regardless of whether the state originating the right has barred suit upon it. Whether or not the action will be held to be barred depends therefore not upon the law of the state which creates the substantive right, but upon the law of the state where suit may be brought. This in turn will depend upon where it may be possible to secure service of process, and thus jurisdiction of the person of the defendant. It may be therefore that because of the plaintiff's inability to find the defendant in the jurisdiction which creates his substantive right, he will be foreclosed of remedy by the sheer necessity of going to the haven of refuge within which the defendant confines its "presence" for jurisdictional purposes. The law of the latter may bar the suit even though suit still would be allowed under the law of the state creating the substantive right.

NOTES AND QUESTIONS

1. If a New York equity court would not grant relief for whatever reason, should a federal court sitting in diversity nevertheless do so on an identical claim? In answering this question, consider Justice Frankfurter's discussion of the difference between recognizing a state-created right and providing a remedy for infringement of that right. Could it not be argued that available remedies actually define the scope of the underlying rights? Compare Sonner v. Premier Nutrition Corp., 971 F.3d 834, 841–44 (9th Cir. 2020) (finding that a federal court cannot award equitable restitution when an adequate legal remedy exists even if state law authorizes such relief "unhampered" by that restriction), with New Mexico ex rel. Balderas v. Real Estate Law Center, P.C., 401 F.Supp.3d 1229, 1348–50 n.93 (D.N.M. 2019) (applying New Mexico's standard for equitable relief even though it was "less stringent" than the federal test).

2. To what extent does *York* require the displacement of a Federal Rule of Civil Procedure in favor of a contrary state practice? Does that result follow from application of the Rules of Decision Act? If not, what is the basis for the Court's holding?

3. Four years after *York*, the Supreme Court decided, all on the same day, a trio of cases involving the *Erie* doctrine:

RAGAN v. MERCHANTS TRANSFER & WAREHOUSE CO., 337 U.S. 530, 69 S.Ct. 1233, 93 L.Ed. 1520 (1949), grew out of a highway accident that occurred on October 1, 1943. On September 4, 1945, Ragan filed a diversity action in a federal court in Kansas. However, service was not made on defendant until December 28. Kansas had a two-year statute of limitations on tort claims. Ragan claimed that according to Federal Rule 3, the suit was commenced (and hence the statute tolled) by the filing of the complaint. Defendant countered that Kansas law dictated that service had to have been made within the two-year period. The Supreme Court held that state law would determine in a diversity action when the statute was tolled. Justice Douglas, writing for the Court, explained:

> [T]here can be no doubt that the suit was properly commenced in the federal court. But in the present case we look to local law to find the cause of action on which suit is brought. Since that cause of action is created by local law, the measure of it is to be found only in local law. It carries the same burden and is subject to the same defense in the federal court as in the state court. * * * It accrues and comes to an end when local law so declares. * * * Where local law qualifies or abridges it, the federal court must follow suit. Otherwise there is a

different measure of the cause of action in one court than in the other, and the principle of Erie * * * is transgressed.

Id. at 533, 69 S.Ct. at 1235, 93 L.Ed. at 1523. Justice Rutledge dissented. Under *Ragan*, does state or federal law determine whether a suit to enforce federal law "was properly commenced in the federal court"?

In WOODS v. INTERSTATE REALTY CO., 337 U.S. 535, 69 S.Ct. 1235, 93 L.Ed. 1524 (1949), the Court held that a Tennessee corporation that had not qualified to do business in Mississippi could not maintain a diversity action in a federal court in that state if, by virtue of its failure to qualify, the Mississippi state courts were closed to it. Justice Douglas, again writing for the Court, explained:

> The York case was premised on the theory that a right which local law creates but which it does not supply with a remedy is no right at all for purposes of enforcement in a federal court in a diversity case; that where in such cases one is barred from recovery in the state court, he should likewise be barred in the federal court. The contrary result would create discriminations against citizens of the State in favor of those authorized to invoke the diversity jurisdiction of the federal courts. It was that element of discrimination that Erie * * * was designed to eliminate.

Id. at 538, 69 S.Ct. at 1237, 93 L.Ed. at 1527. Justices Jackson, Rutledge, and Burton dissented. Does the reasoning in *Woods* require a federal diversity court to apply a state and not federal test for in personam jurisdiction if the effect of the rule would be to open the door of the courthouse while under the federal rule that door would be shut?

Finally, in COHEN v. BENEFICIAL INDUSTRIAL LOAN CORP., 337 U.S. 541, 69 S.Ct. 1221, 93 L.Ed. 1528 (1949), the Court, in an opinion written by Justice Jackson, held that a federal court sitting in diversity must apply a New Jersey statute requiring a plaintiff in a shareholder derivative suit to post a security-for-expenses bond—even though what is now Federal Rule 23.1, which ostensibly governs such cases, did not require a bond. The Court found that regardless of whether the New Jersey statute was classified as procedural or substantive, it created substantive liabilities for expenses. In the Court's view, the federal rule did not contradict the New Jersey statute, but rather addressed independent concerns. Justice Douglas, joined by Justice Frankfurter, dissented on the ground that the New Jersey statute regulated "only the procedure for instituting a particular cause of action and hence need not be applied" in a diversity suit. Justice Rutledge's lengthy dissent "expressed grave doubt" whether *Erie*'s rule that federal diversity courts follow state decisional law rested on "any solid constitutional foundation," and he criticized ceding control of diversity jurisdiction from Congress to the states. Id. at 558, 69 S.Ct. at 1231, 93 L.Ed. at 1543.

4.   Almost any legal rule, whether labeled procedural or substantive, has the potential to affect the outcome of litigation. Does this mean that, after *York*,

a federal court in a diversity case must apply every state legal rule that, if enforced, would affect the lawsuit's result? Does this include housekeeping rules like rules about the size of briefs or the color of paper used? Did Justice Frankfurter mean any rule that could affect the outcome, or would he say that only rules that influence a lawyer's choice of forum at the time of filing are "outcome determinative"?

BYRD v. BLUE RIDGE RURAL ELECTRIC COOPERATIVE, INC.

Supreme Court of the United States, 1958.
356 U.S. 525, 78 S.Ct. 893, 2 L.Ed.2d 953.

Certiorari to the United States Court of Appeals for the Fourth Circuit.

JUSTICE BRENNAN delivered the opinion of the Court.

This case was brought in the District Court for the Western District of South Carolina. Jurisdiction was based on diversity of citizenship. * * * The petitioner, a resident of North Carolina, sued respondent, a South Carolina corporation, for damages for injuries allegedly caused by the respondent's negligence. He had judgment on a jury verdict. The Court of Appeals for the Fourth Circuit reversed and directed the entry of judgment for the respondent. * * *

The respondent is in the business of selling electric power to subscribers in rural sections of South Carolina. The petitioner was employed as a lineman in the construction crew of a construction contractor. The contractor, R.H. Bouligny, Inc., held a contract with the respondent * * * for the building of some * * * power lines, the reconversion to higher capacities of * * * existing lines, and the construction of 2 new substations and a breaker station. The petitioner was injured while connecting power lines to one of the new substations.

One of respondent's affirmative defenses was that under the South Carolina Workmen's Compensation Act, the petitioner—because the work contracted to be done by his employer was work of the kind also done by the respondent's own construction and maintenance crews—had the status of a statutory employee of the respondent and was therefore barred from suing the respondent at law because obliged to accept statutory compensation benefits as the exclusive remedy for his injuries. Two questions concerning this defense are before us: (1) whether the Court of Appeals erred in directing judgment for respondent without a remand to give petitioner an opportunity to introduce further evidence; and (2) whether petitioner, state practice notwithstanding, is entitled to a jury determination of the factual issues raised by this defense.

* * *

[The Supreme Court initially decided to remand the case to the trial court to provide the petitioner an opportunity to introduce evidence on the question of whether the respondent was a statutory employer.]

A question is also presented as to whether on remand the factual issue is to be decided by the judge or by the jury. The respondent argues on the basis of the decision of the Supreme Court of South Carolina in Adams v. Davison-Paxon Co., 230 S.C. 532, 96 S.E.2d 566, that the issue of immunity should be decided by the judge and not by the jury. * * *

The respondent argues that this state-court decision governs the present diversity case and "divests the jury of its normal function" to decide the disputed fact question of the respondent's immunity under § 72–111. This is to contend that the federal court is bound under Erie R. Co. v. Tompkins * * * to follow the state court's holding to secure uniform enforcement of the immunity created by the State.

First. It was decided in Erie R. Co. v. Tompkins that the federal courts in diversity cases must respect the definition of state-created rights and obligations by the state courts. We must, therefore, first examine the rule in Adams v. Davison-Paxon Co. to determine whether it is bound up with these rights and obligations in such a way that its application in the federal court is required. * * *

The Workmen's Compensation Act is administered in South Carolina by its Industrial Commission. The South Carolina courts hold that, on judicial review of actions of the Commission under § 72–111, the question whether the claim of an injured workman is within the Commission's jurisdiction is a matter of law for decision by the court, which makes its own findings of fact relating to that jurisdiction. The South Carolina Supreme Court states no reasons in Adams v. Davison-Paxon Co. why, although the jury decides all other factual issues raised by the cause of action and defenses, the jury is displaced as to the factual issue raised by the affirmative defense under § 72–111. * * * A State may, of course, distribute the functions of its judicial machinery as it sees fit. The decisions relied upon, however, furnish no reason for selecting the judge rather than the jury to decide this single affirmative defense in the negligence action. They simply reflect a policy * * * that administrative determination of "jurisdictional facts" should not be final but subject to judicial review. The conclusion is inescapable that the Adams holding is grounded in the practical consideration that the question had theretofore come before the South Carolina courts from the Industrial Commission and the courts had become accustomed to deciding the factual issue of immunity without the aid of juries. We find nothing to suggest that this rule was announced as an integral part of the special relationship created by the statute. Thus the requirement appears to be merely a form and mode of enforcing the immunity * * * and not a rule intended to be bound up with the definition of the rights and obligations of the parties. * * *

Second. But cases following Erie have evinced a broader policy to the effect that the federal courts should conform as near as may be—in the absence of other considerations—to state rules even of form and mode where the state rules may bear substantially on the question whether the litigation would come out one way in the federal court and another way in the state court if the federal court failed to apply a particular local rule. E.g., Guaranty Trust Co. of New York v. York * * *; Bernhardt v. Polygraphic Co., 350 U.S. 198, 76 S.Ct. 273, 100 L.Ed. 199. Concededly the nature of the tribunal which tries issues may be important in the enforcement of the parcel of rights making up a cause of action or defense, and bear significantly upon achievement of uniform enforcement of the right. It may well be that in the instant personal-injury case the outcome would be substantially affected by whether the issue of immunity is decided by a judge or a jury. Therefore, were "outcome" the only consideration, a strong case might appear for saying that the federal court should follow the state practice.

But there are affirmative countervailing considerations at work here. The federal system is an independent system for administering justice to litigants who properly invoke its jurisdiction. An essential characteristic of that system is the manner in which, in civil common-law actions, it distributes trial functions between judge and jury and, under the influence—if not the command—of the Seventh Amendment, assigns the decisions of disputed questions of fact to the jury. * * * The policy of uniform enforcement of state-created rights and obligations * * * cannot in every case exact compliance with a state rule—not bound up with rights and obligations—which disrupts the federal system of allocating functions between judge and jury. * * * Thus the inquiry here is whether the federal policy favoring jury decisions of disputed fact questions should yield to the state rule in the interest of furthering the objective that the litigation should not come out one way in the federal court and another way in the state court.

We think that in the circumstances of this case the federal court should not follow the state rule. It cannot be gainsaid that there is a strong federal policy against allowing state rules to disrupt the judge-jury relationship in the federal courts. In Herron v. Southern Pacific Co., [283 U.S. 91, 51 S.Ct. 383, 75 L.Ed. 857 (1931),] * * * the trial judge in a personal-injury negligence action brought in the District Court for Arizona on diversity grounds directed a verdict for the defendant when it appeared as a matter of law that the plaintiff was guilty of contributory negligence. The federal judge refused to be bound by a provision of the Arizona Constitution which made the jury the sole arbiter of the question of contributory negligence. This Court sustained the action of the trial judge, holding that "state laws cannot alter the essential character or function of a federal court" because that function "is not in any sense a local matter, and state statutes which would interfere with the appropriate performance of that function are not binding upon the federal court under either the Conformity Act or the 'Rules of Decision' Act." * * * Perhaps even more clearly in light of the influence of the Seventh Amendment, the function assigned to the jury "is an essential factor in the process for which the Federal Constitution provides." * * * Concededly the Herron case was decided before Erie R. Co. v. Tompkins, but even when Swift v. Tyson * * * was governing law and allowed federal courts sitting in diversity cases to disregard state decisional law, it was never thought that state statutes or constitutions were similarly to be disregarded. * * * Yet Herron held that state statutes and constitutional provisions could not disrupt or alter the essential character or function of a federal court. * * *

Third. We have discussed the problem upon the assumption that the outcome of the litigation may be substantially affected by whether the issue of immunity is decided by a judge or a jury. But clearly there is not present here the certainty that a different result would follow * * * or even the strong possibility that this would be the case * * *. There are factors present here which might reduce that possibility. The trial judge in the federal system has powers denied the judges of many States to comment on the weight of evidence and credibility of witnesses, and discretion to grant a new trial if the verdict appears to him to be against the weight of the evidence. We do not think the likelihood of a different result is so strong as to require the federal practice of jury determination of disputed factual issues to yield to the state rule in the interest of uniformity of outcome. * * *

Reversed and remanded.

[JUSTICE WHITTAKER concurred in Part I of the Court's opinion but dissented from Part II on the ground that the South Carolina rule requiring "its courts—not juries—to determine whether jurisdiction over the subject matter of cases like this is vested in its Industrial Commission" should be honored by a federal court. JUSTICE FRANKFURTER and JUSTICE HARLAN dissented on the ground that the evidence required the district court to direct a verdict for the respondent.]

NOTES AND QUESTIONS

1.   The Court's analysis in *Byrd* proceeds in three parts. It starts with an analysis of the South Carolina statute. Do you agree with Justice Brennan's assertion that the South Carolina rule is "merely a form and mode of enforcing the immunity * * * and not a rule intended to be bound up with the definition of the rights and obligations of the parties"? Most states have adopted their worker-compensation schemes only after carefully balancing the equities involved in the typical workplace accident. These statutes are complex and

detailed and often are the result of a political compromise. Does it seem likely, then, that South Carolina randomly would have appropriated to the judge the function of defining a statutory employee?

2.   In the second part of the decision, the Court moved toward a consideration of the importance of the federal interest that is at stake. What does Justice Brennan mean that "the influence * * * if not the command of the Seventh Amendment" determined the result in *Byrd*? If the Seventh Amendment provides a rule of decision for *Byrd*, isn't the Rules of Decision Act inapplicable by its own terms? Indeed, if the Seventh Amendment "commands" that a federal court utilize a jury to decide who is a statutory employee, could the Rules of Decision Act dictate a contrary result? On the other hand, if the Seventh Amendment does not "command" the result in *Byrd*, why should it "influence" the result? Of what relevance is the fact that the Seventh Amendment, unlike other provisions of the Bill of Rights, does not apply to the states through incorporation in the Fourteenth Amendment?

3.   The Court's analysis concludes with an assessment of whether the judge/jury allocation may affect the outcome of the case. Do you agree with the Court's conclusion? Is the analysis consistent with *York*?

4.   Commentators associate *Byrd* with a balancing test for determining when state law should displace federal law in a diversity action. Does the balancing test replace the outcome-determinative test of *York*? If a state rule is "bound up with the definition of the rights and obligations of the parties," does a federal court still engage in balancing?

––––––––

In 1934, Congress passed 28 U.S.C. § 2072, known as the Rules Enabling Act. Read the current version of this Act, which is in the Supplement.

––––––––

HANNA V. PLUMER
Supreme Court of the United States, 1965.
380 U.S. 460, 85 S.Ct. 1136, 14 L.Ed.2d 8.

Certiorari to the United States Court of Appeals for the First Circuit.

CHIEF JUSTICE WARREN delivered the opinion of the Court.

The question to be decided is whether, in a civil action where the jurisdiction of the United States District Court is based upon diversity of citizenship * * *, service of process shall be made in the manner prescribed by state law or that set forth in Rule 4(d)(1) of the Federal Rules of Civil Procedure.[a]

On February 6, 1963, petitioner, a citizen of Ohio, filed her complaint in the District Court for the District of Massachusetts, claiming damages in excess of $10,000 for personal injuries resulting from an automobile accident in South Carolina, allegedly caused by the negligence of one Louise Plumer Osgood, a Massachusetts citizen deceased at the time of the filing of the complaint. Respondent, Mrs. Osgood's executor and also a Massachusetts citizen, was named as defendant. On February 8, service was made by leaving copies of the summons and the complaint with respondent's wife at his residence, concededly in compliance with Rule 4(d)(1) * * *. Respondent filed his answer on February 26, alleging, *inter alia*, that the action could not be maintained because it had been brought "contrary to and in violation of the provisions of Massachusetts General Laws (Ter. Ed.) Chapter 197, Section 9." That section provides:

> Except as provided in this chapter, an executor or administrator shall not be held to answer to an action by a creditor of the deceased which is not commenced within one year from the time of his giving bond for the performance of his trust, or to such an action which is commenced within said year unless before the expiration thereof the writ in such action has been served by delivery in hand upon such executor or administrator or service thereof accepted by him or a notice stating the name of the estate, the name and address of the creditor, the amount of the claim and the court in which the action has been brought has been filed in the proper registry of probate. * * *

On October 17, 1963, the District Court granted respondent's motion for summary judgment * * * [on the ground] that the adequacy of the service was to be measured by § 9, with which, the court held, petitioner had not complied. On appeal, petitioner * * * argued that Rule 4(d)(1) defines the method by which service of process is to be effected in diversity actions. The Court of Appeals for the First Circuit * * * unanimously affirmed. * * *

We conclude that the adoption of Rule 4(d)(1), designed to control service of process in diversity actions, neither exceeded the congressional mandate embodied in the Rules Enabling Act nor transgressed constitutional bounds, and that the Rule is therefore the standard against which the District Court should have measured the adequacy of the service. Accordingly, we reverse the decision of the Court of Appeals.

---

[a] This provision has been amended and renumbered since 1965. Rule 4(e)(1) currently provides that service in federal court may occur by "following state law for serving a summons in an action brought in courts of general jurisdiction in the state where the district court is located or where service is made." See Chapter 3, supra.

* * * Under the cases construing the scope of the Enabling Act, Rule 4(d)(1) clearly passes muster. Prescribing the manner in which a defendant is to be notified that a suit has been instituted against him, it relates to the "practice and procedure of the district courts." * * *

> The test must be whether a rule really regulates procedure,—the judicial process for enforcing rights and duties recognized by substantive law and for justly administering remedy and redress for disregard or infraction of them. Sibbach v. Wilson & Co., [312 U.S. 1, 15, 61 S.Ct. 422, 427, 85 L.Ed. 479, 486 (1941)] * * *.

In Mississippi Pub. Corp. v. Murphree, 326 U.S. 438, 66 S.Ct. 242, 90 L.Ed. 185, this Court upheld Rule 4(f),[b] which permits service of a summons anywhere within the State (and not merely the district) in which a district court sits:

> We think that Rule 4(f) is in harmony with the Enabling Act * * *. Undoubtedly most alterations of the rules of practice and procedure may and often do affect the rights of litigants. Congress' prohibition of any alteration of substantive rights of litigants was obviously not addressed to such incidental effects as necessarily attend the adoption of the prescribed new rules of procedure upon the rights of litigants who, agreeably to rules of practice and procedure, have been brought before a court authorized to determine their rights. * * * The fact that the application of Rule 4(f) will operate to subject petitioner's rights to adjudication by the district court for northern Mississippi will undoubtedly affect those rights. But it does not operate to abridge, enlarge or modify the rules of decision by which that court will adjudicate its rights. Id., at 445–446, 66 S.Ct. at 246.

Thus were there no conflicting state procedure, Rule 4(d)(1) would clearly control. * * * However, respondent, focusing on the contrary Massachusetts rule, calls to the Court's attention another line of cases, a line which—like the Enabling Act—had its birth in 1938. Erie R. Co. v. Tompkins, * * * held that federal courts sitting in diversity cases, when deciding questions of "substantive" law, are bound by state court decisions as well as state statutes. The broad command of *Erie* was therefore identical to that of the Enabling Act: federal courts are to apply state substantive law and federal procedural law. However, as subsequent cases sharpened the distinction between substance and procedure, the line of cases following Erie diverged markedly from the line construing the Enabling Act. * * *

Respondent, by placing primary reliance on York * * *, suggests that the Erie doctrine acts as a check on the Federal Rules * * *, that despite

---

[b] This provision has been renumbered as Rule 4(e)(1).

the clear command of Rule 4(d)(1), Erie and its progeny demand the application of the Massachusetts rule. Reduced to essentials, the argument is: (1) Erie, as refined in York, demands that federal courts apply state law whenever application of federal law in its stead will alter the outcome of the case. (2) In this case, a determination that the Massachusetts service requirements obtain will result in immediate victory for respondent. If, on the other hand, it should be held that Rule 4(d)(1) is applicable, the litigation will continue, with possible victory for petitioner. (3) Therefore, Erie demands application of the Massachusetts rule. The syllogism possesses an appealing simplicity, but is for several reasons invalid.

In the first place, it is doubtful that, even if there were no Federal Rule making it clear that in hand service is not required in diversity actions, the Erie rule would have obligated the District Court to follow the Massachusetts procedure. "Outcome determination" analysis was never intended to serve as a talisman. Byrd v. Blue Ridge Rural Elec. Cooperative * * *. Indeed, the message of York itself is that choices between state and federal law are to be made not by application of any automatic, "litmus paper" criterion, but rather by reference to the policies underlying the Erie rule. * * *

The Erie rule is rooted in part in a realization that it would be unfair for the character or result of a litigation materially to differ because the suit had been brought in a federal court. * * * [N]onsubstantial, or trivial, variations [are] not likely to raise the sort of equal protection problems which troubled the Court in Erie; they are also unlikely to influence the choice of a forum. [The concern that application of a federal rule in place of a state rule will have outcome-determinative effect on the resolution of the dispute]* * * cannot be read without reference to the twin aims of the Erie rule: discouragement of forum-shopping and avoidance of inequitable administration of the laws. * * *

The difference between the conclusion that the Massachusetts rule is applicable, and the conclusion that it is not, is of course at this point "outcome-determinative" in the sense that if we hold the state rule to apply, respondent prevails, whereas if we hold that Rule 4(d)(1) governs, the litigation will continue. But in this sense *every* procedural variation is "outcome-determinative." For example, having brought suit in a federal court, a plaintiff cannot then insist on the right to file subsequent pleadings in accord with the time limits applicable in state courts, even though enforcement of the federal timetable will, if he continues to insist that he must meet only the state time limit, result in determination of the controversy against him. So it is here. Though choice of the federal or state rule will at this point have a marked effect upon the outcome of the litigation, the difference between the two rules would be of scant, if any, relevance to the choice of a forum. Petitioner, in choosing her forum, was not presented with a situation where application of the state rule would wholly bar recovery; rather, adherence to the state rule would have resulted only in altering the way in which process was served. * * * Moreover, it is difficult to argue that permitting service of defendant's wife to take the place of in hand service of defendant himself alters the mode of enforcement of state-created rights in a fashion sufficiently "substantial" to raise the sort of equal protection problems to which the Erie opinion alluded.

There is, however, a more fundamental flaw in respondent's syllogism: the incorrect assumption that the rule of Erie R. Co. v. Tompkins constitutes the appropriate test of the validity and therefore the applicability of a Federal Rule * * *. The Erie rule has never been invoked to void a Federal Rule. It is true that there have been cases where this Court has held applicable a state rule in the face of an argument that the situation was governed by one of the Federal Rules. But the holding of each such case was not that Erie commanded displacement of a Federal Rule by an inconsistent state rule, but rather that the scope of the Federal Rule was not as broad as the losing party urged, and therefore, there being no Federal Rule which covered the point in dispute, Erie commanded the enforcement of state law. * * * (Here, of course, the clash is unavoidable; Rule 4(d)(1) says—implicitly, but with unmistakable clarity—that in hand service is not required in federal courts.) At the same time, in cases adjudicating the validity of Federal Rules, we have not applied the York rule or other refinements of Erie, but have to this day continued to decide questions concerning the scope of the Enabling Act and the constitutionality of specific Federal Rules in light of the distinction set forth in Sibbach. * * *

Nor has the development of two separate lines of cases been inadvertent. The line between "substance" and "procedure" shifts as the legal context changes. * * * It is true that both the Enabling Act and the Erie rule say, roughly, that federal courts are to apply state "substantive" law and federal "procedural" law, but from that it need not follow that the tests are identical. For they were designed to control very different sorts of decisions. When a situation is covered by one of the Federal Rules, the question facing the court is a far cry from the typical, relatively unguided Erie choice: the court has been instructed to apply the Federal Rule, and can refuse to do so only if the Advisory Committee, this Court, and Congress erred in their prima facie judgment that the Rule in question transgresses neither the terms of the Enabling Act nor constitutional restrictions.

We are reminded by the Erie opinion that neither Congress nor the federal courts can, under the guise of formulating rules of decision for federal courts, fashion rules which are not supported by a grant of federal authority contained in Article I or some other section of the Constitution; in such areas state law must govern because there can be no other law. But the opinion in Erie, which involved no Federal Rule and dealt with a question which was "substantive" in every traditional sense * * *, surely neither said nor implied that measures like Rule 4(d)(1) are unconstitutional. For the constitutional provision for a federal court system (augmented by the Necessary and Proper Clause) carries with it congressional power to make rules governing the practice and pleading in those courts, which in turn includes a power to regulate matters which, though falling within the uncertain area between substance and procedure, are rationally capable of classification as either. * * *

Erie and its offspring cast no doubt on the long-recognized power of Congress to prescribe housekeeping rules for federal courts even though some of those rules will inevitably differ from comparable state rules. * * * Thus, though a court, in measuring a Federal Rule against the standards contained in the Enabling Act and the Constitution, need not wholly blind itself to the degree to which the Rule makes the character and result of the federal litigation stray from the course it would follow in state courts, * * * it cannot be forgotten that the Erie rule, and the guidelines suggested in York, were created to serve another purpose altogether. To hold that a Federal Rule * * * must cease to function whenever it alters the mode of enforcing state-created rights would be to disembowel either the Constitution's grant of power over federal procedure or Congress' attempt to exercise that power in the Enabling Act. Rule 4(d)(1) is valid and controls the instant case.

Reversed.

JUSTICE BLACK concurs in the result.

JUSTICE HARLAN, concurring.

* * *

Erie was something more than an opinion which worried about "forum-shopping and avoidance of inequitable administration of the laws," * * * although to be sure these were important elements of the decision. I have always regarded that decision as one of the modern cornerstones of our federalism, expressing policies that profoundly touch the allocation of judicial power between the state and federal systems. Erie recognized that there should not be two conflicting systems of law controlling the primary activity of citizens, for such alternative governing authority must necessarily give rise to a debilitating uncertainty in the planning of everyday affairs. And it recognized that the scheme of our Constitution envisions an allocation of law-making functions between state and federal legislative processes which is undercut if the federal judiciary can make substantive law affecting state affairs beyond the bounds of congressional legislative powers in this regard. * * *

* * * To my mind the proper line of approach in determining whether to apply a state or a federal rule, whether "substantive" or "procedural," is to stay close to basic principles by inquiring if the choice of rule would substantially affect those primary decisions respecting human conduct which our constitutional system leaves to state regulation. If so, Erie and the Constitution require that the state rule prevail, even in the face of a conflicting federal rule.

The Court weakens, if indeed it does not submerge, this basic principle by finding, in effect, a grant of substantive legislative power in the constitutional provision for a federal court system * * *, and through it, setting up the Federal Rules as a body of law inviolate. * * * So long as a reasonable man could characterize any duly adopted federal rule as "procedural," the Court, unless I misapprehend what is said, would have it apply no matter how seriously it frustrated a State's substantive regulation of the primary conduct and affairs of its citizens. Since the members of the Advisory Committee, the Judicial Conference, and this Court who formulated the Federal Rules are presumably reasonable men, it follows that the integrity of the Federal Rules is absolute. Whereas the unadulterated outcome and forum-shopping tests may err too far toward honoring state rules, I submit that the Court's "arguably procedural, *ergo* constitutional" test moves too fast and far in the other direction.

* * *

It remains to apply what has been said to the present case. * * * The evident intent of [the Massachusetts] statute is to permit an executor to distribute the estate which he is administering without fear that further liabilities may be outstanding for which he could be held personally liable. If the Federal District Court in Massachusetts applies Rule 4(d)(1) * * * instead of the Massachusetts service rule, what effect would that have on the speed and assurance with which estates are distributed? As I see it, the effect would not be substantial. It would mean simply that an executor would have to check at his own house or the federal courthouse as well as the registry of probate before he could distribute the estate with impunity. As this does not seem enough to give rise to any real impingement on the vitality of the state policy which the Massachusetts rule is intended to serve, I concur in the judgment of the Court.

NOTES AND QUESTIONS

1.   In *Hanna*, how does Chief Justice Warren treat the distinction between substance and procedure? How does he define that distinction for purposes of the Rules Enabling Act? For purposes of the Rules of Decision Act? Are the definitions the same?

2.   Chief Justice Warren's opinion relied on SIBBACH v. WILSON & CO., 312 U.S. 1, 61 S.Ct. 422, 85 L.Ed. 479 (1941), to define when a rule

complies with the Rules Enabling Act. In *Sibbach*, plaintiff sued in an Illinois federal district court for damages inflicted in Indiana. The Supreme Court affirmed the district court's order that plaintiff undergo a physical examination pursuant to Federal Rule 35, despite an Illinois policy forbidding compulsory physical examinations. The Court concluded that Rule 35 was within the ambit of the rulemaking power granted by Congress since Rule 35 does not "abridge, enlarge, [or] modify substantive rights, in the guise of regulating procedure." The Court rejected plaintiff's argument that the Rules Enabling Act's "substantive rights" limitation prohibited any rules that "deal with important and substantial rights." In an opinion written by Justice Roberts, the Court held:

> * * * If we were to adopt the suggested criterion of the importance of the alleged right we should invite endless litigation and confusion * * *. The test must be whether a rule really regulates procedure— the judicial process for enforcing rights and duties recognized by substantive law and for justly administering remedy and redress for disregard or infraction of them. That the rules in question are such is admitted.

Id. at 14, 61 S.Ct. at 426, 85 L.Ed. at 485. Justice Roberts also emphasized that the Rules Enabling Act empowers Congress to block proposed rules: "[T]he rules were submitted to the Congress so that that body might examine them and veto their going into effect if contrary to the policy of the legislature. * * * That no adverse action was taken by Congress indicates, at least, that no transgression of legislative policy was found." Id. at 14–16, 16 S.Ct. at 427–28, 85 L.Ed. at 485–86.

Justice Frankfurter dissented. He argued that Rule 35, which provides for "the invasion of the person," is quite different from other rules of procedure. He noted, furthermore, that the Rules automatically are effective absent a veto by Congress, so that "to draw any inference of tacit approval from non-action by Congress is to appeal to unreality." In the dissent's view, therefore, "to make the drastic change that Rule 35 sought to introduce would require explicit legislation." Id. at 18, 61 S.Ct. at 428–29, 85 L.Ed. at 487.

3.   Chief Justice Warren asserted that "the Erie rule is rooted in part in a realization that it would be unfair for the character or result of a litigation materially to differ because the suit had been brought in federal court [and] * * * in part a reaction to the practice of forum-shopping." What role does federalism play in his argument? Has he abandoned an important part of *Erie*?

4.   On what basis did Justice Harlan concur? What is meant by "primary" decisions of conduct? Are you convinced that these activities are left by "our constitutional system * * * to state regulation"? Do you share his concern that under the majority opinion in *Hanna* any "arguably procedural" rule would apply "no matter how seriously it frustrated a State's substantive regulation of the primary conduct and affairs of its citizens"? How does Justice Harlan identify and measure state interests for purposes of 28 U.S.C. § 2072?

NOTE ON DETERMINING WHETHER A FEDERAL RULE OR STATUTE IS PERTINENT

In *Hanna*, Chief Justice Warren emphasized that in earlier cases, a state rule applied not because "*Erie* commanded displacement of a Federal Rule by an inconsistent statute," but rather because there was "no Federal Rule which covered the point in dispute." In *Hanna*, however, the "clash" between Federal Rule 4 and the state rule was said to be "unavoidable," p. 338, supra. How should a court determine whether a Federal Rule is pertinent to a dispute? Consider this analysis:

> To understand how *Erie* operates in diversity cases, it is important to distinguish between the *pertinence* of federal rules and their validity. To say a federal rule is "pertinent" means that it was intended or designed to govern the issue at hand—that the rule's purposes would be served by applying it. To say a rule is "valid" means that it has been adopted in conformity with the legal norms controlling the creation of federal law—that it is consistent with the Constitution and other organic statutes regulating the formation of federal law. These combined qualities of pertinence and validity are necessary and sufficient for the proper application of a federal rule: If either quality is absent, a federal rule cannot be lawfully applied; if both are present, the federal rule must be applied.
>
> * * *
>
> Federal rules of civil procedure should be analyzed in the same way as federal statutes, except the rules must satisfy an additional standard of validity. The pertinence analysis is precisely the same for rules as it is for other laws. The court must determine whether the framers of a rule intended that it govern the issue at hand; if so (and if the rule is valid), the rule applies; if not, state law applies.

Westen & Lehman, *Is There Life for* Erie *After the Death of Diversity?*, 78 Mich.L.Rev. 311, 314–15, 342, 359 (1980).

As a first step in the inquiry about pertinence, the Court has stated that the district court must ask whether the federal rule is "sufficiently broad to control the issue before the Court." Walker v. Armco Steel Corp., 446 U.S. 740, 1985, 100 S.Ct. 1978, 64 L.Ed.2d 659, 667 (1980). The Court later explained that the question of pertinence "involves a straightforward exercise in statutory interpretation to determine if the statute covers the point in dispute." Stewart Organization, Inc. v. Ricoh Corp., 487 U.S. 22, 26, 108 S.Ct. 2239, 2242, 101 L.Ed.2d 22, 29 (1988). Whether a federal rule "covers the point," however, does not "mandate that federal law and state law be perfectly coextensive and equally applicable to the issue at hand; rather, the 'direct collision' language, at least where the applicability of a federal statute is at issue, expresses the requirement that the federal statute be sufficiently broad to cover the point in dispute." The Court added: "It would make no sense for the supremacy of federal law to wane precisely because there is no state law directly on point." Id. at 26–27 n.4, 108 S.Ct. at 2242 n.4, 135 L.Ed.2d at 29 n.4. However, in Gasperini v. Center for Humanities, Inc., 518 U.S. 415, 116 S.Ct. 2211, 135 L.Ed.2d 659 (1996), the Court noted that in determining whether a Federal Rule that "is consonant with the Rules Enabling Act" displaces a contrary state rule, "[f]ederal courts have interpreted the Federal Rules * * * with sensitivity to important state interests and regulatory policies." Id. at 427 n.7, 116 S.Ct. at 2219 n.7, 135 L.Ed.2d at 674 n.7. The scope of the Court's "sensitivity" was considered in the next principal case.

SHADY GROVE ORTHOPEDIC ASSOCIATES
v. ALLSTATE INSURANCE CO.
Supreme Court of the United States, 2010.
559 U.S. 393, 130 S.Ct. 1431, 176 L.Ed.2d 311.

Certiorari to the United States Court of Appeals for the Second Circuit.

JUSTICE SCALIA announced the judgment of the Court and delivered the opinion of the Court with respect to Parts I and II-A, an opinion with respect to Parts II-B and II-D, in which THE CHIEF JUSTICE, JUSTICE THOMAS, and JUSTICE SOTOMAYOR join, and an opinion with respect to Part II-C, in which THE CHIEF JUSTICE and JUSTICE THOMAS join.

New York law prohibits class actions in suits seeking penalties or statutory minimum damages. We consider whether this precludes a federal district court sitting in diversity from entertaining a class action under Federal Rule of Civil Procedure 23.

I

The petitioner's complaint alleged the following: Shady Grove Orthopedic Associates, P. A., provided medical care to Sonia E. Galvez for injuries she suffered in an automobile accident. As partial payment for that care, Galvez assigned to Shady Grove her rights to insurance benefits under a policy issued in New York by Allstate Insurance Co. Shady Grove tendered a claim for the assigned benefits to Allstate, which under New York law had 30 days to pay the claim or deny it. * * * Allstate apparently paid, but not on time, and it refused to pay the statutory interest that accrued on the overdue benefits * * *.

Shady Grove filed this diversity suit in the Eastern District of New York to recover the unpaid statutory interest. Alleging that Allstate routinely refuses to pay interest on overdue benefits, Shady Grove sought relief on behalf of itself and a class of all others to whom Allstate owes interest. The District Court dismissed the suit for lack of jurisdiction. * * * It reasoned that N.Y. Civ. Prac. Law Ann. § 901(b), which precludes a suit to recover a "penalty" from proceeding as a class action, applies in diversity suits in federal court, despite Federal Rule * * * 23. * * * And, since Shady Grove conceded that its individual claim (worth roughly $500) fell far short of the amount-in-controversy requirement for individual suits under 28 U.S.C. § 1332(a), the suit did not belong in federal court.

The Second Circuit affirmed. * * *

II

The framework for our decision is familiar. We must first determine whether Rule 23 answers the question in dispute. * * * If it does, it governs—New York's law notwithstanding—unless it exceeds statutory authorization or Congress's rulemaking power. * * * We do not wade into *Erie*'s murky waters unless the federal rule is inapplicable or invalid. * * *

A

The question in dispute is whether Shady Grove's suit may proceed as a class action. Rule 23 provides an answer. It states that "[a] class action may be maintained" if two conditions are met: The suit must satisfy the criteria set forth in subdivision (a) * * *, and it also must fit into one of the three categories described in subdivision (b). * * * By its terms this creates a categorical rule entitling a plaintiff whose suit meets the specified criteria to pursue his claim as a class action. * * * Thus, Rule 23 provides a one-size-fits-all formula for deciding the class-action question. Because § 901(b) attempts to answer the same question—*i.e.*, it states that Shady Grove's suit "may *not* be maintained as a class action" (emphasis added)[c] because of the relief it seeks—it cannot apply in diversity suits unless Rule 23 is ultra vires.

The Second Circuit believed that § 901(b) and Rule 23 do not conflict because they address different issues. Rule 23, it said, concerns only the criteria for determining whether a given class can and should be certified; section 901(b), on the other hand, addresses an antecedent question: whether the particular type of claim is eligible for class treatment in the first place—a question on which Rule 23 is silent. * * *

We disagree. To begin with, the line between eligibility and certifiability is entirely artificial. Both are preconditions for maintaining a class action. Allstate suggests that eligibility must depend on the "particular cause of action" asserted, instead of some other attribute of the suit * * *. But that is not so. Congress could, for example, provide that only claims involving more than a certain number of plaintiffs are "eligible" for class treatment in federal court. In other words, relabeling Rule 23(a)'s prerequisites "eligibility criteria" would obviate Allstate's objection—a sure sign that its eligibility-certifiability distinction is made-to-order.

There is no reason, in any event, to read Rule 23 as addressing only whether claims made eligible for class treatment by some *other* law should be certified as class actions. Allstate asserts that Rule 23 neither explicitly

---

[c] Emphasis in original here and throughout opinion.

nor implicitly empowers a federal court "to certify a class in each and every case" where the Rule's criteria are met. * * * But that is *exactly* what Rule 23 does: It says that if the prescribed preconditions are satisfied "[a] class action *may be maintained*" (emphasis added)—not "*a class action may be permitted.*" Courts do not maintain actions; litigants do. The discretion suggested by Rule 23's "may" is discretion residing in the plaintiff: He may bring his claim in a class action if he wishes. * * *

Allstate points out that Congress has carved out some federal claims from Rule 23's reach * * *—which shows, Allstate contends, that Rule 23 does not authorize class actions for all claims, but rather leaves room for laws like § 901(b). But Congress, unlike New York, has ultimate authority over the Federal Rules * * *; it can create exceptions to an individual rule as it sees fit * * *. * * * The fact that Congress has created specific exceptions to Rule 23 hardly proves that the Rule does not apply generally. In fact, it proves the opposite. * * *

Allstate next suggests that the structure of § 901 shows that Rule 23 addresses only certifiability. Section 901(a), it notes, establishes class-certification criteria roughly analogous to those in Rule 23 (wherefore it agrees *that* subsection is pre-empted). But § 901(b)'s rule barring class actions for certain claims is set off as its own subsection, and where it applies § 901(a) does not. This shows, according to Allstate, that § 901(b) concerns a separate subject. Perhaps it does concern a subject separate from * * * § 901(a). But the question before us is whether it concerns a subject separate from the subject of *Rule 23*—and for purposes of answering *that* question the way New York has structured its statute is immaterial. Rule 23 permits all class actions that meet its requirements, and a State cannot limit that permission by structuring one part of its statute to track Rule 23 and enacting another part that imposes additional requirements. * * *

The dissent argues that § 901(b) has nothing to do with whether Shady Grove may maintain its suit as a class action, but affects only the *remedy* it may obtain if it wins. * * * Accordingly, the dissent says, Rule 23 and New York's law may coexist in peace.

We need not decide whether a state law that limits the remedies available in an existing class action would conflict with Rule 23; that is not what § 901(b) does. * * * Unlike a law that sets a ceiling on damages (or puts other remedies out of reach) in properly filed class actions, § 901(b) says nothing about what remedies a court may award; it prevents the class actions it covers from coming into existence at all. * * *

The dissent asserts that a plaintiff can avoid § 901(b)'s barrier by omitting from his complaint (or removing) a request for statutory penalties. * * * Even assuming all statutory penalties are waivable, the fact that a complaint omitting them could be brought as a class action would not at all prove that § 901(b) is addressed only to remedies. If the state law instead banned class actions for fraud claims, a would-be class-action plaintiff could drop the fraud counts from his complaint and proceed with the remainder in a class action. Yet that would not mean the law provides no remedy for fraud; the ban would affect only the procedural means by which the remedy may be pursued. * * *

The dissent all but admits that the literal terms of § 901(b) address the same subject as Rule 23—*i.e.*, whether a class action may be maintained—but insists the provision's *purpose* is to restrict only remedies. * * * Unlike Rule 23, designed to further procedural fairness and efficiency, § 901(b) (we are told) "responds to an entirely different concern": the fear that allowing statutory damages to be awarded on a class-wide basis would "produce overkill." * * *

* * * [E]vidence of the New York Legislature's purpose is pretty sparse. But even accepting the dissent's account of the Legislature's objective at face value, it cannot override the statute's clear text. * * * The dissent's concern for state prerogatives is frustrated rather than furthered by revising state laws when a potential conflict with a Federal Rule arises; the state-friendly approach would be to accept the law as written and test the validity of the Federal Rule.

The dissent's approach of determining whether state and federal rules conflict based on the subjective intentions of the state legislature is an enterprise destined to produce "confusion worse confounded," *Sibbach* * * * [p. 340, Note 2, supra]. It would mean, to begin with, that one State's statute could survive pre-emption (and accordingly affect the procedures in federal court) while another State's identical law would not, merely because its authors had different aspirations. It would also mean that district courts would have to discern, in every diversity case, the purpose behind any putatively pre-empted state procedural rule, even if its text squarely conflicts with federal law. That task will often prove arduous. Many laws further more than one aim, and the aim of others may be impossible to discern. Moreover, to the extent the dissent's purpose-driven approach depends on its characterization of § 901(b)'s aims as substantive, it would apply to many state rules ostensibly addressed to procedure. Pleading standards, for example, often embody policy preferences about the types of claims that should succeed—as do rules governing summary judgment, pretrial discovery, and the admissibility of certain evidence. Hard cases will abound. It is not even clear that a state supreme court's pronouncement of the law's purpose would settle the issue, since existence of the factual predicate for avoiding federal pre-emption is ultimately a federal question. Predictably, federal judges would be condemned to poring through state legislative history—which may be less easily obtained, less thorough, and less familiar than its federal counterpart * * *.

But while the dissent does indeed artificially narrow the scope of § 901(b) by finding that it pursues only substantive policies, that is not the central difficulty of the dissent's position. The central difficulty is that even artificial narrowing cannot render § 901(b) compatible with Rule 23. *Whatever* the policies they pursue, they flatly contradict each other. * * * Rule 23 unambiguously authorizes *any* plaintiff, in *any* federal civil proceeding, to maintain a class action if the Rule's prerequisites are met. We cannot contort its text, even to avert a collision with state law that might render it invalid. * * *8 What the dissent's approach achieves is not the avoiding of a "conflict between Rule 23 and § 901(b)," * * * but rather the invalidation of Rule 23 * * * to the extent that it conflicts with the substantive policies of § 901. There is no other way to reach the dissent's destination. We must therefore confront head-on whether Rule 23 falls within the statutory authorization.

B

* * *

We have long held that [the limitations on the Rules Enabling Act] means that the Rule must "really regulat[e] procedure,—the judicial process for enforcing rights and duties recognized by substantive law and for justly administering remedy and redress for disregard or infraction of them," *Sibbach* * * *. The test is not whether the rule affects a litigant's substantive rights; most procedural rules do. * * *. What matters is what the rule itself *regulates*: If it governs only "the manner and the means" by which the litigants' rights are "enforced," it is valid; if it alters "the rules of decision by which [the] court will adjudicate [those] rights," it is not. * * *

Applying that test, we have rejected every statutory challenge to a Federal Rule that has come before us. * * * Each of these rules [for example, the service of process rule in *Hanna*, p. 334, supra] had some practical effect on the parties' rights, but each undeniably regulated only the process for enforcing those rights; none altered the rights themselves, the available remedies, or the rules of decision by which the court adjudicated either.

Applying that criterion, we think it obvious that rules allowing multiple claims (and claims by or against multiple parties) to be litigated together are also valid. * * * Such rules neither change plaintiffs' separate entitlements to relief nor abridge defendants' rights; they alter only how the claims are processed. For the same reason, Rule 23—at least insofar as it allows willing plaintiffs to join their separate claims against the same defendants in a class action—falls within § 2072(b)'s authorization. A class action, no less than traditional joinder (of which it is a species), merely

---

8 The cases chronicled by the dissent * * * each involved a Federal Rule that we concluded could fairly be read not to "control the issue" addressed by the pertinent state law, thus avoiding a "direct collision" between federal and state law, *Walker* * * * [p. 342, supra] (internal quotation marks omitted). But here, as in *Hanna* [p. 334, supra], * * * a collision is "unavoidable."

enables a federal court to adjudicate claims of multiple parties at once, instead of in separate suits. And like traditional joinder, it leaves the parties' legal rights and duties intact and the rules of decision unchanged.

Allstate contends that the authorization of class actions is not substantively neutral: Allowing Shady Grove to sue on behalf of a class "transform[s] [the] dispute over a five *hundred* dollar penalty into a dispute over a five *million* dollar penalty." * * *Allstate's aggregate liability, however, does not depend on whether the suit proceeds as a class action. Each of the 1,000-plus members of the putative class could (as Allstate acknowledges) bring a freestanding suit asserting his individual claim. It is undoubtedly true that some plaintiffs who would not bring individual suits for the relatively small sums involved will choose to join a class action. That has no bearing, however, on Allstate's or the plaintiffs' legal rights. The likelihood that some (even many) plaintiffs will be induced to sue by the availability of a class action is just the sort of "incidental effec[t]" we have long held does not violate § 2072(b) * * *.

Allstate argues that Rule 23 violates § 2072(b) because the state law it displaces, § 901(b), creates a right that the Federal Rule abridges— namely, a "substantive right . . . not to be subjected to aggregated class-action liability" in a single suit. * * * To begin with, we doubt that that is so. Nothing in the text of § 901(b) (which is to be found in New York's procedural code) confines it to claims under New York law; and of course New York has no power to alter substantive rights and duties created by other sovereigns. * * * As a fallback argument, Allstate argues that even if § 901(b) is a procedural provision, it was enacted "for *substantive reasons*," * * * (emphasis added)." * * *

The fundamental difficulty with both these arguments is that the substantive nature of New York's law, or its substantive purpose, *makes no difference.* A Federal Rule of Procedure is not valid in some jurisdictions and invalid in others—or valid in some cases and invalid in others— depending upon whether its effect is to frustrate a state substantive law (or a state procedural law enacted for substantive purposes). * * * [*Sibbach* and] *Hanna* unmistakably expressed the same understanding that compliance of a Federal Rule with the Enabling Act is to be assessed by consulting the Rule itself, and not its effects in individual applications * * *.

In sum, it is not the substantive or procedural nature or purpose of the affected state law that matters, but the substantive or procedural nature of the Federal Rule. * * * [T]he validity of a Federal Rule depends entirely upon whether it regulates procedure. * * * If it does, it is authorized by § 2072 and is valid in all jurisdictions, with respect to all claims, regardless of its incidental effect upon state-created rights.

C

A few words in response to the concurrence. * * * The concurrence agrees with us that Rule 23 and § 901(b) conflict * * * and departs from us only with respect to the second part of the test, *i.e.*, whether application of the Federal Rule violates § 2072(b) * * *. Like us, it answers no, but for a reason different from ours. * * *

The concurrence would decide this case on the basis, not that Rule 23 is procedural, but that the state law it displaces is procedural, in the sense that it does not "function as a part of the State's definition of substantive rights and remedies." * * * A state procedural rule is not preempted, according to the concurrence, so long as it is "so bound up with," or "sufficiently intertwined with," a substantive state-law right or remedy "that it defines the scope of that substantive right or remedy" * * *.

This analysis squarely conflicts with *Sibbach*, which established the rule we apply. The concurrence contends that *Sibbach* did not rule out its approach, but that is not so. Recognizing the impracticability of a test that turns on the idiosyncrasies of state law, *Sibbach* adopted and applied a rule with a single criterion: whether the Federal Rule "really regulates procedure." * * * [T]hat rule leaves no room for special exemptions based on the function or purpose of a particular state rule. * * *

In reality, the concurrence seeks not to apply *Sibbach*, but to overrule it (or, what is the same, to rewrite it). Its approach, the concurrence insists, gives short shrift to the statutory text forbidding the Federal Rules from "abridg[ing], enlarg[ing], or modify[ing] any substantive right" * * *. * * * There is something to that. It is possible to understand how it can be determined whether a Federal Rule "enlarges" substantive rights without consulting State law: If the Rule creates a substantive right, even one that duplicates some state-created rights, it establishes a new *federal* right. But it is hard to understand how it can be determined whether a Federal Rule "abridges" or "modifies" substantive rights without knowing what state-created rights would obtain if the Federal Rule did not exist. *Sibbach*'s exclusive focus on the challenged Federal Rule—driven by the very real concern that Federal Rules which vary from State to State would be chaos * * *—is hard to square with § 2072(b)'s terms.[11]

Sibbach has been settled law, however, for nearly seven decades. * * * In all events, Allstate has not even asked us to overrule *Sibbach*, let alone carried its burden of persuading us to do so. * * * Why we should cast aside

---

[11] The concurrence's approach, however, is itself unfaithful to the statute's terms. Section 2072(b) bans abridgement or modification only of "substantive rights," but the concurrence would prohibit pre-emption of "procedural rules that are intimately bound up in the scope of a substantive right or remedy," * * *. This would allow States to force a wide array of parochial procedures on federal courts so long as they are "sufficiently intertwined with a state right or remedy." * * *

our decades-old decision escapes us, especially since (as the concurrence explains) that would not affect the result.[13]

The concurrence also contends that applying *Sibbach* and assessing whether a Federal Rule regulates substance or procedure is not always easy. * * * Undoubtedly some hard cases will arise (though we have managed to muddle through well enough in the 69 years since *Sibbach* was decided). But as the concurrence acknowledges, * * * the basic difficulty is unavoidable: The statute itself refers to "substantive right[s]" * * * so there is no escaping the substance-procedure distinction. What is more, the concurrence's approach does nothing to diminish the difficulty, but rather magnifies it many times over. * * * At the end of the day, one must come face to face with the decision whether or not the state policy (with which a putatively procedural state rule may be "bound up") pertains to a "substantive right or remedy," * * *—that is, whether it is substance or procedure. The more one explores the alternatives to *Sibbach's* rule, the more its wisdom becomes apparent.

D

We must acknowledge the reality that keeping the federal-court door open to class actions that cannot proceed in state court will produce forum shopping. That is unacceptable when it comes as the consequence of judge-made rules created to fill supposed "gaps" in positive federal law. * * * But divergence from state law, with the attendant consequence of forum shopping, is the inevitable (indeed, one might say the intended) result of a uniform system of federal procedure. Congress itself has created the possibility that the same case may follow a different course if filed in federal instead of state court. * * * The short of the matter is that a Federal Rule governing procedure is valid whether or not it alters the outcome of the case in a way that induces forum shopping. To hold otherwise would be to "disembowel either the Constitution's grant of power over federal procedure" or Congress's exercise of it. * * * [*Hanna*].

---

[13] The concurrence is correct * * * that under our disposition any rule that "really regulates procedure," * * * will pre-empt a conflicting state rule, however "bound up" the latter is with substantive law. The concurrence is wrong, however, that that result proves our interpretation of § 2072(b) implausible * * *. The result is troubling only if one stretches the term "substantive rights" in § 2072(b) to mean not only state-law rights themselves, but also any state-law procedures closely connected to them. Neither the text nor our precedent supports that expansive interpretation. The examples the concurrence offers—statutes of limitations, burdens of proof, and standards for appellate review of damages awards—do not make its broad definition of substantive rights more persuasive. They merely illustrate that in rare cases it may be difficult to determine whether a rule "really regulates" procedure or substance. If one concludes the latter, there is no pre-emption of the state rule; the Federal Rule itself is invalid.

The concurrence's concern would make more sense if many Federal Rules that effectively alter state-law rights "bound up with procedures" would survive under *Sibbach*. But as the concurrence concedes, * * * very few would do so. The possible existence of a few outlier instances does not prove *Sibbach's* interpretation is absurd. Congress may well have accepted such anomalies as the price of a uniform system of federal procedure.

* * *

JUSTICE STEVENS concurring in part and concurring in the judgment.

The New York law at issue * * * is a procedural rule that is not part of New York's substantive law. Accordingly, I agree with Justice Scalia that [the] Federal Rule * * * must apply in this case and join Parts I and II-A of the Court's opinion. But I also agree with Justice Ginsburg that there are some state procedural rules that federal courts must apply in diversity cases because they function as a part of the State's definition of substantive rights and remedies.

* * *

* * * When a federal rule appears to abridge, enlarge, or modify a substantive right, federal courts must consider whether the rule can reasonably be interpreted to avoid that impermissible result. * * * And when such a "saving" construction is not possible and the rule would violate the Enabling Act, federal courts cannot apply the rule. * * * A federal rule, therefore, cannot govern a particular case in which the rule would displace a state law that is procedural in the ordinary use of the term but is so intertwined with a state right or remedy that it functions to define the scope of the state-created right. And absent a governing federal rule, a federal court must engage in the traditional Rules of Decision Act inquiry, under the *Erie* line of cases. * * *

Justice Scalia believes that the sole Enabling Act question is whether the federal rule "really regulates procedure," * * * which means, apparently, whether it regulates "the manner and the means by which the litigants' rights are enforced," * * *. I respectfully disagree. This interpretation of the Enabling Act is consonant with the Act's first limitation to "general rules of practice and procedure" * * *. But it ignores the second limitation that such rules also "not abridge, enlarge or modify *any* substantive right" * * *,[8] and in so doing ignores the balance that Congress struck between uniform rules of federal procedure and respect for a State's construction of its own rights and remedies. * * *

Although the plurality appears to agree with much of my interpretation of § 2072 * * *, it nonetheless rejects that approach for two reasons, both of which are mistaken. First, Justice Scalia worries that if federal courts inquire into the effect of federal rules on state law, it will enmesh federal courts in difficult determinations about whether

---

[8]   * * * In some instances, a state rule that appears procedural really is not. A rule about how damages are reviewed on appeal may really be a damages cap. * * * A rule that a plaintiff can bring a claim for only three years may really be a limit on the existence of the right to seek redress. A rule that a claim must be proved beyond a reasonable doubt may really be a definition of the scope of the claim. These are the sorts of rules that one might describe as "procedural," but they nonetheless define substantive rights. Thus, if a federal rule displaced such a state rule, the federal rule would have altered the State's "substantive rights."

application of a given rule would displace a state determination about substantive rights. * * * I do not see why an Enabling Act inquiry that looks to state law necessarily is more taxing than Justice Scalia's. But in any event, that inquiry is what the Enabling Act requires * * *. * * * Although, Justice Scalia may generally prefer easily administrable, bright-line rules, his preference does not give us license to adopt a second-best interpretation of the Rules Enabling Act. * * *

Second, the plurality argues that its interpretation of the Enabling Act is dictated by this Court's decision in *Sibbach*, which applied a Federal Rule about when parties must submit to medical examinations. But the plurality misreads that opinion. * * * The petitioner raised only the facial question whether "Rules 35 and 37 [of the Federal Rules] are . . . within the mandate of Congress to this court" and not the specific question of "the obligation of federal courts to apply the substantive law of a state." * * * The Court, therefore, had no occasion to consider whether the particular application of the Federal Rules in question would offend the Enabling Act.

Nor, in *Sibbach*, was any further analysis necessary to the resolution of the case because the matter at issue, requiring medical exams for litigants, did not pertain to "substantive rights" under the Enabling Act. Although most state rules bearing on the litigation process are adopted for some policy reason, few seemingly "procedural" rules define the scope of a substantive right or remedy. The matter at issue in *Sibbach* reflected competing federal and state judgments about privacy interests. Those privacy concerns may have been weighty and in some sense substantive; but they did not pertain to the scope of any state right or remedy at issue in the litigation. * * *

Notwithstanding the plain language of Rule 23, I understand the dissent to find that Rule 23 does *not* govern the question of class certification in this matter because New York has made a substantive judgment that such a class should not be certified, as a means of proscribing damages. * * *

* * * The dissent would apply the Rules of Decision Act inquiry under *Erie* even to cases in which there is a governing federal rule, and thus the Act, by its own terms, does not apply. * * * [This] approach would, in my view, work an end run around Congress' system of uniform federal rules * * * and our decision in *Hanna*. * * * If my dissenting colleagues feel strongly that § 901(b) is substantive and that class certification should be denied, then they should argue within the Enabling Act's framework. Otherwise, "the Federal Rule applies regardless of contrary state law." * * *

In my view, * * * the bar for finding an Enabling Act problem is a high one. The mere fact that a state law is designed as a procedural rule suggests it reflects a judgment about how state courts ought to operate and not a judgment about the scope of state-created rights and remedies. And for the purposes of operating a federal court system, there are costs involved in attempting to discover the true nature of a state procedural rule and allowing such a rule to operate alongside a federal rule that appears to govern the same question. The mere possibility that a federal rule would alter a state-created right is not sufficient. * * *

The text of CPLR § 901(b) expressly and unambiguously applies not only to claims based on New York law but also to claims based on federal law or the law of any other State. And there is no interpretation from New York courts to the contrary. It is therefore hard to see how § 901(b) could be understood as a rule that, though procedural in form, serves the function of defining New York's rights or remedies. This is all the more apparent because lawsuits under New York law could be joined in federal class actions well before New York passed § 901(b) in 1975, and New York had done nothing to prevent that. * * *

The legislative history, moreover, does not clearly describe a judgment that § 901(b) would operate as a limitation on New York's statutory damages. In evaluating that legislative history, it is necessary to distinguish between procedural rules adopted for *some* policy reason and seemingly procedural rules that are intimately bound up in the scope of a substantive right or remedy. * * * New York clearly crafted § 901(b) with the intent that only certain lawsuits—those for which there were not statutory penalties—could be joined in class actions in New York courts. That decision reflects a policy judgment about which lawsuits should proceed in New York courts in a class form and which should not. * * *

The difference of degree is relevant to the forum shopping considerations that are part of the Rules of Decision Act or *Erie* inquiry. If the applicable federal rule did not govern the particular question at issue (or could be fairly read not to do so), then those considerations would matter, for precisely the reasons given by the dissent. * * * But that is not *this* case. * * *

Because Rule 23 governs class certification, the only decision is whether certifying a class in this diversity case would "abridge, enlarge or modify" New York's substantive rights or remedies. § 2072(b). Although one can argue that class certification would enlarge New York's "limited" damages remedy, * * * such arguments rest on extensive speculation about what the New York Legislature had in mind when it created § 901(b). * * * In order to displace a federal rule, there must be more than just a possibility that the state rule is different than it appears.

Accordingly, I concur in part and concur in the judgment.

JUSTICE GINSBURG, with whom JUSTICE KENNEDY, JUSTICE BREYER, and JUSTICE ALITO join, dissenting.

The Court today approves Shady Grove's attempt to transform a $500 case into a $5,000,000 award, although the State creating the right to recover has proscribed this alchemy. * * *

The Court reads Rule 23 relentlessly to override New York's restriction on the availability of statutory damages. Our decisions, however, caution us to ask, before undermining state legislation: Is this conflict really necessary? * * * Had the Court engaged in that inquiry, it would not have read Rule 23 to collide with New York's legitimate interest in keeping certain monetary awards reasonably bounded. I would continue to interpret Federal Rules with awareness of, and sensitivity to, important state regulatory policies. * * *

I

* * *

Our decisions instruct over and over again that, in the adjudication of diversity cases, state interests—whether advanced in a statute, * * * or a procedural rule * * *—warrant our respectful consideration. Yet today, the Court gives no quarter to New York's limitation on statutory damages and requires the lower courts to thwart the regulatory policy at stake: To prevent excessive damages, New York's law controls the penalty to which a defendant may be exposed in a single suit. * * *

The Court, I am convinced, finds conflict where none is necessary. * * * Rule 23 prescribes the considerations relevant to class certification and postcertification proceedings—but it does not command that a particular remedy be available when a party sues in a representative capacity. * * * Section 901(b), in contrast, trains on that latter issue. Sensibly read, Rule 23 governs procedural aspects of class litigation, but allows state law to control the size of a monetary award a class plaintiff may pursue.

* * * Rule 23 describes a method of enforcing a claim for relief, while § 901(b) defines the dimensions of the claim itself. In this regard, it is immaterial that § 901(b) bars statutory penalties in wholesale, rather than retail, fashion. The New York Legislature could have embedded the limitation in every provision creating a cause of action for which a penalty is authorized; § 901(b) operates as shorthand to the same effect. * * *

The Court single-mindedly focuses on whether a suit "may" or "may not" be maintained as a class action. * * * Putting the question that way, the Court does not home in on the reason *why*. Rule 23 authorizes class treatment for suits satisfying its prerequisites because the class mechanism generally affords a fair and efficient way to aggregate claims for adjudication. Section 901(b) responds to an entirely different concern; it does not allow class members to recover statutory damages because the New York Legislature considered the result of adjudicating such claims en masse to be exorbitant. * * * The fair and efficient *conduct* of class litigation is the legitimate concern of Rule 23; the *remedy* for an infraction of state law, however, is the legitimate concern of the State's lawmakers and not of the federal rulemakers. * * *

* * * The Court suggests that the analysis might differ if the statute "limit[ed] the remedies available in an existing class action," * * * such that Rule 23 might not conflict with a state statute prescribing that "no more than $1,000,000 may be recovered in a class action." There is no real difference in the purpose and intended effect of these two hypothetical statutes. The notion that one directly impinges on Rule 23's domain, while the other does not, fundamentally misperceives the office of Rule 23. * * *

II

* * * I would decide this case by inquiring "whether application of the [state] rule would have so important an effect upon the fortunes of one or both of the litigants that failure to [apply] it would be likely to cause a plaintiff to choose the federal court." *Hanna* * * *.

Seeking to pretermit that inquiry, Shady Grove urges that the class-action bar in § 901(b) must be regarded as "procedural" because it is contained in the CPLR, which "govern[s] the *procedure* in civil judicial proceedings *in all courts of the state.*" * * * Placement in the CPLR is hardly dispositive. The provision held "substantive" for *Erie* purposes in *Gasperini* is also contained in the CPLR * * *, as are limitations periods, * * * prescriptions plainly "substantive" for *Erie* purposes however they may be characterized for other purposes * * *.

* * *

* * * Shady Grove's effort to characterize § 901(b) as simply "procedural" cannot successfully elide this fundamental norm: When no federal law or rule is dispositive of an issue, and a state statute is outcome affective in the sense our cases on *Erie* (pre- and post-*Hanna*) develop, the Rules of Decision Act commands application of the State's law in diversity suits. * * * As the plurality acknowledges, * * * forum shopping will undoubtedly result if a plaintiff need only file in federal instead of state court to seek a massive monetary award explicitly barred by state law. * * *

* * *

III

The Court's erosion of *Erie*'s federalism grounding impels me to point out the large irony in today's judgment. Shady Grove is able to pursue its claim in federal court only by virtue of the recent enactment of the Class Action Fairness Act of 2005 (CAFA) [p. 359, Note 4 and p. 574, Note 2, infra] * * *. In CAFA, Congress opened federal-court doors to state-law-based class actions so long as there is minimal diversity, at least 100 class members, and at least $5,000,000 in controversy. * * * By providing a federal forum, Congress sought to check what it considered to be the overreadiness of some state courts to certify class actions. * * * In other words, Congress envisioned fewer—not more—class actions overall. Congress surely never anticipated that CAFA would make federal courts a mecca for suits of the kind Shady Grove has launched: * * * claims that would be barred from class treatment in the State's own courts. * * *

NOTES AND QUESTIONS

1. In the absence of a majority opinion, does Justice Scalia's plurality or Justice Stevens' concurrence state the rule that federal courts should apply in determining when a state rule is displaced by a Federal Rule? Why? See p. 110, Note 1, supra. The Eleventh Circuit, in Lisk v. Lumber One Wood Preserving, LLC, 792 F.3d 1331 (11th Cir. 2015), held it was not necessary to choose between Justice Scalia's and Justice Stevens' opinions: "Regardless of which *Shady Grove* opinion is binding, the *holding* is binding." Id. at 1335. That holding "controls our case" because "[t]here is no relevant, meaningful distinction between a statutorily created penalty of the kind at issue in *Shady Grove*, on the one hand, and a statutorily created claim for deceptive practices of the kind at issue here." Id. Accordingly, it held that Federal Rule 23 did not alter rights under the Alabama Deceptive Trade Practices Act (ADTPA), and so Alabama's bar on private ADTPA class actions was inapplicable in federal court.

2. How does the plurality's approach to the validity of a Federal Rule under 28 U.S.C. § 2072 differ from that of the concurrence? According to the plurality, does a validly adopted Federal Rule always displace a conflicting state rule?

3. What are the points of disagreement between Justice Stevens in his concurring opinion and Justice Ginsburg in her dissenting opinion? Are you persuaded by the dissent's position that Rule 23 does not conflict with the New York rule? What is the argument?

4. Justice Ginsburg's dissent relied extensively on the legislative history to the New York rule. In ascertaining the meaning and purpose of a state rule, is a court sitting in diversity obliged to follow the state's approach to interpreting legislative history, or can it use its own federal approach? Does the Rules of Decision Act or Rules Enabling Act speak to this question? This topic is discussed in the sections that follow.

5. Would the result in *Shady Grove* have been different if the New York legislature had stated explicitly that CPLR § 901(b) was substantive? In 2016, following the Eleventh Circuit's *Lisk* decision, Note 1, supra, the Alabama legislature enacted a statute stating that its ban on class actions seeking remedies under the ADTPA "is a substantive limitation" and that "allowing a consumer or other person to bring a class action or other representative action for a violation of this chapter would abridge, enlarge, or modify the substantive rights created by this chapter." Ala. Code § 8–19–10(f). Federal courts in

Alabama have found that this language did not change the Eleventh Circuit's conclusion in *Lisk*. See, e.g., Jones v. Coty Inc., 362 F.Supp.3d 1182, 1198–1200 & nn.10–11 (S.D.Ala. 2018) ("Whether the Alabama legislature chooses to label something a 'substantive right' is certainly not dispositive of, and perhaps not even relevant to, * * * whether a substantive right actually is at stake for Rules Enabling Act purposes."). See also Hershkoff, Shady Grove: *Duck-Rabbits, Clear Statements, and Federalism*, 74 Alb.L.Rev. 1703 (2011) (discussing but criticizing the possibility of using "a clear statement rule to determine whether a state law is substantive or procedural for purposes of the Rules of Enabling Act").

Even after *Shady Grove*, however, some federal courts have found state-law class-action bans to be binding in federal court. See, e.g., Fejzulai v. Sam's West, Inc., 205 F.Supp.3d 723, 729 (D.S.C. 2016) (holding that a class prohibition that "is *part of the same sentence* that conveys the substantive right" under the South Carolina Unfair Trade Practices Act (SCUTPA) is binding in federal court, because "the seed from which Plaintiffs' SCUTPA cause of action must germinate simply does not contain the requisite DNA to grow into a class action claim").

6.   *Shady Grove* continues to generate division among the lower federal courts, especially in cases involving rules that are not neatly categorized as procedural or substantive. One particularly challenging issue has been the role of state "SLAPP" laws (Strategic Lawsuits Against Public Participation), which impose special rules for defamation and similar actions that can chill freedom of speech. See, e.g., Cal.Civ.Proc.Code § 425.16(a) (describing the purpose of California's "anti-SLAPP" provisions as addressing "lawsuits brought primarily to chill the valid exercise of the constitutional rights of freedom of speech and petition for the redress of grievances"). Federal courts have had to address whether such state provisions conflict with the Federal Rules governing pleading (Rule 8), motions for sanctions (Rule 11), motions to dismiss (Rule 12), and motions for summary judgment (Rule 56). See, e.g., Carbone v. Cable News Network, Inc., 910 F.3d 1345 (11th Cir. 2018) ("Under [the *Shady Grove*] framework, we cannot apply the dismissal provision of the Georgia anti-SLAPP statute. The question in dispute is whether Carbone's complaint states a claim for relief supported by sufficient evidence to avoid pretrial dismissal. Taken together, Rules 8, 12, and 56 provide an answer."); Planned Parenthood Federation of America, Inc. v. Center for Medical Progress, 890 F.3d 828, 834 (9th Cir.), amended, 897 F.3d 1224 (9th Cir. 2018) (interpreting California's anti-SLAPP provisions to avoid a "stark collision of the state rules of procedure with the governing Federal Rules * * * while in a federal district court"); CoreCivic Inc. v. Candide Grp. LLC, 2021 WL 1267259 (N.D.Cal. 2021) (finding that the anti-SLAPP statute's attorney's fees provisions were binding in federal court, reasoning that there was no procedural conflict with Rule 11 because the statute created a substantive right to recover attorney's fees under specified conditions).

B. THE PROBLEM OF ASCERTAINING STATE LAW

1. DETERMINING WHICH STATE'S LAW GOVERNS

In *Erie*, the parties and the courts appear to have assumed that if state law applied, Pennsylvania tort law would govern even though the action was heard in a federal court in New York. Why did they make this assumption? Was the federal court free to choose the most appropriate state law to govern the dispute? Or was it that New York's choice-of-law rules pointed to an application of Pennsylvania law?

―――――――

KLAXON CO. v. STENTOR ELECTRIC MFG. CO., 313 U.S. 487, 61 S.Ct. 1020, 85 L.Ed. 1477 (1941). The Supreme Court held that in order to promote the uniform application of substantive law within a state, federal courts must apply the conflicts-of-law rules of the states in which they sit. The Court explained:

> * * * Whatever lack of uniformity this may produce between federal courts in different states is attributable to our federal system, which leaves to a state, within the limits permitted by the Constitution, the right to pursue local policies diverging from those of its neighbors. It is not for the federal courts to thwart such local policies by enforcing an independent "general law" of conflict of laws. * * * [T]he proper function of [a] federal court is to ascertain what the state law is, not what it ought to be.

Id. at 496–97, 61 S.Ct. at 1022, 85 L.Ed. at 1480–81.

NOTES AND QUESTIONS

1. Is the *Klaxon* rule constitutionally compelled? Is it required by the Rules of Decision Act?

2. Could Congress enact a statute specifying choice-of-law rules for federal courts in diversity cases? In answering this question, remember that, although today every state contains at least one federal judicial district, there is no constitutional provision that compels this. What if Congress had established only regional courts? Under such a scheme, would Congress or the courts have been forced to establish their own choice-of-law rules?

3. In ALLSTATE INSURANCE CO. v. HAGUE, p. 63, Note 3, supra, the Supreme Court held that a state could apply its substantive law in a case, so long as the state had significant contacts or a significant aggregation of contacts with the parties and the transaction. Doesn't *Hague* encourage plaintiffs to forum shop, with *Klaxon* sealing defendant's fate even in federal court?

4.   The Class Action Fairness Act (CAFA) of 2005 authorizes diversity jurisdiction over multistate state law class actions despite the absence of complete diversity of citizenship. See 28 U.S.C. § 1332(d). Should state or federal conflicts rules apply in class actions under the statute? See Nagareda, *Bootstrapping in Choice of Law After the Class Action Fairness Act*, 74 UMKC L.Rev. 661, 684 (2006). If Congress intended to overrule *Klaxon*, how explicit did CAFA need to be? CAFA is discussed later in these materials, see p. 574, Note 2, infra.

2.   ASCERTAINING STATE LAW

NOTES AND QUESTIONS

1.   It seems fairly clear that when the state's highest court has declared the state law in question, the federal court is required to follow it. Does that mean that the federal court should treat the existing state rule as static, or may it consider lower court decisions and statutory developments to see if the established rule is in flux? See Bernhardt v. Polygraphic Co. of America, 350 U.S. 198, 205, 76 S.Ct. 273, 277, 100 L.Ed. 199, 206 (1956). The general rule is that if the state's highest court has not declared the state law in question, "federal courts must act as 'another court of the State' and choose from a variety of sources, including high court dicta and lower court rulings" in determining the governing law. Kaye & Weissman, *Interactive Judicial Federalism: Certified Questions in New York*, 69 Fordham L.Rev. 373, 376 (2000) (citations omitted). This process is sometimes called making an "*Erie* guess," by which the federal court "must select the rule that it believes the state's highest court, from all that is known about its methods of reaching decisions and the authorities it tends to rely on, is likely to adopt sometime in the not too distant future." 19 Wright & Miller, Federal Practice and Procedure § 4507 (3d ed.). In McKENNA v. ORTHO PHARMACEUTICAL CORP., 622 F.2d 657 (3d Cir.), cert. denied, 449 U.S. 976, 101 S.Ct. 387, 66 L.Ed.2d 237 (1980), the court of appeals emphasized that the process of ascertaining state law is not one of "speculative * * * crystal-ball gazing," but rather requires:

> an examination of all relevant sources of that state's law in order to isolate those factors that would inform its decision. * * * In the absence of authority directly on point, decisions by that court in analogous cases provide useful indications of the court's probable disposition of a particular question of law. * * * Considered dicta by the state's highest court may also provide a federal court with reliable indicia of how the state tribunal might rule on a particular question.

Id. at 662. How "reliable" is this process? Faced with the task of ascertaining state law, Judge Friendly stated: "Our principal task, in this diversity of citizenship case, is to determine what the New York courts would think the California courts would think on an issue about which neither has thought." Nolan v. Transocean Air Lines, 276 F.2d 280, 281 (2d Cir. 1960). Does this task require the diversity court to apply the principles of statutory interpretation of the relevant state? See Gluck, *Intersystemic Statutory Interpretation: Methodology as "Law" and the Erie Doctrine*, 120 Yale L.J. 1898 (2011).

2.   If state law is unclear or unresolved, may the district court conclude "there is simply no law to apply," and rule against the party with the burden on that question? See Clark, *Ascertaining the Laws of the Several States: Positivism and Judicial Federalism After* Erie, 145 U.Pa.L.Rev. 1459, 1462 (1997). Would it ever be appropriate for a diversity court to decline to exercise jurisdiction if state law is clear and resolved? In MEREDITH v. CITY OF WINTER HAVEN, 320 U.S. 228, 234–35, 64 S.Ct. 7, 11, 88 L.Ed. 9, 14 (1943), Chief Justice Stone stated:

> In the absence of some recognized public policy or defined principle guiding the exercise of the jurisdiction conferred, which would in exceptional cases warrant its non-exercise, it has from the first been deemed to be the duty of the federal courts, if their jurisdiction is properly invoked, to decide questions of state law whenever necessary to the rendition of a judgment. * * * When such exceptional circumstances are not present, denial of that opportunity by the federal courts merely because the answers to the questions of state law are difficult or uncertain or have not yet been given by the highest court of the state, would thwart the purpose of the jurisdictional act.

In LOUISIANA POWER & LIGHT CO. v. CITY OF THIBODAUX, 360 U.S. 25, 29, 79 S.Ct. 1070, 1073, 3 L.Ed.2d 1058, 1062 (1959), the Supreme Court upheld the decision of the diversity court, on its own motion, to stay its proceedings to provide Louisiana's highest court an opportunity to interpret a state expropriation statute, citing the "special nature" of eminent domain proceedings. Is abstention inconsistent with the purposes of diversity jurisdiction?

3.   As an alternative to abstention, a district court may invoke a procedure called certification that allows it to petition a state court to answer an unresolved question of state law. Certification postpones the federal court's decision until it has received an answer from the state court. By contrast, abstention results in a dismissal of the federal court action. See Challener, *Distinguishing Certification from Abstention in Diversity Cases: Postponement versus Abdication of the Duty to Exercise Jurisdiction*, 38 Rutgers L.J. 847 (2007). In 1945, Florida became the first state to adopt such a procedure, and its use by the federal courts was endorsed by the Supreme Court in Clay v. Sun Insurance Office Ltd., 363 U.S. 207, 80 S.Ct. 1222, 4 L.Ed.2d 1170 (1960). The procedure now is available in 49 states, the District of Columbia, and Puerto Rico. See Stahle v. CTS Corp., 817 F.3d 96, 113 (4th Cir. 2016) ("North Carolina remains the only state in the nation never to have enacted some form of certification procedure.") (Thacker, J., concurring). Certification procedures vary; some high state courts accept questions only from the Supreme Court, while others also answer questions from lower federal courts and other state courts. See Winship, *Cooperative Interbranch Federalism: Certification of State-Law Questions by Federal Agencies*, 63 Vand.L.Rev. 181 (2010).

The Supreme Court appeared to express a preference for certification in ARIZONANS FOR OFFICIAL ENGLISH v. ARIZONA, 520 U.S. 43, 76, 117 S.Ct. 1055, 1073, 137 L.Ed.2d 170, 199 (1997), because the procedure was assumed to reduce costs and ensure an "authoritative response" from the state. See Thomas-Jensen, *Certification after* Arizonans for Official English v. Arizona*: A Survey of Federal Appellate Courts' Practices*, 87 Denv.U.L.Rev. 139 (2009). In MCKESSON v. DOE, 592 U.S. ___, 141 S.Ct. 48, 208 L.Ed.2d 158 (2020), the Supreme Court declined to decide whether a state-law tort claim against the organizer of a protest would violate the organizer's First Amendment rights. Instead, it held in a per curiam opinion that the Fifth Circuit should have certified to the Louisiana Supreme Court two questions about whether such a tort claim was viable under state law: "the Fifth Circuit should not have ventured into so uncertain an area of tort law—one laden with value judgments and fraught with implications for First Amendment rights— without first seeking guidance on potentially controlling Louisiana law from the Louisiana Supreme Court." Id. at ___, 141 S.Ct. at 51, 208 L.Ed.2d at 162.

4.   In TUNICK v. SAFIR, 228 F.3d 135 (2d Cir. 2000), a photographer challenged the locality's refusal to grant him a permit to conduct a photo shoot of 75 to 100 nude models configured "in an abstract formation" on a residential street in New York City. Tunick claimed that his planned event was exempt from a New York statute that bans public nudity except for "any person entertaining or performing in a play, exhibition, show or entertainment." The Second Circuit Court of Appeals petitioned New York's highest court to resolve the scope of the public nudity ban, emphasizing the need for expedition given the important First Amendment rights at stake in the lawsuit. The New York court declined to answer, explaining that "even with an expedited schedule for new briefing, argument and deliberation, this Court's necessary decisional process would add some months to the life of this case." 94 N.Y.2d 709, 711, 709 N.Y.S.2d 881, 883, 731 N.E.2d 597, 599 (2000). Would the New York court have been obliged to answer a certified question had it come from the Supreme Court?

5.   In SALVE REGINA COLLEGE v. RUSSELL, 499 U.S. 225, 111 S.Ct. 1217, 113 L.Ed.2d 190 (1991), the Court considered the weight a federal appeals court should give to a district court's determination of state law when sitting in diversity, and held that the court of appeals should conduct de novo review, just as it does when questions of federal law are in dispute. Chief Justice Rehnquist authored a strong dissent in which Justice White and Justice Stevens joined:

> Federal courts of appeals perform a different role when they decide questions of state law than they do when they decide questions of federal law. In the former case, these courts are not sources of law but only reflections of the jurisprudence of the courts of a State. While in deciding novel federal questions, courts of appeals are likely to ponder the policy implications as well as the decisional law, only the latter need be considered in deciding questions of state law.

Id. at 242, 111 S.Ct. at 1227, 113 L.Ed.2d at 205. Which approach best promotes the twin aims of *Erie*?

C. FEDERAL "COMMON LAW"

MELTZER, STATE COURT FORFEITURES OF FEDERAL RIGHTS, 99 Harv.L.Rev. 1128, 1167–71 (1986) (footnotes omitted):

Despite *Erie*'s declaration that "[t]here is no federal general common law," courts have fashioned what Judge Friendly has termed "specialized federal common law" to govern a broad range of areas. Unlike the "spurious" federal common law of the era of *Swift v. Tyson*, this new federal common law is binding under the supremacy clause in the state courts.

The proper scope of federal common lawmaking is a matter of considerable uncertainty. If *Erie* held that federal court jurisdiction does not in itself provide the power to fashion common law, then some more specialized source must be found for each example of judicial lawmaking. The lawmaking power of federal courts has been viewed as far more limited than that of Congress, for two reasons extrapolated from the constitutional structure. The first is the idea of separation of powers and the supremacy (in matters not governed by the Constitution) of Congress. But perhaps more important is the view that federal law is and should be interstitial, operating against a background of existing bodies of state law. Restricted federal common lawmaking reduces the number of agencies broadly fashioning federal rules of decision, and preserves the primary role for Congress, in which the interests of the states are more strongly represented—and in which inertia is more powerful. Hence, state law is presumptively operative, and if it is to be displaced, ordinarily it must be Congress that does so.

But these structural concerns do not indicate whether federal common law should be considered altogether illegitimate or simply restricted in scope. And important countervailing arguments support the existence of some common law power in the federal courts. Numerous cases raise issues implicating important federal interests that are not specifically governed by a statutory or constitutional rule. Congress could have enacted a rule governing the issue, but may not have done so, because it lacked time, foresight, or a political consensus. The Court has, accordingly, recognized that federal common law may be a "necessary expedient." Nor does Congress's failure to specify a view on a particular subject indicate that Congress preferred that state rules be followed. Here, as elsewhere, congressional inaction is hardly a clear-cut guide for determining congressional intent, and a failure by a court to make law is itself an important and controversial decision.

Thus, legislative inertia and the political safeguards of federalism are ultimately a double-edged sword. They help explain why the authority to make federal common law is nowhere near so broad as congressional authority to legislate, but also argue that federal common lawmaking may be necessary to fill in the interstices of congressional and constitutional mandates or otherwise to deal with matters of important national concern. Despite extensive discussion in the cases and commentary, no clear standard for judging the appropriateness of federal common law has emerged. * * * I wish * * * to stress some * * * general points that are, I believe, accepted by most cases and commentators.

To begin with, there must be a strong need for the formulation of federal common law in order to justify displacing otherwise operative state rules. Moreover, federal common law, perhaps even more than federal law generally, should be interstitial, building upon the total "corpus juris" of the states. Federal common law fits most easily when it supplements federal constitutional or statutory provisions, providing rules of decision that implement or safeguard the norms embodied in such provisions.

Even where federal interests are implicated, it is often possible, and desirable, to rely upon extant state law for the rule of decision. Such reliance eliminates the need for (and possible difficulties in) fashioning a new rule from scratch, and also promotes intrastate uniformity, which may be of great value. Thus, the decision to formulate federal common law is one of judicial policy, in which a court must find that the advantages of borrowing state law are outweighed by either the need for national uniformity or the inconsistency of state law (either of states generally or of the particular state involved) with federal interests.

Regardless of how the balance is struck in particular cases, it is clear that there is a distinctive body of federal common law, and recognized and defensible authority for its creation. * * *

Federal common law has developed in several broad situations. For example, federal common law is used to resolve cases involving important federal interests. These strong federal interests have emerged in several contexts. When interstate disputes have erupted, federal common law has been adopted where it would be unfair to apply the statutes or decisional law from either state. See, e.g., Hinderlider v. La Plata River & Cherry Creek Ditch Co., 304 U.S. 92, 58 S.Ct. 803, 82 L.Ed. 1202 (1938) (dispute over the apportionment of the water of an interstate stream).

Similarly, federal common law has become firmly established in the admiralty and maritime contexts because the desire for a uniform body of substantive law has long been considered of primary importance. See, e.g., Kossick v. United Fruit Co., 365 U.S. 731, 81 S.Ct. 886, 6 L.Ed.2d 56 (1961). And, cases implicating the international relations of the United States have provided another occasion for resort to federal common law, including cases involving commercial disputes between United States citizens and foreign parties. See, e.g., Banco Nacional de Cuba v. Sabbatino, 376 U.S. 398, 84 S.Ct. 923, 11 L.Ed.2d 804 (1964). The Supreme Court has recently instructed, however, that "before federal judges may claim a new area for common lawmaking, strict conditions must be satisfied"; "one of the most basic" requirements is that, unless there is congressional authorization, federal common law "must be necessary to protect uniquely federal interests." Rodriguez v. FDIC, 589 U.S. ___, ___, 140 S.Ct. 713, 717, 206 L.Ed.2d 62, 67 (2020).

Another important use of federal common law occurs in cases involving the legal activities of the United States. These cases often invoke issues concerning the federal government's contract rights, rights to collect loans and proceeds due to it, or the management of United States bonds and securities.

CLEARFIELD TRUST CO. V. UNITED STATES
Supreme Court of the United States, 1943.
318 U.S. 363, 63 S.Ct. 573, 87 L.Ed. 838.

Certiorari to the Court of Appeals for the Third Circuit.

JUSTICE DOUGLAS delivered the opinion of the Court.

[A check issued by the United States had been mailed, but was not received by its intended recipient. An unknown person, who presumably had stolen the check, cashed it at a J.C. Penney store by signing the name of the intended recipient. J.C. Penney in turn endorsed the check to Clearfield Trust, which accepted it. Clearfield then endorsed the check with a guaranty of all prior endorsements, collected the amount of the check from the Federal Reserve and paid it to J.C. Penney. Neither J.C. Penney nor Clearfield had suspected forgery. Federal officials did not inform any of the interested parties of the forgery until eight months after they had learned that the intended recipient had not received the check.

The United States sued Clearfield on Clearfield's express guaranty of prior endorsements. The district court held that the rights of the parties were to be determined by the law of Pennsylvania. Since the United States had unreasonably delayed giving notice of the forgery, it was barred from recovery under Pennsylvania law and the district court dismissed the complaint. The Court of Appeals for the Third Circuit reversed.]

* * *

We agree with the Circuit Court of Appeals that the rule of Erie R. Co. v. Tompkins * * * does not apply to this action. The rights and duties of the United States on commercial paper which it issues are governed by federal rather than local law. When the United States disburses its funds or pays its debts, it is exercising a constitutional function or power. This check was issued for services performed under the Federal Emergency Relief Act of 1935 * * *. The authority to issue the check had its origin in the Constitution and the statutes of the United States and was in no way dependent on the laws of Pennsylvania or of any other state. * * * The duties imposed upon the United States and the rights acquired by it as a result of the issuance find their roots in the same federal sources.[2] * * * In absence of an applicable Act of Congress it is for the federal courts to fashion the governing rule of law according to their own standards. * * *

In our choice of the applicable federal rule we have occasionally selected state law. * * * But reasons which may make state law at times the appropriate federal rule are singularly inappropriate here. The issuance of commercial paper by the United States is on a vast scale and transactions in that paper from issuance to payment will commonly occur in several states. The application of state law, even without the conflict of laws rules of the forum, would subject the rights and duties of the United States to exceptional uncertainty. It would lead to great diversity in results by making identical transactions subject to the vagaries of the laws of the several states. The desirability of a uniform rule is plain. And while the federal law merchant developed for about a century under the regime of Swift v. Tyson * * * represented general commercial law rather than a choice of a federal rule designed to protect a federal right, it nevertheless stands as a convenient source of reference for fashioning federal rules applicable to these federal questions.

United States v. National Exchange Bank, 214 U.S. 302, 29 S.Ct. 665, 53 L.Ed. 1006 * * * falls in that category. The Court held that the United States could recover as drawee from one who presented for payment a pension check on which the name of the payee had been forged, in spite of a protracted delay on the part of the United States in giving notice of the forgery. * * *

The National Exchange Bank case went no further than to hold that prompt notice of the discovery of the forgery was not a condition precedent to suit. It did not reach the question whether lack of prompt notice might be a defense. We think it may. If it is shown that the drawee on learning of the forgery did not give prompt notice of it and that damage resulted, recovery by the drawee is barred. * * * The fact that the drawee is the United States and the laches those of its employees are not material. * * * The United States as drawee of commercial paper stands in no different light than any other drawee. As stated in National Exchange Bank * * *, "The United States does business on business terms." It is not excepted from the general rules governing the rights and duties of drawees "by the

---

[2] Various Treasury Regulations govern the payment and endorsement of government checks and warrants and the reimbursement of the Treasurer of the United States by Federal Reserve banks and member bank depositories on payment of checks or warrants bearing a forged endorsement. * * * Forgery of the check was an offense against the United States. * * *

largeness of its dealings and its having to employ agents to do what if done by a principal in person would leave no room for doubt." * * * But the damage occasioned by the delay must be established and not left to conjecture. Cases * * * place the burden on the drawee of giving prompt notice of the forgery—injury to the defendant being presumed by the mere fact of delay. * * * But we do not think that he who accepts a forged signature of a payee deserves that preferred treatment. It is his neglect or error in accepting the forger's signature which occasions the loss. * * * He should be allowed to shift that loss to the drawee only on a clear showing that the drawee's delay in notifying him of the forgery caused him damage. * * * No such damage has been shown by Clearfield Trust Co. who so far as appears can still recover from J.C. Penney Co. * * * The inference is that the more prompt the notice the more likely the detection of the forger. But that falls short of a showing that the delay caused a manifest loss. * * * It is but another way of saying that mere delay is enough.

Affirmed.

JUSTICE MURPHY and JUSTICE RUTLEDGE did not participate in the consideration or decision of this case.

NOTES AND QUESTIONS

1.   Why doesn't *Clearfield Trust* rely upon the Rules of Decision Act?

2.   How does the federal common law rule recognized in *Clearfield Trust* differ from the regime of general common law under Swift v. Tyson? Is the former rule binding on the states but the latter rule not? Is your answer constitutionally compelled?

3.   In UNITED STATES v. KIMBELL FOODS, INC., 440 U.S. 715, 99 S.Ct. 1448, 59 L.Ed.2d 711 (1979), the question was whether state or federal law governed the government's priority on loans offered by the Small Business Administration ("SBA") and the Farmers Home Administration ("FHA"). The Court used a two-step analysis. First, the Court interpreted *Clearfield Trust* broadly as permitting federal courts to develop federal law for "questions involving the rights of the United States arising under nationwide federal programs." Thus, the Court held that "the priority of liens stemming from federal lending programs must be determined with reference to federal law" and that the "SBA and FHA unquestionably perform federal functions within the meaning of *Clearfield*."

Having decided that federal law controlled, the Court turned to the second and more challenging task of determining the content of the federal law:

> Controversies directly affecting the operations of federal programs, although governed by federal law, do not inevitably require resort to uniform federal rules. * * * Whether to adopt state law or to fashion a nationwide federal rule is a matter of judicial policy "dependent upon a variety of considerations always relevant to the nature of the

specific governmental interests and to the effects upon them of applying state law." * * *

Undoubtedly, federal programs that "by their nature are and must be uniform in character throughout the Nation" necessitate formulation of controlling federal rules. * * * Conversely, when there is little need for a nationally uniform body of law, state law may be incorporated as the federal rule of decision. Apart from considerations of uniformity, we must also determine whether application of state law would frustrate specific objectives of the federal programs. If so, we must fashion special rules solicitous of those federal interests. Finally, our choice of law inquiry must consider the extent to which application of a federal rule would disrupt commercial relationships predicated on state law. * * *

Id. at 727–29, 99 S.Ct. at 1458–59, 59 L.Ed.2d at 723–24. After weighing these factors with respect to priority rules for the SBA and FHA loans, the Court held that there was no need for an independent federal rule. Thus, the Court chose to adopt the state rule as federal law rather than to develop a separate federal rule.

BOYLE v. UNITED TECHNOLOGIES CORP.

Supreme Court of the United States, 1988.
487 U.S. 500, 108 S.Ct. 2510, 101 L.Ed.2d 442.

Certiorari to the United States Court of Appeals for the Fourth Circuit.

JUSTICE SCALIA delivered the opinion of the Court.

This case requires us to decide when a contractor providing military equipment to the Federal Government can be held liable under state tort law for injury caused by a design defect.

I

On April 27, 1983, David A. Boyle, a United States Marine helicopter copilot, was killed when the CH-53D helicopter in which he was flying crashed off the coast of Virginia Beach, Virginia, during a training exercise. Although Boyle survived the impact of the crash, he was unable to escape from the helicopter and drowned. Boyle's father, petitioner here, brought this diversity action in Federal District Court against the Sikorsky Division of United Technologies Corporation (Sikorsky), which built the helicopter for the United States.

At trial, petitioner presented two theories of liability under Virginia tort law that were submitted to the jury. First, petitioner alleged that Sikorsky had defectively repaired a device called the servo in the helicopter's automatic flight control system, which allegedly malfunctioned and caused the crash. Second, petitioner alleged that Sikorsky had defectively designed the copilot's emergency escape system: the escape hatch opened out instead of in (and was therefore ineffective in a submerged craft because of water pressure), and access to the escape hatch handle was obstructed by other equipment. The jury returned a general verdict in favor of petitioner and awarded him $725,000. The District Court denied Sikorsky's motion for judgment notwithstanding the verdict.

The Court of Appeals reversed and remanded with directions that judgment be entered for Sikorsky. * * * It found, as a matter of Virginia law, that Boyle had failed to meet his burden of demonstrating that the repair work performed by Sikorsky, as opposed to work that had been done by the Navy, was responsible for the alleged malfunction of the flight control system. * * * It also found, as a matter of federal law, that Sikorsky could not be held liable for the allegedly defective design of the escape hatch because, on the evidence presented, it satisfied the requirements of the "military contractor defense," which the court had recognized the same day in *Tozer v. LTV Corp.*, 792 F.2d 403 (CA4 1986). * * *

Petitioner sought review here, challenging the Court of Appeals' decision on three levels: First, petitioner contends that there is no justification in federal law for shielding Government contractors from liability for design defects in military equipment. Second, he argues in the alternative that even if such a defense should exist, the Court of Appeals' formulation of the conditions for its application is inappropriate. Finally, petitioner contends that the Court of Appeals erred in not remanding for a jury determination of whether the elements of the defense were met in this case. We granted certiorari * * *.

II

Petitioner's broadest contention is that, in the absence of legislation specifically immunizing Government contractors from liability for design defects, there is no basis for judicial recognition of such a defense. We disagree. * * * [W]e have held that a few areas, involving "uniquely federal interests," * * * are so committed by the Constitution and laws of the United States to federal control that state law is pre-empted and replaced, where necessary, by federal law of a content prescribed (absent explicit statutory directive) by the courts—so-called "federal common law." * * *

The dispute in the present case borders upon two areas that we have found to involve such "uniquely federal interests." We have held that obligations to and rights of the United States under its contracts are governed exclusively by federal law. * * * The present case does not involve an obligation to the United States under its contract, but rather liability to third persons. That liability may be styled one in tort, but it arises out of performance of the contract—and traditionally has been regarded as sufficiently related to the contract that until 1962 Virginia would generally allow design defect suits only by the purchaser and those in privity with the seller. * * *

Another area that we have found to be of peculiarly federal concern, warranting the displacement of state law, is the civil liability of federal officials for actions taken in the course of their duty. We have held in many contexts that the scope of that liability is controlled by federal law. * * * The present case involves an independent contractor performing its obligation under a procurement contract, rather than an official performing his duty as a federal employee, but there is obviously implicated the same interest in getting the Government's work done.

We think the reasons for considering these closely related areas to be of "uniquely federal" interest apply as well to the civil liabilities arising out of the performance of federal procurement contracts. * * *

Moreover, it is plain that the Federal Government's interest in the procurement of equipment is implicated by suits such as the present one— even though the dispute is one between private parties. * * * The imposition of liability on Government contractors will directly affect the terms of Government contracts: either the contractor will decline to manufacture the design specified by the Government, or it will raise its price. Either way, the interests of the United States will be directly affected.

That the procurement of equipment by the United States is an area of uniquely federal interest does not, however, end the inquiry. That merely establishes a necessary, not a sufficient, condition for the displacement of state law. * * * Displacement will occur only where, as we have variously described, a "significant conflict" exists between an identifiable "federal policy or interest and the [operation] of state law," * * * or the application of state law would "frustrate specific objectives" of federal legislation * * *.

* * *

* * * Here the state-imposed duty of care that is the asserted basis of the contractor's liability (specifically, the duty to equip helicopters with the sort of escape-hatch mechanism petitioner claims was necessary) is precisely contrary to the duty imposed by the Government contract (the duty to manufacture and deliver helicopters with the sort of escape-hatch mechanism shown by the specifications). Even in this sort of situation, it would be unreasonable to say that there is always a "significant conflict" between the state law and a federal policy or interest. If, for example, a federal procurement officer orders, by model number, a quantity of stock helicopters that happen to be equipped with escape hatches opening outward, it is impossible to say that the Government has a significant interest in that particular feature. That would be scarcely more reasonable than saying that a private individual who orders such a craft by model number cannot sue for the manufacturer's negligence because he got precisely what he ordered.

* * *

There is * * * a statutory provision that demonstrates the potential for, and suggests the outlines of, "significant conflict" between federal interests and state law in the context of Government procurement. In the [Federal Tort Claims Act], Congress authorized damages to be recovered against the United States for harm caused by the negligent or wrongful conduct of Government employees, to the extent that a private person would be liable under the law of the place where the conduct occurred. 28 U.S.C. § 1346(b). It excepted from this consent to suit, however,

> "[a]ny claim . . . based upon the exercise or performance or the failure to exercise or perform a discretionary function or duty on the part of a federal agency or an employee of the Government, whether or not the discretion involved be abused." 28 U.S.C. § 2680(a).[d]

We think that the selection of the appropriate design for military equipment to be used by our Armed Forces is assuredly a discretionary function within the meaning of this provision. It often involves not merely engineering analysis but judgment as to the balancing of many technical, military, and even social considerations, including specifically the trade-off between greater safety and greater combat effectiveness. And we are further of the view that permitting "second-guessing" of these judgments * * * through state tort suits against contractors would produce the same effect sought to be avoided by the FTCA exemption. The financial burden of judgments against the contractors would ultimately be passed through, substantially if not totally, to the United States itself, since defense contractors will predictably raise their prices to cover, or to insure against, contingent liability for the Government-ordered designs. To put the point differently: It makes little sense to insulate the Government against financial liability for the judgment that a particular feature of military equipment is necessary when the Government produces the equipment itself, but not when it contracts for the production. In sum, we are of the view that state law which holds Government contractors liable for design defects in military equipment does in some circumstances present a "significant conflict" with federal policy and must be displaced. * * *

Accordingly the judgment is vacated and the case is remanded.

So ordered.

JUSTICE BRENNAN, with whom JUSTICE MARSHALL and JUSTICE BLACKMUN join, dissenting.

* * * We may assume, for purposes of this case, that Lt. Boyle was trapped under water and drowned because respondent United

---

d   Alteration in original.

Technologies negligently designed the helicopter's escape hatch. We may further assume that any competent engineer would have discovered and cured the defects, but that they inexplicably escaped respondent's notice. Had respondent designed such a death trap for a commercial firm, Lt. Boyle's family could sue under Virginia tort law and be compensated for his tragic and unnecessary death. But respondent designed the helicopter for the Federal Government, and that, the Court tells us today, makes all the difference: Respondent is immune from liability so long as it obtained approval of "reasonably precise specifications"—perhaps no more than a rubber stamp from a federal procurement officer who might or might not have noticed or cared about the defects, or even had the expertise to discover them.

If respondent's immunity "bore the legitimacy of having been prescribed by the people's elected representatives," we would be duty bound to implement their will, whether or not we approved. * * * Congress, however, has remained silent—and conspicuously so, having resisted a sustained campaign by Government contractors to legislate for them some defense. * * * The Court—unelected and unaccountable to the people—has unabashedly stepped into the breach to legislate a rule denying Lt. Boyle's family the compensation that state law assures them. This time the injustice is of this Court's own making.

Worse yet, the injustice will extend far beyond the facts of this case, for the Court's newly discovered Government contractor defense is breathtakingly sweeping. It applies not only to military equipment like the CH-53D helicopter, but (so far as I can tell) to any made-to-order gadget that the Federal Government might purchase after previewing plans— from NASA's Challenger space shuttle to the Postal Service's old mail cars. The contractor may invoke the defense in suits brought not only by military personnel like Lt. Boyle, or Government employees, but by anyone injured by a Government contractor's negligent design, including, for example, the children who might have died had respondent's helicopter crashed on the beach. It applies even if the Government has not intentionally sacrificed safety for other interests like speed or efficiency, and, indeed, even if the equipment is not of a type that is typically considered dangerous; thus, the contractor who designs a Government building can invoke the defense when the elevator cable snaps or the walls collapse. And the defense is invocable regardless of how blatant or easily remedied the defect, so long as the contractor missed it and the specifications approved by the Government, however unreasonably dangerous, were "reasonably precise." * * *

In my view, this Court lacks both authority and expertise to fashion such a rule, whether to protect the Treasury of the United States or the coffers of industry. Because I would leave that exercise of legislative power to Congress, where our Constitution places it, I would reverse the Court of Appeals and reinstate petitioner's jury award.

* * *

IV

At bottom, the Court's analysis is premised on the proposition that any tort liability indirectly absorbed by the Government so burdens governmental functions as to compel us to act when Congress has not. That proposition is by no means uncontroversial. The tort system is premised on the assumption that the imposition of liability encourages actors to prevent any injury whose expected cost exceeds the cost of prevention. If the system is working as it should, Government contractors will design equipment to avoid certain injuries (like the deaths of soldiers or Government employees), which would be certain to burden the Government. The Court therefore has no basis for its assumption that tort liability will result in a net burden on the Government (let alone a clearly excessive net burden) rather than a net gain.

Perhaps tort liability is an inefficient means of ensuring the quality of design efforts, but "[w]hatever the merits of the policy" the Court wishes to implement, "its conversion into law is a proper subject for congressional action, not for any creative power of ours." [*United States v. Standard Oil Co. of Calif.*, 332 U.S. 301, 314–15, 67 S.Ct. 1604, 1611, 91 L.Ed. 2067, 2075 (1947)]. * * * If Congress shared the Court's assumptions and conclusion it could readily enact "A BILL [t]o place limitations on the civil liability of government contractors to ensure that such liability does not impede the ability of the United States to procure necessary goods and services," H.R. 4765, 99th Cong., 2d Sess. (1986); see also S. 2441, 99th Cong., 2d Sess. (1986). It has not.

Were I a legislator, I would probably vote against any law absolving multibillion dollar private enterprises from answering for their tragic mistakes, at least if that law were justified by no more than the unsupported speculation that their liability might ultimately burden the United States Treasury. Some of my colleagues here would evidently vote otherwise (as they have here), but that should not matter here. We are judges not legislators, and the vote is not ours to cast.

I respectfully dissent.

JUSTICE STEVENS, dissenting.

When judges are asked to embark on a lawmaking venture, I believe they should carefully consider whether they, or a legislative body, are better equipped to perform the task at hand. There are instances of so-called interstitial lawmaking that inevitably become part of the judicial process. * * * But when we are asked to create an entirely new doctrine— to answer "questions of policy on which Congress has not spoken," * * * we have a special duty to identify the proper decisionmaker before trying to make the proper decision.

When the novel question of policy involves a balancing of the conflicting interests in the efficient operation of a massive governmental program and the protection of the rights of the individual—whether in the social welfare context, the civil service context, or the military procurement context—I feel very deeply that we should defer to the expertise of the Congress. * * *

NOTES AND QUESTIONS

1.   What is the justification for the contractor's immunity? Is it to reduce fiscal costs that might be passed on to the United States? Is it to protect government decisions that affect the military? Should the immunity be extended to manufacturers who produce goods that the government purchases through the general commercial market? See Bellia, Jr., *State Courts and the Making of Federal Common Law*, 153 U.Pa.L.Rev. 825 (2005).

2.   In AMERICAN ELEC. POWER CO., INC. v. CONNECTICUT, 564 U.S. 410, 131 S.Ct. 2527, 180 L.Ed.2d 435 (2011), the Court addressed whether plaintiffs, which included several States, New York City, and three private land trusts, could bring federal common law nuisance claims against four private power companies and the federal Tennessee Valley Authority for their excessive emission of carbon dioxide. Plaintiffs sought an order setting emissions caps for each defendant. The Court acknowledged that environmental protection is within the scope of national power and one in which the federal courts may devise federal rules of decision. However, the Court held that Congress had chosen to assert that power through the Clean Air Act's establishment of the Environmental Protection Agency (EPA). The Court rejected the argument that "federal common law is not displaced until EPA actually exercises its regulatory authority, *i.e.*, until it sets standards governing emissions from the defendants' plants." Id. at 412, 131 S.Ct. at 2531, 180 L.Ed.2d at 441. In her opinion for the Court, Justice Ginsburg explained:

> * * * [T]he relevant question for purposes of displacement is "whether the field has been occupied, not whether it has been occupied in a particular manner." * * * Of necessity, Congress selects different regulatory regimes to address different problems. Congress could hardly preemptively prohibit every discharge of carbon dioxide unless covered by a permit. After all, we each emit carbon dioxide merely by breathing.
>
> The Clean Air Act is no less an exercise of the legislature's "considered judgment" concerning the regulation of air pollution because it permits emissions *until* EPA acts. * * * The critical point is that Congress delegated to EPA the decision whether and how to regulate carbon-dioxide emissions from power plants; the delegation is what displaces federal common law. Indeed, were EPA to decline

to regulate carbon-dioxide emissions altogether at the conclusion of its ongoing * * * rulemaking, the federal courts would have no warrant to employ the federal common law of nuisance to upset the agency's expert determination.

EPA's judgment, we hasten to add, would not escape judicial review. Federal courts * * * can review agency action (or a final rule declining to take action) to ensure compliance with the statute Congress enacted. * * *

Indeed, this prescribed order of decisionmaking—the first decider under the Act is the expert administrative agency, the second, federal judges—is yet another reason to resist setting emissions standards by judicial decree under federal tort law. * * *

Id. at 426, 131 S.Ct. at 2538–39, 180 L.Ed.2d at 448–49. Is it appropriate for an agency's inaction to displace federal judicial common law power?

3.   In RODRIGUEZ v. FDIC, 589 U.S. ___, 140 S.Ct. 713, 206 L.Ed.2d 62 (2020), the Supreme Court rejected the view that federal common law determined which of multiple affiliated corporate entities could claim a particular tax refund. Writing for a unanimous Court, Justice Gorsuch noted that "[j]udicial lawmaking in the form of federal common law plays a necessarily modest role under a Constitution that vests the federal government's 'legislative Powers' in Congress and reserves most other regulatory authority to the States." Id. at ___, 140 S.Ct. at 717, 206 L.Ed.2d at 66. Federal common law was proper when "necessary to protect uniquely federal interests," id., but no such interests were present with respect to this issue. Although "[t]he federal government may have an interest in regulating how it *receives* taxes from corporate groups," it had no "unique interest" in determining how a particular tax refund would be "*distributed* among group members." Id. at ___, 140 S.Ct. at 717–18, 206 L.Ed.2d at 67.

NOTE ON *FEDERAL COMMON LAW PROCEDURE* AND *FEDERAL RULES OF PRECLUSION*

Another area in which federal courts develop common law pertains to procedures that are internal to the courts themselves. The existence of this doctrine is somewhat anomalous. As Justice Amy Coney Barrett (then a law professor) observed:

With few exceptions, this body of law falls outside of the traditional definitions of federal common law. Procedural common law does not generally bind state courts; though developed without congressional authorization, it falls outside of the traditionally recognized enclaves of federal common law; and Congress's ability to abrogate it is often called into question.

Barrett, *Procedural Common Law*, 94 Va.L.Rev. 813, 815 (2008). Examples of procedural common law include the doctrines of forum non conveniens, abstention, stare decisis, and rules of finality. The preclusive effect of a federal judgment, even when the judgment is rendered by a court sitting in diversity, is governed by a federal common law rule. See SEMTEK INTERNATIONAL INC. v. LOCKHEED MARTIN CORPORATION, 531 U.S. 497, 121 S.Ct. 1021, 149 L.Ed.2d 32 (2001), p. 904, infra. In determining the content of the federal rule of preclusion, the federal court may choose to borrow a state rule. See Burbank, Semtek, *Forum Shopping, and Federal Common Law*, 77 Notre Dame L.Rev. 1027 (2002). Why is the creation of a federal common law rule of preclusion consistent with the Rules of Decision Act? See Degnan, *Federalized Res Judicata*, 85 Yale L.J. 741 (1976). Does the Rules Enabling Act delegate to the Court power to adopt a federal rule of preclusion?

D. FEDERAL LAW IN THE STATE COURTS

DICE V. AKRON, CANTON & YOUNGSTOWN R. CO.

Supreme Court of the United States, 1952.
342 U.S. 359, 72 S.Ct. 312, 96 L.Ed. 398.

Certiorari to the Supreme Court of Ohio.

Opinion of the Court by JUSTICE BLACK, announced by JUSTICE DOUGLAS.

Petitioner, a railroad fireman, was seriously injured when an engine in which he was riding jumped the track. Alleging that his injuries were due to respondent's negligence, he brought this action for damages under the Federal Employers' Liability Act, 35 Stat. 65, 45 U.S.C. § 51 et seq., in an Ohio court of common pleas. Respondent's defenses were (1) a denial of negligence and (2) a written document signed by petitioner purporting to release respondent in full for $924.63. Petitioner admitted that he had signed several receipts for payments made him in connection with his injuries but denied that he had made a full and complete settlement of all his claims. He alleged that the purported release was void because he had signed it relying on respondent's deliberately false statement that the document was nothing more than a mere receipt for back wages.

After both parties had introduced considerable evidence the jury found in favor of petitioner and awarded him a $25,000 verdict. The trial judge later entered judgment notwithstanding the verdict. In doing so he reappraised the evidence as to fraud, found that petitioner had been "guilty of supine negligence" in failing to read the release, and accordingly held that the facts did not "sustain either in law or equity the allegations of fraud by clear, unequivocal and convincing evidence." This judgment notwithstanding the verdict was reversed by the Court of Appeals of Summit County, Ohio, on the ground that under federal law, which controlled, the jury's verdict must stand because there was ample evidence to support its finding of fraud. The Ohio Supreme Court, one judge dissenting, reversed * * * and sustained the trial court's action, holding that: (1) Ohio, not federal, law governed; (2) under that law petitioner, a man of ordinary intelligence who could read, was bound by the release even though he had been induced to sign it by the deliberately false statement that it was only a receipt for back wages; and (3) under controlling Ohio law factual issues as to fraud in the execution of this release were properly decided by the judge rather than by the jury. * * *

First. We agree with the Court of Appeals of Summit County, Ohio, and the dissenting judge in the Ohio Supreme Court and hold that validity of releases under the Federal Employers' Liability Act raises a federal question to be determined by federal rather than state law. Congress in § 1 of the Act granted petitioner a right to recover against his employer for damages negligently inflicted. State laws are not controlling in determining what the incidents of this federal right shall be. * * * Manifestly the federal rights affording relief to injured railroad employees under a federally declared standard could be defeated if states were permitted to have the final say as to what defenses could and could not be properly interposed to suits under the Act. Moreover, only if federal law controls can the federal Act be given that uniform application throughout the country essential to effectuate its purposes. * * * Releases and other devices designed to liquidate or defeat injured employees' claims play an important part in the federal Act's administration. * * * Their validity is but one of the many interrelated questions that must constantly be determined in these cases according to a uniform federal law.

Second. In effect the Supreme Court of Ohio held that * * * the negligence of an innocent worker is sufficient to enable his employer to benefit by its deliberate fraud. Application of so harsh a rule to defeat a railroad employee's claim is wholly incongruous with the general policy of the Act to give railroad employees a right to recover just compensation for injuries negligently inflicted by their employers. And this Ohio rule is out of harmony with modern judicial and legislative practice to relieve injured persons from the effect of releases fraudulently obtained. * * * We hold that the correct federal rule is that * * * a release of rights under the Act is void when the employee is induced to sign it by the deliberately false and material statements of the railroad's authorized representatives made to deceive the employee as to the contents of the release. The trial court's charge to the jury correctly stated this rule of law.

Third. Ohio provides and has here accorded petitioner the usual jury trial of factual issues relating to negligence. But Ohio treats factual questions of fraudulent releases differently. It permits the judge trying a negligence case to resolve all factual questions of fraud "other than fraud in the factum." The factual issue of fraud is thus split into fragments, some to be determined by the judge, others by the jury.

It is contended that since a state may consistently with the Federal Constitution provide for trial of cases under the Act by a nonunanimous verdict, Minneapolis & St. Louis R. Co. v. Bombolis, 241 U.S. 211, Ohio may lawfully eliminate trial by jury as to one phase of fraud while allowing jury trial as to all other issues raised. The Bombolis case might be more in point had Ohio abolished trial by jury in all negligence cases including those arising under the federal Act. But Ohio has not done this. It has provided jury trials for cases arising under the federal Act but seeks to single out one phase of the question of fraudulent releases for determination by a judge rather than by a jury. * * *

We have previously held that "The right to trial by jury is 'a basic and fundamental feature of our system of federal jurisprudence' " and that it is "part and parcel of the remedy afforded railroad workers under the Employers' Liability Act." Bailey v. Central Vermont R. Co., 319 U.S. 350, 354. We also recognized in that case that to deprive railroad workers of the benefit of a jury trial where there is evidence to support negligence "is to take away a goodly portion of the relief which Congress has afforded them." It follows that the right to trial by jury is too substantial a part of the rights accorded by the Act to permit it to be classified as a mere "local rule of procedure" for denial in the manner that Ohio has here used. * * *

Reversed and remanded with directions.

JUSTICE FRANKFURTER, whom JUSTICE REED, JUSTICE JACKSON and JUSTICE BURTON join, concurring for reversal but dissenting from the Court's opinion.

Ohio, as do many other States, maintains the old division between law and equity as to the mode of trying issues, even though the same judge administers both. * * * [I]n all cases in Ohio, the judge is the trier of fact on this issue of fraud, rather than the jury. It is contended that the Federal Employers' Liability Act requires that Ohio courts send the fraud issue to a jury in the cases founded on that Act. To require Ohio to try a particular issue before a different fact-finder in negligence actions brought under the Employers' Liability Act from the fact-finder on the identical issue in every other negligence case disregards the settled distribution of judicial power between Federal and State courts where Congress authorizes concurrent enforcement of federally-created rights.

* * *

In 1916 the Court decided without dissent that States in entertaining actions under the Federal Employers' Liability Act need not provide a jury system other than that established for local negligence actions. States are not compelled to provide the jury required of Federal courts by the Seventh Amendment. Minneapolis & St. Louis R. Co. v. Bombolis * * *. In the thirty-six years since * * *, the Bombolis case has often been cited by this Court but never questioned. Until today its significance has been to leave to States the choice of the fact-finding tribunal in all negligence actions, including those arising under the Federal Act. * * *

Although a State must entertain negligence suits brought under the * * * Act if it entertains ordinary actions for negligence, it need conduct them only in the way in which it conducts the run of negligence litigation. The Bombolis case directly establishes that the * * * Act does not impose the jury requirements of the Seventh Amendment on the States *pro tanto* for Employers' Liability litigation. If its reasoning means anything, the Bombolis decision means that, if a State chooses not to have a jury at all, but to leave questions of fact in all negligence actions to a court, certainly the Employers' Liability Act does not require a State to have juries for negligence actions brought under the Federal Act in its courts. Or, if a State chooses to retain the old double system of courts, common law and equity * * *, surely there is nothing in the * * * Act that requires traditional distribution of authority for disposing of legal issues as between common law and chancery courts to go by the board. * * * So long as all negligence suits in a State are treated in the same way, by the same mode of disposing equitable, non-jury, and common law, jury issues, the State does not discriminate against Employers' Liability suits nor does it make any inroad upon substance.

Ohio and her sister States with a similar division of functions between law and equity are not trying to evade their duty under the * * * Act * * *. The States merely exercise a preference in adhering to historic ways of dealing with a claim of fraud; they prefer the traditional way of making unavailable through equity an otherwise valid defense. The State judges and local lawyers who must administer the Federal Employers' Liability Act in State courts are trained in the ways of local practice; it multiplies the difficulties and confuses the administration of justice to require, on purely theoretical grounds, a hybrid of State and Federal practice in the State courts as to a single class of cases. Nothing in the * * * Act or in the judicial enforcement of the Act for over forty years forces such judicial hybridization upon the States. The fact that Congress authorized actions under the * * * Act to be brought in State as well as in Federal courts seems a strange basis for the inference that Congress overrode State procedural arrangements controlling all other negligence suits in a State * * *. Such an inference is admissible, so it seems to me, only on the theory that Congress included as part of the right created by the Employers' Liability Act an assumed likelihood that trying all issues to juries is more favorable to plaintiffs. * * *

Even though the method of trying the equitable issue of fraud which the State applies in all other negligence cases governs Employers' Liability cases, two questions remain for decision: Should the validity of the release be tested by a Federal or a State standard? And if by a Federal one, did the

Ohio courts in the present case correctly administer the standard? If the States afford courts for enforcing the Federal Act, they must enforce the substance of the right given by Congress. They cannot depreciate the legislative currency issued by Congress—either expressly or by local methods of enforcement that accomplish the same result. * * * In order to prevent diminution of railroad workers' nationally-uniform right to recover, the standard for the validity of a release of contested liability must be Federal. * * *

NOTE AND QUESTIONS

How does the right to jury trial in *Dice* relate to the right to jury trial in *Byrd*, see p. 330, supra? Is it inconsistent to hold in *Dice* that a state court adjudicating a federal law claim must follow federal practice regarding jury trials, while holding in *Byrd* that a federal court adjudicating a state law claim may disregard state practice regarding jury trials? Does the Court in *Dice* explain more generally when state courts are obliged to follow federal procedure? See Clermont, *Reverse-Erie*, 82 Notre Dame L.Rev. 1 (2006) (arguing that the role of federal procedure in state court is a function of both formal preemption—when state and federal laws "directly collide"—and a more open-ended "judicial choice-of-law methodology" that seeks to "balance the state's interests in having its legal rule applied in state court" against "the federal interests in having federal law displace the rule of this particular state, while trying to avoid differences in outcome").

CHAPTER 7

MODERN PLEADING

■ ■ ■

This chapter explores modern pleading rules and how they relate to other aspects of pretrial practice. Federal Rule 8, which governs pleading, calls for a short and plain statement of the claim, which, if established, entitles the pleader to relief. This rule, combined with the requirement of a certification under Federal Rule 11 that the pleadings are not frivolous, was considered sufficient to provide notice to defendant, to set out the facts, to narrow the issues, and to deter the filing of baseless claims that may clog a court's calendar and harass an opponent. Over the last two decades, the Supreme Court has reoriented this pleading regime to heighten the complaint's screening function. As you read these materials, consider whether this doctrinal shift reflects an appropriate response to unwarranted litigation or, as Professor Miller has written, an excessive emphasis on cost reduction that in some cases blocks even meritorious *claim with basis?* claims from obtaining relief. See Miller, *Simplified Pleading, Meaningful Days in Court, and Trials on the Merits: Reflections on the Deformation of Federal Procedure*, 88 N.Y.U.L.Rev. 286 (2013).

A. THE COMPLAINT

1. PLEADING AT COMMON LAW

Pleading rules in the United States owe their origins to the manner of allegation that developed in the English royal courts during the medieval period. A person with a grievance against another sought justice from the king, and the king issued a writ, ordering the sheriff to bring the other person before the king's judges to answer the complaint. During the twelfth century, a standard pattern developed and by the sixteenth century, the practice changed from oral to written pleadings. When it became established that the king's courts would hear a particular kind of case, the complainant could obtain a writ from the king's chief minister, the chancellor, as a matter of course. The writ was the document that commenced the action, similar in function to the modern summons. Each writ came to embody a form of action, a concept that governed the method of commencing the suit, the substantive requirements of the case, the manner of trial, and the type of sanction that would attend the eventual judgment. If the writ that did not fit the dispute, the action would fail. See Milsom, Historical Foundations of the Common Law (1969).

NOTES AND QUESTIONS

1. At common law, plaintiff's claim was set forth in the declaration. Stripped of much verbiage, and stated in modern English, it might have said: "Defendant promised to deliver a horse to plaintiff and plaintiff promised to pay $100 for it, but defendant has refused to deliver the horse."

2. A substantive response to a claim, other than an expression of total agreement, would require defendant to demur or to plead. A demurrer would challenge the legal sufficiency of plaintiff's declaration. A defendant who did not demur would respond to the declaration in a plea. Pleas were of two types, dilatory and peremptory. A dilatory plea did not deny the merits of plaintiff's claim, but rather challenged plaintiff's right to have the court hear the case and included pleas to the jurisdiction of the court. A peremptory plea, or plea in bar, was on the merits.

3. If defendant entered a plea, plaintiff had three choices. First, he could demur on the ground that the plea did not state a valid defense. For example, if plaintiff had alleged a breach of contract and defendant's plea was that he was a minor at the time the contract was entered into, the demurrer would raise the question whether defendant's minority was a defense. Second, plaintiff could plead in a replication that defendant had not been a minor. Or, finally, plaintiff might have admitted that defendant had been a minor and pleaded, by way of confession and avoidance, that defendant had lied about his age.

2. DETAIL REQUIRED UNDER THE CODES

The first significant procedural reform in England occurred in the period between 1825 and 1834, when one form of writ was adopted for all three common law courts and all but three real actions were abolished, debt and detinue were reshaped, and the wager of law was ended. The capstone of the reform was a body of new rules of pleading, called the Hilary Rules, which generated new problems. The Common Law Procedure Acts of 1852, 1854, and 1860 weakened the forms of action, expanded joinder, and liberalized pleading. Finally, the Judicature Acts of 1873 and 1875 combined Chancery and the common law courts into one Supreme Court of Judicature, fused law and equity, and abolished the forms of action.

In the United States, New York took the lead in reforming common law pleading. In 1848, that state's legislature enacted a Code of Civil Procedure, commonly called the Field Code. This Code proved to be the prototype for numerous state codes—at one time more than half the states had codes patterned to some degree after the Field Code—and the precursor of the Federal Rules of Civil Procedure. Code pleading differed from the writ system by requiring plaintiffs to provide in the complaint a statement of facts for the elements of each cause of action alleged.

In theory, code pleading operated according to the logic of a syllogism: The allegations provided the minor premise, the law provided the major premise, and the court provided the conclusion. See Julian, *Charles E. Clark and Simple Pleading: Against a "Formalism of Generality,"* 104 Nw.U.L.Rev. 1179, 1186 (2010). In practice, code pleading became mired in technicality, for it was not simple to know what facts to state. Professor Clark, the key architect of the Federal Rules, criticized the codes as resting on a "vain attempt to restrict the pleading to only 'the ultimate facts,' excluding on the one hand evidential facts and on the other legal conclusions." Clark, *Pleading Negligence*, 32 Yale L.J. 483, 484 (1923).

Code pleading persists in some states requiring a "statement of facts" constituting a "cause of action" or demonstrating a "right to relief." Is there a difference between these formulations? Some state provisions call for a statement of "ultimate facts." A number of these code states soften any harsh results of technical enforcement by stating that a pleading is satisfactory if it gives "fair notice" to the opposing party.

COOK, STATEMENTS OF FACT IN PLEADING UNDER THE CODES, 21 Colum.L.Rev. 416, 416–19, 423 (1921) (footnotes omitted):

In * * * [*California Packing Corp. v. Kelly Storage & Distributing Co.*, 228 N.Y. 49, 126 N.E. 269 (1920)] the plaintiff alleged in his complaint that the promise for the breach of which he was suing was made in exchange for "a valuable consideration." The case went to the Court of Appeals upon the question whether this allegation is a "statement of fact" or a "conclusion of law." [The court held it was the former.] * * * An examination of the authorities in [New York and] other code jurisdictions reveals a conflict of authority. * * *

* * *

[Upon careful analysis] * * * it will appear at once that there is no logical distinction between statements which are grouped by the courts under the phrases "statements of fact" and "conclusions of law." It will also be found that many, although by no means all, pleadings held bad because they are said to plead "evidence" rather than "the facts constituting the cause of action" or defense really do nevertheless "state" the operative facts which the pleader will have to prove at the trial, but in a form different from that to which courts and lawyers are accustomed to recognize as a proper method of pleading. * * *

* * *

The facts of life which compose the group of "operative facts" to which the law attaches legal consequences are always *specific* and not *generic*. * * * [I]n an action on the case for, let us say, negligently injuring the plaintiff by the operation of an automobile, the "operative" or "ultimate" facts proved at the trial will always be specific. It will appear that the defendant was driving a particular kind of automobile at some particular rate of speed, *etc., etc.* If now a plaintiff were to state the facts thus specifically in his complaint he would doubtless be told by the average court that he had "pleaded his evidence" and not the "facts constituting the cause of action." This would of course be erroneous. What is according to accepted notions the proper way to plead is merely a mode of stating the facts generically rather than specifically.

It must of course be recognized that at times a pleader really does err by "pleading evidence," *i.e.*, by stating, generically or specifically, facts which do not form part of the group of operative facts, but are merely facts from which by some process of logical inference the existence of the operative facts can be inferred. More often, however, the "error" consists merely in pleading the operative facts more specifically than is usual.

* * * Let us now examine "conclusions of law." The first thing noticed upon analysis is that a so-called "conclusion of law" is a generic statement which can be made only after some legal rule has been applied to some specific group of operative facts. Consider, for example, a statement in a pleading that "defendant owes plaintiff $500." Standing by itself in a pleading this is usually treated as a mere "conclusion of law." It can, however, be made only when one knows certain facts and also the applicable legal rule. It is, in fact, the conclusion of a logical argument: Whenever certain facts, a, b, c, *etc.*, exist, B (defendant) owes A (plaintiff) $500; facts a, b, c, *etc.*, exist; therefore B owes A $500. This being so, when the bare statement is made that "B owes A $500" we may, if we wish, regard it as a statement in generic form that all the facts necessary to create the legal duty to pay money described by the word "owe" are true as between A and B. In dealing, for example, with misrepresentation, such statements are more often than otherwise regarded in exactly this way. The same statement may, however, under proper circumstances be merely a statement as to the law applicable to facts given or known, and so be purely a statement of a "conclusion of law." * * *

* * *

* * * How specific or how generic statements in a pleading may and must be can obviously not be settled by mere logic, but according to notions of fairness and convenience. The pleading should give the adversary and the court reasonable notice of the real nature of the claim or defense; nothing more should be required. * * *

In GILLISPIE v. GOODYEAR SERVICE STORES, 258 N.C. 487, 128 S.E.2D 762 (1963), plaintiff alleged:

> [T]he defendants, without cause or just excuse and maliciously came upon and trespassed upon the premises occupied by the plaintiff as a residence, and by the use of harsh and threatening language and physical force directed against the plaintiff assaulted the plaintiff and placed her in great fear, and humiliated and embarrassed her by subjecting her to public scorn and ridicule, and caused her to be seized and exhibited to the public as a prisoner, and to be confined in a public jail, all to her great humiliation, embarrassment and harm.

Id. at 487, 128 S.E.2d at 763. Under the North Carolina code then in force, plaintiff was required to provide a "plain and concise statement of the facts constituting a cause of action." North Carolina cases interpreting the pleading standard had stated that the complaint must "disclose the issuable facts" and allege "the material, essential and ultimate facts upon which plaintiff's right of action is based." The court held that the allegations were insufficient, noting that the pleading was necessary not only to enable the opposing party to respond but also to enable the court to declare the law upon the facts stated. The court could not do so if "a mere legal conclusion" such as "assault" or "trespass" is stated. The court explained:

> The complaint states no facts upon which * * * legal conclusions may be predicated. Plaintiff's allegations do not disclose what occurred, when it occurred, where it occurred, who did what, the relationships between defendants and plaintiff or of defendants inter se, or any other factual data that might identify the occasion or describe the circumstances of the alleged wrongful conduct of defendants.

Id. at 490, 128 S.E.2d at 766. The court also discussed the sufficiency of pleadings in other types of cases:

> When a complaint alleges defendant is indebted to plaintiff in a certain amount and such debt is due, but does not allege in what manner or for what cause defendant became indebted to plaintiff, it is demurrable for failure to state facts sufficient to constitute a cause of action. * * *
>
> > "In an action or defense based upon negligence, it is not sufficient to allege the mere happening of an event of an injurious nature and call it negligence on the part of the party sought to be charged. This is necessarily so because negligence is not a fact in itself, but is the legal result of certain facts. Therefore, the facts which constitute the negligence charged and also the facts which establish such

> negligence as the proximate cause, or as one of the proximate causes, of the injury must be alleged." Shives v. Sample, 238 N.C. 724, 79 S.E.2d 193.

Id. at 489–90, 128 S.E.2d at 765.

NOTES AND QUESTIONS

1.   Is the court in *Gillispie* legitimately concerned with the inability of defendants to ascertain the claims against them in order that they might answer and prepare their defenses? Can it be said that the pleading in *Gillispie* is unsatisfactory because the trial judge will not know what evidence is or is not relevant?

2.   To what extent might the court in *Gillispie* have been motivated by the notion that a detailed account of the facts might well show that plaintiff did not have a valid claim for relief? Is it significant that at the time of the *Gillispie* decision North Carolina did not have a provision for summary judgment that allowed a party to challenge an opponent's allegations that lack evidentiary support? Has the North Carolina court simply followed a hard and fast line concerning the "fact" pleading requirement, thereby undermining its basic purpose as a device for pretrial communication?

3.   Plaintiff was given leave to amend the complaint after the *Gillispie* decision. Suppose that plaintiff's amended complaint also is deficient. Will she be given leave to amend again? How should the right to amend affect the question of whether a pleading is satisfactory?

3. DETAIL REQUIRED UNDER THE FEDERAL RULES OF CIVIL PROCEDURE

Read Federal Rules of Civil Procedure 8(a), 9(b), and 12(b) and the accompanying material in the Supplement.

In CONLEY v. GIBSON, 355 U.S. 41, 78 S.Ct. 99, 2 L.Ed.2d 80 (1957), the Supreme Court expressed its views on the degree of detail required by Federal Rule 8(a):

> * * * In appraising the sufficiency of the complaint we follow, of course, the accepted rule that a complaint should not be dismissed for failure to state a claim unless it appears beyond doubt that the plaintiff can prove no set of facts in support of his claim which would entitle him to relief. * * *

> * * * [T]he Federal Rules of Civil Procedure do not require a claimant to set out in detail the facts upon which he bases his claim. To the contrary, all the Rules require is "a short and plain

statement of the claim" that will give the defendant fair notice of what the plaintiff's claim is and the grounds upon which it rests. The illustrative forms appended to the Rules plainly demonstrate this. Such simplified "notice pleading" is made possible by the liberal opportunity for discovery and the other pretrial procedures established by the Rules to disclose more precisely the basis of both claim and defense and to define more narrowly the disputed facts and issues. Following the simple guide of Rule 8(f) that "all pleadings shall be so construed as to do substantial justice," we have no doubt that petitioner's complaint adequately set forth a claim and gave the respondents fair notice of its basis. The Federal Rules reject the approach that pleading is a game of skill in which one misstep by counsel may be decisive to the outcome and accept the principle that the purpose of pleading is to facilitate a proper decision on the merits. * * *

Id. at 45–48, 78 S.Ct. 102–03, 2 L.Ed.2d at 84–86.

NOTE ON THE BURDEN OF PLEADING

The burden of pleading determines which party is required to introduce an issue into the litigation by alleging the matter in the pleading. See Hamabe, *Functions of Rule* 12(b)(6) *in the Federal Rules of Civil Procedure: A Categorization Approach*, 15 Campbell L.Rev. 119, 172 (1993). If the burden is assigned to plaintiff, then the complaint must allege the issue, and if plaintiff fails to do so, the complaint is vulnerable to dismissal for failure to state a claim. If the burden is assigned to defendant, then defendant must raise the issue as an affirmative defense, and if defendant fails to do so, defendant will be barred from proving that defense at trial. Generally, the burden of pleading is assigned to the party who has the burden of proof on that issue at trial, but the burdens do not always coincide. It often is said that plaintiff must plead an issue that is essential to the case. Isn't this circular? Should plaintiff have to plead the nonexistence of defenses that defendant potentially has and might raise? See Lee, *Pleading and Proof: The Economics of Legal Burdens*, 1997 B.Y.U.L.Rev. 1.

———

SWIERKIEWICZ v. SOREMA N.A., 534 U.S. 506, 122 S.Ct. 992, 152 L.Ed.2d 1 (2002), addressed whether a complaint in an employment discrimination lawsuit "must contain specific facts establishing a prima facie case of discrimination." In a unanimous opinion for the Court, Justice Thomas wrote, "an employment discrimination complaint need not include such facts and instead must contain only 'a short and plain statement of the claim showing that the pleader is entitled to relief.'" The Court explained:

Petitioner Akos Swierkiewicz is a native of Hungary, who at the time of his complaint was 53 years old. * * * In April 1989, petitioner began working for respondent Sorema N.A., a reinsurance company headquartered in New York and principally owned and controlled by a French parent corporation. Petitioner was initially employed in the position of senior vice president and chief underwriting officer (CUO). Nearly six years later, Francois M. Chavel, respondent's Chief Executive Officer, demoted petitioner to a marketing and services position and transferred the bulk of his underwriting responsibilities to Nicholas Papadopoulo, a 32-year-old who, like Mr. Chavel, is a French national. About a year later, Mr. Chavel stated that he wanted to "energize" the underwriting department and appointed Mr. Papadopoulo as CUO. Petitioner claims that Mr. Papadopoulo had only one year of underwriting experience at the time he was promoted, and therefore was less experienced and less qualified to be CUO than he, since at that point he had 26 years of experience in the insurance industry.

Following his demotion, petitioner contends that he "was isolated by Mr. Chavel ... [and] excluded from business decisions and meetings and denied the opportunity to reach his true potential at SOREMA."[a] * * * Petitioner unsuccessfully attempted to meet with Mr. Chavel to discuss his discontent. Finally, in April 1997, petitioner sent a memo to Mr. Chavel outlining his grievances and requesting a severance package. Two weeks later, respondent's general counsel presented petitioner with two options: He could either resign without a severance package or be dismissed. Mr. Chavel fired petitioner after he refused to resign.

Petitioner filed a lawsuit alleging that he had been terminated on account of his national origin in violation of Title VII of the Civil Rights Act of 1964 * * * and on account of his age in violation of the Age Discrimination in Employment Act of 1967 (ADEA) * * *. The United States District Court for the Southern District of New York dismissed petitioner's complaint because it found that he "ha[d] not adequately alleged a prima facie case, in that he ha[d] not adequately alleged circumstances that support an inference of discrimination." * * * The * * * Second Circuit affirmed * * *. We granted certiorari, * * * and now reverse.

Applying Circuit precedent, the Court of Appeals required petitioner to plead a prima facie case of discrimination in order to survive respondent's motion to dismiss. * * * [P]etitioner was thus required to allege in his complaint: (1) membership in a protected

---

[a] Alteration in original.

group; (2) qualification for the job in question; (3) an adverse employment action; and (4) circumstances that support an inference of discrimination. * * *

The prima facie case * * *, however, is an evidentiary standard, not a pleading requirement. * * * [T]his Court has reiterated that the prima facie case relates to the employee's burden of presenting evidence that raises an inference of discrimination. * * *

This Court has never indicated that the requirements for establishing a prima facie case * * * also apply to the pleading standard that plaintiffs must satisfy in order to survive a motion to dismiss. * * *

* * * [U]nder a notice pleading system, it is not appropriate to require a plaintiff to plead facts establishing a prima facie case because * * * [this] framework does not apply in every employment discrimination case. For instance, if a plaintiff is able to produce direct evidence of discrimination, he may prevail without proving all the elements of a prima facie case. * * * Under the Second Circuit's heightened pleading standard, a plaintiff without direct evidence of discrimination at the time of his complaint must plead a prima facie case of discrimination, even though discovery might uncover such direct evidence. It thus seems incongruous to require a plaintiff, in order to survive a motion to dismiss, to plead more facts than he may ultimately need to prove to succeed on the merits if direct evidence of discrimination is discovered.

* * *

Furthermore, imposing the Court of Appeals' heightened pleading standard in employment discrimination cases conflicts with Federal Rule of Civil Procedure 8(a)(2), which provides that a complaint must include only "a short and plain statement of the claim showing that the pleader is entitled to relief." * * * Such a statement must simply "give the defendant fair notice of what the plaintiff's claim is and the grounds upon which it rests." This simplified notice pleading standard relies on liberal discovery rules and summary judgment motions to define disputed facts and issues and to dispose of unmeritorious claims. * * *

The Court then explained that "Rule 8(a)'s simplified pleading standard applies to all civil actions, with limited exceptions," and that "[o]ther provisions of the Federal Rules * * * are inextricably linked" to this simplified pleading standard. The Court continued:

Applying the relevant standard, petitioner's complaint easily satisfies the requirements of Rule 8(a) because it gives respondent fair notice of the basis for petitioner's claims. Petitioner alleged that he had been terminated on account of his national origin in violation of Title VII and on account of his age in violation of the ADEA. * * * His complaint detailed the events leading to his termination, provided relevant dates, and included the ages and nationalities of at least some of the relevant persons involved with his termination. * * * In addition, they state claims upon which relief could be granted under Title VII and the ADEA.

Respondent argues that allowing lawsuits based on conclusory allegations of discrimination to go forward will burden the courts and encourage disgruntled employees to bring unsubstantiated suits. * * * Whatever the practical merits of this argument, the Federal Rules do not contain a heightened pleading standard for employment discrimination suits. * * * Furthermore, Rule 8(a) establishes a pleading standard without regard to whether a claim will succeed on the merits. "Indeed it may appear on the face of the pleadings that a recovery is very remote and unlikely but that is not the test." [Scheuer v. Rhodes, 416 U.S. 232, 236, 94 S.Ct. 1683, 1686, 40 L.Ed.2d 90, 96 (1974)].

* * *

534 U.S. at 508–12, 122 S.Ct. at 995–99, 152 L.Ed. at 7–11.

NOTES AND QUESTIONS

1.   Would a complaint alleging employment discrimination in violation of Title VII, the statute at issue in *Swierkiewicz*, be sufficient if it alleged, "I was denied employment because of my gender"? See Sparrow v. United Air Lines, Inc., 216 F.3d 1111, 1115 (D.C. Cir. 2000) (complaint is sufficient if it alleges "I was turned down for a job because of my race"). What additional facts did plaintiff in *Swierkiewicz* include in his complaint?

2.   Prior to *Swierkiewicz*, the Court in LEATHERMAN v. TARRANT COUNTY NARCOTICS INTELLIGENCE & COORDINATION UNIT, 507 U.S. 163, 113 S.Ct. 1160, 122 L.Ed.2d 517 (1993), unanimously held that Rule 8 did not impose a heightened pleading standard on civil rights complaints filed under 42 U.S.C. § 1983. The Court made clear that changes to the pleading standard would have to go through the formal process for amending the Federal Rules:

Perhaps if Rules 8 and 9 were rewritten today, claims against municipalities under § 1983 might be subjected to the added specificity requirement of Rule 9(b). But that is a result which must be obtained by the process of amending the Federal Rules, and not by judicial interpretation. In the absence of such an amendment, federal courts and litigants must rely on summary judgment and control of discovery to weed out unmeritorious claims sooner rather than later.

Id. at 168–69, 113 S.Ct. at 1163, 122 L.Ed.2d at 524. See Marcus, *The Puzzling Persistence of Pleading Practice*, 76 Tex.L.Rev. 1749 (1998).

———

Read the complaint in Bell Atlantic Corp. v. Twombly, which is reproduced in the Supplement.

———

BELL ATLANTIC CORP. v. TWOMBLY
Supreme Court of the United States, 2007.
550 U.S. 544, 127 S.Ct. 1955, 167 L.Ed.2d 929.

Certiorari to the United States Court of Appeals for the Second Circuit.

JUSTICE SOUTER delivered the opinion of the Court.

* * *

I

* * *

[Plaintiffs, subscribers to local telephone services, filed a class action against the major telephone companies in the United States sometimes called Incumbent Local Exchange Carriers (hereinafter ILECs), alleging that they had violated § 1 of the Sherman Antitrust Act through efforts (1) to inhibit the growth of Competitive Local Exchange Carriers (hereinafter CLECs) and (2) to eliminate competition among themselves in territories where any one was dominant.]

* * *

The United States District Court for the Southern District of New York dismissed the complaint for failure to state a claim upon which relief can be granted. The District Court acknowledged that "plaintiffs may allege a conspiracy by citing instances of parallel business behavior that suggest an agreement," but emphasized that "while '[c]ircumstantial evidence of consciously parallel behavior may have made heavy inroads into the traditional judicial attitude toward conspiracy[, . . .] "conscious parallelism" has not yet read conspiracy out of the Sherman Act entirely.' " 313 F.Supp.2d 174, 179 (2003) * * *. Thus, the District Court understood that allegations of parallel business conduct, taken alone, do not state a claim under § 1; plaintiffs must allege additional facts that "ten[d] to exclude independent self-interested conduct as an explanation for defendants' parallel behavior." * * * The District Court found plaintiffs' allegations of parallel ILEC actions to discourage competition inadequate because "the behavior of each ILEC in resisting the incursion of CLECs is fully explained by the ILEC's own interests in defending its individual territory." * * * As to the ILECs' supposed agreement against competing with each other, the District Court found that the complaint does not "alleg[e] facts ... suggesting that refraining from competing in other territories as CLECs was contrary to [the ILECs'] apparent economic interests, and consequently [does] not rais[e] an inference that [the ILECs'] actions were the result of a conspiracy." * * *[b]

The Court of Appeals for the Second Circuit reversed, holding that the District Court tested the complaint by the wrong standard. It held that "plus factors are not *required* to be pleaded to permit an antitrust claim based on parallel conduct to survive dismissal." 425 F.3d 99, 114 (2005) (emphasis in original). Although the Court of Appeals took the view that plaintiffs must plead facts that "include conspiracy among the realm of 'plausible' possibilities in order to survive a motion to dismiss," it then said that "to rule that allegations of parallel anticompetitive conduct fail to support a plausible conspiracy claim, a court would have to conclude that there is no set of facts that would permit a plaintiff to demonstrate that the particular parallelism asserted was the product of collusion rather than coincidence." Ibid.

We granted certiorari to address the proper standard for pleading an antitrust conspiracy through allegations of parallel conduct, * * * and now reverse.

II

A

Because § 1 of the Sherman Act "does not prohibit [all] unreasonable restraints of trade ... but only restraints effected by a contract, combination, or conspiracy, * * * [t]he crucial question" is whether the challenged anticompetitive conduct "stem[s] from independent decision or from an agreement, tacit or express," * * *. While a showing of parallel "business behavior is admissible circumstantial evidence from which the fact finder may infer agreement," it falls short of "conclusively establish[ing] agreement or ... itself constitut[ing] a Sherman Act offense."[c] * * * Even "conscious parallelism," a common reaction of "firms in a concentrated market [that] recogniz[e] their shared economic interests and their interdependence with respect to price and output decisions" is "not in itself unlawful." * * *

B

This case presents the antecedent question of what a plaintiff must plead in order to state a claim under § 1 of the Sherman Act. Federal Rule of Civil Procedure 8(a)(2) requires only "a short and plain statement of the claim showing that the pleader is entitled to relief," in order to "give the

---

b   Alteration in original here and in the first paragraph of II.A.

c   Alteration in original.

defendant fair notice of what the . . . claim is and the grounds upon which it rests," *Conley* * * *. While a complaint attacked by a Rule 12(b)(6) motion to dismiss does not need detailed factual allegations * * *, a plaintiff's obligation to provide the "grounds" of his "entitle[ment] to relief" requires more than labels and conclusions, and a formulaic recitation of the elements of a cause of action will not do, see *Papasan v. Allain,* 478 U.S. 265, 286, 106 S.Ct. 2932, 92 L.Ed. 2d 209 (1986) (on a motion to dismiss, courts "are not bound to accept as true a legal conclusion couched as a factual allegation"). Factual allegations must be enough to raise a right to relief above the speculative level, see 5 C. Wright & A. Miller, Federal Practice and Procedure § 1216, pp. 235–236 (3d ed. 2004) (hereinafter Wright & Miller) ("[T]he pleading must contain something more . . . than . . . a statement of facts that merely creates a suspicion [of] a legally cognizable right of action") * * * on the assumption that all the allegations in the complaint are true (even if doubtful in fact) * * *.[d]

In applying these general standards to a § 1 claim, we hold that stating such a claim requires a complaint with enough factual matter (taken as true) to suggest that an agreement was made. Asking for plausible grounds to infer an agreement does not impose a probability requirement at the pleading stage; it simply calls for enough fact to raise a reasonable expectation that discovery will reveal evidence of illegal agreement. And, of course, a well-pleaded complaint may proceed even if it strikes a savvy judge that actual proof of those facts is improbable, and "that a recovery is very remote and unlikely." * * * In identifying facts that are suggestive enough to render a § 1 conspiracy plausible, we have the benefit of the prior rulings and considered views of leading commentators * * * that lawful parallel conduct fails to bespeak unlawful agreement. It makes sense to say, therefore, that an allegation of parallel conduct and a bare assertion of conspiracy will not suffice. Without more, parallel conduct does not suggest conspiracy, and a conclusory allegation of agreement at some unidentified point does not supply facts adequate to show illegality. Hence, when allegations of parallel conduct are set out in order to make a § 1 claim, they must be placed in a context that raises a suggestion of a preceding agreement, not merely parallel conduct that could just as well be independent action.

* * *

We alluded to the practical significance of the Rule 8 entitlement requirement in *Dura Pharmaceuticals, Inc. v. Broudo,* 544 U.S. 336, 125 S.Ct. 1627, 161 L.Ed.2d 577 (2005), when we explained that something beyond the mere possibility of loss causation must be alleged, lest a plaintiff with " 'a largely groundless claim' " be allowed to " 'take up the time of a number of other people, with the right to do so representing an *in*

---

d　　Alteration in original.

terrorem increment of the settlement value.' " *Id.,* at 347, 125 S.Ct. 1627
* * *.

Thus, it is one thing to be cautious before dismissing an antitrust
complaint in advance of discovery * * * but quite another to forget that
proceeding to antitrust discovery can be expensive. As we indicated over 20
years ago * * *, "a district court must retain the power to insist upon some
specificity in pleading before allowing a potentially massive factual
controversy to proceed." * * * That potential expense is obvious enough in
the present case: plaintiffs represent a putative class of at least 90 percent
of all subscribers to local telephone or high-speed Internet service in the
continental United States, in an action against America's largest
telecommunications firms (with many thousands of employees generating
reams and gigabytes of business records) for unspecified (if any) instances
of antitrust violations that allegedly occurred over a period of seven years.

It is no answer to say that a claim just shy of a plausible entitlement
to relief can, if groundless, be weeded out early in the discovery process
through "careful case management," * * * given the common lament that
the success of judicial supervision in checking discovery abuse has been on
the modest side. See, *e.g.,* Easterbrook, *Discovery as Abuse,* 69 B.U. L. Rev.
635, 638 (1989) ("Judges can do little about impositional discovery when
parties control the legal claims to be presented and conduct the discovery
themselves"). And it is self-evident that the problem of discovery abuse
cannot be solved by "careful scrutiny of evidence at the summary judgment
stage," much less "lucid instructions to juries"; * * * the threat of discovery
expense will push cost-conscious defendants to settle even anemic cases
before reaching those proceedings. Probably, then, it is only by taking care
to require allegations that reach the level suggesting conspiracy that we
can hope to avoid the potentially enormous expense of discovery in cases
with no " 'reasonably founded hope that the [discovery] process will reveal
relevant evidence' " to support a § 1 claim. * * *[6]

---

[6] The dissent takes heart in the reassurances of plaintiffs' counsel that discovery would be
" 'phased' " and "limited to the existence of the alleged conspiracy and class certification." * * * But
determining whether some illegal agreement may have taken place between unspecified persons
at different ILECs (each a multibillion dollar corporation with legions of management level
employees) at some point over seven years is a sprawling, costly, and hugely time-consuming
undertaking not easily susceptible to the kind of line drawing and case management that the
dissent envisions. Perhaps the best answer to the dissent's optimism that antitrust discovery is
open to effective judicial control is a more extensive quotation of the authority just cited, a judge
with a background in antitrust law. Given the system that we have, the hope of effective judicial
supervision is slim: "The timing is all wrong. The plaintiff files a sketchy complaint (the Rules of
Civil Procedure discourage fulsome documents), and discovery is launched. A judicial officer does
not know the details of the case the parties will present and in theory *cannot* know the details.
Discovery is used to find the details. The judicial officer always knows less than the parties, and
the parties themselves may not know very well where they are going or what they expect to find.
A magistrate supervising discovery does not—cannot—know the expected productivity of a given
request, because the nature of the requester's claim and the contents of the files (or head) of the
adverse party are unknown. Judicial officers cannot measure the costs and benefits to the
requester and so cannot isolate impositional requests. Requesters have no reason to disclose their

Plaintiffs do not, of course, dispute the requirement of plausibility and the need for something more than merely parallel behavior * * *, and their main argument against the plausibility standard at the pleading stage is its ostensible conflict with an early statement of ours construing Rule 8. Justice Black's opinion for the Court in *Conley v. Gibson* spoke not only of the need for fair notice of the grounds for entitlement to relief but of "the accepted rule that a complaint should not be dismissed for failure to state a claim unless it appears beyond doubt that the plaintiff can prove no set of facts in support of his claim which would entitle him to relief." * * * This "no set of facts" language can be read in isolation as saying that any statement revealing the theory of the claim will suffice unless its factual impossibility may be shown from the face of the pleadings; and the Court of Appeals appears to have read *Conley* in some such way when formulating its understanding of the proper pleading standard * * *.

On such a focused and literal reading of *Conley*'s "no set of facts," a wholly conclusory statement of claim would survive a motion to dismiss whenever the pleadings left open the possibility that a plaintiff might later establish some "set of [undisclosed] facts" to support recovery.[e] So here, the Court of Appeals specifically found the prospect of unearthing direct evidence of conspiracy sufficient to preclude dismissal, even though the complaint does not set forth a single fact in a context that suggests an agreement. * * * It seems fair to say that this approach to pleading would dispense with any showing of a " 'reasonably founded hope' " that a plaintiff would be able to make a case * * *. Mr. Micawber's optimism would be enough.

* * *

* * * [A]fter puzzling the profession for 50 years, this famous observation has earned its retirement. The phrase is best forgotten as an incomplete, negative gloss on an accepted pleading standard: once a claim has been stated adequately, it may be supported by showing any set of facts consistent with the allegations in the complaint. * * * *Conley,* then, described the breadth of opportunity to prove what an adequate complaint claims, not the minimum standard of adequate pleading to govern a complaint's survival.

III

When we look for plausibility in this complaint, we agree with the District Court that plaintiffs' claim of conspiracy in restraint of trade comes

---

own estimates because they gain from imposing costs on rivals (and may lose from an improvement in accuracy). The portions of the Rules of Civil Procedure calling on judges to trim back excessive demands, therefore, have been, and are doomed to be, hollow. We cannot prevent what we cannot detect; we cannot detect what we cannot define; we cannot define 'abusive' discovery except in theory, because in practice we lack essential information." Easterbrook, *Discovery as Abuse,* 69 B.U. L. Rev. 635, 638–639 (1989).

[e] Alteration in original.

up short. To begin with, the complaint leaves no doubt that plaintiffs rest their § 1 claim on descriptions of parallel conduct and not on any independent allegation of actual agreement among the ILECs. * * * Although in form a few stray statements speak directly of agreement, on fair reading these are merely legal conclusions resting on the prior allegations. * * * The nub of the complaint, then, is the ILECs' parallel behavior, consisting of steps to keep the CLECs out and manifest disinterest in becoming CLECs themselves, and its sufficiency turns on the suggestions raised by this conduct when viewed in light of common economic experience.

* * * [T]here is no reason to infer that the companies had agreed among themselves to do what was only natural anyway; so natural, in fact, that if alleging parallel decisions to resist competition were enough to imply an antitrust conspiracy, pleading a § 1 violation against almost any group of competing businesses would be a sure thing.

* * *

Plaintiffs' second conspiracy theory rests on the competitive reticence among the ILECs themselves in the wake of the 1966 Act * * *. * * *

But * * * [a lack of competition is] * * * not suggestive of conspiracy, not if history teaches anything. In a traditionally unregulated industry with low barriers to entry, sparse competition among large firms dominating separate geographical segments of the market could very well signify illegal agreement, but here we have an obvious alternative explanation. * * * In the decade preceding the 1996 Act and well before that, monopoly was the norm in telecommunications, not the exception. * * *. The ILECs were born in that world, doubtless liked the world the way it was, and surely knew the adage about him who lives by the sword. Hence, a natural explanation for the noncompetition alleged is that the former Government-sanctioned monopolists were sitting tight, expecting their neighbors to do the same thing.

In fact, the complaint itself gives reasons to believe that the ILECs would see their best interests in keeping to their old turf. Although the complaint says generally that the ILECs passed up "especially attractive business opportunit[ies]" by declining to compete as CLECs against other ILECs, Complaint ¶ 40 * * *, it does not allege that competition as CLECs was potentially any more lucrative than other opportunities being pursued by the ILECs during the same period, * * * and the complaint is replete with indications that any CLEC faced nearly insurmountable barriers to profitability owing to the ILECs' flagrant resistance to the network sharing requirements of the 1996 Act, id., ¶ 47 * * *. * * *

Plaintiffs say that our analysis runs counter to *Swierkiewicz* * * *. Even though Swierkiewicz's pleadings "detailed the events leading to his termination, provided relevant dates, and included the ages and nationalities of at least some of the relevant persons involved with his termination," the Court of Appeals dismissed the complaint for failing to allege certain additional facts that Swierkiewicz would need at the trial stage to support his claim in the absence of direct evidence of discrimination. * * * We reversed on the ground that the Court of Appeals had impermissibly applied what amounted to a heightened pleading requirement by insisting that Swierkiewicz allege "specific facts" beyond those necessary to state his claim and the grounds showing entitlement to relief. * * *

Here, in contrast, we do not require heightened fact pleading of specifics, but only enough facts to state a claim to relief that is plausible on its face. Because the plaintiffs here have not nudged their claims across the line from conceivable to plausible, their complaint must be dismissed.

* * *

The judgment of the Court of Appeals for the Second Circuit is reversed, and the cause is remanded for further proceedings consistent with this opinion.

It is so ordered.

JUSTICE STEVENS, with whom JUSTICE GINSBURG joins except as to Part IV, dissenting.

* * * If the defendants acted independently, their conduct was perfectly lawful. If, however, that conduct is the product of a horizontal agreement among potential competitors, it was unlawful. Plaintiffs have alleged such an agreement and, because the complaint was dismissed in advance of answer, the allegation has not even been denied. Why, then, does the case not proceed? Does a judicial opinion that the charge is not "plausible" provide a legally acceptable reason for dismissing the complaint? I think not.

Respondents' amended complaint describes a variety of circumstantial evidence and makes the straightforward allegation that petitioners

> "entered into a contract, combination or conspiracy to prevent competitive entry in their respective local telephone and/or high speed internet services markets and have agreed not to compete with one another and otherwise allocated customers and markets to one another." * * * [Amended Complaint ¶ 51].

The complaint explains that, contrary to Congress' expectation when it enacted the 1996 Telecommunications Act, and consistent with their own economic self-interests, * * * [the ILECs] have assiduously avoided infringing upon each other's markets and have refused to permit nonincumbent competitors to access their networks. The complaint quotes

* * * the former chief executive officer of one such ILEC, as saying that competing in a neighboring ILEC's territory " 'might be a good way to turn a quick dollar but that doesn't make it right.' " * * * [Amended Complaint ¶ 42]. * * * Moreover, respondents allege that petitioners "communicate amongst themselves" through numerous industry associations. * * * [Amended Complaint ¶ 46] * * *. In sum, respondents allege that petitioners entered into an agreement that has long been recognized as a classic *per se* violation of the Sherman Act. * * *

* * *

The Court and petitioners' legal team are no doubt correct that the parallel conduct alleged is consistent with the absence of any contract, combination, or conspiracy. But that conduct is also entirely consistent with the *presence* of the illegal agreement alleged in the complaint. And the charge that petitioners "agreed not to compete with one another" is not just one of "a few stray statements" * * *; it is an allegation describing unlawful conduct. As such, the Federal Rules of Civil Procedure, our longstanding precedent, and sound practice mandate that the District Court at least require some sort of response from petitioners before dismissing the case.

Two practical concerns presumably explain the Court's dramatic departure from settled procedural law. Private antitrust litigation can be enormously expensive, and there is a risk that jurors may mistakenly conclude that evidence of parallel conduct has proved that the parties acted pursuant to an agreement when they in fact merely made similar independent decisions. Those concerns merit careful case management, including strict control of discovery, careful scrutiny of evidence at the summary judgment stage, and lucid instructions to juries; they do not, however, justify the dismissal of an adequately pleaded complaint without even requiring the defendants to file answers denying a charge that they in fact engaged in collective decisionmaking. More importantly, they do not justify an interpretation of Federal Rule * * * 12(b)(6) that seems to be driven by the majority's appraisal of the plausibility of the ultimate factual allegation rather than its legal sufficiency.

I

* * *

Under the relaxed pleading standards of the Federal Rules, the idea was not to keep litigants out of court but rather to keep them in. The merits of a claim would be sorted out during a flexible pretrial process and, as appropriate, through the crucible of trial. * * *

II

* * *

Consistent with the design of the Federal Rules, *Conley*'s "no set of facts" formulation permits outright dismissal only when proceeding to discovery or beyond would be futile. Once it is clear that a plaintiff has stated a claim that, if true, would entitle him to relief, matters of proof are appropriately relegated to other stages of the trial process. Today, however, in its explanation of a decision to dismiss a complaint that it regards as a fishing expedition, the Court scraps *Conley*'s "no set of facts" language. Concluding that the phrase has been "questioned, criticized, and explained away long enough," * * * the Court dismisses it as careless composition.

If *Conley*'s "no set of facts" language is to be interred, let it not be without a eulogy. That exact language, which the majority says has "puzzl[ed] the profession for 50 years," * * * has been cited as authority in a dozen opinions of this Court and four separate writings. In not one of those 16 opinions was the language "questioned," "criticized," or "explained away." Indeed, today's opinion is the first by any Member of this Court to express *any* doubt as to the adequacy of the *Conley* formulation. Taking their cues from the federal courts, 26 States and the District of Columbia utilize as their standard for dismissal of a complaint the very language the majority repudiates: whether it appears "beyond doubt" that "no set of facts" in support of the claim would entitle the plaintiff to relief. * * *

Petitioners have not requested that the *Conley* formulation be retired, nor have any of the six *amici* who filed briefs in support of petitioners. I would not rewrite the Nation's civil procedure textbooks and call into doubt the pleading rules of most of its States without far more informed deliberation as to the costs of doing so. Congress has established a process—a rulemaking process—for revisions of that order. * * *

The "pleading standard" label the majority gives to what it reads into the *Conley* opinion—a statement of the permissible factual support for an adequately pleaded complaint—would not, therefore, have impressed the *Conley* Court itself. Rather, that Court would have understood the majority's remodeling of its language to express an *evidentiary* standard, which the *Conley* Court had neither need nor want to explicate. Second, it is pellucidly clear that the *Conley* Court was interested in what a complaint *must* contain, not what it *may* contain. * * *

* * *

* * * *Conley*'s statement that a complaint is not to be dismissed unless "no set of facts" in support thereof would entitle the plaintiff to relief is hardly "puzzling[.]" * * * It reflects a philosophy that, unlike in the days of code pleading, separating the wheat from the chaff is a task assigned to the pretrial and trial process. *Conley*'s language, in short, captures the policy choice embodied in the Federal Rules and binding on the federal courts.

We have consistently reaffirmed that basic understanding of the Federal Rules in the half century since *Conley*. * * *

* * *

Everything today's majority says would * * * make perfect sense if it were ruling on a Rule 56 motion for summary judgment and the evidence included nothing more than the Court has described. But it should go without saying * * * that a heightened production burden at the summary judgment stage does not translate into a heightened pleading burden at the complaint stage. The majority rejects the complaint in this case because—in light of the fact that the parallel conduct alleged is consistent with ordinary market behavior—the claimed conspiracy is "conceivable" but not "plausible[.]" * * * But even if the majority's speculation is correct, its "plausibility" standard is irreconcilable with Rule 8 and with our governing precedents. * * * [F]ear of the burdens of litigation does not justify factual conclusions supported only by lawyers' arguments rather than sworn denials or admissible evidence.

* * *

III

[T]he theory on which the Court permits dismissal is that, so far as the Federal Rules are concerned, no agreement has been alleged at all. This is a mind-boggling conclusion.

* * * I am * * * willing to entertain the majority's belief that any agreement among the companies was unlikely. But the plaintiffs allege in three places in their complaint * * * that the ILECs did in fact agree both to prevent competitors from entering into their local markets and to forgo competition with each other. And as the Court recognizes, at the motion to dismiss stage, a judge assumes "that all the allegations in the complaint are true (even if doubtful in fact)." * * *

The majority circumvents this obvious obstacle to dismissal by pretending that it does not exist. The Court admits that "in form a few stray statements in the complaint speak directly of agreement," but disregards those allegations by saying that "on fair reading these are merely legal conclusions resting on the prior allegations" of parallel conduct. * * * The Court's dichotomy between factual allegations and "legal conclusions" is the stuff of a bygone era * * *. That distinction was a defining feature of code pleading * * *, but was conspicuously abolished when the Federal Rules were enacted in 1938. * * * "Defendants entered into a contract" is no more a legal conclusion than "defendant negligently drove," see Form 9.[f] Indeed it is less of one. * * *

---

[f] Form 9 was renumbered as Form 11. All of the forms were abrogated in 2015, see p. 415, Note 5, infra.

* * *

To be clear, if I had been the trial judge in this case, I would not have permitted the plaintiffs to engage in massive discovery based solely on the allegations in this complaint. On the other hand, I surely would not have dismissed the complaint without requiring the defendants to answer the charge that they "have agreed not to compete with one another and otherwise allocated customers and markets to one another." Even a sworn denial of that charge would not justify a summary dismissal without giving the plaintiffs the opportunity to take depositions from * * * at least one responsible executive representing each of the * * * defendants.

* * *

IV

* * *

* * *Whether the Court's actions will benefit only defendants in antitrust treble-damages cases, or whether its test for the sufficiency of a complaint will inure to the benefit of all civil defendants, is a question that the future will answer. But that the Court has announced a significant new rule that does not even purport to respond to any congressional command is glaringly obvious.

The transparent policy concern that drives the decision is the interest in protecting antitrust defendants—who in this case are some of the wealthiest corporations in our economy—from the burdens of pretrial discovery. * * * Even if it were not apparent that the legal fees petitioners have incurred in arguing the merits of their Rule 12(b) motion have far exceeded the cost of limited discovery, or that those discovery costs would burden respondents as well as petitioners, that concern would not provide an adequate justification for this law-changing decision. For in the final analysis it is only a lack of confidence in the ability of trial judges to control discovery, buttressed by appellate judges' independent appraisal of the plausibility of profoundly serious factual allegations, that could account for this stark break from precedent.

* * *

NOTES AND QUESTIONS

1.   Does *Conley*'s standard of notice pleading survive *Twombly*? If not, what is the new standard under Federal Rule 8(a)? Is this standard consistent with the language of the Federal Rule? Does it mark a return to the requirements of fact pleading under the Codes? Does the new standard reflect an appropriate act of judicial interpretation given the rule amendment process?

2.   Can you explain why the *Twombly* complaint was not "plausible"? Consider the claim of conspiracy. The majority stated that the complaint contained no "independent allegation of actual agreement" among the ILECs, underscoring that the complaint did not allege which ILECs and which employees agreed, or when and where the illicit agreement took place. Why was it not sufficient simply to allege a conspiracy not to compete? Was the allegation about a conspiracy defective because it was alleged on information and belief? Since a conspiracy takes place in secret, was it reasonable to expect plaintiffs, through a presuit investigation but without the benefit of discovery, to uncover the hidden details of a conspiracy? Why did the fact of parallel behavior—that none of the ILECs expanded into new markets—not support an inference of conspiracy? Was the Court's view of implausibility based on a particular theory of market behavior?

3.   What role did the anticipated cost of discovery play in the Court's decision? How did the dissenters in *Twombly* respond to this argument? Is this an appropriate factor to consider at the pleading stage of litigation? See Steinman, *The Pleading Problem*, 62 Stan.L.Rev. 1293, 1351–56 (2010) (discussing the relationship between pleading standards and discovery costs). Professor Epstein has argued that "as the costs of discovery mount, the case for terminating litigation earlier in the cycle gets ever stronger." Epstein, Bell Atlantic v. Twombly: *How Motions To Dismiss Become (Disguised) Summary Judgments*, 25 Wash.U.J.L. & Pol'y 61, 66–67 (2007). Do concerns about the cost of discovery justify extending the plausibility standard of pleading to the many cases that are not discovery-rich? See Dodson, *New Pleading, New Discovery*, 109 Mich.L.Rev. 53 (2010).

––––––––

Read the complaint in Ashcroft v. Iqbal, which is reproduced in the Supplement.

––––––––

ASHCROFT V. IQBAL
Supreme Court of the United States, 2009.
556 U.S. 662, 129 S.Ct. 1937, 173 L.Ed.2d 868.

Certiorari to the United States Court of Appeals for the Second Circuit.

JUSTICE KENNEDY delivered the opinion of the Court.

[Plaintiff-respondent, a Pakistani Muslim man, filed a damages action to redress the violation of his constitutional rights, alleged to have resulted from his pretrial detention in a maximum-security unit where he had been held as a person of "high interest" during the federal government's investigation of the attacks of September 11, 2001. Defendants included John Ashcroft, the Attorney General of the United States, and Robert Mueller, the Director of the Federal Bureau of Investigation (FBI). As to these parties, the complaint alleged that as part of the investigation, they adopted an unconstitutional policy that subjected plaintiff-respondent to harsh conditions on account of his race, religion, or national origin. The district court dismissed the complaint and the Second Circuit Court of Appeals affirmed on an interlocutory appeal.]

IV

A

* * *

To survive a motion to dismiss, a complaint must contain sufficient factual matter, accepted as true, to "state a claim to relief that is plausible on its face." [*Twombly*, p. 391, supra] A claim has facial plausibility when the plaintiff pleads factual content that allows the court to draw the reasonable inference that the defendant is liable for the misconduct alleged. * * * The plausibility standard is not akin to a "probability requirement," but it asks for more than a sheer possibility that a defendant has acted unlawfully. * * * Where a complaint pleads facts that are "merely consistent with" a defendant's liability, it "stops short of the line between possibility and plausibility of 'entitlement to relief.' " * * *

Two working principles underlie our decision in *Twombly*. First, the tenet that a court must accept as true all of the allegations contained in a complaint is inapplicable to legal conclusions. Threadbare recitals of the elements of a cause of action, supported by mere conclusory statements, do not suffice. * * * (Although for the purposes of a motion to dismiss we must take all of the factual allegations in the complaint as true, we "are not bound to accept as true a legal conclusion couched as a factual allegation" (internal quotation marks omitted)). Rule 8 marks a notable and generous departure from the hyper-technical, code-pleading regime of a prior era, but it does not unlock the doors of discovery for a plaintiff armed with nothing more than conclusions. Second, only a complaint that states a plausible claim for relief survives a motion to dismiss. * * * Determining whether a complaint states a plausible claim for relief will, as the Court of Appeals observed, be a context-specific task that requires the reviewing court to draw on its judicial experience and common sense. * * * But where the well-pleaded facts do not permit the court to infer more than the mere possibility of misconduct, the complaint has alleged—but it has not "show[n]"—"that the pleader is entitled to relief." Fed. Rule Civ. Proc. 8(a)(2).

In keeping with these principles a court considering a motion to dismiss can choose to begin by identifying pleadings that, because they are no more than conclusions, are not entitled to the assumption of truth. While legal conclusions can provide the framework of a complaint, they must be supported by factual allegations. When there are well-pleaded factual allegations, a court should assume their veracity and then determine whether they plausibly give rise to an entitlement to relief.

* * *

B

Under *Twombly*'s construction of Rule 8, we conclude that respondent's complaint has not "nudged [his] claims" of invidious discrimination "across the line from conceivable to plausible." * * *

We begin our analysis by identifying the allegations in the complaint that are not entitled to the assumption of truth. Respondent pleads that petitioners "knew of, condoned, and willfully and maliciously agreed to subject [him]" to harsh conditions of confinement "as a matter of policy, solely on account of [his] religion, race, and/or national origin and for no legitimate penological interest." Complaint ¶ 96 * * *. * * * These bare assertions, much like the pleading of conspiracy in *Twombly*, amount to nothing more than a "formulaic recitation of the elements" of a constitutional discrimination claim, * * * namely, that petitioners adopted a policy " 'because of,' not merely 'in spite of,' its adverse effects upon an identifiable group." * * * [Personnel Adm'r of Mass. v. Feeney, 442 U.S. 256, 279, 99 S.Ct. 2282, 2296, 60 L.Ed.2d 870, 888 (1979)]. As such, the allegations are conclusory and not entitled to be assumed true. To be clear, we do not reject these bald allegations on the ground that they are unrealistic or nonsensical. We do not so characterize them any more than the Court in *Twombly* rejected the plaintiffs' express allegation of a " 'contract, combination or conspiracy to prevent competitive entry,' " because it thought that claim too chimerical to be maintained. It is the conclusory nature of respondent's allegations, rather than their extravagantly fanciful nature, that disentitles them to the presumption of truth.

hoped for but impossible to achieve

We next consider the factual allegations in respondent's complaint to determine if they plausibly suggest an entitlement to relief. The complaint alleges that "the [FBI], under the direction of Defendant MUELLER, arrested and detained thousands of Arab Muslim men . . . as part of its investigation of the events of September 11." Complaint ¶ 47 * * *. It further claims that "[t]he policy of holding post-September-11th detainees in highly restrictive conditions of confinement until they were 'cleared' by the FBI was approved by Defendants ASHCROFT and MUELLER in discussions in the weeks after September 11, 2001." Id., ¶ 69 * * *. Taken as true, these allegations are consistent with petitioners' purposefully designating detainees "of high interest" because of their race, religion, or national origin. But given more likely explanations, they do not plausibly establish this purpose.

The September 11 attacks were perpetrated by 19 Arab Muslim hijackers who counted themselves members in good standing of al Qaeda, an Islamic fundamentalist group. Al Qaeda was headed by another Arab Muslim—Osama bin Laden—and composed in large part of his Arab Muslim disciples. It should come as no surprise that a legitimate policy directing law enforcement to arrest and detain individuals because of their suspected link to the attacks would produce a disparate, incidental impact on Arab Muslims, even though the purpose of the policy was to target neither Arabs nor Muslims. On the facts respondent alleges the arrests Mueller oversaw were likely lawful and justified by his nondiscriminatory intent to detain aliens who were illegally present in the United States and who had potential connections to those who committed terrorist acts. As between that "obvious alternative explanation" for the arrests, and the purposeful, invidious discrimination respondent asks us to infer, discrimination is not a plausible conclusion.

But even if the complaint's well-pleaded facts give rise to a plausible inference that respondent's arrest was the result of unconstitutional discrimination, that inference alone would not entitle respondent to relief. It is important to recall that respondent's complaint challenges neither the constitutionality of his arrest nor his initial detention * * *. Respondent's constitutional claims against petitioners rest solely on their ostensible "policy of holding post-September-11th detainees" in the ADMAX SHU [a special unit of the Metropolitan Detention Center in New York known as the Administrative Maximum Special Housing Unit] once they were categorized as "of high interest." Complaint ¶ 69 * * *. To prevail on that theory, the complaint must contain facts plausibly showing that petitioners purposefully adopted a policy of classifying post-September-11 detainees as "of high interest" because of their race, religion, or national origin.

This the complaint fails to do. Though respondent alleges that various other defendants, who are not before us, may have labeled him a person of "of high interest" for impermissible reasons, his only factual allegation against petitioners accuses them of adopting a policy approving "restrictive conditions of confinement" for post-September-11 detainees until they were " 'cleared' by the FBI." Ibid. Accepting the truth of that allegation, the complaint does not show, or even intimate, that petitioners purposefully housed detainees in the ADMAX SHU due to their race, religion, or national origin. All it plausibly suggests is that the Nation's top law enforcement officers, in the aftermath of a devastating terrorist attack, sought to keep suspected terrorists in the most secure conditions available until the suspects could be cleared of terrorist activity. Respondent does not argue, nor can he, that such a motive would violate petitioners' constitutional obligations. He would need to allege more by way of factual content to "nudg[e]" his claim of purposeful discrimination "across the line from conceivable to plausible."

* * *

C

Respondent offers three arguments that bear on our disposition of his case, but none is persuasive.

1

Respondent first says that our decision in *Twombly* should be limited to pleadings made in the context of an antitrust dispute. * * * This argument is not supported by *Twombly* and is incompatible with the Federal Rules * * *. Though *Twombly* determined the sufficiency of a complaint sounding in antitrust, the decision was based on our interpretation and application of Rule 8. * * * That Rule in turn governs the pleading standard "in all civil actions and proceedings in the United States district courts." Fed. Rule Civ. Proc. 1. Our decision in *Twombly* expounded the pleading standard for "all civil actions," * * * and it applies to antitrust and discrimination suits alike. * * *

2

Respondent next implies that our construction of Rule 8 should be tempered where, as here, the Court of Appeals has "instructed the district court to cabin discovery in such a way as to preserve" petitioners' defense of qualified immunity "as much as possible in anticipation of a summary judgment motion." * * * We have held, however, that the question presented by a motion to dismiss a complaint for insufficient pleadings does not turn on the controls placed upon the discovery process. * * *

Our rejection of the careful-case-management approach is especially important in suits where Government-official defendants are entitled to assert the defense of qualified immunity. The basic thrust of the qualified-immunity doctrine is to free officials from the concerns of litigation, including "avoidance of disruptive discovery." *Siegert v. Gilley*, 500 U.S. 226, 236, 111 S.Ct. 1789, 114 L.Ed.2d 277 (1991) (KENNEDY, J., concurring in judgment). There are serious and legitimate reasons for this. If a government official is to devote time to his or her duties, and to the formulation of sound and responsible policies, it is counterproductive to require the substantial diversion that is attendant to participating in litigation and making informed decisions as to how it should proceed. Litigation, though necessary to ensure that officials comply with the law, exacts heavy costs in terms of efficiency and expenditure of valuable time and resources that might otherwise be directed to the proper execution of the work of the Government. The costs of diversion are only magnified when Government officials are charged with responding to * * * "a national and international security emergency unprecedented in the history of the American Republic." * * *

It is no answer to these concerns to say that discovery for petitioners can be deferred while pretrial proceedings continue for other defendants. It is quite likely that, when discovery as to the other parties proceeds, it would prove necessary for petitioners and their counsel to participate in the process to ensure the case does not develop in a misleading or slanted way that causes prejudice to their position. Even if petitioners are not yet themselves subject to discovery orders, then, they would not be free from the burdens of discovery.

We decline respondent's invitation to relax the pleading requirements on the ground that the Court of Appeals promises petitioners minimally intrusive discovery. That promise provides especially cold comfort in this pleading context, where we are impelled to give real content to the concept of qualified immunity for high-level officials who must be neither deterred nor detracted from the vigorous performance of their duties. Because respondent's complaint is deficient under Rule 8, he is not entitled to discovery, cabined or otherwise.

[handwritten margin note: drive, force, or urge to do something]

3

Respondent finally maintains that the Federal Rules expressly allow him to allege petitioners' discriminatory intent "generally," which he equates with a conclusory allegation. It follows, respondent says, that his complaint is sufficiently well pleaded because it claims that petitioners discriminated against him "on account of [his] religion, race, and/or national origin and for no legitimate penological interest." Complaint ¶ 96 * * *. Were we required to accept this allegation as true, respondent's complaint would survive petitioners' motion to dismiss. But the Federal Rules do not require courts to credit a complaint's conclusory statements without reference to its factual context.

It is true that Rule 9(b) requires particularity when pleading "fraud or mistake," while allowing "[m]alice, intent, knowledge, and other conditions of a person's mind [to] be alleged generally." But "generally" is a relative term. In the context of Rule 9, it is to be compared to the particularity requirement applicable to fraud or mistake. Rule 9 merely excuses a party from pleading discriminatory intent under an elevated pleading standard. It does not give him license to evade the less rigid—though still operative—strictures of Rule 8. See 5A C. Wright & A. Miller, Federal Practice and Procedure § 1301, p. 291 (3d ed. 2004) ("[A] rigid rule requiring the detailed pleading of a condition of mind would be undesirable because, absent overriding considerations pressing for a specificity requirement, as in the case of averments of fraud or mistake, the general 'short and plain statement of the claim' mandate in Rule 8(a) . . . should control the second sentence of Rule 9(b)"). And Rule 8 does not empower respondent to plead the bare elements of his cause of action, affix the label "general allegation," and expect his complaint to survive a motion to dismiss.

V

We hold that respondent's complaint fails to plead sufficient facts to state a claim for purposeful and unlawful discrimination against petitioners. The Court of Appeals should decide in the first instance whether to remand to the District Court so that respondent can seek leave to amend his deficient complaint.

The judgment of the Court of Appeals is reversed, and the case is remanded for further proceedings consistent with this opinion.

It is so ordered.

JUSTICE SOUTER with whom JUSTICE STEVENS, JUSTICE GINSBURG, and JUSTICE BREYER join, dissenting.

* * *

I

A

The Court granted certiorari on * * * [two] questions. The first is about pleading; the second goes to the liability standard.

In the first question, Ashcroft and Mueller * * * conceded in their petition for certiorari that they would be liable if they had "actual knowledge" of discrimination by their subordinates and exhibited " 'deliberate indifference' " to that discrimination. * * * [T]hey asked the Court to address whether Iqbal's allegations against them (which they call conclusory) were sufficient to satisfy Rule 8(a)(2), and in particular whether the Court of Appeals misapplied our decision in *Twombly* construing that rule. * * *

In the second question, Ashcroft and Mueller asked this Court to say whether they could be held personally liable for the actions of their subordinates based on the theory that they had constructive notice of their subordinates' unconstitutional conduct. * * * This was an odd question to pose, since Iqbal has never claimed that Ashcroft and Mueller are liable on a constructive notice theory. * * * [T]he second question challenged only one possible ground for imposing supervisory liability * * *. * * *

The briefing at the merits stage was no different. Ashcroft and Mueller argued that the factual allegations in Iqbal's complaint were insufficient to overcome their claim of qualified immunity; they also contended that they could not be held liable on a theory of constructive notice. Again they conceded, however, that they would be subject to supervisory liability if they "had actual knowledge of the assertedly discriminatory nature of the classification of suspects as being 'of high interest' and they were deliberately indifferent to that discrimination." * * * Iqbal argued that the allegations in his complaint were sufficient under Rule 8(a)(2) and

Twombly, and conceded that as a matter of law he could not recover under a theory of respondeat superior. * * * Thus, the parties agreed as to a proper standard of supervisory liability, and the disputed question was whether Iqbal's complaint satisfied Rule 8(a)(2).

Without acknowledging the parties' agreement as to the standard of supervisory liability, the Court asserts that it must sua sponte decide the scope of supervisory liability here. * * * I agree that, absent Ashcroft and Mueller's concession, that determination would have to be made; without knowing the elements of a supervisory liability claim, there would be no way to determine whether a plaintiff had made factual allegations amounting to grounds for relief on that claim. * * * But deciding the scope of supervisory * * * liability in this case is uncalled for. * * *

[handwritten margin note: actions by judges taken without a prior motion or request from parties]

First, Ashcroft and Mueller have * * * made the critical concession that a supervisor's knowledge of a subordinate's unconstitutional conduct and deliberate indifference to that conduct are grounds for * * * liability. Iqbal seeks to recover on a theory that Ashcroft and Mueller at least knowingly acquiesced (and maybe more than acquiesced) in the discriminatory acts of their subordinates; if he can show this, he will satisfy Ashcroft and Mueller's own test for supervisory liability. * * * We do not normally override a party's concession * * *. I would * * * accept Ashcroft and Mueller's concession for purposes of this case and proceed to consider whether the complaint alleges at least knowledge and deliberate indifference.

Second, because of the concession, we have received no briefing or argument on the proper scope of supervisory liability, much less the full-dress argument we normally require. * * *

Finally, the Court's approach is most unfair to Iqbal. He was entitled to rely on Ashcroft and Mueller's concession, both in their petition for certiorari and in their merits briefs, that they could be held liable on a theory of knowledge and deliberate indifference. By overriding that concession, the Court denies Iqbal a fair chance to be heard on the question.

B

The majority, however, does ignore the concession. According to the majority, because Iqbal concededly cannot recover on a theory of *respondeat superior*, it follows that he cannot recover under any theory of supervisory liability. * * * Lest there be any mistake, * * * the majority is not narrowing the scope of supervisory liability; it is eliminating * * * supervisory liability entirely. The nature of a supervisory liability theory is that the supervisor may be liable, under certain conditions, for the wrongdoing of his subordinates, and it is this very principle that the majority rejects. * * *

* * * Even if an employer is not liable for the actions of his employee solely because the employee was acting within the scope of employment,

there still might be conditions to render a supervisor liable for the conduct of his subordinate. * * *

* * *

* * * [W]hat is most remarkable about its foray into supervisory liability is that its conclusion has no bearing on its resolution of the case. The majority says that all of the allegations in the complaint that Ashcroft and Mueller authorized, condoned, or even were aware of their subordinates' discriminatory conduct are "conclusory" and therefore are "not entitled to be assumed true." * * *

II

Given petitioners' concession, the complaint satisfies Rule 8(a)(2). Ashcroft and Mueller admit they are liable for their subordinates' conduct if they "had actual knowledge of the assertedly discriminatory nature of the classification of suspects as being 'of high interest' and they were deliberately indifferent to that discrimination." * * * Iqbal alleges that after the September 11 attacks the Federal Bureau of Investigation (FBI) "arrested and detained thousands of Arab Muslim men," Complaint ¶ 47 * * *, that many of these men were designated by high-ranking FBI officials as being " 'of high interest,' " id., ¶¶ 48, 50 * * *, and that in many cases, including Iqbal's, this designation was made "because of the race, religion, and national origin of the detainees, and not because of any evidence of the detainees' involvement in supporting terrorist activity," id., ¶ 49. The complaint further alleges that Ashcroft was the "principal architect of the policies and practices challenged," id., ¶ 10 * * *, and that Mueller "was instrumental in the adoption, promulgation, and implementation of the policies and practices challenged," id., ¶ 11. According to the complaint, Ashcroft and Mueller "knew of, condoned, and willfully and maliciously agreed to subject [Iqbal] to these conditions of confinement as a matter of policy, solely on account of [his] religion, race, and/or national origin and for no legitimate penological interest." Id., ¶ 96 * * *. The complaint thus alleges, at a bare minimum, that Ashcroft and Mueller knew of and condoned the discriminatory policy their subordinates carried out. Actually, the complaint goes further in alleging that Ashcroft and Mueller affirmatively acted to create the discriminatory detention policy. If these factual allegations are true, Ashcroft and Mueller were, at the very least, aware of the discriminatory policy being implemented and deliberately indifferent to it.

Ashcroft and Mueller argue that these allegations fail to satisfy the "plausibility standard" of *Twombly*. They contend that Iqbal's claims are implausible because such high-ranking officials "tend not to be personally involved in the specific actions of lower-level officers down the bureaucratic chain of command." * * * But this response bespeaks a fundamental misunderstanding of the enquiry that *Twombly* demands. *Twombly* does not require a court at the motion-to-dismiss stage to consider whether the factual allegations are probably true. We made it clear, on the contrary, that a court must take the allegations as true, no matter how skeptical the court may be. * * * The sole exception to this rule lies with allegations that are sufficiently fantastic to defy reality as we know it: claims about little green men, or the plaintiff's recent trip to Pluto, or experiences in time travel. That is not what we have here.

Under *Twombly*, the relevant question is whether, assuming the factual allegations are true, the plaintiff has stated a ground for relief that is plausible. * * * The complaint alleges that FBI officials discriminated against Iqbal solely on account of his race, religion, and national origin, and it alleges the knowledge and deliberate indifference that, by Ashcroft and Mueller's own admission, are sufficient to make them liable for the illegal action. Iqbal's complaint therefore contains "enough facts to state a claim to relief that is plausible on its face." * * *

I do not understand the majority to disagree with this understanding of "plausibility" under *Twombly*. Rather, the majority discards the allegations discussed above with regard to Ashcroft and Mueller as conclusory, and is left considering only two statements in the complaint: that "the [FBI], under the direction of Defendant MUELLER, arrested and detained thousands of Arab Muslim men . . . as part of its investigation of the events of September 11," Complaint ¶ 47 * * *, and that "[t]he policy of holding post-September 11th detainees in highly restrictive conditions of confinement until they were 'cleared' by the FBI was approved by Defendants ASHCROFT and MUELLER in discussions in the weeks after September 11, 2001," id., ¶ 69 * * *. I think the majority is right in saying that these allegations suggest only that Ashcroft and Mueller "sought to keep suspected terrorists in the most secure conditions available until the suspects could be cleared of terrorist activity," * * * and that this produced "a disparate, incidental impact on Arab Muslims," * * *. And I agree that the two allegations selected by the majority, standing alone, do not state a plausible entitlement to relief for unconstitutional discrimination.

But these allegations do not stand alone as the only significant, nonconclusory statements in the complaint, for the complaint contains many allegations linking Ashcroft and Mueller to the discriminatory practices of their subordinates. See Complaint ¶ 10 * * * (Ashcroft was the "principal architect" of the discriminatory policy); id., ¶ 11 (Mueller was "instrumental" in adopting and executing the discriminatory policy); id., ¶ 96 * * * (Ashcroft and Mueller "knew of, condoned, and willfully and maliciously agreed to subject" Iqbal to harsh conditions "as a matter of policy, solely on account of [his] religion, race, and/or national origin and for no legitimate penological interest").

The majority says that these are "bare assertions" that, "much like the pleading of conspiracy in *Twombly*, amount to nothing more than a 'formulaic recitation of the elements' of a constitutional discrimination claim" and therefore are "not entitled to be assumed true." * * * The fallacy of the majority's position, however, lies in looking at the relevant assertions in isolation. The complaint contains specific allegations that, in the aftermath of the September 11 attacks, the Chief of the FBI's International Terrorism Operations Section and the Assistant Special Agent in Charge for the FBI's New York Field Office implemented a policy that discriminated against Arab Muslim men, including Iqbal, solely on account of their race, religion, or national origin. See Complaint ¶¶ 47–53 * * *. Viewed in light of these subsidiary allegations, the allegations singled out by the majority as "conclusory" are no such thing. Iqbal's claim is not that Ashcroft and Mueller "knew of, condoned, and willfully and maliciously agreed to subject" him to a discriminatory practice that is left undefined; his allegation is that "they knew of, condoned, and willfully and maliciously agreed to subject" him to a particular, discrete, discriminatory policy detailed in the complaint. Iqbal does not say merely that Ashcroft was the architect of some amorphous discrimination, or that Mueller was instrumental in an ill-defined constitutional violation; he alleges that they helped to create the discriminatory policy he has described. Taking the complaint as a whole, it gives Ashcroft and Mueller " 'fair notice of what the . . . claim is and the grounds upon which it rests.' " *Twombly* * * * (quoting *Conley* * * *) * * *.

That aside, the majority's holding that the statements it selects are conclusory cannot be squared with its treatment of certain other allegations in the complaint as nonconclusory. For example, the majority takes as true the statement that "[t]he policy of holding post-September-11th detainees in highly restrictive conditions of confinement until they were 'cleared' by the FBI was approved by Defendants ASHCROFT and MUELLER in discussions in the weeks after September 11, 2001." Complaint ¶ 69 * * *. This statement makes two points: (1) after September 11, the FBI held certain detainees in highly restrictive conditions, and (2) Ashcroft and Mueller discussed and approved these conditions. If, as the majority says, these allegations are not conclusory, then I cannot see why the majority deems it merely conclusory when Iqbal alleges that (1) after September 11, the FBI designated Arab Muslim detainees as being of " 'high interest' " "because of the race, religion, and national origin of the detainees, and not because of any evidence of the detainees' involvement in supporting terrorist activity," Complaint ¶¶ 48–50 * * *, and (2) Ashcroft and Mueller "knew of, condoned, and willfully and maliciously agreed" to that discrimination, id., ¶ 96 * * *. By my lights, there is no principled basis for the majority's disregard of the allegations linking Ashcroft and Mueller to their subordinates' discrimination.

* * *

JUSTICE BREYER, dissenting.

I agree with Justice SOUTER and join his dissent. I write separately to point out that, like the Court, I believe it important to prevent unwarranted litigation from interfering with "the proper execution of the work of the Government." * * * But I cannot find in that need adequate justification for the Court's interpretation of * * * *Twombly* and Federal Rule * * * 8. The law, after all, provides trial courts with other legal weapons designed to prevent unwarranted interference. * * * A district court, for example, can begin discovery with lower level government defendants before determining whether a case can be made to allow discovery related to higher level government officials. * * * Neither the briefs nor the Court's opinion provides convincing grounds for finding these alternative case-management tools inadequate, either in general or in the case before us. * * *

NOTES AND QUESTIONS

1.   After *Twombly* and *Iqbal*, which allegations are presumed true when the court decides a motion to dismiss? Does the presumption of truth attach to allegations that are conclusory? Does it attach to allegations that are legal statements in disguise? Does it attach to allegations that are implausible because they are fantastic or unusual? See Steinman, *The Pleading Problem*, 62 Stan.L.Rev. 1293, 1298 (2010).

2.   Recall that the complaint in *Iqbal* alleged that defendants "knew of, condoned, and willfully and maliciously agreed to subject him to harsh confinement as a matter of policy solely on account of * * * religion, race, and/or national origin and for no legitimate penological interest," see First Amended Complaint ¶ 96, reproduced in the Supplement. Why was this allegation treated as conclusory and so ignored? What facts would have transformed this allegation from a "formulaic recitation" to one entitled to the presumption of truth? Must a complaint allege evidentiary facts to survive a motion to dismiss?

3.   Turkmen v. Hasty, 789 F.3d 218 (2d Cir. 2015), reversed in part, vacated in part sub nom. Ziglar v. Abbasi, 582 U.S. ___, 137 S.Ct. 1843, 1864, 194 L.Ed.2d 290, 316 (2017), which was filed—like *Iqbal*—in the aftermath of the 9/11 attacks, alleging that Muslim, South Asian, and Arab non-citizens who were in the United States in violation of immigration laws were unconstitutionally detained on suspicion of terrorism. After the Supreme Court's decision in *Iqbal*, plaintiffs filed a fourth amended complaint, and were able to supplement their allegations with information from two reports of the Office of the Inspector General of the Department of Justice. Motions to dismiss were granted as to some defendants, but denied as to others. On review, the Supreme Court concluded that the complaint plausibly alleged that some defendants showed deliberate indifference to the detainees' brutal

conditions of confinement and abuse sufficient to state a plausible constitutional claim:

> The complaint alleges that guards routinely abused respondents; that the warden encouraged the abuse by referring to respondents as "terrorists"; that he prevented respondents from using normal grievance procedures; that he stayed away from the Unit to avoid seeing the abuse; that he was made aware of the abuse via "inmate complaints, staff complaints, hunger strikes, and suicide attempts"; that he ignored other "direct evidence of [the] abuse, including logs and other official [records]"; that he took no action "to rectify or address the situation"; and that the abuse resulted in the injuries described above * * *. These allegations—assumed here to be true, subject to proof at a later stage—plausibly show the warden's deliberate indifference to the abuse. Consistent with the opinion of every judge in this case to have considered the question, including the dissenters in the Court of Appeals, the Court concludes that the prisoner abuse allegations against Warden Hasty state a plausible ground to find a constitutional violation if a *Bivens* remedy is to be implied.

582 U.S. at ___, 137 S.Ct. at 1864, 194 L.Ed.2d at 316. Without access to the Inspector General's publicly available reports, how could plaintiffs in *Abbasi* have satisfied the plausibility standard prior to discovery? See Reinert, *Pleading as Information-Forcing*, 75 L. & Contemp.Probs. 1 (2012).

4. How does the plausibility standard differ from the heightened pleading standard that the Court rejected in *Swierkiewicz*, p. 387, supra, and in *Leatherman*, p. 390, Note 2, supra? Does the plausibility standard differ from the requirement of fact-pleading under the codes? See Clermont, *Three Myths about* Twombly-Iqbal, 45 Wake Forest L.Rev. 1337, 1346 (2010). Further, to show that the pleader is entitled to relief, must the allegations in the complaint set forth the best explanation, the most likely explanation, a reasonable explanation, a probable explanation, a possible explanation, or the only explanation of the conduct that is alleged to be illicit? The Court in *Iqbal*, quoting *Twombly*, insisted that a plausibility requirement "is not akin to a 'probability requirement,' but it asks for more than a sheer possibility that a defendant has acted unlawfully." See Cavanagh, *Making Sense of* Twombly, 63 S.C.L.Rev. 97, 112 (2011) ("We are left with a sort of Goldilocks approach: probability (too much); possibility (too little); plausibility (just right)."). The Seventh Circuit has said, "What is plausible has a moderately high likelihood of occurring." In re Text Messaging Antitrust Litig., 630 F.3d 622, 629 (7th Cir. 2010) (Posner, J.).

Do you agree that the requirement of plausibility is not "a test for factual detail," but rather for "factual convincingness"? Clermont & Yeazell, *Inventing Tests, Destabilizing Systems*, 95 Iowa L. Rev. 821, 832 (2010). Is that standard consistent with the language of Rule 8?

5.   The original version of the Federal Rules included an Appendix of Forms, accompanying Rule 84. The forms were intended "to indicate, subject to the provisions of these rules, the simplicity and brevity of statement which the rules contemplate." Final Report of the Advisory Committee on Rules for Civil Procedure 55 (Nov. 1937). Rule 84 was amended in 1946 to clarify that the Forms were not mere guides but rather "sufficient to withstand attack under the rules." Advisory Committee Note (1946 amendment). In 2015, Rule 84 and the Appendix of Forms were abrogated; the accompanying Advisory Committee Note states, "The abrogation of Rule 84 does not alter existing pleading standards or otherwise change the requirement of Civil Rule 8." If those forms were sufficient before 2015, and their removal "does not alter existing pleading standards," wouldn't they remain sufficient after 2015? See Steinman, *Notice Pleading in Exile*, 41 Cardozo L.Rev. 1057, 1068–71 (2020). Looking at abrogated Form 11 as a benchmark, which of the following allegations would be sufficient to state a claim? Which are too specific? Which are too vague? Are the allegations sufficient under *Conley*? Under *Twombly/ Iqbal*?

(a)   D is legally liable to P for damages.

(b)   D negligently caused P's injury.

(c)   D negligently caused P's injuries on July 4, 20__, at Dreamworld Amusement Park.

(d)   D negligently operated a roller coaster ride on which P was a passenger on July 4, 20__, at Dreamworld Amusement Park. As a result of this negligence, P suffered a broken arm and was otherwise injured, and P incurred hospital and other medical expenses, and was prevented from transacting business, resulting in damages of $500,000.

(e)   D negligently operated a roller coaster ride on which P was a passenger on July 4, 20__, at Dreamworld Amusement Park. D was negligent because it was operating the roller coaster at excessive speed and the ride was improperly maintained. As a result of this negligence, P suffered a broken arm and was otherwise injured, and P incurred hospital and other medical expenses, and was prevented from transacting business, resulting in damages of $500,000.

(f)   D negligently operated a roller coaster ride on which P was a passenger on July 4, 20__, at Dreamworld Amusement Park. D was negligent because it was operating the roller coaster at excessive speed (the roller coaster was traveling at a speed of thirty-two mph, exceeding the safe speed by five mph) and the ride was improperly maintained. As a result of this negligence, P suffered a broken arm and was otherwise injured, and P incurred hospital and other medical expenses, and was prevented from transacting business, resulting in damages of $500,000.

(g) D negligently operated a roller coaster ride on which P was a passenger on July 4, 20__, at Dreamworld Amusement Park. D was negligent because it was operating the roller coaster at excessive speed (the roller coaster was traveling at a speed of thirty-two mph, exceeding the safe speed by five mph), and the ride was improperly maintained. P was not contributorily negligent. As a result of this negligence, P suffered a broken arm and was otherwise injured, and P incurred hospital and other medical expenses, and was prevented from transacting business, resulting in damages of $500,000.

6. Numerous studies have tried to measure the effects of *Twombly* and *Iqbal* on case-dismissal rates. A study comparing cases in 2006 (before *Twombly*) and 2010 (after *Iqbal*) concluded: "*Iqbal* and *Twombly* are associated with a pleading regime in which plaintiffs do worse at nearly every stage. They are more likely to have their case dismissed, and less likely to proceed to discovery and adjudication of the merits of their claims. Even if they survive dismissal, the cases are less likely to be successful in 2010 than in 2006." Reinert, *Measuring the Impact of Plausibility Pleading*, 101 Va.L.Rev. 2117, 2171 (2015). Another study found "an overall increase in the dismissal rate (as a function of motions) for all claims from 73.3% pre-*Twombly* to 77.2% post-*Iqbal*," and that lawsuits filed by prisoners, in forma pauperis, and pro se are "highly correlative with dismissal-rate increases." Dodson, *A New Look: Dismissal Rates of Federal Civil Claims*, 9 Judicature 127, 132, 134 (2012). The literature also emphasizes the difficulty of using grant rates as a measure of the effects of the new pleading standard. As Professor Gelbach has explained:

> [B]ecause parties can be expected to change their behavior in response to perceived changes in the pleading standard, grant rate changes do not identify judicial behavior effects. Second, even if judicial behavior effects could, somehow, be identified, they are only part of the normatively relevant story of pleading standard changes.

Gelbach, *Can the Dark Arts of the Dismal Science Shed Light on the Empirical Reality of Civil Procedure?*, 2 Stan. J. Complex Litig. 223, 293 (2014). For other studies on the practical impact of *Twombly* and *Iqbal*, see Gelbach, *Material Facts in the Debate Over* Twombly *and* Iqbal, 68 Stan.L.Rev. 369 (2016); Cooper, *King Arthur Confronts TwIqy Pleading*, 90 Or.L.Rev. 955 (2012).

7. State courts are not required to follow the Federal Rules or federal judicial standards governing the sufficiency of a complaint. State courts so far have not unanimously rejected or adopted the *Twombly* or *Iqbal* standards. See, e.g., Warne v. Hall, 373 P.3d 588, 595 (Colo. 2016) (adopting *Twombly* and *Iqbal* in interpreting the pleading standard in the Colorado Rules of Civil Procedure); Walsh v. U.S. Bank, N.A., 851 N.W.2d 598, 603 (Minn. 2014) ("[W]e now decline to engraft the plausibility standard from *Twombly* and *Iqbal* onto our traditional interpretation of Minn.R.Civ.P. 8.01."); McCurry v. Chevy

Chase Bank, 169 Wash.2d 96, 233 P.3d 861 (2010) (declining to apply the plausibility standard and explaining that the federal approach "is predicated on policy determinations specific to the federal trial courts"); Sisney v. Best Inc., 754 N.W.2d 804 (S.D. 2008) (adopting *Twombly* pleading standard for state court pleadings); Colby v. Umbrella, Inc., 184 Vt. 1, 955 A.2d 1082 (2008) (rejecting *Twombly* and retaining *Conley* standard for state court pleadings); Cullen v. Auto-Owners Insurance Co., 218 Ariz. 417, 189 P.3d 344 (2008) (rejecting *Twombly* and *Conley* standards and retaining unique Arizona state pleading requirements). See generally Clopton, *Procedural Retrenchment and the States*, 106 Calif.L.Rev. 411, 424–27 (2018). One empirical study found no systematic increase in the rate of removal in notice-pleading states. See Curry & Ward, *Are* Twombly & Iqbal *Affecting Where Plaintiffs File? A Study Comparing Removal Rates by State*, 45 Tex.Tech.L.Rev. 827 (2013).

8. In JOHNSON v. CITY OF SHELBY, MISS., 574 U.S. 10, 135 S.Ct. 346, 190 L.Ed.2d 309 (2014), the Supreme Court summarily reversed the Fifth Circuit's dismissal of a civil rights suit for failure to invoke 42 U.S.C. § 1983 in the complaint. The Court distinguished *Twombly* and *Iqbal* as pertinent to the factual allegations of a complaint, and not its legal theory:

> Petitioners stated simply, concisely, and directly events that, they alleged, entitled them to damages from the city. Having informed the city of the factual basis for their complaint, they were required to do no more to stave off threshold dismissal for want of an adequate statement of their claim. See Fed. Rules Civ. Proc. 8(a)(2) and (3), (d)(1), (e). For clarification and to ward off further insistence on a punctiliously stated "theory of the pleadings," petitioners, on remand, should be accorded an opportunity to add to their complaint a citation to § 1983. See 5 Wright & Miller, [Federal Practice and Procedure] § 1219, at 277–278 ("The federal rules effectively abolish the restrictive theory of the pleadings doctrine, making it clear that it is unnecessary to set out a legal theory for the plaintiff's claim for relief." * * *).

Id. at 12, 135 S.Ct. at 347, 190 L.Ed.2d at 309. Similarly, in SKINNER v. SWITZER, 562 U.S. 521, 131 S.Ct. 1289, 179 L.Ed.2d 233 (2011), the Supreme Court reversed the dismissal of a complaint filed by a convicted state prisoner seeking DNA testing of crime scene evidence under the federal civil rights statute, 42 U.S.C. § 1983. Justice Ginsburg, for a divided Court, underscored:

> Skinner's complaint is not a model of the careful drafter's art, but under the Federal Rules of Civil Procedure, a complaint need not pin plaintiff's claim for relief to a precise legal theory. Rule 8(a)(2) of the Federal Rules * * * generally requires only a plausible "short and plain" statement of the plaintiff's claim, not an exposition of his legal argument. See 5 C. Wright & A. Miller, Federal Practice & Procedure § 1219, pp. 277–278 (3d ed. 2004 and Supp. 2010).

Id. at 530, 190 S.Ct. at 1296, 179 L.Ed.2d at 241.

NOTE ON PLEADING STANDARDS AND PRO SE LITIGATION

Read the complaint in Erickson v. Pardus, which is reproduced in the Supplement.

ERICKSON v. PARDUS, 551 U.S. 89, 127 S.Ct. 2197, 167 L.Ed.2d 1081 (2007), was decided less than one month after *Twombly*. Plaintiff, an inmate in a Colorado prison, filed a pro se complaint alleging that defendants refused to give him necessary treatment for hepatitis C, thereby putting his life in jeopardy in violation of the Eighth Amendment to the federal Constitution. The district court dismissed the complaint for failing to allege that the denial of treatment caused substantial harm. The court of appeals affirmed, explaining that the complaint made "only conclusionary allegations" of harm. Erickson v. Pardus, 198 Fed.Appx. 694, 698 (10th Cir. 2006). The Supreme Court reversed, per curiam, emphasizing: "Specific facts are not necessary; the statement need only ' "give the defendant fair notice of what the . . . claim is and the grounds on which it rests." ' Bell Atlantic v. Twombly * * * (quoting Conley v. Gibson, * * *)." 551 U.S. at 93, 127 S.Ct. at 2200, 167 L.Ed.2d at 1085.

Can *Erickson* be reconciled with *Twombly* and *Iqbal*? Do you agree that *Erickson* "appeared to exclude pro se cases from the application of *Twombly*"? See Hubbard, *Testing for Change in Procedural Standards with Application to* Bell Atlantic v. Twombly, 42 J. Legal Stud. 35, 61 (2013). Isn't it as reasonable to say that the complaint in *Erickson* satisfied the *Twombly* standard because the statement that the prison refused to treat the inmate's hepatitis C gave defendant fair notice of the claim; provided the basic facts of who-what-where-when-and-how supporting the claim; and read in the light of "judicial experience and common sense," plausibly alleges illicit behavior leading to physical harm?

The Supreme Court traditionally has held that pro se complaints are subject to "less stringent standards than formal pleadings drafted by lawyers." Haines v. Kerner, 404 U.S. 519, 520, 92 S.Ct. 594, 596, 30 L.Ed.2d 652, 654 (1972). However, after *Twombly*, the rate of dismissal of pro se complaints has increased more than the overall dismissal rate. See Schneider, *Illiberal Construction of Pro Se Pleadings*, 159 U.Pa.L.Rev. 585, 605, 617–18 (2011). Is plaintiff's inability or unwillingness to retain counsel suggestive of the implausibility of the claims? For an illuminating discussion of this question by a divided court of appeals, see Merritt v. Faulkner, 823 F.2d 1150, 1155 (7th Cir. 1987) (per curiam). Why might a party with a meritorious claim be unable to secure counsel? See Jefferson, *Brennan Lecture—Liberty and Justice for Some: How the Legal System Falls Short in Protecting Basic Rights*, 88 N.Y.U.L.Rev. 1953 (2013).

4. FORM OF PLEADINGS; ALTERNATIVE AND INCONSISTENT STATEMENTS

Read Federal Rules of Civil Procedure 8(d) and 10(b) and related materials in the Supplement.

NOTES AND QUESTIONS

1.   Can a court reject a pleading for including too much information? Federal Rule 8(d) states that "[e]ach allegation must be simple, concise, and direct." In HEARNS v. SAN BERNADINO POLICE DEPARTMENT, 30 F.3d 1124 (9th Cir. 2008), the Court of Appeals held it was an abuse of discretion to dismiss the first amended complaint solely on the basis of its length. However, in DEYO v. INTERNAL REVENUE SERVICE, 2002 WL 1482517, *1 (D.Conn. 2002), the district court conditionally dismissed a complaint because it was "neither short nor plain," and instead ran for 43 pages including "verbatim dialogue from such things as telephone conversations." In some cases, the pleading defect is not the document's length, but rather the inability of the court and opposing party "to select the relevant material from a mass of verbiage." Salahuddin v. Cuomo, 861 F.2d 40, 42 (2d Cir. 1988). Do the Federal Rules provide a mechanism for striking redundant allegations?

2.   At common law, pleadings were designed to reduce every controversy to a single issue of law or fact. Alternative and hypothetical allegations would have made the search for the single issue impossible and therefore they were forbidden. See McDonald, *Alternative Pleading: I*, 48 Mich.L.Rev. 311 (1950). Despite occasional statements indicating that inconsistent allegations are improper, see, e.g., Sinclair v. Fotomat Corp., 140 Cal. App. 3d 217, 189 Cal. Rptr. 393, 399 (1983) (a case involving verified pleadings), the pleading of inconsistent and alternative statements is permitted if "at least one set of facts" is sufficient to support the plausibility of the pleading. Elena v. Municipality of San Juan, 677 F.3d 1, 8 (1st Cir. 2012). For example, in LEAL v. McHUGH, 731 F.3d 405 (5th Cir. 2013), suit was brought by applicants for federal jobs who had been passed over during the hiring process in favor of another applicant. Plaintiffs alleged age discrimination and personal relationship as the reasons for the selection, and the appeals court held that at the motion to dismiss stage, the pleading of inconsistent allegations was "not fatal to the complaint." Id. at 415.

3.   Rule 8(d) permits the pleading of inconsistent claims, which, as the Eleventh Circuit has explained, allows plaintiff to assert "alternative and contradictory theories of liability." ADINOLFE v. UNITED TECHS. CORP., 768 F.3d 1161, 1175 (11th Cir. 2014). As commentary observes, "[T]he federal rules recognize that inconsistency in the pleadings does not necessarily mean dishonesty, and that frequently a party, after a reasonable inquiry and for

proper purposes, must assert contradictory statements when he or she legitimately is in doubt about the factual background of the case or the legal bases that underlie affirmative recovery or defense." 5 Wright, Miller & Spencer, Federal Practice and Procedure § 1283 (4th ed.).

4. Rule 10(b) requires pleadings to contain separately numbered paragraphs, and provides that "as far as practicable," paragraphs should contain separate counts for claims arising from different transactions. For a criticism, see Tompkins v. Central Laborers' Pension Fund, 2009 WL 3836893 (C.D.Ill. 2009) (calling a requirement that the complaint set out each legal theory in a separate count "a throwback to code pleading, perhaps all the way back to the forms of action"), quoting Bartholet v. Reishauer A.G. (Zurich), 953 F.2d 1073, 1078 (7th Cir. 1992).

5. PLEADING SPECIAL MATTERS

Read Federal Rule of Civil Procedure 9 and the related materials in the Supplement.

KEARNS V. FORD MOTOR COMPANY
United States Court of Appeals, Ninth Circuit, 2009.
567 F.3d 1120.

N.R. SMITH, CIRCUIT JUDGE.

[Plaintiff filed a class action in California state court alleging violations of the California Consumers Legal Remedies Act ("CLRA") and the California Unfair Competition Law ("UCL"). The action was removed to federal court on the basis of diversity jurisdiction and, after unsuccessfully challenging remand, plaintiff filed an amended complaint. Plaintiff claimed that Ford Motor Company and its dealerships acted illegally to increase sales of Certified Pre-Owned ("CPO") vehicles, in violation of the CLRA and UCL. The district court dismissed the amended complaint with leave to amend, and plaintiff filed a Second Amended Complaint. The district court dismissed the Second Amended Complaint, with leave to amend for failing to meet the particularity requirement of Federal Rule 9(b). Plaintiff filed a Third Amended Complaint, which Defendant moved to dismiss. The district court granted the motion with leave to amend. Plaintiff then filed a Notice of Intent Not to File an Amended Complaint, whereupon the district court dismissed the case and Plaintiff timely filed a notice of appeal. The Third Amended Complaint ("TAC") was the operative complaint on appeal.]

* * *

Ford offers potential buyers three classifications of cars to purchase—new, used, and CPO. CPO vehicles are late model used vehicles, which Ford purports to put through a rigorous inspection process in order to certify that the vehicle's safety, reliability, and road-worthiness surpass non-certified used vehicles. Ford advertises and markets these CPO vehicles to purchasers at a premium (above that charged for ordinary used cars).

Ford Motor Company markets and sells the CPO program to its dealerships as a way of repackaging its used car inventory while increasing their profit margin. Ford Motor Company then charges each dealership (1) an annual fee for the program and (2) a per-vehicle fee for each vehicle in the program. Once enrolled, the dealership is supplied with marketing materials, instructional guides, and access to the CPO database, which allows the dealerships to print standard "Maroney-type" window stickers. In addition, Ford Motor Company pays to promote, market, and advertise the CPO program through a variety of print, broadcast, online, and other media. Local dealerships are responsible for the implementation of the sale and service of CPO vehicles.

Kearns makes several allegations concerning the purported benefits of CPO vehicles. Specifically, Kearns contends that Ford makes false and misleading statements concerning the safety and reliability of its CPO vehicles. Kearns claims that, by making such false statements, Ford conspires to mislead class members into believing that the CPO program guarantees a safer, more reliable, and more roadworthy used vehicle. Such statements are allegedly made to get purchasers to rely on the notion that CPO vehicles are safer due to the certification process. Ford engages in such conduct to give the buyers of CPOs "peace of mind," which purportedly costs $1,080 dollars, an amount Kearns claims exceeds the benefit of this "peace of mind."

Kearns also alleges that Ford has failed to disclose the very little oversight it has over the certification process. Kearns claims that Ford misrepresents (1) the quality of the complete repair and accident-history report; (2) the level of training of CPO technicians; and (3) the rigorous certification inspection. Such misrepresentations are claimed to provide the consumer with a sense of security that their CPO has passed a rigorous inspection, has an extended warranty, and therefore is more safe, more reliable, and more roadworthy than a regular used vehicle. Kearns argues that the inspection is not rigorous; the warranty does not cover all components; and the CPO vehicles are not any safer, more reliable, or more roadworthy than a regular used vehicle.

* * *

Kearns argues that his claims should not be subject to Rule 9(b), because (1) California state law precedent is contrary to Rule 9(b); (2) some of his claims are not based in fraud; and (3) the complaint should have been evaluated under the unfairness prong of the UCL instead. * * * We review de novo dismissals under Rule 9(b). * * * Thus, the panel must consider the matter anew, as if no decision previously had been rendered.* * *

* * *

Rule 9(b) demands that the circumstances constituting the alleged fraud "be 'specific enough to give defendants notice of the particular misconduct . . . so that they can defend against the charge and not just deny that they have done anything wrong.' " * * * "Averments of fraud must be accompanied by 'the who, what, when, where, and how' of the misconduct charged." * * * A party alleging fraud must "set forth *more* than the neutral facts necessary to identify the transaction." * * *

Rule 9(b) serves three purposes: (1) to provide defendants with adequate notice to allow them to defend the charge and deter plaintiffs from the filing of complaints "as a pretext for the discovery of unknown wrongs"; (2) to protect those whose reputation would be harmed as a result of being subject to fraud charges; and (3) to "prohibit[ ] plaintiff[s] from unilaterally imposing upon the court, the parties and society enormous social and economic costs absent some factual basis." * * * " '[W]hile a federal court will examine state law to determine whether the elements of fraud have been pled sufficiently to state a cause of action, the Rule 9(b) requirement that the circumstances of the fraud must be stated with particularity is a federally imposed rule.' " [Vess v. Ciba-Geigy Corp. USA, 317 F.3d 1097, 1103 (9th Cir. 2003)] * * *.

A.

Kearns's first argument—that Rule 9(b) does not apply to California's consumer protection statutes because California courts have not applied Rule 9(b) to the Consumer Protection Statutes, which include the CLRA and UCL—is unavailing. It is well-settled that the Federal Rules of Civil Procedure apply in federal court, "irrespective of the source of the subject matter jurisdiction, and irrespective of whether the substantive law at issue is state or federal." * * *

The CLRA prohibits "unfair methods of competition and unfair or deceptive acts or practices undertaken by any person in a transaction intended to result or which results in the sale . . . of goods or services to any consumer." Cal. Civ. Code § 1770. The UCL prohibits "unlawful, unfair or fraudulent business act[s] or practice[s]" and "unfair, deceptive, untrue or misleading advertising." Cal. Bus. & Prof. Code § 17200. Rule 9(b)'s particularity requirement applies to these state-law causes of action. * * *

B.

Kearns next argues that some of his claims are not grounded in fraud, and so should not be subject to Rule 9(b). This argument is also unavailing.

While fraud is not a necessary element of a claim under the CLRA and UCL, a plaintiff may nonetheless allege that the defendant engaged in fraudulent conduct. * * * A plaintiff may allege a unified course of fraudulent conduct and rely entirely on that course of conduct as the basis of that claim. In that event, the claim is said to be 'grounded in fraud' or to 'sound in fraud,' and the pleading * * * as a whole must satisfy the particularity requirement of Rule 9(b). * * *

Reviewing the complaint, Kearns alleges that Ford engaged in a fraudulent course of conduct. Kearns's TAC alleges that Ford Motor Company conspires with its dealerships to misrepresent the benefits of its CPO program to sell more cars and increase revenue. Kearns alleges that Ford's marketing materials and representations led him to believe that CPO vehicles were inspected by specially trained technicians and that the CPO inspections were more rigorous and therefore more safe. Kearns alleges he was exposed to these representations through (1) Ford's televised national marketing campaign; (2) sales materials found at the dealership where he bought his vehicle; and (3) sales personnel working at the dealership where he bought his vehicle. In reliance on these representations, Kearns claims he purchased a CPO vehicle. Therefore he alleges that Ford engaged in a fraudulent course of conduct.

However, Kearns fails to allege in any of his complaints the particular circumstances surrounding such representations. Nowhere in the TAC does Kearns specify what the television advertisements or other sales material specifically stated. Nor did Kearns specify when he was exposed to them or which ones he found material. Kearns also failed to specify which sales material he relied upon in making his decision to buy a CPO vehicle. Kearns does allege that he was specifically told "CPO vehicles were the best used vehicles available as they were individually hand-picked and rigorously inspected used vehicles with a Ford-backed extended warranty." Kearns does not, however, specify who made this statement or when this statement was made. Kearns failed to articulate the who, what, when, where, and how of the misconduct alleged. The pleading of these neutral facts fails to give Ford the opportunity to respond to the alleged misconduct. Accordingly, these pleadings do not satisfy the requirement of Rule 9(b) that "a party must state with particularity the circumstances constituting fraud. . . ." Because Kearns failed to plead his averments of fraud with particularity, we affirm the district court's dismissal of his TAC.

Kearns counters that his entire TAC was not grounded in fraud because all of his allegations were not averments in fraud. For example, Kearns contends that his claims against Ford for their failure to disclose information pertinent to consumers are not based in fraud. * * *

* * *

The court in *Vess* held that "where fraud is not an essential element of a claim, only allegations ('averments') of fraudulent conduct must satisfy the heightened pleading requirements of Rule 9(b)." *Vess*, 317 F.3d at 1105. Applying this rule, the court found that, "[b]ecause Vess's allegations . . . do not rely entirely on a unified fraudulent course of conduct, his claims . . . are not 'grounded in fraud' " as a whole. Id. at 1106. The court found that some of Vess's claims were "not based on fraud . . . neither mention[ing] the word 'fraud,' nor alleg[ing] facts that would necessarily constitute fraud."[g] Id. at 1105–06. The claims of failure to disclose in *Vess* were held to "describe non-fraudulent conduct." Id. at 1106.

However, in *Vess*, this court derived its elements of fraudulent misrepresentation from the California Court of Appeals case, *Hackethal v. National Casualty Co.*, 189 Cal.App.3d 1102, 234 Cal.Rptr. 853, 857 (1987). Id. at 1105, 234 Cal.Rptr. 853 * * *. These elements, however, have been changed by the Supreme Court of California to include nondisclosure. * * * Because the Supreme Court of California has held that nondisclosure is a claim for misrepresentation in a cause of action for fraud, it (as any other fraud claim) must be pleaded with particularity under Rule 9(b). * * * Kearns's claims of nondisclosure were couched in general pleadings alleging Ford's intent to conceal from customers that CPO vehicles were essentially the same as ordinary used vehicles. Such general pleadings do not satisfy the heightened pleading requirements of Rule 9(b). * * *

C.

Finally, Kearns contends that the district court erred by failing to specifically evaluate his complaint under the unfairness prong of the UCL. Specifically, Kearns contends that a determination of whether a business practice violates the unfairness prong is fact intensive and not conducive to resolution on a motion to dismiss. We disagree.

The UCL prohibits unfair competition, which it broadly defines as including "any unlawful, unfair or fraudulent business act or practice and unfair, deceptive, untrue or misleading advertising." * * * Each prong of the UCL is a separate and distinct theory of liability; thus, the "unfair" practices prong offers an independent basis for relief. * * *

We held in *Vess* that if "the claim is said to be 'grounded in fraud' . . . the pleading of that claim as a *whole* must satisfy the particularity requirement of Rule 9(b). Id. at 1103–04 (emphasis added).[h] Kearns's TAC alleges a unified course of fraudulent conduct, namely that Ford Motor Company and its "co-conspirator" dealerships knowingly misrepresent to the public that CPO vehicles are safer and more reliable, with an intent to induce reliance and defraud consumers. Because Kearns's TAC alleges a unified fraudulent course of conduct, his claims against Ford are grounded

---

g   Alteration in original.

h   Alteration in original.

in fraud. His entire complaint must therefore be pleaded with particularity. Thus, the TAC was properly dismissed and no error was committed by not separately analyzing his claims under the unfairness prong of the UCL.

* * *

IV. CONCLUSION

The requirement in Rule 9(b) of the Federal Rules * * * that allegations of fraud be pleaded with particularity applies to claims which are made in federal court under the CLRA and UCL. We hold that Kearns's entire TAC was grounded in fraud. Thus, under Rule 9(b), Kearns's failure to plead his claims with particularity merited that complaint's dismissal. * * *

AFFIRMED.

NOTES AND QUESTIONS

1.   Are you convinced that Rule 9(b) imposes a heightened pleading standard, as the Ninth Circuit held in *Kearns*, on claims that are "grounded in fraud" or "sound in fraud," even when fraud is not an element of the claim? See Fairman, *Heightened Pleading*, 81 Tex.L.Rev. 551 (2002).

2.   *Kearns* held that the Third Amended Complaint was deficient because it failed to allege the specific advertisements that plaintiff saw and relied upon. Under California law, plaintiff can win after trial if the misrepresentations and false statements are a part of an extensive campaign, without proof of individual reliance on a particular advertisement. Some district courts have questioned whether the *Kearns* approach to Rule 9(b) raises problems under the Rules Enabling Act, explaining that to require plaintiffs to plead claims with more particularity "than they are required to prove them at trial would abridge and modify their substantive legal rights." Opperman v. Path, Inc., 84 F.Supp.3d 962, 978 (N.D.Cal. 2015). What is your response? But see Yastrub v. Apple Inc., 173 F.Supp.3d 972 (N.D.Cal. 2016) (particularity required for state consumer claims).

3.   Do the reasons for requiring the heightened pleading of fraud apply as well to claims of mistake? See Richman, Lively & Mell, *The Pleading of Fraud: Rhymes Without Reason*, 60 S.Calif.L.Rev. 959, 979 (1987). According to one court, fraud and mistake share a "common thread" that justifies their similar treatment:

> Unlike other intentional or negligent acts, both fraud and mistake are claims which, by their nature, involve mutual or unilateral confusion and/or delusion. Both claims derive from a party's own subjective misperception, misapprehension or misunderstanding and subsequent reliance. Such claims often may not be readily apparent to others and may appear to contradict existing facts or contracts. Unless defendant and others share plaintiff's view of the situation, they will find it difficult to grasp plaintiff's claim. * * * Allegations of

fraud and mistake seek to undermine the reality of presumed facts and are by their nature unsettling to the parties and their agreements. In conclusion, from the rule's historical foundations, its text, and the nature of fraud and mistake actions, this Court finds that Rule 9(b) applies to actions wherein the major component involves significant delusion or confusion of a party, whether intentional or not.

Breeden v. Richmond Community College, 171 F.R.D. 189, 202 (M.D.N.C. 1997). But see Fairman, *An Invitation to the Rulemakers—Strike Rule* 9(b), 38 U.C.Davis L.Rev. 281 (2004) (questioning whether allegations of mistake pose any reputational injuries).

4. Is it reasonable to require plaintiff, on pain of dismissal, to plead with particularity matters that are within the exclusive custody of defendant? See Sovern, *Reconsidering Federal Civil Rule* 9(b): *Do We Need Particularized Pleading Requirements in Fraud Cases?*, 104 F.R.D. 143 (1985). If the pleading of fraud is special, might there also be a need for special discovery rules that might include limited presuit discovery, mandatory discovery while the motion to dismiss is pending, or cost-shifting? Consider these possibilities in the context of discovery and case management, see Chapters 10 and 11, infra.

6. PLEADING DAMAGES

———

Read Federal Rule of Civil Procedure 9(g) in the Supplement.

———

NOTES AND QUESTIONS

1. Federal Rule 9(g) requires that a claim for special damages "be specifically stated." Does the requirement of specific statement differ from Rule 9(b)'s requirement that the circumstances of a fraud be stated with "particularity"? The Seventh Circuit Court of Appeals has written, "It is hard to know how specific is specific enough, but 'specificity' must be something less than the 'particularity' standard that Rule 9(b) prescribes for allegations of fraud." Pippen v. NBCUniversal Media, LLC, 734 F.3d 610, 614 (7th Cir. 2013).

2. Rule 9(g) does not define what damages are special. A typical definition looks to whether the damages would be "unusual" for the type of claim asserted. For example, in a suit alleging breach of contract, general damages are the benefit of the bargain; special damages would be compensation for additional losses. See Schonfeld v. Hilliard, 218 F.3d 164, 175 (2d Cir. 2000). In an action for trespass, general damages are for injury to the land itself; special damages would be lost profits from plans to use the property. See Weyerhaeuser Co. v. Brantley, 510 F.3d 1256, 1266 (10th Cir. 2007).

Considering the different claims asserted, which of the following items of damages would require specificity in pleading?

(a) Medical bills incurred as a result of personal injuries in a car crash.

(b) Unpaid health insurance benefits for multiple services rendered.

(c) Aggravation of a pre-existing medical condition.

(d) Losses that flow from contractual breach other than the value of the promised performance.

3. The normal consequence of failing to plead special damages is barring the pleader from proving them at trial. However, with regard to a few types of cases, the existence of special damages is an integral part of the claim, and the failure to plead them renders the complaint subject to dismissal. Does the fact that a distinction along these lines is drawn by the courts of the state in which the federal court sits have any relevance to Rule 9(g)? Whether the specificity requirement is met is governed by federal law. See Brown & Williamson Tobacco Corp. v. Jacobson, 713 F.2d 262 (7th Cir. 1983). However, the federal court looks to state law to determine the elements of the claim. Thus, when state law required a libel claim to allege special damages, and the complaint failed to contain this allegation, the complaint was dismissed. See McGowan v. Homeward Residential, Inc., 500 Fed.Appx. 882 (11th Cir. 2012).

4. Is a request for attorney's fees an item of special damages that must be specifically stated in the complaint? In 1993, Rule 54 was amended in order "to provide for a frequently recurring form of litigation not initially contemplated by the rules—disputes over the amount of attorney's fees to be awarded in the large number of actions in which prevailing parties may be entitled to such awards." Fed. R. Civ. P. 54 Advisory Committee Notes. Some courts take the view that a request for attorney's fees is to be raised by motion under Rule 54(d)(2), and that Rule 9(g) does not control, but there is division on this issue. See Riordan v. State Farm. Mut. Auto. Ins. Co., 589 F.3d 999 (9th Cir. 2009).

7. THE PRAYER FOR RELIEF

———

Read Federal Rules of Civil Procedure 8(a)(3) and 54(c) in the Supplement.

———

NOTES AND QUESTIONS

1. What is the relationship between Rule 8(a)(3), which requires the complaint to contain "a demand for the relief sought," and Rule 54(c), which authorizes the court to order a final judgment granting "the relief to which party is entitled, even if the party has not demanded that relief in its

pleading"? In ANHEUSER-BUSCH, INC. v. JOHN LABATT LTD., 89 F.3d 1339, 1349 (8th Cir. 1996), cert. denied, 519 U.S. 1109, 117 S.Ct. 944, 136 L.Ed.2d 833 (1997), plaintiff failed to mention punitive damages in its pleadings or answers to interrogatories. Plaintiff did plead a valid claim for injurious falsehood under state law and requested instructions on punitive damages a week prior to the trial. Over defendant's objection the matter was presented to the jury, which awarded punitive damages in the amount of $5 million. The trial court struck the punitive damage award on the ground that plaintiff had not given sufficient notice of its intent to seek punitive damages. The appellate court affirmed. It did not cite Rules 8(a)(3), 9(g), or 54(c). If the goal is to prevent unfair surprise to defendant, should punitive damages (or some other form of relief) be available even if not specified in the demand for relief, so long as the facts justify such an award and no prejudice is shown? See Bowles v. Osmoste Utilities Services, Inc., 443 F.3d 671, 675 (8th Cir. 2006).

2.   Most states follow the federal rule that relief is not limited by the ad damnum clause, with the exception that default judgments may not exceed the amount of damages sought or include a type of relief not demanded in the complaint. Why should a defendant who defaults be protected by a cap on damages, but a defendant who participates be exposed to damages greater than those pleaded by the plaintiff? Should the remedy cap in Rule 54(c) apply if defendant appears but then does not respond to the complaint or defend the action? The Ninth Circuit has held that Rule 54(c) controls, but there are decisions to the contrary. See Fong v. United States, 300 F.2d 400, 413 (9th Cir. 1962).

B. RESPONDING TO THE COMPLAINT

BACKGROUND NOTE ON FEDERAL RULE 12

After being served with the summons and complaint, defendant must respond to the lawsuit. Federal Rule 12 gives defendant two options. Defendant may file a responsive pleading, called an answer; or, defendant may file a motion that raises one or more of the defenses and objections set out in that rule.

Rule 12(b) sets out seven defenses—some of which are familiar to you from earlier chapters. For example, defendant may challenge the court's subject-matter jurisdiction through a motion to dismiss on that ground under Rule 12(b)(1). What is the consequence of a defendant's failure to raise an objection to subject-matter jurisdiction in its initial Rule 12 motion? See Rule 12(h). By contrast, if defendant omits from the motion defenses listed in Rule 12(b)(2)–(5) (namely, lack of personal jurisdiction, improper venue, insufficient process, and insufficient service of process) those defenses are waived if they were available at the time of the motion. See Rule 12(g)(2) and Rule 12(h)(1). Which other defenses are preserved under Rule 12(h)?

The defenses in Rules 12(b)(1) through 12(b)(5) and 12(b)(7) are essentially modern counterparts to the common-law plea of abatement, which allowed defendant to challenge the pleading by asserting facts outside the record that create an impediment to the suit's going forward. By raising a plea in abatement, the party conceded the merits. See Dodson, *Hybridizing Jurisdiction*, 99 Calif.L.Rev. 1439, 1452 (2011). There never was any doubt that courts may consider extra-pleading material on these motions. For a Rule 12(b)(6) motion, however, the court may consider material outside the pleadings only by treating the motion as one for summary judgment under Rule 56. See Rule 12(d).

1. THE TIME PERMITTED FOR A RESPONSE

Read Federal Rules of Civil Procedure 4(d), 6(b), and 12(a) and (b) and the accompanying materials in the Supplement.

Federal Rule 12(a), as amended in 2009, gives most defendants 21 calendar days from the date of service of the complaint to respond to the complaint either by a Rule 12 motion or by answering the complaint. How does the "waiver of service" provision under Rule 4(d) affect the time period for answering the complaint? The time to respond also may be extended by court order. See Rule 6(b). How does the filing of a Rule 12(b) motion affect the timing for the filings of a responsive pleading? See Rule 12(a)(4).

2. MOTION FOR A MORE DEFINITE STATEMENT AND MOTION TO STRIKE

Read Federal Rules of Civil Procedure 12(e) and 12(f) and the accompanying materials in the Supplement.

GARCIA V. HILTON HOTELS INTERNATIONAL, INC.
United States District Court, District of Puerto Rico, 1951.
97 F.Supp. 5.

ROBERTS, DISTRICT JUDGE. The action here is for damages for defamation brought by plaintiff, a citizen and resident of Puerto Rico, against defendant, a Delaware corporation, in the District Court of Puerto Rico and removed to this Court by defendant corporation. The complaint sets forth two causes of action and the paragraphs considered herein are identical in each cause. Defendant has moved to dismiss the complaint for failure to state a claim upon which relief can be granted and, in the alternative, to strike Paragraphs 5, 6, 7 and 8 and for a more definite statement.

In * * * [support] of its motion to dismiss, defendant contends that no publication of the alleged slanderous statement is alleged and that the complaint, therefore, fails to state a cause of action. This contention will be considered first with respect to Paragraph 4 of the complaint, which reads as follows: "4. On August 22, 1950, the plaintiff was violently discharged by the defendant, being falsely and slanderously accused of being engaged in bringing women from outside the Hotel and introducing them into the rooms thereof for the purpose of developing prostitution in the Hotel and that such women brought by him from outside the Hotel and introduced therein carried on acts of prostitution in said Hotel."

* * *

The controlling question here, with respect to the motion to dismiss, is whether the allegations of Paragraph 4 of the complaint, state a claim upon which relief can be granted. An examination of the authorities is persuasive that [it] does. It is settled, with respect to motions to dismiss for insufficiency of statement, that the complaint is to be construed in the light most favorable to the plaintiff with all doubts resolved in his favor and the allegations accepted as true. If, when a complaint is so considered, it reasonably may be anticipated that plaintiff, on the basis of what has been alleged, could make out a case at trial entitling him to some relief, the complaint should not be dismissed. * * *

In the instant case, it is true that Paragraph 4, of the complaint, fails to state, in so many words, that there was a publication of the alleged slanderous utterance and, to that extent, the cause of action is defectively stated. However, it does not follow that the allegations do not state a claim upon which relief can be granted. It is alleged that plaintiff was "violently discharged" and was "falsely and slanderously accused" of procuring for prostitution. While in a technical sense, this language states a conclusion, it is clear that plaintiff used it intending to charge publication of the slanderous utterance and it would be unrealistic for defendant to claim that it does not so understand the allegations. * * * Clearly, under such allegations it reasonably may be conceived that plaintiff, upon trial, could adduce evidence tending to prove a publication. * * *

In further support of its motion to dismiss, defendant contends that the alleged slanderous utterance was conditionally privileged. Conceding that to be so does not require that a different conclusion be reached with respect to the motion to dismiss. Rule 12(b) requires that every defense in law or fact be asserted in a responsive pleading when one is required or permitted under the rules. The rule, however, enumerates certain defenses which may be asserted by motion to dismiss, all of which go to the jurisdiction except that of failure to state a claim upon which relief can be granted, Rule 12(b)(6). And this latter defense may be asserted successfully by a motion prior to responsive pleading only when it appears to a certainty that plaintiff would be entitled to no relief under any state of fact which could be proved in support of the claim asserted by him. * * *

The conclusiveness of privilege as a defense depends upon whether the privilege involved [is] absolute or conditional. When the privilege involved is absolute, it constitutes a finally determinative or conclusive defense to an action based on the utterance. Consequently, when it appears from a complaint that absolute privilege exists, the defense of failure to state a claim properly may be asserted to accomplish a dismissal on motion under Rule 12(b). It is for the court to determine the existence of privilege and when absolute privilege is found, it constitutes an unassailable defense and, clearly, in such a case, the claim stated is one upon which relief cannot be granted.

But conditional privilege is not a conclusive defense to an action based on a slanderous utterance. It is but a qualified defense which may be lost to the defendant if plaintiff can prove abuse of the privilege or actual malice. * * * When from the allegations contained therein, a complaint indicates the availability of the defense of conditional privilege, it cannot be held therefrom as a matter of law, that there has been a failure to state a claim upon which relief can be granted, such as will warrant dismissal of the complaint on motion under Rule 12(b)(6), for the factual question remains whether defendant abused the privilege or made the communication maliciously. * * *

As has been noted, on motion to dismiss for failure to state a claim [the] complaint must be construed in the light most favorable to plaintiff with all doubts resolved in his favor and the allegation taken as true. That being so, when allegations are sufficient to sustain the defense of conditional privilege they will be, generally, sufficient to permit the introduction of evidence tending to prove abuse of the privilege or actual malice. Save in some extraordinary situation, allegations which are adequate for the admission of evidence to prove the defense of qualified privilege are adequate for the admission of evidence to negative that defense. It appears from the complaint in the instant case that defendant is entitled to raise the defense of conditional privilege. But this defense may be lost to it if plaintiff proves abuse of the privilege or actual malice. And, clearly, plaintiff may introduce evidence under the allegations for the purpose of proving abuse of the privilege or actual malice. Therefore, it is concluded that defendant's motion to dismiss the complaint for failure to state a claim upon which relief can be granted should be denied.

The conclusion to deny defendant's motion to dismiss requires that consideration be given its alternative motion to strike Paragraphs 5, 6, 7 and 8 of the complaint. It is alleged in these paragraphs, in substance, that upon being discharged, plaintiff made claim with the Labor Department of Puerto Rico for severance pay and overtime as is provided for by law (Section 20, Organic Act of Labor Department of Puerto Rico, approved April 14, 1931); that during a hearing on such claim held by the Labor Department, defendant, falsely and slanderously, repeated its charge that plaintiff had been engaged in procuring for prostitution; and, that, after said hearing defendant had compromised plaintiff's claim for severance pay and overtime. As respects defendant's motion to strike, the controlling allegations are contained in Paragraph 7 of this complaint.

Section 4 of "An Act Authorizing Civil Actions to recover Damages for Libel and Slander," enacted by the Legislature of Puerto Rico and approved on February 19, 1902, (Code of Civil Procedure of Puerto Rico, Ed. 1933, page 309) provides in part as follows: "Section 4. A publication or communication shall not be held or deemed malicious when made in any legislative or judicial proceeding or in any other proceeding authorized by law. * * *"

The effect of the above quoted portions of the statute is to confer absolute privilege upon any communication made in any of the proceedings contemplated therein. If the hearing held by the Labor Department on plaintiff's claim for severance pay and overtime, referred to in Paragraph 7 of the complaint, is a proceeding within the meaning of the phrase "or any other proceeding authorized by law" as used in said Section 4 of the Act of February 19, 1902, the utterance was absolutely privileged and such privilege constitutes a conclusive defense in an action based on that utterance.

It appears that the hearing on plaintiff's claim by the Labor Department, referred to in Paragraph 7 of the complaint, is a proceeding "authorized by law" within the meaning of Section 4 of the Act of February 19, 1902. The Labor Department is authorized to hold such a hearing by Act No. 122 of the Legislature of Puerto Rico, approved April 27, 1949, which statute requires the Commissioner of Labor to enforce labor protecting laws. * * *

It appears, upon examination, that this Statute (Act No. 122) has for its purpose the protection of the welfare of the workman and the furtherance of the public good, and that when hearings are held pursuant to its terms it is necessary, if those purposes are to be effectuated, that those called upon to give evidence therein must be protected against liability, civil or criminal, for communications given in evidence at such hearings. And this without regard for the motives of the witness or the truth or falsity of his statements. For otherwise, the giving of full, free and honest testimony, essential to the enforcement of such laws, will be discouraged. Therefore, communications made by witnesses in the course of such hearings, should be absolutely privileged in the same manner and to like extent as those made in the course of a judicial proceeding.

* * *

Clearly, then, the utterance of the defendant made during the Labor Department hearing referred to in Paragraph 7 of the complaint was absolutely privileged and that Paragraph 7 is, therefore, redundant in that it fails to state a claim upon which relief can be granted. It appears then, that defendant's motion to strike Paragraphs 5, 6, 7 and 8 should be granted.

The parties have agreed on hearing in open court that Paragraph 9 of the complaint should be stricken. And this Court being of the opinion that Paragraphs 5, 6, 7 and 8 should be stricken as redundant, defendant's motion for a more definite statement need be considered only with respect to the allegations of Paragraph 4 of the complaint.

As has been noted herein, conditional privilege is an affirmative defense which properly should be raised by its assertion in a responsive pleading. Consequently, when it appears from a complaint that the defense of conditional privilege may be available to a defendant, the allegations thereof should be reasonably adequate to permit the preparation of a responsive pleading asserting such defense. But when, in an action for slander, the complaint fails to set out substantially the utterance alleged to have been slanderously made or the facts relied upon to establish a publication of such utterance, such omission constitutes vagueness such as is a ground for granting a motion for more definite statement within the contemplation of Rule 12(e). Obviously, when such material allegations are insufficient, it would be unreasonable to require the defendant to prepare a responsive pleading without a more definite statement of the pertinent facts.

Considering the allegations of Paragraph 4 of the complaint, * * * [they] suffer from vagueness with respect to the utterance alleged to have been slanderously made and the facts relied upon to establish a publication of the utterance. It is concluded that the defendant here is entitled to a more definite statement setting forth substantially the words alleged to have been slanderously uttered and the facts relied upon to establish a publication thereof.

Defendant's motion to dismiss the complaint for failure to state a claim upon which relief can be granted is denied. Defendant's motion to strike Paragraphs 5, 6, 7 and 8 of the complaint is granted. Defendant's motion for a more definite statement with respect to the matters prescribed in this opinion, is granted. Paragraph 9 of the complaint is ordered stricken. The decisions herein reached are hereby made applicable to the second cause of action set out in the complaint.

NOTES AND QUESTIONS

1.   As originally adopted, Federal Rule 12(e) had two roles. A motion for a more definite statement under the rule could be made when the complaint was so vague or unintelligible as to make the opposing party unable to respond. Rule 12(e) also could operate as a "bill of particulars" to elicit the facts supporting the claim. In that latter role, Rule 12(e) generated a great deal of litigation, and came to be regarded as dilatory and unnecessary given the availability of discovery later in the litigation. Amendments adopted in 1948 eliminated the bill of particulars from federal practice. See Advisory Committee Note to proposed 1948 amendment to Rule 12(e), stating, "The tendency of some courts freely to grant extended bills of particulars has served to neutralize any helpful benefits derived from Rule 8, and has overlooked the intended use of the rules on depositions and discovery."

2.   In defendants' hands, Rule 12(f) provides a mechanism for asking the court "to strike" from the complaint "redundant, immaterial, impertinent, or scandalous matter." The motion is typically not granted absent a showing of prejudice to the movant. See Sheffield v. City of Boston, 319 F.R.D. 52 (D.Mass. 2016). As held in GATEWAY BOTTLING, INC. v. DAD'S ROOTBEER CO., 53 F.R.D. 585, 588 (W.D.Pa. 1971): "To strike material as scandalous it must be obviously false and unrelated to the subject matter of the action. * * * The facts here may be unpleasant for plaintiff to have on the record and they certainly contain charges of reprehensible conduct but the same is true of many facts of life which are entitled to be pleaded as relevant to a cause of action or defense." The question whether allegations really are prejudicial seems to turn on whether the contents of the pleadings will be disclosed to the jury. Because the motion to strike may be used as a dilatory tactic, and the sanction of striking a portion of the complaint may be a drastic remedy, the motion is disfavored and frequently is denied.

3.   Rule 12(f) may not be used to dismiss all or part of a complaint. For example, in WHITTLESTONE, INC. v. HANDI-CRAFT CO., 618 F.3d 970 (9th Cir. 2010), the court of appeals held it was an abuse of discretion for the district court to strike a claim for lost profits and consequential damages from the complaint on the ground that the damages were precluded as a matter of law. Rather, the appropriate mechanism was a motion to dismiss for failure to state a claim under Rule 12(b)(6). Why should the number of the rule and the form of the objection carry such significance?

4.   The court has authority on its own initiative and without a motion by defendant to strike portions of a complaint and so to relieve defendant of responding to the redundant or immaterial allegations. See Simmons v. Abruzzo, 49 F.3d 83, 86–87 (2d Cir. 1995). Before dismissing a complaint that is not concise and direct, see p. 419, Note 1, supra, would it be appropriate for the court initially to strike matters that are prolix or repetitive? See Salahuddin v. Cuomo, 861 F.2d 40 (2d Cir. 1988).

5.   To what extent could plaintiff in *Garcia* have phrased the complaint to avoid the granting of defendant's motions? How should plaintiff in *Garcia*

alter the complaint to satisfy the court's order for a more definite statement? Can he merely eliminate some of the allegations that gave rise to the conditional privilege? Suppose the court had denied defendant's Rule 12(e) motion. How else might defendant have learned the details of the alleged defamatory publication? What are the advantages of the Rule 12(e) motion compared to these other means?

3. MOTION TO DISMISS FOR FAILURE TO STATE A CLAIM

Read Federal Rules of Civil Procedure 12(b)(6) and 12(d) and the materials accompanying them in the Supplement.

a. Historical Antecedents: The Common Law Demurrer

At common law, a party who faced a complaint could either answer, responding to each of the claims, or demur. If defendant demurred, he was not allowed to contest the complaint's facts if the demurrer was overruled. On the other hand, if the demurrer was sustained, plaintiff had no right to replead or amend her complaint. Later, these harsh rules were modified to allow a party to proceed to the merits if the demurrer was overruled and to allow plaintiff to amend her complaint if the demurrer was sustained. The common-law demurrer was incorporated into code pleading. In most code states, a complaint could be dismissed on the pleadings by a motion for failure to state facts sufficient to constitute a cause of action, absence of subject-matter jurisdiction, and deficiencies in the form of the pleading. The demurrer and its code equivalents elevated the importance of technicalities and produced considerable delay and dissatisfaction. The "speaking demurrer," a demurrer that attempted to introduce material outside the pleadings, was not permitted at common law or under the Codes. See Pike, *Objections to Pleadings Under the New Federal Rules of Civil Procedure,* 47 Yale L.J. 50, 51 (1937).

b. Rule 12(b)(6) and Its Relation to Rule 8(a)

Federal Rule 12(b)(6) is the federal system's counterpart to the common-law demurrer. The purpose of the motion is to test the sufficiency of the complaint, and not to prove or disprove the allegations of the complaint. The motion must be made before the filing of a responsive pleading, but the defense is preserved and may be raised even at trial. See Rule 12(h)(2).

Practice under Rule 12(b)(6) must be read in tandem with Rule 8(a). So long as the complaint was expected only to give notice to defendant of plaintiff's claim, the utility of the Rule 12(b)(6) motion was as a screening device for complaints that failed as a pure question of law. The earlier judicial attitude was expressed by the Ninth Circuit in RENNIE & LAUGHLIN, INC. v. CHRYSLER CORP., 242 F.2d 208, 213 (9th Cir. 1957):

> Pretrial conference; the discovery procedures; and motions for a more definite statement, judgment on the pleadings and summary judgment, all provide useful tools for the sifting of allegations and the determination of the legal sufficiency of an asserted claim. The salvaged minutes that may accrue from circumventing these procedures can turn to wasted hours if the appellate court feels constrained to reverse the dismissal of an action. That is one of the reasons why a motion to dismiss is viewed with disfavor in the federal courts. Another is the basic precept that the primary objective of the law is to obtain a determination of the merits of any claim; and that a case should be tried on the proofs rather than the pleadings. * * * This is not to say or imply that a motion to dismiss should never be granted. It is obvious that there are cases which justify and indeed compel the granting of such motion. The line between the totally unmeritorious claims and the others cannot be drawn by scientific instruments but must be carved out case by case by the sound judgment of trial judges. That judgment should be exercised cautiously on such a motion.

The Supreme Court's decisions in *Twombly* and *Iqbal*, p. 391 and p. 402, supra, signaled the increased importance of the Rule 12(b)(6) motion as a mechanism for filtering out pleadings prior to discovery. It was anticipated that *Twombly* and *Iqbal* would encourage defendants' use of Rule 12(b)(6) motions, and that lower courts would more readily grant such motions. Studies underscore the difficulty of measuring these cases' effects on litigant and judicial behavior, but generally they report a higher grant-rate of motions to dismiss. See p. 416, Note 6, supra.

NOTES AND QUESTIONS

1.   In SHAW v. MERRITT-CHAPMAN & SCOTT CORP., 554 F.2d 786 (6th Cir. 1977), cert. denied, 434 U.S. 852, 98 S.Ct. 167, 54 L.Ed.2d 122 (1977), the Sixth Circuit held that absent specific language to the contrary by the district court, a dismissal under Rule 12(b)(6) constitutes an adjudication on the merits, and the dismissal is with prejudice, so further actions on the same claim are barred. It may, however, be an abuse of discretion for a court to grant a Rule 12(b)(6) dismissal without giving plaintiff an opportunity to amend its complaint. See Eminence Capital, LLC v. Aspeon, Inc., 316 F.3d 1048, 1052 (9th Cir. 2003) ("Dismissal with prejudice and without leave to amend is not appropriate unless it is clear on de novo review that the complaint could not be saved by amendment. A

district court's failure to consider the relevant factors and articulate why dismissal should be with prejudice instead of without prejudice may constitute an abuse of discretion."). Without access to discovery, will a curative amendment always be possible?

2.   Does the requirement of plausible pleading apply to defenses raised under Rules 12(b)(1) through (b)(5)? For example, does it supplant the requirement that in a diversity jurisdiction suit, the amount in controversy alleged by plaintiff will be accepted unless the court can determine to a "legal certainty" that recovery is jurisdictionally insufficient? See p. 237, Note 1, supra. See Mallgren v. Microsoft Corp., 975 F.Supp.2d 451 (S.D.N.Y. 2013) (dismissing diversity suit for lack of subject-matter jurisdiction because the allegations of damages were "conclusory").

3.   Recall that the consequence of omitting a defense under Rule 12 depends upon the defense that is omitted. Does a defendant who omits a defense under Rule 12(b)(6) waive that defense? See Rule 12(g)(2) and Rule 12(h)(2). In IN RE APPLE IPHONE ANTITRUST LITIGATION, 846 F.3d 313 (9th Cir. 2017), affirmed on other grounds sub nom., Apple Inc. v. Pepper, 587 U.S. ___, 139 S.Ct. 1514, 203 L.Ed.2d 802 (2019), the district court granted defendant's fourth motion to dismiss, which asserted a ground for Rule 12(b)(6) dismissal that defendant had failed to raise in its earlier motions. The Ninth Circuit reversed the dismissal, but not because of defendant's omission. The appellate court stated that although the district court "may have erred" in considering the motion, the error was harmless, and explained that "a reviewing court * * * should generally be forgiving of a district court's ruling on the merits of a late-filed Rule 12(b)(6) motion." Id. at 316, 319. In its view, "[d]enying late-filed Rule 12(b)(6) motions and relegating defendants to the three procedural avenues specified in Rule 12(h)(2) can produce unnecessary and costly delays, contrary to the direction of Rule 1." Id. at 318. What is your response?

4. ANSWERING THE COMPLAINT

Read Federal Rules of Civil Procedure 8 and 10 in the Supplement.

If defendant has moved under Rule 12(b) or Rule 12(e) but the court denies the motion, defendant must file an answer or otherwise plead in response. What is the current time period in which to respond? See Rule 12(a)(4)(A)–(B). An answer is a kind of pleading, and is governed by Rule 8 and, as to its form, Rule 10.

a. Denials

Federal Rule 8(b) requires a defendant to make one of three responses to the contents of plaintiff's complaint: Defendant may admit, deny, or plead insufficient information in response to each allegation. How will the court treat averments to which defendant does not specifically respond? See Rule 8(b)(6). To avoid an unintended admission, defendants often will include an all-inclusive paragraph in their answers denying each and every averment of the complaint unless otherwise admitted.

Rule 8 (and most state rules) allow the defendant to make a general denial of the complaint, but only if the pleader "intends in good faith to deny all the allegations of the pleading," including jurisdiction. Using a general denial can be risky. If a court decides that a general denial does not "fairly respond to the substance of the allegation," Rule 8(b)(2), it may deem defendant to have admitted plaintiff's specific averments. In addition, a general denial does not put in issue such matters as capacity or conditions precedent, which under Rule 9 defendant must specifically challenge.

a formal *relevant* *by a party*

NOTES AND QUESTIONS

1. An admission in an answer is binding on the party and may not be controverted at trial or on appeal, unless the court allows it to be withdrawn. Further, as explained in Crest Hill Land Development, LLC v. City of Joliet, 396 F.3d 801, 805 (7th Cir. 2005), admitting an allegation in the answer "has the effect of withdrawing the question" from contention.

2. In BIGGS v. PUBLIC SERVICE COORDINATED TRANSPORT, 280 F.2d 311, 313–14 (3d Cir. 1960), a diversity-of-citizenship case, defendant specifically denied that the amount in controversy exceeded the statutory requirement, and entered a qualified general denial that included the paragraph alleging that defendant was incorporated in New Jersey. The court stated:

> We cannot for a moment believe that defendant's counsel was denying in good faith that his client was a New Jersey corporation. We think the only fair interpretation of the pleading in this case is that the denial does not run to the allegation of defendant's citizenship. Therefore, that allegation must be deemed to be admitted.

Even if the allegation is deemed to be admitted, does the court have an independent obligation to determine its subject-matter jurisdiction?

3. To what extent should defendant be permitted to respond that "it neither admits nor denies" plaintiff's allegations? Some states have pleading rules that prohibit "evasive denials." E.g., 2022 Conn. Practice Book (Revision of 1998), § 10–47, Ct. R. Super. Ct. Civ. § 10–47 ("[W]here any matter of fact is alleged with divers circumstances, some of which are untruly stated, it shall

not be sufficient to deny it as alleged, but so much as is true and material should be stated or admitted, and the rest only denied."[i]). Compare the language of Federal Rule 8(b). In KING VISION PAY PER VIEW, LTD. v. J.C. DIMITRI'S RESTAURANT, INC., 180 F.R.D. 332 (N.D.Ill. 1998), defendant responded to several allegations in the complaint with "Neither admit nor deny the allegations of said Paragraph—, but demand strict proof thereof." The court found that this response violated Rule 8(b) and therefore deemed defendant to have admitted those allegations. Id. at 333–34.

4.   Does the plausible pleading standard apply to a denial? Several years ago Professor Miller concluded that the answer is "[s]omewhat uncertain," focusing on the absence from Rule 8(b) of "the magic word 'showing,'" upon which the Court placed emphasis in *Twombly*, and the fact that a defensive pleading typically is alleged "in a formulary, conclusory, and uninformative fashion along the style illustrated in Form 30" (now abrogated with all of the forms, see p. 415, Note 5, supra). He adds:

> If, in fact, plausibility pleading is retained and held to turn strictly on the language of Rule 8(a)(2), federal courts might not extend it to Rules 8(a)(1), 8(a)(3), 8(b), and 8(c). If that proves to be true, the Advisory Committee would have to consider whether to revise Rule 8 in order to correct this pleading burden imbalance in deference to the quest for the metaphorical level litigation playing field. What's good for the goose should be good for the gander. Conversely, if the new pleading structure is applied to all pleading elements by judicial decision or Rule revision, then in theory defensive allegations could be challenged by a Rule 12(f) motion to strike for insufficiency as a corollary to Rule 12(b)(6), although the former now speaks of an "insufficient defense" and the latter of a "failure to state a claim." In reality, any increase in the burden of pleading jurisdiction, the demand for relief, or the plausibility of denials and affirmative defenses, also would cause cost and delay, consequences that would have to be considered in determining whether efficiency and cost savings actually were being realized from the shift to plausibility pleading.

Miller, *From* Conley *to* Twombly *to* Iqbal: *A Double Play on the Federal Rules of Civil Procedure*, 60 Duke L.J. 1, 102–03 (2010).

5.   Some statements are phrased in the negative but imply the affirmative. Suppose plaintiff alleged that defendant owes her $89,000 under a contract. Defendant's denial "that he owes plaintiff $89,000" could be held to be an admission that the amount owed is a penny less than the stated amount. See Thompson v. Hamilton Motor Co., 170 Cal. 737, 151 P. 122 (1915). The cases taking this approach are from the early twentieth century. Is the underlying principle consistent with the requirement of Rule 8(b)(2), that a denial "must fairly respond to the substance of the allegation"? Is it also consistent with the requirements of Federal Rule 8(b)(4), that "[a] party that

---

[i]   As stated in original.

intends in good faith to deny only part of an allegation must admit the part that is true and deny the rest"?

6. A conjunctive denial is a statement in which all propositions considered together are not true, but which does not specifically deny the truth of each proposition alone. See Luse v. U.S., 49 F.2d 241, 244 (9th Cir. 1931) ("It is a familiar rule of pleading that a conjunctive denial is an ineffective denial of the several conjoined statements for the reason that, if any one of them is not true, the conjunctive denial would be true."). Is the insufficiency of a conjunctive denial supported by the Federal Rules?

b. Affirmative Defenses

———

Read Federal Rule of Civil Procedure 8(c) in the Supplement.

———

Defenses under Federal Rule 12(b) may be raised either by a pre-answer motion or responsive pleading. Rule 8(c)(1) instructs that a responding party must "affirmatively state any avoidance or affirmative defense," and then provides a non-exhaustive list of 18 such defenses. The rule's reference to "an avoidance or affirmative defense" generally includes two types of defensive allegations:

> An affirmative defense admits the allegations of the complaint, but challenges plaintiff's legal right to bring the action by suggesting a reason why relief is not available;

> An avoidance avers matters outside the complaint that cannot be raised by denial.

See 5 Wright & Miller, Federal Practice and Procedure § 1271 (4th ed.). The rule does not define when a defensive allegation is to be treated as an avoidance or as an affirmative defense, and a large case law has developed on this question. It traditionally was said that affirmative defenses may be raised only in a responsive pleading.

NOTES AND QUESTIONS

1. If a defense is assigned to defendant and it is not raised as an avoidance or affirmative defense, the defense is waived. Other than with the specific defenses listed in Rule 8(c), how does the court determine on whom to assign the burden of pleading? Review the Note on the Burden of Pleading, p. 387, supra. In INGRAHAM v. UNITED STATES, 808 F.2d 1075 (5th Cir. 1987), the Fifth Circuit explained:

> Determining whether a given defense is "affirmative" within the ambit of Rule 8(c) is not without some difficulty. We find the salient comments of Judge Charles E. Clark, Dean of the Yale Law School,

later Chief Judge of the United States Second Circuit Court of Appeals, and the principal author of the Federal Rules, to be instructive:

> [J]ust as certain disfavored allegations made by the plaintiff . . . must be set forth with the greatest particularity, so like disfavored defenses must be particularly alleged by the defendant. These may include such matters as fraud, statute of frauds . . . , statute of limitations, truth in slander and libel . . . and so on. In other cases the mere question of convenience may seem prominent, as in the case of payment, where the defendant can more easily show the affirmative payment at a certain time than the plaintiff can the negative of nonpayment over a period of time. Again it may be an issue which may be generally used for dilatory tactics, such as the question of the plaintiff's right to sue . . . a vital question, but one usually raised by the defendant on technical grounds. These have been thought of as issues "likely to take the opposite party by surprise," which perhaps conveys the general idea of fairness or the lack thereof, though there is little real surprise where the case is well prepared in advance.

Clark, *Code Pleading,* 2d ed. 1947, § 96 at 609–10, quoted in 5 C. Wright & A. Miller, *Federal Practice and Procedure: Civil, § 1271,* p. 313 (1969).

Also pertinent to the analysis is the logical relationship between the defense and the cause of action asserted by the plaintiff. This inquiry requires a determination (1) whether the matter at issue fairly may be said to constitute a necessary or extrinsic element in the plaintiff's cause of action; (2) which party, if either, has better access to relevant evidence; and (3) policy considerations: should the matter be indulged or disfavored? * * *

Central to requiring the pleading of affirmative defenses is the prevention of unfair surprise. A defendant should not be permitted to "lie behind a log" and ambush a plaintiff with an unexpected defense. * * * The instant cases illustrate this consideration. Plaintiffs submit that, had they known the statute [limiting non-medical damages] would be applied, they would have made greater efforts to prove medical damages which were not subject to the statutory limit. In addition, plaintiffs maintain that they would have had an opportunity and the incentive to introduce evidence to support their constitutional attacks on the statute.

* * *

We view the limitation on damages as an "avoidance" within the intendment of the residuary clause of 8(c). Black's Law Dictionary, 5th ed. 1979, defines an avoidance in pleadings as "the allegation or statement of new matter, in opposition to a former pleading, which, admitting the facts alleged in such former pleading, shows cause why they should not have their ordinary legal effect." Applied to the present discussion, a plaintiff pleads the traditional tort theory of malpractice and seeks full damages. The defendant responds that assuming recovery is in order under the ordinary tort principles, because of the new statutory limitation, the traditional precedents "should not have their ordinary legal effect."

* * * [W]e conclude that the Texas statutory limit on medical malpractice damages is an affirmative defense which must be pleaded timely and that in the cases at bar the defense has been waived.

808 F.2d at 1078–79.

Note, however, that this sort of waiver is not irreversible. A defendant that omits an affirmative defense from its answer might still amend its answer to add the defense—although such an amendment may require permission from either the court or the opposing party. See Chapter 7, Section D, p. 443, infra. Some kind of defenses, however, cannot be saved from waiver. As discussed in the Background Note on Federal Rule 12, p. 428, supra, the defenses listed in Rules 12(b)(2)–(5) (lack of personal jurisdiction, improper venue, insufficient process, and insufficient service of process) can be irretrievably waived if omitted from either a pre-answer motion or defendant's initial answer.

2.   Can the court, sua sponte, consider an affirmative defense that defendant has failed to plead? In DAY v. McDONOUGH, 547 U.S. 198, 126 S.Ct. 1675, 164 L.Ed.2d 376 (2006), the Supreme Court held that district courts may, but are not required to, raise sua sponte the timeliness of a state prisoner's habeas petition when the state defendant has failed to raise the limitations period as an affirmative defense. To mitigate any unfairness, the Court further held that the district court is required to give the parties fair notice and an opportunity to present their positions on why the limitations period should not yield dismissal. Should this practice extend to affirmative defenses that do not have systemic implications for the justice system? Should it matter if plaintiff can show no prejudice or had notice of the defense? Is the approach consistent with the language of Rule 8(c), which provides a party "must affirmatively state" any avoidance or affirmative defense?

3.   Federal Rule 12(f) may be used to strike an affirmative defense from the responsive pleading. Should the motion be granted (with leave to amend) if the affirmative defense fails to meet the standard of plausible pleading otherwise applicable to a pleading? Before *Twombly* and *Iqbal*, an affirmative defense generally was treated as sufficient if it provided notice of the possible existence of the defense and defendant's intention to advance it. Courts are divided on whether affirmative defenses are now subject to the requirement of plausible pleading.

C. THE REPLY

Read Federal Rule of Civil Procedure 7(a) and the accompanying materials in the Supplement.

NOTES AND QUESTIONS

1.   Pleadings basically have two levels in the federal courts, the complaint and the answer. If defendant's answer contains a counterclaim, plaintiff must serve an answer to the counterclaim. See Rule 12(a)(1)(B); Rule 7(a)(3). Otherwise, it is within the discretion of the court to order plaintiff to serve a reply to defendant's answer. See Rule 7(a)(7). If a third party is brought into the action under Federal Rule 14, a third-party complaint will be filed and a third-party answer will be allowed. See Rule 7(a)(5), (6).

2.   Under Federal Rule 7, is a crossclaim a pleading? Is a notice of removal a pleading? Is the answer to a crossclaim a pleading?

3.   Allegations to which a reply is not required are considered avoided or denied and plaintiff may controvert them at trial. See Rule 8(b)(6). Conversely, matters requiring a responsive pleading are taken as admitted if not denied in the reply or if a reply is not filed. See Rule 8(b)(6).

D. AMENDMENTS

Read Federal Rule of Civil Procedure 15 and the accompanying materials in the Supplement.

BEECK v. AQUASLIDE 'N' DIVE CORP.
United States Court of Appeals, Eighth Circuit, 1977.
562 F.2d 537.

BENSON, DISTRICT JUDGE.

* * *

This case is an appeal from the trial court's exercise of discretion on procedural matters in a diversity personal injury action.

Jerry A. Beeck was severely injured on July 15, 1972, while using a water slide. He and his wife, Judy A. Beeck, sued Aquaslide 'N' Dive Corporation (Aquaslide), a Texas corporation, alleging it manufactured the slide involved in the accident, and sought to recover substantial damages on theories of negligence, strict liability and breach of implied warranty.

Aquaslide initially admitted manufacture of the slide, but later moved to amend its answer to deny manufacture; the motion was resisted. The district court granted leave to amend. On motion of the defendant, a separate trial was held on the issue of "whether the defendant designed, manufactured or sold the slide in question." This motion was also resisted by the plaintiffs. The issue was tried to a jury, which returned a verdict for the defendant, after which the trial court entered summary judgment of dismissal of the case. Plaintiffs took this appeal, and stated the issues presented for review to be:

> 1. Where the manufacturer of the product, a water slide, admitted in its Answer and later in its Answer to Interrogatories both filed prior to the running of the statute of limitations that it designed, manufactured and sold the water slide in question, was it an abuse of the trial court's discretion to grant leave to amend to the manufacturer in order to deny these admissions after the running of the statute of limitations?

* * *

I.   Facts

* * *

In 1971 Kimberly Village Home Association of Davenport, Iowa, ordered an Aquaslide product from one George Boldt, who was a local distributor handling defendant's products. The order was forwarded by Boldt to Sentry Pool and Chemical Supply Co. in Rock Island, Illinois, and Sentry forwarded the order to Purity Swimming Pool Supply in Hammond, Indiana. A slide was delivered from a Purity warehouse to Kimberly Village, and was installed by Kimberly employees. On July 15, 1972, Jerry A. Beeck was injured while using the slide at a social gathering sponsored at Kimberly Village by his employer, Harker Wholesale Meats, Inc. Soon after the accident investigations were undertaken by representatives of the separate insurers of Harker and Kimberly Village. On October 31, 1972, Aquaslide first learned of the accident through a letter sent by a representative of Kimberly's insurer to Aquaslide * * *. Aquaslide forwarded this notification to its insurer. Aquaslide's insurance adjuster made an on-site investigation of the slide in May, 1973, and also interviewed persons connected with the ordering and assembly of the slide. An inter-office letter dated September 23, 1973, indicates that Aquaslide's insurer was of the opinion the "Aquaslide in question was definitely manufactured by our insured." The complaint was filed October 15, 1973. Investigators for three different insurance companies, representing Harker, Kimberly and the defendant, had concluded that the slide had been manufactured by Aquaslide, and the defendant, with no information to the contrary, answered the complaint on December 12, 1973, and admitted that it "designed, manufactured, assembled and sold" the slide in question.

The statute of limitations on plaintiff's personal injury claim expired on July 15, 1974. About six and one-half months later Carl Meyer, president and owner of Aquaslide, visited the site of the accident prior to the taking of his deposition by the plaintiff. From his on-site inspection of the slide, he determined it was not a product of the defendant. Thereafter, Aquaslide moved the court for leave to amend its answer to deny manufacture of the slide.

II.   Leave to Amend

* * *

In *Foman v. Davis*, 371 U.S. 178, 83 S.Ct. 227, 9 L.Ed.2d 222 (1962), the Supreme Court had occasion to construe * * * Rule 15(a) * * *:

> Rule 15(a) declares that leave to amend "shall be freely given when justice so requires," this mandate is to be heeded. * * * [This provision was renumbered as Rule 15(a)(2), and the language was altered by the 2007 restyling of the Federal Rules. These changes are not substantive.] If the underlying facts or circumstances relied upon by a plaintiff may be a proper subject of relief, he ought to be afforded an opportunity to test his claim on the merits. In the absence of any apparent or declared reason—such as undue delay, bad faith or dilatory motive on the part of the movant, repeated failure to cure deficiencies by amendments previously allowed, undue prejudice to the opposing party by virtue of allowance of the amendment, futility of amendment, etc.—the leave sought should, as the rules require, be "freely given." Of course, the grant or denial of an opportunity to amend is within the discretion of the District Court * * *.

371 U.S. at 182, 83 S.Ct. at 230. * * *

This Court in *Hanson v. Hunt Oil Co.*, 398 F.2d 578, 582 (8th Cir. 1968), held that "[p]rejudice *must be shown*." (Emphasis added). The burden is on the party opposing the amendment to show such prejudice. In ruling on a motion for leave to amend, the trial court must inquire into the issue of prejudice to the opposing party, in light of the particular facts of the case. * * *

Certain principles apply to appellate review of a trial court's grant or denial of a motion to amend pleadings. First, as noted in *Foman v. Davis*, allowance or denial of leave to amend lies within the sound discretion of the trial court * * * and is reviewable only for an abuse of discretion. * * * The appellate court must view the case in the posture in which the trial court acted in ruling on the motion to amend. * * *

It is evident from the order of the district court that in the exercise of its discretion in ruling on defendant's motion for leave to amend, it searched the record for evidence of bad faith, prejudice and undue delay which might be sufficient to overbalance the mandate of Rule 15(a) * * * and Foman v. Davis, that leave to amend should be "freely given." Plaintiffs had not at any time conceded that the slide in question had not been manufactured by the defendant, and at the time the motion for leave to amend was at issue, the court had to decide whether the defendant should be permitted to litigate a material factual issue on its merits.

In inquiring into the issue of bad faith, the court noted the fact that the defendant, in initially concluding that it had manufactured the slide, relied upon the conclusions of three different insurance companies, each of which had conducted an investigation into the circumstances surrounding the accident. This reliance upon investigations of three insurance companies, and the fact that "no contention has been made by anyone that the defendant influenced this possibly erroneous conclusion," persuaded the court that "defendant has not acted in such bad faith as to be precluded from contesting the issue of manufacture at trial." The court further found "[t]o the extent that 'blame' is to be spread regarding the original identification, the record indicates that it should be shared equally."

In considering the issue of prejudice that might result to the plaintiffs from the granting of the motion for leave to amend, the trial court held that the facts presented to it did not support plaintiffs' assertion that, because of the running of the two year Iowa statute of limitations on personal injury claims, the allowance of the amendment would sound the "death knell" of the litigation. In order to accept plaintiffs' argument, the court would have had to assume that the defendant would prevail at trial on the factual issue of manufacture of the slide, and further that plaintiffs would be foreclosed, should the amendment be allowed, from proceeding against other parties if they were unsuccessful in pressing their claim against Aquaslide. On the state of the record before it, the trial court was unwilling to make such assumptions, and concluded "[u]nder these circumstances, the Court deems that the possible prejudice to the plaintiffs is an insufficient basis on which to deny the proposed amendment." The court reasoned that the amendment would merely allow the defendant to contest a disputed factual issue at trial, and further that it would be prejudicial to the defendant to deny the amendment.

The court also held that defendant and its insurance carrier, in investigating the circumstances surrounding the accident, had not been so lacking in diligence as to dictate a denial of the right to litigate the factual issue of manufacture of the slide.

On this record we hold that the trial court did not abuse its discretion in allowing the defendant to amend its answer.

* * *

NOTES AND QUESTIONS

1. Parties may amend their complaints at various points in a litigation. In *Beeck*, defendant initially moved to amend before the trial took place. Should the court have granted the motion then?

2. Federal Rule 15(a) permits amendment without consent of the court in certain circumstances. What is the justification for this rule? Until 2009, the rule allowed a party to amend as a matter of course only before being served with a responsive pleading. What are the time limits under the current rule?

3. Rule 15(b) permits amendment of the pleadings both during and after trial. How does the procedure described in Rule 15(b)(1) differ from that in Rule 15(b)(2)? What are the consequences of a failure to amend under each subdivision? Keep in mind that Rule 15(b) applies to defenses as well as claims, and may be used to amend a pleading during or after trial to include a defense that was not earlier asserted.

In MOORE v. MOORE, 391 A.2d 762 (D.C. 1978), a custody suit brought by the father, the court granted the mother's post-trial motion to conform the pleadings to the evidence and for attorney's fees, and awarded her custody despite the absence of any request for affirmative relief in her pretrial pleadings. The father argued that it was an abuse of discretion under the state amendment rule for the court to have permitted a post-trial pleading amendment and to award affirmative relief, contending that he did not have notice. In particular, he argued that he did not know that matters contained in the counterclaim were at stake and "he was not prepared, nor given an adequate opportunity, to contest them." Id. at 768. The court rejected these arguments:

> Our treatment of this argument must begin with [District of Columbia] Rule 15(b), which is identical to Fed.R.Civ.Pro. 15(b). Our analysis is accordingly aided by authorities which have interpreted the federal rule. * * * If issues not raised in pleadings are tried by express consent of the parties, there can be no question about the propriety of permitting amendment. The difficult issue arises when, as in most Rule 15(b) cases, "implied consent" is asserted.

> Whether parties have impliedly contested a matter—i.e., whether parties recognize that an issue not stated by the pleadings entered the case * * *—is determined by searching the trial record for indications that the party contesting the amendment received actual notice of the injection of the unpleaded matters, as well as

an adequate opportunity to litigate such matters and to cure any surprise from their introduction. * * *

The clearest indications of a party's implied consent to try an issue lie in the failure to object to evidence, or in the introduction of evidence which is clearly apposite to the new issue but not to other matters specified in the pleadings. * * *

A. Custody

Although at the time of trial only appellant, and not his wife, had filed an action for custody, we conclude—without difficulty—that appellant was on timely notice that the court would decide not merely whether he was entitled to custody but, more broadly, would determine who was entitled to custody. Mrs. Moore asserted in her answer to appellant's complaint that "the best interests of the child" would be served by the child's being in her custody. Moreover, both parties introduced evidence supporting their respective qualifications for custodian. * * *

B. Child Support

The pretrial pleadings do not include a claim for child support. Our determination, therefore, again must be whether the issue was litigated by implied consent. For two reasons we find that it was.

First, and most germane, we believe that the resolution of child support inheres in a custody battle where the best interests of the child are the focal concern. * * * The trial judge recognized this relationship when she opined that a grant of support was required by the court's duty to afford complete relief. Second, our conclusion is bolstered by appellee's introduction of evidence of the financial needs of the child. As appellee points out, this evidence was not contested on relevance grounds; it served to put appellant on notice. * * *

C. Visitation Rights and Bond

Appellant does not dispute that visitation rights are a proper subject for determination as part of the overall custody question. In her Rule 15(b) motion, appellee did not request imposition of a bond covering her husband's visits with Jessica. However, because trial courts are given broad discretion in resolving custody cases, * * * and ought to fashion relief to foster and safeguard a child's best interests, * * * we find no fault with the imposition of a bond upon a parent whose history reflected a capacity for absconding with the child. * * *

D. Attorneys' Fees

This court has determined that even though there is no specific statutory authorization for attorneys' fees awards in child custody cases, courts are empowered to award them to a parent who has enlisted legal assistance to protect the interests of the child. * * *

E. Separate Maintenance

The grant of spousal support is a different matter. The initial pleadings did not mention a claim for separate maintenance, which is not customarily a part of a child custody suit between parents whose marital relationship had not been—and was not being—litigated. While evidence of Mrs. Moore's financial needs was admitted without objection relatively late in the proceedings, we cannot conclude that this evidence was so uniquely pertinent to her support alone, in contrast with the custody or the child support issues, that it justifies our concluding that appellant had adequate, timely notice of, and an opportunity to contest, a claim by his wife for her own support. We find no other indication of record that appellant impliedly consented to try his wife's support claim, Rule 15(b), nor can we conclude that the award was a proper, supportable element of full relief in the child custody action. * * * We therefore find an abuse of trial court discretion in permitting amendment of the pleadings to include separate maintenance and, thereafter, in making such an award.

* * *

391 A.2d at 768–70.

NOTE AND QUESTIONS

What were plaintiff's tactical options in *Moore* in deciding whether to introduce evidence at trial on an issue that clearly was not within the pleadings? The litigant may object and keep the evidence out, but this will induce the other side to request leave to amend, perhaps even to add an issue of which the party seeking amendment previously was not aware. On the other hand, a failure to object may be taken as implied consent to try the issue, thus permitting an amendment to conform to the proof. Whenever a party fails to object in this situation a second dilemma must be faced: whether or not to produce evidence on the point in question. Should the implied consent rule ever be applied in a case like *Moore* when relief is sought by a defendant who failed to file a counterclaim asking for any relief whatsoever? How important was it that the action involved child custody?

NOTE ON THE RELATION BACK DOCTRINE

Federal Rule 15(c) allows amendments that add a new claim or defense to "relate back" to the date of the original pleading, and thus avoid being barred by a statute of limitations. An amendment may relate back under Rule 15(c)(1)(A) (which was added to the rule in 1991), whenever an applicable state statute of limitations would permit relation back. Before Rule 15(c) was amended the circuit courts disagreed whether to characterize relation back as "substantive" or "procedural." In SCHIAVONE v. FORTUNE, 477 U.S. 21, 106 S.Ct. 2379, 91 L.Ed.2d 18 (1986), a diversity case, plaintiffs mistakenly failed to name the correct defendant in the original complaint. Plaintiffs meant to sue the owners of Fortune magazine; however, instead of naming "Time, Incorporated," they named "Fortune," which is not a legal entity. Plaintiffs were unable to serve "Fortune," so they amended their complaint to name "Time, Incorporated." Both the amendment and service of process on "Time, Incorporated" took place after the statute of limitations had run. The Supreme Court applied Rule 15(c) instead of New Jersey's more liberal relation-back rule and dismissed the claims as time barred. The revision to Rule 15(c) makes clear that a pleader gets the benefit of a state limitations rule that is less restrictive than the federal.

Relation back is permitted under Federal Rule 15(c)(1)(B) when the claim or defense that is added arises out of the same conduct, transaction, or occurrence as does the original pleading. In addition, relation back is authorized if the pleader "attempted" to allege the claim or defense, but, for example, amendment is required to cure a deficiency.

Federal Rule 15(c)(1)(C) addresses amendments that seek to change a party after the statute of limitations has expired. Three conditions must be met. The first condition is that the claim that the amendment seeks to assert against the changed party must be transactionally related to the claims in the original pleading, so that Rule 15(c)(1)(B) is met. The second condition is that the changed party must have received notice of the action within the time for serving the summons and complaint under Rule 4(m) (since 2015, 90 days). The notice can be formal or informal, provided the new party "will not be prejudiced" in defending on the merits. The third condition is that the changed party "knew or should have known" that the claim would have been asserted against it, "but for a mistake concerning the proper party's identity." Rule 1(c)(1)(C)(ii).

———

In KRUPSKI v. COSTA CROCIERE S.P.A., 560 U.S. 538, 130 S.Ct. 2485, 177 L.Ed.2d 48 (2010), a cruise passenger sued Costa Cruise, the company that had issued her ticket, for injuries sustained during the cruise. After the limitations period had run, Costa Cruise filed its answer, asserting that it was not the proper defendant, and that it was only the agent for Costa Crociere, an Italian company that was the actual carrier and vessel operator. Costa Cruise then moved for summary judgment, stating that Costa Crociere was the proper defendant. The district court dismissed Costa Cruise from the action, and granted plaintiff leave to amend the complaint to name Costa Crociere as defendant. Costa Crociere, represented by the same counsel as the original defendant, moved to dismiss arguing that the amended complaint did not relate back. The district court dismissed the amended complaint as out of time. The Eleventh Circuit affirmed, but the Supreme Court reversed:

> The Court of Appeals first decided that Krupski either knew or should have known of the proper party's identity and thus determined that she had made a deliberate choice instead of a mistake in not naming Costa Crociere as a party in her original pleading. * * * By focusing on Krupski's knowledge, the Court of Appeals chose the wrong starting point. The question under Rule 15(c)(1)(C)(ii) is not whether Krupski knew or should have known the identity of Costa Crociere as the proper defendant, but whether Costa Crociere knew or should have known that it would have been named as a defendant but for an error. Rule 15(c)(1)(C)(ii) asks what the prospective defendant knew or should have known during the Rule 4(m) period, not what the plaintiff knew or should have known at the time of filing her original complaint. * * *

> Information in the plaintiff's possession is relevant only if it bears on the defendant's understanding of whether the plaintiff made a mistake regarding the * * * proper party's identity. * * *

> Respondent urges that the key issue under Rule 15(c)(1)(C)(ii) is whether the plaintiff made a deliberate choice to sue one party over another. * * * We agree that making a deliberate choice to sue one party instead of another while fully understanding the factual and legal differences between the two parties is the antithesis of making a mistake concerning the proper party's identity. We disagree, however, with respondent's position that any time a plaintiff is aware of the existence of two parties and chooses to sue the wrong one, the proper defendant could reasonably believe that the plaintiff made no mistake. The reasonableness of the mistake is not itself at issue. * * * [A] deliberate but mistaken choice does not foreclose a finding that Rule 15(c)(1)(C)(ii) has been satisfied.

> This reading is consistent with the purpose of relation back: to balance the interests of the defendant protected by the statute of limitations with the preference * * * for resolving disputes on their merits. * * * A prospective defendant who legitimately believed that the limitations period had passed without any attempt to sue him has a strong interest in repose. But repose would be a windfall for a prospective defendant who understood, or who should have understood, that he escaped suit during the limitations period only because the plaintiff misunderstood a

crucial fact about his identity. Because a plaintiff's knowledge of the existence of a party does not foreclose the possibility that she has made a mistake of identity about which that party should have been aware, such knowledge does not support that party's interest in repose.

Our reading is also consistent with the history of Rule 15(c)(1)(C). That provision was added in 1966 to respond to a recurring problem in suits against the Federal Government, particularly in the Social Security context. * * * Individuals who had filed timely lawsuits challenging the administrative denial of benefits often failed to name the party identified in the statute as the proper defendant—the current Secretary of what was then the Department of Health, Education, and Welfare—and named instead the United States; the Department of Health, Education, and Welfare itself; the nonexistent "Federal Security Administration"; or a Secretary who had recently retired from office. * * * By the time the plaintiffs discovered their mistakes, the statute of limitations in many cases had expired, and the district courts denied the plaintiffs leave to amend on the ground that the amended complaints would not relate back. Rule 15(c) was therefore "amplified to provide a general solution" to this problem. * * * It is conceivable that the Social Security litigants knew or reasonably should have known the identity of the proper defendant either because of documents in their administrative cases or by dint of the statute setting forth the filing requirements. * * * Nonetheless, the Advisory Committee clearly meant their filings to qualify as mistakes under the Rule.

560 U.S. at 548, 130 S.Ct. at 2493, 177 L.Ed.2d at 57. The Supreme Court also rejected the argument that plaintiff's delay in filing an amended complaint was grounds for denying relation back, explaining that Rule 15(c) "plainly sets forth an exclusive list of requirements for relation back, and the amending party's diligence is not among them." Plaintiff's conduct is relevant only to the extent it "informs the prospective defendant's understanding of whether the plaintiff initially made a 'mistake concerning the proper party's identity.' " Id. at 540, 130 S.Ct. at 2488, 177 L.Ed.2d at 52.

NOTES AND QUESTIONS

1. Assume that during the course of an arrest two police officers handcuff the detainee and he suffers broken bones. The detainee is later released without being charged. Two years after the event, the detainee sues the Police Department and "two unknown named police officers." After the statute of limitations has run, plaintiff amends his complaint and specifically names the two officers who arrested him, but includes no claim against the

police department. The newly named defendants, represented by the same attorney who represents the police department, move to dismiss the amended complaint on the ground that the statute of limitations has run. The record indicates that the police officers did not know of the lawsuit before the limitations period expired, but they were aware of its pendency within the 90 days for serving the summons and complaint under Federal Rule 4(m).

Does the amendment relate back to the original date of the complaint? Did plaintiff make a "mistake" about the identity of the arresting officers or did he simply not know their identity? Would it be relevant if the officers concealed their identity, and that under state law fraudulent concealment tolls the statute of limitations? See Worthington v. Wilson, 8 F.3d 1253 (7th Cir. 1993).

2.   Assume all of the facts set out in Note 1, except that plaintiff, not knowing the identity of the arresting officers, named in his original complaint the police department and two police officers named as "John Doe" and "Jane Doe" defendants. Would these claims relate back under *Krupski*? See Sherman, *Amending Complaints to Sue Previously Misnamed or Unidentified Defendants after the Statute of Limitations Has Run: Questions Remaining from the* Krupski *Decision*, 15 Nev.L.J. 1329 (2015). Would it matter to the analysis if relation back is timely under state law? See Hogan v. Fischer, 738 F.3d 509 (2d Cir. 2013).

E. SUPPLEMENTAL PLEADINGS

———

Read Federal Rules of Civil Procedure 13(e) and 15(d) in the Supplement.

———

Federal Rule 15(d) provides that the court may allow the filing of a supplemental pleading based on facts not existing when the original complaint was filed. A supplemental pleading can be used to cure defects in the original pleading, to add new claims, or to provide additional facts that update the complaint. The rule's purpose is to promote "as complete an adjudication of the dispute between the parties as possible," William Inglis & Sons Baking Co. v. ITT Continental Baking Co., Inc., 668 F.2d 1014, 1057 (9th Cir. 1981), and "permits the bringing of new claims * * * to permit the economical and speedy disposition of the controversy," Keith v. Volpe, 858 F.2d 467, 473 (9th Cir. 1988), cert. denied, 493 U.S. 813, 110 S.Ct. 61, 107 L.Ed.2d 28 (1989). However, there are limits to this practice, and supplementation may be denied when the pleading introduces a "separate, distinct and new cause of action." Planned Parenthood of S. Ariz. v. Neely, 130 F.3d 400, 402 (9th Cir. 1997).

NOTES AND QUESTIONS

1.   Federal Rule 13(e) permits defendants to use a supplemental pleading to assert counterclaims that arise after serving an answer. As with Rule 15(d), the decision to allow a party to file a supplemental pleading asserting a counterclaim is within the discretion of the district court. See generally 6 Wright, Miller & Kane, Federal Practice and Procedure § 1428 (3d ed.).

2.   Are supplemental pleadings governed by the same relation back analysis as amended pleadings? Rule 15(d) makes no mention of relation back, and courts take divergent approaches. In DAVIS v. PIPER AIRCRAFT CORP., 615 F.2d 606, 609 n.3 (4th Cir. 1980), plaintiff moved to amend his complaint pursuant to Rule 15(a)(1) to reflect his new capacity as ancillary administrator of an estate, which allowed him to go forward with a wrongful death action filed nine months earlier. According to the Court of Appeals, if "the test of Fed.R.Civ.P. 15(c) is met, a supplemental pleading should ordinarily be given the same relation back effect as an amended pleading." Would relation back be appropriate when the supplementation attempts to allege an entirely different transaction by amendment?

F. PROVISIONS TO DETER FRIVOLOUS PLEADINGS

Read Federal Rule of Civil Procedure 11, 28 U.S.C. § 1927, and the accompanying material in the Supplement.

SUROWITZ v. HILTON HOTELS CORP.

Supreme Court of the United States, 1966.
383 U.S. 363, 86 S.Ct. 845, 15 L.Ed.2d 807.

Certiorari to the United States Court of Appeals for the Seventh Circuit.

JUSTICE BLACK delivered the opinion of the Court.

[Petitioner, Dora Surowitz, a stockholder in Hilton Hotels Corporation, filed a derivative action on behalf of herself and other stockholders charging that the officers and directors of the corporation had defrauded it of several million dollars in violation of the Securities Act of 1933, the Securities Exchange Act of 1934, and the Delaware General Corporation Law. The complaint was 60 printed pages and signed by petitioner's counsel in compliance with the then-existing language of Federal Rule 11. Petitioner also verified the complaint pursuant to Rule 23(b) (now Rule

23.1), stating that some of the allegations in the complaint were true and that she "on information and belief" thought that all the other allegations were true. The district court, before requiring defendants to answer, granted their motion to depose petitioner.]

* * *

* * * In this examination Mrs. Surowitz showed in her answers to questions that she did not understand the complaint at all, that she could not explain the statements made in the complaint, that she had a very small degree of knowledge as to what the lawsuit was about, that she did not know any of the defendants by name, that she did not know the nature of their alleged misconduct, and in fact that in signing the verification she had merely relied on what her son-in-law had explained to her about the facts in the case. On the basis of this examination, defendants moved to dismiss the complaint, alleging that "1. It is a sham pleading, and 2. Plaintiff, Dora Surowitz, is not a proper party plaintiff. * * *" In response, Mrs. Surowitz's lawyer, in an effort to cure whatever infirmity the court might possibly find in Mrs. Surowitz's verification in light of her deposition, filed two affidavits which shed much additional light on an extensive investigation which had preceded the filing of the complaint. Despite these affidavits the District Judge dismissed the case holding that Mrs. Surowitz's affidavit was "false," that being wholly false it was a nullity, that being a nullity it was as though no affidavit had been made in compliance with Rule 23, that being false the affidavit was a "sham" and Rule 23(b) required that he dismiss her case, and he did so, "with prejudice."

The Court of Appeals affirmed the District Court's dismissal * * * despite the fact that the charges made against the defendants were viewed as very serious and grave charges of fraud and that "many of the material allegations of the complaint are obviously true and cannot be refuted." 342 F.2d, at 607. We cannot agree with either of the courts below and reverse their judgments. * * *

Mrs. Surowitz, the plaintiff and petitioner here, is a Polish immigrant with a very limited English vocabulary and practically no formal education. For many years she has worked as a seamstress in New York where by reason of frugality she saved enough money to buy some thousands of dollars worth of stocks. She was of course not able to select stocks for herself with any degree of assurance of their value. Under these circumstances she had to receive advice and counsel and quite naturally she went to her son-in-law, Irving Brilliant. Mr. Brilliant had graduated from the Harvard Law School, possessed a master's degree in economics from Columbia University, was a professional investment advisor, and in addition to his degrees and his financial acumen, he wore a Phi Beta Kappa key. In 1957, six years before this litigation began, he bought some stock for his mother-in-law in the Hilton Hotels Corporation, paying a little more than $2,000 of her own money for it. * * *

About December 1962, Mrs. Surowitz received through the mails a notice from the Hilton Hotels Corporation announcing its plan to purchase a large amount of its own stock. Because she wanted it explained to her, she took the notice to Mr. Brilliant. Apparently disturbed by it, he straightway set out to make an investigation. Shortly thereafter he went to Chicago, Illinois, where Hilton Hotels has its home office and talked the matter over with Mr. Rockler. Mr. Brilliant and Mr. Rockler had been friends for many years. * * * The two decided to investigate further, and for a number of months both pursued whatever avenues of information that were open to them. By August of 1963 on the basis of their investigation, both of them had reached the conclusion [that defendants were engaged in a fraudulent scheme, and Mr. Brilliant explained this to Mrs. Surowitz]. * * *

* * * When, on the basis of this conversation, Mrs. Surowitz stated that she agreed that suit be filed in her name, Mr. Rockler prepared a formal complaint which he mailed to Mr. Brilliant. Mr. Brilliant then, according to both his affidavit and Mrs. Surowitz's testimony, read and explained the complaint to his mother-in-law before she verified it. Her limited education and her small knowledge about any of the English language, except the most ordinarily used words, probably is sufficient guarantee that the courts below were right in finding that she did not understand any of the legal relationships or comprehend any of the business transactions described in the complaint. She did know, however, that she had put over $2,000 of her hard-earned money into Hilton Hotels stock, that she was not getting her dividends, and that her son-in-law who had looked into the matter thought that something was wrong. She also knew that her son-in-law was qualified to help her and she trusted him. It is difficult to believe that anyone could be shocked or harmed in any way when, in the light of all these circumstances, Mrs. Surowitz verified the complaint, not on the basis of her own knowledge and understanding, but in the faith that her son-in-law had correctly advised her either that the statements in the complaint were true or to the best of his knowledge he believed them to be true.

* * * Rule 23(b) was not written in order to bar derivative suits. Unquestionably it was originally adopted and has served since in part as a means to discourage "strike suits" by people who might be interested in getting quick dollars by making charges without regard to their truth so as to coerce corporate managers to settle worthless claims in order to get rid of them. * * *

When the record of this case is reviewed in the light of the purpose of Rule 23(b)'s verification requirement, there emerges the plain, inescapable fact that this is not a strike suit or anything akin to it. Mrs. Surowitz was not interested in anything but her own investment made with her own money. Moreover, there is not one iota of evidence that Mr. Brilliant, her son-in-law and counselor, sought to do the corporation any injury in this litigation. In fact his purchases for the benefit of his family of more than $50,000 of securities in the corporation, including a $10,000 debenture, all made years before this suit was brought, manifest confidence in the corporation, not a desire to harm it in any way. The Court of Appeals in affirming the District Court's dismissal, however, indicated that whether Mrs. Surowitz and her counselors acted in good faith and whether the charges they made were truthful were irrelevant once Mrs. Surowitz demonstrated in her oral testimony that she knew nothing about the content of the suit. * * *

We cannot construe Rule 23 or any other one of the Federal Rules as compelling courts to summarily dismiss, without any answer or argument at all, cases like this where grave charges of fraud are shown by the record to be based on reasonable beliefs growing out of careful investigation. The basic purpose of the Federal Rules is to administer justice through fair trials, not through summary dismissals as necessary as they may be on occasion. These rules were designed in large part to get away from some of the old procedural booby traps which common-law pleaders could set to prevent unsophisticated litigants from ever having their day in court. If rules of procedure work as they should in an honest and fair judicial system, they not only permit, but should as nearly as possible guarantee that bona fide complaints be carried to an adjudication on the merits. Rule 23(b), like the other civil rules, was written to further, not defeat the ends of justice. The serious fraud charged here, which of course has not been proven, is clearly in that class of deceitful conduct which the federal securities laws were largely passed to prohibit and protect against. There is, moreover, not one word or one line of actual evidence in this record indicating that there has been any collusive conduct or trickery by those who filed this suit except through intimations and insinuations without any support from anything any witness has said. The dismissal of this case was error. It has now been practically three years since the complaint was filed and as yet none of the defendants have even been compelled to admit or deny the wrongdoings charged. They should be. The cause is reversed and remanded to the District Court for trial on the merits.

Reversed and remanded.

JUSTICE HARLAN, concurring.

Rule 23(b) directs that in a derivative suit "the complaint shall be verified by oath" but nothing dictates that the verification be that of the plaintiff shareholder. * * * In the present circumstances, it seems to me the affidavit of Walter J. Rockler, counsel for Mrs. Surowitz, amounts to an adequate verification by counsel, which I think is permitted by a reasonable interpretation of the Rule at least in cases such as this. On this premise, I agree with the decision of the Court.

NOTES AND QUESTIONS

1.　Given the complexity of contemporary finance, is it realistic to condition the ability to bring suit under Rule 23.1 on the investor's personal knowledge of the transactions that give rise to her injury? Is Justice Harlan's endorsement of third-party verification an appropriate solution to the potential problem of strike suits?

2.　In those state courts in which pleadings generally do not have to be verified, there nevertheless are certain exceptions. Some of the typical ones found in state practice are: petitions for divorce; petitions brought by the state to enjoin a nuisance; and complaints to obtain support of a child born out of wedlock. What makes these actions sufficiently distinctive to require verification?

NOTE ON FEDERAL RULE 11

Rule 11 was adopted as part of the 1938 Federal Rules of Civil Procedure and has been amended a number of times since. In its original version, Rule 11 imposed a signature requirement as a certification that good grounds existed to support a pleading and that the pleading was not interposed for delay. The sanction for violation of the rule was the striking of the pleadings, but the violation had to be willful and the sanction was imposed as a matter of discretion based on a subjective standard of bad faith. Given the severity of the potential sanction, judges appeared disinclined to impose discipline under the rule and the rule was infrequently invoked; as one commentator put it, the original version of Rule 11 was "a paper tiger without any bite." Cavanagh, *Rule 11 of the Federal Rules of Civil Procedure: The Case Against Turning Back the Clock*, 162 F.R.D. 383, 388 (1995). Indeed, between 1938 and 1976, there were only 23 reported cases in which a party moved under Rule 11 to strike a pleading and only nine cases in which violations of the rule were found. See Risinger, *Honesty in Pleading and its Enforcement: Some "Striking" Problems with Federal Rule of Civil Procedure* 11, 61 Minn.L.Rev. 1 (1976).

Rule 11 was amended in 1983 to cure some of its perceived deficiencies. First, the amendments replaced the subjective bad faith standard with an objective standard that required the attorney to "stop and think" before filing suit and to certify that a presuit investigation of both the facts and law had been conducted; this requirement applied not only to the pleadings but also to all court papers (other than discovery, which are covered by Rule 37). Second, the amendments eliminated judicial discretion about whether to impose a sanction and instead made sanctions mandatory. Third, the amendments gave the court discretion to design an appropriate sanction. In practice the amended rule proved to be controversial, and courts, commentators, and practitioners disagreed about the rule's effectiveness, goals, and fairness. See Sanner & Tobias, *Rule 11 and Rule Revision*, 37 Loy.L.A.L.Rev. 573 (2004).

By 1990, amended Rule 11 had generated more than 3,000 proceedings addressing sanctions, and the reported decisions were assumed to compromise only a "fraction" of the sanctions imposed. Zaldivar v. City of Los Angeles, 780 F.2d 823, 829 (9th Cir. 1986). Some commentators expressed concern that sanctions were imposed disproportionately on civil rights litigants and that the rule was having a chilling effect on constitutional enforcement. See Tobias, *The 1993 Revision to Federal Rule* 11, 70 Ind.L.J. 171, 171 (1994). However, the rule also achieved positive effects; lawyers surveyed reported making more rigorous inquiries before filing suit. See Kritzer, Marshall & Zemans, *Rule 11: Moving Beyond the Cosmic Anecdote*, 75 Judicature 269 (1992).

During this period, the Supreme Court decided a number of cases involving different aspects of Rule 11. In PAVELIC & LEFLORE v. MARVEL ENTERTAINMENT GROUP, 493 U.S. 120, 110 S.Ct. 456, 107 L.Ed.2d 438 (1989), the Court held that a law firm could not be sanctioned under the rule for a frivolous pleading signed by a member of the firm, generating a vigorous dissent by Justice Marshall who argued that the Court had effectively created "an immunity" for law firms under the Rule. In COOTER & GELL v. HARTMARX CORP., 496 U.S. 384, 110 S.Ct. 2447, 110 L.Ed.2d 359 (1990), the Court held that sanctions could be imposed upon a party even after the party had taken a voluntary dismissal of the suit, stating that the standard for determining whether sanctions were appropriate was "whether, at the time the attorney filed the pleading or other paper, his legal argument would have appeared plausible." Id. at 403–04, 110 S.Ct. at 2459–60, 110 L.Ed.2d at 380–81.

In BUSINESS GUIDES, INC. v. CHROMATIC COMMUNICATIONS ENTERPRISES, INC., 498 U.S. 533, 111 S.Ct. 922, 112 L.Ed.2d 1140 (1991), the Court held that Rule 11 imposed an objective standard of reasonable injury on a represented party who signed papers, whether the signatures were required or voluntary. Business Guides, Inc. sought a temporary restraining order through its law firm against the publication of a directory by Chromatic Communications Enterprises, Inc., on the ground that Chromatic had copied phone listings from the Business Guides, Inc. guide. Business Guides claimed to know of the copying because Chromatic had "reprinted" ten seeded listings, i.e., listings that Business Guides had deliberately printed incorrectly in order to be able to prove the copying. When the judge's law clerk asked to check the listings, however, Business Guides retracted its claim that three of the ten listings were seeds. The clerk, after calling the numbers, discovered that nine of the ten supposedly incorrect listings were actually valid numbers and thus were not valid proof of copying. Although Chromatic did not in the end pursue sanctions against the law firm because the firm had become insolvent, a magistrate recommended that both Business Guides and the law firm be sanctioned (the firm for not investigating further when the first three listings were retracted by Business Guides), and the Supreme Court upheld the sanctions imposed against Business Guides. The Court equated the standards applicable to attorneys with those of represented parties. Justice Kennedy dissented, arguing it is an abuse of discretion to sanction a represented party "who acts in good faith but errs as to the facts." Id. at 555, 111 S.Ct. at 935, 112 L.Ed.2d at 1161.

In 1993, Rule 11 again was amended and this version remains in effect. The amendment made significant changes to Rule 11 and abrogated Supreme Court decisions that were regarded as wrong:

(a) The amendment eliminated mandatory sanctions and restored a regime of discretionary sanctions. Rule 11(c)(1).

(b) The amendment introduced a "safe harbor provision," requiring a separate motion for sanctions that may not be filed for at least 21 days after service of the challenged paper. Rule 11(c)(2).

(c) The amendment clarified that sanctions are for deterrence, not compensation, and may include non-monetary sanctions. Rule 11(c)(4).

(d) The amendment provided that "[a]bsent exceptional circumstances," a law firm "must be held jointly responsible" for a violation of the rule committed by a partner, associate, or employee. Rule 11(c)(1).

(e) The amendment allowed the court, on its own initiative, to order a party or attorney to show cause that Rule 11 has not been violated. Rule 11(c)(3).

The 1993 amendment preserved the signature requirement not just for pleadings but also for any written motion and "other paper" (except discovery), and requires the court to strike an unsigned paper "unless the omission is promptly corrected after being called to the attorney's or party's attention." Rule 11(a). The rule also applies to "later advocating" of a position to the court based on the offending paper. Rule 11(b).

Justice Scalia dissented from the adoption of the 1993 amendment:

The proposed revision would render the Rule toothless, by allowing judges to dispense with sanction, by disfavoring compensation for litigation expenses, and by providing a 21-day "safe harbor". * * * The Rules should be solicitous of the abused (the courts and the opposing party), and not of the abuser. Under the revised Rule, parties will be able to file thoughtless, reckless, and harassing pleadings, secure in the knowledge that they have nothing to lose: If objection is raised, they can retreat without penalty. The proposed revision contradicts what this court said only three years ago: "Baseless filing puts the machinery of justice in motion, burdening courts and individuals alike with needless expense and delay." Cooter & Gell [p. 459, supra].

Order of the Supreme Court Amending the Federal Rules of Civil Procedure (April 22, 1993), reprinted in 146 F.R.D. 404, 507 (1993) (Scalia, J., dissenting).

NOTES AND QUESTIONS

1.   What constitutes a "reasonable" inquiry under Rule 11(b)(2)? In GOLDEN EAGLE DISTRIBUTING CORP. v. BURROUGHS CORP., 801 F.2d 1531 (9th Cir. 1986), rehearing denied with a dissenting opinion, 809 F.2d 584 (9th Cir. 1987), plaintiff's counsel cited a 1965 California Supreme Court case supporting its argument but had not cited a 1979 California Supreme Court opinion that was inconsistent with the 1965 case. Counsel distinguished the latter case in its reply brief after it had been cited by the opposition, arguing that the 1965 case had not been overruled. Counsel did not address two intermediate court opinions that discussed the effect of the 1979 opinion on the 1965 opinion. The district court held that Rule 11 sanctions were appropriate for counsel's failing to cite adverse authority, on the view that "[t]here would be little point to Rule 11 if it tolerated counsel making an argument for the extension of existing law disguised as one based on existing law." 103 F.R.D. 124, 127 (1984). The Ninth Circuit reversed.

> The text of the Rule, however, does not require that counsel differentiate between a position which is supported by existing law and one that would extend it. The Rule on its face requires that the motion be either one or the other. Moreover, there is nothing in any of the statements of the proponents of the amended Rule or in the authorities we have surveyed since its adoption which suggests such a requirement.

801 F.2d at 1539–40. Does the 1993 amendment change the result?

2.   Does the standard of plausible pleading affect Rule 11? The consensus is that under the 1993 version of Rule 11, sanctions are not warranted simply because a complaint does not survive a Rule 12(b)(6) motion. However, one commentator reports that post-*Iqbal*, "there has been a veritable explosion of threatened sanctions," observing that "one district judge has been citing Rule 11 alongside *Twombly* and *Iqbal* [p. 391 and p. 402, supra] as the standard governing the sufficiency of a plaintiff's complaint." Cooper, *Iqbal's Retro Revolution*, 46 Wake Forest L.Rev. 937, 964 (2011). In addition, questions have been raised whether the plausibility standard forecloses the kind of complaints that were assumed to be permissible under Rule 11(b)(3)— in particular, when plaintiff alleges that specifically identified factual contentions "will likely have evidentiary support." Should the test for plausible pleading be linked "to the likelihood of discovery producing evidentiary support"? Hartnett, *Taming* Twombly, *Even After* Iqbal, 158 U.Pa.L.Rev. 473, 506 (2010).

3.   Congress has authorized claim-specific sanctions in particular statutes. Sanctions under the Private Securities Litigation Reform Act, 15 U.S.C. § 78u–4, closely resemble those available under the 1983 version of Rule 11 and are mandatory once a violation of the sanction provision is found. Congress also has authorized courts to award attorney's fees to a prevailing defendant in a civil rights case if plaintiff's claim is found to be frivolous,

unreasonable, or groundless. See § 706(k) of Title VII of the Civil Rights Act of 1964, 42 U.S.C. § 2000e–5(k) (employment discrimination actions).

4. Courts have statutory authority under 28 U.S.C. § 1927 to impose excess costs on an attorney "who so multiplies the proceedings in any case unreasonably and vexatiously." Courts also have inherent power to sanction parties, and this power is neither constrained nor supplanted by Rule 11 or 28 U.S.C. § 1927. In CHAMBERS v. NASCO, INC., 501 U.S. 32, 111 S.Ct. 2123, 115 L.Ed.2d 27 (1991), the Supreme Court held, five-to-four, in an opinion authored by Justice White, that the district court properly imposed sanctions as a matter of inherent power when the offending party engaged in bad faith activity that abused the judicial process. Justice Kennedy dissented and criticized the use of inherent authority in this situation: "By inviting district courts to rely on inherent authority as a substitute for attention to the careful distinctions contained in the rules and statutes, today's decision will render these sources of authority superfluous in many instances." Id. at 67, 111 S.Ct. at 2144, 115 L.Ed.2d at 59.

Although Rule 11 sanctions have declined since 1993, there appears to be an uptick in sanctions imposed either as a matter of inherent authority or under 28 U.S.C. § 1927 in situations in which the procedural protections of Rule 11 "have not been or could not be met." Hart, *And the Chill Goes On— Federal Civil Rights Plaintiffs Beware: Rule* 11 *vis-á-vis* 28 U.S.C. § 1927 *and the Court's Inherent Power*, 37 Loy.L.A.L.Rev. 645, 647–48 (2004). Moreover, although there is circuit disagreement as to whether sanctions may be imposed on pro se litigants under 28 U.S.C. § 1927, some courts elide the statutory barrier by relying on their inherent authority. See Whitt, *The Split on Sanctioning Pro Se Litigants under* 28 U.S.C. § 1927: *Choose Wisely When Picking a Side, Eighth Circuit*, 73 Mo.L.Rev. 1365 (2008).

5. Does a court have inherent authority to award attorney's fees as a sanction absent a showing of bad faith? In WILSON v. CITIGROUP, 702 F.3d 720 (2d Cir. 2012), the Second Circuit reversed an order of attorney's fees imposed on counsel for filing opposition papers four days after the court-ordered deadline but consistent with a schedule to which all parties had consented. The appeals court found that the party had done "nothing to warrant a sanction," underscoring that he had "disobeyed no order of the district court and caused no prejudice to opposing counsel." Moreover, the appeals court underscored that it was an abuse of discretion to impose sanctions without first making a finding of bad faith and giving counsel notice:

> Our case law is clear that a district court may not impose attorney's fees as a sanction without first making an explicit finding that the sanctioned party, whether a party or a party's counsel, acted in bad faith in engaging in the sanctionable conduct. * * * Here, it is undisputed that the district court made no "explicit finding" that * * * [the] untimely submission of its opposition papers * * * was in bad faith. * * *

Id. at 724.

6. In KING v. WHITMER, 556 F.Supp.3d 680 (E.D.Mich. 2021), plaintiffs filed an unsuccessful suit against the Michigan Governor and Secretary of State—among others—alleging violations of federal and state law in connection with the 2020 presidential election. After the case was dismissed voluntarily, the district court imposed sanctions on nine of the plaintiffs' attorneys under 28 U.S.C. § 1927, Rule 11, and the court's inherent authority. The court's 110-page opinion began by observing:

> This lawsuit represents a historic and profound abuse of the judicial process. * * * Individuals may have a right (within certain bounds) to disseminate allegations of fraud unsupported by law or fact in the public sphere. But attorneys cannot exploit their privilege and access to the judicial process to do the same. And when an attorney has done so, sanctions are in order. * * * The attorneys who filed the instant lawsuit abused the well-established rules applicable to the litigation process by proffering claims not backed by law; proffering claims not backed by evidence (but instead, speculation, conjecture, and unwarranted suspicion); proffering factual allegations and claims without engaging in the required prefiling inquiry; and dragging out these proceedings even after they acknowledged that it was too late to attain the relief sought."

The sanctions ordered by the district court included: (1) an obligation to complete 12 hours of continuing legal education—six hours on pleading standards and six hours on election law; (2) a referral for investigation and possible suspension or disbarment to the appropriate authorities in Michigan and the states in which they were admitted to practice; and (3) an award of attorneys' fees and costs, which the court ultimately calculated to be over $175,000. See King v. Whitmer, 2021 WL 5711102 (E.D.Mich. 2021). As of this writing, the sanctions ruling is on appeal to the Sixth Circuit.

7. Rule 11 remains hotly debated. Some commentators see a social value in "meritless" litigation as a spur to legal innovation. See Reinert, *Screening Out Innovation: The Merits of Meritless Litigation*, 89 Ind.L.J. 1191 (2014). Indeed, some economists have argued that even frivolous lawsuits may have a positive effect on deterrence. See Stone & Miceli, *The Impact of Frivolous Lawsuits on Deterrence: Do They Have Some Redeeming Value?*, 10 J.L.Econ. & Pol'y 301 (2014). Still other commentators question whether litigation abuse is a widespread problem, and emphasize the democratic value of keeping the courts open for redress. See Miller, *Are the Federal Courthouse Doors Closing? What's Happened to the Federal Rules of Civil Procedure?*, 43 Tex.Tech.L.Rev. 587 (2011). On the other hand, some lawmakers continue to argue that litigation is too expensive, and have urged a return to mandatory sanctions. See Lawsuit Abuse Reduction Act of 2017, S. 237, 115th Cong. (proposing to withdraw Rule 11's 21-day safe harbor provision and to mandate sanctions).

CHAPTER 8

JOINDER OF CLAIMS AND PARTIES: EXPANDING THE SCOPE OF THE CIVIL ACTION

■ ■ ■

This chapter examines procedures that allow multiple claims and parties to be combined in one lawsuit. Common law procedure stayed close to a bilateral model in which one plaintiff sued one defendant on one cause of action. See Sunderland, *Joinder of Actions*, 18 Mich.L.Rev. 571 (1920). As social and commercial relations became increasingly complex and disputes more intricate, new procedures were needed to avoid the cost, delay, and potential unfairness of piecemeal litigation. Broadly speaking, joinder rules today fall into one of two categories: permissive rules, which give a litigant the option of joining parties and claims in a single lawsuit; and mandatory rules, which require a litigant to do so. It is important to remember that the question of joinder is separate from whether the court may exercise jurisdiction over the claim or party to be joined. See Federal Rule 82.

A. IDENTIFYING PARTIES WHO MAY SUE AND BE SUED

Read Federal Rule of Civil Procedure 17 in the Supplement.

NOTES AND QUESTIONS

1. The real-party-in-interest rule is justified by the need to foreclose duplicative lawsuits, to assert all defenses in one action, and to avoid prejudice. See The Ezra Charitable Trust v. Rent-Way, Inc., 136 F.Supp.2d 435, 443 (W.D. Pa. 2001). How does Rule 17 achieve these goals? Is the rule redundant of the governing applicable substantive law? Some courts and commentators see no need for the rule and have argued for its elimination. See Virginia Elec. & Power Co. v. Westinghouse Elec. Corp., 485 F.2d 78, 83 (4th Cir. 1973) (" 'Rule 17(a) is a barnacle on the federal practice ship. It ought to be scraped away.' ") (quoting Kennedy, *Federal Rule 17(a): Will the Real Party in Interest*

Please Stand?, 51 Minn.L.Rev. 675, 724 (1967)). See Entman, *More Reasons for Abolishing Federal Rule of Civil Procedure* 17(a): *The Problem of the Proper Plaintiff and Insurance Subrogation*, 68 N.C.L.Rev. 893 (1990).

2. Apart from Rule 17, two other concepts are relevant to determining who may sue or be sued—"capacity" and "standing."

Capacity refers to the ability of a party to enforce rights or to be sued by others. Capacity rules are designed to protect a party by ensuring that the party's interests are adequately represented. Real-party-in-interest rules serve to protect the opposing party's interests by ensuring that only the litigant who has a true stake in the outcome can sue or be sued. This prevents situations in which a person first might be sued by the person who holds the nominal title to a claim, and after successfully defending that claim, is subjected to a second action by the real party in interest. The federal system and many states have special rules to deal with suits by or against minors and mental incompetents. See Rules 17(b) and 17(c).

Standing is a constitutional requirement under Article III of the United States Constitution for actions in federal court and focuses on who may invoke the power of the Court to redress an injury. State judicial systems have similar requirements derived from state law. See Hershkoff, *State Courts and the "Passive Virtues": Rethinking the Judicial Function*, 114 Harv.L.Rev. 1833 (2001). Federal doctrine requires plaintiff to allege a "personal injury fairly traceable to the defendant's allegedly unlawful conduct and likely to be redressed by the requested relief." Allen v. Wright, 468 U.S. 737, 751, 104 S.Ct. 3315, 3324, 82 L.Ed.2d 556, 569 (1984). The requirement of standing reflects constitutional limits on judicial power and helps to ensure adversarial presentation by insisting upon a party with an actual injury.

It is possible to have a case in which a real party in interest (the beneficiary of a will, for example) lacks capacity to sue (perhaps because the party is a minor). Moreover, even if this hypothetical beneficiary has capacity to sue, standing to raise particular claims might be lacking.

B. JOINDER OF CLAIMS

1. HISTORICAL LIMITATIONS ON THE PERMISSIVE JOINDER OF CLAIMS

At common law, a plaintiff generally could join claims in a single lawsuit only if they were a part of the same writ and so belonged to the same form of action. Although the codes were somewhat more liberal, the typical code provision authorized joinder of claims only when they fell within one of several statutory classes, which ordinarily included the following:

(a) Contracts express or implied;

(b) Injuries to the person;

(c) Injuries to character;

(d) Injuries to property;

(e) Actions to recover real property, with or without damages;

(f) Actions to recover chattels, with or without damages; and

(g) Actions arising out of the same transaction or transactions connected with the same subject of the action.

Is the code approach to joinder of claims any less formalistic than at common law? See Blume, *A Rational Theory for Joinder of Causes of Action and Defences, and for the Use of Counterclaims,* 26 Mich.L.Rev. 1 (1927).

2. PERMISSIVE JOINDER OF CLAIMS BY PLAINTIFFS UNDER FEDERAL RULE 18

———

Read Federal Rule of Civil Procedure 18 in the Supplement.

———

NOTES AND QUESTIONS

1. Federal Rule 18 removes all obstacles to the joinder of claims and permits the joinder of both legal and equitable matters. The only restriction on the claims that may be joined is imposed by jurisdictional requirements. What are the advantages of permitting the liberal joinder of claims? Are there any disadvantages? How much credence should we give to the efficiency rationale? If each claim is different, are there material efficiency gains?

2. Rule 18 describes the claims that a party is allowed to assert in a single action against an opposing party, but it does not compel joinder. What are the arguments for a rule of compulsory joinder of all related claims existing between a plaintiff and a defendant? See Friedenthal, *Joinder of Claims, Counterclaims and Cross-Complaints: Suggested Revision of the California Provisions,* 23 Stan.L.Rev. 1, 11–17 (1970).

3. Rule 18 generally applies at the pleading stage of the lawsuit and is subject to the rules that govern pleadings. At the pleading stage, there is no doctrine of misjoinder of claims. However, Rule 42(b) allows the court to sever claims and to authorize separate trials of claims or issues. Does the availability of severance of claims eliminate all of the objections to permitting unrestricted joinder of claims as an initial matter? To what extent does the court's power to sever claims prevent the system from achieving the objectives of a liberal joinder rule?

4. The doctrine of claim preclusion, addressed in Chapter 15, infra, may create incentives for the joinder of related claims even in the absence of a rule of compulsory joinder. See Blume, *Required Joinder of Claims,* 45 Mich.L.Rev.

797 (1947). Thus, for example, if A and B are involved in an automobile accident in which A suffers both bodily injury and damage to her automobile, the risk of claim preclusion in a system that defines the claim in terms of transactional relation may lead A to join both claims in one action, even though Federal Rule 18 does not require this result.

5.   In SPORN v. HUDSON TRANSIT LINES, 265 A.D. 360, 38 N.Y.S.2d 512 (1st Dep't 1942), the court had before it an attempt to join five causes of action for negligence resulting in personal injuries with one cause of action for malicious prosecution. It stated:

> The causes of action for negligence and for malicious prosecution are essentially different in nature; each type involves different rules of law; each requires different testimony to establish a case and each carries a different measure of damages. If a single jury were to try both types of action at the one time, there is a strong likelihood that confusion would exist in the minds of the jurors as to the rules of law to be applied to the respective actions and they would undoubtedly entertain much difficulty in applying the various parts of testimony introduced to the appropriate cause of action.

Id. at 361, 38 N.Y.S.2d at 514. Would the result in *Sporn* have been different if the action had been brought in a federal court?

C. ADDITION OF CLAIMS BY DEFENDANT

1. COUNTERCLAIMS

The counterclaim in its present form did not exist at common law, although it had well-recognized precursors in set-off and recoupment and in equity practice. The philosophy underlying set-off and recoupment was the common sense view that someone should not be compelled to pay one moment what the party will be entitled to recover back the next. Judge Clark outlined the development and theory of set-off and recoupment as follows:

> * * * At first * * * [recoupment] was limited to a showing of payment, or of former recovery. Later, recoupment was developed so as to allow a defendant to show for the purpose of reducing the plaintiff's recovery any facts arising out of the transaction sued upon or connected with the subject thereof, which facts might have founded an independent action in favor of the defendant against the plaintiff. * * * It was not necessary that the opposing claims be liquidated, or that they be of the same character; i.e., a claim in "tort" could be set off against one in "contract." It was essential, however, that the claims of both plaintiff and defendant involve the same "subject-matter," or arise out of the "same transaction" * * *.

But where the defendant's claims arose out of a transaction different from that sued upon, the common-law recoupment was unavailable. The defendant, therefore, was compelled to bring a separate suit in order to satisfy his claim against the plaintiff. Equity, at an early date, relieved the defendant of this hardship by allowing a set-off of claims [arising out of a transaction different from the plaintiff's claim] * * *.

Under the set-off * * *, it was necessary that the demands either be liquidated, or arise out of contract or judgment. It was necessary, also, that the demands be due the defendant in his own right against the plaintiff, or his assignor, and be not already barred by the statute of limitations * * *.

Clark, Code Pleading § 100, at 634–36 (2d ed. 1947). The utility of recoupment was limited because defendant was not permitted to recover affirmative relief; the claim could be used only to reduce or "net out" plaintiff's recovery. Set-off likewise was limited because the claim had to be for a liquidated amount.

The movement for procedural reform in the mid-nineteenth century gave passing attention to the problem of defendant's claims against plaintiff; the original New York Field Code of 1848 made no provision for counterclaims. Amendments in 1852 corrected this omission and permitted as a counterclaim:

1. A cause of action arising out of the contract or transaction set forth in the complaint, as the foundation of the plaintiff's claim, or connected with the subject of the action; and

2. In an action arising on contract, any other cause of action arising on contract, and existing at the commencement of the action.

See Blume, *A Rational Theory for Joinder of Causes of Action and Defences, and for the Use of Counterclaims*, 26 Mich.L.Rev. 1, 48 (1927). The English Judicature Act of 1873 eliminated the historic limitations on defendant's ability to assert claims against plaintiff. Then, at the beginning of this century, a number of states amended their codes to adopt the English practice.

———

Read Federal Rules of Civil Procedure 13(a)–(f) and the accompanying materials in the Supplement.

———

NOTES AND QUESTIONS

1.   Federal Rule 13(a) goes beyond the English and code practice by *requiring* a party to assert certain counterclaims. Is this rule unduly harsh? See Wright, *Estoppel by Rule: The Compulsory Counterclaim Under Modern Pleading*, 38 Minn.L.Rev. 423, 465 (1954), arguing that adoption of the rule was "an important part of the movement to end a multiplicity of litigation." However, critics argued that a rule of compulsory counterclaim could be justified only "when the counterclaim operates by way of defense to the principal claim." Millar, Civil Procedure of the Trial Court in Historical Perspective 138 (1952).

2.   The critical question in applying Rule 13(a) is: What constitutes a transaction or occurrence? The classic test is found in MOORE v. NEW YORK COTTON EXCHANGE, 270 U.S. 593, 46 S.Ct. 36, 70 L.Ed. 750 (1926). In *Moore*, plaintiff sought to compel defendant to install a price quotation ticker in plaintiff's place of business. Defendant counterclaimed for damages, alleging that although plaintiff had been denied permission to use quotations from defendant's exchange, plaintiff "was purloining them and giving them out." In the course of holding defendant's counterclaim compulsory under former Equity Rule 30, the Court said:

> * * * "Transaction" is a word of flexible meaning. It may comprehend a series of many occurrences, depending not so much upon the immediateness of their connection as upon their logical relationship. The refusal to furnish the quotations is one of the links in the chain which constitutes the transaction upon which appellant here bases its cause of action. It is an important part of the transaction constituting the subject-matter of the counterclaim. It is the one circumstance without which neither party would have found it necessary to seek relief. Essential facts alleged by appellant enter into and constitute in part the cause of action set forth in the counterclaim. That they are not precisely identical, or that the counterclaim embraces additional allegations, as, for example, that appellant is unlawfully getting the quotations, does not matter. To hold otherwise would be to rob this branch of the rule of all serviceable meaning, since the facts relied upon by the plaintiff rarely, if ever, are, in all particulars, the same as those constituting the defendant's counterclaim. * * *

Id. at 610, 46 S.Ct. at 371, 70 L.Ed. at 757. How similar is this test to the *Gibbs* approach for determining whether pendent claim jurisdiction may be asserted, p. 260, supra?

3.   Judicial decisions suggest four interrelated but different tests for determining whether a claim arises out of the same "transaction or occurrence":

(a)   Are the issues of fact and law raised by the claim and counterclaim largely the same?

a third person who is required within the meaning of Rule 19 and over whom defendant cannot obtain jurisdiction, is assertion of the claim mandatory? See Rule 13(a)(1)(B).

(c) If, five days after defendant has served the answer, defendant is assigned a claim that arises out of the same transaction or occurrence as plaintiff's claim against defendant, must defendant amend the answer to allege a counterclaim? See Rule 13(e).

Further assume a federal lawsuit in which defendant fails to raise a compulsory counterclaim. Does the failure to bring the claim in federal court prevent defendant from raising it in a subsequent state court action? What if defendant brings suit on the unasserted claim in a state court before the federal action is terminated? Should the state court hearing the counterclaim grant a motion to dismiss based on the assertion that Federal Rule 13(a) bars the state action? Should the federal court hearing plaintiff's suit restrain further proceedings in the state court? The answer to these questions is not clear from the language of Rule 13 and implicates the federal court's power to enjoin state proceedings, see 28 U.S.C. § 2283.

4. In SOUTHERN CONSTRUCTION CO. v. PICKARD, 371 U.S. 57, 83 S.Ct. 108, 9 L.Ed.2d 31 (1962), the Southern Construction Company was the prime contractor on contracts with the United States for the rehabilitation of certain barracks at Fort Campbell, Tennessee, and Fort Benning, Georgia. The plumbing and heating subcontractor on both projects was the respondent Samuel J. Pickard, doing business as Pickard Engineering Company. Pickard's primary supplier on both projects was the Atlas Supply Company.

Pickard filed suit against Southern in district courts in both Georgia and Tennessee under the Miller Act for amounts due on the contracts. Defendant elected to assert its counterclaim for the amount paid in settlement to Atlas in the Tennessee suit, the second of the two suits commenced. Pickard answered that the counterclaim was barred for failure to raise it in the first suit as a compulsory counterclaim.

The Supreme Court accepted the district court's ruling that the $35,000 settlement had not been allocated as between the Tennessee and Georgia projects and that it therefore could have been asserted in either action. It stated, however, that Rule 13(a) does not operate to prohibit its use in the later Tennessee action. The Court found the policy of preventing multiplicity of actions and achieving resolution in a single lawsuit of all disputes arising out of common matters to be inapplicable in these circumstances:

> * * * The Rule was particularly directed against one who failed to assert a counterclaim in one action and then instituted a second action in which that counterclaim became the basis of the complaint. * * *

> It is readily apparent that this policy has no application here. In this instance, the plaintiff-respondent, who originally sought to combine all his claims in a single suit, correctly concluded that he was

required by statute to split those claims and to bring two separate actions in two different districts. The fragmentation of these claims, therefore, was compelled by federal law, and the primary defendant in both actions was thus for the first time confronted with the choice of which of the two pending suits should be resorted to for the assertion of a counterclaim common to both. Under these circumstances, we hold that Rule 13(a) did not compel this counterclaim to be made in whichever of the two suits the first responsive pleading was filed. Its assertion in the later suit, to which Southern, not without reason, considered it more appurtenant * * * , by no means involved the circuity of action that Rule 13(a) was aimed at preventing. * * *

Id. at 60–61, 83 S.Ct. at 110, 9 L.Ed.2d at 34–35. Should the *Pickard* exception to Rule 13(a) be limited to the situation in which the governing substantive law requires that related claims be pled as separate actions in separate districts?

2. CROSSCLAIMS

———

Read Federal Rules of Civil Procedure 13(g) and (h) and the accompanying materials in the Supplement.

———

NOTES AND QUESTIONS

1.   Generally, a crossclaim is permissive so that the failure to raise it does not bar suit in a subsequent action. Why should this be so? Doesn't this lead to a multiplicity of suits? Should the rule be different if the crossclaim is transactionally related to plaintiff's original claim? Isn't judicial economy fostered by hearing all transactionally related claims in one suit? Or, is it unfair to force defendants to file crossclaims in a forum not of their own choosing?

2.   Do the Federal Rules define "coparty" for purposes of a crossclaim? In EARLE M. JORGENSON CO. v. T.I. UNITED STATES, LTD., 133 F.R.D. 472 (E.D. Pa. 1991), plaintiff filed suit to recover cleanup costs and other damages arising from environmental contamination of real property. T.I. United States, one of seven defendants, impleaded a third-party defendant, Tosti. Another one of the original defendants, Reed, then crossclaimed against Tosti for indemnity and contribution. Tosti moved to dismiss, arguing that he as a third-party defendant and Reed as an original defendant were not "coparties." The court found that Reed and Tosti were coparties, not opposing parties, defining "opposing parties" as "parties that formally oppose each other on a pleaded claim, such as plaintiffs and original defendants, or third-party plaintiffs and the third-party defendants they have joined," and on this ground

held that the original defendant could crossclaim against Tosti. Id. at 475. Whether an original defendant and a third-party defendant are coparties for purposes of Rule 13 remains unsettled, but *Jorgenson*'s approach comports with the structure of the Federal Rules.

3.   Can a plaintiff crossclaim against a co-plaintiff? In DANNER v. ANSKIS, 256 F.2d 123 (3d Cir. 1958), the driver and passenger of one car sued the driver of a second car for damages arising out of a two-car collision. The passenger-plaintiff also attempted to crossclaim for her injuries against the driver-plaintiff. The Third Circuit upheld dismissal of the crossclaim, on the view that "Rule 13(g) does not authorize a plaintiff to state as a crossclaim against a co-plaintiff a claim arising out of the transaction or occurrence which also is the subject matter of their common complaint against the defendant." The court added that a contrary reading of the rule "could have the effect of extending the jurisdiction of the district court to controversies not within the federal judicial power." Id. at 124. Is the court's reasoning consistent with the language of Rule 13(g)? If the concern is that plaintiffs are engaged in jurisdictional collusion, couldn't the crossclaim be dismissed under 28 U.S.C. § 1359? How does supplemental jurisdiction under 28 U.S.C. § 1367 affect the analysis?

4.   When does Rule 13(h) authorize joinder of a party? Can the rule be used to assert a crossclaim against a person who is not already a party to the original action? Can a person who already is a party to the action be made an additional party under Rule 13(h)? Should the rule be read liberally as to encourage judicial economy? May a federal court exercise supplemental jurisdiction under 28 U.S.C. § 1367 over parties joined under Rule 13(h) to a compulsory counterclaim?

D. CLAIMS INVOLVING MULTIPLE PARTIES

1. PERMISSIVE JOINDER OF PARTIES

Read Federal Rules of Civil Procedure 20, 21, and 42(a) and the accompanying materials in the Supplement.

---

a. Historical Limitations on Permissive Joinder of Parties

At common law, the forms of action—not convenience or economy—controlled whether parties could be joined in a lawsuit. Plaintiffs asserting joint rights were compelled to join their claims in a single action, but a notion of permissive joinder of claims that were not joint did not exist. The rules for joinder of defendants were somewhat more liberal: joint tortfeasors and defendants whose contract obligations were both joint and several could be joined at the plaintiff's option. The equity courts adopted a more flexible approach to the permissive joinder of parties by allowing all persons having an interest in the subject matter of the action or in the relief demanded to join in a single proceeding. The early state codes adopted the equity rule as a general provision, but many state courts read it as imposing a two-part conjunctive test requiring an interest in both the subject matter and the relief requested. See Bone, *Mapping the Boundaries of the Dispute: Conceptions of Ideal Lawsuit Structure from the Field Code to the Federal Rules*, 89 Colum.L.Rev. 1 (1989). Code provisions relating to the joinder of causes of action, which typically required all parties to be interested in each of the causes, further limited joinder of defendants. For a history of the development of American joinder rules, see Blume, *Free Joinder of Parties, Claims, and Counterclaims*, 2 F.R.D. 250 (1943); *Legislation: Recent Trends in Joinder of Parties, Causes, and Counterclaims*, 37 Colum.L.Rev. 462 (1937). For an early comparative view, see Millar, *The Joinder of Actions in Continental Civil Procedure*, 28 Ill.L.Rev. 26 (1933).

b.   Permissive Joinder Under Rule 20

MOSLEY V. GENERAL MOTORS CORP.

United States Court of Appeals, Eighth Circuit, 1974.
497 F.2d 1330.

ROSS, CIRCUIT JUDGE.

Nathaniel Mosley and nine other persons joined in bringing this action individually and as class representatives alleging that their rights guaranteed under 42 U.S.C. § 2000e et seq. and 42 U.S.C. § 1981 were denied by General Motors and Local 25, United Automobile, Aerospace and Agriculture Implement Workers of America (Union) by reason of their color and race. * * *

In each of the first eight counts of the twelve-count complaint, eight of the ten plaintiffs alleged that General Motors, Chevrolet Division, had engaged in unlawful employment practices by: "discriminating against Negroes as regards promotions, terms and conditions of employment"; "retaliating against Negro employees who protested actions made unlawful by Title VII of the Act and by discharging some because they protested said unlawful acts"; "failing to hire Negro employees as a class on the basis of race"; "failing to hire females as a class on the basis of sex"; "discharging Negro employees on the basis of race"; and "discriminating against Negroes and females in the granting of relief time." Each additionally charged that the defendant Union had engaged in unlawful employment practices "with respect to the granting of relief time to Negro and female employees" and "by failing to pursue 6a grievances."[a] The remaining two plaintiffs made similar allegations against General Motors, Fisher Body Division. All of the individual plaintiffs requested injunctive relief, back pay, attorneys fees and costs. Counts XI and XII of the complaint were class action counts against the two individual divisions of General Motors. They also sought declaratory and injunctive relief, back pay, attorneys fees and costs.

General Motors moved to strike portions of each count of the twelve-count complaint * * *. The district court ordered that "insofar as the first ten counts are concerned, those ten counts shall be severed into ten separate causes of action," and each plaintiff was directed to bring a separate action based upon his complaint, duly and separately filed. The court also ordered that the class action would not be dismissed, but rather would be left open "to each of the plaintiffs herein, individually or collectively . . . to allege a separate cause of action on behalf of any class of persons which such plaintiff or plaintiffs may separately or individually represent."

In reaching this conclusion on joinder, the district court followed the reasoning of Smith v. North American Rockwell Corp., 50 F.R.D. 515 (N.D.Okla.1970), which, in a somewhat analogous situation, found there was no right to relief arising out of the same transaction, occurrence or series of transactions or occurrences, and that there was no question of law or fact common to all plaintiffs sufficient to sustain joinder under Federal Rule of Civil Procedure 20(a). Similarly, the district court here felt that the plaintiffs' joint actions against General Motors and the Union presented a variety of issues having little relationship to one another; that they had only one common problem, i.e. the defendant; and that as pleaded the joint actions were completely unmanageable. * * *

* * * [Under Federal Rules 20(b) and 42(b)] the scope of the civil action is made a matter for the discretion of the district court, and a determination on the question of joinder of parties will be reversed on appeal only upon a showing of abuse of that discretion. * * * To determine whether the district court's order was proper herein, we must look to the policy and law that have developed around the operation of Rule 20.

The purpose of the rule is to promote trial convenience and expedite the final determination of disputes, thereby preventing multiple lawsuits. * * * Single trials generally tend to lessen the delay, expense and inconvenience to all concerned. * * *

Permissive joinder is not, however, applicable in all cases. The rule imposes two specific requisites to the joinder of parties: (1) a right to relief must be asserted by, or against, each plaintiff or defendant relating to or arising out of the same transaction or occurrence, or series of transactions

---

[a]   A grievance under a collective bargaining agreement claiming discrimination is referred to as a "6a" grievance.

or occurrences; and (2) some question of law or fact common to all the parties must arise in the action.

In ascertaining whether a particular factual situation constitutes a single transaction or occurrence for purposes of Rule 20, a case by case approach is generally pursued. * * * No hard and fast rules have been established under the rule. However, construction of the terms "transaction or occurrence" as used in the context of Rule 13(a) counterclaims offers some guide to the application of this test. * * * [A]ll "logically related" events entitling a person to institute a legal action against another generally are regarded as comprising a transaction or occurrence. * * * The analogous interpretation of the terms as used in Rule 20 would permit all reasonably related claims for relief by or against different parties to be tried in a single proceeding. Absolute identity of all events is unnecessary.

This construction accords with the result reached in United States v. Mississippi, 380 U.S. 128 (1965), a suit brought by the United States against the State of Mississippi, the election commissioners, and six voting registrars of the State, charging them with engaging in acts and practices hampering and destroying the right of black citizens of Mississippi to vote. The district court concluded that the complaint improperly attempted to hold the six county registrars jointly liable for what amounted to nothing more than individual torts committed by them separately against separate applicants. In reversing, the Supreme Court said

> But the complaint charged that the registrars had acted and were continuing to act as part of a state-wide system designed to enforce the registration laws in a way that would inevitably deprive colored people of the right to vote solely because of their color. On such an allegation the joinder of all the registrars as defendants in a single suit is authorized by Rule 20(a) * * *. * * * These registrars were alleged to be carrying on activities which were part of a series of transactions or occurrences the validity of which depended to a large extent upon "question(s) of law or fact common to all of them."

Id. at 142–143.

Here too, then, the plaintiffs have asserted a right to relief arising out of the same transactions or occurrences. Each of the ten plaintiffs alleged that he had been injured by the same general policy of discrimination on the part of General Motors and the Union. Since a "state-wide system designed to enforce the registration laws in a way that would inevitably deprive colored people of the right to vote" was determined to arise out of the same series of transactions or occurrences, we conclude that a company-wide policy purportedly designed to discriminate against blacks in employment similarly arises out of the same series of transactions or occurrences. Thus the plaintiffs meet the first requisite for joinder under Rule 20(a).

The second requisite necessary to sustain a permissive joinder under the rule is that a question of law or fact common to all the parties will arise in the action. The rule does not require that all questions of law and fact raised by the dispute be common. Yet, neither does it establish any qualitative or quantitative test of commonality. * * *

The right to relief here depends on the ability to demonstrate that each of the plaintiffs was wronged by racially discriminatory policies on the part of the defendants General Motors and the Union. The discriminatory character of the defendants' conduct is thus basic to each plaintiff's recovery. The fact that each plaintiff may have suffered different effects from the alleged discrimination is immaterial for the purposes of determining the common question of law or fact. Thus, we conclude that the second requisite for joinder under Rule 20(a) is also [met] by the complaint.

For the reasons set forth above, we conclude that the district court abused its discretion in severing the joined actions. The difficulties in ultimately adjudicating damages to the various plaintiffs are not so overwhelming as to require such severance. If appropriate, separate trials may be granted as to any particular issue after the determination of common questions.

The judgment of the district court disallowing joinder of the plaintiffs' individual actions is reversed and remanded with directions to permit the plaintiffs to proceed jointly. * * *

NOTE AND QUESTION

Mosley, although decided in 1974, remains a leading case and sets forth a liberal approach to the permissive joinder of parties under Federal Rule 20. Is it significant that Rule 20(b) and Rule 42(b) authorize protective measures to avoid prejudice from plaintiff's joinder decisions? In addition, Rule 21, which speaks to misjoinder, permits the judge to authorize severance "at any time, on just terms," and courts have done so even when parties are properly joined. What are the tactical factors that must be considered before attempting to join multiple defendants? See Friedenthal, *Whom to Sue—Multiple Defendants,* 5 Am.Jur. Trials 1 (1966). Why would the plaintiffs in *Mosley* have wanted to litigate together?

2. MANDATORY JOINDER OF PARTIES

a. The Traditional Concept of "Indispensable" Parties

Before the adoption of Federal Rule 19, the principle of mandatory joinder was a judicially created doctrine. SHIELDS v. BARROW, 58 U.S.

(17 How.) 130, 15 L.Ed. 158 (1854), established the notion that parties could be classified as necessary or indispensable depending on the nature of their substantive rights ("joint" or "severable"). The consequences of this classification were extremely important. If an absent party who was not subject to the jurisdiction of the court or whose joinder would destroy the pre-existing diversity of citizenship was labeled indispensable, the entire action had to be dismissed. On the other hand, if the absentee merely was necessary, the court could exercise its discretion in determining whether or not to continue without that person. Because plaintiff might have been deprived of any remedy if a party was found to be indispensable, courts often strained to avoid that conclusion. As might be suspected, this method had a debilitating effect on the standard for classification.

b.   Joinder of Required Persons Under Rule 19

Read Federal Rule of Civil Procedure 19 and the accompanying materials in the Supplement.

PROVIDENT TRADESMENS BANK & TRUST CO. v. PATTERSON

Supreme Court of the United States, 1968.
390 U.S. 102, 88 S.Ct. 733, 19 L.Ed.2d 936.

Certiorari to the United States Circuit Court of Appeals for the Third Circuit.

JUSTICE HARLAN delivered the opinion of the Court.

This controversy, involving in its present posture the dismissal of a declaratory judgment action for nonjoinder of an "indispensable" party, began nearly 10 years ago with a traffic accident. An automobile owned by Edward Dutcher, who was not present when the accident occurred, was being driven by Donald Cionci, to whom Dutcher had given the keys. John Lynch and John Harris were passengers. The automobile crossed the median strip of the highway and collided with a truck being driven by Thomas Smith. Cionci, Lynch, and Smith were killed and Harris was severely injured.

Three tort actions were brought. Provident Tradesmens Bank, the administrator of the estate of passenger Lynch and petitioner here, sued the estate of the driver, Cionci, in a diversity action. Smith's administratrix, and Harris in person, each brought a state-court action against the estate of Cionci, Dutcher, the owner, and the estate of Lynch. These Smith and Harris actions, for unknown reasons, have never gone to

against Lynch the passenger?

trial and are still pending. The Lynch action against Cionci's estate was settled for $50,000, which the estate of Cionci, being penniless, has never paid.

Dutcher, the owner of the automobile and a defendant in the as yet untried tort actions, had an automobile liability insurance policy with Lumbermens Mutual Casualty Company, a respondent here. That policy had an upper limit of $100,000 for all claims arising out of a single accident. This fund was potentially subject to two different sorts of claims by the tort plaintiffs. First, Dutcher himself might be held vicariously liable as Cionci's "principal"; the likelihood of such a judgment against Dutcher is a matter of considerable doubt and dispute. Second, the policy by its terms covered the direct liability of any person driving Dutcher's car with Dutcher's "permission."

The insurance company had declined, after notice, to defend in the tort action brought by Lynch's estate against the estate of Cionci, believing that Cionci had not had permission and hence was not covered by the policy. The facts allegedly were that Dutcher had entrusted his car to Cionci, but that Cionci had made a detour from the errand for which Dutcher allowed his car to be taken. The estate of Lynch, armed with its $50,000 liquidated claim against the estate of Cionci, brought the present diversity action for a declaration that Cionci's use of the car had been "with permission" of Dutcher. The only named defendants were the company and the estate of Cionci. The other two tort plaintiffs were joined as plaintiffs. Dutcher, a resident of the State of Pennsylvania as were all the plaintiffs, was not joined either as plaintiff or defendant. The failure to join him was not adverted to at the trial level.

The major question of law contested at trial was a state-law question. * * * The District Court * * * directed verdicts in favor of the two estates. * * * The jury * * * found that Cionci had had permission, and hence awarded a verdict to Harris also.

Lumbermens appealed the judgment to the Court of Appeals for the Third Circuit, raising various state-law questions. * * * The Court of Appeals did not reach any of these issues. Instead, after reargument *en banc,* it decided, 5–2, to reverse on two alternative grounds neither of which had been raised in the District Court or by the appellant.

The first of these grounds was that Dutcher was an indispensable party. The court held that the "adverse interests" that had rendered Dutcher incompetent to testify under the Pennsylvania Dead Man Rule also required him to be made a party. The court did not consider whether the fact that a verdict had already been rendered, without objection to the nonjoinder of Dutcher, affected the matter. Nor did it follow the provision of Rule 19 of the Federal Rules of Civil Procedure that findings of "indispensability" must be based on stated pragmatic considerations. It held, to the contrary, that the right of a person who "may be affected" by the judgment to be joined is a "substantive" right, unaffected by the federal rules; that a trial court "may not proceed" in the absence of such a person; and that since Dutcher could not be joined as a defendant without destroying diversity jurisdiction the action had to be dismissed.

* * * Concluding that the inflexible approach adopted by the Court of Appeals in this case exemplifies the kind of reasoning that the Rule was designed to avoid, we reverse.

I.

* * *

We may assume, at the outset, that Dutcher falls within the category of persons who, under [Rule 19] (a), should be "joined if feasible." The action was for an adjudication of the validity of certain claims against a fund. Dutcher, faced with the possibility of judgments against him, had an interest in having the fund preserved to cover that potential liability. Hence there existed, when this case went to trial, at least the possibility that a judgment might impede Dutcher's ability to protect his interest, or lead to later relitigation by him.

The optimum solution, an adjudication of the permission question that would be binding on all interested persons, was not "feasible," however, for Dutcher could not be made a defendant without destroying diversity. Hence the problem was the one to which Rule 19(b) appears to address itself: in the absence of a person who "should be joined if feasible," should the court dismiss the action or proceed without him? Since this problem emerged for the first time in the Court of Appeals, there were also two subsidiary questions. First, what was the effect, if any, of the failure of the defendants to raise the matter in the District Court? Second, what was the importance, if any, of the fact that a judgment, binding on the parties although not binding on Dutcher, had already been reached after extensive litigation? The three questions prove, on examination, to be interwoven.

We conclude, upon consideration of the record and applying the "equity and good conscience" test of Rule 19(b), that the Court of Appeals erred in not allowing the judgment to stand.

Rule 19(b) suggests four "interests" that must be examined in each case to determine whether, in equity and good conscience, the court should proceed without a party whose absence from the litigation is compelled. Each of these interests must, in this case, be viewed entirely from an appellate perspective since the matter of joinder was not considered in the trial court. First, the plaintiff has an interest in having a forum. Before the trial, the strength of this interest obviously depends upon whether a satisfactory alternative forum exists. On appeal, if the plaintiff has won, he has a strong additional interest in preserving his judgment. Second, the defendant may properly wish to avoid multiple litigation, or inconsistent relief, or sole responsibility for a liability he shares with another. After trial, however, if the defendant has failed to assert this interest, it is quite proper to consider it foreclosed.

Third, there is the interest of the outsider whom it would have been desirable to join. Of course, since the outsider is not before the court, he cannot be bound by the judgment rendered. This means, however, only that a judgment is not *res judicata* as to, or legally enforceable against, a nonparty. It obviously does not mean either (a) that a court may never issue a judgment that, in practice, affects a nonparty or (b) that (to the contrary) a court may always proceed without considering the potential effect on nonparties simply because they are not "bound" in the technical sense. Instead, as Rule 19(a) expresses it, the court must consider the extent to which the judgment may "as a practical matter impair or impede his ability to protect" his interest in the subject matter.[b] When a case has reached the appeal stage the matter is more complex. The judgment appealed from may not in fact affect the interest of any outsider even though there existed, before trial, a possibility that a judgment affecting his interest would be rendered. When necessary, however, a court of appeals should, on its own initiative, take steps to protect the absent party, who of course had no opportunity to plead and prove his interest below.

Fourth, there remains the interest of the courts and the public in complete, consistent, and efficient settlement of controversies. We read the Rule's third criterion, whether the judgment issued in the absence of the nonjoined person will be "adequate," to refer to this public stake in settling disputes by wholes, whenever possible, for clearly the plaintiff, who himself chose both the forum and the parties defendant, will not be heard to complain about the sufficiency of the relief obtainable against them. After trial, considerations of efficiency of course include the fact that the time and expense of a trial have already been spent.

Rule 19(b) also directs a district court to consider the possibility of shaping relief to accommodate these four interests. Commentators had argued that greater attention should be paid to this potential solution to a joinder stymie, and the Rule now makes it explicit that a court should consider modification of a judgment as an alternative to dismissal. Needless to say, a court of appeals may also properly require suitable modification as a condition of affirmance.

Had the Court of Appeals applied Rule 19's criteria to the facts of the present case, it could hardly have reached the conclusion it did. We begin with the plaintiffs' viewpoint. It is difficult to decide at this stage whether they would have had an "adequate" remedy had the action been dismissed before trial for nonjoinder: we cannot here determine whether the plaintiffs

---

[b]   This provision is now Rule 19(a)(1)(B)(i) and the language has been altered.

could have brought the same action, against the same parties plus Dutcher, in a state court. After trial, however, the "adequacy" of this hypothetical alternative, from the plaintiffs' point of view, was obviously greatly diminished. Their interest in preserving a fully litigated judgment should be overborne only by rather greater opposing considerations than would be required at an earlier stage when the plaintiffs' only concern was for a federal rather than a state forum.

Opposing considerations in this case are hard to find. The defendants had no stake, either asserted or real, in the joinder of Dutcher. They showed no interest in joinder until the Court of Appeals took the matter into its own hands. This properly forecloses any interest of theirs, but for purposes of clarity we note that the insurance company, whose liability was limited to $100,000, had or will have full opportunity to litigate each claim on that fund against the claimant involved. Its only concern with the absence of Dutcher was and is to obtain a windfall escape from its defeat at trial.

The interest of the outsider, Dutcher, is more difficult to reckon. The Court of Appeals, concluding that it should not follow Rule 19's command to determine whether, as a practical matter, the judgment impaired the nonparty's ability to protect his rights, simply quoted the District Court's reasoning on the Dead Man issue as proof that Dutcher had a "right" to be joined:

 The subject matter of this suit is the coverage of Lumbermens' policy issued to Dutcher. Depending upon the outcome of this trial, Dutcher may have the policy all to himself or he may have to share its coverage with the Cionci Estate, thereby extending the availability of the proceeds of the policy to satisfy verdicts and judgments in favor of the two Estate plaintiffs. Sharing the coverage of a policy of insurance with finite limits with another, and thereby making that policy available to claimants against that other person is immediately worth less than having the coverage of such policy available to Dutcher alone. By the outcome in the instant case, to the extent that the two Estate plaintiffs will have the proceeds of the policy available to them in their claims against Cionci's estate, Dutcher will lose a measure of protection. Conversely, to the extent that the proceeds of this policy are not available to the two Estate plaintiffs Dutcher will gain. * * * It is sufficient for the purpose of determining adversity [of interest] that it appears clearly that the measure of Dutcher's protection under this policy of insurance is dependent upon the outcome of this suit. That being so, Dutcher's interest in these proceedings is adverse to the interest of the two Estate plaintiffs, the parties who represent, on this record, the interests of the deceased persons in the matter in controversy.[11]

There is a logical error in the Court of Appeals' appropriation of this reasoning for its own quite different purposes: Dutcher had an "adverse" interest * * * because he would have been benefited by a ruling in favor of the insurance company; the question before the Court of Appeals, however, was whether Dutcher was harmed by the judgment against the insurance company.

The two questions are not the same. If the three plaintiffs had lost to the insurance company on the permission issue, that loss would have ended the matter favorably to Dutcher. If, as has happened, the three plaintiffs obtain a judgment against the insurance company on the permission issue, Dutcher may still claim that as a nonparty he is not estopped by that judgment from relitigating the issue. At that point it might be argued that Dutcher should be bound by the previous decision because, although technically a nonparty, he had purposely bypassed an adequate opportunity to intervene. We do not now decide whether such an argument would be correct under the circumstances of this case. If, however, Dutcher is properly foreclosed by his failure to intervene in the present litigation, then the joinder issue considered in the Court of Appeals vanishes, for any rights of Dutcher's have been lost by his own inaction.

If Dutcher is not foreclosed by his failure to intervene below, then he is not "bound" by the judgment in favor of the insurance company and, in theory, he has not been harmed. There remains, however, the practical question whether Dutcher is likely to have any need, and if so will have any opportunity, to relitigate. The only possible threat to him is that if the fund is used to pay judgments against Cionci the money may in fact have disappeared before Dutcher has an opportunity to assert his interest. Upon examination, we find this supposed threat neither large nor unavoidable.

The state-court actions against Dutcher had lain dormant for years at the pleading stage by the time the Court of Appeals acted. Petitioner asserts here that under the applicable Pennsylvania vicarious liability law there is virtually no chance of recovery against Dutcher. We do not accept this assertion as fact, but the matter could have been explored below. Furthermore, even in the event of tort judgments against Dutcher, it is unlikely that he will be prejudiced by the outcome here. The potential claimants against Dutcher himself are identical with the potential claimants against Cionci's estate. Should the claimants seek to collect from Dutcher personally, he may be able to raise the permission issue defensively, making it irrelevant that the actual monies paid from the fund may have disappeared: Dutcher can assert that Cionci did not have his

---

[11]   218 F.Supp. 802, 805–806, quoted [by the Third Circuit Court of Appeals] at 365 F.2d, at 805.

permission and that therefore the payments made on Cionci's behalf out of Dutcher's insurance policy should properly be credited against Dutcher's own liability. Of course, when Dutcher raises this defense he may lose, either on the merits of the permission issue or on the ground that the issue is foreclosed by Dutcher's failure to intervene in the present case, but Dutcher will not have been prejudiced by the failure of the District Court here to order him joined.

If the Court of Appeals was unconvinced that the threat to Dutcher was trivial, it could nevertheless have avoided all difficulties by proper phrasing of the decree. The District Court, for unspecified reasons, had refused to order immediate payment on the Cionci judgment. Payment could have been withheld pending the suits against Dutcher and relitigation (if that became necessary) by him. In this Court, furthermore, counsel for petitioners represented orally that they, the tort plaintiffs, would accept a limitation of all claims to the amount of the insurance policy. Obviously such a compromise could have been reached below had the Court of Appeals been willing to abandon its rigid approach and seek ways to preserve what was, as to the parties, subject to the appellants' other contentions, a perfectly valid judgment.

The suggestion of potential relitigation of the question of "permission" raises the fourth "interest" at stake in joinder cases—efficiency. It might have been preferable, at the trial level, if there were a forum available in which both the company and Dutcher could have been made defendants, to dismiss the action and force the plaintiffs to go elsewhere. Even this preference would have been highly problematical, however, for the actual threat of relitigation by Dutcher depended on there being judgments against him and on the amount of the fund, which was not revealed to the District Court. By the time the case reached the Court of Appeals, however, the problematical preference on efficiency grounds had entirely disappeared: there was no reason then to throw away a valid judgment just because it did not theoretically settle the whole controversy.

II.

Application of Rule 19(b)'s "equity and good conscience" test for determining whether to proceed or dismiss would doubtless have led to a contrary result below. The Court of Appeals' reasons for disregarding the Rule remain to be examined. The majority of the court concluded that the Rule was inapplicable because "substantive" rights are involved, and substantive rights are not affected by the Federal Rules. Although the court did not articulate exactly what the substantive rights are, or what law determines them, we take it to have been making the following argument: (1) there is a category of persons called "indispensable parties"; (2) that category is defined by substantive law and the definition cannot be modified by rule; (3) the right of a person falling within that category to participate in the lawsuit in question is also a substantive matter, and is absolute.

With this we may contrast the position that is reflected in Rule 19. Whether a person is "indispensable," that is, whether a particular lawsuit must be dismissed in the absence of that person, can only be determined in the context of particular litigation. There is a large category, whose limits are not presently in question, of persons who, in the Rule's terminology, should be "joined if feasible," and who, in the older terminology, were called either necessary or indispensable parties. Assuming the existence of a person who should be joined if feasible, the only further question arises when joinder is not possible and the court must decide whether to dismiss or to proceed without him. To use the familiar but confusing terminology, the decision to proceed is a decision that the absent person is merely "necessary" while the decision to dismiss is a decision that he is "indispensable." The decision whether to dismiss (i.e., the decision whether the person missing is "indispensable") must be based on factors varying with the different cases, some such factors being substantive, some procedural, some compelling by themselves, and some subject to balancing against opposing interests. Rule 19 does not prevent the assertion of compelling substantive interests; it merely commands the courts to examine each controversy to make certain that the interests really exist. To say that a court "must" dismiss in the absence of an indispensable party and that it "cannot proceed" without him puts the matter the wrong way around: a court does not know whether a particular person is "indispensable" until it has examined the situation to determine whether it can proceed without him.

The Court of Appeals concluded, although it was the first court to hold, that the 19th century joinder cases in this Court created a federal, common-law, substantive right in a certain class of persons to be joined in the corresponding lawsuits. At the least, that was not the way the matter started. The joinder problem first arose in equity and in the earliest case giving rise to extended discussion the problem was the relatively simple one of the inefficiency of litigation involving only some of the interested persons. [Elmendorf v. Taylor, 23 U.S. (10 Wheat.) 152, 6 L.Ed. 289 (1825).] * * *

Following this case there arose three cases, also in equity, that the Court of Appeals here held to have declared a "substantive" right to be joined. It is true that these cases involved what would now be called "substantive" rights. This substantive involvement of the absent person with the controversy before the Court was, however, in each case simply an inescapable fact of the situation presented to the Court for adjudication. The Court in each case left the outsider with no more "rights" than it had already found belonged to him. The question in each case was simply whether, given the substantive involvement of the outsider, it was proper to proceed to adjudicate as between the parties.

* * *

The most influential of the cases in which this Court considered the question whether to proceed or dismiss in the absence of an interested but not joinable outsider is Shields v. Barrow, 17 How. 130, referred to in the opinion below. There the Court attempted, perhaps unfortunately, to stage general definitions of those persons without whom litigation could or could not proceed. In the former category were placed

> Persons having an interest in the controversy, and who ought to be made parties, in order that the court may act on that rule which requires it to decide on, and finally determine the entire controversy, and do complete justice, by adjusting all the rights involved in it. These persons are commonly termed necessary parties; but if their interests are separable from those of the parties before the court, so that the court can proceed to a decree, and do complete and final justice, without affecting other persons not before the court, the latter are not indispensable parties.

The persons in the latter category were

> Persons who not only have an interest in the controversy, but an interest of such a nature that a final decree cannot be made without either affecting that interest, or leaving the controversy in such a condition that its final termination may be wholly inconsistent with equity and good conscience.

These generalizations are still valid today, and they are consistent with the requirements of Rule 19, but they are not a substitute for the analysis required by that Rule. Indeed, the second *Shields* definition states, in rather different fashion, the criteria for decision announced in Rule 19(b). One basis for dismissal is prejudice to the rights of an absent party that "*cannot*" be avoided in issuance of a final decree. Alternatively, if the decree can be so written that it protects the interests of the absent persons, but as so written it leaves the controversy so situated that the outcome may be inconsistent with "equity and good conscience," the suit should be dismissed.

The majority of the Court of Appeals read Shields v. Barrow to say that a person whose interests "may be affected" by the decree of the court is an indispensable party, and that all indispensable parties have a "substantive right" to have suits dismissed in their absence. We are unable to read *Shields* as saying either. It dealt only with persons whose interests must, unavoidably, be affected by a decree and it said nothing about substantive rights. Rule 19(b), which the Court of Appeals dismissed as an ineffective attempt to change the substantive rights stated in *Shields,* is, on the contrary, a valid statement of the criteria for determining whether to proceed or dismiss in the forced absence of an interested person. It takes, for aught that now appears, adequate account of the very real, very substantive claims to fairness on the part of outsiders that may arise in some cases. This, however, simply is not such a case.

* * *

The judgment is vacated and the case is remanded to the Court of Appeals * * *.

NOTES AND QUESTIONS

1.   *Provident Tradesmens* interpreted the 1966 version of Federal Rule 19. Examine the Advisory Committee's Note to Rule 19, which is set out in the Supplement. What impact did the 1966 amendment have on the distinction between "persons required to be joined if feasible," of Rule 19(a), and "a person who is required to be joined if feasible cannot be joined," of Rule 19(b)? Given the amendment, what is the purpose of Rule 12(b)(7)? Of Rule 12(h)?

2.   Consider the following comments in an article written shortly after the Third Circuit decision dismissing the action:

> * * * How has Dutcher been affected? The judgment declaring that Cionci was driving with permission does not bind Dutcher legally, since he was not a party. Dutcher is free to contest the point with all, including the insurer. Be it noted that although he testified in the action, Dutcher made no attempt to intervene; as the minority suggests, he might have reasonably preferred to stay out of the action. Whereas a judgment declaring Cionci to be an insured did not bind Dutcher, a judgment the other way would very likely have inured to Dutcher's benefit * * *.

Kaplan, *Continuing Work of the Civil Committee: 1966 Amendments of the Federal Rules of Civil Procedure* (I), 81 Harv.L.Rev. 356, 373 (1967).

3.   In what ways might the court shape relief in order to lessen any prejudice under Rule 19(b)? Is the court free simply to grant a remedy other than the one originally requested—for example, by awarding money damages when specific performance might have a detrimental impact on the absentee? Of what importance is the availability of another forum in determining whether the action must be dismissed in the absence of someone whose joinder is not feasible?

4.   What weight should be given to the various factors listed in Rule 19? Because there is no precise formula for determining whether a particular nonparty must be joined under Rule 19(a), the decision has to be made in light of the general policies of the rule. Can you articulate what those policies are? For example, what is the difference between the Rule 19(a)(1)(A) standard that in the absence of the nonparty "the court cannot accord complete relief among existing parties," and the factor listed in Rule 19(b)(3), "whether a judgment

rendered in the person's absence would be adequate"? How do these factors differ from the focus in Rule 19(a)(1)(B) on the prejudicial effect of not joining the absentee?

5.   REPUBLIC OF THE PHILIPPINES v. PIMENTEL, 553 U.S. 851, 128 S.Ct. 2180, 11 L.Ed.2d 131 (2008), involved the intersection of Rule 19(b), statutory interpleader, and sovereign immunity. See p. 500, infra.

E. IMPLEADER

Read Federal Rule of Civil Procedure 14 and the accompanying materials in the Supplement.

1. THE HISTORICAL USE OF IMPLEADER

Impleader has its roots in "vouching to warranty," a common law procedure "whereby a person whose title to land had been attacked could notify his vendor of the attack if the latter had warranted the title. The vendor, whether or not he chose to participate, would then be bound by the prior determination in a subsequent suit by his vendee":

> When A sues B, there is often a third party, C, who may ultimately be liable to B for all or some part of the damages which A might recover. This liability * * * may be based on such legal relationships as those which arise from a contract of indemnity for loss or liability or a right to contribution from a joint tortfeasor. If it were necessary for B to institute a separate action to recover reimbursement from C, the issue of B's liability to A would often have to be relitigated between B and C, since C, not a party to the original litigation, would generally not be bound by the prior determination. * * * Even if B could obtain a wholly consistent result against C, the courts would have been burdened by two trials and B might have been seriously handicapped by having to satisfy A's judgment long before his recovery over from C. * * *

Developments in the Law—Multiparty Litigation in the Federal Courts, 71 Harv.L.Rev. 877, 906–07 (1958). See Neiderman & Reed, *Vouching In Under the U.C.C.: Its History, Modern Use, and Questions About Its Continued Viability,* 23 J.L. & Com. (2003).

2. THIRD-PARTY PRACTICE UNDER RULE 14

JEUB V. B/G FOODS, INC.

United States District Court, District of Minnesota, 1942.
2 F.R.D. 238.

Rule 14

NORDBYE, DISTRICT JUDGE. The facts are briefly these: The complainants seek to recover damages from the defendant, B/G Foods, Inc., on the grounds that, in one of the restaurants operated by this defendant, they were served with certain ham which was contaminated, unwholesome, and deleterious to the health, causing complainants to become sick and distressed to their damage. * * * Prior to the service of the answer, on application of the defendant, an ex parte order was obtained, making Swift and Company a third-party defendant. The third-party complaint set forth that the ham served was canned "Swift Premium Ham", a product of Swift and Company, and purchased in a sealed can by B/G Foods the day preceding the serving of the ham to the complainants. It is asserted that B/G Foods was entirely free from any blame or negligence in connection therewith. It is further alleged in the third-party complaint that "if any of said ham was unwholesome, poisonous, deleterious or otherwise in any way unfit for human consumption, such condition was caused solely and entirely by negligence and carelessness and unlawful conduct on the part of Swift and Company." Further, that "Swift and Company is liable to indemnify and reimburse B/G Foods, Inc., for the whole amount of any recovery made by plaintiff, * * * against B/G Foods, Inc., on account of said ham being served to her in its food shop. * * *" Judgment is prayed that any recovery be against Swift and Company and not B/G Foods, Inc., and that B/G Foods, Inc., have judgment against Swift and Company for any and all sums which may be adjudged against B/G Foods, Inc., in favor of the plaintiff.

The motion to vacate the order is based on the showing that plaintiffs have not amended, and have refused to amend, their complaints to state any cause of action against Swift and Company. It is therefore the position of the third-party defendant that no relief can be granted against it in this proceeding; that [Federal] Rule 14 * * * is merely procedural and does not create any substantive rights; that no right of contribution or indemnity exists under the Minnesota law merely because a suit has been commenced; and that the party must have suffered some loss or paid more than his share of the loss before any rights will inure. It is pointed out that, as yet, the B/G Foods has suffered no loss and has made no payment growing out of the incident in question.

That the rights over and against Swift and Company, which B/G Foods may have by reason of any loss sustained by it, must be governed by the substantive laws of this State is entirely clear. The invoking of the third-party procedural practice must not do violence to the substantive rights of the parties. However, an acceleration or an expedition of the presentation of such rights does not conflict with any Minnesota law. Rule 14 * * * permits the impleader of a party "who is or may be liable."[c] The fact that an independent action for money recovery could not be brought at this time does not militate against B/G Foods' right to invoke a procedure which will determine rights of the parties concurrently with that of the basic proceeding, and if and when any loss has been sustained as to which Swift and Company is liable over, the laws of this State in regard thereto may be made effective. * * * Rule 14 is not restricted to the rights of indemnity or contribution which are presently * * * [enforceable] * * *.

to have weight or effect

The apparent purpose of Rule 14 is to provide suitable machinery whereby the rights of all parties may be determined in one proceeding. Manifestly if Swift and Company is liable over to B/G Foods, Inc., for any or all damages sustained by reason of the tortious act alleged, no cogent reason is suggested why the original defendant should not avail itself of this rule. Otherwise, B/G Foods, Inc., would be required to await the outcome of the present suit, and then if plaintiffs recover, to institute an independent action for contribution or indemnity. The rule under consideration was promulgated to avoid this very circuity of proceeding. Neither is any good reason suggested why the determination of the entire controversy in one proceeding will prejudice the rights of any of the parties. Certainly, plaintiffs cannot complain. They have not availed themselves of the opportunity to join Swift and Company as a party defendant. To require the same jury to determine the controversy between the third-party plaintiff and third-party defendant will not harm or jeopardize their rights or position before these triers of fact. The rights of Swift and Company are likewise not prejudiced by being made a third-party defendant. If it is liable over, it is concerned with the payment by B/G Foods, Inc., of any loss or damage obtained by these plaintiffs. However, the recognition or preservation of that right presents no particular difficulty. Any judgment against it by way of contribution or indemnity may be stayed until the judgment in the original proceeding against the B/G Foods, Inc., is paid or satisfied. One jury impaneled to determine the entire controversy may not only save time and expense, but it is fair to assume that the ends of justice will be served by disposition of the entire matter through the facilities of one jury. * * *

The motion, therefore, to vacate the order making Swift and Company a third-party defendant in each of the above-entitled cases, is denied. * * *

---

[c] In 2007, the provision was renumbered as Rule 14(a)(1).

NOTES AND QUESTIONS

1.   Federal Rule 14 avoids circuity of actions by permitting a defending party to add a party who is or may be liable for all or part of the claim against it. See 6 Wright, Miller & Kane, Federal Practice and Procedure § 1443 (3d ed.). Rule 14 does not authorize the joinder of a party who is liable on a separate or independent claim; rather, the liability must be derivative of the original claim. The original version of Rule 14 limited the availability of third-party practice:

> Permission to the defendant to implead a person, not originally a party, asserted to be liable to the defendant for all or part of the plaintiff's claim against the defendant, was something of an innovation when it was brought into the civil practice on a general basis in 1938. Perhaps by reason of its novelty, this "third-party practice" of Rule 14 was closely guarded. The defendant seeking impleader had always to apply to the court for leave: he might move ex parte if he had not yet served his answer; after answer, the more common case, he was obliged to give notice to the plaintiff.

Kaplan, *Amendments of the Federal Rules of Civil Procedure,* 1961–1963 (II), 77 Harv.L.Rev. 801, 801 (1964). Amendments in 1963 permitted the third party to be impleaded without court permission if the impleader complaint is filed shortly after defendant's answer in the original suit is served. What are the advantages of the current approach?

2.   Rule 14 does not allow a defendant to implead an existing defendant. See Horton v. Continental Can Co., 19 F.R.D. 429 (D. Neb. 1956). But there are at least two other possible procedures for a defendant to assert its claims against an existing defendant. What are they? What difference does it make if a defendant's claim is brought under Rule 14 or some "other appropriate procedure"? What is the logic of Rules 13(a), (b), and (g) permitting or requiring counterclaims and crossclaims to be asserted against persons who already are parties and Rule 14(a) denying impleader in that context?

F. INTERPLEADER IN THE FEDERAL COURTS

———

Read Federal Rule of Civil Procedure 22 and 28 U.S.C. §§ 1335, 1397, and 2361 and the accompanying materials in the Supplement.

———

Interpleader is a device designed to enable a party who might be exposed to multiple claims to money or property under the party's control to settle the controversy in a single proceeding. For example, if two people claim that each is the sole beneficiary of a life insurance policy, the insurance company, in the absence of a joinder device such as interpleader, would be required to defend against both in two actions. Not only would the company be forced to incur the expense of additional litigation, but it would be faced with the possibility that, in separate lawsuits, *both* claimants might win. See 7 Wright, Miller & Kane, Federal Practice and Procedure § 1702 (3d ed.).

STATE FARM FIRE & CASUALTY CO. V. TASHIRE

Supreme Court of the United States, 1967.
386 U.S. 523, 87 S.Ct. 1199, 18 L.Ed.2d 270.

Certiorari to the United States Court of Appeals for the Ninth Circuit.

JUSTICE FORTAS delivered the opinion of the Court.

[This case arose out of a collision between a Greyhound bus and a pickup truck in Shasta County, California in September, 1964. Two of the bus passengers were killed and 33 others were injured, as were the bus driver, the driver of the truck, and its passenger. One of the dead and ten of the injured passengers were Canadians; the rest of the individuals were citizens of five American states.

Four of the injured passengers filed suit in California state courts seeking damages in excess of $1,000,000 and naming as defendants: Greyhound Lines, Inc.; Nauta, the bus driver; Clark, the driver of the truck; and Glasgow, the truck passenger who apparently was its owner. Each of the individual defendants was a citizen of Oregon; Greyhound was a California corporation. Before the California cases came to trial and before any other suits were filed, petitioner, State Farm Fire & Casualty Company, an Illinois corporation, brought this interpleader action in the United States District Court for the District of Oregon.

State Farm asserted that at the time of the collision it had in force an insurance policy covering Clark, the driver of the truck, for bodily injury liability up to $10,000 per person and $20,000 per occurrence. State Farm further asserted that the aggregate damages sought in actions already filed in California and other anticipated actions far exceeded the amount of its maximum liability under the policy. Accordingly, it paid into court the sum of $20,000 and asked the court (1) to require all claimants to establish their claims against Clark and his insurer in the Oregon proceeding and in no other action, and (2) to discharge State Farm from all further obligations under its policy. Alternatively, State Farm requested a decree that the insurer owed no duty to Clark and was not liable on the policy, and asked the court to refund the $20,000 deposit. State Farm joined as defendants Clark, Glasgow, Nauta, Greyhound, and each of the prospective claimants. Jurisdiction was predicated both upon the Federal Interpleader Act and general diversity of citizenship. Personal service was effected on each of the American defendants and registered mail was employed to give notice to the 11 Canadian claimants.

The Oregon District Court issued an order requiring each of the defendants to show cause why he should not be restrained from filing or prosecuting any proceeding affecting the property or obligation involved in the interpleader action. In response, several of the defendants contended that the policy did cover the accident and advanced various arguments for the position that interpleader was inappropriate.

When a temporary injunction along the lines sought by State Farm issued, the respondents moved to dismiss and, in the alternative, sought a change of venue to the district in which the collision had occurred. After a hearing, the District Court declined to dissolve the temporary injunction but continued the motion for a change of venue. Later, the temporary injunction was broadened so that all suits against Clark, State Farm, Greyhound, and Nauta had to be prosecuted in the interpleader proceeding.

On interlocutory appeal, the Ninth Circuit reversed on the ground that in states, such as Oregon, that do not permit a "direct action" against an insurance company until a judgment is obtained against the insured, State Farm could not invoke federal interpleader until the claims against the insured had been reduced to judgment. The Court of Appeals held that prior to that time claimants with unliquidated tort claims are not "claimants" within the meaning of Section 1335 of Title 28 and are not "persons having claims against the plaintiff" within the meaning of Federal Rule 22.[d] The Ninth Circuit directed that the temporary injunction be dissolved and the action be dismissed. The Supreme Court granted certiorari.]

* * *

I

Before considering the issues presented by the petition for certiorari, we find it necessary to dispose of a question neither raised by the parties nor passed upon by the courts below. Since the matter concerns our jurisdiction, we raise it on our own motion. * * * The interpleader statute * * * has been uniformly construed to require only "minimal diversity," that is, diversity of citizenship between two or more claimants, without regard to the circumstance that other rival claimants may be co-citizens. The language of the statute, the legislative purpose broadly to remedy the problems posed by multiple claimants to a single fund, and the consistent judicial interpretation tacitly accepted by Congress, persuade us that the statute requires no more. There remains, however, the question whether such a statutory construction is consistent with Article III of our Constitution * * *. In Strawbridge v. Curtiss * * * [p. 220, supra], this Court held that the diversity of citizenship statute required "complete

---

d   The language of Rule 22 has since been altered without any substantive change.

diversity": where co-citizens appeared on both sides of a dispute, jurisdiction was lost. But Chief Justice Marshall there purported to construe only "The words of the act of Congress," not the Constitution itself. And in a variety of contexts this Court and the lower courts have concluded that Article III poses no obstacle to the legislative extension of federal jurisdiction, founded on diversity, so long as any two adverse parties are not co-citizens. Accordingly, we conclude that the present case is properly in the federal courts.

II

We do not agree with the Court of Appeals that, in the absence of a state law or contractual provision for "direct action" suits against the insurance company, the company must wait until persons asserting claims against its insured have reduced those claims to judgment before seeking to invoke the benefits of federal interpleader. * * *

Considerations of judicial administration demonstrate the soundness of this view which, in any event, seems compelled by the language of the present statute, which is remedial and to be liberally construed. Were an insurance company required to await reduction of claims to judgment, the first claimant to obtain such a judgment or to negotiate a settlement might appropriate all or a disproportionate slice of the fund before his fellow claimants were able to establish their claims. The difficulties such a race to judgment pose for the insurer, and the unfairness which may result to some claimants, were among the principal evils the interpleader device was intended to remedy.

III

The fact that State Farm had properly invoked the interpleader jurisdiction under § 1335 did not, however, entitle it to an order both enjoining prosecution of suits against it outside the confines of the interpleader proceeding and also extending such protection to its insured, the alleged tortfeasor. Still less was Greyhound Lines entitled to have that order expanded so as to protect itself and its driver, also alleged to be tortfeasors, from suits brought by its passengers in various state or federal courts. Here, the scope of the litigation, in terms of parties and claims, was vastly more extensive than the confines of the "fund," the deposited proceeds of the insurance policy. In these circumstances, the mere existence of such a fund cannot, by use of interpleader, be employed to accomplish purposes that exceed the needs of orderly contest with respect to the fund.

There are situations, of a type not present here, where the effect of interpleader is to confine the total litigation to a single forum and proceeding. One such case is where a stakeholder, faced with rival claims to the fund itself, acknowledges—or denies—his liability to one or the other of the claimants. In this situation, the fund itself is the target of the claimants. It marks the outer limits of the controversy. It is, therefore, reasonable and sensible that interpleader, in discharge of its office to protect the fund, should also protect the stakeholder from vexatious and multiple litigation. In this context, the suits sought to be enjoined are squarely within the language of 28 U.S.C. § 2361 * * *.

But the present case is another matter. Here, an accident has happened. Thirty-five passengers or their representatives have claims which they wish to press against a variety of defendants: the bus company, its driver, the owner of the truck, and the truck driver. The circumstance that one of the prospective defendants happens to have an insurance policy is a fortuitous event which should not of itself shape the nature of the ensuing litigation. * * * [A]n insurance company whose maximum interest in the case cannot exceed $20,000 and who in fact asserts that it has no interest at all, should not be allowed to determine that dozens of tort plaintiffs must be compelled to press their claims—even those claims which are not against the insured and which in no event could be satisfied out of the meager insurance fund—in a single forum of the insurance company's choosing. There is nothing in the statutory scheme, and very little in the judicial and academic commentary upon that scheme, which requires that the tail be allowed to wag the dog in this fashion.

State Farm's interest in this case * * * receives full vindication when the court restrains claimants from seeking to enforce against the insurance company any judgment obtained against its insured, except in the interpleader proceeding itself. To the extent that the District Court sought to control claimants' lawsuits against the insured and other alleged tortfeasors, it exceeded the powers granted to it by the statutory scheme.

We recognize, of course, that our view of interpleader means that it cannot be used to solve all the vexing problems of multiparty litigation arising out of a mass tort. But interpleader was never intended to perform such a function, to be an all-purpose "bill of peace." Had it been so intended, careful provision would necessarily have been made to insure that a party with little or no interest in the outcome of a complex controversy should not strip truly interested parties of substantial rights—such as the right to choose the forum in which to establish their claims, subject to generally applicable rules of jurisdiction, venue, service of process, removal, and change of venue. None of the legislative and academic sponsors of a modern federal interpleader device viewed their accomplishment as a "bill of peace," capable of sweeping dozens of lawsuits out of the various state and federal courts in which they were brought and into a single interpleader proceeding. * * *

In light of the evidence that federal interpleader was not intended to serve the function of a "bill of peace" in the context of multiparty litigation arising out of a mass tort, of the anomalous power which such a construction of the statute would give the stakeholder, and of the thrust of the statute and the purpose it was intended to serve, we hold that the interpleader statute did not authorize the injunction entered in the present case. Upon remand, the injunction is to be modified consistently with this opinion.

IV

The judgment of the Court of Appeals is reversed * * *.

[JUSTICE DOUGLAS dissented on the ground that the litigants were not "claimants" to the fund as required by the Federal Interpleader Act. He pointed out that the insurance policy specifically provided that no action could be brought against the company until the insured's obligation was determined. Furthermore, both California and Oregon law did not permit a direct action against the insurer until after final judgment against the insured. The dissent also took issue with the majority's construction of the words "may claim" in the Interpleader Act.]

NOTES AND QUESTIONS

1. The common law bill of interpleader was subject to a number of "historical limitations" that impeded its utility as an expeditious procedure. Among others, the requirement that the party wishing to institute an interpleader action show that competing claims were "identical in every respect and without the slightest degree of variation" posed a difficult barrier to hurdle. See Hancock Oil Co. v. Indep. Distrib. Co., 24 Cal.2d 497, 503–04, 150 P.2d 463, 466 (1944). The limits of a court's personal jurisdiction also often made it difficult to obtain power over all of the claimants consistent with constitutional requirements, and this inhibition likewise curtailed the availability of interpleader in federal courts. See NEW YORK LIFE INS. CO. v. DUNLEVY, 241 U.S. 518, 36 S.Ct. 613, 60 L.Ed. 1140 (1916).

Partially in response to the *Dunlevy* decision, Congress passed the Federal Interpleader Act in 1917. The statute was successively broadened and now appears as 28 U.S.C. §§ 1335, 1397, and 2361. The present act permits venue to be laid in any judicial district in which one or more of the claimants resides; allows for nationwide service of process; and provides for a federal forum when the stake is worth $500 and there is diversity of citizenship between two or more claimants. Interpleader also is available under Rule 22, but rule interpleader is subject to the usual rules of venue and jurisdiction. See Pan American Fire & Casualty Co. v. Revere, 188 F.Supp. 474 (E.D.La. 1960); Doernberg, *What's Wrong with This Picture?: Rule Interpleader, the Anti-Injunction Act, In Personam Jurisdiction, and M.C. Escher*, 67 U.Colo.L.Rev. 551 (1996).

2. In TREINIES v. SUNSHINE MINING CO., 308 U.S. 66, 60 S.Ct. 44, 84 L.Ed. 85 (1939), the Supreme Court held that a federal court could constitutionally assert jurisdiction under the Federal Interpleader Act despite the cocitizenship of the stakeholder and one of the claimants. In arriving at

this conclusion, the Court said that the stakeholder's "disinterestedness as between the claimants and as to the property in dispute" was demonstrated by his deposit of the fund in the court, and his discharge, which left the dispute to be ironed out between the "adverse claimants." Id. at 72, 60 S.Ct. at 48, 84 L.Ed. at 90. Was it realistic for the Court to treat the stakeholder as a nominal party for diversity purposes?

3.   In *Tashire*, on what basis did the Supreme Court decide that cocitizenship between adverse claimants does not destroy diversity jurisdiction? Would the result have been different had there been a lack of diversity between State Farm and the named defendants and an absence of "complete diversity" among all of the claimants?

4.   In *Tashire*, the Court concluded that an insurer may invoke statutory interpleader before claimants have reduced their insurance claims to judgment. However, the existence of the interpleader action was not a sufficient basis to stay all other actions involving claims of liability. According to the Court, what kinds of litigation would be appropriate for the interpleader-court to enjoin under 28 U.S.C. § 2361? Is this approach consistent with the Court's view that interpleader is not "an all-purpose 'bill of peace' "? Do you agree that a stay would be appropriate when the fund is "the target of entire litigation"? See Buckeye State Mut. Ins. Co. v. Moens, 944 F.Supp.2d 678, 695 (N.D. Iowa 2013).

5.   In GRIFFIN v. McCOACH, 313 U.S. 498, 61 S.Ct. 1023, 85 L.Ed. 1481 (1941), the Supreme Court held that in a statutory interpleader suit based on diversity jurisdiction a federal court is bound by the *Erie* doctrine to apply the conflict-of-law rules of the state in which it sits. The case was decided on the same day as *Klaxon*, p. 358, supra. Yet, in certain statutory interpleader actions, the courts of the forum state might never have been able to hear a comparable case due to Fourteenth Amendment limitations on their personal jurisdiction. Should federal courts be able to develop their own conflicts rules when a federal act extends service of process beyond what is permitted a state by the Constitution? See *Developments in the Law—Multiparty Litigation in the Federal Courts*, 71 Harv.L.Rev. 877, 924–26 (1958). Are there any other arguments to suggest the inapplicability of *Erie* and *Klaxon* in statutory interpleader cases? Relatedly, can a federal court grant interpleader under Rule 22 when the state courts would deny interpleader because the stakeholder alleges a personal interest in the outcome of the case?

6.   Consider the statement in *Tashire* that "our view of interpleader means that it cannot be used to solve all the vexing problems of multiparty litigation arising out of a mass tort." 386 U.S. at 535, 87 S.Ct. at 1206, 18 L.Ed.2d at 278. How far does this limitation extend? Should it prohibit crossclaims between interpleader claimants, the assertion of an unrelated claim by a disinterested stakeholder against a claimant, and a counterclaim by a claimant against the stakeholder? In the case that follows, what are the barriers that impede the utility of the interpleader proceeding?

REPUBLIC OF THE PHILIPPINES v. PIMENTEL, 553 U.S. 851, 128 S.Ct. 2180, 171 L.Ed.2d 131 (2008). The holder of $35 million transferred to a Panamanian company by Ferdinand Marcos, the former President of the Republic of the Philippines, brought a statutory interpleader action to determine ownership of the assets. Claimants included the Republic of the Philippines ("Republic"); the Philippine Presidential Commission on Good Governance ("Commission"); a class of persons who had suffered human rights abuses during the Marcos regime (known as the "Pimentel class"), seeking to enforce a $2 billion judgment entered by a federal court in the United States; and other judgment creditors. On a parallel track, the Republic and the Commission were requesting a declaration from the Sandiganbayan, a Philippine court of special jurisdiction over corruption cases, that any assets Marcos had obtained through misuse of office were forfeited to the Republic. The Republic and the Commission moved to dismiss the interpleader action, asserting that they were entitled to sovereign immunity and that under Rule 19 the action could not go forward in their absence because they were required parties. After complicated proceedings, the District Court awarded the assets to the Pimentel class, and the Ninth Circuit affirmed. The Supreme Court granted certiorari and held that the Republic and the Commission were required parties and that the interpleader action could not proceed without them, ordering that the action be dismissed.

No party contested that Rule 19(a) applied to the case. The Republic and the Commission were considered required because "their interests in the subject matter" were not protected if they were not present as parties. Id. at 864, 128 S.Ct. at 2189, 171 L.Ed.2d at 144 (internal citation omitted). The harder question was whether the case could go forward in their absence under Rule 19(b). On this point, the Supreme Court held that the Court of Appeals committed reversible error by giving insufficient weight to the absentees' assertion of sovereign immunity. The absentees would suffer prejudice to their sovereign status, which gave them, among other things, a "unique interest" in resolving ownership of the contested assets "and in determining if, and how, the assets should be used to compensate those persons who suffered grievous injury." Id. at 866, 128 S.Ct. at 2190, 171 L.Ed.2d at 145. In the Court's view, the absentees' comity interest in using Philippine courts to resolve the disputed claims offset any interest of the Pimentel class in recovering damages or any international concerns in combating public corruption. Moreover, the use of an alternative remedy could not lessen the prejudice to the absentees under Rule 19(b)(2)—no alternative remedies had "been proposed * * * or appear[ed] to be available." Id. at 870, 128 Sup.Ct. at 2192, 171 L.Ed.2d at 148. Nor would the judgment be adequate without the absentees under Rule 19(b)(3). On this factor, the Court explained, the Ninth Circuit erred by equating adequacy with "satisfaction of the Pimentel class' claims." To the contrary, adequacy referred to the " 'public stake in settling disputes by wholes, whenever possible,'" and in this case the judgment would not be adequate because it would not bind the absentees. Finally, it was also error to focus on the Pimentel class claimants, and not Merrill Lynch, in determining "whether the plaintiff would have an adequate remedy if the [interpleader] action were dismissed for nonjoinder," because Merrill Lynch as stakeholder was the plaintiff in the interpleader action. See Rule 19(b)(4). In the Supreme Court's view, dismissing the interpleader action would protect the stakeholder-bank by providing "an effective defense against piecemeal litigation and inconsistent, conflicting judgments"; moreover, any prejudice to the stakeholder was "outweighed by prejudice to the absent entities invoking sovereign immunity." Id. at 872, 128 S.Ct. at 2193–94, 171 L.Ed.2d at 149 (internal citation omitted).

The Court concluded:

> The Court of Appeals' failure to give sufficient weight to the likely prejudice to the Republic and the Commission should the interpleader proceed in their absence would, in the usual course, warrant reversal and remand for further proceedings. In this case, however, that error and our further analysis under the additional provisions of Rule 19(b) lead us to conclude the action must be dismissed. This leaves the Pimentel class, which has waited for years now to be compensated for grievous wrongs, with no immediate way to recover on its judgment against Marcos. And it leaves * * * [the stakeholder] without a judgment.

> The balance of equities may change in due course. One relevant change may occur if it appears that the Sandiganbayan cannot or will not issue its ruling within a reasonable period of time. Other changes could result when and if there is a ruling. * * * We do note that if [the stakeholder or other parties] * * * elect to commence further litigation in light of changed circumstances, it would not be necessary to file the new action in the District Court where this action arose, provided venue and jurisdictional requirements are satisfied elsewhere. The present action, however, may not proceed.

Id. at 872–73, 128 S.Ct. at 2194, 171 L.Ed.2d at 149–50. Justice Stevens dissented in part. He criticized the Court for taking "a more 'inflexible approach'" to the question of mandatory parties than required by Rule 19 and for ignoring the parties' interest "in the prompt resolution" of their claims. Id. at 879, 128 S.Ct. at 2197, 171 L.Ed.2d at 153.

NOTES AND QUESTIONS

1.   Sovereign immunity is a doctrine that insulates the government from suit unless it gives it consent to be sued. The immunity of a foreign government to suit in United States courts is governed by the Foreign Sovereign

Immunities Act, codified at Title 28, §§ 1330, 1332, 1391(f), 1441(d), and 1602–11 of the United States Code. A course in Constitutional Law or Federal Courts typically covers the doctrine in detail.

2.   One commentator has singled out the majority decision in *Pimentel* as an "obvious" example of "dismal reasoning." Ides, *Foreword: A Critical Appraisal of the Supreme Court's Decision in* J. McIntyre Machinery, Ltd. v. Nicastro, 45 Loy.L.A.L.Rev. 341, 386 n.175 (2012). Did the *Pimentel* Court misapprehend the requirements of interpleader and, in particular, the "required" party condition under Rule 19? Or was the problem that the substantive law of sovereign immunity impeded the utility of these procedural devices? See Issacharoff, *Private Claims, Aggregate Rights*, 2008 Sup.Ct.Rev. 183.

3.   Commentators note that a "near-categorical" rule has developed that an entire case is to be dismissed under Rule 19 when a party considered to be necessary cannot be joined because of sovereign immunity. For example, in WICHITA & AFFILIATED TRIBES OF OKLAHOMA v. HODEL, 788 F.2d 765, 776 (D.C. Cir. 1986), the court determined that it was impossible to shape the relief so as to avoid prejudice to absent parties, in this case, Indian tribes invoking sovereign immunity. See Fletcher, *The Comparative Rights of Indispensable Sovereigns*, 40 Gonz.L.Rev. 1 (2005). Should dismissal ever be appropriate when no alternative forum exists to provide adequate relief? See Florey, *Making Sovereigns Indispensable:* Pimentel *and the Evolution of Rule 19*, 58 UCLA L.Rev. 667 (2011); Andre, *Compulsory (Mis)joinder: The Untenable Intersection of Sovereign Immunity and Federal Rule of Civil Procedure 19*, 60 Emory L.J. 1157 (2011). Should the public importance of the litigation be an explicit factor in determining whether the suit ought to be dismissed? See Tobias, *Rule 19 and the Public Rights Exception to Party Joinder*, 65 N.C.L.Rev. 745 (1987).

G. INTERVENTION

———

Read Federal Rule of Civil Procedure 24 in the Supplement.

———

Federal Rule 24, which governs intervention, differs from the joinder rules so far studied in an important respect: The rule allows a stranger to a lawsuit to interject itself into the action. A noted commentator has explained:

> A civil action, in the Anglo-American tradition, has usually been thought of as a private controversy between plaintiff and defendant. Although outsiders were sometimes permitted to take part in order to protect their interests, they were more often regarded by the court and the parties as undesired intermeddlers

who should be required to protect themselves—if they could—by bringing a lawsuit of their own. Indeed after courts of admiralty, and later of equity, recognized intervention as a proper means of asserting an interest in property in the custody of the court, there remained considerable uncertainty for many years about whether, and to what extent, intervention could be permitted in a routine action at law.

But in recent decades the increased complexity of litigation and the growing number of cases involving the public interest or a wide variety of private interests have been accompanied by a steady change in the attitude toward intervention. Both intervention of right and permissive intervention were given new vitality in the federal system by adoption of [R]ule 24 of the Federal Rules * * * in 1938, and subsequent amendments have broadened their scope.

Shapiro, *Some Thoughts on Intervention Before Courts, Agencies, and Arbitrators,* 81 Harv.L.Rev. 721, 721–22 (1968) (footnotes omitted); see 7C Wright, Miller & Kane, Federal Practice and Procedure § 1901 (3d ed.).

SMUCK V. HOBSON

United States Court of Appeals, District of Columbia Circuit, 1969.
132 U.S. App. D.C. 372, 408 F.2d 175.

BAZELON, CHIEF JUDGE.

[In Hobson v. Hansen, 269 F.Supp. 401 (D.D.C. 1967), a class action brought on behalf of Black and poor children, the court found that plaintiffs were being denied their constitutional rights to equal educational opportunities because the District of Columbia schools were being operated on a basis that was racially and economically discriminatory. The Board of Education voted not to appeal and ordered Dr. Carl Hansen, the Superintendent of Schools, not to appeal. Nonetheless, Dr. Hansen and Carl Smuck, one of the dissenting Board members, filed notices of appeal. In addition, motions to intervene were made in the district court and in the Court of Appeals by Dr. Hansen and 20 parents who said they "dissent from" the court's decision. The court of appeals decided to hold the direct appeals in abeyance and remanded the intervention motions for a hearing. The district court granted the motions to intervene, even though neither Hansen nor the parents had shown a substantial interest that could be protected only through intervention, "in order to give the Court of Appeals an opportunity to pass on the intervention questions raised here, and the questions to be raised by the appeal on the merits * * *." Hobson v. Hansen,

44 F.R.D. 18, 33 (D.D.C. 1968). The court of appeals then considered the matter *en banc.*]

* * * These appeals challenge the findings of the trial court that the Board of Education has in a variety of ways violated the Constitution in administering the District of Columbia schools. Among the facts that distinguish this case from the normal grist of appellate courts is the absence of the Board of Education as an appellant. Instead, the would-be appellants are Dr. Carl F. Hansen, the resigned superintendent of District schools, who appeals in his former official capacity and as an individual; Carl C. Smuck, a member of the Board of Education, who appeals in that capacity; and the parents of certain school children who have attempted to intervene in order to register on appeal their "dissent" from the order below.

* * * Whatever standing he might have possessed to appeal as a named defendant in the original suit * * * disappeared when Dr. Hansen left his official position. Presumably because he was aware of this, he subsequently moved to intervene under Rule 24(a)[e] * * * in order to appeal as an individual. * * * He does not claim that a reversal or modification of the order by this Court would make his return to office likely. Consequently, the supposed impact of the decision upon his tenure is irrelevant insofar as an appeal is concerned, since a reversal would have no effect. Dr. Hansen thus has no "interest relating to the property or transaction which is the subject of the action" sufficient for Rule 24(a), and intervention is therefore unwarranted.

We also find that Mr. Smuck has no appealable interest as a member of the Board of Education. While he was in that capacity a named defendant, the Board of Education was undeniably the principal figure and could have been sued alone as a collective entity. Appellant Smuck had a fair opportunity to participate in its defense, and in the decision not to appeal. Having done so, he has no separate interest as an individual in the litigation. The order directs the board to take certain actions. But since its decisions are made by vote as a collective whole, there is no apparent way in which Smuck as an individual could violate the decree and thereby become subject to enforcement proceedings.

The motion to intervene by the parents presents a more difficult problem requiring a correspondingly more detailed examination of the requirements for intervention of right.

* * *

The phrasing of Rule 24(a)(2) as amended parallels that of Rule 19(a)(2)[f] concerning joinder. But the fact that the two rules are entwined

---

[e] The rule is now Rule 24(a)(2).

[f] The rule is now Rule 19(a)(1)(B).

does not imply that an "interest" for the purpose of one is precisely the same as for the other. The occasions upon which a petitioner should be allowed to intervene under Rule 24 are not necessarily limited to those situations when the trial court should compel him to become a party under Rule 19. And while the division of Rule 24(a) and (b) into "Intervention of Right" and "Permissible Intervention" might superficially suggest that only the latter involves an exercise of discretion by the court, the contrary is clearly the case.

The effort to extract substance from the conclusory phrase "interest" or "legally protectable interest" is of limited promise. Parents unquestionably have a sufficient "interest" in the education of their children to justify the initiation of a lawsuit in appropriate circumstances, as indeed was the case for the plaintiff-appellee parents here. But in the context of intervention the question is not whether a lawsuit should be begun, but whether already initiated litigation should be extended to include additional parties. The 1966 amendments to Rule 24(a) have facilitated this, the true inquiry, by eliminating the temptation or need for tangential expeditions in search of "property" or someone "bound by a judgment." It would be unfortunate to allow the inquiry to be led once again astray by a myopic fixation upon "interest." Rather, as Judge Leventhal recently concluded for this Court, "[A] more instructive approach is to let our construction be guided by the policies behind the 'interest' requirement. * * * [T]he 'interest' test is primarily a practical guide to disposing of lawsuits by involving as many apparently concerned persons as is compatible with efficiency and due process."[12]

The decision whether intervention of right is warranted thus involves an accommodation between two potentially conflicting goals: to achieve judicial economies of scale by resolving related issues in a single lawsuit, and to prevent the single lawsuit from becoming fruitlessly complex or unending. Since this task will depend upon the contours of the particular controversy, general rules and past decisions cannot provide uniformly dependable guides. The Supreme Court, in its only full-dress examination of Rule 24(a) since the 1966 amendments, found that a gas distributor was entitled to intervention of right although its only "interest" was the economic harm it claimed would follow from an allegedly inadequate plan for divestiture approved by the Government in an antitrust proceeding.[14] While conceding that the Court's opinion granting intervention in Cascade Natural Gas Corp. v. El Paso Natural Gas Co. "is certainly susceptible of a very broad reading," the trial judge here would distinguish the decision on the ground that the petitioner "did show a strong direct economic interest, for the new company [to be created by divestiture] would be its sole

---

[12] Nuesse v. Camp, 128 U.S. App. D.C. 172, 385 F.2d 694, 700 (1967).

[14] Cascade Natural Gas Corp. v. El Paso Natural Gas Co., 386 U.S. 129, 132–136, 87 S.Ct. 932, 17 L.Ed.2d 814 (1967).

supplier." Yet while it is undoubtedly true that "*Cascade* should not be read as a carte blanche for intervention by anyone at any time," there is no apparent reason why an "economic interest" should always be necessary to justify intervention. The goal of "disposing of lawsuits by involving as many apparently concerned persons as is compatible with efficiency and due process" may in certain circumstances be met by allowing parents whose only "interest" is the education of their children to intervene. In determining whether such circumstances are present, the first requirement of Rule 24(a)(2), that of an "interest" in the transaction, may be a less useful point of departure than the second and third requirements, that the applicant may be impeded in protecting his interest by the action and that his interest is not adequately represented by others.

This does not imply that the need for an "interest" in the controversy should or can be read out of the rule. But the requirement should be viewed as a prerequisite rather than relied upon as a determinative criterion for intervention. If barriers are needed to limit extension of the right to intervene, the criteria of practical harm to the applicant and the adequacy of representation by others are better suited to the task. If those requirements are met, the nature of his "interest" may play a role in determining the sort of intervention which should be allowed—whether, for example, he should be permitted to contest all issues, and whether he should enjoy all the prerogatives of a party litigant.

Both courts and legislatures have recognized as appropriate the concern for their children's welfare which the parents here seek to protect by intervention. While the artificiality of an appeal without the Board of Education cannot be ignored, neither can the importance of the constitutional issues decided below. The relevance of substantial and unsettled questions of law has been recognized in allowing intervention to perfect an appeal. And this Court has noted repeatedly, "obviously tailored to fit ordinary civil litigation, [the provisions of Rule 24] require other than literal application in atypical cases."[20] We conclude that the interests asserted by the intervenors are sufficient to justify an examination of whether the two remaining requirements for intervention are met.

* * *

[The court then determined that the disposition of the action might impair the applicants' ability to protect their interests if they were not allowed to intervene.]

The remaining requirement for intervention is that the applicant not be adequately represented by others. No question is raised here but that the Board of Education adequately represented the intervenors at the trial below; the issue rather is whether the parents were adequately represented

---

[20] Textile Workers Union, etc. v. Allendale Co., 226 F.2d 765, 767 (D.C. Cir. 1955) (en banc), cert. denied, Allendale Co. v. Mitchell, 351 U.S. 909, 76 S.Ct. 699, 100 L.Ed. 1444 (1956) * * *.

by the school board's decision not to appeal. The presumed good faith of the board in reaching this decision is not conclusive. * * * As the conditional wording of Rule 24(a)(2) suggests in permitting intervention "unless the applicant's interest is adequately represented by existing parties," "the burden [is] on those opposing intervention to show the adequacy of the existing representation." In this case, the interests of the parents who wish to intervene in order to appeal do not coincide with those of the Board of Education. The school board represents all parents within the District. The intervening appellants may have more parochial interests centering upon the education of their own children. While they cannot of course ask the Board to favor their children unconstitutionally at the expense of others, they like other parents can seek the adoption of policies beneficial to their own children. Moreover, considerations of publicity, cost, and delay may not have the same weight for the parents as for the school board in the context of a decision to appeal. And the Board of Education, buffeted as it like other school boards is by conflicting public demands, may possibly have less interest in preserving its own untrammeled discretion than do the parents. It is not necessary to accuse the board of bad faith in deciding not to appeal or of a lack of vigor in defending the suit below in order to recognize that a restrictive court order may be a not wholly unwelcome haven.

* * *

Our holding that the appellants would be practically disadvantaged by a decision without appeal in this case and that they are not otherwise adequately represented necessitates a closer scrutiny of the precise nature of their interest and the scope of intervention that should accordingly be granted. The parents who seek to appeal do not come before this court to protect the good name of the Board of Education. Their interest is not to protect the board, or Dr. Hansen, from an unfair finding. Their asserted interest is rather the freedom of the school board—and particularly the new school board recently elected—to exercise the broadest discretion constitutionally permissible in deciding upon educational policies. Since this is so, their interest extends only to those parts of the order which can fairly be said to impose restraints upon the Board of Education. And because the school board is not a party to this appeal, review should be limited to those features of the order which limit the discretion of the old or new board.

* * *

[A partial concurring opinion by JUDGE MCGOWAN and dissenting opinions by JUDGES DANAHER and BURGER are omitted.]

NOTES AND QUESTIONS

1.   Inadequate representation has been found when the applicant's interests are not represented at all, see Purnell v. City of Akron, 925 F.2d 941 (6th Cir. 1991); when the interests of the applicant are antagonistic to those of the attorney who supposedly represents the interests of the applicant, see United States v. C.M. Lane Lifeboat Co., 25 F.Supp. 410 (E.D.N.Y. 1938), but see Stadin v. Union Elec. Co., 309 F.2d 912 (8th Cir. 1962), cert. denied, 373 U.S. 915, 83 S.Ct. 1298, 10 L.Ed.2d 415 (1963) (minority stockholder was not entitled to intervention as of right when there was a showing of difference of opinion as to how the litigation should be conducted but no showing of plaintiff's failure in its duty to its shareholders); and when there is collusion between the representative and the adverse parties, see Virginia Elec. & Power Co. v. Westinghouse Elec. Corp., 542 F.2d 214 (4th Cir. 1976).

2.   In NATURAL RESOURCES DEFENSE COUNCIL, INC. v. NEW YORK STATE DEPARTMENT OF ENVIRONMENTAL CONSERVATION, 834 F.2d 60 (2d Cir. 1987), the American Petroleum Institute (API) appealed a district court order denying its motion to intervene in a "citizen suit" brought by the Natural Resources Defense Council, Inc. and other groups concerned with air pollution against the New York State Department of Environmental Conservation, the United States Environmental Protection Agency, and the administrators of both agencies. The court of appeals affirmed:

> * * * API contends that in this suit it too has an interest different from that of New York. API's interest, it urges, is economic, whereas the State's interest is governmental.
>
> We think API misperceives the concept of an interest "adequately represented" within the meaning of Rule 24. A putative intervenor does not have an interest not adequately represented by a party to a lawsuit simply because it has a motive to litigate that is different from the motive of an existing party. So long as the party has demonstrated sufficient motivation to litigate vigorously and to present all colorable contentions, a district judge does not exceed the bounds of discretion by concluding that the interests of the intervenor are adequately represented. * * *

Id. at 61–62. Is the decision consistent with *Smuck*? See Vreeland, *Public Interest Groups, Public Law Litigation, and Federal Rule 24(a)*, 57 U.Chi.L.Rev. 279 (1990).

3.   In TRBOVICH v. UNITED MINE WORKERS OF AMERICA, 404 U.S. 528, 928 S.Ct. 630, 30 L.Ed.2d 686 (1972), a union member who filed an initial complaint with the Secretary of Labor wished to intervene in a suit brought by the Secretary under the Labor-Management Reporting and Disclosure Act of 1959 to set aside the election of officers of the union. The Act made suit by the Secretary the exclusive post-election remedy for violation of the statute, and the Court held that it did not bar intervention by a union member, provided the intervenor was limited to the claims of illegality

presented by the Secretary's complaint. Moreover, the Court held that Rule 24(a)(2) is satisfied "if the applicant shows that representation of his interest 'may be' inadequate, and the burden of making that showing should be treated as minimal." Id. at 538 n.10, 928 S.Ct. at 636 n.10, 30 L.Ed.2d at 694 n.10. The applicant met this burden by showing that "[e]ven if the Secretary is performing his duties, broadly conceived, as well as can be expected, the union member may have a valid complaint about the performance of 'his lawyer.' " Id. at 539, 928 S.Ct. at 637, 30 L.Ed.2d at 695.

4.   Are there circumstances when intervention by a private litigant might undermine regulatory goals or create unnecessary expense? See Black, *Trashing the Presumption: Intervention on the Side of the Government*, 39 Envtl.L. 481 (2009). Could this concern explain why some courts, despite the "minimal burden standard," require the proposed intervenor to make a "strong showing" of inadequate representation by the government? See United States v. Hooker Chemicals & Plastics Corp., 749 F.2d 968 (2d Cir. 1984) (Friendly, J.). Even if intervention is granted, isn't there the possibility that the interests of private litigants will be sidelined in the government's suit? See Holley, *Narrative Highground: The Failure of Intervention as a Procedural Device in Affirmative Action Litigation*, 54 Case W.Res.L.Rev. 103 (2003).

5.   The United States has an unconditional right to intervene in actions challenging the constitutionality of an act of Congress. See 28 U.S.C. § 2403(a). Section 2403(b) extends the intervention right to states in actions involving the constitutionality of state statutes. In addition, the Civil Rights Act of 1964, 42 U.S.C. § 2000h–2, provides the federal government an unconditional right to intervene in a suit seeking relief against a denial of equal protection under the Fourteenth Amendment on account of race, color, religion, sex, or national origin. How might the intervention of the United States affect the interests of the original litigants?

6.   Does intervention require an independent basis for subject-matter jurisdiction? Before Congress enacted 28 U.S.C. § 1367, an independent jurisdictional basis generally was not required for intervention as of right, but was required for permissive actions. Compare Lenz v. Wagner, 240 F.2d 666 (5th Cir. 1957), with Reedsburg Bank v. Apollo, 508 F.2d 995 (7th Cir. 1975). How does the codification of supplemental jurisdiction affect the analysis? May supplemental jurisdiction be exercised under 28 U.S.C. § 1367(b) over a non-diverse applicant? See 7C Wright, Miller & Kane, Federal Practice and Procedure § 1917 (3d ed.). Relatedly, in TOWN OF CHESTER, N.Y. v. LAROE ESTATES, INC., 137 S.Ct. 1645, 1651, 198 L.Ed.2d 64, 71 (2017), the Supreme Court held that a party seeking to intervene as of right must have standing "when it seeks additional relief beyond that which the plaintiff requests."

7.   Rule 24 treats intervention as a permissive joinder device, so that the "outsider" to the litigation has the option of joining the lawsuit or not. Are there circumstances when intervention ought to be compulsory? The Supreme Court considered that question in MARTIN v. WILKS, 490 U.S. 755, 109 S.Ct. 2180, 104 L.Ed.2d 835 (1989). The case involved a challenge by white firefighters to

hiring decisions taken by the City of Birmingham pursuant to consent decrees that resolved discrimination claims by Black individuals who alleged that they had been denied employment or promotion because of their race. The district court dismissed the firefighters' lawsuit, holding, in part, that because they had not intervened in the prior cases, they could not collaterally challenge the decrees. The Supreme Court, five-to-four, held that "[k]nowledge of a lawsuit" does not obligate a party to intervene in a lawsuit; "a party seeking a judgment binding on another cannot obligate that person to intervene; he must be joined." Id. at 763–65, 109 S.Ct. at 2185–86, 104 L.Ed.2d at 846–47. Justice Stevens, in a dissent, underscored that "in complex litigation this Court has squarely held that a sideline-sitter may be bound as firmly as an actual party if he had adequate notice and a fair opportunity to intervene and if the judicial interest in finality is sufficiently strong." Id. at 793, 109 S.Ct. at 2200–01, 104 L.Ed.2d at 863. Why did Rule 19 not require the joinder of the firefighters in the earlier discrimination suits? Are you persuaded that permissive party-initiated joinder is a better approach than a rule of mandatory intervention? See Brunet, *The Triumph of Efficiency and Discretion Over Competing Complex Litigation Policies*, 10 Rev.Litig. 273 (1991).

H. JOINDER, CONSOLIDATION, AND "AGGREGATE" LITIGATION

———

Read Federal Rule of Civil Procedure 42 and 28 U.S.C. § 1407 in the Supplement.

———

The Federal Rules eliminated many of the historical limitations on the joinder of parties and claims and today hundreds and even thousands of parties and claims can be bundled together in a single lawsuit. Rule 42 encourages this trend toward aggregation by allowing for the consolidation of actions. Rule 42(a) permits a district judge to consolidate actions pending before the court when they involve common questions of law or fact. The court may consolidate the actions for all purposes, or limited pretrial proceedings; the basis for consolidation turns on the law and facts that the lawsuits share, and does not require an identity of parties. The court has authority to order a separate trial of one or more separate issues. See Rule 42(b).

Generally, actions consolidated under Rule 42 retain their separate identity. In a decision that predates the adoption of Rule 42, the Supreme Court stated that consolidation "does not merge the suits into a single cause or change the rights of the parties, or make those who are parties in one suit parties in another," but rather is "permitted as a matter of convenience and economy in administration." JOHNSON v. MANHATTAN

RY. CO., 289 U.S. 479, 496–97, 53 S.Ct. 721, 727, 77 L.Ed. 1331, 1345 (1932). In HALL v. HALL, 138 S.Ct. 1118, 200 L.Ed.2d 399 (2018), the Court held that consolidated cases retain their independence for purposes of finality and appealability.

Consolidation under Rule 42 is limited to actions pending in the same district. However, cases that are pending in different districts that share common questions of fact may be consolidated by the Judicial Panel on Multidistrict Litigation ("MDL") and transferred to a single district, as provided for under 28 U.S.C. § 1407, see p. 294, supra. As the Supreme Court has explained:

> * * * Enacted in 1968 in response to a growing number of complex but related cases filed in multiple districts, § 1407 authorizes the Judicial Panel on Multidistrict Litigation (JPML) to transfer civil actions * * * in order to "promote the just and efficient conduct of such actions." § 1407(a); see H.R.Rep. No. 1130, 90th Cong., 2d Sess., 2 (1968) (§ 1407 codified procedures used in the early 1960's to resolve more than 1,800 separate actions filed against electrical equipment manufacturers in 33 District Courts, all of the actions seeking damages for antitrust law violations).

> Transfer under § 1407 aims to "eliminate duplication in discovery, avoid conflicting rulings and schedules, reduce litigation cost, and save the time and effort of the parties, the attorneys, the witnesses, and the courts." Manual for Complex Litigation § 20.131, p. 220 (4th ed. 2004). "Each action" transferred pursuant to § 1407, the provision instructs, "shall be remanded by the panel at or before the conclusion of . . . pretrial proceedings to the district from which it was transferred unless it shall have been previously terminated." § 1407(a).

GELBOIM v. BANK OF AMERICA CORP., 574 U.S. 405, 410, 135 S.Ct. 897, 903, 190 L.Ed.2d 789, 795 (2015). In practice, only about three percent of MDL cases are remanded to the transferor court; the overwhelming majority are resolved by settlement or summary judgment. See Burch, *Remanding Multidistrict Litigation*, 75 La.L.Rev. 399, 399–402 (2014). MDL suits now command a great deal of federal judicial attention—since 1968, the Panel has decided millions of individual claims. See Redish & Karaba, *One Size Doesn't Fit All: Multidistrict Litigation, Due Process, and the Dangers of Procedural Collectivism*, 95 B.U.L.Rev. 109 (2015). By one count MDL cases comprise 39 percent of open cases on the federal docket. See Burch, *Monopolies in Multidistrict Litigation*, 70 Vand.L.Rev. 67, 72 (2017).

The extensive use of Section 1407 consolidation has led to profound changes in federal court practice. MDL judges are said to have "an outsized role" given the scope of their law-making discretion and authority to create rules of practice for transferred cases. Gluck, *Unorthodox Civil Procedure: Modern Multidistrict Litigation's Place in the Textbook Understandings of Procedure*, 165 U.Pa.L.Rev. 1669 (2017). This discretion extends to the appointment of lead counsel for the MDL consolidated suit and has led to the emergence of a specialized bar for actions before the Panel and transferee courts. See Coleman, *One Percent Procedure*, 91 Wash.L.Rev. 1005 (2016). Is there a danger, as Professor Miller has suggested, of "mega-cases" involving "so much money on the table that professional judgment and client loyalty are sometimes compromised"? See Miller, *What Are Courts For? Have We Forsaken the Procedural Gold Standard?*, 78 La.L.Rev. 739, 742–43 (2018).

NOTES AND QUESTIONS

1.   In 1994, the American Law Institute completed and published its Complex Litigation Project, which contains a study and recommendations for handling large-scale cases in the federal system. Fifteen years later, the ALI adopted the Principles of the Law of Aggregate Litigation, which covers procedures for resolving multiparty disputes that "combine claims or defenses held by many persons for unified resolution." See American Law Institute, Principles of the Law of Aggregate Litigation. § 1.02, cmt. a (2010). Adoption of the ALI Principles signaled what one commentator called "the normalization of aggregation" and further erosion of the day-in-court ideal. See Resnik, *Compared to What?: ALI Aggregation and the Shifting Contours of Due Process and of Lawyers' Powers*, 79 Geo.Wash.L.Rev. 628, 633 (2011).

2.   As civil actions become ever larger and more complex, some courts have found it important to streamline litigation into "smaller pieces" through procedures like putting cases on "fast tracks" or trying "bellwether" cases, and then having the decision in one or two cases drive the settlement of the others. See Cavanagh, *Issue Preclusion in Complex Litigation*, 29 Rev.Litig. 859 (2010). At least one commentator predicts that "disaggregation" will be the driver of procedural innovation. See Dodge, *Disaggregative Mechanisms: Mass Claims Resolution Without Class Actions*, 63 Emory L.J. 1253 (2014).

3.   State courts have joinder and consolidation rules that are similar to those of the federal system. However, cases pending in different states cannot be consolidated in the court of one state. A case may be removed to federal court and then undergo transfer and consolidation, but only if subject-matter jurisdiction is available. See Glover, *Mass Litigation Governance in the Post-Class Action Era: The Problems and Promise of Non-Removable State Actions in Multi-District Litigation*, 6 J. Tort L. 3 (2014).

4.   The tension between consolidation and litigant autonomy can be illustrated by the relatively simple state court decision in TANBRO FABRICS CORP. v. BEAUNIT MILLS, INC., 4 A.D.2d 519, 521–26, 167 N.Y.S.2d 387, 388–93 (1957). *Tanbro* involved three lawsuits arising out of a business dispute among the seller of the goods, the purchaser of the goods, and the processor of

the goods. The buyer moved to consolidate, and the seller and processor opposed the motion on appeal from a grant of the motion.

> Both the seller and the processor * * * do so on the ground that each had a separate and different relationship to the buyer, and that each was involved in a separate and independent contract. Therefore, they say, there is not involved the "same transaction or occurrence," nor any common question of law or fact to sustain either a joinder of parties or a consolidation of the actions. They stress that the buyer * * * wishes to pit against each other the seller and the processor on the issue of responsibility for the alleged defect, while the buyer sits back free from the obligation to prove a full case, as it would otherwise have to do in separate actions against the seller and the processor. The buyer, on the other hand, argues that what is identical to the cases are the goods and the defect, with the common question of who is responsible for the defect. The buyer concedes that it would have to prove the defect, and also prove that the defect must have been caused by either the seller or the processor or both of them; that, therefore, this involves a single transaction or occurrence and involves a common question of fact [as required by New York's Civil Practice Act].

* * *

> A reading of the [Act's] section by itself would suggest little or no difficulty in permitting a joinder of parties in the buyer's main action or a consolidation of the three actions. * * * [A lengthy discussion of the statute's legislative history is omitted.]

> * * * It should be beyond argument, by now, that it is no longer a bar to joinder, and, by parallel reasoning, *a fortiori*, to consolidation, that there is not an identity of duty or contract upon which to assert alternative liability. It is still necessary, of course, that there be a finding that the alternative liability arises out of a common transaction or occurrence involving common questions of fact and law. But this is not a rigid test. It is to be applied with judgment and discretion, in the balancing of convenience and justice between the parties involved * * *. Indeed, the buyer's situation prompted * * * [the lower court] to comment that the buyer, Tanbro, "is in the unenviable position of not knowing possibly which of its contracting parties is responsible and in separate actions may find itself confronted with defeat in each event though the product as finally delivered may be defective."

* * *

> The right of joinder and the privilege to obtain consolidation is always counterbalanced, of course, by the power of the court to grant a severance, or to deny a consolidation, if prejudice or injustice appear. In this case, the danger of separate trials, leading, perhaps, to an

unjust and illogical result, is a possibility well worth avoiding. The buyer is entitled to a less hazardous adjudication of his dispute, so long as he is able to make out a prima facie case of alternative liability.

5.   The increasing tendency to bundle claims and parties together in a single lawsuit is not unique to the United States. European and English judicial systems likewise now utilize forms of aggregate litigation that range from the English group litigation orders, to the Dutch collective settlement action, to the German model case in securities litigation. For a catalogue of aggregate procedures used abroad, see Chase, Hershkoff, Silberman, Sorabji, Stürner, Taniguchi & Varano, Civil Litigation in Comparative Context 504–62 (Chase & Hershkoff, eds., 2d ed. 2017).

CHAPTER 9

CLASS ACTIONS

■ ■ ■

This chapter introduces the complex yet fascinating topic of the class action, probably the most innovative but controversial feature of United States civil procedure. The materials examine the history and justification for the class action, the operation of Federal Rule 23, the emergence of the settlement class, and the policy questions that the practice raises. For many years the class action was viewed as a uniquely American device, unlikely to take root abroad. However, forms of collective action increasingly are being adopted outside the United States, influenced by, but not fully embracing, the American form. As you read these materials, consider whether the class action enhances access to justice given the scope of mass harms in contemporary life, or whether the practice deviates too far from the individualistic values of the adversarial system.

A. OVERVIEW AND THEMES

The class action allows a named plaintiff to litigate claims and defenses of similarly situated persons in a single lawsuit, and the resulting judgment binds all of the "unnamed" parties who are members of the class. In some sense, the class action is simply another form of joinder device; the procedure aggregates claims and defenses that the named representative and class members share in common, but which any individual litigant alone might not be able to pursue because of the expense and inconvenience of litigation. However, unlike other joinder devices, all of the parties in a class action do not appear in person before the court. Rather, the named "representative" acts as a proxy for strangers who do not initially know that a lawsuit has been filed, yet may be barred by the class action judgment from further litigation on their claims. The legitimacy of the class action turns on whether the named party will fully and fairly represent the interests of the absentee class members in the proceedings before the court. See Hutchinson, *Class Actions: Joinder or Representational Device?*, 1983 Sup.Ct.Rev. 459. The class action differs from other joinder devices in another important respect, as well: The use of the procedure gives rise to a new entity—the "class"—which did not exist prior to the litigation and which imposes new practical and ethical burdens on the parties, lawyers, and court. See Shapiro, *Class Actions: The Class as Party and Client*, 73 Notre Dame L.Rev. 913 (1998). The joinder and representative models of the class action often are in tension, and shifts in the Supreme Court's interpretation of Federal Rule 23—and restrictions imposed on the rule's operation—may reflect greater emphasis on one model rather than the other. Whether the class action is best viewed as a joinder or a representative device implicates all of the doctrines so far covered in this course, including subject-matter jurisdiction, personal jurisdiction, and venue, as well as topics still to be studied—in particular, claim and issue preclusion. See Chapter 15, infra.

Rule 23 was substantially revised in 1966 and became a critical vehicle for challenging racial segregation. Use of the rule, as Professor Miller has chronicled, quickly extended "to other constitutional and public policy contexts. These included the reapportionment of legislative bodies, free speech, prisoner rights, the environment, various governmental programs and benefits, due process and equal protection issues, even the legality of the Vietnam War." Miller, *Keynote Address: The American Class Action: From Birth to Maturity*, 19 Theoretical Inq. in Law 1 (2018). In addition, lawyers enlisted the class action to redress injuries caused by mass torts— particularly, large-scale accidents and product liability suits. In some of these actions, individuals claimed significant monetary damages. But in others, the stakes for each absentee were small and given the costs of individual litigation, the injuries likely would have gone unremedied. In these cases, class-wide relief was important because "[a]lthough each individual who [was] harmed [won] only a small amount, the public benefit [was] substantial. The costs of the large public harm [were] borne by the person or firm responsible for it, and incentives to commit future transgressions [were] removed." Bronsteen & Fiss, *The Class Action Rule*, 78 Notre Dame L.Rev. 1419, 1419 (2003).

The class action has come to serve a public role by providing a private means for redressing broad-scale problems that Congress or the states may be unwilling or unable to address, or when the costs of private lawsuits are less than that of bureaucratic enforcement. In the process, the procedure has expanded democratic access, influenced policymaking, and secured compensation for injured parties. Rule 23 also has generated controversy about its legitimacy, scope, and effectiveness.

NOTES AND QUESTIONS

1.   The class action can be traced to the English "bill of peace" utilized by the Courts of Chancery in the seventeenth century. The "bill" allowed an action to be brought by or against representative parties when (1) the number of persons involved was too large to permit joinder, (2) all the members of the group possessed a joint interest in the question being adjudicated, and (3) the named parties adequately represented the interests of those who were not present. If these three conditions were met, the judgment that ultimately was entered was binding on all the members of the represented group. See Yeazell, From Medieval Group Litigation to the Modern Class Action (1987).

2. The various state codes and Federal Equity Rules provided for class actions based upon the English procedure. Federal Rule 23, as adopted in 1938, made the class action available in both legal and equitable actions in the federal courts. The justification for the class action was associated with the increasing complexity yet routinization of social and market relations. As an early commentary explained:

> Modern society seems increasingly to expose men [and all persons] to * * * group injuries for which individually they are in a poor position to seek legal redress, either because they do not know enough or because such redress is disproportionately expensive. If each is left to assert his rights alone if and when he can, there will at best be a random and fragmentary enforcement, if there is any at all. This result is not only unfortunate in the particular case, but it will operate seriously to impair the deterrent effect of the sanctions which underlie much contemporary law. The problem of fashioning an effective and inclusive group remedy is thus a major one.

Kalven & Rosenfield, *The Contemporary Function of a Class Suit*, 8 U.Chi.L.Rev. 684, 686 (1941).

3. The original Rule 23 attempted to describe when a class action was proper in a highly conceptualized way. Briefly, the categories were as follows: A "true" class action was involved when the class members possessed joint and common interests in the subject matter of the action; a "hybrid" class action was present when several claims to the same property were being litigated; and what was described as a "spurious" class action existed when persons possessing independent interests joined together in the suit. This structure proved to be confusing to apply and made the procedure less effective than was desirable.

4. In 1966, a completely rewritten Rule 23 was amended to substitute functional tests for the conceptual categories and to provide procedural guidance for the courts about handling class actions. The amendments made clear that a judgment in a class action is binding on all class members, except in those cases in which the right to opt-out of the lawsuit applies and has been exercised. The 1966 amendments generated increased use of the class action, particularly in public law cases seeking injunctive relief. The 1966 amendments also spurred debates about the utility of the practice, especially in cases involving mass torts when the remedy sought was money damages. The extremes of that debate, summarized by Professor Miller about a decade after the 1966 amendments, persist today:

> * * * Opinions regarding the effect of the revision range over an amazing gamut. Class action adherents would have us believe it is a panacea for a myriad of social ills, which deters unlawful conduct and compensates those injured by it. Catch phrases such as "therapeutic" or "prophylactic" and "[taking] care of the smaller guy" are frequently trumpeted. Its opponents have rallied around characterizations of the procedure as a form of "legalized blackmail" or a "Frankenstein

Monster" They also have charged widespread abuse of the rule by lawyers and litigants on both sides of the "v.," including unprofessional practices relating to attorneys' fees, "sweetheart" settlement deals, dilatory motion practice, harassing discovery, and misrepresentations to judges. Finally, some have questioned the wisdom of imposing the burdens of class actions on an already overtaxed federal judiciary. They assert that many Rule 23 cases are unmanageable and inordinately protracted by opposing counsel, creating a certain millstone or dinosaur character that diverts federal judges from matters more worthy of their energies.

* * *

Yet despite the attention that has been riveted on Rule 23, we have precious little empiric evidence as to how it actually has been functioning, in terms of either its alleged benefits or supposed blasphemies. Even if the negative effects of class actions were assumed, they would have to be balanced against the societal benefits derived from deterring socially proscribed conduct and providing small claim rectification—considerations that thus far have escaped measurement and perhaps always will.

Miller, *Of Frankenstein Monsters and Shining Knights: Myth, Reality, and the "Class Action Problem,"* 92 Harv.L.Rev. 664, 665 (1979).

5.   Eight years after he wrote his Harvard Law Review article, Professor Miller served as the Reporter for a study of complex litigation for the American Law Institute. In that study, he wrote:

Class actions have proven to be the most effective legal technique for avoiding piecemeal litigation and preserving legal resources. Nevertheless, the class action suit continues to be eyed with suspicion by many courts. In complex cases, the goals of the class action device have been frustrated by strict adherence to the requirements of Rule 23. Often, complex multiparty, multiforum cases are denied class action treatment. Certification of large scale tort action classes is rare. Courts deny certification based on decisions that the commonality of interest requirement is not satisfied and based on fear that the size of the class would make the litigation unwieldy and inefficient.

* * *

The usefulness of the class action device for future complex litigation raises two issues concerning the suitability of class actions to modern litigation needs. The first issue is whether the scope of the class action should be broadened to include more types of litigation. The second is whether courts should increase the frequency with which they certify mandatory classes. Presently, class actions are used relatively infrequently in many multiparty, multiforum litigation

> contexts. With some adjustments the class action device could be
> made a valuable litigation tool.

Am. Law Inst., Preliminary Study of Complex Litigation, Report 61–70 (1987).
The Preliminary Study was followed by a comprehensive exploration of the
subject, which led to the American Law Institute's formal approval of Complex
Litigation: Statutory Recommendations and Analysis (1994).

6. In 1996, the Research Division of the Federal Judicial Center
conducted an empirical study of Rule 23 proceedings in four federal districts.
See Willging, Hooper & Niemic, *An Empirical Analysis of Rule 23 to Address
the Rulemaking Challenges*, 71 N.Y.U.L.Rev. 74 (1996). It was a surprise to
some that the study found that not all applications of Rule 23 were difficult;
indeed, there were a significant number of "routine" class actions, particularly
in the securities and civil rights contexts. The study also seemed to
demonstrate that attorney's fees were not disproportionate to class recoveries.
As with most civil litigation, class actions followed the general pattern of
settlement in lieu of trial.

7. Since 1966, defendant groups have issued unabated calls for a radical
revision of the rule. See Burbank & Farhang, *Class Actions and the
Counterrevolution Against Federal Litigation*, 165 U.Pa.L.Rev. 1495 (2017).
Although Rule 23 underwent amendment in 1998, 2003, 2007, and 2009, it still
retains the basic "architecture" of the 1966 version. However, the universe of
class-action practice has become much more complicated since 1966. Parallel
to Rule 23, Congress has created special rules for discrete kinds of claims, most
notably the Private Securities Litigation Reform Act, 15 U.S.C. § 78u–4. In
addition, Congress has carved out certain claims from the operation of Rule 23
(for example, those filed by a lawyer funded through the Legal Services
Corporation) and shifted state law class actions into federal court relying on a
concept of minimal diversity. See 28 U.S.C. § 1332(d). Moreover, the Supreme
Court and a number of court of appeals decisions have tightened up the
application of Rule 23. See Klonoff, *Class Actions Part* II: *A Respite from the
Decline*, 92 N.Y.U.L.Rev. 971, 972, 996 (2017). During this period, other forms
of group actions, in particular, multidistrict pretrial proceedings under 28
U.S.C. § 1407, see p. 294 and p. 510, supra, have emerged as complementary
procedural devices for harms that involve multiple claimants.

8. Significantly, 50 years after the 1966 amendments brought modern
class action practice into being, the legal community continues to lack the
"empiric" information that Professor Miller called for—or a consensus on the
role of the class action in a society where harms are mass produced, litigation
is expensive, and small claimants are pushed out of court and into arbitration:

> More than three decades onwards from Professor Arthur Miller's
> attempt to demolish the dueling depictions of Rule 23 class actions as
> "Frankenstein monsters" and "shining knights," we still do not have
> sufficient data to know what the 1966 revision of Rule 23 effected. As
> I discuss further, assessing the character of class actions—are they
> monsters or knights?—presents challenging empirical problems. But

the monster appellation connotes something large and out of control, which in turn suggests that the sheer number of class action filings should disturb us, regardless of their character. It seems odd, therefore, that we have gone so long without knowing how many class action filings there are.

Hensler, *Happy 50th Anniversary, Rule 23! Shouldn't We Know You Better After All This Time?*, 165 U.Pa.L.Rev. 1599, 1604 (2017).

B. DUE PROCESS CONSIDERATIONS

HANSBERRY V. LEE
Supreme Court of the United States, 1940.
311 U.S. 32, 61 S.Ct. 115, 85 L.Ed. 22.

Certiorari to the Supreme Court of the State of Illinois.

JUSTICE STONE delivered the opinion of the Court.

[This suit was brought in an Illinois state court in 1937 on behalf of a class of landowners to enforce a racially restrictive covenant that covered properties on approximately 27 blocks in the Washington Park neighborhood of the City of Chicago. The covenant provided that it would not go into effect unless signed by the "owners of 95 per centum of the frontage" and filed with the office of the Recorder of Deeds of Cook County, Illinois, by December 31, 1928. Plaintiffs sought an injunction to block the sale of a restricted property to Hansberry, a Black man, as a breach of the covenant by an owner who had signed the agreement. Plaintiffs alleged that the validity of the covenant had been established in an earlier Illinois state court action holding that owners of 95 percent of the area's street frontage had signed the agreement. In response, defendants pleaded that they were not bound by the earlier judgment because they had not been joined as parties to that suit and were not successors in interest or in privity with any of the parties to that action. Thus they argued it would be a denial of due process to hold them to the first decree.

The Illinois Circuit Court found that owners representing only about 54 percent of the frontage actually had signed the agreement and that the previous judgment rested on a "false and fraudulent" stipulation of the parties. Nevertheless, the court held that defendants were bound by the prior judgment on the issue of the covenant's validity. The Supreme Court of Illinois affirmed. It found that although the stipulation was untrue it was not fraudulent or collusive. The Illinois court then went on to conclude that the first action had been a "class" or "representative" suit, that it was therefore binding on all the class members unless reversed or set aside on direct proceedings, that Hansberry and the persons who had sold the land to him were members of the class represented in the first action, and that consequently the defendants were bound by the decree in the prior suit.]

The question is whether the Supreme Court of Illinois, by its adjudication that petitioners in this case are bound by a judgment rendered in an earlier litigation to which they were not parties, has deprived them of the due process of law guaranteed by the Fourteenth Amendment.

* * *

* * * [W]hen the judgment of a state court, ascribing to the judgment of another court the binding force and effect of res judicata, is challenged for want of due process it becomes the duty of this Court to examine the course of procedure in both litigations to ascertain whether the litigant whose rights have thus been adjudicated has been afforded such notice and opportunity to be heard as are requisite to the due process which the Constitution prescribes. * * *

It is a principle of general application in Anglo-American jurisprudence that one is not bound by a judgment *in personam* in a litigation in which he is not designated as a party or to which he has not been made a party by service of process. Pennoyer v. Neff * * * [p. 37, supra]. A judgment rendered in such circumstances is not entitled to the full faith and credit which the Constitution and statute of the United States * * * prescribe * * * and judicial action enforcing it against the person or property of the absent party is not that due process which the Fifth and Fourteenth Amendments requires. * * *

To these general rules there is a recognized exception that, to an extent not precisely defined by judicial opinion, the judgment in a "class" or "representative" suit, to which some members of the class are parties, may bind members of the class or those represented who were not made parties to it. * * *

The class suit was an invention of equity to enable it to proceed to a decree in suits where the number of those interested in the subject of the litigation is so great that their joinder as parties in conformity to the usual rules of procedure is impracticable. Courts are not infrequently called upon to proceed with causes in which the number of those interested in the litigation is so great as to make difficult or impossible the joinder of all because some are not within the jurisdiction or because their whereabouts is unknown or where if all were made parties to the suit its continued abatement by the death of some would prevent or unduly delay a decree. In such cases where the interests of those not joined are of the same class as the interests of those who are, and where it is considered that the latter fairly represent the former in the prosecution of the litigation of the issues in which all have a common interest, the court will proceed to a decree. * * *

It is evident that the considerations which may induce a court thus to proceed, despite a technical defect of parties, may differ from those which must be taken into account in determining whether the absent parties are bound by the decree or, if it is adjudged that they are, in ascertaining whether such an adjudication satisfies the requirements of due process and of full faith and credit. Nevertheless there is scope within the framework of the Constitution for holding in appropriate cases that a judgment rendered in a class suit is res judicata as to members of the class who are not formal parties to the suit. Here, as elsewhere, the Fourteenth Amendment does not compel state courts or legislatures to adopt any particular rule for establishing the conclusiveness of judgments in class suits; * * * nor does it compel the adoption of the particular rules thought by this court to be appropriate for the federal courts. With a proper regard for divergent local institutions and interests * * *, this Court is justified in saying that there has been a failure of due process only in those cases where it cannot be said that the procedure adopted, fairly insures the protection of the interests of absent parties who are to be bound by it. * * *

It is familiar doctrine of the federal courts that members of a class not present as parties to the litigation may be bound by the judgment where they are in fact adequately represented by parties who are present, or where they actually participate in the conduct of the litigation in which members of the class are present as parties * * * or where the interest of the members of the class, some of whom are present as parties, is joint, or where for any other reason the relationship between the parties present and those who are absent is such as legally to entitle the former to stand in judgment for the latter. * * *

In all such cases, * * * we may assume for present purposes that such procedure affords a protection to the parties who are represented though absent, which would satisfy the requirements of due process and full faith and credit. * * * Nor do we find it necessary for the decision of this case to say that, when the only circumstance defining the class is that the determination of the rights of its members turns upon a single issue of fact or law, a state could not constitutionally adopt a procedure whereby some of the members of the class could stand in judgment for all, provided that the procedure were so devised and applied as to insure that those present are of the same class as those absent and that the litigation is so conducted as to insure the full and fair consideration of the common issue. * * * We decide only that the procedure and the course of litigation sustained here by the plea of res judicata do not satisfy these requirements.

The restrictive agreement did not purport to create a joint obligation or liability. If valid and effective its promises were the several obligations of the signers and those claiming under them. The promises ran severally to every other signer. It is plain that in such circumstances all those alleged to be bound by the agreement would not constitute a single class in any litigation brought to enforce it. Those who sought to secure its benefits by enforcing it could not be said to be in the same class with or represent those whose interest was in resisting performance, for the agreement by its terms imposes obligations and confers rights on the owner of each plot of land who signs it. If those who thus seek to secure the benefits of the agreement were rightly regarded by the state Supreme Court as constituting a class, it is evident that those signers or their successors who are interested in challenging the validity of the agreement and resisting its performance are not of the same class in the sense that their interests are identical so that any group who had elected to enforce rights conferred by the agreement could be said to be acting in the interest of any others who were free to deny its obligation.

Because of the dual and potentially conflicting interests of those who are putative parties to the agreement in compelling or resisting its performance, it is impossible to say, solely because they are parties to it, that any two of them are of the same class. Nor without more, and with the due regard for the protection of the rights of absent parties which due process exacts, can some be permitted to stand in judgment for all.

It is one thing to say that some members of a class may represent other members in a litigation where the sole and common interest of the class in the litigation, is either to assert a common right or to challenge an asserted obligation. * * * It is quite another to hold that all those who are free alternatively either to assert rights or to challenge them are of a single class, so that any group, merely because it is of the class so constituted, may be deemed adequately to represent any others of the class in litigating their interests in either alternative. Such a selection of representatives for purposes of litigation, whose substantial interests are not necessarily or even probably the same as those whom they are deemed to represent, does not afford that protection to absent parties which due process requires. The doctrine of representation of absent parties in a class suit has not hitherto been thought to go so far. * * * Apart from the opportunities it would afford for the fraudulent and collusive sacrifice of the rights of absent parties, we think that the representation in this case no more satisfies the requirements of due process than a trial by a judicial officer who is in such situation that he may have an interest in the outcome of the litigation in conflict with that of the litigants. * * *

The plaintiffs in the [first] case sought to compel performance of the agreement in behalf of themselves and all others similarly situated. They did not designate the defendants in the suit as a class or seek any injunction or other relief against others than the named defendants, and the decree which was entered did not purport to bind others. In seeking to enforce the agreement the plaintiffs in that suit were not representing the petitioners here whose substantial interest is in resisting performance. The defendants in the first suit were not treated by the pleadings or decree as representing others or as foreclosing by their defense the rights of others, and even though nominal defendants, it does not appear that their interest in defeating the contract outweighed their interest in establishing its validity. For a court in this situation to ascribe to either the plaintiffs or defendants the performance of such functions on behalf of petitioners here, is to attribute to them a power that it cannot be said that they had assumed to exercise, and a responsibility which, in view of their dual interests it does not appear that they could rightly discharge.

Reversed.

NOTES AND QUESTIONS

1. *Hansberry* is an important decision about due process and the legitimacy of the class action. The case is equally important for its substantive contribution to civil rights and racial equality. The use of racially restrictive covenants became widespread after the Supreme Court's decision in Buchanan v. Warley, 245 U.S. 60, 38 S. Ct. 16, 62 L.Ed. 149 (1917), which struck down a city's racially restrictive zoning ordinance as a violation of the Due Process Clause of the Fourteenth Amendment. White property owners then turned to covenants—considered a form of private ordering free of constitutional limitations, unlike public zoning laws—to circumvent *Buchanan*. The lawfulness of racially restrictive covenants, however, continued to be challenged in the lower courts. Although ultimately decided on procedural grounds, *Hansberry* also presented to the Supreme Court the question whether judicial enforcement of a racially restrictive covenant violated the Fourteenth Amendment. The Court finally reached that question several years later and held that enforcement of those covenants was indeed unconstitutional. See Shelley v. Kraemer, 334 U.S. 1, 68 S.Ct. 836, 92 L.Ed. 1161 (1948). For background on racially restrictive covenants and the legal challenges to them, see Brooks & Rose, Saving the Neighborhood: Racially Restrictive Covenants, Law, and Social Norms (2013), and Long & Johnson, People v. Property: Race Restrictive Covenants in Housing (1947).

Beyond its legal significance, *Hansberry* is a remarkable personal story. Lorraine Hansberry, author of A Raisin in the Sun, was the daughter of Carl A. Hansberry, the named party in the case. The family was evicted from their home when the Cook County Circuit Court in July 1937 entered a preliminary injunction to enforce the ugly covenant that was said to bar her father from purchasing property in a Chicago neighborhood. That covenant stated, "[N]o part of said premises shall be sold, given, conveyed or leased to any negro or negroes, and no permission or license to use or occupy any part thereof shall be given to any negro except house servants or janitors or chauffeurs employed thereon." See Tidmarsh, *The Story of* Hansberry: *The Rise of Modern Class Actions, in* Civil Procedure Stories 217, 222 (Clermont ed., 2d ed. 2008). See also Kamp, *The History Behind* Hansberry v. Lee, 20 U.C. Davis L.Rev. 481 (1987).

2. Was the problem in *Hansberry* a lack of consent by the seller and purchaser of the restricted property or their absence from the earlier lawsuit? In *Mullane*, p. 173, supra, the Supreme Court held that before absent parties

could be bound by a judgment, due process required that individual notice be given to those parties whose names and addresses were known, and constructive notice if that information was not reasonably available. See Leubsdorf, *Unmasking* Mullane: *Due Process, Common Trust Funds, and the Class Action Wars*, 66 Hastings L.J. 1693 (2015). Did *Hansberry* rely on notice and consent to justify the preclusive effect of the prior judgment? If not, what was the Court's rationale?

3.   *Hansberry* acknowledged that the Due Process Clause does not require states to adopt federal procedures for class actions adjudicated in state courts. Why was the Illinois procedure nevertheless constitutionally defective? What did the Court mean when it said that because of the "dual and potentially conflicting interests" of those who signed the covenant, the signators could not "be deemed adequately to represent any others of the class"?

4.   Does *Hansberry* require that as a constitutional matter all members of the class must agree with the actions of the named plaintiffs if the class is to be deemed adequately represented and a resulting judgment treated as binding upon the absentees? Is it reasonable to assume complete agreement on all issues by members of the class? Which types of intra-class conflicts ought to have constitutional significance?

5.   Did *Hansberry* treat the named class plaintiff as an agent of the unnamed class members? Of what relevance is the fact that the named plaintiff was a self-selected representative and not appointed by the seller or purchaser of the restricted property? Consider this analysis:

> The class action is in fact a representative lawsuit * * * but it employs a peculiar concept of representation: self-appointment. Contrary to the situation where I appoint someone as my agent, in the class action the named plaintiff appoints himself or herself as the representative of the class. Self-appointment is not unheard of in the world of politics and other social domains. * * * Yet there is no denying that self-appointment is as anomalous form of representation, only justified, if at all, by the most exceptional circumstances.

Fiss, *The Political Theory of the Class Action*, 53 Wash. & Lee L.Rev. 21, 25 (1996). According to *Hansberry*, what "exceptional circumstances" allow one party to represent the interests of another? Why were those circumstances absent in the principal case?

C. OPERATION OF THE CLASS ACTION DEVICE

Read Federal Rule of Civil Procedure 23 in the Supplement.

Rule 23 authorizes the class action in federal court and has influenced state judicial practice. Although there are defendant class actions, they are rather unusual, and these materials use the far more common plaintiff class action as the model for discussion. A class action, like all lawsuits, is commenced by the filing of a complaint and the service of a summons. The caption specifies the name of the representative plaintiff and also indicates that the lawsuit is being filed on behalf of a class. The complaint alleges the claims of the named plaintiff and sets forth classwide allegations of the unnamed class members. Special rules pertaining to subject-matter jurisdiction, personal jurisdiction, and venue apply to the class action. See p. 573, infra.

1. RULE 23(a): PREREQUISITES OF CERTIFICATION

Rule 23(a) sets forth four conditions that an action must meet to be certified as a class action. These prerequisites to bringing a class action apply to all actions certified under Rule 23, and the party seeking to invoke the rule has the burden of showing by a preponderance of the evidence that the requirements are met. See 7A Wright, Miller & Kane, Federal Practice and Procedure § 1759 (4th ed.).

WAL-MART STORES, INC. V. DUKES

Supreme Court of the United States, 2011.
564 U.S. 338, 131 S.Ct. 2541, 180 L.Ed.2d 374.

Certiorari to the United States Court of Appeals for the Ninth Circuit.

JUSTICE SCALIA delivered the opinion of the Court, in which THE CHIEF JUSTICE, JUSTICE KENNEDY, JUSTICE THOMAS, and JUSTICE ALITO joined, and, with respect to Parts I and III, in which JUSTICE GINSBURG, JUSTICE BREYER, JUSTICE SOTOMAYOR, and JUSTICE KAGAN joined.

We are presented with one of the most expansive class actions ever. The District Court and the Court of Appeals approved the certification of a class comprising about one and a half million plaintiffs, current and former female employees of petitioner Wal-Mart who allege that the discretion exercised by their local supervisors over pay and promotion matters violates Title VII by discriminating against women. In addition to injunctive and declaratory relief, the plaintiffs seek an award of backpay. * * *

A

Petitioner Wal-Mart is the Nation's largest private employer. * * * In all, Wal-Mart operates approximately 3,400 stores and employs more than one million people.

Pay and promotion decisions at Wal-Mart are generally committed to local managers' broad discretion, which is exercised "in a largely subjective manner." * * * Local store managers may increase the wages of hourly employees (within limits) with only limited corporate oversight. As for salaried employees, such as store managers and their deputies, higher corporate authorities have discretion to set their pay within preestablished ranges.

Promotions work in a similar fashion. Wal-Mart permits store managers to apply their own subjective criteria when selecting candidates as [managers]. * * * [E]xcept for [limited] requirements, regional and district managers have discretion to use their own judgment when selecting candidates for management training. Promotion to higher office * * * is similarly at the discretion of the employee's superiors after prescribed objective factors are satisfied.

B

* * *

Betty Dukes began working * * * as a cashier, but later sought and received a promotion to customer service manager. After a series of disciplinary violations, however, Dukes was demoted back to cashier and then to greeter. Dukes concedes she violated company policy, but contends that the disciplinary actions were in fact retaliation for invoking internal complaint procedures and that male employees have not been disciplined for similar infractions. Dukes also claims two male greeters in the Pittsburgh store are paid more than she is.

Christine Kwapnoski * * * has held a number of positions, including a supervisory position. She claims that a male manager yelled at her frequently and screamed at female employees, but not at men. The manager in question "told her to 'doll up,' to wear some makeup, and to dress a little better." * * *

* * * Edith Arana * * * approached the store manager on more than one occasion about management training, but was brushed off. Arana concluded she was being denied opportunity for advancement because of her sex. She initiated internal complaint procedures, whereupon she was told to apply directly to the district manager if she thought her store manager was being unfair. Arana, however, decided against that and never applied for management training again. * * * [S]he was fired for failure to comply with Wal-Mart's timekeeping policy.

* * *

* * * [Respondents] do not allege that Wal-Mart has any express corporate policy against the advancement of women. Rather, they claim that their local managers' discretion over pay and promotions is exercised disproportionately in favor of men, leading to an unlawful disparate impact on female employees. * * * And, respondents say, because Wal-Mart is aware of this effect, its refusal to cabin its managers' authority amounts to disparate treatment. * * *

Importantly for our purposes, respondents claim that the discrimination to which they have been subjected is common to all Wal-Mart's female employees. The basic theory of their case is that a strong and uniform "corporate culture" permits bias against women to infect, perhaps subconsciously, the discretionary decisionmaking of each one of Wal-Mart's thousands of managers—thereby making every woman at the company the victim of one common discriminatory practice. Respondents therefore wish to litigate the Title VII claims of all female employees at Wal-Mart's stores in a nationwide class action.

C

* * *

* * * [R]espondents moved the District Court to certify a plaintiff class consisting of " '[a]ll women employed at any Wal-Mart domestic retail store at any time since December 26, 1998, who have been or may be subjected to Wal-Mart's challenged pay and management track promotions policies and practices.' " * * * As evidence that there were indeed "questions of law or fact common to" all the women of Wal-Mart, as Rule 23(a)(2) requires, respondents relied chiefly on three forms of proof: statistical evidence about pay and promotion disparities between men and women at the company, anecdotal reports of discrimination from about 120 of Wal-Mart's female employees, and the testimony of a sociologist, Dr. William Bielby, who conducted a "social framework analysis" of Wal-Mart's "culture" and personnel practices, and concluded that the company was "vulnerable" to gender discrimination. * * *

Wal-Mart unsuccessfully moved to strike much of this evidence. * * *

D

A divided en banc Court of Appeals substantially affirmed the District Court's certification order. * * * The majority concluded that respondents' evidence of commonality was sufficient to "raise the common question whether Wal-Mart's female employees nationwide were subjected to a single set of corporate policies (not merely a number of independent discriminatory acts) that may have worked to unlawfully discriminate against them in violation of Title VII." * * *

II

* * * The Rule's four requirements—numerosity, commonality, typicality, and adequate representation—"effectively 'limit the class claims to those fairly encompassed by the named plaintiff's claims.' " *General Telephone Co. of Southwest v. Falcon*, 457 U.S. 147, 156, 102 S.Ct. 2364, 72 L.Ed.2d 740 (1982). * * *

A

The crux of this case is commonality—the rule requiring a plaintiff to show that "there are questions of law or fact common to the class." Rule 23(a)(2).[5] That language is easy to misread, since "[a]ny competently crafted class complaint literally raises common 'questions.'" Nagareda, Class Certification in the Age of Aggregate Proof, 84 N.Y.U.L.Rev. 97, 131–132 (2009). For example: Do all of us plaintiffs indeed work for Wal-Mart? Do our managers have discretion over pay? Is that an unlawful employment practice? What remedies should we get? Reciting these questions is not sufficient to obtain class certification. Commonality requires the plaintiff to demonstrate that the class members "have suffered the same injury," *Falcon, supra,* at 157, 102 S.Ct. 2364. This does not mean merely that they have all suffered a violation of the same provision of law. Title VII, for example, can be violated in many ways—by intentional discrimination, or by hiring and promotion criteria that result in disparate impact, and by the use of these practices on the part of many different superiors in a single company. Quite obviously, the mere claim by employees of the same company that they have suffered a Title VII injury, or even a disparate-impact Title VII injury, gives no cause to believe that all their claims can productively be litigated at once. Their claims must depend upon a common contention—for example, the assertion of discriminatory bias on the part of the same supervisor. That common contention, moreover, must be of such a nature that it is capable of classwide resolution—which means that determination of its truth or falsity will resolve an issue that is central to the validity of each one of the claims in one stroke.

> "What matters to class certification ... is not the raising of common 'questions'—even in droves—but, rather the capacity of a classwide proceeding to generate common *answers* apt to drive the resolution of the litigation. Dissimilarities within the proposed class are what have the potential to impede the generation of common answers." Nagareda, *supra,* at 132.

Rule 23 does not set forth a mere pleading standard. A party seeking class certification must affirmatively demonstrate his compliance with the Rule—that is, he must be prepared to prove that there are *in fact* sufficiently numerous parties, common questions of law or fact, etc. We

---

[5] We have previously stated in this context that "[t]he commonality and typicality requirements of Rule 23(a) tend to merge. Both serve as guideposts for determining whether under the particular circumstances maintenance of a class action is economical and whether the named plaintiff's claim and the class claims are so interrelated that the interests of the class members will be fairly and adequately protected in their absence. Those requirements therefore also tend to merge with the adequacy-of-representation requirement, although the latter requirement also raises concerns about the competency of class counsel and conflicts of interest." *General Telephone Co. of Southwest v. Falcon,* 457 U.S. 147, 157–158, n. 13, 102 S.Ct. 2364, 72 L.Ed.2d 740 (1982). In light of our disposition of the commonality question, however, it is unnecessary to resolve whether respondents have satisfied the typicality and adequate-representation requirements of Rule 23(a).

recognized in *Falcon* that "sometimes it may be necessary for the court to probe behind the pleadings before coming to rest on the certification question," 457 U.S., at 160, 102 S.Ct. 2364, and that certification is proper only if "the trial court is satisfied, after a rigorous analysis, that the prerequisites of Rule 23(a) have been satisfied," [id., at 161, 102 S.Ct. 2364]. * * * Frequently that "rigorous analysis" will entail some overlap with the merits of the plaintiff's underlying claim. That cannot be helped. * * *[6] Nor is there anything unusual about that consequence: The necessity of touching aspects of the merits in order to resolve preliminary matters, *e.g.*, jurisdiction and venue, is a familiar feature of litigation. * * *

In this case, proof of commonality necessarily overlaps with respondents' merits contention that Wal-Mart engages in a *pattern or practice* of discrimination.[7] That is so because, in resolving an individual's Title VII claim, the crux of the inquiry is "the reason for a particular employment decision," *Cooper v. Federal Reserve Bank of Richmond*, 467 U.S. 867, 876, 104 S.Ct. 2794, 81 L.Ed.2d 718 (1984) [p. 590, infra] Here respondents wish to sue about literally millions of employment decisions at once. Without some glue holding the alleged *reasons* for all those decisions together, it will be impossible to say that examination of all the class members' claims for relief will produce a common answer to the crucial question *why was I disfavored.*

B

This Court's opinion in *Falcon* describes how the commonality issue must be approached. There an employee who claimed that he was deliberately denied a promotion on account of race obtained certification of a class comprising all employees wrongfully denied promotions and all applicants wrongfully denied jobs. * * * We rejected that composite class for lack of commonality and typicality, explaining:

> "Conceptually, there is a wide gap between (a) an individual's claim that he has been denied a promotion [or higher pay] on discriminatory grounds, and his otherwise unsupported allegation that the company has a policy of discrimination, and (b) the existence of a class of persons who have suffered the same injury

---

[6] A statement in one of our prior cases, *Eisen v. Carlisle & Jacquelin*, 417 U.S. 156, 177, 94 S.Ct. 2140, 40 L.Ed.2d 732 (1974), is sometimes mistakenly cited to the contrary: "We find nothing in either the language or history of Rule 23 that gives a court any authority to conduct a preliminary inquiry into the merits of a suit in order to determine whether it may be maintained as a class action." But in that case, the judge had conducted a preliminary inquiry into the merits of a suit * * * in order to shift the cost of notice required by Rule 23(c)(2) from the plaintiff to the defendants. To the extent the quoted statement goes beyond the permissibility of a merits inquiry for any other pretrial purpose, it is the purest dictum and is contradicted by our other cases. * * *

[7] In a pattern-or-practice case, the plaintiff tries to "establish by a preponderance of the evidence that . . . discrimination was the company's standard operating procedure[,] the regular rather than the unusual practice." *Teamsters v. United States*, 431 U.S. 324, 358, 97 S.Ct. 1843, 52 L.Ed.2d 396 (1977). * * * If he succeeds, that showing will support a rebuttable inference that all class members were victims of the discriminatory practice * * *.

as that individual, such that the individual's claim and the class claim will share common questions of law or fact and that the individual's claim will be typical of the class claims." *Id.*, at 157–158, 102 S.Ct. 2364.

Falcon suggested two ways in which that conceptual gap might be bridged. First, if the employer "used a biased testing procedure to evaluate both applicants for employment and incumbent employees, a class action on behalf of every applicant or employee who might have been prejudiced by the test clearly would satisfy the commonality and typicality requirements of Rule 23(a)." *Id.*, at 159, n. 15, 102 S.Ct. 2364. Second, "[s]ignificant proof that an employer operated under a general policy of discrimination conceivably could justify a class of both applicants and employees if the discrimination manifested itself in hiring and promotion practices in the same general fashion, such as through entirely subjective decisionmaking processes." *Ibid.* We think that statement precisely describes respondents' burden in this case. The first manner of bridging the gap obviously has no application here; Wal-Mart has no testing procedure or other companywide evaluation method that can be charged with bias. * * *

The second manner of bridging the gap requires "significant proof" that Wal-Mart "operated under a general policy of discrimination." That is entirely absent here. Wal-Mart's announced policy forbids sex discrimination, * * * and as the District Court recognized the company imposes penalties for denials of equal employment opportunity. * * * The only evidence of a "general policy of discrimination" respondents produced was the testimony of Dr. William Bielby, their sociological expert. Relying on "social framework" analysis, Bielby testified that Wal-Mart has a "strong corporate culture," that makes it " 'vulnerable' " to "gender bias." * * * He could not, however, "determine with any specificity how regularly stereotypes play a meaningful role in employment decisions at Wal-Mart. At his deposition ... Dr. Bielby conceded that he could not calculate whether 0.5 percent or 95 percent of the employment decisions at Wal-Mart might be determined by stereotyped thinking." * * * Bielby's testimony does nothing to advance respondents' case. "[W]hether 0.5 percent or 95 percent of the employment decisions at Wal-Mart might be determined by stereotyped thinking" is the essential question on which respondents' theory of commonality depends. If Bielby admittedly has no answer to that question, we can safely disregard what he has to say. It is worlds away from "significant proof" that Wal-Mart "operated under a general policy of discrimination."

C

The only corporate policy that the plaintiffs' evidence convincingly establishes is Wal-Mart's "policy" of *allowing discretion* by local supervisors over employment matters. On its face, of course, that is just the opposite of a uniform employment practice that would provide the commonality needed for a class action; it is a policy *against having* uniform employment practices. * * *

To be sure, we have recognized that, "in appropriate cases," giving discretion to lower-level supervisors can be the basis of Title VII liability under a disparate-impact theory—since "an employer's undisciplined system of subjective decisionmaking [can have] precisely the same effects as a system pervaded by impermissible intentional discrimination." * * * But the recognition that this type of Title VII claim "can" exist does not lead to the conclusion that every employee in a company using a system of discretion has such a claim in common. To the contrary, left to their own devices most managers in any corporation—and surely most managers in a corporation that forbids sex discrimination—would select sex-neutral, performance-based criteria for hiring and promotion that produce no actionable disparity at all. Others may choose to reward various attributes that produce disparate impact—such as scores on general aptitude tests or educational achievements. * * * And still other managers may be guilty of intentional discrimination that produces a sex-based disparity. In such a company, demonstrating the invalidity of one manager's use of discretion will do nothing to demonstrate the invalidity of another's. A party seeking to certify a nationwide class will be unable to show that all the employees' Title VII claims will in fact depend on the answers to common questions.

Respondents have not identified a common mode of exercising discretion that pervades the entire company—aside from their reliance on Dr. Bielby's social frameworks analysis that we have rejected. * * * Respondents attempt to make that showing by means of statistical and anecdotal evidence, but their evidence falls well short.

The statistical evidence consists primarily of regression analyses performed by Dr. Richard Drogin, a statistician, and Dr. Marc Bendick, a labor economist. * * * After considering regional and national data, Drogin concluded that "there are statistically significant disparities between men and women at Wal-Mart . . . [and] these disparities . . . can be explained only by gender discrimination." * * * Bendick compared work-force data from Wal-Mart and competitive retailers and concluded that Wal-Mart "promotes a lower percentage of women than its competitors." * * *

Even if they are taken at face value, these studies are insufficient to establish that respondents' theory can be proved on a classwide basis. * * * As Judge Ikuta observed in her dissent, "[i]nformation about disparities at the regional and national level does not establish the existence of disparities at individual stores, let alone raise the inference that a company-wide policy of discrimination is implemented by discretionary decisions at the store and district level." * * * A regional pay disparity, for example, may be attributable to only a small set of Wal-Mart stores, and cannot by itself establish the uniform, store-by-store disparity upon which the plaintiffs' theory of commonality depends.

There is another, more fundamental, respect in which respondents' statistical proof fails. Even if it established (as it does not) a pay or promotion pattern that differs from the nationwide figures or the regional figures in *all* of Wal-Mart's 3,400 stores, that would still not demonstrate that commonality of issue exists. Some managers will claim that the availability of women, or qualified women, or interested women, in their stores' area does not mirror the national or regional statistics. And almost all of them will claim to have been applying some sex-neutral, performance-based criteria—whose nature and effects will differ from store to store. In the landmark case of ours which held that giving discretion to lower-level supervisors can be the basis of Title VII liability under a disparate-impact theory, the plurality opinion *conditioned* that holding on the corollary that merely proving that the discretionary system has produced a racial or sexual disparity *is not enough*. "[T]he plaintiff must begin by identifying the specific employment practice that is challenged." * * * That is all the more necessary when a class of plaintiffs is sought to be certified. Other than the bare existence of delegated discretion, respondents have identified no "specific employment practice"—much less one that ties all their 1.5 million claims together. Merely showing that Wal-Mart's policy of discretion has produced an overall sex-based disparity does not suffice.

Respondents' anecdotal evidence suffers from the same defects, and in addition is too weak to raise any inference that all the individual, discretionary personnel decisions are discriminatory. In *Teamsters v. United States*, 431 U.S. 324, 97 S.Ct. 1843, 52 L.Ed.2d 396 (1977) * * * the [plaintiff] produced about 40 specific accounts of racial discrimination * * *. * * * That number was significant because * * * [t]he 40 anecdotes * * * represented roughly one account for every eight members of the class. Moreover, * * * the anecdotes came from individuals "spread throughout" the company who "for the most part" worked at the company's operational centers that employed the largest numbers of the class members. * * * Here, by contrast, respondents filed some 120 affidavits reporting experiences of discrimination—about 1 for every 12,500 class members—relating to only some 235 out of Wal-Mart's 3,400 stores. * * * More than half of these reports are concentrated in only six States * * *; half of all States have only one or two anecdotes; and 14 States have no anecdotes about Wal-Mart's operations at all. * * * Even if every single one of these accounts is true, that would not demonstrate that the entire company "operate[s] under a general policy of discrimination," * * * which is what respondents must show to certify a companywide class.

The dissent misunderstands the nature of the foregoing analysis. It criticizes our focus on the dissimilarities between the putative class members on the ground that we have "blend[ed]" Rule 23(a)(2)'s commonality requirement with Rule 23(b)(3)'s inquiry into whether common questions "predominate" over individual ones. * * * That is not so. We quite agree that for purposes of Rule 23(a)(2) " '[e]ven a single [common] question' " will do. * * * We consider dissimilarities not in order to determine (as Rule 23(b)(3) requires) whether common questions *predominate*, but in order to determine (as Rule 23(a)(2) requires) whether there is "[e]ven a single [common] question." And there is not here. Because respondents provide no convincing proof of a companywide discriminatory pay and promotion policy, we have concluded that they have not established the existence of any common question. * * *

In sum, we agree with Chief Judge Kozinski that the members of the class:

"held a multitude of different jobs, at different levels of Wal-Mart's hierarchy, for variable lengths of time, in 3,400 stores, sprinkled across 50 states, with a kaleidoscope of supervisors (male and female), subject to a variety of regional policies that all differed . . . . Some thrived while others did poorly. They have little in common but their sex and this lawsuit." 603 F.3d, at 652 (dissenting opinion).

* * *

The judgment of the Court of Appeals is

Reversed.

JUSTICE GINSBURG, with whom JUSTICE BREYER, JUSTICE SOTOMAYOR, and JUSTICE KAGAN join, concurring in part and dissenting in part.

* * *

* * * [T]he Court * * * disqualifies the class at the starting gate, holding that the plaintiffs cannot cross the "commonality" line set by Rule 23(a)(2). In so ruling, the Court imports into the Rule 23(a) determination concerns properly addressed in a Rule 23(b)(3) assessment.

I

A

* * *

A "question" is ordinarily understood to be "[a] subject or point open to controversy." American Heritage Dictionary 1483 (3d ed.1992). * * * Thus, a "question" "common to the class" must be a dispute, either of fact or of law, the resolution of which will advance the determination of the class members' claims.[3]

B

The District Court, recognizing that "one significant issue common to the class may be sufficient to warrant certification," * * * found that the plaintiffs easily met that test. * * *

* * * The named plaintiffs * * * propose to litigate, on behalf of the class, allegations that Wal-Mart discriminates on the basis of gender in pay and promotions. * * * Wal-Mart permits those prejudices to infect personnel decisions, the plaintiffs contend, by leaving pay and promotions in the hands of "a nearly all male managerial workforce" using "arbitrary and subjective criteria." * * * Further alleged barriers to the advancement of female employees include the company's requirement, "as a condition of promotion to management jobs, that employees be willing to relocate." * * * Absent instruction otherwise, there is a risk that managers will act on the familiar assumption that women, because of their services to husband and children, are less mobile than men. * * *

Women fill 70 percent of the hourly jobs in the retailer's stores but make up only "33 percent of management employees." * * * "[T]he higher one looks in the organization the lower the percentage of women." * * * The plaintiffs'" largely uncontested descriptive statistics" also show that women working in the company's stores "are paid less than men in every region" and "that the salary gap widens over time even for men and women hired into the same jobs at the same time." * * *

The District Court identified "systems for . . . promoting in-store employees" that were "sufficiently similar across regions and stores" to conclude that "the manner in which these systems affect the class raises issues that are common to all class members." * * * The selection of employees for promotion to in-store management "is fairly characterized as a 'tap on the shoulder' process," in which managers have discretion about whose shoulders to tap. * * * Vacancies are not regularly posted; from among those employees satisfying minimum qualifications, managers choose whom to promote on the basis of their own subjective impressions. * * *

Wal-Mart's compensation policies also operate uniformly across stores, the District Court found. The retailer leaves open a $2 band for every position's hourly pay rate. Wal-Mart provides no standards or criteria for

---

[3] The Court suggests Rule 23(a)(2) must mean more than it says. * * * If the word "questions" were taken literally, the majority asserts, plaintiffs could pass the Rule 23(a)(2) bar by "[r]eciting . . . questions" like "Do all of us plaintiffs indeed work for Wal-Mart?" * * * Sensibly read, however, the word "questions" means disputed issues, not any utterance crafted in the grammatical form of a question.

setting wages within that band, and thus does nothing to counter unconscious bias on the part of supervisors. * * *

Wal-Mart's supervisors do not make their discretionary decisions in a vacuum. The District Court reviewed means Wal-Mart used to maintain a "carefully constructed . . . corporate culture," such as frequent meetings to reinforce the common way of thinking, regular transfers of managers between stores to ensure uniformity throughout the company, monitoring of stores "on a close and constant basis," and "Wal-Mart TV," "broadcas[t] . . . into all stores." * * *

The plaintiffs' evidence, including class members' tales of their own experiences,[4] suggests that gender bias suffused Wal-Mart's company culture. Among illustrations, senior management often refer to female associates as "little Janie Qs." * * * One manager told an employee that "[m]en are here to make a career and women aren't." * * * A committee of female Wal-Mart executives concluded that "[s]tereotypes limit the opportunities offered to women." * * *

Finally, the plaintiffs presented an expert's appraisal to show that the pay and promotions disparities at Wal-Mart "can be explained only by gender discrimination and not by . . . neutral variables." * * * Using regression analyses, their expert, Richard Drogin, controlled for factors including, *inter alia*, job performance, length of time with the company, and the store where an employee worked. * * *.[5] * * *

C

The District Court's identification of a common question, whether Wal-Mart's pay and promotions policies gave rise to unlawful discrimination, was hardly infirm. The practice of delegating to supervisors large discretion to make personnel decisions, uncontrolled by formal standards, has long been known to have the potential to produce disparate effects. Managers, like all humankind, may be prey to biases of which they are unaware. The risk of discrimination is heightened when those managers are predominantly of one sex, and are steeped in a corporate culture that perpetuates gender stereotypes.

* * *

---

[4] The majority purports to derive from *Teamsters v. United States* * * * a rule that a discrimination claim, if accompanied by anecdotes, must supply them in numbers proportionate to the size of the class. * * * *Teamsters* * * * instructs that statistical evidence alone may suffice * * *; that decision can hardly be said to establish a numerical floor before anecdotal evidence can be taken into account.

[5] The Court asserts that Drogin showed only average differences at the "regional and national level" between male and femaile emplyees. * * * In fact, his regression analysis showed there were disparities *within* stores. The majority's contention to the contrary reflects only an arcane disagreement about statistical method—which the District Court resolved in the plaintiffs' favor. Appellate review is no occasion to disturb a trial court's handling of factual disputes of this order.

We have held that "discretionary employment practices" can give rise to Title VII claims, not only when such practices are motivated by discriminatory intent but also when they produce discriminatory results. See *Watson v. Fort Worth Bank & Trust*, 487 U.S. 977, 988, 991, 108 S.Ct. 2777, 101 L.Ed.2d 827 (1988). * * *

Aware of "the problem of subconscious stereotypes and prejudices," we held that the employer's "undisciplined system of subjective decisionmaking" was an "employment practic[e]" that "may be analyzed under the disparate impact approach." *Id.*, at 990–991, 108 S.Ct. 2777. * * *

The plaintiffs' allegations state claims of gender discrimination in the form of biased decisionmaking in both pay and promotions. The evidence reviewed by the District Court adequately demonstrated that resolving those claims would necessitate examination of particular policies and practices alleged to affect, adversely and globally, women employed at Wal-Mart's stores. Rule 23(a)(2), setting a necessary but not a sufficient criterion for class-action certification, demands nothing further.

II

A

The Court gives no credence to the key dispute common to the class: whether Wal-Mart's discretionary pay and promotion policies are discriminatory. * * *

The Court blends Rule 23(a)(2)'s threshold criterion with the more demanding criteria of Rule 23(b)(3), and thereby elevates the (a)(2) inquiry so that it is no longer "easily satisfied," 5 J. Moore et al., Moore's Federal Practice § 23.23[2], p. 23–72 (3d ed.2011).[7] Rule 23(b)(3) certification requires * * * determinations that "questions of law or fact common to class members predominate over any questions affecting only individual members" and that "a class action is superior to other available methods for . . . adjudicating the controversy."

The Court's emphasis on differences between class members mimics the Rule 23(b)(3) inquiry into whether common questions "predominate" over individual issues. And by asking whether the individual differences "impede" common adjudication, * * * the Court duplicates 23(b)(3)'s question whether "a class action is superior" to other modes of adjudication. * * * "The Rule 23(b)(3) predominance inquiry" is meant to "tes[t] whether proposed classes are sufficiently cohesive to warrant adjudication by

---

[7]   The Court places considerable weight on *General Telephone Co. of Southwest v. Falcon* * * *. That case has little relevance to the question before the Court today. There were "*no* common questions of law or fact" between the claims of the lead plaintiff and the applicant class. 457 U.S., at 162, 102 S.Ct. 2364 (Burger, C. J., concurring in part and dissenting in part) (emphasis added). The plaintiff-employee alleged that the defendant-employer had discriminated against him intentionally. The applicant class claims, by contrast, were "advanced under the 'adverse impact' theory," *ibid.*, appropriate for facially neutral practices. * * * Here the same practices touch and concern all members of the class.

representation." * * * If courts must conduct a "dissimilarities" analysis at the Rule 23(a)(2) stage, no mission remains for Rule 23(b)(3).

Because Rule 23(a) is also a prerequisite for Rule 23(b)(1) and Rule 23(b)(2) classes, the Court's "dissimilarities" position is far reaching. Individual differences should not bar a Rule 23(b)(1) or Rule 23(b)(2) class, so long as the Rule 23(a) threshold is met. * * *

B

The "dissimilarities" approach leads the Court to train its attention on what distinguishes individual class members, rather than on what unites them. * * *

Wal-Mart's delegation of discretion over pay and promotions is a policy uniform throughout all stores. The very nature of discretion is that people will exercise it in various ways. A system of delegated discretion * * * is a practice actionable under Title VII when it produces discriminatory outcomes. * * * A finding that Wal-Mart's pay and promotions practices in fact violate the law would be the first step in the usual order of proof for plaintiffs seeking individual remedies for company-wide discrimination. * * * That each individual employee's unique circumstances will ultimately determine whether she is entitled to backpay or damages * * * should not factor into the Rule 23(a)(2) determination.

* * *

NOTES AND QUESTIONS

1. In *Wal-Mart*, the large number of class members clearly made joinder impracticable for purposes of satisfying Rule 23(a)(1), but the Court raised other concerns about the appropriateness of Rule 23 certification. Generally, the test for numerosity has both a quantitative and a qualitative aspect. A class of 20 members is likely to be too small; a class of 40 is likely to be sufficient. Moreover, joinder does not have to be "impossible—only that the difficulty or inconvenience of joining all members of the class make use of the class action appropriate." Novella v. Westchester County, 661 F.3d 128, 144 (2d Cir. 2011). Was it significant to the decision in *Wal-Mart*, as one commentator observed, that "[n]o class action of this magnitude had ever been certified"? Sherry, *Hogs Get Slaughtered at the Supreme Court*, 2011 Sup.Ct.Rev. 1, 22.

2. Prior to *Wal-Mart*, courts tended to give Rule 23(a)(2)'s "commonality" requirement a "permissive application." 7A Wright, Miller & Kane, Federal Practice and Procedure § 1763 (4th ed.). Even in a mass tort action, the threshold for commonality was "not high" and instead was "relatively easy to satisfy." In re Telectronics Pacing Sys., Inc., 164 F.R.D. 222, 228 (S.D.Ohio 1995) (the class was later decertified and then recertified). The majority in *Wal-Mart* toughened the commonality standard to require a showing and proof of a "common contention" that is "capable of classwide resolution." Under this standard should it be sufficient for the class complaint

to allege that defendant has engaged in a systemic violation of the law that harms the absentees? In Wallace B. Roderick Revocable Living Tr. v. XTO Energy, Inc., 725 F.3d 1213 (10th Cir. 2013), royalty owners of natural gas wells brought a class action against the lessee, challenging the adequacy of their royalty payments. The Tenth Circuit held that commonality was not established by the lessee's use of a uniform methodology to determine the royalty payments. What additional showing does the *Wal-Mart* standard require?

3.   In deciding whether "commonality" was shown, the majority in *Wal-Mart* examined the merits of plaintiffs' claims on the ground that doing so was necessary to probe whether the requirements of Rule 23(a) had been satisfied. Before *Wal-Mart*, the Court had limited the district court's authority to weigh the merits as part of the class certification calculus. Justice Powell, in a unanimous opinion in Eisen v. Carlisle & Jacquelin, 417 U.S. 156, 94 S.Ct. 2140, 40 L.Ed.2d 732 (1974), explained: "We find nothing in either the language or history of Rule 23 that gives a court any authority to conduct a preliminary inquiry into the merits of a suit in order to determine whether it may be maintained as a class action." Id. at 177, 94 S.Ct. at 2152, 40 L.Ed.2d at 748–49. Because the district court in *Eisen* had sought expressly to encourage certification (on the ground that the class was likely to prevail on its claims), the *Wal-Mart* majority read that statement in Justice Powell's opinion narrowly. After *Wal-Mart*, the Court in Comcast Corp. v. Behrend, 569 U.S. 27, 34, 133 S.Ct. 1426, 1433, 185 L.Ed.2d 515, 522 (2013), reaffirmed that consideration of the merits may be "pertinent" to the Rule 23(a) inquiry and it would be an abuse of discretion for the district court not to take them into consideration. However, in AMGEN v. CONNECTICUT RETIREMENT PLANS AND TR. FUNDS, 568 U.S. 455, 133 S.Ct. 1184, 184 L.Ed.2d 308 (2013), the Court, six-to-three, clarified the relationship between a review of the merits and the certification inquiry. In *Amgen*, the question was whether proof of materiality—an essential element of plaintiff's fraud-on-the-market securities case—was a prerequisite to class certification, and the Court answered that it was not:

> Although we have cautioned that a court's class-certification analysis must be "rigorous" and may "entail some overlap with the merits of the plaintiff's underlying claim," [*Wal-Mart*, p. 526, supra], Rule 23 grants courts no license to engage in free-ranging merits inquiries at the certification stage. Merits questions may be considered to the extent—but only to the extent—that they are relevant to determining whether the Rule 23 prerequisites for class certification are satisfied.
> * * *

Id. at 465–66, 133 S.Ct. at 1194–95, 184 L.Ed.2d at 320–21. Requiring plaintiffs to prove materiality before the certification decision, the Court stated, "put[s] the cart before the horse"; a "certification ruling is not to adjudicate the case; rather it is to select the 'metho[d]" best suited to adjudication of the controversy 'fairly and efficiently.'" Id. at 460, 133 S.Ct. at 1191, 184 L.Ed.2d at 316 (alteration in original).

4. The Court in *Wal-Mart* noted in dicta a relationship between the typicality requirement of Rule 23(a)(3) and that of commonality, calling them "guideposts" for whether a class suit would be "economical" and adequate representation could be ensured. As the Third Circuit has explained, the typicality inquiry looks to whether "the class representatives are sufficiently similar to the rest of the class—in terms of their legal claims, factual circumstances, and stake in the litigation—so that certifying those individuals to represent the class will be fair to the rest of the proposed class." In re Schering Plough Corp. ERISA Litig., 589 F.3d 585, 597 (3d Cir. 2009).

5. Will typicality be defeated if the claims of the named representative are not identical to those of the absentees? In GENERAL TELEPHONE CO. OF SOUTHWEST v. FALCON, 457 U.S. 147, 156, 102 S.Ct. 2364, 72 L.Ed.2d 740 (1982), relied upon in *Wal-Mart*, the Court stated that a named representative must have the same interest and suffer the same injury as the class. The Court then found that the named plaintiff, who alleged that defendant had discriminated against him in its employment *promotion* practices, could not represent the interests of absent class members alleging discrimination in employment *hiring*. However, in GRATZ v. BOLLINGER, 539 U.S. 244, 123 S.Ct. 2411, 156 L.Ed.2d 257 (2003), a challenge to a public university's use of racial criteria in the selection of students for undergraduate admission, the Court held that the named plaintiff, a transfer student, could represent students who had applied in the regular admission process; their difference in application status was irrelevant because the university used the same criteria to select entry and transfer students. As the Seventh Circuit has explained, "The lesson we take from that is that there must be enough congruence between the named representative's claim and that of the unnamed members of the class to justify allowing the named party to litigate on behalf of the group." Spano v. Boeing Co., 633 F.3d 574, 586 (7th Cir. 2011). Why was this congruence not present in *Falcon*?

6. Rule 23(a)(4) requires that the named plaintiff "fairly and adequately protect the interests of the class." In AMCHEM PRODS., INC. v. WINDSOR, 521 U.S. 591, 117 S.Ct. 2231, 138 L.Ed.2d 689 (1997), a proposed global settlement of "hundreds of thousands, perhaps millions" of claims arising from exposure to asbestos, the Court explained that the purpose of the adequacy requirement is "to uncover conflicts of interest between named parties and the class they seek to represent." Id. at 625, 117 S.Ct. at 2250, 138 L.Ed.2d at 714. Finding that common claims did not predominate, the Court did not discuss adequacy issues "discretely," but observed that the class members had diverse medical conditions, were exposed to different asbestos-containing products, had different prospects for physical injury and death, and had different preferences for immediate or long term payment. As the Court concluded,

> The settling parties, in sum, achieved a global compromise with no structural assurance of fair and adequate representation for the diverse groups and individuals affected. Although the named parties alleged a range of complaints, each served generally as representative for the whole, not for a separate constituency.

Id. at 609, 626–27, 117 S.Ct. at 2243, 2251, 138 L.Ed.2d at 704, 714–15. *Amchem* makes clear that potentially conflicting interests do not inevitably doom class certification; however, they do require the district court to take steps at the outset of the lawsuit to protect absentee interests (for example, by ordering provisional certification of subclasses with independent counsel for groups with different interests). See Ratner, *Class Conflicts*, 92 Wash.L.Rev. 78 (2017). Settlement classes are discussed later in this Chapter, see p. 557, infra.

7.   In addition to monitoring intra-class conflict, the adequacy inquiry examines the "zeal and competence" of the named party and the party's lawyer, as well as "the willingness and ability of the representative to take an active role in and control the litigation and to protect the interests of absentees." Jones v. Singing River Health Serv. Found., 865 F.3d 285, 294 (5th Cir. 2017) (citation omitted), cert. denied, 138 S.Ct. 1000 (2017). For example, in Monroe v. City of Charlottesville, 579 F.3d 380 (4th Cir. 2009), cert. denied, 559 U.S. 992, 130 S.Ct. 1740, 176 L.Ed.2d 213 (2010), the court found the class representative to be inadequate when the party could not recognize the complaint and was unaware that the lawsuit had been filed in his name until reading about it in a newspaper.

2.   RULE 23(b): THE TYPES OF CLASS ACTIONS

The party seeking class certification must show that the case falls within one of the three types of actions set forth in Rule 23(b). Certification of the case as one type rather than another imposes specific and different duties on counsel and the court, and affects the ability of the unnamed class members to disassociate themselves from the binding effect of a resulting class judgment. Two critical differences among the types of class actions are whether the absentee class members must be given an opportunity to "opt-out" of the class; and whether and when individual notice must be given to each absentee at the certification stage about claims, defenses, exit rights, and other matters. Federal Rule 23(b)(1) and (b)(2) generally—but not always—do not require notice at the certification stage and do not provide opt-out rights to absentees. For this reason they are sometimes referred to as "mandatory" class actions. Rule 23(b)(3) requires notice and opt-out rights in all cases.

As you read the descriptions that follow, consider which type of class action best fits this fact pattern:

Pacemakers containing allegedly defective wires and leads to the heart were implanted into more than 10,000 patients in 48 states throughout the United States. Because of the defect, the pacemakers were prone to break in some instances and cause injury to the heart or blood vessels. Approximately 8,500 of the patients are still alive. Implantees filed suit in the Eastern

District of California alleging negligence, products liability, breach of warranty, intentional misrepresentation, and infliction of emotional distress. As relief, they sought (a) notice to all implantees of the potential danger from continued use of the pacemaker; (b) creation of a medical monitoring program for the purpose of providing ongoing diagnosis and treatment to implantees; (c) creation of a medical monitoring fund to pay all other future medical expenses in any way related to the defective product, with the amount of the fund limited to defendant's profits from its manufacturer and distribution of the defective product; (d) creation of a medical research fund to investigate innovative treatment for implantees; (e) classwide punitive damages for deceit; and (f) compensatory damages for intentional infliction of emotional distress.

———

a.   *"Prejudice" Class Actions*: Rule 23(b)(1) authorizes a class from which members cannot exit in order to avoid prejudice that could result from the pursuit of individual lawsuits. The rule has two subparts: Subdivision (A) focuses on prejudice to defendant; Subdivision (B) focuses on prejudice to the absentees.

Rule 23(b)(1)(A) deals with the risk that individual actions would create "incompatible standards of conduct" for the party opposing the class. Certification under Subdivision (A) is not appropriate when plaintiffs primarily seek monetary damages; a defendant does not face incompatible standards of conduct simply because damages are to be paid to one claimant and not to another. Rather, certification would be appropriate only when the class primarily seeks relief that typically acts as an injunction or declaration, and a series of individual lawsuits would place defendant in a position of uncertainty, not knowing how to treat other members of the class. Thus, for example, certification under Rule 23(b)(1)(A) was appropriate in a suit by football players against the National Football League for violations of antitrust laws; "[t]he need to revise or to eliminate past rules and practices of professional football" embraced the possibility "that adjudications of separate actions could set incompatible standards of conduct." Reynolds v. National Football League, 584 F.2d 280, 284 (8th Cir. 1978). If defendant is willing to risk incompatible adjudications, should the court refuse to certify the class? See Gallagher, *Vetoing Class Actions*, 24 Rev.Litig. 527 (2005).

Rule 23(b)(1)(B) focuses on the potential for prejudice to the absentees and authorizes certification when individual actions "would be dispositive of the interests" or "substantially impair or impede" the ability of nonparties to protect their interests. The classic example involves multiple claimants to a limited fund, such as insurance proceeds. Individual lawsuits by those with competing claims would create the risk that those who sue first will deplete the fund and leave nothing for the latecomers, subjecting them to practical prejudice. The Court has emphasized that the fund must have "definitely, ascertained limits, all of which would be distributed to satisfy all those with liquidated claims"; "the shared character of rights claimed or relief awarded entails that any individual adjudication by a class member disposes of, or substantially affects, the interests of absent class members." Ortiz v. Fibreboard Corp., 527 U.S. 815, 834, 841, 119 S.Ct. 2295, 2309, 2312, 144 L.Ed.2d 715, 733, 737 (1999).

    b.   Injunctive and Declaratory Relief: Class actions under Rule 23(b)(2) seek injunctive or declaratory relief to change defendant's conduct prospectively rather than to provide individual compensation to the class members for past harms. For an action to fall within Rule 23(b)(2), defendant's conduct need only apply generally to the class; perfect harmony among the class members is not required. See Gilles & Friedman, *The Radical Majoritarianism of Rule* 23(b)(2), 65 U.Kan.L.Rev. 989 (2017). The 1966 amendment that created Rule 23(b)(2) had in mind school desegregation cases, but the injunctive class action has been used in a broad range of substantive areas. See Marcus, *Flawed But Noble: Desegregation Litigation and Its Implications for the Modern Class Action*, 6 Fla.L.Rev. 657 (2011).

    c.   Damages Class Actions: Class suits seeking damages for injuries caused by the same defendant are candidates for certification under Rule 23(b)(3). The rule requires the class members to share questions of law or fact that predominate over any questions affecting only individual members; moreover, class treatment must be shown to be a superior mode of adjudication. Rule 23(b)(3) sets forth four factors pertinent to finding predominance and superiority. Rule 23(b)(3)(A)–(D). Members of a class certified under this provision are permitted to opt-out of the action. These conditions are intended to insure that the proposed class is "sufficiently cohesive to warrant adjudication by representation." Amchem Products, Inc. v. Windsor, 521 U.S. 591, 623, 117 S.Ct. 2231, 2249, 138 L.Ed.2d 689, 712 (1997).

    In CASTANO v. AMERICAN TOBACCO CO., 84 F.3d 734 (5th Cir. 1996), the appeals court decertified a class defined as:

    (a) All nicotine-dependent persons in the United States . . . who have purchased and smoked cigarettes manufactured by the defendants;

    (b) The estates, representatives, and administrators of these nicotine-dependent cigarette smokers; and

    (c) The spouses, children, relatives and "significant others" of these nicotine-dependent cigarette smokers as their heirs or survivors.

Id. at 737 (alteration in original). In the appellate court's view, class certification was not appropriate because the claims were governed by the laws of different states and the theories of liability were considered "novel and wholly untested." Id. at 737. See McGovern, *Resolving Mature Mass Tort Litigation*, 69 B.U.L.Rev. 659 (1989). After the *Castano* class failed and legislative reform of the tobacco industry proved unlikely, over 40 states filed lawsuits against tobacco companies to recover expenditures made for tobacco-related illnesses. The companies negotiated a settlement with the Attorneys General of these states, and in November 1998, the settlement was accepted by 46 states, the District of Columbia, and five territories. This settlement included payments to the states totaling $206 billion to be paid over the next 25 years. Why was this approach to claims-resolution superior to a class action by the consumers themselves? See Lemos, *Aggregate Litigation Goes Public: Representative Suits by State Attorneys General*, 126 Harv.L.Rev. 486 (2012).

The Supreme Court's decision in Erie R.R. v. Tompkins, p. 314, supra, complicates certification decisions in Rule 23(b)(3) cases because numerous state laws often must be applied in multi-state and national class actions, making satisfaction of the Rule's predominance requirement more difficult. In Klay v. Humana, Inc., 382 F.3d 1241, 1261 (11th Cir. 2004), cert. denied, 543 U.S. 1081, 125 S.Ct. 172, 160 L.Ed.2d 825 (2004), the Court stated: "It goes without saying that class certification is impossible where the fifty states truly establish a large number of different legal standards governing a particular claim." See also In the Matter of Rhone-Poulenc Rorer, Inc., 51 F.3d 1293, 1300–02 (7th Cir. 1995), cert. denied, 516 U.S. 867, 116 S.Ct. 184, 133 L.Ed.2d 122 (1995).

NOTE ON "HYBRID" CLASS ACTIONS

In some class actions, the representative parties may wish to pursue class-wide injunctive relief as well as money damages. In that case, what type of class action should be certified? In Wal-Mart Stores, Inc. v. Dukes, p. 526, supra, the Court held that claims for monetary relief may not be certified under Federal Rule 23(b)(2) when the "the monetary relief is not incidental to the injunctive or declaratory relief":

> * * * [W]e think it clear that individualized monetary claims belong in Rule 23(b)(3). The procedural protections attending the (b)(3) class—predominance, superiority, mandatory notice, and the right to opt out—are missing from (b)(2) not because the Rule considers them unnecessary, but because it considers them unnecessary *to a (b)(2) class*. When a class seeks an indivisible injunction benefitting all its members at once, there is no reason to undertake a case-specific inquiry into whether class issues predominate or whether class action is a superior method of adjudicating the dispute. * * * But with respect to each class member's individualized claim for money, that

is not so—which is precisely why (b)(3) requires the judge to make findings about predominance and superiority before allowing the class. Similarly, (b)(2) does not require that class members be given notice and opt-out rights, presumably because it is thought (rightly or wrongly) that notice has no purpose when the class is mandatory, and that depriving people of their right to sue in this manner complies with the Due Process Clause. In the context of a class action predominantly for money damages we have held that absence of notice and opt-out violates due process. * * * While we have never held that to be so where the monetary claims do not predominate, the serious possibility that it may be so provides an additional reason not to read Rule 23(b)(2) to include the monetary claims here.

* * *

Respondents' predominance test * * * creates perverse incentives for class representatives to place at risk potentially valid claims for monetary relief. In this case, for example, the named plaintiffs declined to include employees' claims for compensatory damages in their complaint. That strategy of including only backpay claims made it more likely that monetary relief would not "predominate." But it also created the possibility * * * that individual class members' compensatory-damages claims would be *precluded* by litigation they had no power to hold themselves apart from. * * * That possibility underscores the need for plaintiffs with individual monetary claims to decide *for themselves* whether to tie their fates to the class representatives' or go it alone—a choice Rule 23(b)(2) does not ensure that they have.

* * *

* * * We need not decide in this case whether there are any forms of "incidental" monetary relief that are consistent with the interpretation of Rule 23(b)(2) we have announced and that comply with the Due Process Clause. Respondents do not argue that they can satisfy this standard, and in any event they cannot.

Id. at 362–66, 131 S.Ct. at 2558–60, 180 L.Ed.2d at 397–400.

Are you persuaded by the Court's statement that a single injunction would not benefit all class members? What forms of monetary relief should be treated as "incidental" under Rule 23(b)(2)? In Allison v. Citgo Petro. Corp., 151 F.3d 402, 415 (5th Cir. 1998), the Fifth Circuit defined incidental monetary relief as "damages that flow directly from liability to the class as a whole on the claims forming the basis of the injunctive or declaratory relief." In that situation, "incidental damage should not require additional hearings to resolve the disparate merits of each individual's case; it should neither introduce new substantial legal or factual issues, nor entail complex individualized determinations." Id. See Malveaux, *Class Actions at the Crossroads: An Answer to* Wal-Mart v. Dukes, 5 Harv.L. & Pol'y Rev. 375 (2011).

3. RULE 23(c): CERTIFICATION DECISIONS

"[A]t an early practicable time" the district court must issue a certification order granting or denying certification and defining the class. The scope of the class may change as discovery goes forward and the court retains authority to amend the order "before final judgment" Rule 23(c)(1)(A), (C). Under Rule 23(c)(4), the court also may choose to certify an "issue class"—that is, it may permit the case to be "maintained as a class action with respect to particular issues." See Burch, *Constructing Issue Classes*, 10 Va.L.Rev. 1855 (2015). For example, although a controversial approach, a judge in a products liability suit could certify for class treatment solely the issue of whether the manufacturer knew of the product's adverse effects before taking it to market. Finally, the certification order addresses the notice that is to be given to the absent class members and appoints class counsel under Rule 23(g). These requirements are discussed in the materials that follow.

a. Defining the Class

As amended in 2003, Rule 23(c)(1)(B) states that the order certifying the class "must define the class and the class claims, issues, or defenses." The original Rule 23 did not specify this condition, and prior to the amendment there was no hard-and-fast rule governing class definition. Generally, courts required the definition to "be precise, objective, and presently ascertainable," and that it "not depend on subjective criteria or the merits of the case or require extensive factual inquiry to determine who is a class member." In re Copper Antitrust Litig., 196 F.R.D. 348, 353 (W.D.Wis. 2000) (citations omitted). Under this standard, class definitions failed if they were too broad (e.g., "all learning disabled children in the state of Texas"); too specific (e.g., "all people with Spanish surnames having Spanish, Mexican, or Indian ancestry who spoke Spanish as a primary or secondary language"); too vague (e.g., "all users of drug X who suffered medical problems"); or too amorphous (e.g., "all recipients of unsolicited spam messages"). Having a clear class definition protects absentees by identifying the recipients of notice when required; it protects the parties and the court by facilitating claim preclusion; and it saves judicial resources by making the definition easy to administer. See Marcus v. BMW of N. Am., LLC, 687 F.23d 583, 593 (3d Cir. 2012).

The circuits are divided on the standard to use in reviewing a district court's class definition. The battle lines are between those circuits that impose a "heightened ascertainability" requirement, at least in cases certified under Rule 23(b)(3), and those that do not. In rejecting the heightened standard, the Seventh Circuit has explained:

> Nothing in Rule 23 mentions or implies this heightened requirement under Rule 23(b)(3), which has the effect of skewing

the balance that district courts must strike when deciding whether to certify classes. The policy concerns motivating the heightened ascertainability requirement are better addressed by applying carefully the explicit requirements of Rule 23(a) and especially (b)(3). * * *

Mullins v. Dir. Dig., LLC, 795 F.3d 654, 657–58 (7th Cir. 2015). See Moore, *The Heightened Standard of Ascertainability: An Unnecessary Hurdle to Class Action Certification*, 122 Penn. St.L.Rev. 247 (2017). Are there any advantages to insisting on closer scrutiny of the class definition early in the lawsuit?

b. Notice in Different Types of Classes

i. *The Court's Role and the Timing of Notice*

Rule 23 authorizes notice to class members at the time of certification, see Rule 23(c)(2); during the conduct of the action, see Rule 23(d)(1)(B); and at the time of "settlement, voluntary dismissal, or compromise." Rule 23(e). The question of notice to absent class members has tremendous theoretical and practical importance. As a matter of due process, the absence of or a defect in notice may open a classwide judgment to a collateral challenge. As a practical matter, the costs of notice can be high and are borne by plaintiffs.

Rule 23 sets out two different requirements for notice at the certification stage. Notice is discretionary in so-called "mandatory" class actions under Rule 23(b)(1) and (b)(2) from which absentees may not opt-out. The assumption in these types of classes is that the suits are sufficiently cohesive to ensure the adequacy of representation needed to meet due process and day-in-court values. However, notice is required in Rule 23(b)(3) classes, from which absentees may opt-out. Moreover, the notice provided must be "the best notice that is practicable under the circumstances, including individual notice to all members who can be identified through reasonable effort." Rule 23(c)(2).

Rule 23 does not specifically address notice when the suit is a "hybrid" class action, combining, for example, equitable claims for apportionment of a limited fund and individual claims to damages. In the context of a state class action, the Court has held that due process requires notice and an opportunity for exit if the claims involve "money damages or similar relief at law." Phillips Petroleum Co. v. Shutts, p. 577, infra; see also Ortiz v. Fibreboard Corp., p. 564, infra. See Klonoff, *Class Actions for Monetary Relief Under Rule* 23(b)(1)(A) *and* (b)(1)(B): *Does Due Process Require Notice and Opt-out Rights?*, 82 Geo.Wash.L.Rev. 798 (2014).

The notice requirements at the back-end of the lawsuit—at the time of settlement or dismissal—apply to all types of class actions but are less demanding than at the front-end when certification is ordered. See Rule 23(e).

ii. The Content and Delivery of Notice

If notice is to serve its function, the information that it provides must be intelligible to the person who receives it. See Wheatman & LeClercq, *Majority of Class Action Publication Notices Fail to Satisfy Rule* 23 *Requirements*, 30 Rev.Litig. 53 (2010). Over the years questions have been raised whether the class notice adequately informs absentees of their rights or whether class members understand their options. Rule 23 was amended in 2003 to address some of the problems that had been uncovered in practice. The rule now specifies the categories of information that must be discussed in the class notice, as well as the form of the information—the notice must be clear, concise, and written in plain language that is "easily understood." Rule 23(c)(2)(B).

What constitutes the best notice practicable in the Internet era? E-mail and websites have become common means of providing notice to class members, particularly in consumer class actions. See Klonoff, *Making Class Actions Work: The Untapped Potential of the Internet*, 69 U.Pitt.L.Rev. 727 (2008). How might the increasing accessibility and popularity of the Internet affect the due process analysis? See Mirfasihi v. Fleet Mortg. Corp., 356 F.3d 781, 786 (2004) ("[I]n this age of electronic communications, newspaper notice alone is not always an adequate alternative to individual notice."). Some commentators believe that technological advances have enhanced the legitimacy of the class action by making it easier for class members who receive notice to monitor class counsel and to communicate concerns through social media. See Cabraser & Issacharoff, *The Participatory Class Action*, 92 N.Y.U.L.Rev. 846 (2017).

Back-end notice—when the lawsuit is settled, dismissed, or otherwise resolved—differs from front-end notice in two important ways: first, notice must be given to all class members, and second, the notice must be directed "in a reasonable manner"—not the "best notice that is practicable," as required under Rule 23(c)(2). See Rule 23(e). When parties seek simultaneously to certify a settlement class and to settle the class action, see p. 557, infra, courts typically combine the elements of Rule 23(c) notice with that of Rule 23(e). Notice must be complete and accurate, but courts have held that due process does not require the notice to advise absentees of every ground upon which an objection might be mounted to the settlement. Rather, the notice must provide enough information—or opportunities to access information—so that the unnamed class members "may come to their own conclusions about whether the settlement serves their interests." Grunin v. Int'l House of Pancakes, 513 F.2d 114, 122 (8th Cir. 1975). On this basis, the Sixth Circuit held that "the due-process baseline" was met when the notice provided an address, phone number, and website to obtain more information about the proposed settlement. See Gooch v. Life Inv'rs Ins. Co. of Am., 62 F.3d 402 (6th Cir. 2012).

iii. The Cost of Notice

The Court has held that the costs of providing certification notice must be borne by the party seeking class treatment. EISEN v. CARLISLE & JACQUELIN, 417 U.S. 156, 94 S.Ct. 2140, 40 L.Ed.2d 732 (1974). *Eisen* involved antitrust and securities law claims by "odd-lot" stock traders on the New York Stock Exchange; the proposed class was said to include six million individuals, institutions, and intermediaries, and with "reasonable effort" it was thought possible to identify two million investors by name and address. After conducting a preliminary inquiry into the merits and finding that plaintiff was "more than likely" to prevail, the district court allocated a share of the cost of notice to defendants. The Supreme Court reversed, finding that individual notice had to be provided to class members who could be identified with reasonable effort, and that Rule 23 did not authorize shifting the cost of such notice from plaintiff to defendant. Id. at 178–79, 94 S.Ct. at 2153, 40 L.Ed.2d at 749. The named plaintiff's claim in *Eisen* involved an individual stake of $70; the cost of notice was estimated to exceed $20,000. The Court acknowledged that "[e]conomic reality dictates that petitioner's suit proceed as a class action or not at all." Id. at 161, 94 S.Ct. at 2144, 40 L.Ed.2d at 739.

In OPPENHEIMER FUND, INC. v. SANDERS, 437 U.S. 340, 98 S.Ct. 2380, 57 L.Ed.2d 253 (1978), the Court held that Rule 23 authorized a district court "to order one of the parties to perform the tasks necessary to send notice," and that *Eisen* did not foreclose apportioning some of the costs of those tasks to defendant as part of the court's order. The Court admonished that "courts must not stray too far from the principle underlying [*Eisen*] that the representative plaintiff should bear all costs relating to the sending of notice because it is he who seeks to maintain the suit as a class action." Id. at 359, 98 S.Ct. at 2393, 57 L.Ed.2d at 270. However, the Court made clear that in some circumstances, the cost of carrying out the task will be so insubstantial as to make it administratively inconvenient to shift the charge to plaintiff; moreover, some tasks are carried out by defendant "in any event in the ordinary course of its business" and the expense should not be shifted to plaintiff. In *Oppenheimer Fund*, the information requested was contained in documents in the hands of a third-party transfer agent, and the representative party was required to pay the costs of extracting the information from the documents.

The cost question is different at the settlement stage of the class suit, when liability has been established. At this point, defendant typically reimburses the cost of notice. As the Ninth Circuit explained in 2009:

> So far as we are aware, no appellate court has addressed in a
> published opinion whether a district court's determination that a
> class action defendant is liable on the merits entitles the district

court to shift notice costs to that defendant. This absence of authority is not surprising. Because the losing party in a class action typically is responsible for class notice costs, there is no need for an appellate court reviewing a final merits judgment also to review a notice cost order that is based on a party's liability.

Hunt v. Imperial Merch. Servs., Inc., 560 F.3d 1137, 1142 (9th Cir. 2009). In some cases, courts have shifted notice costs to defendant if the representative party has shown some success on the merits, for example, through a preliminary injunction or partial summary judgment. Id. at 1143.

c. Appointing Class Counsel

The 1966 version of Rule 23 did not discuss the appointment of class counsel. The rule was amended in 2003 to require that the court's certification order make such an appointment. See Rule 23(g). The court also has authority to designate interim counsel before determining whether to certify the action. The amendment responded to concerns about conflicts between class counsel and the class. Compare Coffee, Jr., *Class Action Accountability: Reconciling Exit, Voice, and Loyalty in Representative Litigation*, 100 Colum.L.Rev. 370 (2000), with Gilles & Friedman, *Exploding the Class Action Agency Costs Myth: The Social Utility of Entrepreneurial Lawyers*, 155 U.Pa.L.Rev. 103 (2006).

At the core of the concern is the uneasy fit between the traditional conception of the attorney-client relationship and the class action. In an individual lawsuit, it is assumed that (1) the attorney gives advice to the client and the client makes final decisions about litigation strategy, and (2) the attorney acts with virtually unmitigated loyalty to the client and in the client's best interest. Class action litigation strains both of these notions. Class action attorneys exercise unusually significant control over decisions made on behalf of the class, and has authority—subject to court approval—to settle an action. But what is "loyalty to the client" when it is not clear who the "client" is? Should the attorney give complete loyalty to the interests and wishes of the class representative? To those of each member of the class? To the attorney's conception of the best interests of the class as a whole? Another complication is that class actions may involve a large number of independent lawyers or legal teams representing interests that might be in tension with each other even if they do not raise a conflict sufficient to defeat class certification. See Kane, *Of Carrots and Sticks: Evaluating the Role of the Class Action Lawyer*, 66 Tex.L.Rev. 385, 390 (1987).

The rule sets out factors that must be considered in making the appointment, and essentially codifies practice as it had developed under the 1966 rule. See Manesh, *The New Class Action Rule: Procedural Reforms in an Ethical Vacuum*, 18 Geo.J. Legal Ethics 923, 929–31 (2005). The 2003 amendment to Rule 23(g) does not replace methods for class-counsel selection under federal statutes. One such statute is the Private Securities Litigation Reform Act of 1995, under which courts occasionally have used an "auction" to select lead counsel. See Harel & Stein, *Auctioning for Loyalty: Selection and Monitoring of Class Counsel*, 22 Yale L. & Pol'y Rev. 69 (2004).

4. RULE 23(f): INTERLOCUTORY APPEALS FROM CERTIFICATION ORDERS

Certification is among the most critical stages in the life of a class action. In particular, most class actions are settled before they go to trial, and certification determines the relative leverage that the parties bring to the negotiation table. For the party opposing the class, a certification order also threatens unfavorable publicity and other adverse reputational effects. Rule 23(f) was added in 1998 to allow interlocutory appeal from an order granting or denying class certification. The decision to grant the appeal rests with the court of appeals. The Advisory Committee Note accompanying Rule 23(f) states:

> * * * [M]any suits with class-action allegations present familiar and almost routine issues that are not more worthy of immediate appeal than many other interlocutory rulings. Yet several concerns justify expansion of present opportunities to appeal. An order denying certification may confront the plaintiff with a situation in which the only sure path to appellate review is by proceeding to final judgment on the merits of an individual claim that, standing alone, is far smaller than the costs of litigation. An order granting certification, on the other hand, may force a defendant to settle rather than incur the costs of defending a class action and run the risk of potentially ruinous liability.

See Solimine & Hines, *Deciding To Decide: Class Action Certification and Interlocutory Review by the United States Courts of Appeals under Rule 23(f)*, 41 Wm. & Mary L.Rev. 1531, 1599 (2000).

Courts typically consider three factors in deciding whether to grant or deny an appeal. As the First Circuit has explained:

> * * * First, an appeal ordinarily should be permitted when a denial of class status effectively ends the case (because, say, the named plaintiff's claim is not of a sufficient magnitude to warrant the costs of stand-alone litigation). Second, an appeal ordinarily should be permitted when the grant of class status raises the stakes of the litigation so substantially that the defendant likely will feel irresistible pressure to settle. Third, an appeal ordinarily should be permitted when it will lead to clarification of a fundamental issue of law.

Waste Mgmt. Holdings, Inc. v. Mowbray, 208 F.3d 288, 293 (1st Cir. 2000). Other circuits have expressed "caution against routinely granting appellate review" under Rule 23(f), out of concern that the district court "may feel constrained from revisiting the issue and thereby potentially triggering a new round of appellate proceedings with the inevitable delay and effort of such proceedings." Prado-Steiman v. Bush, 221 F.3d 1266, 1272–73 (11th Cir. 2000).

Rule 23(f) requires that a petition to appeal be filed within 14 days after the order granting or denying certification is entered (under the original rule, the time period was ten days). The courts of appeals take different views on whether the time-period is jurisdictional or whether it may be enlarged if good cause is shown. Compare Lambert v. Nutraceutical Corp., 870 F.3d 1190 (9th Cir. 2017), with Fleischman v. Albany Med. Ctr., 639 F.3d 28 (2d Cir. 2011). In NUTRACEUTICAL CORP. v. LAMBERT, 586 U.S. ___, 139 S.Ct. 710, 203 L.Ed.2d 43 (2019), the Supreme Court held that this time-period is not jurisdictional, but rather is a claim-processing rule (because it is found in a rule of procedure promulgated by the Supreme Court and not enacted by Congress). The Court also held, however, that the 14-day appeal period cannot be equitably tolled. The Court relied primarily on Federal Rule of Appellate Procedure 26(b), which generally allows for extensions of time limits for good cause but specifically prohibits an extension of time to file for permission to appeal. The Court distinguished cases allowing appeals when a motion for reconsideration had been filed within 14 days of the decertification decision on the ground that until such a motion was decided, there was no final order by the trial court to trigger the start of the 14-day appeal period.

In MICROSOFT v. BAKER, 137 S.Ct. 1702, 198 L.Ed.2d 132 (2017), plaintiffs chose to stipulate to a dismissal of their individual claims after the denial of their Rule 23 certification motion and of their request to appeal. Final judgment in hand, plaintiffs then appealed from the denial of class certification. The Ninth Circuit heard the appeal, and reversed the district court's denial of class certification. The Supreme Court held that the Ninth Circuit lacked appellate jurisdiction, finding that the use of a voluntary dismissal worked an impermissible end-run around Rule 23(f). However, in Brown v. Cinemark USA, Inc., 876 F.3d 1199 (9th Cir. 2017), the Ninth Circuit held that Microsoft v. Baker did not bar it from considering an appeal of a case in which the district court denied class certification and dismissed some individual claims, and the parties then settled the remaining individual claims. The settlement explicitly reserved the representative's right to appeal the district court's judgment denying certification and dismissing individual claims. Finding no evidence of "sham tactics to achieve an appealable final judgment," the Ninth Circuit distinguished a "mutual settlement" from the kind of "unilateral dismissal" that attempted "to sidestep Rule 23(f)." Id. at 1201.

5. RULE 23(d): ORDERS REGULATING THE CONDUCT OF PRETRIAL AND TRIAL PROCEEDINGS

Rule 23(d) authorizes the district court to issue orders regulating the conduct of class action proceedings. To illustrate, the court may create a timetable for discovery and for the presentation of issues at trial; set time limits on oral presentations made by counsel; establish a committee of counsel (consisting of the attorneys representing various members of the class) to make decisions about the prosecution of the class case; and regulate the substantive aspects of discovery (for example, by determining the parties from whom discovery may be sought and the items which may be requested).

Frequently, courts will issue the management orders after they have held a pretrial conference. See Rule 16, discussed in Chapter 11, infra. In this regard, consider how the timing of the court's certification order under Rule 23(c) affects its later management of the lawsuit. The 2003 amendment to Rule 23(c) requires the court to order a denial or grant of certification "at an early practicable time," replacing the prior requirement that certification be made "as soon as practicable." Postponing the timing of certification affords the court an opportunity, as needed, to examine the merits and even to order discovery prior to an early dispositive motion.

As part of their orders conducting the action, courts in some cases have developed supplementary proceedings to "individualize" aspects of a class suit that vary with the relief sought. See Garth, *Conflict and Dissent in Class Actions: A Suggested Perspective*, 77 Nw.U.L.Rev. 492, 518–20 (1982). For example, class suits for damages inevitably create problems that are not present in traditional binary litigation. The court in these damage class actions must complete three analytically separate tasks: it must determine if defendant is liable; it must calculate the amount of damages to the class; and, it must distribute the proper share of the award to individual class members. One or more of these tasks may demand fragmentation or "individualization" of the class. See Edelman, Nagareda & Silver, *The Allocation Problem in Multiple-Claimant Representations*, 14 Sup.Ct.Econ.Rev. 95 (2006); Rosenberg, *Individual Justice and Collectivizing Risk-Based Claims in Mass-Exposure Cases*, 71 N.Y.U.L.Rev. 210 (1996).

Courts have approached the task of individualization in different ways and are continuing to develop judicial techniques to assure efficiency and fairness. One approach is to use a single trial to determine defendant's liability (if any) and the amount of damages. These determinations are based on the representative's individual claims, which in some cases are supplemented by statistics and expert testimony. When liability and the amount of damages are set, the court determines how to distribute the class award among individual class members. A related approach is that of the "single issue" class action under Rule 23(c)(4), although the question remains whether the provision is an independent basis for certification. See Hines, *Codifying the Issue of Class Action*, 16 Nev.L.J. 625 (2016).

Another approach is that of the bifurcated trial. The first trial considers only the issue of liability, using the same evidence techniques as would be used in an ordinary proceeding. The second trial, which occurs only if defendant is found liable, addresses the amount of damages. This second proceeding may be a highly individualized one (involving, for example, mini-trials on individual damages claims, or administrative proceedings on individual claims), or it may be a general proceeding designed to calculate the damages to the class as a whole.

A third approach, known as "sampling," involves the judge selecting some individual cases at random to adjudicate and then combining the outcomes of these sample cases to yield results for the larger class population. The sample cases receive their actual awards, but the others all receive the statistically determined sum. The Supreme Court disapproved a variation of the "sampling" approach in *Wal-Mart*, p. 526, supra, because it was said to deprive defendant of its right to employ statutory defenses to defeat individual claims, thereby violating the Rules Enabling Act.

Courts sometimes use a fourth approach—the "fluid class recovery"—in cases in which the costs of identifying and distributing the award exceed the award due each class member, or when the amount of money that can be distributed to class members does not exhaust the amount of defendant's liability as determined at trial. In such cases, the class award is used to provide a general benefit to class members spread evenly, rather than individual compensation. For example, in Daar v. Yellow Cab Co., 67 Cal.2d 695, 63 Cal.Rptr. 724, 433 P.2d 732 (1967), a class action was brought against a taxi company to recover alleged overcharges to customers. Since it was impossible to identify each person who had been overcharged, the court ordered defendant to lower its prices to all riders for a certain period of time. Other courts have used a cy pres distribution. See Bone, *Justifying Class Action Limits: Parsing the Debates Over Ascertainability and Cy Pres*, 65 U.Kan.L.Rev. 913 (2017). The American Law Institute has proposed that unclaimed funds should be used for further distributions to participating class members unless the amounts are too small for individual distributions to be administered economically. Only then would a cy pres distribution be used, with approval of the court. American Law Institute, Principles of the Law of Aggregate Litigation § 3.07 (2010).

For discussions of different judicial techniques, see Bone, *Statistical Adjudication: Rights, Justice, and Utility in a World of Process Scarcity*, 46 Vand.L.Rev. 561 (1993); Cheng, *When* 10 *Trials Are Better than* 1000: *An*

Evidentiary Perspective on Trial Sampling, 160 U.Pa L.Rev. 955 (2012); Fallon, Grabill & Wynne, *Bellwether Trials in Multidistrict Litigation*, 82 Tul.L.Rev. 2323 (2008).

6. RULE 23(e): THE SETTLEMENT OR COMPROMISE OF A CLASS SUIT

Rule 23(e) imposes a virtually unique obligation on the district court to approve any decision to settle, dismiss, or compromise a class action. Rule 23(e) reflects the same philosophical concerns that already have been discussed in connection with adequacy of representation. First, due process demands that the absent class members be protected from an unfair settlement made because the representative parties have lost their enthusiasm for the litigation or are themselves receiving a substantial benefit at the expense of the absentees. In addition, the efficiency and economy objectives of Rule 23 would be subverted if the judgment produced by the settlement proves to be vulnerable to collateral attack, a situation that might arise if the settlement does not take proper account of the rights of the absent class members. Because notice is required at this stage, the absentees have an opportunity to assess the terms of the proposed judgment before they are bound by it, and the court must hold a hearing and make findings before making a final disposition. The settlement of class actions remains one of the most controversial features of Rule 23 practice. See Rubenstein, *The Fairness Hearing: Adversarial and Regulatory Approaches*, 53 UCLA L.Rev. 1435 (2006); Rutherglen, *Better Late Than Never: Notice and Opt Out at the Settlement Stage of Class Actions*, 71 N.Y.U.L.Rev. 258 (1996).

NOTES AND QUESTIONS

1.   Proponents of a settlement have the burden of satisfying Rule 23(e)(2). Generally, in assessing whether a proposed settlement is fair, reasonable, and adequate, the district court assesses a variety of factors, which include: the merits of the case weighed against the terms of the settlement; defendant's financial condition; the expense and complexity of continuing to litigate the suit; and opposition to the settlement. See Marshall v. National Football League, 787 F.3d 502 (8th Cir. 2015). Additional factors may include the experience and views of counsel; the extent of discovery; and the presence of a government participant. Hanlon v. Chrysler Corp., 150 F.3d 1011 (9th Cir. 1998).

2.   Whether the class as a whole favors the proposed settlement is an extremely important consideration in the court's assessment. The preference of any particular class member, however, is not dispositive. Settlements can be approved over the objections of the class representatives, as well as those of absent class members who have received and responded to the settlement notice. Objecting class members are free to appeal the court's decision

approving the settlement when a judgment based on it is entered. See Issacharoff & Nagareda, *Class Settlements Under Attack*, 156 U.Pa.L.Rev. 1649 (2008); Leslie, *The Significance of Silence: Collective Action Problems and Class Action Settlements*, 59 Fla.L.Rev. 71 (2007).

3.   What weight ought a court give to bonus payments—known as "incentive awards"—made to the representative party as part of a proposed settlement? Such awards are a fairly typical feature of a class settlement, and are ordered because of the party's vigilance in securing compensation for the class; contribution to the public interest in redressing legal violations that might otherwise have gone unredressed; or assumption of reputational risk associated with the action. See Eisenberg & Miller, *Incentive Awards to Class Action Plaintiffs: An Empirical Study*, 53 UCLA L.Rev. 1303 (2006). Should the court also scrutinize such awards to ensure against intra-class conflict and self-serving representation? In Staton v. Boeing Co., 327 F.3d 938 (9th Cir. 2003), the Ninth Circuit disapproved a settlement agreement when the bonus payments suggested that the representatives were "more concerned with maximizing [their own] incentives than with judging the adequacy of the settlement as it applies to class members at large." Id. at 977–78. The Eleventh Circuit has gone further to hold that incentive payments to class representatives—notwithstanding their ubiquity—are prohibited. See Johnson v. NPAS Solutions, LLC, 975 F.3d 1244, 1255–61 (11th Cir. 2020).

4.   The Class Action Fairness Act (CAFA) see p. 574, Note 2, infra, imposes special requirements on settlements that rely on "coupons." See 28 U.S.C. § 1712. Coupons typically permit the class members to purchase goods at a discount from defendant. See Leslie, *The Need to Study Coupon Settlements in Class Action Litigation*, 18 Geo.J. Legal Ethics 1395 (2005). Although CAFA does not prohibit coupon settlements, the statute limits the award of attorney's fees to class counsel with respect to the portion of a settlement that will be distributed as a coupon payment. See 28 U.S.C. § 1712(a)–(c). What concerns do coupon settlements raise? See Klonoff & Herman, *The Class Action Fairness Act: An Ill-Conceived Approach to Class Settlements*, 80 Tul.L.Rev. 1695 (2006).

7.   RULE 23(h): ATTORNEY'S FEES

Federal Rule 23(h), adopted in 2003, authorizes the court to award a reasonable attorney's fee in any action certified as a class action. Long before the amendment made this power explicit, courts routinely awarded fees to the attorney of the prevailing representative party. Fees also are available under specific statutes. See, e.g., 42 U.S.C. § 1988(b); 42 U.S.C. § 2000e–5(k). In other contexts, courts have awarded attorney's fees out of the "common fund" created for the benefit of class members by the recovery from defendant due to class counsel's efforts. The Supreme Court has rejected the argument that fee awards under a common fund theory are impermissible. Boeing Co. v. Van Gemert, 444 U.S. 472, 100 S.Ct. 745, 62 L.Ed.2d 676 (1980).

Courts use different approaches to set the amount of the fee. See Resnik, Curtis & Hensler, *Individuals within the Aggregate: Relationships, Representation, and Fees*, 71 N.Y.U.L.Rev. 296 (1996). In a case that produces a common fund recovery, the court may apply a percentage to the fund to determine the amount that should be awarded, an approach generally endorsed by the American Law Institute. See Masters v. Wilhelmina Model Agency, Inc., 473 F.3d 423 (2d Cir. 2007); American Law Institute, Principles of the Law of Aggregate Litigation § 3.13 (2010). An alternative approach, referred to as the "lodestar," looks to the number of hours expended by each lawyer on the case, multiplied by a "normal billing rate," and adjusted, up or down, for discretionary factors such as the riskiness of the lawsuit and the quality of the attorney's performance. The Supreme Court has discouraged the use of risk multipliers in lawsuits involving statutory fee provisions. See Perdue v. Kenny A. ex rel. Winn, 559 U.S. 542, 130 S.Ct. 1662, 176 L.Ed.2d 494 (2010).

Fee awards in some cases have generated media attention, especially when the attorney's fee exceeds the benefit accorded to any individual class member. However, empirical studies suggest that large fees are awarded when the case presented a high risk and produced a large recovery for the class. See Eisenberg, Miller & Germano, *Attorneys' Fees in Class Actions: 2009–2013*, 92 N.Y.U.L.Rev. 937 (2017); see also Eisenberg & Miller, *Attorney Fees in Class Action Settlements: An Empirical Study*, 1 J. Empirical Legal Stud. 27 (2004); Willging, Hooper & Niemic, *An Empirical Analysis of Rule 23 to Address the Rulemaking Challenges*, 71 N.Y.U.L.Rev. 74 (1996). Indeed, some commentators suggest that fee awards in small-stakes class actions are too low to have sufficient deterrent effects. See Fitzpatrick, *Do Class Action Lawyers Make Too Little?*, 158 U.Pa.L.Rev. 2043 (2010). Nevertheless, in some cases, the appeals court has overturned a settlement because the ratio of attorney's fees to the class recovery suggested inadequacy of representation. See Redman v. RadioShack Corp., 768 F.3d 622 (7th Cir. 2014), cert. denied, 135 S.Ct. 1429, 191 L.Ed.2d 366 (2015).

D. SETTLEMENT CLASSES

A class action based on a mass tort or statutory violation a potentially involves hundreds of thousands of individual injuries. As such, defendant faces exposure for a large number of claims. At the same time, plaintiffs suffer the cost of injuries that may involve loss of income, medical bills, and emotional distress. If the class suit is litigated to judgment, both parties are exposed to large and unpredictable transaction costs but achieve finality that results from the preclusive effect of the judgment. Under these circumstances, it may be economically rational for the parties to use the filing of a class action as the occasion to negotiate a global settlement of claims in order to reduce costs and uncertainty.

In AMCHEM PRODS., INC. v. WINDSOR, 521 U.S. 591, 117 S.Ct. 2231, 138 L.Ed.2d 689 (1997), the Court considered whether a diversity class action filed for the purpose of securing a "global settlement" of all current and future asbestos-related claims by millions of individuals was appropriately certified under Rule 23. The complaint was accompanied by a stipulation of settlement intended to bar all class members, whether or not represented by class counsel, from litigating claims not filed before a specified date for all "for present and future asbestos-related personal injury or death." Id. at 603, 117 S.Ct. at 2240, 138 L.Ed.2d at 701. The stipulation contemplated establishment of an administrative mechanism for carrying out and monitoring relief, and set out a schedule of payments for qualifying injuries; the amounts were not adjustable for inflation and could not be revised even if state law recognized the claim. Under the terms of the settlement, class members were to be precluded by the decree "in perpetuity," but defendants could withdraw from the settlement after ten years. Id. at 605, 117 S.Ct. at 2241, 138 L.Ed.2d at 701. Although claimants had a right to opt-out, this option was limited and those who chose to litigate were barred from seeking punitive damages or asserting any claim for increased risk of cancer. The settlement also provided for monitoring and for attorney's fees. The district court approved the settlement, rejecting all objections and declining to create subclasses for claimants with different injuries. The Third Circuit reversed and decertified the class settlement, and the Supreme Court affirmed.

First, the Supreme Court made clear that "[s]ettlement is relevant to a class certification," id. at 619, 117 S.Ct. at 2248, 138 L.Ed.2d at 710, and that when faced with a settlement-only class certification motion, the district court is required to consider the provisions of Rule 23(a) and (b); it may not confine its review to a fairness inquiry under Rule 23(e). Justice Ginsburg explained:

> Confronted with a request for settlement-only class certification, a district court need not inquire whether the case, if tried, would present intractable management problems, * * * for the proposal is that there be no trial. But other specifications of the Rule— those designed to protect absentees by blocking unwarranted or overbroad class definitions—demand undiluted, even heightened, attention in the settlement context. Such attention is of vital importance, for a court asked to certify a settlement class will lack the opportunity, present when a case is litigated, to adjust the class, informed by the proceedings as they unfold. * * *

Id. at 620, 117 S.Ct. at 2248, 138 L.Ed.2d at 710–11.

Turning next to the predominance requirement of Rule 23(b)(3), the Court considered and rejected the district court's conclusion that commonality was satisfied by the class members' "shared experience of asbestos exposure" and their common interest in receiving prompt compensation. Id. at 622, 117 S.Ct. at 2248, 138 L.Ed.2d at 710–11. The Court also declined to find commonality based on whether the settlement itself was fair:

> The benefits asbestos-exposed persons might gain from the establishment of a grand-scale compensation scheme is a matter fit for legislative consideration, * * * but it is not pertinent to the predominance inquiry. That inquiry trains on the legal or factual questions that qualify each class member's case as a genuine controversy, questions that preexist any settlement. * * *
>
> The Rule 23(b)(3) predominance inquiry tests whether proposed classes are sufficiently cohesive to warrant adjudication by representation. See 7A Wright, Miller, & Kane 518–519. * * * The inquiry appropriate under Rule 23(e), on the other hand, protects unnamed class members "from unjust or unfair settlements affecting their rights when the representatives become fainthearted before the action is adjudicated or are able to secure satisfaction of their individual claims by a compromise." See 7B Wright, Miller, & Kane § 1797, at 340–341. But it is not the mission of Rule 23(e) to assure the class cohesion that legitimizes representative action in the first place. If a common interest in a fair compromise could satisfy the predominance requirement of Rule 23(b)(3), that vital prescription would be stripped of any meaning in the settlement context.

Id. at 623, 117 S.Ct. at 2249–50, 138 L.Ed.2d at 712–13. The members of the class, in the Court's view, were separated by "disparate questions"; differences in state law governing the class members' claims compounded these disparities. Id. at 624, 117 S.Ct. at 2250, 138 L.Ed.2d at 713–14. Exposure-only claimants, for example, lacked commonality with claimants who had present injuries and faced current medical expenses. The Court made clear, however, that in some situations, a settlement class could meet the commonality test:

> * * * Predominance is a test readily met in certain cases alleging consumer or securities fraud or violations of the antitrust laws. * * * Even mass tort cases arising from a common cause or disaster may, depending upon the circumstances, satisfy the predominance requirement. The Advisory Committee for the 1966 revision of Rule 23, it is true, noted that "mass accident" cases are likely to present "significant questions, not only of damages but of liability and defenses of liability, . . . affecting the individuals in different ways." * * * And the Committee advised that such cases are "ordinarily not appropriate" for class treatment. * * * But the text of the Rule does not categorically exclude mass tort cases from

class certification, and District Courts, since the late 1970's, have been certifying such cases in increasing number. * * * The Committee's warning, however, continues to call for caution when individual stakes are high and disparities among class members great. As the Third Circuit's opinion makes plain, the certification in this case does not follow the counsel of caution. That certification cannot be upheld, for it rests on a conception of Rule 23(b)(3)'s predominance requirement irreconcilable with the Rule's design.

Id. at 624–25, 117 S.Ct. at 2250, 138 L.Ed.2d at 713–14.

The Court also found that the class did not meet the adequacy requirement of Rule 23(a)(4):

As the Third Circuit pointed out, named parties with diverse medical conditions sought to act on behalf of a single giant class rather than on behalf of discrete subclasses. In significant respects, the interests of those within the single class are not aligned. Most saliently, for the currently injured, the critical goal is generous immediate payments. That goal tugs against the interest of exposure-only plaintiffs in ensuring an ample, inflation-protected fund for the future. * * *

The disparity between the currently injured and exposure-only categories of plaintiffs, and the diversity within each category are not made insignificant by the District Court's finding that petitioners' assets suffice to pay claims under the settlement. * * * Although this is not a "limited fund" case certified under Rule 23(b)(1)(B), the terms of the settlement reflect essential allocation decisions designed to confine compensation and to limit defendants' liability. For example, as earlier described, * * * the settlement includes no adjustment for inflation; only a few claimants per year can opt out at the back end; and loss-of-consortium claims are extinguished with no compensation.

The settling parties, in sum, achieved a global compromise with no structural assurance of fair and adequate representation for the diverse groups and individuals affected. Although the named parties alleged a range of complaints, each served generally as representative for the whole, not for a separate constituency. * * *

Id. at 627, 117 S.Ct. at 2251, 138 L.Ed.2d at 715. Finally, although the Court recognized the need for a nationwide administrative solution to the problem of asbestos-exposure injuries, in its view Rule 23 did not support the parties' global solution:

The argument is sensibly made that a nationwide administrative claims processing regime would provide the most secure, fair, and efficient means of compensating victims of asbestos [exposure] * * *. Congress, however, has not adopted such a solution. And Rule 23, which must be interpreted with fidelity to the Rules Enabling Act and applied with the interests of absent class members in close view, cannot carry the large load * * * heaped upon it. As this case exemplifies, the rulemakers' prescriptions for class actions may be endangered by "those who embrace [Rule 23] * * * too enthusiastically just as [they are by] those who approach [the Rule] * * * with distaste." C. Wright, Law of Federal Courts 508 (5th ed.1994) * * *.

Id. at 628, 117 S.Ct. at 2252, 138 L.Ed.2d at 716.

Justice Breyer, joined by Justice Stevens, concurred in part and dissented in part.

Although I agree with the Court's basic holding that "[s]ettlement is relevant to a class certification," * * * I find several problems in its approach that lead me to a different conclusion. First, I believe that the need for settlement in this mass tort case, with hundreds of thousands of lawsuits, is greater than the Court's opinion suggests. Second, I would give more weight than would the majority to settlement-related issues for purposes of determining whether common issues predominate. Third, I am uncertain about the Court's determination of adequacy of representation, and do not believe it appropriate for this Court to second-guess the District Court on the matter without first having the Court of Appeals consider it. Fourth, I am uncertain about the tenor of an opinion that seems to suggest the settlement is unfair. And fifth, in the absence of further review by the Court of Appeals, I cannot accept the majority's suggestions that "notice" is inadequate.

These difficulties flow from the majority's review of what are highly fact-based, complex, and difficult matters, matters that are inappropriate for initial review before this Court. The law gives broad leeway to district courts in making class certification decisions, and their judgments are to be reviewed by the court of appeals only for abuse of discretion. * * * Indeed, the District Court's certification decision rests upon more than 300 findings of fact reached after five weeks of comprehensive hearings. Accordingly, I do not believe that we should in effect set aside the findings of the District Court. That court is far more familiar with the issues and litigants than is a court of appeals or are we * * *. * * *

I do not believe that we can rely upon the Court of Appeals' review of the District Court record, for that review, and its ultimate conclusions, are infected by a legal error. * * * There is no evidence that the Court of Appeals at any point considered the settlement as something that would help the class meet Rule 23. I find, moreover, the fact-related issues presented here sufficiently close to warrant further detailed appellate court review under the correct legal standard. * * *

I

First, I believe the majority understates the importance of settlement in this case. Between 13 and 21 million workers have been exposed to asbestos in the workplace—over the past 40 or 50 years—but the most severe instances of such exposure probably occurred three or four decades ago. * * * This exposure has led to several hundred thousand lawsuits, about 15% of which involved claims for cancer and about 30% for asbestosis. * * * About half of the suits have involved claims for pleural thickening and plaques—the harmfulness of which is apparently controversial. * * * Some of those who suffer from the most serious injuries, however, have received little or no compensation. * * * These lawsuits have taken up more than 6% of all federal civil filings in one recent year, and are subject to a delay that is twice that of other civil suits. * * *

The District Court, when approving the settlement, concluded that it improved the plaintiffs' chances of compensation and reduced total legal fees and other transaction costs by a significant amount. * * * The court believed the settlement would create a compensation system that would make more money available for plaintiffs who later develop serious illnesses.

I mention this matter because it suggests that the settlement before us is unusual in terms of its importance, both to many potential plaintiffs and to defendants, and with respect to the time, effort, and expenditure that it reflects. All of which leads me to be reluctant to set aside the District Court's findings without more assurance than I have that they are wrong. * * *

Second, the majority, in reviewing the District Court's determination that common "issues of fact and law predominate," says that the predominance "inquiry trains on the legal or factual questions that qualify each class member's case as a genuine controversy, questions that preexist any settlement." * * * I find it difficult to interpret this sentence in a way that could lead me to the majority's conclusion. * * *

The settlement is relevant because it means that these common features and interests are likely to be important in the proceeding that would ensue—a proceeding that would focus primarily upon whether or not the proposed settlement fairly and properly satisfied the interests class members had in common. That is to say, the settlement underscored the importance of (a) the common fact of exposure, (b) the common interest in receiving some compensation for certain rather than running a strong risk of no compensation, and (c) the common interest in avoiding large legal fees, other transaction costs, and delays. * * *

Of course, as the majority points out, there are also important differences among class members. * * * The relevant question, however, is *how much* these differences matter in respect to the legal proceedings that lie ahead. Many, if not all, toxic tort class actions involve plaintiffs with such differences. And the differences in state law are of diminished importance in respect to a proposed settlement in which the defendants have waived all defenses and agreed to compensate all those who were injured. * * *

These differences might warrant subclasses * * *. Or these differences may be too serious to permit an effort at group settlement. This kind of determination, as I have said, is one that the law commits to the discretion of the district court—reviewable for abuse of discretion by a court of appeals. I believe that we are far too distant from the litigation itself to reweigh the fact-specific Rule 23 determinations and to find them erroneous without the benefit of the Court of Appeals first having restudied the matter with today's legal standard in mind.

Third, the majority concludes that the "representative parties" will not "fairly and adequately protect the interests of the class." Rule 23(a)(4). It finds a serious conflict between plaintiffs who are now injured and those who may be injured in the future because "for the currently injured, the critical goal is generous immediate payments," a goal that "tugs against the interest of exposure-only plaintiffs in ensuring an ample, inflation-protected fund for the future." * * *

I agree that there is a serious problem, but it is a problem that often exists in toxic tort cases. * * * And it is a problem that potentially exists whenever a single defendant injures several plaintiffs, for a settling plaintiff leaves fewer assets available for the others. With class actions, at least, plaintiffs have the consolation that a district court, thoroughly familiar with the facts, is charged with the responsibility of ensuring that the interests of no class members are sacrificed.

But this Court cannot easily safeguard such interests through review of a cold record. "What constitutes adequate representation is a question of fact that depends on the circumstances of each case." 7A Wright, Miller, & Kane, Federal Practice and Procedure § 1765, at 271. * * * The majority's use of the lack of an inflation adjustment as evidence of inadequacy of representation for future plaintiffs * * * is one example of this difficulty. An inflation adjustment might not be as valuable as the majority assumes if most plaintiffs are old and not worried about receiving compensation decades from now. There are, of course, strong arguments as to its value. But that disagreement is one that this Court is poorly situated to resolve.

* * *

Fourth, I am more agnostic than is the majority about the basic fairness of the settlement. * * * The District Court's conclusions rested upon complicated factual findings that are not easily cast aside. It is helpful to consider some of them, such as its determination that the settlement provided "fair compensation . . . while reducing the delays and transaction costs endemic to the asbestos litigation process" and that "the proposed class action settlement is superior to other available methods for the fair and efficient resolution of the asbestos-related personal injury claims of class members." * * * Indeed, the settlement has been endorsed as fair and reasonable by the AFL-CIO (and its Building and Construction Trades Department), which represents a " 'substantial percentage' " of class members, * * * and which has a role in monitoring implementation of the settlement * * *. I do not intend to pass judgment upon the settlement's fairness, but I do believe that these matters would have to be explored in far greater depth before I could reach a conclusion about fairness. And that task, as I have said, is one for the Court of Appeals.

Id. at 629–640, 117 S.Ct. at 2252–58, 138 L.Ed.2d at 716–23.

In ORTIZ v. FIBREBOARD CORP., 527 U.S. 815, 119 S.Ct. 2295, 144 L.Ed.2d 715 (1999), the Supreme Court again faced the question of the propriety of a settlement class and again decertified the class. Fibreboard was the subject of many personal injury lawsuits arising from exposure to its asbestos products. It already had settled some 45,000 claims, when it decided, together with its insurers and a group of plaintiffs' lawyers, on a "Global Settlement" of the majority of its remaining liability. Under the plan, Fibreboard and its insurers would put up $1.535 billion for asbestos claimants who would file a Rule 23(b)(1)(B) class action, based on the notion that there was a "limited fund" to pay members of the class.

At the time of the settlement talks, litigation was pending in California state court concerning Fibreboard's insurance coverage. As a condition of the Global Settlement, plaintiffs' counsel insisted that Fibreboard and two of its insurers settle the coverage dispute by separate agreement. The resulting "Trilateral Settlement Agreement" required the insurers to create a $2 billion fund for damage payments to plaintiffs should the Global Settlement not receive judicial approval. Plaintiffs then filed a class action lawsuit in federal court in the Eastern District of Texas.

The Global Settlement required Fibreboard and its insurers to place the agreed upon amount in a trust. Individual claimants were provided with a process for settling their claims with the trust. If no settlement could be reached, claimants were required to engage in mediation, arbitration, and a mandatory settlement conference. After exhausting that process a claimant could bring a court proceeding against the trust, but there would be a $500,000 limit on recovery, and punitive damages and prejudgment interest would be barred. The class did not cover all claimants. Some 45,000 individuals who had settled their claims were excluded, along with some 53,000 individuals with pending lawsuits. The trial court, after extensive hearings, found that the class action met the requirements of Rule 23(a) and that it fell within the "limited fund" provision of Rule 23(b)(1)(B). It determined that the plan provided a "fair, reasonable, and adequate" settlement under Rule 23(e). On appeal the Fifth Circuit affirmed both the certification of the class and the adequacy of the settlement.

Justice Souter, writing for the Court, reversed:

> The inherent tension between representative suits and the day-in-court ideal is only magnified if applied to damage claims gathered in a mandatory class. Unlike Rule 23(b)(3) class members, objectors to the collectivism of a mandatory subdivision (b)(1)(B) action have no inherent right to abstain. The legal rights of absent class members (which in a class like this one would include claimants who by definition may be unidentifiable when the class is certified) are resolved regardless either of their consent, or, in a class with objectors, their express wish to the contrary. * * * And in settlement-only class actions the procedural protections built into the Rule to protect the rights of absent class members during litigation are never invoked in an adversarial setting * * *.

> * * *

> The defect of certification going to the most characteristic feature of a limited fund action was the uncritical adoption by both the District Court and the Court of Appeals of figures agreed upon by the parties in defining the limits of the fund and demonstrating its inadequacy. * * * [I]n an action such as this the settling parties must present not only their agreement, but evidence on which the district court may ascertain the limit and the insufficiency of the fund, with support in findings of fact following a proceeding in which the evidence is subject to challenge * * *.

* * * Although we might assume, *arguendo*, that prior judicial experience with asbestos claims would allow a court to make a sufficiently reliable determination of the probable total, the District Court here apparently thought otherwise, concluding that "there is no way to predict Fibreboard's future asbestos liability with any certainty." * * * Nothing turns on this conclusion, however, since there was no adequate demonstration of the second element required for limited fund treatment, the upper limit of the fund itself, without which no showing of insufficiency is possible.

The "fund" in this case comprised both the general assets of Fibreboard and the insurance assets provided by the two policies * * *. As to Fibreboard's assets exclusive of the contested insurance, the District Court and the Fifth Circuit concluded that Fibreboard had a then-current sale value of $235 million that could be devoted to the limited fund. While that estimate may have been conservative, * * * at least the District Court heard evidence and made an independent finding at some point in the proceedings. The same, however, cannot be said for the value of the disputed insurance. * * *

We do not, of course, know exactly what an independent valuation of the limit of the insurance assets would have shown. * * * [O]bjecting and unidentified class members alike are entitled to have the issue settled by specific evidentiary findings independent of the agreement of defendants and conflicted class counsel.

* * *

The explanation of need for independent determination of the fund has necessarily anticipated our application of the requirement of equity among members of the class. There are two issues, the inclusiveness of the class and the fairness of distributions to those within it. On each, this certification for settlement fell short.

The definition of the class excludes myriad claimants with causes of action, or foreseeable causes of action, arising from exposure to Fibreboard asbestos. While the class includes those with present claims never filed, present claims withdrawn without prejudice, and future claimants, it fails to include those who had previously settled with Fibreboard while retaining the right to sue again "upon development of an asbestos related malignancy," plaintiffs with claims pending against Fibreboard at the time of the initial announcement of the Global Settlement Agreement, and the plaintiffs in the "inventory" claims settled as a supposedly necessary step in reaching the global settlement * * *. The number of those outside the class who settled with a reservation of rights may be uncertain, but there is no such uncertainty about the significance of the settlement's exclusion of the 45,000 inventory plaintiffs and the plaintiffs in the unsettled present cases, estimated by the Guardian Ad Litem at more than 53,000 as of August 27, 1993 * * *. It is a fair question how far a natural class may be depleted by prior dispositions of claims and still qualify as a mandatory limited fund class, but there can be no question that such a mandatory settlement class will not qualify when in the very negotiations aimed at a class settlement, class counsel agree to exclude what could turn out to be as much as a third of the claimants that negotiators thought might eventually be involved, a substantial number of whom class counsel represent * * *.

Might such class exclusions be forgiven if it were shown that the class members with present claims and the outsiders ended up with comparable benefits? * * * [E]ven ostensible parity between settling nonclass plaintiffs and class members would be insufficient to overcome the failure to provide the structural protection of independent representation as for subclasses with conflicting interests.

On the second element of equity within the class, the fairness of the distribution of the fund among class members, the settlement certification is likewise deficient. Fair treatment in the older cases was characteristically assured by straightforward pro rata distribution of the limited fund. * * * While equity in such a simple sense is unattainable in a settlement covering present claims not specifically proven and claims not even due to arise, if at all, until some future time, at the least such a settlement must seek equity by providing for procedures to resolve the difficult issues of treating such differently situated claimants with fairness as among themselves.

First, it is obvious after *Amchem* that a class divided between holders of present and future claims (some of the latter involving no physical injury and to claimants not yet born) requires division into homogeneous subclasses under Rule 23(c)(4)(B),[a] with separate representation to eliminate conflicting interests of counsel. * * * No such procedure was employed here, and the conflict was as contrary to the equitable obligation entailed by the limited fund rationale as it was to the requirements of structural protection applicable to all class actions under Rule 23(a)(4).

---

[a] The rule is now Rule 23(c)(5).

Second, the class included those exposed to Fibreboard's asbestos products both before and after 1959. The date is significant, for that year saw the expiration of Fibreboard's insurance policy with Continental, the one which provided the bulk of the insurance funds for the settlement. Pre-1959 claimants accordingly had more valuable claims than post-1959 claimants * * *, the consequence being a second instance of disparate interests within the certified class. While at some point there must be an end to reclassification with separate counsel, these two instances of conflict are well within the requirement of structural protection recognized in *Amchem*.

* * *

A third contested feature of this settlement certification that departs markedly from the limited fund antecedents is the ultimate provision for a fund smaller than the assets understood by the Court of Appeals to be available for payment of the mandatory class members' claims; most notably, Fibreboard was allowed to retain virtually its entire net worth. Given our treatment of the two preceding deficiencies of the certification, there is of course no need to decide whether this feature of the agreement would alone be fatal to the Global Settlement Agreement. To ignore it entirely, however, would be so misleading that we have decided simply to identify the issue it raises, without purporting to resolve it at this time.

Fibreboard listed its supposed entire net worth as a component of the total (and allegedly inadequate) assets available for claimants, but subsequently retained all but $500,000 of that equity for itself. * * * On the face of it, the arrangement seems irreconcilable with the justification of necessity in denying any opportunity for withdrawal of class members whose jury trial rights will be compromised, whose damages will be capped, and whose payments will be delayed. With Fibreboard retaining nearly all its net worth, it hardly appears that such a regime is the best that can be provided for class members. Given the nature of a limited fund and the need to apply its criteria at the certification stage, it is not enough for a District Court to say that it "need not ensure that a defendant designate a particular source of its assets to satisfy the class' claims; [but only that] the amount recovered by the class [be] fair." * * *

The District Court in this case seems to have had a further point in mind, however. One great advantage of class action treatment of mass tort cases is the opportunity to save the enormous transaction costs of piecemeal litigation, an advantage to which the settlement's proponents have referred in this case. * * * Although the District Court made no specific finding about the transaction cost saving likely from this class settlement, estimating the amount in the "hundreds of millions" * * *, it did conclude that the amount would exceed Fibreboard's net worth as the Court valued it * * * (Fibreboard's net worth of $235 million "is considerably less than the likely savings in defense costs under the Global Settlement"). If a settlement thus saves transaction costs that would never have gone into a class member's pocket in the absence of settlement, may a credit for some of the savings be recognized in a mandatory class action as an incentive to settlement? It is at least a legitimate question, which we leave for another day.

Id. at 846–61, 119 S.Ct. at 2315–22, 144 L.Ed.2d at 740–49.

NOTES AND QUESTIONS

1.   Chief Justice Rehnquist concurred in *Ortiz*, stating that the problem of asbestos-exposure "cries out for a legislative solution." Justice Ginsburg, writing for the Court in Norfolk & Western Ry. Co. v. Ayers, 538 U.S. 135, 166, 123 S.Ct. 1210, 1229, 155 L.Ed.2d 261, 187 (2003), echoed this view, as she did in *Amchem.* See Stengel, *The Asbestos End-Game,* 62 N.Y.U.Ann. Surv. Am.L. 223 (2006). Does legislative inaction heighten the need for judicial intervention or undermine its democratic legitimacy? See Carrington, *Asbestos Lessons: The Consequences of Asbestos Litigation,* 26 Rev.Litig. 583, 611–12 (2007).

2.   In decertifying the settlement class in *Ortiz,* the Supreme Court criticized Fibreboard's "constructive bankruptcy" (defendant was still a solvent corporation) because it allowed defendant to circumvent the substantive and procedural requirements of federal bankruptcy law. Because the Bankruptcy Code did not actually apply, Fibreboard did not have to accord all its creditors equal treatment, and it was able to place its shareholders ahead of its tort creditors. Thus, Fibreboard was required only to contribute a small sum ($10 million) in comparison to the insurers' contributions to the fund. The dramatic increase in the company's stock price that followed the announcement of the settlement terms suggests that the gains conferred upon its stockholders were substantial.

A more common practice has been for corporations to use bankruptcy proceedings as a way of resolving extensive future liability. See, e.g., In re Johns-Manville Corp., 78 F.3d 764 (2d Cir. 1996). Under this approach, the corporation reorganizes its assets to create a trust for which all claimants compete on equal footing. In *Johns-Manville,* where the company used a bankruptcy proceeding to resolve asbestos-related mass tort claims, the trust was funded by a mix of cash, insurance proceeds, and shares in the reorganized debtor. (Although the company faced significant liability due to its past sales of asbestos products, the contemporary business enterprise remained profitable.) As a result, the tort creditors' claims were to be satisfied by giving them an "evergreen" source of payments from an ownership stake in the company. However, this approach is not without its problems; settlement funds may be depleted by present claimants entirely, leaving future claimants without recovery. See McKenzie, *Toward a Bankruptcy Model for Nonclass Aggregate Litigation*, 87 N.Y.U.L.Rev. 960 (2012).

3. The decertification orders in *Amchem* and *Ortiz* raised a number of important questions about the future of class action practice. In particular, observers disagreed whether the Court indirectly had announced that class certification was not appropriate for certain mass tort claims, or whether the potential for intra-class conflict necessitated closer management of the mass tort class action through the provisional certification of sub-classes and appointment of independent counsel for absentees with different interests. Compare Nagareda, *Autonomy, Peace, and Put Options in the Mass Tort Class Action*, 115 Harv.L.Rev. 747 (2002), with Rosenberg, *Mandatory-Litigation Class Action: The Only Option for Mass Tort Cases*, 115 Harv.L.Rev. 831 (2002). Settlement classes have evolved in response to the Court's concerns and remain significant. To borrow from Mark Twain, reports of the death of the settlement class action are highly exaggerated—"class actions, and especially settlement classes, continue to thrive." Cabraser & Issacharoff, *The Participatory Class Action*, 92 N.Y.U.L.Rev. 846, 848 (2017).

NOTE ON THE NFL CONCUSSION LITIGATION

Starting in 2002, researchers began uncovering evidence that repeated football concussions, and even repeated subconcussive hits, were linked to long term neurological problems. Researchers began diagnosing deceased players with Chronic Traumatic Encephalopathy (CTE), a degenerative brain disease that can only be diagnosed after death. The NFL initially discredited the research, telling players that the evidence of the long term effects of repeated concussions was inconclusive. By 2009, the NFL was forced to acknowledge the link between repeated head injuries and long term neurological problems. The NFL issued new rules to reduce head injuries, including stricter return-to-play guidelines, stating that any player that exhibits symptoms of a concussion should not return to play the same day.

In 2011 former Atlanta Falcons safety Ray Easterling filed the first "concussion lawsuit" against the NFL. He committed suicide the next year, and after his death was diagnosed with CTE. Eventually, more than 4,500 other former players also filed actions in state courts alleging that the NFL had failed to inform them of, and protect them from, the risks of football head injuries. The NFL removed the lawsuits to federal court, and they were consolidated under 28 U.S.C. § 1407 in the Eastern District of Pennsylvania. In 2013, the NFL began requiring that an independent neurologist be available on the sidelines at every game. These new rules did not satisfy retired players, who faced an unusually high number of neurological problems.

The transferee court ordered mediation before a retired federal judge, and after the terms of a settlement framework were developed, the court appointed a Special Master to assist in assessing the financial terms of settlement. In 2014, plaintiffs filed a class action complaint, and the parties applied to the court for class certification and approval of the settlement. The proposed class included all living NFL football players who retired before July 7, 2014, as well as their representative claimants (those authorized by law to assert the claims of deceased or incapacitated players) and derivative claimants (those who have a legal right to the income of retired players). The class was divided into two subclasses, which were each represented by their own counsel: one class was composed of retired players who had already received a qualifying diagnosis under the proposed settlement, and the second was composed of retired players who had not yet received a qualifying diagnosis. The proposed settlement was composed of three parts: $75 million for neurological assessments of retired NFL players, $675 million to compensate retired players with qualifying diagnoses, and a $10 million education fund to educate players about the dangers of head injuries.

In January 2014, the district court denied preliminary approval of the settlement. In re Nat'l Football League Players Concussion Injury Litig., 961 F.Supp.2d 708 (E.D.Pa.2014). The court's key concern was that not all retired NFL players with qualifying diagnoses would be compensated before the $ 675 monetary fund was exhausted:

> * * * More specifically, the Settlement contemplates a $675 million Monetary Award Fund with a 65-year lifespan for a Settlement Class of approximately 20,000 people. Retired NFL Football Players with a Qualifying Diagnosis of Parkinson's Disease, for example, are eligible for a maximum award of $3.5 million; those with a Qualifying Diagnosis of [Amyotrophic Lateral Sclerosis] may receive up to $5 million. Even if only 10 percent of Retired NFL Football Players eventually receive a Qualifying Diagnosis, it is difficult to see how the Monetary Award Fund would have the funds available over its lifespan to pay all claimants at these significant award levels.

Id. at 715.

Five months later, the parties reached a revised settlement agreement with an uncapped monetary award fund, which the court approved as a Rule 23(b)(3) class. In re Nat'l Football League Players Concussion Injury Litig., 307 F.R.D. 351 (E.D.Pa.2015). The revised, uncapped monetary award fund provided varying levels of compensation to players who are required to submit proof of certain diagnoses. Awards were to be adjusted for the age of the player when diagnosed, and the number of seasons the player played in the NFL. The fund would remain in place for 65 years, and every class member who registered and qualified during the lifetime of the fund would receive an award.

Two hundred and two class members opted out of the settlement (out of a proposed class of about 22,000) and 205 class members joined objections, which were consolidated before the Third Circuit. The Third Circuit affirmed the district court's decision to certify the class and approve the classwide settlement. In re Nat'l Football League Players Concussion Injury Litig., 821

F.3d 410, 425 (3d Cir. 2016), cert. denied, 137 S.Ct. 607, 196 L.Ed.2d 473 (2016).

In reviewing the district court's decision to certify the class, the appeals court responded to objections about commonality and the adequacy of representation. Objectors argued that the commonality requirement was not met because different players had played different numbers of seasons (which would affect their monetary award) and had played under different conditions. The court distinguished *Wal-Mart*, p. 526, supra, because the NFL allegedly caused injury to all class members through the same course of conduct, failing to provide players with information about the effects of head injuries or create rules in a timely manner to reduce head injuries. Regarding the adequacy of representation, objectors argued that the class should be decertified on the same grounds as in *Amchem*—there was a fundamental conflict between those who already had a qualifying diagnosis and those who might receive one in the future. The court distinguished the analysis in *Amchem*, finding that the subclass structure of the negotiations adequately balanced the interests of each group. The court also dismissed concerns that counsel for one of the subclasses represented plaintiffs from both subclasses, creating a conflict of interest.

Objectors also raised fairness concerns about the approval of the settlement. The court found that the settlement was reasonable in light of several factors, including the preceding negotiations and the risks of further litigation. On the issue of discovery, objectors argued that the settlement was not entitled to a presumption of fairness because there had been no formal discovery—the Third Circuit rejected this argument, noting that avoiding the expense of formal discovery was an in important bargaining chip for plaintiffs that the court would not do away with.

The final issue reviewed was attorney's fees. The district court deferred that issue until the class was certified and the settlement approved. Objectors argued that this deprived class members of due process of rights. The court found that deferring the fee decision did not violate class members' due process rights, but that the best practice was for the notice to class members to include information about attorney's fees. Objectors also raised concerns about the settlement's "clear sailing provision," a stipulation by the NFL that they would not object to an attorney's fee up to $112.5 million. Objectors argued that this raised concerns about collusion between plaintiffs' attorneys and the NFL. The court found that the clear sailing provisions did not per se prevent approval, although they did warrant close scrutiny.

The Third Circuit found that the subclasses in this case adequately dealt with the type of class conflicts that prevented certification in *Amchem*. This was true even though the appointment of subclass counsel was made after negotiations had begun, and that counsel for one subclass represented plaintiffs from both classes. The NFL litigation responded to the concerns expressed in *Amchem* and *Ortiz* about class conflicts by establishing judicially monitored, structural solutions designed to ensure representational legitimacy and substantive fairness. For example, the district court denied approval to the initial proposed settlement because it capped monetary award funds, and the court was concerned that the cap would unfairly impact players who had not yet received a qualifying diagnosis but might in the future. Some authors have highlighted the importance of electronic communication in the litigation, emphasizing the role that the absentees played as informal monitors in the suit, and the unusually high number of benefits claims that were filed, even before the appeals process concluded. See Cabraser & Issacharoff, *The Participatory Class Action*, 92 N.Y.U.L.Rev. 846 (2017). Others have focused on the court's role in managing a process that encouraged the parties' disclosure of information and the monitoring of intra-group conflicts. See Bradt & Rave, *The Information-Forcing Role of the Judge in Multidistrict Litigation*, 106 Calif.L.Rev. 1259 (2017). What is clear is that the court, subclass counsel, and parties actively engaged with each other to balance and account for the interests of the different players affected by the NFL's conduct. See Deubert, Cohen & Lynch, *Protecting and Promoting the Health of NFL Players: Legal and Ethical Analysis and Recommendations*, 7 Harv.J.Sports & Ent.L. 1 (2016).

E. JURISDICTION AND VENUE

1. SUBJECT-MATTER JURISDICTION

NOTES AND QUESTIONS

1. A class action based upon a federal question usually does not raise any special problems of subject-matter jurisdiction. A class action based upon diversity, however, does raise two special questions: first, to which class members should the court look in determining whether there is diversity of citizenship and, second, to which class members should the court look in calculating the jurisdictional-amount requirement?

In SUPREME TRIBE OF BEN-HUR v. CAUBLE, 255 U.S. 356, 41 S.Ct. 338, 65 L.Ed. 673 (1921), the Court held that determinations of diversity of citizenship in class actions should be based on the citizenship of the named parties only. How does this rule apply to a class action brought by an unincorporated association?

In SNYDER v. HARRIS, 394 U.S. 332, 89 S.Ct. 1053, 22 L.Ed.2d 319 (1969), Snyder, a shareholder of Missouri Fidelity Union Trust Life Insurance Co., brought suit in federal court against members of the company's board of directors. Since the petitioner's allegations showed that she sought for herself only $8,740 in damages, the respondent moved to dismiss on the ground that the matter in controversy did not exceed $10,000 (the requisite jurisdictional amount at the time). Petitioner contended that her claim should be aggregated with those of the other members of her class, approximately 4,000 shareholders of the company stock. If all 4,000 potential claims were aggregated, the amount-in-controversy would be approximately $1,200,000. The Supreme Court held that separate and distinct claims could not be aggregated. It noted that "[a]ggregation has been permitted only (1) in cases in which a single plaintiff seeks to aggregate two or more of his claims against a single defendant and (2) in cases where two or more plaintiffs unite to enforce a single title or right in which they have a common or undivided interest." Id. at 335, 89 S.Ct. at 1056, 22 L.Ed.2d at 323.

In ZAHN v. INTERNATIONAL PAPER CO., 414 U.S. 291, 94 S.Ct. 505, 38 L.Ed.2d 511 (1973), owners of property fronting on Lake Champlain in Orwell, Vermont, brought a diversity action seeking damages from International Paper Co., a New York corporation, for allegedly polluting the waters of the lake and damaging the value and utility of the surrounding properties. The claims of each of the named plaintiffs were found to satisfy the then-required $10,000 jurisdictional amount, but the district court was convinced "to a legal certainty" that not every individual owner in the class had suffered pollution damages in excess of $10,000. The Court held that each plaintiff in a Rule 23(b)(3) class action must satisfy the jurisdictional-amount requirement. Again, the majority opinion rested on the traditional rules that courts had used for aggregating claims.

However, in EXXON MOBIL CORP. v. ALLAPATTAH SERVICES, INC., pp. 267–268, Note 7, supra, the Court held, five-to-four, that the 1990 enactment of the supplemental jurisdiction statute, 28 U.S.C. § 1367, effectively overruled *Zahn*. The Court explained that when the complaint includes "at least one claim that satisfies the amount in controversy requirement, and there are no other relevant jurisdictional defects, the district court, beyond all question, has original jurisdiction over that claim," and that the court then "can turn to the question whether it has a constitutional and statutory basis for exercising supplemental jurisdiction over the other claims in the action." The Court found "[n]othing in the text of § 1367(b)" that could be read to withhold "supplemental jurisdiction over the claims of plaintiffs certified as class-action members pursuant to Rule 23." 545 U.S. at 559–60, 125 S.Ct. at 2620–21, 162 L.Ed.2d at 521–22. Does *Allapattah* affect the result in Snyder v. Harris?

2. In 2005, Congress enacted the Class Action Fairness Act ("CAFA"), and special subject-matter jurisdiction rules apply to classes certified under that statute and to what are called "mass actions," defined as actions seeking to try jointly monetary relief claims involving common questions of law or fact for 100 or more persons. See 28 U.S.C. § 1332(d)(11).

Amount-in-Controversy Requirement: CAFA authorizes federal jurisdiction over class actions in which the amount in controversy exceeds the sum of $5 million. 28 U.S.C. § 1332(d)(2). Importantly, CAFA allows for the aggregation of individual claims to meet the amount-in-controversy requirement. 28 U.S.C. § 1332(d)(6). What if a named plaintiff files a class action in state court and signs a binding stipulation limiting the damages sought to less than $5 million? Will such a stipulation defeat removal under CAFA? The Supreme Court has held that a stipulation of this sort is not binding on absent class members and therefore will not preclude federal

relief to any uninjured plaintiff, class action or not." *Tyson Foods, Inc. v. Bouaphakeo*, 577 U.S. 442, 466 (2016) (Roberts, C.J., concurring).

594 U.S. at ___, 141 S.Ct. at 2207–08, 210 L.Ed.2d at 587. The Court noted, however, that its decision did not "address the distinct question whether every class member must demonstrate standing *before* a court certifies a class." Id. at ___, 141 S.Ct. at 2208 n.4, 210 L.Ed.2d at 588 n.4.

Justice Thomas, joined by three other justices, dissented on the ground that all class members had suffered a violation of private rights granted by Congress to each consumer under the FCRA, and so had standing under Article III to assert their claims.

2. PERSONAL JURISDICTION

PHILLIPS PETROLEUM CO. V. SHUTTS
Supreme Court of the United States, 1985.
472 U.S. 797, 105 S.Ct. 2965, 86 L.Ed.2d 628.

Certiorari to the Supreme Court of Kansas.

JUSTICE REHNQUIST delivered the opinion of the Court.

[During the 1970s, Phillips Petroleum produced or purchased natural gas from leased land located in eleven states. Shutts and several other royalty owners possessing rights to leases from which Phillips Petroleum produced the gas brought a class action against the company in a Kansas state court, seeking to recover interest on royalty payments that had been delayed. The trial court certified a class consisting of 33,000 royalty owners. The class representative provided each class member with a notice by first-class mail describing the action and informing each member that he could appear in person or by counsel, that otherwise he would be represented by the named royalty owners, and that class members would be included in the class and bound by the judgment unless they "opted out" of the action by returning a "request for exclusion." The final class consisted of more than 28,000 members, who resided in all 50 states, the District of Columbia, and several foreign countries. Notwithstanding that over 99 percent of the gas leases in question and some 97 percent of the plaintiff class members had no apparent connection to Kansas except for the lawsuit, the trial court applied Kansas contract and equity law to every claim and found Phillips Petroleum liable for interest on the suspended royalties to all class members. The Kansas Supreme Court affirmed despite the company's contentions that the Due Process Clause of the Fourteenth Amendment prevented Kansas from adjudicating the claims of all the class members, and that the Due Process Clause and the Full Faith and Credit Clause prohibited application of Kansas law to all of the transactions between it and the class members.]

* * *

I

* * *

* * * As a class-action defendant petitioner is in a unique predicament. If Kansas does not possess jurisdiction over this plaintiff class, petitioner will be bound to 28,100 judgment holders scattered across the globe, but none of these will be bound by the Kansas decree. Petitioner could be subject to numerous later individual suits by these class members because a judgment issued without proper personal jurisdiction over an absent party is not entitled to full faith and credit elsewhere and thus has no res judicata effect as to that party. Whether it wins or loses on the merits, petitioner has a distinct and personal interest in seeing the entire plaintiff class bound by res judicata just as petitioner is bound. The only way a class action defendant like petitioner can assure itself of this binding effect of the judgment is to ascertain that the forum court has jurisdiction over every plaintiff whose claim it seeks to adjudicate, sufficient to support a defense of res judicata in a later suit for damages by class members.

While it is true that a court adjudicating a dispute may not be able to predetermine the res judicata effect of its own judgment, petitioner has alleged that it would be obviously and immediately injured if this class-action judgment against it became final without binding the plaintiff class. We think that such an injury is sufficient to give petitioner standing on its own right to raise the jurisdiction claim in this Court.

* * *

II

Reduced to its essentials, petitioner's argument is that unless out-of-state plaintiffs affirmatively consent, the Kansas courts may not exert jurisdiction over their claims. Petitioner claims that failure to execute and return the "request for exclusion" provided with the class notice cannot constitute consent of the out-of-state plaintiffs; thus Kansas courts may exercise jurisdiction over these plaintiffs only if the plaintiffs possess the sufficient "minimum contacts" with Kansas as that term is used in cases involving personal jurisdiction over out-of-state defendants. *E.g., International Shoe Co. v. Washington* * * * [p. 52, supra]. Since Kansas had no prelitigation contact with many of the plaintiffs and leases involved, petitioner claims that Kansas has exceeded its jurisdictional reach and thereby violated the due process rights of the absent plaintiffs.

In *International Shoe* we were faced with an out-of-state corporation which sought to avoid the exercise of personal jurisdiction over it as a defendant by a Washington state court. We held that the extent of the defendant's due process protection would depend "upon the quality and nature of the activity in relation to the fair and orderly administration of the laws * * *." We noted that the Due Process Clause did not permit a

State to make a binding judgment against a person with whom the State had no contacts, ties, or relations. * * * If the defendant possessed certain minimum contacts with the State, so that it was "reasonable and just, according to our traditional conception of fair play and substantial justice" for a State to exercise personal jurisdiction, the State could force the defendant to defend himself in the forum, upon pain of default, and could bind him to a judgment. * * *

The purpose of this test, of course, is to protect a defendant from the travail of defending in a distant forum, unless the defendant's contacts with the forum make it just to force him to defend there. As we explained in *Woodson* * * * [p. 71, supra] the defendant's contacts should be such that "he should reasonably anticipate being haled" into the forum. * * * In *Insurance Corp. of Ireland v. Compagnie des Bauxites de Guinee* * * * [p. 135, supra] we explained that the requirement that a court have personal jurisdiction comes from the Due Process Clause's protection of the defendant's personal liberty interest, and said that the requirement "represents a restriction on judicial power not as a matter of sovereignty, but as a matter of individual liberty." * * *

Although the cases like *Shaffer* [p. 147, supra] and *Woodson* which petitioner relies on for a minimum contacts requirement all dealt with out-of-state defendants or parties in the procedural posture of a defendant, * * * petitioner claims that the same analysis must apply to absent class-action plaintiffs. In this regard petitioner correctly points out that a chose in action is a constitutionally recognized property interest possessed by each of the plaintiffs. * * * An adverse judgment by Kansas courts in this case may extinguish the chose in action forever through res judicata. Such an adverse judgment, petitioner claims, would be every bit as onerous to an absent plaintiff as an adverse judgment on the merits would be to a defendant. Thus, the same due process protections should apply to absent plaintiffs: Kansas should not be able to exert jurisdiction over the plaintiffs' claims unless the plaintiffs have sufficient minimum contacts with Kansas.

We think petitioner's premise is in error. The burdens placed by a State upon an absent class-action plaintiff are not of the same order or magnitude as those it places upon an absent defendant. An out-of-state defendant summoned by a plaintiff is faced with the full powers of the forum State to render judgment *against* it. The defendant must generally hire counsel and travel to the forum to defend itself from the plaintiff's claim, or suffer a default judgment. The defendant may be forced to participate in extended and often costly discovery, and will be forced to respond in damages or to comply with some other form of remedy imposed by the court should it lose the suit. The defendant may also face liability for court costs and attorney's fees. These burdens are substantial, and the minimum contacts requirement of the Due Process Clause prevents the forum State from unfairly imposing them upon the defendant.

A class-action plaintiff, however, is in quite a different posture. The Court noted this difference in *Hansberry v. Lee* * * * [p. 520, supra] which explained that a "class" or "representative" suit was an exception to the rule that one could not be bound by judgment *in personam* unless one was made fully a party in the traditional sense. * * * As the Court pointed out in *Hansberry*, the class action was an invention of equity to enable it to proceed to a decree in suits where the number of those interested in the litigation was too great to permit joinder. The absent parties would be bound by the decree so long as the named parties adequately represented the absent class and the prosecution of the litigation was within the common interest. * * *

Modern plaintiff class actions follow the same goals, permitting litigation of a suit involving common questions when there are too many plaintiffs for proper joinder. Class actions also may permit the plaintiffs to pool claims which would be uneconomical to litigate individually. For example, this lawsuit involves claims averaging about $100 per plaintiff; most of the plaintiffs would have no realistic day in court if a class action were not available.

In sharp contrast to the predicament of a defendant haled into an out-of-state forum, the plaintiffs in this suit were not haled anywhere to defend themselves upon pain of a default judgment. As commentators have noted, from the plaintiffs' point of view a class action resembles a "quasi-administrative proceeding, conducted by the judge." * * *

A plaintiff class in Kansas and numerous other jurisdictions cannot first be certified unless the judge, with the aid of the named plaintiffs and defendant, conducts an inquiry into the common nature of the named plaintiffs' and the absent plaintiffs' claims, the adequacy of representation, the jurisdiction possessed over the class, and any other matters that will bear upon proper representation of the absent plaintiffs' interest. * * * Unlike a defendant in a civil suit, a class-action plaintiff is not required to fend for himself. * * * The court and named plaintiffs protect his interests. Indeed, the class-action defendant itself has a great interest in ensuring that the absent plaintiffs' claims are properly before the forum. In this case, for example, the defendant sought to avoid class certification by alleging that the absent plaintiffs would not be adequately represented and were not amenable to jurisdiction. * * *

The concern of the typical class-action rules for the absent plaintiffs is manifested in other ways. Most jurisdictions, including Kansas, require that a class action, once certified, may not be dismissed or compromised without the approval of the court. In many jurisdictions such as Kansas the court may amend the pleadings to ensure that all sections of the class are represented adequately. * * *

Besides this continuing solicitude for their rights, absent plaintiff class members are not subject to other burdens imposed upon defendants. They need not hire counsel or appear. They are almost never subject to counterclaims or cross-claims, or liability for fees or costs. Absent plaintiff class members are not subject to coercive or punitive remedies. Nor will an adverse judgment typically bind an absent plaintiff for any damages, although a valid adverse judgment may extinguish any of the plaintiff's claims which were litigated.

Unlike a defendant in a normal civil suit, an absent class-action plaintiff is not required to do anything. He may sit back and allow the litigation to run its course, content in knowing that there are safeguards provided for his protection. In most class actions an absent plaintiff is provided at least with an opportunity to "opt out" of the class, and if he takes advantage of that opportunity he is removed from the litigation entirely. This was true of the Kansas proceedings in this case. The Kansas procedure provided for the mailing of a notice to each class member by first-class mail. The notice, as we have previously indicated, described the action and informed the class member that he could appear in person or by counsel, in default of which he would be represented by the named plaintiffs and their attorneys. The notice further stated that class members would be included in the class and bound by the judgment unless they "opted out" by executing and returning a "request for exclusion" that was included in the notice.

Petitioner contends, however, that the "opt out" procedure provided by Kansas is not good enough, and that an "opt in" procedure is required to satisfy the Due Process Clause of the Fourteenth Amendment. Insofar as plaintiffs who have no minimum contacts with the forum State are concerned, an "opt in" provision would require that each class member affirmatively consent to his inclusion within the class.

Because States place fewer burdens upon absent class plaintiffs than they do upon absent defendants in nonclass suits, the Due Process Clause need not and does not afford the former as much protection from state-court jurisdiction as it does the latter. The Fourteenth Amendment does protect "persons," not "defendants," however, so absent plaintiffs as well as absent defendants are entitled to some protection from the jurisdiction of a forum State which seeks to adjudicate their claims. In this case we hold that a forum State may exercise jurisdiction over the claim of an absent class-action plaintiff, even though that plaintiff may not possess the minimum contacts with the forum which would support personal jurisdiction over a defendant. If the forum State wishes to bind an absent plaintiff concerning a claim for money damages or similar relief at law,[3] it must provide

---

[3]   Our holding today is limited to those class actions which seek to bind known plaintiffs concerning claims wholly or predominately for money judgments. We intimate no view concerning other types of class action lawsuits, such as those seeking equitable relief. Nor, of course, does our

minimal procedural due process protection. The plaintiff must receive notice plus an opportunity to be heard and participate in the litigation, whether in person or through counsel. The notice must be the best practicable, "reasonably calculated, under all the circumstances, to apprise interested parties of the pendency of the action and afford them an opportunity to present their objections." * * * The notice should describe the action and the plaintiffs' rights in it. Additionally, we hold that due process requires at a minimum that an absent plaintiff be provided with an opportunity to remove himself from the class by executing and returning an "opt out" or "request for exclusion" form to the court. Finally, the Due Process Clause of course requires that the named plaintiff at all times adequately represent the interests of the absent class members. * * *

We reject petitioner's contention that the Due Process Clause of the Fourteenth Amendment requires that absent plaintiffs affirmatively "opt in" to the class, rather than be deemed members of the class if they do not "opt out." We think that such a contention is supported by little, if any, precedent, and that it ignores the differences between class action plaintiffs, on the one hand, and defendants in non-class civil suits on the other. Any plaintiff may consent to jurisdiction. * * * The essential question, then, is how stringent the requirement for a showing of consent will be.

We think that the procedure followed by Kansas, where a fully descriptive notice is sent first-class mail to each class member, with an explanation of the right to "opt out," satisfies due process. Requiring a plaintiff to affirmatively request inclusion would probably impede the prosecution of those class actions involving an aggregation of small individual claims, where a large number of claims are required to make it economical to bring suit. * * * The plaintiff's claim may be so small, or the plaintiff so unfamiliar with the law, that he would not file suit individually, nor would he affirmatively request inclusion in the class if such a request were required by the Constitution. * * * If, on the other hand, the plaintiff's claim is sufficiently large or important that he wishes to litigate it on his own, he will likely have retained an attorney or have thought about filing suit, and should be fully capable of exercising his right to "opt out."

In this case over 3,400 members of the potential class did "opt out," which belies the contention that "opt out" procedures result in guaranteed jurisdiction by inertia. Another 1,500 were excluded because the notice and "opt out" form was undeliverable. We think that such results show that the "opt out" procedure provided by Kansas is by no means *pro forma*, and that the Constitution does not require more to protect what must be the somewhat rare species of class member who is unwilling to execute an "opt out" form, but whose claim is nonetheless so important that he cannot be

---

discussion of personal jurisdiction address class actions where the jurisdiction is asserted against a defendant class.

presumed to consent to being a member of the class by his failure to do so. Petitioner's "opt in" requirement would require the invalidation of scores of state statutes and of the class-action provision of the Federal Rules of Civil Procedure, * * * and for the reasons stated we do not think that the Constitution requires the State to sacrifice the obvious advantages in judicial efficiency resulting from the "opt out" approach for the protection of the *rara avis* portrayed by petitioner.

We therefore hold that the protection afforded the plaintiff class members by the Kansas statute satisfies the Due Process Clause. The interests of the absent plaintiffs are sufficiently protected by the forum State when those plaintiffs are provided with a request for exclusion that can be returned within a reasonable time to the court. * * * Both the Kansas trial court and the Supreme Court of Kansas held that the class received adequate representation, and no party disputes that conclusion here. We conclude that the Kansas court properly asserted personal jurisdiction over the absent plaintiffs and their claims against petitioner.

III

The Kansas courts applied Kansas contract and Kansas equity law to every claim in this case, notwithstanding that over 99% of the gas leases and some 97% of the plaintiffs in the case had no apparent connection to the State of Kansas except for this lawsuit. * * * Petitioner protested that the Kansas courts should apply the laws of the States where the leases were located, or at least apply Texas and Oklahoma law because so many of the leases came from those States. The Kansas courts disregarded this contention and found petitioner liable for interest on the suspended royalties as a matter of Kansas law, and set the interest rates under Kansas equity principles.

Petitioner contends that total application of Kansas substantive law violated the constitutional limitations on choice of law mandated by the Due Process Clause of the Fourteenth Amendment and the Full Faith and Credit Clause of Article IV, § 1. We must first determine whether Kansas law conflicts in any material way with any other law which could apply. There can be no injury in applying Kansas law if it is not in conflict with that of any other jurisdiction connected to this suit.

Petitioner claims that Kansas law conflicts with that of a number of States connected to this litigation, especially Texas and Oklahoma. These putative conflicts range from the direct to the tangential, and may be addressed by the Supreme Court of Kansas on remand under the correct constitutional standard. * * *

The conflicts on the applicable interest rates, alone—which we do not think can be labeled "false conflicts" without a more thorough-going treatment than was accorded them by the Supreme Court of Kansas— certainly amounted to millions of dollars in liability. We think that the

Supreme Court of Kansas erred in deciding on the basis that it did that the application of its laws to all claims would be constitutional.

Four Terms ago we addressed a similar situation in *Allstate Ins. Co. v. Hague* * * * [p. 63, Note 3, supra]. In that case we were confronted with two conflicting rules of state insurance law. Minnesota permitted the "stacking" of separate uninsured motorist policies while Wisconsin did not. Although the decedent lived in Wisconsin, took out insurance policies and was killed there, he was employed in Minnesota and after his death his widow moved to Minnesota for reasons unrelated to the litigation, and was appointed personal representative of his estate. She filed suit in Minnesota courts, which applied the Minnesota stacking rule.

The plurality in *Allstate* noted that a particular set of facts giving rise to litigation could justify, constitutionally, the application of more than one jurisdiction's laws. The plurality recognized, however, that the Due Process Clause and the Full Faith and Credit Clause provided modest restrictions on the application of forum law. These restrictions required "that for a State's substantive law to be selected in a constitutionally permissible manner, that State must have a significant contact or significant aggregation of contacts, creating state interests, such that choice of its law is neither arbitrary nor fundamentally unfair." * * * The dissenting Justices were in substantial agreement with this principle. * * *

The plurality in *Allstate* affirmed the application of Minnesota law because of the forum's significant contacts to the litigation which supported the State's interest in applying its law. * * * Kansas' contacts to this litigation, as explained by the Kansas Supreme Court, can be gleaned from the opinion below.

Petitioner owns property and conducts substantial business in the State, so Kansas certainly has an interest in regulating petitioner's conduct in Kansas. * * * Moreover, oil and gas extraction is an important business to Kansas, and although only a few leases in issue are located in Kansas, hundreds of Kansas plaintiffs were affected by petitioner's suspension of royalties; thus the court held that the State has a real interest in protecting "the rights of these royalty owners both as individual residents of [Kansas] and as members of this particular class of plaintiffs." * * *

Kansas must have a "significant contact or significant aggregation of contacts" to the claims asserted by each member of the plaintiff class, contacts "creating state interests" in order to ensure that the choice of Kansas law is not arbitrary or unfair. * * * Given Kansas' lack of "interest" in claims unrelated to that State, and the substantive conflict with jurisdictions such as Texas, we conclude that application of Kansas law to every claim in this case is sufficiently arbitrary and unfair as to exceed constitutional limits. * * *

When considering fairness in this context, an important element is the expectation of the parties. There is no indication that when the leases involving land and royalty owners outside of Kansas were executed, the parties had any idea that Kansas law would control. Neither the Due Process Clause nor the Full Faith and Credit Clause requires Kansas "to substitute for its own [laws], applicable to persons and events within it, the conflicting statute of another state," * * * but Kansas "may not abrogate the rights of parties beyond its borders having no relation to anything done or to be done within them." * * *

Here the Supreme Court of Kansas took the view that in a nationwide class action where procedural due process guarantees of notice and adequate representation were met, "the law of the forum should be applied unless compelling reasons exist for applying a different law." * * * Whatever practical reasons may have commended this rule to the Supreme Court of Kansas, for the reasons already stated we do not believe that it is consistent with the decisions of this Court. We make no effort to determine for ourselves which law must apply to the various transactions involved in this lawsuit, and we reaffirm our observation in *Allstate* that in many situations a state court may be free to apply one of several choices of law. But the constitutional limitations laid down in cases such as *Allstate* * * * must be respected even in a nationwide class action.

We therefore affirm the judgment of the Supreme Court of Kansas insofar as it upheld the jurisdiction of the Kansas courts over the plaintiff class members in this case, and reverse its judgment insofar as it held that Kansas law was applicable to all of the transactions which it sought to adjudicate. We remand the case to that court for further proceedings not inconsistent with this opinion.

It is so ordered.

JUSTICE POWELL took no part in the decision of this case.

[JUSTICE STEVENS wrote an opinion concurring in Parts I and II of the Court's opinion and dissenting from Part III.]

NOTES AND QUESTIONS

1. On remand to the Kansas courts after the Supreme Court's decision in *Shutts,* Phillips Petroleum continued to press the argument that the laws of five states (Louisiana, New Mexico, Oklahoma, Texas, and Wyoming) differed in important respects from the law of Kansas—in particular on the issue of liability for interest on suspended royalties and on the issue of the applicable interest rate where liability is found. These two issues constituted the heart of the legal controversy in the case, and the five identified states embraced 97 percent of the leases involved. In addressing this argument, the Kansas Supreme Court first analyzed the Supreme Court's decision in *Shutts*:

* * * As to the choice of law question, however, it was ruled the application of Kansas law to all of the investors' claims for interest violated the due process and full faith and credit clauses. In its analysis, the Court first noted that if the law of Kansas was not in conflict with any of the other jurisdictions connected to the suit, then there would be no injury in applying the law of Kansas. * * * The Court then cited differences in the laws of Kansas, Texas, and Oklahoma which Phillips *contended* existed. It appears, however, no analysis was made by the Court to determine whether these differences existed in fact. * * *

Shutts v. Phillips Petroleum Co., 240 Kan. 764, 767, 732 P.2d 1286, 1291 (1987), cert. denied, 487 U.S. 1223, 108 S.Ct. 2883, 101 L.Ed.2d 918 (1988) (emphasis in original).

The Kansas court then examined the laws of the five states—only to conclude that *none* of the five was in conflict with the law of Kansas. It therefore entered a new judgment reflecting no change in the original outcome of the case regarding liability and the applicable prejudgment interest rate. See Miller & Crump, *Jurisdiction and Choice of Law in Multistate Class Actions After* Phillips Petroleum Co. v. Shutts, 96 Yale L.J. 1 (1986).

2.   In Shaffer v. Heitner, p. 147, supra, the Court stated that "all assertions of state-court jurisdiction must be evaluated according to the standards set forth in *International Shoe* and its progeny." Does *Shutts* mean that class plaintiffs are not entitled to this protection? Or is *Shutts* based upon the inference of consent from a class member's failure to opt-out of the class? If so, is that inference accurate or appropriate? Compare Wolff, *Federal Jurisdiction and Due Process in the Era of the Nationwide Class Action*, 156 U.Pa.L.Rev. 2035, 2086–89 (2008), with Kahan & Silberman, Matsushita *and Beyond: The Role of State Courts in Class Actions Involving Exclusive Federal Claims*, 1996 Sup.Ct.Rev. 219, 263–64. What are the implications of *Shutts* for class actions in which class members reside abroad? Should such cases require an affirmative opt-in? See Bassett, *Implied "Consent" to Personal Jurisdiction in Transnational Class Litigation*, 2004 Mich. St.L.Rev. 619. Do you agree?

3.   Consider the requirement of personal jurisdiction in its conventional context—the power of the court to enter a judgment against a defendant. *Bristol-Myers Squibb Co.,* p. 122, supra, held that the California court could not exercise specific jurisdiction over claims by non-Californians whose injuries did not arise out of defendant's in-state activity. *Bristol-Myers* involved complex joinder, but was not a class action. Does the decision foreclose a nationwide class filed anywhere other than defendant's home state of incorporation or principal place of business?

The Supreme Court has yet to address the issue, but the lower courts have begun to do so.

In MUSSAT v. IQVIA, INC., 953 F. 3d 441 (7th Cir. 2020), plaintiff, an Illinois resident, sued defendant, a Delaware corporation with its principal place of business in Pennsylvania, for violations of the Telephone Consumer Protection Act, 47 U.S.C. § 227. Plaintiff filed the case in the Northern District of Illinois and sought to represent a nationwide class of similarly situated persons. Because it was not subject to general personal jurisdiction in Illinois, defendant moved to strike the class allegations on the ground that the district court did not have personal jurisdiction over the claims of the non-Illinois class members. The district court agreed with defendant and held, based on *Bristol-Myers*, that each class member had to show minimum contacts between defendant and Illinois with respect to that class member's claim. The Seventh Circuit granted an interlocutory appeal under Rule 23(f) and reversed because "the principles announced in *Bristol-Myers* do not apply to the case of a nationwide class action filed in federal court under a federal statute." 953 F. 3d at 443. The court explained why the class action context was different from the mass joinder involved in *Bristol-Myers*:

> Although *Bristol-Myers* arose in the context of consolidated individual suits, the district court in our case thought that the *Bristol-Myers* approach to personal jurisdiction should be extended to certified class actions. It held that the Due Process Clause of the Fourteenth Amendment precludes the exercise of personal jurisdiction over a defendant where "nonresident, absent members [of a class] seek to aggregate their claims with an in-forum resident, even though the defendant allegedly injured the nonresidents outside of the forum." * * * This meant, the court realized, that nationwide class actions will, as a practical matter, be impossible any time the defendant is not subject to general jurisdiction. This would have been far from the routine application of personal-jurisdiction rules that *Bristol-Myers* said it was performing. * * *

> Procedural formalities matter, however, as the Supreme Court emphasized in *Taylor v. Sturgell*, 553 U.S. 880, 128 S.Ct. 2161, 171 L.Ed.2d 155 (2008), where it stressed the importance of class certification as a pre-requisite for binding a nonparty (including an unnamed class member) to the outcome of a suit. * * * With that in mind, it rejected the notion of "virtual representation" as an end-run around the careful procedural protections outlined in Rule 23. * * * Class actions, in short, are different from many other types of aggregate litigation, and that difference matters in numerous ways for the unnamed members of the class.

> *Bristol-Myers* neither reached nor resolved the question whether, in a Rule 23 class action, each unnamed member of the class must separately establish specific personal jurisdiction over a defendant. In holding otherwise, the district court failed to recognize the critical distinction between this case and *Bristol-Myers*. The *Bristol-Myers* plaintiffs brought a coordinated mass action, which * * * does not involve any absentee litigants. * * * [A]ll of the plaintiffs are named parties to the case. * * * In a Rule 23 class action, by contrast, the lead plaintiffs earn the right to represent the interests of absent class

members by satisfying all four criteria of Rule 23(a) and one branch of Rule 23(b). The absent class members are not full parties to the case for many purposes.

The proper characterization of the status of absent class members depends on the issue. As the Supreme Court [has] recognized * * * "[n]onnamed class members . . . may be parties for some purposes and not for others. The label 'party' does not indicate an absolute characteristic, but rather a conclusion about the applicability of various procedural rules that may differ based on context." * * *. For example, absent class members are not considered parties for assessing whether the requirement of diverse citizenship under 28 U.S.C. § 1332 has been met. * * * As long as the named representative meets the amount-in-controversy requirement, jurisdiction exists over the claims of the unnamed members. * * * Nor are absent class members considered when a court decides whether it is the proper venue. * * * We see no reason why personal jurisdiction should be treated any differently from subject-matter jurisdiction and venue: the named representatives must be able to demonstrate either general or specific personal jurisdiction, but the unnamed class members are not required to do so.

* * *

The rules for class certification support a focus on the named representative for purposes of personal jurisdiction. Rule 23(b)(3), for example, governs damages class actions. Among the factors it lists is "the desirability or undesirability of concentrating the litigation of the claims in the particular forum." The Committee Note to this provision mentions that a court should consider the desirability of the forum "in contrast to allowing the claims to be litigated separately in forums to which they would ordinarily be brought." * * * These provisions recognize that a class action may extend beyond the boundaries of the state where the lead plaintiff brings the case. And nothing in the Rules frowns on nationwide class actions, even in a forum where the defendant is not subject to general jurisdiction.

Finally, it is worth recalling that the Supreme Court in *Bristol-Myers* expressly reserved the question whether its holding extended to the federal courts at all. 137 S. Ct. at 1784 * * *. In addition, the opinion does not reach the question whether its holding would apply to a class action. *Id.* at 1789 n.4 (Sotomayor, J., dissenting) * * *. Fitting this problem into the broader edifice of class-action law, we are convinced that * * * the absentees are more like nonparties, and thus there is no need to locate each and every one of them and conduct a separate personal-jurisdiction analysis of their claims.

As the *Mussat* opinion explains, absent class members are taken into consideration for some procedural requirements but not others. Is there a coherent explanation for when a court does or does not look beyond the named representatives in a class action? Is it sensible that each class member must have Article III standing (a jurisdictional requirement in federal court), see *TransUnion,* p. 576, Note 3, supra, but that absent class members are not considered when a court determines if it has diversity jurisdiction or if venue is proper? Does the role of absent class members in these threshold procedural determinations depend on whether the class action is best viewed as a joinder or a representative device?

3. VENUE

NOTES AND QUESTIONS

1.   When venue is based on residence, 28 U.S.C. § 1391(b)(1), does it make sense to look only at the residence of the named representative and not that of the absent class members? See 7A Wright, Miller & Kane, Federal Practice and Procedure § 1757 (4th ed.).

2.   Where to locate venue was a significant threshold question in *Wal-Mart,* p. 526, supra, involving employment discrimination claims under the Title VII of the Civil Rights Act of 1964, which has a special venue provision. Plaintiffs filed their suit in the Northern District of California, and defendant countered by moving to dismiss for improper venue or, alternatively, for transfer to the Western District of Arkansas, where its headquarters is located. The district court denied the motion. Although four of the six named plaintiffs did not satisfy Title VII's venue requirements, the court cured the defect by dismissing them from the action. Dukes v. Wal-Mart, Inc., 2001 WL 1902806, *9–10 (N.D.Cal. 2001). Could the improperly venued plaintiffs have rejoined the class as absent class members? In a nationwide class action, would a geographically diverse set of named plaintiffs better represent the interests of absent class members? See Hoffman, *How Many Plaintiffs Are Enough? Venue in Title VII Class Actions*, 42 U.Mich.J.L. Reform 843 (2009).

3.   Should the named plaintiff's choice of venue be given deference when defendant moves to transfer under 28 U.S.C. § 1404(a)? Why not? See Roling v. E*Trade Sec., LLC, 756 F.Supp.2d 1179, 1185 (N.D.Cal.2010); Glass v. S & M NuTec, LLC, 456 F.Supp.2d 498, 504 (S.D.N.Y.2006).

F. THE PRECLUSIVE EFFECT OF A CLASS ACTION JUDGMENT

COOPER V. FEDERAL RESERVE BANK OF RICHMOND
Supreme Court of the United States, 1984.
467 U.S. 867, 104 S.Ct. 2794, 81 L.Ed.2d 718.

Certiorari to the United States Court of Appeals for the Fourth Circuit.

JUSTICE STEVENS delivered the opinion of the Court.

The question to be decided is whether a judgment in a class action determining that an employer did not engage in a general pattern or practice of racial discrimination against the certified class of employees precludes a class member from maintaining a subsequent civil action alleging an individual claim of racial discrimination against the employer.

I

On March 22, 1977, the Equal Employment Opportunity Commission commenced a civil action against respondent, the Federal Reserve Bank of Richmond. * * * Respondent operates a branch in Charlotte, N.C. (the Bank), where during the years 1974–1978 it employed about 350–450 employees in several departments. The EEOC complaint alleged that the Bank was violating § 703(a) of Title VII of the Civil Rights Act of 1964 by engaging in "policies and practices" that included "failing and refusing to promote *blacks* because of race." * * *

Six months after the EEOC filed its complaint, four individual employees * * * were allowed to intervene as plaintiffs. * * * In due course, the District Court entered an order conditionally certifying the following class pursuant to Federal Rules of Civil Procedure 23(b)(2) and (3):

> "All black persons who have been employed by the defendant at its Charlotte Branch Office at any time since January 3, 1974 * * * who have been discriminated against in promotion, wages, job assignments and terms and conditions of employment because of their race." * * *

After certifying the class, the District Court ordered that notice be published in the Charlotte newspapers and mailed to each individual member of the class. The notice described the status of the litigation, and plainly stated that members of the class "will be bound by the judgment or other determination" if they did not exclude themselves by sending a written notice to the Clerk. * * * Among the recipients of the notice were Phyllis Baxter and five other individuals employed by the Bank. * * * It is undisputed that these individuals—the Baxter petitioners—are members of the class represented by the intervening plaintiffs and that they made no attempt to exclude themselves from the class.

At the trial the intervening plaintiffs, as well as the Baxter petitioners, testified. The District Court found that the Bank had engaged in a pattern and practice of discrimination from 1974 through 1978 by failing to afford black employees opportunities for advancement and assignment equal to opportunities afforded white employees in pay grades 4 and 5. Except as so specified, however, the District Court found that "there does not appear to be a pattern and practice of discrimination pervasive enough for the court to order relief." * * * Finally, the court somewhat cryptically stated that although it had an opinion about "the entitlement to relief of some of the class members who testified at trial," it would defer decision of such matters to a further proceeding. * * *

Thereafter, on March 24, 1981, the Baxter petitioners moved to intervene, alleging that each had been denied a promotion for discriminatory reasons. * * * The District Court stated: "The court has found no proof of any classwide discrimination above grade 5 and, therefore, they are not entitled to participate in any Stage II proceedings in this case." * * * The court added that it could "see no reason why, if any of the would be intervenors are actively interested in pursuing their claims, they cannot file a Section 1981 suit next week. . ." * * *.

A few days later the Baxter petitioners filed a separate action against the Bank alleging that each of them had been denied a promotion because of their race in violation of 42 U.S.C. § 1981. The Bank moved to dismiss the complaint on the ground that each of them was a member of the class that had been certified in the Cooper litigation, that each was employed in a grade other than 4 or 5, and that they were bound by the determination that there was no proof of any classwide discrimination above grade 5. The District Court denied the motion to dismiss, but certified its order for interlocutory appeal under 28 U.S.C. § 1292(b). The Bank's interlocutory appeal from the order was then consolidated with the Bank's pending appeal in the Cooper litigation.

The United States Court of Appeals for the Fourth Circuit reversed the District Court's judgment on the merits in the Cooper litigation, concluding that (1) there was insufficient evidence to establish a pattern or practice of racial discrimination in grades 4 and 5, and (2) two of the intervening plaintiffs had not been discriminated against on account of race. *EEOC v. Federal Reserve Bank of Richmond*, 698 F.2d 633 (4th Cir. 1983). The court further held that under the doctrine of res judicata, the judgment in the Cooper class action precluded the Baxter petitioners from maintaining their individual race discrimination claims against the Bank. The court thus reversed the order denying the Bank's motion to dismiss in the Baxter action, and remanded for dismissal of the Baxter complaint. We granted certiorari to review that judgment * * *, and we now reverse.

II

Claims of two types were adjudicated in the Cooper litigation. First, the individual claims of each of the four intervening plaintiffs have been finally decided in the Bank's favor. * * * Those individual decisions do not, of course, foreclose any other individual claims. Second, the class claim that the Bank followed "policies and practices" of discriminating against its employees has also been decided. * * * It is that decision on which the Court of Appeals based its res judicata analysis.

There is of course no dispute that under elementary principles of prior adjudication a judgment in a properly entertained class action is binding on class members in any subsequent litigation. * * * Basic principles of res judicata (merger and bar or claim preclusion) and collateral estoppel (issue preclusion) apply. A judgment in favor of the plaintiff class extinguishes their claim, which merges into the judgment granting relief. A judgment in favor of the defendant extinguishes the claim, barring a subsequent action on that claim. A judgment in favor of either side is conclusive in a subsequent action between them on any issue actually litigated and determined, if its determination was essential to that judgment.

III

* * *

The crucial difference between an individual's claim of discrimination and a class action alleging a general pattern or practice of discrimination is manifest. The inquiry regarding an individual's claim is the reason for a particular employment decision, while "at the liability stage of a pattern-or-practice trial the focus often will not be on individual hiring decisions, but on a pattern of discriminatory decisionmaking." * * *

This distinction was critical to our holding in *General Telephone Co. of Southwest v. Falcon*, 457 U.S. 147, 102 S.Ct. 2364, 72 L.Ed.2d 740 (1982), that an individual employee's claim that he was denied a promotion on racial grounds did not necessarily make him an adequate representative of a class composed of persons who had allegedly been refused employment for discriminatory reasons.

* * *

Falcon thus holds that the existence of a valid individual claim does not necessarily warrant the conclusion that the individual plaintiff may successfully maintain a class action. It is equally clear that a class plaintiff's attempt to prove the existence of a companywide policy, or even a consistent practice within a given department, may fail even though discrimination against one or two individuals has been proved. The facts of this case illustrate the point.

The District Court found that two of the intervening plaintiffs, Cooper and Russell, had both established that they were the victims of racial discrimination but, as the Court of Appeals noted, they were employed in grades higher than grade 5 and therefore their testimony provided no support for the conclusion that there was a practice of discrimination in grades 4 and 5. * * * Given the burden of establishing a prima facie case of a pattern or practice of discrimination, it was entirely consistent for the District Court simultaneously to conclude that Cooper and Russell had valid individual claims even though it had expressly found no proof of any classwide discrimination above grade 5. It could not be more plain that the rejection of a claim of classwide discrimination does not warrant the conclusion that no member of the class could have a valid individual claim. "A racially balanced work force cannot immunize an employer from liability for specific acts of discrimination." *Furnco Construction Corp. v. Waters,* 438 U.S., at 579, 98 S.Ct., at 2950–2951.

* * *

The Court of Appeals was correct in generally concluding that the Baxter petitioners, as members of the class represented by the intervening plaintiffs in the Cooper litigation, are bound by the adverse judgment in that case. The court erred, however, in the preclusive effect it attached to that prior adjudication. That judgment (1) bars the class members from bringing another class action against the Bank alleging a pattern or practice of discrimination for the relevant time period and (2) precludes the class members in any other litigation with the Bank from relitigating the question whether the Bank engaged in a pattern and practice of discrimination against black employees during the relevant time period. The judgment is not, however, dispositive of the individual claims the Baxter petitioners have alleged in their separate action. Assuming they establish a prima facie case of discrimination * * *, the Bank will be required to articulate a legitimate reason for each of the challenged decisions, and if it meets that burden, the ultimate questions regarding motivation in their individual cases will be resolved by the District Court. Moreover, the prior adjudication may well prove beneficial to the Bank in the Baxter action: the determination in the Cooper action that the Bank had not engaged in a general pattern or practice of discrimination would be relevant on the issue of pretext. * * *

The Bank argues that permitting the Baxter petitioners to bring separate actions would frustrate the purposes of Rule 23. We think the converse is true. The class-action device was intended to establish a procedure for the adjudication of common questions of law or fact. If the Bank's theory were adopted, it would be tantamount to requiring that every member of the class be permitted to intervene to litigate the merits of his individual claim.

* * *

The judgment of the Court of Appeals is reversed, and the case is remanded for further proceedings consistent with this opinion.

It is so ordered.

JUSTICE MARSHALL concurs in the judgment.

JUSTICE POWELL took no part in the decision of this case.

NOTES AND QUESTIONS

1. Conceptually, why should a class action judgment ever bind an absent member whose interests were not adequately represented in the lawsuit?

2. Should a class action judgment be given collateral estoppel effect in favor of a plaintiff who elected to opt-out of the class action and filed an individual lawsuit? If allowed, wouldn't this practice enable plaintiffs to benefit from a favorable judgment but not be barred by an unfavorable judgment—even as to the very matter determined in the class action itself? Would this undermine the opt-out procedure? See Wolff, *Preclusion in Class Action Litigation,* 105 Colum.L.Rev. 717 (2005).

G. CLASS ACTION WAIVERS

In AT&T MOBILITY LLC v. CONCEPCION, 563 U.S. 333, 131 S.Ct. 1740, 179 L.Ed.2d 742 (2011), a California telephone customer sued a telephone company for advertising free phone service when in fact sales tax of about $30 was charged. The contract provided for arbitration of all disputes between the customer and the company and mandated that any claims be brought in an "individual capacity, and not as a plaintiff or class member in any purported class or representative proceeding." Id. at 336, 131 S.Ct. at 1744, 179 L.Ed.2d at 749. The company moved to compel arbitration, but under a California rule the ban on class treatment was nonenforceable as an unconscionable term. The Supreme Court, five-to-four, held that the Federal Arbitration Act ("FAA") preempted the state rule:

> Although we have had little occasion to examine classwide arbitration, our decision in *Stolt-Nielson [S.A. v. Animalfeeds International Corp.* 559 U.S. 662, 130 S.Ct. 1758, 176 L.Ed.2d 605 (2010)]* is instructive. In that case we held that an arbitration panel exceeded its power * * * by imposing class procedures based on policy judgments rather than the arbitration agreement itself * * *. * * * We then held that the agreement at issue, which was silent on the question of class procedures, could not be interpreted to allow them because the "changes brought about by the shift from bilateral arbitration to class-action arbitration" are

"fundamental." * * * [Id. at 686, 130 S.Ct. at 1776, 176 L.Ed.2d at 625]. This is obvious as a structural matter: Classwide arbitration includes absent parties, necessitating additional and different procedures and involving higher stakes. Confidentiality becomes more difficult. And while it is theoretically possible to select an arbitrator with some expertise relevant to the class-certification question, arbitrators are not generally knowledgeable in the often-dominant procedural aspects of certification, such as the protection of absent parties. * * * [C]lass arbitration, to the extent it is * * * [not] consensual, is inconsistent with the FAA.

First, the switch from bilateral to class arbitration sacrifices the principal advantage of arbitration—its informality—and makes the process slower, more costly, and more likely to generate procedural morass than final judgment. "In bilateral arbitration, parties forgo the procedural rigor and appellate review of the courts in order to realize the benefits of private dispute resolution: lower costs, greater efficiency and speed, and the ability to choose expert adjudicators to resolve specialized disputes." * * * But before an arbitrator may decide the merits of a claim in classwide procedures, he must first decide, for example, whether the class itself may be certified, whether the named parties are sufficiently representative and typical, and how discovery for the class should be conducted. * * *

Second, class arbitration requires procedural formality. * * * If procedures are too informal, absent class members would not be bound by the arbitration. For a class-action money judgment to bind absentees in litigation, class representatives must at all times adequately represent absent class members, and absent members must be afforded notice, an opportunity to be heard, and a right to opt out of the class. * * * At least this amount of process would presumably be required for absent parties to be bound by the results of arbitration.

We find it unlikely that in passing the FAA Congress meant to leave the disposition of these procedural requirements to an arbitrator. Indeed, class arbitration was not even envisioned by Congress when it passed the FAA in 1925 * * *. * * * And it is at the very least odd to think that an arbitrator would be entrusted with ensuring that third parties' due process rights are satisfied.

Third, class arbitration greatly increases risks to defendants. Informal procedures do of course have a cost: The absence of multilayered review makes it more likely that errors will go uncorrected. Defendants are willing to accept the costs of these errors in arbitration, since their impact is limited to the size of individual disputes, and presumably outweighed by savings from avoiding the courts. But when damages allegedly owed to tens of thousands of potential claimants are aggregated and decided at once, the risk of an error will often become unacceptable. Faced with even a small chance of a devastating loss, defendants will be pressured into settling questionable claims. * * * Other courts have noted the risk of "in terrorem" settlements that class actions entail * * * and class arbitration would be no different.

Arbitration is poorly suited to the higher stakes of class litigation. * * * [Section 10 of the FAA] allows a court to vacate an arbitral award only where [there was evidence of fraud, partiality, or misconduct on the part of the arbitrators]. The AAA rules do authorize judicial review of certification decisions, but this review is unlikely to have much effect given these limitations; review under § 10 focuses on misconduct rather than mistake. * * * We find it hard to believe that defendants would bet the company with no effective means of review, and even harder to believe that Congress would have intended to allow state courts to force such a decision. * * *

The Concepcions contend that because parties may and sometimes do agree to aggregation, class procedures are not necessarily incompatible with arbitration. But the same could be said about procedures that the Concepcions admit States may not superimpose on arbitration: Parties could agree to arbitrate pursuant to the Federal Rules of Civil Procedure, or pursuant to a discovery process rivaling that in litigation. Arbitration is a matter of contract, and the FAA requires courts to honor parties' expectations. * * * But what the parties in the aforementioned examples would have agreed to is not arbitration as envisioned by the FAA, lacks its benefits, and therefore may not be required by state law.

The dissent claims that class proceedings are necessary to prosecute small-dollar claims that might otherwise slip through the legal system. * * * But States cannot require a procedure that is inconsistent with the FAA, even if it is desirable for unrelated reasons. * * *

Id. at 347–51, 131 S.Ct. at 1751–53, 179 L.Ed.2d at 756–58.

Justice Breyer, joined by Justice Ginsburg, Justice Sotomayor, and Justice Kagan, dissented:

* * * [T]he majority highlights the disadvantages of class arbitrations, as it sees them. * * * But class proceedings have countervailing advantages. In general agreements that forbid the

consolidation of claims can lead small-dollar claimants to abandon their claims rather than to litigate. * * *

What rational lawyer would have signed on to represent the Concepcions in litigation for the possibility of fees stemming from a $30.22 claim? * * * In California's perfectly rational view, nonclass arbitration over such sums will also sometimes have the effect of depriving claimants of their claims (say, for example, where claiming the $30.22 were to involve filling out many forms that require technical legal knowledge or waiting at great length while a call is placed on hold). *Discover Bank* [*v. Superior Court*, 36 Cal. 4th 148, 30 Cal.Rptr.3d 76, 113 P.3d 1100 (2005),] sets forth circumstances in which the California courts believe that the terms of consumer contracts can be manipulated to insulate an agreement's author from liability for its own frauds by "deliberately cheat[ing] large numbers of consumers out of individually small sums of money." * * * Why is this kind of decision—weighing the pros and cons of all class proceedings alike—not California's to make?

Id. at 365, 131 S.Ct. at 1760–61, 179 L.Ed.2d at 767.

NOTES AND QUESTIONS

1.   One commentary has called *Concepcion* a "coup de grace" signaling the effective death of consumer class actions; indeed, the authors predicted that commercial counsel face malpractice liability if they fail to include boilerplate class action waivers in consumer contracts. See Gilles & Friedman, *After Class: Aggregate Litigation in the Wake of* AT&T Mobility v. Concepcion, 79 U.Chi.L.Rev. 623, 627, 632 (2012). Do you agree with that assessment? Are there situations when a company would prefer classwide resolution of claims? See Nagareda, *The Litigation-Arbitration Dichotomy Meets the Class Action*, 86 Notre Dame L.Rev. 1069 (2011).

2.   Does *Concepcion* leave open the possibility of voiding class action waivers based on generally applicable contract defenses that do not discriminate against arbitration? On this basis, some courts have continued to invalidate waivers on individualized findings of unconscionability. See Wolff, *Is There Life After* Concepcion? *State Courts, State Law, and the Mandate of Arbitration*, 56 St. Louis U.L.J. 1269 (2012). However, in AMERICAN EXPRESS CO. v. ITALIAN COLORS RESTAURANT, 570 U.S. 228, 133 S.Ct. 2304, 186 L.Ed.2d 417 (2013), an antitrust suit by merchants who use American Express cards, the Court held that a California court could not treat as unconscionable an arbitration clause that barred class proceedings. The Court rejected the argument that the clause effectively blocked plaintiffs from pursuing federal relief because the costs of individually arbitrating the claims exceeded the potential recovery.

3. Should *Concepcion's* rationale apply to agreements that bar class actions under Rule 23 to redress federal claims? Professor Miller has commented:

> This decision effectively replaces judges and juries with one-by-one arbitrators in many contexts better served by class actions or other forms of claim aggregation. As a result, powerful economic entities can impose no-class-action-arbitration clauses on people with little or no bargaining position—through adhesion contracts involving securities accounts, credit cards, mobile phones, car rentals, and many other social amenities and necessities. * * * The effect, of course, is that the vast majority of people who would comprise a judicial or arbitration class and possibly secure legal relief are not in a position to invoke their contractual "right" to arbitrate. As a result, these people remain remediless, leaving the challenged conduct undeterred.

Miller, *Simplified Pleading, Meaningful Days in Court, and Trials on the Merits: Reflections on the Deformation of Federal Procedure*, 88 N.Y.U.L.Rev. 286, 322–23 (2013).

NOTE ON CLASS ACTIONS ABROAD

The class action traditionally has been regarded as "a uniquely American procedural device." See Sherman, *Group Litigation Under Foreign Legal Systems: Variations and Alternatives to American Class Actions*, 52 DePaul L.Rev. 401, 401 (2002). Civil law systems were presumed to be resistant to the class action. Even in common law systems, mass joinder rules, such as the English group litigation order, did not embrace representative litigation. See Rowe, *Debates over Group Litigation in Comparative Perspective: What Can We Learn from Each Other?*, 11 Duke J.Comp. & Int'l L. 157 (2001). Legal systems abroad, however, have begun to show "greater receptiveness" toward aggregate litigation, although many countries still stop short of adopting United States-style class actions:

> Looking across the European landscape, one can situate within the broad rubric of "aggregate litigation" such differing procedures as Dutch collective settlement actions, English group litigation orders, German model cases in securities litigation, and Italian class actions, among other procedures. Additional moves in the offing suggest a similar openness to possible reforms in the direction of more rather than less aggregate litigation. These include major studies by the European Commission of new measures for aggregate redress in antitrust and consumer litigation and by the Civil Justice Council of England and Wales on reform of collective redress.

Nagareda, *Aggregate Litigation Across the Atlantic and the Future of American Exceptionalism*, 62 Vand.L.Rev. 1, 4–5 (2009). In 2009, the European Union issued a directive that permits injunctions in consumer class actions. See Directive 2009/22/EC of the European Parliament and of the Council of 23

April 2009 on injunctions for the protection of consumers' interests. Earlier, Italy had introduced a new damages class action for consumers, also permitting certain consumer associations to bring injunctive claims. See Consumer code of 2005, art. 139 and 140-bis, as amended by the laws n. 99 of July 23, 2009. Israel's class action regime became effective in 2008, and it now has a higher rate of class action filings per capita than the United States. See Hensler, *From Sea to Shining Sea: How and Why Class Actions Are Spreading Globally*, 65 U.Kan.L.Rev. 965, 986 (2017). For other nation-specific examples, see Chase, Hershkoff, Silberman, Sorabji, Stürner, Taniguchi & Varano, Civil Litigation in Comparative Context, ch. 8 (Chase & Hershkoff, eds., 2d ed. 2017).

CHAPTER 10

PRETRIAL DEVICES FOR OBTAINING INFORMATION: DEPOSITIONS AND DISCOVERY

■ ■ ■

This chapter examines how parties obtain information to pursue lawsuits and to defend against them. The original Federal Rules made information broadly discoverable provided it was not privileged and was relevant to the subject matter of the dispute. Moreover, in keeping with the spirit of an adversary system that values party autonomy, the Federal Rules placed the discovery process in the litigants' hands with little judicial oversight. As Professor Miller has commented, "Discovery was designed to let each side have access to * * * information so that the litigation playing field would be level to promote more informed settlements and trials." Miller, *Are the Federal Courthouse Doors Closing? What's Happened to the Federal Rules of Civil Procedure?*, 43 Tex.Tech.L.Rev. 587, 596 (2011). Amendments to the Federal Rules have subjected the discovery process to greater judicial control; now mandate the disclosure of certain types of information without a party's request or court order; and make discoverable only information relevant to the claims and defenses in the lawsuit—not the subject matter—when disclosure is proportional to the needs of the case. Commentators disagree whether these changes legitimately rein in discovery practices that have become exorbitant, expensive, and burdensome, or whether they needlessly impede efforts to prove meritorious claims. The rules also have been amended to account for electronic forms of information that are now a standard part of personal communication and business practice.

A. INTRODUCTION

Facts are essential to a common law system based on adversarial values:

> Our adversary system for the resolution of disputes rests on the unshakable foundation that truth is the object of the system's process which is designed for the purpose of dispensing justice. However, because no one has an exclusive insight into truth, the process depends on the adversarial presentation of evidence, precedent and custom, and argument to reasoned conclusions—

all directed with unwavering effort to what, in good faith, is
believed to be true on matters material to the disposition.

U.S. v. Shaffer Equipment Co., 11 F.3d 450, 457 (4th Cir. 1993). As the
Supreme Court stated almost a decade after adoption of the Federal Rules,
"Mutual knowledge of all the relevant facts gathered by both parties is
essential to proper litigation. To that end, either party may compel the
other to disgorge whatever facts he has in his possession." Hickman v.
Taylor, 329 U.S. 495, 507, 67 S.Ct. 385, 392, 91 L.Ed. 451, 460 (1947). The
original Federal Rules saw an important connection between discovery and
the truth-function of litigation—in particular, the need to avoid "trial by
ambush." Klonoski v. Mahlab, 156 F.3d 255, 271 (1st Cir. 1998).
Commentators also emphasize that discovery produces indirect public
benefits by enabling lawsuits that encourage regulatory compliance and
deter future wrongdoing. See Burbank, *Proportionality and the Social
Benefits of Discovery: Out of Sight and Out of Mind?*, 34 Rev.Litig. 647
(2015).

During the 1970s discovery practice began to come under attack as
critics raised concerns about the costs and burdens of litigation. See Reda,
*The Cost-and-Delay Narrative in Civil Justice Reform: Its Fallacies and
Functions*, 90 Or.L.Rev. 1085 (2012). For the most part, empirical studies
showed that discovery "operate[d] effectively in most lawsuits." Tobias, *The
2000 Federal Civil Rules Revisions*, 38 San Diego L.Rev. 875, 884 (2001).
To the extent discovery abuse did exist, it appeared confined to complex
cases that involved high stakes damage awards. See Mullenix, *The
Pervasive Myth of Pervasive Discovery Abuse: The Sequel*, 39 B.C.L.Rev.
683, 684 (1998). Nevertheless, the perception of discovery practice as a
"fishing expedition"—aimed at extorting unfair settlements—has persisted
and has influenced changes in the Court's approach to pleading, motions to
dismiss, and summary judgment. See Thornburg, *Just Say "No Fishing":
The Lure of Metaphor*, 40 U.Mich.J.L. Reform 1 (2006).

B. FACT-GATHERING PRIOR TO FILING SUIT

The Federal Rules impose a duty on the parties and their counsel to
investigate the facts before filing a lawsuit or presenting factual
contentions to the court. See p. 458, Note on Rule 11, supra. For the most
part, presuit investigation takes place outside the formal discovery rules—
the only exception is the limited opportunity under Federal Rule 27 to
perpetuate testimony. See p. 603, infra. Even in a simple case a litigant
may face obstacles to obtaining critical information needed for a complaint
to survive an early dismissal under Rule 12(b)(6). The problems are
compounded when the claim is based on defendant's concealment of the
truth—as in a securities fraud case—or rests on an intent or purpose that
only defendant knows—as in an employment discrimination case.

Fact-gathering prior to filing suit requires creativity, resources, and diligence. Increasingly, a prospective litigant will attempt to probe publicly available sources of information—such as government data bases or agency websites—as part of a presuit investigation. See Reardon, *Note, Pleading in the Information Age*, 85 N.Y.U.L.Rev. 2170 (2010). In addition, lawyers may hire private investigators to ferret out hidden facts. See Schaller, *Secrets of the Trade: Tactical and Legal Considerations from the Trade Secret Plaintiff's Perspective*, 29 Rev.Litig. 729 (2010). Efforts to interview key witnesses might produce a "whistleblower," although in some situations the source will insist upon confidentiality and additional evidence likely will be needed for corroboration. See, e.g., Makor Issues & Rights, Ltd. v. Tellabs, Inc., 513 F.3d 702 (7th Cir. 2008). Court filings and consent decrees in other cases may be a source of information or lead to information that can be alleged. See, e.g., In re National Ass'n of Music Merchants, Musical Instruments and Equipment Antitrust Litigation, 2011 WL 3702453 (S.D.Cal. 2011); see also Garrett, *The Public Interest in Corporate Settlements*, 58 B.C.L.Rev. 1483 (2017). Counsel can file requests under the Freedom of Information Act or under state Public Records Acts. For an example of this strategy, see Carpenter, *Family Farm Advocacy and Rebellious Lawyering*, 24 Clinical L.Rev. 79 (2017); see also Becker v. Carney, 2017 WL 4264229 (W.D.Wash. 2017). Finally, advocates increasingly are turning to social media that enable access to hundreds and even thousands of strangers and "friends" who may be sources of relevant information or lead to information. See Robertson, *The Facebook Disruption: How Social Media May Transform Civil Litigation and Facilitate Access to Justice*, 65 Ark.L.Rev. 75 (2012).

Whether these forms of presuit investigation will be sufficient to allow meritorious claims to withstand a challenge under Rule 12(b)(6) remains to be seen; no study has yet fully assessed the overall effects of tightened pleading rules and reduced access to discovery. See Gelbach & Kobayashi, *The Law and Economics of Proportionality in Discovery*, 50 Ga.L.Rev. 1093 (2016). Moreover, the availability of information through presuit investigation may also depend on the effect of restrictions that bar the sharing of pertinent information, such as non-disclosure agreements contained in settlements or other contracts.

———

Read Federal Rule of Civil Procedure 27 and the accompanying materials in the Supplement.

———

A request under Federal Rule 27 does not substitute for discovery and cannot be treated as a first step in a litigant's presuit investigation. To the contrary, the requestor must be able to file a verified petition that sets forth specific information, as listed in Rule 27(a)(1)(A)–(E), and is filed in the district court for the district where an expected adverse party resides. What must a requestor for presuit discovery show as a condition of invoking Federal 27? Is it sufficient that evidence will be lost? Or must the requestor show that without discovery a lawsuit cannot be filed? Will a delay in bringing a lawsuit tilt in favor of a Rule 27 request?

IN RE PETITION OF SHEILA ROBERTS FORD

United States District Court, Middle District of Alabama, 1997.
170 F.R.D. 504.

THOMPSON, CHIEF JUDGE.

* * *

On November 15, 1996, Ford filed, through counsel, her petition pursuant to [Federal] Rule 27. In the petition, Ford asks "for leave to proceed with the deposition of Elmore County Sheriff Bill Franklin." She alleges that she "expects to be a party to an action in the United States District Court for the Middle District of Alabama, Northern Division, but is presently unable to bring said action"; that the "anticipated action surrounds the shooting death of Fred William Roberts by law-enforcement officers of Elmore County on November 8, 1996"; that she "is the Administratrix of the Estate of Fred William Roberts"; that she "intends to establish who the appropriate party defendants to the anticipated action are through the testimony of Elmore County Sheriff Bill Franklin"; that she "is unable to determine the appropriate party defendants and the basic facts surrounding the death of Fred William Roberts without the testimony of Sheriff Franklin" and "needs to establish an accurate account of the events that took place . . . before the memories of those involved fade or become dist[or]ted by publicity"; and that she is "requesting the deposition of . . . Franklin" because he "was the commanding officer of the Elmore County deputies believed to be involved in the shooting of . . . Roberts" and he "is expected to identify the facts involved in Mr. Roberts' shooting death as well as the identity of the law enforcement officers involved." Ford also gave the names, addresses, and descriptions of the persons she expected to be adverse parties.

* * *

A hearing was held on the petition on December 13. At the hearing, Sheriff Franklin appeared through counsel and stated that he opposed the petition because it was not authorized by Rule 27. Ford responded by reaffirming that she needed to take Sheriff Franklin's deposition in order "to determine . . . the basic facts surrounding the death of Fred William Roberts." Without this information, she said, she could not determine whom to sue. She did not know whether Sheriff Franklin or one of his deputies shot Roberts and whether the shooting was justified.

* * *

Admittedly, Ford * * * asserts in her petition a desire to preserve testimony; she states that she "needs to establish an accurate account of the events that took place . . . before the memories of those involved fade or become dist[or]ted by publicity." This reason is not credible, however. Ford can do this by simply filing suit today. She presented no evidence that Sheriff Franklin's testimony is in imminent danger of being lost because he is gravely ill or about to leave the country. Ford therefore wishes only to discover or uncover what happened on November 8. The simple question for the court is whether Rule 27 authorizes such relief.

* * * [T]he first and obvious place to look to determine whether Rule 27 authorizes pre-complaint discovery is the language of the rule itself. If the language of the rule is unambiguous and dispositive and is reasonable within its context, then the court should go no further and simply should enforce the language. Here, Rule 27 meets this straightforward test.

Subsection (a)(1) of Rule 27 provides, as stated, that "A person who desires to *perpetuate* testimony regarding any matter that may be cognizable in any court of the United States may file a verified petition." (Emphasis added.) Subsection (a)(3) then provides that an order allowing examination may be entered only "If the court is satisfied that the *perpetuation* of the testimony may prevent a failure or delay of justice." (Emphasis added.)[a] Rule 27's coverage therefore extends only to the "perpetuation" of testimony. The term "perpetuate" is defined as "to make perpetual," "preserve from extinction," or "cause to last indefinitely." Webster's Third International Dictionary, unabridged 1685 (1976); see also Black's Law Dictionary 1027 (5th ed. 1979) ("perpetuating testimony" is a "means . . . for *preserving* the testimony of witness, which might otherwise be lost before the trial in which it is intended to be used") (emphasis added). Here, Ford seeks to discover or uncover testimony, not to perpetuate it. She seeks pre-complaint discovery of evidence, not pre-complaint perpetuation of it. There is nothing before the court to indicate that Sheriff Franklin's testimony is in imminent danger of being lost. Rather, Ford simply wants to know who shot Roberts and why. Rule 27 simply does not provide for such discovery.

* * *

Ford also argues that Rule 27 should be read in conjunction with Rule 11 * * *. The problem, however, is that Rule 27 is not a vehicle for compliance with Rule 11. As stated, the language in

---

[a]   The language of Rule 27 was altered by the 2007 restyling of the Federal Rules but the changes were not substantive.

Rule 27 is clear that the rule authorizes the perpetuation of evidence, not the discovery or uncovering of it. * * *

The court is not without sympathy for Ford. She is understandingly deeply troubled by and concerned about the shooting death of her father. If a law enforcement officer was at fault she desires to have him or her held accountable in a court of law. But, under Rule 11, she cannot file suit against any one without first having uncovered some "evidentiary support" for holding the person liable or having obtained some preliminary evidence that there is likely to be some "evidentiary support after a reasonable opportunity for further investigation or discovery."[b] Similarly, the defense of qualified immunity protects law enforcement officials from federal suit in the absence of detailed factual allegations of a violation of a clearly established federal right. * * * However, without the discovery incident to litigation, Ford is without the means to uncover whether her father was a victim of foul play in violation of a clearly established federal right. Her predicament is a "Catch 22." Indeed, she must feel that, under the rules established by our civil justice system, a law enforcement officer can get away with murder. This court has no answer for her, however, other than that Rule 27 does not offer an avenue of relief.

* * *

It is further ORDERED that costs are taxed against petitioner Ford, for which execution may issue.

NOTES AND QUESTIONS

1.   The Southern District of New York has put forward a three-part test for invoking Rule 27 discovery:

> In order to prevail on their Rule 27 petition, the petitioners must satisfy three elements. First, they must furnish a focused explanation of what they anticipate any testimony would demonstrate. Such testimony cannot be used to discover evidence for the purpose of filing a complaint. Second, they must establish in good faith that they expect to bring an action cognizable in federal court, but are presently unable to bring it or cause it to be brought. Third, petitioners must make an objective showing that without a Rule 27 hearing, known testimony would otherwise be lost, concealed or destroyed.

In re Petition of Allegretti, 229 F.R.D. 93, 96 (S.D.N.Y. 2005). In Penn Mut. Life Ins. Co. v. U.S., 68 F.3d 1371 (D.C.Cir. 1995), the appellate court found that presuit discovery was warranted when a potential witness's advanced age presented a significant risk that he would be unavailable to testify at a trial. However, the court denied discovery when the potential witness simply had retired from his job and might forget information.

---

[b]   The language as changed now appears in Rule 11(b)(3).

2.   Presuit discovery is available in some states either by rule or through an equitable action for a bill of discovery. See Dodson, *Federal Pleading and State Presuit Discovery*, 14 Lewis & Clark L.Rev. 43 (2010) (collecting examples). Is it significant that some states condition the filing of a medical malpractice claim on presuit discovery, anticipating that early fact gathering will deter the filing of meritless claims? See Florida Hosp. Waterman v. Stoll, 855 So.2d 271 (Fla.App. 2003).

3.   Should Rule 27 be amended to allow presuit discovery when facts are needed to frame a complaint? See Dodson, *New Pleading, New Discovery*, 109 Mich.L.Rev. 53, 74 (2010). To avoid abuse, what kind of showing ought to be required? See Hoffman, *Using Presuit Discovery to Overcome Barriers to the Courthouse*, 34 Litigation 31 (2008). A potential model is the Texas presuit discovery rule which permits a presuit deposition in order to "investigate a potential claim or suit." Tex.R.Civ.P. 202.1(a)–(b); see In re Reed, 2016 WL 5660421 (S.D.Tex. 2016).

C. THE SCOPE OF DISCOVERY: RELEVANCE AND PROPORTIONALITY

Discovery helps to preserve relevant information that might not be available at trial. The earliest discovery procedures in the federal courts were designed primarily for this purpose. See *Developments in the Law—Discovery*, 74 Harv.L.Rev. 940, 949 (1961). Discovery also helps to isolate those issues that actually are in controversy between the parties. In addition, discovery serves important public purposes. Discovery promotes transparency by uncovering information about government and business practices that may be illegal, and potentially makes that information available to a broader set of individuals than just the parties to the suit. See City of Greenville, Ill. v. Syngenta Crop Protection, LLC, 764 F.3d 695 (7th Cir. 2014). Discovery also promotes the work of "private attorneys general" who, through private litigation, help to enforce the law and deter wrongdoing. See Carrington, *Renovating Discovery*, 49 Ala.L.Rev. 51, 54 (1997).

Once a lawsuit has commenced, the Federal Rules enable the parties to obtain information from each other and from third parties, but generally discovery cannot begin until the parties have conferred and devised a discovery plan. See Rule 26(f). Drafting a discovery plan requires cooperation, strategic thinking, and attention to the multi-faceted aspects of the discovery process, each of which is discussed in this chapter:

(1)   The permissible scope of discovery in terms of the governing concepts of relevance and proportionality;

(2)   The discovery schedule, the possibility of expedition, the timing of automatic disclosure, and the duty of supplementation;

(3) The availability and utility of different discovery devices, including the use of experts, and the limits that the Rules place on discovery requests that are cumulative or redundant and that may involve thousands of items of electronically stored information;

(4) The role of evidentiary privileges that protect information from disclosure, even if relevant and proportional to the needs of the case;

(5) The procedures for objecting to discovery requests or compelling discovery responses, and the power of the court to regulate the discovery process and to sanction parties who do not cooperate, do not provide required supplementation, or cause undue burden or expense; and

(6) The scope of the parties' autonomy to disclose, and retain, information under seal or otherwise to keep information revealed during the litigation from public view.

———

Read Federal Rule of Civil Procedure 26(b)(1) in the Supplement.

———

FASSETT V. SEARS HOLDINGS CORP.
United States District Court, Middle District of Pennsylvania, 2017.
319 F.R.D. 143.

BRANN, UNITED STATES DISTRICT JUDGE.

Some personal injury cases spring from highly questionable circumstances, and others from undeniably life-altering events. Setting aside ultimate questions of liability and damages, this litigation is tragically one of the latter. When Plaintiff Daniel Fassett heard sputtering sounds emitting from his lawnmower, he attempted to relieve the pressure in its fuel tank by loosening the cap. As he did so, gasoline sprayed from the machine onto his body, igniting in flames. Mr. Fassett sustained serious injuries and shortly thereafter initiated this products liability action.

Although the litigation has progressed in a timely fashion since its inception in May 2015, the parties have recently reached a rather technical impasse. That quandary involves, among other questions, the extent to which material about alternative fuel cap designs and distinct lawnmower layouts may be discoverable. In other words, the parties have struggled to define the outer bounds of discovery in this case: what, if anything, can be discovered about parts or mowers not involved in the subject fire? By presenting such a question, this dispute necessarily calls upon the Court to apply the proportionality provision of recently amended Federal Rule * * * 26 to the case's technologically nuanced facts.

* * * I hold that in a products liability suit such as this one * * * material corresponding to alternative designs or components that exhibit significant similarities to the design or component at issue should be discoverable in the greatest quantities and for the most varied purposes; however, material corresponding to alternative designs or components that share less in common with the contested design or component should be incrementally less discoverable—and for more limited purposes—as those similarities diminish.

* * *

"To determine the scope of discoverable information under Rule 26(b)(1), the Court looks initially to the pleadings." * * *

* * *

* * * From the outset, I note that the Court is mindful of Defendants' concerns about the mounting expense of unbridled discovery. Nevertheless, I cannot agree with the threshold assertion that what is discoverable is strictly limited to material that is ultimately relevant or otherwise admissible. As the parties well know, Rule 26(b)(1) envisions a broader universe of discoverable material than that. It makes clear, for instance, that "[i]nformation within this scope of discovery need not be admissible in evidence to be discoverable."

At the same time, however, "[t]his concept of relevance is tempered . . . by principles of proportionality." * * *

* * *

Considering the factors set forth at Rule 26(b)(1), the parties' access to relevant information is undeniably lop-sided in this case: Defendants are repeat players in this genre of litigation, and they consequently enjoy the benefits of sweeping protective orders. * * * On the other hand, the Plaintiffs lack nearly all avenues other than judicially-sanctioned ones to obtain the requisite records that rest in Defendants' possession.

Moreover, the importance of the issues at stake in the litigation militates slightly in Plaintiffs' favor. Although this is not a case involving, for instance, constitutional rights or matters of national significance, to these particular litigants, it is a matter of grave import. Further, its outcome may impact the marketability of a widely sold piece of home machinery or some of its components.

Just as important, I believe that the utility of the proposed discovery outweighs its attendant expenses. Certainly, the Defendants can readily produce electronically stored records relevant to the aforementioned models and can engage in a good faith effort to gather whatever data might not have been documented electronically. In the same vein, I am confident that production of the requested material will bear directly upon resolution of the [core] issues in this case. It may also clarify any lingering issues as to the most appropriate defendants.

Turning now to Rule 26(b)(1)'s application in product liability cases, the Plaintiffs here allege negligence and strict liability claims, two theories whose proof necessarily entails such questions as: what the Defendants knew or foresaw * * *; what safety tests they conducted * * *; and what designs they considered. * * *

The touchstone used to distinguish discoverable inputs from others in products liability cases was set forth in Fine v. Facet Aerospace Prods. Co., 133 F.R.D. 439 (S.D.N.Y. 1990) * * *. The *Fine* decision outlined the following test:

> In product liability actions it is frequently difficult to judge which of a manufacturer's products are sufficiently similar to the allegedly defective product to be subject to discovery. Generally, different models of a product will be relevant if they share with the accident-causing model those characteristics pertinent to the legal issues raised in the litigation. For example, where a plaintiff alleged that three-wheel all-terrain vehicles are inherently unstable, he was entitled to discovery with respect to each of the manufacturer's models. * * * Similarly, an injured party who contended that the redesigned motor mounts that had failed in his vehicle had not eliminated the defects of earlier models was granted discovery concerning the predecessor versions. * * * Finally, a plaintiff arguing that the left front spring main leaf on his vehicle failed could obtain discovery regarding all types of vehicles with that component, not merely the identical model. * * *

Id. at 441.

Moreover, the *Fine* court explained that "a plaintiff who raises a design defect claim is entitled to broader discovery than, for example, if the claim were solely one of negligent manufacture," so long as the requested materials "are truly alternatives and that they are potentially safer." * * * This does not require the moving party to prove its case on the merits at the discovery stage. * * * Instead, this threshold showing might be satisfied by, for example, the affidavit of an expert in engineering. * * *

* * *

* * * Although the hallmark factor in my analysis is the extent to which the sought-after discovery shared those relevant characteristics with the accident-causing component, I also weighed several additional factors

in arriving at what I determined was the appropriate scope of discovery.
* * *[1]

The first factor—the extent to which the contested discovery can achieve the same functionality as the accident-causing part—speaks, in many ways, directly to the core issue here. In particular, [defendant] contends that the only type of gas cap design about which the Plaintiffs may discover information is the open design, because that is the cap design used on Mr. Fassett's lawnmower. Although not outlandish, that suggestion is likely overly restrictive. "[A] party should not be limited by its opponent's theory of the case in determining what is discoverable." * * *

Of great weight is the deposition testimony of Michael J. Holtz, a corporate designee and the gas cap's product design and engineering manager. * * * In addition to the open style vent cap, Mr. Holtz identified three other variations: the screw vent cap, the duckbill cap, and the covered vent cap. * * * Although the three variations are distinguishable from an open vent cap in that they possess different structural designs, all of these caps could function at a partly open setting. * * * In fact, Mr. Holtz testified that each cap was designed to be placed on an open setting while the lawnmower was activated, but closed while it was shut off and being transported. * * *

The second factor that I considered was the extent to which the contested discovery could be safety tested using the same procedures and standards as would be used for the accident-causing part. That was true here, and in my view, that fact goes a long way in making the test results as to all of those design caps discoverable. As the reasoning goes, testing using the same protocol makes the results comparable and therefore relevant to such issues as the existence of a safer alternative design and the Defendants' prior knowledge. * * * This protocol could be applied to all free venting caps, including screw, closed, and duckbill designs.

The third factor I considered was whether, compared with the accident-causing part, the contested discovery was an interchangeable component or a distinct system. As to the discovery sought from [defendant], the requested discovery materials are components that could be easily interchanged with the accident-causing parts. Their use on the accident-causing model would not require, for instance, wholesale refurbishing of the entire lawnmower or total replacement of its fuel unit. Barring some surface-level adjustments, distinct fuel cap designs can easily be substituted. This factor is highly relevant in cases such as these: if the various components are readily interchangeable, then the cost of exchanging dangerous parts with safer ones is comparatively low.

---

[1] This Court's use of the term "accident-causing" is in no way meant as an assignment of fault. Rather, it is merely the way I distinguish the unit or component used by the complainant at the time of the accident from other units or components under consideration.

The final factor that I evaluated was the extent to which the moving party supported its technical assertions with testimony by a witness who possesses adequate knowledge of the design, development, and functionality of the contested components. Again, as to [these] * * * requests, the considerations underlying that factor have been satisfied as by Plaintiffs' citations to the deposition testimony of Michael J. Holtz, a corporate designee and the gas cap's product design and engineering manager.

* * *

Because application of all of the aforementioned factors reveals that warranty information, testing data, and any other materials evidencing over-pressurization or geysering corresponding to each of the enumerated free venting caps designs (open, screw, covered, and duckbill) are relevant to a number of Plaintiffs' theories, those materials are discoverable so long as they are not work product. * * *

My conclusion is different, however insofar as Plaintiffs' requests for claims and other litigation material in all cases involving every variety of the free venting cap. "In products liability cases evidence of prior accidents involving the same product under similar circumstances is admissible to show notice to the defendant of the danger, to show existence of the danger, and to show the cause of the accident." * * * That being said, "[t]he almost universal requirement, however, is that the prior occurrence must involve facts and circumstances which are substantially similar to those involved in the case under consideration or they will be excluded." * * *

At a superficial level, it appears that all of the contested cap designs could be characterized generally as "free venting caps" because they contain a specified orifice that allows air to permeate them in some fashion or another. * * * Nevertheless, based upon Mr. Holtz's characterization of the different cap designs, the screw and covered vent caps appear most like the open vent cap in design and operation, with the duckbill being the most distinct as a consequence of its unique shaping. The notion that information relating to all prior free venting claims is discoverable because all of those accidents involved failed venting is much too high a level of abstraction.

As for screw, covered, and duckbill caps, the differences in design and what tend to be the distinct factual circumstances render them beyond the scope of discovery. Specifically, each prior claim is capable of differing on a number of grounds: the age and prior history of the lawnmower; whether the lawnmower was a riding or push unit; the period of time for which [the] lawnmower had been running on the date of the accident; the atmospheric conditions at the site of the accident; and the varied actions of the accident victims. * * *

* * * Plaintiffs have not met their burden of showing substantial similarity as to the accidents involving these other designs. * * *

I consider this outcome to be an amenable compromise between the two overbroad and underinclusive proposals that have been presented. So often, discovery is not properly construed as an all-or-nothing game. Rather, it is a means for uncovering truth—the strengths and weaknesses of one's case—rationally bounded by efficiency and cost concerns. It is that dynamic that makes discovery a trade-off between knowledge and expenditure. The district court's role under Rule 26, then, is to discern that middle ground between two countervailing pressures, the optimal solution to the information-cost equations. * * *

* * *

Another issue central to this discussion is the proper temporal scope of discovery. In particular, Plaintiffs' proposed order seeking discovery from [defendant] requests discovery from as early as 1970. Mr. Fassett purchased the subject lawnmower on or around March 2, 2007, * * * and the Defendants approximate that this particular mower was manufactured between February 16, 2005 and June 29, 2005. * * * As such, requiring the production of documents dating back to the 1970s would appear excessive in comparison with the needs of the case.

* * * Though the appropriate bounds will vary depending on the specific circumstances of each case, courts in this Circuit have often taken the default position of limiting discovery to no earlier than five years from the date on which the allegedly tortious conduct occurred. * * *

I find this tendency to follow the so-called "five-year rule" instructive, though I would modify it slightly for its application in the products liability setting. In regard to such lawsuits where a defendant is alleged to have knowingly designed, manufactured, or sold a defective product when safer, feasible alternatives existed, I hold that the temporal bounds of discoveries should be set not from the date of the accident but from the time period during which the product was manufactured and sold.

* * * [T]he tortious conduct is more properly construed as having occurred at the point of defective manufacture, design, or sale than at the point of injury. Further, a plaintiff should be able to gather information regarding a defendant's decision-making process, as the propriety of that risk-utility analysis occupies the core of such disputes. * * *

* * *

NOTES AND QUESTIONS

1.   Relevant information is discoverable under Rule 26(b)(1) even if it would not be admissible in evidence at trial. The Federal Rules do not define "relevance," and courts have tended to look to Federal Rule of Evidence 401 for

guidance: "Evidence is relevant if: (a) it has any tendency to make a fact more or less probable than it would be without the evidence; and (b) the fact is of consequence in determining the action." Mora v. Zeta Interactive Corp., 2017 WL 1187710, *3 (E.D.N.Y. 2017).

2.   Prior to 2015, Rule 26(b)(1) set forth a two-tier approach to discoverability of relevant information. The first tier defined relevance with respect to any claim or defense of a party, and information was discoverable without a court order. The second tier defined relevance with respect to the subject matter of the dispute, and disclosure required a court order upon a showing of good cause. The two-tier approach, which was adopted in 2000, replaced earlier language that had allowed discovery, without a court order, of information relevant to the subject matter of the dispute. The 2015 amendment eliminated any reference to subject-matter discovery and the court no longer has discretion to order disclosure of such information. However, the Advisory Committee Note to the 2015 amendment states that the rule change does not foreclose discovery of information "not directly pertinent to the incident" as the Advisory Committee had explained when it adopted the two-tier approach in 2000.

3.   Even if information is relevant, it is discoverable only if disclosure is proportional to the needs of the case in light of factors set forth in Rule 26(b)(1). The proportionality factors trace back to the 1983 amendments to the Federal Rules. The 2015 amendment essentially moved the proportionality factors from a separate provision in Rule 26(b) to its current place. The Advisory Committee Notes to the 2015 amendment emphasize that the relocation of the proportionality factors to Rule 26(b)(1) "does not change the existing responsibilities of the court and the parties to consider proportionality, and the change does not place on the party seeking discovery the burden of addressing all proportionality considerations."

An empirical analysis of the courts' application of proportionality factors during the period prior to and after the 2015 amendment found that the relocation of the requirement "may have fostered real change"; the study reports that "parties and court are applying proportionality more than four times more frequently than before the amendment, and that courts are narrowing discovery on proportionality grounds more than four times more frequently post-amendment." Baicker-McKee, *Mountain or Molehill?*, 55 Duq.L.Rev. 307, 313 (2017).

4.   In MARRESE v. AMERICAN ACADEMY OF ORTHOPAEDIC SURGEONS, 726 F.2d 1150 (7th Cir. 1984), reversed on other grounds, 470 U.S. 373, 105 S.Ct. 1327, 84 L.Ed.2d 274 (1985), two orthopedic surgeons initially sued in state court alleging that they were refused membership in the Academy without a hearing. Although membership in the Academy is not necessary to practice as an orthopedic surgeon, it was alleged to confer some degree of professional advantage. Finding membership in the Academy was not an "economic necessity," the state court dismissed the complaint on the ground that no valid state law claim was stated. Plaintiffs then sued in federal

court, alleging violations of the antitrust laws. In the course of discovery, plaintiffs demanded that the Academy produce correspondence and other documents relating to denials of membership applications between 1970 and 1980. The court ordered the Academy to produce the documents pursuant to an order protecting their confidentiality. The Academy refused to comply with the order, was held in criminal contempt, and was fined $10,000. It appealed, and the Seventh Circuit reversed with directions to dismiss the contempt proceedings. Among other things, the appellate court held that the protective order did not adequately protect the privacy interests of the Academy's members, and that the court could have fashioned discovery in a way that "prevented the plaintiffs from abusing the discovery process, without denying them any information essential to developing their case." Id. at 1162. How would the discovery dispute be decided under the proportionality factors in the 2015 version of Rule 26(b)(1)?

D. PLANNING FOR DISCOVERY

Read Federal Rule of Civil Procedure 26(f) in the Supplement.

1. THE DUTY TO CONFER AND PLAN DISCOVERY

The Federal Rules have been amended a number of times to encourage party cooperation and to impose judicial oversight on the discovery process. Currently the parties are obliged "to confer as soon as practicable" after the commencement of the suit—and at least 21 days before a Rule 16(b) scheduling conference—to devise a discovery plan. Rule 26(f)(1). The discovery plan is to include the "views and proposals" of the parties concerning the range of proposed discovery requests, including issues of automatic disclosure, privilege, electronic information, and the schedule for production. The plan must be in writing and submitted to the court within 14 days of the discovery conference. Rule 26(f)(3). As one district court has observed, "[T]he cooperation that is necessary [to confer and devise the discovery plan] * * * enhances the legitimate goals of the adversary system, by facilitating discovery of the facts needed to support the claims and defenses that have been raised, at a lesser cost, and expediting the time when the case may be resolved on its merits, or settled." Mancia v. Mayflower Textile Servs. Co., 253 F.R.D. 354, 365 (D.Md. 2008). The *Mancia* court, like some other district courts, urged the parties to be cooperative and drew attention to the Sedona Conference's "Cooperation Proclamation." The Sedona Conference, a non-profit, educational research institute, "propose[d] to develop 'a detailed understanding and full articulation of the issues and changes needed to obtain cooperative fact-finding,' as well as '[d]evelop[ ] and distribut[e] practical "toolkits" to train and support lawyers, judges, other professionals, and students in techniques of discovery cooperation, collaboration, and transparency.' " Id. at 363. Courts also look to Rule 1, which was amended in 2015 to emphasize the role of parties, as a basis for the duty to cooperate. See Hyatt v. Rock, 2016 WL 6820378, *2 (N.D.N.Y. 2016).

NOTES AND QUESTIONS

1. Discovery generally may not begin before the Rule 26(f) discovery conference, although amendments adopted in 2015 allow the parties to serve early Rule 34 document requests. See Note 2, p. 664, infra. The parties may stipulate to discovery earlier than the Rule 26(f) conference, but if all parties do not agree, the court must give permission. Expedited discovery most typically is granted to resolve threshold issues such as subject-matter jurisdiction, personal jurisdiction, and qualified immunity. For example, in Strike 3 Holdings, LLC v. Doe subscriber assigned IP address 108.51.209.163, 2018 WL 385418 (D.D.C. 2018), a copyright infringement action, the court granted plaintiff expedited discovery to "learn Defendant's identity, investigate Defendant's role in the infringement, and effectuate service." The court applied a "good cause" standard" requiring the requestor to show the necessity of discovery for the suit to progress and a good faith belief that discovery would demonstrate the basis for the court's jurisdiction over defendant.

2. Would it be appropriate for a district court to expedite discovery on issues pertaining to the merits prior to the filing of a Rule 12(b)(6) motion? Could "plausibility" discovery be incorporated into a Rule 26(f) discovery plan and discussed at a Rule 16 conference? See Malveaux, *Front Loading and Heavy Lifting: How Pre-Dismissal Discovery Can Address the Detrimental Effect of* Iqbal *on Civil Rights Cases*, 14 Lewis & Clark L.Rev. 65 (2010).

2. AUTOMATIC DISCLOSURE

———

Read Federal Rule of Civil Procedure 26(a) and the accompanying materials in the Supplement.

———

The 1993 amendments to Federal Rule 26(a)(1), requiring automatic disclosure of specified categories of information, were controversial when promulgated. Justice Scalia filed a dissenting statement, joined by Justice Thomas and in part by Justice Souter, on the ground that the proposal introduced "into the trial process an element that is contrary to the nature of our adversary system." Amendments to Federal Rules of Civil Procedure, 146 F.R.D. 401, 507 (1993). See Bell, Varner & Gottschalk, *Automatic Disclosure in Discovery—The Rush to Reform*, 27 Ga.L.Rev. 1 (1992). Concerns also were expressed that the rule would increase cost and delay and decrease incentives to settle. See Issacharoff & Loewenstein,

Unintended Consequences of Mandatory Disclosure, 73 Tex.L.Rev. 753 (1995). In 2000, the duty of automatic disclosure was limited to information that the party intends to use. See Huang, *Mandatory Disclosure: A Controversial Device with No Effects*, 21 Pace L.Rev. 203 (2000).

In CUMMINGS v. GENERAL MOTORS CORP., 365 F.3d 944, 953–54 (10th Cir. 2004), abrogated on other grounds by Unitherm Food Systems, Inc. v. Swift-Eckrich, Inc., 546 U.S. 394, 126 S.Ct. 980, 163 L.Ed.2d 974 (2006), plaintiffs were car owners who had been severely injured in a car accident. They sued the manufacturer of their car's seat belt, alleging that it was defective and had been improperly designed. After a jury verdict for defendant, plaintiffs learned that defendant had videos of safety seat acceleration tests that it had conducted and failed to disclose under Rule 26(a), but had produced in an unrelated trial. On appeal, they argued that defendant violated its discovery obligation. The Tenth Circuit disagreed:

> The magistrate ruled the newest version of Rule 26 would govern in this case, including the 2000 amendments, * * * and the Cummings did not object to this holding. Under the 2000 amendments, a party's "initial disclosure obligation . . . has been narrowed." Fed. R. Civ. P. 26 advisory committee's note, 2000 amends. Rule 26(a)(1) only requires automatic disclosure of "the name and, if known, the address and telephone number of each individual likely to have discoverable information that the disclosing party may use to support its claims or defenses" * * *. Under this rule, a party is not obligated "to disclose witnesses or documents, whether favorable or unfavorable, that it does not intend to use." Fed. R. Civ. P. 26 advisory committee's note, 2000 amends.; see Gluck v. Ansett Austl. Ltd., 204 F.R.D. 217, 221–22 (D.D.C. 2001) (holding under the new version of Rule 26 that the opposing party was not required to produce information with regard to potential witnesses because "the essential inquiry is whether the disclosing party intends to use the witness.").

As you read more about the mechanics of discovery, see p. 619, infra, consider how a party should follow-up an adversary's automatic disclosures with information requests under the Rules.

NOTES AND QUESTIONS

1.   Does Federal Rule 26(a) require the actual production of documents? Should the court compel further disclosure if the disclosing party provides redacted copies of documents?

2.   Automatic disclosure is required of the computation of each category of damages claimed by the disclosing party, who also must disclose documents "on which each computation is based." Rule 26(a)(1)(A)(iii). In City and County of San Francisco v. Tutor-Saliba Corp., 218 F.R.D. 219 (N.D.Cal. 2003),

plaintiffs provided damage estimates and identified supporting documents, but defendants moved to compel further supplementation. Acknowledging that Rule 26 "does not elaborate on the level of specificity required in the initial damages disclosure," the district court said that the standard for adequacy "must be gleaned from Rule 26(a)'s purpose: to 'accelerate the exchange of basic information' that is 'needed in most cases to prepare for trial or make an informed decision about settlement,'" quoting from the 1993 Advisory Committee notes. An additional factor in the court's view was the role of early disclosure "to assist the parties in focusing and prioritizing their organization of discovery." Given these purposes, plaintiff was required to provide "some analysis and not just a "lump sum statement of the damages allegedly sustained" to enable defendants to understand the scope of their exposure to liability "and make informed decisions as to settlement and discovery." Id. at 220–22.

3. Until 1970, insurance agreements were not discoverable under Rule 26. The rule was amended in favor of disclosure to "enable counsel for both sides to make the same realistic appraisal of the case, so that settlement and litigation strategy are based on knowledge and not speculation." Proposed Amendments to the Federal Rules of Civil Procedure Relating to Discovery, reprinted at 48 F.R.D. 487, 499 (1969–70). How does Rule 26(a)(1)(iv) currently treat disclosure of insurance policies?

4. What types of proceedings are exempt from automatic disclosure? Are they actions in which there is little need for discovery? Or in which one of the parties is likely to appear pro se? Does the court have discretion to mandate disclosure in these cases? See Subrin, *Uniformity in Procedural Rules and the Attributes of a Sound Procedural System: The Case for Presumptive Limits*, 49 Ala.L.Rev. 79 (1997).

5. Some state discovery rules require automatic disclosure of categories of information. See Allen, Price & Donison, *Federal Discovery under the* 2000 *Amendments to Rule* 26, 3 Sedona Conf.J. 211 (2002) (Arizona); Moskowitz, *Rediscovering Discovery: State Procedural Rules and the Level Playing Field*, 54 Rutgers L.Rev. 595 (2002) (Arizona, Colorado, Illinois, and Texas). West Virginia, although it models its discovery rules on those of the federal system, elected not to require automatic disclosure. See Olds, *Give It to Me Uniformly: West Virginia Wants Initial Disclosure*, 115 W.Va.L.Rev. 363 (2012).

3. CERTIFICATION AND THE DUTY TO SUPPLEMENT

The parties have a duty to cooperate throughout the discovery process that is enforced through the signature requirement of Federal Rule 26(g). Specifically, "Rule 26(g) imposes an affirmative duty to engage in pretrial discovery in a responsible manner that is consistent with the spirit and purposes of rules 26 through 37." Heller v. City of Dallas, 303 F.R.D. 466, 476 (N.D.Tex. 2014) (quoting the Advisory Committee's note to Rule 26(g) (1983)).

Consistent with this obligation, Rule 26(g) operates as the discovery analogue to Rule 11. Every automatic disclosure, every party-initiated request for discovery, every response to discovery, and every objection must be signed by at least one counsel of record or by the party if not represented by counsel. The signature certifies that to the best of the signer's knowledge, information, and belief, the document presented is accurate and complete and is being served for a proper purpose. Moreover, the proponent is certifying that a reasonable inquiry has been made before submitting the document. Unsigned discovery documents are to be stricken unless the proponent provides substantial justification for the omission. Moreover, the court has authority to impose a sanction on a party that violates the requirement, including dismissal of the action.

Finally, Rule 26(e) imposes a self-executing duty to supplement automatic disclosures and discovery responses. The duty is triggered even if the original disclosure or response was accurate when made; the duty is to provide information or documents that are obtained later and is a "continuing obligation." Robbins & Myers, Inc. v. J.M. Huber Corp., 274 F.R.D. 63, 79 (W.D.N.Y. 2011). A failure to supplement is subject to sanctions. Sanctions are discussed later in this chapter, see p. 662, infra.

E. THE MECHANICS OF REQUESTED DISCOVERY

1. DEPOSITIONS

———

Read Federal Rules of Civil Procedure 26(d), 30, and 31 and the accompanying materials in the Supplement.

———

An oral deposition allows a party to question any person (the "deponent"), whether a party or not, under oath. The Federal Rules spell out in detail when, how, before whom, and on what notice as to time and place a deposition may be taken. See Rules 28, 29, 30, 31, and 32(d). Invariably, the parties designate as officer the reporter who records the questions, the answers, and any objections made by the parties or by the witness. See Rule 30(b)(5). Under Rule 30(d)(1), "a deposition is limited to 1 day of 7 hours," but the court may authorize additional time "if needed to fairly examine the deponent or if the deponent, another person, or any other circumstance impedes or delays the examination." When the deposition is concluded, the reporter prepares a transcript, which the deponent then is called upon to sign. Federal Rule 30(a)(2)(A)(i) currently sets a presumptive limit of ten depositions for each party.

An attorney schedules a deposition by serving a notice on the opposing attorney. The notice must include the name and address of the deponent, if known, and the date, time, and place of the deposition. If the deponent is a party, the notice is sufficient to require the party's appearance, and a subpoena is unnecessary. The notice may include a demand that the party produce documents and other items of evidence at the deposition, in which case the procedure of Rule 34 applies.

Under Federal Rule 30(b)(6) a party may seek, by notice or subpoena, the deposition of a corporation or association and require it to produce a person or persons who will testify on behalf of the organization. Of course, the party seeking the information must, with "reasonable particularity," detail the issues that are to be explored in order for the organization to ascertain which witness or witnesses have the relevant knowledge. Witnesses who do not already have knowledge of the topics that will be the subject of the deposition must be educated with documents and other "information known or reasonably available to the organization." This form of corporate deposition is especially useful when the party taking the deposition is unaware of which individual or individuals within a large organization have the information that is needed. Amendments to Rule 30(b)(6) in 2020 direct the parties to confer "in good faith about the matters for examination" either "[b]efore or promptly after" the notice of deposition or subpoena is served. If the deponent is not a party, the notice of deposition will not be sufficient to compel the nonparty's appearance. There is no requirement that a nonparty be subpoenaed to a deposition. However, a nonparty who is not subpoenaed and does not appear, or if does appear but fails to bring requested documents or other items, is not subject to sanction. A person who fails to respond to a subpoena will be subject to a citation for contempt of court. In addition, if a party notices a deposition but does not subpoena the witness and the witness fails to appear, that party may be ordered to pay the reasonable expenses, including attorney's fees, of any other party for wasted time appearing at the place where the deposition was to be taken. Thus, unless full cooperation of the nonparty witness is certain, the use of a subpoena is advisable.

The usual expectation is that a deposition will proceed without court involvement. The deponent usually will answer even those questions to which counsel object, unless the deponent's counsel instructs the deponent not to answer. Objections are interposed at depositions to preserve a right to object to another party's use of the deposition's transcript at trial. Counsel must object at the deposition if the ground for the objection is one that might be corrected at the time. Under Rule 30(c)(2), a deponent may be instructed not to answer only when necessary "to preserve a privilege, to enforce a limitation ordered by the court, or to present a motion under Rule 30(d)(3)" to terminate or limit an examination that is oppressive or conducted in bad faith. Moreover, Rule 30(d)(2) authorizes the imposition of costs and attorney's fees to sanction any culpable individual who "impedes, delays, or frustrates the fair examination of the deponent."

POLYCAST TECHNOLOGY CORP. V. UNIROYAL, INC.

United States District Court, Southern District of New York, 1990.
1990 WL 138968.

FRANCIS IV, UNITED STATES MAGISTRATE.

In October, 1986, Uniroyal, Inc. ("Uniroyal") sold its wholly-owned subsidiary, Uniroyal Plastics Company, Inc. ("Plastics") to Polycast Technology Corporation ("Polycast"). In this action, Polycast alleges that it entered into this transaction on the basis of misleading financial information that Uniroyal provided about Plastics. * * *

The parties to this action have taken substantial discovery from a non-party, Deloitte & Touche ("Deloitte"). In its incarnation as Deloitte Haskins & Sells, Deloitte had performed auditing services for both Uniroyal and Polycast prior to the sale of Plastics. After the transaction was completed, Deloitte continued as Polycast's independent auditors, reviewing Plastics' operations.

* * *

The second pending discovery issue concerns the proposed deposition of Gregory Durant, a Deloitte employee who was the on-site manager of an audit of Plastics that commenced immediately after the acquisition of that entity by Uniroyal on October 31, 1986. Deloitte now seeks a protective order barring Mr. Durant's deposition on the grounds that the information obtained would not be relevant and that it would, in any event, be duplicative of the deposition testimony of Michael Bowman, Deloitte's engagement partner on the audit.

Orders barring the taking of * * * depositions altogether are both unusual and disfavored. * * * On the other hand, non-party witnesses may be subject to somewhat greater protection against costly but marginally relevant discovery than are the parties. * * *

However, even if some heightened consideration should be paid to Deloitte as a non-party witness, it would still be inappropriate to foreclose the deposition of Mr. Durant. Polycast alleges that it bought Plastics in reliance on a representation in October, 1986, that the year-end earnings of Plastics would be approximately $13.3 million. According to Polycast, the actual 1986 earnings for Plastics were $5.25 million, and Polycast therefore contends that it paid an inflated price for Plastics based on Uniroyal's misrepresentations. Uniroyal argues, however, that Polycast has understated the actual earnings of Plastics for 1986. Since the $5.5 million figure is derived at least in part from the audit conducted by Deloitte for the first ten months of that year, that audit is an entirely proper subject of inquiry. Moreover, the fact that Mr. Bowman has provided substantial deposition testimony about the audit does not relieve Deloitte of the obligation of producing Mr. Durant for examination. There were some gaps in Mr. Bowman's testimony, attributable to a quite understandable inability to recall every detail of the audit process. More significantly, Mr. Durant was present at the location where the audit was conducted and is in a better position to describe the workings of the audit team and its interactions with Plastics' employees. His deposition will therefore go forward.

At the same time, Uniroyal has already obtained from other Deloitte witnesses as well as from discovery of the parties substantial evidence concerning the audit. Mr. Durant's role will largely be to fill in the interstices in a picture that should otherwise be substantially complete. Accordingly, the parties' examination of him shall be limited to one full day of deposition.

* * *

NOTES AND QUESTIONS

1.   The oral deposition has been called "[t]he most important of the discovery devices":

> It is the only significant discovery device that may be directed against any person and is not confined to parties to the action. It is the only discovery device that permits examination and cross-examination of a live witness by counsel, where there is no opportunity to reflect and carefully shape the information given. Thus, despite its expense, it is the most valuable device if the deponent has important information.

Wright & Kane, Law of Federal Courts § 84 (8th ed.). Under the 1938 version of Federal Rule 30, the parties competed to take the first deposition, in an attempt to pin down an opponent before submitting himself or his own witnesses to the discovery process. How has deposition strategy changed under the amended discovery rules?

2.   When the Federal Rules were first adopted, depositions typically were recorded by court reporters using stenography. In 1970, the Rules were amended to allow for the taking of videotaped depositions by stipulation of the parties or by court order. The 1993 amendment gives the party noticing the deposition a right to choose how the deposition will be memorialized. Numerous advantages are attached to videotaped depositions: "Video depositions can markedly increase accuracy and trustworthiness. In addition, to the extent that a video deposition reduces tedium, the fact-finder's concentration and attention will be enhanced, again to the benefit of the decision process." Rice's Toyota World, Inc. v. Southeast Toyota Distributors, Inc., 114 F.R.D. 647, 649 (M.D.N.C. 1987). Why might a written transcript be useful?

2. DEPOSITION BY WRITTEN QUESTIONS

Federal Rule 31 authorizes the taking of depositions by written questions from parties and nonparties. The answers are given orally after the "officer" puts the questions to the deponent. In practice, written depositions are rarely used. Rule 31 saves the expense of travel, but the procedure is said to be "cumbersome" relative to an oral deposition. Wright & Kane, Law of Federal Courts § 85 (8th ed.). Unlike interrogatories to parties under Rule 33, which are also written, depositions by written questions may be propounded to "any person," including a nonparty.

A deposition upon written questions was used in WATSON v. LOWCOUNTRY RED CROSS, 974 F.2d 482 (4th Cir. 1992), a wrongful death action on behalf of an infant who died from HIV following a blood transfusion. The suit alleged that the Red Cross had negligently screened the blood donor, and sought discovery from the donor. To preserve confidentiality, the court permitted plaintiff to submit written questions to the donor's lawyer, to which the Red Cross could object. Questions included:

1. On how many occasions in your life have you donated blood?

* * *

5. When you gave blood on February 26 or 27, 1985, were you asked about any diseases or behaviors or experiences that put you at risk for these diseases? * * *

9. On February 26 or 27, 1985, in the course of your preparing to give blood, did the Red Cross staff or volunteers give you any written or verbal information about AIDS risks? * * *

13. On February 26 & 27, 1985 could you read? * * *

Id. at 490. Why might defendant's counsel have preferred a Rule 31 deposition rather than an oral one? Why was this approach used rather than Rule 33 interrogatories?

3. INTERROGATORIES TO PARTIES

Read Federal Rule of Civil Procedure 33 and the accompanying materials in the Supplement.

Written interrogatories allow one party to send to another a series of questions to be answered under oath within a specific time. The procedure is extremely simple. No court order is required and no officers need be appointed; the entire exchange is accomplished by mail. If a question is thought to be improper, the responding party may say so rather than answering. The interrogating party then has the option of seeking a court order requiring an answer. An important advantage of interrogatories exists to the extent that a party has a duty to respond to interrogatories not only on the basis of her own knowledge but also with regard to the knowledge of other persons, including her lawyers, employees, and other agents, that reasonably can be obtained through investigation. Under Federal Rule 33(b)(1)(B) such an obligation clearly exists for a party who is a public or private corporation, an association, or a government entity. What is the obligation of an individual under Rule 33(b)(1)(A)?

Interrogatories had been cited as the most abused of the available discovery devices and the Federal Rules have been amended a number of times to police the process. In 1980, then Rule 33(c) (now Rule 33(d)), was amended to require a party exercising the option to produce its business records to specify the records from which the answer can be found in sufficient detail to permit the interrogating party to locate and to identify them as readily as can the party served. The clarification sought to prevent the party served with interrogatories from directing the party who propounded them to a mass of business records or by offering to make all their records available.

In 1993, Rule 33(a) was amended to impose a presumptive limit on the number of interrogatories, including discrete parts, that a party can serve. Although the requirement cannot be evaded through use of subparts, the Notes of the Advisory Committee indicate that "a question asking about communications of a particular type should be treated as a single interrogatory" even though it asks for a number of specific details regarding the particular communication.

Rule 33 interrogatories have several advantages relative to depositions. Typically their use is less expensive, and can help narrow and frame issues in the dispute. Moreover, they are effective when requesting technical, statistical, or logistical information. Nevertheless, interrogatories often are the target of criticism and are said to be "tailor-made for abuse." Rennie, *The End of Interrogatories: Why* Twombly *and* Iqbal *Should Finally Stop Rule* 33 *Abuse*, 15 Lewis & Clark L.Rev. 191, 263 (2011). One particular problem has been the use of boilerplate objections that do not advance and instead delay the proceedings. See Jarvey, *Boilerplate Discovery Objections: How They Are Used, Why They Are Wrong, and What We Can Do About Them*, 61 Duke L.Rev. 913 (2013). How might greater judicial oversight reduce abusive interrogatory practice?

CABLE & COMPUTER TECHNOLOGY, INC.
v. LOCKHEED SAUNDERS, INC.

United States District Court, Central District of California, 1997.
175 F.R.D. 646.

CHAPMAN, UNITED STATES MAGISTRATE JUDGE.

[The complaint alleged breach of contract, fraud, and other claims in connection with loss of a contract to provide radar simulators to the Air Force in favor of defendant's affiliated entities.]

* * *

The defendants seek to compel responses to defendant Lockheed Martin Corp.'s (hereafter defendant Lockheed) First Set of Special Interrogatories, interrogatory nos. 1, 5 through 11, and 14 through 16.[3] The plaintiff has objected to all of these interrogatories on the grounds they are "contention interrogatories" and, therefore, improper, citing In re Convergent Technologies Securities Litigation, 108 F.R.D. 328, 345–49 (N.D.Cal.1985).

> [T]he phrase 'contention interrogatory' is used imprecisely to refer to many different kinds of questions. Some people would classify as a contention interrogatory any question that asks another party to indicate what it contends. Some people would define contention interrogatories as embracing only questions that ask another party whether it makes some specified contention. . . . Another kind of question . . . asks an opposing party to state all the facts on which it bases some specified contention. Yet another form of this category of interrogatory asks an opponent to state all the evidence on which it bases some specified contention. Some contention interrogatories ask the responding party to take a position, and then to explain or defend that position, with respect to how the law applies to facts. A variation on this theme involves interrogatories that ask parties to spell out the legal basis for, or theory behind, some specified contention.

Id. at 332.

The Advisory Committee Notes to the 1970 amendment of Rule 33(b) (now Rule 33(c)), explain succinctly the reason for Rule 33(c), as it now reads:

---

[3] Interrogatory no. 1 asks plaintiff to describe "each component of damages YOU claim YOU have suffered as a result of the acts or omissions YOU allege in the Complaint, including, but not limited, stating the dollar amount of each, and how much was calculated."

Interrogatory nos. 5, 6, 7, 10, 11, 14, 15 and 16 ask plaintiff to state all facts upon which a particular, specified allegation in the Complaint is based.

Interrogatory nos. 8 and 9 ask plaintiff to identify documents, statements or actions specifically and particularly alleged in the Complaint.

There are numerous and conflicting decisions on the question whether and to what extent interrogatories are limited to matters 'of fact,' or may elicit opinions, contentions, and legal conclusions. [¶] Rule 33 is amended to provide that an interrogatory is not objectionable merely because it calls for an opinion or contention that relates to fact or the application of law to fact. Efforts to draw sharp lines between facts and opinions have been invariably unsuccessful, and the clear trend of the cases is to permit 'factual' opinions. . . .

* * * Further, if the concern in answering a contention interrogatory before discovery has been completed, or even substantially done, is that the answer to the interrogatory may limit the party's proof at trial, that concern is misplaced in that, among other things, the trial court may permit the withdrawal or amendment of an answer to an interrogatory. Wright, Miller & Marcus, Federal Practice and Procedure: Civil § 2181 at 344 (2d ed.1994) * * *.

* * *

In *Convergent Technologies*, Judge Wayne D. Brazil, in a very thoughtful opinion, held that the 1983 amendments to Fed.R.Civ.P. 26(b) compelled his conclusion that the "wisest course is not to preclude entirely the early use of contention interrogatories, but to place a burden of justification on the party who seeks answers to these kinds of questions before substantial documentary or testimonial discovery has been completed* * *." More recently, however, Judge Brazil has modified his position, noting that contention interrogatories may in certain cases be the most reliable and cost-effective discovery device, which would be less burdensome than depositions at which contention questions are propounded. * * *

Applying the foregoing principles, this Court prefers to consider contention interrogatories in the same manner it would consider any interrogatory, placing the burden on the party opposing discovery rather than shifting the burden to the proponent of the contention interrogatories to justify their propoundment. Thus, although it is too early for plaintiff to provide expert opinions on the subject of damages, plaintiff may, at this time, answer interrogatory no. 1 based on the information it has to date. Of course, plaintiff may later amend its answer with leave of Court or supplement it, as it has an obligation to do under Fed.R.Civ.P. 26(e). The other disputed interrogatories, interrogatory nos. 5 through 11 and 14 through 16, are straightforward "factual" contention interrogatories which plaintiff should also be able to answer now. Requiring the answer to these "factual" contention interrogatories is * * * [consistent with Rule 11]."

4. DISCOVERY AND PRODUCTION OF PROPERTY

———

Read Federal Rules of Civil Procedure 34 and 45 and the accompanying materials in the Supplement.

———

Federal Rule 34 allows a party to request other parties to produce documents, electronically stored information, and tangible things in their possession or control. The Rule also allows a party entry to the other parties' land or property for such activities as inspection, survey, or measurement. A request must describe the items to be discovered "with reasonable particularity," a standard that varies with circumstances. Rule 34(b)(1)(D) and (E) address the production of electronically stored information.

Most courts allow discovery of general categories of items if the description is easily understood (e.g., all written communications between plaintiff and defendant from July 1 to September 1, 2015). Many attorneys combine Rule 33 interrogatories that ask the opposing party to identify documents with a Rule 34 request that the party produce "all documents identified" in the opposing party's answers to the interrogatories. Although the standard for requesting documents is a flexible one, the writing of a request calls for a great deal of precision.

A request must specify a reasonable time, place, and manner for the inspection. The time usually is set at least 30 days after service of the request because the opposing party generally has at least 30 days to respond. The place typically designated for production of documents is the office of the requesting party's attorney, unless it is more convenient to examine the documents where they are kept or to have them copied at some other place. Since 1980, Rule 34 has required that the producer of documents for inspection "shall produce them in the usual course of business or shall organize and label them to correspond with the categories of the request."

The party that receives a request serves a written response on the requesting party, as well as any other parties to the lawsuit, within the time specified by Rule 34. The response states the responding party's objections, if any, to part or all of the requested production or inspection. Absent objection, the responding party must produce the documents as requested, or admit counsel to its premises for the scheduled inspection. Amendments adopted in 2015 make clear that objections to document production must be stated with particularity.

Although Rule 34 is limited to parties, amendments to Rule 45 (adopted in 1991) set forth a similar procedure to obtain material from nonparties. If the request for production of documents or inspection of premises is addressed to a nonparty, the litigant must serve a subpoena pursuant to Rule 45. Rule 45 now provides that an attorney may issue a subpoena commanding any person to give testimony, to produce and permit inspection and copying of designated records or other tangible objects, or to permit inspection of premises.

NOTES AND QUESTIONS

1.   Federal Rule 34 originally was limited to the production of documents and things "material to any matter involved in the action" and only on a showing of "good cause," but currently is governed by the relevance and proportionality factors of Rule 26(b). See 8B Wright, Miller & Marcus, Federal Practice and Procedure § 2201 (3d ed.).

2.   Rule 34 allows discovery of documents and things in the "possession, custody, or control" of a party. Does a client control information that is in its counsel's hands? Courts have held that because a client has the right "to obtain copies of documents gathered or created by its attorneys pursuant to their representation of that client, such documents are clearly within the client's control." Am. Soc. For Prevention of Cruelty to Animals v. Ringling Bros. and Barnum & Bailey Circus, 233 F.R.D. 209, 212 (D.D.C. 2006). Would a party be considered to control documents in the following circumstances?

(a)   The party has given the documents to the party's insurance carrier;

(b)   The documents are in the custody of the party's wholly-owned subsidiary;

(c)   The documents are in the custody of the party's former corporate employee; or

(d)   The documents are in the custody of a foreign-based subsidiary.

Should the touchstone be legal control over the custodian of the documents or some other factor?

3.   How might a party sequence its use of discovery to ensure that document requests are made with the requisite specificity? Amendments adopted in 2015 allow the parties to serve early Rule 34 document requests prior to the Rule 26(f) conference, but responses are not due until 30 days after the conference has taken place. How might the early service of a document request aid the parties in devising their discovery plan?

4.   The Federal Rules were adopted before the computers and other electronic devices came into existence. The rules, however, have been adapted and amended to deal with technological change. In 1970, Federal Rule 34 was amended to include "data compilations from which information can be obtained" as among the documents that can be requested under the rule. Rule 34 was amended in 2006 to make clear that under Rule 34(a) electronically stored information is discoverable when "stored in any medium" from which it

can be obtained, "translated, if necessary" into a "reasonably usable form." Allman, *Conducting E-Discovery After the Amendments: The Second Wave*, 10 Sedona Conf.J. 215, 216 (2009). Electronic information is discoverable even when it is transitory or temporary.

5.   Rule 26(b)(2)(B) limits the burden of electronic discovery by identifying a category of information that is "not reasonably accessible." The Advisory Committee's Note to the 2006 amendments explains:

> The decision whether to require a responding party to search for and produce information that is not reasonably accessible depends not only on the burdens and costs of doing so, but also on whether those burdens and costs can be justified in the circumstances of the case. Appropriate considerations may include: (1) the specificity of the discovery request; (2) the quantity of information available from other and more easily accessed sources; (3) the failure to produce relevant information that seems likely to have existed but is no longer available on more easily accessed sources; (4) the likelihood of finding relevant, responsive information that cannot be obtained from other, more easily accessed sources; (5) predictions as to the importance and usefulness of the further information; (6) the importance of the issues at stake in the litigation; and (7) the parties' resources.

The Advisory Committee drew guidance from the district court's decision in ZUBULAKE v. UBS WARBURG LLC, 217 F.R.D. 309 (S.D.N.Y. 2003), an employment discrimination suit. Plaintiff sought discovery of emails exchanged by defendants' employees that were stored on backup tapes and optical disks. Each employee received about 200 emails a day, and, under federal securities law, defendant was required to preserve all communications for a fixed number of years. Defendant resisted producing the materials, arguing that "restoring those e-mails would cost approximately $175,000.00, exclusive of attorney time in reviewing the e-mails." Id. at 312. The district court identified seven factors to consider in assessing whether to require disclosure but to shift the costs of discovery:

1.   The extent to which the request is specifically tailored to discover relevant information;

2.   The availability of such information from other sources;

3.   The total cost of production, compared to the amount-in-controversy;

4.   The total cost of production, compared to the resources available to each party;

5.   The relative ability of each party to control costs and its incentive to do so;

6.   The importance of the issues at stake in the litigation; and

7.   The relative benefits to the parties of obtaining the information.

Id. at 322. Are any other factors relevant to the analysis?

6. Complicated discovery issues have arisen with respect to metadata, which essentially are data that describe other data. Metadata range from useful to absolutely necessary in the interpretation of original data. Before computers, metadata were included in library cards describing books, naming the author, publishing company and date, length of the book, and so on. In digital data, metadata might be descriptive; for an image file, it might include the resolution of the picture, the date and location and type of camera on which it was taken, while metadata of a text file might include a word count and the name of the author. This can be particularly important in looking at database files—without metadata, a database could look like hundreds of thousands of entries of seemingly random numbers, but with metadata, those numbers could be interpreted as dates, times, employee ID numbers, dollar amounts, ISBNs, or other meaningful information.

7. "Predictive coding," sometimes referred to as "technology assisted review ("TAR"), is a computerized process by which a random sampling of documents is reviewed manually and determined to be responsive or unresponsive to the discovery request. See Yablon & Landsman-Roos, *Predictive Coding: Emerging Questions and Concerns*, 64 S.C.L.Rev. 633 (2013). Predictive coding algorithms and heuristics are applied to analyze the sample set, and the data are used to create a programming protocol that can be applied to the rest of the discovery materials. Using that protocol, a computer program combs through the remaining materials and labels documents responsive or unresponsive based on the sample data. An influential example of this method is reported in Moore v. Publicis Groupe SA, 2012 WL 2574742 (S.D.N.Y. 2012). For an empirical analysis of the costs of discovery responses in cases involving digital information, see Pace & Zakaras, Where the Money Goes: Understanding Litigant Expenditures for Producing Electronic Discovery, RAND Institute for Civil Justice (2012). For an example of how courts resolve disputes between parties about the use of particular methods of TAR, see Livingston v. City of Chicago, 2020 WL 5253848 (N.D.Ill. Sept. 3, 2020).

8. The explosion in the volume of electronically stored information has meant that parties in litigation often confer on search terms to narrow the range of items, such as emails, that must be reviewed for responsiveness to a document request. This approach to document requests involving electronic documents is consistent with Rule 26(f)(3)(C), which requires a discovery plan to address "issues about disclosure, discovery, or preservation of electronically stored information," but the rules do not directly require it. Nonetheless, courts can react harshly when litigants do not cooperate in formulating search terms for electronic discovery.

In PYLE v. SELECTIVE INSURANCE CO. OF AMERICA, 2016 WL 5661749 (W.D.Pa. Sept. 30, 2016), an employment discrimination case, plaintiff served defendant with a document request for "all emails, correspondence, memorandum, and/or other documents" relating to her employment and receipt of disability benefits, and to the termination of her employment. Defendant's counsel asked plaintiff's counsel for a "suggested list of search terms . . . so that we can agree on a common set of terms so that the electronic records [defendant] has gathered can be searched for relevance." Id. at *1. Plaintiff's counsel would not offer search terms to defendant and argued that there was no authority to support the request. The district court granted defendant's motion to compel:

> Plaintiff's argument totally misses the mark; in fact, it borders on being incomprehensible. Far from being baseless, Defendant's request is entirely consistent with both the letter and spirit of the Federal Rules of Civil Procedure regarding the discovery of electronically stored information and this Court's Local Rules. It is well settled by now that "electronic discovery should be a party-driven process." Romero v. Allstate Ins. Co., 271 F.R.D. 96, 109 (E.D. Pa. 2010) (internal citation omitted). The Federal Rules expressly require counsel to meet and confer on "any issues about disclosure, discovery, or preservation of electronically stored information, including the form or forms in which it should be produced[.]" Fed. R. Civ. P. 26(f)(3)(C). "Among the items about which the court expects counsel to 'reach practical agreement' without the court having to micro-manage e-discovery are 'search terms, date ranges, key players and the like.' " Romero, 271 F.R.D. at 109 * * * . Indeed, this principle is incorporated into this Court's Local Rules, which direct counsel to "meet and confer, and attempt to agree, on the discovery of ESI, including . . . an ESI search protocol, including methods to filter data, such as application of search terms or date ranges." LCvR 26.2(C). Accordingly, Defendant's motion is GRANTED insofar as it seeks to compel Plaintiff to confer and come to an agreement on the search terms Defendant will use to cull through the additional email archives that Defendant has identified as having been retrieved. * * *

Id. at *2.

5. PHYSICAL AND MENTAL EXAMINATIONS

———

Read Federal Rule of Civil Procedure 35 and the accompanying materials in the Supplement.

———

In many lawsuits, a party will need to have its own medical professionals physically examine an adverse party whose condition is in controversy. However, a compelled medical examination involves an intrusion on a person's privacy, and some medical tests can entail discomfort and pain. Federal Rule 35 requires a court order for an examination and imposes strict standards. A court can force a party to submit to examination or to make persons under their legal custody or control available for examination. But the person's physical or mental condition must be in controversy, and the movant must show "good cause" to compel the examination. The determination of good cause involves weighing the pain, danger, or intrusiveness of the examination against the need for, or usefulness of, the information to be gained.

In practice, most physical and mental examinations occur as a result of agreements between attorneys. The primary effect of Rule 35 is to encourage parties to stipulate to examinations. Examinations are routine in personal injury actions, as well as in litigation involving issues of paternity, incompetence, and undue influence. Of course, the Rule is available in those cases in which the parties cannot agree. Stipulations typically address questions concerning the time and place of the examination, and the procedures to be used. Rule 35 gives the examined party the right to a copy of the examiner's report, even if he or she submitted to an examination without the compulsion of a court order.

SCHLAGENHAUF V. HOLDER

Supreme Court of the United States, 1964.
379 U.S. 104, 85 S.Ct. 234, 13 L.Ed.2d 152.

Certiorari to the United States Court of Appeals for the Seventh Circuit.

JUSTICE GOLDBERG delivered the opinion of the Court.

This case involves the validity and construction of Rule 35(a) of the Federal Rules of Civil Procedure as applied to the examination of a defendant in a negligence action. * * *

An action based on diversity of citizenship was brought in the District Court seeking damages arising from personal injuries suffered by passengers of a bus which collided with the rear of a tractor-trailer. The named defendants were The Greyhound Corporation, owner of the bus; petitioner, Robert L. Schlagenhauf, the bus driver; Contract Carriers, Inc., owner of the tractor; Joseph L. McCorkhill, driver of the tractor; * * * and National Lead Company, owner of the trailer. Answers were filed by each of the defendants denying negligence.

Greyhound then cross-claimed against Contract Carriers and National Lead for damage to Greyhound's bus, alleging that the collision was due solely to their negligence in that the tractor-trailer was driven at an unreasonably low speed, had not remained in its lane, and was not equipped with proper rear lights. Contract Carriers filed an answer to this cross-claim denying its negligence and asserting "[t]hat the negligence of the driver of the * * * bus [petitioner Schlagenhauf] proximately caused and contributed to * * * Greyhound's damages."

* * *

Contract Carriers and National Lead then petitioned the District Court for an order directing petitioner Schlagenhauf to submit to both mental and physical examinations by one specialist in each of the following fields:

(1) Internal medicine;

(2) Ophthalmology;

(3) Neurology; and

(4) Psychiatry.

For the purpose of offering a choice to the District Court of one specialist in each field, the petition recommended two specialists in internal medicine, ophthalmology, and psychiatry, respectively, and three specialists in neurology—a total of nine physicians. The petition alleged that the mental and physical condition of Schlagenhauf was "in controversy" as it had been raised by Contract Carriers' answer to Greyhound's cross-claim. This was supported by a brief of legal authorities and an affidavit of Contract Carriers' attorney stating that Schlagenhauf had seen red lights 10 to 15 seconds before the accident, that another witness had seen the rear lights of the trailer from a distance of three-quarters to one-half mile, and that Schlagenhauf had been involved in a prior accident.

* * *

While disposition of this petition was pending, National Lead filed its answer to Greyhound's cross-claim and itself "cross-claimed" against Greyhound and Schlagenhauf for damage to its trailer. * * *

The District Court, on the basis of the petition filed by Contract Carriers, and without any hearing, ordered Schlagenhauf to submit to nine examinations—one by each of the recommended specialists—despite the fact that the petition clearly requested a total of only four examinations.

Petitioner applied for a writ of mandamus in the Court of Appeals against the respondent, the District Court Judge, seeking to have set aside the order requiring his mental and physical examinations. The Court of Appeals denied mandamus, one judge dissenting * * *.

We granted certiorari to review undecided questions concerning the validity and construction of Rule 35. * * *

Rule 35 on its face applies to all "parties," which under any normal reading would include a defendant. Petitioner contends, however, that the application of the Rule to a defendant would be an unconstitutional invasion of his privacy, or, at the least, be a modification of substantive rights existing prior to the adoption of the Federal Rules of Civil Procedure and thus beyond the congressional mandate of the Rules Enabling Act.

These same contentions were raised [and rejected] in Sibbach v. Wilson & Co. * * * [p. 340, Note 2, supra] by a plaintiff in a negligence action who asserted a physical injury as a basis for recovery. * * * Petitioner does not challenge the holding in Sibbach as applied to plaintiffs. He contends, however, that it should not be extended to defendants. We can see no basis * * * for such a distinction. * * * Issues cannot be resolved by a doctrine of favoring one class of litigants over another.

We recognize that, insofar as reported cases show, this type of discovery in federal courts has been applied solely to plaintiffs, and that some early state cases seem to have proceeded on a theory that a plaintiff who seeks redress for injuries in a court of law thereby "waives" his right to claim the inviolability of his person. * * *

[The Court then rejected the "waiver" theory on the basis of language in the *Sibbach* case.] The chain of events leading to an ultimate determination on the merits begins with the injury of the plaintiff, an involuntary act on his part. Seeking court redress is just one step in this chain. If the plaintiff is prevented or deterred from this redress, the loss is thereby forced on him to the same extent as if the defendant were prevented or deterred from defending against the action.

* * *

Petitioner contends that even if Rule 35 is to be applied to defendants, which we have determined it must, nevertheless it should not be applied to him as he was not a party in relation to Contract Carriers and National Lead—the movants for the mental and physical examinations—at the time the examinations were sought. * * * While it is clear that the person to be examined must be a party to the case,[12] we are of the view that * * * Rule 35 only requires that the person to be examined be a party to the "action," not that he be an opposing party *vis-à-vis* the movant. There is no doubt that Schlagenhauf was a "party" to this "action" by virtue of the original complaint. * * * Insistence that the movant have filed a pleading against the person to be examined would have the undesirable result of an unnecessary proliferation of cross-claims and counterclaims and would not be in keeping with the aims of a liberal, nontechnical application of the Federal Rules. * * *

While the Court of Appeals held that petitioner was not a party *vis-à-vis* National Lead or Contract Carriers at the time the examinations were first sought, it went on to hold that he had become a party *vis-à-vis* National Lead by the time of a second order entered by the District Court

---

[12] Although petitioner was an agent of Greyhound, he was himself a party to the action. He is to be distinguished from one who is not a party but is, for example, merely the agent of a party.

and thus was a party within its rule. This second order, identical in all material respects with the first, was entered on the basis of supplementary petitions filed by National Lead and Contract Carriers. These petitions gave no new basis for the examinations, except for the allegation that petitioner's mental and physical condition had been additionally put in controversy by the National Lead answer and cross-claim, which had been filed subsequent to the first petition for examinations. Although the filing of the petition for mandamus intervened between these two orders, we accept, for purposes of this opinion, the determination of the Court of Appeals that this second order was the one before it and agree that petitioner was clearly a party at this juncture under any test.

Petitioner next contends that his mental or physical condition was not "in controversy" and "good cause" was not shown for the examinations, both as required by the express terms of Rule 35.

* * *

It is notable * * * that in none of the other discovery provisions is there a restriction that the matter be "in controversy," and only in Rule 34 is there Rule 35's requirement that the movant affirmatively demonstrate "good cause."[c]

This additional requirement of "good cause" was reviewed by Chief Judge Sobeloff in Guilford National Bank v. Southern R. Co., 297 F. 2d 921, 924 (C.A. 4th Cir.), in the following words:

> "* * * The specific requirement of good cause would be meaningless if good cause could be sufficiently established by merely showing that the desired materials are relevant, for the relevancy standard has already been imposed by Rule 26(b). Thus, by adding the words '* * * good cause * * *,' the Rules indicate that there must be greater showing of need under Rules 34 and 35 than under the other discovery rules."

The courts of appeals in other cases * * * have also recognized that Rule 34's good-cause requirement is not a mere formality, but is a plainly expressed limitation on the use of that Rule. This is obviously true as to the "in controversy" and "good cause" requirements of Rule 35. They are not met by mere conclusory allegations of the pleadings—nor by mere relevance to the case—but require an affirmative showing by the movant that each condition as to which the examination is sought is really and genuinely in controversy and that good cause exists for ordering each particular examination. Obviously, what may be good cause for one type of examination may not be so for another. The ability of the movant to obtain the desired information by other means is also relevant.

---

[c]   The "good cause" requirement was eliminated from Rule 34 in 1970.

Rule 35, therefore, requires discriminating application by the trial judge, who must decide, as an initial matter in every case, whether the party requesting a mental or physical examination or examinations has adequately demonstrated the existence of the Rule's requirements of "in controversy" and "good cause," which requirements, as the Court of Appeals in this case itself recognized, are necessarily related. 321 F.2d, at 51.* * *

Of course, there are situations where the pleadings alone are sufficient to meet these requirements. A plaintiff in a negligence action who asserts mental or physical injury * * * places that mental or physical injury clearly in controversy and provides the defendant with good cause for an examination to determine the existence and extent of such asserted injury. This * * * applies equally to a defendant who asserts his mental or physical condition as a defense to a claim, such as, for example, where insanity is asserted as a defense to a divorce action. * * *

Here, however, Schlagenhauf did not assert his mental or physical condition either in support of or in defense of a claim. His condition was sought to be placed in issue by other parties. Thus, under the principles discussed above, Rule 35 required that these parties make an affirmative showing that petitioner's mental or physical condition was in controversy and that there was good cause for the examinations requested. This, the record plainly shows, they failed to do.

The only allegations in the pleadings relating to this subject were the general conclusory statement in Contract Carriers' answer to the cross-claim that "Schlagenhauf was not mentally or physically capable of operating" the bus at the time of the accident and the limited allegation in National Lead's cross-claim that, at the time of the accident, "the eyes and vision of * * * Schlagenhauf was [sic] impaired and deficient."

The attorney's affidavit attached to the petition for the examinations provided:

> "That * * * Schlagenhauf, in his deposition * * * admitted that he saw red lights for 10 to 15 seconds prior to a collision with a semi-tractor trailer unit and yet drove his vehicle on without reducing speed and without altering the course thereof.

> The only eye-witness to this accident known to this affiant * * * testified that immediately prior to the impact between the bus and truck that he had also been approaching the truck from the rear and that he had clearly seen the lights of the truck for a distance of three-quarters to one-half mile to the rear thereof.

> * * * Schlagenhauf has admitted in his deposition * * * that he was involved in a [prior] similar type rear end collision. * * *"

This record cannot support even the corrected order which required one examination in each of the four specialties of internal medicine, ophthalmology, neurology, and psychiatry. * * * Nothing in the pleadings or affidavit would afford a basis for a belief that Schlagenhauf was suffering from a mental or neurological illness warranting wide-ranging psychiatric or neurological examinations. Nor is there anything stated justifying the broad internal medicine examination. * * *

The only specific allegation made in support of the four examinations ordered was that the "eyes and vision" of Schlagenhauf were impaired. Considering this in conjunction with the affidavit, we would be hesitant to set aside a visual examination if it had been the only one ordered. * * * However, as the case must be remanded to the District Court because of the other examinations ordered, it would be appropriate for the District Judge to reconsider also this order in light of the guidelines set forth in this opinion.

* * *

Accordingly, the judgment of the Court of Appeals is vacated and the case remanded to the District Court to reconsider the examination order in light of the guidelines herein formulated and for further proceedings in conformity with this opinion.

Vacated and remanded.

JUSTICE BLACK, with whom JUSTICE CLARK joins, concurring in part and dissenting in part.

* * *

In a collision case like this one, evidence concerning very bad eyesight or impaired mental or physical health which may affect the ability to drive is obviously of the highest relevance. It is equally obvious, I think, that when a vehicle continues down an open road and smashes into a truck in front of it although the truck is in plain sight and there is ample time and room to avoid collision, the chances are good that the driver has some physical, mental or moral defect. When such a thing happens twice, one is even more likely to ask, "What is the matter with that driver? Is he blind or crazy?" Plainly the allegations of the other parties were relevant and put the question of Schlagenhauf's health and vision "in controversy." * * *

JUSTICE DOUGLAS, dissenting in part.

* * * When the defendant's doctors examine plaintiff, they are normally interested only in answering a single question: did plaintiff in fact sustain the specific injuries claimed? But plaintiff's doctors will naturally be inclined to go on a fishing expedition in search of *anything* which will tend to prove that the defendant was unfit to perform the acts which resulted in the plaintiff's injury. And a doctor for a fee can easily discover

something wrong with any patient—a condition that in prejudiced medical eyes might have caused the accident. Once defendants are turned over to medical or psychiatric clinics for an analysis of their physical well-being and the condition of their psyche, the effective trial will be held there and not before the jury. There are no lawyers in those clinics to stop the doctor from probing this organ or that one, to halt a further inquiry, to object to a line of questioning. And there is no judge to sit as arbiter. The doctor or the psychiatrist has a holiday in the privacy of his office. The defendant is at the doctor's (or psychiatrist's) mercy; and his report may either overawe or confuse the jury and prevent a fair trial.

* * *

Neither the Court nor Congress up to today has determined that any person whose physical or mental condition is brought into question during some lawsuit must surrender his right to keep his person inviolate. Congress did, according to *Sibbach*, require a plaintiff to choose between his privacy and his purse; but before today it has not been thought that any other "party" had lost this historic immunity. Congress and this Court can authorize such a rule. But a rule suited to purposes of discovery against defendants must be carefully drawn in light of the great potential of blackmail.

* * *

[JUSTICE HARLAN's dissenting opinion is omitted.]

NOTE AND QUESTIONS

In Torres v. Time Manufacturing Company, 2012 WL 13006155, *3 (E.D.Mich. 2012), the district court ordered an independent medical examination and denied a request to have a third party present or a recording taken, finding no special need or good reason for either condition. The court underscored that "Rule 35(a) is silent on the question of whether a recording of the examination or observers should be allowed." Does Rule 35 permit counsel to be present at a Rule 35 examination? A friend? A personal physician? Under what circumstances might a court order these persons present at an examination? See Wyatt & Bales, *The Presence of Third Parties at Rule 35 Examinations*, 71 Temp.L.Rev. 103 (1998).

6.   REQUESTS TO ADMIT

Read Federal Rule of Civil Procedure 36 and the accompanying materials in the Supplement.

Federal Rule 36 authorizes a party to serve on another party written requests to admit the truth of certain matters of fact or of the application of law to fact, or the genuineness of a document or other evidence that may be used at trial. Rule 36 is not a true discovery device since it does not require the responding party to disclose information. Requests for admissions are used to shape information already known into statements that expedite the trial by limiting the issues in dispute and by obviating some of the formalities that control the introduction of evidence at trial. Although responses to other discovery devices are not conclusive proof and may be contradicted at trial, responses to Rule 36 requests constitute conclusive evidence, unless withdrawn, and cannot be contradicted at trial. However, requests for admissions may function as a discovery device if a party uses them early enough in the litigation to help identify the issues not in dispute and to target the remaining issues for discovery.

A request for admission may be served without the necessity of a court order at any time after the parties have conferred in accordance with Rule 26(d), although usually not later than thirty days before a fixed trial date. Rule 36 provides that each matter of admission must be set forth separately, but says nothing else about the format for requests. However, the now-abrogated Form 51 appended to the Federal Rules of Civil Procedure, which is reproduced in the Supplement, provides an illustration of a request for admissions.

The party who receives a request to admit must respond under oath and in timely fashion, admitting or denying each matter for which an admission is requested, or providing a detailed explanation why it cannot admit or deny the matter. The responding party also may object to a request because improperly phrased (as "vague," "ambiguous," "a compound sentence," or otherwise defectively drafted), or because it seeks privileged or protected information. The responding party may request a court to extend its time to respond. Rule 29 provides that counsel may stipulate to extend the time limits set forth in Rule 36 unless the stipulation would "interfere with the time set for completing discovery, for hearing a motion, or for trial."

If the party who receives a request to admit does nothing, the matter in the request is deemed admitted. The effects of Rule 36, unlike other discovery rules, are self-executing. Once the time to respond has passed, the requesting party can rely on the matters admitted and take no further discovery on those issues. If a party serves a late response, and the opponent refuses to accept it, a court may excuse the party's failure to respond in a timely manner. Likewise, a court may permit a party to withdraw or modify an admission in a timely response. In either situation, the court's decision turns on the degree of prejudice the requesting party will suffer because of its reliance on the admission. Because courts so frequently granted a responding party's request for relief from its failure to respond, leaving requesting parties uncertain about the validity of the admission, and, hence, the necessity of developing evidence for trial, Rule 36(a) was amended in 1970 to permit a requesting party to move for an order deeming the matter to be admitted. Thus, a litigant takes a serious risk by failing to respond to Requests for Admissions. The court may well find that the failure was not justified, that the admissions have been made, and that, as a result, summary judgment is appropriate.

Although Rule 36 and its state counterparts can be enormously useful, in practice requests for admissions are the least used of the discovery devices.

NOTES AND QUESTIONS

1.   Federal Rule 36 formerly limited requests for admissions to matters of "fact." The Rule was amended in 1970 and now permits requests for admissions to inquire into matters relating to facts, the application of law to fact, or opinions about either, and the genuineness of any described documents. A great deal of information can be learned about an opposing party through social media sites. Can a party use a request to admit in order to determine whether a party maintains a social media site, and then to secure authentication of the site for purposes of admissibility?

2.   What is a "reasonable inquiry" under Rule 36 and when is information not "readily obtainable" by an answering party? In Kay v. Lamar Advertising of South Dakota, Inc., 2008 WL 5221083 (D.S.D. 2008), the court held that before a responding party "gives the answer 'I don't know,'" it is required under the rule "to state that it has made reasonable inquiry to attempt to find out the answer to the request to admit and that it still cannot admit or deny the question after having sought information readily available to it." Id. at *6. The duty of reasonable investigation applies even if discovery is at its early stages. See Tolton v. Marty, 2011 WL 4625994 (D.S.D. 2011).

3.   Armour v. Knowles, 512 F.3d 147 (5th Cir. 2007), involved a copyright infringement suit against the popular musician known as Beyoncé for her song "Baby Boy." The district court granted summary judgment for defendant. The Fifth Circuit affirmed on an alternative ground that plaintiff had failed to show that defendant had access to the disputed song and so could not have copied it. The basis for the affirmance was plaintiff's answer to defendant's request for admission stating when he had sent a demo tape of the disputed song to Beyoncé.

F. SPECIAL PROBLEMS REGARDING THE SCOPE OF DISCOVERY

1. MATERIALS PREPARED IN ANTICIPATION OF TRIAL

Read Federal Rule of Civil Procedure 26(b)(3)' and the accompanying materials in the Supplement.

HICKMAN V. TAYLOR

Supreme Court of the United States, 1947.
329 U.S. 495, 67 S.Ct. 385, 91 L.Ed. 451.

Certiorari to the Circuit Court of Appeals for the Third Circuit.

JUSTICE MURPHY delivered the opinion of the Court.

This case presents an important problem under the Federal Rules * * * as to the extent to which a party may inquire into oral and written statements of witnesses, or other information, secured by an adverse party's counsel in the course of preparation for possible litigation after a claim has arisen. Examination into a person's files and records, including those resulting from the professional activities of an attorney, must be judged with care. It is not without reason that various safeguards have been established to preclude unwarranted excursions into the privacy of a man's work. At the same time, public policy supports reasonable and necessary inquiries. Properly to balance these competing interests is a delicate and difficult task.

On February 7, 1943, the tug "J.M. Taylor" sank while engaged in helping to tow a car float of the Baltimore & Ohio Railroad across the Delaware River at Philadelphia. The accident was apparently unusual in nature, the cause of it still being unknown. Five of the nine crew members were drowned. Three days later the tug owners and the underwriters employed a law firm, of which respondent Fortenbaugh is a member, to defend them against potential suits by representatives of the deceased crew members and to sue the railroad for damages to the tug.

A public hearing was held on March 4, 1943, before the United States Steamboat Inspectors, at which the four survivors were examined. This testimony was recorded and made available to all interested parties. Shortly thereafter, Fortenbaugh privately interviewed the survivors and took statements from them with an eye toward the anticipated litigation; the survivors signed these statements on March 29. Fortenbaugh also interviewed other persons believed to have some information relating to the accident and in some cases he made memoranda of what they told him. At the time when Fortenbaugh secured the statements of the survivors, representatives of two of the deceased crew members had been in communication with him. Ultimately claims were presented by representatives of all five of the deceased; four of the claims, however, were settled without litigation. The fifth claimant, petitioner herein, brought suit in a federal court under the Jones Act on November 26, 1943, naming as defendants the two tug owners, individually and as partners, and the railroad.

One year later, petitioner filed 39 interrogatories directed to the tug owners. The 38th interrogatory read: "State whether any statements of the members of the crews of the Tugs 'J.M. Taylor' and 'Philadelphia' or of any other vessel were taken in connection with the towing of the car float and the sinking of the Tug 'John M. Taylor'. Attach hereto exact copies of all such statements if in writing, and if oral, set forth in detail the exact provisions of any such oral statements or reports."

Supplemental interrogatories asked whether any oral or written statements, records, reports or other memoranda had been made concerning any matter relative to the towing operation, the sinking of the tug, the salvaging and repair of the tug, and the death of the deceased. If the answer was in the affirmative, the tug owners were then requested to set forth the nature of all such records, reports, statements or other memoranda.

The tug owners, through Fortenbaugh, answered all of the interrogatories except No. 38 and the supplemental ones just described. While admitting that statements of the survivors had been taken, they declined to summarize or set forth the contents. They did so on the ground that such requests called "for privileged matter obtained in preparation for litigation" and constituted "an attempt to obtain indirectly counsel's private files." It was claimed that answering these requests "would involve practically turning over not only the complete files, but also the telephone records and, almost, the thoughts of counsel."

In connection with the hearing on these objections, Fortenbaugh made a written statement and gave an informal oral deposition explaining the circumstances under which he had taken the statements. But he was not expressly asked in the deposition to produce the statements. The District Court for the Eastern District of Pennsylvania, sitting en banc, held that the requested matters were not privileged. 4 F.R.D. 479. The court then decreed that the tug owners and Fortenbaugh, as counsel and agent for the tug owners forthwith "Answer Plaintiff's 38th interrogatory and supplemental interrogatories; produce all written statements of witnesses obtained by Mr. Fortenbaugh, as counsel and agent for Defendants; state in substance any fact concerning this case which Defendants learned through oral statements made by witnesses to Mr. Fortenbaugh whether or not included in his private memoranda and produce Mr. Fortenbaugh's memoranda containing statements of fact by witnesses or to submit these memoranda to the Court for determination of those portions which should be revealed to Plaintiff." Upon their refusal, the court adjudged them in contempt and ordered them imprisoned until they complied.

The Third Circuit Court of Appeals, also sitting en banc, reversed the judgment of the District Court. 153 F.2d 212. It held that the information here sought was part of the "work product of the lawyer" and hence privileged from discovery under the Federal Rules of Civil Procedure. The importance of the problem, which has engendered a great divergence of views among district courts, led us to grant certiorari. * * *

There is an initial question as to which of the deposition-discovery rules is involved in this case. Petitioner, in filing his interrogatories, thought that he was proceeding under Rule 33.

* * * [I]t does not appear from the record that petitioner filed a motion under Rule 34 for a court order directing the production of the documents in question. Indeed, such an order could not have been entered as to Fortenbaugh since Rule 34, like Rule 33, is limited to parties to the proceeding, thereby excluding their counsel or agents.

Thus to the extent that petitioner was seeking the production of the memoranda and statements gathered by Fortenbaugh in the course of his activities as counsel, petitioner misconceived his remedy. Rule 33 did not permit him to obtain such memoranda and statements as adjuncts to the interrogatories addressed to the individual tug owners. A party clearly cannot refuse to answer interrogatories on the ground that the information sought is solely within the knowledge of his attorney. But that is not this case. Here production was sought of documents prepared by a party's attorney after the claim has arisen. Rule 33 does not make provision for such production, even when sought in connection with permissible interrogatories. Moreover, since petitioner was also foreclosed from securing them through an order under Rule 34, his only recourse was to take Fortenbaugh's deposition under Rule 26 and to attempt to force Fortenbaugh to produce the materials by use of a subpoena duces tecum in accordance with Rule 45. * * * But despite petitioner's faulty choice of action, the District Court entered an order, apparently under Rule 34, commanding the tug owners and Fortenbaugh, as their agent and counsel, to produce the materials in question. Their refusal led to the anomalous result of holding the tug owners in contempt for failure to produce that which was in the possession of their counsel and of holding Fortenbaugh in contempt for failure to produce that which he could not be compelled to produce under either Rule 33 or Rule 34.

But under the circumstances we deem it unnecessary and unwise to rest our decision upon this procedural irregularity, an irregularity which is not strongly urged upon us and which was disregarded in the two courts below. * * * [T]he basic question at stake is whether any of those devices may be used to inquire into materials collected by an adverse party's counsel in the course of preparation for possible litigation. The fact that the petitioner may have used the wrong method does not destroy the main thrust of his attempt. * * * [I]n the present circumstances, for the purposes of this decision, the procedural irregularity is not material. * * *

In urging that he has a right to inquire into the materials secured and prepared by Fortenbaugh, petitioner emphasizes that the deposition-discovery portions of the Federal Rules of Civil Procedure are designed to enable the parties to discover the true facts and to compel their disclosure wherever they may be found. It is said that inquiry may be made under these rules, epitomized by Rule 26, as to any relevant matter which is not privileged; and since the discovery provisions are to be applied as broadly and liberally as possible, the privilege limitation must be restricted to its narrowest bounds. On the premise that the attorney-client privilege is the one involved in this case, petitioner argues that it must be strictly confined to confidential communications made by a client to his attorney. And since the materials here in issue were secured by Fortenbaugh from third persons rather than from his clients, the tug owners, the conclusion is reached that these materials are proper subjects for discovery under Rule 26.

As additional support for this result, petitioner claims that to prohibit discovery under these circumstances would give a corporate defendant a tremendous advantage in a suit by an individual plaintiff. Thus in a suit by an injured employee against a railroad or in a suit by an insured person against an insurance company the corporate defendant could pull a dark veil of secrecy over all the pertinent facts it can collect after the claim arises merely on the assertion that such facts were gathered by its large staff of attorneys and claim agents. At the same time, the individual plaintiff, who often has direct knowledge of the matter in issue and has no counsel until some time after his claim arises could be compelled to disclose all the intimate details of his case. By endowing with immunity from disclosure all that a lawyer discovers in the course of his duties, it is said, the rights of individual litigants in such cases are drained of vitality and the lawsuit becomes more of a battle of deception than a search for truth.

But framing the problem in terms of assisting individual plaintiffs in their suits against corporate defendants is unsatisfactory. Discovery concededly may work to the disadvantage as well as to the advantage of individual plaintiffs. Discovery, in other words, is not a one-way proposition. It is available in all types of cases at the behest of any party, individual or corporate, plaintiff or defendant. The problem thus far transcends the situation confronting this petitioner. And we must view that problem in light of the limitless situations where the particular kind of discovery sought by petitioner might be used.

We agree, of course, that the deposition-discovery rules are to be accorded a broad and liberal treatment. No longer can the time-honored cry of "fishing expedition" serve to preclude a party from inquiring into the facts underlying his opponent's case. Mutual knowledge of all the relevant facts gathered by both parties is essential to proper litigation. To that end, either party may compel the other to disgorge whatever facts he has in his possession. The deposition-discovery procedure simply advances the stage at which the disclosure can be compelled from the time of trial to the period preceding it, thus reducing the possibility of surprise. But discovery, like all matters of procedure, has ultimate and necessary boundaries. As indicated by Rules 30(b) and (d) and 31(d), limitations inevitably arise when it can be shown that the examination is being conducted in bad faith or in such a manner as to annoy, embarrass or oppress the person subject to the inquiry.[d] And as Rule 26(b) provides, further limitations come into existence when the inquiry touches upon the irrelevant or encroaches upon the recognized domains of privilege.

We also agree that the memoranda, statements and mental impressions in issue in this case fall outside the scope of the attorney-client privilege and hence are not protected from discovery on that basis. * * *

But the impropriety of invoking that privilege does not provide an answer to the problem before us. Petitioner has made more than an ordinary request for relevant, non-privileged facts in the possession of his adversaries or their counsel. He has sought discovery as of right of oral and written statements of witnesses whose identity is well known and whose availability to petitioner appears unimpaired. He has sought production of these matters after making the most searching inquiries of his opponents as to the circumstances surrounding the fatal accident, which inquiries were sworn to have been answered to the best of their information and belief. Interrogatories were directed toward all the events prior to, during and subsequent to the sinking of the tug. Full and honest answers to such broad inquiries would necessarily have included all pertinent information gleaned by Fortenbaugh through his interviews with the witnesses. Petitioner makes no suggestion, and we cannot assume, that the tug owners or Fortenbaugh were incomplete or dishonest in the framing of their answers. In addition, petitioner was free to examine the public testimony of the witnesses taken before the United States Steamboat Inspectors. We are thus dealing with an attempt to secure the production of written statements and mental impressions contained in the files and the mind of the attorney Fortenbaugh without any showing of necessity or

---

[d]   These matters are now covered by Rule 26(c).

any indication or claim that denial of such production would unduly prejudice the preparation of petitioner's case or cause him any hardship or injustice. For aught that appears, the essence of what petitioner seeks either has been revealed to him already through the interrogatories or is readily available to him direct from the witnesses for the asking.

* * *

In our opinion, neither Rule 26 nor any other rule dealing with discovery contemplates production under such circumstances. That is not because the subject matter is privileged or irrelevant, as those concepts are used in these rules. Here is simply an attempt, without purported necessity or justification, to secure written statements, private memoranda and personal recollections prepared or formed by an adverse party's counsel in the course of his legal duties. As such, it falls outside the arena of discovery and contravenes the public policy underlying the orderly prosecution and defense of legal claims. Not even the most liberal of discovery theories can justify unwarranted inquiries into the files and the mental impressions of an attorney.

Historically, a lawyer is an officer of the court and is bound to work for the advancement of justice while faithfully protecting the rightful interests of his clients. In performing his various duties, however, it is essential that a lawyer work with a certain degree of privacy, free from unnecessary intrusion by opposing parties and their counsel. Proper preparation of a client's case demands that he assemble information, sift what he considers to be the relevant from the irrelevant facts, prepare his legal theories and plan his strategy without undue and needless interference. That is the historical and the necessary way in which lawyers act within the framework of our system of jurisprudence to promote justice and to protect their clients' interests. This work is reflected, of course, in interviews, statements, memoranda, correspondence, briefs, mental impressions, personal beliefs, and countless other tangible and intangible ways—aptly though roughly termed by the Circuit Court of Appeals in this case (153 F.2d 212, 223) as the "work product of the lawyer." Were such materials open to opposing counsel on mere demand, much of what is now put down in writing would remain unwritten. An attorney's thoughts, heretofore inviolate, would not be his own. Inefficiency, unfairness and sharp practices would inevitably develop in the giving of legal advice and in the preparation of cases for trial. The effect on the legal profession would be demoralizing. And the interests of the clients and the cause of justice would be poorly served.

We do not mean to say that all written materials obtained or prepared by an adversary's counsel with an eye toward litigation are necessarily free from discovery in all cases. Where relevant and non-privileged facts remain hidden in an attorney's file and where production of those facts is essential to the preparation of one's case, discovery may properly be had. Such written statements and documents might, under certain circumstances, be admissible in evidence or give clues as to the existence or location of relevant facts. Or they might be useful for purposes of impeachment or corroboration. And production might be justified where the witnesses are no longer available or can be reached only with difficulty. Were production of written statements and documents to be precluded under such circumstances, the liberal ideals of the deposition-discovery portions of the Federal Rules * * * would be stripped of much of their meaning. But the general policy against invading the privacy of an attorney's course of preparation is so well recognized and so essential to an orderly working of our system of legal procedure that a burden rests on the one who would invade that privacy to establish adequate reasons to justify production through a subpoena or court order. That burden, we believe, is necessarily implicit in the rules as now constituted.

Rule 30(b), as presently written, gives the trial judge the requisite discretion to make a judgment as to whether discovery should be allowed as to written statements secured from witnesses. But in the instant case there was no room for that discretion to operate in favor of the petitioner. No attempt was made to establish any reason why Fortenbaugh should be forced to produce the written statements. There was only a naked, general demand for these materials as of right and a finding by the District Court that no recognizable privilege was involved. That was insufficient to justify discovery under these circumstances and the court should have sustained the refusal of the tug owners and Fortenbaugh to produce.

But as to oral statements made by witnesses to Fortenbaugh, whether presently in the form of his mental impressions or memoranda, we do not believe that any showing of necessity can be made under the circumstances of this case so as to justify production. Under ordinary conditions, forcing an attorney to repeat or write out all that witnesses have told him and to deliver the account to his adversary gives rise to grave dangers of inaccuracy and untrustworthiness. No legitimate purpose is served by such production. The practice forces the attorney to testify as to what he remembers or what he saw fit to write down regarding witnesses' remarks. Such testimony could not qualify as evidence; and to use it for impeachment or corroborative purposes would make the attorney much less an officer of the court and much more an ordinary witness. The standards of the profession would thereby suffer.

Denial of production of this nature does not mean that any material, nonprivileged facts can be hidden from the petitioner in this case. He need not be unduly hindered in the preparation of his case, in the discovery of facts or in his anticipation of his opponents' position. Searching interrogatories directed to Fortenbaugh and the tug owners, production of written documents and statements upon a proper showing and direct interviews with the witnesses themselves all serve to reveal the facts in Fortenbaugh's possession to the fullest possible extent consistent with public policy. Petitioner's counsel frankly admits that he wants the oral statements only to help prepare himself to examine witnesses and to make sure that he has overlooked nothing. That is insufficient under the circumstances to permit him an exception to the policy underlying the privacy of Fortenbaugh's professional activities. If there should be a rare situation justifying production of these matters, petitioner's case is not of that type.

We fully appreciate the wide-spread controversy among the members of the legal profession over the problem raised by this case. * * * But until some rule or statute definitely prescribes otherwise, we are not justified in permitting discovery in a situation of this nature as a matter of unqualified right. When Rule 26 and the other discovery rules were adopted, this Court and the members of the bar in general certainly did not believe or contemplate that all the files and mental processes of lawyers were thereby opened to the free scrutiny of their adversaries. And we refuse to interpret the rules at this time so as to reach so harsh and unwarranted a result.

We therefore affirm the judgment of the Circuit Court of Appeals.

Affirmed.

JUSTICE JACKSON, concurring.

* * *

To consider first the most extreme aspect of the requirement in litigation here, we find it calls upon counsel, if he has had any conversations with any of the crews of the vessels in question or of any other, to "set forth in detail the exact provision of any such oral statements or reports." Thus the demand is not for the production of a transcript in existence but calls for the creation of a written statement not in being. But the statement by counsel of what a witness told him is not evidence when written. Plaintiff could not introduce it to prove his case. What, then, is the purpose sought to be served by demanding this of adverse counsel?

Counsel for the petitioner candidly said on argument that he wanted this information to help prepare himself to examine witnesses, to make sure he overlooked nothing. He bases his claim to it in his brief on the view that the Rules were to do away with the old situation where a law suit developed into "a battle of wits between counsel." But a common law trial is and always should be an adversary proceeding. Discovery was hardly intended to enable a learned profession to perform its functions either without wits or on wits borrowed from the adversary.

The real purpose and the probable effect of the practice ordered by the district court would be to put trials on a level even lower than a "battle of wits." I can conceive of no practice more demoralizing to the Bar than to require a lawyer to write out and deliver to his adversary an account of what witnesses have told him. Even if his recollection were perfect, the statement would be his language permeated with his inferences. Every one who has tried it knows that it is almost impossible so fairly to record the expressions and emphasis of a witness that when he testifies in the environment of the court and under the influence of the leading question there will not be departures in some respects. Whenever the testimony of the witness would differ from the "exact" statement the lawyer had delivered, the lawyer's statement would be whipped out to impeach the witness. Counsel producing his adversary's "inexact" statement could lose nothing by saying, "Here is a contradiction, gentlemen of the jury. I do not know whether it is my adversary or his witness who is not telling the truth, but one is not." Of course, if this practice were adopted, that scene would be repeated over and over again. The lawyer who delivers such statements often would find himself branded a deceiver afraid to take the stand to support his own version of the witness's conversation with him, or else he will have to go on the stand to defend his own credibility—perhaps against that of his chief witness, or possibly even his client.

Every lawyer dislikes to take the witness stand and will do so only for grave reasons. This is partly because it is not his role; he is almost invariably a poor witness. But he steps out of professional character to do it. He regrets it; the profession discourages it. But the practice advocated here is one which would force him to be a witness, not as to what he has seen or done but as to other witnesses' stories, and not because he wants to do so but in self-defense.

And what is the lawyer to do who has interviewed one whom he believes to be a biased, lying or hostile witness to get his unfavorable statements and know what to meet? He must record and deliver such statements even though he would not vouch for the credibility of the witness by calling him. Perhaps the other side would not want to call him either, but the attorney is open to the charge of suppressing evidence at the trial if he fails to call such a hostile witness even though he never regarded him as reliable or truthful.

Having been supplied the names of the witnesses, petitioner's lawyer gives no reason why he cannot interview them himself. If an employee-witness refuses to tell his story, he, too, may be examined under the Rules. He may be compelled on discovery as fully as on the trial to disclose his version of the facts. But that is his own disclosure—it can be used to impeach him if he contradicts it and such a deposition is not useful to promote an unseemly disagreement between the witness and the counsel in the case.

It is true that the literal language of the Rules would admit of an interpretation that would sustain the district court's order. * * * But all such procedural measures have a background of custom and practice which was assumed by those who wrote and should be by those who apply them. * * * Certainly nothing in the tradition or practice of discovery up to the time of these Rules would have suggested that they would authorize such a practice as here proposed.

The question remains as to signed statements or those written by witnesses. Such statements are not evidence for the defendant. * * * Nor should I think they ordinarily could be evidence for the plaintiff. But such a statement might be useful for impeachment of the witness who signed it, if he is called and if he departs from the statement. There might be circumstances, too, where impossibility or difficulty of access to the witness or his refusal to respond to requests for information or other facts would show that the interests of justice require that such statements be made available. Production of such statements are governed by Rule 34 and on "Showing good cause therefore" the court may order their inspection, copying or photographing. No such application has here been made; the demand is made on the basis of right, not on showing of cause.[e]

I agree to the affirmance of the judgment of the Circuit Court of Appeals which reversed the district court.

JUSTICE FRANKFURTER joins in this opinion.

NOTES AND QUESTIONS

1.   Federal Rule 26(b)(3), adopted in 1970, provides limited protection for work product from discovery. How does the scope of the Rule differ from the doctrine set out in *Hickman*? Does *Hickman* survive adoption of Rule 26(b)(3)? See Clermont, *Surveying Work Product*, 68 Cornell L.Rev. 755 (1983).

2.   Protection under Rule 26(b)(3) is relatively clear when the documents have a "single purpose" in the sense of having been prepared in anticipation of litigation or trial by or for another party or by that other party's representative. See In re Grand Jury Subpoena (Mark Torf/Torf Environmental Management), 357 F.3d 900, 907 (9th Cir. 2004). Does protection attach if the documents have a "dual purpose," for example, they also were prepared in response to regulatory or business requirements? Many circuits have adopted a "because of" standard:

> The "because of" standard does not consider whether litigation was a primary or secondary motive behind the creation of a document. Rather, it considers the totality of the circumstances and affords protection when it can fairly be said that the "document was created because of anticipated litigation, and would not have been created in substantially similar form but for the prospect of that litigation[.]"

Id. at 908 (internal citation omitted).

---

[e]   The requirement of "good cause" was removed by the 1970 amendment to Rule 34.

3. Would it be preferable to apply a "primary purpose" test? Or a narrower "for use in anticipation of litigation" test? Which test would Hickman v. Taylor support? Under each of these standards, explain whether work-product protection should attach in the circumstances that follow:

(a) A company prepares a memorandum about a contemplated transaction recognizing that the transaction may result in litigation;

(b) A company is engaged in merger discussions with another company, which requests a candid assessment of the likelihood of success in pending litigations; or

(c) A company prepares financial statements for its executives, including reserves for projected litigation.

4. Is Rule 26(b)(3)(B), which protects "against disclosure of the mental impressions, conclusions, opinions or legal theories of a party's attorney or other representative concerning litigation," consistent with the availability of contention interrogatories and requests for admission? Consider these problems:

(a) Should a party have to disclose the selection of documents made by counsel to prepare a witness for deposition?

(b) Can a party depose the opposing party's attorney to determine whether discovery production has been completed?

See Waltz, *Opinion Work Product: A Critical Analysis of Current Law and a New Analytical Framework*, 73 Or.L.Rev. 385 (1994).

5. Rule 26(b)(3)(C) does not protect a party's own prior statement concerning the action. Why? Rule 26(b)(3)(C) permits a nonparty witness to obtain a copy of its statement upon request. Should a party and nonparty witness be treated the same? Might a court usefully postpone release of a witness statement until after the witness is deposed?

2. PRIVILEGES AND WORK PRODUCT— THE EXTENT OF PROTECTION

Rule 26(b)(1) limits discovery to "any nonprivileged matter," and the usual view has been that the same rules of privilege generally apply to discovery as apply at the trial. A privilege rule gives a person a right to refuse to disclose information that he otherwise would be required to provide. It also may give a person the right to prevent someone else from disclosing information, or it may give its possessor a right to refuse to become a witness. A rule of privilege is a counterweight to the general power of courts to compel testimony. Modern pretrial discovery involves an extension of the judicial power to compel disclosure and has been met by the expansion of old privileges and the creation of new ones that will check this power.

One rule of privilege that all American courts recognize is the attorney-client privilege. They also agree on its basic contours. For the privilege to attach to a communication, four elements must be present:

> (1) [T]he asserted holder of the privilege is or sought to be a client; (2) the person to whom the communication was made (a) is a member of the bar of a court, or his subordinate and (b) in connection with this communication is acting as a lawyer; (3) the communication relates to a fact of which the attorney was informed (a) by his client (b) without the presence of strangers (c) for the purpose of securing primarily either (i) an opinion on law or (ii) legal services or (iii) assistance in some legal proceeding, and not (d) for the purpose of committing a crime or tort; and (4) the privilege has been (a) claimed and (b) not waived by the client.

UNITED STATES v. UNITED SHOE MACHINERY CORP., 89 F.Supp. 357, 358–59 (D.Mass. 1950).

Because the attorney-client privilege results in the suppression of relevant facts, courts tend to construe it narrowly and to resolve doubtful cases against a finding of privilege. One observer has said:

> While often unexpressed, the crucial factor limiting the privilege's availability is not the past law of the privilege but the developing rules of liberal discovery. * * * At least when precedent is not absolutely clear, whether a party can assert the privilege will often depend less on the jurisdiction's law of privilege than on the particular judge's attitude toward liberal discovery.

Bartell, *The Attorney-Client Privilege and the Work-Product Doctrine*, in ALI-ABA Civil Procedure and Litigation in Federal and State Courts, vol. I, at 507 (1987).

UPJOHN CO. V. UNITED STATES

Supreme Court of the United States, 1981.
449 U.S. 383, 101 S.Ct. 677, 66 L.Ed.2d 584.

Certiorari to the United States Court of Appeals for the Sixth Circuit.

JUSTICE REHNQUIST delivered the opinion of the Court.

We granted certiorari in this case to address important questions concerning the scope of the attorney-client privilege in the corporate context and the applicability of the work-product doctrine in proceedings to enforce tax summonses. * * * With respect to the privilege question the parties and various *amici* have described our task as one of choosing between two "tests" which have gained adherents in the courts of appeals. We are acutely aware, however, that we sit to decide concrete cases and not abstract propositions of law. We decline to lay down a broad rule or series of rules to govern all conceivable future questions in this area, even were we able to do so. We can and do, however, conclude that the attorney-client privilege protects the communications involved in this case from compelled disclosure and that the work-product doctrine does apply in tax summons enforcement proceedings.

I

Petitioner Upjohn Co. manufactures and sells pharmaceuticals here and abroad. In January 1976 independent accountants conducting an audit of one of Upjohn's foreign subsidiaries discovered that the subsidiary made payments to or for the benefit of foreign government officials in order to secure government business. The accountants so informed Mr. Gerard Thomas, Upjohn's Vice President, Secretary, and General Counsel. * * * He consulted with outside counsel and R. T. Parfet, Jr., Upjohn's Chairman of the Board. It was decided that the company would conduct an internal investigation of what were termed "questionable payments." As part of this investigation the attorneys prepared a letter containing a questionnaire which was sent to "All Foreign General and Area Managers" over the Chairman's signature. The letter began by noting recent disclosures that several American companies made "possibly illegal" payments to foreign government officials and emphasized that the management needed full information concerning any such payments made by Upjohn. The letter indicated that the Chairman had asked Thomas, identified as "the company's General Counsel," "to conduct an investigation for the purpose of determining the nature and magnitude of any payments made by the Upjohn Company or any of its subsidiaries to any employee or official of a foreign government." The questionnaire sought detailed information concerning such payments. Managers were instructed to treat the investigation as "highly confidential" and not to discuss it with anyone other than Upjohn employees who might be helpful in providing the requested information. Responses were to be sent directly to Thomas. Thomas and outside counsel also interviewed the recipients of the questionnaire and some 33 other Upjohn officers or employees as part of the investigation.

On March 26, 1976, the company voluntarily submitted a preliminary report to the Securities and Exchange Commission on Form 8BK disclosing certain questionable payments. A copy of the report was simultaneously submitted to the Internal Revenue Service, which immediately began an investigation to determine the tax consequences of the payments. Special agents conducting the investigation were given lists by Upjohn of all those interviewed and all who had responded to the questionnaire. On November 23, 1976, the Service issued a summons pursuant to 26 U.S.C. § 7602 demanding production of:

All files relative to the investigation conducted under the supervision of Gerard Thomas to identify payments to employees of foreign governments and any political contributions made by the Upjohn Company or any of its affiliates since January 1, 1971 and to determine whether any funds of the Upjohn Company had been improperly accounted for on the corporate books during the same period.

The records should include but not be limited to written questionnaires sent to managers of the Upjohn Company's foreign affiliates, and memoranda or notes of the interviews conducted in the United States and abroad with officers and employees of the Upjohn Company and its subsidiaries. * * *

The company declined to produce the documents specified in the second paragraph on the grounds that they were protected from disclosure by the attorney-client privilege and constituted the work product of attorneys prepared in anticipation of litigation. On August 31, 1977, the United States filed a petition seeking enforcement of the summons under 26 U.S.C. §§ 7402(b) and 7604(a) in the United States District Court for the Western District of Michigan. That court adopted the recommendation of a Magistrate who concluded that the summons should be enforced. Petitioners appealed to the Court of Appeals for the Sixth Circuit which rejected the Magistrate's finding of a waiver of the attorney-client privilege, * * * but agreed that the privilege did not apply "[t]o the extent that the communications were made by officers and agents not responsible for directing Upjohn's actions in response to legal advice * * * for the simple reason that the communications were not the 'client's.' " * * * The court reasoned that accepting petitioner's claim for a broader application of the privilege would encourage upper-echelon management to ignore unpleasant facts and create too broad a "zone of silence." Noting that Upjohn's counsel had interviewed officials such as the Chairman and President, the Court of Appeals remanded to the District Court so that a determination of who was within the "control group" could be made. In a concluding footnote the court stated that the work-product doctrine "is not applicable to administrative summonses issued under 26 U.S.C. § 7602." * * *

II

Federal Rule of Evidence 501 provides that "the privilege of a witness * * * shall be governed by the principles of the common law as they may be interpreted by the courts of the United States in light of reason and experience." The attorney-client privilege is the oldest of the privileges for confidential communications known to the common law. 8 J. Wigmore, Evidence § 2290 (McNaughton rev. 1961). Its purpose is to encourage full and frank communication between attorneys and their clients and thereby promote broader public interests in the observance of law and administration of justice. The privilege recognizes that sound legal advice or advocacy serves public ends and that such advice or advocacy depends upon the lawyer's being fully informed by the client. * * * Admittedly complications in the application of the privilege arise when the client is a corporation, which in theory is an artificial creature of the law, and not an individual; but this Court has assumed that the privilege applies when the client is a corporation. * * *

The Court of Appeals, however, considered the application of the privilege in the corporate context to present a "different problem," since the client was an inanimate entity and "only the senior management, guiding and integrating the several operations, . . .ᶠ can be said to possess an identity analogous to the corporation as a whole." * * * Such a view, we think, overlooks the fact that the privilege exists to protect not only the giving of professional advice to those who can act on it but also the giving of information to the lawyer to enable him to give sound and informed advice. * * * The first step in the resolution of any legal problem is ascertaining the factual background and sifting through the facts with an eye to the legally relevant.* * *

In the case of the individual client the provider of information and the person who acts on the lawyer's advice are one and the same. In the corporate context, however, it will frequently be employees beyond the control group as defined by the court below—"officers and agents . . . [omission in original] responsible for directing [the company's] actions in response to legal advice"—who will possess the information needed by the corporation's lawyers. Middle-level—and indeed lower-level—employees can, by actions within the scope of their employment, embroil the corporation in serious legal difficulties, and it is only natural that these employees would have the relevant information needed by corporate counsel if he is adequately to advise the client with respect to such actual or potential difficulties. * * *

The control group test adopted by the court below thus frustrates the very purpose of the privilege by discouraging the communication of relevant information by employees of the client to attorneys seeking to render legal advice to the client corporation. The attorney's advice will also frequently be more significant to noncontrol group members than to those who officially sanction the advice, and the control group test makes it more difficult to convey full and frank legal advice to the employees who will put into effect the client corporation's policy. * * *

The narrow scope given the attorney-client privilege by the court below not only makes it difficult for corporate attorneys to formulate sound advice when their client is faced with a specific legal problem but also threatens to limit the valuable efforts of corporate counsel to ensure their client's compliance with the law. In light of the vast and complicated array of

---

ᶠ   Alteration in original.

regulatory legislation confronting the modern corporation, corporations, unlike most individuals, "constantly go to lawyers to find out how to obey the law[.]" * * * [I]f the purpose of the attorney-client privilege is to be served, the attorney and client must be able to predict with some degree of certainty whether particular discussions will be protected. An uncertain privilege, or one which purports to be certain but results in widely varying applications by the courts, is little better than no privilege at all. The very terms of the test adopted by the court below suggest the unpredictability of its application. The test restricts the availability of the privilege to those officers who play a "substantial role" in deciding and directing a corporation's legal response. * * *

The communications at issue were made by Upjohn employees to counsel for Upjohn acting as such, at the direction of corporate superiors in order to secure legal advice from counsel. * * * Information, not available from upper-echelon management, was needed to supply a basis for legal advice concerning compliance with securities and tax laws, foreign laws, currency regulations, duties to shareholders, and potential litigation in each of these areas. The communications concerned matters within the scope of the employees' corporate duties, and the employees themselves were sufficiently aware that they were being questioned in order that the corporation could obtain legal advice. The questionnaire identified Thomas as "the company's General Counsel" and referred in its opening sentence to the possible illegality of payments such as the ones on which information was sought. * * * A statement of policy accompanying the questionnaire clearly indicated the legal implications of the investigation. The policy statement was issued "in order that there be no uncertainty in the future as to the policy with respect to the practices which are the subject of this investigation." It began "Upjohn will comply with all laws and regulations," and stated that commissions or payments "will not be used as a subterfuge for bribes or illegal payments" and that all payments must be "proper and legal." Any future agreements with foreign distributors or agents were to be approved "by a company attorney" and any questions concerning the policy were to be referred "to the company's General Counsel." * * * This statement was issued to Upjohn employees worldwide, so that even those interviewees not receiving a questionnaire were aware of the legal implications of the interviews. Pursuant to explicit instructions from the Chairman of the Board, the communications were considered "highly confidential" when made, * * * and have been kept confidential by the company. Consistent with the underlying purposes of the attorney-client privilege, these communications must be protected against compelled disclosure.

The Court of Appeals declined to extend the attorney-client privilege beyond the limits of the control group test for fear that doing so would entail severe burdens on discovery and create a broad "zone of silence" over corporate affairs. Application of the attorney-client privilege to communications such as those involved here, however, puts the adversary in no worse position than if the communications had never taken place. The privilege only protects disclosure of communications; it does not protect disclosure of the underlying facts by those who communicated with the attorney * * *. Here the Government was free to question the employees who communicated with Thomas and outside counsel. Upjohn has provided the IRS with a list of such employees, and the IRS has already interviewed some 25 of them. While it would probably be more convenient for the Government to secure the results of petitioner's internal investigation by simply subpoenaing the questionnaires and notes taken by petitioner's attorneys, such considerations of convenience do not overcome the policies served by the attorney-client privilege. As Justice Jackson noted in his concurring opinion in Hickman v. Taylor * * *: "Discovery was hardly intended to enable a learned profession to perform its functions . . . on wits borrowed from the adversary."[g]

* * *

III

Our decision that the communications by Upjohn employees to counsel are covered by the attorney-client privilege disposes of the case so far as the responses to the questionnaires and any notes reflecting responses to interview questions are concerned. * * * To the extent that the material subject to the summons is not protected by the attorney-client privilege as disclosing communications between an employee and counsel, we must reach the ruling by the Court of Appeals that the work-product doctrine does not apply to summonses issued under 26 U.S.C. § 7602.[6]

The Government concedes, wisely, that the Court of Appeals erred and that the work-product doctrine does apply to IRS summonses. * * * This doctrine was announced by the Court over 30 years ago in Hickman v. Taylor * * *. * * * The Court noted that "it is essential that a lawyer work with a certain degree of privacy" * * *. The "strong public policy" underlying the work-product doctrine * * * has been substantially incorporated in Federal Rule * * * 26(b)(3). * * * Nothing in the language of the IRS summons provisions or their legislative history suggests an intent on the part of Congress to preclude application of the work-product doctrine. Rule 26(b)(3) codifies the work-product doctrine, and the Federal Rules of Civil Procedure are made applicable to summons enforcement proceedings by Rule 81(a)(3).[h] * * * While conceding the applicability of the work-product

---

[g]   Alteration in original.

[6]   The following discussion will also be relevant to counsels' notes and memoranda of interviews with the seven former employees should it be determined that the attorney-client privilege does not apply to them. * * *

[h]   The rule is now renumbered as Rule 81(a)(5).

doctrine, the Government asserts that it has made a sufficient showing of necessity to overcome its protections. * * * The Government stresses that interviewees are scattered across the globe and that Upjohn has forbidden its employees to answer questions it considers irrelevant. The above-quoted language from *Hickman*, however, did not apply to "oral statements made by witnesses . . .[i] whether presently in the form of [the attorney's] mental impressions or memoranda." * * * As to such material the Court did "not believe that any showing of necessity can be made under the circumstances of this case so as to justify production * * *." * * * Forcing an attorney to disclose notes and memoranda of witnesses' oral statements is particularly disfavored because it tends to reveal the attorney's mental processes * * *.

Rule 26 accords special protection to work product revealing the attorney's mental processes. The Rule permits disclosure of documents and tangible things constituting attorney work product upon a showing of substantial need and inability to obtain the equivalent without undue hardship. * * * Rule 26 goes on, however, to state that "[i]n ordering discovery of such materials when the required showing has been made, the court shall protect against disclosure of the mental impressions, conclusions, opinions or legal theories of an attorney or other representative of a party concerning the litigation." [This language has been altered but its substance has not been changed.] Although this language does not specifically refer to memoranda based on oral statements of witnesses, the *Hickman* court stressed the danger that compelled disclosure of such memoranda would reveal the attorney's mental processes. It is clear that this is the sort of material the draftsmen of the Rule had in mind as deserving special protection. * * *

* * * It is clear that the Magistrate applied the wrong standard when he concluded that the Government had made a sufficient showing of necessity to overcome the protections of the work-product doctrine. The Magistrate applied the "substantial need" and "without undue hardship" standard articulated in the first part of Rule 26(b)(3). The notes and memoranda sought by the Government here, however, are work product based on oral statements. If they reveal communications, they are, in this case, protected by the attorney-client privilege. To the extent they do not reveal communications, they reveal the attorneys' mental processes in evaluating the communications. As Rule 26 and *Hickman* make clear, such work product cannot be disclosed simply on a showing of substantial need and inability to obtain the equivalent without undue hardship.

While we are not prepared at this juncture to say that such material is always protected by the work-product rule, we think a far stronger showing of necessity and unavailability by other means * * * would be necessary to compel disclosure. * * *

---

[i]   Alteration in original.

Accordingly, the judgment of the Court of Appeals is reversed, and the case remanded for further proceedings.

[The concurring opinion of CHIEF JUSTICE BURGER is omitted.]

NOTES AND QUESTIONS

1. What is the scope of the attorney-client privilege after *Upjohn*? Although the Court declined to announce standards to govern the privilege, would you agree that the factors to be considered include: 1) the communication must be one that would not have been made but for the contemplation of legal services; 2) the content of the communication must relate to the legal services being rendered; 3) the information-giver must be an employee, agent, or independent contractor with a significant relationship to the corporation and the corporation's involvement in the transaction that is the subject of legal services; 4) the communication must be made in confidence; and 5) the privilege may be asserted either by the corporation or by the information-giver. See Sexton, *A Post-*Upjohn *Consideration of the Corporate Attorney-Client Privilege*, 57 N.Y.U.L.Rev. 443, 487 (1982).

2. Explain whether the privilege would attach in the following situations:

   (a) A former employee speaks to the corporation's attorney in the course of an internal investigation concerning accounting practices and admits to embezzling funds;

   (b) An inventor speaks to a lawyer before filing an application for the patent and the statements are not entirely technical;

   (c) A client gives documents to his attorney that were created by and received from an unrelated third party;

   (d) A taxpayer gives canceled checks and bank statements to his attorney; or

   (e) An insured sends a report to a liability insurer pertinent to a matter covered by the liability policy.

See 8 Wright, Miller & Marcus, Federal Practice and Procedure § 2017 (3d ed.).

3. Rule 26(b)(5) establishes a process for asserting the privilege, requiring that the claim be made expressly and that the nature of the withheld material be described in a way that enables the other parties to test the assertion of the privilege. Failure to comply can result not only in the loss of the privilege but also in sanctions under Rule 37. Filing a "privilege log" has become a standard way to assert the privilege. See Smith v. Café Asia, 256 F.R.D. 247, 250–51 (D.D.C. 2009). Assertion of the privilege also involves a timeliness requirement. In MOLONEY v. UNITED STATES, 204 F.R.D. 16 (D.Mass. 2001), defendant's counsel blocked testimony during a deposition by asserting work product and attorney-client privilege. In response to plaintiff's motion to compel, counsel raised and briefed protection under different

privileges. The district court ordered production: "[I]t defies logic to permit counsel to assert one privilege so as to preclude testimony at a deposition, but thereafter research and claim an entirely different privilege in response to a motion to compel. Such conduct most assuredly circumvents both the letter and the spirit of Rules 26(b)(5) and 30(d)(1)." Id. at 21. (Rule 30(d)(1) is now numbered as Rule 30(c)(2).)

4.   Rule 26(b)(5)(B) allows for the "clawback" of privileged information that is inadvertently disclosed. Traditionally, the privilege was waived by a party's voluntary disclosure of the communication. Moreover, once waived, the party could be forced to disclose not only the specific communication but also all communications involving the same subject matter. See Duplan Corp. v. Deering Milliken, Inc., 397 F.Supp. 1146 (D.S.C. 1974). The danger of an inadvertent disclosure resulting in a waiver has increased exponentially in e-discovery cases that potentially involve millions of documents. See The Sedona Conference, *Best Practices Commentary on the Use of Search and Information Retrieval Methods in E-Discovery*, 8 Sedona Conf.J. 189 (2007). Under the rule what steps must be taken if a party believes that privileged information has been inadvertently handed over to the opposing party?

5.   Does a party waive attorney-client privilege forever by disclosing privileged documents to the federal government in response to an agency subpoena? The circuits are divided on whether a rule of selective waiver ought to apply. Compare In re Pacific Pictures Corp., 679 F.3d 1121 (9th Cir. 2012), with Diversified Industries, Inc. v. Meredith, 572 F.2d 596 (8th Cir. 1978). In addition, legislative efforts to adopt a theory of selective waiver have not succeeded.

6.   Evidentiary privileges other than that of the attorney-client also exist at common law. Among the most widely recognized is the spousal privilege that protects communications between parties to a marriage. The Constitution is the source of several privileges—for example, the Fifth Amendment privilege against self-incrimination. Other privileges struggle for recognition—for example, a privilege for communications between accountants and their clients. See generally *Developments in the Law—Privileged Communication*, 98 Harv.L.Rev. 1450 (1985).

7.   In state courts, privileges are a matter of state law, and state courts are not bound by the *Upjohn* approach to the attorney-client privilege. In federal courts, privilege is governed by federal law, except that Federal Rule of Evidence 501 directs a federal district court sitting in a diversity case to apply the privilege law of the state in which it sits. See Valente v. Pepsico, Inc., 68 F.R.D. 361, 366 n.10 (D.Del. 1975).

8.   It has become commonplace in large cases for parties to stipulate to protective orders negotiated by opposing counsel. And judges generally assent to these agreements, in large part to move cases along and avoid controversy. The stipulations typically provide for "umbrella" protection for confidential information, which is defined as any information that is designated "confidential" by the producing party. The result of these orders is that

virtually all nonpublic documents are designated confidential without any individualized review. See Moskowitz, *Discovering Discovery: Non-Party Access to Pretrial Information in the Federal Courts 1938–2006*, 78 U.Colo.L.Rev. 817, 871 (2007). Why have these orders become so common? What is the strategic significance for a defendant of a confidentiality order? Does disclosure to third persons open the door to misuse of the court system for blackmail or extortion through the threat of suits involving sensitive issues? What does a plaintiff's attorney gain by agreeing to a broad protective order? What standard should a court use if asked to modify an existing protective order to give nonparties access to discovery material? Is it relevant that the matter shielded may have an impact on public health and safety? What is the "right amount of confidentiality" in discovery requests or settlement agreements? See Levmore & Fagan, *Semi-Confidential Settlements in Civil, Criminal, and Sexual Assault Cases*, 103 Cornell L.Rev. 311 (2018). For a discussion of these issues, see Miller, *Confidentiality, Protective Orders, and Public Access to the Courts*, 105 Harv.L.Rev. 427 (1991). On protective orders generally, see Friedenthal, *Secrecy in Civil Litigation: Discovery and Party Agreements*, 9 J.L. & Pol'y 61 (2000). For a range of views on the subject, see Symposium: *Secrecy in Litigation*, 81 Chi.-Kent L.Rev. 305 (2006).

3.   EXPERT INFORMATION

———

Read Federal Rule of Civil Procedure 26(a)(2)–(3) and 26(b)(4) and the accompanying materials in the Supplement.

———

Discovery of expert witnesses has undergone significant change under the Federal Rules. Until 1993, expert discovery was limited to using interrogatories, unless otherwise ordered by the court, and could be directed only at experts called to testify. Expert discovery now begins with mandatory disclosure under Rule 26(a). Without a discovery request the parties must identify any witness who "may" be used at trial to present expert evidence and produce an expert report. What must the report contain? See Rule 26(a)(2)(B)(i)–(vi). As to witnesses who are not "retained or specially employed to provide expert testimony," the party must disclose the subject matter on which the witness is expected to present testimony and a summary of the facts and opinions to which the witness is expected to testify. See Rule 26(a)(2)(C). The court can set the timing of these disclosures; if there is no court order or stipulation, when must the disclosures be made? See Rule 26(d)(i). Mandatory disclosure of experts whose reports must be disclosed is subject to the duty of on-going supplementation, and this duty extends to an expert's responses during a deposition. See Rule 26(e). Finally, Rule 26(a)(3) requires disclosure of all witnesses who may testify at trial.

Rule 26(b)(4) also regulates the timing and scope of party-initiated expert discovery. Depositions may be taken of experts identified as trial witnesses, but cannot take place until the mandatory report is received. Different rules apply to the discovery of non-testifying experts. In that context, the requestor must demonstrate exceptional circumstances. See Rule 26(b)(4)(D)(ii). Is any discovery permitted of experts who are not retained but simply informally consulted? The rule also allocates the cost of expert discovery by requiring the court to impose a fee on the party interposing a discovery request unless an injustice would result. See Rule 26(b)(4)(E).

NOTES AND QUESTIONS

1.   Why doesn't discovery under Rule 26(b)(4) pertain to experts who participated in the events that form the basis for their knowledge? Is it appropriate to subject these "experts" to full discovery and to withhold fees from their participation in discovery?

2.   Are drafts of expert reports protected from disclosure? See Rule 26(b)(4). What is the rationale for this rule?

3.   Are the communications between a lawyer and a retained expert protected as work-product? Is the protection absolute or qualified? See Rule 26(b)(4)(C).

G. JUDICIAL SUPERVISION OF DISCOVERY

———

Read Federal Rules of Civil Procedure 26(c) and 37 and the accompanying Advisory Committee's Notes in the Supplement.

———

Discovery disputes come to the court's attention through a number of pathways.

The court on its own must limit discovery that is not relevant or proportional to the needs of the case or for other reasons, including excessive burden or expense. The court may impose expenses on a party or party's counsel for failure to cooperate in devising a discovery plan, see p. 615, supra, but only after giving notice and an opportunity to be heard. Courts also have inherent authority to sanction discovery misconduct. See ROADWAY EXPRESS, INC. v. PIPER, 447 U.S. 752, 100 S.Ct. 2455, 65 L.Ed.2d 488 (1980).

In addition, the parties or a person from whom discovery is sought may request the court's involvement. First, a party requesting information may move for an order compelling discovery when the potential respondent objects to answering an interrogatory or a question at a deposition, serving a response to a document request, or providing supplementation. Rule 37(c). If the court grants the motion, and enters an order under Rule 37 to compel discovery, it may impose attorney's fees unless it finds that the respondent's actions were substantially justified. If the respondent then fails to comply with the Rule 37(a) order, the court may impose a sanction. Rule 37(b).

Second, a party seeking information may immediately move for sanctions if there has been a complete failure to comply—for example, the respondent fails to attend its own deposition or respond to a request for inspection. Rule 37(d). If the court grants the motion to compel, sanctions immediately can be imposed; there is no requirement of noncompliance with the court order and the only limitation on the sanction is that it be "just." Rule 37(b)(2). Rule 37(e) was amended significantly in 2015 to toughen the potential sanctions for a failure to preserve electronically stored information.

Finally, a party or a person from whom discovery is sought may move for a protective order. Rule 26(c); Rule 37. Special procedures govern when a respondent seeks to withhold information based on a claim of privilege or work product. In particular, the respondent must assert the reason for nondisclosure with particularity. See Rule 26(b)(5); Rule 37.

NOTES AND QUESTIONS

1.   Under the original Federal Rules, courts rarely imposed sanctions for discovery abuse. A 1981 survey reported the following:

> The typical pattern of sanctioning that emerges from the reported cases is one in which the delay, obfuscation, contumacy, and lame excuses on the part of litigants and their attorneys are tolerated without any measured remedial action until the court is provoked beyond endurance. At that point the court punishes one side or the other with a swift and final termination of the lawsuit by dismissal or default. This "all or nothing" approach to sanctions results in considerable laxity in the day-to-day application of the rules. Attorneys are well aware that sanctions will be imposed only in the most flagrant situations.

Rodes, Ripple & Mooney, Sanctions Imposable for Violations of the Federal Rules of Civil Procedure 85 (Fed.Jud. Center 1981).

In NATIONAL HOCKEY LEAGUE v. METROPOLITAN HOCKEY CLUB, INC., 427 U.S. 639, 96 S.Ct. 2778, 49 L.Ed.2d 747 (1976), the Supreme Court found that there was no abuse of discretion in the district court's dismissal of a complaint for plaintiff's failure to comply with a discovery order. In the wake of *National Hockey*, lower courts increasingly imposed sanctions in a much wider variety of discovery situations. See American Bar Association, Sanctions: Rule 11 and Other Powers 34–36, 46–48, 61–70, 79–82, 97–101,

115–16, 128–29, 138–42, 158–60, 170, 175–77, 182, 186–87 (2d ed. 1988) (surveying decisions); see also American Law Institute-American Bar Association, Sanctions in Civil Litigation: A Review of Sanctions by Rule, Statute, and Inherent Power (2007). A survey of decisions involving the discovery of electronic information before the 2006 amendments found that courts granted sanctions in about two-thirds of the cases, most often when a party had willfully destroyed documents in violation of a court order or caused prejudice to the opposing party. See Scheindlin & Wangkeo, *Electronic Discovery Sanctions in the Twenty-First Century*, 11 Mich.Telecomm. & Tech.L.Rev. 71, 73 (2004).

2. "Spoliation" refers to the "destruction or alteration of evidence or to the failure to preserve property for another." Silvestri v. General Motors Corp., 271 F.3d 583, 590 (4th Cir. 2001). The Federal Rules do not create the duty to preserve; that duty is based on the common law and statute and generally arises "when a party should have known that the evidence may be relevant to future litigation." Kronisch v. United States, 150 F.3d 112, 126–27 (2d Cir. 1998). Courts have discretion to devise a sanction for spoliation; in the Second Circuit, the aim is to: "(1) deter parties from engaging in spoliation; (2) place the risk of an erroneous judgment on the party who wrongfully created the risk; and (3) restore 'the prejudiced party to the same position he would have been in absent the wrongful destruction of evidence by the opposing party.'" West v. Goodyear Tire & Rubber Co., 167 F.3d 776, 779 (2d Cir. 1999), citation omitted.

In 2015 the Federal Rules were amended to add Rule 37(e) dealing with sanctions for the spoliation of electronically stored information ("ESI"). Sanctions may be imposed if the court finds a party was prejudiced by the loss of ESI and the respondent had a duty to preserve the ESI, the party failed to take reasonable steps to preserve the ESI and it was lost, and the ESI cannot be recovered or replaced. More severe sanctions may be imposed if the court finds that the respondent intentionally sought to deprive the opposing party of the ESI. Under the prior version of Rule 37, "absent exceptional circumstances," sanctions were barred for the loss of ESI "resulting from the routine, good-faith operation of an electronic information system." Advisory Committee Note to 2015 amendment. Prior to the 2015 amendment, courts acknowledged authority in extreme circumstances to order an adverse-inference instruction against a party that lost ESI through "negligent and possibly reckless" conduct, upon a showing that the lost evidence was relevant to and would be favorable to the claim or defense of the requestor. Zubulake v. UBS Warburg LLC, 220 F.R.D. 212, 221 (S.D.N.Y. 2003). Even after the 2015 amendment, some district courts have emphasized that they retain "broad discretion" to do so: "Without limitation, litigation misconduct may also be otherwise sanctioned by the inherent power of the court." DVComm, LLC v. Hotwire Communications, LLC, 2016 WL 6246824, *7 (E.D.Pa. 2016). Why should Rule 37(e) be limited to ESI and not to all discoverable information?

3. In GOODYEAR TIRE & RUBBER CO. v. HAEGER, 137 S.Ct. 1178, 197 L.Ed.2d 585 (2017), a unanimous eight-person Court held that a court can

impose attorney's fees on a party for bad faith discovery conduct under its inherent powers, but the award must be "limited to the fees the innocent party incurred solely because of the misconduct—or put another way, to the fees that party would not have incurred but for the bad faith." The lower court did not apply that standard, and so the award of $2.7 million in fees to plaintiffs was reversed. Discovery sanctions under Rule 37 were not available because the suit already had settled. The Court explained that a civil sanction must be compensatory, not punitive, so only those fees incurred because of the misconduct can be shifted to the sanctioned party. In this case, the Court found, plaintiffs had failed to show that Goodyear's "non-disclosure so permeated" the suit as to make that misconduct a but-for cause of every subsequent legal expense; nor did they show that the litigation would have settled once the information was disclosed. Id. at 1189, 197 L.Ed.2d at 597. On remand, the district court found that Goodyear had waived objections to an alternative sanction award of $2 million and that it was vicariously liable for the acts of its attorneys. See Haeger v. Goodyear Tire and Rubber Co., 2018 WL 1182551 (D. Ariz. 2018).

4.   In KLIPSCH GROUP, INC. v. ePRO E-COMMERCE LTD., 880 F.3d 620 (2d Cir. 2018), the Second Circuit Court of Appeals affirmed the award of $2.7 million of discovery sanctions, including attorney's fees, to compensate plaintiff for having to undertake corrective action:

> * * * [D]efendant engaged in persistent discovery misconduct: it failed to timely disclose the majority of the responsive documents in its possession, restricted a discovery vendor's access to its electronic data, and failed to impose an adequate litigation hold even after the court directed it to do so, which omission allowed custodians of relevant electronic data to delete thousands of documents and significant quantities of data, sometimes permanently.

Id. at 623. The district court relied upon its inherent authority, not Rule 37, as authority for the award. The appellate court, affirmed, stating:

> [W]e emphasize that discovery sanctions should be commensurate with the costs unnecessarily created by the sanctionable behavior. A monetary sanction in the amount of the cost of discovery efforts that appeared to be reasonable to undertake *ex ante* does not become impermissibly punitive simply because those efforts did not ultimately uncover more significant spoliation and fraud, or increase the likely damages in the underlying case.

Id. Moreover, in the appellate court's view, the sanction was not punitive merely because it may appear out of proportion "to the likely ultimate value of the case." To the contrary, the costs were incurred because defendant had failed to comply with discovery obligations, and compliance is "not optional or negotiable; rather, the integrity of our civil litigation process requires that the parties before us, although adversarial to one another, carry out their duties to maintain and disclose the relevant information in their possession in good faith."

5.   What if a corporate party whose deposition is noticed under Rule 30(b)(6) deliberately selects a person to testify to appear for the deposition but who lacks information sufficient to respond to the questions asked? The circuits are divided on when and whether sanctions should be imposed. In the First Circuit, sanctions generally are available only when the deponent "literally fails to show up for a deposition session." Baker v. St. Paul Travelers Ins. Co., 670 F.3d 119 (1st Cir. 2012) (internal quotations omitted). By contrast the Fifth Circuit has held that because a corporation controls whom to designate for a Rule 30(b)(6) deposition, the corporation should be subject to sanctions if it designates a deponent who is not knowledgeable about the relevant facts. See Resolution Trust Corp. v. Southern Union Co., Inc., 985 F.2d 196 (5th Cir. 1993).

6.   Although trial judges have broad discretion to manage discovery matters, excessive judicial limits on discovery constitute an abuse of discretion. In MILLER v. SAM HOUSTON STATE UNIVERSITY, 986 F.3d 880 (5th Cir. 2021), the Fifth Circuit reversed a grant of summary judgment in favor of defendants due, in part, to the trial judge's discovery rulings against the plaintiff. Plaintiff, who was denied tenure at a public university in Texas, brought related suits under Title VII of the Civil Rights Act of 1964 and the Equal Pay Act against various defendants in the Texas public university systems. From the outset of the litigation, the district judge "effectively stifled [plaintiff's] attempts at discovery" by issuing orders that "foreclosed the parties from propounding written discovery or noticing depositions 'without court approval.'" Id. at 886. The district court then ordered the parties to exchange certain information, including plaintiff's "performance and personnel records, her pay records, names of relevant parties, and organizational charts." The district judge also attended and participated in a key deposition in the case. The court of appeals concluded that the judge's rulings denied plaintiff a full and fair opportunity to discover information essential to opposing defendants' summary judgment motions:

> * * * "[A]lthough the district court is customarily accorded wide discretion in handling discovery matters, we will not uphold a ruling which has failed to adhere to the liberal spirit of the Rules." Coughlin v. Lee, 946 F.2d 1152, 1159 (5th Cir. 1991). * * * [T]he district judge here permitted only [plaintiff's] deposition to be taken before summary judgment briefing and argument—and then actually participated in the deposition. By contrast, the court repeatedly denied [plaintiff] the opportunity to depose any witnesses, relenting only after summary judgment briefing was complete to allow [plaintiff] one deposition * * * . And that deposition was limited to "two hours, at most." To put it simply, the court's discovery restrictions suffocated any chance for [plaintiff] fairly to present her claims. While the Universities offer that Miller was not prejudiced because she had already received voluminous documentation from a pre-suit Texas Public Information Act request, we are not persuaded given the district court's inflexible denials of both her written

discovery requests and her requests to take depositions. * * * Even given the deference afforded to district courts when deciding discovery matters, the restrictions here * * * were "arbitrary or clearly unreasonable." * * * Although we are never quick to second-guess a district court's management of discovery, we must do so here.

Id. at 891–92.

H. USE OF DISCOVERY AT TRIAL

———

Read Federal Rules of Civil Procedure 32, 33(c), and 36(b) and the accompanying materials in the Supplement.

———

Attorneys can use the discovery devices simply to find out information, but commonly they anticipate using an adversary's or a witness's answers at trial: as admissions, to refresh a witness's recollection, or to provide a basis for cross-examination or impeachment. And sometimes a response to discovery can be used in lieu of or in addition to live testimony. The use of discovery responses at trial is governed by two sets of rules: the rules of procedure, governing whether the discovery material can be used at all at trial; and the rules of evidence, governing whether the matters are admissible at trial.

TATMAN V. COLLINS

United States Court of Appeals, Fourth Circuit, 1991.
938 F.2d 509.

NIEMEYER, CIRCUIT JUDGE:

During the course of trial in this personal injury litigation, the district court excluded the deposition of a treating physician offered by the plaintiff because (1) it had been taken only for discovery purposes, and (2) the witness was within 100 miles of the borders of the district (although more than 100 miles from the courthouse). Because the plaintiff's other critical expert testimony was dependent on the excluded deposition, the court struck that testimony and directed a verdict for the defendants. For the reasons that follow, we conclude that Fed.R.Civ.P. 32 was misapplied to exclude the deposition, and we reverse and remand the case for a new trial.

I

On April 15, 1986, near Winfield, West Virginia, Monte L. Tatman, while in an automobile, was struck from the rear by a tractor-trailer driven by Bobby Wayne Collins. Tatman was treated by Dr. Joseph Amico, a doctor located in Columbus, Ohio, for injuries to his neck, back, shoulder and head. Almost a year later, Tatman was hospitalized with a cerebral aneurysm. He died on March 12, 1987, when the aneurysm ruptured.

In March 1988, Rebecca Tatman, Monte's wife, filed suit against Collins and his employer, H & T Trucking Services, Inc., in the Southern District of West Virginia, sitting in Charleston. The complaint alleges that Monte Tatman's death was causally linked to the injuries sustained in the accident. It alleges that the accident caused an uncontrollable rise and fall in Monte Tatman's blood pressure, which, in turn, caused the rupture of the aneurysm.

During discovery, the defendants took the deposition of Dr. Amico who testified to Tatman's treatment and gave an opinion that there was a causal connection between the injuries sustained in the accident and the subsequent rupturing of the aneurysm. When a scheduling conflict prevented Dr. Amico from coming to the trial, the plaintiff sought to introduce the deposition of Dr. Amico, pointing out the conflict in his schedule and noting that he was more than 100 miles from the courthouse. The court excluded the deposition because it was taken early in the case as a discovery deposition and the defense counsel should not be "chargeable" with it. The court also concluded that the deposition could not be used because Columbus, Ohio, where Dr. Amico was located, was within 100 miles of the northern border of the Southern District of West Virginia, even though more than 100 miles from the courthouse. * * * Because the only other witness linking Tatman's aneurysm with the accident, Dr. Cyril Wecht, relied on the testimony of Dr. Amico, the court struck Dr. Wecht's testimony and granted defendant's motion for a directed verdict on the wrongful death claim. The jury returned a verdict on the survivor's claim, finding Collins negligent but finding that Tatman's injury was not caused by the accident.

II

In refusing to admit the deposition of Dr. Amico because it was a "discovery" deposition rather than one taken for use at trial, the district court stated, "the deposition that's involved here is a discovery deposition; it is one that was taken by the defense counsel at an early juncture in the case; it is one that the defense counsel should not be chargeable with at last minute—at the trial because plaintiff's counsel did not produce the physician." * * *

The Federal Rules of Civil Procedure make no distinction for use of a deposition at trial between one taken for discovery purposes and one taken for use at trial (de bene esse). See Rule 32 (use of depositions in court proceedings). Moreover, we are unaware of any authority which makes that distinction. * * * United States v. IBM Corp., 90 F.R.D. 377 (S.D.N.Y.1981). In IBM Corp. the court provided a historical explanation of how any distinction between a "discovery" deposition and a "de bene esse" deposition was deliberately eliminated from the rule:

> Prior to the revision of the Federal Rules of Civil Procedure in 1970, Rule 26(a) provided that depositions could be taken "for the purpose of discovery or for use as evidence in the action or for both purposes." Rule 26(d), the predecessor of Rule 32(a), which governed the use of depositions at trial, did not, however, state any distinction between discovery and evidentiary depositions. Recognizing a possible ambiguity in the rule, courts nevertheless refused to recognize a distinction between "discovery" and "evidentiary" depositions with regard to admissibility at trial. When the subject matter of Rule 26(a) was transferred to Rule 30(a) in the 1970 revision of the rules, the language authorizing depositions "for the purpose of discovery or for use as evidence in the action or for both purposes" was omitted.

90 F.R.D. at 381 n. 7 (citations omitted).

Fed.R.Civ.P. 32 provides that a deposition may be offered at trial, subject to the rules of evidence, as though the witness were present and testifying, and no distinction is now made in the rule with respect to the purpose for which the deposition was taken. While the rule makes distinctions in the circumstances when depositions of parties and witnesses may be used, it provides in section (a)(3) that when a witness is unavailable as therein provided, the deposition of the witness may be used for any purpose. Parties cognizable of the rule can overcome limitations of the deposition format and its timing in the discovery process by appropriate cross-examination, objections, and motions as permitted by Rules 30 and 32 (both of which govern depositions), Rule 29 (regarding stipulations), and Rule 26 (governing discovery in general). When, as here, the witness' deposition was duly noticed and all parties had the opportunity to attend (and did attend), it may be introduced at trial, subject to the rules of evidence, if the witness is unavailable as described in Rule 32(a)(3). It is irrelevant to the issue that one party or the other initiated the deposition, that it was initiated only for discovery purposes, or that it was taken before other discovery was completed.

The district court, of course, is afforded broad discretion to admit or exclude any deposition testimony by applying the rules of evidence. But it cannot exclude deposition testimony on the basis that the defendant intended that the deposition be taken for discovery purposes and did not expect that it would be used at trial.

III

The district court also excluded Dr. Amico's deposition because Columbus, where Dr. Amico was located, is within 100 miles of the border of the Southern District of West Virginia, although more than 100 miles from the courthouse in Charleston where the trial was taking place. This interpretation of Rule 32 is also one with which we do not agree.

Rule 32(a)(3)(B) provides that a deposition may be admitted if the witness is "at a greater distance than 100 miles from the *place of trial*" (emphasis added). We hold that for purposes of applying the rule the place of trial is the courthouse where the trial takes place. It is apparent that the rule is intended to protect the convenience of the witness and the parties, and that the limit of convenience is measured by the 100-mile distance. To measure a distance from the borders of the district, as defendants argue, rather than from the courthouse, would provide a variable standard of convenience, depending on the size of the district, the location of the trial, and the location of the witness. Had the drafters of the rule intended that the calculation of the 100 miles be made from the borders of the district they could have so specified. It is noteworthy that the language defining the scope of the subpoena power under Rule 45(e) distinguishes itself from Rule 32(a)(3)(B) by permitting service within 100 miles of the place of trial *or* anywhere within the district (even if it is more than 100 miles). That distinction suggests that the "place of trial" as used in Rule 32(a)(3)(B) is a locus more definite than the entire district. * * *

Although few courts have specifically addressed the meaning of "place of trial," several cases dealing with Rule 32 have interchanged "courthouse" for the "place of trial." *See, e.g.*, United States v. Vespe, 868 F.2d 1328, 1339 (3rd Cir. 1989) (Rule 32 "permits the deposition of a witness who is more than one hundred miles from the *courthouse*.") (emphasis added) * * *.

Because Dr. Amico was beyond 100 miles of the courthouse and no showing was made that his absence was procured by a party (on the contrary, his professional commitment prevented his coming), his deposition was not properly excludable on the ground that he was within 100 miles of the borders of the district.

* * *

REVERSED AND REMANDED.

K.K. HALL, CIRCUIT JUDGE, dissenting:

I agree with the salient legal points of the majority opinion. The district court misstated the "100-mile" rule, and there is no categorical exclusion of "discovery" depositions at trial.

On the other hand, the district court has broad discretion on questions of admissibility of evidence and broad power over the management of litigation before it. In order to avoid disputes like this one, the district court required the parties to prepare an integrated pretrial order. Plaintiff disclosed that Dr. Amico would be a witness, but did not propose to offer his deposition. The defendants had no notice of plaintiff's intention to use the deposition; the deposition was taken at the earliest stages of the litigation. The rules of civil procedure permit the admission of Amico's deposition, but they do not require it. The district court concluded that it would be unfair to ambush the defendants with the deposition at the last moment. I do not believe that this ruling was an abuse of discretion.

* * *

NOTES AND QUESTIONS

1.   What is the rationale for permitting the use of testimony by deposition at trial, rather than insisting on live testimony? Does the format of the deposition, whether videotaped or by written transcript, affect its use under Rule 32?

2.   How do the circumstances for use of deposition testimony under Rule 32(a)(2) differ from those of Rule 32(a)(3)?

3.   Can a party use deposition testimony selectively, offering only portions of the transcript or videotape? See Rule 32(a)(6).

4.   Why is there no longer a distinction drawn between "discovery" and other depositions? Strategically, what steps should a party take with respect to her discovery plan once she knows that the opposing party plans to use a deposition transcript at trial?

5.   Why is the 100-mile rule calculated differently for purposes of a witness's availability under Rule 32(a)(4) than for a subpoena under Rule 45? Is the 100-mile rule an appropriate proxy for unavailability given the different cost and convenience of different modes of travel? See Sloan & Gotfryd, *Eliminating the* 100 *Mile Limit for Civil Trial Witnesses: A Proposal to Modernize Civil Trial Practice*, 140 F.R.D. 33, 37 (1992).

6.   Does absence from the jurisdiction because of military service count as being "unavailable" under Rule 32(a)(4)(C)? See generally Allred, *Depositions and a Case Called* Savard, 63 A.F.L.Rev. 1 (2009).

CHAPTER 11

CASE MANAGEMENT

■ ■ ■

This chapter examines the history, theory, and practice of judicial case management techniques. One of the hallmark features of the adversary system is its reliance on the parties to initiate the action and to move the proceeding toward its resolution. The increased importance of case management, including the centrality of Rule 16 pretrial conferences, in part reflects shifting attitudes about the burdens and benefits of civil litigation and concerns about rising dockets and increased costs. Disagreements about the efficacy of case management are at the center of procedural debates involving pleading, discovery, and summary judgment. As you read the materials that follow, consider the values that ought to inform the practice of case management and whether it might be reformed to improve its utility and fairness.

A. THE DEVELOPMENT OF CASE MANAGEMENT TECHNIQUES

Read Federal Rule of Civil Procedure 16 and the accompanying materials in the Supplement.

MILLER, THE PRETRIAL RUSH TO JUDGMENT: ARE THE "LITIGATION EXPLOSION," "LIABILITY CRISIS," AND EFFICIENCY CLICHÉS ERODING OUR DAY IN COURT AND JURY TRIAL COMMITMENTS?, 78 N.Y.U.L.Rev. 982, 1003 (2003) (footnotes omitted):

Federal district judges began utilizing management techniques on an ad hoc basis in the years following the Second World War. These experimental procedures were organized under the aegis of the Handbook of Recommended Procedure for the Trial of Protracted Cases and then the Manual on Complex Litigation, which first appeared in the 1960s. Their principles were given greater prominence and officially sanctioned in 1983, and then embellished further in 1993 by amendments to Rule 16; prior to these amendments the Rule described a discretionary and rather simple eve-of-trial conference. Given that by the early 1980s only an estimated six percent of cases actually reached trial and the lion's share of resource expenditures occurred pretrial, the Rule was of little help in reducing the institution-to-termination litigation timeframe, let alone achieving any systemic economy. Recognizing that judicial intervention should occur shortly after commencement, Rule 16 was transformed into a provision that encouraged—and in time effectively mandated—judicial management throughout the pretrial proceedings.

SHAPIRO, FEDERAL RULE 16: A LOOK AT THE THEORY AND PRACTICE OF RULEMAKING, 137 U.Pa.L.Rev. 1969, 1981–84 (1989) (footnotes omitted):

* * * Rule [16 was] designed to substitute for formal pleadings the less formal processes of discussion and exchange as ways of narrowing issues for trial and of expediting proof. But because flexibility and discretion were the watchwords, judges were not instructed to do anything; they would only be encouraged to act. At the same time, they were not given express power to act coercively in any way not authorized by other, more formal procedures, and the comments of several important figures in the drafting of the rules left little doubt of their resistance to the coercive use of the conference.

* * *

* * * [A]n extraordinary range of practices * * * developed within the framework of the Rule [as promulgated in 1938]. While in some districts judges made relatively little use of the Rule, and seldom required pretrial conferences, other districts promulgated elaborate local rules that required pretrial conferences in most or all cases and/or imposed heavy burdens on counsel to confer in advance and to prepare detailed pretrial orders for the judge's consideration. Some judges held pretrial conferences early and often, and were encouraged to do so in complex cases by the Manual for Complex Litigation. Some judges saw the pretrial conference as the chance to compel the parties to produce information that had not been (and perhaps could not be) sought in routine pretrial discovery; others saw the occasion as an opportunity to rid the case of frivolous or insubstantial issues of fact or law, whether or not requested to do so by one of the parties in an appropriate motion; still others saw the conference as a device to facilitate settlement, and saw the judge as a major player in that process.

* * *

At a more general level, the major development during this period was a sea-change in the attitude of many, perhaps most, judges toward their role in the pretrial period—a change that occurred with surprisingly little concern for the purposes and limitations of Rule 16. Judges began to see themselves less as neutral adjudicators—deciding what the parties brought to them for decision and proceeding at a pace to be determined by the parties—and more as managers of a costly and complicated process. Many district courts began to assign judges to a case from the beginning, and many judges, encouraged by this system and by the increased availability of magistrates and other support staff, began to manage their cases with a firm hand. Crowded dockets, costly discovery, and delay were seen as problems not just for the litigants but for the system, and even the litigants were thought of as frequent victims of their lawyers' self-interest. The role of the judge, then, was to keep cases moving at a reasonable pace, and to see that cases not be needlessly tried. Indeed, the concept of disposition without trial began to embrace a variety of inventive techniques other than simple mediation and settlement.

* * *

NOTE ON FEDERAL RULE 16

Federal Rule 16 was based on the experience of pretrial conferences in the Wayne County Circuit Court, in Michigan. The rationale for this innovation was explained by a leading commentator and member of the original Advisory Committee:

> Every issue which can * * * be withdrawn from the trial agenda will result in a net gain for all parties concerned. It will save time for the court and jury, save expense for the parties to the action, save trouble for the witnesses, diminish the risk of error by simplifying the proceedings, and reduce the labor and cost of an appeal by curtailing the size of the record. If the admissions go far enough, or the evidence is clear enough, no trial at all may be necessary.

Sunderland, *The Theory and Practice of Pre-Trial Procedure*, 36 Mich.L.Rev. 215, 219 (1937). The rule was designed to be broad and flexible. As was emphasized, "This flexibility calls for discriminating between the cases that need the full treatment and those that do not warrant the full scope of the requirements." Pollack, *Pretrial Conferences*, 50 F.R.D. 451, 465 (1970).

As the excerpt from Professor Miller's article explains, developments in case management techniques were influenced by the emergence of the "big case" and the pressures that large scale discovery and multiple parties placed on the court. In the late 1960s a committee of federal judges, known as the Coordinating Committee for Multiple Litigation of the United States District Courts, together with legal scholars and representatives of the bar, drafted a manual of suggested procedures for dealing with "protracted cases." The manual, which has been revised and updated from time to time, and is now the Manual for Complex Litigation (Fourth) (Federal Judicial Center 2012), traces its origins to the Handbook of Recommended Procedures for the Trial of Protracted Cases, 25 F.R.D. 351 (1960), and also to the Prettyman Report on Procedure in Anti-Trust and Other Protracted Cases, 13 F.R.D. 62 (1951). The

Manual deals with many contemporary procedural devices that are now also used in less complex cases.

In 1983, Rule 16 was substantially revised. As the Advisory Committee Notes explain, the amendment was aimed at making "scheduling and case management an express goal of pretrial procedure," shifting the emphasis of the pretrial conference from preparation for trial to a "process of judicial management that embraces the entire pretrial phase, especially motions and discovery." In particular, amended Rule 16(b) made a scheduling order mandatory in every case, although it also authorized the district courts to promulgate local rules exempting certain categories of cases from the requirement. In cases not exempted, the assumption was that the judge or a magistrate would take "some action in every case within 120 days after the complaint is filed." In addition, Rule 16(c) expanded the topics to be discussed at a pretrial conference; subdivision (7) included discussion of settlement and of using alternative dispute mechanisms to resolve the suit short of trial. Rule 16(f) specifically provided for the imposition of sanctions on parties and their counsel who failed to comply with a management order. Proponents defended judicial case management on efficiency grounds, contending that the adversary system had become "too costly and inefficient a device for resolving civil disputes." Miller, *The Adversary System: Dinosaur or Phoenix*, 69 Minn.L.Rev. 1, 20 (1984).

Amendments in 1993 aimed at strengthening the judge's managerial authority. The amended rule set deadlines for specific litigation activities, made explicit and expanded the topics to be discussed at the pretrial conference, provided for greater supervision of discovery, allowed for earlier consideration of pretrial dispositive motions (such as summary judgment), and confirmed that the judge has authority to facilitate settlement by ordering the parties to be present at pretrial conferences. The amendment aligned the deadline for the initial scheduling order with the period for service of process, and clarified the scope of the trial court's discretion to impose sanctions for such derelictions as failing to comply with a scheduling order or failing to attend or prepare for a pretrial conference. For discussion of Rule 16 by an experienced trial judge who urged greater use of case management techniques, see Richey, *Rule 16 Revised, and Related Rules: Analysis of Recent Developments for the Benefit of Bench and Bar*, 157 F.R.D. 69 (1994). See also Kelleher, *The December 1993 Amendments to the Federal Rules of Civil Procedure—A Critical Analysis*, 12 Touro L. Rev. 7, 80 (1995).

The 2006 amendment to Rule 16(b) addressed a variety of discovery issues that may be discussed at a pretrial conference, including the discovery or disclosure of electronically stored information. Rule 26(f), which requires the parties to meet and confer to develop a discovery plan, was amended at the same time in order to dovetail with Rule 16(b).

The 2015 amendment required the scheduling conference to be held in person, by telephone, or by electronic means, thus ruling out conferring by mail. In addition, the rule reduced the time to issue the scheduling order (consistent with the shortening of time to effect service under Rule 4(m)), although the court retains discretion to extend the time. Further, the amendment again expanded the list of topics that may be included in the pretrial order, see Rule 16(b)(3)(B), largely concerning preservation of electronically stored information.

Early critics of case management emphasized its incompatibility with features of the adversary system, such as party autonomy, litigant initiative, and judicial neutrality. They also warned that judicial management would be less transparent than traditional judging, and that the practice would be susceptible to bias, yet evade appellate oversight. See Resnik, *Managerial Judges*, 96 Harv.L.Rev. 374, 376–78 (1982). Even some proponents of case management voiced concern that the rule's emphasis on expedition and flexibility could cut too far against court access, the civil jury right, and due process. See Schuh, *Curbing Judicial Discretion in Pretrial Conferences*, 20 Lewis & Clark L. Rev. 647 (2016). Other commentators have questioned whether the civil litigation system is as costly and slow as the conventional wisdom assumes. See Reda, *The Cost-and-Delay Narrative in Civil Justice Reform: Its Fallacies and Functions*, 90 Ore.L.Rev. 1085 (2012).

The pressures of "big cases" resolved through multidistrict consolidation or class-wide settlement have served as accelerants in the acceptance of case management and the development of new techniques. It is not clear, however, that all or even the majority of cases are of a size or complexity to benefit from active case management. See Subrin, *Reflections on the Twin Dreams of Simplified Procedure and Useful Empiricism*, 35 W.St.U.L.Rev. 173 (2007). Nor can one safely quantify the negative effects of active judicial supervision on an adversarial system that values litigant autonomy and relies on judicial interpretation for the creation of democratic norms:

> The important resource that the judiciary provides is a forum for the integration of law and fact. When the parties settle a case prior to trial or when a judge terminates a case prior to a trial, the process of integrating law and fact is truncated. When this process is abbreviated systematically, the mandate of substantive law is compromised; false negatives and, to a lesser extent, false positives, surely follow. Trials, in particular, are the paradigmatic integration of law and fact. Importantly, when trials vanish, the *shadow* of trials also vanish. The shadow of a trial is critical for parties engaged in settlement negotiations: if trial is not a realistic alternative to a negotiated settlement, the only realistic alternative is a motion terminating the case.

Main, *Procedural Constants: How Delay Aversion Shapes Reform*, 15 Nev.L.J. 1597, 1628 (2015) (footnotes omitted).

In recent years, a number of states have developed management practices modelled after those in the federal courts. E.g., Jokela & Herr, *Special Masters in State Court Complex Litigation: An Available and Underused Case Management Tool*, 31 Wm. Mitchell L.Rev. 1299 (2005). However, state practice varies a great deal. For a survey, see Oakley, *A Fresh Look at the Federal Rules in State Courts*, 3 Nev.L.J. 354 (2002/03).

The appropriate role of case management cannot be assessed in isolation. As one commentator has observed, "Case management is a part of the larger, interwoven fabric of our dispute-resolution system. It is inextricably bound up with policy debates about the role of judges and with fundamental questions about the proper design of pretrial procedure." Gensler, *Judicial Case Management: Caught in the Crossfire*, 60 Duke L.J. 669, 672–73 (2010). Civil law systems, such as in Germany and France, have long relied on the judge to take an active role in superintending the disposition of a lawsuit. See Langbein, *The German Advantage in Civil Procedure*, 82 U.Chi.L.Rev. 823 (1985). It probably is significant that the training and selection of first-tier judges in continental Europe differs from that of judges in the United States. See Dodson & Klebba, *Global Civil Procedure Trends in the Twenty-First Century*, 34 B.C. Int'l & Comp.L.Rev. 1 (2011).

B. THE OPERATION OF RULE 16

Read Federal Rule of Civil Procedure 16, the sample pretrial scheduling order, and the sample Standing Order set out in the Supplement.

---

1. CASE MANAGEMENT TECHNIQUES

NICK V. MORGAN'S FOODS, INC.
United States Court of Appeals, Eighth Circuit, 2001.
270 F.3d 590.

MCMILLIAN, CIRCUIT JUDGE.

[The district court imposed a monetary sanction on defendant and its counsel for failing to participate in good faith in court-ordered alternative dispute resolution in an effort to settle the lawsuit.]

* * *

* * * Nick filed suit against appellant on June 15, 1998, alleging sexual harassment and retaliation in violation of Title VII of the Civil Rights Act of 1964, as amended, 42 U.S.C. § 2000e *et seq.* At that time, appellant was represented by outside counsel Robert Seibel, but all business decisions were made by appellant's in-house counsel Barton Craig. Pursuant to Fed. R. Civ. P. 16(f),[a] a pretrial scheduling conference was held on May 20, 1999.

---

[a]   The rule is now Rule 16(b)1)(B).

The parties consented to ADR with a court-appointed mediator pursuant to E.D. Mo. L.R. 6.01—6.05 ("the local rules"), and agreed to report back to the district court with the results of the ADR by September 30, 1999. On August 2, 1999, the district court issued an Order Referring Case to Alternate Dispute Resolution ("Referral Order") mandating that the ADR process be conducted in compliance with the local rules and listing other specific requirements. * * * These requirements included, *inter alia*, that, at least seven days before the first ADR conference, each party shall supply the mediator with a memorandum presenting a summary of the disputed facts and its position on liability and damages; that all parties, counsel, corporate representatives and claims professionals with settlement authority shall attend all mediation conferences and participate in good faith; and that noncompliance with any court deadline could result in the imposition of sanctions against the appropriate party or parties.

On appellant's request, the district court agreed to postpone the first ADR conference until October 18, 1999. Appellant did not file the memorandum that was required to be filed at least seven days before the first ADR conference. In attendance at the conference on October 18, 1999 was the court-appointed mediator; Nick; Nick's counsel; appellant's outside counsel, Seibel; and a corporate representative of appellant who had no independent knowledge of the facts of the case and had permission to settle only up to $500. Any settlement offer over $500 had to be relayed by telephone to Craig, who chose not to attend the ADR conference on the advice of outside counsel Seibel. During the ADR conference, Nick twice made offers of settlement that were rejected without a counteroffer by appellant. The ADR conference ended shortly thereafter without a settlement having been reached.

After the ADR conference, the mediator informed the district court of appellant's minimal level of participation, and the district court issued an order directing appellant to show cause why it should not be sanctioned for its failure to participate in good faith in the court-ordered ADR process. In an October 29, 1999 response, appellant asserted that the Referral Order was only a set of nonbinding guidelines and admitted that it decided not to comply with the guidelines because doing otherwise would be a waste of time and money. On the same day, Nick moved to sanction appellant for failing to participate in good faith in the ADR process and requested attorneys' fees and costs arising out of her participation in the mediation.

The district court held a hearing on its show cause order and Nick's motion for sanctions on December 1, 1999, at which time Seibel confirmed that appellant's corporate representative at the ADR conference had only $500 settlement authority; that any change in appellant's position could only be made by Craig, who was not present but available by telephone; and that counsel had indeed failed to file the pre-ADR conference memorandum. After hearing argument by both parties, the district court concluded that appellant failed to participate in good faith in the court-ordered ADR process and sanctioned appellant $1,390.63 and appellant's outside counsel $1,390.62. These sanctions were calculated to cover the cost of the ADR conference fees ($506.25) and Nick's attorneys' fees ($2,275.00). The court also ordered appellant to pay a $1,500.00 fine to the Clerk of the District Court as a sanction for failing to prepare the required memorandum and for its decision to send a corporate representative with limited authority to settle to the ADR conference. The district court ordered appellant and appellant's outside counsel each to pay $30.00 to Nick for the costs she incurred attending the ADR conference.

On December 20, 1999, appellant filed a Motion for Reconsideration and Vacation of the Court's Order Granting Plaintiff's Motion for Sanctions (motion for reconsideration). The district court denied the motion for reconsideration and imposed additional sanctions against appellant and appellant's counsel in the amount of $1,250.00 each to be paid to the Clerk of the District Court for vexatiously increasing the costs of litigation by filing a frivolous motion. This appeal followed. Appellant appeals the sanctions levied against it that are to be paid to the Clerk of the District Court; Appellant does not contest the sanctions levied against it that are to be paid to Nick and her counsel.

* * *

Appellant argues that, whereas Rule 11 * * * authorizes monetary fines payable to the court, Rule 16 does not. * * * Rule 16(f) expressly permits a judge to impose any other sanction the judge deems appropriate in addition to, or in lieu of, reasonable expenses. * * * Here, the district court judge acted well within his discretion by imposing a monetary fine payable to the Clerk * * * as a sanction for failing to prepare the required memorandum, deciding to send a corporate representative with limited authority to the ADR conference, and for vexatiously increasing the costs of litigation by filing a frivolous motion for reconsideration.

* * *

Appellant urges that the "uncontroverted facts on the record conclusively establish that all of the conduct which irritated the Trial Court was the exclusive product of Appellant's trial lawyer and unknown to Appellant." * * * Appellant argues that the affidavits of Craig and Seibel establish that it had no knowledge that its conduct was sanctionable and that its outside counsel was solely responsible for the noncompliance. * * * Appellant claims that Seibel did not pass along to Craig the necessity for a memorandum, and that, although Seibel advised Craig of the district court's Referral Order and the relevant local rules, Craig read neither and relied instead on the advice of Seibel. * * * Appellant further claims that Seibel advised Craig that his attendance at the ADR conference was not necessary. * * * For this reason, appellant argues that the district court abused its discretion in imposing the sanctions against it and not solely against its outside counsel.

* * *4

It is a well-established principle in this Circuit that a party may be held responsible for the actions of its counsel. * * * While forcing parties to answer for their attorneys' behavior may seem harsh, * * * litigants who are truly misled and victimized by their attorneys have recourse in malpractice actions. * * * [T]he sanction imposed by the district court need only be proportionate to the litigant's transgression. * * *

* * *

In sum, we hold that the district court did not abuse its discretion in imposing monetary sanctions against appellant for its lack of good faith participation in the ADR process, for its failure to comply with the district court's August 2, 1999, Referral Order, and for vexatiously increasing the costs of litigation by filing a frivolous motion for reconsideration. The order of the district court is affirmed.

NOTES AND QUESTIONS

1.   As *Nick* illustrates, Rule 16 anticipates that the judge will play an energetic role in encouraging the parties to settle their dispute. See Glover, *The Federal Rules of Civil Settlement*, 87 N.Y.U.L.Rev. 1713 (2012). That role often includes, as in *Nick*, facilitating settlement by directing the parties toward the use of alternative dispute resolution. For practice prior to the 1993 amendment, see G. Heileman Brewing Co. v. Joseph Oat Corp., 871 F.2d 648 (7th Cir. 1989) (en banc). Does the facilitation of settlement undermine its ability to decide the case on the merits? Does your answer depend on whether the trial is to a jury or to the bench? Would it be preferable to refer all settlement discussions to a third party? For suggestions on how to reform settlement conferences to protect against "unbounded, unbridled, and virtually unfettered" judicial discretion, see Parness, *Improving Judicial Settlement Conferences*, 39 U.C. Davis L.Rev. 1891, 1891–92 (2006).

2.   Rule 16 provides the district courts with an arsenal of tools for managing a judicial proceeding. As one commentator puts it, the rule offers federal judges "more managerial arrows than can fit in an ordinary quiver." See Rowe, *Authorized Managerialism Under the Federal Rules—And the Extent of Convergence with Civil-Law Judging*, 36 Sw.U.L.Rev. 191, 196 (2007). Rule 16 authority embraces such orders as the court's dismissing a party from the lawsuit, blocking the presentation of testimony at trial, and

---

4   Appellant argues that its counsel, Seibel, failed to inform appellant that Craig was required to attend the mediation and instead erroneously assured appellant that sending its highest ranking manager in Missouri was sufficient. * * * This argument incorrectly frames the issue because the problem was not the rank of the corporate representative but the corporate representative's ability to meaningfully participate in the ADR conference and to reconsider the company's position on settlement at that conference.

enforcing the waiver of claims or defenses. Illustrative is Freeman v. Astrue, 405 Fed.Appx. 148, 150–51 (9th Cir. 2010) (no abuse of discretion by excluding evidence filed 34 minutes after the court-imposed deadline). But a court's powers to manage each stage of litigation, including pretrial discovery, are not limitless and will exceed permissible bounds if used to impose undue restrictions on the process of fact gathering and adjudication. For an example of a judge's use of managerial authority that was deemed an abuse of discretion, see Miller v. Sam Houston State University, 986 F.3d 880 (5th Cir. 2021), discussed p. 666, Note 6, supra.

3.   Rule 16 permits the imposition of monetary sanctions on a party or the party's counsel. Should these sanctions be compensatory—to reimburse the opposing party or the court for the added litigation costs—or a deterrent? How do Rule 16 sanctions differ from those imposed under Rule 11? See p. 458, Note on Federal Rule 11, supra. Are monetary sanctions always preferable to the relatively drastic sanction of dismissal?

4.   The liberal pleading amendment standard of Rule 15 does not generally apply to modification of a pretrial scheduling order:

> The pretrial scheduling order is designed to allow the district court to better manage its calendar and to facilitate the more efficient disposition of cases by settlement or by trial. *See Johnson v. Mammoth Recreations, Inc.*, 975 F.2d 604, 607–08 (9th Cir. 1992). A scheduling order is not "a frivolous piece of paper, idly entered, which can be cavalierly disregarded by counsel without peril." *Id.* at 610 (citation and quotation marks omitted). Rather, a scheduling order may be changed only with the court's consent and for "good cause." Fed. R. Civ. P. 16(b)(4). But, the "good cause" standard requires less than the "manifest injustice" test used to modify a final pretrial order. *See* Fed. R. Civ. P. 16(e). *See also* Fed. R. Civ. P. 16, 1983 Advisory Committee Notes ("Since the scheduling order is entered early in the litigation, this standard seems more appropriate than a 'manifest injustice' or 'substantial hardship' test.").

> When litigants move to alter the schedule, the court's inquiry focuses primarily on the diligence of the moving party * * *. Essentially, "[t]he district court may modify the pretrial schedule 'if it cannot reasonably be met despite the diligence of the party seeking the extension'. . . . [i]f that party was not diligent, the inquiry should end." *Johnson*, 975 F.2d at 609 (internal citation omitted). Ultimately, a district court has "broad discretion" to alter the schedule. *United States v. Flynt*, 756 F.2d 1352, 1358 (9th Cir. 1985).

Stoddart v. Express Services, 2017 WL 3333994 (E.D. Cal. 2017).

To determine whether the party seeking modification was diligent, courts in the Ninth Circuit look primarily at three factors:

> [T]he movant may be required to show the following: (1) that she was diligent in assisting the Court in creating a workable Rule 16 order

* * *; (2) that her noncompliance with a Rule 16 deadline occurred or will occur, notwithstanding her diligent efforts to comply, because of the development of matters which could not have been reasonably foreseen or anticipated at the time of the Rule 16 scheduling conference * * *; and (3) that she was diligent in seeking amendment of the Rule 16 order, once it became apparent that she could not comply with the order * * *.

Jackson v. Laureate, Inc., 186 F.R.D. 605, 608 (E.D. Cal. 1999). The Sixth Circuit relies upon a four-factor test:

(1)   the explanation for the failure to timely move for leave to amend;

(2)   the importance of the amendment;

(3)   potential prejudice in allowing the amendment; and

(4)   the availability of a continuance to cure such prejudice.

Fahim v. Marriott Hotel Services, Inc., 551 F.3d 344, 348 (5th Cir. 2008). How do these standards differ, if at all?

5.   KASSNER v. 2nd AVENUE DELICATESSEN, INC., 496 F.3d 229 (2d Cir. 2007), an employment discrimination action, plaintiff moved to amend the complaint before defendant had filed an answer, but one month after the date specified in the Rule 16(b) scheduling order as the final date for the amendment of the pleadings. The court of appeals held that the more stringent "good cause" standard of Rule 16(b), and not Rule 15(a), applied:

* * * The advisory committee notes [to the 1983 amendments] provide that "[i]tem (1) assures that at some point both the parties and the pleadings will be fixed, by setting a time within which joinder of parties shall be completed and the pleadings amended." * * * This objective would be frustrated by an interpretation of the first sentence of Rule 15(a) that precludes a district court from exercising any discretion to specify the time period during which a party may effect the first amendment of its complaint prior to the serving of a responsive pleading. Rule 16(b), in allowing modifications of scheduling orders only for good cause, provides the district courts discretion to ensure that limits on time to amend pleadings do not result in prejudice or hardship to either side. * * *

Id. at 243–44. Other circuits also have held that Rule 15 governs a timely motion to amend a complaint, but that Rule 16(b) governs a post-deadline motion. E.g., Public Health Equipment & Supply Co., Inc. v. Clarke Mosquito Control Systems, Inc., 410 Fed.Appx. 738 (5th Cir. 2010); Sosa v. Airprint Systems, Inc., 133 F.3d 1417, 1419 (11th Cir. 1998) ("If we considered only Rule 15(a) without regard to Rule 16(b), we would render scheduling orders meaningless and effectively would read Rule 16(b) and its good cause requirement out of the Federal Rules of Civil Procedure.").

6.   An appellate court will accord deference to the trial court's managerial decisions, including whether to impose a sanction. The First

Circuit has warned that it is "folly" to treat case management orders as "polite suggestions rather than firm directives," and that a party who ignores an order does so on peril of dismissal:

> Administering a bustling docket is hard work. * * *

> Of course, dismissal does not follow automatically from every failure to abide by a case-management order. When a party fails to obey such an order, the selection of an appropriate sanction is peculiarly within the province of the district court. In making this selection, a district judge "must work a complicated equation, balancing fairness to the parties with the need to manage crowded dockets." *Macaulay v. Anas,* 321 F.3d 45, 51 (1st Cir. 2003). Given the trial court's "intimate knowledge of the variables that enter into the equation, appellate review of sanctions orders is deferential." *Id.* * * * "[W]e focus our review particularly on whether a material factor deserving significant weight was ignored, whether an improper factor was relied upon, or whether when all proper and no improper factors were assessed the court made a serious mistake in weighing them." *United States v. One 1987 BMW 325,* 985 F.2d 655, 657–58 (1st Cir. 1993) * * *. Absent an error of law—and we discern none here—the party challenging a sanction faces an uphill climb in persuading a reviewing court that the trial court abused its discretion. *Id.* at 657.

Mulero-Abreu v. Puerto Rico Police Dept., 675 F.3d 88, 89, 91–92 (1st Cir. 2012).

7. Note that the sanctions imposed by the district court against the appellant in *Nick* stemmed in part from counsel's failure to adhere to requirements set forth in the Eastern District of Missouri's local rules. Those local rules governed the referral of cases to court-ordered alternative dispute resolution. In some district courts, local rules impose duties on litigants or counsel, in furtherance of case management, that are not found in the Federal Rules. These can include provisions that expand the Rule 16 concept of encouraging planning and consensual resolution, such as local rules requiring parties to meet and confer before filing motions. See, e.g., D. Minn. R. 7.1.

2. THE FINAL PRETRIAL ORDER

PAYNE V. S. S. NABOB
United States Court of Appeals, Third Circuit, 1962.
302 F.2d 803.

MCLAUGHLIN, CIRCUIT JUDGE.

In this personal injury admiralty action libellant filed a pretrial memorandum stating that he was relying upon the condition of a winch to prove his cause of action. The judge's pretrial report noted that. Sometime later the suit went to trial. Libellant's attorney included in his opening the fact that the loading had been handled improperly as an important element of his proof of unseaworthiness. The impleaded stevedore employer objected as it was outside the scope of the pretrial memorandum and report. The trial court sustained the objection. Two witnesses on behalf of the libellant, not listed in his pretrial memorandum, were not allowed to testify. Libellant's attorney moved for a continuance and this was denied.

* * *

Appellant * * * would have it that the Standing Order [local rule adopting Rule 16] did not furnish any ground for the court's barring of the unseaworthy allegation and of the witnesses not mentioned in the appellant's pretrial memorandum or the court's pretrial report. This seems to be founded on the thought that a pretrial memorandum is merely preparatory to the conference and that the court's pretrial order is the sole proof of the results of the pretrial procedure. In this instance, goes the contention, the function of appellant's memorandum was exhausted at the conference and since no pretrial "order" was made there were no binding results of the pretrial steps. [Padovani v. Bruchhausen, 293 F.2d 546 (2d Cir. 1961)] * * * is cited for this, where it states:

> "Nothing in the rule [16] affords basis for clubbing the parties into admissions they do not willingly make; but it is a way of advancing the trial ultimately to be had by setting forth points on which the parties are agreed after a conference directed by a trained judge."

Appellant was not clubbed into admissions he did not willingly make. It was his own voluntary statement of the basis of his claim that was included in the pretrial report of the judge. The report was never objected to as incorrectly outlining appellant's pretrial statement.

The position now taken that the pretrial report of the trial judge because it is not titled as an "order" does not comply with Rule 16 is without merit. Appellant's pretrial memorandum was filed. In accordance with the Standing Order it contained a "brief summary statement of both the facts of this case and counsel's contention as to the liability of defendant." It also contained "The names and addresses of all witnesses (except rebuttal) whom the plaintiff expects to call to testify at the time of trial." The pretrial conference was held in due course and attended by the attorneys for the parties. Based on the pretrial memoranda and the conference, the district judge drew and filed his report. There was no complaint concerning it or any part of it down to and including the trial until libellant's attorney was stopped in his opening as he went beyond his pretrial outline of alleged liability. The pretrial "report"[2] drawn, signed and filed by the pretrial judge

---

[2] "Pre-Trial Report of Judge Van Dusen

Date Pre-Trial Held: 9/21/59 No. on Consolidated List: 2109 303 of 1958 in Admiralty

Case Title: Hosea Payne v. S.S. Nabob & North German Lloyd v. Lavino Shipping Co.

1. Trial Counsel: LC Philip Dorfman, Esq. & Saul C. Waldbaum, Esq.

R—Robert A. Hauslohner, Esq. (T. Mount will try)

properly and fully (having the particular litigation and its requirements in mind) complies with the requirements of Rule 16. It, including its references to the pretrial memoranda, succinctly fulfilled the letter and spirit of pretrial. It reduced the action to essentials, eliminated surplusage, enabled the parties and the court to prepare for a trial of stated issues, named witnesses and contained no hidden charms. The argument to the contrary, depending as it does on a quibble over the word "report", is rootless.

It is asserted on behalf of the appellant that the Standing Order can only be construed as a request to stipulate, that counsel had no intention of stipulating and that no warning or notice was given by the Standing Order that failure to list the requirements ordered would constitute a stipulation or a waiver of all other theories. Rule 16 gives as the first purpose of pretrial "The simplification of issues".[b] Under the Standing Order counsel were asked to furnish "A brief summary of both the facts of the case and counsel's contentions as to the liability of the defendant." That was done. Libellant's contentions as to the liability of the defendant were inserted into the Court's Report with the note "See pre-trial memo". The Report was filed September 28, 1959. The trial did not commence until March 14, 1960, a five and a half months interval during which no effort was made to change the signed and filed contentions of the libellant regarding the liability of the defendant or to add names of witnesses. The facts that the situation was plain on its face and that the practice was well settled by then, (the Standing Order having been in effect since October 23, 1958), set the tone for this contention on behalf of appellant. Krieger v. Ownership Corporation, 270 F.2d 265 (3 Cir. 1959), relied upon by appellant is inapposite. We there held that disputed issues of fact *actually raised* at the pretrial stage could not be resolved by the trial court on motion for summary judgment. It has long been the law that attorneys at the pretrial stage "owe a duty to the court and opposing counsel to make a full and fair disclosure of their views as to what the real issues at the trial will be." Cherney v. Holmes, 185 F.2d 718, 721 (7th Cir. 1950) * * *. It is

---

IR—F. Hastings Griffin, Jr., Esq. (P. Price will try)

2. Amendments: If IR wishes to amend pre-trial memo, notice to be given to undersigned.

3. Discovery: Respondent will answer impleaded respondent's interrogatories (unexecuted copies to be furnished counsel by September 23).

4. L's Claim: Ship unseaworthy due to improper port winch on after side at #2 hatch. Brakes would not hold when set in neutral. Port winch on house-fall did not work from early hours of morning. See pre-trial memo.

5. R's Claim: Sole cause of injuries was L's negligence and that of his fellow workmen. Two men pushed draft into L and 2 other men said nothing was defective in winches. See pre-trial memo. IR's position—see pre-trial memo.

6. Stipulations:

7. Issues:

8. Legal Issues:

9. Trial Time: 6 days

Francis L. Van Dusen, J."

b   This language has been altered without any substantive change.

through such disclosure at pretrial that trial prejudice can be avoided. The awareness of appellant's attorney to the trial situation is apparent in his request for a continuance when he told the court "I think under the circumstances I would move for a continuance of the case to give *the other side* ample time, because actually this is a question of surprise." (Emphasis supplied.)

It is argued also that the court abused its discretion by refusing to permit amendment of the pretrial memorandum. This was not an easy decision for the trial judge. His inclination clearly, as is habitual with judges, was to help. And help he would have if, in his opinion, he could have done so fairly. But he was confronted with the realization that if he granted the request or allowed a continuance of the trial he was repudiating the whole pretrial theory and system as understood and followed in the Eastern District at a crucial period of its existence. Pretrial was finally on a firm foundation there. The judges had all given it generous and complete attention. This, with the gradual realization of the bar that pretrial was here to stay as a vital element of litigation practice and its resultant full cooperation, had made pretrial procedure routine in the Eastern District. One consequence was that directly and indirectly enormous relief was given the badly clogged trial list. It was admittedly vitally important to make sure that pretrial procedure would continue to function properly. One necessary phase of attaining that objective was, as expressed by the trial judge, "We have come to the point of enforcing it very strictly." In the circumstances he considered himself obliged to deny the motions to amend the pretrial memorandum with respect to liability allegations and witnesses. The refusal of appellant's motion for a continuance is in the same category.

Beyond all doubt the judge acted entirely within his discretion. It was difficult for him, it took courage but it was what this sound, experienced judge had to do as he saw it, in accordance with his judicial obligation.

The decree of the district court will be affirmed.

NOTES AND QUESTIONS

1.   The general rule makes the final pretrial order, together with all stipulations, agreements, and statements of counsel made at the final pretrial conference, binding for purposes of trial. See Kona Technology Corp. v. Southern Pacific Transportation Co., 225 F.3d 595, 604 (5th Cir. 2000). Certainly the benefits of case management depend on the court's efficient resolution of each stage of the proceeding and development of a clear plan for final disposition.

2.   The practical significance of the final pretrial order cannot be overstated. In HOWARD v. KERR GLASS MFG. CO., 699 F.2d 330 (6th Cir. 1983), the Sixth Circuit ruled that the final pretrial order prevailed over the

original pleadings and that the trial judge had erred in refusing to admit evidence on issues included in the final pretrial order but not in the pleadings. Conversely, omission of an issue from a pretrial order in other cases has proved fatal. In McLEAN CONTRACTING CO. v. WATERMAN S.S. CORP., 277 F.3d 477 (4th Cir. 2002), plaintiff had made it clear that defendant's liability depended upon the fact that a third company had acted as defendant's agent. Defendant intended to dispute the agency but failed to have it included as an issue in the pretrial order. The appellate court held it was not an abuse of discretion to refuse defendant's evidence on the issue; to the contrary, the court underscored that "[c]ounsel bear a substantial responsibility for assisting the court in identifying the factual issues worthy of trial. If counsel fails to identify an issue to the court, the right to have the issue tried is waived." Id. at 480.

C. NON-ARTICLE III JUDICIAL PERSONNEL

Read Federal Rules of Civil Procedure 53, 72, and 73, and the materials accompanying Rule 53 in the Supplement.

The managerial authority of federal judges is bolstered by the assistance of non-Article III decision-makers such as magistrate judges and masters. The contribution of these judicial adjuncts, who serve for a fixed statutory term or by appointment, is quite significant. Magistrate Judges can preside over civil trials with the parties' consent and often serve as the initial adjudicator of a dispute. In 2016, magistrate judges disposed of 1,087,249 matters, and held 57,660 pretrial conferences in civil actions. See United States Courts, U.S. Magistrate Judges—Judicial Business 2016, available at: http://www.uscourts.gov/statistics-reports/us-magistrate-judges-judicial-business-2016. Masters also play a critical role as adjuncts in the federal courts, assigned such tasks as supervising discovery, overseeing disputes about attorney's fees, and managing other aspects of complex cases. The selection of magistrates and masters falls within the authority of the district judges within guidelines that are general and differ among districts.

1. MAGISTRATE JUDGES

NOTES AND QUESTIONS

1. The use of extra-judicial personnel is not a new phenomenon, but the practice in civil cases initially was disfavored. See Silberman, *Masters and Magistrates, Part I: The English Model*, 50 N.Y.U.L.Rev. 1070 (1975); Silberman, *Masters and Magistrates, Part II: The American Analogue*, 50 N.Y.U.L.Rev. 1297 (1975). The modern office of magistrate judge dates to the 1968 enactment of the Federal Magistrates Act, which replaced a system of

commissioners who carried out ministerial tasks for the federal judges. See Foschio, *A History of the Development of the Office of United States Commissioner and Magistrate Judge System*, 1999 Fed.Cts.L.Rev. 4 (1999); Weinstein & Wiener, *Of Sailing Ships and Seeking Facts: Brief Reflections on Magistrates and the Federal Rules of Civil Procedure*, 62 St. John's L.Rev. 429 (1988).

2.   Magistrate judges are judicial officers who serve as adjuncts to the district court. Unlike Article III judges who are appointed by the President after confirmation by the Senate and have the protection of life tenure, magistrate judges are appointed by the district judges of their court and serve for fixed terms. The work of a magistrate judge comports with the requirements of Article III under the theory that an assigned case "belongs to the district judge throughout," Conetta v. National Hair Care Centers, 236 F.3d 67, 74 (1st Cir. 2001), and the "Article III courts firmly 'control' each magistrate." Orsini v. Wallace, 913 F.2d 474, 477–79 (8th Cir. 1990), cert. denied, 498 U.S. 1128, 111 S.Ct. 1093, 112 L.Ed.2d 1197 (1991). At bottom, the use of magistrate judges is justified on efficiency grounds:

> A preference for magistrate judges can be explained by considering the comparative "prices" of a life-tenured judgeship and of a magistrate judgeship. Not only are Article III judges more expensive in dollar terms, they also create possibilities for party patronage and for conflicts between Congress and the Executive. Further, Article III judgeships typically require lag time from judicial request to congressional authorization and executive appointment. In contrast, magistrate judge lines can be created directly by the judiciary, which remains dependent on Congress for funding but not for appointing or allocating positions.

Resnik, *Trial as Error, Jurisdiction as Injury: Transforming the Meaning of Article* III, 113 Harv.L.Rev. 924, 990–91 (2000). See also Resnik, *Judicial Selection and Democratic Theory: Demand, Supply, and Life Tenure*, 26 Cardozo L.Rev. 579 (2005).

3.   What kinds of determinations may be assigned to a magistrate judge under 28 U.S.C. § 636(b)(1)? Can you identify the motions that are excepted under the statute? What is the scope of the magistrate's authority regarding "dispositive" motions? What is the procedure for objecting to a magistrate judge's recommendations and determinations? Would it be constitutional for a magistrate judge to terminate a case before trial without de novo review by an Article III judge? Likewise, should a magistrate judge's imposition of sanctions be subject to de novo review? See Bell, *The Power to Award Sanctions: Does It Belong in the Hands of Magistrate Judge*s, 61 Alb.L.Rev. 433 (1997).

4.   The surge in the number of litigants who appear pro se has raised questions about the complexity of court procedure and the fairness of having parties navigate the litigation process without counsel. See Swank, *The Pro Se Phenomenon*, 19 BYU J.Pub.L. 373 (2005). The Eastern District of New York created a magistrate judge position to hear many categories of pro se matters.

See Bloom & Hershkoff, *Federal Courts, Magistrate Judges, and the Pro Se Plaintiff*, 16 Notre Dame J.L. Ethics & Pub.Pol'y 475 (2002). Do you see any benefits to this approach? Disadvantages? See Stancil, *Substitute Equality and Procedural Justice*, 102 Iowa L.Rev. 1633 (2017).

2. MASTERS

Prior to the adoption of Federal Rule 53 in 1938, the Supreme Court recognized that in "exceptional circumstances" a court had authority to appoint a master "to aid judges in the performance of specific judicial duties, as they may arise in the progress of a cause." La Buy v. Howes Leather Co., 352 U.S. 249, 256, 77 S.Ct. 309, 313, 1 L.Ed.2d 290, 297 (1957) (internal citations omitted). What circumstances ought to count as exceptional? Does Rule 53 incorporate that limitation? Does the appointment of a master depend on the parties' consent?

NOTES AND QUESTIONS

1.   Rule 53 was amended in 2003 making it easier to appoint a master in a jury case. See Fellows & Hardock, *Federal Court Special Masters: A Vital Resource in the Era of Complex Litigation*, 31 Wm. Mitchell L.Rev. 1269, 1272–73 (2005); Scheindlin & Redgrave, *The Evolution and Impact of the New Federal Rule Governing Special Masters*, 51 Fed.Law. 34 (Feb. 2004).

2.   What are the key differences between a magistrate judge and a special master?

3.   IN RE WORLD TRADE CENTER DISASTER SITE LITIG., 521 F.3d 169 (2d Cir. 2008), involved litigation by more than 9,000 plaintiffs, including New York City fire fighters, against 200 defendants for injuries allegedly caused by exposure to toxic chemicals during the clean-up effort that followed the destruction of the World Trade Center on September 11, 2001. The district judge appointed two special masters to oversee "bellwether" trials but settlements were reached before the trials took place. See Lahav, *The Case for "Trial by Formula*," 90 Tex.L.Rev. 571, 610–12 (2012). The use of special masters in this litigation is to be distinguished from the special master who administered the September 11th Victim Compensation Fund, which was established under the Air Transportation Safety and System Stabilization Act, and who reported to the Attorney General of the United States.

CHAPTER 12

ADJUDICATION WITHOUT TRIAL OR BY SPECIAL PROCEEDING

■ ■ ■

This chapter examines procedures that may dispose of a lawsuit without a trial. The main focus is Federal Rule 56, which allows a court to enter judgment as a matter of law if there are no material issues of fact in dispute. The chapter also covers voluntary and involuntary dismissals and default judgments. Initially, courts used Rule 56 cautiously, only "to weed out frivolous and sham cases, and cases for which the law had a quick and definitive answer." Wald, *Summary Judgment at Sixty*, 76 Tex.L.Rev. 1897, 1897 (1998). However, in 1986, the Supreme Court decided a trilogy of cases that encouraged greater use of summary judgment with a resulting decline in the number of civil trials—Celotex v. Catrett, 477 U.S. 317, 106 S.Ct. 2548, 91 L.Ed.2d 265; Anderson v. Liberty Lobby, Inc., 477 U.S. 242, 106 S.Ct. 2505, 91 L.Ed.2d 202; and Matsushita Electric Industrial Co. v. Zenith Radio Corp., 475 U.S. 574, 106 S.Ct. 1348, 89 L.Ed.2d 538. See Langbein, *The Disappearance of Civil Trial in the United States*, 122 Yale L.J. 522 (2012). Unquestionably, summary disposition can save time and money. However, critics warn that a "hyperactive" use of Rule 56 and other short-cut procedures "threatens longstanding constitutional values." Miller, *The Pretrial Rush to Judgment: Are the "Litigation Explosion," "Liability Crisis," and Efficiency Clichés Eroding Our Day in Court and Jury Trial Commitments?*, 78 N.Y.U.L.Rev. 982, 983 (2003).

A. SUMMARY JUDGMENT

Read Federal Rule of Civil Procedure 56 and the accompanying materials in the Supplement.

---

1. SUMMARY JUDGMENT: A SHORT HISTORY

FRIEDENTHAL & GARDNER, JUDICIAL DISCRETION TO DENY SUMMARY JUDGMENT IN THE ERA OF MANAGERIAL JUDGING, 31 Hofstra L.Rev. 91, 96 (2002) (footnotes omitted):

Modern summary judgment has its root in nineteenth century English law. Both the 1855 Summary Procedure on Bills of Exchange Act, more commonly known as Keating's Act, and the Judicature Act of 1873 allowed plaintiffs summary adjudication in their collection of liquidated claims when they demonstrated no dispute as to the terms of an agreement to provide goods or services, the actual provision of those goods or services, and nonpayment. The purpose of these acts was to "reduce delay and expense resulting from frivolous defenses." Although forms of summary proceedings existed in the United States as early as 1769, several states enacted summary judgment statutes based on the English model in the late 1800s. These American statutes were similar to the English Acts in that they were limited to use by plaintiffs and could only be used for claims appropriately resolved by documentary proof. Initially, judges expressed reluctance in granting summary judgment motions, viewing summary judgment as a drastic remedy. Yet by the mid-1920s, judges granted more than half of such motions before them.

MILLER, THE PRETRIAL RUSH TO JUDGMENT: ARE THE "LITIGATION EXPLOSION," "LIABILITY CRISIS," AND EFFICIENCY CLICHÉS ERODING OUR DAY IN COURT AND JURY TRIAL COMMITMENTS?, 78 N.Y.U.L.Rev. 982, 1019–23 (2003) (footnotes omitted):

Since its promulgation, Rule 56 has been the subject of periodic debate, as first exemplified in the 1940s by the opinions of two extremely distinguished Second Circuit judges, Charles E. Clark and Jerome N. Frank, in Arnstein v. Porter, [154 F.2d 464 (2d Cir. 19460,] an action charging one of America's greatest songwriters with the infringement of musical copyrights of an apparently litigious plaintiff. Judge Frank, writing for the majority, decided against summary judgment and in favor of trial, stating that the "[p]laintiff must not be deprived of the invaluable privilege of cross-examining the defendant—the 'crucial test of credibility'—in the presence of the jury." Although finding composer Ira Arnstein's theory about Cole Porter's plagiarism to be highly implausible, Judge Frank held that it raised a credibility question requiring a jury's determination, and that summary judgment should not be granted when there was the "slightest doubt as to the facts." He was concerned that liberal utilization of the motion would allow judges to usurp the role of juries, and would "favor unduly the party with the more ingenious and better paid lawyer." * * * He also expressed the sentiment that use of summary procedures in the name of clearing crowded dockets unjustly deprived litigants of their day in court.

Conversely, Judge Clark argued that summary judgment was "more necessary in the system of simple pleading now enforced in the federal courts" to avoid useless and unnecessary trials. He disagreed with an across-the-board limitation on summary judgment that would prevent it from being granted whenever credibility issues were crucial, and he accused his colleague of judicially amending the Rules, stating that "the clear-cut provisions of F.R. 56 conspicuously do not contain either a restriction on the kinds of actions to which it is applicable (unlike most state summary procedures) or any presumption against its use." He also mounted a vigorous assault on Judge Frank's "slightest doubt" standard, commenting in a later writing that "a slight doubt can be developed as to practically all things human." A narrow construction of the Rule, in his view, would encourage trials for the purpose of harassment and mean that the federal courts were endorsing the "obvious tendency to force settlement of the claim not because it is just, but because contesting it has become too costly or too inconvenient."

* * *

The Supreme Court seemed to adopt Judge Frank's philosophy of discouraging summary judgment by urging courts to apply it cautiously, keeping in mind the importance of jury trial, and calling for even greater restraint in lawsuits involving state-of-mind questions and complex issues. The paradigm case, Poller v. CBS, Inc., involved a private antitrust action brought against CBS alleging conspiracy to restrain and monopolize trade in violation of the Sherman Act by canceling its affiliation with a UHF station to drive the plaintiff out of business.[221] The District of Columbia District Court granted the defendant's summary judgment motion alleging lack of the illicit motive required to prove a Sherman Act violation. * * * The Court of Appeals for the District of Columbia affirmed, * * * but the Supreme Court reversed, with Justice Clark writing that:

> [S]ummary procedures should be used sparingly in complex antitrust litigation where motive and intent play leading roles, the proof is largely in the hands of the alleged conspirators, and hostile witnesses thicken the plot. It is only when the witnesses are present and subject to cross-examination that their credibility and the weight to be given their testimony can be appraised. Trial by affidavit is no substitute for trial by jury which so long has been the hallmark of "even handed justice."

* * * *Poller* had a decidedly dampening effect on summary judgment in the federal courts; indeed, the reported decisions reveal few cases of any complexity adjudicated under Rule 56 during the succeeding two decades.

---

[221] 368 U.S. 464 (1962).

2. THE MOTION FOR SUMMARY JUDGMENT UNDER RULE 56

The fact that a complaint survives a Rule 12(b)(6) motion to dismiss for failure to state a claim does not mean that plaintiff will prevail in the action. It means only that plaintiff has the opportunity to move to discovery and to trial. At trial plaintiff must produce evidence establishing the truth of the allegations set out in the complaint and persuade the decision-maker of an entitlement to relief. Thus, in order to win, plaintiff must meet the trial burden of production and burden of persuasion. The Rule 56 motion tests whether facts are in dispute and so a trial is needed to resolve them. As the First Circuit has put it, summary judgment is "a means of avoiding full-dress trials in unwinnable cases, thereby freeing courts to utilize scarce judicial resources in more beneficial ways." Mesnick v. Gen. Elec. Co., 950 F.2d 816, 822 (1st Cir. 1991).

Any party—plaintiff or defendant, claimant, crossclaimant, or counter-claimant—may move for summary judgment under Federal Rule 56. Judgment can be sought as to the entire claim or defense, or parts of a claim or defense. In either situation, the motion directs the court to evidence, drawn from the discovery record and affidavits, but it is not intended to replace the trial. Consistent with the Seventh Amendment, the court is expected to draw reasonable inferences in favor of the party opposing the motion, but is not permitted to weigh the evidence or assess its credibility.

NOTE ON RULE 56 BURDENS

The Rule 56 movant carries an initial burden of showing the absence of a genuine dispute about a material issue of fact, but otherwise the Rule 56 burdens track the trial burdens of production and persuasion. The Supreme Court has explained that "the mere existence of some alleged factual dispute between the parties will not defeat an otherwise properly supported motion for summary judgment." Rather, what is material is determined by the substantive law that governs the claim. "Only disputes over facts that might affect the outcome of the suit under the governing law will properly preclude the entry of summary judgment." Anderson v. Liberty Lobby, Inc., 477 U.S. 242, 247–48, 106 S.Ct. 2505, 2510, 91 L.Ed.2d 202, 21 (1986).

a. Burden of Production

In a civil action, the burden of production, sometimes called the burden of proof or of going forward, usually is placed on plaintiff in civil actions. This means that plaintiff is responsible for "producing" a certain threshold amount of evidence to raise a claim. However, defendant must normally meet the burden of production with respect to affirmative defenses. The threshold is defined as the minimum amount of evidence needed to satisfy the standard of proof and, thus, win the case. Put another way, one has met the burden of production if the party has produced enough evidence for a reasonable jury to decide in its favor. Therefore, one can meet the burden of production even if all the evidence produced is refuted by the opposing party.

Meeting the burden of production does not ensure victory—one must still "persuade" the fact finder—but failing to meet it will ensure defeat. If the party charged with the burden of production has failed to adduce enough evidence, a summary judgment motion (prior to trial) or a motion for judgment as a matter of law (at trial) will be granted. The burden of production must be met if the case is to be decided by the trier of fact.

b. Burden of Persuasion

If the burden of production is met, the case can move forward to the stage of persuasion. Once there is enough evidence for plaintiff to win, the defendant will try to cast doubt on the credibility or reliability of that evidence, in addition to bringing forth evidence of its own. Each party will try to persuade the trier of fact that its evidence is more weighty than the other's. If plaintiff has the burden of persuasion, and does not convince the jury (or judge, in a bench trial) by the standard of proof required, the jury must rule for the defendant. Even if plaintiff has satisfied the burden of production and the defendant brings forth no evidence of his own, if the jury is not persuaded that plaintiff's evidence is sufficiently reliable or credible, the defendant must prevail.

ADICKES v. S. H. KRESS & CO., 398 U.S. 144, 90 S.Ct. 1598, 26 L.Ed.2d 142 (1970), involved a civil rights claim filed by a white New York City school teacher who had volunteered to teach at a "Freedom School" in Hattiesburg, Mississippi during the summer of 1964. The district court found the following undisputed facts:

> On August 14, 1964, plaintiff and six Negro students sought to integrate the Hattiesburg Public Library, but were refused the use of its facilities and shortly thereafter the library was closed by the Chief of Police of Hattiesburg. On leaving the library, plaintiff and the six students proceeded to a Woolworth store for the purposes of eating lunch and, on the way, plaintiff observed policemen following them. Since the Woolworth store was crowded, the plaintiff and her group went to defendant's store and sat down in two lunch booths and ordered lunch. The waitress took the orders of the six Negroes, but refused to take plaintiff's order. The six Negroes refused to eat unless plaintiff was served. They left the store and had proceeded only a short distance when a police officer, previously observed by plaintiff, arrested her for vagrancy.

Adickes v. S. H. Kress & Co., 252 F.Supp. 140, 142 (S.D.N.Y. 1966). Plaintiff's complaint raised two claims: first, that the denial of restaurant service violated her civil rights; and second, that the refusal to serve and her subsequent arrest were the result of a conspiracy between defendant and the town police.

Kress moved for summary judgment, and supported its motion with affidavits from the store manager, the chief of police, and the arresting officers denying the existence of a pre-arranged scheme to arrest Adickes after she was denied service. The store manager's affidavit also stated that he had arranged for Adickes not to be served because he believed a riot would otherwise take place. In opposing the motion, Adickes responded by pressing her circumstantial case. She noted the allegation in the complaint that the policeman who arrested her had earlier been in the store, and pointed out that defendant had failed to dispute this allegation. She adduced her sworn deposition testimony that one of her students had seen a policeman come into the restaurant and she offered an unsworn statement by a Kress employee (given by Kress to Adickes in discovery) stating that the officer who arrested Adickes once she was outside the restaurant had been in the store before she was refused service. Adickes also submitted an affidavit disputing the store manager's statement that serving her would have created a riot.

The district court denied the motion with respect to the first count, but granted summary judgment on the second, finding that there was "no evidence in the complaint or in the affidavits and other papers from which a 'reasonably-minded person' might draw an inference of conspiracy." Id. at 144. The Second Circuit affirmed. 409 F.2d 121, 126–27 (2d Cir. 1968). The Supreme Court reversed, finding that the movant had not met its procedural burden of showing "the absence of any disputed material fact." 398 U.S. at 148, 90 S.Ct. at 1603, 26 L.Ed.2d at 149. The Court stated:

> * * * [Kress] did not carry its burden because of its failure to foreclose the possibility that there was a policeman in the Kress store while petitioner was awaiting service, and that this policeman reached an understanding with some Kress employee that petitioner not be served.

> It is true that * * * [the store manager] claimed in his deposition that he had not seen or communicated with a policeman prior to his tacit signal to * * * the supervisor of the food counter [not to serve Adickes]. But respondent did not submit any affidavits from * * * [the supervisor of the food counter], or from * * * the waitress who actually refused petitioner service, either of whom might well have seen and communicated with a policeman in the store. Further, we find it particularly noteworthy that the two officers involved in the arrest each failed in his affidavit to foreclose the

possibility (1) that he was in the store while petitioner was there; and (2) that, upon seeing petitioner with Negroes, he communicated his disapproval to a Kress employee, thereby influencing the decision not to serve petitioner.

Given these unexplained gaps in the materials submitted by respondent, we conclude that respondent failed to fulfill its initial burden of demonstrating what is a critical element in this aspect of the case—that there was no policeman in the store. If a policeman were present, we think it would be open to a jury, in light of the sequence that followed, to infer from the circumstances that the policeman and a Kress employee had a "meeting of the minds" and thus reached an understanding that petitioner should be refused service. Because "[o]n summary judgment the inferences to be drawn from the underlying facts contained in [the moving party's] materials must be viewed in the light most favorable to the party opposing the motion," * * * we think respondent's failure to show there was no policeman in the store requires reversal.

Id. at 158, 90 S Ct. at 1609, 26 L.Ed.2d at 159.

The Court rejected Kress's argument that because the form of plaintiff's evidence did not satisfy Rule 56(e)[a]—for example, the deposition was hearsay and the waitress's statement was unsworn—plaintiff could not avoid summary judgment.

If respondent had met its initial burden by, for example, submitting affidavits from the policemen denying their presence in the store at the time in question, Rule 56(e) would then have required petitioner to have done more than simply rely on the contrary allegation in her complaint. To have avoided conceding this fact for purposes of summary judgment, petitioner would have had to come forward with either (1) the affidavit of someone who saw the policeman in the store or (2) an affidavit under Rule 56(f)[b] explaining why at that time it was impractical to do so. Even though not essential here to defeat respondent's motion, the submission of such an affidavit would have been the preferable course for petitioner's counsel to have followed.

Id. at 159–60, 90 S.Ct. at 1609–10, 26 L.Ed.2d at 155–56.

---

[a]   The rule was amended and currently is Rule 56(c).

[b]   The rule was amended and currently is Rule 56(d).

NOTES AND QUESTIONS

1.   In *Adickes* what facts were material to the Rule 56 motion? Are these the same facts that plaintiff had to allege to survive a motion to dismiss? Are they the same facts that plaintiff must prove in order to win her case?

2.   What burden did *Adickes* place on the defendant moving for summary judgment? Was summary judgment denied because defendant failed to "foreclose the possibility" of a material fact? By imposing this burden on the movant did the court effectively shift the trial burden onto defendant by requiring that party to negate the existence of material issues? See Louis, *Federal Summary Judgment Doctrine: A Critical Analysis*, 83 Yale L.J. 745, 751–53 (1974).

3.   After *Adickes*, district courts generally asked whether a movant who did not have the trial burden had "sufficiently established the non-existence of any material fact." According to Professor Friedenthal:

> The moving party had been obligated to come forward with some information, in most cases affidavits containing testimony that would be presented at trial. The responding party was then permitted to avoid summary judgment without showing that he or she could meet the burden of production at trial, merely by attacking the veracity of the moving party's affiants or the form of the moving party's supporting papers.

Friedenthal, *Cases on Summary Judgment: Has There Been a Material Change in Standards?*, 63 Notre Dame L.Rev. 770, 776 (1988). Why should even a minimal burden be placed under Rule 56 on the movant who does not have the trial burden? Consider this explanation:

> There would appear to be two reasons for placing some requirements on a moving party who does not have the burden of production at trial. First, there are many cases, undoubtedly the vast majority, in which the litigants are fully aware that the party with the burden of production is able to call witnesses on its behalf who will carry its burden of producing evidence. Any 'automatic' rule requiring all such parties to make a showing would be extremely wasteful. If one party could, merely by filing an unsupported motion, force an opponent to make a substantial showing, there would be a strong incentive to make such a filing, if for no other reason than to harass the other party and raise its costs of litigation. The purpose of summary judgment is to save the courts and the litigants from the burdens of trying cases where no genuine dispute exists, not to raise the stakes by meaningless procedural devices. Second, there are a number of actions in which the party with the burden of proof can only establish its case through circumstantial evidence—a painstaking, item-by-item, process. It would be costly and unfair to require the responding party to go through that process at the pretrial stage, by taking numerous depositions of reluctant witnesses, obtaining affidavits

from a large number of cooperating witnesses, and preparing documents for admission into evidence, unless there is some sound reason to doubt that the respondent will be able to establish such a case at trial.

Id. at 776–77. Does the language of the rule impose this burden? Is the requirement a matter of policy? Does it reflect the influence even if not the command of the Seventh Amendment?

4.   Does the question of the existence of a conspiracy, which turns on the state of mind of the participants, inevitably depend on credibility issues that ought to be decided by the jury?

5.   Did *Adickes* address the burden placed on the party opposing the motion for summary judgment? Of what significance is the dictum that defendant's uncontroverted affidavit denying the officer's presence in the store would have required summary judgment for defendant, unless plaintiff came forward with evidence to refute defendant's showing? In the wake of *Adickes*, an important commentator urged that Rule 56 be amended "to make clear that a motion for summary judgment, without more, puts an opposing party with the burden of proof to the task of producing evidence sufficient to sustain a favorable verdict." As he explained:

> [T]he *Adickes* dictum that an uncontradicted affidavit asserting the policeman's absence would have justified summary judgment seems correct in policy but not, as the Court intimated, because such an affidavit would have foreclosed a jury finding that a policeman was in the store. Rather, although a jury might have been entitled to disbelieve the arguably interested testimony of a policeman or of a store employee, its doing so would nevertheless have left the plaintiff subject to a directed verdict for failure to satisfy her burden of proof.

See Currie, *Thoughts on Directed Verdicts and Summary Judgments*, 45 U. Chi.L.Rev. 72, 78 (1977).

CELOTEX CORP. V. CATRETT
Supreme Court of the United States, 1986.
477 U.S. 317, 106 S.Ct. 2548, 91 L.Ed.2d 265.

Certiorari to the United States Court of Appeals for the District of Columbia Circuit.

JUSTICE REHNQUIST delivered the opinion of the Court.

* * *

[Respondent Myrtle Nell Catrett filed suit in the U.S. District Court for the District of Columbia in September 1980, alleging that the death in 1979 of her husband, Louis H. Catrett, resulted from his exposure to products containing asbestos manufactured or distributed by 15 named corporations, including Petitioner Celotex. Catrett's complaint sounded in negligence, breach of warranty, and strict liability. In September 1981, Celotex moved for summary judgment on the ground that Catrett had "failed to produce evidence that any [Celotex] product * * * was the proximate cause of the injuries alleged within the jurisdictional limits of [the District] Court." In support of its summary judgment motion, Celotex noted that Catrett had failed to identify, in answering interrogatories specifically requesting such information, any witnesses who could testify about Louis Catrett's exposure to Celotex's asbestos products.

Catrett opposed the motion by producing three documents that she claimed would "demonstrate that there is a genuine material factual dispute" as to whether Louis Catrett had been exposed to Celotex's asbestos products. The first document was a transcript of Louis Catrett's testimony in a worker's compensation proceeding wherein he indicated his exposure to a product called "Firebar," which was manufactured by a corporate predecessor of Celotex, when he worked for a company named Anning-Johnson. The second document was a letter from T.R. Hoff, the Assistant Secretary of Anning-Johnson, to an Aetna insurance agent reporting on Catrett's employment with Anning-Johnson. The third document was a letter from the Aetna agent, O'Keefe, to Mrs. Catrett's counsel essentially restating the contents of Hoff's letter. Catrett argued that, because Celotex supplied the asbestos used by Anning-Johnson, all three documents tended to establish her husband's exposure to Celotex's product.

The district court granted Celotex's motion because "there [was] no showing that the plaintiff was exposed to the defendant Celotex's product in the District of Columbia or elsewhere within the statutory period." On appeal, a divided panel of the D.C. Circuit reversed and held that Celotex's summary judgment motion was rendered "fatally defective" by the fact that Celotex "made no effort to adduce *any* evidence, in the form of affidavits or otherwise, to support its motion." The panel majority read Rule 56 and the Supreme Court's decision in Adickes v. S.H. Kress & Co. to establish that "the party opposing the motion for summary judgment bears the burden of responding *only after* the moving party has met its burden of coming forward with proof of the absence of any genuine issues of material fact." The majority therefore declined to consider Celotex's argument that none of the evidence produced by Catrett in opposition to the motion for summary judgment would have been admissible at trial.]

* * *

We think that the position taken by the majority of the Court of Appeals is inconsistent with the standard for summary judgment set forth in Rule 56(c) * * *.c In our view, the plain language of [the] Rule * * * mandates the entry of summary judgment, after adequate time for discovery and upon motion, against a party who fails to make a showing

---

c   The rule was changed and the substance now appears in Rule 56(a).

sufficient to establish the existence of an element essential to that party's case, and on which that party will bear the burden of proof at trial. * * *

Of course, a party seeking summary judgment always bears the initial responsibility of informing the district court of the basis for its motion, and identifying those portions of "the pleadings, depositions, answers to interrogatories, and admissions on file, together with the affidavits, if any," which it believes demonstrate the absence of a genuine issue of material fact. But unlike the Court of Appeals, we find no express or implied requirement in Rule 56 that the moving party support its motion with affidavits or other similar materials *negating* the opponent's claim. * * * [R]egardless of whether the moving party accompanies its summary judgment motion with affidavits, the motion may, and should, be granted so long as whatever is before the district court demonstrates that the standard for the entry of summary judgment * * * is satisfied. One of the principal purposes of the summary judgment rule is to isolate and dispose of factually unsupported claims or defenses, and we think it should be interpreted in a way that allows it to accomplish this purpose.

Respondent argues, however, that Rule 56 * * *, by its terms, places on the nonmoving party the burden of coming forward with rebuttal affidavits, or other specified kinds of materials, only in response to a motion for summary judgment "made and supported as provided in this rule." According to respondent's argument, since petitioner did not "support" its motion with affidavits, summary judgment was improper in this case. * * * In cases like the instant one, where the nonmoving party will bear the burden of proof at trial on a dispositive issue, a summary judgment motion may properly be made in reliance solely on the "pleadings, depositions, answers to interrogatories, and admissions on file." Such a motion, whether or not accompanied by affidavits, will be "made and supported as provided in this rule," and Rule 56(e)[d] therefore requires the nonmoving party to go beyond the pleadings and by her own affidavits, or by the "depositions, answers to interrogatories, and admissions on file," designate "specific facts showing that there is a genuine issue for trial."

* * *

The Court of Appeals in this case felt itself constrained, however, by language in our decision in *Adickes* * * *. In the course of its opinion, the *Adickes* Court said that "both the commentary on and the background of the 1963 Amendment conclusively show that it was not intended to modify the burden of the moving party ... to show initially the absence of a genuine issue concerning any material fact." * * * We think that this statement is accurate in a literal sense, since we fully agree with the *Adickes* Court that the 1963 Amendment to Rule 56 * * * was not designed to modify the burden of making [such a] * * * showing * * *. It also appears

---

d   The practice is now subject to current Rule 56(c).

to us that, on the basis of the showing before the Court in *Adickes*, the motion for summary judgment in that case should have been denied. But we do not think the *Adickes* language quoted above should be construed to mean that the burden is on the party moving for summary judgment to produce evidence showing the absence of a genuine issue of material fact, even with respect to an issue on which the nonmoving party bears the burden of proof. Instead, as we have explained, the burden on the moving party may be discharged by "showing"—that is, pointing out to the District Court—that there is an absence of evidence to support the nonmoving party's case.

* * *

Respondent commenced this action in September 1980, and petitioner's motion was filed in September 1981. The parties had conducted discovery, and no serious claim can be made that respondent was in any sense "railroaded" by a premature motion for summary judgment. Any potential problem with such premature motions can be adequately dealt with under Rule 56(f),[e] which allows a summary judgment motion to be denied, or the hearing on the motion to be continued, if the nonmoving party has not had an opportunity to make full discovery.

In this Court, respondent's brief and oral argument have been devoted as much to the proposition that an adequate showing of exposure to petitioner's asbestos products was made as to the proposition that no such showing should have been required. But the Court of Appeals declined to address either the adequacy of the showing made by respondent in opposition to petitioner's motion for summary judgment, or the question whether such a showing, if reduced to admissible evidence, would be sufficient to carry respondent's burden of proof at trial. We think the Court of Appeals with its superior knowledge of local law is better suited than we are to make these determinations in the first instance.

The Federal Rules of Civil Procedure have for more than 50 years authorized motions for summary judgment upon proper showings of the lack of a genuine, triable issue of material fact. Summary judgment procedure is properly regarded not as a disfavored procedural shortcut, but rather as an integral part of the Federal Rules as a whole, which are designed "to secure the just, speedy and inexpensive determination of every action." * * * Before the shift to "notice pleading" accomplished by the Federal Rules, motions to dismiss a complaint or to strike a defense were the principal tools by which factually insufficient claims or defenses could be isolated and prevented from going to trial with the attendant unwarranted consumption of public and private resources. But with the advent of "notice pleading," the motion to dismiss seldom fulfills this function any more, and its place has been taken by the motion for summary

---

e   The rule currently is Rule 56(d)(2) and (e)(1).

judgment. Rule 56 must be construed with due regard not only for the rights of persons asserting claims and defenses that are adequately based in fact to have those claims and defenses tried to a jury, but also for the rights of persons opposing such claims and defenses to demonstrate in the manner provided by the Rule, prior to trial, that the claims and defenses have no factual basis.

The judgment of the Court of Appeals is accordingly reversed, and the case is remanded for further proceedings consistent with this opinion.

It is so ordered.

JUSTICE WHITE, concurring.

I agree that the Court of Appeals was wrong in holding that the moving defendant must always support his motion with evidence or affidavits showing the absence of a genuine dispute about a material fact. I also agree that the movant may rely on depositions, answers to interrogatories and the like to demonstrate that the plaintiff has no evidence to prove his case and hence that there can be no factual dispute. But the movant must discharge the burden the rules place upon him: It is not enough to move for summary judgment without supporting the motion in any way or with a conclusory assertion that the plaintiff has no evidence to prove his case.

* * *

Petitioner Celotex does not dispute that if respondent has named a witness to support her claim, summary judgment should not be granted without Celotex somehow showing that the named witness' possible testimony raises no genuine issue of material fact. * * * It asserts, however, that respondent has failed on request to produce any basis for her case. Respondent, on the other hand, does not contend that she was not obligated to reveal her witnesses and evidence but insists that she has revealed enough to defeat the motion for summary judgment. Because the Court of Appeals found it unnecessary to address this aspect of the case, I agree that the case should be remanded for further proceedings.

JUSTICE BRENNAN, with whom THE CHIEF JUSTICE and JUSTICE BLACKMUN join, dissenting.

This case requires the Court to determine whether Celotex satisfied its initial burden of production in moving for summary judgment on the ground that the plaintiff lacked evidence to establish an essential element of her case at trial. I do not disagree with the Court's legal analysis. The Court clearly rejects the ruling of the Court of Appeals that the defendant must provide affirmative evidence disproving the plaintiff's case. Beyond this, however, the Court has not clearly explained what is required of a moving party seeking summary judgment on the ground that the non-moving party cannot prove its case. This lack of clarity is unfortunate: district courts must routinely decide summary judgment motions, and the

Court's opinion will very likely create confusion. For this reason, even if I agreed with the Court's result, I would have written separately to explain more clearly the law in this area. However, because I believe that Celotex did not meet its burden of production under Federal Rule * * * 56, I respectfully dissent from the Court's judgment.

I

* * * The burden of establishing the nonexistence of a "genuine issue" is on the party moving for summary judgment. * * * This burden has two distinct components: an initial burden of production, which shifts to the nonmoving party if satisfied by the moving party; and an ultimate burden of persuasion, which always remains on the moving party. * * * The court need not decide whether the moving party has satisfied its ultimate burden of persuasion unless and until the court finds that the moving party has discharged its initial burden of production.

* * *

The manner in which this showing can be made depends upon which party will bear the burden of persuasion on the challenged claim at trial. If the *moving* party will bear the burden of persuasion at trial that party must support its motion with credible evidence—using any of the material specified in Rule 56(c)—that would entitle it to a directed verdict if not controverted at trial. * * * Such an affirmative showing shifts the burden of production to the party opposing the motion and requires that party either to produce evidentiary materials that demonstrate the existence of a "genuine issue" for trial or to submit an affidavit requesting additional time for discovery. * * *

If the burden of persuasion at trial would be on the *non-moving* party, the party moving for summary judgment may satisfy Rule 56's burden of production in either of two ways. First, the moving party may submit affirmative evidence that negates an essential element of the nonmoving party's claim. Second, the moving party may demonstrate to the Court that the nonmoving party's evidence is insufficient to establish an essential element of the nonmoving party's claim. * * * If the nonmoving party cannot muster sufficient evidence to make out its claim, a trial would be useless and the moving party is entitled to summary judgment as a matter of law. * * *

Where the moving party adopts this second option and seeks summary judgment on the ground that the nonmoving party—who will bear the burden of persuasion at trial—has no evidence, the mechanics of discharging Rule 56's burden of production are somewhat trickier. Plainly, a conclusory assertion that the nonmoving party has no evidence is insufficient. * * * Such a "burden" of production is no burden at all and would simply permit summary judgment procedure to be converted into a tool for harassment. * * * Rather, as the Court confirms, a party who moves for summary judgment on the ground that the nonmoving party has no evidence must affirmatively show the absence of evidence in the record. * * * This may require the moving party to depose the nonmoving party's witnesses or to establish the inadequacy of documentary evidence. If there is literally no evidence in the record, the moving party may demonstrate this by reviewing for the court the admissions, interrogatories and other exchanges between the parties that are in the record. Either way, however, the moving party must affirmatively demonstrate that there is no evidence in the record to support a judgment for the nonmoving party.

If the moving party has not fully discharged this initial burden of production, its motion for summary judgment must be denied, and the Court need not consider whether the moving party has met its ultimate burden of persuasion. Accordingly, the nonmoving party may defeat a motion for summary judgment that asserts that the nonmoving party has no evidence by calling the Court's attention to supporting evidence already in the record that was overlooked or ignored by the moving party.

* * *

II

I do not read the Court's opinion to say anything inconsistent with or different than the preceding discussion. My disagreement with the Court concerns the application of these principles to the facts of this case.

* * *

On these facts, there is simply no question that Celotex failed to discharge its initial burden of production. Having chosen to base its motion on the argument that there was no evidence in the record to support plaintiff's claim, Celotex was not free to ignore supporting evidence that the record clearly contained. Rather, Celotex was required, as an initial matter, to attack the adequacy of this evidence. Celotex' failure to fulfill this simple requirement constituted a failure to discharge its initial burden of production under Rule 56, and thereby rendered summary judgment improper.

* * *

[A dissenting opinion by JUSTICE STEVENS is omitted.]

NOTES AND QUESTIONS

1. On remand to the court of appeals, a divided panel found that plaintiff had produced sufficient evidence of exposure and, therefore, that summary judgment was inappropriate. See Catrett v. Johns-Manville Sales Corp., 826 F.2d 33 (D.C. Cir. 1987), cert. denied, 484 U.S. 1066, 108 S.Ct. 1028, 98 L.Ed.2d 992 (1988). Celotex argued that the three documents relied on by

Mrs. Catrett—the transcript of Louis Catrett's testimony in the worker's compensation proceeding, the Hoff letter, and the O'Keefe letter—were inadmissible hearsay, out-of-court statements that are inadmissible at trial, and thus should not be considered on the Rule 56 motion. The panel majority rejected that argument with respect to the Hoff letter. Judge Starr, writing for the majority, stated:

> In the circumstances of this case, we believe that the Hoff letter should be considered. The inadmissibility of the letter, despite Celotex's contention to the contrary, is by no means obvious (although we need not and do not pass judgment on its admissibility). Mrs. Catrett argues that the letter is admissible * * * as falling within the business records exception to the hearsay rule. See Fed.R.Evid. 803(6). *More importantly, Celotex never objected to the District Court's consideration of the Hoff letter.* * * * Since it is well established that "inadmissible documents may be considered by the court if not challenged [at trial]," * * * we are satisfied that the Hoff letter is properly (at this stage) to be considered in assessing whether a genuine issue of fact exists.

> * * * [Moreover, i]n her supplemental interrogatory responses, Mrs. Catrett listed Hoff as a witness. There can, of course, be no doubt that this response is properly considered in ruling on a summary judgment motion. * * * Taking this response together with the Hoff letter, the record, dispassionately viewed, reflects the existence of a witness who can testify with respect to Mr. Catrett's exposure to Firebar. Thus, even if the Hoff letter itself would not be admissible at trial, Mrs. Catrett has gone on to indicate that the substance of the letter is reducible to admissible evidence in the form of trial testimony. * * *

Id. at 37–38 (emphasis in original). Judge Bork, in dissent, wrote:

> * * * [P]laintiff has not identified "specific facts" that would indicate such exposure occurred, and I certainly think that plaintiff has not made the kind of showing necessary to defeat a directed verdict motion. I would therefore grant defendant's motion for summary judgment.

> * * * [T]he mere listing of a potential witness, without more, does not constitute setting forth specific facts. Here plaintiff has never claimed that Mr. Hoff has any personal knowledge that her husband was exposed to asbestos during his year of work at this company, and indeed did not specify the grounds of his possible testimony at all, except to say that he would be able to testify about "facts relevant to the subject matter of this lawsuit." * * * On the other hand, plaintiff has failed ever to answer interrogatories served by defendant that asked for a variety of specific items of information she might have about her husband's possible exposure to asbestos on any occasion. * * *

The majority concludes, however, that we should interpret plaintiff's listing of Mr. Hoff as a witness in light of his letter to the insurance company, thereby finding enough evidence to stave off the equivalent of a motion for directed verdict on causation. This conclusion is incorrect for two reasons. First, the sum total of all this "evidence" falls far short of showing, or even suggesting, that anyone has been identified who can testify from personal knowledge about any asbestos exposure. That lack alone requires that defendant's motion for summary judgment be granted.

In addition, and also dispositive, the letter itself is inadmissible as evidence and thus cannot be considered by this court in evaluating the summary judgment motion. * * * It is settled law that the judge may consider only these specific materials or other evidence that would be admissible at trial. Inadmissible evidence is not to be considered unless, like an affidavit, it is "otherwise provided for" in Rule 56.

Id. at 41.

2.　According to the *Celotex* majority, a Rule 56 movant who does not have the burden of production at trial "bears the initial responsibility" of "informing" the court of the grounds for the motion and "identifying those portions" of the discovery record that show the absence of a material issue of fact. Is this description of the movant's burden consistent with *Adickes*? Consider the following analysis:

* * * [A] party may satisfy the standard for summary judgment by one or both of two methods. First, the movant may, by submitting affirmative evidence, negate an element essential to the opposing party's claim or defense. Second, the movant may show that the opposing party lacks sufficient evidence to establish an essential element of its claim or defense. *Celotex* involved the second method exclusively; *Adickes*, arguably, involved a combination of the two methods. The defendant in *Adickes* offered affirmative evidence in the form of the deposition of the store manager and affidavits from the involved officers. In addition, the defendant pointed to statements in the plaintiff's deposition that the plaintiff lacked any knowledge of communications between the police and Kress employees. The inadequacy of Kress's motion was not its failure to offer affirmative evidence, but rather that the affirmative evidence it offered was insufficient to establish the absence of a genuine issue of a material fact. *Adickes*, therefore, should not be read as requiring the moving party to negate an essential element of the opposing party's case by affirmative evidence in every instance. Rather, the decision may be viewed as stating the proposition that the moving party is required to sustain its burden of proving the absence of a genuine issue of a material fact by affirmative evidence only if it must utilize the first method, or a combination of the two methods, of obtaining summary

judgment. If the moving party is able to use the second method exclusively, it is only required to show that the opposing party has failed to establish sufficient evidence of an essential element of its claim or defense. *Celotex*, viewed in this light, is therefore consistent with the *Adickes* decision. By failing to fully explain this distinction, however, Justice Rehnquist's statements, while correct in the context of the *Celotex* decision, appear to eviscerate *Adickes* and may promote rather than resolve doctrinal confusion.

Foremaster, *The Movant's Burden in a Motion for Summary Judgment*, 1987 Utah L.Rev. 731, 748–49.

3.   Under *Celotex*, can a party who does not have the trial burden move for summary judgment and do no more than insist that the opposing party show that it can meet its trial burden? Or does *Celotex* impose an initial burden on the movant to review the discovery record and identify for the court deficiencies in plaintiff's evidence? Notice that Justice White's concurring opinion stated that the movant must do more than support the motion with "a conclusory assertion" that plaintiff lacks evidence. In 2010, Rule 56 was amended. How does the current version of Rule 56(c)(3) affect your answer? Note also that the current version of the rule expressly recognizes the court's power to grant summary judgment sua sponte—independent of any motion by a party—after "giving notice and a reasonable time to respond." See Rule 56(f).

4.   *Celotex* focused primarily on what a party moving for summary judgment must show in order to shift the Rule 56 burden to the opposing party. As the First Circuit has explained, the nonmovant can forestall summary judgment only by presenting "definite, competent evidence," "sufficiently probative that, if it is credited, a fact finder could resolve the case in favor of the nonmovant." Murray v. Kindred Nursing Centers West LLC, 789 F.3d 20, 25 (1st Cir. 2015) (internal quotation omitted).

5.   Does a court have any discretion to deny a properly supported summary judgment motion? Before Rule 56 was restyled in 2007, its text provided that summary judgment "shall be rendered" when the rule's requirements are satisfied. In the revised version of what is now Rule 56(a), the Advisory Committee replaced that phrase (in keeping with a style convention that sought to eliminate the word "shall" from the Federal Rules) with "should be rendered." The choice of "should" rather than "must" reflected a line of cases recognizing a degree of discretion to deny summary judgment. See Friedenthal & Gardner, *Judicial Discretion to Deny Summary Judgment in the Era of Managerial Judging*, 31 Hofstra L.Rev. 91, 104–110 (2002). The Advisory Committee Note accompanying the restyled rule cautioned, however, that "courts will seldom exercise the discretion to deny summary judgment when there is no genuine issue as to any material fact." In 2010, Rule 56(a) was amended to restore the use of "shall," a decision that recognized a division in the case law on whether a district court has such discretion. The Advisory Committee explained that "shall" in Rule 56 had "acquired significance over many decades of use" and that eliminating it "created an unacceptable risk of

changing the summary-judgment standard." Would it be appropriate for a district court to deny summary judgment on the ground that resolution of a legal issue would benefit from the development of the record at trial? Would it matter if a court concludes that resolving the summary judgment motion will be as time-consuming as a trial? See 10A Wright & Miller, Federal Practice and Procedure § 2728 (4th ed.).

———

The Court's decision in *Celotex* framed the moving party's burden of production on the summary judgment motion in light of that party's ultimate burden at trial. In a similar way, the second case in the Court's summary judgment trilogy, Anderson v. Liberty Lobby, Inc., 477 U.S. 242, 106 S.Ct. 2505, 91 L.Ed.2d 202, instructed courts to view the summary judgment record through the lens of the applicable standard of proof at trial. The standard for meeting the burden of persuasion represents the quantity and quality of evidence a party must produce at trial to prevail. The three most common standards are (1) preponderance of the evidence, (2) clear and convincing evidence, and (3) beyond a reasonable doubt. These standards usually are not defined any more specifically than their plain meaning suggests, although a "preponderance" is considered to be "more than fifty percent," and the clear and convincing standard lies somewhere between a preponderance and "beyond a reasonable doubt." In most civil cases, the party bearing the burden of persuasion must prove by a preponderance of the evidence that she is entitled to the relief requested. On a Rule 56 motion, how should the court decide whether a genuine dispute exists if the trial standard would require clear and convincing evidence?

———

ANDERSON v. LIBERTY LOBBY, INC., 477 U.S. 242, 106 S.Ct. 2505, 91 L.Ed.2d 202 (1986). Liberty Lobby, a non-profit organization, and its founder filed a libel suit against The Investigator magazine, its publisher, and chief executive officer, alleging that defendants published false statements that portrayed plaintiffs as "neo-Nazi, anti-Semitic, racist, and Fascist." Id. at 245, 106 S.Ct. at 2508, 91 L.Ed.2d at 210. Following discovery, defendants moved for summary judgment on the ground that plaintiffs could not prove by clear and convincing evidence that defendants had acted with knowledge that the statements were false or that they had been made with reckless disregard of whether they were true or false (this is known as the "actual malice" standard and is required in libel cases against public figures under New York Times Co. v. Sullivan, 376 U.S. 254, 84 S.Ct. 710, 11 L.Ed.2d 686 (1964)). In support of the motion, defendants submitted an affidavit from the author, stating that he had spent a substantial amount of time doing research and writing. His affidavit detailed sources for each of the statements alleged to be false, and affirmed that he believed the facts he reported to be true. Plaintiffs responded to the motion by pointing to numerous claimed inaccuracies in the articles. On the issue of malice, plaintiffs showed that one of the author's sources was a 12-year-old article published in Time magazine that had been the subject of an earlier libel suit by plaintiff, which had resulted in a settlement by which Time published a favorable article about Liberty Lobby and paid money to its founder, and that one of the co-authors of the Time article was an editor of The Investigator. Plaintiffs also showed that another source was a freelance journalist whom the author had never met and who was not asked to, and never did, identify his sources. Finally, they showed that another editor of The Investigator had told the magazine's president that the articles were "terrible" and "ridiculous."

The district court granted the motion for summary judgment. The court of appeals reversed, ruling that it was irrelevant on a motion for summary judgment that the standard for proving actual malice was clear and convincing evidence, rather than a preponderance of evidence. In an opinion written by Justice White, the Court reversed:

> * * * [I]n ruling on a motion for summary judgment, the judge must view the evidence presented through the prism of the substantive evidentiary burden. This conclusion is mandated by the nature of this determination. The question here is whether a jury could reasonably find either that the plaintiff proved his case by the quality and quantity of evidence required by the governing law or that he did not. Whether a jury could reasonably find for either party, however, cannot be defined except by the criteria governing what evidence would enable the jury to find for either the plaintiff or the defendant: It makes no sense to say that a jury could reasonably find for either party without some benchmark as to what standards govern its deliberations and within what boundaries its ultimate decision must fall, and these standards and boundaries are in fact provided by the applicable evidentiary standards.

> Our holding that the clear-and-convincing standard of proof should be taken into account does not denigrate the role of the jury. It by no means authorizes trial on affidavits. Credibility determinations, the weighing of the evidence, and the drawing of legitimate inferences from the facts are jury functions, not those of a judge, whether he is ruling on a motion for summary judgment or for a directed verdict. The evidence of the non-movant is to be believed, and all justifiable inferences are to be drawn in his favor. * * * Neither do we suggest that the trial courts should act other than with caution in granting summary judgment or that the trial court may not deny summary judgment in a case

where there is reason to believe that the better course would be to proceed to a full trial. * * *

Id. at 254–56, 106 S.Ct. at 2513–14, 91 L.Ed.2d at 215–16.

———

On a summary judgment motion, the court must view the record in the light most favorable to the nonmoving party. The third decision in the trilogy, Matsushita Electric Industrial Co. v. Zenith Radio Corp., 475 U.S. 574, 106 S.Ct. 1348, 89 L.Ed.2d 538, addressed the extent to which a court may draw particular inferences from the record. Consistent with *Celotex* and *Anderson*, the Supreme Court in *Matsushita* instructed lower courts to bear in mind the substantive law that would govern at trial when assessing the permissible inferences that can be drawn from a factual record. In doing so, the Court linked the role of a district court when deciding a pretrial motion for summary judgment under Rule 56 to the court's role when deciding a motion for judgment as a matter of law at trial under Rule 50. See Chapter 13, infra.

———

MATSUSHITA ELECTRIC INDUSTRIAL CO. v. ZENITH RADIO CORP., 475 U.S. 574, 106 S.Ct. 1348, 89 L.Ed.2d 538 (1986). Plaintiffs, a group of American television manufacturers, alleged that a group of 21 Japanese manufacturers and distributors conspired to fix prices in an effort to monopolize the American market. The trial court granted defendant's motion for summary judgment, but the Third Circuit reversed. The appeals court found that because there was direct evidence of concerted action, as well as circumstantial evidence that concerted action may have occurred, a fact finder reasonably could have found a conspiracy to engage in predatory pricing. The Supreme Court reversed, emphasizing that antitrust law limits the range of permissible inferences that may be drawn in favor of the nonmovant, and that when a claim is factually improbable, the nonmovant must come forward with more persuasive evidence than usual to defeat summary judgment:

> To survive petitioners' motion for summary judgment, respondents must establish that there is a genuine issue of material fact as to whether petitioners entered into an illegal conspiracy that caused respondents to suffer a cognizable injury. * * * This showing has two components. First, respondents must show more than a conspiracy in violation of the antitrust laws; they must show an injury to them resulting from the illegal conduct. Respondents charge petitioners with a whole host of conspiracies in restraint of trade. * * * Except for the alleged conspiracy to monopolize the American market through predatory pricing, these alleged conspiracies could not have caused

respondents to suffer an "antitrust injury," * * * because they actually tended to benefit respondents. * * * Therefore, unless, in context, evidence of these "other" conspiracies raises a genuine issue concerning the existence of a predatory pricing conspiracy, that evidence cannot defeat petitioners' summary judgment motion.

Second, the issue of fact must be "genuine." * * * When the moving party has carried its burden * * *, its opponent must do more than simply show that there is some metaphysical doubt as to the material facts. * * *

It follows from these settled principles that if the factual context renders respondents' claim implausible—if the claim is one that simply makes no economic sense—respondents must come forward with more persuasive evidence to support their claim than would otherwise be necessary. * * *

Respondents correctly note that "[o]n summary judgment the inferences to be drawn from the underlying facts . . . must be viewed in the light most favorable to the party opposing the motion." * * * But antitrust law limits the range of permissible inferences from ambiguous evidence in a § 1 case. * * * To survive a motion for summary judgment or for a directed verdict, a plaintiff seeking damages for a violation of § 1 [of the Sherman Act] must present evidence "that tends to exclude the possibility" that the alleged conspirators acted independently. * * * Respondents in this case, in other words, must show that the inference of conspiracy is reasonable in light of the competing inferences of independent action or collusive action that could not have harmed respondents. * * *

* * *

[T]he absence of any plausible motive to engage in the conduct charged is highly relevant to whether a "genuine issue for trial" exists * * *. Lack of motive bears on the range of permissible conclusions that might be drawn from ambiguous evidence: if petitioners had no rational economic motive to conspire, and if their conduct is consistent with other, equally plausible explanations, the conduct does not give rise to an inference of conspiracy. * * * In sum, in light of the absence of any rational motive to conspire, neither petitioner's (respondent's) pricing practices, nor their conduct in the Japanese market, nor their agreements respecting prices and distribution in the American market, suffice to create a "genuine issue for trial." * * *

Id. at 585–88, 596–97, 106 S.Ct. at 1355–57, 1361, 89 L.Ed.2d at 552–53, 558–59.

NOTE AND QUESTIONS

Would a rational decision-maker find that a genuine dispute exists if presented with the following evidence?

(a) Two cars enter an intersection at right angles and strike one another, killing both drivers and all passengers. There are no eyewitnesses to the accident. The only evidence available is that there was a working traffic light; thus one of the drivers, but only one, had to go through a red light.

(b) X must take a certain pill once a day to remain alive. The pill is highly toxic. To take two within twenty-four hours is fatal. X is found dead in his bedroom and the evidence is clear that he took two pills that day. If X died by accident, his estate will receive a large sum of insurance money; if he committed suicide, the amount will be substantially reduced. Several hours before his death, X made out a new will, substantially different from the one previously in force. It also shows that at about the same time, X made plans to accompany several friends on a fishing trip on the following day.

Problems adapted from: Friedenthal, *Cases on Summary Judgment: Has There Been a Material Change in Standards?*, 63 Notre Dame L.Rev. 770, 784–86 (1988).

———

SCOTT v. HARRIS, 550 U.S. 372, 127 S.Ct. 1769, 167 L.Ed.2d 686 (2007). Plaintiff Harris suffered severe physical injuries when his vehicle was forced off the road during a police chase by defendant Scott, a deputy police officer. Plaintiff alleged that the officer violated his Fourth Amendment rights by using excessive force. Defendant moved for summary judgment raising the defense of qualified immunity, an issue on which he would bear the burden of proof at trial. The district court denied the motion and the Court of Appeals for the Eleventh Circuit affirmed.

The Supreme Court reversed as follows:

[Plaintiff's] * * * version of events (unsurprisingly) differs substantially from * * * [defendant's] version. When things are in such a posture courts are required to view the facts and draw reasonable inferences "in the light most favorable to the party opposing the [summary judgment] motion." * * * In qualified immunity cases, this usually means adopting (as the Court of Appeals did here) the plaintiff's version of the facts.

There is, however, an added wrinkle in this case: existence in the record of a videotape capturing the events in question. There are no allegations or indications that this videotape was doctored or altered in any way, nor any contention that what it depicts differs from what actually happened. The videotape quite clearly contradicts the version of the story told by * * * [plaintiff] and adopted by the Court of Appeals. * * * Indeed, reading the lower court's opinion, one gets the impression that * * * [plaintiff], rather than fleeing from police, was attempting to pass his driving test * * *.

The videotape tells quite a different story. * * * Far from [plaintiff] being the cautious and controlled driver the lower court depicts, what we see on the video more closely resembles a Hollywood-style car chase of the most frightening sort, placing police officers and innocent bystanders alike at great risk of serious injury.

At the summary judgment stage, facts must be viewed in the light most favorable to the nonmoving party only if there is a "genuine" dispute as to those facts. * * * When opposing parties tell two different stories, one of which is blatantly contradicted by the record, so that no reasonable jury could believe it, a court should not adopt that version of the facts for purposes of ruling on a motion for summary judgment.

That was the case here with regard to the factual issue whether respondent was driving in such fashion as to endanger human lie. Respondent's version of events is so utterly discredited by the record that no reasonable jury could have believed him. The Court of Appeals should not have relied on such visible fiction; it should have viewed the facts in the light depicted by the videotape.

* * *

The car chase that * * * [plaintiff] initiated in this case posed a substantial and immediate risk of serious physical injury to others; no reasonable jury could conclude otherwise. Scott's attempt to terminate the chase by forcing respondent off the road was reasonable, and Scott is entitled to summary judgment.

Id. at 378–81, 127 S.Ct. at 1774–76, 1779, 167 L.Ed.2d at 692–95, 697. Justices Ginsburg and Breyer separately concurred. Justice Stevens, in a dissenting opinion, criticized the other members of the Court for usurping the jury's role:

Relying on a de novo review of a videotape of a portion of a nighttime chase on a lightly traveled road in Georgia where no pedestrians or other "bystanders" were present, buttressed by uninformed speculation about the possible consequences of discontinuing the chase, eight of the jurors on this Court reach a verdict that differs from the views of the judges on both the District Court and the Court of Appeals who are surely more familiar with the hazards of driving on Georgia roads than we are. The Court's justification for this unprecedented departure from our well-settled standard of review of factual determinations made by a district court and affirmed by a court of appeals is based on its mistaken view that the Court of Appeals' description of the facts was "blatantly contradicted by the record" and that respondent's version of the events was "so utterly discredited by the record that no reasonable jury could have believed him." * * *

Rather than supporting the conclusion that what we see on the video "resembles a Hollywood-style car chase of the most frightening sort," * * * the tape actually confirms, rather than contradicts, the lower courts' appraisal of the factual questions at issue. More importantly, * * * it surely does not provide a principled basis for depriving the respondent of his right to have a jury evaluate the question whether the police officers' decision to use deadly force to bring the chase to an end was reasonable.

Id. at 389–90, 127 S.Ct. at 1781–82, 167 L.Ed.2d at 700.

NOTES AND QUESTIONS

1.   The video at issue in *Scott* is available on the Supreme Court's website: see http://www.supremecourt.gov/media/media.aspx/ (site last accessed Dec. 19, 2021). After viewing the video, do you agree with the Court's statement that "no reasonable juror" could find that the driver's flight did not pose a danger to the public?

2.   A study based on a sample of more than 1,300 viewers of the *Scott* video found that although a "fairly substantial majority did interpret the facts the way the Court did," this view generally was not shared by African Americans, low-income workers, residents of the Northeast, and persons who identified themselves as Democrats, who tended to view the facts in a light more favorable to the plaintiff. Based on these findings, the authors have criticized the decision in *Scott* for terminating the case on summary judgment:

> * * * Although an admitted minority of American society, citizens disposed to see the facts differently from the *Scott* majority share a perspective founded on common experiences and values. By insisting that a case like *Scott* be decided summarily, the Court not only denied those citizens an opportunity, in the context of jury deliberations, to inform and possibly change the view of citizens endowed with a different perspective. It also needlessly bound the result in the case to a process of decisionmaking that deprived the decision of any prospect of legitimacy in the eyes of that subcommunity whose members saw the facts differently.

Kahan, Hoffman & Braman, *Whose Eyes Are You Going To Believe? Scott v. Harris and the Perils of Cognitive Illiberalism*, 122 Harv.L.Rev. 837, 841–42 (2009).

3.   TOLAN v. COTTON, 134 S.Ct 1861, 188 L.Ed.2d 895 (2014), was a civil rights action against a police officer alleging the use of excessive force in violation of the Fourth Amendment. Defendant moved for summary judgment; the district court granted the motion and the court of appeals affirmed. The Supreme Court, per curiam, vacated and remanded:

decision by a court in whole not specifically by judges

> * * * [T]he court below credited the evidence of the party seeking summary judgment and failed properly to acknowledge key evidence offered by the party opposing that motion. And while "this Court is not equipped to correct every perceived error coming from the lower federal courts," * * * we intervene here because the opinion below reflects a clear misapprehension of summary judgment standards in light of our precedents. * * *

> The witnesses on both sides come to this case with their own perceptions, recollections, and even potential biases. It is in part for that reason that genuine disputes are generally resolved by juries in our adversarial system. By weighing the evidence and reaching factual inferences contrary to Tolan's competent evidence, the court below neglected to adhere to the fundamental principle that at the summary judgment stage, reasonable inferences should be drawn in favor of the nonmoving party.

> Applying that principle here, the court should have acknowledged and credited Tolan's evidence with regard to the lighting, his mother's demeanor, whether he shouted words that were an overt threat, and his positioning during the shooting. This is not to say, of course, that these are the only facts that the Fifth Circuit should consider, or that no other facts might contribute to the reasonableness of the officer's actions as a matter of law. Nor do we express a view as to whether Cotton's actions violated clearly established law. We instead vacate the Fifth Circuit's judgment so that the court can determine whether, when Tolan's evidence is properly credited and factual inferences are reasonably drawn in his favor, Cotton's actions violated clearly established law.

Id. at 1867, 188 L.Ed.2d 895. Justice Alito, joined by Justice Scalia, concurred in the judgment:

> In my experience, a substantial percentage of the civil appeals heard each year by the courts of appeals present the question whether the evidence in the summary judgment record is just enough or not quite enough to support a grant of summary judgment. The present case falls into that very large category. There is no confusion in the courts of appeals about the standard to be applied in ruling on a summary judgment motion, and the Court of Appeals invoked the correct

standard here. * * * Thus, the only issue is whether the relevant evidence, viewed in the light most favorable to the nonmoving party, is sufficient to support a judgment for that party. In the courts of appeals, cases presenting this question are utterly routine. There is no question that this case is important for the parties, but the same is true for a great many other cases that fall into the same category.

On the merits of the case, while I do not necessarily agree in all respects with the Court's characterization of the evidence, I agree that there are genuine issues of material fact and that this is a case in which summary judgment should not have been granted.

Id. at 1868–69, 188 L.Ed.2d at 904. By contrast, in PLUMHOFF v. RICKARD, 572 U.S. 765, 134 S.Ct. 2012, 188 L.Ed.2d 1056 (2014), also a civil rights action alleging excessive use of force by a police officer, the Supreme Court reversed the denial of the officer's motion for summary judgment. For a discussion of the Court's approach to video evidence in these cases, see Wasserman, *Mixed Signals on Summary Judgment*, 2014 Mich.St.L.Rev. 1331 (2015).

4. The Supreme Court has characterized the standard for avoiding summary judgment as "relatively lenient." AMGEN INC. v. CONNECTICUT RETIREMENT PLANS AND TRUST FUNDS, 568 U.S. 455, 480, 135 S.Ct. 1184, 1203, 185 L.Ed.2d 308, 328 (2013). Some studies suggest that there has not been a significant increase in the grant of summary judgment motions in the wake of *Celotex, Anderson*, and *Matsushita*, but this may be because Rule 12(b)(6) now plays an early and robust role in filtering out cases pretrial. See Eisenberg & Clermont, *Plaintiphobia in the Supreme Court*, 100 Cornell L.Rev. 193 (2014). Moreover, the trilogy has had an uneven effect; civil rights claims, for example, appear to be disproportionately terminated by Rule 56 motions. See Gertner, *Losers' Rules*, 122 Yale L.J. Online 109 (2012); Schneider, *The Dangers of Summary Judgment: Gender and Federal Litigation*, 59 Rutgers L.Rev. 705 (2007); see also Pfautz, *What Would a Reasonable Jury Do? Jury Verdicts Following Summary Judgment Reversals*, 115 Colum.L.Rev. 1255 (2015). What is clear, as Professor Miller has written, is the fact that the "three decisions in one term sent a clear signal to the legal profession that Rule 56 provides a useful mechanism for disposing of cases short of trial when the district judge feels the plaintiff's case is not plausible. Many courts responded to this invitation with considerable receptivity." Miller, *From* Conley *to* Twombly *to* Iqbal: *A Double Play on the Federal Rules of Civil Procedure*, 60 Duke L.J. 1, 10 (2010).

NOTE ON THE TIMING OF A RULE 56 MOTION

Federal Rule 56(b) permits the filings of a summary judgment motion "until 30 days after the close of discovery," unless another time is ordered by the court or specified by local rule. This means that a motion for summary judgment may be filed before defendant has filed an answer or before discovery has commenced or completed. However, the Court in *Celotex* warned that a Rule 56 motion should be granted only if the nonmovant has had adequate time for discovery. The district court, using its Rule 16 managerial authority, may set a scheduling order for the filing of summary judgment motions and for discovery. See Gensler & Rosenthal, *Managing Summary Judgment*, 43 Loy.Chi.L.J. 517 (2012). In addition, Rule 56(d) provides safeguards for a nonmovant who requires additional time to marshal facts in opposition to a summary judgment motion. Although the general presumption is that a continuance should be liberally granted, Rule 56(d) requests are not automatically granted—the rule "is designed to minister to the vigilant, not to those who slumber upon perceptible rights." Pina v. Children's Place, 740 F.3d 785, 794 (1st Cir. 2014) (internal quotation omitted). In some circuits, the party seeking Rule 56(d) relief must submit an affidavit, and the motion "must: 1) be timely; 2) be authoritative; 3) show good cause for failure to discover the relevant facts earlier; 4) establish a plausible basis for believing that the specified facts probably exist, and 5) indicate how those facts will influence the outcome of summary judgment." Id.

B. DISMISSAL OF ACTIONS

Read Federal Rule of Civil Procedure 41 and the accompanying materials in the Supplement.

1. VOLUNTARY DISMISSAL

Rule 41 allows a plaintiff to extricate itself from a lawsuit before significant resources have been expended by the court and an opposing party. Generally, a voluntary dismissal places the parties in the positions they occupied before the lawsuit began and does not affect plaintiff's legal rights. Are there situations when a voluntary dismissal should have the preclusive effect of an adjudication on the merits? Should it ever toll the statute of limitations? See 9 Wright & Miller, Federal Practice and Procedure §§ 2361–68 (4th ed.). Is there a danger that a party might use the strategy of repeated voluntary dismissals as a way to harass an opponent?

McCANTS v. FORD MOTOR CO., 781 F.2d 855 (11th Cir. 1986). McCants, a member of the United States Army Reserve on a two-week active duty training mission, was killed while riding in a military jeep built by Ford. His administratrix commenced a wrongful death suit in federal district court in Alabama. After discovery had proceeded for about a year, interrogatories were served and answered, and defendant had moved for summary judgment based on Alabama's one-year general statute of limitations, plaintiff moved for voluntary dismissal of the action without prejudice under Rule 41(a)(2), in order to file a new suit in Mississippi, where the controlling statute of limitations had not expired. The district court granted the motion to dismiss, and simultaneously denied Ford's motion for summary judgment. The Eleventh Circuit vacated the order and remanded to determine whether conditions ought to have been attached to the order of dismissal. The court of appeals explained that "in most cases a [voluntary] dismissal should be granted unless the defendant will suffer clear legal prejudice, *other than the mere prospect of a subsequent lawsuit,* as a result," emphasizing that the district court is to "bear in mind principally the interests of the defendant, for it is the defendant's position that the court should protect." Id. at 856–57. When defendant "has been put to considerable expense," then dismissal is not warranted except on condition that plaintiff reimburse defendant for a portion of his expenses, including attorney's fees. Id. at 860.

———

WOJTAS v. CAPITAL GUARDIAN TRUST CO., 477 F.3d 924 (7th Cir. 2007). Plaintiff, the owner of an Individual Retirement Account, instructed the custodian to roll over the investment into a new IRA managed by a successor custodian. An employee at the successor custodian converted the funds and later was convicted of mail fraud. Plaintiff sued the original custodian for breach of fiduciary duty and negligence, alleging that defendant had failed to verify that the successor custodian was legally qualified. Defendant answered and moved for judgment on the pleadings, arguing that both claims were time-barred under Wisconsin's two-year statute of limitations, and, in the alternative, that plaintiff failed to state a claim upon which relief could be granted. Plaintiff responded to the latter argument but also moved for a voluntary dismissal without prejudice, in order to refile the action in Illinois, where the controlling statute of limitations was longer. The district court denied the motion for voluntary dismissal and granted the motion for judgment on the pleadings. The court of appeals affirmed, finding that plaintiff's failure to respond to the statute of limitations argument constituted a waiver, and that it would be an abuse of the district court's discretion to permit voluntary dismissal when "the defendant would suffer 'plain legal prejudice' as a result.'" Id. at 927.

NOTES AND QUESTIONS

1. At common law, plaintiff was permitted, at any time prior to judgment, to dismiss a case voluntarily and without prejudice to refiling the action. Today the right to dismiss voluntarily generally is governed by a rule or statute that typically permits a dismissal before "trial" or "commencement" of trial. These provisions have raised many problems of interpretation regarding the meaning of the words "trial" and "commencement." A few courts have held that "before trial" means at any time prior to submission of the case to the jury or court for decision. Can you explain this distinction?

2. In *McCants*, plaintiff moved to dismiss after defendant had made a motion for summary judgment. Could any plaintiff simply move to dismiss before losing such a motion and refile in another, possibly more sympathetic, court? Could plaintiff do this repeatedly? Would it be appropriate for the court to attach conditions to a Rule 41 dismissal? What might those conditions be? See Solimine & Lippert, *Deregulating Voluntary Dismissals*, 36 U.Mich.J.L. Reform 367, 367 (2003), calling unilateral dismissal under Rule 41(a) "an anachronism in an age of managerial judging."

3. In ESPOSITO v. PIATROWSKI, 223 F.3d 497 (7th Cir. 2000), plaintiff voluntarily dismissed his initial case against defendant. Plaintiff was ordered to reimburse defendant the costs of that proceeding. Subsequently plaintiff sued on the same cause, joining other defendants with the original defendant. Because plaintiff never did comply with the order to pay costs, the trial court, under Rule 41(b), dismissed the second case, not only against the original defendant but against all the defendants. The court of appeals affirmed. Is the decision consistent with the spirit of Rule 41(b) and (d)?

4. Courts are divided as to whether attorney fees can be awarded to a defendant as costs when a plaintiff has voluntarily dismissed an action and later refiles it. Compare Rogers v. Wal-Mart Stores, Inc., 230 F.3d 868 (6th Cir. 2000), cert. denied, 532 U.S. 953, 121 S.Ct. 1428, 149 L.Ed.2d 367 (2001) (fees cannot be awarded under Rule 41(d)), with Andrews v. America's Living Centers, LLC, 827 F.3d 306 (4th Cir. 2016) (fees can be awarded).

2. DISMISSAL FOR FAILURE TO PROSECUTE

It is accepted that courts possess inherent discretionary power to dismiss an action if plaintiff does not proceed to trial with "due diligence." Exactly when this power should be invoked has been a matter about which judges have disagreed. Should simple delay by plaintiff be sufficient to justify dismissal, or should prejudice to defendant also be required? In MESSENGER v. UNITED STATES, 231 F.2d 328, 331 (2d Cir. 1956),[f] the court said: "The operative condition of the Rule is lack of due diligence on the part of the plaintiff—not a showing by the defendant that it will be prejudiced by denial of its motion. * * * It may well be that the latter factor may be considered by the court, especially in cases of moderate or excusable neglect, in the formulation of its discretionary ruling." Does this standard make sense? Does it have any practical utility as a guide for the trial judge? What is its effect on appellate-court review of the trial court's exercise of discretion?

Some jurisdictions control dismissals for want of prosecution by statute. In the federal system, Rule 41(b) "allows dismissal for the plaintiff's failure to prosecute, [and] is intended as a safeguard against

---

[f]   *Messenger* was superseded on other grounds by the addition in 1983 of Rule 4(j), as stated in Frasca v. United States, 921 F.2d 450, 452 (2d Cir. 1990). Rule 4(j) was later redesignated as Rule 4(m).

delay in litigation and harassment of a defendant." 9 Wright & Miller, Federal Practice and Procedure § 2370 (4th ed.). If the court has power under Rule 41(b) to dismiss the action, does it have an implied authority to fashion other, less onerous sanctions? Does Rule 16 affect your analysis?

LINK v. WABASH RAILROAD CO., 370 U.S. 626, 629–30, 633–34, 82 S.Ct. 1386, 1388, 1390–91, 8 L.Ed.2d 734, 737–38, 739–40 (1962). Petitioner appealed a *sua sponte* dismissal of his diversity negligence action after petitioner and his counsel failed to attend a pretrial conference. The trial date had been set some six years after the action had been commenced, during which two other fixed trial dates had been postponed. The Seventh Circuit affirmed, after which the Supreme Court, in an opinion by Justice Harlan, affirmed, holding:

> The authority of a federal trial court to dismiss a plaintiff's action with prejudice because of his failure to prosecute cannot seriously be doubted. The power to invoke this sanction is necessary in order to prevent undue delays in the disposition of pending cases and to avoid congestion in the calendars of the District Courts. The power is of ancient origin, having its roots in judgments of *nonsuit* and *non prosequitur* entered at common law, e.g., 3 Blackstone, Commentaries (1768), 295–296, and dismissals for want of prosecution of bills in equity * * *. It has been expressly recognized in Federal Rule of Civil Procedure 41(b) * * *.
>
> * * *
>
> Accordingly, when circumstances make such action appropriate, a District Court may dismiss a complaint for failure to prosecute even without affording notice of its intention to do so or providing an adversary hearing before acting. Whether such an order can stand on appeal depends not on power but on whether it was within the permissible range of the court's discretion.
>
> On this record we are unable to say that the District Court's dismissal of this action for failure to prosecute, as evidenced only partly by the failure of petitioner's counsel to appear at a duly scheduled pretrial conference, amounted to an abuse of discretion. * * *
>
> There is certainly no merit to the contention that dismissal of petitioner's claim because of his counsel's unexcused conduct imposes an unjust penalty on the client. Petitioner voluntarily chose this attorney as his representative in the action, and he cannot now avoid the consequences of the acts or omissions of this freely selected agent. Any other notion would be wholly inconsistent with our system of representative litigation, in which

each party is deemed bound by the acts of his lawyer-agent and is considered to have "notice of all facts, notice of which can be charged upon the attorney." * * *

We need not decide whether unexplained absence from a pretrial conference would *alone* justify a dismissal with prejudice if the record showed no other evidence of dilatoriness on the part of the plaintiff. For the District Court in this case relied on *all* the circumstances that were brought to its attention, including the earlier delays.

In his dissent, Justice Black argued that it was unfair to impose such a harsh penalty upon plaintiff for the misconduct of his or her attorney. The Justice suggested that numerous other sanctions were available in this instance that could have served the purpose of penalizing the attorney without resorting to a dismissal of the action, thus barring forever plaintiff's right to recovery for his injuries.

NOTE AND QUESTIONS

Lengthy delays do not necessarily lead to a dismissal for failure to prosecute. In GCIU EMPLOYER RETIREMENT FUND v. CHICAGO TRIBUNE, 8 F.3d 1195 (7th Cir. 1993), the court held that a dismissal with prejudice for failure to prosecute was improper, despite a 22-month delay, because during that period the litigants were actively negotiating. What other factors should affect the court's decision? Is the district court required to give a warning before dismissing the case?

C. DEFAULT JUDGMENT

Read Federal Rule of Civil Procedure 55 in the Supplement.

COULAS V. SMITH
Supreme Court of Arizona, 1964.
96 Ariz. 325, 395 P.2d 527.

UDALL, CHIEF JUSTICE. This is an appeal from an order of the Superior Court of Pima County, denying a motion to set aside a judgment entered against the appellant.

* * *

The plaintiff filed a complaint against the defendant and cross-claimant on two counts. The first count was for $ 669.32 on an open account. The second count was on a promissory note upon which $ 3,666.67

was alleged to be due. The cross-claimant answered individually by his attorney and denied any liability to the plaintiff on either count and thereafter filed a cross-claim against the defendant in which he sought judgment against the defendant for any sums or amounts which the plaintiff may obtain against him by virtue of the judgment; for the sum of $ 4,000 on a debt alleged to be owed by the defendant to him, and $ 500 attorney's fees. The defendant appeared individually by his attorneys and answered the complaint of the plaintiff, answered the cross-claim of the cross-claimant, and counterclaimed against the plaintiff, seeking damages in the sum of $ 18,000. The plaintiff replied to the defendant's counterclaim.

On July 11, 1958, the lower court made an order setting the case for trial on October 10, 1958. All counsel were notified by the clerk of the court. On October 6, 1958, counsel for the plaintiff and counsel for the cross-claimant stipulated that the trial be set for December 10, 1958. The lower court ordered that the prior trial date be vacated and the case be reset for trial on December 10, 1958. All counsel were regularly notified by the clerk of the new trial setting. The defendant's counsel was not present before the court on October 6, 1958, and did not participate in the stipulation vacating the original trial setting and resetting the case for trial on December 10, 1958. The defendant and defendant's counsel deny ever receiving any notice from the clerk concerning the new trial date.

On December 10, 1958, the new trial date, the case came on regularly to be heard. The defendant did not appear either in person or by counsel. The court made the following minute entry during the course of the trial:

* * *

"The plaintiff Smith and the defendant Bray announce ready for trial.

"William J. Bray is sworn, cross-examined, and examined.

"Plaintiff's Exhibit 1, being a promissory note in the sum of $4,000.00 dated February 14, 1955, is marked for identification and admitted in evidence.

"Nicholas Coulas having failed to appear at this time either in person or by counsel, and it further appearing that this case was previously set for trial both as to the issues framed by the complaint and answer thereto of the defendant Nicholas Coulas and as to the cross-claim filed by the defendant William J. Bray, Jr., against the defendant Nicholas Coulas,

"IT IS HEREBY ORDERED that the default of the said defendant Nicholas Coulas be entered as to said complaint and as to said cross-claim and the court proceeding to hear evidence pertaining to said complaint and cross-claim and being fully advised in the premises,

"IT IS THEREFORE ORDERED that judgment is hereby rendered * * * against the defendant Nicholas Coulas * * *."

The plaintiff obtained judgment against the defendant on both counts and against the cross-claimant as to count two (the promissory note). The cross-claimant obtained judgment against the defendant on the promissory note. The judgment was entered on December 11, 1958.

On October 29, 1960, nearly two years later, the defendant filed a motion to set aside and vacate the judgment. The trial court denied this motion. * * *

The defendant subsequently filed this appeal.

The defendant contends that the "default" judgment entered against him was void, since he did not receive 3 days' notice of the application for judgment by default pursuant to Rule 55(b) of the Arizona Rules of Civil Procedure * * *. The defendant's contention would be valid if the judgment below was a judgment by default. A default judgment obtains when a defendant fails to plead or otherwise defend. Rule 55. If he has made an appearance in the case, he must be given 3 days' notice of application for judgment by default. * * *

However, the defendant's contention is invalid here since the judgment below was not a default judgment. It should be noted that the defendant did plead to the merits. He answered the complaint and filed a counterclaim. He then failed to appear at the trial in person or by counsel. The trial proceeded, evidence was heard, and a judgment on the merits of the plaintiff's and counter-claimant's claims was entered. The judgment was not by default within the meaning of Rule 55. Therefore Rule 55(b) with its 3-day notice requirement is not applicable. In fact, the trial court would have erred if a default was entered, since the case was at issue. Bass v. Hoagland, 172 F.2d 205 (5th Cir. 1949), cert. denied, 338 U.S. 816, 70 S.Ct. 57, 94 L.Ed. 494 (1949) * * *.

The following language is from Bass v. Hoagland * * * concerning the applicability of Rule 55:

"Rule 55(a) authorizes the clerk to enter a default * * *. This does not require that to escape default the defendant must not only file a sufficient answer to the merits, but must also have a lawyer or be present in court when the case is called for a trial. The words 'otherwise defend' refer to attacks on the service, or motions to dismiss, or for better particulars, and the like, which may prevent default without presently pleading to the merits. *When Bass by his attorney filed a denial of the plaintiff's case neither the clerk nor the judge could enter a default against him.*

The burden of proof was put on the plaintiff in any trial. When neither Bass nor his attorney appeared at the trial, no default was generated; the case was not confessed. The plaintiff might proceed, but he would have to prove his case." 172 F.2d p. 210 (emphasis added).

* * *

* * * It should * * * be stated that once an answer on the merits is filed and the case is at issue, a default judgment is not proper, and if the defendant fails to appear at the trial a judgment on the merits may be entered against him upon proper proof.

* * *

The contention of the defendant that he did not receive notice of the new trial date is not substantiated by the minutes. The record indicates that the clerk of the superior court notified all counsel of all of the orders and judgment pursuant to Rule 77(h) * * *. It is well settled that in the absence of a showing to the contrary a public officer, such as the clerk of the court in this case, is presumed to have performed the duty imposed upon him by law. * * * In addition, if the defendant's counsel did not receive the notice of the change of the trial date to December 10, 1958, he certainly would have learned of the change in the trial date when he appeared for trial on the earlier date, October 10, 1958.

Since the judgment of the lower court is merely voidable, at most, Rule 60(c) * * * prevents the defendant from attacking the judgment more than six months after it was entered. The defendant attempted to attack the judgment nearly two years after it was entered. * * * The lower court properly denied defendant's motion to set aside and vacate the judgment.

Judgment affirmed.

NOTES AND QUESTIONS

1. In BASS v. HOAGLAND, which is relied upon in *Coulas*, a default judgment was rendered in favor of plaintiff after defendant's counsel, who had filed an answer, had withdrawn from the case. The judgment recited that defendant had been informed of the withdrawal. Defendant did not appeal but collaterally attacked the judgment when enforcement was sought against him in another jurisdiction. Defendant claimed that he did not know of the counsel's withdrawal from the case and was not aware that the adverse judgment had been rendered. A majority of the Fifth Circuit held that, since an answer had been filed, defendant was not in default under Rule 55, that the entry of judgment without trial by jury, which had been demanded, was a violation of the Due Process Clause of the Fifth Amendment, and that the judgment was void. The court indicated that even if the case fell within Rule 55, the failure to give notice under Rule 55(b)(2) might render the judgment void, although in

that event no jury trial would be required. The dissenting judge took the position that defendant, by not attending trial, was in default, that no jury trial was required, and therefore that the decision was not void and not subject to collateral attack.

2.   Federal Rule 54(c) provides that plaintiff may recover all the relief to which he is entitled except that plaintiff is limited to the amount prayed for in the case of a default judgment. Suppose at trial in Coulas v. Smith plaintiff's evidence showed that defendant was liable for $10,000, although only $4,000 had been claimed. Would the court have been justified in awarding plaintiff the full amount?

3.   What activities, short of a formal challenge to the jurisdiction or the pleadings, constitute an appearance for purposes of Rule 55(b)(2)? Consider these situations:

(a)   There are oral and written communications between counsel for the parties with a view toward settlement, and a letter by plaintiff to defendant that he would apply for a default judgment if defendant did not answer.

(b)   There are oral and written communications between counsel for the parties, and both parties intended to contest the suit if settlement negotiations broke down.

(c)   Defendant executes a waiver of service of process.

See 10A Wright, Miller, Kane & Marcus, Federal Practice and Procedure § 2686 (4th ed.).

4.   A defendant's default does not automatically entitle plaintiff to a court-ordered default judgment; the decision to grant or deny the application rests in the court's discretion. In making the determination, the Ninth Circuit relies on the following factors:

(1) the possibility of prejudice to the plaintiff, (2) the merits of plaintiff's substantive claim, (3) the sufficiency of the complaint, (4) the sum of money at stake in the action, (5) the possibility of a dispute concerning the material facts, (6) whether the default was due to excusable neglect, and (7) the strong policy underlying the Federal Rules of Civil Procedure favoring decisions on the merits.

Eitel v. McCool, 782 F.2d 1470, 1471–72 (9th Cir. 1986). For a discussion of the appropriate standard in debt collection cases, see Bearden, *Employing the Prima Facie Standard in Third Party Debt Collection Default Judgments*, 48 Urb. Law. 365 (2016).

5.   A special type of default judgment can be imposed on a party who has appeared and contested the matters at issue but willfully violated the rules of procedure or disobeyed an order of the court. Normally, this penalty is invoked against a party who is defending a claim; if the complaining party is guilty of comparable violations, the most typical remedy is to dismiss the case with prejudice. See Federal Rule 41(b). The penalty default can be used to sanction

discovery violations. Federal Rules 37(b)(2)(A) and 37(d) and their state counterparts specifically permit default judgments in these situations. The Seventh Circuit has stated "that the ultimate sanction of dismissal should be involved only in extreme situations, when there is a clear record of delay or contumacious conduct, or when other less drastic sanctions have proven unavailable." Rice v. City of Chicago, 333 F.3d 780, 785–86 (7th Cir. 2003) (internal quotations omitted).

6.   Default judgments represent a significant portion of the civil dockets of the state courts. Typically, defendant is an unrepresented individual, often in a consumer debt case, who does not make an appearance. Although many defendants choose to default because they have no defense on the merits, examples of abusive default judgments—entered without proper notice due to "sewer service"—are common. One study of consumer debt litigation reported that in the limited number of state courts that had been studied, more than 70 percent of all debt-collection cases ended in default judgments. The Pew Charitable Trusts, *How Debt Collectors Are Transforming the Business of State Courts*, May 2020, at 15–16. In New York, where more than 100,000 debt collection suits were filed each year as of 2014, the state court system responded to concerns about abusive default judgments by requiring that: (1) debt collectors provide additional notice explaining the consequences of defaulting to defendants before a default judgment may be entered; (2) debt collectors submit affidavits evidencing their right to collect on the debt in question; and (3) counsel for debt collectors represent by affirmation that the applicable statute of limitations on the debt has not expired. See, e.g., 22 N.Y.C.R.R. §§ 202.27–a & 202.27–b. See also McKinley, *Top State Judge Tightens Rules on Debt Collection*, N.Y. Times, May 1, 2014, at A20. Should a properly functioning procedural system be expected to produce such a high number of default judgments?

CHAPTER 13

TRIAL

■ ■ ■

Prior chapters have explored the ways in which litigants initiate actions, prepare for trial, and (when possible) avoid trial. But trials do take place, and it is important to discuss and analyze how they proceed, how decisions ultimately are reached, and whether the process is a fair one. The chapter begins with a discussion of jury trials. Next, attention is given to the nature of a trial in which a judge hears the case without a jury. Finally, the materials explore the ways in which errors, omissions, and improper tactics may result in the reversal of a decision and an order for a new trial. For several reasons, the primary focus is on these matters as they pertain to the federal courts. First, each state has its own rules and procedures, and it would be impossible to deal with each of them in any meaningful detail. Second, the federal system is a sound prototype for study since most states, generally speaking, employ procedures that follow those of the federal courts.

One might think that a trial is the natural destination for a case in the civil justice system. In reality, trials have become rare today in both the federal and state courts. In the 1930s, about 20 percent of civil cases in federal court concluded with a trial. See Yeazell, *The Misunderstood Consequences of Modern Civil Process*, 1994 Wis.L.Rev. 631, 633 n.3. That number dropped to about 9 percent in 1972, to 3.5 percent in 1992, and to about 2 percent in 2002. See Gallanter, *The Vanishing Trial: An Examination of Trials and Related Matters in Federal and State Courts*, 1 J. Empirical Legal Stud. 459, 462–63 tbl.1 (2004). A similar trend happened in the state courts, where the vast majority (perhaps 98 percent) of civil trials occur. Burns, The Death of the American Trial 85 (2011). One survey found that in 2005 about 3 percent of civil cases in the state courts were concluded by trial. See Langton & Cohen, Bureau of Justice Statistics, U.S. Dep't of Justice, *Civil Bench and Jury Trials in State Courts*, 2005, at 9 & tbl.10 (2008) (revised Apr. 9, 2009). More recent data confirm a continuation of this downward trend. In 2016, only 1 percent of civil cases in the federal courts concluded with a trial, and the portion of civil cases going to trial in a sample of state courts (covering almost half the states) ranged from 0.05 percent to 0.5 percent. See Nora Freeman Engstrom, *The Diminished Trial*, 86 Fordham L.Rev. 2131, 2131–32 (2018).

Scholars and policymakers have attempted to explain the causes of the "vanishing trial." There is a large literature exploring many theories for the phenomenon, but a few prominent ones bear mention. One theory points to the procedural model adopted by the Federal Rules as contributing to the decline. To be sure, at the time of their adoption "many believed that the Federal Rules represented a Gold Standard that envisioned a trial and, when appropriate, one before a jury." Miller, *What Are Courts For? Have We Forsaken the Procedural Gold Standard?*, 78 La.L.Rev. 739, 740 (2018). Because the rules provide for robust pre-trial discovery, however, cases now develop a deeper factual record than would have been typical on the eve of trial in an earlier era. As a result, liberal discovery under the rules facilitates settlement by the parties or summary judgment by the court rather than disposition at trial. See Langbein, *The Disappearance of Civil Trial in the United States*, 122 Yale L.J. 522, 544– 53 (2012). That effect is intensified by the rise of "managerial judging," the drive toward active judicial case management from the commencement of litigation, which has been said to limit contested issues and produce a greater likelihood of settlement. Id. Some commentators go beyond the details of Rule 16 (and similar case management tools developed over the years) and point to a longterm change in judicial mood accompanying active case management—a shift toward the view that the civil justice system has failed when a case gets to trial. See Resnik, *Trial as Error, Jurisdiction as Injury: Transforming the Meaning of Article III*, 113 Harv.L.Rev. 924 (2000). That shift, it is said, encourages judges to avoid trial in favor of resolution by settlement or dispositive motion. See generally Miller, *The Pretrial Rush to Judgment: Are the "Litigation Explosion," "Liability Crisis," and Efficiency Cliches Eroding Our Day in Court and Jury Trial Commitments?*, 78 N.Y.U.L.Rev. 982 (2003).

The documented decline in trial rates has sparked renewed interest in countering the trend. The arguments in favor of encouraging trials fall generally into three categories. First, some commentators believe the decline of civil trials undermines the role of the jury as a democratic institution—"the New England town meeting writ large"—in the administration of justice. Young, *Vanishing Trials, Vanishing Juries, Vanishing Constitution*, 40 Suffolk L.Rev. 67, 69 (2006).

Second, others suggest that a trial may be a more cost effective path to resolving cases than motion-dependent litigation. On this view, the certainty of a looming trial actually enhances efficiency by limiting overreliance on time-consuming motion practice and forcing parties to streamline discovery, which is now viewed "as the battleground where the adversary process is played out." Anderson, *Where Have You Gone, Spot Mozingo? A Trial Judge's Lament over the Demise of the Civil Jury Trial*, 4 Fed.Cts.L.Rev. 99, 99 (2010); see also Inst. for the Advancement of the Am. Legal Sys., A Return to Trials: Implementing Effective Short, Summary, and Expedited Civil Action Programs 3–5 (2012). In 2012, Texas adopted rules for expedited civil actions designed to proceed to trial within one year of filing. The expedited action rules provide for more constricted discovery and impose a firm date for trial. See Tex. R. Civ. P. 169. A number of other states have explored the adoption of similar rules. The evidence is unclear whether this approach increases resort to trials or simply prompts earlier settlement. See National Center for State Courts, Call to Action: Achieving Civil Justice for All, app. D at 7–8 (2016).

Third, some commentators fear that advocacy skills in the legal profession will deteriorate due to the rarity of civil trials. Judge Joseph F. Anderson, Jr., describes the concern this way:

> With a dramatic decline in trials, courtroom skills atrophy, the Rules of Evidence become an unnecessary annoyance and the well-read, flamboyant trial lawyer—an advocate in the truest sense of the term—goes the way of the dodo bird. Young lawyers lose the once-considered indispensable opportunity to observe attorneys in the courtroom. The phenomenon then feeds on itself as more and more lawyers—having no courtroom experience—settle cases, at least in part, because of the fear of going to trial. With the growth in unseasoned trial lawyers, it follows that in the not too distant future, judges as well will occupy the bench with little trial experience.

Anderson, *Where Have You Gone, Spot Mozingo? A Trial Judge's Lament over the Demise of the Civil Jury Trial*, 4 Fed.Cts.L.Rev. 99, 110 (2010).

Whether or not the rate of civil trials increases, litigants and their counsel must appreciate the dynamics of a potential trial when choosing their litigation strategy. Accordingly, the materials in this chapter provide a comprehensive discussion of the trial process.

A. TRIAL BY JURY

1. THE INSTITUTION OF TRIAL BY JURY

The jury trial established itself as central to the process of adjudication under the common law. As one commentator has observed, "the main features of the Anglo-American civil trial developed * * * as a consequence of the jury system, in which panels of lay persons were used to decide cases." Langbein, *The Disappearance of Civil Trial in the United States*, 122 Yale L.J. 522, 527 (2012). Indeed, before the middle of the nineteenth century, trial by jury was the only form of trial used in any common law court. Id.

During its formative period, the jury was an activist group that both investigated the facts and judged the evidence. A famous example of the work of the early jury is the Domesday Book, compiled in the twelfth century, setting forth an inventory of William the Conqueror's realm. The Domesday "jury" viewed the land and formed its own judgments without using witnesses. The revered status of the jury trial at common law is evidenced by Blackstone's statement that the right to trial by jury "has been, and I trust ever will be, looked upon as the glory of the English law * * * and * * * it is the most transcendent privilege which any subject can enjoy or wish for, that he not be affected either in his property, his liberty, or his person, but by unanimous consent of twelve of his neighbors and equals." 3 Blackstone, Commentaries on the Laws of England *378 (1765–1769). Yet in modern English practice, trial by jury in civil actions has been abandoned except in rare cases.

2.   THE RIGHT TO A JURY TRIAL

Read the Seventh Amendment of United States Constitution and the accompanying state materials in the Supplement.

---

a.   The Nature of the Right Under the United States Constitution

The federal Constitution and most state constitutions do not "create" a right to jury trial. Rather, they "preserve" the right as it existed at common law, either in 1791, the date of the Seventh Amendment's ratification, or, in the case of some states, as of the time the state constitution was adopted. Because the Seventh Amendment was assumed to incorporate the jury trial practice as of 1791, federal courts have applied a historical test for determining whether the civil jury right attaches. Critics argue that the historical test is difficult to apply and inappropriate for novel, hybrid actions. See 9 Wright & Miller, Federal Practice and Procedure § 2302 (4th ed.).

b.   The Effect of the Single Form of Action on the Jury Right

The formal elimination under Federal Rule 2 of separate actions in law and equity and the adoption of other procedural innovations have raised a number of challenging issues regarding the historic right to a trial by jury. Cases at law—those that were brought in courts of law in 1791—continue to carry the right to trial by jury in cases in federal courts. Suits in equity, historically decided by the chancellor, sitting without a jury, continue to be decided by judges, although judges can, in their discretion, employ an advisory jury. See Federal Rule 39(c).

i.   Maintenance of the Law-Equity Distinction

The law-equity distinction is based primarily on the nature of the relief sought. Relief at law generally is limited to compensatory damages along with the ejectment of a defendant who wrongfully is occupying plaintiff's land. Equity provides remedies when the law does not, including injunctions, restitution, rescission, and reformation of contracts.

ii.   Cases Involving Both Equitable and Legal Relief

In simple cases, plaintiff, by designating the right to relief sought, was able to control whether or not a jury trial is required. See Thomas, *A Limitation on Congress: "In Suits at Common Law,"* 71 Ohio St.L.J. 1071 (2010). However, the merger of law and equity has complicated the application of the jury trial right because today a party may enter a single court with both legal and equitable claims. Even if a plaintiff brings claims of only one type, a defendant, by way of counterclaim, may introduce the other type.

The "mixed" remedies case was not completely unknown in 1791. Long before merger, equity developed the so-called "clean-up" doctrine, which allowed an equity court that had obtained jurisdiction over a suit primarily of an equitable character to decide any incidental legal issues that arose in the course of the litigation. See Levin, *Equitable Clean-up and the Jury: A Suggested Orientation*, 100 U.Pa.L.Rev. 320, 320–21 (1951).

BEACON THEATRES, INC. V. WESTOVER
Supreme Court of the United States, 1959.
359 U.S. 500, 79 S.Ct. 948, 3 L.Ed.2d 988.

Certiorari to the United States Court of Appeals for the Ninth Circuit.

JUSTICE BLACK delivered the opinion of the Court.

Petitioner, Beacon Theatres, Inc., sought by mandamus to require a district judge in the Southern District of California to vacate certain orders alleged to deprive it of a jury trial of issues arising in a suit brought against it by Fox West Coast Theatres, Inc. The Court of Appeals for the Ninth Circuit refused the writ, holding that the trial judge had acted within his proper discretion in denying petitioner's request for a jury. * * *

Fox had asked for declaratory relief against Beacon alleging a controversy arising under the Sherman Antitrust Act, 26 Stat. 209, as amended, 15 U.S.C. §§ 1, 2, and under the Clayton Act, 38 Stat. 731, 15 U.S.C. § 15, which authorizes suits for treble damages against Sherman Act violators. According to the complaint Fox operates a movie theatre in

San Bernardino, California, and has long been exhibiting films under contracts with movie distributors. These contracts grant it the exclusive right to show "first run" pictures in the "San Bernardino competitive area" and provide for "clearance"—a period of time during which no other theatre can exhibit the same pictures. After building a drive-in theatre about 11 miles from San Bernardino, Beacon notified Fox that it considered contracts barring simultaneous exhibitions of first-run films in the two theatres to be overt acts in violation of the antitrust laws. Fox's complaint alleged that this notification, together with threats of treble damage suits against Fox and its distributors, gave rise to "duress and coercion" which deprived Fox of a valuable property right, the right to negotiate for exclusive first-run contracts. Unless Beacon was restrained, the complaint continued, irreparable harm would result. Accordingly, while its pleading was styled a "Complaint for Declaratory Relief," Fox prayed both for a declaration that a grant of clearance between the Fox and Beacon theatres is reasonable and not in violation of the antitrust laws, and for an injunction, pending final resolution of the litigation, to prevent Beacon from instituting any action under the antitrust laws against Fox and its distributors arising out of the controversy alleged in the complaint. Beacon filed an answer, a counterclaim against Fox, and a cross-claim against an exhibitor who had intervened. These denied the threats and asserted that there was no substantial competition between the two theatres, that the clearances granted were therefore unreasonable, and that a conspiracy existed between Fox and its distributors to manipulate contracts and clearances so as to restrain trade and monopolize first-run pictures in violation of the antitrust laws. Treble damages were asked.

Beacon demanded a jury trial of the factual issues in the case as provided by Federal Rule * * * 38(b). The District Court, however, viewed the issues raised by the "Complaint for Declaratory Relief," including the question of competition between the two theatres, as essentially equitable. Acting under the purported authority of Rules 42(b) and 57, it directed that these issues be tried to the court before jury determination of the validity of the charges of antitrust violations made in the counterclaim and cross-claim. A common issue of the "Complaint for Declaratory Relief," the counterclaim, and the cross-claim was the reasonableness of the clearances granted to Fox, which depended, in part, on the existence of competition between the two theatres. Thus the effect of the action of the District Court could be, as the Court of Appeals believed, "to limit the petitioner's opportunity fully to try to a jury every issue which has a bearing upon its treble damage suit," for determination of the issue of clearances by the judge might "operate either by way of res judicata or collateral estoppel so as to conclude both parties with respect thereto at the subsequent trial of the treble damage claim." * * *

The District Court's finding that the Complaint for Declaratory Relief presented basically equitable issues draws no support from the Declaratory Judgment Act, 28 U.S.C. §§ 2201, 2202; Fed.Rules Civ.Proc. 57. * * * That statute, while allowing prospective defendants to sue to establish their nonliability, specifically preserves the right to jury trial for both parties. It follows that if Beacon would have been entitled to a jury trial in a treble damage suit against Fox it cannot be deprived of that right merely because Fox took advantage of the availability of declaratory relief to sue Beacon first. Since the right to trial by jury applies to treble damage suits under the antitrust laws, and is, in fact, an essential part of the congressional plan for making competition rather than monopoly the rule of trade * * *, the Sherman and Clayton Act issues * * * were essentially jury questions.

Nevertheless the Court of Appeals * * * held that the question of whether a right to jury trial existed was to be judged by Fox's complaint read as a whole. In addition to seeking a declaratory judgment, the court said, Fox's complaint can be read as making out a valid plea for injunctive relief, thus stating a claim traditionally cognizable in equity. A party who is entitled to maintain a suit in equity for an injunction, said the court, may have all the issues in his suit determined by the judge without a jury regardless of whether legal rights are involved. The court then rejected the argument that equitable relief, traditionally available only when legal remedies are inadequate, was rendered unnecessary in this case by the filing of the counterclaim and cross-claim which presented all the issues necessary to a determination of the right to injunctive relief. Relying on American Life Ins. Co. v. Stewart, 300 U.S. 203, 215, 57 S.Ct. 377, 380, 81 L.Ed. 605, decided before the enactment of the Federal Rules * * *, it invoked the principle that a court sitting in equity could retain jurisdiction even though later a legal remedy became available. In such instances the equity court had discretion to enjoin the later lawsuit in order to allow the whole dispute to be determined in one case in one court. Reasoning by analogy, the Court of Appeals held it was not an abuse of discretion for the district judge, acting under Federal Rule * * * 42(b), to try the equitable cause first even though this might, through collateral estoppel, prevent a full jury trial of the counterclaim and cross-claim which were as effectively stopped as by an equity injunction.[6]

Beacon takes issue with the holding of the Court of Appeals that the complaint stated a claim upon which equitable relief could be granted. As initially filed the complaint alleged that threats of lawsuits by petitioner against Fox and its distributors were causing irreparable harm to Fox's

---

[6]   252 F.2d at page 874. In Ettelson v. Metropolitan Life Ins. Co., 317 U.S. 188, 192, 63 S.Ct. 163, 164, 87 L.Ed. 176, this Court recognized that orders enabling equitable causes to be tried before legal ones had the same effect as injunctions. In City of Morgantown, W.Va. v. Royal Ins. Co., 337 U.S. 254, 69 S.Ct. 1067, 93 L.Ed. 1347, the Court denied at least some such orders the status of injunctions for the purposes of appealability. It did not, of course, imply that when the orders came to be reviewed they would be examined any less strictly than injunctions. * * *

business relationships. The prayer for relief, however, made no mention of the threats but asked only that pending litigation of the claim for declaratory judgment, Beacon be enjoined from beginning any lawsuits under the antitrust laws against Fox and its distributors arising out of the controversy alleged in the complaint. Evidently of the opinion that this prayer did not state a good claim for equitable relief, the Court of Appeals construed it to include a request for an injunction against threats of lawsuits. * * * But this fact does not solve our problem. Assuming that the pleadings can be construed to support such a request and assuming additionally that the complaint can be read as alleging the kind of harassment by a multiplicity of lawsuits which would *traditionally* have justified equity to take jurisdiction and settle the case in one suit, we are nevertheless of the opinion that, under the Declaratory Judgment Act and the Federal Rules * * *, neither claim can justify denying Beacon a trial by jury of all the issues in the antitrust controversy.

The basis of injunctive relief in the federal courts has always been irreparable harm and inadequacy of legal remedies. At least as much is required to justify a trial court in using its discretion under the Federal Rules to allow claims of equitable origins to be tried ahead of legal ones, since this has the same effect as an equitable injunction of the legal claims. And it is immaterial, in judging if that discretion is properly employed, that before the Federal Rules and the Declaratory Judgment Act were passed, courts of equity, exercising a jurisdiction separate from courts of law, were, in some cases, allowed to enjoin subsequent legal actions between the same parties involving the same controversy. This was because the subsequent legal action, though providing an opportunity to try the case to a jury, might not protect the right of the equity plaintiff to a fair and orderly adjudication of the controversy. * * * Under such circumstances the legal remedy could quite naturally be deemed inadequate. Inadequacy of remedy and irreparable harm * * * today must be determined, not by precedents decided under discarded procedures, but in the light of the remedies now made available by the Declaratory Judgment Act and the Federal Rules.

Viewed in this manner, the use of discretion by the trial court under Rule 42(b) to deprive Beacon of a full jury trial on its counterclaim and cross-claim, as well as on Fox's plea for declaratory relief, cannot be justified. Under the Federal Rules the same court may try both legal and equitable causes in the same action. * * *

Thus any defenses, equitable or legal, Fox may have to charges of antitrust violations can be raised either in its suit for declaratory relief or in answer to Beacon's counterclaim. On proper showing, harassment by threats of other suits, or other suits actually brought, involving the issues being tried in this case, could be temporarily enjoined pending the outcome of this litigation. Whatever permanent injunctive relief Fox might be entitled to on the basis of the decision in this case could, of course, be given by the court after the jury renders its verdict. In this way the issues between these parties could be settled in one suit giving Beacon a full jury trial of every antitrust issue. * * * By contrast, the holding of the court below while granting Fox no additional protection unless the avoidance of jury trial be considered as such, would compel Beacon to split his antitrust case, trying part to a judge and part to a jury. Such a result, which involves the postponement and subordination of Fox's own legal claim for declaratory relief as well as of the counterclaim which Beacon was compelled by the Federal Rules to bring, is not permissible.

Our decision is consistent with the plan of the Federal Rules and the Declaratory Judgment Act to effect substantial procedural reform while retaining a distinction between jury and nonjury issues and leaving substantive rights unchanged. Since in the federal courts equity has always acted only when legal remedies were inadequate, the expansion of adequate legal remedies provided by the Declaratory Judgment Act and the Federal Rules necessarily affects the scope of equity. Thus, the justification for equity's deciding legal issues once it obtains jurisdiction, and refusing to dismiss a case, merely because subsequently a legal remedy becomes available, must be re-evaluated in the light of the liberal joinder provisions of the Federal Rules which allow legal and equitable causes to be brought and resolved in one civil action. Similarly the need for, and therefore, the availability of such equitable remedies as Bills of Peace, *Quia Timet* and Injunction must be reconsidered in view of the existence of the Declaratory Judgment Act as well as the liberal joinder provision of the Rules. * * *

If there should be cases where the availability of declaratory judgment or joinder in one suit of legal and equitable causes would not in all respects protect the plaintiff seeking equitable relief from irreparable harm while affording a jury trial in the legal cause, the trial court will necessarily have to use its discretion in deciding whether the legal or equitable cause should be tried first. Since the right to jury trial is a constitutional one, however, while no similar requirement protects trials by the court, that discretion is very narrowly limited and must, wherever possible, be exercised to preserve jury trial. * * * [O]nly under the most imperative circumstances, circumstances which in view of the flexible procedures of the Federal Rules we cannot now anticipate, can the right to a jury trial of legal issues be lost through prior determination of equitable claims. * * *

As we have shown, this is far from being such a case.

* * *

The judgment of the Court of Appeals is reversed.

Reversed.

JUSTICE FRANKFURTER took no part in the consideration or decision of this case.

JUSTICE STEWART, with whom JUSTICE HARLAN and JUSTICE WHITTAKER concur, dissenting.

* * *

I.

The Court suggests that "the expansion of adequate legal remedies provided by the Declaratory Judgment Act * * * necessarily affects the scope of equity." Does the Court mean to say that the mere availability of an action for a declaratory judgment operates to furnish "an adequate remedy at law" so as to deprive a court of equity of the power to act? That novel line of reasoning is at least implied in the Court's opinion. But the Declaratory Judgment Act did not "expand" the substantive law. That Act merely provided a new statutory remedy, neither legal nor equitable, but available in the areas of both equity and law. When declaratory relief is sought, the right to trial by jury depends upon the basic context in which the issues are presented. * * * If the basic issues in an action for declaratory relief are of a kind traditionally cognizable in equity, e.g., a suit for cancellation of a written instrument, the declaratory judgment is not a "remedy at law." If, on the other hand, the issues arise in a context traditionally cognizable at common law, the right to a jury trial of course remains unimpaired, even though the only relief demanded is a declaratory judgment.

Thus, if in this case the complaint had asked merely for a judgment declaring that the plaintiff's specified manner of business dealings with distributors and other exhibitors did not render it liable to Beacon under the antitrust laws, this would have been simply a "juxtaposition of parties" case in which Beacon could have demanded a jury trial. But the complaint * * * presented issues of exclusively equitable cognizance, going well beyond a mere defense to any subsequent action at law. Fox sought from the court protection against Beacon's allegedly unlawful interference with its business relationships—protection which this Court seems to recognize might not have been afforded by a declaratory judgment, unsupplemented by equitable relief. The availability of a declaratory judgment did not, therefore, operate to confer upon Beacon the right to trial by jury with respect to the issues raised by the complaint.

II.

* * * [T]he Court holds, quite apart from its reliance upon the Declaratory Judgment Act, that Beacon by filing its counterclaim and cross-claim acquired a right to trial by jury of issues which otherwise would have been properly triable to the court. Support for this position is found in the principle that, "in the federal courts equity has always acted only when legal remedies were inadequate. * * *" Yet that principle is not employed in its traditional sense as a limitation upon the exercise of power by a court of equity. This is apparent in the Court's recognition that the allegations of the complaint entitled Fox to equitable relief—relief to which Fox would not have been entitled if it had had an adequate remedy at law. Instead, the principle is employed today to mean that because it is possible under the counterclaim to have a jury trial of the factual issue of substantial competition, that issue must be tried by a jury, even though the issue was primarily presented in the original claim for equitable relief. This is a marked departure from long-settled principles.

It has been an established rule "that equitable jurisdiction existing at the filing of a bill is not destroyed because an adequate legal remedy may have become available thereafter." * * * [American Life Ins. Co. v. Stewart, 300 U.S. 203, 215, 57 S.Ct. 377, 380, 81 L.Ed. 605 (1937)]. * * * It has also been long settled that the District Court in its discretion may order the trial of a suit in equity in advance of an action at law between the same parties, even if there is a factual issue common to both. * * *

III.

The Court today sweeps away these basic principles as "precedents decided under discarded procedures." It suggests that the Federal Rules * * * have somehow worked an "expansion of adequate legal remedies" so as to oust the District Courts of equitable jurisdiction, as well as to deprive them of their traditional power to control their own dockets. But obviously the Federal Rules could not and did not "expand" the substantive law one whit.

Like the Declaratory Judgment Act, the Federal Rules preserve inviolate the right to trial by jury in actions historically cognizable at common law, as under the Constitution they must. They do not create a right of trial by jury where that right "does not exist under the Constitution or statutes of the United States." Rule 39(a).[a] Since Beacon's counterclaim was compulsory under the Rules, see Rule 13(a), it is apparent that by filing it Beacon could not be held to have waived its jury rights. * * * But neither can the counterclaim be held to have transformed Fox's original complaint into an action at law. * * *

The Rules make possible the trial of legal and equitable claims in the same proceeding, but they expressly affirm the power of a trial judge to determine the order in which claims shall be heard. Rule 42(b). Certainly the Federal Rules were not intended to undermine the basic structure of equity jurisprudence, developed over the centuries and explicitly recognized in the United States Constitution.

---

[a] Comparable language is now found in Federal Rule 38(a).

For these reasons I think the petition for a writ of mandamus should have been dismissed.

NOTES AND QUESTIONS

1. DAIRY QUEEN, INC. v. WOOD, 369 U.S. 469, 82 S.Ct. 894, 8 L.Ed.2d 44 (1962), arose out of a licensing agreement entered into by respondents, owners of the trademark "Dairy Queen," under which petitioner agreed to pay $150,000 for the exclusive right to use that trademark in certain parts of Pennsylvania. The contract provided for a small initial payment, with the remaining payments to be made at the rate of 50 percent of all amounts received by petitioner on sales and franchises to deal with the trademark; minimum annual payments were to be made regardless of petitioner's receipts. In August, 1960, respondents wrote petitioner a letter in which they claimed that the latter had committed "a material breach of that contract" by defaulting on the contract's payment provisions and notified petitioner that the contract would be terminated unless the claimed default was remedied immediately. When petitioner continued to deal with the trademark, respondents brought an action for breach of contract praying for: (1) temporary and permanent injunctions to restrain petitioner from any future use of or dealing in the franchise and the trademark; (2) an accounting to determine the exact amount of money owed by petitioner and a judgment for that amount; and (3) an injunction pending an accounting to prevent petitioner from collecting any money from "Dairy Queen" stores in the territory.

The Eastern District of Pennsylvania granted a motion to strike petitioner's demand for a jury trial on the alternative grounds that either the action was "purely equitable" or, if not purely equitable, the legal issues were "incidental" to equitable issues, and, in either case, no right to trial by jury existed. The Third Circuit refused to mandamus the district judge to vacate this order. The Supreme Court reversed.

The Court first disposed of the District Court's conclusion that there is no right to jury trial on legal issues that are "incidental" to equitable issues.

> * * * The holding in *Beacon Theatres* * * * applies whether the trial judge chooses to characterize the legal issues presented as "incidental" to equitable issues or not. Consequently, * * * *Beacon Theatres* requires that any legal issues for which a trial by jury is timely and properly demanded be submitted to a jury. * * *

Id. at 472–73, 82 S.Ct. at 897, 8 L.Ed.2d at 48.

As to the lower court's conclusion that the action was "purely equitable," the Court said:

> * * * The most natural construction of the respondents' claim for a money judgment would seem to be that it is a claim that they are entitled to recover whatever was owed them under the contract as of the date of its purported termination plus damages for infringement of their trademark since that date. * * * As an action on a debt

allegedly due under a contract, it would be difficult to conceive of an action of a more traditionally legal character. And as an action for damages based upon a charge of trademark infringement, it would be no less subject to cognizance by a court of law.

The respondents' contention that this money claim is "purely equitable" is based primarily upon the fact that their complaint is cast in terms of an "accounting," rather than in terms of an action for "debt" or "damages." But the constitutional right to trial by jury cannot be made to depend upon the choice of words used in the pleadings. The necessary prerequisite to the right to maintain a suit for an equitable accounting, like all other equitable remedies, is, as we pointed out in *Beacon Theatres*, the absence of an adequate remedy at law. Consequently, in order to maintain such a suit on a cause of action cognizable at law, as this one is, the plaintiff must be able to show that the "accounts between the parties" are of such a "complicated nature" that only a court of equity can satisfactorily unravel them. In view of the powers given to District Courts by Federal Rule * * * 53(b) to appoint masters to assist the jury in those exceptional cases where the legal issues are too complicated for the jury adequately to handle alone, the burden of such a showing is considerably increased and it will indeed be a rare case in which it can be met. * * * A jury, under proper instructions from the court, could readily determine the recovery, if any, to be had here, whether the theory finally settled upon is that of breach of contract, that of trademark infringement, or any combination of the two. * * *

Id. at 476–79, 82 S.Ct. at 899–900, 8 L.Ed.2d at 50–52.

2. ROSS v. BERNHARD, 396 U.S. 531, 90 S.Ct. 733, 24 L.Ed.2d 729 (1970). Plaintiffs brought a derivative suit in federal court against the directors of a closed-end investment company of which they were shareholders and joined the company's brokers, alleging that the company had been charged excessive brokerage fees. Plaintiffs' demand for jury trial, granted by the trial court but set aside by the Second Circuit, was upheld by the Supreme Court in a five-to-three decision:

Derivative suits posed no Seventh Amendment problems where the action against the directors and third parties would have been by a bill in equity had the corporation brought the suit. Our concern is with cases based upon a legal claim of the corporation against directors or third parties. Does the trial of such claims at the suit of a stockholder and without a jury violate the Seventh Amendment?

* * * The heart of the action is the corporate claim. If it presents a legal issue, one entitling the corporation to a jury trial under the Seventh Amendment, the right to a jury is not forfeited merely because the stockholder's right to sue must first be adjudicated as an equitable issue triable to the court. *Beacon* and *Dairy Queen* require no less.

Id. at 538–39, 90 S.Ct. at 739, 24 L.Ed.2d at 736.

A footnote in the majority opinion in *Ross* provided some guidance on the categorization of issues as legal or equitable for Seventh Amendment purposes:

> As our cases indicate, the "legal" nature of an issue is determined by considering, first, the pre-merger custom with reference to such questions; second, the remedy sought; and, third, the practical abilities and limitations of juries. * * *

396 U.S. at 538 n.10, 90 S.Ct. at 738 n.10, 24 L.Ed.2d at 736 n.10.

Some lower federal courts read the third "consideration" mentioned in the *Ross* footnote as a basis for denying a jury trial in cases in which the number of parties, complexity of the issues, or conceptual sophistication of the evidence and applicable substantive law support a finding that a jury would not be a rational and capable fact finder. See In re Japanese Electronic Prods. Antitrust Litigation, 631 F.2d 1069 (3d Cir. 1980), affirmed in part and reversed in part on other grounds following summary judgment 723 F.2d 238, 319 (3d Cir. 1983), reversed on other grounds Matsushita Elec. Indus. Co. v. Zenith Radio Corp., 475 U.S. 574, 106 S.Ct. 1348, 89 L.Ed.2d 538 (1986).

iii. Newly Established Court-Based Rights to Relief

CURTIS V. LOETHER
Supreme Court of the United States, 1974.
415 U.S. 189, 94 S.Ct. 1005, 39 L.Ed.2d 260.

Certiorari to the United States Court of Appeals for the Seventh Circuit.

JUSTICE MARSHALL delivered the opinion of the Court.

Section 812 of the Civil Rights Act of 1968, 82 Stat. 88, 42 U.S.C. § 3612, authorizes private plaintiffs to bring civil actions to redress violations of Title VIII, the fair housing provisions of the Act * * *. The question presented in this case is whether the Civil Rights Act or the Seventh Amendment requires a jury trial upon demand by one of the parties in an action for damages and injunctive relief under this section.

Petitioner, a Negro woman, brought this action under § 812, claiming that respondents, who are white, had refused to rent an apartment to her because of her race * * *. In her complaint she sought only injunctive relief and punitive damages; a claim for compensatory damages was later added. After an evidentiary hearing, the District Court granted preliminary injunctive relief, enjoining the respondents from renting the apartment in question to anyone else pending the trial on the merits. This injunction was dissolved some five months later with the petitioner's consent, after she had finally obtained other housing, and the case went to trial on the issues of actual and punitive damages.

Respondents made a timely demand for jury trial in their answer. The District Court * * * denied the jury request. * * * After trial on the merits, the District Judge found that respondents had in fact discriminated against petitioner on account of her race. Although he found no actual damages, * * * he awarded $250 in punitive damages, denying petitioner's request for attorney's fees and court costs.

The Court of Appeals reversed on the jury trial issue. * * * In view of the importance of the jury trial issue in the administration and enforcement of Title VIII and the diversity of views in the lower courts on the question, we granted certiorari * * *. We affirm.

* * * [W]e think it is clear that the Seventh Amendment entitles either party to demand a jury trial in an action for damages in the federal courts under § 812.

* * * Although the thrust of the Amendment was to preserve the right to jury trial as it existed in 1791, it has long been settled that the right extends beyond the common-law forms of action recognized at that time. * * *

Petitioner nevertheless argues that the Amendment is inapplicable to new causes of action created by congressional enactment. As the Court of Appeals observed, however, we have considered the applicability of the constitutional right to jury trial in actions enforcing statutory rights "as a matter too obvious to be doubted." * * * The Seventh Amendment does apply to actions enforcing statutory rights, and requires a jury trial upon demand, if the statute creates legal rights and remedies, enforceable in an action for damages in the ordinary courts of law.

NLRB v. Jones & Laughlin Steel Corp., 301 U.S. 1, 57 S.Ct. 615, 81 L.Ed. 893 (1937), relied on by petitioner, lends no support to her statutory-rights argument. The Court there upheld the award of back pay without jury trial in an NLRB unfair labor practice proceeding, rejecting a Seventh Amendment claim on the ground that the case involved a "statutory proceeding" and "not a suit at common law or in the nature of such a suit." Id. at 48[, 57 S.Ct. at 629, 81 L.Ed. at 918]. *Jones & Laughlin* merely stands for the proposition that the Seventh Amendment is generally inapplicable in administrative proceedings, where jury trials would be incompatible with the whole concept of administrative adjudication and would substantially interfere with the NLRB's role in the statutory scheme. * * * These cases uphold congressional power to entrust enforcement of statutory rights to an administrative process or specialized court of equity free from the strictures of the Seventh Amendment. But when Congress provides for enforcement of statutory rights in an ordinary civil action in the district courts, where there is obviously no functional justification for denying the jury trial right, a jury trial must be available if the action involves rights and remedies of the sort typically enforced in an action at law.

We think it is clear that a damages action under § 812 is an action to enforce "legal rights" within the meaning of our Seventh Amendment decisions. See, *e.g.*, Ross v. Bernhard * * * [p. 741, Note 2, supra]; Dairy Queen, Inc. v. Wood * * * [p. 740, Note 1, supra]. A damages action under the statute sounds basically in tort—the statute merely defines a new legal duty, and authorizes the courts to compensate a plaintiff for the injury caused by the defendant's wrongful breach. As the Court of Appeals noted, this cause of action is analogous to a number of tort actions recognized at common law.[10] More important, the relief sought here—actual and punitive damages—is the traditional form of relief offered in the courts of law.

We need not, and do not, go so far as to say that any award of monetary relief must necessarily be "legal" relief. * * * A comparison of Title VIII with Title VII of the Civil Rights Act of 1964, where the courts of appeals have held that jury trial is not required in an action for reinstatement and back pay, is instructive, although we of course express no view on the jury trial issue in that context. In Title VII cases the courts of appeals have characterized back pay as an integral part of an equitable remedy, a form of restitution. But the statutory language on which this characterization is based—

> [T]he court may enjoin the respondent from engaging in such unlawful employment practice, and order such affirmative action as may be appropriate, which may include, but is not limited to, reinstatement or hiring of employees, with or without back pay * * *, or any other equitable relief as the court deems appropriate, 42 U.S.C. § 2000e–5(g) (1970 ed., Supp. II)—

contrasts sharply with § 812's simple authorization of an action for actual and punitive damages. In Title VII cases, also, the courts have relied on the fact that the decision whether to award back pay is committed to the discretion of the trial judge. There is no comparable discretion here: if a plaintiff proves unlawful discrimination and actual damages, he is entitled to judgment for that amount. Nor is there any sense in which the award here can be viewed as requiring the defendant to disgorge funds wrongfully withheld from the plaintiff. Whatever may be the merit of the "equitable" characterization in Title VII cases, there is surely no basis for characterizing the award of compensatory and punitive damages here as equitable relief.

---

[10] For example, the Court of Appeals recognized that Title VIII could be viewed as an extension of the common-law duty of innkeepers not to refuse temporary lodging to a traveler without justification, a duty enforceable in a damages action triable to a jury, to those who rent apartments on a long-term basis. See 467 F.2d at 1117. An action to redress racial discrimination may also be likened to an action for defamation or intentional infliction of mental distress. * * *

We are not oblivious to the force of petitioner's policy arguments. Jury trials may delay to some extent the disposition of Title VIII damages actions. But Title VIII actions seeking only equitable relief will be unaffected, and preliminary injunctive relief remains available without a jury trial even in damages actions, Dairy Queen, Inc. v. Wood * * *. Moreover, the statutory requirement of expedition of § 812 actions * * * applies equally to jury and nonjury trials. We recognize, too, the possibility that jury prejudice may deprive a victim of discrimination of the verdict to which he or she is entitled. Of course, the trial judge's power to direct a verdict, to grant judgment notwithstanding the verdict, or to grant a new trial provides substantial protection against this risk, and respondents' suggestion that jury trials will expose a broader segment of the populace to the example of the federal civil rights laws in operation has some force. More fundamentally, however, these considerations are insufficient to overcome the clear command of the Seventh Amendment. The decision of the Court of Appeals must be affirmed.

Affirmed.

NOTE AND QUESTIONS

TULL v. UNITED STATES, 481 U.S. 412, 107 S.Ct. 1831, 95 L.Ed.2d 365 (1987), further considered how a federal court should decide whether a modern-day statutory action is entitled to a trial by jury. In *Tull* the Government sued in federal court to impose a statutory monetary penalty on defendant for alleged violations of the Clean Water Act. Defendant demanded a jury trial, arguing that the action was akin to an historical action in debt decided by the law courts. The Government countered with arguments that the action was basically one in equity to abate a nuisance. The Supreme Court noted that in making its decision it first must "compare the statutory action to 18th-century actions brought in the courts of England prior to the merger of the courts of law and equity * * * [and then] examine the remedy sought and determine whether it is legal or equitable in nature." Id. at 417–18, 107 S.Ct. at 1835, 95 L.Ed.2d at 373. However, the Court went on to state "that characterizing the relief sought is '[m]ore important' than finding a precisely analogous common law cause of action in determining whether the Seventh Amendment guarantees a jury trial." Id. at 421, 107 S.Ct. at 1837, 95 L.Ed.2d at 375 (internal citation omitted). The Court then found that a civil penalty was a remedy enforced by the law courts and thus entitled to a trial by jury. Does the Court's two-part "test" make sense? If the nature of the remedy is "more important" than the characterization of the action, what is the value of the latter determination? See the concurring opinion of Justice Brennan in Chauffers, Teamsters & Helpers, Local 391 v. Terry, p. 748, infra.

iv. *Decisions by Non-Article III Tribunals*

In ATLAS ROOFING CO. v. OCCUPATIONAL SAFETY & HEALTH REVIEW COMMISSION, 430 U.S. 442, 97 S.Ct. 1261, 51 L.Ed.2d 464

(1977), the Court held that Congress may create new statutory rights—
"public rights"—and "assign their adjudication to an administrative agency
with which a jury trial would be incompatible, without violating the
Seventh Amendment's injunction that jury trial is to be 'preserved' in 'suits
at common law.'" Does *Atlas* create an exception only for "public rights"
cases? Could the legislature provide that ordinary personal injury actions
are to be decided by an administrative tribunal because existing remedies
are "inadequate"? Are there any limits on Congress's power to replace
common law claims with statutory claims and to assign adjudication of the
latter to administrative tribunals?

In GRANFINANCIERA, S.A. v. NORDBERG, 492 U.S. 33, 109 S.Ct.
2782, 106 L.Ed.2d 26 (1989), Nordberg, the bankruptcy trustee for the
debtor, Chase & Sanborn Corporation, brought an adversary proceeding
under the Bankruptcy Code, 11 U.S.C. §§ 548 & 550 against
Granfinanciera to recover funds fraudulently transferred to
Granfinanciera by the debtor before bankruptcy. In addition to avoiding
(that is, unwinding) the transfers, the trustee's fraudulent conveyance
action sought damages, costs, expenses, and interest. Granfinanciera's
request for a jury trial was denied on the ground that the bankruptcy
courts, like administrative agencies, are outside the Seventh Amendment.
The Supreme Court disagreed. Applying the two-stage analysis set out in
Tull the Court determined, first, that the jury trial right attached to an
action to recover a fraudulent conveyance, and, second, that the public
rights exception was not implicated in private tort, contract, and property
cases:

> * * * Congress may devise novel causes of action involving public
> rights free from the strictures of the Seventh Amendment if it
> assigns their adjudication to tribunals without statutory
> authority to employ juries as factfinders. But it lacks the power to
> strip parties contesting matters of private right of their
> constitutional right to a trial by jury. * * *

> In certain situations, of course, Congress may fashion causes of
> action that are closely analogous to common-law claims and place
> them beyond the ambit of the Seventh Amendment by assigning
> their resolution to a forum in which jury trials are unavailable.
> * * * Congress' power to do so is limited, however, just as its power
> to place adjudicative authority in non-Article III tribunals is
> circumscribed. * * *

> * * * If a statutory right is not closely intertwined with a federal
> regulatory program Congress has power to enact, and if the right
> neither belongs to nor exists against the Federal Government,
> then it must be adjudicated by an Article III court. If the right is

legal in nature, then it carries with it the Seventh Amendment's guarantee of a jury trial.

Id. at 55–63, 109 S.Ct. at 2797–802, 106 L.Ed.2d at 49–54. The Court then considered whether the jury trial right attached to an action in the bankruptcy court:

> * * * Although the issue admits of some debate, a bankruptcy trustee's right to recover a fraudulent conveyance under 11 U.S.C. 548(a)(2) seems to us more accurately characterized as a private rather than a public right as we have used those terms in our Article III decisions. * * * There can be little doubt that fraudulent conveyance actions by bankruptcy trustees * * * are quintessentially suits at common law that more nearly resemble state-law contract claims brought by a bankrupt corporation to augment the bankruptcy estate than they do creditors' hierarchically ordered claims to a pro rata share of the bankruptcy res. They therefore appear matters of private rather than public right. * * *
>
> * * * It may be that providing jury trials in some fraudulent conveyance actions—if not in this particular case, because respondent's suit was commenced after the bankruptcy court approved the debtor's plan of reorganization—would impede swift resolution of bankruptcy proceedings and increase the expense of Chapter 11 reorganizations. But "these considerations are insufficient to overcome the clear command of the Seventh Amendment." * * *

Id. at 55–63, 109 S.Ct. at 2797–802, 106 L.Ed.2d at 49–54.

In footnote 4 of the majority opinion in *Granfinanciera*, the Court commented:

> This quite distinct inquiry into whether Congress has permissibly entrusted the resolution of certain disputes to an administrative agency or specialized court of equity, and whether jury trials would impair the functioning of the legislative scheme, appears to be what the Court contemplated when, in *Ross* v. *Bernhard* * * * it identified "the practical abilities and limitations of juries" as an additional factor to be consulted in determining whether the Seventh Amendment confers a jury trial right. * * *

Id. at 42 n.4, 109 S.Ct. at 2791 n.4, 106 L.Ed.2d at 41 n.4.

NOTE AND QUESTION

Granfinanciera left open whether a bankruptcy judge may preside over a jury trial, and the lower courts divided in their response to this question. In 1994, Congress authorized bankruptcy courts to conduct jury trials in core matters with the express consent of the parties; however, a party that submits a claim against the bankruptcy estate waives the right to a civil jury trial. 28 U.S.C. § 157(e). See 17 Wright, Miller & Amar, Federal Practice and Procedure § 4106 (3d ed.).

v. The Modern Effect of Historical Equity Jurisdiction Based on a Party's Legal Status

CHAUFFEURS, TEAMSTERS AND HELPERS LOCAL 391 V. TERRY

Supreme Court of the United States, 1990.
494 U.S. 558, 110 S.Ct. 1339, 108 L.Ed.2d 519.

Certiorari to the United States Court of Appeals for the Fourth Circuit.

JUSTICE MARSHALL delivered the opinion of the Court except as to Part III-A.

This case presents the question whether an employee who seeks relief in the form of backpay for a union's alleged breach of its duty of fair representation has a right to trial by jury. We hold that the Seventh Amendment entitles such a plaintiff to a jury trial.

I

McLean Trucking Company and the Chauffeurs, Teamsters, and Helpers Local Union No. 391 were parties to a collective-bargaining agreement that governed the terms and conditions of employment at McLean's terminals. The 27 respondents were employed by McLean as truckdrivers in bargaining units covered by the agreement, and all were members of the Union.

* * * Claiming a violation of their seniority rights, respondents filed a * * * grievance with the Union, but the Union declined to refer the charges to a grievance committee on the ground that the relevant issues had been determined in * * * prior proceedings.

In July 1983, respondents filed an action in District Court, alleging * * * that the Union had violated its duty of fair representation * * * [and] sought, inter alia, compensatory damages for lost wages and health benefits. * * *

Respondents had requested a jury trial in their pleadings. The Union moved to strike the jury demand on the ground that no right to a jury trial exists in a duty of fair representation suit. The District Court denied the motion to strike. After an interlocutory appeal, the Fourth Circuit affirmed the trial court, holding that the Seventh Amendment entitled respondents to a jury trial of their claim for monetary relief. 863 F.2d 334 (1988). We granted the petition for certiorari to resolve a circuit conflict on this issue * * * and now affirm the judgment of the Fourth Circuit.

II

The duty of fair representation is inferred from unions' exclusive authority under the National Labor Relations Act, 49 Stat. 449, 29 U.S.C. § 159(a) (1982 ed.), to represent all employees in a bargaining unit. * * * The duty requires a union "to serve the interests of all members without hostility or discrimination toward any, to exercise its discretion with complete good faith and honesty, and to avoid arbitrary conduct." * * *

III

* * *

To determine whether a particular action will resolve legal rights, we examine both the nature of the issues involved and the remedy sought. "First, we compare the statutory action to 18th-century actions brought in the courts of England prior to the merger of the courts of law and equity. Second, we examine the remedy sought and determine whether it is legal or equitable in nature." *Tull* * * * [p. 745, supra]. The second inquiry is the more important in our analysis. * * *

A

An action for breach of a union's duty of fair representation was unknown in 18th-century England; in fact, collective bargaining was unlawful. * * * We must therefore look for an analogous cause of action that existed in the 18th century to determine whether the nature of this duty of fair representation suit is legal or equitable.

The Union contends that this duty of fair representation action resembles a suit brought to vacate an arbitration award because respondents seek to set aside the result of the grievance process. In the 18th century, an action to set aside an arbitration award was considered equitable. * * *

The arbitration analogy is inapposite, however, to the Seventh Amendment question posed in this case. No grievance committee has considered respondents' claim that the Union violated its duty of fair representation; the grievance process was concerned only with the employer's alleged breach of the collective-bargaining agreement. Thus, respondents' claim against the Union cannot be characterized as an action to vacate an arbitration award * * *.

The Union next argues that respondents' duty of fair representation action is comparable to an action by a trust beneficiary against a trustee for breach of fiduciary duty. Such actions were within the exclusive jurisdiction of courts of equity. * * * This analogy is far more persuasive than the arbitration analogy. Just as a trustee must act in the best interests of the beneficiaries, * * * a union, as the exclusive representative of the workers, must exercise its power to act on behalf of the employees in good faith * * *. Moreover, just as a beneficiary does not directly control the actions of a trustee, * * * an individual employee lacks direct control over a union's actions taken on his behalf * * *.

The trust analogy extends to a union's handling of grievances. In most cases, a trustee has the exclusive authority to sue third parties who injure the beneficiaries' interest in the trust, * * * including any legal claim the trustee holds in trust for the beneficiaries, * * *. The trustee then has the sole responsibility for determining whether to settle, arbitrate, or otherwise dispose of the claim. * * * Similarly, the union typically has broad discretion in its decision whether and how to pursue an employee's grievance against an employer. * * * Just as a trust beneficiary can sue to enforce a contract entered into on his behalf by the trustee only if the trustee "improperly refuses or neglects to bring an action against the third person," * * * so an employee can sue his employer for a breach of the collective-bargaining agreement only if he shows that the union breached its duty of fair representation in its handling of the grievance * * *.

Respondents contend that their duty of fair representation suit is less like a trust action than an attorney malpractice action, which was historically an action at law * * *.

The attorney malpractice analogy is inadequate in several respects. Although an attorney malpractice suit is in some ways similar to a suit alleging a union's breach of its fiduciary duty, the two actions are fundamentally different. The nature of an action is in large part controlled by the nature of the underlying relationship between the parties. Unlike employees represented by a union, a client controls the significant decisions concerning his representation. Moreover, a client can fire his attorney if he is dissatisfied with his attorney's performance. This option is not available to an individual employee who is unhappy with a union's representation, unless a majority of the members of the bargaining unit share his dissatisfaction. * * * Thus, we find the malpractice analogy less convincing than the trust analogy.

Nevertheless, the trust analogy does not persuade us to characterize respondents' claim as wholly equitable. The Union's argument mischaracterizes the nature of our comparison of the action before us to 18th-century forms of action. As we observed in *Ross v. Bernhard* * * *, "The Seventh Amendment question depends on the nature of the *issue* to be tried rather than the character of the overall action." * * * [T]o recover from the Union here, respondents must prove both that McLean violated § 301 by breaching the collective-bargaining agreement and that the Union breached its duty of fair representation. When viewed in isolation, the duty of fair representation issue is analogous to a claim against a trustee for breach of fiduciary duty. The § 301 issue, however, is comparable to a breach of contract claim—a legal issue.

Respondents' action against the Union thus encompasses both equitable and legal issues. The first part of our Seventh Amendment inquiry, then, leaves us in equipoise as to whether respondents are entitled to a jury trial.

B

Our determination under the first part of the Seventh Amendment analysis is only preliminary. * * * In this case, the only remedy sought is a request for compensatory damages representing backpay and benefits. Generally, an action for money damages was "the traditional form of relief offered in the courts of law." *Curtis* v. *Loether* * * * [p. 742, supra]. This Court has not, however, held that "any award of monetary relief must *necessarily* be 'legal' relief." *Ibid.* (emphasis added). * * * [B]ecause we conclude that the remedy respondents seek has none of the attributes that must be present before we will find an exception to the general rule and characterize damages as equitable, we find that the remedy sought by respondents is legal.

First, we have characterized damages as equitable where they are restitutionary, such as in "action[s] for disgorgement of improper profits," *Tull* * * *. * * * The backpay sought by respondents is not money wrongfully held by the Union, but wages and benefits they would have received from McLean had the Union processed the employees' grievances properly. Such relief is not restitutionary.

Second, a monetary award "incidental to or intertwined with injunctive relief" may be equitable. *Tull* * * *. * * * Because respondents seek only money damages, this characteristic is clearly absent from the case.[8]

The Union argues that the backpay relief sought here must nonetheless be considered equitable because this Court has labeled backpay awarded under Title VII, 42 U.S.C. § 2000e *et seq.* (1982 ed.), as equitable. * * *

The Court has never held that a plaintiff seeking backpay under Title VII has a right to a jury trial. See *Lorillard* v. *Pons*, 434 U.S. 575, 581–

---

[8] Both the Union and the dissent argue that the backpay award sought here is equitable because it is closely analogous to damages awarded to beneficiaries for a trustee's breach of trust. * * * Such damages were available only in courts of equity because those courts had exclusive jurisdiction over actions involving a trustee's breach of his fiduciary duties. * * *

The Union's argument, however, conflates the two parts of our Seventh Amendment inquiry. Under the dissent's approach, if the action at issue were analogous to an 18th-century action within the exclusive jurisdiction of the courts of equity, we would necessarily conclude that the remedy sought was also equitable because it would have been unavailable in a court of law. This view would, in effect, make the first part of our inquiry dispositive. We have clearly held, however, that the second part of the inquiry—the nature of the relief—is more important to the Seventh Amendment determination. * * * The second part of the analysis, therefore, should not replicate the "abstruse historical" inquiry of the first part, *Ross* * * *, but requires consideration of the general types of relief provided by courts of law and equity.

582[, 98 S.Ct. 866, 870–871, 55 L.Ed.2d 40] (1978). Assuming, without deciding, that such a Title VII plaintiff has no right to a jury trial, the Union's argument does not persuade us that respondents are not entitled to a jury trial here. Congress specifically characterized backpay under Title VII as a form of "equitable relief." * * * Congress made no similar pronouncement regarding the duty of fair representation. Furthermore, the Court has noted that backpay sought from an employer under Title VII would generally be restitutionary in nature, see *Curtis* v. *Loether* * * *, in contrast to the damages sought here from the union. Thus, the remedy sought in this duty of fair representation case is clearly different from backpay sought for violations of Title VII.

* * *

We hold, then, that the remedy of backpay sought in this duty of fair representation action is legal in nature. Considering both parts of the Seventh Amendment inquiry, we find that respondents are entitled to a jury trial on all issues presented in their suit.

* * *

It is so ordered.

JUSTICE BRENNAN, concurring in part and concurring in the judgment.

I agree with the Court that respondents seek a remedy that is legal in nature and that the Seventh Amendment entitles respondents to a jury trial on their duty of fair representation claims. * * * I do not join that part of the opinion which reprises the particular historical analysis this Court has employed to determine whether a claim is a "Suit at common law" under the Seventh Amendment, * * * because I believe the historical test can and should be simplified.

The current test * * * requires a court to compare the right at issue to 18th-century English forms of action to determine whether the historically analogous right was vindicated in an action at law or in equity, and to examine whether the remedy sought is legal or equitable in nature. However, this Court, in expounding the test, has repeatedly discounted the significance of the analogous form of action for deciding where the Seventh Amendment applies. I think it is time we dispense with it altogether. I would decide Seventh Amendment questions on the basis of the relief sought. If the relief is legal in nature, *i.e.*, if it is the kind of relief that historically was available from courts of law, I would hold that the parties have a constitutional right to a trial by jury—unless Congress has permissibly delegated the particular dispute to a non-Article III decisionmaker and jury trials would frustrate Congress' purposes in enacting a particular statutory scheme.

* * *

We have long acknowledged that, of the factors relevant to the jury trial right, comparison of the claim to ancient forms of action, "requiring extensive and possibly abstruse historical inquiry, is obviously the most difficult to apply." *Ross* v. *Bernhard* * * * [p. 741, Note 2, supra]. Requiring judges, with neither the training nor time necessary for reputable historical scholarship, to root through the tangle of primary and secondary sources to determine which of a hundred or so writs is analogous to the right at issue has embroiled courts in recondite controversies better left to legal historians. * * *

To rest the historical test required by the Seventh Amendment solely on the nature of the relief sought would not, of course, offer the federal courts a rule that is in all cases self-executing. Courts will still be required to ask which remedies were traditionally available at law and which only in equity. But this inquiry involves fewer variables and simpler choices, on the whole, and is far more manageable than the scholasticist debates in which we have been engaged. Moreover, the rule I propose would remain true to the Seventh Amendment, as it is undisputed that, historically, "[j]urisdictional lines [between law and equity] were primarily a matter of remedy." McCoid, Procedural Reform and the Right to Jury Trial: A Study of *Beacon Theaters, Inc.* v. *Westover*, 116 U. Pa. L. Rev. 1 (1967). * * *

This is not to say that the resulting division between claims entitled to jury trials and claims not so entitled would exactly mirror the division between law and equity in England in 1791. But it is too late in the day for this Court to profess that the Seventh Amendment preserves the right to jury trial only in cases that would have been heard in the British law courts of the 18th century. See, e.g., * * * *Ross* v. *Bernhard* * * *.

JUSTICE STEVENS, concurring in part and concurring in the judgment.

Because I believe the Court has made this case unnecessarily difficult by exaggerating the importance of finding a precise common-law analogue to the duty of fair representation, I do not join Part III-A of its opinion. * * *

* * * Duty of fair representation suits are for the most part ordinary civil actions involving the stuff of contract and malpractice disputes. There is accordingly no ground for excluding these actions from the jury right.

In my view, the evolution of this doctrine through suits tried to juries, the useful analogy to common-law malpractice cases, and the well-recognized duty to scrutinize any proposed curtailment of the right to a jury trial "with the utmost care," * * * provide a plainly sufficient basis for the Court's holding today. * * *

JUSTICE KENNEDY, with whom JUSTICE O'CONNOR and JUSTICE SCALIA join, dissenting.

* * *

I disagree with the analytic innovation of the Court that identification of the trust action as a model for modern duty of fair representation actions is insufficient to decide the case. The Seventh Amendment requires us to determine whether the duty of fair representation action "is more similar to cases that were tried in courts of law than to suits tried in courts of equity." *Tull* v. *United States*. Having made this decision in favor of an equitable action, our inquiry should end. Because the Court disagrees with this proposition, I dissent.

* * *

II

The Court relies on two lines of precedents to overcome the conclusion that the trust action should serve as the controlling model. The first consists of cases in which the Court has considered simplifications in litigation resulting from modern procedural reforms in the federal courts. Justice Marshall asserts that these cases show that the Court must look at the character of individual issues rather than claims as a whole. * * * The second line addresses the significance of the remedy in determining the equitable or legal nature of an action for the purpose of choosing the most appropriate analogy. Under these cases, the Court decides that the respondents have a right to a jury because they seek money damages. * * * These authorities do not support the Court's holding.

A

In * * * [*Beacon Theatres, Dairy Queen,* and *Ross*] we have found a right to trial by jury where there are legal claims that, for procedural reasons, a plaintiff could have or must have raised in the courts of equity before the systems merged. * * *

These three cases responded to the difficulties created by a merged court system. * * * They stand for the proposition that, because distinct courts of equity no longer exist, the possibility or necessity of using former equitable procedures to press a legal claim no longer will determine the right to a jury. Justice Marshall reads these cases to require a jury trial whenever a cause of action contains legal issues and would require a jury trial in this case because the respondents must prove a breach of the collective-bargaining agreement as one element of their claim. * * *

I disagree. The respondents, as shown above, are asserting an equitable claim. Having reached this conclusion, the *Beacon, Dairy Queen,* and *Ross* cases are inapplicable. Although we have divided self-standing legal claims from equitable declaratory, accounting, and derivative procedures, we have never parsed legal elements out of equitable claims absent specific procedural justifications. Actions which, beyond all question, are equitable in nature may involve some predicate inquiry that would be submitted to a jury in other contexts. For example, just as the plaintiff in a duty of fair representation action against his union must show breach of the collective-bargaining agreement as an initial matter, in an action against a trustee for failing to pursue a claim the beneficiary must show that the claim had some merit. * * * But the question of the claim's validity, even if the claim raises contract issues, would not bring the jury right into play in a suit against a trustee.

* * *

B

The Court also rules that, despite the appropriateness of the trust analogy as a whole, the respondents have a right to a jury trial because they seek money damages. * * * The nature of the remedy remains a factor of considerable importance in determining whether a statutory action had a legal or equitable analog in 1791, but we have not adopted a rule that a statutory action permitting damages is by definition more analogous to a legal action than to any equitable suit. In each case, we look to the remedy to determine whether, taken with other factors, it places an action within the definition of "suits at common law."

In *Curtis* * * *, for example, we ruled that the availability of actual and punitive damages made a statutory antidiscrimination action resemble a legal tort action more than any equitable action. We made explicit that we did not "go so far as to say that any award of monetary relief must necessarily be 'legal' relief." * * * Although monetary damages might cause some statutory actions to resemble tort suits, the presence of monetary damages in this duty of fair representation action does not make it more analogous to a legal action than to an equitable action. Indeed, as shown above, the injunctive and monetary remedies available make the duty of fair representation suit less analogous to a malpractice action than to a suit against a trustee.

* * *

III

The Court must adhere to the historical test in determining the right to a jury because the language of the Constitution requires it. The Seventh Amendment "preserves" the right to jury trial in civil cases. We cannot preserve a right existing in 1791 unless we look to history to identify it. * * *

I would hesitate to abandon or curtail the historical test out of concern for the competence of the Court to understand legal history. We do look to history for the answers to constitutional questions. * * * Although opinions will differ on what this history shows, the approach has no less validity in the Seventh Amendment context than elsewhere.

* * *

NOTE AND QUESTION

In footnote 8 of his opinion in *Terry*, does Justice Marshall provide an adequate explanation for continuing to employ a two-prong test that values the second prong more than the first? Or does the historical analysis "needlessly convolute our Seventh Amendment jurisprudence," as Justice Brennan argues? Justices Marshall and Stevens and the dissenters all disagree on the appropriate historical model for a "duty of fair representation" action. Is this disagreement in favor of severing the historical analysis from the Seventh Amendment test, or favor keeping the analysis as it is?

3. THE PROVINCE OF JUDGE AND JURY

WEINER, THE CIVIL JURY AND THE LAW-FACT DISTINCTION, 54 Calif.L.Rev. 1867, 1867–68 (1966):

> The categories of "questions of law" and "questions of fact" have been the traditional touchstones by which courts have purported to allocate decision-making between judge and jury. * * * Many statutes in effect today echo * * * [the] dichotomy, utilizing the law and fact terminology to identify the respective provinces of the judge and the jurors in a civil case. None of these statutes, however, attempts to define what is meant by a question of law or a question of fact. Nor have the courts shown any inclination to fashion definitions which can serve as useful guidelines. Indeed, when faced with a dispute as to whether a specific issue should be resolved by the judge or the jury, the typical appellate opinion today does no more than label the question as one of law or of fact, perhaps citing some authorities which are equally devoid of any more detailed consideration of the point. * * * A question of law or a question of fact is a mere synonym for a judge question or a jury question.

MARKMAN V. WESTVIEW INSTRUMENTS, INC.

Supreme Court of the United States, 1996.
517 U.S. 370, 116 S.Ct. 1384, 134 L.Ed.2d 577.

Certiorari to the United States Court of Appeals for the Federal Circuit.

JUSTICE SOUTER delivered the opinion of the Court.

The question here is whether the interpretation of a so-called patent claim, the portion of the patent document that defines the scope of the patentee's rights, is a matter of law reserved entirely for the court, or subject to a Seventh Amendment guarantee that a jury will determine the meaning of any disputed term of art about which expert testimony is offered. We hold that the construction of a patent, including terms of art within its claim, is exclusively within the province of the court.

[The dispute involved competing claims to a patent used to monitor clothing in a dry-cleaning establishment. Both systems used a keyboard and data processor and generated records including bar codes. Westview argued that Markman's patent was not infringed because Westview's patent merely recorded an inventory of receivables by tracking invoices, rather than an inventory of articles of clothing.]

* * * Part of the dispute hinges upon the meaning of the word "inventory," a term found in Markman's independent claim 1, which states that Markman's product can "maintain an inventory total" and "detect and localize spurious additions to inventory." The case was tried before a jury, which heard, among others, a witness produced by Markman who testified about the meaning of the claim language.

After the jury compared the patent to Westview's device, it found an infringement of Markman's claim 1 * * *. The District Court nevertheless granted Westview's deferred motion for judgment as a matter of law, one of its reasons being that the term "inventory" in Markman's patent encompasses "both cash inventory and the actual physical inventory of articles of clothing." * * * Under the trial court's construction of the patent, the production, sale, or use of a tracking system for dry cleaners would not infringe Markman's patent unless the product was capable of tracking articles of clothing throughout the cleaning process and generating reports about their status and location. Since Westview's system cannot do these things, the District Court directed a verdict * * *.

Markman appealed, arguing it was error for the District Court to substitute its construction of the disputed claim term "inventory" for the construction the jury had presumably given it. The United States Court of Appeals for the Federal Circuit affirmed, holding the interpretation of claim terms to be the exclusive province of the court and the Seventh Amendment to be consistent with that conclusion. * * * Markman sought our review on each point, and we granted certiorari. * * *

* * *

III

Since evidence of common law practice at the time of the Framing does not entail application of the Seventh Amendment's jury guarantee to the construction of the claim document, we must look elsewhere to characterize this determination of meaning in order to allocate it as between court or jury. We accordingly consult existing precedent and consider both the relative interpretive skills of judges and juries and the statutory policies that ought to be furthered by the allocation.

A.

* * * [The Court examined the few cases that were alleged to be relevant and found them to be inconclusive. The Court indicated that, if anything, they supported the view that a jury determination of the issue was not required.]

B.

Where history and precedent provide no clear answers, functional considerations also play their part in the choice between judge and jury to define terms of art. We said in *Miller v. Fenton*, 474 U.S. 104, 114[, 106 S.Ct. 445, 451, 88 L.Ed.2d 405, 413] (1985), that when an issue "falls somewhere between a pristine legal standard and a simple historical fact, the fact/law distinction at times has turned on a determination that, as a matter of sound administration of justice, one judicial actor is better positioned than another to decide the issue in question." So it turns out here, for judges, not juries, are the better suited to find the acquired meaning of patent terms.

The construction of written instruments is one of those things that judges often do and are likely to do better than jurors unburdened by training in exegesis. Patent construction in particular "is a special occupation, requiring, like all others, special training and practice. The judge, from his training and discipline, is more likely to give a proper interpretation to such instruments than a jury, and he is, therefore, more likely to be right, in performing such a duty, than a jury can be expected to be." *Parker* v. *Hulme*, 18 F. Cas., at 1140. Such was the understanding nearly a century and a half ago, and there is no reason to weigh the respective strengths of judge and jury differently in relation to the modern claim; quite the contrary, for "the claims of patents have become highly technical in many respects as the result of special doctrines relating to the proper form and scope of claims that have been developed in the courts and the Patent Office." Woodward, Definiteness and Particularity in Patent Claims, 46 Mich.L.Rev. 755, 765 (1948).

Markman would trump these considerations with his argument that a jury should decide a question of meaning peculiar to a trade or profession simply because the question is a subject of testimony requiring credibility determinations, which are the jury's forte. It is, of course, true that credibility judgments have to be made about the experts who testify in patent cases, and in theory there could be a case in which a simple credibility judgment would suffice to choose between experts whose testimony was equally consistent with a patent's internal logic. But our own experience with document construction leaves us doubtful that trial courts will run into many cases like that. In the main, we expect, any credibility determinations will be subsumed within the necessarily sophisticated analysis of the whole document, required by the standard construction rule that a term can be defined only in a way that comports with the instrument as a whole. * * * Thus, in these cases a jury's capabilities to evaluate demeanor, * * * to sense the "mainsprings of human conduct," * * * or to reflect community standards, * * * are much less significant than a trained ability to evaluate the testimony in relation to the overall structure of the patent. The decisionmaker vested with the task of construing the patent is in the better position to ascertain whether an expert's proposed definition fully comports with the specification and claims and so will preserve the patent's internal coherence. We accordingly think there is sufficient reason to treat construction of terms of art like many other responsibilities that we cede to a judge in the normal course of trial, notwithstanding its evidentiary underpinnings.

C

Finally, we see the importance of uniformity in the treatment of a given patent as an independent reason to allocate all issues of construction to the court. As we noted in *General Elec. Co. v. Wabash Appliance Corp.*, 304 U.S. 364, 369[, 58 S.Ct. 899, 902, 82 L.Ed. 1402, 1405] (1938), "[t]he limits of a patent must be known for the protection of the patentee, the encouragement of the inventive genius of others and the assurance that the subject of the patent will be dedicated ultimately to the public." Otherwise, a "zone of uncertainty which enterprise and experimentation may enter only at the risk of infringement claims would discourage invention only a little less than unequivocal foreclosure of the field," *United Carbon Co. v. Binney & Smith Co.*, 317 U.S. 228, 236[, 63 S.Ct. 165, 170, 87 L.Ed. 232, 237] (1942), and "[t]he public [would] be deprived of rights supposed to belong to it, without being clearly told what it is that limits these rights." *Merrill v. Yeomans*, 94 U.S. 568, 573[, 24 L.Ed. 235, 237] (1877). * * *

Uniformity would, however, be ill served by submitting issues of document construction to juries. Making them jury issues would not, to be sure, necessarily leave evidentiary questions of meaning wide open in every new court in which a patent might be litigated, for principles of issue preclusion would ordinarily foster uniformity. * * * But whereas issue preclusion could not be asserted against new and independent infringement defendants even within a given jurisdiction, treating interpretive issues as purely legal will promote (though it will not guarantee) intrajurisdictional certainty through the application of stare decisis on those questions not yet subject to interjurisdictional uniformity under the authority of the single appeals court.

* * *

Accordingly, we hold that the interpretation of the word "inventory" in this case is an issue for the judge, not the jury, and affirm the decision of the Court of Appeals for the Federal Circuit.

It is so ordered.

NOTE AND QUESTIONS

1.   When an issue is classified as one of "law," the rule binds litigants in subsequent cases. When is the need for a precise legal standard sufficient to justify withdrawing the matter from the jury? Consider the question of whether a posting on the Internet is obscene. Should the decision to give the question of obscenity to the judge or jury depend on the need for legal certainty, or should consideration be given to the desirability of a judgment by the community as reflected by several juries passing on the question in different locales? Compare Solomon, *The Political Puzzle of the Civil Jury*, 61 Emory L.J. 1331 (2012), with Miller, *The Pretrial Rush to Judgment: Are the "Litigation Explosion," "Liability Crisis," and Efficiency Clichés Eroding Our Day in Court and Jury Trial Commitments?*, 78 N.Y.U.L.Rev. 982, 1094–1126 (2003).

2.   In MERCK SHARP & DOHME CORP. v. ALBRECHT, 587 U.S. ___, 139 S.Ct. 1668, 203 L.Ed.2d 822 (2019), the Court considered whether a judge or jury should decide if a failure-to-warn drug labeling claim under state law was preempted by the Federal Food, Drug, and Cosmetic Act. In a prior case, Wyeth v. Levine, 555 U.S. 555, 129 S.Ct. 1187, 173 L.Ed.2d 51 (2009), the Court had held that for preemption to apply there must be "clear evidence" that the Federal Food and Drug Administration (which administers the statute) would not have approved a change in a label required by state law. The trial judge in the *Merck* case held that it was for the judge; the court of appeals reversed, holding it was a question for the jury. The Supreme Court agreed that the question was for the judge, although the Court noted its complexity, falling somewhere between a clear legal standard and a simple historical fact. Drawing on *Markman*, the Court analyzed the situation as follows:

> The complexity of the * * * law [pertaining to when federal law preempts state law] helps to illustrate why we answer this question by concluding that the question is a legal one for the judge, not a jury. The question often involves the use of legal skills to determine whether agency disapproval fits facts that are not in dispute. Moreover, judges, rather than lay juries, are better equipped to evaluate the nature and scope of an agency's determination. Judges are experienced in "[t]he construction of written instruments," such as those normally produced by a federal agency to memorialize its considered judgments. *Markman* v. *Westview Instruments, Inc.*, [p. 756, supra]. And judges are better suited than are juries to understand and to interpret agency decisions in light of the governing statutory and regulatory context. * * * To understand the question as a legal question for judges makes sense given the fact that judges are normally familiar with principles of administrative law. Doing so should produce greater uniformity among courts; and greater

uniformity is normally a virtue when a question requires a determination concerning the scope and effect of federal agency action. * * *

We understand that sometimes contested brute facts will prove relevant to a court's legal determination about the meaning and effect of an agency decision. For example, if the FDA rejected a drug manufacturer's supplemental application to change a drug label on the ground that the information supporting the application was insufficient to warrant a labeling change, the meaning and scope of that decision might depend on what information the FDA had before it. Yet in litigation between a drug consumer and a drug manufacturer (which will ordinarily lack an official administrative record for an FDA decision), the litigants may dispute whether the drug manufacturer submitted all material information to the FDA.

But we consider these factual questions to be subsumed within an already tightly circumscribed legal analysis. And we do not believe that they warrant submission alone or together with the larger pre-emption question to a jury. Rather, in those contexts where we have determined that the question is "for the judge and not the jury," we have also held that "courts may have to resolve subsidiary factual disputes" that are part and parcel of the broader legal question. *Teva Pharmaceuticals USA, Inc.* v. *Sandoz, Inc.*, [574 U.S. 318, 327, 135 S.Ct. 831, 838, 190 L.Ed.2d 719, 730] (2015). And, as in contexts as diverse as the proper construction of patent claims and the voluntariness of criminal confessions, they create a question that " 'falls somewhere between a pristine legal standard and a simple historical fact.' " *Markman*, 517 U.S. at 388, 116 S.Ct. 1384 (quoting *Miller* v. *Fenton*, 474 U.S. 104, 114, 106 S.Ct. 445, 88 L.Ed.2d 405 (1985)). In those circumstances, " 'the fact/law distinction at times has turned on a determination that, as a matter of the sound administration of justice, one judicial actor is better positioned than another to decide the issue in question.' " *Markman*, 517 U.S. at 388, 116 S.Ct. 1384 (quoting *Miller*, 474 U.S. at 114, 106 S.Ct. 445). In this context, that "better positioned" decisionmaker is the judge.

587 U.S. at ___, 139 S.Ct. at 1680, 203 L.Ed.2d 822, 837–38 (2019).

3. How should decisionmaking be divided between judge and jury when an issue is a mixed question of law and fact—that is, when there is underlying factfinding that informs the application of a legal standard? In GOOGLE LLC v. ORACLE AMERICA, INC., 593 U.S. ___, 141 S.Ct. 1183, 209 L.Ed.2d 311 (2021), the Supreme Court held that the Seventh Amendment jury trial right is not violated when a judge decides whether a defendant in a copyright dispute has established "fair use," a defense to copyright infringement. The Court treated the defense as an equitable one; although informed by the jury's factfinding, the ultimate fair use determination could be resolved by the judge.

4. DEMAND AND WAIVER OF TRIAL BY JURY

———

Read Federal Rules of Civil Procedure 38 and 39 and the accompanying materials in the Supplement.

———

NOTES AND QUESTIONS

1. The district court's discretion under Federal Rule 39(b) to grant a motion excusing an untimely jury demand is broad. Courts typically consider such factors as: the length of the delay in making the jury demand, the reasons for the delay, prejudice to the nonmovant, and the effect on the court's docket. See Olympia Express, Inc. v. Linee Aeree Italiane, S.P.A., 509 F.3d 347 (7th Cir. 2007). Additional factors may include whether the case "involves issues which are best tried to a jury." TG Plastics Trading Co., Inc. v. Toray Plastics (America), Inc., 775 F.3d 31, 36 (1st Cir. 2014).

2. Waiver of a constitutional right usually requires a voluntary, intentional, and knowing decision. Can a jury waiver that is made before a dispute arises meet this standard? Compare National Equip. Rental, Ltd. v. Hendrix, 565 F.2d 255 (2d Cir. 1977), with Bank South, N.W. v. Howard, 264 Ga. 339, 444 S.E.2d 799 (1994). Should an agreement to arbitrate a dispute, assented to before the dispute has arisen, be interpreted as an implicit waiver of the jury trial right? Is it relevant that the clause appears in a form contract, rather than as the result of an arms-length negotiation between evenly matched business entities? See Sternlight, *Mandatory Binding Arbitration and the Demise of the Seventh Amendment Right to a Jury Trial*, 16 Ohio St.J.Disp. Resol. 669 (2001). In practice, whether the arbitration clause mentions the waiver of jury right specifically is of little consequence to the court's finding of waiver. See Snowden v. CheckPoint Check Cashing, 290 F.3d 631 (4th Cir. 2002).

5. SELECTION AND COMPOSITION OF THE JURY

a. Size

At common law, a trial jury consisted of twelve members. In Patton v. United States, 281 U.S. 276, 288, 50 S.Ct. 253, 254, 74 L.Ed. 854, 858 (1930), a criminal case, the Court said that the phrase "trial by jury" incorporated "all the essential elements" of such a trial "as they were recognized in this country and England when the Constitution was adopted," including "[t]hat the jury should consist of twelve men, neither more nor less." However, in Williams v. Florida, 399 U.S. 78, 90 S.Ct. 1893, 26 L.Ed.2d 446 (1970), the Court held that a state constitutionally might use a jury with six (or perhaps fewer) members in a criminal case without violating the Sixth Amendment's jury trial guarantee, as applied to the states through the Fourteenth Amendment. In the years following *Williams*, numerous district courts seized upon its holding and transferred its analysis to the civil-jury guarantee in the Seventh Amendment, using their Rule 83 power to promulgate local rules to provide that ordinary civil actions shall be tried by six-member juries.

b. Empaneling the Jury

Jury selection is a two-stage process. First, a list of potential jurors, the venire, is compiled and they are assembled. A number of them, equal to the number who will serve are then selected at random to sit as a tentative jury. In 1991, Federal Rule 48 was amended to permit a court to decide the size of the jury so long as it consists of at least six and no more than 12 members. Prior to the amendment, the Rule merely allowed parties to stipulate that the jury could consist of any number less than 12. See Resnik, *Changing Practices, Changing Rules: Judicial and Congressional Rulemaking on Civil Juries, Civil Justice, and Civil Judging*, 49 Ala.L.Rev. 133 (1997).

Second, these tentative jurors are questioned by the judge and/or by the attorneys to determine whether each of them can decide the case fairly and appropriately. This questioning is called "voir dire." If one of them is dismissed, his or her place is taken by another member of the venire, selected at random, who is in turn subject to questioning. This process continues until the final panel is in place. For a summary of the empirical literature about voir dire, see Zalman & Tsoudis, *Plucking Weeds from the Garden: Lawyers Speak About Voir Dire*, 51 Wayne L.Rev. 163 (2005).

NOTES AND QUESTIONS

1. The Report of the Committee on the Operation of the Jury System of the Judicial Conference of the United States, on which the present federal jury selection statute is based, appears at 42 F.R.D. 353 (1967). See 28 U.S.C. §§ 1861–66. Qualifications for jury service vary from state to state but may include such factors as citizenship, residence, criminal history, and the ability to use and understand English. See Mize, Hannaford-Agor & Waters, National Center for State Courts, The State-of-the-States Survey of Jury Improvement Efforts: A Compendium Report 21–22 (2007).

2. The most common method for creating jury lists is by relying on voter registration records, with supplemental sources used to promote fair representation. See 28 U.S.C. § 1863(b). These other sources can include driver's license or public utilities lists, state tax rolls, or telephone lists. Because of the under-representation of minority and low-income persons in voter registration records, as well as the low percentage of voters overall, many have argued that use of multiple lists should be constitutionally compelled. For an examination of how jury selection methods may lead to unrepresentative

juries, see Rose & Abramson, *Data, Race, and the Courts: Some Lessons on Empiricism from Jury Representation Cases*, 2011 Mich.St.L.Rev. 911.

3.   The "blue ribbon" jury, which is composed of people who are specially selected because of their level of education, is an attempt to meet concerns that the ordinary juror is incompetent to deal with the complex problems of modern litigation. See Strier, *The Educated Jury: A Proposal for Complex Litigation*, 47 DePaul L.Rev. 49 (1997). Is a "blue ribbon" jury consistent with 28 U.S.C. § 1862, which bars exclusion of citizens on account of "economic status"? See Fisher, *Going for the Blue Ribbon: The Legality of Expert Juries in Patent Litigation*, 2 Colum. Sci. & Tech.L.Rev. 1 (2001).

4.   Do nationwide cases require a jury drawn from a nationwide pool? See Dooley, *National Juries for National Cases: Preserving Citizen Participation in Large-Scale Litigation*, 83 N.Y.U.L.Rev. 411 (2008).

c.   Challenging Individual Jurors

Challenges to individual jurors—sometimes called challenges to the polls—are of two kinds: for cause and peremptory. Challenges for cause permit a prospective juror to be rejected when partiality can be shown. Peremptory challenges permit rejection of jurors without any statement of reason and usually are based on an assumed partiality that may not be susceptible of proof.

An unlimited number of challenges for cause are permitted each party. These challenges are determined by the trial judge, although some states have experimented with so-called "triers"—independent officials who have the responsibility of determining challenges for cause. The number of peremptory challenges allowed each side varies among the states. In the federal courts each side is permitted three. See 28 U.S.C. § 1870.

NOTES AND QUESTIONS

1.   In EDMONSON v. LEESVILLE CONCRETE COMPANY, INC., 500 U.S. 614, 111 S.Ct. 2077, 114 L.Ed.2d 660 (1991), the Supreme Court held that in a civil case tried in federal court the Due Process Clause of the Fifth Amendment bars a private litigant from using preemptory challenges to exclude jurors on account of their race. Justice O'Connor, joined by the Chief Justice and Justice Scalia, dissented, arguing that the government was not responsible for the racist acts of private litigants and therefore the Due Process Clause did not apply.

2.   In J.E.B. v. ALABAMA EX REL. T.B., 511 U.S. 127, 114 S.Ct. 1419, 128 L.Ed.2d 89 (1994), the State of Alabama, on behalf of the mother of a minor child, brought suit in a state court against the defendant for paternity and child support. The state used nine of its ten peremptory challenges to remove male jurors, with the result that the jury consisted solely of women. The Alabama courts rejected defendant's objection that the use of peremptory challenges solely to exclude persons on the basis of gender violated the

Fourteenth Amendment's Equal Protection Clause. A divided Supreme Court reversed. Justice Blackmun, writing for himself and three others, stated:

> Discrimination in jury selection, whether based on race or on gender, causes harm to the litigants, the community and the individual jurors who are wrongfully excluded from participation in the judicial process. * * *

> * * * All persons, when granted the opportunity to serve on a jury, have the right not to be excluded summarily because of discriminatory and stereotypical presumptions that reflect and reinforce patterns of historical discrimination. Striking individual jurors on the assumption that they hold particular views simply because of their gender is "practically a brand upon them, affixed by the law, an assertion of their inferiority." *Strauder* v. *West Virginia*, 100 U.S. 303, 308, 25 L.Ed. 664, 666 (1880).

> Our conclusion that litigants may not strike potential jurors solely on the basis of gender does not imply the elimination of all peremptory challenges. * * * Parties still may remove jurors who they feel might be less acceptable than others on the panel; gender simply may not serve as a proxy for bias. * * * Even strikes based on characteristics that are disproportionately associated with one gender [e.g., employment in the military or as nurses] could be appropriate, absent a showing of pretext.

Id. at 140–43, 114 S.Ct. at 1427–29, 128 L.Ed.2d at 104–06.

> Justice Kennedy concurred. He wrote:

> There is no doubt under our precedents * * * that the Equal Protection Clause prohibits sex discrimination in the selection of jurors. * * * For purposes of the Equal Protection Clause, an individual denied jury service because of a peremptory challenge exercised against her on account of her sex is no less injured than the individual denied jury service because of a law banning members of her sex from serving as jurors.

Id. at 152–53, 114 S.Ct. at 1433–34, 128 L.Ed.2d at 111–12.

> Justice O'Connor concurred in a separate opinion. She wrote:

> Today's decision severely limits a litigant's ability to act on * * * intuition, for the import of our holding is that any correlation between a juror's gender and attitudes is irrelevant as a matter of constitutional law. * * * [T]o say that gender makes no difference as a matter of law is not to say that gender makes no difference as a matter of fact. * * * In extending [our holdings on race] * * * to gender we have * * * taken a step closer to eliminating the peremptory challenge, and diminishing the ability of litigants to act on sometimes accurate gender-based assumptions about juror attitudes.

* * *

Accordingly, I adhere to my position that the Equal Protection Clause does not limit the exercise of peremptory challenges by private civil litigants * * *. This case itself presents no state action dilemma for here the State of Alabama itself filed the paternity suit. * * * But what of the next case? Will we, in the name of fighting gender discrimination, hold that the battered wife—on trial for wounding her abusive husband—is a state actor? Will we preclude her from using her peremptory challenges to ensure that the jury of her peers contains as many women members as possible? I assume we will, but I hope we will not.

Id. at 149–51, 114 S.Ct. at 1432–33, 128 L.Ed.2d at 109–10.

Justice Scalia, writing for himself and two other Justices, dissented. Essentially he agreed with Justice O'Connor's assessment of the importance of the peremptory challenge system and argued that even in the case before the Court no one was denied equal protection of the laws.

d. Conducting the Voir Dire

Rules concerning the extent to which the judge or the lawyers conduct voir dire vary among jurisdictions. Federal Rule 47(a) leaves the matter entirely in the district judge's discretion. For the range of state practices, see Mize, Hannaford-Agor & Waters, National Center for State Courts, The State-of-the-States Survey of Jury Improvement Efforts: A Compendium Report 28 (2007).

B. THE SCOPE AND ORDER OF TRIAL

1. SETTING THE CASE FOR TRIAL

Trial will take place only after one of the parties or the court takes steps to have the case placed on the appropriate trial calendar and the court disposes of all the cases previously on that calendar. The Federal Rules contemplate that the trial judge, after consulting the parties, may schedule the date of trial. See Federal Rule 16(b)(3)(B)(vi) and (c)(2)(G). It is impossible to pinpoint case scheduling with total certainty, but case management techniques and computers have helped to increase the predictability of the flow of business through the courts.

2. ORDER OF TRIAL

Trial courts have the ability to divide cases into discrete portions, trying claims or issues separately whenever that is convenient, economical, or avoids prejudice to a party or parties.

a. Jury Cases

When a particular case or aspect of a case comes before a jury, the court invariably has discretion to determine the order of trial, but a judge usually will not deviate from standard practice, which is as follows:

1. Plaintiff's opening statement

2. Defendant's opening statement

3. Plaintiff's presentation of direct evidence

4. Defendant's presentation of direct evidence

5. Plaintiff's presentation of rebuttal evidence

6. Defendant's presentation of rebuttal evidence

7. Opening final argument by plaintiff

8. Defendant's final argument

9. Closing final argument by plaintiff

10. Giving instructions to the jury.

b. Non-Jury Cases

Although jury and non-jury cases generally are handled in the same way, there are a number of significant differences in scope. For example, the court often will dispense with the opening statement and the closing argument, and, of course, there is never a need to give instructions. Some jurisdictions provide that an attorney has an absolute right to argue, even in non-jury cases. Rarely will that right be exercised, however, if the judge, as is often the situation, makes clear that she believes an argument to be unnecessary.

3. THE BURDEN OF PROOF

Review pp. 694–695, Note on Rule 56 Burdens, supra.

The burdens of production and persuasion usually fall on the same party at trial, either plaintiff or defendant. But there are times when the burden of production is placed on one party and the burden of persuasion on the other. In these cases, once the burden of production is satisfied, the burden of persuasion "shifts" to the other party.

One example of a type of action in which the burden shifts is an employment discrimination action alleging disparate impact of systemic disparate treatment under Title VII of the Civil Rights Act of 1964. In proceedings under this statute, the employee must make out a prima facie case that there was intentional discrimination. At that point, the burden of production falls on the employer, who must explain the non-discriminatory basis for the adverse employment action in question. If the employer offers a legitimate explanation for the action, then plaintiff must show that the reason given for the employer's action is merely pretextual— that the action was, in fact, taken for discriminatory reason. The burden of persuasion remains with plaintiff, but the intermediate burden of production that falls on defendant serves an important function. As the Supreme Court has explained, the shifting of burdens allows the employer the opportunity to rebut plaintiff's claims and helps "to frame the factual issue with sufficient clarity so that the plaintiff will have a full and fair opportunity to demonstrate pretext." See Texas Dep't of Comm'y Affairs v. Burdine, 450 U.S. 248, 255–56, 101 S.Ct. 1089, 1095, 67 L.Ed.2d 207, 217– 18 (1981).

C. TAKING THE CASE FROM THE JURY— MOTIONS FOR JUDGMENT AS A MATTER OF LAW

———

Read Federal Rule of Civil Procedure 50 in the Supplement.

———

Various procedural devices enable a judge to insure that the jury carries out its functions. Rule 50(a) permits the judge, after the witnesses have testified and the evidence has been presented, to withhold the case from the jury and instead to enter judgment as a matter of law if there is not sufficient evidence to raise a genuine factual dispute and a particular result is required under the governing law (until 1991, this procedure was known as a "directed verdict"). Rule 50(b) authorizes a similar procedure for cases that have been submitted to the jury once the jurors have already reached a verdict. If the judge in this situation decides that judgment as a matter of law should have been granted, the court may set aside the verdict and enter judgment (until 1991, this procedure was known as a "judgment notwithstanding the verdict" or "j.n.o.v."—for "judgment non obstante veredicto").

1. THE CONSTITUTIONAL ISSUES

In GALLOWAY v. UNITED STATES, 319 U.S. 372, 63 S.Ct. 1077, 87 L.Ed. 1458 (1943), the Supreme Court faced directly the charge that taking a case away from a jury on the ground that a plaintiff had not met its burden of production at trial was a violation of the Seventh Amendment jury trial right. The Court held as follows:

> If the intention is to claim generally that the Amendment deprives the federal courts of power to direct a verdict for insufficiency of evidence, the short answer is the contention has been foreclosed by repeated decisions made here consistently for nearly a century.

> More recently the practice has been approved explicitly in the promulgation of the Federal Rules of Civil Procedure. * * * The objection therefore comes too late.

Justice Black, with whom Justices Douglas and Murphy concurred, wrote a dissenting opinion:

> The call for the true application of the Seventh Amendment is not to words, but to the spirit of honest desire to see that Constitutional right preserved. Either the judge or the jury must decide facts and to the extent that we take this responsibility, we lessen the jury function. Our duty to preserve this one of the Bill of Rights may be peculiarly difficult, for here it is our own power which we must restrain. * * * As for myself, I believe that a verdict should be directed, if at all, only when, without weighing the credibility of the witnesses, there is in the evidence no room whatever for honest difference of opinion over the factual issue in controversy. * * *

Id. at 397–407, 63 S.Ct. at 1089–96, 87 L.Ed. 1474–81.

NEELY v. MARTIN K. EBY CONSTRUCTION CO., 386 U.S. 317, 321–22, 87 S.Ct. 1072, 1076–77, 18 L.Ed.2d 75, 80–81 (1967). Plaintiff brought a wrongful death action against defendant, claiming that defendant's negligent construction, maintenance, and supervision of a missile silo proximately caused the death of plaintiff's father, who died when he fell from a platform while working at the silo. At the close of plaintiff's case and again at the close of all the evidence, defendant moved unsuccessfully for a directed verdict. The jury returned a $25,000 verdict for plaintiff, and the trial judge entered judgment for plaintiff after denying defendant's Rule 50(b) motion or, alternatively, its motion for a new trial.

On appeal, the Court of Appeals for the Tenth Circuit found the evidence insufficient to establish negligence or proximate cause, and reversed the district court's ruling on defendant's Rule 50(b) motion. Plaintiff appealed to the Supreme Court, arguing that she had had no opportunity to raise claims for a new trial, and therefore an appellate court could not dismiss the case without running afoul of the Seventh Amendment jury trial right. Justice White wrote:

> * * * The question here is whether the Court of Appeals, after reversing the denial of a defendant's Rule 50(b) motion * * *, may itself order dismissal or direct entry of judgment for defendant. As far as the Seventh Amendment's right to jury trial is concerned, there is no greater restriction on the province of the jury when an appellate court enters judgment n.o.v. than when a trial court

does; consequently, there is no constitutional bar to an appellate court granting judgment n.o.v. * * *

NOTES AND QUESTIONS

1.   In Weisgram v. Marley Co., 528 U.S. 440, 120 S.Ct. 1011, 145 L.Ed.2d 958 (2000), a wrongful death action, plaintiff introduced expert testimony over defendant's objection and won a jury verdict. On appeal, the Eighth Circuit held that the district court erred in admitting the expert testimony, and found that the remainder of the evidence in the record was insufficient to support the verdict. The Supreme Court held that the appeals court under *Neeley* could direct entry of judgment as a matter of law for the verdict-loser, if "on excision of testimony erroneously admitted, there remains insufficient evidence to support the jury's verdict." Id. at 457, 120 S.Ct. at 1022, 145 L.Ed.2d at 974.

2.   For a criticism of *Galloway* and other Supreme Court cases upholding procedures that impinge on the jury right, see Thomas, The Missing American Jury: Restoring the Fundamental Constitutional Role of the Criminal, Civil, and Grand Juries (2016); Thomas, *The Seventh Amendment, Modern Procedure, and the English Common Law*, 82 Wash.U.L.Q. 687 (2004).

2.   STANDARDS FOR A MOTION FOR JUDGMENT AS A MATTER OF LAW

REEVES V. SANDERSON PLUMBING PRODUCTS, INC.

Supreme Court of the United States, 2000.
530 U.S. 133, 120 S.Ct. 2097, 147 L.Ed.2d 105.

Certiorari to the United States Court of Appeals for the Fifth Circuit.

JUSTICE O'CONNOR delivered the opinion of the Court.

This case concerns the kind and amount of evidence necessary to sustain a jury's verdict that an employer unlawfully discriminated on the basis of age. Specifically, we must resolve whether a defendant is entitled to judgment as a matter of law when the plaintiff's case consists exclusively of a prima facie case of discrimination and sufficient evidence for the trier of fact to disbelieve the defendant's legitimate, nondiscriminatory explanation for its action. * * *

* * * [In age discrimination cases, the courts of appeals generally first require plaintiff to establish a prima facie case of discrimination, and then the burden of production shifts to defendant to present evidence supporting a legitimate, nondiscriminatory reason for the job action. Petitioner satisfied this burden, and the burden shifted to respondent.] Respondent met this burden by offering admissible evidence sufficient for the trier of fact to conclude that petitioner was fired because of his failure to maintain accurate attendance records. * * * Accordingly, * * * the sole remaining issue was "discrimination *vel non*" * * *.

Although intermediate evidentiary burdens shift back and forth under this framework, "[t]he ultimate burden of persuading the trier of fact that the defendant intentionally discriminated against the plaintiff remains at all times with the plaintiff." * * * And in attempting to satisfy this burden, the plaintiff—once the employer produces sufficient evidence to support a nondiscriminatory explanation for its decision—must be afforded the "opportunity to prove by a preponderance of the evidence that the legitimate reasons offered by the defendant were not its true reasons, but were a pretext for discrimination." * * * That is, the plaintiff may attempt to establish that he was the victim of intentional discrimination "by showing that the employer's proffered explanation is unworthy of credence." * * * Moreover, although the presumption of discrimination "drops out of the picture" once the defendant meets its burden of production, * * * the trier of fact may still consider the evidence establishing the plaintiff's prima facie case "and inferences properly drawn therefrom . . . [omission in original] on the issue of whether the defendant's explanation is pretextual" * * *.

In this case, the evidence supporting respondent's explanation for petitioner's discharge consisted primarily of testimony by [the supervisor and others] * * * of petitioner's alleged "shoddy record keeping." * * *

Petitioner, however, made a substantial showing that respondent's explanation was false. First, petitioner offered evidence that he had properly maintained the attendance records. * * *

Petitioner similarly cast doubt on whether he was responsible for any failure to discipline late and absent employees. * * * [The company admitted that petitioner was not responsible for disciplining employees, and conceded that there had never been a union grievance or employee complaint about petitioner's recordkeeping, and there was testimony about the absence of overpayments.]

Based on this evidence, the Court of Appeals concluded that petitioner "very well may be correct" that "a reasonable jury could have found that [respondent's] explanation for its employment decision was pretextual." * * * Nonetheless, the court held that this showing, standing alone, was insufficient to sustain the jury's finding of liability: "We must, as an essential final step, determine whether Reeves presented sufficient evidence that his age motivated [respondent's] employment decision." * * * And in making this determination, the Court of Appeals ignored the evidence supporting petitioner's prima facie case and challenging respondent's explanation for its decision. * * * The court confined its review of evidence favoring petitioner to that evidence showing that * * * [the supervisor] had directed derogatory, age-based comments at petitioner, and that * * * [the supervisor] had singled out petitioner for harsher treatment than younger employees. * * * It is therefore apparent that the court believed that only this additional evidence of discrimination was relevant to whether the jury's verdict should stand. That is, the Court of Appeals proceeded from the assumption that a prima facie case of discrimination, combined with sufficient evidence for the trier of fact to disbelieve the defendant's legitimate, nondiscriminatory reason for its decision, is insufficient as a matter of law to sustain a jury's finding of intentional discrimination.

In so reasoning, the Court of Appeals misconceived the evidentiary burden borne by plaintiffs who attempt to prove intentional discrimination through indirect evidence. * * * [T]he factfinder's rejection of the employer's legitimate, nondiscriminatory reason for its action does not *compel* judgment for the plaintiff. * * *

* * * [H]owever, * * * it is *permissible* for the trier of fact to infer the ultimate fact of discrimination from the falsity of the employer's explanation. * * *

Proof that the defendant's explanation is unworthy of credence is simply one form of circumstantial evidence that is probative of intentional discrimination, and it may be quite persuasive. * * * In appropriate circumstances, the trier of fact can reasonably infer from the falsity of the explanation that the employer is dissembling to cover up a discriminatory purpose. * * * Moreover, once the employer's justification has been eliminated, discrimination may well be the most likely alternative explanation, especially since the employer is in the best position to put forth the actual reason for its decision. * * * Thus, a plaintiff's prima facie case, combined with sufficient evidence to find that the employer's asserted justification is false, may permit the trier of fact to conclude that the employer unlawfully discriminated.

This is not to say that such a showing by the plaintiff will *always* be adequate to sustain a jury's finding of liability. Certainly there will be instances where, although the plaintiff has established a prima facie case and set forth sufficient evidence to reject the defendant's explanation, no rational factfinder could conclude that the action was discriminatory. * * *

Whether judgment as a matter of law is appropriate in any particular case will depend on a number of factors. Those include the strength of the plaintiff's prima facie case, the probative value of the proof that the employer's explanation is false, and any other evidence that supports the employer's case and that properly may be considered on a motion for judgment as a matter of law. * * * For purposes of this case, we need not— and could not—resolve all of the circumstances in which such factors would entitle an employer to judgment as a matter of law. It suffices to say that, because a prima facie case and sufficient evidence to reject the employer's explanation may permit a finding of liability, the Court of Appeals erred in proceeding from the premise that a plaintiff must always introduce additional, independent evidence of discrimination.

* * *

The remaining question is whether, despite the Court of Appeals' misconception of petitioner's evidentiary burden, respondent was nonetheless entitled to judgment as a matter of law [under Federal Rule 50]. * * * The Courts of Appeals have articulated differing formulations as to what evidence a court is to consider in ruling on a Rule 50 motion. * * * Some decisions have stated that review is limited to that evidence favorable to the nonmoving party, * * * while most have held that review extends to the entire record, drawing all reasonable inferences in favor of the nonmovant * * *.

On closer examination, this conflict seems more semantic than real. Those decisions holding that review under Rule 50 should be limited to evidence favorable to the nonmovant appear to have their genesis in *Wilkerson* v. *McCarthy,* 336 U.S. 53[, 69 S.Ct. 413, 93 L.Ed. 497] (1949). * * * In *Wilkerson,* we stated that "in passing upon whether there is sufficient evidence to submit an issue to the jury we need look only to the evidence and reasonable inferences which tend to support the case of" the nonmoving party. * * * But subsequent decisions have clarified that this passage was referring to the evidence to which the trial court should *give credence,* not the evidence that the court should *review.* In the analogous context of summary judgment under Rule 56, we have stated that the court must review the record "taken as a whole." *Matsushita* * * * [p. 711, supra]. And the standard for granting summary judgment "mirrors" the standard for judgment as a matter of law, such that "the inquiry under each is the same." *Anderson* v. *Liberty Lobby* * * * [p. 709, supra]. It therefore follows that, in entertaining a motion for judgment as a matter of law, the court should review all of the evidence in the record.

In doing so, however, the court must draw all reasonable inferences in favor of the nonmoving party, and it may not make credibility determinations or weigh the evidence. * * * "Credibility determinations, the weighing of the evidence, and the drawing of legitimate inferences from the facts are jury functions, not those of a judge." * * * Thus, although the court should review the record as a whole, it must disregard all evidence favorable to the moving party that the jury is not required to believe. * * * That is, the court should give credence to the evidence favoring the nonmovant as well as that "evidence supporting the moving party that is uncontradicted and unimpeached, at least to the extent that that evidence comes from disinterested witnesses." * * *

* * *

Applying this standard here, it is apparent that respondent was not entitled to judgment as a matter of law. In this case, in addition to establishing a prima facie case of discrimination and creating a jury issue as to the falsity of the employer's explanation, petitioner introduced additional evidence that * * * [the supervisor] was motivated by age-based animus and was principally responsible for petitioner's firing. * * *

Further, petitioner introduced evidence that [the supervisor] was the actual decisionmaker behind his firing. * * *

* * * Again, the court disregarded critical evidence favorable to petitioner * * *. The court also failed to draw all reasonable inferences in favor of petitioner. For instance, while acknowledging "the potentially damning nature" of * * * [the supervisor's] age-related comments, the court discounted them on the ground that they "were not made in the direct context of Reeves's termination." * * * And the court discredited petitioner's evidence that * * * [the supervisor] was the actual decisionmaker by giving weight to the fact that there was "no evidence to suggest that any of the other decision makers were motivated by age." * * * In concluding that these circumstances so overwhelmed the evidence favoring petitioner that no rational trier of fact could have found that petitioner was fired because of his age, the Court of Appeals impermissibly substituted its judgment concerning the weight of the evidence for the jury's.

* * * Given the evidence in the record supporting petitioner, we see no reason to subject the parties to an additional round of litigation before the Court of Appeals rather than to resolve the matter here. * * * Given that petitioner established a prima facie case of discrimination, introduced enough evidence for the jury to reject respondent's explanation, and produced additional evidence of age-based animus, there was sufficient evidence for the jury to find that respondent had intentionally discriminated. The District Court was therefore correct to submit the case to the jury, and the Court of Appeals erred in overturning its verdict.

For these reasons, the judgment of the Court of Appeals is reversed.

It is so ordered.

[A concurring opinion of JUSTICE GINSBURG is omitted.]

NOTES AND QUESTIONS

1.   The Court in *Reeves* resolved a conflict in the circuits concerning the portion of the evidence a court is to consider in ruling on a motion under Rule 50. Some of the circuits had examined all of the evidence in a manner most favorable to the nonmoving party; others considered only the evidence that supports the verdict winner; still others considered uncontradicted, unimpeached evidence from disinterested witnesses. See Schwimmer

Electronics Co. v. Sony Corp., 459 U.S. 1007, 103 S.Ct. 362, 74 L.Ed.2d 398 (1982) (White, J., dissenting from the denial of certiorari). Do you agree with the majority's statement in *Reeves* that these various standards reflect only "semantic" differences? What did the Court mean when it stated the "the court should give credence to the evidence favoring the nonmovant as well as that 'evidence supporting the moving party that is uncontradicted and unimpeached, at least to the extent that that evidence comes from disinterested witnesses' "? For a discussion, see Childress, *Standards of Review Primer: Federal Civil Appeals*, 293 F.R.D. 156 (2013).

2.   In deciding *Reeves*, the Court analogized a motion for judgment as a matter of law under Rule 50 to a motion for summary judgment under Rule 56 because "the standard for granting summary judgment 'mirrors' the standard for judgment as a matter of law." For a discussion of the operation of summary judgment motions, see Chapter 12, supra. The interaction between Rule 50 and Rule 56 can be complicated when the court denies a motion for summary judgment and the case then proceeds to trial. In ORTIZ v. JORDAN, 562 U.S. 180, 131 S.Ct. 884, 178 L.Ed.2d 703 (2011), the Supreme Court held that challenges to the sufficiency of the record at summary judgment are not preserved for appeal after trial. Instead, the Court explained that defendants needed to file a motion for judgment as a matter of law under Rule 50(b) in order to raise a sufficiency-of-the-evidence issue that they had pursued unsuccessfully in a pretrial summary judgment motion. Id. at 191–92, 131 S.Ct. at 893, 178 L.Ed.2d at 708. What purpose does this requirement serve?

3.   Either party may move for a judgment as a matter of law under Rule 50(a). If plaintiff's motion is denied, what are defendant's next steps in the litigation? What if it is defendant's motion that has been denied?

3. THE MOTION FOR JUDGMENT AS A MATTER OF LAW AFTER THE VERDICT (J.N.O.V.)

Why is there a need for a judgment as a matter of law after the jury has rendered its verdict? If a case has not been made during the presentation of the evidence, shouldn't the court have dismissed the case without submission to the jury? In fact, it is extremely rare that a court will grant a motion for judgment as a matter of law at the end of all of the evidence. Instead it will wait until after the jury has made its decision. Why is this so? In this context consider the situation if the trial judge is held to be incorrect in granting the motion and the appellate court reverses. What is the posture of the case at that point? Do the same considerations obtain when the court grants such a motion at an earlier time, e.g., at the end of plaintiff's case?

D. CHALLENGING ERRORS: NEW TRIAL

1. THE NATURE AND THE SCOPE OF THE POWER TO GRANT A NEW TRIAL

———

Read Federal Rules of Civil Procedure 59 and 61 and the accompanying materials in the Supplement.

———

NOTE ON THE RANGE OF THE TRIAL COURT'S DISCRETION

Errors committed during the course of a trial may be categorized as follows: (i) those that would result in reversal if the case were to be appealed; (ii) those that may have had an impact on the verdict, but do not justify reversal of the case on appeal, and (iii) those that did not significantly affect the outcome. Obviously errors that do not have any impact on the decision are harmless and it would be an abuse of discretion for the trial court to predicate a new trial on them. On the other hand, errors that would justify a reversal by an appellate court demand remedial measures at the trial level. A judge should not force a litigant to pay the costs of prosecuting an appeal as well as the costs of the new trial to which he is entitled.

The district court has discretion to decide whether a new trial is appropriate only with regard to errors that affect the result in the case but would not lead to reversal on appeal. However, the court's power to grant a new trial is greater than it might otherwise seem to be. First, an aggrieved litigant may decide to stand or fall on the motion for new trial since the case simply may not be worth the added cost of an appeal or the litigant may not have sufficient funds to continue fighting. Second, in many jurisdictions, the grant of a new trial, not being a final judgment, cannot be appealed. Thus the cost of a new trial will have to be absorbed before an appeal is even possible. Third, the very question of what constitutes reversible error on appeal often is affected by the ruling of the trial judge on the motion for new trial. In those jurisdictions in which a motion for a new trial is a prerequisite for appeal, the denial of a new trial certainly will influence the appellate court in deciding whether the error is harmless for purposes of appeal if the effect of the error in question can better be determined by the trial judge. Even when a motion for a new trial is not required, and when, theoretically, the appellate court should not penalize a litigant for having so moved, knowledge that the trial judge has rejected the alleged error as harmless may have an impact on the decision of the appellate court. Finally, in some jurisdictions the trial judge may grant a new trial without specifying or without actually relying on any precise grounds. Obviously this narrows the scope of review of such decisions.

———

GINSBERG v. WILLIAMS, 270 Minn. 474, 135 N.W.2d 213 (1965). Plaintiff brought suit for damages received in an automobile accident. The jury rendered a verdict for defendant and plaintiff moved for a new trial. The court granted the motion "in the interests of justice," giving no other basis for its ruling. Defendant sought a writ of prohibition to restrain enforcement of the ruling, claiming that the trial court is empowered to grant a new trial only for one of the grounds specifically set forth in Rule 59.01 of the Minnesota Rules of Civil Procedure. The Minnesota Supreme Court granted the writ, holding as follows:

> * * * The causes enumerated in Rule 59.01 are so comprehensive that they include every conceivable reason for which a new trial ought to be ordered. Those causes requiring the exercise of discretion, such as 59.01(1) (irregularities depriving the moving party of a fair trial) and 59.01(8) (insufficiency of the evidence), vest the broadest possible discretionary power in the trial court. To permit granting a new trial "in the interests of justice" would invite an arbitrary exercise of power over which appellate review is not now available. Even if it were, it would be difficult to fashion any effective rules to control arbitrary action since the basis for such an order would necessarily be subjective, varying from judge to judge. Further, each of the causes enumerated is designed to promote justice and prevent injustice. It is one thing to order a new trial "on the ground that on the evidence substantial justice has not been done" or in the interest of justice on the ground that the evidence does not justify the verdict, and quite another thing to order a new trial simply "in the interests of justice." It is difficult to conceive how such a general ground would add anything to the grounds enumerated in our rules unless it is desirable to restore the common-law power of granting a new trial when the judge is personally dissatisfied with the verdict.

Id. at 483–84, 135 N.W.2d at 220.

2.   INCOHERENT JURY VERDICTS

DUK v. MGM GRAND HOTEL, INC.

United States Court of Appeals for the Ninth Circuit, 2003.
320 F.3d 1052.

HAWKINS, CIRCUIT JUDGE.

Fernando Duk ("Duk") appeals the judgment arising from a defense verdict in favor of MGM Grand Hotel, Inc. ("MGM") in Duk's personal injury action in which there were two trials and three verdicts. MGM cross-appeals the district court's decision to resubmit the first verdict to the jury for clarification. Because we find that the court was within its discretion in resubmitting the first verdict, but erred in ordering a new trial upon receipt of the second verdict, we reverse and remand with instructions to enter judgment in Duk's favor consistent with the first jury's second verdict.

* * *

* * * The first jury trial was held in 1998. Because Nevada's comparative negligence scheme awards damages only to those plaintiffs who are found to be 50% negligent or less, the jury was presented with a special verdict form in which it was asked to determine the relative negligence of each party. Nev.Rev.Stat. § 41.141. Question 5 of the verdict form asked the jury to allot a percentage of the total negligence to the plaintiff and to the defendant. Following question 5, the jury was instructed that if it found the plaintiff to be more than 50% negligent, it should "sign and return [the] [in original] verdict" and judgment would be entered for the defendant. However, if in question 5 the jury found the plaintiff's negligence to be 50% or less, it was instructed to answer question 6, which asked for a determination of damages. Despite these instructions, the verdict form returned by the jury ("the first verdict") attributed 65% of the negligence to Duk and 35% to MGM, but still went on to award Duk $3.3 million in damages.

The district court reviewed the first verdict and, before announcing it, resubmitted the verdict form to the jury, informing the jury that the verdict contained an inconsistency and asking it to "continue [its] deliberations." Following 20 minutes of deliberation, the jury returned with a new verdict ("the second verdict"), apportioning 51% of the fault to MGM and 49% to Duk, but leaving the award of damages the same. The court granted MGM's subsequent motion for a new trial based on the inconsistency between the two verdicts.

* * *

At the second trial, the jury returned a verdict for MGM. Duk appeals the new trial grant and the judgment based upon the MGM verdict in the second trial, claiming that the second verdict was legitimate. * * * MGM cross-appeals, claiming that the trial court should not have resubmitted the original inconsistent verdict, but should have discarded the damages award and entered judgment for MGM. In the alternative, MGM argues that a new trial was properly ordered. * * *

* * * Although Rule 49(a), dealing with special verdicts such as this one, does not explicitly provide for resubmission in case of an inconsistency, we have held that, because the rule does not prohibit it, special verdicts are also subject to the practice. * * *

* * * [E]mbrace of the practice is based on the notion that resubmission "promotes both fairness and efficiency." * * * That principle was reaffirmed in *Larson* v. *Neimi,* 9 F.3d 1397 (9th Cir. 1993), when we held that the resubmission of an inconsistent special verdict to a jury, with a request for clarification, was within the district court's discretion. * * * *Id.* at 1402. * * *

Here, the inconsistency arose when the jury awarded damages to Duk, even though it found him more than 50% responsible for his own injuries. MGM argues that the jury contravened the verdict form's instructions to "sign and return [the] verdict" if Duk were found to be more than 50% negligent and, as a result, resubmission was barred by *Floyd* v. *Laws,* 929 F.2d 1390, 1397 (9th Cir. 1991) (responses in special verdict given in violation of a "stop here" instruction should be disregarded).

Floyd involved a 42 U.S.C. § 1983 suit and pendent state tort claims brought by a mother and her children against a municipality and its police chief. *Id.* at 1392. The jury was given a special verdict form addressing each of the claims, and found the police chief liable for assault and false imprisonment. *Id.* However, after the jury had been discharged, the defendant's counsel pointed out that the jury's answers to two of the questions were apparently inconsistent with one another. The jury answered "no" to question 13, which asked whether the plaintiffs were damaged as a result of the chief's actions. Following question 13 was an instruction which read: "If your answer to question 13 is 'No,' do not answer any further questions, but proceed to the end of this form and sign the verdict. If you answered 'Yes' to question 13, proceed to question 14." *Id.* at 1392–93. Question 14 asked the jury to award damages, which it did, awarding the plaintiffs $7,500. *Id.* at 1393. The trial court declared the answer to question 14 to be surplusage and entered judgment for the defendants. *Id.*

We upheld the trial court's decision, holding that, "as in the case of parenthetical comments, special findings issued in violation of the trial court's express instructions do not constitute legitimate or viable findings of fact." *Id.* at 1397. Because the trial court was "bound by law to disregard any answer to question 14 as surplusage," the damages award "never became a part of the special verdict, and the trial court was faced with no apparent inconsistency." *Id.* at 1399–1400.

Floyd, however, does not address the situation where the jury is still available when the inconsistency is recognized. *Id.* at 1392. * * * Because the jury had already been dismissed, the trial court in *Floyd* was left with the option of either disregarding the jury's answers following the "stop here" instruction or ordering a new trial. Thus, we had no occasion to consider whether resubmission, if it were possible, would *also* be within a trial court's discretion.

* * *

* * * [W]hen the jury is still available, resubmitting an inconsistent verdict best comports with the fair and efficient administration of justice. Allowing the jury to correct its own mistakes conserves judicial resources and the time and convenience of citizen jurors, as well as those of the parties. It also allows for a resolution of the case according to the intent of the original fact-finder, while that body is still present and able to resolve the matter. An entirely different situation is present where the jury has been dismissed. There, dismissal of surplusage * * * makes sense. It is certainly preferable to ordering a new trial, and is very probably the best available instrument to determine the jury's intent.

Resubmission, of course, leaves open the possibility that the jury will reach an improper "compromise" verdict. * * * However, we presume that citizen jurors will properly perform the duties entrusted them and will not construe resubmission as an invitation to subvert the law and contort findings of fact in favor of a desired result.

* * *

A trial court, is rarely entitled to disregard jury verdicts that are supported by substantial evidence. The Supreme Court has held that a trial court has a duty to attempt to harmonize seemingly inconsistent answers to special verdict interrogatories, "if it is possible under a fair reading of them." * * * A court may not disregard a jury's verdict and order a new trial until it "attempt[s] to reconcile the jury's findings, by exegesis if necessary." * * *

[T]here is little authority addressing the question whether harmonization is required *across different verdicts,* where a verdict has been resubmitted for clarification. Indeed, resubmission necessarily means that there might well be a difference between the first verdict and that reached after resubmission. Such an "inconsistency" will usually be considered a proper correction of a mistake in the original verdict. However, even if the second verdict appears to the trial court to be an improper compromise, the Seventh Amendment requires the court to seek a legitimate explanation for a verdict that is not contrary to the weight of the evidence.* * * Further, verdicts rendered pursuant to resubmission are readily amenable to the harmonization requirement. In this case, the second verdict is flatly inconsistent with the first because it apportions liability differently. However, this discrepancy is easily explained by the process of redeliberation.

* * *

Resubmission of an inconsistent verdict is done with the sole purpose of allowing a jury to reconcile inconsistencies. This process is not simply restricted to correcting transcription errors, but also envisions a process of redeliberation. * * * Such a result is possible only where the jury is allowed to resume its deliberations. Some inconsistencies may only be resolved if the jury reconsiders its answers in light of the instructions given to determine how its legally inconsistent answers can be properly reconciled according to its view of the facts.

Once this premise is accepted, it becomes clear that a post-resubmission verdict can easily be harmonized with its earlier counterpart by reference to a wholly proper process of redeliberation. In this case, the second verdict was not internally inconsistent. The only reason the district court expressed in finding that a new trial was required was that the second verdict was the product of a "manipulation of negligence percentages." The court did not consider the possibility that the jury came to a different conclusion as to the facts because it engaged in further deliberations and legitimately came to new findings of fact. This is precisely what the trial court instructed the jury to do. When the court resubmitted the verdict to the jury, it twice instructed the jurors to "continue [their] deliberations."

* * *

* * * [H]owever, the amount of damages remained unchanged from the first verdict to the second. Therefore, it is still quite plausible that the jury changed the apportionment of liability because it redeliberated and either changed its mind or clarified its thinking. It cannot be said here that the jury was clearly seeking a predetermined result. * * * As we have stated, the trial court has a duty to reconcile the verdicts "on *any reasonable theory* consistent with the evidence." * * * Because it is possible to explain the inconsistency in a way that comports with the law, the district court's decision to disregard the second verdict and order a new trial was an abuse of discretion.

* * *

* * * We order reinstatement of the second verdict and entry of judgment for the plaintiff, including such interest thereon as calculated by the district court.

NOTE AND QUESTIONS

Are there practical difficulties to resubmission in jurisdictions that do not require jurors to remain together constantly once the case has been submitted? Before allowing the jurors to separate, the court normally will warn them not to discuss the case with anyone outside the jury room and not to inspect sites referred to in the testimony or otherwise to obtain evidence. See Steckler, Management of the Jury, 28 F.R.D. 190, 191 (1960). Is it realistic to expect jurors not to have some discussions of a case with other jurors or with their families? What should the court do if it learns that discussions have occurred?

3. JURY MISCONDUCT AND THE INTEGRITY OF THE VERDICT

Should a juror be permitted to impeach his own verdict? Under Lord Mansfield's rule, courts were barred from relying on jurors' affidavits to revisit a verdict. See Vaise v. Delaval, 1 Term Rep. 11, 99 Eng. Rep. 944 (K.B. 1785). In 1866, the Iowa Supreme Court became the first state to deviate from the Mansfield rule, holding that "affidavits of jurors may be received for the purpose of avoiding a verdict, to show any matter occurring during the trial or in the jury room, which does not essentially inhere in the verdict." Wright v. Illinois & Mississippi Telegraph Co., 20 Iowa 195, 210 (1866).

NOTE AND QUESTIONS

Federal Rule of Evidence 606 addresses a juror's competency as a witness. Subsection (b) is set out below.

(b) During an Inquiry into the Validity of a Verdict or Indictment.

> **(1)** *Prohibited Testimony or Other Evidence.* During an inquiry into the validity of a verdict or indictment, a juror may not testify about any statement made or incident that occurred during the jury's deliberations; the effect of anything on that juror's or another juror's vote; or any juror's mental processes concerning the verdict or indictment. The court may not receive a juror's affidavit or evidence of a juror's statement on these matters.
>
> **(2)** *Exceptions.* A juror may testify about whether:
>
> > **(A)** extraneous prejudicial information was improperly brought to the jury's attention;
> >
> > **(B)** an outside influence was improperly brought to bear on any juror; or
> >
> > **(C)** a mistake was made in entering the verdict on the verdict form.

Does Rule 606(b) follow the Mansfield or the Iowa rule? In PENA-RODRIGUEZ v. COLORADO, 137 S.Ct. 855, 197 L.Ed.2d 107 (2017), a Colorado jury convicted petitioner of harassment and unlawful sexual contact on a child. The empaneled jurors did not express any reservations based on racial or any other bias after repeatedly being asked if they could be fair and impartial in the case. Petitioner moved for a new trial based on affidavits of two of the jurors that during deliberations, a third juror had made statements establishing that his vote to convict was based on racial bias against petitioner and an alibi witness. The Colorado courts rejected the affidavits under Colorado's Rule of Evidence 606(b) (virtually identical to Federal Rule 606(b)) that prohibits juror testimony as to statements made during deliberations to overturn a verdict. The Supreme Court, by a five-to-three decision, reversed. Although the Court generally praised Rule 606(b), it held that in the special case of racial bias in a criminal action, the Sixth Amendment required the rule to give way to permit consideration of the affidavits. Should this same approach be taken in civil cases, where the Sixth Amendment does not apply? See Harden v. Hillman, 993 F.3d 465, 481 (6th Cir. 2021) (holding that "the Fourteenth Amendment's guarantee of 'equal protection of the laws' provides a sufficient basis to extend *Pena-Rodriguez* to civil cases").

————

In MCDONOUGH POWER EQUIPMENT, INC. v. GREENWOOD, 464 U.S. 548, 104 S.Ct. 845, 78 L.Ed.2d 663 (1984), the respondent was injured in an accident involving a power mower manufactured by the petitioner. During the *voir dire* before the empaneling of the six-member jury, the respondents' attorney asked a panel of prospective jurors how many of them had sustained or had immediate family members who had sustained any severe injury. The man who would become the foreman of the jury did not respond. The jury ultimately found for the petitioner. After judgment was entered for the petitioner, the respondents' attorney questioned the jurors and discovered that the son of the foreman of the jury had been injured some time before by the explosion of a truck tire, sustaining a broken leg. During the post-judgment interview, the foreman said that "having accidents are a part of life," and that "all his children have been involved in accidents." Id. at 553 n.3, 104 S.Ct. at 848 n.3, 78 L.Ed.2d at 669 n.3. When the respondents' motion for a new trial reached the Supreme Court, it held that:

> To invalidate the result of a 3-week trial because of a juror's mistaken, though honest, response to a question, is to insist on something closer to perfection than our judicial system can be expected to give. A trial represents an important investment of private and social resources, and it ill serves the important end of finality to wipe the slate clean simply to recreate the peremptory challenge process because counsel lacked an item of information which objectively he should have obtained from a juror on *voir dire* examination. * * * We hold that to obtain a new trial in such a situation, a party must first demonstrate that a juror failed to answer honestly a material question on *voir dire,* and then further show that a correct response would have provided a valid basis for a challenge for cause. * * *

Id. at 555–56, 104 S.Ct. at 849–50, 78 L.Ed.2d at 671.

Justice Blackmun, joined by Justices Stevens and O'Connor, concurred, stressing that the decision should not be understood as "foreclos[ing] the normal avenue of relief available to a party who is asserting that he did not have the benefit of an impartial jury." Id. at 556, 104 S.Ct. at 850, 78 L.Ed.2d at 672. Justice Brennan, joined by Justice Marshall, concurred in the judgment, proposing a different legal standard:

> * * * In my view, the proper focus when ruling on a motion for new trial in this situation should be on the bias of the juror and the resulting prejudice to the litigant. More specifically, to be awarded a new trial, a litigant should be required to demonstrate that the juror incorrectly responded to a material question on *voir dire,* and that, under the facts and circumstances surrounding the particular case, the juror was biased against the moving litigant. * * *

> * * * [F]or a court to determine properly whether bias exists, it must consider at least two questions: are there any facts in the case suggesting that bias should be conclusively presumed; and, if not, is it more probable than not that the juror was actually biased against the litigant. Whether the juror answered a particular question on *voir dire* honestly or dishonestly, or whether an inaccurate answer was inadvertent or intentional, are simply factors to be considered in this latter determination of actual bias. * * *

Id. at 557–58, 104 S.Ct. at 851, 78 L.Ed.2d at 672–73.

4.   NEW TRIAL BECAUSE THE VERDICT IS AGAINST THE WEIGHT OF THE EVIDENCE

————

Read Federal Rule of Civil Procedure 59 and the accompanying state materials in the Supplement.

————

AETNA CASUALTY & SURETY CO. V. YEATTS
United States Circuit Court of Appeals, Fourth Circuit, 1941.
122 F.2d 350.

PARKER, CIRCUIT JUDGE.

This is the second appeal in a suit originally instituted to obtain a declaratory judgment with respect to the coverage of a policy of indemnity insurance. * * * The company denied liability on the ground that the defendant Yeatts was engaged in the performance of a criminal abortion at the time he incurred the liability for which the recovery was had against him, and that such liability was expressly excluded from the coverage of the policy. The question as to whether the defendant Yeatts was engaged in such criminal conduct was submitted to the jury, and from verdict and judgment in his favor the plaintiff brings this appeal.

There was testimony below from which the jury would have been amply justified in finding in favor of the plaintiff insurance company on the issue submitted; but the defendant himself was examined as a witness and, if his testimony is believed, he was guilty of no criminal act. No motion for directed verdict was made by the plaintiff, nor was the sufficiency of the evidence to sustain a finding in favor of the defendant challenged in any other way before verdict. After verdict, plaintiff moved for judgment non obstante veredicto and also for a new trial, on the ground that the verdict was contrary to the credible evidence in the case; and exceptions directed to denial of these motions constitute the only points presented by the appeal.

Even if a motion for directed verdict had been made by plaintiff, it is clear that same should have been denied as should also, any motion for judgment non obstante veredicto based thereon * * *.

The motion to set aside the verdict and grant a new trial was a matter of federal procedure, governed by Rule * * * 59 and not subject in any way to the rules of state practice. On such a motion it is the duty of the judge to set aside the verdict and grant a new trial, if he is of opinion that the verdict is against the clear weight of the evidence, or is based upon evidence which is false, or will result in a miscarriage of justice, even though there may be substantial evidence which would prevent the direction of a verdict. The exercise of this power is not in derogation of the right of trial by jury but is one of the historic safeguards of that right. * * * The matter was well put by Mr. Justice Mitchell, speaking for the Supreme Court of Pennsylvania in Smith v. Times Publishing Co., * * * [178 Pa. 481, 501, 36 A. 296, 298 (1897)], as follows: "The authority of the common pleas in the control and revision of excessive verdicts through the means of new trials was firmly settled in England before the foundation of this colony, and has always existed here without challenge under any of our constitutions. It is a power to examine the whole case on the law and the evidence, with a view to securing a result, not merely legal, but also not manifestly against justice,—a power exercised in pursuance of a sound judicial discretion, *without which the jury system would be a capricious and intolerable tyranny,* which no people could long endure. This court has had occasion more than once recently to say that it was *a power the courts ought to exercise unflinchingly."* (Italics supplied).

In the same case, Mr. Justice Williams, in a concurring opinion, traces the history of the exercise of this power and sums up his conclusion as follows:

* * *

As early * * * as 1665, the courts at Westminster did precisely what we have done in this case, and for the same reason. The right of trial by jury was not then supposed to give to a successful party the right to insist on an advantage due to the mistake or the willful misconduct of the jury, no matter how grossly unjust and oppressive the result might be; but the supervisory control of the court in banc, sitting as a court of review, was promptly exercised to relieve against the miscarriage of justice. The exercise of this power was then thought to be in aid of trial by jury. * * *

[Id. at 508–09, 36 A. at 309.]

* * *

The distinction between the rules to be followed in granting a new trial and directing a verdict were stated by us with some care in Garrison v. United States, 4 Cir., 62 F.2d 41, 42, * * * as follows: "Where there is substantial evidence in support of plaintiff's case, the judge may not direct a verdict against him, even though he may not believe his evidence or may think that the weight of the evidence is on the other side; for, under the constitutional guaranty of trial by jury, it is for the jury to weigh the evidence and pass upon its credibility. He may, however, set aside a verdict supported by substantial evidence where in his opinion it is contrary to the clear weight of the evidence, or is based upon evidence which is false; for, even though the evidence be sufficient to preclude the direction of a verdict, it is still his duty to exercise his power over the proceedings before him to prevent a miscarriage of justice. * * *"

It is equally well settled, however, that the granting or refusing of a new trial is a matter resting in the sound discretion of the trial judge, and that his action thereon is not reviewable upon appeal, save in the most exceptional circumstances. * * * The rule and the reason therefor is thus stated by Mr. Justice Brandeis in Fairmount Glass Works v. Cub Fork Coal Co., * * * [287 U.S. 474, 481, 53 S.Ct. 252, 254, 77 L.Ed. 439, 443 (1933)]: "The rule that this Court will not review the action of a federal trial court in granting or denying a motion for a new trial for error of fact has been settled by a long and unbroken line of decisions * * *. The rule precludes likewise a review of such action by a Circuit Court of Appeals. Its early formulation by this Court was influenced by the mandate of the Judiciary Act of 1789, which provided in section 22 that there should be 'no reversal in either (circuit or Supreme) court on such writ of error * * * for any error in fact.' Sometimes the rule has been rested on that part of the Seventh Amendment which provides that 'no fact tried by a jury, shall be otherwise reexamined in any court of the United States than according to the rules of the common law'. More frequently the reason given for the denial of review is that the granting or refusing of a motion for a new trial is a matter within the discretion of the trial court."

While an examination of the record has led us to the conclusion that the trial judge might very properly have granted the motion for new trial, we cannot say that his denial of the motion amounted to an abuse of discretion on his part or that there are present any of the special circumstances which would subject his action to review by this court. The judgment appealed from will accordingly be affirmed.

Affirmed.

NOTES AND QUESTIONS

1.   How does the standard for granting a motion for a judgment as a matter of law (formerly called a motion for a directed verdict) differ from that of a motion for a new trial? In DYER v. MacDOUGALL, 201 F.2d 265, 271 (2d Cir. 1952), Judge Frank, concurring, said:

> * * * The well-settled rule is that, in passing on a motion for a directed verdict, the trial judge always must utterly disregard his own views of witnesses' credibility, and therefore of their demeanor; that he believes or disbelieves some of the testimony is irrelevant. When asked to direct a verdict for the defendant, the judge must assume that, if he lets the case go to the jury, the jurymen will believe all evidence—including "demeanor evidence"—favorable to the plaintiff. In other words, the judge must not deprive plaintiff of any advantage that plaintiff might derive from having the jury pass upon the oral testimony. Indeed, the important difference between a trial judge's power on a motion for a new trial and on a motion for a directed verdict is precisely that on a new-trial motion he may base his action on his belief or disbelief in some of the witnesses, while on a directed-verdict motion he may not.

See also Bowditch v. City of Boston, 101 U.S. (11 Otto) 16, 18, 25 L.Ed. 980, 980–81 (1879): "It is now a settled rule in the courts of the United States that whenever, in the trial of a civil case, it is clear that the state of the evidence is such as not to warrant a verdict for a party, and that if such a verdict were rendered the other party would be entitled to a new trial, it is the right and duty of the judge to direct the jury to find according to the views of the court." The *Bowditch* case is but one of many with language of this kind.

2.   It often is said that the grant of a new trial is largely unappealable; in those systems that adhere to the final-judgment rule, it can be reviewed by appealing from the judgment on the second trial, but in that case the appellant presumably will have lost the verdict in the second trial, and it will be difficult to argue that the grant of a new trial was an abuse of discretion. Some commentators have called for more robust review of judgments granting or denying a motion for a new trial. See Robertson, *Judging Jury Verdicts*, 83 Tul.L.Rev. 157, 217–18 (2008).

5. THE POWER TO GRANT CONDITIONAL AND PARTIAL NEW TRIALS

FISCH V. MANGER

Supreme Court of New Jersey, 1957.
24 N.J. 66, 130 A.2d 815.

JACOBS, J.

The plaintiff suffered serious injuries in an automobile accident and, after trial, received a jury verdict in the sum of $3,000. He applied for a new trial because of the inadequacy of the verdict but his application was denied when the defendants consented that the damages awarded to the plaintiff be increased to the sum of $7,500. The plaintiff appealed and we thereafter certified on our own motion.

* * *

The plaintiff's actual expenditures to doctors and nurses and for drugs and hospitalization exceeded $2,200. And although he received most of his normal earnings despite his temporary incapacity, there was a loss of wages approximating $620. While the jury's verdict of $3,000 just about took care of the plaintiff's actual monetary losses, it awarded substantially nothing for his suffering and permanent injuries. Its gross inadequacy was recognized by the trial judge who pointed out that "there was no dispute but that the plaintiff suffered excruciating pain, and was rendered totally helpless for a considerable period of time." On June 28, 1956 the trial judge wrote to the parties advising that unless the defendants filed a consent in writing that the verdict be increased from $3,000 to $7,500, "then the verdict heretofore rendered will be set aside and a new trial granted limited to damages only." The consent was filed by the defendants and on June 30, 1956 a formal order was entered dismissing the plaintiff's motion for a new trial. * * *

The first point which he urges in support of his appeal is that once the trial court had concluded that the damages awarded by the verdict were inadequate it had no legal power whatever to condition the grant of a new trial upon the defendants' failure to consent to a prescribed increase in the verdict. * * * The term *remittitur* is used to describe an order denying the defendant's application for new trial on condition that the plaintiff consent to a specified reduction in the jury's award, whereas the term *additur* is used to describe an order denying the plaintiff's application for a new trial on condition that the defendant consent to a specified increase in the jury's award. While it is now recognized that the two practices are logically and realistically indistinguishable, *remittiturs* have been recognized almost everywhere, whereas *additurs* are still outlawed in some, though by no means all, of the states. * * *

The English precedents prior to the American Revolution are somewhat obscure and they are discussed in the majority and minority opinions in Dimick v. Schiedt, 293 U.S. 474, 55 S.Ct. 296, 302, 79 L.Ed. 603 (1935). There Justice Sutherland, speaking for a majority of five (with Justice Stone, joined by Chief Justice Hughes and Justices Brandeis and Cardozo, dissenting) held that although *remittitur* is permissible in the federal courts, *additur* is prohibited by * * * the Seventh Amendment * * *. Justice Sutherland in the Dimick case * * * declined to upset the *remittitur* practice, first approved by Justice Story in Blunt v. Little, 3 Fed.Cas.760, No. 1,578 (C.C.Mass.1822), and since reaffirmed in many federal decisions. * * *

The majority opinion in Dimick has been the subject of much criticism and it is doubtful whether the Supreme Court would still subscribe to it; in any event, the Seventh Amendment differs somewhat from our constitutional provision and has no application to proceedings in our state courts. * * * We must look primarily to our own history and precedents in ascertaining whether the highly desirable practices of *remittitur* and *additur* may be adhered to in our State * * *.

The *remittitur* practice has been recognized in New Jersey since early days. * * * [In 1917] the Court of Errors and Appeals had occasion to deal with a negligence case in which the practice of *additur* had been invoked. * * * Chancellor Walker, speaking for the entire court, had this to say ([Gaffney v. Illingsworth,] 90 N.J.L. at page 492, 101 A. at page 243):

> The power of the court in granting a new trial upon the ground that the damages are *excessive,* upon terms that a new trial shall be had unless the plaintiff will accept a certain sum named, less than that awarded by a verdict, is too well established to be questioned. It would seem to follow, by parity of reasoning, that when a new trial is granted because the damages are inadequate, the court may impose like terms, that is, terms to the effect that if the defeated party will pay a certain sum, greater than that awarded by the verdict, the rule will be discharged, subject, doubtless, to the power of an appellate court to vacate any such terms when they appear to be an abuse of discretion. * * *

* * *

* * *[W]e are satisfied that the practices of *remittitur* and *additur* violate none of our constitutional interdictions and, if fairly invoked, serve the laudable purpose of avoiding a further trial where substantial justice may be attained on the basis of the original trial. * * * Accordingly, we reject the first point urged by the plaintiff and come now to his meritorious contention that, in any event, the prescribed increase to $7,500 was "grossly inadequate and should be set aside." * * * In the instant matter, we believe that the trial judge had a mistaken notion of the evidence which

led to his prescribing the scanty sum of $7,500. He stated that the plaintiff was not entitled to a "great sum, because he certainly did have a back condition before this accident occurred"; but the evidence in the record points to the view that whatever "back condition" the plaintiff had as a result of the 1950 accident had cleared up and had no relation to the very severe injuries resulting from the 1953 accident. Under these highly special circumstances, we believe that the trial court's action should not be permitted to stand and that the interests of justice will best be served by permitting a second jury to pass on the issue of damages. The separable issue of liability was clearly and properly decided against the defendants; under the evidence it could hardly have been determined otherwise and need not be submitted for redetermination. * * *

Reversed, with direction for a new trial on the issue of damages.

HEHER, J. (concurring in result). * * *

As is shown by Justice Sutherland's analysis of the case history in Dimick v. Schiedt * * *, there was no power in the English courts at the time of the adoption of the New Jersey Constitution of 1776 to increase, either absolutely or conditionally, the damages fixed by a jury in a case such as this. * * *

* * * Justice Sutherland concluded, and with unquestionable authority, that "while there was some practice to the contrary in respect of *decreasing* damages, the established practice and the rule of the common law, as it existed in England at the time of the adoption of the Constitution, forbade the court to *increase* the amount of damages awarded by a jury in actions such as that here under consideration." * * *

The "controlling distinction between the power of the court and that of the jury," said Justice Sutherland, "is that the former is the power to determine the law and the latter to determine the facts," and while the *remittitur* practice in the case of an excessive verdict "is not without plausible support in the view that what remains is included in the verdict along with the unlawful excess,—in the sense that it has been found by the jury,—and that the *remittitur* has the effect of merely lopping off an excrescence," yet where an inadequate verdict is increased by the court there is a "bald addition of something which in no sense can be said to be included in the verdict," and if that be done with the consent of the defendant alone, the plaintiff is compelled to forego his "constitutional right to the verdict of a jury and accept 'an assessment partly made by a jury which has acted improperly, and partly by a tribunal which has no power to assess.' "

* * *

NOTES AND QUESTIONS

1.   For an argument that the practice of remittitur is not constitutional under the Seventh Amendment, see Thomas, *Re-Examining the Constitutionality of Remittitur Under the Seventh Amendment*, 64 Ohio St.L.J. 731 (2003).

2.   Should a trial court have discretion to set a reasonable remittitur figure somewhere between the highest and lowest possible verdicts? Would it make more sense to require, as the alternative to a new trial, the highest amount an unprejudiced jury properly could have awarded plaintiff?

6. REQUIREMENT AND TIMELINESS OF REQUESTS FOR A NEW TRIAL

Reread Federal Rules of Civil Procedure 50 and 59 in the Supplement.

UNITHERM FOOD SYSTEMS, INC. v. SWIFT-ECKRICH, INC., 546 U.S. 394, 126 S.Ct. 980, 163 L.Ed.2d 974 (2006). Defendant moved at the end of the evidence under Federal Rule 50(a) for judgment as a matter of law. The motion was denied, and the case was submitted to the jury, which found for plaintiff. Defendant failed either to renew the motion for judgment as a matter of law or to move for a new trial. The court of appeals held that although the failure to file a renewed motion for judgment as a matter of law precluded a court from entering judgment as a matter of law, an appeals court nevertheless could grant a new trial as long as a preverdict motion for judgment as a matter of law had been filed.

The Supreme Court reversed as follows:

* * * The text of Rule 50(b) confirms that respondent's preverdict Rule 50(a) motion did not present the District Court with the option of granting a new trial. That text provides that a district court may only order a new trial on the basis of issues raised in a preverdict 50(a) motion when "ruling on a renewed motion" under Rule 50(b). Accordingly, even if the District Court was inclined to grant a new trial on the basis of arguments raised in respondents's preverdict motion, it was without the power to do so under Rule 50(b) absent a postverdict motion pursuant to that Rule. Consequently the Court of Appeals was similarly powerless.

* * * [T]he District Court's denial of respondent's preverdict motion cannot form the basis of respondent's appeal, because the denial of that motion was not in error. It was merely an exercise of the District Court's discretion, in accordance with the text of the Rule and the accepted practice of permitting the jury to make

an initial judgment about the sufficiency of the evidence. The only error here was counsel's failure to file a post-verdict motion pursuant to Rule 50(b).

Id. at 404, 126 S.Ct. at 988, 163 L.Ed.2d at 986.

Justice Stevens, in his dissent, argued that counsel's error did not oust the appellate court of its authority to correct plain error:

> Murphy's law applies to trial lawyers as well as pilots. Even an expert will occasionally blunder. For that reason Congress has preserved the federal appeals courts' power to correct plain error, even though trial counsel's omission will ordinarily give rise to a binding waiver. This is not a case, in my view, in which the authority of the appellate court is limited by an explicit statute or controlling rule. The spirit of the Federal Rules * * * favors preservation of a court's power to avoid manifestly unjust results in exceptional cases.

Id. at 407, 126 S.Ct. at 988, 163 L.Ed.2d at 987.

NOTES AND QUESTIONS

1. *Does Unitherm* affect motions for a new trial under Federal Rule 59? Is it significant that the text of Rule 59 does not require any preverdict motion? Does *Unitherm* bar appeals based on legal error unless a post-verdict motion is filed? The Eighth Circuit has explained:

> The *Unitherm* opinion includes language that, when read out of context, indicates that an appeal may never be taken unless a postverdict motion is filed * * * ("[A] party is not entitled to pursue a new trial on appeal unless that party makes an appropriate postverdict motion in the district court."). However, in addressing whether this language extends to all post-trial appeals, appeals courts have uniformly limited it to sufficiency of the evidence challenges where parties fail to file a postverdict motion under Rule 50(b) after the *denial* of a Rule 50(a) preverdict motion.* * * Reading *Unitherm* more broadly would dramatically alter the well-accepted rule that an objection at trial generally preserves an issue for review on appeal.* * *

LINDEN v. CNH AMERICA, LLC, 673 F.3d 829, 832–33 (8th Cir. 2012).

2. The time period for filing a motion under Rule 50, 52, and 59 is 28 days after the entry of judgment. The period is treated as jurisdictional so the district court is without power to extend it. See Hulson v. Atchison, Topeka & Santa Fe Railway, 289 F.2d 726 (7th Cir.), cert. denied, 368 U.S. 835, 82 S.Ct. 61, 7 L.Ed.2d 36 (1961).

7. THE POWER TO SET ASIDE A JUDGMENT

Read Federal Rule of Civil Procedure 60 in the Supplement.

a. Mistake and Excusable Neglect

BRIONES v. RIVIERA HOTEL & CASINO, 116 F.3d 379 (9th Cir. 1997). Plaintiff sued his former employer for unlawful discharge. Defendant filed a Federal Rule 12(b) motion to dismiss for lack of jurisdiction and lack of proper service, to which plaintiff failed to respond. The court thus granted the motion. Plaintiff, who was appearing *pro se* and was not proficient in English, moved for relief under Federal Rule 60(b)(1) on the ground that the court had never informed him that his case might be dismissed and he had failed to notify his translator and typist of the deadline for filing his opposition papers. The trial court denied the Rule 60(b) motion. At that time case law had seemed to establish as a *per se* rule that a motion under Rule 60(b) could not be utilized to cure a failure to comply with court rules. See, e.g., Hulson v. Atchison, Topeka & Santa Fe Ry., p. 792, Note 2, supra. However the appeals court noted that the Supreme Court in PIONEER INV. SERVS. CO. v. BRUNSWICK ASSOCIATES LTD. PARTNERSHIP, 507 U.S. 380, 113 S.Ct. 1489, 123 L.Ed.2d 74 (1993), addressing the filing of untimely claims under the Bankruptcy Code, had analyzed the term "excusable neglect" and referred to Rules 6(b) and 60(b) as follows

> Although inadvertence, ignorance of the rules, or mistakes construing the rules do not usually constitute "excusable" neglect, it is clear the "excusable neglect" under Rule 6(b) is a somewhat "elastic concept" and is not limited strictly to omissions caused by circumstances beyond the control of the movant. * * * [A]t least for purposes of Rule 60(b), "excusable neglect" is understood to encompass situations in which the failure to comply with a filing deadline is attributable to negligence.

Id. at 392, 113 S.Ct. at 1496, 123 L.Ed.2d at 87. The Supreme Court in *Pioneer* listed four factors to be considered in deciding whether neglect was "excusable": (1) the danger of prejudice to the opposing party, (2) the length of the delay and its potential impact on the judicial proceedings, (3) the reason for the delay, and (4) whether the moving party acted in good faith. In view of the *Pioneer* opinion, the *Briones* court remanded the case to the trial court to determine whether plaintiff's negligence was "excusable" under all the circumstances.

In Pincay v. Andrews, 351 F.3d 947, 951–52 (9th Cir. 2003), the Ninth Circuit held that excusable neglect to extend the time for filing an appeal was not present when defendant's lawyer relied upon his firm's calendar clerk to calculate the filing and the calculation was in error:

> We do not have a pro se plaintiff as in *Briones.* * * * It is consonant with *Pioneer*'s teaching that "ignorance of the rules or mistakes construing the rules do not usually constitute 'excusable' neglect." * * * Here there was ignorance of the rules, compounded by delegation of knowledge of the rules to a nonlawyer for whom responsibility was not accepted.

See Simpson-Wood, *A Litmus Test for Pioneer: Ethical Considerations and the Delegation Situation*, 31 J.Legal Prof. 171 (2007).

b.   Newly Discovered Evidence; Fraud

PATRICK v. SEDWICK, 413 P.2d 169 (Alaska 1966). Plaintiff brought an action for medical malpractice, alleging permanent physical injuries. The case was tried in October 1961 without a jury. In February 1962, the trial judge rendered findings on the issues of liability. These findings were subject to a lengthy appeal and it was not until more than two years later that the appellate court directed the trial court to enter findings for plaintiff on all issues of liability and to proceed to determine damages. The trial judge fixed the amount of damages on the basis of the evidence that had been presented at the trial and entered judgment on January 12, 1965. On January 22, 1965, defendant moved for a new trial on the ground that in 1963 a Dr. Robert Lewy had devised a new treatment that would ameliorate plaintiff's injuries and therefore should reduce his damages. The trial court denied the motion. The judge rejected the significance of the new treatment since there was no assurance that any improvement it might bring would be permanent.

The appellate court affirmed the denial of a new trial with the following explanation:

> * * * [A] motion for new trial on the grounds of newly discovered evidence must meet the following requirements before it [can] be granted:
>
> (1) must be such as would probably change the result on a new trial; (2) must have been discovered since the trial; (3) must be of such a nature that it could not have been discovered before trial by due diligence; (4) must be material; (5) must not be merely cumulative or impeaching.
>
> In addition to the foregoing requirements, it is established that for any evidence to come within the category of "newly discovered"

such evidence must relate to facts which were in existence at the time of the trial. * * *

We hold, under the authorities referred to, that the trial court did not abuse its discretion in denying appellee's motion for a new trial on the grounds of newly discovered evidence. It is clear from the record that Dr. Lewy's discovery of the Teflon technique did not occur until a considerable period of time had elapsed after the case was tried in October 1961. Thus, the Lewy technique was not in existence at the time the trial took place and under the above authorities would not qualify as newly discovered evidence.

Id. at 177.

NOTES AND QUESTIONS

1.   The standard for "newly discovered evidence" is similar under the federal rule. In American Civil Liberties Union v. Department of Defense, 406 F.Supp.2d 330 (S.D.N.Y. 2005), plaintiffs sought documents under the Freedom of Information Act pertaining to the treatment of detainees and to interrogation methods used against top Al-Qaeda members. The government declined to confirm or deny the existence of any documents, on the ground that their existence was itself classified. The court entered a judgment in favor of the government. After the CIA acknowledged in the press that its agents had participated in the interrogation of detainees, plaintiffs moved under Rule 60(b)(2) and (b)(6) for relief from the judgment based on newly discovered evidence. The court denied the motion:

> * * * To prevail on a Rule 60(b)(2) motion, the party must show that " '(1) newly discovered evidence is of facts existing at the time of [the prior decision]; (2) the moving party is excusably ignorant of the facts despite using due diligence to learn about them; (3) the newly discovered evidence is admissible and probably effective to change the result of the former ruling; and (4) the newly discovered evidence is not merely cumulative . . . of evidence already offered.' " * * * To prevail under the catch-all provision of a Rule 60(b)(6) motion, the party must show that the asserted grounds for relief are other than those recognized in clauses one through five of Rule 60, in addition to showing extraordinary circumstances justify relief.* * *

Id. at 332. The court found that the media reports would not have changed its earlier ruling, and were merely cumulative of evidence already submitted. As a result, relief was not available under Rule 60(b)(2). Nor did Rule 60(b)(6) provide a catch-all basis for relief. "Because the asserted grounds for relief, 'newly discovered evidence,' are recognized in clause two of Rule 60, relief under clause 6 of Rule 60 is unavailable." Id.

2.   In TITLE v. UNITED STATES, 263 F.2d 28, 31 (9th Cir. 1959), cert. denied, 359 U.S. 989, 79 S.Ct. 1118, 3 L.Ed.2d 978 (1959), appellant sought to set aside a judgment of denaturalization on the ground that some two years

thereafter the United States Supreme Court, in a different case, interpreted the immigration act in such a way as to demonstrate that the original decision in *Title* was erroneous. Appellant relied on Rules 60(b)(4) and (5). The trial court denied the motions and the court of appeals affirmed: "Rule 60(b) was not intended to provide relief for error on the part of the court or to afford a substitute for appeal. * * * Nor is a change in the judicial view of applicable law after a final judgment sufficient basis for vacating such judgment entered before announcement of the change." Assume that the change in the law is announced after the trial court has rendered judgment but before the time for appeal has run? Now should it be open to a party to seek relief under Rule 60(b)? Which subdivision would be the appropriate basis? See Visa Intern. Service Ass'n v. JSL Corp., 590 F.Supp.2d 1306 (D.Nev.2008).

––––––––––

In HAZEL-ATLAS GLASS CO. v. HARTFORD-EMPIRE CO., 322 U.S. 238, 245–46, 64 S.Ct. 997, 1001, 88 L.Ed. 1250, 1255–56 (1944), plaintiff brought an action in the court of appeals to set aside a judgment rendered against it some nine years earlier. The first action had turned on the validity of a patent held by defendant. Both the issuance of that patent by the Patent Office and the determination of its validity by the federal Court of Appeals for the Third Circuit in the prior action had been affected by an article offered by defendant, ostensibly written by a disinterested expert, but actually prepared by defendant's own officials, to the effect that the machine under patent was a "revolutionary device." One of the attorneys who presented defendant's case in the first action also had participated in the scheme to prepare and publish the fraudulent article. The court of appeals refused to set aside the judgment; the Supreme Court reversed:

> Every element of the fraud here disclosed demands the exercise of the historic power of equity to set aside fraudulently begotten judgments. This is not simply a case of a judgment obtained with the aid of a witness who, on the basis of after-discovered evidence, is believed possibly to have been guilty of perjury. Here, even if we consider nothing but Hartford's sworn admissions, we find a deliberately planned and carefully executed scheme to defraud not only the Patent Office but the Circuit Court of Appeals. * * *

> The Circuit Court did not hold that Hartford's fraud fell short of that which prompts equitable intervention, but thought Hazel had not exercised proper diligence in uncovering the fraud and that this should stand in the way of its obtaining relief. We cannot easily understand how, under the admitted facts, Hazel should have been expected to do more than it did to uncover the fraud. But even if Hazel did not exercise the highest degree of diligence, Hartford's fraud cannot be condoned for that reason alone. This matter does not concern only private parties. There are issues of

great moment to the public in a patent suit. * * * Furthermore, tampering with the administration of justice in the manner indisputably shown here involves far more than an injury to a single litigant. It is a wrong against the institutions set up to protect and safeguard the public, institutions in which fraud cannot complacently be tolerated consistently with the good order of society. Surely it cannot be that preservation of the integrity of the judicial process must always wait upon the diligence of litigants. The public welfare demands that the agencies of public justice be not so impotent that they must always be mute and helpless victims of deception and fraud.

NOTES AND QUESTIONS

1. Does *Hazel-Atlas* stand for the proposition that a court on its own motion may set aside a judgment obtained by fraud on the court? Was it proper for the Court to find that there had been a fraud on the lower court? Different circuits have set out similar tests of what constitutes fraud on the court meriting the setting aside of a verdict. The Third Circuit, for example, requires the showing of an intentional act, by an officer of the court, directed at the court itself, which in fact deceives the court. See Herring v. United States, 424 F.3d 384 (3d Cir. 2005).

2. In PEACOCK RECORDS, INC. v. CHECKER RECORDS, INC., 365 F.2d 145, 147 (7th Cir. 1966), cert. denied, 385 U.S. 1003, 87 S.Ct. 707, 17 L.Ed.2d 542 (1967), the court of appeals reversed the denial of a Rule 60(b) motion as an abuse of discretion:

> * * * We hold that where it appears that perjured testimony may have played some part in influencing the court to render a judgment, the perjury will not be *weighed,* on a motion to set aside the judgment. This seems self evident. * * * [If the judgment was obtained in part by the use of perjury] then it was clearly the duty of the district court to set aside the judgment, because poison had permeated the fountain of justice.

However, in Philos Technologies, Inc. v. Philos & D, Inc., 802 F.2d 905 (7th Cir. 2015), the Seventh Circuit emphasized that the showing of fraud for Rule 60(b) relief must be clear and convincing, referring to *Peacock* as a case in which the basis for the motion was "incontrovertible * * * evidence of perjury," because "the witnesses were willing to testify that they had perjured themselves." Id. at 918.

c. The Independent Action to Obtain Relief from a Prior Judgment

---

Reread Federal Rule of Civil Procedure 60(d) and the accompanying materials in the Supplement.

NOTES AND QUESTIONS

1. Federal Rule 60(d) is a "savings clause" that permits an independent action to be brought to attack a judgment that is older than one year. As the Sixth Circuit has explained:

> * * * Independent actions for relief under this section "must, if Rule 60(b) is to be interpreted as a coherent whole, be reserved for those cases of 'injustice which, in certain instances, are deemed sufficiently gross to demand a departure' from rigid adherence to the doctrine of *res judicata.*" [United States v. Beggerly, 524 U.S. 38, 46, 118 S.Ct. 1862, 1867, 141 L.Ed.2d 32, 40 (1998) (quoting Hazel-Atlas Glass Co. v. Hartford-Empire Co., 322 U.S. 238, 244, 64 S.Ct. 997, 1000, 88 L.Ed.1250, 1255 (1944)).]

> We have set forth the elements of such an independent cause of action as:

> (1) a judgment which ought not, in equity and good conscience, to be enforced; (2) a good defense to the alleged cause of action on which the judgment is founded; (3) fraud, accident, or mistake which prevented the defendant in the judgment from obtaining the benefit of his defense; (4) the absence of fault or negligence on the part of the defendant; and (5) the absence of any adequate remedy at law.

MARCELLI v. WALKER, 313 Fed.Appx. 839 (6th Cir. 2009), citing Barrett v. Sec'y of Health & Human Servs., 840 F.2d 1259, 1263 (6th Cir. 1987) (citations omitted).

2. Many jurisdictions permit an independent action in equity to set aside a judgment. Fraud is one of the substantive grounds upon which relief may be granted in such an action. Suppose that instead of putting forth false information, a party merely conceals facts of which she has direct knowledge that would have a definite bearing on the outcome of the case. Does this constitute fraud? Does the distinction between extrinsic and intrinsic fraud affect whether the motion will be granted? For an extensive analysis of the bases for a Rule 60(d) motion, see Benham, Twombly *and* Iqbal *Should (Finally!) Put the Distinction Between Intrinsic and Extrinsic Fraud Out of Its Misery,* 64 SMU L.Rev. 649 (2011). Should the plausible pleading standard

apply to such an independent action? See Hague, *Fraud on the Court and Abusive Discovery*, 16 Nev.L.J. 707 (2016).

CHAPTER 14

APPELLATE REVIEW

■ ■ ■

This chapter considers appellate review on a number of levels. First, there is the question of timing. When can a litigant obtain review of a court order? Must the appellant await a final decision in the action or may the matter be reviewed at once? Second, there is the question of who may seek review of a court decision. To what extent, for example, should a person who prevailed in a case be able to appeal an adverse determination of the court, one made along the way, that could have an impact on future cases? Should the right to appeal be limited to parties who originally litigated a case? Third, there is the question of the appellate court's jurisdiction and the standard of review to be used. As you read these materials consider how the availability of appellate review affects other aspects of the judicial proceeding, such as discovery, case management, and sanctions.

A. THE PRINCIPLE OF FINALITY

1. APPLICATION OF THE BASIC CONCEPT

———

Read 28 U.S.C. §§ 1291 and 1292 in the Supplement.

———

COOPER, EXTRAORDINARY WRIT PRACTICE IN CRIMINAL CASES: ANALOGIES FOR THE MILITARY COURTS, 98 F.R.D. 593, 594–96 (1983):

A truly final judgment is one that marks the completion of all the events that will occur in a trial court. Nothing more remains to be done, unless it be execution of a judgment against the defendant.

The advantages that may be gained by deferring appeals until entry of a truly final judgment are familiar, and can be summarized in short order. Immediate review of every ruling made by a trial court could not be tolerated. Repeated interruptions and delays could put the trial process beyond any reasonable control, even if appeals were taken only when there was a good faith and reasonable belief that the court was wrong. The opportunities for less honorable delay and harassment of an adversary also would not go entirely unexploited. More limited opportunities for interlocutory review would not be so disastrous, but would carry some part of the same costs. The possible advantages to be set against these costs arise from the opportunity to correct a wrong ruling. These advantages, however, are reduced by the prospects that most trial court rulings are correct; that wrong rulings often are corrected by the trial court; and that uncorrected wrong rulings will not, in the end, taint the final judgment.

The price that is paid for a final judgment rule, however, can be high. An erroneous ruling may taint everything that follows. If appeal must be delayed until final judgment, it may become necessary to repeat the entire trial proceeding. The costs of repeating the trial go beyond the obvious costs of expense and anxiety. The further proceedings will be held later, and may suffer from lapses of memory, inconsequential inconsistencies that are blown into exaggerated importance, and actual loss of evidence. Beyond these defects, the retrial proceedings often will be affected by lessons learned at the first trial. * * * The problem is more than one of boredom; strategies have been revealed and must be revised, opportunities to sustain truth by impeachment are diminished, and so on.

* * *

Beyond the impact on individual cases, loss of the opportunity for interlocutory review means that some areas of law must develop without much opportunity for appellate guidance. Questions of discovery, for example, may confuse and divide trial courts for years without the guidance and uniformity that appeals could provide.

NOTE AND QUESTIONS

Appellate review serves a number of purposes. One goal is to correct errors made by the court of original jurisdiction. A related goal is to develop a consistent body of law to be followed in future cases. See Shavell, *The Appeals Process as a Means of Error Correction*, 24 J. Legal Stud. 379, 379–80, 416, 425–26 (1995). Yet a third goal is to meet the public's "demand for justice," which assumes that "important grievances [will] be heard and resolved by the highest possible governmental authority." Kelso, *A Report on the California Appellate System*, 45 Hastings L.J. 433, 434–35 (1994) How does the requirement of finality promote or undermine these goals?

2. THE NEW YORK APPROACH

New York allows appeals as of right to the state's intermediate appellate court—the Appellate Division—in a great many situations in which no final judgment has been rendered. Read the New York provision, N.Y.C.P.L.R. 5701, which is found in the Supplement following 28 U.S.C. § 1292.

KORN, CIVIL JURISDICTION OF THE NEW YORK COURT OF
APPEALS AND APPELLATE DIVISIONS, 16 Buffalo L.Rev. 307, 332
(1967):

> Today * * * it is well known that there is hardly a question of
> practice that cannot be appealed; and, if a matter is said to be
> addressed to the court's discretion or favor, this may mean a more
> limited scope of review but will rarely affect appealability.
> Appeals on practice matters are legion, ranging far and wide over
> questions of venue, parties, consolidation and joint trial, pleading
> and pre-trial disclosure. The only meaningful method of inquiry
> as to the content of the present standards is to examine the types
> of orders that have been held *not* to involve some part of the merits
> or affect a substantial right.

NOTE AND QUESTIONS

In refusing to allow an appeal from an interlocutory order, an unnecessary
appellate hearing may be avoided; in allowing an appeal, an unnecessary trial
may be avoided, either by disposing of the case at that stage or by correcting
in advance of trial an error that might otherwise require a new trial. Is there
any basis for supposing that the appellate hearing is more likely to prove
unnecessary than the trial? Is it relevant that the trial judge, hopefully, will
be correct in his rulings more often than he is wrong? Is it better to resolve the
question of allowing an interlocutory appeal by weighing the advantages and
disadvantages against each other in the abstract or by considering them as
they apply in each case?

Even if it is assumed that a reversal of the trial court's order by the
appellate court is as probable as its affirmance and consideration is taken of
the possibility that trial may demand more time of lawyers and judges than an
appeal, does it follow that interlocutory appeals should be freely allowed?
Consider the effect of the following factors:

(1)   In the course of a single lawsuit there may be many interlocutory
      orders from which one of the parties would like to appeal; thus,
      if finality is required, several appeals may be saved for every
      trial saved under the other approach.

(2)   Not every reversal of an interlocutory order will terminate the
      case without trial.

(3)   The number of appellate courts cannot be increased as readily
      as can the number of trial courts in order to take care of heavier
      calendars. There will be a serious problem as long as it is the
      function of appellate courts not only to review trial court
      decisions but also to establish and maintain a degree of
      uniformity in the law.

3. DEPARTURES FROM THE FINAL JUDGMENT RULE IN THE FEDERAL COURTS

a. Defining "Finality"

i. *Cases Involving Multiple Claims*

———

Read Federal Rule of Civil Procedure 54(b) and the accompanying materials in the Supplement.

———

SEARS, ROEBUCK & CO. v. MACKEY, 351 U.S. 427, 76 S.Ct. 895, 100 L.Ed. 1297 (1956). Mackey brought suit for damages against Sears, Roebuck under the Sherman Antitrust Act (Counts I and II) and under common law for unlawfully inducing a breach of contract (Count III) and unfair competition and patent infringement (Count IV). The district court dismissed only those claims presented in Counts I and II. On appeal to the Court of Appeals for the Seventh Circuit, the court upheld its appellate jurisdiction under 28 U.S.C. § 1291. The Supreme Court affirmed.

The Court noted that before the promulgation of the Federal Rules, no appeal would have been allowed from the final determination of Counts I and II since the district court's judgment was not a final decision of the whole case. However, with the adoption of the Federal Rules and the subsequent increase in multiple-claim actions, the promulgators recognized the need to ameliorate the standard that "*all* claims had to be finally decided before an appeal could be entertained from a final decision upon any of them." Id. at 434, 76 S.Ct. at 899, 100 L.Ed. at 1305. Consequently, Rule 54(b) was adopted.

> * * * [Rule 54(b), as amended in 1946,] does not relax the finality required of each decision, as an individual claim, to render it appealable, but it does provide a practical means of permitting an appeal to be taken from one or more final decisions on individual claims, in multiple claims actions, without waiting for final decisions to be rendered on *all* the claims in the case. * * *

> To meet the demonstrated need for flexibility, the District Court is used as a "dispatcher." It is permitted to determine, in the first instance, the appropriate *time when each "final decision"* upon "one or more but less than all" of the claims in a multiple claims action is ready for appeal. This arrangement already has lent welcome certainty to the appellate procedure. Its "negative effect" has met with uniform approval. The effect so referred to is the rule's specific requirement that for "one or more but less than all"

multiple claims to become appealable, the District Court must make both "an express determination that there is no just reason for delay" and "an express direction for the entry of judgment." A party adversely affected by a final decision thus knows that his time for appeal will *not* run against him until this certification has been made.

* * *

In the case before us, there is no doubt that each of the claims dismissed is a "claim for relief" within the meaning of Rule 54(b), or that their dismissal constitutes a "final decision" on individual claims. Also, it cannot well be argued that the claims stated in Counts I and II are so inherently inseparable from, or closely related to, those stated in Counts III and IV that the District Court has abused its discretion in certifying that there exists no just reason for delay. They certainly *can* be decided independently of each other.

* * *

* * * The District Court *cannot,* in the exercise of its discretion, treat as "final" that which is not "final" within the meaning of § 1291. But the District Court *may,* by the exercise of its discretion in the interest of sound judicial administration, release for appeal final decisions upon one or more, but less than all, claims in multiple claims actions. The timing of such a release is, with good reason, vested by the rule primarily in the discretion of the District Court as the one most likely to be familiar with the case and with any justifiable reasons for delay. * * *

* * * [Rule 54] does not supersede any statute controlling appellate jurisdiction. It scrupulously recognizes the statutory requirement of a "final decision" under § 1291 as a basic requirement for an appeal to the Court of Appeals. It merely administers that requirement in a practical manner in multiple claims actions and does so by rule instead of by judicial decision. By its negative effect, it operates to restrict in a valid manner the number of appeals in multiple claims actions.

We reach a like conclusion as to the validity of the amended rule where the District Court acts affirmatively and thus assists in properly timing the release of final decisions in multiple claims actions. The amended rule adapts the single judicial unit theory so that it better meets the current needs of judicial administration. Just as Rule 54(b), in its original form, resulted in the release of some decisions on claims in multiple claims actions before they otherwise would have been released, so amended Rule 54(b) now makes possible the release of more of such decisions subject to judicial supervision. The amended rule preserves the historic federal policy against piecemeal appeals in many cases more effectively than did original rule.

Id. at 435–38, 76 S.Ct. at 899–901, 100 L.Ed. at 1306–07.

NOTES AND QUESTIONS

1.　In the principal case, the Court declined to provide a hard and fast definition of claim for purposes of Rule 54(b). Would it be best to conform the definition to the test used under Rule 8 for pleading? Under 28 U.S.C. § 1367 for supplemental jurisdiction? Under Rule 20 for claim joinder? Under the doctrine of claim preclusion?

2.　The Supreme Court has not yet provided a generally accepted test for whether one claim or multiple claims are before the trial court. However, lower court decisions provide some insight. The Fifth Circuit, for example, has held that certification is not available "where a court disposes of an affirmative defense, or even every affirmative defense raised by the defendant" unless the court "makes an express holding as to liability"; "where the district court rules on some issues concerning a claim," but does not complete the analysis because of outstanding factual issue;" and where the district court has resolved a threshold issue relevant to a claim, but has not resolved the claim itself. Tetra Technologies, Inc. v. Continental Ins. Co., 755 F.3d 222, 230 (5th Cir. 2014).

ii.　Decisions Involving "Collateral Orders"

In COHEN v. BENEFICIAL INDUSTRIAL LOAN CORP., 337 U.S. 541, 69 S.Ct. 1221, 93 L.Ed. 1528 (1949), see, pp. 328–329, Note 3, supra, Cohen brought a shareholder's derivative suit in a New Jersey federal court. The district court denied Beneficial's motion to require Cohen to post security for costs pursuant to a New Jersey statute, holding the statute inapplicable to an action in a federal court. The court of appeals reversed, and the Supreme Court affirmed that decision. The Justices addressed the question of appealability in the following passage:

> * * * Appeal gives the upper court a power of review, not one of intervention. So long as the matter remains open, unfinished or inconclusive, there may be no intrusion by appeal. But the District Court's action upon this application was concluded and closed and its decision final in that sense before the appeal was taken.
>
> Nor does the statute permit appeals, even from fully consummated decisions, where they are but steps towards final judgment in which they will merge. The purpose is to combine in one review all stages of the proceeding that effectively may be reviewed and corrected if and when final judgment results. But this order of the District Court did not make any step toward final

disposition of the merits of the case and will not be merged in final judgment. When that time comes, it will be too late effectively to review the present order and the rights conferred by the statute, if it is applicable, will have been lost, probably irreparably. We conclude that the matters embraced in the decision appealed from are not of such an interlocutory nature as to affect, or to be affected by, decision of the merits of this case.

This decision appears to fall in that small class which finally determine claims of right separable from, and collateral to, rights asserted in the action, too important to be denied review and too independent of the cause itself to require that appellate consideration be deferred until the whole case is adjudicated. The Court has long given this provision of the statute this practical rather than a technical construction. * * *

We hold this order appealable because it is a final disposition of a claimed right which is not an ingredient of the cause of action and does not require consideration with it. * * * Here it is the right to security that presents a serious and unsettled question. If the right were admitted or clear and the order involved only an exercise of discretion as to the amount of security, a matter the statute makes subject to reconsideration from time to time, appealability would present a different question.

Id. at 545, 69 S.Ct. at 1225, 93 L.Ed. at 1536.

NOTES AND QUESTIONS

1.   In MOHAWK INDUSTRIES, INC. v. CARPENTER, 558 U.S. 100, 130 S.Ct. 599, 175 L.Ed.2d 258 (2009), the Court held that a discovery order compelling a defendant to disclose information it claimed was protected by the attorney-client privilege did not qualify for immediate appeal under the collateral order doctrine; the Court reasoned that litigants could be sufficiently protected by post-judgment appeal. There are numerous other examples of the unavailability of appeal based on the collateral order doctrine despite hardship for the party seeking an appeal and the potential waste of resources. For example, in WILL v. HALLOCK, 546 U.S. 345, 126 S.Ct. 952, 163 L.Ed.2d 836 (2006), the Supreme Court held that an order rejecting the judgment bar of the Federal Tort Claims Act as a defense by federal officials was not immediately appealable.

2.   When a party refuses to obey a court order and has been held in criminal contempt the issue is so distinct from the underlying case, and so important, that an appeal will be permitted under the collateral order doctrine. See United States v. Ryan, 402 U.S. 530, 91 S.Ct. 1580, 29 L.Ed.2d 85 (1971). Indeed, in UNITED STATES v. NIXON, 418 U.S. 683, 690–92, 94 S.Ct. 3090, 3098–99, 41 L.Ed.2d 1039, 1053–55 (1974), interlocutory appeal was permitted even though there was no contempt. The case involved an order that the

President of the United States produce tape recordings for examination by a federal judge. The President had not refused to comply and thus had not been held in contempt. The Court explained: "To require a President of the United States to place himself in the posture of disobeying an order of a court merely to trigger the procedural mechanism for review of the ruling would be unseemly, and would present an unnecessary occasion for constitutional confrontation between two branches of Government." Does *Nixon* stand for a unique exception, or might other situations be so exceptional as to warrant an immediate appeal without a finding of contempt?

3.   In COOPERS & LYBRAND v. LIVESAY, 437 U.S. 463, 98 S.Ct. 2454, 57 L.Ed.2d 351 (1978), the Court held that the denial of class certification under Federal Rule 23 is not appealable under the collateral order doctrine. The Court explained:

> To come within the "small class" of decisions excepted from the final-judgment rule by *Cohen*, the order must conclusively determine the disputed question, resolve an important issue completely separate from the merits of the action, and be effectively unreviewable on appeal from a final judgment. * * * An order passing on a request for class certification does not fall in that category. First, such an order is subject to revision in the District Court. * * * Second, the class determination generally involves considerations that are "enmeshed in the factual and legal issues comprising the plaintiff's cause of action." * * * Finally, an order denying class certification is subject to effective review after final judgment at the behest of the named plaintiff or intervening class members. * * *

Id. at 468–69, 98 S.Ct. at 2458, 57 L.Ed.2d at 378–58. See p. 551, supra, for a discussion of Federal Rule 23(f), which now permits discretionary interlocutory appeal of class certification decisions.

iii. Decisions Based on "Pragmatic Finality"

In BROWN SHOE CO. v. UNITED STATES, 370 U.S. 294, 82 S.Ct. 1502, 8 L.Ed.2d 510 (1962), the district court found defendant had violated the antitrust laws and directed divestiture of a subsidiary, but it reserved its ruling on a specific plan of divestiture. On a direct appeal by the shoe company, the Supreme Court held the divestiture decree was sufficiently final to be appealable even though a specific plan had not been formulated. Its own past practice, said the Court, had been to hear such appeals in antitrust cases; the substantive aspects of the case had been fully determined and to delay decision on the merits would chill the "careful, and often extended, negotiation and formulation" of the final divestiture order.

NOTE AND QUESTIONS

In UNITED STATES v. COPAR PUMICE CO., INC., 714 F.3d 1197 (10th Cir. 2013), an action against a mine operator and others for the wrongful removal of undersized pumice from their mine, defendants sought to appeal the denial of a protective order for documents from law firms that had provided legal advice about mining. The Tenth Circuit held that an interlocutory appeal was not available under the collateral order doctrine as interpreted in *Mohawk Industries*, p. 807, Note 1, supra, or under the doctrine of pragmatic finality:

> * * * Defendants attempt to distinguish *Mohawk* by focusing on whether the subpoenaed documents were sought from a nonparty, or from a party to the litigation. * * *

> Defendants' quote omits the remaining part of the sentence. The Supreme Court stated that "litigants confronted with a particularly injurious or novel privilege ruling have *several potential avenues of review* apart from collateral order appeal." * * * Specifically, the Court delineated three potential avenues: 1) the party could ask the district court to certify an appeal under 28 U.S.C. § 1292(b); 2) the party could petition the court of appeals for a writ of mandamus; and 3) the party could defy the disclosure order and incur sanctions or be held in contempt when "characterized as a criminal punishment." * * * While the third avenue of review is arguably unavailable to Defendants because they were not the custodian of the subpoenaed documents, the first and second avenues of review are available. Defendants do not mention these available avenues, or explain how the unavailability of one of these three avenues would render *Mohawk* wholly distinguishable.

> * * *

> Finally, Defendants argue that jurisdiction is proper pursuant to the pragmatic finality doctrine. Under this doctrine, a "court may assume jurisdiction where the danger of injustice by delaying appellate review outweighs the inconvenience and costs of piecemeal review." * * * This court has described the pragmatic finality doctrine as "more subjective" than the collateral order doctrine, involving "ad hoc adjustments to the final decision requirement of § 1291." * * *

> To the extent this doctrine is still recognized, it must be "invoked only in truly 'unique instances,'" and not when the dispute can be adequately reviewed on appeal from a final judgment. * * * We have questioned the pragmatic finality doctrine's "continued viability for the last fifteen [plus] years," and continue to do so after *Mohawk*. * * *

> Defendants argue that the present appeal is a unique or exceptional circumstance because this court has not decisively answered whether federal or state law governs the privilege asserted. However, Defendants neither explain the importance of deciding this legal issue on immediate appeal, nor have Defendants shown that the danger of injustice by delaying appellate review outweighs the inconvenience and costs of piecemeal review. Defendants' interests in immediate review center on their desire to prevent information they

deem privileged from disclosure, but the Supreme Court has already found such interests insufficient to warrant immediate appeal. * * *

Id. at 1204–06, 1209–10.

b. Avoidance or Evasion of the Basic Concept—Mandamus

Read 28 U.S.C. § 1651(a) in the Supplement.

NOTES AND QUESTIONS

1.   In SCHLAGENHAUF v. HOLDER, 379 U.S. 104, 85 S.Ct. 234, 13 L.Ed.2d 152 (1964), the substantive aspects of which are set out at p. 632, supra, the Court upheld the use of mandamus to review an order requiring defendant to submit to a physical and mental examination:

> It is, of course, well settled that the writ is not to be used as a substitute for appeal * * * even though hardship may result from delay and perhaps unnecessary trial * * *. The writ is appropriately issued, however, when there is "usurpation of judicial power" or a clear abuse of discretion * * *.

> [T]he challenged order * * * appears to be the first of its kind in any reported decision in the federal courts under Rule 35 * * *.

> * * * It is thus appropriate for us to determine on the merits the issues presented and to formulate the necessary guidelines in this area. * * *

> This is not to say, however, that following the setting of guidelines in this opinion, any future allegation that the District Court was in error in applying these guidelines to a particular case makes mandamus an appropriate remedy.

Id. at 110–12, 85 S.Ct. at 238–39, 13 L.Ed.2d at 156–60.

2.   Many of the Supreme Court's decisions regarding mandamus concern discovery disputes. In CHENEY v. UNITED STATES DISTRICT COURT, 542 U.S. 367, 124 S.Ct. 2576, 159 L.Ed.2d 459 (2004), the Vice President of the United States sought a writ of mandamus to halt discovery of the National Energy Policy Development Group, an Executive Branch task force charged with making policy recommendations to the President. The court of appeals declined to issue the writ because it regarded the possible assertion of executive privilege as an available avenue of relief. The Supreme Court reversed and set out a three-part test for issuance of the writ of mandamus: there must be "no other adequate means" to attain the relief sought; the movant bears the burden of showing that the right to relief is "clear and indisputable"; and the issuing court in its discretion "must be satisfied that the

writ is appropriate under the circumstances." Id. at 380–81, 124 S.Ct. at 2587, 159 L.Ed.2d at 477–78 (internal quotations and citations omitted). Would a discovery dispute not involving a high ranking official ever meet this test? See Fullerton, *Exploring the Far Reaches of Mandamus*, 49 Brooklyn L.Rev. 1131, 1152 (1983).

3.   Mandamus relief as a form of interlocutory review is used sparingly, and, as a result, many intermediate procedural decisions by the district court that may have profound implications for the lawsuit are not reviewed until a final judgment is entered. These interlocutory decisions include: change of venue under 28 U.S.C. § 1404; declining to exercise supplemental jurisdiction under 28 U.S.C. § 1367(c); and legal rulings rendered in multidistrict litigation under 28 U.S.C. § 1407. Which of these issues seems most pressing from the perspective of the goals of appellate review—error correction, legal uniformity, and public trust? Would it be appropriate to provide a method of appeal other than mandamus for these issues?

c.   Displacement of the Basic Concept—Discretionary Appeals

———

Read 28 U.S.C. §§ 1292(b) and 1292(e) in the Supplement.

———

ATLANTIC CITY ELECTRIC CO. v. GENERAL ELECTRIC CO.
United States Court of Appeals, Second Circuit, 1964.
337 F.2d 844.

PER CURIAM. The district court has certified pursuant to Section 1292(b) * * * that its order, sustaining objections to interrogatories designed to discover whether damages were actually sustained by plaintiffs who may have shifted such damages, if any, to their customers of electricity, involves a controlling question of law in these litigations and that there is substantial ground for differences of opinion. * * *

In sustaining the objections to the interrogatories posed, the district court has, in effect, foreclosed defendants from pre-trial discovery of facts relating to a defense that plaintiffs have "passed-on" to their customers any damages incurred by plaintiffs and hence are not entitled to recover to the extent that defendants can prove such passing-on.

Upon this application for leave to appeal it would not be appropriate to isolate and endeavor to decide before an appeal from any final judgment this particular question of law. Pre-trial leave to appeal applications must be decided against the background of the entire case. Many important questions of law will undoubtedly arise in these cases but the problem now confronting us is the feasibility and advisability of trying to decide this particular question in advance of trial.

If pre-trial discovery were allowed as defendants request it could easily develop into a multitude of full scale rate cases which could dwarf in time and testimony the already extensive pre-trial proceedings. If the district court is in error * * * defendants will have full opportunity in the event of an adverse judgment, if based in whole or in part upon this error, to have it corrected upon appeal together with any other errors which may be urged. It is doubtful that any discoveries or hearings required to establish the extent of any damages, if the passing-on-doctrine applies, would be more burdensome than now. Since defendants' rights to this defense are not being taken away or prejudiced on any ultimate appeal by denial of the pre-trial appeal now sought, we believe that the ultimate disposition of these cases would be delayed rather than advanced by granting this application.

Application denied.

NOTES AND QUESTIONS

1.   Under 28 U.S.C. § 1292(b) the court considers many of the same factors used to determine whether there is "no just reason for delay" for the issuance of a Federal Rule 54(b) certificate. In what respects do the two statutes differ?

2.   When is a question of law considered to be "controlling" or subject to a "substantial ground for disagreement"? Must the issue be "dispositive" of the lawsuit in order to be considered controlling? Is it sufficient that the issue could produce "reversible error" on final appeal? Does the party's "strong disagreement" with the district court's ruling deserve any weight? For a discussion of these questions and an emphasis on the exceptional nature of review under 28 U.S.C. § 1292(b), see In re Cement Antitrust Litigation, 673 F.2d 1020 (9th Cir. 1982).

3.   Is review limited to the question that the trial court identifies in its certified order? In YAMAHA MOTOR CORP. v. CALHOUN, 516 U.S. 199, 116 S.Ct. 619, 133 L.Ed.2d 578 (1996), involved the death of a 12-year-old in the territorial waters off Puerto Rico while riding a jet ski manufactured by petitioner. The district court certified the question of whether particular items of damages were available under the federal maritime wrongful death action. The Third Circuit granted interlocutory review, but then considered the antecedent question of whether state remedies remained available in maritime accidents of this sort. The Supreme Court held that although a jurisdiction under 28 U.S.C. § 1292(b) is limited to the order certified by the district court, it "is not tied to the particular question formulated by the district court." Rather, "the appellate court may address any issue fairly included within the certified order," because it is the order—and not the controlling question—that is appealable. Id. at 205, 116 S.Ct. at 623, 133 L.Ed.2d at 585. However, in UNITED STATES v. STANLEY, 483 U.S. 669, 677, 107 S.Ct. 3054, 3060, 97 L.Ed.2d 550, 563 (1987), a damages action brought by a former serviceman, the Supreme Court appeared to hold that appellate jurisdiction is limited to

the certified order and does not reach "any other orders that may have been entered in the case." The Court has relied on *Yamaha's* reasoning to justify appellate review under 28 U.S.C. § 1447(d) of all bases for an order remanding a case to state court even though only one ground for removal would independently support appellate jurisdiction. See p. 276, Note 3, supra.

4.   Since 1992 the Supreme Court has had power pursuant to 28 U.S.C. § 1292(e) to promulgate rules permitting interlocutory appeals from any orders that it deems appropriate. So far, the Court has used this power only once, to add Federal Rule 23(f) for the interlocutory appeal of an order granting or denying class certification. How would Rule 23(f) affect the result in *Coopers & Lybrand*, p. 808, Note 3, supra? How does Rule 23(f) differ from 28 U.S.C. § 1292(b)?

In MICROSOFT CORP. v. BAKER, 137 S.Ct. 1702, 198 L.Ed.2d 132 (2017), consumers filed a putative class action. After the district court denied class certification as well as permission to appeal the denial under Federal Rule 23(f), plaintiffs voluntarily dismissed their individual claims with prejudice but reserved the right to revive the claims if the district court order was reversed on appeal. The Supreme Court held that the voluntary dismissal did not qualify as a final order under 28 U.S.C. § 1291, and that allowing an appeal would undermine "Rule 23(f)'s careful calibration." Id. at 1715, 198 L.Ed.2d at 146. See p. 551, supra.

5.   Should the Court's rulemaking power be used to authorize mandatory interlocutory review for the situations identified in p. 811, Note 3, supra? See Glynn, *Discontent and Indiscretion: Discretionary Review of Interlocutory Orders*, 77 Notre Dame L.Rev. 175, 180 (2001). Would it be advisable to limit such review to questions of unsettled law?

d.   An Historical Footnote to the Basic Concept—Injunctions

———

Read 28 U.S.C. § 1292(a)(1) and Federal Rules of Civil Procedure 65(a) and (b) in the Supplement.

———

SMITH v. VULCAN IRON WORKS, 165 U.S. 518, 525, 17 S.Ct. 407, 410, 41 L.Ed. 810, 812 (1897):

> The manifest intent of this provision, read in the light of the previous practice in the courts of the United States, contrasted with the practice in courts of equity of the highest authority elsewhere, appears to this court to have been, not only to permit the defendant to obtain immediate relief from an injunction, the continuance of which throughout the progress of the cause might seriously affect his interests, but also to save both parties from the expense of further litigation, should the appellate court be of

opinion that the plaintiff was not entitled to an injunction because his bill had no equity to support it.

NOTES AND QUESTIONS

1.   What is the justification for allowing appeals from interlocutory orders granting or refusing injunctions? Do these reasons apply to orders granting or denying preliminary injunctions? Would it work just as well to relegate the parties to discretionary appeals under 28 U.S.C. § 1292(b)? Why is it significant that injunctive orders are outside the scope of Federal Rule 54(b)?

2.   Is the grant or denial of a temporary restraining order under Federal Rule 65(b) appealable? See 28 U.S.C. § 1292(a)(1). Are the differences between preliminary injunctions and temporary restraining orders relevant to the question whether appeal should be permitted in the case of the former and not permitted in the case of the latter? In close cases it may be difficult to tell the difference between a preliminary injunction and a temporary restraining order.

In UNITED STATES v. WOOD, 295 F.2d 772 (5th Cir. 1961), cert. denied, 369 U.S. 850, 82 S.Ct. 933, 8 L.Ed.2d 9 (1962), a Black man who was active in voter registration in Mississippi was arrested for disturbing the peace and ordered to trial in fifteen days. Two days before trial, the United States, moving under 42 U.S.C. § 1971 and alleging that the prosecution would intimidate African-Americans in the exercise of their voting rights, brought suit to restrain the criminal action. A temporary restraining order was denied and the Government appealed. The court of appeals held that it had jurisdiction under Section 1291. Inasmuch as the case would quickly become moot if the restraining order was not issued, the court said, its denial was "a final disposition of the * * * claimed right. * * * [T]o call this de facto dismissal a nonappealable interlocutory order is to preclude review altogether." Id. at 777.

In GULFSTREAM AEROSPACE CORP. v. MAYACAMAS CORP., 485 U.S. 271, 108 S.Ct. 1133, 99 L.Ed.2d 296 (1988), the Supreme Court resolved that a district court's denial of a motion to stay or dismiss legal proceedings on equitable grounds is not automatically appealable under 28 U.S.C. § 1291(a)(1). Under *Gulfstream*, an order that has the practical effect of granting or denying an injunction is appealable under 28 U.S.C. § 1292(a) if it has serious, irreparable consequence.

B.   THE NOTICE AND TIME TO APPEAL

———

Read Federal Rule of Civil Procedure 58; Federal Rules of Appellate Procedure 3, 4, and 5; and the accompanying material in the Supplement.

———

NOTES AND QUESTIONS

1.   Under Appellate Rule 3, what must the notice of appeal include? In SMITH v. BARRY, 502 U.S. 244, 112 S.Ct. 678, 116 L.Ed.2d 678 (1992), an inmate, without consulting counsel, filed a notice of appeal while a motion for judgment notwithstanding the verdict was pending in his civil rights suit. The clerk for the court of appeals responded to the notice of appeal by sending all of the parties copies of the "informal brief" that the court uses in pro se appeals, and appellant returned his informal brief to the appellate court within the deadline for filing a notice of appeal. After appointment of counsel for appellant, the Fourth Circuit dismissed the appeal for want of jurisdiction. The Supreme Court reversed, holding that an appellate brief may serve as a notice of appeal under Appellate Rule 3 when it gives notice of the litigant's intent to seek review. On remand, the appeals court held that the informal brief sufficed as a notice of appeal with respect to six prison guards, but not to a prison psychologist. The informal brief asked for a "new trial on all issues triable by Jury," but did not mention the doctor and so notice was not provided. Smith v. Barry, 985 F.2d 180, 184 (4th Cir. 1993), cert. denied, 510 U.S. 874, 114 S.Ct. 207, 126 L.Ed.2d 164.

2.   In TORRES v. OAKLAND SCAVENGER CO., 487 U.S. 312, 108 S.Ct. 2405, 101 L.Ed.2d 285 (1988), the Court held that the court of appeals lacked jurisdiction over a litigant in a purported class action when the notice of appeal under Appellate Rule 3(c) used the term "et al." rather than listing the names of all of the appellants. The fact that the omission was due to a clerical error by the secretary employed by the litigant's attorney did not provide grounds for waiver. Although Appellate Rule 3(c) was amended in 1979 to add that an appeal "shall not be dismissed for informality of form or title of the notice of appeal," the Court emphasized that "[t]he failure to name a party in a notice of appeal is more than excusable 'informality'; it constitutes a failure of that party to appeal." Does the failure to list the parties' names in the notice of appeal raise due process concerns?

3.   What is the effect of a notice of appeal if it is filed before entry of judgment? See Appellate Rule 4(a)(2). The leading case on the effect of a premature notice of appeal, at least when the appeal is taken under 28 U.S.C. § 1291, is FIRSTIER MORTGAGE CO. v. INVESTORS MORTGAGE INSURANCE CO., 498 U.S. 269, 111 S.Ct. 648, 112 L.Ed.2d 743 (1991). The Court stated:

> In our view, Rule 4(a)(2) permits a notice of appeal from a nonfinal decision to operate as a notice of appeal from the final judgment only when a district court announces a decision that would be appealable if immediately followed by the entry of judgment. In these instances, a litigant's confusion is understandable, and permitting the notice of appeal to become effective when judgment is entered does not catch the appellee by surprise. * * *

Id. at 276, 111 S.Ct. at 653, 112 L.Ed.2d at 753. However, the Court went on to say that Rule 4(a)(2) does not permit a premature notice of appeal from a "clearly interlocutory decision—such as a discovery ruling or a sanction order under Rule 11" because a "belief that such a decision is a fatal judgment would *not* be reasonable." Id. at 276, 111 S.Ct. 648, 112 L.Ed.2d at 753.

4.   How does the filing of a post-judgment motion affect the time to file an appeal? See Appellate Rule 4(a)(4). Whether a motion falls within the rule has generated a great deal of confusion. In BUDINICH v. BECTON DICKINSON & CO., 486 U.S. 196, 108 S.Ct. 1717, 100 L.Ed.2d 178 (1988), the District Court determined plaintiff's new trial motion on May 14, leaving only the amount of attorney's fees to be decided. That motion was decided August 1, and plaintiff filed a notice of appeal on August 29. Citing, among other cases, *Brown Shoe,* p. 808, supra, the Court found that the May 14 order was a final judgment and dismissed the appeal as to all issues other than attorney's fees:

> We are not inclined to adopt a disposition that requires the merits or nonmerits status of each attorney's fee provision to be clearly established before [finality can be determined]. Courts and litigants are best served by the bright-line rule, which accords with traditional understanding, that a decision on the merits is a "final decision" for purposes of § 1291 whether or not there remains for adjudication a request for attorney's fees attributable to the case.

Id. at 202, 108 S.Ct. at 1722, 100 L.Ed.2d at 185. Appellate Rule 4(a)(4) was later amended to conform to *Budinich.* As the Advisory Committee Note explains, the revised rule "exclude[s] motions for attorney's fees from the class of motions that extend the filing time unless a district court, acting under Rule 58, enters an order extending the time for appeal."

5.   Appellate Rule 4(a)(5) permits the district court to extend the filing period, but only upon a finding of excusable neglect or good cause. PIONEER INVESTMENT SERVS. CO. v. BRUNSWICK ASSOC. LTD. PARTNERSHIP, 507 U.S. 380, 113 S.Ct. 1489, 123 L.Ed.2d 74 (1993), concerned the late filing of a proof of claim in the bankruptcy court. The Supreme Court found excusable neglect on the basis of a balancing of four factors: the party's good faith; the absence of any danger of prejudice to the opposing party; the length of the filing delay and its effect on the proceeding; and the reason for the delay. However, in BOWLES v. RUSSELL, 551 U.S. 205, 127 S.Ct. 2360, 168 L.Ed.2d 96 (2007), the Supreme Court made clear that the district court's authority to grant an extension of time is limited by the time periods set out in statute, and rejected as untimely a notice of appeal filed outside the statutory period but in conformity with the district court's order. The *Bowles* rationale is grounded in separation of powers, and does not apply to time limits set out in court rules, which are treated as claim-processing rules and may be subject to forfeiture. See Hamer v. Neighborhood Services of Chicago, 583 U.S. ___, 138 S.Ct. 13, 199 L.Ed.2d 249 (2017).

6.   In 1963 and again in 2002, Federal Rule 58 was amended to clarify when a judgment is considered entered and thus the time for appeal begins to run. When is a separate document not required for a judgment?

C. THE AMBIT OF APPELLATE REVIEW

1. ISSUES SUBJECT TO REVIEW

There are a number of well-defined limits on the scope of appellate review. First, the alleged errors must appear in the trial court record. Thus it is vital during the course of pretrial preparation as well as during trial itself that an attorney make certain that all rulings and evidence that might form the basis for an appeal be formally recorded. Second, an aggrieved party must have objected promptly to the trial court regarding rulings or events that the judge could have corrected or ameliorated. Normally an error is waived unless a proper objection was taken. Third, even if the issue that the appellant seeks to have reviewed has been presented properly below and has not been waived, it must not constitute "harmless error"—that is, it must have affected substantial rights. See Federal Rule 61. Fourth, an alleged error must be presented to the appellate court in appellant's brief and the relevant portions of the trial court record must be brought to the appellate court's attention. Finally, even when the issues have been preserved properly in the trial court and presented to the appellate court for review, an appellate court generally will not entertain an appeal by the party who, at least ostensibly, won below. See ELECTRICAL FITTINGS CORP. v. THOMAS & BETTS CO., 308 U.S. 241, 59 S.Ct. 860, 83 L.Ed. 1263 (1939).

In JENNINGS v. STEPHENS, 574 U.S. 271, 135 S.Ct. 793, 190 L.Ed.2d 662 (2015), the Supreme Court emphasized the difference between a court's adjudication of different theories for relief and its adjudication of different forms of relief. The petitioner sought habeas relief in the district court on grounds of ineffective assistance of counsel during the sentencing phase of his state court capital murder trial. He advanced three theories for why his trial counsel had been constitutionally ineffective. The district court ruled in petitioner's favor on the first two theories but rejected the third; the court then entered judgment ordering the state to give petitioner a new sentencing hearing or commute his sentence or else release him. When the state appealed to the Fifth Circuit, petitioner defended the district court's ruling on the first two theories but also argued that the district court should have granted habeas relief on the third theory as well. The court of appeals rejected the district court's decision on the first two theories and declined to consider petitioner's arguments on the third theory because he had not filed a cross-appeal.

The Supreme Court reversed and held that petitioner was not required to take a cross-appeal in order for the court of appeals to consider his arguments on the third theory. Justice Scalia, writing for the Court, explained that "[a] prevailing party seeks to enforce not a district court's reasoning, but the court's judgment." Petitioner had not sought on appeal to enlarge the relief ordered by the district court or otherwise to alter the rights granted by the district court's judgment. The district court had entered judgment in his favor, and there was nothing for him to cross-appeal, because petitioner, "whether prevailing on a single theory or all three, sought the same, indivisible relief: a new sentencing hearing." Id. at 282, 135 S.Ct. at 802, 190 L.Ed. at 671.

2. REVIEW OF FACT FINDING

Read Federal Rules of Civil Procedure 52 and 59 and the Seventh Amendment to the United States Constitution in the Supplement.

a. Fact Finding in Cases Decided by a Jury

CORCORAN V. CITY OF CHICAGO
Supreme Court of Illinois, 1940.
373 Ill. 567, 27 N.E.2d 451.

MURPHY, JUSTICE. John F. Corcoran * * * began a suit * * * against the city of Chicago * * * to recover damages for personal injuries alleged to have been caused by the negligent acts of the defendant. The cause was tried with a jury and resulted in a verdict for the plaintiff for $5,000. A motion for new trial was overruled and judgment entered on the verdict. On appeal, the Appellate Court for the First District reversed the judgment and remanded the cause for another trial. The plaintiff filed a motion in the Appellate Court asking that the remanding part of the order be stricken [in order that on appeal to the state Supreme Court, that court could then order that the initial verdict be reinstated]. * * * The motion was granted * * *.

The negligence charged was that defendant had carelessly and negligently permitted certain streets to be and remain in an unsafe condition for travel * * *. The evidence was conflicting. The Appellate Court found the verdict was against the manifest weight of the evidence and reversed the judgment for that reason.

It is conceded the power which the Appellate Court assumed to exercise in reviewing the evidence and setting aside the verdict is found in section 92(3b) of the Civil Practice Act * * * which provides that Appellate Courts may review "error of fact, in that the judgment, decree or order appealed from is not sustained by the evidence or is against the weight of the evidence." Plaintiff's position is that such provision, as applied to facts found by a jury upon conflicting evidence, as in the instant case, is unconstitutional, in that the findings of the Appellate Court * * * take from him the right to a trial by jury as guaranteed by section 5 of article 2 of the [Illinois] Constitution * * *.

* * *

Prior to 1837, the law of this state was that the granting or refusal of a motion for a new trial rested in the sound discretion of the trial court and the ruling thereon could not be urged as error in the court of review. * * * In 1837, an act was passed which provided "exceptions taken to opinions or decisions of circuit court overruling motions in arrest of judgment, motions for new trials and for continuance of causes shall hereafter be allowed and the party excepting may assign for error any opinion so excepted to, any usage to the contrary notwithstanding." The substance of the act * * * has been the statutory law of this state since 1837.

* * *

The effect of the operation of the statute was considered in Chicago & Rock Island Railroad Co. v. McKean, 40 Ill. 218, a case where the trial court had overruled a motion for new trial and error was assigned on such ruling. Mr. Justice Breese, speaking for the court, said: "An appellate court was, before the passage of that act, judge of the law only * * *. The old and honored maxim once was, 'the judges respond to the law, the jury to the facts,' but now, by this innovation, the judges of an appellate court have as much power over the facts as the jury had in the first instance, for it is undeniable this court may set aside a verdict if the facts fail to satisfy it of its propriety. * * *"

Plaintiff contends that on all questions of fact where the evidence is conflicting the verdict of the jury can not be set aside as being against the weight of the evidence except by the court that tried the case, and asserts that such was the practice at common law. * * *

From the authorities cited and others which have been examined, we conclude that there was a practice at common law which authorized courts exercising appellate jurisdiction to set aside verdicts on the grounds the findings of fact were not supported by the evidence. * * *

Judgment affirmed.

NOTES AND QUESTIONS

1.   How does the reviewing court's role differ when the trial court has denied the motion for a new trial on the weight of the evidence and when it has granted the motion? See Carrington, *The Power of District Judges and the Responsibility of Courts of Appeals*, 3 Ga.L.Rev. 507 (1969); Schnapper, *Judges Against Juries—Appellate Review of Federal Civil Jury Verdicts*, 1989 Wis.L.Rev. 237, 298–313.

2.   In the federal system, the appellate court applies an abuse of discretion standard in reviewing the district court's denial of a Rule 59(a) motion for a new trial based upon the alleged excessiveness of the jury's compensatory damage award, giving "the benefit of every doubt to the judgment of the trial judge." Gasperini v. Center for Humanities, Inc., 518 U.S. 415, 438–39, 116 S.Ct. 2211, 2225, 135 L.Ed.2d 659, 680–81 (1996). Whether a jury award is excessive is considered to be a question of law. See Cooper Industries, Inc. v. Leatherman Tool Group, Inc., 532 U.S. 424, 121 S.Ct. 1678, 149 L.Ed.2d 674 (2001), in which the Court stated, "Because the jury's award of punitive damages does not constitute a finding of 'fact,' appellate review of the district court's determination that an award is consistent with due process does not implicate the Seventh Amendment * * *." Id. at 437, 121 S.Ct. at 1687, 149 L.Ed.2d at 687–88.

3.   GOOGLE LLC v. ORACLE AMERICA, INC., 593 U.S. ___, 141 S.Ct. 1183, 209 L.Ed.2d 311 (2021), considered the role of an appellate court when reviewing a jury verdict that involves mixed questions of law and fact.

When developing Android, a computer operating system designed for smartphones and other mobile devices, Google copied roughly 11,500 lines of computer code (out of 2.86 million lines) from the software platform for the Java programming language. Oracle, which acquired the copyright to Java, sued Google in federal court for infringement of that copyright. In response, Google argued, among other things, that its copying of the Java code was protected by the "fair use" defense to liability under the Copyright Act of 1976. See 17 U.S.C. § 107. The statutory defense includes a non-exclusive list of factors to be considered to determine whether use of a copyrighted work constitutes infringement. After a weeklong jury trial, the district court asked the jury to determine whether Google had shown, by a preponderance of the evidence, that its copying of the Java code "constitutes a 'fair use' under the Copyright Act." The jury returned a verdict finding that Google had established fair use as an affirmative defense, and the district court entered judgment accordingly. Oracle appealed to the U.S. Court of Appeals for the Federal Circuit, which reversed. The court of appeals assumed that all factual issues had been resolved in Google's favor but treated the issue whether those facts constituted fair use under the Copyright Act as a question of law subject to de novo review. On that question, the Federal Circuit concluded Google's copying was not fair use and remanded for a new trial on damages. The Supreme Court reversed the Federal Circuit's fair use decision.

Although the Court disagreed with the Federal Circuit's ultimate conclusion about the merits of Google's fair use defense, it did agree with the court of appeals that fair use should be treated as a mixed question of law and fact, "leaving factual determinations to the jury and reviewing the ultimate question, a legal question, de novo." The Court explained:

> * * * We have said, "[f]air use is a mixed question of law and fact." We have explained that a reviewing court should try to break such a question into its separate factual and legal parts, reviewing each

according to the appropriate legal standard. But when a question can be reduced no further, we have added that "the standard of review for a mixed question all depends—on whether answering it entails primarily legal or factual work."

In this case, the ultimate "fair use" question primarily involves legal work. "Fair use" was originally a concept fashioned by judges. Our cases still provide legal interpretations of the fair use provision. And those interpretations provide general guidance for future cases.

593 U.S. at ___, 141 S. Ct. at 1199–1200, 209 L.Ed.2d at 331.

The Court also rejected Google's arguments that the Federal Circuit's approach violated the Reexamination Clause of the Seventh Amendment or the underlying right to trial by jury preserved by the Seventh Amendment. There was no reexamination concern because "[i]t does not violate the Reexamination Clause for a court to determine the controlling law in resolving a challenge to a jury verdict, as happens any time a court resolves a motion for judgment as a matter of law." The Court similarly rejected the argument, based on trial practice in eighteenth century English copyright cases, that the right to trial by jury under the Seventh Amendment included the right to have a jury resolve a fair use defense. The Seventh Amendment guarantees the common law jury trial right as it existed in 1791, when the amendment was adopted. But, the Court explained, "we have described the [fair use] doctrine as an 'equitable,' not a 'legal,' doctrine." Id. at ___, 141 S. Ct. at 1200, 209 L.Ed.2d at 331–32. In light of the Supreme Court's holding in *Google*, how should an appellate court disentangle the portions of a mixed question of law and fact that are subject to de novo review? Would it be better for appellate courts to adopt a standard analogous to Rule 50, which governs motions for judgment as a matter of law at trial and after trial? See Chapter 14, Section C, supra.

b. Fact Findings in a Non-Jury Case

NOTES AND QUESTIONS

1. In PULLMAN v. SWINT, 456 U.S. 273, 102 S.Ct. 1781, 72 L.Ed.2d 66 (1982), an employment discrimination suit, the district court upheld the validity of the employer's seniority system, and the Court of Appeals reversed. The Supreme Court held that the question of whether the differential impact of the seniority system reflected an intent to discriminate was a pure question of fact, subject to the clearly erroneous standard of review under Rule 52(a). In this case, the Court of Appeals found that the district court failed to make a finding because of an erroneous view of the law, but then erroneously failed to remand to permit the trial court to determine the facts in the first instance. See Cooper, *Civil Rule* 52(a): *Rationing and Rationalizing the Resources of Appellate Review*, 63 Notre Dame L.Rev. 645, 664–666 (1988).

2. If the trial court faces two permissible views of the weight of the evidence, and chooses one, may the appeals court reverse under the Rule 52(a)

standard? In ANDERSON v. CITY OF BESSEMER, 470 U.S. 564, 105 S.Ct. 1504, 84 L.Ed.2d 518 (1985), the Court held:

> In Pullman-Standard v. Swint * * *, we held that a District Court's finding of discriminatory intent in an action brought under Title VII of the Civil Rights Act of 1964 * * * is a factual finding that may be overturned on appeal only if it is clearly erroneous. In this case, the Court of Appeals for the Fourth Circuit concluded that there was clear error in a District Court's finding of discrimination and reversed. Because our reading of the record convinces us that the Court of Appeals misapprehended and misapplied the clearly-erroneous standard, we reverse.
>
> * * *
>
> Although the meaning of the phrase "clearly erroneous" is not immediately apparent, certain general principles governing the exercise of the appellate court's power to overturn findings of a district court may be derived from our cases. The foremost of these principles * * * is that "[a] finding is 'clearly erroneous' when although there is evidence to support it, the reviewing court on the entire evidence is left with the definite and firm conviction that a mistake has been committed." * * * This standard plainly does not entitle a reviewing court to reverse the finding of the trier of fact simply because it is convinced that it would have decided the case differently. The reviewing court oversteps the bounds of its duty under Rule 52(a) if it undertakes to duplicate the role of the lower court. * * * If the district court's account of the evidence is plausible in light of the record viewed in its entirety, the court of appeals may not reverse it even though convinced that had it been sitting as the trier of fact, it would have weighed the evidence differently. Where there are two permissible views of the evidence, the factfinder's choice between them cannot be clearly erroneous. * * *

The Court clarified that this standard applies even when the findings are not based on credibility determinations:

> The rationale for deference to the original finder of fact is not limited to the superiority of the trial judge's position to make determinations of credibility. The trial judge's major role is the determination of fact, and with experience in fulfilling that role comes expertise. Duplication of the trial judge's efforts in the court of appeals would very likely contribute only negligibly to the accuracy of fact determination at a huge cost in diversion of judicial resources. In addition, the parties to a case on appeal have already been forced to concentrate their energies and resources on persuading the trial judge that their account of the facts is the correct one; requiring them to persuade three more judges at the appellate level is requiring too much. As the Court has stated in a different context, the trial on the merits should be "the 'main event' . . . rather than a 'tryout on the

road.' " * * *. For these reasons, review of factual findings under the clearly-erroneous standard—with its deference to the trier of fact—is the rule, not the exception.

Id. at 575, 105 S.Ct. at 1512, 84 L.Ed.2d at 529. In 1985, Rule 52 was amended and Rule 52(a)(6) now states that findings, "whether based on oral or other evidence," are not to be set aside unless they are found by the reviewing court to be clearly erroneous. See 9C Wright & Miller, Federal Practice and Procedure § 2587 (3d ed.).

NOTES AND QUESTIONS

1.   Compare the provisions for direct appeal to the Supreme Court of California and to the Court of Appeals of New York that are set out in the Supplement following 28 U.S.C. § 1254. How do the provisions differ?

2.   Appellate review by state high courts shows a shift from mandatory to discretionary jurisdiction, but in some states all review continues to be mandatory or mandatory in categories of cases. For a collection of state jurisdictional provisions, see Eisenberg & Miller, *Reversal, Dissent, and Variability in State Supreme Courts: The Centrality of Jurisdictional Source*, 89 B.U.L.Rev. 1451 (2009).

3.   Appellate review by the Supreme Court of the United States likewise has shown a shift from mandatory to discretionary jurisdiction. During the first hundred years of its existence, the Supreme Court's appellate jurisdiction was mandatory and it had no discretion to choose among cases. See Hartnett, *Questioning Certiorari: Some Reflections Seventy-five Years After the Judge's Bill*, 100 Colum.L.Rev. 1643 (2000). In 1988, Congress eliminated almost all of the Court's mandatory jurisdiction, continuing a trend that began in 1921 with the introduction of the writ of certiorari. See Act of June 27, 1988, 100th Cong., 2d Sess., Pub. L. 100–352, 102 Stat. 662. The only general provision retained permits direct appeal from some decisions of three-judge district courts. See 28 U.S.C. § 1253. Note that the Supreme Court can effect a direct appeal in any case in which certiorari would lie by taking up the case as soon as it is docketed in the court of appeals and before that court considers it, but this power rarely has been exercised.

CHAPTER 15

THE BINDING EFFECT OF PRIOR DECISIONS: RES JUDICATA AND COLLATERAL ESTOPPEL

■ ■ ■

This chapter focuses on the binding effect on prior judgments and the twin doctrines of res judicata and collateral estoppel—now known as claim preclusion and issue preclusion. The materials examine the doctrine, its history, and the policies that support the concept of finality. The chapter opens by examining the reach of claim and issue preclusion within a single court system and closes by widening the scope to the inter-system effects of a judgment, surely one of the most difficult and vexing questions in the entire Procedure course. As you learn about preclusion, consider this insightful statement about the doctrine: "Courts can only do their best to determine the truth on the basis of the evidence, and the first lesson one must learn on the subject of res judicata is that judicial findings must not be confused with absolute truth." Currie, *Mutuality of Collateral Estoppel: Limits of the* Bernhard *Doctrine*, 9 Stan.L.Rev. 281, 315 (1957).

A. TERMINOLOGY

Although the doctrine of former adjudication is complex, four common sense principles explain it. First, a party ordinarily gets only one chance to litigate a "claim"; if a party litigates only a portion of a claim the first time around, the party risks losing the chance to litigate the rest. Second, a party generally gets only one chance to litigate a factual or a legal "issue"; once litigated, a party cannot ask a second court to decide it differently at a later point. Third, a party typically is entitled to at least one "full and fair" chance to litigate before being barred from having the claims and issues heard by a court. And fourth, the defense of preclusion may be waived unless it is raised at an early stage of the litigation.

The effects of a former adjudication have been discussed in varying and occasionally conflicting terminology. Although a single vocabulary is still not used, substantial progress has been made toward a convention:

"Res judicata" is used * * * as a general term referring to all of the ways in which one judgment will have a binding effect on another. That usage is and doubtless will continue to be common, but it lumps under a single name two quite different effects of judgments. The first is the effect of foreclosing any litigation of

matters that never have been litigated, because of the
determination that they should have been advanced in an earlier
suit. The second is the effect of foreclosing relitigation of matters
that have once been litigated and decided. The first of these,
preclusion of matters that were never litigated, has gone under
the name, "true res judicata," or the names, "merger and bar."
* * * The second doctrine, preclusion of matters that have once
been decided, has usually been called "collateral estoppel."
Professor Allen Vestal has long argued for use of the names "claim
preclusion" and "issue preclusion" for these two doctrines, * * *
and this usage is increasingly employed by the courts as it is by
Restatement Second of Judgments. * * *

Wright & Kane, Law of Federal Courts § 100A (8th ed.).

Another useful summary is the following:

* * * "Res judicata" is the term traditionally used to describe two
discrete effects: (1) what we now call claim preclusion (a valid final
adjudication of a claim precludes a second action on that claim or
any part of it), see Restatement (Second) of Judgments §§ 17–19
(1982); and (2) issue preclusion, long called "collateral estoppel"
(an issue of fact or law, actually litigated and resolved by a valid
final judgment, binds the parties in a subsequent action, whether
on the same or a different claim), see *id.*, at § 27.

BAKER v. GENERAL MOTORS CORP., 522 U.S. 222, 233 n.5, 118 S.Ct.
657, 664 n.5, 139 L.Ed.2d 580, 592 n.5 (1998). See 18 Wright, Miller &
Cooper, Federal Practice and Procedure §§ 4401–15 (3d ed.); Shapiro, Civil
Procedure: Preclusion in Civil Actions (2001).

B. CLAIM AND DEFENSE PRECLUSION

It is difficult to give a precise definition of the doctrine of claim
preclusion, but it is possible to sketch its general form. One formulation is:
In certain circumstances, when a second suit is brought, the judgment from
a prior suit will be considered conclusive, both on the parties to the
judgment and on those in privity with them, as to matters that actually
were litigated or should have been litigated in the first suit. Justice Field
has provided a more detailed formulation of the same basic rule:

* * * [A] judgment, if rendered upon the merits, constitutes an
absolute bar to a subsequent action. It is a finality as to the claim
or demand in controversy, concluding parties and those in privity
with them, not only as to every matter which was offered and
received to sustain or defeat the claim or demand, but as to any
other admissible matter which might have been offered for that
purpose. Thus, for example, a judgment rendered upon a

promissory note is conclusive as to the validity of the instrument and the amount due on it, although it be subsequently alleged that perfect defences actually existed, of which no proof was offered, such as forgery, want of consideration, or payment. * * * The judgment is as conclusive, so far as future proceedings at law are concerned, as though the defences never existed. * * *

CROMWELL v. COUNTY OF SAC, 94 U.S. (4 Otto) 351, 352–53, 24 L.Ed. 195, 197–98 (1876).

For claim preclusion to operate, three elements must be present. First, only judgments that are "final," "valid," and "on the merits" have preclusive effect. Second, the parties in the subsequent action must be identical to or in privity with those in the first. This requirement is one of the most important distinctions between claim preclusion and its sister doctrine, issue preclusion. Third, the claim in the second suit must involve matters properly considered to have been included in the first action. This last requirement is the focus of the case that follows.

1. CLAIM PRECLUSION

RUSH v. CITY OF MAPLE HEIGHTS
Supreme Court of Ohio, 1958.
167 Ohio St. 221, 147 N.E.2d 599,
cert. denied, 358 U.S. 814, 79 S.Ct. 21, 3 L.Ed.2d 57.

HERBERT, JUDGE.

[Plaintiff was injured in a fall from a motorcycle. She brought an action in the Municipal Court of Cleveland for damage to her personal property; that court found that defendant city was negligent in maintaining its street and that this negligence was the proximate cause of plaintiff's damages, which were fixed at $100. Defendant appealed and the judgment was affirmed by the Ohio Court of Appeals and Supreme Court. Plaintiff also brought this action in the Court of Common Pleas of Cuyahoga County for personal injuries she incurred in the same accident; her motion to set trial on the issue of damages alone was granted on the ground that the defendant was precluded from contesting the issue of negligence because of the municipal court action; judgment was entered in plaintiff's favor on a verdict for $12,000, and the court of appeals affirmed.]

The eighth error assigned by the defendant is that "the trial and appellate courts committed error in permitting plaintiff to split her cause of action * * *."

* * *

In the case of Vasu v. Kohlers, Inc., 145 Ohio St. 321, 61 N.E.2d 707, 709, 166 A.L.R. 855, plaintiff operating an automobile came into collision with defendant's truck, in which collision he suffered personal injuries and also damage to his automobile. At the time of collision, plaintiff had coverage of a $50 deductible collision policy on his automobile. The insurance company paid the plaintiff a sum covering the damage to his automobile, whereupon, in accordance with a provision of the policy, the plaintiff assigned to the insurer his claim for such damage.

In February 1942, the insurance company commenced an action * * * against Kohlers, Inc., * * * to recoup the money paid by it to cover the damage to Vasu's automobile.

In August 1942, Vasu commenced an action in the same court against Kohlers, Inc., to recover for personal injuries which he suffered in the same collision.

In March 1943, in the insurance company's action, a verdict was rendered in favor of the defendant, followed by judgment.

Two months later an amended answer was filed in the Vasu case, setting out as a bar to the action * * * the judgment rendered in favor of defendant in the insurance company case. A motion to strike that defense * * * [was] sustained * * *. A trial of the action resulted in a verdict for plaintiff, upon which judgment was entered.

On appeal to the Court of Appeals the defendant claimed that the Court of Common Pleas erred in sustaining plaintiff's motion to strike from the defendant's answer the defense of *res judicata* claimed to have arisen by reason of the judgment in favor of the defendant in the action by the insurance company.

The Court of Appeals reversed the judgment of the Court of Common Pleas and entered final judgment in favor of defendant.

This court reversed the judgment of the Court of Appeals, holding in the syllabus, in part, as follows:

* * *

"4. Injuries to both person and property suffered by the same person as a result of the same wrongful act are infringements of different rights and give rise to distinct causes of action, with the result that the recovery or denial of recovery of compensation for damages to the property is no bar to an action subsequently prosecuted for the personal injury, unless by an adverse judgment in the first action issues are determined against the plaintiff which operate as an estoppel against him in the second action.

* * *

"6. Where an injury to person and to property through a single wrongful act causes a prior contract of indemnity and subrogation as to the injury to property to come into operation for the benefit of the person injured, the indemnitor may prosecute a separate action against the party causing such injury for reimbursement for indemnity monies paid under such contract.

"7. Parties in privy, in the sense that they are bound by a judgment, are those who acquired an interest in the subject matter after the beginning of the action or the rendition of the judgment; and if their title or interest attached before that fact, they are not bound unless made parties.

"8. A grantor or assignor is not bound, as to third persons, by any judgment which such third persons may obtain against his grantee or assignee adjudicating the title to or claim for the interest transferred unless he participated in the action in such manner as to become, in effect, a party."

* * *

* * * The sixth, seventh and eighth paragraphs deal with the factual situation which existed in the Vasu case, i.e., a prior contract of indemnity and subrogation. Although, as discussed *infra*, it was not actually necessary to the determination of the issue in that case, attention centers on the fourth paragraph.

* * *

* * * [Subsequent] cases, distinguishing and explaining the Vasu case, have not changed the rule established in paragraph four of the syllabus * * *.

However, it is contended here that that rule is in conflict with the great weight of authority in this country and has caused vexatious litigation.

* * *

Upon examination of decisions of courts of last resort, we find that the majority rule is followed in the following cases in each of which the action was between the person suffering injury and the person committing the tort, and where insurers were not involved, as in the case here. * * * [The court cited cases from 20 states forming the majority and five states forming the minority.]

The reasoning behind the majority rule seems to be well stated in the case of Mobile & Ohio Rd. Co. v. Matthews * * * [115 Tenn. 172, 91 S.W. 194 (1906)], as follows:

"The negligent action of the plaintiff in error constituted but one tort. The injuries to the person and property of the defendant in error were the several results and effects of one wrongful act. A single tort can be the basis of but one action. It is not improper to

declare in different counts for damages to the person and property
when both result from the same tort, and it is the better practice
to do so where there is any difference in the measure of damages,
and all the damages sustained must be sued for in one suit. This
is necessary to prevent multiplicity of suits, burdensome expense,
and delays to plaintiffs, and vexatious litigation against
defendants. * * *

"Indeed, if the plaintiff fail to sue for the entire damage done him
by the tort, a second action for the damages omitted will be
precluded by the judgment in the first suit brought and tried."

The minority rule would seem to stem from the English case of
Brunsden v. Humphrey (1884), 14 Q.B. 141. The facts in that case are set
forth in the opinion in the Vasu case * * * concluding with the statement:

"The Master of the Rolls, in his opinion, stated that the test is
'whether the same sort of evidence would prove the plaintiff's case
in the two actions' and that, in the action relating to the cab, 'it
would be necessary to give evidence of the damage done to the
plaintiff's vehicle. In the present action it would be necessary to
give evidence of the bodily injury occasioned to the plaintiff, and
of the sufferings which he has undergone, and for this purpose to
call medical witnesses. This one test shows that the causes of
action as to the damage done to the plaintiff's cab, and as to the
injury occasioned to the plaintiff's person, are distinct."

The fallacy of the reasoning in the English court is best portrayed in
the dissenting opinion of Lord Coleridge, as follows:

"* * * [I]t seems to me a subtlety not warranted by law to hold that
a man cannot bring two actions, if he is injured in his arm and in
his leg, but can bring two, if besides his arm and leg being injured,
his trousers which contain his leg, and his coat-sleeve which
contains his arm, have been torn."

There appears to be no valid reason in these days of code pleading to
adhere to the old English rule as to distinctions between injuries to the
person and damages to the person's property resulting from a single tort.
It would seem that the minority rule is bottomed on the proposition that
the right of bodily security is fundamentally different from the right of
security of property and, also, that, in actions predicated upon a negligent
act, damages are a necessary element of each independent cause of action
and no recovery may be had unless and until actual consequential damages
are shown.

Whether or not injuries to both person and property resulting from the
same wrongful act are to be treated as injuries to separate rights or as

separate items of damage, * * * a plaintiff may maintain only one action to enforce his rights existing at the time such action is commenced.

The decision of the question actually in issue in the Vasu case is found in paragraphs six, seven and eight of the syllabus, as it is quite apparent from the facts there that the first judgment, claimed to be *res judicata* in Vasu's action against the defendant, was rendered against Vasu's insurer in an action initiated by it after having paid Vasu for the damages to his automobile. * * *

Upon further examination of the cases from other jurisdictions, it appears that in those instances where the courts have held to the majority rule, a separation of causes of action is almost universally recognized where an insurer has acquired by an assignment or by subrogation the right to recover for money it has advanced to pay for property damage.

* * *

In the light of the foregoing, it is the view of this court that the so-called majority rule conforms much more properly to modern practice, and that the rule declared in the fourth paragraph of the syllabus in the Vasu case, on a point not actually at issue therein, should not be followed.

* * *

Judgment reversed and final judgment for defendant.

STEWART, JUDGE (concurring). * * * If it had been necessary [in *Vasu*] to decide the question whether a single tort gives rise to two causes of action as to the one injured by such tort, I would be reluctant to disturb that holding. However, neither the discussion in the Vasu case as to whether a single or double cause of action arises from one tort nor the language of the fourth paragraph of the syllabus was necessary to decide the issue presented in the case, and obviously both such language and such paragraph are obiter dicta and, therefore, are not as persuasive an authority as if they had been appropriate to the question presented.

* * *

* * * This court is justified in departing from the obiter dicta of the Vasu case.

ZIMMERMAN, JUDGE (dissenting). I am not unalterably opposed to upsetting prior decisions of this court where changing conditions and the lessons of experience clearly indicate the desirability of such course, but, where those considerations do not obtain, established law should remain undisturbed in order to insure a stability on which the lower courts and the legal profession generally may rely with some degree of confidence.

* * *

NOTES AND QUESTIONS

1. The *Rush* case illustrates the important and by now familiar concept of stare decisis. Although neither party in *Rush* had been a party to Vasu v. Kohler's, Inc., both of the lower Ohio courts as well as the dissenting judge in the Supreme Court of Ohio regarded that case as controlling in *Rush*. Of course, as *Rush* itself demonstrates, the binding force of stare decisis is not absolute, and the parties to a later action are free to argue that the law announced in an earlier case should be changed. But a court will not lightly depart from precedent even though the parties who are before it were not represented in the case that established the precedent.

Stare decisis is a judicial doctrine that helps the courts fashion and preserve a system of laws based upon rational principle. The Supreme Court has explained:

> The obligation to follow precedent begins with necessity, and a contrary necessity marks its outer limit. With Cardozo, we recognize that no judicial system could do society's work if it eyed each issue afresh in every case that raised it. See B. Cardozo, The Nature of the Judicial Process 149 (1921). Indeed, the very concept of the rule of law underlying our own Constitution requires such continuity over time that a respect for precedent is, by definition, indispensable. * * * At the other extreme, a different necessity would make itself felt if a prior judicial ruling should come to be seen so clearly as error that its enforcement was for that very reason doomed.

PLANNED PARENTHOOD OF SOUTHEASTERN PENNSYLVANIA v. CASEY, 505 U.S. 833, 854, 112 S.Ct. 2791, 2808, 120 L.Ed.2d 674, 699–700 (1992).

2. The results of res judicata sometimes may seem harsh, but the doctrine is supported by a number of important policy goals. The Supreme Court has emphasized that "res judicata and collateral estoppel relieve parties of the cost and vexation of multiple lawsuits, conserve judicial resources, and, by preventing inconsistent decisions, encourage reliance on adjudication." Allen v. McCurry, 449 U.S. 90, 94, 101 S.Ct. 411, 415, 66 L.Ed.2d 308, 313 (1980). Why are these goals so important?

3. Was the critical language in *Vasu* a holding or dictum? Consider the following:

> "[I]t is often difficult to determine whether statements in a court's opinion constitute an alternative ground for the decision or merely dicta." * * * Black's Law Dictionary defines "obiter dictum" as a statement "made during the course of delivering a judicial opinion, but one that is unnecessary to the decision in the case and therefore not precedential (though it may be considered persuasive)." * * * However, "where a decision rests on two or more grounds, none can be relegated to the category of obiter dictum."

Best Life Assur. Co. of California v. Comm'r of Internal Revenue, 281 F.3d 828, 833–34 (9th Cir. 2002) (internal citations omitted). See Dorf, *Dicta and Article III*, 142 U.Pa.L.Rev. 1997 (1994) ("A holding consists of those propositions along the chosen decisional path or paths of reasoning that (1) are actually decided, (2) are based upon the facts of the case, and (3) lead to the judgment. If not a holding, a proposition stated in a case counts as dicta."); Leval, *Judging Under the Constitution: Dicta About Dicta*, 81 N.Y.U.L.Rev. 1249, 1256 (2006) ("A dictum is an assertion in a court's opinion of a proposition of law which does not explain why the court's judgments goes in favor of the winner.")?

4. Why might plaintiff in *Rush* have wanted to sue first on the claim for property damage and then separately for personal injuries?

5. In making his decision, Judge Herbert in *Rush* asked "[w]hether or not injuries to both person and property resulting from the same wrongful act are to be treated as injuries to separate rights or as separate items of damage," explaining that "a plaintiff may maintain only one action to enforce his rights existing at the time such action is commenced." Is this test the same as asking whether the injuries are based on shared operative facts or common factual groupings? If not, how do the tests differ?

The tests for determining the scope of claim preclusion have undergone significant change since the beginning of the twentieth century:

> * * * In defining claim to embrace all the remedial rights of the plaintiff against the defendant growing out of the relevant transaction (or series of connected transactions), * * * [Section 24 of the Restatement (Second)] responds to modern procedural ideas which have found expression in the Federal Rules of Civil Procedure and other procedural systems.

> "Claim," in the context of res judicata, has never been broader than the transaction to which it related. But in the days when civil procedure still bore the imprint of the forms of action and the division between law and equity, the courts were prone to associate claim with a single theory of recovery, so that, with respect to one transaction, a plaintiff might have as many claims as there were theories of the substantive law upon which he could seek relief against the defendant. Thus, defeated in an action based on one theory, the plaintiff might be able to maintain another action based on a different theory, even though both actions were grounded upon the defendant's identical act or connected acts forming a single life-situation. In those earlier days there was also some adherence to a view that associated claim with the assertion of a single primary right as accorded by the substantive law, so that, if it appeared that the defendant had invaded a number of primary rights conceived to be held by the plaintiff, the plaintiff had the same number of claims, even though they all sprang from a unitary occurrence. There was difficulty in knowing which rights were primary and what was their extent, but a primary right and the corresponding claim might turn out to be

narrow. Thus it was held by some courts that a judgment for or against the plaintiff in an action for personal injuries did not preclude an action by him for property damage occasioned by the same negligent conduct on the part of the defendant—this deriving from the idea that the right to be free of bodily injury was distinct from the property right. Still another view of claim looked to sameness of evidence; a second action was precluded where the evidence to support it was the same as that needed to support the first. Sometimes this was made the sole test of identity of claim; sometimes it figured as a positive but not as a negative test; that is, in certain situations a second action might be precluded although the evidence material to it varied from that in the first action. Even so, claim was not coterminous with the transaction itself.

The present trend is to see claim in factual terms and to make it coterminous with the transaction regardless of the number of substantive theories, or variant forms of relief flowing from those theories, that may be available to the plaintiff; regardless of the number of primary rights that may have been invaded; and regardless of the variations in the evidence needed to support the theories or rights. The transaction is the basis of the litigative unit or entity which may not be split.

Restatement (Second), Judgments § 24, comment *a* (1982).

6.   In VANOVER v. NCO FINANCIAL SERVICES, INC., 857 F.3d 833 (11th Cir. 2017), a debtor sued a debt collector in Florida federal court, alleging a violation of the federal Telephone Consumer Protection Act. One year later, the same debtor sued the same defendant in Florida state court, again alleging violations of the federal law. Defendant removed to federal court, and the district court granted defendant's motion to dismiss the federal action for improper claim splitting. The Eleventh Circuit affirmed. Noting that the doctrine of claim splitting applies "where the second suit has been filed before the first suit has reached a final judgment," the appeals court explained that although claim splitting is related to res judicata, its application does not require a final judgment. Instead, the inquiry is two-fold: "(1) whether the case involves the same parties and their privies, and (2) whether separate cases arise from the same transaction or series of transactions." Id. at 841–42 (internal citations omitted). The rationale for the doctrine is fairness and efficiency: The claim-splitting doctrine "ensures that a plaintiff may not 'split up his demand and prosecute it by piecemeal, or present only a portion of the grounds upon which relief is sought, and leave the rest to be presented in a second suit, if the first fails.' " Id. at 841 (citation omitted). See Clermont, *Res Judicata as Requisite for Justice*, 68 Rutgers U.L. Rev. 1067, 1109 (2016) (explaining that under the transactional approach to claim preclusion, "[a]ny plaintiff who asserts only a part of the claim is said to have impermissibly split the claim").

MATHEWS V. NEW YORK RACING ASSOCIATION, INC.

United States District Court, Southern District of New York, 1961.
193 F.Supp. 293.

MACMAHON, DISTRICT JUDGE. Defendants move for summary judgment, pursuant to Rule 56(b),[a] Federal Rules * * *, on the ground that a judgment in a prior action in this court is res judicata as to the claim alleged in the complaint.

New York Racing Association Inc. is a New York corporation which operates Jamaica Race Track. It employs defendant Thoroughbred Racing Protective Association Inc., a private detective agency, for security purposes.

Plaintiff brings this action against the Association and Thoroughbred alleging that on April 4, 1958, at Jamaica Race Track, he was "assaulted," "kidnapped," "falsely arrested," and "falsely imprisoned" by employees of Thoroughbred. He further alleges that the defendants charged him with disorderly conduct and maliciously caused him to be prosecuted and convicted in the Magistrate's Court of the City of New York on April 10, 1958. He prays for relief in the form of money damages and an injunction restraining the defendants from interfering with his attendance at race tracks, from publication of libelous statements, and from acting as peace officers.

The prior judgment on which defendants rely was entered in this court on June 30, 1960 following a trial before Judge Palmieri sitting without a jury. The complaint in that action alleged, among other matters, that plaintiff was assaulted by the defendant's private investigators at Jamaica Race Track on April 4, 1958. It also alleged that the employees of the defendants had made libelous statements concerning the plaintiff on several occasions, including plaintiff's trial for disorderly conduct on April 10, 1958. The relief prayed for in that action was also money damages and an injunction from further interference with plaintiff's attendance at race tracks within the United States. The earlier action named three individuals as defendants. The only two properly served were employees of the defendants named in the present suit.

* * *

* * * [T]he question is whether the claim alleged in this complaint is the same as that in the suit concluded earlier. The term "claim" refers to a group of facts limited to a single occurrence or transaction without particular reference to the resulting legal rights. It is the facts surrounding the occurrence which operate to make up the claim, not the legal theory upon which a plaintiff relies. * * *

---

[a]   The rule was changed and the substance now appears in Rule 56(a).

The facts relevant to [plaintiff's current lawsuit] * * * along with three other separate claims based on different facts, were tried to a conclusion in the earlier suit. There, the plaintiff relied on the acts of the agents occurring on April 4, 1958 as the basis of a claim against them on the theory of assault. Now, he asserts these same acts as the basis of a claim against the agents' principals on the theory of false arrest. In the earlier action, plaintiff relied on the statements of the agents made on April 10, 1958 as the basis of a claim against them on the theory of libel. Now, he asserts those same statements as the basis of a claim against their principals on the theory of malicious prosecution. Clearly, any liability of the defendants for the acts or statements of their agents must be predicated upon the familiar principle of respondeat superior. Thus, if the agents committed no actionable wrong against the plaintiff, neither did their principals. * * *

The plaintiff cannot be permitted to splinter his claim into a multiplicity of suits and try them piecemeal at his convenience. * * * "The plaintiff having alleged operative facts which state a cause of action because he tells of defendant's misconduct and his own harm has had his day in court. He does not get another day after the first lawsuit is concluded by giving a different reason than he gave in the first for recovery of damages for the same invasion of his rights. The problem of his rights against the defendant based upon the alleged wrongful acts is fully before the court whether all the reasons for recovery were stated to the court or not." * * *

The court is cognizant of the fact that plaintiff appears pro se, but as the law provides a beginning for litigation, it must also provide an end. * * *

NOTES AND QUESTIONS

1.   In *Rush*, plaintiff won her first suit for property damage, and the court held that any claims she had for personal injuries were "merged" into the judgment and so extinguished. In *Mathews*, plaintiff lost the first suit. Since the basic factual setting of the claim in the second suit was the same as in the first, the court held that the allegations were "barred" by the earlier judgment. By using a different definition of a "claim," could you make an argument that the second suit should not have been precluded?

2.   One of the benefits of the transaction approach to claim preclusion is its flexibility. But flexibility comes at a price. Because a court may interpret the claim presented in the first lawsuit more broadly than a litigant does, the litigant unknowingly may forfeit parts of his action by failing to raise them. It is said that litigants thus learn "by trial and error in the harsh school of experience" of the need to raise all possibly connected allegations in the first proceeding. Cleary, *Res Judicata Reexamined*, 57 Yale L.J. 339, 340 (1948). This may well mean that parties will advance claims that they otherwise might not have brought to court. Recall that in *Mathews*, plaintiff was appearing pro

se. Should the sophistication of the litigant be considered in deciding the scope of claim preclusion?

3.   Should the test for claim preclusion be the same as the test for supplemental jurisdiction under 28 U.S.C. § 1367 or for whether a counterclaim is compulsory? See p. 267, Notes 4 and 5, supra. How are these situations different?

4.   Consider how the transaction test would affect the preclusive effect of a judgment in the following situations:

(a)   An abused spouse sues for divorce. Does the divorce judgment bar the party from later filing a tort action for spousal abuse? Should it matter whether the abuse was claimed as the basis for the divorce in the earlier suit? Or that it took place during the course of the marriage? Assume the former spouses later cross-move to modify a child custody agreement entered following the final judgment of divorce. Will claim preclusion bar the modification? See Aviel, *Family Law and the New Access to Justice*, 86 Fordham L. Rev. 2279 (2018).

(b)   An individual who was exposed to toxic chemicals sues for damages and seeks reimbursement for the expense of on-going medical monitoring. Years later, plaintiff experiences physical injury greater and qualitatively different than initially anticipated or diagnosed. Does claim preclusion bar a new lawsuit?

———

FEDERATED DEPARTMENT STORES, INC. v. MOITIE, 452 U.S. 394, 101 S.Ct. 2424, 69 L.Ed.2d 103 (1981). Respondents Moitie and Brown were two of seven plaintiffs to file separate antitrust actions against petitioner (*Moitie* I and *Brown* I). The actions were consolidated in the district court after which they were dismissed for failure to allege an "injury" to their "business or property" within the meaning of Section 4 of the Clayton Act. The other five plaintiffs appealed to the Ninth Circuit. Moitie and Brown, however, did not appeal, but, instead, refiled their actions in state court (*Moitie* II and *Brown* II). The actions were removed to federal court and then dismissed on res judicata grounds. Meanwhile, the five appeals cases were reversed and remanded to the district court to be reconsidered in light of an intervening Supreme Court opinion. When *Moitie* II and *Brown* II reached the Ninth Circuit on appeal, the court held that, although a strict application of res judicata would preclude the second action, an exception should be made when the dismissal rested on a case that had been effectively overruled. The Supreme Court disagreed:

The Court of Appeals * * * rested its opinion in part on what it viewed as "simple justice." But we do not see the grave injustice which would be done by the application of accepted principles of res judicata. "Simple justice" is achieved when a complex body of law developed over a period of years is evenhandedly applied. The doctrine of res judicata serves vital public interests beyond any individual judge's ad hoc determination of the equities in a particular case. There is simply "no principle of law or equity which sanctions the rejection by a federal court of the salutary principle of *res judicata*." * * * The Court of Appeals' reliance on "public policy" is similarly misplaced. This Court has long recognized that "[p]ublic policy dictates that there be an end of litigation; that those who have contested an issue shall be bound by the result of the contest, and that matters once tried shall be considered forever settled as between the parties." *Baldwin* v. *Traveling Men's Association*, 283 U.S. 522, 525[, 51 S.Ct. 517, 518, 75 L.Ed. 1244] (1931). We have stressed that "[the] doctrine of *res judicata* is not a mere matter of practice or procedure inherited from a more technical time than ours. It is a rule of fundamental and substantial justice, 'of public policy and of private peace,' which should be cordially regarded and enforced by the courts * * *." *Hart Steel Co.* v. *Railroad Supply Co.*, 244 U.S. 294, 299[, 37 S.Ct. 506, 507, 61 L.Ed. 1148] (1917). * * *

Id. at 401–02, 101 S.Ct. at 2429–30, 69 L.Ed.2d at 110–11.

NOTES AND QUESTIONS

1.   In spite of the harsh language of *Moitie*, there are situations in which considerations of justice and fairness dictate that prior judgments not be given preclusive effect. When the prior judgment was obtained by the use of fraud, courts generally will not consider it binding. See, e.g., McCarty v. First of Georgia Ins. Co., 713 F.2d 609 (10th Cir. 1983). Similarly, when there was a clear and fundamental jurisdictional defect that should have prevented the first court from hearing the suit, courts often will hold that the judgment has no preclusive effect. However, would you agree that by its logic and language *Moitie* forecloses a general fairness exception to claim preclusion? See 18 Wright, Miller & Cooper, Federal Practice and Procedure § 4415 (3d ed.).

2.   Claim preclusion requires a final judgment. Is a judgment final if an appeal is pending? The general rule in the federal system and most states is that a pending appeal does not defeat the claim preclusive effect of a judgment. See Deposit Bank of Frankfort v. Board of Councilmen of City of Frankfort, 191 U.S. 499, 24 S.Ct. 154, 48 L.Ed. 276 (1903). The rule can create a great deal of mischief if the second appeal relies upon a first judgment that is later reversed. Restatement (Second), Judgments § 13, comment *f* (1982), suggests that, if possible, the second panel ought to postpone consideration of preclusion until the first appeal is concluded. See U.S. v. 5 Unlabeled Boxes, 572 F.3d 169 (3d Cir. 2009).

3.   In *Moitie*, defendants removed the actions to federal court on the basis of federal question jurisdiction, and the cases subsequently were dismissed due to the preclusive effect of the prior judgment. In a similar case, RIVET v. REGIONS BANK, 522 U.S. 470, 118 S.Ct. 921, 139 L.Ed.2d 912 (1998), the dispute involved only state issues, but defendants, relying on *Moitie*, sought to remove the case to federal court on the ground that the action was precluded by a prior federal judgment. The Supreme Court rejected this interpretation of *Moitie*, holding that claim preclusion does not create an exception to the rule that removal under 28 U.S.C. § 1441(b) cannot be based upon a federal defense. On *Moitie*, see Miller, *Artful Pleading: A Doctrine in Search of Definition*, 76 Tex.L.Rev. 1781 (1998).

JONES V. MORRIS PLAN BANK OF PORTSMOUTH

Supreme Court of Appeals of Virginia, 1937.
168 Va. 284, 191 S.E. 608.

GREGORY, JUSTICE.

William B. Jones instituted an action for damages against the Morris Plan Bank of Portsmouth for the conversion of his automobile. * * *

After the plaintiff had introduced all of his evidence and before the defendant had introduced any evidence on its behalf, the latter's counsel moved to strike the evidence of the plaintiff and the court sustained the motion. A verdict for the defendant resulted.

The facts are that the plaintiff purchased from J.A. Parker, a dealer in automobiles, a Plymouth sedan, agreeing to pay therefor $595. He paid a part of the purchase price by the delivery of a used car to Parker of the agreed value of $245 and after crediting that amount on the purchase price and adding a finance charge of $78.40, there remained an unpaid balance due the dealer of $428. This latter amount was payable in 12 monthly installments of $35.70 each and evidenced by one note in the principal sum of $428.40. The note contained this provision: "The whole amount of this note (less any payments made hereon) becomes immediately due and payable in the event of nonpayment at maturity of any installment thereof." The note was secured by the usual conditional sales contract * * * in which it was agreed that the title to the car would be retained by the dealer until the entire purchase price was paid in full. * * * [T]he contract was assigned to the defendant * * * and the note was indorsed by Parker and delivered to the defendant at the same time.

Installment payments due on the note for May and June were not made when payable and for them an action was instituted in the civil and police court of the city of Suffolk. No appearance was made by the defendant (Jones) in that action and judgment was obtained against him for the two payments. Execution issued upon the judgment and it was satisfied * * * by Jones * * *.

Later the defendant instituted another action against Jones in the same court for the July installment which had become due and was unpaid, and to that action Jones filed a plea of res adjudicata, whereupon the * * * [Bank] took a nonsuit.

* * * [T]he defendant * * * took possession of the automobile without the consent of the plaintiff and later sold it and applied the proceeds upon the note.

Afterwards, the plaintiff instituted the present action for conversion to recover damages for the loss of the automobile. His action in the court below was founded upon the theory that when the May and June installments became due and were unpaid, then under the acceleration clause in the note, the entire balance due thereon matured and at once became due and the defendant having elected to sue him for only two installments instead of the entire amount of the note, and having obtained a judgment for the two installments and satisfaction of the execution issued thereon, it waived its right to collect the balance. He also contends that the note was satisfied in the manner narrated and that the conditional sales contract, the sole purpose of which was to secure the payment of the note, served its purpose and ceased to exist, and, therefore, the title to the automobile was no longer retained, but upon the satisfaction of the note, passed to the plaintiff and was his property when the agent of the defendant removed it and converted it to its own use.

The position of the defendant is that * * * the title to the automobile, which was the subject of the alleged conversion, was not vested in the plaintiff at the time of the action, nor since, because the condition in the contract was that the title should be retained by the seller (whose rights were assigned to the defendant) until the entire purchase price was paid, and that the purchase price had never been paid * * *.

The defendant also contends that the note and conditional sales contract were divisible; that successive actions could be brought upon the installments as they matured; and that it was not bound, at the risk of waiving its right to claim the balance, to sue for all installments in one action.

* * *

We decide that under the unconditional acceleration provision in the note involved here and in the absence of the usual optional provision reserved to the holder, the entire amount due upon the note became due and payable when default was made in paying an installment. * * *

Was it essential that the defendant here institute an action for all of the installments then due, or could it institute its action for only two of the installments and later institute another action for other installments? The answer to that question depends upon the nature of the transaction. If a transaction is represented by one single and indivisible contract and the breach gives rise to one single cause of action, it cannot be split into distinct parts and separate actions maintained for each.

On the other hand, if the contract is divisible giving rise to more than one cause of action, each may be proceeded upon separately.

Was the contract here single and indivisible or was it divisible? Our answer is that the note and conditional sales contract constituted one single contract. The sole purpose of the conditional sales contract was to retain the title in the seller until the note was paid. When that condition was performed, the contract ended.

One of the principal tests in determining whether a demand is single and entire, or whether it is several, so as to give rise to more than one cause of action, is the identity of facts necessary to maintain the action. If the same evidence will support both actions, there is but one cause of action.

In the case at bar, all of the installments were due. The evidence essential to support the action on the two installments for which the action was brought would be the identical evidence necessary to maintain an action upon all of the installments. All installments having matured at the time the action was begun, under well-settled principles, those not embraced in that action are now barred.

* * * At the time the defendant lost its right to institute any action for the remaining installments, the title to the automobile passed to the plaintiff. He was the owner at the time the agent of the defendant took possession of it and exposed it to sale.

It follows that the judgment of the court below will be reversed, and the case will be remanded for the sole purpose of determining the quantum of damages.

Reversed and remanded.

NOTES AND QUESTIONS

1.   When a debt is secured by a series of notes or when a bond includes a number of interest coupons, an action on one of the notes or coupons, even though others are due, does not bar a subsequent action on those others. Restatement, Judgments § 62, comment *i* (1942); Restatement (Second), Judgments § 24, comment *d* (1982). Cf. Nesbit v. Riverside Independent District, 144 U.S. 610, 619, 12 S.Ct. 746, 748, 36 L.Ed. 562, 565 (1892):

> Each matured coupon is a separable promise, and gives rise to a separate cause of action. It may be detached from the bond and sold by itself. Indeed, the title to several matured coupons of the same bond may be in as many different persons, and upon each a distinct and separate action be maintained. So, while the promises of the bond and of the coupons in the first instance are upon the same paper, and

the coupons are for interest due upon the bond, yet the promise to
pay the coupon is as distinct from that to pay the bond as though the
two promises were placed in different instruments, upon different
paper.

2.   It can be difficult to define the scope of a prior judgment in
controversies involving continuing or renewed conduct. Restatement (Second),
Judgments § 24 (1982) lists some relevant considerations, and suggests
evaluating "whether the facts are related in time, space, origin, or motivation,
whether they form a convenient trial unit, and whether their treatment as a
unit conforms to the parties' expectations or business understanding or usage."

Suits asserting claims for nuisance commonly involve continuing conduct.
Judgments involving "permanent" nuisances are considered to have full
preclusive effect; those involving "temporary" nuisances are not considered to
preclude later litigation involving the same behavior. Courts are not always
consistent in their classification of nuisances. For a further discussion of claims
that involve continuing and renewed conduct, see 18 Wright, Miller & Cooper,
Federal Practice and Procedure § 4409 (3d ed.).

3.   As the previous Notes suggest, often the underlying substantive law
will affect the definition of the claim for purposes of preclusion. For example,
if one party to a contract commits a material breach that is neither
accompanied nor followed by a repudiation, the law of contracts teaches that
the other party is free, on the one hand, to treat the contract as binding and
sue for the damages or, on the other hand, to treat the contract as ended. If the
aggrieved party chooses the former option and then suffers further material
breaches, a later suit for damages not sought in the first suit will not be barred.
See Restatement (Second), Judgments § 26, comment *g* (1982).

The expectations of the parties also may be decisive in determining the
scope of the prior judgment. Imagine that a wholesale distributor regularly
ships goods to a retailer on credit. If the parties conceive of their relationship
as a series of discrete transactions, a suit by the creditor seeking to recover any
one of the payments would not bar subsequent suits for other payments. If,
however, the parties believe they have a single running account, the creditor
would have to seek to recover the entire balance then due.

2.   DEFENSE PRECLUSION

Thus far we have looked at claim preclusion from the perspective of
plaintiff. However, defendants also need to take the doctrine into account,
typically in one of three situations:

The first two situations involve a second action in which a former
defendant seeks to advance a claim against the original plaintiff.
In one, the claim involves matters that were not advanced in the
first action; in the other, the claim involves matters that were
advanced in the first action but are not foreclosed by issue
preclusion. The third situation involves a second action by the

original plaintiff in which the defendant seeks to raise defenses that were equally available in the first action but were not advanced there.

18 Wright, Miller & Cooper, Federal Practice and Procedure § 4414 (3d ed.). "The third situation" is referred to as "defense preclusion," and the scope of the doctrine is implicated in the case that follows.

MITCHELL V. FEDERAL INTERMEDIATE CREDIT BANK

Supreme Court of South Carolina, 1932.
165 S.C. 457, 164 S.E. 136.

STABLER, J.

[An action for an accounting against defendant bank for proceeds of a crop of potatoes. Plaintiff alleged that in order to obtain loans from defendant he had—at the behest of defendant's agent—sold his potatoes through a growers' association and assigned the proceeds as security for two notes, totaling $9,000, which had been discounted with defendant; that the potatoes had netted $18,000, but that he had never received any of this, and that the proceeds had been received by defendant or an agent of defendant. In a previous action by defendant on the notes, plaintiff had pleaded in the answer the same facts now the basis of an affirmative claim, but had not counterclaimed or asked for relief; judgment had been for him in that action. In the present suit, defendant contended that plaintiff's claim was merged in the earlier judgment. This contention was upheld by the trial court.]

* * *

We now come to the main question presented by the appeal, namely, Was the circuit judge in error in sustaining the plea in bar to plaintiff's action? Turning to appellant's answer in the federal court case * * * we find that the facts there pleaded by him as a defense to the bank's recovery on its notes are the same as those set out by him in his complaint as the basis of his action in the case at bar, it being alleged that the total amount paid to the bank was in excess of all sums advanced to him on the notes or otherwise, and as a result of the transaction the notes sued upon were fully paid and discharged. In addition, we find in the record of the case before us the following statement by appellant as an admission of fact on his part: "* * * The indebtedness of the bank to Mitchell arising from the embezzlement of the proceeds of the crop was used pro tanto as an offset to the claim of the bank in the Federal Court. The case at bar seeks recovery of the surplusage, over the offset, of the proceeds of the same crop lost by the same embezzlement. The appellant, however, is not seeking to recover in this action the same money that has already been used as an offset."

* * *

In support of his position * * * appellant cites certain decisions of this court, which he claims to be conclusive of the issue, relying especially upon Kirven v. Chemical Co., 77 S.C. 493, 58 S.E. 424, 426.

* * * [T]he record shows that Kirven had bought from the Chemical Company $2,228 worth of fertilizers and had given his note for that amount. The company, upon maturity of the note, brought action against him on his obligation. He at first filed an answer setting up three defenses, the third of which was that the fertilizers furnished were deleterious and destructive to the crops, and that there was an entire failure of consideration for the note. Later, he was permitted to file a supplemental answer in which he withdrew the third defense. On trial in the federal court, the jury rendered a verdict for the Chemical Company. Thereafter, Kirven brought an action against the company * * * alleging that the defendant caused damage to his crop in the sum of $1,995 by reason of the deleterious effect of the fertilizers furnished. The company set up the defense that the issues in this action were or could have been adjudicated in the [first] suit * * *. A verdict was given Kirven in the amount prayed for, and on appeal * * * it was pointed out that the question raised in the state court was not *actually* litigated and determined in the federal action, and it appears that the court, for that reason, took the view that a bar or estoppel did not exist. Mr. Justice Woods, in his concurring opinion, took the view that, as Kirven elected not to use, as a defense, the fact of *worthlessness,* which might have been available in the action of the company against him, "he was not precluded from using the very different facts of deleteriousness and positive injury caused by appellant's alleged negligence in the manufacture of the fertilizer as the basis of an independent cause of action."

We think the facts of the case at bar, however, present a different situation. * * *

O'Connor v. Varney, 10 Gray (Mass.) 231, was an action on contract to recover damages for Varney's failure to build certain additions to a house according to the terms of a written agreement between the parties. The defendant set up as a defense "a judgment recovered by O'Connor in an action brought by Varney against him on that contract to recover the price therein agreed to be paid for the work, in defence of which O'Connor relied on the same nonperformance by Varney, and in which an auditor to whom the case was referred * * * found that Varney was not entitled to recover under the agreement," as the work had been so imperfectly done that it would require a greater sum than the amount sued for to make it correspond with the contract. At the trial of the second action, the trial judge ruled that the judgment in the first suit was a bar, and directed a verdict for the defendant. The plaintiff O'Connor thereupon appealed.

Chief Justice Shaw, who rendered the opinion of the court, said: "The presiding judge rightly ruled that the former judgment was a bar to this action. A party against whom an action is brought on a contract has two modes of defending himself. He may allege specific breaches of the contract declared upon, and rely on them in defence. But if he intends to claim, by way of damages for nonperformance of the contract, more than the amount for which he is sued, he must not rely on the contract in defence, but must bring a cross action, and apply to the court to have the cases continued so that the executions may be set off. He cannot use the same defence, first as a shield, and then as a sword. * * *"

It will be noted that Varney was not entitled to recover in the first suit because his dereliction amounted to more than he sued for. This would seem to be exactly the situation in the case at bar.

* * * When the bank sued * * * [Mitchell] on his two notes, amounting to about $9,000, he had the option to interpose his claim as a defense to that suit or to demand judgment against the bank, by way of counterclaim, for the amount owing him by it. * * * The transaction out of which the case at bar arises is the same transaction that Mitchell pleaded as a defense in the federal suit. He might, therefore, "have recovered in that action, upon the same allegations and proofs which he there made, the judgment which he now seeks, if he had prayed for it." He did not do this, but attempted to split his cause of action, and to use one portion of it for defense in that suit and to reserve the remainder for offense in a subsequent suit, which, under applicable principles, could not be done. * * *

The judgment of the circuit court is affirmed.

NOTES AND QUESTIONS

1.   The federal courts and majority of the state courts require a party to include a compulsory counterclaim in the answer. See Federal Rule 13(a). Can a party raise the omitted claim in a separate action? See Peterson, *The Misguided Law of Compulsory Counterclaims in Default Cases*, 50 Ariz.L.Rev. 1107 (2008). Professor Wright has written that "it has never been doubted in any of the jurisdictions which have adopted such a rule that the pleader who fails to comply therewith is prohibited from subsequent assertion of his claim." Wright, *Estoppel by Rule: The Compulsory Counterclaim Under Modern Pleading*, 38 Minn.L.Rev. 423, 449 n.121 (1954). Is the preclusion a result of waiver or res judicata?

2.   At common law, would Mitchell's defense in the first action have been in the nature of a recoupment or a set-off? Consider the following definitions:

At common law the term "recoupment" described a claim that defendant could assert against plaintiff only if it arose from the same transaction as plaintiff's claim. It was purely defensive in its character and could be used only to defeat or diminish plaintiff's recovery; recoupment could not be the basis for affirmative relief. "Setoff," on the other hand, referred to a claim by defendant that was unrelated to plaintiff's claim. Moreover, unlike recoupment, setoff permitted defendant to assert an affirmative claim for relief. But the utility of setoff was limited by the requirement that the claim either be for a liquidated amount or arise out of a contract of judgment.

6 Wright, Miller & Kane, Federal Practice and Procedure § 1401 (3d ed.). Assuming that the defense would have been one or the other, would this have made a difference to Mitchell's right to bring a later suit for the excess?

3.   The Supreme Court cast doubt on defense preclusion as an independent doctrine separate from ordinary principles of claim and issue preclusion in LUCKY BRAND DUNGAREES, INC. v. MARCEL FASHIONS GROUP INC., 590 U.S. ___, 140 S.Ct. 1589, 206 L.Ed.2d 893 (2020). The parties, competitors in the fashion industry, both used the word "Lucky" as part of their marks on jeans and other apparel. They were involved in three rounds of trademark litigation. In a 2003 settlement, Lucky Brand agreed to stop using the phrase "Get Lucky"—a trademark claimed by Marcel Fashions—and Marcel Fashions agreed to release any claims regarding Lucky Brand's use of its own trademarks. Then, in a 2005 action, Lucky Brand sued Marcel Fashions for trademark infringement involving use of "Lucky" marks on a new line of clothing sold under a license from Marcel. In that lawsuit, Marcel Fashions filed counterclaims turning on Lucky Brand's alleged continued use of the "Get Lucky" mark. In its motion to dismiss the counterclaims and in its answer, Lucky Brand initially raised the 2003 settlement as a defense, but it did not press that defense again as the litigation proceeded through summary judgment and trial. The 2005 action concluded when the court permanently enjoined Lucky Brand from copying or imitating the "Get Lucky" mark, and a jury found against Lucky Brand on the remaining counterclaims.

In a 2011 action, Marcel Fashions sued Lucky Brand for trademark infringement involving "Lucky" marks but involving conduct that postdated the 2005 case. This time, Lucky Brand argued as a defense that Marcel Fashions had released any infringement claims concerning Lucky Brand's marks in the 2003 settlement agreement. Marcel Fashions countered that Lucky Brand was precluded from raising the release defense because it could have pursued that defense in the 2005 action and failed to do so. The district court disagreed with Marcel and granted Lucky Brand's motion to dismiss. But the Second Circuit vacated and remanded, concluding that, because Lucky Brand could have asserted the release defense in the 2005 action, the doctrine of defense preclusion barred it from asserting the defense in the new case.

A unanimous Supreme Court reversed. Because the 2011 action challenged different conduct and raised different claims from the 2005 action, the Court held that Lucky Brand could not be precluded in the later action from raising defenses that it had not litigated in the prior action. In an opinion by Justice Sotomayor, the Court emphasized that it had never recognized a doctrine of defense preclusion "as a standalone category of res judicata, unmoored from the two guideposts of issue preclusion and claim preclusion." Rather, the Court rested its decision on the fact that the parties agreed that issue preclusion did not apply, so Lucky Brand could be barred only if the requirements of claim preclusion were met. (In an extended footnote, the Court questioned whether claim preclusion ought ever to apply to defenses, but explicitly did not decide the question.)

The Court then held that claim preclusion did not apply because the two suits did not share a common nucleus of operative facts. To the contrary, "the two suits here were grounded on different conduct, involving different marks, occurring at different times." Nor could it be argued that allowing the assertion of defenses in the 2011 action would "impair or destroy" the judgment in the prior action, for the "lawsuits involved both different conduct and different trademarks." Indeed, the challenged conduct in the 2011 action occurred after the 2005 action had concluded, and "preclusion generally does not bar claims that are predicated on events that postdate the filing of the initial complaint." 590 U.S. at ___, 140 S.Ct. at 1596, 206 L.Ed.2d at 901–02 (internal quotation marks omitted). The Court emphasized the importance of this principle "in the trademark context, where the enforceability of a mark and likelihood of confusion between marks often turns on extrinsic facts that change over time."

The Court also distinguished cases involving judgment enforcement or a collateral attack on a prior judgment. The Court questioned whether these cases could be said to "stand for anything more than traditional claim- or issue-preclusion principles," and, in any event, they did not apply to Lucky Brand's defense of release. Id. at ___, 140 S.Ct. at 1597, 206 L.Ed.2d at 902–03.

4.   Generally, defendant's failure to raise a counterclaim that is not compulsory does not preclude a later action. However, as is suggested in the Supreme Court's decision in *Lucky Brand Dungarees*, Note 3, supra, the rule is more complicated when the claim that defendant seeks to assert would impair or nullify rights established in the first action. In Rudell v. Comprehensive Accounting Corp., 802 F.2d 926, 929 (7th Cir. 1986), cert. denied, 480 U.S. 907, 107 S.Ct. 1351, 94 L.Ed.2d 521 (1987), franchisees were barred from challenging a franchise agreement as procured by fraud, when that defense could have been raised in a prior arbitration proceeding. As the court of appeals explained, allowing the party to raise the fraud claim in a later action "could now serve to undermine or nullify the prior decision of the district court confirming the arbitration award."

———

Restatement (Second), Judgments § 20(1) (1982) sets out a nonexhaustive list of valid and final judgments that are not preclusive: (a) dismissal for lack of jurisdiction, dismissal for improper venue, dismissal for nonjoinder or misjoinder of parties; and (b) election or direction of a nonsuit. How should dismissals that are not expressly listed be treated?

———

COSTELLO v. UNITED STATES, 365 U.S. 265, 287, 81 S.Ct. 534, 545, 5 L.Ed.2d 551, 565 (1961), concerned an order dismissing a denaturalization proceeding on the ground that the government had failed to file an affidavit of good cause. Although the order did not specify that the dismissal was "without prejudice," the Supreme Court held that the dismissal was "for lack of jurisdiction" within the meaning of Federal Rule 41(b) and did not bar a subsequent denaturalization proceeding by the government. The Court explained:

> At common law dismissal on a ground not going to the merits was not ordinarily a bar to a subsequent action on the same claim. * * *

> We do not discern in Rule 41(b) a purpose to change this common-law principle with respect to dismissals in which the merits could not be reached for failure of the plaintiff to satisfy a precondition. * * * Although a sua sponte dismissal is not an enumerated ground, here * * * the defendant has been put to the trouble of preparing his defense because there was no initial bar to the Court's reaching the merits. * * *

> In contrast, the failure of the Government to file the affidavit of good cause in a denaturalization proceeding does not present a situation calling for the application of the policy making dismissals operative as adjudications on the merits. The defendant is not put to the necessity of preparing a defense because the failure of the Government to file the affidavit with the complaint require the dismissal of the proceeding.

Id. at 545–46, 81 S.Ct. at 287–88, 5 L.Ed.2d at 566.

The general rule in the federal system and in most state systems is that a dismissal for failure to state a claim carries claim preclusive effect. But that is not always the case. In the federal courts, an order granting a motion to dismiss a complaint under Rule 12(b)(6) for failure to state a claim is a dismissal with prejudice unless it contains specific language to the contrary. In some state courts, including New York, the presumption is reversed. Why should a later claim ever be barred if the pleading defect is curable? See Shreve, *Preclusion and Federal Choice of Law*, 64 Tex.L.Rev. 1209, 1218, n.44 (1986). The Restatement (Second) justifies the majority approach as follows:

> * * * [Claim preclusion] is warranted by the ease with which pleadings may be amended, normally at least once as a matter of course, and by the unfairness of requiring the defendant to submit to a second action (often initiated long after the first has come to an end) when no such amendment is sought, or when no appeal has been taken from an erroneous denial of leave to amend.

Restatement (Second) of Judgments § 19, comment *d* (1982).

C. ISSUE PRECLUSION

One of the most frequently quoted descriptions of what once was called collateral estoppel and is now referred to as issue preclusion was provided by the first Justice Harlan in Southern Pacific Railroad Co. v. United States, 168 U.S. 1, 48–49, 18 S.Ct. 18, 27, 42 L.Ed. 355, 377 (1897):

> The general principle announced in numerous cases is that a right, question, or fact distinctly put in issue and directly determined by a court of competent jurisdiction, as a ground of recovery, cannot be disputed in a subsequent suit between the same parties or their privies; and, even if the second suit is for a different cause of action, the right, question, or fact once so determined must, as between the same parties or their privies, be taken as conclusively established, so long as the judgment in the first suit remains unmodified.

As this passage reveals, there is a critical difference between claim preclusion and issue preclusion. Under the doctrine of claim preclusion, a claim may be "merged" or "barred" by a party's failure to raise the claim in a prior action. Issue preclusion, however, applies only to matters argued and decided in an earlier lawsuit.

For issue preclusion to exist, a proceeding must involve the identical issue that was present in a previous suit. However, more than a mere duplication of issues is required. It is necessary to examine the nature of the first action and the treatment that the issue received in it. Just as for claim preclusion, the judgment in the first action must have been of a certain "quality"—that is, it must have been valid, final, and on the merits (the "on the merits" requirement does not apply if the issue being precluded is exclusively a procedural issue). Moreover, the issue raised in a second suit must have been actually litigated in the first action, and must have been decided by the first court. In addition, determination of that issue must have been necessary to the court's judgment.

Some courts require still more before they will allow a party to invoke issue preclusion. For example, some demand that the issue have occupied a high position in the hierarchy of legal rules applied in the first action—that it was important. Others require "mutuality"—that is, that the party invoking preclusion would have been bound by an unfavorable judgment in the first suit. However, fewer and fewer courts now impose these latter two conditions, and the mutuality requirement in particular is no longer required if certain conditions are met.

A party may invoke issue preclusion in different procedural contexts. Two main situations are presented. First, the plaintiff in a second action may invoke issue preclusion offensively, in order to preclude litigation of an issue that was decided favorably to that party in a prior action. Second, the defendant in a second suit may seek to preclude relitigation of an issue that was decided in that party's favor in a prior suit. Some courts and commentators further distinguish between "direct" and "collateral" preclusion or estoppel—depending upon whether the second proceeding involves the same cause of action as the first. When the two suits involve the same cause of action, issue preclusion sometimes is referred to as direct estoppel. When the second suit involves a new claim or cause of action, issue preclusion sometimes is referred to as collateral estoppel.

1. ACTUALLY LITIGATED

CROMWELL V. COUNTY OF SAC
Supreme Court of the United States, 1876.
94 U.S. (4 Otto) 351, 24 L.Ed. 195.

Error to the Circuit Court of the United States for the District of Iowa.

JUSTICE FIELD delivered the opinion of the court.

This was an action on four bonds * * * each for $1,000, and four coupons for interest, attached to them, each for $100. The bonds were issued in 1860, and were made payable to bearer, in the city of New York, in the years 1868, 1869, 1870, and 1871, respectively, with annual interest at the rate of ten per cent a year.

To defeat this action, the defendant relied upon the estoppel of a judgment rendered in favor of the county in a prior action brought by one Samuel C. Smith upon certain earlier maturing coupons on the same bonds, accompanied with proof that the plaintiff Cromwell was at the time the owner of the coupons in that action, and that the action was prosecuted for his sole use and benefit.

* * *

In considering the operation of this judgment, it should be borne in mind * * * that there is a difference between the effect of a judgment as a bar or estoppel against the prosecution of a second action upon the same claim or demand, and its effect as an estoppel in another action between the same parties upon a different claim or cause of action. In the former case, the judgment, if rendered upon the merits, constitutes an absolute bar to a subsequent action.[b] [* * * The language * * * which is so often used, that a judgment estops not only as to every ground of recovery or defence actually presented in the action, but also as to every ground which might

---

[b] The Court's description of claim preclusion appears at p. 827, supra.

have been presented, is strictly accurate, when applied to the demand or claim in controversy. * * *

But where the second action between the same parties is upon a different claim or demand, the judgment in the prior action operates as an estoppel only as to those matters in issue or points controverted, upon the determination of which the finding or verdict was rendered. In all cases, therefore, where it is sought to apply the estoppel of a judgment rendered upon one cause of action to matters arising in a suit upon a different cause of action, the inquiry must always be as to the point or question actually litigated and determined in the original action, not what might have been thus litigated and determined. Only upon such matters is the judgment conclusive in another action.

The difference in the operation of a judgment in the two classes of cases mentioned is seen through all the leading adjudications upon the doctrine of estoppel. Thus, in the case of *Outram* v. *Morewood*, 3 East, 346, the defendants were held estopped from averring title to a mine, in an action of trespass for digging out coal from it, because, in a previous action for a similar trespass, they had set up the same title, and it had been determined against them. In commenting upon a decision cited in that case, Lord Ellenborough, in his elaborate opinion, said: "It is not the recovery, but the matter alleged by the party, and upon which the recovery proceeds, which creates the estoppel. The recovery of itself in an action of trespass is only a bar to the future recovery of damages for the same injury; but the estoppel precludes parties and privies from contending to the contrary of that point or matter of fact, which, having been once distinctly put in issue by them, or by those to whom they are privy in estate or law, has been, on such issue joined, solemnly found against them."

* * *

Various considerations, other than the actual merits, may govern a party in bringing forward grounds of recovery or defence in one action, which may not exist in another action upon a different demand, such as the smallness of the amount or the value of the property in controversy, the difficulty of obtaining the necessary evidence, the expense of the litigation, and his own situation at the time. A party acting upon considerations like these ought not to be precluded from contesting in a subsequent action other demands arising out of the same transaction. * * *

If, now, we consider the main question presented for our determination * * * its solution will not be difficult. It appears from the findings in the original action of Smith, that the county of Sac, by a vote of its people, authorized the issue of bonds to the amount of $10,000, for the erection of a court-house; that bonds to that amount were issued by the county judge, and delivered to one Meserey, with whom he had made a contract for the erection of the court-house; that immediately upon receipt of the bonds the contractor gave one of them as a gratuity to the county judge; and that the court-house was never constructed by the contractor, or by any other person pursuant to the contract. It also appears that the plaintiff had become, before their maturity, the holder of twenty-five coupons, which had been attached to the bonds, but there was no finding that he had ever given any value for them. * * * The case coming here on writ of error, this court held that the facts disclosed by the findings were sufficient evidence of fraud and illegality in the inception of the bonds to call upon the holder to show that he had given value for the coupons; and, not having done so, the judgment was affirmed. Reading the record of the lower court by the opinion and judgment of this court, it must be considered that the matters adjudged in that case were these: that the bonds were void as against the county in the hands of parties who did not acquire them before maturity and give value for them, and that the plaintiff, not having proved that he gave such value, was not entitled to recover upon the coupons. * * * The finding and judgment upon the invalidity of the bonds, as against the county, must be held to estop the plaintiff here from averring to the contrary. But as the bonds were negotiable instruments * * * they would be held as valid obligations against the county in the hands of a *bona fide* holder taking them for value before maturity * * *. If, therefore, the plaintiff received the bond and coupons in suit before maturity for value, as he offered to prove, he should have been permitted to show that fact. There was nothing adjudged in the former action in the finding that the plaintiff had not made such proof in that case which can preclude the present plaintiff from making such proof here. The fact that a party may not have shown that he gave value for one bond or coupon is not even presumptive, much less conclusive, evidence that he may not have given value for another and different bond or coupon. The exclusion of the evidence offered by the plaintiff was erroneous * * *.

Judgment reversed, and cause remanded for a new trial.

[The dissenting opinion of JUSTICE CLIFFORD is omitted.]

NOTES AND QUESTIONS

1.   Restatement (Second), Judgments § 27 (1982) adopted the actually litigated requirement as a condition for issue preclusion. What is the justification for the requirement? Consider this criticism:

> The Restatement Second offers several reasons to support its adoption of the "actually litigated" requirement. First, the Comment * * * states that an action may involve "so small an amount that litigation of the issue may cost more than the value of the lawsuit."[c] This is a rather curious rationale. It does not support the "actually

---

[c]   All quotations in the excerpt are from: Restatement (Second) of Judgments § 68, Comment *e* (Tent. Draft No. 4, 1977) [§ 27].

litigated" requirement; rather it supports a rejection of issue preclusion under any circumstances. If there is insufficient incentive to litigate a matter, then there should be no issue preclusion. Litigation in small claims courts or prosecutions for misdemeanors cannot give rise to issue preclusion because often those actions provide litigants with inadequate incentive to litigate. Although the line is not clearly defined, it seems reasonable to conclude that prosecutions for felonies and civil litigation involving substantial amounts will give rise to issue preclusion. The burden properly falls on the presumably precluded party to show why issue preclusion should not apply.

* * * [A second argument used to justify the actually litigated requirement is] that "the forum may be an inconvenient one in which to produce the necessary evidence or in which to litigate at all." If a valid judgment is going to be handed down, then this forum must have jurisdiction over the defendant and it is the forum of choice of the plaintiff. As the forum of choice of the plaintiff, it is proper to hold that the plaintiff should be bound by any adverse decision reached by the court. It is only in the case of the defendant that he might be able to assert that he should not be bound because it is inconvenient.

In light of (a) the present constitutional limitations on the exercise of jurisdiction over defendants, (b) the fact that the suit by definition involves a substantial interest, and (c) the availability of procedures to get and present the relevant evidence, this justification is not very persuasive. Would it not be better to hold for issue preclusion, and then permit the apparently precluded party to explain why preclusion should not apply?

The [Restatement's] Comment also gives as a reason for the "actually litigated" rule that a rule to the contrary "might serve to discourage compromise, to decrease the likelihood that the issues in an action would be narrowed by stipulation, and thus to intensify litigation." This litigation, where there is the incentive to litigate, must involve substantial interests on the part of the parties. The issue preclusion that may flow from the judgment does not change the suit from unimportant to important. The suit is, by definition, important. If a compromise is going to be discouraged, it probably will be by the size of the present suit. If there is going to be a refusal to stipulate and thus narrow issues, in all probability it will be because of the importance of the instant suit and not because of the issue preclusion that may flow from the decision.

Vestal, *The Restatement (Second) of Judgments: A Modest Dissent*, 66 Cornell L.Rev. 464, 473–74 (1981).

2. Should an issue be considered actually litigated simply because it is included in the pleadings? Consider this analysis:

A good case can be made for saying that if a matter is distinctly put
in issue and formally admitted, the party making the admission
should be bound by it in subsequent litigation. This was the old
formulation of the rule of "judicial estoppel," as it was then called:
"The former verdict is conclusive only as to facts directly and
distinctly put in issue * * *." But how can a matter be "directly and
distinctly put in issue"? Obviously, by actual litigation. Another way
is through pleadings. In a pleading system where matters are
"distinctly put in issue," it makes sense to say that if a proposition is
clearly asserted, and if a party is called upon solemnly to admit or
deny the proposition, and if the stakes are high enough to assure that
the party is serious in dealing with the issue, and if the party then
admits or fails to deny the proposition, then he ought to be estopped
from controverting it on some other occasion, particularly if that
other occasion involves essentially the same transaction. The clearest
case for such an estoppel is where a defendant pleads guilty to a
substantial criminal charge and then seeks in civil litigation
concerning the same transaction to assert that he did not commit the
criminal act. Particularly galling is the situation where a criminal
convicted on his own guilty plea seeks as plaintiff in a subsequent
civil action to claim redress based on a repudiation of the confession.
* * *

The same principle could apply when an issue is put forward and
admitted "distinctly"—that is, clearly and solemnly—in a civil case.
It is therefore appropriate to impose an estoppel based on a formal
admission in a civil case, and the law of evidence does so. A judicial
admission is considered in subsequent litigations as prima facie
evidence that the admitted matter is true.

* * *

Professor Vestal says there should be an estoppel because, where
there is an incentive to deny, failure to deny constitutes an
admission. This turns the notion of incentive to litigate on its head.
The "incentive to litigate" formula, as used in most of the cases and
in the *Restatement Second,* allows a party who *did* litigate an issue
to relitigate it if the party can show that the original litigation was a
side show rather than a struggle to the finish. [See Restatement
(Second), Judgments § 28, comment *j* (1982).] The *Restatement
Second* allows a party to rebut the inference naturally drawn from
the fact that the issue was actually litigated—the inference that the
party had treated the issue with entire seriousness in the first
litigation. In Professor Vestal's system, however, "incentive to
litigate" allows a court to conjecture that the party probably had
reason to litigate the issue in the first action, and to conjecture
further that the failure to litigate is an admission of a proposition not
litigated. Professor Vestal's "opportunity" theory allows the court to

infer that the issue was important to a party whose behavior indicates he thought the issue was unimportant, and, having done that, to convict the party by his silence. * * *

Hazard, *Revisiting the Second Restatement of Judgments: Issue Preclusion and Related Problems*, 66 Cornell L.Rev. 564, 577–79, 584 (1981).

3. Should a default judgment be given issue preclusive effect? Restatement (First) treated the default as an implied admission of the truth of the allegations, but Restatement (Second) withholds preclusive effect because the implied admission is seen as only a fiction and the issue was not actually litigated. See Noland, *Finding Fault with Defaults: New York Courts' Inconsistent Application of Issue Preclusion to Default Judgments*, 31 Cardozo L.Rev. 941, 953 (2010). Not all states follow the rule of Restatement (Second) on this question.

Generally, a penalty dismissal (for example, imposed under Federal Rule 37) carries claim preclusive effect but not issue preclusive effect, because the dismissal does not in and of itself actually litigate any of the issues. However, the procedural context and the purposes of the sanction can affect the court's decision. In In re Bush, 62 F.3d 1319 (11th Cir. 1995), the Eleventh Circuit, on an issue of first impression, considered whether in a bankruptcy discharge exception proceeding, a default judgment based on allegations of fraud may be used to establish conclusively the elements of fraud and prevent discharge of the judgment debt. In this context, the appeals court held that a default judgment entered as a sanction for the deliberate refusal to participate in discovery carried issue preclusive effect. The court explained:

> Where a party has substantially participated in an action in which he had a full and fair opportunity to defend on the merits, but subsequently chooses not to do so, and even attempts to frustrate the effort to bring the action to judgment, it is not an abuse of discretion * * * for a district court to apply the doctrine of collateral estoppel to prevent further litigation of the issues resolved by the default judgment in the prior action.

Id. at 1326. There is division on this question. E.g., In re Martel, 332 B.R. 922 (M.D.Fla. 2005).

4. What is the preclusive effect of a guilty plea in a subsequent civil lawsuit? Not surprisingly, Professor Vestal has argued that a guilty plea should be given preclusive effect unless the defendant can show that an adequate opportunity or incentive to litigate the issue was not present in the first lawsuit. Restatement (Second), Judgments § 85, comment *b* (1982) does not exempt a guilty plea from the "actually litigated" requirement and withholds issue preclusive effect, but notes that a guilty plea is admissible into evidence in later civil suits. Despite the *Restatement*'s position, some courts, without always setting forth a clear rationale, have granted preclusive effect to guilty pleas in subsequent suits involving the essential elements of the

crime. See Shapiro, *Should a Guilty Plea Have Preclusive Effect?*, 70 Iowa L.Rev. 27 (1984).

5.   How should a court determine what was actually decided in a prior litigation? Will the difficulty of this task be affected by whether the case was tried to a judge or to a jury? Are there any procedural rules that can play a role in defining what a suit has decided? Consider, in particular, Federal Rule 49 (special verdict) and Federal Rule 52 (findings and conclusions). The proponent of the defense has the burden to plead and prove it. In making that showing, the record of the prior trial, as well as extraneous evidence, may be used to prove what issues actually were decided. See 18 Wright, Miller & Cooper, Federal Practice and Procedure § 4420 (3d ed.).

6.   Should a judgment carry issue preclusive effect when an appeal is pending? Isn't there the problem of inconsistency if a judgment is given issue preclusive effect and then is reversed on appeal? On the other hand, isn't there a danger that the losing party will seek appeal only to delay allowing the prevailing party to benefit from her judgment? Should a judgment that cannot be appealed trigger issue preclusive effect? For a discussion of these and other issues relevant to issue preclusion, see Cavanagh, *Issue Preclusion in Complex Litigation*, 29 Rev.Litig. 859 (2010).

2.   NECESSARILY DECIDED

RIOS V. DAVIS

Court of Civil Appeals of Texas, Eastland, 1963.
373 S.W.2d 386.

COLLINGS, JUSTICE.

Juan C. Rios brought this suit against Jessie Hubert Davis in the District Court to recover damages * * * alleged to have been sustained as a result of personal injuries received * * * in an automobile collision. Plaintiff alleged that his injuries were proximately caused by negligence on the part of the defendant. The defendant answered alleging that Rios was guilty of contributory negligence. Also, among other defenses, the defendant urged a plea of res judicata and collateral estoppel based upon the findings and the judgment entered * * * in a suit between the same parties in the County Court at Law of El Paso County. The plea of res judicata was sustained and judgment was entered in favor of the defendant * * *.

It is shown by the record that * * * Popular Dry Goods Company brought suit against appellee Davis * * * seeking to recover for damages to its truck in the sum of $443.97, alleged to have been sustained in the same collision here involved. Davis answered alleging contributory negligence on the part of Popular and joined appellant Juan C. Rios as a third party defendant and sought to recover from Rios $248.50, the alleged amount of damages to his automobile. The jury * * * found that Popular Dry Goods Company and Rios were guilty of negligence proximately causing the collision. However, the jury also found that Davis was guilty of negligence proximately causing the collision, and judgment was entered * * * denying Popular Dry Goods any recovery against Davis and denying Davis any recovery against Rios.

Appellant Rios in his third point contends that the District Court erred in sustaining appellee's plea of res judicata based upon the judgment of the County Court at Law because the findings on the issues regarding appellant's negligence and liability * * * were immaterial because the judgment entered in that case was in favor of appellant. We sustain this point. * * * The sole basis for the judgment * * * as between Rios and Davis was the findings concerning the negligence of Davis. The finding that Rios was negligent was not essential or material to the judgment and the judgment was not based thereon. On the contrary, the finding * * * that Rios was negligent proximately causing the accident would, if it had been controlling, led [sic] to a different result. Since the judgment was in favor of Rios he had no right or opportunity to complain of or to appeal from the finding that he was guilty of such negligence even if such finding had been without any support whatever in the evidence. The right of appeal is from a judgment and not from a finding. * * * In the case of Word v. Colley, Tex.Civ.App., 173 S.W. 629, at page 634 of its opinion (Error Ref.), the court stated as follows:

> It is the judgment, and not the verdict or the conclusions of fact, filed by a trial court which constitutes the estoppel, and a finding of fact by a jury or a court which does not become the basis or one of the grounds of the judgment rendered is not conclusive against either party to the suit.

* * *

The judgment is, therefore, reversed, and the cause is remanded.

NOTES AND QUESTIONS

1. The verdict in the earlier action in *Rios* reflects the consistent practice, utilized in some states, of submitting a case to the jury on "special issues." Does *Rios* offer a reason for special verdicts to be used more frequently?

2. In *Rios,* even though the jury gave a special verdict, certain issues were not given preclusive effect because the outcome did not depend upon those findings. However, multiple findings have been found preclusive when the jury could not have arrived at the same judgment without each of those findings. See, e.g., Patterson v. Saunders, 194 Va. 607, 74 S.E.2d 204 (1953).

3. The court in *Rios* held that the judgment in the earlier case did not estop Rios from denying his own negligence. Should the earlier judgment estop Davis from denying his own negligence?

4.   The court in *Rios* supported its view by noting that Rios could not appeal the finding of his negligence in the earlier action. See also Restatement (Second), Judgments § 28(1) (1982). Should the prevailing party in the earlier action be permitted in a later action to attack a finding that was necessary to the judgment in the earlier action? Such a situation will not be common.

5.   How would you justify each of these statements?

(a)   When a judgment is supported by multiple independent grounds, all of the grounds may be relitigated. See Halpern v. Schwartz, 426 F.2d 102, 106 (2d Cir. 1970).

(b)   When a judgment is supported by multiple independent grounds, none of the grounds may be relitigated. See In re Westgate-California Corp., 642 F.2d 1174 (9th Cir. 1981).

(c)   When a judgment is supported by multiple independent grounds, the primary issue may not be relitigated, but secondary issues are not barred. See National Satellite Sports, Inc. v. Eliadis, Inc., 253 F.3d 900 (6th Cir. 2001).

For a full discussion of each approach, see Brownewell, Note, *Rethinking the Restatement View (Again!): Multiple Independent Holdings and the Doctrine of Issue Preclusion*, 37 Val.U.L.Rev. 879 (2003), in which the author recounts the following shift in the position of the Restatement with respect to the collateral estoppel effect of multiple alternative holdings:

> The American Law Institute ("ALI") completely reversed its position on the proper procedure for multiple independent holdings and collateral estoppel between the 1942 edition and the 1982 edition. According to the Restatement of Judgments section 68, comment *n*, when a judgment is based on alternative grounds, the "judgment is determinative on both grounds." The Second Restatement, however, mandates that, when there are multiple independent holdings in the first decision, the judgment is not conclusive to either issue alone.

> The Second Restatement compares a judgment on multiple independent grounds to that of a nonessential determination. One of the main reasons for this shift was that in 1977, when the Tentative Draft Number Four of the Second Restatement of Judgments was published, *Halpern v. Schwartz* [p. 858, Note 5(a), supra] was the most recent decision on the question of issue preclusion and multiple independent grounds for a decision. The rationale behind the Second Restatement's position is that determinations in the alternative may not have been as carefully considered as a judgment based on one holding. The second justification deals with the issue of appeal. The losing party, who is entitled to take an appeal from both determinations, might be dissuaded from appealing because there is a likelihood that at least one of the determinations would be upheld, although the other determination would not even be analyzed by the appellate court. The Second Restatement emphasizes that, "in the

interest of predictability and simplicity," the result of nonpreclusion should be uniform.

Id. at 892–93 (citations omitted). Is it appropriate to analogize multiple independent holdings to nonessential holdings? Is it significant that the multiple holdings are appealable?

3. DEFINING AND CHARACTERIZING THE ISSUE

UNITED STATES v. MOSER, 266 U.S. 236, 45 S.Ct. 66, 69 L.Ed. 262 (1924). Moser was a captain when he retired from the Navy. In his first action, he won a ruling that service as a Naval Academy cadet during the Civil War constituted service during the war that entitled him to be retired with the rank and three-fourths of the sea pay of the next higher grade. Although the Court of Claims changed its mind about the interpretation of the pension statutes, he won his next two actions for later installments of his pay on grounds of preclusion. In his fourth action for still later installments, the Court of Claims ruled both that its initial interpretation of the statute had been correct and that in any event he was entitled to rely on preclusion. The Supreme Court affirmed solely on the res judicata ground:

> * * * The question expressly and definitely presented in this suit is the same as that definitely and actually litigated and adjudged in favor of the claimant in the three preceding suits, viz. whether he occupied the status of an officer who had served during the Civil War.
>
> The contention of the government seems to be that the doctrine of res judicata does not apply to questions of law; and, in a sense, that is true. It does not apply to unmixed questions of law. Where, for example, a court in deciding a case has enunciated a rule of law, the parties in a subsequent action upon a different demand are not estopped from insisting that the law is otherwise, merely because the parties are the same in both cases. But a *fact, question* or *right* distinctly adjudged in the original action cannot be disputed in a subsequent action, even though the determination was reached upon an erroneous view or by an erroneous application of the law. That would be to affirm the principle in respect of the thing adjudged but, at the same time, deny it all efficacy by sustaining a challenge to the grounds upon which the judgment was based. * * *

Id. at 241–42, 45 S.Ct. at 67, 69 L.Ed. at 264.

NOTES AND QUESTIONS

1. *Moser* held that "unmixed questions of law" are not subject to issue preclusion. In UNITED STATES v. STAUFFER CHEMICAL CO., 464 U.S.

165, 172, 104 S.Ct. 575, 579, 78 L.Ed.2d 388, 394 (1984), the Court acknowledged that "the purpose underlying the exception for 'unmixed questions of law' in successive actions on unrelated claims is far from clear." Rather than engaging in the virtually impossible task of delineating the boundary between an issue of fact, law, or mixed fact and law, the Court adopted the more pragmatic approach suggested in Restatement (Second), Judgments § 28, comment *b* (1982):

> When the claims in two separate actions between the same parties are the same or are closely related * * * it is not ordinarily necessary to characterize an issue as one of fact or of law for purposes of issue preclusion. * * * In such a case, it is unfair to the winning party and an unnecessary burden on the courts to allow repeated litigation of the same issue in what is essentially the same controversy, even if the issue is regarded as one of "law."

Why isn't the doctrine of stare decisis an adequate protection against the undue burden of relitigation of issues of "law"? Further, is it appropriate, as a noted commentator has asked, for "the law to remain static as between two litigants in a prior case if it is subject to change in any other litigation"? Shapiro, Civil Procedure: Preclusion in Civil Actions 54 (2001).

2. In HERRERA v. WYOMING, 587 U.S. ___, 139 S.Ct. 1686, 203 L.Ed.2d 846 (2019), the Supreme Court concluded that a change in law justified an exception to issue preclusion. Herrera, a member of the Crow Tribe, was convicted in a Wyoming state court of taking elk off-season and without a Wyoming hunting license. He based his defense on an 1868 Treaty in which the Crow Indian Nation ceded lands to the United States in exchange for the right to hunt on unoccupied portions of those lands. Wyoming argued that the treaty had been terminated when the state was admitted to the Union. Wyoming invoked issue preclusion based on a prior judgment in Crow Tribe of Indians v. Repsis, 73 F.3d 982 (10th Cir. 1995), a case that had involved the same treaty and had been argued on behalf of the Crow Tribe. *Repsis* determined that the treaty rights did not survive statehood.

In a five-to-four decision, the Supreme Court held that *Repsis* did not preclude Herrera from asserting a defense under the treaty. Although *Repsis* involved the same treaty and the same tribe, it relied on the reasoning of an older Supreme Court case, Ward v. Race Horse, 163 U.S. 504, 16 S.Ct. 1076, 41 L.Ed.2d 244 (1896), which the Court had repudiated—after the *Repsis* decision—in Minnesota v. Mille Lac Band of Chippewa Indians, 526 U.S. 172, 119 S.Ct. 1187, 143 L.Ed.2d 270 (1999). The majority explained that under the change-in-law exception to issue preclusion, *Repsis* was not a bar to litigating whether the treaty's grant of hunting rights survived Wyoming's statehood:

> Because this Court's intervening decision in *Mille Lacs* repudiated the reasoning on which the Tenth Circuit relied in *Repsis*, *Repsis* does not preclude Herrera from arguing that the 1868 Treaty right survived Wyoming's statehood.

Under the doctrine of issue preclusion, "a prior judgment ... foreclos[es] successive litigation of an issue of fact or law actually litigated and resolved in a valid court determination essential to the prior judgment." *New Hampshire* v. *Maine*, 532 U.S. 742, 748–749, 121 S. Ct. 1808, 149 L.Ed. 2d 968 (2001). Even when the elements of issue preclusion are met, however, an exception may be warranted if there has been an intervening " 'change in [the] applicable legal context.' " *Bobby* v. *Bies*, 556 U.S. 825, 834, 129 S. Ct. 2145, 173 L.Ed. 2d 1173 (2009) (quoting Restatement (Second) of Judgments § 28, Comment *c* (1980)) * * * ; *Commissioner* v. *Sunnen*, 333 U.S. 591, 599, 68 S. Ct. 715, 92 L.Ed. 898 (1948) * * *. The change-in-law exception recognizes that applying issue preclusion in changed circumstances may not "advance the equitable administration of the law." *Bobby*, 556 U.S., at 836–837, 129 S. Ct. 2145, 173 L.Ed.2d 1173.

* * * We conclude that a change in law justifies an exception to preclusion in this case. * * * Although we recognize that it may be difficult at the margins to discern whether a particular legal shift warrants an exception to issue preclusion, this is not a marginal case. At a minimum, a repudiated decision does not retain preclusive force.

587 U.S. ___, 139 S.Ct. at 1697–98, 203 L.Ed.2d at 858–59.

In dissent, Justice Alito contended that *Repsis* also relied on another ground for decision—namely, that the lands in question were occupied and no longer subject to Crow hunting rights under the treaty—and that this ground was not disturbed by *Mille Lacs*. (In a footnote, the majority rejected the argument that the Wyoming state courts gave issue preclusive effect to that ground for decision.) As to the scope of the change-in-law exception to issue preclusion, the dissent stated:

* * * There is support in the Restatement (Second) of Judgments for the general proposition that a change in law may alter a judgment's preclusive effect, § 28, Comment *c*, p. 276 (1980), and in a prior case, *Bobby* v. *Bies* * * * , we invoked that provision. But we have never actually held that a prior judgment lacked preclusive effect on this ground. Nor have we ever defined how much the relevant "legal context" must change in order for the exception to apply. If the exception is applied too aggressively, it could dangerously undermine the important interests served by issue preclusion. So caution is in order in relying on that exception here.

The majority thinks that the exception applies because *Mille Lacs* effectively overruled *Race Horse*, even though it did not say that in so many words. But that is a questionable interpretation. The fact of the matter is that the *Mille Lacs* majority held back from actually overruling *Race Horse*, even though the dissent claimed that it had effectively done so. * * * And while the opinion of the Court repudiated one of the two grounds that the *Race Horse* Court gave for its decision * * * , it is by no means clear that *Mille Lacs* also rejected the second ground (the conclusion that the terms of the Act admitting Wyoming to the Union manifested a congressional intent not to burden the State with the right created by the 1868 Treaty). * * *

On this reading, it appears that *Mille Lacs* did not reject the second ground for the decision in *Race Horse* but simply found it inapplicable to the facts of the case at hand. I do not claim that this reading of *Mille Lacs* is indisputable, but it is certainly reasonable, and if it is correct, *Mille Lacs* did not change the legal context as much as the majority suggests. * * *

The majority cites no authority holding that a decision like *Mille Lacs* is sufficient to deprive a prior judgment of its issue-preclusive effect. * * *

587 U.S. ___, 139 S.Ct. at 1707–08, 203 L.Ed.2d at 870.

———

THE EVERGREENS DOCTRINE. In addition to limiting collateral estoppel to identical issues, courts sometimes have distinguished between "ultimate" and "mediate" facts when determining whether issues decided in one suit will be viewed as preclusive in a later one. The most influential explanation of this distinction is found in Judge Learned Hand's opinion in THE EVERGREENS v. NUNAN, 141 F.2d 927 (2d Cir. 1944), cert. denied, 323 U.S. 720, 65 S.Ct. 49, 89 L.Ed. 579 (1944). The gist of the doctrine is simple: imagine a lawsuit as a logical structure resembling a pyramid. At its base are the facts introduced into evidence. From these facts are drawn conclusions that, when combined with other deductions or evidence, lead eventually to "ultimate facts" that establish a legal right, duty, or status. The ultimate facts are the summit of the structure; all that supports them are "mediate data." *The Evergreens* held that only matters constituting ultimate facts in the second action are subject to preclusion by collateral estoppel.

The controversy in *The Evergreens* turned on the value for tax purposes of cemetery lots appropriated by the City of New York. The lots were of two kinds, improved and unimproved. An earlier proceeding had determined the value of the improved lots, and that determination was accepted in the later action without dispute. The earlier proceeding also had fixed the cost of upgrading the unimproved lots to "improved" status. Plaintiff maintained that these two findings taken together should determine the value of the unimproved lots: the uncontested value of the improved lots minus the cost of improving them should be taken as the value of the unimproved lots.

The Second Circuit rejected this argument, relying on the distinction between ultimate and mediate facts. Judge Hand first noted that authorities differed concerning whether mediate facts or only ultimate

18 Wright, Miller & Cooper, Federal Practice and Procedure § 4424 (3d ed.).

D. THE REQUIRED QUALITY OF JUDGMENT

Only judgments of a certain quality will give rise to preclusion. The traditional words used to describe that quality was that the judgment must be valid, final, and on the merits. Keep in mind that courts enter judgments that are regarded as "on the merits" although reached without a full adjudicatory proceeding. In addition, courts increasingly are faced with the prior determinations of state or federal administrative agencies that act in a quasi-judicial capacity. This Section highlights some of the difficult questions the "quality of judgment" requirement raises.

1. JUDGMENTS OF JUDICIAL TRIBUNALS

HANOVER LOGANSPORT, INC. V. ROBERT C. ANDERSON, INC.

Court of Appeals of Indiana, Third District, 1987.
512 N.E.2d 465.

STATON, JUDGE.

[Hanover Logansport, Inc. ("Hanover") and Robert C. Anderson, Inc. ("Anderson") entered into an agreement pursuant to which Hanover agreed to lease certain property to Anderson for use as a liquor store. Hanover failed to deliver the premises on the agreed upon date, and Anderson filed suit for breach of the lease. Before trial, Hanover offered to deliver the real estate to Anderson, and Anderson accepted with the following reservation: "[T]he offer is only accepted for purposes of mitigation of damages and not in settlement of damages arising to Plaintiff caused by Defendants' breach of contract."

The parties filed a stipulation that "the judgment as stipulated to by the Defendants herein should be recorded of record in the judgment record book of the County of St. Joseph." Anderson took possession of the premises, and, after several months, Hanover moved to dismiss the earlier breach action. The trial court denied the motion, and Hanover appealed, arguing that the prior consent judgment precluded any further litigation based on the same cause of action.]

* * *

Hanover makes the following argument:

1.   The complaint seeks specific performance of the lease or *in the alternative* money damages for loss of profits *over the term of the lease.*

2.   Hanover made an offer of real estate pursuant to [Indiana Trial Rule 68] consistent with one of the alternatives—specific performance—in the complaint.[d]

3.   Anderson accepted the offer.

4.   Under T.R. 68, the clerk is required to enter judgment.

5.   Anderson took possession of the real estate.

6.   By accepting the offer of real estate and taking possession of the premises, Anderson chose its remedy and is now barred by law from continuing the litigation.

Anderson argues that (1) an offer of judgment under T.R. 68 may be in part or in whole; and (2) both Hanover and the trial court were on notice that the offer of judgment did not address and dispose of the whole of its claim. Anderson points to the portion of its acceptance which states: " * * * Further, the offer is only accepted for purposes of mitigation of damages and not in settlement of damages arising to Plaintiff caused by Defendants' breach of contract." In its brief, Anderson states: "The acceptance of said offer specifically states that the lease between the parties would be as contracted, subject to the conditions in the lease, but that the Plaintiff did not waive damages for breach of contract which arose due to the failure of Defendant to honor its contract *between the date the offer was signed and the date the Court entered an Order approving the settlment [sic]* [in original] *as to possession*." (Emphasis added.)

Thus, we address the following issue: Whether, by law, a plaintiff, who accepts an offer of judgment which conforms to one of the alternative prayers for relief contained in his complaint, may then seek additional damages arising from the same cause of action.

* * *

A consent judgment has a dual aspect. It represents an agreement between the parties settling the underlying dispute and providing for the entry of judgment in a pending or contemplated action. See James, *Consent Judgments as Collateral Estoppel*, 108 U.Pa.L.Rev. 173, 175 (1959). It also represents the entry of such a judgment by a court—with all that this means in the way of committing the force of society to implement the judgment of its courts. Id.

As a result of this dual aspect, some courts and commentators focus on the contractual aspect of a consent judgment, thus determining whatever

---

[d]   Indiana Rule 68: Offer of judgment

* * * An offer not accepted shall be deemed withdrawn and evidence thereof is not admissible except in a proceeding to determine costs. If the judgment finally obtained by the offeree is not more favorable than the offer, the offeree must pay the costs incurred after the making of the offer. The fact that an offer is made but not accepted does not preclude a subsequent offer. * * *

its preclusive effect may be by ascertaining the intent of the parties—in the same way courts construe other agreements. * * *

Yet, other courts and commentators focus on the entry of a consent judgment by a court and argue that such a judgment possesses the same force with regard to *res judicata* and collateral estoppel as a judgment entered after a trial on the merits. * * *

Proponents of the consent-judgment-as-contract theory argue that if consent judgments are given preclusive effect regardless of the intent of the parties, such a rule would lessen the chance of compromise between them. This, they argue, is true for two reasons. First, in many cases, the application of such a rule (at least in regard to the collateral estoppel aspect of the rule) would be unforeseeable—it would reach into all possible future disputes among the parties, no matter how hard it may be to predict them at the outset of the first litigation. Second, if all issues and claims must be negotiated and dealt with in a consent judgment or foregone forever, parties will be reluctant to enter into such an agreement for fear that they will "miss" something.

But, proponents of the consent-judgment-as-final judgment theory counter that the preclusive effect of a consent judgment serves several objectives. Among them, economy is achieved in the use of judicial resources, the harassment of parties avoided, and the possibility of inconsistent results is eliminated. * * *

We note that T.R. 68 is intended to encourage settlements, discourage vexatious suits, and avoid protracted litigation. See 12 Wright & Miller, *Federal Practice and Procedure,* § 3001. Therefore, the result we reach should serve those purposes.

Because we agree that if all issues and claims must be negotiated and dealt with in a consent judgment or foregone forever, parties will be reluctant to enter into such agreements, we adopt the consent-judgment-as-contract theory and hold that the preclusive effect of a consent judgment must be measured by the intent of the parties. However, it must be clear that *both* parties have agreed to reserve an issue or claim. *And,* it must be precisely stated what issues or claims are being reserved.

* * *

[I]n order to insure that both parties have agreed to reserve a claim or issue[9] and that the reserved claim or issue is clearly apparent to both parties, we hold that (1) the reservation must be incorporated into the offer of judgment itself and (2) it must be an inherent part of the original complaint. Thus, for example, before a party may reserve an additional

---

9   Here, we are dealing with the reservation of a claim for damages. However, there may be cases where a party desires to reserve an issue or another cause of action. The same rule would apply in those situations.

cause of action in a consent judgment, that cause of action must have been originally set out on the face of the complaint. Because Anderson did not include a claim for damages for delay in tendering the real estate in its Complaint, it is precluded from reserving such a claim in the consent judgment.[10] * * *

[T]his rule will avoid protracted litigation, since it requires plaintiffs to reserve a claim or issue both in the complaint and in the consent judgment. If we were to require such a reservation only in the consent judgment (as Anderson asks us to do here), the potential for protracted litigation would be too great. For example, in a situation where A and B have entered a consent judgment and B thinks the controversy has ended, such a rule would allow A: (1) to argue that it had no intention of ending the controversy and (2) to proceed on the alleged balance of its claim. This could potentially allow the litigation to continue on and on through the years.

But, under the rule we have set forth here, A would not be allowed to make such a claim unless it was shown that a reservation was made in A's complaint and in the consent judgment. In this way, courts can be assured it was also B's intention to continue the litigation.

Therefore, we reverse and remand to the trial court, with instructions to enter a judgment on the offer of judgment and to grant Hanover's motion to dismiss.

Reversed and remanded.

NOTES AND QUESTIONS

1.   Should the agreement between Hanover and Anderson be considered a court judgment, or is it more properly characterized as a contract? If it is merely a contract, should the intent of the parties as to its preclusive effect be dispositive? Did the parties require the approval of the court in the form of a judgment to make a new contract? Do you agree that a rule that did not make the intent of the parties dispositive would have the effect of discouraging consent judgments? See Easterbrook, *Justice and Contract in Consent Judgments*, 1987 U.Chi.Legal F. 19.

2.   Even if a consent decree has claim preclusive effect, should it also have issue preclusive effect? Doesn't collateral estoppel doctrine require that

---

[10]   Indiana Rules of Procedure, Trial Rule 12(B) states, in part:

" * * * When a motion to dismiss is sustained for failure to state a claim under subdivision (B)(6) of this rule the pleading may be amended once as of right pursuant to Rule 15(A) within ten [10] days after service of notice of the court's order sustaining the motion and thereafter with permission of the court pursuant to such rule. * * *"

However, Anderson may not take advantage of this rule by amending the complaint, then arguing it has met the requirements set out by this opinion. Obviously, the claim or issue must be in the complaint at the time the parties reach an agreement or enter a judgment.

an issue be "actually litigated"? In ARIZONA v. CALIFORNIA, 530 U.S. 392, 120 S.Ct. 2304, 147 L.Ed.2d 374 (2000), the Supreme Court explained:

> * * * [S]ettlements ordinarily occasion no *issue preclusion* (sometimes called collateral estoppel), unless it is clear * * * that the parties intend their agreement to have such an effect. * * * "In most circumstances, it is recognized that consent agreements ordinarily are intended to preclude any further litigation on the claim presented but are not intended to preclude further litigation on any of the issues presented. Thus consent judgments ordinarily support claim preclusion but not issue preclusion." * * * This differentiation is grounded in basic res judicata doctrine. It is the general rule that issue preclusion attaches only "[w]hen an issue of fact or law is actually litigated and determined by a valid and final judgment, and the determination is essential to the judgment." Restatement (Second) of Judgments, § 27 * * * (1982). "In the case of a judgment entered by confession, consent, or default, none of the issues is actually litigated. * * *."

Id. at 414, 120 S.Ct. at 2319, 147 L.Ed.2d at 395–96 (internal citation omitted).

3.   Should a final judgment be stripped of its preclusive effect if both parties consent to that result on appeal? A stipulated reversal allows parties seeking to facilitate settlement during the pendency of an appeal to join in asking the appellate court to set aside a trial court judgment, rather than dismissing the appeal, thereby avoiding the preclusive effect of a final judgment. In U.S. BANCORP MORTGAGE CO. v. BONNER MALL PARTNERSHIP, 513 U.S. 18, 115 S.Ct. 386, 130 L.Ed.2d 233 (1994), the Supreme Court unanimously denied petitioner's motion to vacate a judgment of a court of appeals in a case that had become moot by reason of settlement after certiorari was sought, but the Court recognized that vacatur could be granted in "extraordinary circumstances." Id. at 29, 115 S.Ct. at 393, 130 L.Ed.2d at 244. What circumstances might count as "extraordinary"?

Two years earlier, in NEARY v. REGENTS OF THE UNIVERSITY OF CALIFORNIA, 3 Cal.4th 273, 10 Cal.Rptr.2d 859, 834 P.2d 119 (1992), the California Supreme Court held that stipulated reversals are consistent with the policy in favor of peaceful settlements and should be granted *absent* a showing of extraordinary circumstances warranting an exception to this general rule. What did the California court mean by "extraordinary circumstances"? The California legislature during its 1999–2000 session modified California Code of Civil Procedure § 128(a)(8) to provide that an appellate court shall not permit a stipulated reversal absent a finding of two specified conditions:

(a)   There is no reasonable possibility that the interests of nonparties or the public will be adversely affected by the reversal.

(b)   The reasons of the parties for requesting reversal outweigh the
erosion of public trust that may result from the nullification of a
judgment and the risk that the availability of stipulated reversal
will reduce the incentive for pretrial settlement.

See City of Palmdale v. State Bd. of Equalization, 206 Cal.App.4th 329, 141
Cal.Rptr.3d 719 (2012) (motion to vacate judgment that exposed an agency's
deficiencies denied because it would adversely affect the public interest). For a
discussion of issues raised by *Bancorp* and *Neary*, see Resnik, *Whose
Judgment? Vacating Judgments, Preferences for Settlement, and the Role of
Adjudication at the Close of the Twentieth Century,* 41 UCLA L.Rev. 1471
(1994).

4.   Suppose that rather than settling the dispute in *Hanover*, the parties
merely stipulated most of the material facts concerning the lease agreement.
The case went to trial, further factual findings were made, and a decision was
rendered for Hanover against Anderson. Should the admissions in those
stipulations be available in a subsequent suit between the parties? What if the
suit is between another plaintiff and Hanover, and the complaint is based upon
the same alleged breach of the lease? What light does the last sentence of Rule
36(b) shed on this problem? Do stipulated facts constitute an "adjudication on
the merits"?

2.   JUDGMENTS OF NONJUDICIAL TRIBUNALS

HOLMBERG v. STATE, DIVISION OF RISK MANAGEMENT
Supreme Court of Alaska, 1990.
796 P.2d 823.

MOORE, JUSTICE.

Karen Holmberg asks us to reverse the Alaska Workers' Compensation
Board ("AWCB") decision denying her permanent total disability benefits
on the ground that a later decision of the Public Employees Retirement
Board ("PERB") conclusively determined that she was not physically able
to perform her duties as an employee of the State of Alaska. * * *

I.

Karen Holmberg began working for the State of Alaska, Division of
Risk Management ("Risk Management") in 1979. She has a history of back
injuries dating to the early 1960s. * * *

* * * On February 18, 1988, AWCB awarded Holmberg temporary total
disability benefits, but denied her claim for permanent total disability
benefits. Holmberg appealed AWCB's denial of permanent total disability
benefits to the superior court in March 1988.

Holmberg also sought disability benefits from [the Public Employees
Retirement System ("PERS")]. The Division of Retirement and Benefits

("Retirement and Benefits"), which administers PERS, awarded her non-occupational disability benefits. However, the Disability Review Board denied her claim for occupational disability benefits. Holmberg appealed this initial decision to PERB. On April 20, 1988, after AWCB had denied her claim for permanent total disability benefits, PERB found that Holmberg was permanently and totally disabled as a result of accidents at work, and accordingly, awarded her occupational disability benefits.

Holmberg supplemented the record in her appeal from the prior AWCB decision with the new PERB decision. In the proceedings before the superior court, Holmberg argued that the AWCB decision should be reversed because of the preclusive effect of the later PERB decision. The superior court affirmed the AWCB decision and Holmberg appealed.

II.

Holmberg's primary contention is that PERB's factual determination that she was physically unable to perform her duties at Risk Management should be given binding effect in this appeal of the AWCB decision against her.[2] * * *

Although res judicata principles were developed in judicial settings, they "may be applied to adjudicative determinations made by administrative agencies." Jeffries v. Glacier State Tel. Co., 604 P.2d 4, 8 (Alaska 1979) * * *. Of course, "[a]n administrative decision commands preclusive effects only if it resulted from a procedure that seems an adequate substitute for judicial procedure." * * * [18 Wright, Miller and Cooper, Federal Practice and Procedure: Jurisdiction and Related Matters § 4475 (2d ed.)].

Recently, we held that AWCB decisions may have preclusive effect. * * * We see no reason why PERB decisions should not also be given preclusive effect. First, like AWCB proceedings, PERB hearings include many of the procedural safeguards of a judicial hearing including the right to introduce evidence, call witnesses, and cross-examine opposing witnesses. * * * Second there is no indication in the PERS enabling statute * * * that a PERB determination should not preclude an independent judicial determination.

The state does not contend that PERB decisions should not be given preclusive effect. Rather, the state argues that preclusive effect should not be given to PERB determinations in AWCB proceedings. We have not addressed the question how res judicata principles apply between different

---

[2] * * * Holmberg recognizes that the question whether she was disabled for purposes of PERS is not the same question as whether she was disabled for purposes of the Alaska Workers' Compensation Act. * * * Holmberg limits her collateral estoppel claim to the narrower factual question whether she was physically able to work at Risk Management. However, she maintains that the resolution of this factual issue in her favor is tantamount to a finding that she was permanently and totally disabled for purposes of workers' compensation because the state conceded as much in the AWCB proceeding.

agencies. The Supreme Court has held that litigation conducted before one agency or official is generally binding on another agency or official of the same government because officers of the same government are in privity with each other. *Sunshine Anthracite Coal Co. v. Adkins,* 310 U.S. 381, 402–03, 60 S.Ct. 907, 916–17, 84 L.Ed. 1263 (1940). The Court stated that "[t]he crucial point is whether or not in the earlier litigation the representative of the United States had authority to represent its interests in a final adjudication of the issue in controversy." 310 U.S. at 403, 60 S.Ct. at 917. * * *

The United States Court of Appeals has applied this authority principle in appropriate cases. In *Safir v. Gibson,* 432 F.2d 137 (2d Cir.), *cert. denied,* 400 U.S. 850, 91 S.Ct. 57, 27 L.Ed.2d 88 (1970), the court relied on the authority principle in holding that the Federal Maritime Commission's determination that the rates of a conference of common carriers were unfair and unjustly discriminatory precluded the independent Maritime Administration from relitigating the issue. * * * In *Porter & Dietsch, Inc. v. FTC,* 605 F.2d 294 (7th Cir. 1979), *cert. denied,* 445 U.S. 950, 100 S.Ct. 1597, 63 L.Ed.2d 784 (1980), the court refused to give preclusive effect to a Postal Service factual determination concerning the safety of a diet pill in a Federal Trade Commission proceeding. The court found that there was "a clear and convincing need for a new determination of the issue ... because of the potential impact of the determination on the public interest or the interests of persons not themselves parties to the initial action." 605 F.2d at 300.

The court's holding in *Porter & Dietsch* illustrates the principle that preclusion may be defeated by finding such an important difference in the functions of different agencies that one does not have authority to represent the interests of the other. * * *

In this case, it does not appear that PERB has any more expertise than AWCB in making factual determinations of a person's physical ability to work at a particular job. Therefore, there is no affirmative reason why the PERB decision should be given preclusive effect as * * * [the agency's] decision was in *Safir.* The state makes several arguments why granting PERB determinations preclusive effect in AWCB proceedings would be inconsistent with the Alaska Workers Compensation Act * * * [but this argument] stems from the false premise that Holmberg seeks to preclude AWCB's ultimate disability determination instead of its factual determination that Holmberg was physically able to perform her job duties.[3]

---

[3] For example, the State's argument that collateral estoppel is not properly invoked between two independent tribunals which have statutory discretion to fashion separate remedies confuses issue preclusion with claim preclusion. * * * AWCB's authority to fashion a separate remedy is no argument against precluding the relitigation of identical factual issues decided in an earlier PERB proceeding. * * *

The state argues that the different functions of the workers compensation system and PERS prevent the application of collateral estoppel. * * * [The court noted that different standards govern the two agencies' disability determinations, but went on to state that these differences] * * * provide no substantial reason why AWCB should be allowed to relitigate the narrow factual question whether Holmberg is physically able to continue performing her job with Risk Management. Although the value of collateral estoppel may be low in light of the [different] * * * disability inquiry under AWCA, that is not a substantial reason to allow relitigation.* * *

III.

[The court then determined whether the two agencies are in privity with each other as to allow issue preclusion against a nonparty to a judgment.]

* * *

A.

* * * Privity exists between different agencies of the same government unless "there are important differences in the authority of the respective agencies." Briggs v. State, 732 P.2d 1078, 1082 (Alaska 1987). This is the same test that determines whether the decision of one agency binds another agency. In the privity context, however, the question is not whether the forum agencies are in privity, but whether the agencies appearing before them are. * * *

* * * Holmberg * * * argues that Retirement and Benefits is in privity with Risk Management because "the interests of the two agencies are virtually identical for purposes of [her] claims, and Retirement and Benefits had every incentive to vigorously defend the PERS claim."

Holmberg's error is in identifying Retirement and Benefits as the party against which PERB entered judgment. Retirement and Benefits is charged with administrative responsibility for PERS. The significance of this is that when Retirement and Benefits appears before PERB, it represents the interests of PERS, not the interests of the state. Thus, while Retirement and Benefits contested Holmberg's claim before PERB, the state is correct in saying that the party against which PERB entered judgment is the system itself.

* * *

* * * PERS is not a state agency but an independent retirement plan in which public employees are members and in which their employers participate. * * * While a state agency administers PERS and represents it during appeals, the state as employer is just one participant. The state

treasury is affected by a benefit determination only insofar as the state is an employer participant. * * *

* * * The question is not whether PERS is bound by an AWCB decision against one of its members, but whether one of its members is bound by a decision against PERS. The questions are not symmetrical. The PERS constituency is not represented at all in a workers' compensation proceeding. The employer-participant, however, is at least nominally represented in the PERS proceeding to the extent that it has an interest in the PERS fund. At the same time, this nominal representation is not sufficient to assure that the participant has had adequate notice and opportunity to be heard and that its rights and interests have been protected. We therefore hold that the state as a participant in PERS is not in privity with PERS.

B.

Our holding that the state is not in privity with PERS is sufficient to deny affording any preclusive effect to the PERB decision as against the state. However, even if the state and PERS were in privity, the PERB decision would not preclude any issues raised in the earlier AWCB proceeding because the PERB decision was not the first final judgment addressing those issues. Holmberg observes that "[t]his case presents the collateral estoppel issue in a somewhat unusual procedural context." AWCB reached its decision first. While that decision was on appeal, PERB entered a contrary decision which was not appealed. Holmberg argues that the PERB decision was the first final judgment for the res judicata purposes and therefore precludes AWCB's contrary decision because the AWCB decision was appealed.

We disagree. A final judgment retains all of its res judicata effects pending resolution of an appeal of the judgment. * * * This rule respects the principle of repose inherent in the doctrine of res judicata. If a judgment was denied its res judicata effects merely because an appeal was pending, a litigant could refile an identical case in another trial court creating duplicative litigation. This case well illustrates the point. Having lost on the issue whether she was physically able to perform her job duties in the AWCB proceeding, Holmberg appealed the decision and then successfully relitigated the issue before PERB. Retirement and Benefits did not argue that PERB was precluded from relitigating the issue that AWCB already had decided. Now Holmberg asks us to reverse the earlier AWCB determination simply because of the later PERB determination. * * * To reward relitigation of an issue by reversing the original determination is completely at odds with the purpose of collateral estoppel to prevent relitigation of issues that already have been decided.

* * *

In this case, the AWCB decision was the first final judgment even though it was appealed. The later PERB determination that Holmberg was not physically able to perform her duties at Risk Management cannot preclude AWCB's earlier contrary determination. Indeed, if the other requirements of collateral estoppel were satisfied, Retirement and Benefits could have precluded Holmberg from relitigating the issue already decided by AWCB.

* * *

The decision of the superior court is AFFIRMED.

NOTE AND QUESTIONS

1.   The Supreme Court opened the door of the federal courts to administrative preclusion in UNITED STATES v. UTAH CONSTRUCTION & MINING CO., 384 U.S. 394, 86 S.Ct. 1545, 16 L.Ed.2d 642 (1966), in which the Court said: "When an administrative agency is acting in a judicial capacity and resolves disputed issues of fact properly before it which the parties have had an adequate opportunity to litigate, the courts have not hesitated to apply res judicata * * *." Id. at 422, 86 S.Ct. at 1560, 16 L.Ed.2d at 661. *Holmberg* likewise examined whether the adjudication was sufficiently judicial to warrant issue preclusion. What factors might be appropriate to make that determination? Restatement (Second), Judgments § 83(2) (1982) suggests the following:

(2)   An adjudicative determination by an administrative tribunal is conclusive under the rules of res judicata only insofar as the proceeding resulting in the determination entailed the essential elements of adjudication, including:

(a)   Adequate notice to persons who are to be bound by the adjudication * * *;

(b)   The right on behalf of a party to present evidence and legal argument in support of the party's contentions and fair opportunity to rebut evidence and argument by opposing parties;

(c)   A formulation of issues of law and fact in terms of the application of rules with respect to specified parties concerning a specific transaction, situation, or status, or a specific series thereof;

(d)   A rule of finality, specifying a point in the proceeding when presentations are terminated and a final decision is rendered; and

(e)   Such other procedural elements as may be necessary to constitute the proceeding a sufficient means of conclusively determining the matter in question, having regard for the magnitude and complexity of the matter in question, the urgency

with which the matter must be resolved, and the opportunity of
the parties to obtain evidence and formulate legal contentions
* * *.

2.   What role did privity play in the court's decision in *Holmberg*? Privity
recognizes that certain substantive relationships justify extending the
preclusive effect of a judgment to a nonparty. These relationships include that
of a partnership and its members, successors in interest to property, and a
corporation and its officers. Restatement (Second) of Judgments §§ 41, 54, 59–
60 (1982). Privity has been criticized as an "elusive" concept that is more
conclusory than explanatory:

> * * * [T]he term privity in itself does not state a reason for either
> including or excluding a person from the binding effect of a prior
> judgment, but rather it represents a legal conclusion that the
> relationship between the one who is a party on the record and the
> non-party is sufficiently close to afford application of the principle of
> preclusion.

Southwest Airlines Co. v. Texas Int'l Airlines, 546 F.2d 84, 95 (5th Cir. 1977),
cert. denied, 434 U.S. 832, 98 S.Ct. 117, 54 L.Ed.2d 93 (1977) (citation omitted).
See also 18A Wright, Miller & Cooper, Federal Practice and Procedure § 4449
(3d ed.). What factors did the court in *Holmberg* consider in determining
whether the two government agencies were in privity? Should these same
factors apply when the question is whether natural persons are in privity?

E. PERSONS BENEFITED AND PERSONS BOUND BY PRECLUSION

1. THE TRADITIONAL MODEL

The traditional rule of issue preclusion was that persons benefitted
from a prior judgment only if they also were bound by it. "This rule, known
as the rule of mutuality, established a pleasing symmetry—a judgment was
binding only on parties and persons in privity with them, and a judgment
could be invoked only by parties and their privies." 18A Wright, Miller &
Cooper, Federal Practice and Procedure § 4463 (3d ed.). The modern trend
has been an erosion in the requirement of mutuality—"followed more
recently by second thoughts about whether the erosion is sufficiently
justified." Shapiro, Civil Procedure: Preclusion in Civil Actions 102–03
(2001).

Indemnification relations provided the earliest basis for an exception
from the rule of mutuality. See First Nat. Bank v. City Nat. Bank, 182
Mass. 130, 65 N.E. 24 (1902). The policy rationale was rooted in the
substantive obligation created by the relation:

> * * * [D]enial of preclusion would force an impossible choice
> between unacceptable alternatives. If a second action can be

maintained against the indemnitee, either the indemnitee must be allowed to assert his right of indemnification or the right must be defeated by the judgment in favor of the indemnitor. To allow the right of indemnification would be to destroy the victory won by the indemnitor in the first action. To deny the right of indemnification would be to destroy the indemnitee's right by the result of an action in which he took no part.

18A Wright, Miller & Cooper, Federal Practice and Procedure § 4463 (3d ed.).

2. THE DECLINE OF THE MUTUALITY DOCTRINE

BERNHARD v. BANK OF AMERICA NAT. TRUST & SAVINGS ASS'N

Supreme Court of California, 1942.
19 Cal.2d 807, 122 P.2d 892.

TRAYNOR, JUSTICE.

In June, 1933, Mrs. Clara Sather, an elderly woman, made her home with Mr. and Mrs. Charles O. Cook in San Dimas, California. Because of her failing health, she authorized Mr. Cook and Dr. Joseph Zeiler to make drafts jointly against her commercial account in the Security First National Bank of Los Angeles. On August 24, 1933, Mr. Cook opened a commercial account at the First National Bank of San Dimas in the name of "Clara Sather by Charles O. Cook." * * * Thereafter, a number of checks drawn by Cook and Zeiler on Mrs. Sather's commercial account in Los Angeles were deposited in the San Dimas account * * *.

On October 26, 1933, a teller from the Los Angeles Bank called on Mrs. Sather at her request to assist in transferring her money from the Los Angeles Bank to the San Dimas Bank. In the presence of this teller, the cashier of the San Dimas Bank, Mr. Cook, and her physician, Mrs. Sather signed by mark an authorization directing the Security First National Bank of Los Angeles to transfer the balance of her savings account in the amount of $4,155.68 to the First National Bank of San Dimas * * * "for credit to the account of Mrs. Clara Sather." The order was credited by the San Dimas Bank to the account of "Clara Sather by Charles O. Cook." Cook withdrew the entire balance from that account and opened a new account in the same bank in the name of himself and his wife. * * *

Mrs. Sather died in November, 1933. Cook qualified as executor of the estate and proceeded with its administration. After a lapse of several years he filed an account at the instance of the probate court accompanied by his resignation. The account made no mention of the money transferred by Mrs. Sather to the San Dimas Bank; and Helen Bernhard * * * [and other] beneficiaries under Mrs. Sather's will, filed objections to the account for this reason. After a hearing on the objections the court settled the account, and as part of its order declared that the decedent during her lifetime had made a gift to Charles O. Cook of the amount of the deposit in question.

After Cook's discharge, Helen Bernhard was appointed administratrix with the will annexed. She instituted this action against defendant, the Bank of America, successor to the San Dimas Bank, seeking to recover the deposit on the ground that the bank was indebted to the estate for this amount because Mrs. Sather never authorized its withdrawal. In addition to a general denial, defendant pleaded two affirmative defenses: (1) That the money on deposit was paid out to Charles O. Cook with the consent of Mrs. Sather and (2) that this fact is res judicata by virtue of the finding of the probate court * * *. The trial court * * * gave judgment for defendant on the ground that Cook's ownership of the money was conclusively established by the finding of the probate court. * * *

Plaintiff contends that the doctrine of res judicata does not apply because the defendant who is asserting the plea was not a party to the previous action nor in privity with a party to that action and because there is no mutuality of estoppel.

* * *

Many courts have stated the facile formula that the plea of res judicata is available only when there is privity and mutuality of estoppel. * * * Under the requirement of privity, only parties to the former judgment or their privies may take advantage of or be bound by it. * * * A party in this connection is one who is "directly interested in the subject matter, and had a right to make defense, or to control the proceeding, and to appeal from the judgment." * * * A privy is one who, after rendition of the judgment, has acquired an interest in the subject matter affected by the judgment through or under one of the parties, as by inheritance, succession, or purchase. * * * The estoppel is mutual if the one taking advantage of the earlier adjudication would have been bound by it, had it gone against him. * * *

The criteria for determining who may assert a plea of res judicata differ fundamentally from the criteria for determining against whom a plea of res judicata may be asserted. The requirements of due process of law forbid the assertion of a plea of res judicata against a party unless he was bound by the earlier litigation in which the matter was decided. * * * He is bound by that litigation only if he has been a party thereto or in privity with a party thereto. * * * There is no compelling reason, however, for requiring that the party asserting the plea of res judicata must have been a party, or in privity with a party, to the earlier litigation.

No satisfactory rationalization has been advanced for the requirement of mutuality. Just why a party who was not bound by a previous action should be precluded from asserting it as res judicata against a party who was bound by it is difficult to comprehend. * * * Many courts have abandoned the requirement of mutuality and confined the requirement of privity to the party against whom the plea of res judicata is asserted. * * * The commentators are almost unanimously in accord. * * * The courts of most jurisdictions have in effect accomplished the same result by recognizing a broad exception to the requirements of mutuality and privity, namely, that they are not necessary where the liability of the defendant asserting the plea of res judicata is dependent upon or derived from the liability of one who was exonerated in an earlier suit brought by the same plaintiff upon the same facts. * * * Typical examples of such derivative liability are master and servant, principal and agent, and indemnitor and indemnitee. Thus, if a plaintiff sues a servant for injuries caused by the servant's alleged negligence within the scope of his employment, a judgment against the plaintiff * * * [on] the grounds that the servant was not negligent can be pleaded by the master as res judicata if he is subsequently sued by the same plaintiff for the same injuries. Conversely, if the plaintiff first sues the master, a judgment against the plaintiff on the grounds that the servant was not negligent can be pleaded by the servant as res judicata if he is subsequently sued by the plaintiff. In each of these situations the party asserting the plea of res judicata was not a party to the previous action nor in privity with such a party * * *. Likewise, the estoppel is not mutual since the party asserting the plea, not having been a party or in privity with a party to the former action, would not have been bound by it had it been decided the other way. The cases justify this exception on the ground that it would be unjust to permit one who has had his day in court to reopen identical issues by merely switching adversaries.

In determining the validity of a plea of res judicata three questions are pertinent: Was the issue decided in the prior adjudication identical with the one presented in the action in question? Was there a final judgment on the merits? Was the party against whom the plea is asserted a party or in privity with a party to the prior adjudication?

* * * Since the issue as to the ownership of the money is identical with the issue raised in the probate proceeding, and since the order of the probate court settling the executor's account was a final adjudication of this issue on the merits * * *, it remains only to determine whether the plaintiff in the present action was a party or in privity with a party to the earlier proceeding. The plaintiff has brought the present action in the capacity of administratrix of the estate. In this capacity she represents the very same persons and interests that were represented in the earlier hearing on the executor's account. In that proceeding plaintiff and the other legatees who objected to the executor's account represented the estate of the decedent. They were seeking not a personal recovery but, like the plaintiff in the present action, as administratrix, a recovery for the benefit of the legatees

and creditors of the estate, all of whom were bound by the order settling the account. * * *

The judgment is affirmed.

NOTES AND QUESTIONS

1.   In *Bernhard*, a new defendant sought to bar a plaintiff who lost on an issue decided in defendant's favor from relitigating the issue in a second lawsuit—a form of preclusion now called "nonmutual defensive collateral estoppel." For a classic discussion, see Currie, *Civil Procedure: The Tempest Brews*, 53 Calif.L.Rev. 25, 38–46 (1965); and, Currie, *Mutuality of Collateral Estoppel—Limits of the* Bernhard *Doctrine*, 9 Stan.L.Rev. 281 (1957).

2.   In which of the following situations would preclusion be available under *Bernhard*?

(a)   Three cars, driven by A, B, and C, respectively, collide at an intersection in a jurisdiction without a compulsory joinder statute. Driver A, believing that C does not have enough money to satisfy the judgment, institutes a negligence action against B. At trial B is exonerated, the court holding that A's injuries were solely the result of A's own negligence. A then discovers that C actually does have enough money to make it worthwhile to sue, and promptly files suit against C. Can C invoke the judgment in A's prior action against B to preclude recovery by A in the second suit?

(b)   Assume the same fact pattern as above. Could C assert the judgment in the prior suit as the basis to recover on a counterclaim against A?

(c)   A bus owned and driven by D is in an accident. Passenger P1 sues D, alleging that the accident was caused by D's negligent driving. The trial court finds for P1. Passenger P2 then files a lawsuit against D, also alleging damages as a result of D's negligence. Is preclusion available to P2? Can you articulate how this fact pattern differs from that of (b)?

(d)   What if, on the facts of (c), the bus driver/owner had prevailed in the first suit? When P2 brought the second litigation, could D then use the first suit's judgment as a defense to the second action?

———

In BLONDER-TONGUE LABORATORIES, INC. v. UNIVERSITY OF ILLINOIS FOUNDATION, 402 U.S. 313, 91 S.Ct. 1434, 28 L.Ed.2d 788 (1971), a patent infringement action, the Supreme Court expressed the following views on the propriety of nonmutual preclusion:

The cases and authorities discussed * * * connect erosion of the mutuality requirement to the goal of limiting relitigation of issues where that can be achieved without compromising fairness in particular cases. The courts have often discarded the rule while commenting on crowded dockets and long delays preceding trial. Authorities differ on whether the public interest in efficient judicial administration is a sufficient ground in and of itself for abandoning mutuality, but it is clear that more than crowded dockets is involved. The broader question is whether it is any longer tenable to afford a litigant more than one full and fair opportunity for judicial resolution of the same issue. The question in these terms includes as part of the calculus the effect on judicial administration, but it also encompasses the concern exemplified by Bentham's reference to the gaming table in his attack on the principle of mutuality of estoppel. In any lawsuit where a defendant, because of the mutuality principle, is forced to present a complete defense on the merits to a claim which the plaintiff has fully litigated and lost in a prior action, there is an arguable misallocation of resources. To the extent the defendant in the second suit may not win by asserting, without contradiction, that the plaintiff had fully and fairly, but unsuccessfully, litigated the same claim in the prior suit, the defendant's time and money are diverted from alternative uses—productive or otherwise—to relitigation of a decided issue. And, still assuming that the issue was resolved correctly in the first suit, there is reason to be concerned about the plaintiff's allocation of resources. Permitting repeated litigation of the same issue as long as the supply of unrelated defendants holds out reflects either the aura of the gaming table or "a lack of discipline and of disinterestedness on the part of the lower courts, hardly a worthy or wise basis for fashioning rules of procedure." *Kerotest Mfg. Co. v. C-O-Two Co.*, 342 U.S. 180, 185[, 72 S.Ct. 219, 222, 96 L.Ed. 200] (1952). Although neither judges, the parties, nor the adversary system performs perfectly in all cases, the requirement of determining whether the party against whom an estoppel is asserted had a full and fair opportunity to litigate is a most significant safeguard.

Some litigants—those who never appeared in a prior action—may not be collaterally estopped without litigating the issue. They have never had a chance to present their evidence and arguments on the claim. Due process prohibits estopping them despite one or more existing adjudications of the identical issue which stand squarely against their position. * * * Also, the authorities have been more willing to permit a defendant in a second suit to invoke an estoppel against a plaintiff who lost on the same claim in an earlier suit than they have been to allow a plaintiff in the second suit to use offensively a judgment obtained by a different plaintiff in a prior suit against the same defendant. But the case before us involves neither due process nor "offensive use" questions. Rather, it depends on the considerations weighing for and against permitting a patent holder to sue on his patent after it has once been held invalid following opportunity for full and fair trial.

Id. at 328–33, 91 S.Ct. at 1442–43, 28 L.Ed.2d at 799–800.

The Court emphasized that the district court retained discretion to accept or reject a plea of collateral estoppel:

* * * [W]e do not suggest, without legislative guidance, that a plea of estoppel by an infringement or royalty suit defendant must automatically be accepted once the defendant in support of his plea identifies the issue in suit as the identical question finally decided against the patentee or one of his privies in previous litigation. * * * Rather, the patentee-plaintiff must be permitted to demonstrate, if he can, that he did not have "a fair opportunity procedurally, substantively and evidentially to pursue his claim the first time." * * * This element in the estoppel decision will comprehend, we believe, the important concerns about the complexity of patent litigation and the posited hazard that the prior proceedings were seriously defective.

Determining whether a patentee has had a full and fair chance to litigate the validity of his patent in an earlier case is of necessity not a simple matter. In addition to * * * considerations of choice of forum and incentive to litigate * * *, certain other factors immediately emerge. For example, if the issue is nonobviousness, appropriate inquiries would be whether the first validity determination purported to employ the [appropriate legal] standards * * *; whether the opinions filed by the District Court and the reviewing court, if any, indicate that the prior case was one of those relatively rare instances where the courts wholly failed to grasp the technical subject matter and issues in suit; and whether without fault of his own the patentee was deprived of crucial evidence or witnesses in the first litigation. But as so often is the case, no one set of facts, no one collection of words or phrases will provide an automatic formula for proper rulings on estoppel pleas. In the end, decision will necessarily rest on the trial courts' sense of justice and equity.

Id. at 332–34, 91 S.Ct. at 1445, 28 L.Ed.2d at 802.

The Court underscored that relaxing the mutuality requirement in patent cases would produce cost savings for the federal courts:

* * *[A]lthough patent trials are only a small portion of the total amount of litigation in the federal courts, they tend to be of disproportionate length. * * *

* * * [I]t is clear that abrogation of [the mutuality rule in patent cases] * * * will save *some* judicial time if even a few relatively lengthy patent suits may be fairly disposed of on pleas of estoppel. More fundamentally, while the cases do discuss reduction in dockets as an effect of elimination of the mutuality requirement, they do not purport to hold that predictions about the actual amount of judicial time that will be saved under such a holding control decision of that question.

Id. at 348–49, 91 S.Ct. at 1452–53, 28 L.Ed.2d at 810–11.

NOTES AND QUESTIONS

1.   Do you find the justification for relaxing the mutuality requirement in patent cases persuasive? Does the *Blonder-Tongue* rule "merely shift the focus of litigation from the merits of the dispute to the question whether the party to be estopped had a full and fair opportunity to litigate his claim in the first action"? *Blonder-Tongue*, 402 U.S. at 347, 91 S.Ct. at 1452, 28 L.Ed.2d at 810. Does this inquiry really save time and resources?

2.   Although *Blonder-Tongue* could be read as limited to patent actions, lower courts have cited to it as authority for nonmutual preclusion in suits involving different types of substantive claims. Is it clear that relaxing the mutuality requirement in these other contexts will produce cost savings?

3.   Is it feasible or fair to require extensive party joinder in a single lawsuit? Is it possible that the presence of too many defendants in an action will undermine the quality of decision making in the first action? See 18A Wright, Miller & Cooper, Federal Practice and Procedure § 4464 (3d ed.).

4.   Does the *Bernhard* test for nonmutual collateral estoppel differ from that of the Supreme Court in *Blonder-Tongue*? In what ways? Which test is preferable?

5.   In both *Bernhard* and *Blonder-Tongue* the party against whom the preclusion defense was asserted had instituted the first action. Should this be an important factor in determining whether nonmutual preclusion is appropriate? Or should the only relevant consideration be whether the party against whom preclusion is asserted have had a full and fair opportunity to litigate? For a criticism of nonmutual issue preclusion, see Waggoner, *Fifty Years of* Bernhard v. Bank of America *Is Enough: Collateral Estoppel Should Require Mutuality But Res Judicata Should Not*, 12 Rev. Litig. 391 (1993), arguing:

That nonmutual collateral estoppel is unfair emerges from the fact that litigation involves a substantial element of chance * * *.

The risk in litigation is much like the risk in a coin flip, even though the court system by a variety of mechanisms tries to resolve disputes accurately, and even though each side tries by retention of skilled counsel and by diligent preparation to make the odds as much as possible favor it. In such a coin flip you put up your money and you abide by the result, win or lose. That seems fair. Now suppose a bystander who has watched the coin flip but who has not risked his cash were to approach the loser and say, "Pay me, too." Such a demand would be laughed away, it is so obviously unfair. Yet such demands are now commonly enforced under the doctrine of nonmutual collateral estoppel.

Id. at 416.

PARKLANE HOSIERY CO. V. SHORE

Supreme Court of the United States, 1979.
439 U.S. 322, 99 S.Ct. 645, 58 L.Ed.2d 552.

Certiorari to the United States Court of Appeals for the Second Circuit.

JUSTICE STEWART delivered the opinion of the Court.

* * *

The respondent brought this stockholder's class action against the petitioners in a federal district court. The complaint alleged that the petitioners * * * had issued a materially false and misleading proxy statement in connection with a merger. * * * The complaint sought damages, rescission of the merger, and recovery of costs.

Before this action came to trial, the SEC filed suit against the same defendants in a federal district court, alleging that the proxy statement that had been issued by Parklane was materially false and misleading in essentially the same respects as those that had been alleged in the respondent's complaint. Injunctive relief was requested. After a four-day trial, the District Court found that the proxy statement was materially false and misleading in the respects alleged, and entered a declaratory judgment to that effect. * * * The Court of Appeals for the Second Circuit affirmed * * *.

The respondent in the present case then moved for partial summary judgment against the petitioners, asserting that the petitioners were collaterally estopped from relitigating the issues that had been resolved against them in the action brought by the SEC. The District Court denied the motion on the ground that such an application of collateral estoppel would deny the petitioners their Seventh Amendment right to a jury trial.

The Court of Appeals for the Second Circuit reversed * * *. Because of an intercircuit conflict,[3] we granted certiorari.

I

The threshold question to be considered is whether, quite apart from the right to a jury trial under the Seventh Amendment, the petitioners can be precluded from relitigating facts resolved adversely to them in a prior equitable proceeding with another party under the general law of collateral estoppel. Specifically, we must determine whether a litigant who was not a party to a prior judgment may nevertheless use that judgment "offensively" to prevent a defendant from relitigating issues resolved in the earlier proceeding.[4]

* * *

B

The *Blonder-Tongue* case involved defensive use of collateral estoppel * * *. The present case, by contrast, involves offensive use of collateral estoppel—a plaintiff is seeking to estop a defendant from relitigating the issues which the defendant previously litigated and lost against another plaintiff. In both the offensive and defensive use situations, the party against whom estoppel is asserted has litigated and lost in an earlier action. Nevertheless, several reasons have been advanced why the two situations should be treated differently.

First, offensive use of collateral estoppel does not promote judicial economy in the same manner as defensive use does. Defensive use of collateral estoppel precludes a plaintiff from relitigating identical issues by merely "switching adversaries." * * * Thus defensive collateral estoppel gives a plaintiff a strong incentive to join all potential defendants in the first action if possible. Offensive use of collateral estoppel, on the other hand, creates precisely the opposite incentive. Since a plaintiff will be able to rely on a previous judgment against a defendant but will not be bound by that judgment if the defendant wins, the plaintiff has every incentive to adopt a "wait and see" attitude, in the hope that the first action by another plaintiff will result in a favorable judgment. * * * Thus offensive use of collateral estoppel will likely increase rather than decrease the total

---

[3] The position of the Court of Appeals for the Second Circuit is in conflict with that taken by the Court of Appeals for the Fifth Circuit in *Rachal* v. *Hill*, 435 F.2d 59.

[4] In this context, offensive use of collateral estoppel occurs when the plaintiff seeks to foreclose the defendant from litigating an issue the defendant has previously litigated unsuccessfully in an action with another party. Defensive use occurs when a defendant seeks to prevent a plaintiff from asserting a claim the plaintiff has previously litigated and lost against another defendant.

amount of litigation, since potential plaintiffs will have everything to gain
and nothing to lose by not intervening in the first action.[13]

A second argument against offensive use of collateral estoppel is that
it may be unfair to a defendant. If a defendant in the first action is sued for
small or nominal damages, he may have little incentive to defend
vigorously, particularly if future suits are not foreseeable. * * * Allowing
offensive collateral estoppel may also be unfair to a defendant if the
judgment relied upon as a basis for the estoppel is itself inconsistent with
one or more previous judgments in favor of the defendant. Still another
situation where it might be unfair to apply offensive estoppel is where the
second action affords the defendant procedural opportunities unavailable
in the first action that could readily cause a different result.[15]

C

We have concluded that the preferable approach for dealing with these
problems in the federal courts is not to preclude the use of offensive
collateral estoppel, but to grant trial courts broad discretion to determine
when it should be applied. The general rule should be that in cases where
a plaintiff could easily have joined in the earlier action or where, either for
the reasons discussed above or for other reasons, the application of
offensive estoppel would be unfair to a defendant, a trial judge should not
allow the use of offensive collateral estoppel.

In the present case, however, none of the circumstances that might
justify reluctance to allow the offensive use of collateral estoppel is present.
The application of offensive collateral estoppel will not here reward a
private plaintiff who could have joined in the previous action, since the
respondent probably could not have joined in the injunctive action brought
by the SEC even had he so desired.[17] Similarly, there is no unfairness to
the petitioners in applying offensive collateral estoppel in this case. First,
in light of the serious allegations made in the SEC's complaint against the
petitioners, as well as the foreseeability of subsequent private suits that
typically follow a successful government judgment, the petitioners had

---

[13] The Restatement (Second) of Judgments (Tent. Draft No. 2, 1975) § 88(3), provides that
application of collateral estoppel may be denied if the party asserting it "could have effected joinder
in the first action between himself and his present adversary."

[15] If, for example, the defendant in the first action was forced to defend in an inconvenient
forum and therefore was unable to engage in full scale discovery or call witnesses, application of
offensive collateral estoppel may be unwarranted. Indeed, differences in available procedures may
sometimes justify not allowing a prior judgment to have estoppel effect in a subsequent action even
between the same parties, or where defensive estoppel is asserted against a plaintiff who has
litigated and lost. The problem of unfairness is particularly acute in cases of offensive estoppel,
however, because the defendant against whom estoppel is asserted typically will not have chosen
the forum in the first action. See * * * [Restatement (Second) of Judgments (Tentative Draft No.
2, 1975) § 88(2)] and Comment *d.*

[17] *SEC* v. *Everest Management Corp.*, 475 F.2d 1236, 1240 (CA2) ("[T]he complicating effect
of the additional issues and the additional parties outweighs any advantage of a single disposition
of the common issues."). Moreover, consolidation of a private action with one brought by the SEC
without its consent is prohibited by statute. 15 U.S.C. § 78u(g).

every incentive to litigate the SEC lawsuit fully and vigorously. Second, the judgment in the Commission action was not inconsistent with any previous decision. Finally, there will in the respondent's action be no procedural opportunities available to the petitioner that were unavailable in the first action of a kind that might be likely to cause a different result.[19]

We conclude, therefore, that none of the considerations that would justify a refusal to allow the use of offensive collateral estoppel is present in this case. Since the petitioners received a "full and fair" opportunity to litigate their claims in the SEC action, the contemporary law of collateral estoppel leads inescapably to the conclusion that the petitioners are collaterally estopped from relitigating the question of whether the proxy statements were materially false and misleading.

II

The question that remains is whether, notwithstanding the law of collateral estoppel, the use of offensive collateral estoppel in this case would violate the petitioners' Seventh Amendment right to a jury trial.

A

* * *

Recognition that an equitable determination could have collateral estoppel effect in a subsequent legal action was the major premise of this Court's decision in *Beacon Theatres* v. *Westover* * * * [p. 733, supra].

It is clear that the Court in the *Beacon Theatres* case thought that if an issue common to both legal and equitable claims was first determined by a judge, relitigation of the issue before a jury might be foreclosed by res judicata or collateral estoppel. * * *

B

* * * The petitioners contend that since the scope of the Amendment must be determined by reference to the common law as it existed in 1791, and since the common law permitted collateral estoppel only where there was mutuality of parties, collateral estoppel cannot constitutionally be applied when such mutuality is absent.

The petitioners have advanced no persuasive reason, however, why the meaning of the Seventh Amendment should depend on whether or not mutuality of parties is present. A litigant who has lost because of adverse factual findings in an equity action is equally deprived of a jury trial whether he is estopped from relitigating the factual issues against the

---

[19] It is true, of course, that the petitioners in the present action would be entitled to a jury trial of the issues bearing on whether the proxy statement was materially false and misleading had the SEC action never been brought—a matter to be discussed in Part II of this opinion. But the presence or absence of a jury as factfinder is basically neutral, quite unlike, for example, the necessity of defending the first lawsuit in an inconvenient forum.

same party or a new party. In either case, the party against whom estoppel is asserted has litigated questions of fact, and has had the facts determined against him in an earlier proceeding. In either case there is no further factfinding function for the jury to perform, since the common factual issues have been resolved in the previous action. * * *

The Seventh Amendment has never been interpreted in the rigid manner advocated by the petitioners. On the contrary, many procedural devices developed since 1791 that have diminished the civil jury's historic domain have been found not to be inconsistent with the Seventh Amendment. * * *

The law of collateral estoppel, like the law in other procedural areas defining the scope of the jury's function, has evolved since 1791. * * * [T]hese developments are not repugnant to the Seventh Amendment simply for the reason that they did not exist in 1791. Thus if, as we have held, the law of collateral estoppel forecloses the petitioners from relitigating the factual issues determined against them in the SEC action, nothing in the Seventh Amendment dictates a different result, even though because of lack of mutuality there would have been no collateral estoppel in 1791.

The judgment of the Court of Appeals is

Affirmed.

JUSTICE REHNQUIST, dissenting.

It is admittedly difficult to be outraged about the treatment accorded by the federal judiciary to petitioners' demand for a jury trial in this lawsuit. Outrage is an emotion all but impossible to generate with respect to a corporate defendant in a securities fraud action, and this case is no exception. But the nagging sense of unfairness as to the way petitioners have been treated, engendered by the *imprimatur* placed by the Court of Appeals on respondent's "heads I win, tails you lose" theory of this litigation, is not dispelled by this Court's antiseptic analysis of the issues in the case. It may be that if this Nation were to adopt a new Constitution today, the Seventh Amendment guaranteeing the right of jury trial in civil cases in federal courts would not be included among its provisions. But any present sentiment to that effect cannot obscure or dilute our obligation to enforce the Seventh Amendment, which *was* included in the Bill of Rights in 1791 and which has not since been repealed in the only manner provided by the Constitution for repeal of its provisions.

* * *

The Seventh Amendment requires that the right of trial by jury be "preserved." Because the Seventh Amendment demands preservation of the jury trial right, our cases have uniformly held that the content of the right must be judged by historical standards. * * * If a jury would have been impaneled in a particular kind of case in 1791, then the Seventh Amendment requires a jury trial today, if either party so desires.

* * *

To say that the Seventh Amendment does not tie federal courts to the exact procedure of the common law in 1791 does not imply, however, that any nominally "procedural" change can be implemented, regardless of its impact on the functions of the jury. * * *

Judged by the foregoing principles, I think it is clear that petitioners were denied their Seventh Amendment right to a jury trial in this case. Neither respondents nor the Court doubt that at common law as it existed in 1791, petitioners would have been entitled in the private action to have a jury determine whether the proxy statement was false and misleading in the respects alleged. The reason is that at common law in 1791, collateral estoppel was permitted only where the parties in the first action were identical to, or in privity with, the parties to the subsequent action. * * * [D]evelopments in the judge-made doctrine of collateral estoppel, however salutary, cannot, consistent with the Seventh Amendment, contract in any material fashion the right to a jury trial that a defendant would have enjoyed in 1791. * * *

* * * [T]he Court seems to suggest that the offensive use of collateral estoppel in this case is permissible under the limited principle set forth above that a mere procedural change that does not invade the province of the jury and a defendant's right thereto to a greater extent than authorized by the common law is permissible. But the Court's actions today constitute a far greater infringement of the defendant's rights than it ever before has sanctioned. * * * The procedural devices of summary judgment and directed verdict are direct descendants of their common-law antecedents. They accomplish nothing more than could have been done at common law, albeit by a more cumbersome procedure. * * *

By contrast, the development of nonmutual estoppel is a substantial departure from the common law and its use in this case completely deprives petitioners of their right to have a jury determine contested issues of fact. * * *

Even accepting, *arguendo,* the majority's position that there is no violation of the Seventh Amendment here, I nonetheless would not sanction the use of collateral estoppel in this case. * * * In my view, it is "unfair" to apply offensive collateral estoppel where the party who is sought to be estopped has not had an opportunity to have the facts of his case determined by a jury. Since in this case petitioners were not entitled to a jury trial in the Securities and Exchange Commission (SEC) lawsuit, I would not estop them from relitigating the issues determined in the SEC suit before a jury in the private action. I believe that several factors militate in favor of this result.

First, the use of offensive collateral estoppel in this case runs counter to the strong federal policy favoring jury trials, even if it does not, as the majority holds, violate the Seventh Amendment. * * *

Second, I believe that the opportunity for a jury trial in the second action could easily lead to a different result from that obtained in the first action before the court and therefore that it is unfair to estop petitioners from relitigating the issues before a jury. * * *

The ultimate irony of today's decision is that its potential for significantly conserving the resources of either the litigants or the judiciary is doubtful at best. That being the case, I see absolutely no reason to frustrate so cavalierly the important federal policy favoring jury decisions of disputed fact questions. The instant case is an apt example of the minimal savings that will be accomplished by the Court's decision. As the Court admits, even if petitioners are collaterally estopped from relitigating whether the proxy was materially false and misleading they are still entitled to have a jury determine whether respondents were injured by the alleged misstatements and the amount of damages, if any, sustained by respondents. * * * Thus, a jury must be impaneled in this case in any event. The time saved by not trying the issue of whether the proxy was materially false and misleading before the jury is likely to be insubstantial.[24] It is just as probable that today's decision will have the result of coercing defendants to agree to consent orders, or settlements in agency enforcement action in order to preserve their right to jury trial in the private actions. In that event, the Court, for no compelling reason, will have simply added a powerful club to the administrative agencies' arsenals that even Congress was unwilling to provide them.

NOTES AND QUESTIONS

1.   Offensive nonmutual collateral estoppel is the term used to describe a case in which "a plaintiff seeks to preclude a defendant from relitigating an issue which defendant previously litigated and lost against a different plaintiff." 47 Am. Jur.2d Judgments § 647 (2d ed.). How does this situation differ from the defensive use of collateral estoppel in *Bernhard* and *Blonder-Tongue*?

2.   *Parklane* permits but limits a stranger's offensive use of nonmutual issue preclusion against a party to a prior judgment. Professor Currie, in an important article, recommended two distinct limits on the nonmutual application of collateral estoppel:

---

[24] Much of the delay in jury trials is attributed to the jury selection, voir dire and the charge. See H. Zeisel, H. Kalven, & B. Buchholtz, Delay in the Court 79 (1959). None of these delaying factors will be avoided by today's decision.

(a) that one not a party to the prior action should not be allowed to assert the prior judgment against one who was a party thereto unless the person against whom the judgment is asserted in fact had a full, fair and effective opportunity to contest the issue; and (b) that the please should not be allowed where its allowance would result in intolerable anomalies in the administration of justice.

Currie, *Mutuality of Collateral Estoppel: The Limits of the* Bernhard *Doctrine*, 9 Stan.L.Rev. 281, 322 (1957). One important exception involves what Professor Currie called the "multiple-claimant anomaly":

An express train speeds through the night. Suddenly, as it enters a curve, the locomotive leaves the rails, followed by half a dozen tumbling passenger cars. Fifty passengers are injured. Fifty actions for personal injuries are filed against the railroad—some in California courts, some in federal courts in California, some in other state and federal courts. The first of these to be reached for trial is in a California court. A full trial is had on the issue of the railroad's negligence, and the result is a verdict and judgment for the plaintiff. The judgment becomes final. What is the status of the forty-nine remaining actions?

* * *

Suppose, that, in a case like our railroad case, the first injured passenger to sue loses his action against the railroad. The railroad cannot plead that judgment against the next passenger to sue, because the second passenger was not a party to the first action, nor in privity with the first passenger. Nevertheless, let us say that the second passenger also loses, and indeed that twenty-five passengers, in twenty-five separate actions, all fail to establish negligence on the part of the railroad. Then passenger No. 26 wins his action. Are we to understand that the remaining twenty-four passengers can plead the judgment in the case of No. 26 as conclusively establishing that the railroad was guilty of negligence, while the railroad can make no reference to the first twenty-five cases which it won?

There is only one possible answer to this question: no such absurdity would be tolerated for a moment. The indefensibility of such a result seems obvious * * *.

* * *

Our aversion to the twenty-sixth judgment as a conclusive adjudication stems largely from the feeling that such a judgment in such a series must be an aberration, but we have no warrant for assuming that the aberrational judgment will not come as the first in the series.

Id. at 281 & 285–86.

3.   What if before a case settles it yields a judicial finding that conflicts with a prior adjudication of the same issue? Such a finding may result, for example, when a motion to dismiss is denied before a settlement is reached. Does that finding create sufficient inconsistency to block offensive issue preclusion? In JACK FAUCETT ASSOCS. v. AMERICAN TELEPHONE & TELEGRAPH CO., 744 F.2d 118 (D.C.Cir. 1984), cert. denied, 469 U.S. 1196, 105 S.Ct. 980, 83 L.Ed.2d 982 (1985), Judge Mikva wrote for the court: "Parklane Hosiery does not hold that only inconsistent final judgments can preclude offensive estoppel." Id. at 130. Rather, according to Judge Mikva, the issue was whether "the inconsistency undermines the court's confidence in the correctness of the prior decision." Id.

In the *Jack Faucett* case, the court found another factor weighing against allowing the plea of offensive issue preclusion. The prior decision upon which the party seeking preclusion sought to rely had been affirmed by the Second Circuit. However, the appeals court held that one of the trial judge's evidentiary rulings was erroneous, although harmless. The District of Columbia Circuit found that the presence of even "harmless" error in the rulings of the trial court constituted a "serious obstacle" to offensive issue preclusion. Id. at 128.

4.   What issue preclusive effect should be given to a guilty verdict? Obviously, became plaintiff in a subsequent civil action did not have the opportunity to join in the criminal case, the concern that plaintiff will bring repetitious litigation is not present. On the other hand, are the issues necessary to resolve the civil case the same as those that are central to the criminal case? Does the criminal defendant have the same range of discovery as a civil litigant? Are the burdens of persuasion the same? In deciding whether or not to allow the civil plaintiff to employ offensive collateral estoppel, courts consider the incentives defendant had to litigate the first action vigorously, the procedural opportunities available, and any other factors that weigh on fairness. See, e.g., Doe v. Tobias, 715 N.E.2d 829 (Ind.1999) (allowing plaintiff rape victim to assert offensive collateral estoppel against defendant, who had been convicted of the offense in a prior criminal trial).

5.   Suits against the federal government represent an important exception to the extension of offensive nonmutual collateral estoppel. However, the scope of the exception is not clear. In UNITED STATES v. MENDOZA, 464 U.S. 154, 162, 104 S.Ct. 568, 573, 78 L.Ed.2d 379, 386 (1984) the Court held "that nonmutual offensive collateral estoppel simply does not apply against the Government in such a way as to preclude relitigation of issues such as those involved in this case." The Court justified this result on the ground that offensive issue preclusion "would thwart the development of important questions of law by freezing the first decision rendered on a particular legal issue." Id. at 160, 104 S.Ct. at 572, 78 L.Ed.2d at 385. However, in UNITED STATES v. STAUFFER CHEMICAL CO., 464 U.S. 165, 173, 104 S.Ct. 575, 580, 78 L.Ed.2d 388, 395 (1984), decided the same day as Mendoza, the Court clarified that this rationale "is persuasive only to prevent the application of collateral estoppel against the Government in the absence of mutuality. When

estoppel is applied in a case where the Government is litigating the same issue arising under virtually identical facts against the same party * * * the Government's argument loses its force."

3. BINDING NONPARTIES

Often, formal substantive relationships between persons may justify nonparty preclusion. For example, when a guardian litigates a suit on behalf of a minor, the minor in the usual situation will be bound by that suit's outcome. However, a relationship between parties need not always be so formal as to justify nonparty preclusion. In MONTANA v. UNITED STATES, 440 U.S. 147, 99 S.Ct. 970, 59 L.Ed.2d 210 (1979), the Supreme Court held that when nonparties assume control over litigation in which they have a direct financial or pecuniary interest, they may be precluded from relitigating issues that the earlier suit resolved. The state of Montana gave contractors different tax treatment depending on whether they contracted to build public or private projects. A contractor on a federal construction project brought a state court action challenging the constitutionality of this practice. The United States directed and financed the litigation for the contractor, but it also brought a federal court action challenging the practice. After the Montana Supreme Court upheld Montana's system of taxation, the United States continued with its federal action. But Montana argued that the federal government was bound by the state court judgment. When the case reached the United States Supreme Court, Justice Marshall, writing for the Court, observed that "although not a party, the United States plainly had a sufficient laboring oar in the conduct of the state-court litigation to actuate principles of estoppel." Id. at 154–55, 99 S.Ct. at 974, 59 L.Ed.2d at 217–18.

Are there other types of informal relations or litigation conduct that arguably justify nonparty preclusion? What if individuals agree that a case will serve as a test case? See Lahav, *Bellwether Trials*, 76 Geo.Wash.L.Rev. 576 (2008). Certain proceedings, such as bankruptcy and probate actions, bind nonparties, making use of special procedures to insure that due process is satisfied. See *Mullane*, p. 173, supra.

TAYLOR V. STURGELL
Supreme Court of the United States, 2008.
553 U.S. 880, 128 S.Ct. 2161, 171 L.Ed.2d 155.

Certiorari to the United States Court of Appeals for the District of Columbia.

JUSTICE GINSBURG delivered the opinion of the Court for a unanimous Court.

[Taylor filed a lawsuit under the Freedom of Information Act in the District Court for the District of Columbia seeking documents from the

Federal Aviation Administration related to a vintage airplane manufactured by the Fairchild Engine and Airplane Corporation. Greg Herrick, his friend, had previously filed an unsuccessful suit in the District of Wyoming seeking the same documents. In the earlier lawsuit, the FAA successfully argued that the documents contained trade secrets and were therefore exempt from disclosure under FOIA. When Herrick appealed to the Tenth Circuit, the court of appeals affirmed the district court's judgment against him but noted that Herrick had not raised two legal issues concerning whether the documents still qualified for the trade secret exemption.

Taylor and Herrick had no legal relationship, and there was no evidence that Taylor controlled, financed, participated in, or had notice of Herrick's lawsuit. But Taylor's suit, which was filed shortly after the Tenth Circuit's decision in Herrick's case, raised the two unresolved legal issues about the trade secret exemption that had been noted by the Tenth Circuit. The district court did not address those issues and instead granted summary judgment to defendants, holding that Taylor was barred by the District of Wyoming judgment because his interests had been virtually represented by a party in that suit, Herrick. In reaching this result, the district court relied on the Eighth Circuit's seven-factor test for virtual representation that requires an identity of interests between the nonparty and the party to the judgment, and six other factors that are relevant but not required: (1) a close relationship between the present party and a party to the judgment alleged to be preclusive; (2) participation in the prior litigation by the present party; (3) the present party's apparent acquiescence to the preclusive effect of the judgment; (4) the present party's deliberate maneuvering to avoid the preclusive effect of the prior judgment; (5) adequate representation of the present party by a party to the prior adjudication; and (6) a suit raising a public law (such as a constitutional question) rather than a private law issue.]

* * *

The D.C. Circuit affirmed. It observed, first, that other Circuits "vary widely" in their approaches to virtual representation. * * * In this regard, the D.C. Circuit contrasted the multifactor balancing test applied by the Eighth Circuit and the D.C. District Court with the Fourth Circuit's narrower approach, which "treats a party as a virtual representative only if the party is 'accountable to the nonparties who file a subsequent suit' and has 'the tacit approval of the court' to act on the nonpart[ies'] behalf." * * *

Rejecting both of these approaches, the D.C. Circuit announced its own five-factor test. The first two factors—"identity of interests" and "adequate representation"—are necessary but not sufficient for virtual representation. * * * In addition, at least one of three other factors must be established: "a close relationship between the present party and his putative representative," "substantial participation by the present party in the first case," or "tactical maneuvering on the part of the present party to avoid preclusion by the prior judgment." * * *

Applying this test to the record in Taylor's case, the D.C. Circuit found both of the necessary conditions for virtual representation well met. * * *

* * *

We granted certiorari * * * to resolve the disagreement among the Circuits over the permissibility and scope of preclusion based on "virtual representation." * * *

II

* * *

Taylor's case presents an issue of first impression in this sense: Until now, we have never addressed the doctrine of "virtual representation" adopted (in varying forms) by several Circuits and relied upon by the courts below. Our inquiry, however, is guided by well-established precedent regarding the propriety of nonparty preclusion. We review that precedent before taking up directly the issue of virtual representation.

* * *

A person who was not a party to a suit generally has not had a "full and fair opportunity to litigate" the claims and issues settled in that suit. The application of claim and issue preclusion to nonparties thus runs up against the "deep-rooted historic tradition that everyone should have his own day in court." * * * [*Richards v. Jefferson County*, 517 U.S. 793, 798, 116 S.Ct. 1761, 1766, 135 L.Ed.2d 76, 82 (1996)].

B

Though hardly in doubt, the rule against nonparty preclusion is subject to exceptions. For present purposes, the recognized exceptions can be grouped into six categories. * * *

[The Court summarized the exceptions as: (1) a nonparty may agree to be bound by a judgment and is bound by the terms of the agreement; (2) certain substantive relationships, traditionally referred to by the term privity, may justify preclusion of a nonparty; (3) a nonparty may be bound if its interests are represented adequately by a party to the suit, citing as examples class actions and suits by trustees and guardians; (4) a nonparty who has assumed control over a lawsuit, as in *Montana*, p. 893, supra, may be precluded; (5) a nonparty who has colluded to avoid the preclusive effect of a judgment by litigating through a proxy may be bound; and (6) special statutory schemes, such as bankruptcy, or other suits that are brought "only on behalf of the public at large," see *Richards*, may bind a nonparty.]

III

Reaching beyond these six established categories, some lower courts have recognized a "virtual representation" exception to the rule against nonparty preclusion. Decisions of these courts, however, have been far from consistent. * * *

The D.C. Circuit, the FAA, and Fairchild have presented three arguments in support of an expansive doctrine of virtual representation. We find none of them persuasive.

A

[The D.C. Circuit argued that] * * * a person may be bound by a judgment if she was adequately represented by a party to the proceeding yielding that judgment. * * * But the D.C. Circuit's definition of "adequate representation" strayed from the meaning our decisions have attributed to that term.

* * * [Our precedent has] established that representation is "adequate" for purposes of nonparty preclusion only if (at a minimum) one of * * * two circumstances is present. [The Court described the two circumstances as when (1) the court uses "special procedures to protect the nonparties' interests" or (2) "an understanding by the concerned parties that the first suit was brought in a representative capacity."] * * *

* * *

B

Fairchild and the FAA do not argue that the D.C. Circuit's virtual representation doctrine fits within any of the recognized grounds for nonparty preclusion. Rather, they ask us to abandon the attempt to delineate discrete grounds and clear rules altogether. Preclusion is in order, they contend, whenever "the relationship between a party and a non-party is 'close enough' to bring the second litigant within the judgment." * * * Courts should make the "close enough" determination, they urge, through a "heavily fact-driven" and "equitable" inquiry. * * * Only this sort of diffuse balancing, Fairchild and the FAA argue, can account for all of the situations in which nonparty preclusion is appropriate.

We reject this argument for three reasons. First, our decisions emphasize the fundamental nature of the general rule that a litigant is not bound by a judgment to which she was not a party. * * * Accordingly, we have endeavored to delineate discrete exceptions that apply in "limited circumstances." * * * Respondents' amorphous balancing test is at odds with the constrained approach to nonparty preclusion our decisions advance.

* * *

Our second reason for rejecting a broad doctrine of virtual representation rests on the limitations attending nonparty preclusion based on adequate representation. A party's representation of a nonparty is "adequate" for preclusion purposes only if, at a minimum: (1) the interests of the nonparty and her representative are aligned, see *Hansberry* [p. 520, supra]; and (2) either the party understood herself to be acting in a representative capacity or the original court took care to protect the interests of the nonparty * * *. In addition, adequate representation sometimes requires (3) notice of the original suit to the persons alleged to have been represented * * *. In the class-action context, these limitations are implemented by the procedural safeguards contained in Federal Rule * * * 23.

An expansive doctrine of virtual representation, however, would "recogniz[e], in effect, a common-law kind of class action." *Tice* [v. American Airlines, Inc., 162 F.3d 966, 972 (7th Cir. 1988)] * * *. That is, virtual representation would authorize preclusion based on identity of interests and some kind of relationship between parties and nonparties, shorn of the procedural protections [that are grounded in due process and] prescribed in *Hansberry, Richards*, and Rule 23. * * *

Third, a diffuse balancing approach to nonparty preclusion would likely create more headaches than it relieves. Most obviously, it could significantly complicate the task of district courts faced in the first instance with preclusion questions. An all-things-considered balancing approach might spark wide-ranging, time-consuming, and expensive discovery tracking factors potentially relevant under seven- or five-prong tests. And after the relevant facts are established, district judges would be called upon to evaluate them under a standard that provides no firm guidance. * * * Preclusion doctrine, it should be recalled, is intended to reduce the burden of litigation on courts and parties. * * * "In this area of the law," we agree, " 'crisp rules with sharp corners' are preferable to a round-about doctrine of opaque standards." *Bittinger* v. *Tecumseh Products Co.*, 123 F.3d 877, 881 (C.A.6 1997).

C

Finally, * * * the FAA maintains that nonparty preclusion should apply more broadly in "public-law" litigation than in "private-law" controversies. To support this position, the FAA offers two arguments. First, the FAA urges * * * the plaintiff has a reduced interest in controlling the litigation "because of the public nature of the right at issue." * * *

Taylor's FOIA action falls within * * * the [public-law] category * * *, the FAA contends, because "the duty to disclose under FOIA is owed to the public generally." * * * The Act, however, instructs agencies receiving FOIA requests to make the information available not to the public at large, but rather to the "person" making the request. * * * Thus, in contrast to

* * * public-law litigation * * *, a successful FOIA action results in a grant of relief to the individual plaintiff, not a decree benefiting the public at large.

Furthermore, * * * States are free to adopt procedures limiting repetitive litigation [of public-law claims]. * * * It hardly follows, however, that *this Court* should proscribe or confine successive FOIA suits by different requesters. Indeed, Congress' provision for FOIA suits with no statutory constraint on successive actions counsels against judicial imposition of constraints through extraordinary application of the common law of preclusion.

But we are not convinced that this risk justifies departure from the usual rules governing nonparty preclusion. First, *stare decisis* will allow courts swiftly to dispose of repetitive suits brought in the same circuit. Second, even when *stare decisis* is not dispositive, "the human tendency not to waste money will deter the bringing of suits based on claims or issues that have already been adversely determined against others." Shapiro[, Civil Procedure: Preclusion in Civil Actions] 97 [(2001)]. This intuition seems to be borne out by experience: The FAA has not called our attention to any instances of abusive FOIA suits in the Circuits that reject the virtual-representation theory respondents advocate here.

IV

For the foregoing reasons, we disapprove the theory of virtual representation on which the decision below rested. * * *

Although references to "virtual representation" have proliferated in the lower courts, our decision is unlikely to occasion any great shift in actual practice. Many opinions use the term "virtual representation" in reaching results at least arguably defensible on established grounds. * * *

In some cases, however, lower courts have relied on virtual representation to extend nonparty preclusion beyond the latter doctrine's proper bounds. We now turn back to Taylor's action to determine whether his suit is such a case, or whether the result reached by the courts below can be justified on one of the recognized grounds for nonparty preclusion.

A

It is uncontested that * * * [there] is no indication that Taylor agreed to be bound by Herrick's litigation, that Taylor and Herrick have any legal relationship, that Taylor exercised any control over Herrick's suit, or that this suit implicates any special statutory scheme limiting relitigation. Neither the FAA nor Fairchild contends otherwise.

It is equally clear that preclusion cannot be justified on the theory that Taylor was adequately represented in Herrick's suit. Nothing in the record indicates that Herrick understood himself to be suing on Taylor's behalf, that Taylor even knew of Herrick's suit, or that the Wyoming District Court took special care to protect Taylor's interests. Under our pathmarking precedent, therefore, Herrick's representation was not "adequate." * * *

That leaves only the * * * [possibility of] preclusion because a nonparty to an earlier litigation has brought suit as a representative or agent of a party who is bound by the prior adjudication. Taylor is not Herrick's legal representative and he has not purported to sue in a representative capacity. He concedes, however, that preclusion would be appropriate if respondents could demonstrate that he is acting as Herrick's "undisclosed agen[t]." * * *

Respondents argue here, as they did below, that Taylor's suit is a collusive attempt to relitigate Herrick's action. * * * The D.C. Circuit considered a similar question in addressing the "tactical maneuvering" prong of its virtual representation test. * * * The Court of Appeals did not, however, treat the issue as one of agency, and it expressly declined to reach any definitive conclusions due to "the ambiguity of the facts." * * * We therefore remand to give the courts below an opportunity to determine whether Taylor, in pursuing the instant FOIA suit, is acting as Herrick's agent. Taylor concedes that such a remand is appropriate. * * *

We have never defined the showing required to establish that a nonparty to a prior adjudication has become a litigating agent for a party to the earlier case. Because the issue has not been briefed in any detail, we do not discuss the matter elaboratively here. We note, however, that courts should be cautious about finding preclusion on this basis. A mere whiff of "tactical maneuvering" will not suffice; instead, principles of agency law are suggestive. They indicate that preclusion is appropriate only if the putative agent's conduct of the suit is subject to the control of the party who is bound by the prior adjudication. * * *

B

On remand, Fairchild suggests, Taylor should bear the burden of proving he is not acting as Herrick's agent. * * *

We reject Fairchild's suggestion. Claim preclusion, like issue preclusion, is an affirmative defense. * * * Ordinarily, it is incumbent on the defendant to plead and prove such a defense, * * * and we have never recognized claim preclusion as an exception to that general rule * * *. We acknowledge that direct evidence justifying nonparty preclusion is often in the hands of plaintiffs rather than defendants. * * * But "[v]ery often one must plead and prove matters as to which his adversary has superior access to the proof." * * * In these situations, targeted interrogatories or deposition questions can reduce the information disparity. We see no greater cause here than in other matters of affirmative defense to disturb the traditional allocation of the proof burden.

* * *

For the reasons stated, the judgment of the United States Court of Appeals for the District of Columbia Circuit is vacated, and the case is remanded for further proceedings consistent with this opinion.

It is so ordered.

NOTES AND QUESTIONS

1.   Why might the trend toward nonparty preclusion apply more broadly in public law cases than in private law cases? Are there some substantive areas of law, such as those involving property, in which the need for finality and predictability ought to outweigh an individual's autonomy interests? Professor Nagareda has urged that the law recognize a concept of "embedded aggregation" which would permit a judgment, even in a traditional one-on-one litigation, to have a binding effect on a mass scope. See Nagareda, *Embedded Aggregation in Civil Litigation*, 95 Cornell L.Rev. 1105 (2010). Would recognition of this concept avoid the need for establishing safeguards of the type discussed by the Court in *Taylor*? Or would it simply change the nature of the safeguards that are needed?

2.   Under what circumstances would *Taylor* bar issue preclusion against a nonparty to a prior litigation? In Lynch v. Merrell-National Labs. Div. of Richardson-Merrell, Inc., 646 F.Supp. 856 (D.Mass.1986), affirmed on other grounds, 830 F.2d 1190 (1st Cir. 1987), plaintiff sought damages for injuries sustained by her child's exposure during gestation to a prescription drug manufactured by defendant. Plaintiff had elected not to participate in earlier consolidated trials raising identical claims against the drug company. The court held that plaintiff was issue precluded by the earlier judgment from proving causation. Is *Lynch* at odds with the day-in-court ideal that informs the Court's decision in *Taylor*? Or can the decision be explained by the fairness and efficiency concerns that informed the Court's decision in *Parklane*?

3.   In MARTIN v. WILKS, 490 U.S. 755, 109 S.Ct. 2180, 104 L.Ed.2d 835 (1989), the Supreme Court held that nonparties to discrimination suits under Title VII of the Civil Rights Act could challenge employment decisions taken under consent decrees resolving the actions, even though the nonparties had declined to intervene in the original actions. The specific holding of *Martin* was legislatively overruled by Section 108 of the Civil Rights Act of 1991, Pub.L.No. 102–166, tit. I, § 108, 105 Stat. 1071, 1076. The 1991 Act prohibits challenges to employment consent decrees by individuals who had actual notice of the lawsuit and a reasonable opportunity to intervene in it, or whose interests were represented adequately. What problems do you see with a rule requiring intervention by persons who are aware of litigation that could potentially affect their interests? Suppose a nonparty becomes aware of litigation that will affect its interests, but the litigation is taking place in a jurisdiction where the party would not be subject to in personam jurisdiction. Are there due process concerns? The preclusion issues addressed in Martin generated much

commentary, See, e.g., Bone, *Rethinking the "Day in Court" Ideal and Nonparty Preclusion*, 67 N.Y.U.L.Rev. 193 (1992); Kramer, *Consent Decrees and the Rights of Third Parties*, 87 Mich.L.Rev. 321 (1988).

4.   Is the doctrine of stare decisis, see p. 832, Note 1, supra, inconsistent with the Court's rationale against nonparty preclusion in *Taylor*? Isn't there a strong societal interest in allowing individuals to plan and shape conduct in reliance on legal precedent? For a discussion of this argument, Minzer, *Saving Stare Decisis: Preclusion, Precedent, and Procedural Due Process*, 2010 BYU L.Rev. 597 (2010).

F. INTERSYSTEM PRECLUSION

Taylor v. Sturgell considered the preclusive effect of a federal court judgment upon another court in the federal system. Often, however, questions of preclusion are presented to a court that is part of a different judicial system than that of the rendering court. How should this factor affect the preclusive effect accorded the prior judgment?

Read Article IV, § 1 of the United States Constitution and 28 U.S.C. § 1738 in the Supplement.

------

1. INTERSTATE PRECLUSION

The Full Faith and Credit Clause of the Constitution requires one state to honor the final judgment of a sister state to the same extent that the courts of the rendering state would honor it. This is true even though the decision was clearly against the policy of the second state, which would not have given the same judgment had the case been brought there initially. See Fauntleroy v. Lum, 210 U.S. 230, 28 S.Ct. 641, 52 L.Ed. 1039 (1908). It follows, of course, that if the initial decision is modifiable in the rendering state, such as in the case of a child support order, then it is subject to modification in the second state. There has been considerable debate over whether a court can rest nonmutual preclusion on the judgment of a court that would itself require mutuality. See Restatement (Second), Judgments § 86, Comment *g* (1982).

NOTES AND QUESTIONS

1.   In BAKER v. GENERAL MOTORS CORP., 522 U.S. 222, 118 S.Ct. 657, 139 L.Ed.2d 580 (1998), the Bakers subpoenaed Elwell, a former GM engineering analyst, to testify in a wrongful death action brought in Missouri against the automobile company. GM asserted Elwell's testimony was barred by a prior Michigan court settlement and permanent injunction generally prohibiting Elwell from testifying in any litigation involving GM. Reversing

the Eighth Circuit, the Supreme Court, in an opinion authored by Justice Ginsburg, held Elwell may testify "without offense" to the Full Faith and Credit requirement: "Recognition, under full faith and credit, is owed to dispositions Michigan has authority to order. But a Michigan decree cannot command obedience elsewhere on a matter the Michigan court lacks authority to resolve." Id. at 240–41, 118 S.Ct. at 667–68, 139 L.Ed.2d at 597. The Court held that Michigan "lacks authority" to dictate evidentiary issues in courts of other states, in the context of actions brought by strangers to the Michigan litigation. However, the Court noted that this exception is a narrow one: "If the Bakers had been parties to the Michigan proceedings and had actually litigated the privileged character of Elwell's testimony, the Bakers would of course be precluded from relitigating that issue in Missouri." Id. at 239 n.12, 118 S.Ct. at 667 n.12, 139 L.Ed.2d at 596 n.12 (internal citations omitted).

2.   In V.L. v. E.L., 577 U.S. 404, 136 S.Ct. 1017, 194 L.Ed.2d 92 (2016), the Supreme Court held that the Alabama Supreme Court erred in refusing to enforce a Georgia adoption decree involving the child of a same-sex couple that later separated. The Alabama court held that it was not required to accord Full Faith and Credit to the Georgia judgment because the Georgia court lacked subject-matter jurisdiction to enter an adoption decree while still recognizing the parental rights of the non-adoptive party. The Supreme Court rejected that argument. Although a court, before according recognition to a sister state's judgment, may inquire into the decree's jurisdictional basis, in this case the Georgia judgment "on its face" appeared under Georgia law to have been entered by a court with jurisdiction and therefore warranted respect. Id. at 407–08, 136 S.Ct. at 1022, 194 L.Ed.2d at 96.

2.   STATE-FEDERAL PRECLUSION

It generally is agreed that the Full Faith and Credit Clause applies only to state courts. However, Congress in enacting 28 U.S.C. § 1738 has imposed the same general principles on the federal courts, requiring them to accord Full Faith and Credit to the judgments of state courts. Because the requirement is statutory and not constitutional, it may be supervened. Moreover, the writ of habeas corpus, which is authorized by the federal Constitution and by statute, 28 U.S.C. §§ 2241–55, provides a federal forum in which people who have been convicted of crimes in state court may litigate constitutional claims arising out of their prosecutions. Under traditional rules of preclusion, this subsequent action would be prevented.

What other circumstances might justify departing from the usual rules of intersystem preclusion? Consider, for example, cases involving federal issues. Should a federal court give preclusive effect to a state court's determination of federal law? What about circumstances in which the federal claim arises only by way of defense, and thus the original action could not have been removed to federal court? What if the issue falls within an area, such as copyright, within the exclusive jurisdiction of the federal courts?

NOTES AND QUESTIONS

1. In MIGRA v. WARREN CITY SCHOOL DISTRICT BOARD OF EDUCATION, 465 U.S. 75, 104 S.Ct. 892, 79 L.Ed.2d 56 (1984), the Court found that a prior state court adjudication precluded plaintiff's subsequent federal civil rights action under 42 U.S.C. § 1983 because she could have, but did not, raise her constitutional claims in the prior action. Justice Blackmun wrote for the Court:

> In the present litigation, petitioner does not claim that the state court would not have adjudicated her federal claims had she presented them in her original suit in state court. Alternatively, petitioner could have obtained a federal forum for her federal claim by litigating it first in a federal court. Section 1983, however, does not override state preclusion law and guarantee petitioner a right to proceed to judgment in state court on her state claims and then turn to federal court for adjudication of her federal claims. We hold, therefore, that petitioner's state-court judgment in this litigation has the same claim preclusive effect in federal court that the judgment would have in the Ohio state courts.

Id. at 84, 104 S.Ct. at 898, 79 L.Ed.2d at 64.

2. In MARRESE v. AMERICAN ACADEMY OF ORTHOPAEDIC SURGEONS, 470 U.S. 373, 105 S.Ct. 1327, 84 L.Ed.2d 274 (1985), a case arising under the Sherman Act, Justice O'Connor set forth a two-step approach for determining the preclusive effect of a state court judgment in a subsequent suit over which federal courts have exclusive jurisdiction. First, applying the Full Faith and Credit Statute, the federal court must determine whether *state* claim preclusion law would preclude the federal suit. If not, there is no preclusion. If the state would bar the federal action, then, as a second step, the federal court must determine whether the relevant federal law contains an implied or explicit exception to 28 U.S.C. § 1738. The Supreme Court has since applied the *Marrese* test in Matsushita Electric Industrial Co. v. Epstein, 516 U.S. 367, 116 S.Ct. 873, 134 L.Ed.2d 6 (1996), involving a judgment of a Delaware state court settling a shareholder class action. Justice Thomas held that under Section 1738, the Delaware judgment was entitled to Full Faith and Credit even though it settled state law claims as well as federal securities claims that could not have been litigated in state court because they were within the exclusive subject-matter jurisdiction of the federal courts. Writing separately, Justice Ginsburg dissented in part on the ground that the denial of an opportunity to raise exclusively federal issues raised due process concerns.

3. FEDERAL-STATE PRECLUSION

Must a state court grant preclusive effect to a prior federal court judgment? The general requirement that federal judgments be given Full Faith and Credit in state courts never has been challenged seriously, even though the constitutional clause does not apply to the situation, and most courts agree that Section 1738 is inapplicable as well. Commentators invoke various provisions of the Constitution (including the Supremacy Clause and the "case or controversy" doctrine of Article III) to support binding state courts to federal court judgments.

The conclusion that state courts are obliged to grant preclusive effect to federal court judgments does not determine which rules of preclusion the state should apply. There is almost universal agreement that federal preclusion rules usually apply in a state court when the prior federal-court judgment involved a federal question. Should federal preclusion rules define the effect of a prior federal judgment deciding state-law claims? Arguably, the *Erie* doctrine, p. 314, supra, requires the court to treat a prior federal determination of the claim in the same way that it would treat a prior state determination of the claim; under Section 1738, that would mean the application of the preclusion rules of the state in which the rendering federal court sits.

SEMTEK INTERNATIONAL INC. V. LOCKHEED MARTIN CORP.

Supreme Court of the United States, 2001.
531 U.S. 497, 121 S.Ct. 1021, 149 L.Ed.2d 32.

Certiorari to the Court of Special Appeals of Maryland.

JUSTICE SCALIA delivered the opinion for a unanimous Court.

[Petitioner sued respondent in a California state court, alleging breach of contract and various business torts. After removal to the United States District Court for the Central District of California on the basis of diversity of citizenship, the action was dismissed "on the merits and with prejudice" because it was barred by California's two-year statute of limitations. The Ninth Circuit affirmed. Petitioner also brought suit against respondent in the Circuit Court for Baltimore City, Maryland, alleging the same causes of action, which were not time barred under Maryland's three-year statute of limitations. Respondent asked the California federal court to enjoin this action; it also removed the Maryland state court action on federal question grounds (diversity grounds were not available because Lockheed "is a Maryland citizen"). The California federal court denied the requested relief, and the Maryland federal court remanded the case to state court because the federal question arose only by way of defense. The Maryland state court granted Lockheed's motion to dismiss on the ground of res judicata. Petitioner appealed the Maryland trial court's order of dismissal to the Maryland Court of Special Appeals. That court affirmed, holding that, regardless of whether California would have accorded claim preclusive effect to a statute of limitations dismissal by one of its own courts, the dismissal by the California federal court barred the Maryland complaint since the res judicata effect of federal diversity judgments is prescribed by federal law, under which the earlier dismissal was "on the merits" and claim preclusive. The Maryland Court of Appeals declined to review the case.]

* * *

II

Petitioner contends that the outcome of this case is controlled by *Dupasseur* v. *Rochereau*, 21 Wall. 130, 135 (1874), which held that the res judicata effect of a federal diversity judgment "is such as would belong to judgments of the State courts rendered under similar circumstances," and may not be accorded any "higher sanctity or effect." Since, petitioner argues, the dismissal of an action on statute-of-limitations grounds by a California state court would not be claim preclusive, it follows that the similar dismissal of this diversity action by the California federal court cannot by claim preclusive. While we agree that this would be the result demanded by *Dupasseur*, the case is not dispositive because it was decided under the Conformity Act of 1872, 17 Stat. 196, which required federal courts to apply the procedural law of the forum State in nonequity cases.

Respondent, for its part, contends that the outcome of this case is controlled by Federal Rule * * * 41(b), which provides as follows:

> * * * Unless the court in its order for dismissal otherwise specifies, a dismissal under this subdivision and any dismissal not provided for in this rule, other than a dismissal for lack of jurisdiction, for improper venue, or for failure to join a party under Rule 19, operates as an adjudication upon the merits.

Since the dismissal here did not "otherwise specify" (indeed, it specifically stated that it was "on the merits"), and did not pertain to the excepted subjects of jurisdiction, venue, or joinder, it follows, respondent contends, that the dismissal "is entitled to claim preclusive effect."e * * * Implicit in this reasoning is the unstated minor premise that all judgments denominated "on the merits" are entitled to claim-preclusive effect. That premise is not necessarily valid. The original connotation of an "on the merits" adjudication is one that actually "pass[es] directly on the substance of [a particular] claim" before the court. Restatement § 19, Comment *a*, at 161. That connotation remains common to every jurisdiction of which we are aware. See *ibid*. * * * And it is, we think, the meaning intended in those many statements to the effect that a judgment "on the merits" triggers the doctrine of res judicata or claim preclusion. * * *

But over the years the meaning of the term "judgment on the merits" "has gradually undergone change," R. Marcus, M. Redish, & E. Sherman, Civil Procedure: A Modern Approach 1140–1141 (3d ed. 2000), and it has

---

e   The quoted language was altered in 2007 without substantive effect.

come to be applied to some judgments (such as the one involved here) that do *not* pass upon the substantive merits of a claim and hence do *not* (in many jurisdictions) entail claim-preclusive effect. * * * That is why the Restatement of Judgments has abandoned the use of the term—"because of its possibly misleading connotations," Restatement § 19, Comment *a*, at 161.

In short, it is no longer true that a judgment "on the merits" is necessarily a judgment entitled to claim-preclusive effect; and there are a number of reasons for believing that the phrase "adjudication upon the merits" does not bear that meaning in Rule 41(b). To begin with, Rule 41(b) sets forth nothing more than a default rule for determining the import of a dismissal (a dismissal is "upon the merits," with the three stated exceptions, unless the court "otherwise specifies"). This would be a highly peculiar context in which to announce a federally prescribed rule on the complex question of claim preclusion, saying in effect, "All federal dismissals (with three specified exceptions) preclude suit elsewhere, unless the court otherwise specifies."

And even apart from the purely default character of Rule 41(b), it would be peculiar to find a rule governing the effect that must be accorded federal judgments by other courts ensconced in rules governing the internal procedures of the rendering court itself. Indeed, such a rule would arguably violate the jurisdictional limitation of the Rules Enabling Act: that the Rules "shall not abridge, enlarge or modify any substantive right" * * *. In the present case, for example, if California law left petitioner free to sue on this claim in Maryland even after the California statute of limitations had expired, the federal court's extinguishment of that right (through Rule 41(b)'s mandated claim-preclusive effect of its judgment) would seem to violate this limitation.

Moreover, as so interpreted, the rule would in many cases violate the federalism principle of *Erie* * * * [p. 314, supra] by engendering " 'substantial' variations [in outcomes] between state and federal litigation" which would "likely . . . influence the choice of a forum," *Hanna* * * * [p. 334, supra]. With regard to the claim-preclusion issue involved in the present case, for example, the traditional rule is that expiration of the applicable statute of limitations merely bars the remedy and does not extinguish the substantive right, so that dismissal on that ground does not have claim-preclusive effect in other jurisdictions with longer, unexpired limitation periods. * * * Out-of-state defendants sued on stale claims in California and in other States adhering to this traditional rule would systematically remove state-law suits brought against them to federal court—where, unless otherwise specified, a statute-of-limitations dismissal would bar suit everywhere.

Finally, if Rule 41(b) did mean what respondent suggests, we would surely have relied upon it in our cases recognizing the claim-preclusive effect of federal judgments in federal-question cases. Yet for over half a century since the promulgation of Rule 41(b), we have not once done so. * * *

We think the key to a more reasonable interpretation of the meaning of "operates as an adjudication upon the merits" in Rule 41(b) is to be found in Rule 41(a), which, in discussing the effect of voluntary dismissal by the plaintiff, makes clear than an "adjudication upon the merits" is the opposite of a "dismissal without prejudice" * * *. * * * The primary meaning of "dismissal without prejudice," we think, is dismissal without barring the defendant from returning later, to the same court, with the same underlying claim. That will also ordinarily (though not always) have the consequence of not barring the claim from *other* courts, but its primary meaning relates to the dismissing court itself. Thus, Black's Law Dictionary (7th ed. 1999) defines "dismissed without prejudice" as "removed from the court's docket in such a way that the plaintiff may refile the same suit on the same claim," * * * and defines "dismissal without prejudice" as "[a] dismissal that does not bar the plaintiff from refiling the lawsuit within the applicable limitations period," *ibid.*

We think, then, that the effect of the "adjudication upon the merits" default provision of Rule 41(b)—and, presumably, of the explicit order in the present case that used the language of that default provision—is simply that, unlike a dismissal "without prejudice," the dismissal in the present case barred refiling of the same claim in the United States District Court for the Central District of California. That is undoubtedly a necessary condition, but it is not a sufficient one, for claim-preclusive effect in other courts.

III

Having concluded that the claim-preclusive effect, in Maryland, of this California federal diversity judgment is dictated neither by *Dupasseur* v. *Rochereau*, as petitioner contends, nor by Rule 41(b), as respondent contends, we turn to consideration of what determines the issue. Neither the Full Faith and Credit Clause * * * [and] no other federal textual provision, neither of the Constitution nor of any statute, addresses the claim-preclusive effect of a judgment in a federal diversity action.

It is also true, however, that no federal textual provision addresses the claim-preclusive effect of a federal-court judgment in a federal-question case, yet we have long held that States cannot give those judgments merely whatever effect they would give their own judgments, but must accord them the effect that this Court prescribes. * * * The reasoning of that line of cases suggests, moreover, that even when States are allowed to give federal judgments * * * no more than the effect accorded to state judgments, that disposition is by direction of *this* Court, which has the last word on the claim-preclusive effect of *all* federal judgments * * *. In other words, in *Dupasseur* the State was allowed (indeed, required) to give a federal diversity judgment no more effect than it would accord one of its own judgments only because reference to state law was the *federal rule that this Court deemed appropriate*. In short, federal common law governs the claim-preclusive effect of a dismissal by a federal court sitting in diversity. * * *

It is left to us, then, to determine the appropriate federal rule. And despite the sea change that has occurred in the background law since *Dupasseur* was decided * * * we think the result decreed by *Dupasseur* continues to be correct for diversity cases. Since state, rather than federal, substantive law is at issue there is no need for a uniform federal rule. And indeed, nationwide uniformity in the substance of the matter is better served by having the same claim-preclusive rule (the state rule) apply whether the dismissal has been ordered by a state or a federal court. This is, it seems to us, a classic case for adopting, as the federally prescribed rule of decision, the law that would be applied by state courts in the State in which the federal diversity court sits. * * * As we have alluded to above, any other rule would produce the sort of "forum-shopping . . . and . . . inequitable administration of the laws" that *Erie* seeks to avoid * * * since filing in, or removing to, federal court would be encouraged by the divergent effects that the litigants would anticipate from likely grounds of dismissal. * * *

This federal reference to state law will not obtain, of course, in situations in which the state law is incompatible with federal interests. * * * No such conflict with potential federal interests exists in the present case. Dismissal of this state cause of action was decreed by the California federal court only because the California statute of limitations so required; and there is no conceivable federal interest in giving that time bar more effect in other courts than the California courts themselves would impose.

* * *

Because the claim-preclusive effect of the California federal court's dismissal "upon the merits" of petitioner's action on statute-of-limitations grounds is governed by a federal rule that in turn incorporates California's law of claim preclusion (the content of which we do not pass upon today), the Maryland Court of Special Appeals erred in holding that the dismissal necessarily precluded the bringing of this action in the Maryland courts. The judgment is reversed * * *.

It is so ordered.

NOTES AND QUESTIONS

1. The rule in *Semtek* requires courts to apply federal common law to determine the preclusive effect of an earlier judgment of a federal court that exercised diversity jurisdiction, but the federal common law rule adopts the rule of preclusion of the state in which the federal diversity court sat. Will this rule, as Justice Scalia posits, really reduce forum shopping? Is *Semtek*'s approach consistent with the principles set out in *Erie* and *Klaxon*, p. 314 and p. 358, supra?

2. In what circumstances might the Supreme Court conclude that a federal interest is "incompatible" with the application of a state preclusion standard?

3. *Semtek* decided the appropriate rule of claim preclusion to apply to a diversity judgment. Should the same rule apply to determine the issue preclusive effect of a diversity judgment? And what rule of preclusion should a diversity court apply to the judgment of a prior diversity court of another state? See CSX Transportation, Inc. v. General Mills, Inc., 846 F.3d 1333 (11th Cir. 2017), adopting Georgia's rule denying nonmutual issue preclusion as the federal common law rule for determining the preclusive effects of a prior federal diversity judgment based on Florida law.

NOTE ON INTERSYSTEM ADMINISTRATIVE PRECLUSION

The Supreme Court has held that 28 U.S.C. § 1738 is limited to the judgments of courts, and does not apply to the decisions of administrative agencies. More and more, states are moving toward giving preclusive effect *within the state court system* to the decisions of state administrative agencies. What preclusive effect should a federal court give to the determination of a state administrative agency?

In UNIVERSITY OF TENNESSEE v. ELLIOTT, 478 U.S. 788, 106 S.Ct. 3220, 92 L.Ed.2d 635 (1986), plaintiff was discharged as an employee of the University. He commenced an action in federal court alleging that the discharge was racially motivated and violated Title VII of the Civil Rights Act of 1964 and 42 U.S.C. § 1983. While the federal lawsuit was pending, a state administrative law judge found that the discharge was not racially motivated, and the University moved for summary judgment in the federal action on the ground of issue preclusion. The Sixth Circuit denied preclusion on both the Title VII and the Section 1983 claims. The Supreme Court affirmed the ruling as to Title VII and reversed as to Section 1983.

On both points, the Court looked to congressional intent, and found that Title VII showed a clear legislative intent not to accord unreviewed state administrative proceedings preclusive effect on a later-filed Title VII discrimination claim. However, no such intent was present in the history of 42 U.S.C. § 1983; neither was there evidence that Congress "wished to foreclose the adaption of traditional principles of preclusion to such subsequent developments as the burgeoning use of administrative adjudication in the 20th century." Id. at 797, 106 S.Ct. at 3225, 92 L.Ed.2d at 645. Rather, following the policy developed in *Utah Construction & Mining Co.*, p. 875, Note 1, supra, the Court held that it was appropriate to devise a federal common law rule of preclusion for administrative fact finding, so that when a state administrative agency is acting in a judicial capacity and gives the parties an adequate opportunity to litigate disputed issues of fact, the agency's fact finding will receive the same preclusive effect as would be accorded in the state's courts. The Court remanded for a determination of whether the agency provided the litigant the necessary opportunity to be heard.

NOTES AND QUESTIONS

1.   Once the Supreme Court found, based on legislative intent, that certain claims could not be precluded by state agency findings of fact (Title VII claims) but that others could be precluded (Section 1983 claims), the federal courts were left to decide which federal statutes fell into each category. In ASTORIA FEDERAL SAVINGS & LOAN ASSOCIATION v. SOLIMINO, 501 U.S. 104, 111 S.Ct. 2166, 115 L.Ed.2d 96 (1991), the Supreme Court provided some guidance as to what level of congressional intent is required to defeat the presumption in favor of administrative preclusion. The Court rejected a test that would have required a "clear statement" by Congress, and held that the presumption would apply unless "administrative preclusion would be inconsistent with Congress' intent in enacting the particular statute." The "clear statement" test would have provided more certainty to lower courts trying to determine when administrative preclusion should apply. Why then did the Court reject the "clear statement" test in favor of a less certain test that requires congressional intent to be discerned by inference?

2.   Assume that a state establishes a Personnel Court to decide employment discrimination disputes. Is the state's characterization of the decisionmaker as judicial dispositive for purposes of 28 U.S.C. § 1738? See McINNES v. CALIFORNIA, 943 F.2d 1088 (9th Cir. 1991), in which the Ninth Circuit explained:

> [F]ederal law, not state law, ultimately governs the question of what constitutes a "court" within the meaning of section 1738. Section 1738 is a federal statute, and as such its interpretation is a matter of federal law. Section 1738 requires the federal courts to follow state preclusion law under certain circumstances—for example, when a prior judgment has been rendered by a state court and is sufficiently authenticated—but whether the conditions for preclusion exist is a question of federal law. We look to state law to identify the attributes and functions of an entity, and the state's characterization of the entity is entitled to some deference, but federal law ultimately determines whether the entity is a court for purposes of section 1738.
> * * *

Id. at 1094–95. Does *Solimino*, Note 1, supra, support or undermine this analysis?

3. In arbitration, the parties agree by contract to be bound by the decision of a third party. It is more informal than judicial adjudication, but uses some adversarial procedures. Arbitration is studied in Chapter 16, infra. Should arbitral determinations be given claim or issue preclusive effect in a judicial proceeding? See Carlisle, *Getting a Full Bite of the Apple: When Should the Doctrine of Issue Preclusion Make an Administrative or Arbitral Determination Binding in a Court of Law?*, 55 Fordham L.Rev. 63 (1986). Does the answer to the question turn exclusively on the parties' intent as reflected in their contract, or should the court in its discretion consider the procedural character of the arbitral proceeding and the substantive policies at stake? See Shell, *Res Judicata and Collateral Estoppel Effects of Commercial Arbitration*, 35 UCLA L.Rev. 623 (1988). Should it matter that in some settings (such as employment), arbitration is a mandatory and not a negotiated feature of the commercial relationship? See Kim, *Arbitrating Statutory Rights in the Union Setting: Breaking the Collective Interest Problem Without Damaging Labor Relations*, 65 U.Chi.L. Rev. 225 (1998).

CHAPTER 16

ALTERNATIVE DISPUTE RESOLUTION

■ ■ ■

This chapter examines alternative dispute resolution ("ADR"), an umbrella term for private decision-making mechanisms that include arbitration, mediation, and negotiation. The use of ADR became widespread after the 1970s in response to perceived defects in litigation and adversarial process. Over the last generation, courts have integrated ADR into their adjudicative procedures, and consumer and employment contracts now routinely mandate ADR should disputes arise. The institutionalization of ADR, including its enforcement by state-sponsored power, has raised concerns about the absence of meaningful consent to its use and the fairness of its procedures. To the extent that ADR does not function as a freely negotiated system of private dispute resolution, critics argue that it should be publicly regulated and not automatically exempt from the requirements of the Due Process Clause, the jury trial right, or other public laws. What new problems, as well as new possibilities, does ADR present for the fair and efficient resolution of disputes?

A. ADR AND THE CRITIQUE OF ADVERSARIAL JUSTICE

ADR is the collective shorthand for a cluster of privately organized practices that offer an alternative to adjudication. When the push for ADR began, proponents argued that the traditional lawsuit had become too expensive and was too emotionally enervating given its reliance on legal formality, procedural regularity, and elite third-party decision-makers. Chief Justice Burger posed the problem in the title of his article, *Isn't There a Better Way?*, 68 A.B.A.J. 274 (1982). Later, the Chief Justice bluntly stated that litigation "is too costly, too painful, too destructive, too inefficient for a truly civilized people." Burger, Remarks at the Midyear Meeting of the American Bar Association (Feb. 13–14, 1984), reprinted in 52 U.S.L.W. 2471 (Feb. 28, 1984). Proponents of ADR responded to this critique by offering innovative procedures for use outside of the court system. See Reynolds, *Games, Dystopia, and ADR*, 27 Ohio St.J. on Disp. Resol. 477 (2012). In this earlier period, ADR was characterized as an informal and inexpensive process that could expedite dispute resolution, enhance relationships, and reduce decision-making costs.

ADR now is understood to offer not a single alternative to court-centered adjudication but rather multiple processes that are practiced in a variety of private as well as public places. See Sternlight, *Is Binding Arbitration a Form of ADR?: An Argument That the Term "ADR" Has Begun To Outlive Its Usefulness*, 2000 J.Disp. Resol. 97, 99. As one commentator has explained, "The first obstacle to an understanding of the role of ADR is the sheer breadth and diversity of activities to be taken into account, a breathtaking range of approaches and strategies that we lump under the heading of 'ADR' (an outmoded acronym that survives as a matter of convenience)." Stipanowich, *ADR and the "Vanishing Trial": The Growth and Impact of "Alternative Dispute Resolution,"* 1 J. Empirical Legal Stud. 843, 845 (2004). New terms such as "litigotiation" have been coined for practices that combine elements of ADR and traditional adjudication. Galanter, *Worlds of Deals: Using Negotiation to Teach about Legal Process*, 34 J. Legal Educ. 268, 268 (1984). In place of the transsubstantive procedure of the federal courts, commentators now speak of the need for "appropriate" (rather than alternative) modes of resolution specific to the dispute. See Sternlight, *ADR Is Here: Preliminary Reflections on Where It Fits in a System of Justice*, 3 Nev.L.J. 289, 295 (2002–03).

Since the 1970s, ADR has moved outside the commercial and family context and is now a routine and mandatory feature of consumer and employment contracts. See *Developments in the Law—The Paths of Civil Litigation*, 113 Harv.L.Rev. 1851 (2000). Critics warn that the increasing use of ADR is having negative effects on public life, pointing to the elimination of the jury right, downward pressures on due process, and unknowing, uninformed, or mandated waivers of federal statutory protections. Professor Miller has observed, "Compelled private adjudication essentially is now competing with the public adjudicatory system and replacing access to the courts, the possibility of jury trial, and any process transparency." Miller, *Simplified Pleading, Meaningful Days in Court, and Trials on the Merits: Reflections on the Deformation of Federal Procedure*, 88 N.Y.U.L.Rev. 286, 328–29 (2013).

This section introduces the basic forms of ADR and identifies the features that distinguish them from court-based adjudication. As you read these materials, consider whether ADR mechanisms differ qualitatively from adjudication or whether they really are only different points on a procedural spectrum. In particular, focus carefully on these questions:

Who presides over the dispute? Possibilities include: a judge, an officer of the state with professional education in the law; a lawyer with similar professional training; an expert in the field in which the dispute arose with no legal training; a representative of the community; the disputants with the help of a neutral third party; the disputants themselves.

What is the source of the standard for resolution? Possibilities include: rules established by legislatures and courts ("law"); the prior practice of those similarly situated; community values; standards developed by the disputants themselves.

Who speaks for the disputants? Possibilities include: lawyers; persons without professional legal training (including friends, relatives, or neighbors); the disputants themselves.

What is the nature and extent of fact finding and norm creation? Possibilities include: no fact finding or norm creation; monopolization of these tasks by a third party; the sharing of these tasks by a third party and the disputants and their representatives; responsibility in the disputants and their representatives alone.

Who decides the dispute? Possibilities include: a third party privately chosen by the disputants; a third party mandated by the state; the parties themselves; the parties through their lawyers.

What remedies are available, awarded, and enforced? Possibilities include: compensatory damages; punitive damages; group monetary awards; individual equitable relief; class-wide or group remedies; company- or industry-wide structural reforms.

What is the binding effect of any resolution? Possibilities include: binding on the parties through coercive sanctions; binding on the parties in an advisory or precatory sense; binding on nonparties; binding on the parties in ways that they decide themselves; binding when enforced through a court's coercive power.

Who pays for the decision-making process? Possibilities include: taxpayers; industry groups; the claimant; the parties to the dispute; the losing party.

Who can access the process and its decisional results? Possibilities include: the parties; industry groups; the public; the courts.

NOTES AND QUESTIONS

1.   At the start of the ADR movement, commentators suggested establishing a Dispute Resolution Center that would match disputes to the decision-making mechanism "best suited for the resolution of the particular controversy":

Take, for example, a case involving a minor assault by one neighbor against another growing out of increasing anger over a trespassing dog. Presently such a dispute would probably wind up in criminal court because that is the tag society has placed on this type of conflict.

But since the parties really want help in resolving this interpersonal problem, not a determination of whether A struck B, the case might well be sent to mediation, at least in the first instance. Similar treatment might be accorded to a landlord-tenant dispute over the adequacy of the services provided by the landlord. But if the landlord sought to raise questions about the constitutionality of the rent-control law, then obviously that case would have to be sent to the regular court. * * *

Sander, *Varieties of Dispute Processing*, in The Pound Conference: Perspectives on Justice in the Future 65 (Levin & Wheeler eds. 1979); see also Sander, *The Multidoor Courthouse*, National Forum, Vol. LXIII, No. 4, Fall 1983. For a criticism of the view that disputes can be resolved by matching them to different processing techniques, see Sarat, *The "New Formalism" in Disputing and Dispute Processing*, 21 Law & Soc'y Rev. 695 (1987–1988).

2.   ADR presumes that private parties should have wide authority to design the procedures and substantive rules that govern their disputes. Is there a danger that a stronger party will impose an unfair process or one-sided rules that work to its advantage? Won't some private arrangements negatively affect individuals who are not parties to the dispute and have no say in its resolution? See Davis & Hershkoff, *Contracting for Procedure*, 53 Wm. & Mary L.Rev. 507, 513 (2011). Should the public be able to access ADR decisions that relate to dangerous products; employers who are sexual predators; or other matters that pertain to health and safety?

B. FORMS OF ALTERNATIVE DISPUTE PROCESS

1. NEGOTIATION

Negotiation is a process that allows the parties to choose both the procedures and standards that will help them reach a settlement of their dispute. Negotiation can take place in a variety of places and can be conceptualized along a temporal continuum. Some cases may reach a settlement before litigation is ever commenced. In this setting, a lawsuit reflects a failed negotiation, and each party, for different reasons, may believe he can achieve better results through a formal, law-based process supervised by an impartial judge. The filing of a lawsuit, however, often precipitates a new round of negotiation, this time under the auspices of the court. In the federal system, a judge may invoke Rule 16 managerial authority to encourage and even to require the disputants to attempt to negotiate a settlement during the pretrial phase of the litigation or once trial has begun. In some settlements, information gained through the discovery process may shift some of the power imbalance that might have existed at the commencement of the suit. Although in the early stages of some disputes the parties may represent themselves, once a lawsuit is commenced it is likely that lawyers will take charge of negotiations; both counsel and a party who has settlement authority will be expected to attend judicially mandated settlement conferences.

Proponents of negotiation cast it as an alternative to the "win-lose" mentality of litigation. Because negotiation is said to focus on the parties' interests, rather than on their positions, theoretically it creates a procedural space that distances the parties from the problem that divides them and potentially creates a "win-win" situation that maximizes overall gain. See Fisher & Ury, Getting to Yes: Negotiating Agreement Without Giving In 73 (1981). A commentator has explained:

> In contrast [to adjudication], the universe and operation of norms in dispute-negotiation is typically open-ended. Thus it is characteristic of dispute-negotiation that when norms collide account is taken of both, although the eventual settlement may reflect an adjustment for relative applicability and weight. Similarly, the parties in dispute-negotiation may accord partial or even full recognition to a norm that is generally deemed subordinate or even legally invalid, so that a negligent plaintiff who has no "right" to prevail in a tort action because of the doctrine of contributory negligence may nevertheless make a favorable settlement by reason of the legally invalid but socially real principle of comparative negligence. Finally, parties to dispute-negotiation can and frequently do take person-oriented norms into account as freely as act-oriented norms.

Eisenberg, *Private Ordering Through Negotiation: Dispute-Settlement and Rulemaking*, 89 Harv.L.Rev. 637, 644–45 (1976). Studies indicate that the parties' success in reaching and accepting a negotiated solution frequently turns on perceptions of fairness, as well as compliance with substantive law. See Hollander-Blumoff & Tyler, *Procedural Justice in Negotiation: Procedural Fairness, Outcome Acceptance, and Integrative Potential*, 33 Law & Soc. Inq'y 473 (2008). An influential commentary emphasizes that negotiation takes place "in the shadow of the law," which sets the parameters and terms of an acceptable deal even when the parties do not seek judicial intervention. See Mnookin & Kornhauser, *Bargaining in the Shadow of the Law: The Case of Divorce*, 88 Yale L.J. 950 (1979).

2. MEDIATION

Mediation is a process that uses a third party as a "go-between" to assist the disputants in reaching a settlement of their differences. Mediation differs from "lawyers only" bargaining sessions in that the mediator functions as a neutral party with no personal interest in the outcome of the case and is not empowered to render a decision. See Tarpley, *ADR, Jurisprudence, and Myth*, 17 Ohio St.J. on Disp. Resol. 113, 116 (2001). The mediator's role is to help the parties find common ground and to identify potential paths to resolution. Proponents underscore the potential of mediation to encourage the parties' self-determination and autonomous decision-making. See Welsh, *The Thinning Vision of Self-Determination in Court-Connected Mediation: The Inevitable Price of Institutionalization?*, 6 Harv. Negot.L.Rev. 1, 4 (2001).

Mediation lacks any discovery mechanism to force the opposing side to reveal information (for example, about finances) that may be critical to a full and fair evaluation of the dispute. Although the disputants decide themselves the standard for resolution, other values, such as those of the mediator or the community, also come into play. Disputants often but do not always represent themselves; some mediators actively discourage the presence of lawyers and witnesses. Mediation is considered to be most appropriate when the disputants have equal bargaining power, when they engage in the process voluntarily, and when they have a relationship that they believe is important to preserve. In its ideal form, rather than attempting to assess blame for past conduct, mediation focuses on the future and encourages prospective changes in behavior. Mediators come from a variety of backgrounds and often have differing conceptions of their proper role. See Daiker, *No J.D. Required: The Critical Role and Contributions of Non-Lawyer Mediators*, 24 Rev.Litig. 499 (2005); see also Alberstein, *Forms of Mediation and Law: Cultures of Dispute Resolution*, 22 Ohio St.J. on Disp. Resol. 321 (2007). The mediator might be a former attorney, someone familiar with the norms of a particular industry, someone specially trained as a mediator, or simply a member of the community. Mediators also use a variety of approaches, broadly categorized as facilitative, transformative, and evaluative. Thus, some mediators actively intervene to suggest possible grounds for settlement and to persuade the disputants to settle. If successful, mediation results in a signed agreement that defines the parties' future behavior and may be enforceable in court.

Proponents saw mediation as an appropriate process to resolve disputes between neighbors or family members, and early mediation programs often were located in family courts and "community justice centers." Hensler, *Our Courts, Ourselves: How the Alternative Dispute Resolution Movement Is Re-Shaping Our Legal System*, 108 Penn St.L.Rev. 165, 172 (2003); see also Brazil, *Hosting Mediations as a Representative of the System of Civil Justice*, 22 Ohio St.J. on Disp. Resol. 227, 237 (2007). Critics questioned whether in practice mediation benefited claimants from subordinated groups, such as women, people of color, consumers, and workers. See Grillo, *The Mediation Alternative: Process Dangers for Women*, 100 Yale L.J. 1545 (1991). Some research has suggested that once litigation has commenced, women have a greater preference than men for mediation in the two types of lawsuits studied, "slip and fall" and pay discrimination cases. See Wofford, *The Effect of Gender and Relational*

Distance on Plaintiff Decision Making in the Litigation Process, 51 Law & Soc'y Rev. 966 (2017).

Over time, mediation has emerged in many contexts that seem at odds with the core notion of voluntarism and autonomy. For example, "court-annexed mediation" programs directing the parties to mediation now have become entrenched within civil court systems. See Ward, *Mandatory Court-Annexed Alternative Dispute Resolution in the United States Federal Courts: Panacea or Pandemic?*, 81 St. John's L.Rev. 77 (2007). Proponents of this development argue that it relieves courts of caseload burdens. See Brazil, *Should Court-Sponsored ADR Survive?*, 21 Ohio St.J. on Disp. Resol. 241, 245 (2006). Mediation also has gained wide acceptance in private commercial contexts. See Nolan-Haley, *Mediation: The "New Arbitration,"* 17 Harv. Negot.L.Rev. 61, 68 (2012). According to one report, 96 percent of major corporations utilize mediation for a range of matters including employment and consumer disputes. See Lipsky, *How Corporate America Uses Conflict Management: The Evidence from a New Survey of the Fortune* 1000, 30 Alternatives to High Cost Litig. 139, 140 (2012); see also Lande, *Getting the Faith: Why Business Lawyers and Executives Believe in Mediation*, 5 Harv. Negot.L.Rev. 137 (2000). Although some companies mandate mediation, the practice is criticized. See Quek, *Mandatory Mediation: An Oxymoron? Examining the Feasibility of Implementing a Court-Mandated Mediation Program*, 11 Cardozo J. Conflict Resol. 479 (2010).

3. ARBITRATION

Arbitration is the form of ADR with which the American legal system has had the longest experience. The parties select an arbitrator or arbitrators, who conduct hearings and then reach a decision. The arbitration hearing is an adversarial proceeding, in which each of the parties presents its case, with full opportunity for cross-examination and rebuttal. Lawyers often represent the disputants, and are responsible for gathering and presenting evidence and arguments. Frequently, the decision of the arbitrator, called an "award," is then entered in court, much as a judgment in a formally adjudicated case is entered. In each case, both parties are bound to abide by the award, even though in certain limited circumstances, either or both parties may seek to challenge, modify, or even vacate the award in a court. Arbitration thus is a form of adversarial adjudication that is conducted largely outside the courts.

As a general matter, arbitration is contractual: the parties will either enter a written agreement before a dispute arises to submit the possible dispute to arbitration, or they will enter into an agreement to submit an existing dispute to arbitration. Arbitration achieved widespread acceptance after World War II, having first developed in the commercial area, then moved to the labor-management field, and then extending to industries in which disputants share roughly equal bargaining power, such as securities broker agreements and construction contracts. Federal and state statutes play a significant role in shaping the context in which arbitration occurs. The Federal Arbitration Act, 9 U.S.C. §§ 1 et seq., and Article 75 of New York's Civil Practice Law and Rules are the most notable statutes of this type, and both have served as models for other states' arbitration statutes.

Arbitration's procedural structure depends largely on the pre-dispositions of the arbitrator conducting a given hearing; the arbitrator is relatively free to shape the hearing as it sees fit and has three broad areas of responsibility: (1) the pre-hearing phase; (2) the hearing; and (3) the award and the opinion (if an opinion is thought necessary). Patterns of practice tend to become associated with particular types of arbitration. For example, commercial arbitrators follow a practice of receiving written briefs; by contrast, labor arbitrators tend to discourage them. Pre-hearing discovery often is limited to what the parties voluntarily disclose, but arbitrators are empowered at the request of either party to subpoena documents and persons for the hearing, and counsel generally can agree on a procedure to review the subpoenaed documents in advance of the hearing. Further, arbitration in the securities industry offers formalized discovery in the pre-hearing phase that permits the parties themselves to serve written requests for information or documents on other parties to the arbitration. The arbitrator is the sole judge of the relevance and materiality of evidence offered and need not conform to the legal rules of evidence. However, some arbitrators believe that at least some compliance with traditional rules of evidence is necessary and beneficial. Because the arbitrator has such broad discretion to choose to admit or exclude evidence or to hear or refuse to hear witnesses, its power to find facts and decide questions of law virtually is unlimited. The final phase of arbitration produces the award. The arbitrator's award need not contain anything more than a statement of the rights and obligations of the parties to that dispute. However, the parties may request a written statement of decision.

In addition to this standard form, arbitration also may be of the final-form or one-way variety. Final-offer arbitration plays an important role in contexts in which it is important not to interrupt the disputants' relation. It is used, for example, to set the terms of contracts, rather than to interpret and apply contractual provisions, and has figured prominently in setting the salaries of major league baseball players and some public employees. See Carrell & Bales, *Considering Final Offer Arbitration to Resolve Public Sector Impasses in Times of Concession Bargaining*, 28 Ohio St.J. on Disp. Resol. 1 (2013). Each party proposes a final offer of settlement, and the neutral must choose between the two. The process encourages the parties to be reasonable in the positions they advocate and to engage in serious negotiation. Fact finding can be more limited because the arbitrator need only choose between two positions rather than find and justify one particular result out of many that are possible. In one-way arbitration only one party agrees to be bound.

Arbitration's presumed flexibility, confidentiality, and expertise traditionally have made it an attractive alternative for resolving commercial disputes outside of courts. See Stipanowich, *Arbitration: The "New Litigation,"* 2010 U.Ill.L.Rev. 1, 4. Numerous private organizations have emerged to facilitate use of arbitration, to provide procedural default rules, and to maintain lists of possible arbitrators. The American Arbitration Association is now the preferred arbitration forum for construction and other commercial disputes, while the Financial Industry Regulatory Authority handles a large number of securities disputes. Arbitration has become pervasive in international matters; in that context transnational parties rely on the International Chamber of Commerce or the London Court of International Arbitration to provide a neutral forum. Arbitration also has assumed an important role in resolving disputes that arise out of religious contracts. See Mohammedi, *Sharia-Compliant Wills: Principles, Recognition, and Enforcement,* 57 N.Y.L.Sch.L.Rev. 259 (2012/2013).

What is distinctive about practice in the United States is the expansion and great growth of arbitration in the consumer and employment settings. See Resnik, *The Privatization of Process: Requiem for and Celebration of the Federal Rules of Civil Procedure at* 75, 162 U.Pa.L.Rev. 1793 (2014). Professor Miller has written:

> Many businesses and employers now insist on private dispute resolution with their customers and employees through the widespread use of contractual mandatory arbitration provisions that expressly forbid resort to the courts; many of these provisions also prohibit the use of any form of law and affect a range of consumer, financing, employment, and small business transactions. These activities are engaged in by millions of people. Thus, dispute resolution is being privatized by a process that is invisible, under the control of industry, not constrained by rules of evidence or procedure, and lacks any meaningful judicial or other review.

Miller, *What Are Courts For? Have We Forsaken the Procedural Gold Standard?,* 78 La.L.Rev. 739, 773 (2018).

4. PRIVATE JUDGING

Disputants who can afford it may utilize private judging in order to avoid the delays of the court system. The disputants agree, after the dispute has arisen and been filed in court, to hire a private judge, often someone who has retired from the public court system. The court then refers the case to that judge. The standard for resolution is the applicable legal principles and the proceedings are conducted in much the same manner as a bench trial, although in an expedited and simplified manner. Unlike an arbitrator's award, the decision can be appealed as if the court referring it to the private judge had made the decision itself. Thus the disputants can ensure that the resolution will be in accordance with the law, while bypassing the backlog in the trial courts. In California, which served as a model for other states, the process is well established (particularly in family law disputes), and parties may pursue private adjudication before referees or designated "temporary judges." See Cal. Civ. Proc. Code §§ 638–645 (providing for appointment of referees by agreement of the parties or on the court's own motion); Cal. Const. art. VI § 21 (providing that "on stipulation of the parties litigant the court may order a cause to be tried by a temporary judge who is a member of the State Bar, sworn and empowered to act until final determination of the cause").

Unlike a civil trial, the process of private judging can be much faster and the proceedings generally take place outside the public gaze. As such, although the process protects the privacy of the participants, it fails to generate precedent in the same way as a dispute before a court and lacks the transparency needed for public accountability. Concerns also have been raised whether the process creates "a two-tiered system of justice that benefits the wealthy at the expense of others." Nagaraj, Comment, *The Marriage of Family Law and Private Judging in California*, 116 Yale L.J. 1615, 1621 (2007).

5. NEUTRAL FACT FINDING AND OMBUDSPERSONS

Neutral fact finding is a generic term for the use of a third party to gather information relevant to the settlement of a dispute. One of the most common institutional instances of a neutral fact finder is the ombudsperson. An ombudsperson is a third party who receives and investigates complaints aimed at an institution by its constituents, clients, or employees. The ombudsperson may take actions such as bringing an apparent injustice to the attention of high-level officials, advising the complainant of available options and resources, proposing a settlement of the dispute, or proposing systemic changes within the institution. A neutral fact finder often is employed by the institution against which the complaint is made. In government, an ombudsperson can serve the important function of steering a complaint through a tangled bureaucracy.

Ombudspersons are most likely to be hired in closely regulated institutions, fields in which customer satisfaction is critical, and institutions concerned with resolving disputes internally. Universities frequently use ombudspersons to enforce a set of rules that may be different from those applicable to people generally. Some independent ombudspersons are employed by local media and use publicity as their major tool. The disputants are responsible for resolving the dispute, although the ombudsperson can pressure them to settle. The source of the standard for resolution is either internal policy or commonly shared values. The ombudsperson acts as a representative of the complainant, investigating and presenting the facts for her as well as reminding the high-level officials of the policies they have set or the community's shared values.

6. EARLY NEUTRAL EVALUATION

It has been observed that parties often do not settle at an early stage in the litigation process because they fail to evaluate the case adequately until the trial process requires them to do so. Early neutral evaluation ("ENE") is a mechanism designed to respond to this problem. ENE involves the factual and legal presentation of a dispute to a neutral selected by the parties or a court. On the basis of this presentation the neutral, often an experienced lawyer, arbitrator, or former judge, provides the parties with an open assessment of their respective positions. This can have the effect of encouraging settlement, but at the very least it should help to focus the issues for the litigation process and assist in its efficient management. Roughly one-third of the district courts are authorized to refer parties to ENE, but it is less clear how often this process is utilized. See Judicial Conference of the United States, Civil Litigation Management Manual 69 (2d ed. 2010).

7. MINI-TRIALS

Similar to early neutral evaluation, but procedurally more complex, the mini-trial is a privately developed method of helping to bring about a negotiated settlement in lieu of protracted litigation. The procedural contours of mini-trials are tailored individually in accordance with the desires of the disputants. A typical mini-trial is a confidential process that entails a period of limited discovery after which attorneys for each side present an abbreviated version of the case before a panel consisting of managers with authority to settle and a neutral advisor. The neutral advisor is often a retired judge or respected lawyer. The managers then enter settlement negotiations.

Thus the parties resolve the dispute aided by the assessment of the neutral advisor as to the likely outcome should the matter go to court. The advisor's impartial appraisal of the conflict encourages the parties to adopt more realistic goals in negotiating a settlement. The source of the resolution standard is the disputants, despite the presence of the neutral legal advisor. Facts and standards are researched and presented by the disputants' lawyers, although in an abbreviated way. Mini-trials have been used successfully in disputes that were bogged down in discovery and motion practice by reconverting what had become a lawyer's problem back into a business problem. See *Recent Developments in Alternative Forms of Dispute Resolution*, 100 F.R.D. 512 (1984).

8.   SUMMARY JURY TRIALS

A summary jury trial is a nonbinding process used for cases ready to be tried before a jury. Instead of presenting a formal case before a full jury panel, the lawyers for the parties present an abbreviated case before a panel of six jurors. The presentations usually last less than a week and the resulting "verdict"—although not binding on the parties—provides a basis for settlement. The practice was introduced in the 1980s and is defended as a useful procedure when the parties hold highly divergent views of the likely outcome of the case and settlement efforts have been futile. See Lambros, *The Summary Jury Trial and Other Alternative Methods of Dispute Resolution*, 103 F.R.D. 481 (1984). Some states limit the summary jury trial to small claims. See Croley, *Summary Jury Trials in Charleston County, South Carolina*, 41 Loy.L.A.L.Rev. 1585 (2008). Early critics argued that in practice the procedure yielded little or no cost savings. See Posner, *The Summary Jury Trial and Other Alternative Methods of Alternative Dispute Resolution: Some Cautionary Observations*, 53 U.Chi.L.Rev. 366 (1986).

NOTES AND QUESTIONS

1.   ADR responds to a number of repeated criticisms of adversarial process as practiced in United States courts: that it is too costly and takes too long; that it cannot work because of litigant inequality; and that it is impersonal and disempowering.

Cost and Delay: Whether an actual litigation crisis exists in the United States remains a contested and unresolved question. Professor Miller has remarked "that the supposed litigation crisis is the product of assumption; that reliable empirical data is in short supply; and that data exist that support any proposition." Miller, *The Pretrial Rush to Judgment: Are the "Litigation Explosion," "Liability Crisis," and Efficiency Clichés Eroding Our Day in Court and Jury Trial Commitments?*, 78 N.Y.U.L.Rev. 982, 996 (2003); see also Reda, *The Cost-and-Delay Narrative in Civil Justice Reform: Its Fallacies and Functions*, 90 Or.L.Rev. 1085 (2012).

How much delay might be attributable to the rules of procedure, evidence, and appellate review that govern traditional adjudication? Rules of procedure are designed to protect litigants and to enforce the integrity of judicial decision-making. However, they generate strategic behavior by lawyers depending on the case and client. For certain litigants, delay may produce serious injustice—directly, because justice delayed may be justice denied, and indirectly, because the threat of delay may create an artificial pressure on one of the litigants to settle on less than fair terms. In addition, because delay might increase the cost of litigation, some individuals with meritorious claims may be discouraged from pursuing litigation or find themselves "out litigated" by an opponent with greater resources.

In theory, ADR introduces elements of informality that tend to expedite the process, resulting in faster and cheaper resolution. For example, arbitration's traditional hallmarks are its limited discovery and motion practice, the arbitrator's subject-matter expertise, and the finality of the award. Together, these factors provide a streamlined process that is intended to accelerate resolution. See Sussman, *Why Arbitrate? The Benefits and Savings*, N.Y.St.B.J. 20 (Oct. 2009). Expedition, however, may produce error or unfairness. Moreover, to the extent ADR adopts adjudicative-like procedures, won't cost and delay increase too, but without public accountability? See Stipanowich, *Arbitration: The "New Litigation,"* 2010 U.Ill.L.Rev. 1, 4. Indeed, it is now not unusual for disputants to litigate the results of ADR, challenging such issues as costs, confidentiality, and the size of awards. See Coben & Thompson, *Disputing Irony: A Systematic Look at Litigation About Mediation*, 11 Harv.Negot.L.Rev. 43 (2006).

Litigant Inequality: Another criticism of the adversarial system is that it does not work properly because disputants are not evenly matched in terms of resources, representation, and information. See Kruse, *Learning from Practice: What ADR Needs from a Theory of Justice*, 5 Nev.L.J. 389, 390–92 (2004–2005). Adjudication thus is said to contain a structural bias that tilts in favor of some groups more than others. See Nader, *Controlling Processes in the Practice of Law: Hierarchy and Pacification in the Movement to Re-Form Dispute Ideology*, 9 Ohio St.J. on Disp.Resol. 1 (1993).

ADR responds to this problem by attempting to level the playing field and having the parties depend less on counsel and procedural rules. See Edwards, *Alternative Dispute Resolution: Panacea or Anathema?*, 99 Harv.L.Rev. 668, 671 (1986); see also Kovach, *Privatization of Dispute Resolution: In the Spirit of Pound, But Mission Incomplete: Lessons Learned and a Possible Blueprint for the Future*, 48 S.Tex.L.Rev. 1003 (2007). However, this cure is a double-edged sword; diluting procedural protection may magnify resource and political disparities between disputants. See Oliver, Jr., *Alternate Dispute Resolution and Minorities in the Federal Courts*, 39 Cap.U.L.Rev. 805 (2011).

Impersonal Formalism: Litigation builds on a professional model of attorney representation and so tends to remove the parties from direct and personal control of decisions and solutions. Litigation also may polarize the parties, decreasing opportunities for future cooperation and straining the social fabric. This is particularly problematic when disputants have an ongoing relationship, as in the case of neighbors or family members and even in commercial settings. All of these factors may combine in some situations to obstruct disputants from reaching optimal outcomes. Professor Menkel-Meadow explains:

> The "culture of adversarialism" and the rules that enforce this culture often (not always) distort how we think about legal and human problem solving by assuming there are only two sides to an issue or

question, that "truth" about either what happened factually or what is correct legally can best be resolved by vigorous contestations between two fully armed advocates and decided by a third-party judge who is separate from the parties and appointed by the state. * * * Often, what is most important to parties may be excluded from consideration, as irrelevant or inadmissible, according to our well-worn legal principles, which may protect other important interests (like privileges, trade secrets, bias and prejudice, or constitutional rights).

Menkel-Meadow, *The Lawyer as Problem Solver and Third-Party Neutral: Creativity and Non-Partisanship in Lawyering*, 72 Temple L.Rev. 785, 788–89 (1999) (citations omitted).

ADR builds on a different conceptual model of dispute resolution that is not dependent on legal formality, attorney representation, or coercive power. See Welsh, *Musings on Mediation, Kleenex, and (Smudged) White Hats*, 33 U. La Verne L.Rev. 5 (2011). However, does arbitration, which in many respects closely resembles litigation, really solve the problems associated with the impersonal legalism of adjudication? Does it overcome or exacerbate power differentials between the disputants? Relatedly, can non-voluntary mediation, in which the mediator speaks for the parties, truly be said to promote personal empowerment? See Harper, *Mediator as Peacemaker: The Case for Activist Transformative-Narrative Mediation*, 2006 J.Disp. Resol. 595; see also Rack, *A Letter to My Successor*, 26 Ohio St.J. on Disp. Resol. 429, 432 (2011).

2. The literature on procedural justice, discussed in p. 4, Note 1, supra, repeatedly has found that participants favor adjudicative procedure because of its perceived fairness and its related capacity to generate satisfaction and trust. See Thibaut & Walker, Procedural Justice (1975). However, procedural preferences also are affected by the size and scale of the dispute. A psychological study of small civil law disputants observed that participants favor processes that offer "control": "(a) control over the decision such that a neutral third party would help disputants arrive at their own resolution; (b) a process that granted disputants control over the presentation of evidence (rather than using a representative to do so); and (c) either a set of rules that both disputants would have agreed to in advance of the resolution process, or the well-established rules used in a court of law." See Shestowsky, *Procedural Preferences in Alternative Dispute Resolution*, 10 Psychol. Pub. Pol'y & L. 211, 233 (2004). What other information might be relevant to ensuring the fairness and accuracy of dispute resolution mechanisms? See Hensler, *Suppose It's Not True: Challenging Mediation Ideology*, 2002 J.Disp. Resol. 81 (urging more empirical examination).

3. How might the financial stakes of a dispute affect the parties' preference for different forms of procedure? In the aftermath of the attack on the World Trade Center on September 11, 2001, Congress created a Victim Compensation Fund ("VCF") to ensure the payment of damages to individuals who suffered loss. Compensation was conditioned on the claimant's waiver of

damage claims associated with the attack. See Berkowitz, *The Problematic Role of the Special Master: Undermining the Legitimacy of the September 11th Compensation Fund*, 24 Yale L. & Pol'y Rev. 1, 5–7 (2006). The VCF paid out more than $7.048 billion for about 5,500 claims, and only 95 lawsuits were filed on behalf of 96 claimants. See In re September 11 Litigation, 600 F.Supp.2d 549, 552 (S.D.N.Y. 2009). These lawsuits were judicially managed to secure a mediated, coordinated settlement, and the aggregate amount that was approved by the district court totaled $500 million. The district court noted the different reasons for the claimants' decision to litigate rather than accept a cash payment from the VCF:

> Some, the successors of victims with very high incomes or income potential, believed that the Fund would not compensate them adequately in relation to lost income, and filed suits instead. Others filed suits to avoid having to deduct their life insurance recoveries and other collateral source payments * * *. Still others wanted to tell their stories, participate in forcing facts into the public domain, or avail themselves of traditional remedies for other reasons. And some could not free themselves from the shadows and despair of the September 11 tragedy to do anything on a timely basis, even though the Special Master [of the VCF] made special efforts to reach such people and relaxed the Fund's requirements to accommodate such claimants.

Id. at 561, citing *Report of the Mediator on the Mediation and the Settlement Efforts of the Parties in the Cases Previously Docketed Under 21 MC 97.* All but three lawsuits settled. See Hadfield, *Framing the Choice Between Cash and the Courthouse: Experiences with the 9/11 Victim Compensation Fund*, 42 Law & Soc'y Rev. 645 (2008).

C. ADR AND CIVIL LITIGATION

———

Read Federal Rules of Civil Procedure 16, 54(a), 54(d), and 68 and 28 U.S.C. § 1920 in the Supplement.

———

1. THE INSTITUTIONALIZATION OF ADR WITHIN THE COURT AND ADMINISTRATIVE SYSTEM

Over the last generation ADR has become an integral and mandatory feature of the public system of courts and agency administration. This development raises new and important questions about the fairness and efficiency of ADR when the parties no longer play a role in its design or voluntarily accede to its use.

An important first step toward the institutionalization of ADR within the court and administrative system occurred with the enactment of the Civil Justice Reform Act of 1990, requiring federal courts to consider ADR mechanisms as a way to reduce litigation expense and delay. 28 U.S.C. §§ 471 et seq. In 1998, this "invitation" was upgraded to a requirement under the Alternative Dispute Resolution Act, 28 U.S.C. § 651, that federal courts implement ADR programs and mandate participation. See Crowne, *The Alternative Dispute Resolution Act of 1998: Implementing a New Paradigm of Justice*, 76 N.Y.U.L.Rev. 1768 (2001). Congress also authorized administrative agencies to use alternative means of dispute resolution, and agencies have responded by establishing large-scale ADR programs. See Administrative Dispute Resolution Act, 5 U.S.C. §§ 571–583; Marcus & Senger, *ADR and the Federal Government: Not Such Strange Bedfellows After All*, 66 Mo.L.Rev. 709 (2001). On a parallel track, states incorporated ADR into their judicial systems. See, e.g., Dana, Jr., *Court-Connected Alternative Dispute Resolution in Maine*, 57 Me.L.Rev. 349 (2005). For a comprehensive assessment of court-annexed ADR, see Shestowsky, *Disputants' Preferences for Court-Connected Dispute Resolution Procedures: Why We Should Care and Why We Know So Little*, 23 Ohio St.J. on Disp. Resol. 549 (2008).

Court-annexed arbitration builds upon the standard model of arbitration except that the parties have not previously agreed to arbitrate their dispute. Instead, certain disputes, usually those in which the amount in controversy is less than a certain dollar figure, must be referred to an arbitrator before the court will hear them. The arbitrator thus is less likely to have expertise in the subject area in which the conflict arose. Moreover, since the source of the standard for resolution is the law, the arbitrator typically will be a lawyer. The nature and extent of fact finding and standard-finding are not substantially different from adjudication, although discovery may be limited and the rules of evidence may be relaxed. If a disputant is dissatisfied with the arbitrator's decision, he can demand a trial de novo, but if the disputant fails to obtain a better result at trial, he may be required to pay the costs of the opposing party. See Boyarin, *Court-Connected ADR—A Time of Crisis, A Time of Change*, 95 Marq.L.Rev. 993 (2012).

Some observers predicted that the institutionalization of ADR would subvert its claim to flexibility, voluntary participation, and cooperative resolution. See Menkel-Meadow, *Pursuing Settlement in an Adversary Culture: A Tale of Innovation Co-opted or "The Law of ADR,"* 19 Fla.St.U.L.Rev. 1 (1990). Others warned that mainstreaming ADR would cause it to become mass-produced, more expensive, and subject to delay, yet it would remain less protective of litigant rights. See Sabatino, *ADR as "Litigation Lite": Procedural and Evidentiary Norms Embedded Within Alternative Dispute Resolution*, 47 Emory L.J. 1289 (1998). See generally

Reuben, *Public Justice: Toward a State Action Theory of Alternative Dispute Resolution*, 85 Calif.L.Rev. 579 (1997).

As the institutionalization of ADR has become more conventional, a persistent criticism is that court-annexed ADR functions as no more than settlement conferences that push disputants to a quick disposition rather than a consensual working out of grievances. See Brown, *A Community of Court ADR Programs: How Court-Based ADR Programs Help Each Other Survive and Thrive*, 26 Just. Sys.J. 327, 330 (2005). Typical is the following concern:

> Those who established court-annexed mandatory mediation programs and those who run them appear to have a very clear agenda—to settle cases. Legislatures that have been persuaded to support such programs have viewed them as a cost-effective way of dealing with rising judicial caseloads. The chief criterion for providing funds has been the number of settlements arranged. * * * When settlement is king, the idea of self-determination is likely to be undercut—the only determination that is acceptable is the one that ends the case.

Landsman, *Nothing for Something? Denying Legal Assistance to Those Compelled to Participate in ADR Proceedings*, 37 Fordham Urb.L.J. 273, 286–87 (2010). Critics also have questioned whether ADR should ever be mandatory.

Proponents of ADR have argued that courts should be more aggressive in adopting streamlined procedures that have proven useful in practice. These techniques include narrowing the scope of discovery and restricting the use of expert submissions. See Welsh, *The Current Transitional State of Court-Connected ADR*, 95 Marq.L.Rev. 873 (2012). Other analysts have asked, again drawing on the ADR experience, whether courts should use non-uniform procedural rules and, if so, how these rules ought to be designed. See Tidmarsh, *Exiting Litigation*, 41 Loy.U.Chi.L.J. 263, 283 (2010).

It is difficult to assess the effects of court-annexed ADR on litigants, the court system, or ADR. One commentator has referred to the "exodus from and transformation of American civil litigation," and the consequent movement from a trial-centered process in which disputes are resolved and public norms are announced, to a system that emphasizes efficiency, settlement, and pre-discovery disposition. See Freer, *Exodus from and Transformation of American Civil Litigation*, 65 Emory L.J. 1491 (2016). What further consequences do you see if courts increasingly recede from their law-declaring and information-disclosing functions?

2.   CHANGING JUDICIAL ATTITUDES TOWARD ADR: THE EXAMPLE OF BINDING ARBITRATION

Congress enacted the Federal Arbitration Act ("FAA") in 1925 in part to overcome common law hostility to arbitration. Initially, the Supreme Court refused to enforce pre-dispute arbitration agreements when their use would dilute statutory protections. For example, in WILKO v. SWAN, 346 U.S. 427, 74 S.Ct. 182, 98 L.Ed. 168 (1953), the Supreme Court held that the Securities Act of 1933 barred a mandatory arbitration clause that was included in a brokerage margin agreement.

Since then, the Court's approach to arbitration has undergone a radical change with far-reaching social effects. In 1983, in MOSES H. MEMORIAL CONE HOSPITAL v. MERCURY CONSTRUCTION CORP., 460 U.S. 1, 103 S.Ct. 927, 74 L.Ed.2d 765 (1983), the Court held that a district court could adjudicate a petition to compel arbitration even though a state court was considering the claims that the federal plaintiff sought to arbitrate, relying upon a "liberal federal policy favoring arbitration agreements." Id. at 24, 103 S.Ct. at 941, 74 L.Ed.2d at 785.

After *Moses H. Cone*, the Court steadily expanded the reach of the FAA. A sea change came in SOUTHLAND CORP. v. KEATING, 465 U.S. 1, 104 S.Ct. 852, 79 L.Ed.2d 1 (1984). *Southland* involved individual and class actions brought in a state court by convenience store franchisees under state law; the trial court ordered arbitration of all claims but the California Supreme Court held that statutory claims were not arbitrable. The Supreme Court reversed, holding that the FAA preempted state law and withdrew from the states any power to require a judicial forum for claims that the parties agreed to resolve by arbitration. Then, in RODRIGUEZ DE QUIJAS v. SHEARSON/AMERICAN EXPRESS, 490 U.S. 477, 484, 109 S.Ct. 1917, 1922, 104 L.Ed.2d 526, 536 (1989), the Court, five-to-four, overruled *Wilko*, holding that it "was incorrectly decided" and at odds with other federal statutes that in the interim had been interpreted to permit pre-dispute agreements to arbitrate.

In keeping with *Rodriguez de Quijas*, the Court has rejected attempts to use other federal statutes to displace the FAA's policy favoring arbitration. In EPIC SYSTEMS CORP. v. LEWIS, 584 U.S. ___, 138 S.Ct. 1612, 200 L.Ed.2d 889 (2018), employees brought wage-and-hour claims against their employers under federal and state law. Although they were bound by pre-dispute arbitration agreements that required individualized arbitration, plaintiffs sought to litigate their claims as collective actions and class actions, relying on Section 7 of the National Labor Relations Act (NLRA), which guarantees to workers the right to engage in "concerted activities for the purpose of collective bargaining or other mutual aid or protection." The Court nevertheless concluded that the NLRA did not overcome the presumption in favor of arbitration because it did "not mention class or collective action procedures or even hint at a clear and manifest wish to displace the Arbitration Act." Id. at ___, 138 S.Ct. at 1617, 200 L.Ed.2d at 902. The result in *Epic Systems* is consistent with the Court's view that the FAA embodies not only a policy in favor of arbitration but also in favor of *individualized* arbitration. In LAMPS PLUS, INC. v. VARELA, 587 U.S. ___, 139 S.Ct. 1407, 203 L.Ed.2d 636 (2019), the Court held that an arbitration agreement must have clear, express language permitting class arbitration. In so holding, the Court rejected application of the doctrine of *contra proferentem*—the contract law principle that an ambiguous contractual provision should be interpreted against the drafter.

The Court currently accords a strong presumption of validity to arbitration agreements, even when the clauses are adhesive, not voluntary, and curtail jury and other public rights. In AT&T MOBILITY v. CONCEPCION, p. 594, supra, the Court held that the FAA preempts state laws that treat class-action waivers as unconscionable. See Gilles & Friedman, *After Class: Aggregate Litigation in the Wake of* AT&T Mobility v. Concepcion, 79 U.Chi.L.Rev. 623 (2012). Then, in DIRECTV, INC. v. IMBURGIA, 136 S.Ct. 463, 193 L.Ed.2d 365 (2015), the Court held that an arbitration clause providing it would be invalid if the "law of your state" made the waiver of class-wide arbitration unenforceable, did not include a California law that was valid at the time the contract was entered into, but later ruled preempted in *Concepcion*. Justice Thomas dissented, on the view that the FAA "does not require state courts to order arbitration." Id. at 471, 193 L.Ed.2d at 375. Justice Ginsburg also dissented, joined by Justice Sotomayor, criticizing the majority as having usurped the state court's role in the interpretation of state contract law, for depriving consumers of choice in the laws that govern their arbitration agreements; and for insulating "powerful economic interests from liability." Id. at 477, 193 L.Ed.2d at 381.

The Supreme Court also upheld a contractual ban on class-wide arbitration in AMERICAN EXPRESS CO. v. ITALIAN COLORS RESTAURANT, 570 U.S. 228, 133 S.Ct. 2304, 186 L.Ed.2d 417 (2013), see p. 597, Note 2, supra. At issue was a merchant agreement with a credit card company that barred merchants from bringing a group or collective action. The Court explicitly rejected plaintiffs' argument that the class-bar was unenforceable even though the cost of individual arbitration exceeded any individual's potential recovery.

In KINDRED NURSING CENTERS LIMITED PARTNERSHIP v. CLARK, 137 S.Ct. 1421, 197 L.Ed.2d 806 (2017), the estates of two nursing home residents sued the nursing home in state court alleging substandard care leading to wrongful death, personal injuries, and violation of the Kentucky Long Term Care Facilities Act. The Kentucky court denied defendant's motion to dismiss and to compel arbitration. The Kentucky Supreme Court affirmed, holding that under Kentucky law, a power of attorney must include a specific statement that the attorney-in-fact has authority to waive the principal's state constitutional rights to access to the courts and to a jury trial. The Supreme Court reversed, holding that the Kentucky rule disfavored arbitration agreements and was preempted by the FAA. Id. at 1426, 197 L.Ed.2d at 812. Again, Justice Thomas dissented, emphasizing his view that the FAA does not apply in state court. Id. at 1429, 197 L.Ed.2d at 815.

NOTES AND QUESTIONS

1.   Arbitrators do not receive any in-depth professional training or briefing on their task, but they exercise broad discretion in their decision-making. Is there a danger that their method of selection might create a potential for bias, particularly among arbitrators who receive repeat appointments by one company or by one segment of a regulated industry? See Rossein & Hope, *Disclosure and Disqualification Standards for Neutral Arbitrators: How Far to Cast the Net and What Is Sufficient to Vacate Award*, 81 St. John's L.Rev. 203 (2007). An empirical study found a perception of pro-industry bias among securities-industry arbitrators, leading customers to "express a consistently negative impression of the overall arbitration process." Gross, *When Perception Changes Reality: An Empirical Study of Investors' Views of the Fairness of Securities Arbitration*, 2008 J.Disp.Resol. 349, 389. Is there also a danger that informality will permit bias or prejudice to go unchecked? See Delgado, Dunn, Brown, Lee & Hubbert, *Fairness and Formality: Minimizing the Risk of Prejudice in Alternative Dispute Resolution*, 1985 Wis.L.Rev. 1359.

2.   Arbitration decisions need not be based on statute or common law. For this reason some commentators view arbitration as "lawless." Black & Gross, *Making It Up As They Go Along: The Role of Law in Securities Arbitration*, 23 Cardozo L.Rev. 991 (2002). Does that view fairly account for the important autonomy interests arguably promoted by arbitration? In recent years it has become common practice for arbitral parties to circulate arbitration awards and decisions, and forms of nonbinding precedent have emerged. See Weidemaier, *Toward a Theory of Precedent in Arbitration*, 51 Wm. & Mary L.Rev. 1895 (2010); see also Weidemaier, *Judging-Lite: How Arbitrators Use and Create Precedent*, 90 N.C.L.Rev. 1091 (2012). Might the diversion of disputes to arbitration proceedings make it more difficult for the courts to create precedent in important fields of law? See Scodro, Note, *Arbitrating Novel Legal Questions: A Recommendation for Reform*, 105 Yale L.J. 1927 (1996).

3.   The expansion of international trade and commercial transactions in the past 50 years has created a need for private international commercial dispute resolution. Many commercial parties are uncomfortable adjudicating disputes in foreign court systems because they are unfamiliar with the procedures and law of foreign forums and fear favoritism to nationals. The demand for mechanisms for private commercial dispute resolution has led to

the development of international commercial arbitration rules (such as the International Chamber of Commerce Rules). These are applied in international arbitration centers around the world. Using these accepted rules and forums, private parties are able to arbitrate and resolve their commercial disputes without submitting the dispute to a foreign forum. Enforcement of these arbitration awards can then be sought in court under the Convention on the Recognition and Enforcement of Foreign Arbitral Awards (commonly known as the New York Convention), a treaty that has been ratified by most countries, including the United States. Given these resources, why might parties still prefer to resolve their dispute in court? Should an international commercial arbitration decision be enforceable in any forum in the world?

4. Arbitration has spread from disputes between evenly matched corporate entities seeking a private, expeditious, and industry-specific resolution to a wide range of employment and consumer disputes in which its use is mandated by an adhesive term in a boilerplate contract. See Sternlight, *Rethinking the Constitutionality of the Supreme Court's Preference for Binding Arbitration: A Fresh Assessment of Jury Trial, Separation of Powers, and Due Process Concerns*, 72 Tul.L.Rev. 1 (1997); see also Eisenberg, Miller & Sherwin, *Arbitrator's Summer Soldiers: An Empirical Study of Arbitration Clauses in Consumer and Nonconsumer Contracts*, 41 U.Mich.J.L.Reform. 871, 86 (2008). The Supreme Court through its interpretation of the Federal Arbitration Act has encouraged this development. See Wasserman, *Legal Process in a Box, or What Class Action Waivers Teach Us About Law-Making*, 44 Loy.U.Chi.L.J. 391, 399–400 (2012). Critics have warned that in these new contexts arbitration inevitably tilts in favor of the commercial party that, as a repeat player, enjoys strategic advantages. See Kapeliuk, *The Repeat Appointment Factor: Exploring Decision Patterns of Elite Investment Arbitrators*, 96 Cornell L.Rev. 47 (2010).

Justice Ginsburg underscored that other industrialized, democratic nations ban mandatory arbitration clauses in consumer contracts of adhesion:

> A 1993 European Union Directive forbids binding consumers to unfair contractual terms, defined as those "not . . . individually negotiated" that "caus[e] a significant imbalance in the parties' rights and obligations . . . to the detriment of the consumer." Coun. Directive 93/13, Art. 3, 1993 O.J. (L. 95) 31. A subsequent EU Recommendation interpreted this Directive to bar enforcement of one-party-dictated mandatory consumer arbitration agreements. Comm'n Recommendation 98/257, 1998 O.J. (L. 115) 34 ("The consumer's recourse to the out-of-court procedure may not be the result of a commitment prior to the materialisation of the dispute, where such commitment has the effect of depriving the consumer of his right to bring an action before the courts for the settlement of the dispute."). As a result of this Directive and Recommendation, disputes between providers and consumers in the EU are arbitrated only when the parties mutually agree to arbitration on a "post-dispute basis." Sternlight, Is the U.S. Out on a Limb? Comparing the U.S. Approach

to Mandatory Consumer and Employment Arbitration to That of the Rest of the World, 56 U. Miami L. Rev. 831, 847–848 (2002) (emphasis deleted); *see id.*, at 852 (enforcement of mandatory arbitration clauses in consumer contracts of adhesion "is quite rare, if not nonexistent," outside the United States).

Id. at 478, 193 L.Ed.2d at 383. See Resnik, *A2J/A2K: Access to Justice, Access to Knowledge, and Economic Inequalities in Open Courts and Arbitrations*, 96 N.C.L.Rev. 605 (2018).

5. Because arbitration is private, it has been difficult to obtain information needed to assess disputant satisfaction. Available information has shown an uneven pattern across parties and industries. See Landsman, *ADR and the Cost of Compulsion*, 57 Stan.L.Rev. 1593 (2005). One study of publicly held companies suggested that although arbitration clauses are common in consumer contracts, sophisticated companies prefer litigation to arbitration when they deal with peers. See Eisenberg & Miller, *The Flight from Arbitration: An Empirical Study of Ex Ante Arbitration Clauses in the Contracts of Publicly Held Companies*, 56 DePaul L.Rev. 335 (2007). A study commissioned by the U.S. Chamber of Commerce's Institute for Law Reform, based on a dataset of approximately 100,000 arbitrations between 2014 and 2020, claims that consumers prevailed more often in arbitration than in comparable court proceedings. See Pham & Donovan, Fairer, Faster, Better II: An Empirical Assessment of Consumer Arbitration (2020). A close examination of consumer arbitration data, however, strongly suggests that very few individual consumers file standalone arbitration cases. Resnik, Garlock & Wang, *Collective Preclusion and Inaccessible Arbitration: Data, Nondisclosure, and Public Knowledge*, 24 Lewis & Clark L.Rev. 611 (2020). Instead, the bulk of consumer arbitration cases result from the de facto aggregation of claims by "[l]awyers and other entities [that] enable groups of consumers and workers to file individual claims against the same respondents." Id. at 615.

The Consumer Financial Protection Bureau prepared an extensive report for Congress in 2015 on the prevalence of pre-dispute arbitration clauses in consumer agreements. The report confirmed that tens of millions of consumers use financial products or services that are subject to mandatory arbitration. Surveys of credit card users indicated that these consumers generally were unaware that their contracts included mandatory arbitration clauses and wrongly believed they could sue in court. Moreover, although some agreements—most typically for storefront payday loans—provided a right to pursue a claim in small claims court, consumers generally were unaware of their rights. See Consumer Financial Protection Bureau, Arbitration Study: Report to Congress Pursuant to Dodd-Frank Wall Street Reform and Consumer Protections Act (March 2015), http://files.consumerfinance.gov/f/201503_cfpb_arbitration-study-report-to-congress-2015.pdf.

6. Critics of arbitration argue that it effectively deprives consumers and other weaker parties of regulatory protections by "changing rules of evidence, the availability of aggregation, burdens of production and proof, and other

features of the dispute resolution process." See Noll, *Regulating Arbitration*, 105 Calif.L.Rev. 985, 990 (2017). Professor Miller has cautioned:

> [T]he great expansion of contractual limitations on private law enforcement by consumers through the insertion of arbitration clauses into agreements that are often adhesive—and the validation by the Supreme Court of such clauses—may be seen as part of an overall campaign to reduce the effectiveness of federal regulatory law and public enforcement proceedings. These clauses impair citizen access to a judicial forum with the possibility of jury trial. And quite recently the Supreme Court indicated that the availability of the class action in arbitration may be extremely limited, potentially impairing the effectiveness of consumer remedies in various contexts.

Miller, *From* Conley *to* Twombly *to* Iqbal*: A Double Play on the Federal Rules of Civil Procedure*, 60 Duke L.J. 1, 12–13 (2010).

7.   It is not only an arbitrator's decision on the merits of a dispute that enjoys a high degree of insulation from court scrutiny. The Supreme Court has interpreted the FAA to permit the parties to assign to the arbitrator, rather than the court, the power to decide the threshold question whether a dispute is subject to an arbitration agreement in the first instance. In HENRY SCHEIN, INC. v. ARCHER & WHITE SALES, INC., 586 U.S. ___, 139 S.Ct. 524, 202 L.Ed.2d 480 (2019), the parties entered into a contract requiring arbitration of disputes under or related to the contract, except for actions seeking injunctive relief. Respondent brought suit against petitioner in federal district court alleging violations of federal and state antitrust laws and seeking both money damages and injunctive relief. When petitioner moved to compel arbitration, respondent argued that the case was not subject to the arbitration agreement because respondent sought, in part, injunctive relief. Petitioner argued that the arbitrator, and not the court, should decide whether the dispute was subject to arbitration. The district court, without deciding if the contract called for arbitration of the threshold question, denied arbitration on the ground that the arguments for arbitration were "wholly groundless," and the Fifth Circuit affirmed. In a unanimous opinion, the Supreme Court vacated the judgment, holding that if a contract delegates the question whether a dispute is subject to arbitration to an arbitrator, the court may not override that delegation, even if it thinks that the argument favoring arbitration is "wholly groundless." According to the Court, the "wholly groundless" doctrine, which some lower courts had recognized, was inconsistent with the FAA. The Court remanded the case to permit the Fifth Circuit to determine whether the arbitration contract, by its terms, in fact delegated the question of arbitrability to the arbitrator.

Note, however, that parties cannot agree to more expansive judicial review of an arbitrator's decision than the narrow and deferential post-arbitral review provided under the FAA. In HALL STREET ASSOCIATES, L.L.C. v. MATTEL, INC., 552 U.S. 576, 128 S.Ct. 1396, 170 L.Ed.2d 254 (2008), the

Court read the text of the FAA to mean that the statute provides the exclusive grounds for vacating or modifying an arbitral award:

> Hall Street is certainly right that the FAA lets parties tailor some, even many * * * features of arbitration by contract, including the way arbitrators are chosen, what their qualifications should be, which issues are arbitrable, along with procedure and choice of substantive law. But to rest this case on the general policy of treating arbitration agreements as enforceable as such would be to beg the question, which is whether the FAA has textual features at odds with enforcing a contract to expand judicial review following the arbitration.

Id. at 586, 128 S.Ct. at 1404, 170 L.Ed.2d at 264.

3. ADR AND THE JUDICIAL PREFERENCE FOR SETTLEMENT

———

Read Federal Rule of Civil Procedure 68 and the accompanying materials in the Supplement.

———

In DELTA AIR LINES, INC. v. AUGUST, 450 U.S. 346, 101 S.Ct. 1146, 67 L.Ed.2d 287 (1981), Rosemary August filed suit against Delta Air Lines seeking $20,000 in back pay for violation of Title VII of the Civil Rights Act of 1964. Delta made a formal settlement offer of $450, which August rejected. At trial, judgment was for Delta and the district court directed that each party bear its own costs. The court held that Federal Rule 68, which directs that a plaintiff who rejects a formal settlement offer must pay post-offer costs if the "judgment that the offeree finally obtains is not more favorable than the unaccepted offer," was not applicable since Delta's offer of $450 was not a reasonable, good faith attempt to settle the case. The Court of Appeals for the Seventh Circuit affirmed on the same grounds.

The Supreme Court affirmed the result, although it rejected the reasoning of the lower courts. In an opinion written by Justice Stevens, the Court held that Rule 68's reference to "judgment * * * obtained by the offeree" did not encompass a judgment against the offeree:

> Our interpretation of the Rule is consistent with its purpose. The purpose of Rule 68 is to encourage the settlement of litigation. In all litigation, the adverse consequences of potential defeat provide both parties with an incentive to settle in advance of trial. Rule 68 provides an additional inducement to settle in those cases in which there is a strong probability that the plaintiff will obtain a judgment but the amount of recovery is uncertain. Because

prevailing plaintiffs presumptively will obtain costs under Rule 54(d), Rule 68 imposes a special burden on the plaintiff to whom a formal settlement offer is made. If a plaintiff rejects a Rule 68 settlement offer, he will lose some of the benefits of victory if his recovery is less than the offer. Because costs are usually assessed against the losing party, liability for costs is a normal incident of defeat. Therefore, a nonsettling plaintiff does not run the risk of suffering additional burdens that do not ordinarily attend a defeat, and Rule 68 would provide little, if any, additional incentive if it were applied when the plaintiff loses.

Defendant argues that Rule 68 does provide such an incentive, because it operates to deprive the district judge of the discretion vested in him by Rule 54(d). According to this reasoning, Rule 68 is mandatory, and a district judge must assess costs against a plaintiff who rejects a settlement offer and then either fails to obtain a judgment or recovers less than the offer. * * *

* * * If, as defendant argues, Rule 68 applies to defeated plaintiffs, any settlement offer, no matter how small, would apparently trigger the operation of the Rule. Thus any defendant, by performing the meaningless act of making a nominal settlement offer, could eliminate the trial judge's discretion under Rule 54(d). We cannot reasonably conclude that the drafters of the Federal Rules intended on the one hand affirmatively to grant the district judge discretion to deny costs to the prevailing party under Rule 54(d) and then on the other hand to give defendants—and only defendants—the power to take away that discretion by performing a token act. Moreover, if the Rule operated as defendant argues, we cannot conceive of a reason why the drafters would have given only defendants, and not plaintiffs, the power to divest the judge of his Rule 54(d) discretion. * * * When Rule 68 is read literally, however, it is evenhanded in its operation. As we have already noted, it does not apply to judgments in favor of the defendant or to judgments in favor of the plaintiff for an amount greater than the settlement offer. In both of those extreme situations the trial judge retains his Rule 54(d) discretion. * * * Thus unless we assume that the Federal Rules were intended to be biased in favor of defendants, we can conceive of no reason why defendants—and not plaintiffs—should be given an entirely risk-free method of denying trial judges the discretion that Rule 54(d) confers regardless of the outcome of the litigation.

The Court of Appeals, perceiving the anomaly of allowing defendants to control the discretion of district judges by making sham offers, resolved the problem by holding that only reasonable offers trigger the operation of Rule 68. But the plain language of the Rule makes it unnecessary to read a reasonableness requirement into the Rule. * * *

Id. at 352–55, 101 S.Ct. at 1150–52, 67 L.Ed.2d at 292–95.

———

MAREK v. CHESNY, 473 U.S. 1, 105 S.Ct. 3012, 87 L.Ed.2d 1 (1985), involved three police officers, who, in answering a call on a domestic disturbance, shot and killed Alfred Chesny's son. Chesny, on his own behalf and as administrator of his son's estate, filed suit against the officers in federal district court under 42 U.S.C. § 1983 and state tort law. Prior to trial, the police officers made a timely offer of settlement of $100,000, expressly including accrued costs and attorney's fees, but Chesny did not accept the offer. The case went to trial and Chesny was awarded $5,000 on the state-law claim, $52,000 for the Section 1983 violation, and $3,000 in punitive damages. Chesny then filed a request for attorney's fees under 42 U.S.C. § 1988, which provides that a prevailing party in a Section 1983 action may be awarded attorney's fees "as part of the costs." The claimed attorney's fees included fees for work performed subsequent to the settlement offer. The district court declined to award these latter fees pursuant to Rule 68. The court of appeals reversed, but the Supreme Court agreed with the district court.

The Court held first that the officers' offer was valid under Rule 68. As the Court read it, the Rule does not require that a defendant's offer itemize the respective amounts being tendered for settlement of the underlying substantive claim and for costs. In reaching this result, Chief Justice Burger, writing for the majority, asserted that the drafters' concern was not so much with the particular components of offers, but with the judgments to be allowed against defendants. Whether or not the offer recites that costs are included or specifies an amount for costs, the offer allows judgment to be entered against the defendant both for damages caused by the challenged conduct and for costs. In the Chief Justice's view, this construction of Rule 68 furthers its objective of encouraging settlements.

He next noted that the drafters of Rule 68 were aware of the various federal statutes that, as an exception to the "American Rule," authorize an award of attorney's fees to prevailing parties as part of the costs in particular cases. From this, he concluded that the term "costs" in the Rule was intended to refer to all costs properly awardable under the relevant substantive statute. Thus, when the underlying statute defines "costs" to include attorney's fees, the fees are to be included as costs for purposes of Rule 68. Since Section 1983 expressly includes attorney's fees as "costs" available to a prevailing plaintiff in a suit under the statute, those fees are subject to the cost-shifting provision of Rule 68. As Chief Justice Burger saw it, rather than "cutting against the grain" of Section 1983, applying

Rule 68 in the context of a Section 1983 action is consistent with Section 1988's policies and objectives of encouraging plaintiffs to bring meritorious civil rights suits; Rule 68 simply encourages settlements.

Justice Brennan filed a vigorous dissent for himself and Justices Marshall and Blackmun.

NOTES AND QUESTIONS

1. The majority in *Marek* argued that the effect of Rule 68 is neutral because settlements serve the interest of plaintiffs as well as defendants. However, because the rule is available only to defendants, might its use tend to lower settlement offers? See Miller, *An Economic Analysis of Rule* 68, 15 J. Legal Stud. 93 (1986); Rowe, *Predicting the Effects of Attorney Fee Shifting*, 47 Law & Contemp.Probs. 139 (1984).

2. Implicit in the attempt to encourage settlement is an assumption that a negotiated resolution of a dispute is more desirable than that of a judicial disposition. Consider the contrary position of Professor Fiss, who has emphasized the public role of litigation as "an institutional arrangement for using state power to bring a recalcitrant reality closer to our chosen ideals":

> I do not believe that settlement as a generic practice is preferable to judgment or should be institutionalized on a wholesale and indiscriminate basis. It should be treated instead as a highly problematic technique for streamlining dockets. Settlement is for me the civil analogue of plea bargaining: Consent is often coerced; the bargain may be struck by someone without authority; the absence of a trial and judgment renders subsequent judicial involvement troublesome; and although dockets are trimmed, justice may not be done. Like plea bargaining, settlement is a capitulation to the conditions of mass society and should be neither encouraged nor praised.

Fiss, *Against Settlement*, 93 Yale L.J. 1073, 1075, 1089 (1984) (citations omitted). See Cohen, *Revisiting* Against Settlement*: Some Reflections on Dispute Resolution and Public Values*, 78 Fordham L.Rev. 1143 (2009).

3. Settlement terms may be drafted to protect the privacy of the parties to the contract. Retaining the confidentiality of information may be desirable for the parties, but is it desirable for society as a whole? See Macklin, *Promoting Settlement, Foregoing the Facts*, 14 N.Y.U.Rev.L. & Soc. Change 579 (1986) (stressing the value of judicial fact finding as "a source of tested facts" for use in public policy discussion and planning). Is it appropriate for settlement agreements to block the public from learning about defective products, employment discrimination, and other forms of illegality that reasonably can be expected to harm nonparties? See Levmore & Fagan, *Semi-Confidential Settlements in Civil, Criminal, and Sexual Assault Cases*, 103 Cornell L.Rev. 311 (2018); Resnik, *Uncovering, Disclosing, and Discovering*

How the Public Dimensions of Court-Based Processes Are at Risk, 81 Chi.-Kent L.Rev. 521 (2006).

4.   How does judicial participation in the settlement process affect the judge's traditional role as decision-maker? Some judges delegate the task of negotiating a settlement to an extrajudicial officer. Other judges may conduct a mediation conference with the goal of settling the dispute. See Brunet, *Judicial Mediation and Signaling,* 3 Nev.L.Rev. 233 (2002–2003). Is there a danger that judicial mediation will undermine the judge's ability to be a neutral decisionmaker? See Shweder, *Judicial Limitations on ADR: The Role and Ethics of Judges Encouraging Settlements,* 20 Geo.J.Legal Ethics 51 (2007).

D. ASSESSING ADR AND THE ROLE OF CIVIL LITIGATION IN AMERICAN SOCIETY

ADR promises an alternative to the public system of courts that is flexible, participatory, expeditious, and cheaper. Whether ADR succeeds on its own terms remains an open question given limited data about a set of processes that are private and shielded from public scrutiny. See Landsman, *ADR and the Cost of Compulsion,* 57 Stan.L.Rev. 1593 (2005). Equally important, the success of ADR may come at the expense of democratic values which are difficult to quantify. As Professor Hensler has explained:

> The public spectacle of civil litigation gives life to the "rule of law." * * * In a democracy where many people are shut out of legislative power either because they are too few in number, or too dispersed to elect representatives, or because they do not have the financial resources to influence legislators, collective litigation in class or other mass form provides an alternative strategy for group action. Private individualized dispute resolution extinguishes the possibility of such collective litigation. Conciliation has much to recommend it. But the visible presence of institutionalized and legitimized conflict, channeled productively, teaches citizens that it is not always better to compromise and accept the status quo because, sometimes, great gains are to be had by peaceful contest.

Hensler, *Our Courts, Ourselves: How the Alternative Dispute Resolution Movement Is Re-Shaping Our Legal System,* 108 Penn St.L.Rev. 165 (2003). In what ways might a parallel system of private justice affect the operation of the public courts? See Horton, *Arbitration as Delegation,* 86 N.Y.U.L.Rev. 437 (2011). A noted federal judge has expressed these concerns:

> Widespread privatization of dispute resolution has the potential to stunt the common law's development as entire areas of law are removed from the courts; deprive the public of important

information, such as news of a product's harmful effects; deny
plaintiffs the therapeutic benefit of having their "day in court;"
degrade constitutional guarantees of the right to a jury trial; and
prevent public debate and consensus-building in cases with
national public policy implications.

Weinstein, *Some Benefits and Risks of Privatization of Justice Through
ADR*, 11 Ohio St.J. on Disp. Resol. 241, 246 (1996).

Recall the question posed at the outset of this book: "What is the test
of a good system of procedure?" See p. 4, supra. What is the relevance of
this question to your assessment of ADR?

INDEX